P9-BHU-241

FOR REFERENCE

Do Not Take From This Room

Nineteenth-Century
Literature Criticism

Guide to Gale Literary Criticism Series

For criticism on	Consult these Gale series
Authors now living or who died after December 31, 1959	*CONTEMPORARY LITERARY CRITICISM (CLC)*
Authors who died between 1900 and 1959	*TWENTIETH-CENTURY LITERARY CRITICISM (TCLC)*
Authors who died between 1800 and 1899	*NINETEENTH-CENTURY LITERATURE CRITICISM (NCLC)*
Authors who died between 1400 and 1799	*LITERATURE CRITICISM FROM 1400 TO 1800 (LC)* *SHAKESPEAREAN CRITICISM (SC)*
Authors who died before 1400	*CLASSICAL AND MEDIEVAL LITERATURE CRITICISM (CMLC)*
Black writers of the past two hundred years	*BLACK LITERATURE CRITICISM (BLC)*
Authors of books for children and young adults	*CHILDREN'S LITERATURE REVIEW (CLR)*
Dramatists	*DRAMA CRITICISM (DC)*
Hispanic writers of the late nineteenth and twentieth centuries	*HISPANIC LITERATURE CRITICISM (HLC)*
Native North American writers and orators of the eighteenth, nineteenth, and twentieth centuries	*NATIVE NORTH AMERICAN LITERATURE (NNAL)*
Poets	*POETRY CRITICISM (PC)*
Short story writers	*SHORT STORY CRITICISM (SSC)*
Major authors from the Renaissance to the present	*WORLD LITERATURE CRITICISM, 1500 TO THE PRESENT (WLC)*

ISSN 0732-1864

Volume 47

Nineteenth-Century Literature Criticism

Excerpts from Criticism of the
Works of Novelists, Poets, Playwrights,
Short Story Writers, Philosophers, and Other
Creative Writers Who Died between 1800
and 1899, from the First Published Critical
Appraisals to Current Evaluations

Joann Cerrito
Marie Lazzari
Editors

Catherine C. Dominic
Jelena O. Krstović
Associate Editors

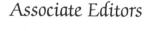 **Gale Research Inc.**

An International Thomson Publishing Company

I(T)P

NEW YORK • LONDON • BONN • BOSTON • DETROIT • MADRID
MELBOURNE • MEXICO CITY • PARIS • SINGAPORE • TOKYO
TORONTO • WASHINGTON • ALBANY NY • BELMONT CA • CINCINNATI OH

APR '95
Riverside Community College
Library
4800 Magnolia Avenue
Riverside, California 92506

Ref
PN
761
N3

STAFF

Joann Cerrito, Marie Lazzari, *Editors*

Catherine C. Dominic, Jelena O. Krstović, *Associate Editors*

Matthew C. Altman, Dana Barnes, Mary L. Onorato, Paul Sassalos, *Assistant Editors*

Marlene H. Lasky, *Permissions Manager*
Margaret A. Chamberlain, Linda M. Pugliese, *Permissions Specialists*
Susan Brohman, Diane Cooper, Maria L. Franklin, Pamela A. Hayes,
Arlene Johnson, Josephine M. Keene, Michele Lonoconus, Maureen Puhl,
Shalice Shah, Kimberly F. Smilay, Barbara A. Wallace, *Permissions Associates*
Edna Hedblad, Tyra A. Phillips, *Permissions Assistants*

Victoria B. Cariappa, *Research Manager*
Barbara McNeil, *Research Specialist*
Frank Vincent Castronova, Eva M. Felts, Mary Beth McElmeel, Donna Melnychenko,
Tamara C. Nott, Tracie A. Richardson, Norma Sawaya, *Research Associates*
Alicia Noel Biggers, Maria E. Bryson, Julia C. Daniel, Shirley Gates,
Michele P. Pica, Amy Terese Steel, Amy Beth Wieczorek, *Research Assistants*

Mary Beth Trimper, *Production Director*
Mary Kelley, *Production Associate*

Cynthia Baldwin, *Product Design Manager*
Barbara J. Yarrow, *Graphic Services Supervisor*
Sherrell Hobbs, *Macintosh Artist*
Willie F. Mathis, *Camera Operator*

Since this page cannot legibly accommodate all copyright notices, the acknowledgments constitute an extension of the copyright notice.

While every effort has been made to ensure the reliability of the information presented in this publication, Gale Research Inc. neither guarantees the accuracy of the data contained herein nor assumes any responsibility for errors, omissions or discrepancies. Gale accepts no payment for listing; and inclusion in the publication of any organization, agency, institution, publication, service, or individual does not imply endorsement of the editors or publisher. Errors brought to the attention of the publisher and verified to the satisfaction of the publisher will be corrected in future editions.

The paper used in this publication meets the minimum requirements of American National Standard for Information Sciences—Permanence Paper for Printed Library Materials, ANSI Z39.48-1984. ∞™

This publication is a creative work fully protected by all applicable copyright laws, as well as by misappropriation, trade secret, unfair competition, and other applicable laws. The authors and editors of this work have added value to the underlying factual material herein through one or more of the following: unique and original selection, coordination, expression, arrangement, and classification of the information.

All rights to this publication will be vigorously defended.

Copyright © 1995
Gale Research Inc.
835 Penobscot Building
Detroit, MI 48226-4094

All rights reserved including the right of reproduction in whole or in part in any form.

Library of Congress Catalog Card Number 84-643008
ISBN 0-8103-8938-X
ISSN 0732-1864

Printed in the United States of America

10 9 8 7 6 5 4 3 2 1

Contents

Preface vii

Acknowledgments xi

Preface

Since its inception in 1981, *Nineteenth-Century Literature Criticism* has been a valuable resource for students and librarians seeking critical commentary on writers of this transitional period in world history. Designated an "Outstanding Reference Source" by the American Library Association with the publication of its first volume, *NCLC* has since been purchased by over 6,000 school, public, and university libraries. The series has covered more than 300 authors representing 26 nationalities and over 15,000 titles. No other reference source has surveyed the critical reaction to nineteenth-century authors and literature as thoroughly as *NCLC*.

Scope of the Series

NCLC is designed to introduce students and advanced readers to the authors of the nineteenth century, and to the most significant interpretations of these authors' works. The great poets, novelists, short story writers, playwrights, and philosophers of this period are frequently studied in high school and college literature courses. By organizing and reprinting commentary written on these authors, *NCLC* helps students develop valuable insight into literary history, promotes a better understanding of the texts, and sparks ideas for papers and assignments. Each entry in *NCLC* presents a comprehensive survey of an author's career or an individual work of literature and provides the user with a multiplicity of interpretations and assessments. Such variety allows students to pursue their own interests; furthermore, it fosters an awareness that literature is dynamic and responsive to many different opinions.

Every fourth volume of *NCLC* is devoted to literary topics that cannot be covered under the author approach used in the rest of the series. Such topics include literary movements, prominent themes in nineteenth-century literature, literary reaction to political and historical events, significant eras in literary history, prominent literary anniversaries, and the literatures of cultures that are often overlooked by English-speaking readers.

NCLC continues the survey of criticism of world literature begun by Gale's *Contemporary Literary Criticism (CLC)* and *Twentieth-Century Literary Criticism (TCLC)*, both of which excerpt and reprint commentary on authors of the twentieth century. For additional information about *TCLC, CLC,* and Gale's other criticism series, users should consult the Guide to Gale Literary Criticism Series preceding the title page in this volume.

Coverage

Each volume of *NCLC* is carefully compiled to present:

- criticism of authors, or literary topics, representing a variety of genres and nationalities
- both major and lesser-known writers and literary works of the period
- 7-10 authors or 4-6 topics per volume
- individual entries that survey critical response to an author's work or a topic in literary history, including early criticism to reflect initial reactions, later criticism to represent any rise or decline in reputation, and current retrospective analyses.

Organization

An author entry consists of the following elements: author heading, biographical and critical introduction, list of principal works, excerpts of criticism (each preceded by an annotation and followed by a bibliographic citation), and a bibliography of further reading.

- The **Author Heading** consists of the name under which the author most commonly wrote, followed by birth and death dates. If an author wrote consistently under a pseudonym, the pseudonym will be listed in the author heading and the real name given in parentheses on the first line of the biographical and critical introduction. Also located at the beginning of the introduction to the author entry are any name variations under which an author wrote, including transliterated forms for an author whose language uses a nonroman alphabet.

- The **Biographical and Critical Introduction** outlines the author's life and career, as well as the critical issues surrounding his or her work. References are provided to past volumes of *NCLC* in which further information about the author may be found.

- Most *NCLC* entries include a **Portrait** of the author. Many entries also contain reproductions of materials pertinent to an author's career, including manuscript pages, title pages, dust jackets, letters, and drawings, as well as photographs of important people, places, and events in an author's life.

- The list of **Principal Works** is chronological by date of first publication and identifies the genre of each work. In the case of foreign authors with both foreign-language publications and English translations, the English-language version is given in brackets. Unless otherwise indicated, dramas are dated by first performance, not first publication.

- **Criticism** in each author entry is arranged chronologically to provide a perspective on changes in critical evaluation over the years. All titles of works by the author featured in the entry are printed in boldface type to enable the user to easily locate discussion of particular works. Also for purposes of easier identification, the critic's name and the publication date of the essay are given at the beginning of each piece of criticism. Unsigned criticism is preceded by the title of the journal in which it appeared. Publication information (such as publisher names and book prices) and parenthetical numerical references (such as footnotes or page and line references to specific editions of works) have been deleted at the editors' discretion to provide smoother reading of the text.

- Critical excerpts are prefaced by **Annotations** providing the reader with information about both the critic and the criticism that follows. Included are the critic's reputation, individual approach to literary criticism, and particular expertise in an author's works. Also noted are the relative importance of a work of criticism, the scope of the excerpt, and the growth of critical controversy or changes in critical trends regarding an author. In some cases, these annotations cross-reference excerpts by critics who discuss each other's commentary.

- A complete **Bibliographic Citation** designed to facilitate location of the original essay or book follows each piece of criticism.

- An annotated list of **Further Reading** appearing at the end of each entry suggests secondary sources on the author. In some cases it includes essays for which the editors could not obtain reprint rights.

Cumulative Indexes

■ Each volume of *NCLC* contains a cumulative **Author Index** listing all authors who have appeared in Gale's Literary Criticism Series, along with cross-references to such biographical series as *Contemporary Authors* and *Dictionary of Literary Biography*. Useful for locating authors within the various series, this index is particularly valuable for those authors who are identified with a certain period but who, because of their death dates, are placed in another, or for those authors whose careers span two periods. For example, Fyodor Dostoevsky is found in *NCLC,* yet Leo Tolstoy, another major nineteenth-century Russian novelist, is found in *TCLC* because he died after 1899.

■ Each *NCLC* volume includes a cumulative **Nationality Index** which lists all authors who have appeared in *NCLC*, arranged alphabetically under their respective nationalities, as well as Topics volume entries devoted to particular national literatures.

■ Each new volume in Gale's Literary Criticism Series includes a cumulative **Topic Index**, which lists all literary topics treated in *NCLC, TCLC, LC 1400-1800*, and the *CLC* Yearbook.

■ Each new volume of *NCLC*, with the exception of the Topics volumes, contains a **Title Index** listing the titles of all literary works discussed in the volume. In response to numerous suggestions from librarians, Gale has also produced a **Special Paperbound Edition** of the *NCLC* title index. This annual cumulation lists all titles discussed in the series since its inception and is issued with the first volume of *NCLC* published each year. Additional copies of the index are available on request. Librarians and patrons have welcomed this separate index: it saves shelf space, is easy to use, and is recyclable upon receipt of the following year's cumulation. Titles discussed in the Topics volume entries are not included in the *NCLC* cumulative index.

Citing *Nineteenth-Century Literature Criticism*

When writing papers, students who quote directly from any volume in Gale's Literary Criticism Series may use the following general forms to footnote reprinted criticism. The first example pertains to material drawn from periodicals, the second to material reprinted from books:

[1]T.S. Eliot, "John Donne," *The Nation and Athenaeum*, 33 (9 June 1923), 321-32; excerpted and reprinted in *Literature Criticism from 1400-1800,* Vol. 10, ed. James E. Person, Jr. (Detroit: Gale Research, 1989), pp. 28-9.

[2]Clara G. Stillman, *Samuel Butler: A Mid-Victorian Modern* (Viking Press, 1932); excerpted and reprinted in *Twentieth-Century Literary Criticism,* Vol. 33, ed. Paula Kepos (Detroit: Gale Research, 1989), pp. 43-5.

Suggestions Are Welcome

In response to suggestions, several features have been added to *NCLC* since the series began, including annotations to excerpted criticism, a cumulative index to authors in all Gale literary criticism series, entries devoted to criticism on a single work by a major author, more illustrations, and a title index listing all literary works discussed in the series.

Readers who wish to suggest authors or topics to appear in future volumes, or who have other suggestions, are cordially invited to write the editors.

Acknowledgments

The editors wish to thank the copyright holders of the excerpted criticism included in this volume and the permissions managers of many book and magazine publishing companies for assisting us in securing reprint rights. We are also grateful to the staffs of the Detroit Public Library, the Library of Congress, the University of Detroit Mercy Library, Wayne State University Purdy/Kresge Library Complex, and the University of Michigan Libraries for making their resources available to us. Following is a list of the copyright holders who have granted us permission to reprint material in this volume of *NCLC*. Every effort has been made to trace copyright, but if omissions have been made, please let us know.

COPYRIGHTED EXCERPTS IN *NCLC*, VOLUME 47, WERE REPRINTED FROM THE FOLLOWING PERIODICALS:

Audubon, v. 87, May, 1985. Copyright © 1985 by the National Audubon Society.—*Early American Literature,* v. VIII, Winter, 1974 for "The Case of Drake and Halleck" by Joseph Slater. Copyright, 1974, by the University of Massachusetts. Reprinted by permission of the publisher and the author.—*Essays in French Literature,* n. 13, November, 1976. © Department of French Studies, The University of Western Australia. Reprinted by permission of the publisher.—*MLN,* v. 92, December, 1977. © copyright 1977 by The Johns Hopkins University Press. All rights reserved. Reprinted by permission of the publisher.—*Neophilologue,* v. LXXV, October, 1991 for "Sade and the Problem of Closure: Keeping Philosophy in the Bedroom" by Scott Carpenter. © 1991 by H. D. Tjeenk Willink. Reprinted by permission of the publisher and the author.—*The New York Review of Books,* v. VII, December 1, 1966. Copyright © 1966 Nyrev, Inc. Reprinted with permission from *The New York Review of Books.*—*The New Yorker,* v. LXVII, February 25, 1991 for "Audubon's Passion" by Adam Gopnik. © 1991 by the author. Reprinted by permission of the publisher.—*Representations,* n. 36, Fall, 1991 for "Sade and the Pornographic Legacy" by Frances Ferguson. © 1991 by The Regents of the University of California. Reprinted by permission of the publisher and the author.—*Russian Literature,* v. XI, February 15, 1982 for "Dramatic Genre as a Tool of Characterization in Lermontov's 'A Hero of Our Time' " by Gary D. Cox. © 1982, Elsevier Science Publishers B. V. (North-Holland). All rights reserved. Reprinted by permission of the publisher and the author.—*Russian Literature Triquarterly,* n. 10, Fall, 1974. © 1974 by Ardis Publishers. Reprinted by permission of the publisher.—*Studies on Voltaire and the Eighteenth Century,* v. LXXXVIII, 1972; v. XCVIII, 1972; v. 249, 1987; v. 265, 1989. All reprinted by permission of the publisher.—*Texas Studies in Literature and Language,* v. XXXII, Winter, 1990 for "Fate and Narrative Structure in Lermontov's 'A Hero of Our Time' " by R. L. Kesler. Copyright © 1990 by the University of Texas Press. Reprinted by permission of the publisher and the author.

COPYRIGHTED EXCERPTS IN *NCLC*, VOLUME 47, WERE REPRINTED FROM THE FOLLOWING BOOKS:

Cahalane, Victor H. From an introduction to *The Imperial Collection of Audubon Animals: The Quadrupeds of North America.* Edited by Victor H. Cahalane. Hammond Incorporated, 1967.—Calder, Angus. From *Russian Discovered: Nineteenth-Century Fiction from Pushkin to Chekhov.* Barnes and Noble Books, 1976. © Angus Calder 1976. Reprinted by permission of the Peters Frasers & Dunlop Group Ltd.—Carter, Angela. From *The Sadeian Woman and the Ideology of Pornography.* Pantheon Books, 1978. Copyright © 1978 by Angela Carter. All rights reserved. Reprinted by permission of Pantheon Books, a Division of Random House, Inc.—DeJean, Joan. From *Literary Fortifications: Rousseau, Laclos, Sade.* Princeton University Press, 1984. Copyright © 1984 by Princeton University Press. All rights reserved. Reprinted by permission of the publisher.—DiPiero, Thomas. From *Dangerous Truths & Criminal Passions: The Evolution of the French Novel, 1569-1791.* Stanford University Press, 1992. Copyright © 1992 by the Board of Trustees of Leland Stanford Junior University. Reprinted by permission of the publishers, Stanford University Press.—Dworkin, Andrea. From *Pornography: Men Possessing Women*. The Women's Press, 1981. Copyright © Andrea Dworkin, 1979, 1980, 1981. All rights reserved. Reprinted by permission of the author. In U.K. and British Commonwealth by The Women's Press Ltd.—Foote, Paul. From an introduction to *A Hero of Our Time*. By M. Yu. Lermontov, translated by Paul Foote. Penguin Books 1966. Copyright © Paul Foote, 1966. All rights reserved. Reproduced by permission of Penguin Books Ltd.—Freeborn, Richard. From *The Rise of the Russian Novel: Studies in the Russian Novel from "Eugene Onegin" to "War and Peace."* Cambridge University Press, 1973. © Cambridge University Press 1973. Reprinted by permission of the publisher and the author.—Garrard, John H. From "Old Wine in New Bottles: The Legacy of Lermontov," in *Poetica Slavica: Studies in Honour of Zbigniew Folejewski*. Edited by J. Douglas Clayton and Gunter Schaarschmidt. University of Ottawa Press, 1981. © University of Ottawa Press, 1981. Reprinted by permission of the publisher.—Griscom, Ludlow. From an introduction to *Audubon's Birds of America*. By John James Audubon. The Macmillan Company, 1950. Copyright , 1950, renewed 1977, by Macmillan Publishing Company. All rights reserved. Reprinted with permission of the publisher.—Hayes, Julie Candler. From *Identity and Ideology: Diderot, Sade, and the Serious Genre*. John Benjamins Publishing Company, 1991. © copyright 1991 —John Benjamins B. V. Reprinted by permission of the publisher.—Keith, W. J. From *Richard Jefferies: A Critical Study*. University of Toronto Press, 1965. © University of Toronto Press 1965. Reprinted by permission of University of Toronto Press Incorporated.—Krasner, James. From *The Entangled Eye: Visual Perception and the Representation of Nature in Post-Darwinian Narrative*. Oxford University Press, 1992. Copyright © 1992 by Oxford University Press, Inc. All rights reserved.—Leavis, Q. D. From *Collected Essays, Vol 3*. Edited by G. Singh. Cambridge University Press, 1989. © Cambridge University Press, 1989. Reprinted with permission of the publisher.—Lynch, Lawrence W. From *The Marquis de Sade*. Twayne, 1984. Copyright © 1984 by G. K. Hall & Company. All rights reserved. Reprinted with the permission of Twayne Publishers, an imprint of Macmillan Publishing Company.—Mabey, Richard. From an introduction to *Landscape with Figures*. By Richard Jefferies, edited by Richard Mabey. Penguin Books, 1983. Introduction copyright © Richard Mabey, 1983. All rights reserved. Reproduced by permission of Penguin Books Ltd.—Meyer, Priscilla. From "Lermontov's Reading of Pushkin: 'The Tales of Belkin' and 'A Hero of Our Time'," in *The Golden Age of Russian Literature and Thought*. Edited by Derek Offord. St. Martin's Press, 1992. © International Council for Soviet and East European Studies, and Derek Offord, 1992. All rights reserved. Reprinted by permission of St. Martin's Press, Incorporated.—Morris, David B. From "Marquis de Sade and the Discourses of Pain: Literature and Medicine at the Revolution," in *The Languages of Psyche: Mind and Body in Enlightenment Thought, Clark Library Lectures 1985-1986*. Edited by G. S. Rousseau. University of California Press, 1990. Copyright © 1990 by The Regents of the University of California. Reprinted by permission of the publisher and the author.—Peattie, Donald Culross, Robert Cushman Murphy, and Mark Van Doren. From "John James Audubon: American Scenery and Character," in *The New Invitation to Learning*. Edited by Mark Van Doren. Random House, 1942. Copyright 1942 by the Columbia Broadcasting System, Inc. Renewed 1970 by Mark Van Doren. Reprinted by permission of the Literary Estate of Mark Van Doren.—Poovey, Mary. From *Uneven Developments: The Ideological Work of Gender in Mid-Victorian England*. The University of Chicago Press, 1988. © 1988 by The University of Chicago. All rights reserved. Reprinted by permission of the publisher.—Pritchett, V. S. From *A Man of Letters: Selected Essays*. Random House, 1985. Copyright © 1985 by V. S. Pritchett. All rights reserved. Reprinted by permission of Random House, Inc. In Canada by Sterling Lord Literistic, Inc.—Reeve, F. D. From *The Russian Novel*. Frederick Muller, 1967. Copyright © F.D. Reeve, 1966. Reprinted by permission of the author.—Richards, D. J. From "Lermontov: 'A Hero of Our Time'," in *The Voice of a Giant: Essays on Seven Russian Prose Classics*. Edited by Roger Cockrell and David Richards. University of Exeter, 1985. © 1985 Department of Russian University of Exeter. Reprinted by permission of the publisher.—Rosenshield, Gary. From "Fatalism in 'A Hero of Our Time': Cause or Commonplace?" in *The Supernatural in Slavic and Baltic Literature: Essays in Honor of Victor Terras*. Edited by Amy Mandelker and Roberta Reeder. Slavic Publishers, Inc. 1988. Each contribution copyright © 1988 by its author. All rights reserved. Reprinted by permission of the author.—Rowe, W. W. From *Nabokov & Others: Patterns in Russian Literature*. Ardis, 1979. Copyright © 1979 by Ardis. Reprinted by permission of the publisher.—Taylor, Brian. From *Richard Jefferies*. Twayne, 1982. Copyright © 1982 by G. K. Hall & Company. Reprinted with the permission of Twayne Publishers, an imprint of Macmillan Publishing Company.

John James Audubon

1785-1851

(Born Jean Jacques Fougère Rabin) American naturalist, artist, and non-fiction writer.

INTRODUCTION

Audubon is chiefly remembered as a painter of birds. His masterwork is the collection of prints entitled *The Birds of America.* He was also an important early American naturalist writer, and his *Ornithological Biography,* a written supplement to *The Birds of America*, is valued by historians and literary enthusiasts for its vivid descriptions of bird behavior and of frontier life.

Biographical Information

Audubon was born on the island of Santo Domingo (now Haiti) in 1785, the illegitimate child of a French Navy captain and a local woman. He was later brought to France and adopted by his father. At the age of eighteen Audubon travelled to Pennsylvania to manage his father's American estate outside Philadelphia. There he married and began his studies of American birds. In 1807 he moved to Kentucky and embarked on a number of business ventures, all of which failed. During this time, the study of birds became Audubon's all-consuming passion; he undertook expeditions along still-unexplored portions of the Ohio and Mississippi rivers in search of new specimens to paint. Audubon conceived of a comprehensive guidebook to American birds which would showcase his paintings. He traveled to England and France to secure subscriptions and find an engraver for the project. Here Audubon adopted the role of American frontiersman, dressing in buckskins and entertaining potential patrons with demonstrations of native American language, bird calls, and stories of frontier life. Adam Gopnik noted that: "Audubon understood that while in America it paid him to be very French, in France it paid him to be very American. . . . In the salons of Paris, Audubon at last became an American." *The Birds of America* began publication in 1827 and reached completion in 1838, comprising a total of four volumes which sold for $1000. A less expensive edition was published from 1840 to 1844. The work brought Audubon fame and financial security. The remaining years of his life were devoted to compiling a study of mammals, *The Viviparous Quadrupeds of North America*, in collaboration with his sons and the naturalist John Bachman. The work began publication in 1846 and was completed in 1854, three years after Audubon's death.

Major Works

Prior to Audubon, bird paintings generally resembled the stiffly mounted museum specimens that were commonly used as models. In *The Birds of America,* Audubon paint-

ed birds that appeared full of motion and life. Although Audubon too sketched and painted dead birds, he manipulated his models into life-like poses using threads and wires, based on extensive field observation of their actual behavior. Audubon was also the first to depict birds in their natural habitats, foreshadowing the wildlife dioramas found in modern natural history museums. Publication of *The Birds of America* was a massive undertaking. Nearly all of Audubon's paintings were reproduced life-size, requiring sheets of paper known as "double elephant," measuring 29½ by 39½ inches. Each of the four volumes of the first edition weighs between forty and forty-five pounds. The 435 engraved plates were each hand-colored. *The Birds of America* was followed by a written companion, *Ornithological Biography*, in which Audubon gives detailed descriptions of the behavior, migration patterns, mating habits, and anatomy of every bird he had painted. The *Biography* established Audubon's reputation as a scientist. Scott Russell Sanders has pointed out that Charles Darwin cited only two other authorities more often than Audubon. Interspersed with the descriptions of birds are chapters entitled "Episodes," where Audubon reports on the places he had visited and the customs of the people he met. These sketches are noted for their colorful depictions of nature and society in early eighteenth-century America. Observed nature writer Robert Cushman Murphy, "He saw America when it was still an Eden, the last garden of that sort remaining in the temperate world. . . . There is no other such picture of the dawn of history in the United States." Audubon's last major endeavor was the compilation of *The Viviparous Quadrupeds of North America*. Less popular and well known than his catalogue of birds, the study nevertheless remains a classic of nineteenth-century natural history, and some commentators regard Audubon's paintings of mammals to be his best work.

Critical Reception

As a naturalist, Audubon was responsible for the discovery of many new species of North American birds and mammals. He also was the first ornithologist to use banding as a method for tracking bird migration. Scientists have noted, however, that his descriptions of natural phenomena often lack technical sophistication, particularly in regard to animal classification. As a painter, Audubon was reproached in his own day by naturalists who charged that his representations of birds and animals were anthropomorphized. Audubon is perhaps more a nature writer than an objective scientist. Scott Russell Sanders has placed him at the beginning of a tradition that includes Henry David Thoreau, John Muir, and Rachel Carson. "All these writers confront nature not as aloof observers, seeking facts; but as human participants in nature, seeking meaning. This was Audubon's strength as a writer, not system-building, but reporting and collecting, bearing his keen sensibility through uncharted territory." In the twentieth century, Audubon is most commonly associated with the National Audubon Society. First organized in 1886 in the interests of bird protection, it has become one of the largest and most respected conservation societies in the world.

PRINCIPAL WORKS

The Birds of America. 4 vols. (nonfiction) 1827-38; also published as *The Birds of America*. 7 vols. 1840-44
Ornithological Biography. 5 vols. (nonfiction) 1831-39; also published as *Delineations of American Scenery and Character*, 1926
The Viviparous Quadrupeds of North America [with John Bachman]. 5 vols. (nonfiction) 1846-54

CRITICISM

John James Audubon   (essay date 1838?)
SOURCE: "My Style of Drawing Birds," in *Audubon and*

His Journals, by Maria R. Audubon, Charles Scribner's Sons, 1897, pp. 522-27.

[*In the following essay, originally published at the time* The Birds of America *appeared, Audubon explains his techniques for making his bird paintings appear lifelike.*]

When, as a little lad, I first began my attempts at representing birds on paper, I was far from possessing much knowledge of their nature, and, like hundreds of others, when I had laid the effort aside, I was under the impression that it was a finished picture of a bird because it possessed some sort of a head and tail, and two sticks in lieu of legs; I never troubled myself with the thought that abutments were requisite to prevent it from falling either backward or forward, and oh! what bills and claws I did draw, to say nothing of a perfectly straight line for a back, and a tail stuck in anyhow, like an unshipped rudder.

Many persons besides my father saw my miserable attempts, and so many praised them to the skies that perhaps no one was ever nearer being completely wrecked than I by these mistaken, though affectionate words. My father, however, spoke very differently to me; he constantly impressed upon me that nothing in the world possessing life and animation was easy to imitate, and that as I grew older he hoped I would become more and more alive to this. He was so kind to me, and so deeply interested in my improvement that to have listened carelessly to his serious words would have been highly ungrateful. I listened less to others, more to him, and his words become my law.

The first collection of drawings I made were from European specimens, procured by my father or myself, and I still have them in my possession. They were all represented *strictly ornithologically,* which means neither more nor less than in stiff, unmeaning profiles, such as are found in most works published to the present day. My next set was begun in America, and there, without my honored mentor, I betook myself to the drawing of specimens hung by a string tied to one foot, having a desire to show every portion, as the wings lay loosely spread, as well as the tail. In this manner I made some pretty fair signs for poulterers.

One day, while watching the habits of a pair of Pewees at Mill Grove, I looked so intently at their graceful attitudes that a thought struck my mind like a flash of light, that nothing, after all, could ever answer my enthusiastic desires to represent nature, except to copy her in her own way, alive and moving! Then I began again. On I went, forming, literally, hundreds of outlines of my favorites, the Pewees; how good or bad I cannot tell, but I fancied I had mounted a step on the high pinnacle before me. I continued for months together, simply outlining birds as I observed them, either alighted or on the wing, but could finish none of my sketches. I procured many individuals of different species, and laying them on the table or on the ground, tried to place them in such attitudes as I had sketched. But, alas! they were *dead,* to all intents and purposes, and neither wing, leg, nor tail could I place according to my wishes. A second thought came to my assistance; by means of threads I raised or lowered a head, wing, or tail, and by fastening the threads securely, I had something like life before me; yet much was wanting.

When I saw the living birds, I felt the blood rush to my temples, and almost in despair spent about a month without drawing, but in deep thought, and daily in the company of the feathered inhabitants of dear Mill Grove.

I had drawn from the "manikin" whilst under David, and had obtained tolerable figures of our species through this means, so I cogitated how far a manikin of a bird would answer. I labored with wood, cork, and wires, and formed a grotesque figure, which I cannot describe in any other words than by saying that when set up it was a tolerable-looking Dodo. A friend roused my ire by laughing at it immoderately, and assuring me that if I wished to represent a tame gander it might do. I gave it a kick, broke it to atoms, walked off, and thought again.

Young as I was, my impatience to obtain my desire filled my brains with many plans. I not infrequently dreamed that I had made a new discovery; and long before day, one morning, I leaped out of bed fully persuaded that I had obtained my object. I ordered a horse to be saddled, mounted, and went off at a gallop towards the little village of Norristown, distant about five miles. When I arrived there not a door was open, for it was not yet daylight. Therefore I went to the river, took a bath, and, returning to the town, entered the first opened shop, inquired for wire of different sizes, bought some, leaped on my steed, and was soon again at Mill Grove. The wife of my tenant, I really believe, thought that I was mad, as, on offering me breakfast, I told her I only wanted my gun. I was off to the creek, and shot the first Kingfisher I met. I picked the bird up, carried it home by the bill, sent for the miller, and bade him bring me a piece of board of soft wood. When he returned he found me filing sharp points to some pieces of wire, and I proceeded to show him what I meant to do. I pierced the body of the fishing bird, and fixed it on the board; another wire passed above his upper mandible held the head in a pretty fair attitude, smaller ones fixed the feet according to my notions, and even common pins came to my assistance. The last wire proved a delightful elevator to the bird's tail, and at last—there stood before me the *real* Kingfisher.

Think not that my lack of breakfast was at all in my way. No, indeed! I outlined the bird, aided by compasses and my eyes, colored it, finished it, without a thought of hunger. My honest miller stood by the while, and was delighted to see me pleased. This was what I shall call my first drawing actually from nature, for even the eye of the Kingfisher was as if full of life whenever I pressed the lids aside with my finger.

In those happy days of my youth I was extremely fond of reading what I still call the delightful fables of La Fontaine. I had frequently perused the one entitled *"L'hirondelle et les petits oiseaux",* and thought much of the meaning imparted in the first line, which, if I now recollect rightly, goes on to say that *"Quiconque a beaucoup vu, peut avoir beaucoup retenu."* To me this meant that to study Nature was to ramble through her domains late and early, and if I observed all as I should, that the memory of what I saw would at least be of service to me.

"Early to bed, and early to rise," was another adage which I thought, and still think, of much value; 't is a pity that instead of being merely an adage it has not become a general law; I have followed it ever since I was a child, and am ever grateful for the hint it conveyed.

As I wandered, mostly bent on the study of birds, and with a wish to represent all those found in our woods, to the best of my powers, I gradually became acquainted with their forms and habits, and the use of my wires was improved by constant practice. Whenever I produced a better representation of any species the preceding one was destroyed, and after a time I laid down what I was pleased to call a constitution of my manner of drawing birds, formed upon natural principles, which I will try to put briefly before you.

The gradual knowledge of the forms and habits of the birds of our country impressed me with the idea that each part of a family must possess a certain degree of affinity, distinguishable at sight in any one of them. The Pewees, which I knew by experience were positively Flycatchers, led me to the discovery that every bird truly of that genus, when standing, was usually in a passive attitude; that they sat uprightly, now and then glancing their eyes upwards or sideways, to watch the approach of their insect prey; that if in pursuit of this prey their movements through the air were, in each and all of that tribe, the same, etc., etc.

Gallinaceous birds I saw were possessed of movements and positions peculiar to them. Amongst the waterbirds also I found characteristic manners. I observed that the Herons walked with elegance and stateliness, that, in fact, every family had some mark by which it could be known; and, after having collected many ideas and much material of this kind, I fairly began, in greater earnest than ever, the very collection of ***Birds of America,*** which is now being published.

The better I understood my subjects, the better I became able to represent them in what I hoped were natural positions. The bird, once fixed with wires on squares, I studied as a lay figure before me, its nature, previously known to me as far as habits went, and its general form having been frequently observed. Now I could examine more thoroughly the bill, nostrils, eyes, legs, and claws, as well as the structure of the wings and tail; the very tongue was of importance to me, and I thought the more I understood all these particulars, the better representations I made of the originals.

My drawings at first were made altogether in watercolors, but they wanted softness and a great deal of finish. For a long time I was much dispirited at this, particularly when vainly endeavoring to imitate birds of soft and downy plumage, such as that of most Owls, Pigeons, Hawks, and Herons. How this could be remedied required a new train of thought, or some so-called accident, and the latter came to my aid.

One day, after having finished a miniature portrait of the one dearest to me in all the world, a portion of the face was injured by a drop of water, which dried where it fell; and although I labored a great deal to repair the damage, the blur still remained. Recollecting that, when a pupil of David, I had drawn heads and figures in different colored

Barn owl by Audubon.

chalks, I resorted to a piece of that material of the tint required for the part, applied the pigment, rubbed the place with a cork stump, and at once produced the desired effect.

My drawings of Owls and other birds of similar plumage were much improved by such applications; indeed, after a few years of patience, some of my attempts began almost to please me, and I have continued the same style ever since, and that now is for more than thirty years.

Whilst travelling in Europe as well as America, many persons have evinced the desire to draw birds in my manner, and I have always felt much pleasure in showing it to any one by whom I hoped ornithological delineations or portraitures would be improved.

A. Innes Shand   (essay date 1898)

SOURCE: "A Great Naturalist," in *Blackwood's Edinburgh Magazine,* Vol. CLXIV, No. DCCCCXCIII, July, 1898, pp. 58-69.

[*In the following review, the critic commends the interest of Audubon's published journals.*]

Biographies of all sorts are the craze of the day, but not many of them have the intense human and sensational fascination of these journals and "Episodes" by Audubon, piously edited by his granddaughter [Maria R. Audubon]. They come as a tardy sequel to the great ornithological works—like these, they are eminently autobiographical and self-revealing—which won him a world-wide fame some seventy years ago. For his graphic style is always inspired by a delightful and innocently unconscious egoism. The numerous portraits in the volumes give us the measure of the man: his character is stamped upon his face in the most legible of large print. As we see him in his prime, he is something between "Christopher North" and a peregrine falcon. There is the lofty forehead and the aquiline nose, though the flashing search-light in the hawk-like eye is tempered by a mild benignity. By the way, Audubon is an old acquaintance of 'Maga,'—an intimate in the inner circle of the directorate. During a prolonged residence in Edinburgh, which he loved beyond all European cities, he was drawn to Wilson, not only by congenial tastes and habits, but by previous acquaintance with the Professor's brother, who had devoted himself, like Audubon, to American bird-lore. He was mentioned at a "Noctes" in terms of the highest admiration, and two eloquent eulogies of his works appeared immediately afterwards in the Magazine. Like Christopher, he had a constitution of iron, which he never spared; but in one point there was little resemblance between them. Christopher took his liquor like a man, though the potations pottle-deep at Ambrose's were the flights of a poetical imagination. Audubon prides himself on never having tasted wine or spirits before his marriage, although he learned later to carry a flask as a companion in his multifarious and malarious wanderings. For, like Christopher and the peregrine, he was a born rover, with eyes that were ever on the alert for each movement of animated nature. The son of a Frenchman, and Spanish on the mother's side, he was early naturalised as an American citizen. Oddly enough, though his descen-

dants have religiously preserved all memorials of him, the date and circumstances of his birth are mysterious as those of Melchizedek. His granddaughter cannot pretend to fix it within several years; but she strikes the most probable average about 1780. It is certain that he was a schoolboy in France during the Reign of Terror; and while heads were falling under the guillotine in Paris, and Carrier was perpetrating his grotesque atrocities on the Loire, little John James Laforest was playing truant on the lower banks of the river, bird-nesting and collecting eggs and specimens. Already "I had upwards of 200 drawings, all bad enough, yet they were representations of birds, and I felt pleased with them."

He came to America, where his father had good properties, and, about the time of attaining his majority, launched out as a gay young Pennsylvanian squire. He tells us he was extremely extravagant, with neither vices nor high aims. It was but natural that he should be fond of shooting, and lavish money on a costly stud. And as irrepressible genius will break out, it was as natural he should indulge his taste for drawing, in the intervals of the graver occupations of picnicking, music, and dancing. But the man whose daily wear was to be homespun or deerskins was then so finished and fantastic a dandy that he went shooting in satin small-clothes, silk stockings, and ruffled shirts.

A happy marriage with a charming English girl made, reformed, and beggared him. His father-in-law insisted that he should go into trade, and like many another unlucky man of business, he never discovered his true vocation till he was ruined. His partners may have been honest; but they may be excused if they were disgusted and inclined to take advantage of him. They might tempt him to venture his all in risky speculation, but they could never keep him to the inside of the countinghouse. He was keen to break away to the woods and fields, as any falcon fettered to the perch. Fancy the feelings of a respectable New Englander, intent on "making his pile," when coming on such a passage as this in his associate's note-books: "Were I to tell you that once when travelling and driving several horses before me, laden with goods and dollars, I lost sight of the packsaddles and the cash they bore, to watch the motions of a warbler, I should only repeat occurrences which happened a hundred times and more in those days." And the locations in which the speculators settled offered him rare opportunities and temptations irresistible. He was first at the rising township of Louisville on the Ohio; afterwards at Henderson, a hundred miles lower down the river. The woods, the wolves, and the Indians came up to the skirts of the settlement: the country was sparsely dotted over with squatters, who lived chiefly by their guns. What was bred in the bone would come out, and Audubon was always playing truant as when at school, and picking up respectable, but unprofitable, acquaintances. The inevitable results followed. The Pennsylvanian plantation was sold, his debts were paid, and he was left without a dollar. "Was I inclined to cut my throat in foolish despair? No.! I *had* talents, and to them I instantly resorted." He stood then at the parting of the ways, and immediately he struck into the path which was to lead him to fame and reasonable affluence. In the meantime, however, he had to resign himself to dire extremities. Here is an incident which shows the careless *viveur* of civilised Pennsylvania, the man who was to be welcomed as an honoured guest in the most intellectual society of Western Europe, reduced to the condition of the meanest tramp, and with no previous hardening to stoical endurance. It is in an autobiographical sketch bequeathed to his children:—

> After our dismal removal, one morning when all of us were sadly desponding, I took you both from Shippingport to Louisville. I had purchased a loaf of bread and some apples: before you reached Louisville you were all hungry, and by the riverside we sat down and ate our scanty meal. On that day the world was with me as a blank and my heart was sorely heavy, for scarcely had I enough to keep my dear ones alive, and yet through those dark ways I was being led to a development of the talents I loved, and which have brought so much enjoyment to us *all*.

He goes on characteristically:—

> One of the most extraordinary things among all these adverse circumstances was, that I never for a day gave up listening to the songs of our birds or watching their peculiar habits or delineating them in the best way I could: nay, during my deepest troubles, I frequently would wrench myself from the persons around me and retire to some secluded part of our noble forests; and many a time, at the sound of the woodthrush's melodies, have I fallen on my knees and there prayed earnestly to our God.

These touching extracts may serve to indicate the nervous simplicity of his graphic style. He was no drawer of landscapes, except in pen and ink; but he was equally effective in portraiture with pen, pencil, and brush. As an animal-artist, for truth and spirit he stands unrivalled, except perhaps by Joseph Wolf of the Rhineland, and by Bewick in wood-engraving; though in gratitude for our mercies we should not forget our own Thorburn and Millais. Candid almost to a fault in his criticisms as he was frank in his speech, he ridicules the best work of Sneiders, Hondiko-eter, and Edwin Landseer, for their fanciful travesties of the truthful reality. At the same time, he expresses his unbounded admiration of their colouring and of the technique to which he dare never hope to attain. Considering that, save for a few lessons, he was virtually self-taught, his presentations of all the animal creation are marvellous. In the meantime, being thrown back, as he says, on his talents, he has to draw the wild creatures for his pleasure and his fellow-creatures for a living. *Où la vanité va-t-elle se nicher?* Happily for him, the rough backwoodsmen and the scarcely less rude *bourgeois* of the rising frontier townships had a *penchant,* and even a passion, for having the family portraits. And they paid liberally, according to their limited ideas, often not only replenishing an empty purse, but giving a surplus to draw upon for weeks of wanderings. So, thanks to these pot-boilers, he kept adding to the collection, which sent him reluctantly to Europe in 1826 to hunt up wealthy subscribers to the *magnum opus.*

The early journals seem to have perished in a great fire at New York, when the premises in which they were stored were blown up to isolate the conflagration. But we do not know that anything was really lost by that, for there is a good deal of technical prolixity in the naturalist's notes. On the other hand, when he "let himself go," no one could write with more spirit or with more vivid originality, and the "Episodes" which nearly fill the second of these volumes reflect all that was most picturesque in the adventurous life, when "he was making himself," as Shortreed said of Walter Scott. Incidentally we are for ever being reminded of the changes which have been transforming the Union since the beginning of the century. Western Pennsylvania was then as wild as anything to be found now in Oregon or on the frontiers of New Mexico. Now the rich coalfields of the Lehigh district are blackened with the fumes of the pits and iron-works: they are covered with populous towns and grimy villages, and traversed by railways ingeniously constructed on the stiffest practicable gradients. Then, though the mineral wealth had been suspected, the freshness of the virgin forests was unsoiled; and Audubon lived for weeks in an outlying mining-camp, the approaches through almost inaccessible defiles being slowly pioneered by the axes of the lumberers. The weekly consignments of bread and pork were lowered into the depths of the gorge by a rope 300 feet long. Then the Ohio formed the boundary of civilisation beyond Kentucky, and, as we have said, when he had his homes in Louisville or Henderson, he could make a mixed bag of everything from a bear to a tomtit in woods and prairieland coming up to his door. The wandering traders who supplied the stores generally bought a horse for the journey, and took pack-mules to carry the goods. There were neither inns nor regular resting-places, and the travellers either hobbled their beasts and bivouacked, or sought the casual hospitality of some squatter's cabin. Even so late as in 1843, describing his voyage on a Mississippi steamer, he treats his compatriots far more cavalierly than Dickens in *Martin Chuzzlewit* or the *American Notes.* It may be worth while quoting a passage or two, to show that the much abused Englishman's satire was well within bounds:—

> Such a steamer as we have come in!—the very filthiest of all old rattraps I have ever travelled in, and the fare worse, certainly much worse, and so scanty withal, that our worthy commander could not have given us another meal, had we been detained a night longer. . . . Our *compagnons de voyage,* about 150, were composed of Buckeyes, Wolverines, Suckers, Hoosiers and gamblers, with drunkards of every denomination, their ladies and babies of the same nature, and specifically the dirtiest of the dirty. We had to dip the water for washing from the river in tin basins, soap ourselves from the same cake, and wipe the whole 150 with the same solitary towel rolling over a pin, until it would have been difficult to say whether it was manufactured of hemp, flax, or cotton.

Audubon objected more to dirt than to discomfort, and to danger in its many forms he had habituated himself. In the woods beyond the Ohio, no man ever parted with his firearms: they were indispensable for personal security as for supplying the daily meals. Ruffians of all kinds had sought a refuge in the wilderness and were next-door neighbours—at a distance of many miles—of honest, respectable, and hard-working settlers. When a wanderer knocked at a door in the dusk, he had to take his chance of his reception. One thrilling escape of the naturalist brought him into touch with the Regulators, self-constituted satellites of the law, who anticipated the constitutional sheriffs. The naturalist was belated and lost in the woods, when, guided by the flicker of a light, he came to a log cabin. He had a gruff greeting from a formidable-looking virago. Appearances at the best were not reassuring, and within was seated a wounded Indian, who made significant signs of warning to the new arrival, whenever the lady's back was turned. Audubon foolishly showed the woman a gold watch, and her covetous glances made him regret his folly. However, he supped heartily on buffalo-meat and venison; lying down under his blanket, he tucked himself in with his dog, and felt that his gun was ready to his hand. But fresh looks of warning from the Indian had kept his senses on the alert. Presently the door opened, and two stalwart youths entered. There was no mistaking the evil meaning of their whispered conversation with their mother; but in the meantime they were gorging themselves with venison and whisky. The old woman drank freely also, but she was a seasoned vessel:—

> Judge of my astonishment when I saw this incarnate fiend take a large carving-knife and go to the grind-stone to whet its edge. . . . Her task finished, she walked to her reeling sons and said, 'There, that'll soon settle him! Boys, kill you——, and then for the watch.' . . . All was ready. The infernal hag was advancing slowly, probably contemplating the best way of despatching me, while her sons should be engaged with the Indian.

He was lying with finger on the trigger, ready to fire, when the door opened and two travellers walked in. His tale was told: the Indian "fairly danced with joy": the half-drunken family was secured, when, "having used them as Regulators were wont to use such delinquents, we set fire to the cabin." We should have fancied that to be a delicate paraphrase for stringing them up to any convenient bough. But it appears from the sequel that the mild-mannered Regulators in these parts practised less summary methods. When a habit-and-repute criminal made himself exceptionally objectionable by repeated atrocities, they led him into the solitude of the forest, searched the woods, and surrounded them with a mounted cordon, and then flogged the victim within an inch of his life—or beyond—in the certainty that no one would hear his yells. If he survived, it was a broad hint to be off—the rather that they had proceeded to burn his cabin. If he took the hint, good and well; if not, and he were charged with offences again, the bare suspicion sufficed to hang him.

These Regulators were law-enforcing folk, but naturally the naturalist often found himself in more doubtful company. Before he associated with *voyageurs* and mountainmen on the Upper Missouri, he had made acquaintance among others with Florida wreckers, Tortugas turtlers, and Labrador eggers. The business of the wreckers lay among those keys and creeks in the Mexican Gulf of which we shall hear more in the next few months, now that war has broken out between the Union and Spain.

Shoals, reefs, and shallows make the coasts perilously dangerous, and those wreckers drove a thriving trade, though it could scarcely be called an honourable industry. But they did not, like the Cornishmen or Bretons, lure ships ashore by false lights: they only plundered the vessels that had already come to grief. Audubon found them a very decent set of fellows,—eager to welcome him on board as a passenger, and keen to assist his zoological collections. To his surprise, their vessels were swift, clean, and commodious: they seem to have resembled our fruiterers of thirty years ago, which used to run between the Channel and the Azores. He speaks very differently of the eggers of Labrador; but two of a trade can never agree. The eggers followed a legal business, but they were unmitigated ruffians and inveterate drunkards. Their ill-found sloops were as sea-worn and filthy as any whaler that has been cruising for years in Antarctic waters, without putting into port. They made descents on the breeding-places to freight their barks with fresh eggs,—which might have been legitimate enough. But what roused Audubon's indignation was the ruthless brutality with which they smashed every egg they came across, and trampled the helpless fledglings underfoot. The stench of those breeding-places at the best is bad; but after a visit from those marauders it was simply pestilential. It was some comfort that in their jealousy and by retributive justice, when two gangs met, they invariably fought, making use of their guns as well as, cudgels. Yet the warfare generally wound up with a debauch which made the drunkards the best of friends for the time being. The chapter on the turtlers takes us to the Tortugas, renowned in the annals of pirates and buccaneers, and gives us the most vivid account we have read of the haunts and habits of the turtle. Monsters that ran to several hundred weights were turned by several men with the help of hand-spikes, for the sake of the valuable shells. They would have been ignominiously rejected at "The Ship and Turtle" in Leadenhall Street, and even in Tortugas the flesh sold for less than that of the delicate 30-pounders. One curious fact is recorded. The turtles when surprised invariably made a scramble for the sea, and fought and snapped viciously when intercepted. But when the lady-fish, as Tom Cringle calls her, is depositing her eggs by the score, she lets nothing interfere with that important business. Apparently she must finish her *accouchement coûte qu'il coûte,* and so she falls an easy victim.

The naturalist's outfit for those wanderings in the woods was of the slightest, and characteristic. No wonder that the backwoodsfolk who saw him unpack his bundle of a night were puzzled as to his objects. It contained a shirt, a few powder-canisters, some pounds of shot, a package of drawing-paper, and a box of colours. In all circumstances, unless it were raining hard, he would sit down to sketch, and then sit up of a night over the smouldering log-fire to write up his journal or preserve a skin. Besides the risks he ran from outlaws and Indians, his hairbreadth escapes were innumerable from the accidents and convulsions of the wilderness. Repeatedly he went astray in the woods, when the game had seemed perversely to elude him, and he was brought to the verge of starvation. He fled before forest-fires, entangled among pitfalls and fallen trees, till the distant crackling and subdued but ominous murmur had swelled into an appalling roar, and the fiery blasts from the furnace had become almost intolerable. On one occasion he just intrenched himself in time behind a lagoon, to escape scathless except for scorched skin and burned hair. There are companion pictures of hurricanes in the woods and on the water, which are filled in with extraordinary force, for the scenes seem most realistically to present themselves. In the former case, the hurricane had swept by him, almost within gunshot, following a narrow belt as clearly defined as the track of the cholera-demon through an Indian cantonment. The tornado that cracked the strongest timber like pipe-stems carried with it "a mingled mass of twigs and foliage that obscured the view." When all was over, "the mass of branches, twigs, foliage, and dust was whirled onwards like a cloud of feathers, and on passing disclosed a wide space filled with fallen trees, naked stumps, and heaps of shapeless ruins, which marked the path of the tempest."

Even more impressive, perhaps, is the description of the Florida storm which fortunately surprised him when within half a cable's length of the beach. "The waters drifted like snow: the tough mangroves hid their tops among their roots, and the loud roaring of the waves driven among them blended with the howl of the tempest." Then, by way of contrast and before taking leave of these varied episodes, we may turn to the softer poetry of a forest sunset, for the naturalist has the true inspiration of the poet:—

> The sun was setting with a fiery aspect, and by degrees it sunk in its full circular form, as if giving warning of a sultry morrow. Myriads of insects, delighted at its departure, now filled the air on buzzing wings. Each piping frog arose from the muddy pool in which it had concealed itself: the squirrel retired to its hole, the crow to its roost, and far above, the harsh, croaking voice of the heron announced that, full of anxiety, it was wending its way towards the miry interior of some distant swamp. Now the woods began to resound to the shrill cries of the owl; and the breeze, as it swept among the columnar stems of the forest trees, came laden with heavy and chilling dews.

In short, he makes us understand and sympathise with no little of the fascination of swamp and forest for the born woodsman. There could hardly be a more startling change of habits when most reluctantly he came over to Europe to tout for subscriptions for his great ornithological work. But Americans, at once cultured and rich, were few, and there was no help for it. Doubtless he was partly actuated by honourable ambition, but it was chiefly by a grave sense of duty. In some respects he was an indifferent husband. His wife could never tie the rover to her apron-strings, and as for sticking to the desk and counting-house, that was altogether out of the question. Nevertheless, he was the most affectionate of husbands and the most doating of fathers. Now he saw his way, though a very disagreeable one, to making satisfactory provision for them. We are safe to say it needed more constancy, if not more courage, than all the perils and hardships he had faced in the woods. He came to England, whither his fame had preceded him, with good introductions, which were hospitably honoured. He found a host of congenial spirits in ama-

teurs, artists, and men of science. Wherever he went, almost without exception, he was offered a home, and he need seldom have put up at a hotel or dined alone in his lodgings. Moreover, he found generous friends and patrons, nor had he any of the unpleasant experiences of Johnson in the anteroom of Lord Chesterfield. But never was man more heartily home-sick: he even looked back with fond longing to the pestilential Floridan lagoons, where alligators were the stepping-stones and watersnakes the foot-snares. The deerskin shirt was easier wear than the swallow-tail coat; if there was one thing he did detest, it was a ceremonial dinner; and he looked forward with the apprehension of a shy schoolboy to meeting a statesman or even a great nobleman. Yet there was not a touch of vulgarity in that: it was merely a want of familiarity and the imaginative dread of the unknown. Audubon was intensely imaginative and emotional: the nerves that never failed him before savage or bear were tremulous in the Horrors of ceremonious society. But he kept these inner secrets for his private note-books, and was stoical in society to appearance, as an Indian at the stake. Frequently there was the surprise of delightful reaction. Like Roland Graeme when ushered into the presence of Murray, he had much dreaded a visit to the descendant of the Regent's trusted ally at Dalmahoy, for Lord Morton had held high office at Court. He was greatly relieved to find that the veteran courtier, confined to his bath-chair by rheumatism and gout, was an object of compassion rather than terror. Yet it would be a mistake to fancy that he ever showed awkwardness. He had all the easy grace of his French parentage, and the stately dignity of his Spanish blood. And he had the dignity, besides, of a self-respecting man, with a discriminating sense of his own gifts and superiority. He knew well where he excelled, as he was equally alive to his artistic shortcomings.

We have spoken of his "touting" for subscriptions, and the trivial expression is at once applicable and misleading. Needless to say that he never stooped to humiliation, still less to servility. But, on the other hand, he experienced the mortifications, the disappointments, and the delays which always await those who must stoop to make attacks on other men's purses. Rich squires and stately nobles who were free with their dinners and their wines were slow to come forward as subscribers. Curators of museums and college librarians, eloquent of praise of his drawings, regretted the narrow means which compelled their institutions to severe economy. Subscribers who had signed engagements in moments of expansion, shamelessly repudiated them. On the whole, he did fairly well in that travelling business; but sometimes a sojourn in such a town as York was a dead loss, and he was detained in Paris for many weeks waiting the good pleasure or the caprice of royal patrons.

The impressions which the England of seventy years ago made on a quick-sighted American are curiously interesting. On the long voyage, delayed by baffling winds and protracted calms, he had beguiled the time by studying the habits of sharks, porpoises, and dolphins, of sea-birds and migrants. But he was heartily tired of it all when he sighted Cape Clear, and his soul was gladdened by the hedgerows of Wales, as the vessel tacked up the Irish Channel.

Landing at Liverpool, he found himself, at once one of the family in the hospitable households of the Rathbones and Roscoes. In their houses he made useful and agreeable acquaintances; but the first of his meetings with really illustrious Englishmen was that with Lord Stanley. His feelings before it came off are eminently illustrative of his temperament. His lordship was the statesman and future Premier; but he seems to have been nearly as enthusiastic a naturalist as his father the thirteenth Earl, who made the famous collections at Knowsley. "My head was full of Lord Stanley. I am a very poor fool, to be sure, to be troubled at the idea of meeting an English *gentleman,* when those I have met have been in kindness, manners, talent, all I could desire." When his lordship entered the room, "my hair, and I have enough, stood on end, I am sure." Lord Stanley cordially shook hands, saying easily—as might have been expected—"I am glad to see you;" and "the words and manner put me at once at my ease." A few minutes more and the dreaded visitor was kneeling on the carpet, turning over the drawings. "He is a great naturalist; and in an instant he was exclaiming, 'Fine!' 'Beautiful!' . . . I forgot he was Lord Stanley. I knew only he too loved nature." Indeed Audubon was a very singular compound of nervous modesty and innocent vanity. He reminds us of Fanny Burney over the *début* of *Evelina,* in the sensitiveness to criticism, unaffected in his case, and in the voluptuous modesty with which he eagerly reports all the civil and flattering things that were said to him.

Liverpool and Manchester were made tolerable by cordial welcomes and by sojourns in rural mansions in the neighbourhoods. But during his long stay in the British Isles, Edinburgh was his residence of predilection: Scott himself scarcely expresses greater affection or admiration for "mine own romantic town." Indeed Audubon came to it steeped in adoration of Scott, for he had been under the spell of the Magician since his boyhood. He stood up on the roof of the Hawick mail, vainly stretching his neck for one glimpse of the chimneys of Abbotsford. He wishes patriotically that he could have transplanted the Wizard to Kentucky, to have immortalised in romance its semi-tropical woodlands, with the magnolias and the deer, the eagles and the songsters, before they are swept away in the rising flood of industry, commerce, and agriculture. Nor can we have a more striking proof of the intellectual lustre of the Edinburgh of that radiant day than in the constellation of remarkable personages that sparkle in those journals. There is nothing to compare to it in the writer's reminiscences of London or Paris, though undoubtedly that may be due in some measure to the more concrete society of the smaller northern capital. There the illustrious stranger was launched at once in an intellectual world, where he saw all that was worth the seeing. We make a few selections and extracts which should have special interest for Scots, though we should be glad to quote the journal almost *in toto.* Comfortably established in lodgings in George Street, his lifelong enthusiasm for Scott sent him straight to the theatre to see *Rob Roy.* We presume that Murray was personating the Bailie, and that Mackay was playing in the part of the Dougal Creature. At any rate, Audubon was delighted: the Highland drama was put on the stage just as he had imagined it; he protests that *Rob Roy* should always be seen in Auld Reekie as *Tartuffe*

at the Français. Next day he goes to leave a letter for Jeffrey: being Sunday, Jeffrey was probably at Craigcrook. But he was shown into his sanctum, where he was staggered by the masses of books and letters, the beautiful paintings, and, above all, by the piles of unopened parcels addressed to the editor of the *Edinburgh.* " 'What have I done,' I thought, 'compared to what this man has done and has to do? I much long to see the famous critic.' " When he did see him, he was disappointed. "His looks were shrewd, but I thought his eyes almost cunning. . . . He never came near me, and I never went near him, for if he was Jeffrey, I was Audubon." And he was annoyed besides, because as Basil Hall, who was contemplating his American tour, persistently turned the conversation in that direction, so Jeffrey always adroitly diverted it to indifferent subjects. But Audubon had been one of the victims of the Edinburgh Reviewers; the men had no love for each other. While he worshipped the romantic genius of Scott, he had little sympathy with the cold intellect of the critic.

In an important interview he made the acquaintance of Lizars, who first undertook the engraving for him, though subsequently their relations were strained or interrupted. "I slowly unbuckled my portfolio, and with my heart like a stone, held up a drawing. Mr Lizars rose from his seat, exclaiming, 'My God, I never saw anything like this before!' " Next came James Wilson, that other American ornithologist, and Sir William Jardine and Mr Selby—with the two last he had much friendly and ornithological intercourse—and afterwards "the famous Professor Wilson of *Blackwood* fame, I might almost say the author of *Blackwood's Magazine,*" and the elder brother of the ornithologist. Thereupon he ejaculates, in genuine Boswellian vein, "How proud I feel that in Edinburgh, the seat of learning, science, and solidity of judgment, I am liked and am received so kindly!" He returned the Professor's call next day:—

> I did not even ask if Professor Wilson was in. No; I simply told the man to say that Mr Audubon from America wished to speak with him. In a moment I was conducted to a room where I wished that all that had been written in it was my own to remember, to enjoy, to profit by; but I had not been here many minutes before a sweet child, a happy daughter of this great man, asked me to go up-stairs, saying, "Papa, will be there in a minute;" and truly, almost at once, the Professor came in, with freedom and kindness of manner, life in his eye and benevolence in his heart.

There is a humorously amusing account of a banquet on St Andrew's Day, when the American was introduced to the Scottish *cuisine* of the olden time, followed by a second substantial dinner *à l'Anglaise.* There he was made temporarily miserable by the prospect of having to return thanks for his health, which he did in the fewest possible words; and then no less a person than Sir William Allan entertained the company by imitating the humming of a bumblebee, and chasing it about the room, in the manner of John Ballantyne with the souter and his blackbird. *Autres temps, autres moeurs!* Apropos to buzzing bees, Audubon writes a fortnight afterwards that, much as he found to enjoy, the dissipation, the painting, and his incessant correspondence makes his head feel like an immense hornet's-nest. It was little wonder. He still allowed himself only four hours' sleep, and worked indefatigably at his easel, even in the dark northern December. His rapidity and facility were marvellous. He tells us he finished an otter, which had a great success, in thirteen hours. The laborious work sounds like drudgery, yet he always gave soul and character to the birds and beasts. There is an infinity of suggestive romance in the pathos and comedy of his sylvan studies. Like Joseph Wolf, he knew the art of enveloping the night-prowlers in shadow, dim moonlight, and mystery. As a tangible and material proof of his mastership, for drawings that had cost him but a day or two of toil £100 or even £200 were offered. He did well as it was; but it would seem he might have made his fortune had he renounced scientific ambition for lucrative engagements.

He was sufficiently nervous when he made the acquaintance of Dr Brewster. Reading to him, on the first introduction, a paper on the habits of the carrion crow, "About midway, my nervousness affected my respiration. I paused a moment, and he was good enough to say it was highly interesting. . . . I felt the penetrating looks and keen observation of the learned man before me, so that the cold sweat started from me." But that was nothing to his excitement and emotion when at length he saw the author of *Waverley* in the flesh. The meeting had been looked forward to, and longed for, and deferred, like that of Boswell with Johnson. Here is the entry in the journal on that memorable Monday:—

> I was painting diligently when Captain Hall came in and said, "Put on your coat and come with me to Sir Walter Scott: he wishes to see you now." In a moment I was ready, for I really believe my coat and hat came to me instead of my going to them. My heart trembled. I longed for the meeting, yet wished it over. Had not his wondrous pen penetrated my soul with the consciousness that here was a genius from God's hand? . . . Sir Walter came forward, pressed my hand, and said "he was glad to have the honour of meeting me." His long, loose, silvery locks struck me: he looked like. Franklin at his best. He also reminded me of Benjamin West: he had the great benevolence of William Roscoe about him, and a kindness most prepossessing. I watched his movements as I would those of a celestial being: his long, heavy, white eyebrows struck me forcibly. . . . There was much conversation. I talked little, but, believe me, I listened and observed.

On the following day, when Sir Walter shook hands with him at a meeting of the Royal Society, "the mark of attention was observed by other members, who looked at me as if I had been a distinguished stranger." One other extract, and, reluctantly as Audubon, we must tear ourselves away from Edinburgh. Indeed, there is nothing of equal interest recorded elsewhere, except when he met Bewick at Newcastle, and perhaps when he was presented to Cuvier in Paris. Although he seems to have preferred worshipping in the woods to services in temples made with hands, he went to church in George Street on one noteworthy occasion:—

> But Sydney Smith preached. Oh, what a soul there must be in the body of that great man! What sweet yet energetic thoughts, what goodness he must possess! It was a sermon to *me*. He made me smile, and he made me think deeply. He pleased me at times by painting my foibles with due care, and again I felt the colour come to my cheeks as he portrayed my sins. I left the church, full of veneration not only towards God, but towards the wonderful man who so beautifully illustrates his noblest handiwork.

Much as we admire Sydney Smith's versatile talents, we must say, as Dugald Dalgetty said to Argyle in the marquis's dungeon, that we never heard so much good of him as a preacher before.

The most eloquent and sympathetic tribute of a compatriot to the wonderful creative genius of the peasant-born Bewick is to be found in Howitt's "Visits to Remarkable Places"; but Audubon, with his deeper and more technical acquaintance with nature, does not yield to Howitt in unstinted admiration for "the wonderful man. I call him wonderful because I am sincerely of opinion that his work on wood is superior to anything ever attempted in ornithology." For the sake of Bewick the banks of Tyne had been as much enchanted ground to him as those of Tweed for the love of Scott. He saw the venerable engraver for the first time, and several times afterwards, in "a half-clean cotton nightcap, tinged with the smoke of the place," and he was not disenchanted. From the first they met and talked on the footing of old and familiar friends, for each had studied and appreciated the work of the other. His reception by Cuvier and Geoffrey St Hilaire in Paris, though courteous and even cordial, was less gratifying. It was mortifying to the American "woodsman" to find that these illustrious French *savants* had never heard of him or of his ornithological labours; but French appreciation is not cosmopolitan, and is limited by its ignorance of foreign languages.

We shall not touch on the elaborate journals kept faithfully as ever on the Upper Missouri and in Labrador. Though full of incident and abounding in reminiscences of perils, from storm and flood, from fevers and dysenteries, from wild Indians and wild animals, they merely amplify in somewhat monotonous detail the picturesque retrospects of the "Episodes." Temperate habits, iron health, and long days in the open air stood the great naturalist in good stead to the last. Whatever the date of his birth may have been, he was certainly well over the threescore years and ten when he died in New York in 1851, of no active disease, but of a sudden and easy collapse. He lies in a beautiful suburban cemetery, among the flowers and beneath the trees he loved so well, and under a stately monument erected to his memory by the New York Academy of Sciences.

Francis H. Herrick (essay date 1926)

SOURCE: An introduction to *Delineations of American*

Audubon's wife, Lucy Bakewell.

Scenery and Character, by John James Audubon, G. A. Baker & Co., 1926, pp. ix-xix.

[*In the following excerpt, Herrick discusses Audubon's life and works, focusing on the "Episodes" in his* Ornithological Biography.]

Beyond a doubt John James Audubon was one of the most versatile and striking characters that has ever appeared in our history. In ardor and enthusiasm for the study of nature perhaps no one has ever surpassed him, and no one can measure the influence which his talents and devotion have exerted upon his favorite pursuits.

Until recent years Audubon had been regarded as the Melchizedek of American natural history, nothing having been certainly known up to that time concerning his birth, his parentage and early life. Then the personal letters and family documents of his father, Lieutenant Jean Audubon, were suddenly discovered in surprising abundance at Couëron in France, where, in a villa on the right bank of the Loire, they had lain unnoticed for nearly an hundred years. The veil of mystery which had so completely enveloped the life of his illustrious son was suddenly lifted and we were enabled to form a more just estimate of his character and work.

"America, my country," whose life and scenery Audubon

never tired of celebrating, has not forgotten him. A lofty peak in the Rocky Mountains, American counties and towns, as well as parks and streets in American cities now bear his name; and the far-famed and beneficent National Association of Audubon Societies for the Protection of Wild Birds and Animals in recent years has made his name a household word throughout the land which he loved and whose bird and wild life he has depicted in unfading colors.

Notwithstanding Audubon's great fame and success as an animal painter and descriptive writer, the public has never had access to his work in cheap editions. It should be noticed that his accounts of the birds were much more detailed than those of his famous contemporary, Alexander Wilson, and that his publications were projected on a large and expensive scale. It is therefore hardly surprising that no reprint of even the smaller edition of his **Birds** has been made for half a century.

Audubon's greatest monument in the fields of natural history and the graphic arts is the series of four-hundred and thirty-five double elephant folio plates that was published in Edinburgh and London from 1826 to 1838 and called **The Birds of America,** together with the five volumes of text entitled **Ornithological Biography,** which accompanied this and were issued at Edinburgh in 1831-39. Audubon had represented on his plates 1,065 life-size figures of 489 supposedly distinct species of American birds, besides hundreds of examples of American plants, insects and other animals.

To relieve the tedium of descriptive ornithology Audubon introduced articles of a general nature into his Biographies, and called them "Episodes," or "Delineations of American Scenery and Character," one such following every five articles which described the species of birds depicted in a corresponding "part" of his plates. . . .

These off-hand sketches mainly relate to events between 1808 and 1834, and as sidelights on pioneer life in America, particularly of the Ohio and Mississippi Vallies, they have a perennial interest. The reader will find numerous tales of adventure in the wilderness and on the frontier, particularly in Kentucky, which for local coloring, vivid presentment and personal charm have seldom been equalled. Audubon was a keen observer of men and things as well as of birds and animal life, and when writing down his experiences on the spot, as was his invariable custom after 1820, he was as truthful with his pen as with his pencil and brush. There is a wild and placid beauty in this description of the Ohio, his favorite river,—*La Belle Rivière* as the compatriots of his ancestors had called it at an earlier day:

> As night came, sinking in darkness the broader portions of the river, our minds became affected by strong emotions, and wandered far beyond the present moments. The tinkling of bells told us that the cattle which bore them were gently roving from valley to valley in search of food, or returning to their distant homes. The hooting of the Great Owl, or the muffled noise of its wings as it sailed smoothly over the stream, were matters of interest to us; so was the sound of the

boatman's horn, as it came winding more and more softly from afar. When daylight returned, many songsters burst forth with echoing notes, more and more mellow to the listening ear. Here and there the lonely cabin of a squatter struck the eye, giving note of commencing civilization. The crossing of the stream by a deer foretold how soon the hills would be covered with snow.

With wonderful vividness also can we see the interior of the log-cabin in Kentucky, where he and his young son sought refuge on a stormy night in the forest, and to which the hospitable young woodsman had just brought his bride; the coon-hunter loading his rifle, or the bells with their beaux at "A Ball in Newfoundland." When returning from St. Geneviève in what is now Missouri, in the spring of 1811, with his knapsack, gun and dog as his only baggage and companions, and when following the old Indian trails, he met with an adventure which he thought had nearly cost him his life; and that, he said, was the only instance, during upwards of twenty-five years in which his wanderings extended to every part of the country, that he felt his life to have been in danger from his fellow man. "Will you believe," he said when writing in 1839, "that not many miles from the place where this adventure happened, and where fifteen years ago no habitation belonging to civilized man was to be expected, and very few ever seen, large roads are now laid out, cultivation has converted the woods into fertile fields, taverns have been erected, and much of what we Americans call comfort is to be met with. So fast does improvement proceed in our abundant and free country."

Audubon foresaw with great concern the alteration which cultivation would produce along the delightful banks of his favorite stream, as he beheld "the surplus population of Europe coming to assist in the destruction of the forest" then "fast disappearing under the axe by day and the fire by night"; and he longed to have his incomparable country adequately portrayed by competent hands ere it was too late and when, as he would say, it was fresh from the Creator's own hand. He, at least, would do all in his power to portray the birds of his adopted land in their characteristic attitudes and environments, whether moving or at rest, amid appropriate foliage, flowers and fruits,—all holding up the mirror to nature in the accuracy of truth and in beauty as well. These "Delineations" were to be added also to give his work a more intimate and human touch as well as to beguile the reader. Such an ambition was enough to call out all of the man's ardent enthusiasm, resourcefulness and iron tenacity of purpose; but the canvass was too large, and Audubon was obliged to give up his intercalated sketches in order to make way for the new materials relating more directly to ornithology, which were constantly growing under his hand.

When Audubon, through dint of many failures and hard knocks, had come to the full realization of his mission, and when, at the age of thirty-five, his serious travels over the New and later over the Old World began, he turned every experience to good account. Wherever he slept, whether in the forest or in the settlements, there for the time he was at home and there his "observatory nerves" and pencil were at work. At commercial book-keeping he had proved

a total failure, but in the care with which he posted his "books of nature" he had few equals. Every night, in spite of bodily fatigue or the many plausible excuses which are ever ready at hand, he would write out in pen and ink a full and careful record of his experiences of the day. Audubon was always the observer and the doer, and perhaps at times the actor as well, rather than the thinker, but he kept an honest record of himself, and the power of expression which he thus attained stood him in good stead when at the age of forty-six he came to produce his Bird-Biographies in Europe.

One hundred years from the day and date on which this is written, John James Audubon was at sea, aboard the schooner Delos, captain Joseph Hatch, of Kennebunk, Maine, which had sailed from New Orleans on the seventh of May and was bound for Liverpool with a cargo of cotton. Though he had then attained his forty-first year he was known to but few of his countrymen, yet his handsome face and French accent, aside from his flowing hair and nether garments of liberal dimensions, would have marked him anywhere as an unusual character. He had fortified himself with valuable letters, but his most important credentials were the fruits of a life's campaign,—his original paintings of American birds, contained in sundry large portfolios that constituted his principal baggage. Having been denied the encouragement and recognition which he craved in the land of his adoption mainly through the jealousy of a few individuals at Philadelphia, who could not brook a rival to the fame of Alexander Wilson, Audubon had now resolutely turned his face to the Old World, and in London or Paris he hoped to find an engraver of his drawings as well as patrons through whose aid he could bring his labors to the light of day.

The story of this unknown foreigner's struggles and eventual success in the Europe of that period, which in an economic sense still belonged essentially to the eighteenth century, is one of the strangest romances in the history of science and literature of the past hundred years. In less than a week after his landing in Liverpool, unheralded and not over supplied with funds, he was invited to exhibit his pictures at the Royal Institution and was immediately proclaimed as a great American genius. It was not long before this artist-naturalist from the woods of the New World became the social lion of the day. At Edinburgh he attracted the ablest scientific and literary characters of the British Athens and he was liberally patronized by the aristocracy. There Lizars engraved the first of his mammoth plates,—the American Turkey Cock,—and showed him a proof of it on the twenty-eighth of November, 1826. Good copies of this, the most sought after, and possibly the rarest, of all Audubon's plates, together with number eleven, the "Great American Hen and Young," which was engraved by Lizars also, have brought upwards of five hundred dollars in America in recent years. Audubon was compelled to transfer his publication to London, where under the Havells, father and son, it took a fresh start in the spring of 1827, and where under the skilful hands of Robert Havell, Junior, it was brought to a successful completion eleven years later.

After Audubon had weathered the critical summer of

1827 his prospects brightened and honors came to him in rapid succession. In 1828 he was elected a member of the Linnaean Society, and a fellow of the Royal Society in 1830. In the latter year he brought his wife to England, and in 1832 his elder son, Victor, took charge of his publication in London. Audubon's return with his wife, who was English born and bred, marked one of the happiest periods of his life. For ten years she had worked for the support and upbringing of their children in order that her husband's hands might be free to follow his true vocation; never for a moment had she doubted his genius, and was not her judgment now vindicated before all the world? It is safe to say that without the sterling qualities of Lucy Audubon her husband's name would not have reached far beyond the scenes of his trading ventures of the South and West.

Audubon learned much from his early experience in writing for publication in 1827, when he was bitterly assailed, as many thought, by those who had poured cold water on his plans at Philadelphia in 1824; but this and other attacks which followed probably helped him in the end. At all events, in his powers of expression, Audubon was not at this time the illiterate novice that certain antagonists had intimated, as his journalizing will amply testify. John Wilson, or "Christopher North," who recognized Audubon's great talents from the first, and gave him much needed literary advice, devoted fifty pages of Blackwood's Magazine to eulogistic reviews of the first volume of the *Ornithological Biography.* "Audubon," he said, "who had written but little even in his native tongue, under a powerful motive took to writing English; and he was not long in learning to write it well, not only with fluency, but eloquence. . . . Not a particle of jealousy is in his composition; a sin, that, alas! seems too easily to beset too many of the most gifted spirits in literature and science."

Wilson was essentially right in his estimate of Audubon with whom, as with every one else, more than genius was needed for good writing; his checkered career had been rich in experience; he had gone to nature, the fountainhead, for his materials, and once his mission was clearly seen the spur to fulfil it was never lacking; but having been denied an education in either the sciences or the classics, he stood in need of aid as well as advice. Both he later received in full measure from William Macgillivray, who in addition to correcting his letterpress supplied the anatomical details of the *Ornithological Biography;* and the aid thus received was acknowledged in a way satisfactory to both.

In the course of an interrupted residence of thirteen years in the British Isles Audubon made three extended journeys through the United States, which occupied nearly five years (1829-30, 1831-34 and 1836-37) in search of new birds and subscribers. In 1833 he chartered his own vessel and sailed for Labrador with five assistants, while the spring of 1837 found him aboard a Government vessel bound from New Orleans for Galveston in the newly established Republic of Texas.

In the earlier and more critical years of his undertaking Audubon constantly resorted to his palette and brush and painted his way to liberty, or to what was then its equivalent, freedom from debt. "There are moments," he said in 1835, "and they are not far between, when, thinking of my present enormous undertaking, I wonder how I have been able to support the extraordinary amount of monies paid for the work alone, without taking cognizance of my family and my expeditions, which ever and anon travelling as we are from place to place and country to country are also very great." Yet Audubon supported himself and his family during their long residence aboard, met all the obligations incurred in the publication of a work which cost upwards of one hundred thousand dollars to produce, a sum that meant a large fortune in the first third of the last century, and with fame and a modest competence returned to the land of his choice in 1839.

Audubon's great work was now accomplished and he anticipated a well earned leisure at home; but his restless energy still drove him on and he entered at once upon two formidable tasks, the bringing out of his "small" or octavo revised edition of *The Birds,* and the beginning of the delineation of *The Quadrupeds,* in which he was aided by his two sons, and the accompanying text of which was written by his friend Bachman. In 1842 he settled upon his estate in what is now the portion of New York City called Audubon Park, which he deeded to his wife and named for her "Minnie's land"; the name, said his granddaughter, coming from the fact that her father and uncle always used the Scotch name "Minnie" for mother. This was in Carmansville, later known as Washington Heights, where he purchased between thirty and forty acres of land which extended a thousand feet along the Hudson River from the present One hundred and Fifty-fifth to One hundred and Fifty-eighth Streets, and reached to the easterly limits of the village at the old Bloomingdale Road, near the present Amsterdam Avenue.

Though feeling the weight of his laborious years and discouraged by his family, who felt for his safety, in March, 1843, Audubon set out with four friends and assistants for one of his greatest journeys, to the region of the Upper Missouri and Yellowstone Rivers, then little known; and although unable to attain his long contemplated goal, the Rocky Mountains, he returned in the autumn with many new birds and mammals. To judge from his portraits, Audubon aged greatly between 1848 and 1850, when at the age of sixty-five he had the appearance of a broken and feeble man; and he died at "Minnie's Land" on January 27, 1851, before the completion of his sixty-sixth year. His grave, now in Trinity Cemetery, New York, is marked by a beautiful Runic cross in white marble which was erected by popular subscription and dedicated in 1893.

To revert to the mystery that was so successfully spread over the early life of John James Audubon that probably not a single member of his family in America ever learned the facts: Audubon at one time declared that he belonged to every country, at another that the precise period of his birth was a complete enigma to him, and, stranger yet, he was not adverse to being considered much older than he really was. The first definite date which he gave of his own history was that of his marriage to Lucy Bakewell on June 12, 1808. His granddaughter, Maria R. Audubon, accepted the late tradition, without a shred of historical evidence in support of it, that he was a Louisianian by birth and first saw light on a certain plantation on the north side of Lake Pontchartrain about 1780. Fables, like traditions are commonly of slow growth, but when they have become entrenched in the popular mind by a process of gradual absorption their tenacity of life is remarkable. No doubt the false halo of mystery and tradition which has gathered about the life of this remarkable man will be cherished and repeated by the uninformed for many years to come.

Audubon's life offers a striking example of the power which circumstance and environment can exert in awakening dormant capacity and in calling into action every talent which heredity has supplied. Long thought to be indolent by some of his neighbors because he did not stick behind the counter or follow their pursuits, and also "suthin' peculiar-some," as Dennis Hanks said of young Abe Lincoln, Audubon at the age of forty suddenly emerges from obscurity and is soon recognized as one of the great workers of the world. Who can say whether his success in the end was not due as much to a winning personality and enthusiasm as to his remarkable talents?

Donald Culross Peattie, Robert Cushman Murphy, and Mark Van Doren   (dialogue date 1942)

SOURCE: "John James Audubon: American Scenery and Character," in *The New Invitation to Learning,* edited by Mark Van Doren, Random House, 1942, pp. 297-310.

[*Murphy and Peattie were American nature writers. Van Doren was an influential American writer and critic. In the following dialogue, originally broadcast on CBS Radio as part of the* Invitation to Learning *series, they discuss the "Episodes" of Audubon's* Ornithological Biography, *collected in 1926 under the title* Delineations of American Scenery and Character.]

John James Audubon is best known for his paintings of birds, but he was also a writer who had something unique to say. In his **Ornithological Biography,** which followed the great folio entitled **Birds of America,** he alternated descriptions of birds with descriptions of the country which they beautified; and it is these latter sketches, called by him **Delineations of American Scenery and Character,** that will survive along with his plates of the wild turkey and the swallow-tailed kite, the humming bird and the downy woodpecker. Audubon, coming in his youth from France to America, saw the New World in its golden age of maximum promise. The time was the early nineteenth century, when the country, feverish with expansion and ecstatic over its liberty, shone everywhere with confident hope in a limitless future. Audubon in fact saw this America more clearly than any of its natives did; for he brought with him the legends of a bright new world which Europe had been repeating for centuries, and which no experience with the reality had been permitted to tarnish. Many Americans at the moment were already tired and disillusioned, but Audubon never was. Traveling on foot and by horse or boat through the valley of the Ohio, through the then frontier, he saw everything in Homeric proportions, as if this were indeed the age of gold and these the progenitors of a perfect race to come. The result is his **Delinea-**

tions, than which no more infectious description survives of America in her golden morning. . . .

DONALD CULROSS PEATTIE

ROBERT CUSHMAN MURPHY

MARK VAN DOREN

Van Doren: Audubon is a great man for many reasons. One is this book we are discussing today, although I am sure our discussion will go far beyond the **Delineations.** It is to me one of the most interesting of all books that describe America. It describes both the landscape and the people of America as of a century and a quarter ago, and it has a quality of admiration, love, energy, which has always endeared the author to me. But I am not an ornithologist, I am not a natural historian, and so I do not have the perspective which enables me to be confident that this is even an important aspect of Audubon. Mr. Murphy, is it so to you?

Murphy: There is no more important aspect of Audubon from the standpoint of American history, because of all the nature writers who pictured the country in its pristine days no one has left us the composite picture of Audubon. He saw America when it was still an Eden, the last garden of that sort remaining in the temperate world. He shows us by what he records that the destructive changes of the first two centuries matched in no way the damage that has been done since his time. There is no other such picture of the dawn of history in the United States.

Van Doren: Mr. Peattie, Mr. Murphy praises Audubon chiefly for his historical value, for being accurate—I dare say a little more than accurate—in his description of an America which once existed. I don't know whether I am quoting you properly or not, Mr. Murphy.

Murphy: Yes, that is quite correct.

Van Doren: Your emphasis was upon his accuracy with respect to a vanished America.

Murphy: Precisely.

Van Doren: Mr. Peattie, do you think that his description continues to have special interest or validity?

Peattie: It is still very true. I know that there are types of Americans which have vanished. We're not going to meet Daniel Boone anywhere, and we're not going to meet his exact like. But as you read in Audubon, in his **Delineations of American Character and Scenery,** you realize that though the scenery has changed somewhat, and sometimes for the worse, the American character is still there, and I am happy to say that the American character is no worse. In some respects it is better, but it is the same character.

Van Doren: Do you say so from personal observation—from having lived in certain places—or is it a faith that you have? I happen to agree with you, but I was wondering what your evidence is.

Peattie: It doesn't matter where you live or what experiences you have. Human character, American character, could be found just as well in a cross-section of modern

America as in his time; you could find it in Brooklyn or you could find it in Oregon. If Audubon is telling a true story it should be the same, and our measure of whether he was telling a true story or not is our own observation—yours and mine. What is it like when you talk to a taxi-driver? Audubon never saw a taxi-driver, but just the same he is a human being, and Audubon was himself an intensely human person. He had all the human faults in excess, and he had the human virtues in excess. He was so human a being that he wore himself out at a comparatively early age and died without his full mental faculties. He burnt himself out in the some sixty-five years that he lived; he consumed himself in passionate living.

Van Doren: In these **Delineations** he obviously is very much in love with the people that he finds, as he is in love with the birds.

Peattie: He loved everybody.

Van Doren: In other words, he is inclined to give the benefit of every doubt to the individuals and the groups whom he meets.

Peattie: That is right. And at the same time if you read his original journals—the notes he kept from day to day—you find him often in a highly crotchety state of mind. He hasn't any money, his shoes are worn out, his feet are wet, he has no powder for his gun, the drawing he is making of a bird is spoiled—everything has gone wrong that day, and a great many people have insulted him. He was excessively sensitive to insult, being an artist.

Murphy: He says himself that no one could keep him down, that the only time in all his life when he was depressed for more than a few moments was when he lost his daughter and his daughter-in-law, or when the rats ate up his 120 or more drawings at Henderson, Kentucky. That, of course, was an advantage in the end, because he did them over much better than they were done the first time.

Van Doren: Nothing could ever discourage him.

Peattie: Well, not quite. Dr. Murphy and I were very interested to discover that in a Japanese book there was a description of Audubon and his experience with the rats.

Murphy: It was a translation of Samuel Smiles's old book, *Self Help.*

Peattie: That's right. And therefore it is a universal story; it appeals to all peoples at all times. When he had met with an adversity, he simply was made the stronger by overcoming it.

Van Doren: Mr. Peattie, you seem to refer to two stages of an account written by Audubon. You refer to his own journals, kept currently with his explorations, and to these **Delineations,** many of which seem clearly to have been written years afterwards.

Peattie: They were written years afterward, and the two accounts seem almost to contradict each other at times. Then you say: Which is the true one? And of course they're both true. The point is that when we have encounters on the street and someone is rude and we're out of

money and jostled along, we are experiencing things that we wish we were out of at the moment, but at the same time we are living that experience. Say it is on Fifth Avenue. Years later, were you to describe Fifth Avenue, you wouldn't stress the fact that you had no money that day and that somebody was cross to you and you were jostled on the street. You would describe how the flags were lifted by the wind that is forever sweeping up it and how the crowds are forever surging backward and forward. Well, just so did Audubon, when describing American nature and American people, have the actual experiences of intimate contact; then, many years later, he recollected the scene and did what any good artist should do, he selected and composed. That is why we have two separate accounts. It wasn't until recently that most of the original journals, the ones that I might call the almost annoyed ones, came to life.

Van Doren: A man describing a people is always describing himself, isn't he?

Peattie: Oh, very distinctly. He is describing his own moods. But then so was Keats when he was listening to the nightingale. You wouldn't have the faintest idea how a nightingale sang, but you know a lot more about Keats. Well, Audubon was completely an artist by temperament. He became a scientist by training, and consequently he is forever describing himself.

Murphy: He took out what he put in.

Peattie: That's right.

Murphy: And he was a man of very rapid combustion, as you said before.

Peattie: But is that not true of all artists?

Murphy: It is true of all creative individuals.

Peattie: Sinclair Lewis describes the American scene, and his description is true; it is called "photographically accurate," and so it is. But it is also the most accurate photograph of Sinclair Lewis. That's why we read it. Let me point out, Mr. Van Doren, what I feel is very important here—that Audubon was an artist. I mean a graphic artist, a painter. Therefore, he was taught or he taught himself to observe with the most minute detail. Very few writers, myself included, know how to observe in that way. It so happens that he was also able to write. I don't mean that he was a great writer. He merely had a great subject. But it is just because he was taught to observe like a scientist and an artist, minutely, that he is a much better depicter of the American scene than most ordinary writers would be.

Van Doren: I should say, incidentally, challenging you, that your own books are very brilliant at description and they all seem to me accurate. But you refer to him as a great artist. We have not, so far, even mentioned the fact that most people know him for his **Birds of America,** which is a volume or a series of volumes containing pictures of birds. Would you say, Mr. Murphy, that he is a great artist in general or that he is merely a good painter of birds?

Murphy: I think he is a great artist whose work with birds has never been surpassed, and I believe that artists today, including those who belong even to the most modernist schools, have a constantly continuing appreciation of Audubon's work. Frank Benson, who is known the world over as a painter and etcher of birds among other subjects, a man with the finest academic training as an artist, says that Audubon as a painter of birds, by and large, has never been equaled; and Paul Manship, the sculptor, feels exactly the same way about him. He has many of his birds of prey on the walls of his own studio.

Van Doren: That judgment is a judgment of Audubon apart from his subject matter?

Murphy: As an artist. Precisely!

Peattie: Well, we can't forget that Audubon was a painter of mammals and of sporting scenes, of still life and of portraits.

Van Doren: What about his paintings of other subjects? Not that we want to get away from the birds; we shall come back to them. Have you seen very many such paintings?

Murphy: I've seen portraits and I've seen the mammals. There is a large oil, a deer, at the Brooklyn Museum, and there are many smaller paintings in the American Museum of Natural History, in several media.

Peattie: I know some of those, and I also know some of his portrait work. It is true that he never set up to be a great portraitist. He painted portraits merely in order to make enough money to be able to go on painting birds. But he loved painting the portraits just the same. Whether or not he loved the subject when he started out, he got excited about it; and he is a very vigorous portrait painter.

Van Doren: You mentioned once his having to do all sorts of painting, even on sidewalks, for a living or for money to go on with his explorations.

Peattie: I don't mean he painted on the sidewalks. I mean that he sat by the side of the road and would paint anybody who came by. Or he would ask some picturesque old codger around town to sit for him; that would attract a crowd, and then he would begin selling his pictures; that would give him enough to go on 100 miles and see more birds.

Van Doren: He would do anything in order to get on with his birds. I remember, I think from your *Life of Audubon,* the fact that even at the age of nine he was being beaten by his father, in France, because he insisted upon drawing birds rather than studying Latin or whatever it was that his father then wanted him to study. I suppose there are few examples in history of a man more completely given, almost from birth, to an idea.

Peattie: Very few, and particularly to that idea. Then it must be pointed out that he was a dual genius of art and science. There have been very few in the entire history of the world. Goethe was one and Leonardo da Vinci was another. But while each excelled Audubon in certain respects, I wouldn't say that they were more completely dual than he. He had those two great and almost incompatible gifts exquisitely balanced in him.

Van Doren: The gift of knowing a bird as a scientist would know it and of knowing a bird as an artist would know it. I wonder what the difference is? That interests me a great deal, because some time ago, when we were discussing the *Notebooks* of Leonardo here, we found it rather difficult to disentangle the kind of interest the scientist has in a natural fact from the kind of interest an artist has.

Peattie: And just after telling me it's so difficult, you ask me to venture upon the task.

Van Doren: Yes, I beg you to say what we couldn't say. Many people would suppose it was a very easy distinction to state, because in most people's minds the scientist and the artist are very far apart.

Peattie: I'm willing to try—and fall down on my nose in front of everyone.

Van Doren: Go ahead.

Peattie: I would say that science knows its way toward reality, and art feels its way toward reality. One is emotion and the other is knowing.

Van Doren: Or could you put it this way: That both know, perhaps, but the scientist knows the abstract, knows the general, knows the laws involved—the classes and species involved—whereas the artist is always concerned with the individual thing.

Murphy: No, it is not a matter of concern; it is a matter of the impression with which you're to be left.

Van Doren: Yes, but Audubon, painting a particular turkey or particular sandpiper or swallow-tailed kite, seems to have that individual thing before him.

Peattie: That is right. He had a very, very strong sense of exactly what species was to be described, and there must be no other in his mind. I have heard a modernist artist say he didn't care whether the object in his picture was taken for a cow or a Chinaman, just so long as you were interested in the shape.

Van Doren: But I don't assume that it was enough for Audubon to have the species in mind. A scientist thinks in terms of species; he wants his knowledge to be sound with respect to the kind of thing being described or painted or what not. The artist on the other hand is a man who can lose himself, so to speak, in the individual before him. Isn't that true? For instance, take a philosopher and a poet. It is perhaps the same sort of difference. The philosopher is interested in truth everywhere; the artist, the poet, is interested in the truth here and now; it is as if no other man had ever existed before.

Peattie: Exactly, but now you bring us to the point of what Audubon intended you to come away with when you'd seen one of his pictures, and I'll show you why I think he was such a perfectly balanced dual genius. He painted the bird not as most artists would do, as an impression of that bird; he painted every single barb on every single pinion; you can count them if you want to, and they come out correctly. Every feather lies just where it should to please the most exacting ornithologist, and it lies as it looks on the living bird, not on a dusty museum specimen 150 years

The ivory-billed woodpecker, now believed to be extinct.

old. All right, so far it is scientific illustration; it is an illustration from which you could identify the bird at any time, and he will stop and give you in enlarged detail the finest details of the bill or the feet or some form even of the viscera of the animal. But when you have looked at the picture, even if you are not an ornithologist, you come away with a feeling that makes you think: I never saw a picture of an eagle that was more like an eagle in all my life—that is the most eaglish thing ever done. Or if it's a duck, it's the most ducklike; and if it is a small singing bird, everything is there but the sound. The bird is singing, the tree is flowering, the day is spring, the dew is on the landscape, and you feel as though it were the morning of all the world. That is where he is a great artist; he does both things at the same time. No other individual, either by combining science and painting or science and description or science and anything else, has ever more perfectly blended those two things.

Murphy: I agree entirely with that.

Van Doren: Your emphasis is still upon the certainty the spectator will have that he is face to face with a species. Would you go further and say that it is a particular day which seems to be rendered, Mr. Murphy? A particular

day with dew on it, and a particular member of the species of sandpiper?

Murphy: Oh, decidedly. Everything is a factual experience. Audubon had seen the bird in his setting; in most cases, he had shot it himself.

Van Doren: Then it was one bird.

Murphy: It was one bird and one place and one time.

Peattie: So much so, Mr. Van Doren, that when he found a bird in a very peculiar attitude and he delightedly painted the bird going through that strange antic, fellow scientists, already enraged by his breaking all the holy taboos of science, said that he was a nature-faker and that no bird had ever been seen to do that before. But in actual experience every picture I know of that represents a peculiar attitude, or something else that might make you a little doubtful of its reality, has been substantiated later on. He was constantly doing individual scenes, individual days, and animals that were just those animals of all in the world. That is why he is a complete artist, at the same time that he is a complete scientist.

Murphy: It is a commonplace remark among taxidermists, who also know nature: "If I should ever mount a bird in that position, the Museum wouldn't put it on exhibition!" That's the sort of thing that Audubon illustrates and demonstrates.

Van Doren: But Audubon didn't worry.

Murphy: Not a bit. And he had of course a peculiar gift of observation. In his rambles near New Orleans in 1821, he heard a note and immediately pricked up his ears; he followed the bird until he obtained it, and he said: "I instantly recognized the note as one I had never heard before." He always knew that.

Van Doren: What was the bird, do you remember?

Murphy: I don't recall. It was a warbler, but I'm not sure what it was.

Van Doren: I suppose the birds he is most likely to render in fantastic postures are the long-legged ones and long-necked ones. It has always seemed to me that long-legged and long-necked birds can look sillier upon occasion than any other living thing.

Murphy: Well, he had to fit them into a plate. He chose a plate impression that would accommodate the whooping crane and the trumpeter swan and the turkey-cock, the largest species found in North America, and that meant that he had to use little tricks and conventions. In a few cases, the bill of the bird projects beyond the plate impression, or a bit of the tail makes an attractive artistic effect.

Van Doren: I have one rather naive question to ask both of you. I am sure you'll think it's naive. Why are birds so important? I'm convinced they are very important, and I assume that one of the reasons the world admires and loves Audubon so much is that he seemed to understand their indeed almost mystical importance. Can you say anything about this, or is it an embarrassing question?

Murphy: Dr. Chapman once said: "Birds are the most eloquent expression of nature's beauty, joy, and freedom." They've probably been the most observed members of the fauna of the world from the very earliest days, whether the observation was done in forecasting or whether for purely esthetic reasons, or for practical reasons other than augury.

Van Doren: It is in them that nature seems most alive.

Peattie: Mr. Van Doren, ask anybody on the street what he would rather be if not a man, and you'll get the answer why birds are important.

Van Doren: All right.

Peattie: They are important to our emotions.

Van Doren: And also, in a way, to our understanding of what everything is about. We can so easily believe that if we were birds we should have a power which would enable us to enjoy all the necessary, all the important experience.

Peattie: Dr. Murphy brought up a moment ago a point that would be interesting to pursue a little further, that is, the size of the plates. Audubon was making a uniform book. There were to be 500 plates, and every bird in North America was to be represented on it life-sized. It didn't matter if it was a titmouse or a great horned owl or a flamingo. They all had to be life-sized, so he had to take the largest possible size of paper he could get and fit his birds onto it, no matter how difficult that might seem at first flush. But what he accomplished is something that has never been surpassed in America, in science or in art, so far as I know. He did a book of 500 elephant-folio-sized plates. Now, that book sold for $1,000 when it came out, which was a staggering price. It would still be a staggering price.

Van Doren: I should think so.

Peattie: Yes, $1,000 for a book about birds. But do you realize that if you had one today you could sell it for $10,000?

Murphy: $15,000. Within a month, in New York City.

Peattie: But what happens to them is this: The plates are so valuable individually that as soon as one of these copies comes up for sale in an auction room, some one buys up the entire set, then breaks it up and sells it plate by plate.

Van Doren: By the way, does that seem horrible to you? Every now and then it appalls me to think of the book being broken up.

Peattie: No, it is not horrible, I'm sure, because as they are broken up they reach a larger number of people.

Murphy: Precisely.

Peattie: Were they all immediately bought up by brownstone-front institutions and put deep in a vault where you had to sign something before you were allowed to look at them, very few people would ever see them.

Murphy: It is the breaking up of the books that has created knowledge of Audubon and made him popular. There were probably 177 issued, or some number very close to

that, and it is believed now that about 100 have been distributed.

Van Doren: And of course we can count upon all the plates that are taken out of them being preserved somewhere. Clearly people would want to preserve them.

Peattie: Correct. Now, if you want to buy an Audubon plate and you want to be sure of getting one of the originals and not one of the later reproductions, look in the lower right-hand corner. If it says "Lizars—Edinburgh" or "Havell—London," then you have one of the originals, and it is worth quite a good deal of money. If it says anything else, then it is not one of the original copper-plated, aquatinted plates; it is a modern or comparatively modern chromo-lithograph, and should sell for very much less.

Murphy: But well worth possessing.

Peattie: Well worth possessing nevertheless.

Van Doren: We are talking now of the book which most people associate with Audubon: ***The Birds of America.*** I should like to go back at the end to his ***Delineations,*** to a passage which I think is typical of that book for its tone, for its accent of one who is describing Paradise. He is describing the Ohio River by day and by night:

> The days were yet warm; the sun had assumed a rich and glowing hue, which at that season produces the singular phenomenon called there 'the Indian Summer.' The moon had rather passed the meridian at her grandeur. We glided down the river, meeting no other ripple of the water than that formed by the propulsion of our boat. Leisurely we moved along, gazing all day on the grandeur and beauty of the wild scenery around us. As night came, sinking in darkness the broader portions of the river, our minds became affected by strong emotions and wandered far beyond the present moment. The tinkling of bells told us that the cattle which bore them were gently roving from valley to valley in search of food or returning to their distant homes. The hooting of the great owl or the muffled noise of its wings, as it sailed smoothly over the stream, were matters of interest to us. So was the sound of the boatsman's horn as it came winding more and more softly from afar. When daylight returned, many songsters burst forth with echoing notes, more and more mellow to the listening ear. Here and there the lonely cabin of a squatter struck the eye, giving note of commencing civilization. The crossing of the stream by deer foretold how soon the hills would be covered with snow.

Ludlow Griscom   (essay date 1950)

SOURCE: An introduction to *Audubon's Birds of America,* by John James Audubon, The Macmillan Company, 1950, pp. 15-30.

[*In the following essay, Griscom discusses Audubon as a painter and ornithologist.*]

It is now almost a century since the death of John James Audubon (1785-1851). Not only has his reputation lasted, but if anything, his fame and renown have increased with

An excerpt from *Ornithological Biography*

When I think of these times, and call back to my mind the grandeur and beauty of those almost uninhabited shores; when I picture to myself the dense and lofty summits of the forest, that everywhere spread along the hills, and overhung the margins of the stream, unmolested by the axe of the settler; when I know how dearly purchased the safe navigation of that river has been by the blood of many worthy Virginians; when I see that no longer any Aborigines are to be found there, and that the vast herds of elks, deer and buffaloes which once pastured on these hills and in these valleys, making for themselves great roads to the several salt-springs, have ceased to exist; when I reflect that all this grand portion of our Union, instead of being in a state of nature, is now more or less covered with villages, farms, and towns, where the din of hammers and machinery is constantly heard; that the woods are fast disappearing under the axe by day, and the fire by night; that hundreds of steam-boats are gliding to and fro, over the whole length of the majestic river, forcing commerce to take root and to prosper at every spot; when I see the surplus population of Europe coming to assist in the destruction of the forest, and transplanting civilization into its darkest recesses;— when I remember that these extraordinary changes have all taken place in the short period of twenty years, I pause, wonder, and, although I know all to be fact, can scarcely believe its reality.

Whether these changes are for the better or for the worse, I shall not pretend to say. . . .

John James Audubon, from Delineations of American Scenery and Character, *edited by Francis Hobart Herrick, 1926.*

dubon was no exception to this rule. The son of a French naval officer and a creole woman of Santo Domingo, he was probably illegitimate, but never admitted it. Howbeit, the father was a man of some substance, and young Audubon had a spoiled and petted boyhood on an estate in France, early developing both a talent for drawing, and a love of the outdoors, natural history and birds in particular, which he could not control, and which motivated his entire life.

When about seventeen years of age, he was sent to North America to take charge of a property near Philadelphia, and thenceforth adopted his new country wholeheartedly. Here he met and married Lucy Bakewell, and began a series of commercial ventures with his patrimony, which took him to Kentucky in 1808 and to New Orleans in 1812. As Audubon could not restrain himself from a continual hunting, shooting and drawing, all these ventures failed, until finally he had practically nothing left except a wife, gun, and the precious drawings of his beloved birds. By 1822 most people in the pioneer settlements from the Ohio to New Orleans regarded him as an incompetent madman.

In the meantime his dream, to publish a series of paintings of every North American bird, had been crystallizing, and he determined to devote his time, talents and energy to the attainment of this goal, no matter what the cost. He was encouraged by his devoted and unselfish wife, who believed in his genius and a final triumphant success. For years Audubon led a truly remarkable life. Supporting himself by painting, portraiture, and teaching drawing, separated from his wife for years at a time, in some incredible manner he always got where he wanted to go, and attained all his objectives. He solicited subscriptions to his great work in the principal eastern cities, going back and forth to Edinburgh, London and Paris, most of the time leading a hand-to-mouth existence. In 1831 he made his famous expedition to the Florida Keys, the next year going to Labrador, then travelling through the southern states to the independent republic of Texas, always seeking out wilderness areas. In between trips he wrote the volumes of the text, and the whole work was completed in 1838 at a cost of about $100,000, the total number of sets issued being under two hundred, at $1,000 a set. The project had taken just about twenty-five years to complete, his wife's faith was justified, success and renown were his.

This success would have been impossible without the possession of qualities, many of which the world properly regards as magnificent. Audubon had enormous confidence in himself, inflexible determination, and the capacity of never admitting failure or becoming really discouraged. His physical endurance and energy were extraordinary, and some of his adventures required great bravery. His dealings with others were aided by a magnetic personality, he was remarkably handsome with beautiful eyes, and practised the arts of self-dramatization and salesmanship instinctively. The American Woodsman became a sensational success in the houses of the great and near great. Audubon's life has been described as a typical success story; he just could not be stopped.

Audubon's later life further illustrates his remarkable en-

the passage of time. It, perhaps, might be worth while to pause and enquire why this is so. He is a perpetual source of study, discussion and debate, and much ink has been spilled over whether his claim to fame was primarily as an ornithologist or an artist. In my opinion much of this debate is second rate or even trivial, and misses the major point.

Actually he was both, and it is an irrelevant detail to consider in which field he may have excelled, for the moment. Moreover, his biography, letters, and delineations of the American scenery and manners of his day have acquired increasing value and historical interest with the years, and make good reading for people with no knowledge of birds whatever. To my view his greatest claims to fame and glory were first, the versatility of his talents and gifts, and second that the completion of his main ambition, the original elephant folio of paintings of 435 species of American birds against overwhelming odds was a *tour de force,* of a kind which has never again been equalled in history.

It is perhaps trite to remark that men who accomplish a *tour de force* usually lead extraordinary lives, and display characteristics not possessed by the humdrum citizen. Au-

ergy. In 1840 he began work on the octavo edition of his *Birds of America,* completing the text of the seven volumes in only four years, and taking time out for his last and most perilous expedition to the Great Plains and Rocky Mountains when he was nearly sixty. Moreover, shortly prior to 1846, he had completed all 155 paintings of the quadrupeds of North America. By the irony of fate his health and mind began to fail rapidly in 1848, and he became totally blind before he died in 1851.

In this [essay] we are chiefly concerned with Audubon as an artist and ornithologist, and we pass to a critique of his stature in these two fields. There can be no question of his place as an artist. He is one of the American immortals, his originals are priceless, and only the very rich can afford the earlier octavo editions. It is high time that bird-lovers were reminded again of what Audubon set out to do and what his contribution was. Illustrations of birds prior to him were mostly incredibly crude. The artist drew the stuffed and mounted specimen, about which he knew nothing, often faithfully reproducing the unnatural lumps in the outline of the body, and foreshortening the neck and tail. The colors faithfully showed any fading or dirt on the mount, and little effort was made to indicate the fact that the bird's body was coated with feathers. Finally the bird was placed on a conventionalized perch or twig, not in the least resembling any twig existing in nature.

Audubon's paintings were life-sized portraits in natural attitudes, in a natural habitat, or perched on a flower or tree of a species actually existing and instantly recognizable. Only the well-informed ornithologist can criticize some of his work. He dramatized his birds as well as himself. The colors of some are too bright, the poses of others are too striking, or they are in startling attitudes which the bird actually never adopts in life. We happen to live in an age of extreme exactitude, bird portraits in color are hopelessly expensive, and the goal of most illustration today is scientific delineation, measured out to the last millimeter, as an aid to identification and recognition. Thus Audubon's Bald Eagle is easily seen to have eleven tail feathers, whereas eagles possess twelve. No modern illustrator of birds would dream of making so unimportant a slip, which of course in no way detracts from the artistic as well as lifelike effect.

If a sort of Gallup poll were held, and the question were asked—"Can you mention the name of some noted ornithologist?," it is my best guess that a substantial percentage of the better educated Americans would answer, "Audubon" without hesitation. It is equally my guess that only those with a special interest in birds would ever have heard of any other!

Various competent ornithologists have given critiques of Audubon, and have, quite fairly, pointed out his limitations. He did indeed discover many new birds, and he added greatly to our knowledge of many others, but he was not at all scientifically minded in technical directions, and made no effort to improve the classification of birds in the higher categories of genera and families. In many directions his artistic side dominated the scientific. The ornithologist who discovers and describes new birds, or who finds others in America for the first time, invariably prizes

and preserves the specimen as a permanent voucher or proof of his discovery. To Audubon, the precious possession to which he clung no matter what the adversity of his circumstances, was his painting. Throughout most of his life he threw the specimens away after the painting was completed, never supposing that his integrity or fidelity to nature would be questioned. He has, therefore, left behind him a certain number of insoluble mysteries. On the one hand he claims to have seen or shot and painted some well known European birds, never seen or heard of in the New World again. On the other hand, he discovered, described and painted several "new" species, also never heard of again, none of which can be explained away as hybrids, freaks, or a plumage variation of any bird we know. Needless to say, in these last cases particularly, modern science would give anything to have the original specimen preserved and available for study. Finally, some of Audubon's "errors" were really due to the misinformation of friends and correspondents in whom he had confidence. Thus specimens of certain sea birds were sent him, purporting to come from the "mouth of the Columbia River" in Oregon, which actually were collected at Cape Horn, or near it.

Other criticisms of Audubon reflect chiefly on the critics. It is common sense that we have learned a lot about the birds of eastern North America since Audubon's day, and are still adding to knowledge about them. Moreover, every corner of a great continent has now been explored, half of which Audubon never penetrated, containing birds of whose existence he remained unaware. It is obviously no reflection on this remarkable man that there was plenty to find out after his death. Think of the handicaps and difficulties under which he labored, the difficulties of transportation and travel, the lack of field glasses, to mention only a few. We consequently find that his knowledge was most incomplete with the small forest and tree-top birds that he could not observe from the ground, and that he shot on a few occasions only by pure chance. In common with all early or pioneer ornithologists, he could not work out the relationships of technically very difficult groups of birds like the gulls, terns, small flycatchers and certain thrushes. His experience was inadequate to determine that some of his species were nothing but the immature or winter plumages of birds well known to him only in their adult plumages. He was unable to unravel the puzzling color phases of certain hawks. There is little merit in attempting to depreciate him because he did not know certain things that it took two generations of ornithologists after him to find out.

In spite of various things Audubon did not know about American birds, the passage of time has rendered some of the things he did know and some of the things he saw of ever increasing interest and historical value. He foretold the inevitable disappearance of the wilderness, and remarked on the rapid decrease of various birds in his own lifetime. Actually he could never have even conceived of the rapid acceleration of tempo with which scientific inventions have enabled our civilization to take possession of the country, exploit its natural resources, utterly change the landscape, and destroy the natural habitats which nature had provided. Never in history has a native continental fauna ever been called on to endure so sudden and catastrophic a change, and endeavor to survive. Added to this, a large list of birds suffered intense persecution from sport, market gunning, the plume trade, cage-bird traffic and other reasons. There were practically no game laws worthy of the name in the whole country, and they could not be enforced in unsettled regions. No sentiment of any kind in favor of most birds existed. Hawks, crows, owls, and all large water and marsh birds were natural targets for hunters and travellers on which to practise marksmanship. Small boys learned to shoot by popping away at the birds on the lawn. We must also remember that in Audubon's time even robins and blackbirds were regarded as game, while the poor gathered gulls' and terns' eggs for food.

The results can easily be appreciated. Several famous American birds are extinct. Two, the Labrador Duck and Great Auk, were little known even in Audubon's time, but the Carolina Paroquet was common, and the Passenger Pigeon existed in such spectacular multitudes that it was one of the great wonders of the living world. Several others are on the verge of extinction. The game supply of the continent was decimated beyond recovery, roughly speaking only about 10 per cent of it surviving into modern times. A large number of other birds greatly decreased by reason of the destruction of the forests, the drainage of marshes, and the spoiling of much country by civilization. Audubon has left us accounts of these rare and vanished birds. The numbers of some of the game birds he saw were so prodigious as to appear incredible to the present generation of bird-lovers. Thus a two-day October flight of woodcock down the Ohio River was estimated by him to consist of between thirty and forty thousand. It is problematical if any expert devoting himself to hunting this bird could manage to see that many in a lifetime today.

One of the many points of interest about birds is a characteristic which may loosely be termed "powers of adaptation." This is in marked contrast to lower or less evolved groups of animals, as well as the plants, which are the unconscious victims of blind chance; these live or perish according to whether their circumstances are favorable or unfavorable. But most birds can take some steps to mitigate or improve their lot. They can leave an area where they are hunted, acquire wariness under persecution, adopt new habitats, abandon their natural shyness and suspicion upon learning that it is uncalled for. Birds put up with or even adopt the vicinity of man if he does them no harm. In other words they can adapt themselves to new or changed conditions, whether for better or for worse.

American birds began adapting themselves to the changes brought about by the white man in early colonial times. The robin, swallows, chimney swift, and martin became familiar dooryard birds. Audubon took for granted that a great variety of common birds were characteristic of gardens, orchards, fields and pastures, without stopping to think that these habitats had never previously existed. They were created by the white man deliberately, involving the destruction of the original primeval forest. This event serves to illustrate and explain a fundamental principle in natural history and biology. It is *impossible* to destroy one habitat without automatically creating another.

The destruction of the forest may well involve the loss or disappearance of some or most of those birds and animals requiring it as a habitat, and we may well mourn their decrease or extinction. But some at least of these forest birds adapted themselves to the new conditions. The robin, for instance, was originally a forest bird, and still is in remote parts of the continent. The chimney swift nested in hollow trees in the forest before there were any chimneys.

It consequently follows that the changes brought about by the white man created a great boon for those birds requiring or preferring forest edges, sprout woods, thickets, and open country of every kind. At least one hundred species are now common, well known, and widely distributed, which were absent or else rare and local in most of the forested northern and eastern states in early colonial times. Our final debt to Audubon is that he left us some invaluable data on this subject. In certain cases he has told us what type of country a certain bird inhabited in his time, now found in radically different environments. Even more interesting are those cases, where the bird was rare and little known to him, but a species now common and widely distributed. Several warblers preferring second-growth woodlands will illustrate this category, and we have a definite historic record of their arrival in and gradual spread over much of the Northeast since Audubon's time.

Audubon's name has become indelibly associated with the popular movement to protect and conserve American birds. Some seventy years ago thoughtful and high class sportsmen, appalled at the increasingly rapid decimation of game, began to agitate for the absolute necessity for restrictive legislation. At this period practically no bird received any legal protection whatever. In a few states certain game birds had a brief closed season during most of or a part of their breeding season only, and there were virtually no bag limits whatever. Moreover, any method was legal, including the most destructive, such as night shooting, fire lighting, netting and trapping. The last great nesting flock of Passenger Pigeons in Michigan was so unmercifully raided that over one hundred million birds were shipped to city markets. Chesapeake Bay was a noted paradise for waterfowl. Market gunning began there in 1795, was pursued throughout the season (September 15-April 15) at a steadily increasing tempo, so that by 1870, up to fifteen thousand ducks were killed in a day. As the same activity was going on in every other locality where waterfowl were numerous, the decimation in numbers of this group of birds can be imagined. The plume trade reduced the egrets and most terns to the verge of extinction.

The various state, and, finally (1904) the National, Audubon societies were an outgrowth of the original bird protection committee of the American Ornithologists Union (1883). These societies were led by thoughtful sportsmen and ornithologists, but their rise to power, influence and adequate financing was chiefly due to the rise of popular interest in birds, which began about 1895 and has been going on ever since. The era of bird protection was rapidly and triumphantly successful. By 1920 every North American bird was protected, the federal government had taken over the control of all migratory birds, any form of commercial use of native birds was illegal, a large number of birds had been permanently removed from the game list, and the open season and permissible take on the remainder had been drastically reduced, and this reduction has still been going on. The results have been most gratifying. Over one hundred species of North American birds have greatly increased in numbers, and some are already as numerous as at any time in the historical period.

The one possible criticism the naturalist can make of the extensive literature of the bird protection era was its uniformly pessimistic tone. It was probably necessary for arousing a supine public, but was not entirely true. It was indeed very true that from 1850-1900 far more birds were rapidly decreasing than the few which were increasing. It is human nature to sigh for what has been lost, and to take what one has for granted. The other natural error of this era was the general belief that the rapid decrease of many birds was due wholly to overshooting.

This fallacy is now being gradually corrected by time and experience, but must still be sold to the vast number of Americans interested in birds. We now know that many of the birds completely protected for many years will never regain their former numbers, or anything anywhere near it. The reason is that our civilization has destroyed too large a percentage of their required habitat, and they

The first plate in The Birds of America: *The American turkey.*

lack the necessary powers of adaptation to adopt a new one or make some compromise. This leads to a second great general principle in natural history. The total number of existing individuals of any bird or animal can never be greater than the amount of favorable habitat existing or remaining, and the total amount of the necessary food.

We speak of marsh and water birds without stopping to think that they have to have marshes and water. Our civilization has drained millions of acres of marshland, and is continuing to do so at a rapid rate. Innumerable streams are polluted or dried up by a century of building operations. Ponds and lakes are now surrounded by cabins and camps, and covered with boats and canoes for parts of each year. For many water birds such a lake has become a total loss. It transpires that food cannot be taken for granted. The Brant Goose feeds on eel-grass almost exclusively, and was so seriously reduced when a disease struck this plant that it had to be removed from the game list for some years. The Ivory-billed Woodpecker is almost certainly about to become extinct in the near future, because highly specialized food habits require a substantial acreage of primeval forest to keep one pair alive. As civilization has eliminated the southern primeval forest, the few surviving individuals are doomed.

Along the lines of this exposition the era of bird protection passed rapidly but imperceptibly into the era of conservation. Our birds are protected, but still need to be conserved. The Golden Age has not arrived because we have stopped shooting. Never are all of them prospering and doing well at any one time. Particularly hard pressed are our few remaining game birds, whose foes, the sporting fraternity, are increasing by leaps and bounds, as leisure, means, and facilities of transportation increase. But all the birds are being put under constant strain and difficulty by the multiple and rapid changes which an expanding technological civilization is making on the face of our land. Forest fires, lumbering, and oil wells ruin vast stretches of country yearly; the prairies are fenced in and overgrazed by cattle and sheep; intercoastal canals bring salt water into fresh water bays and landlocked sounds, ruining and disrupting the native plants and animals. Fields and pastures are plowed up and planted to corn or vegetables; some farmer's woodlot of last summer is cut down for firewood during the winter; every year some local marsh is used as a town dump and gradually filled in. Every one of these habitats supported a rich community of bird life. Where do they go?

Conservation consequently involves an intelligent and successful effort to preserve major habitats and types of country, in as natural a state as possible. Hence the great development of national and state parks, national and state forests, and the great chain of federal wild life refuges. A new profession of wild life management has arisen, an outlet for young naturalists. The refuge area must be maintained and guarded; it can also be improved. Dams can be built, artificial ponds can be created, the more desirable food plants can be introduced, and water levels preserved. The manager and his staff can count and note the increase in the wild life, observe the relative success of the breeding season. The plants, animals and birds requiring all these types of country are almost automatically conserved for the enjoyment of posterity. One good proof of the overall success of this movement is the steadily increasing number of campers, tourists and visitors, the money involved supporting a variety of industries in the economic sense. A forceful and able executive staff is also essential. The appropriations must be secured from Congress, and above all the constant effort to raid the parks, forests, and refuges for other interests must be fought off. Our civilization is now so complex that it is almost impossible to do anything without hurting some one else's interest. The army and navy are looking for bombing ranges in wilderness areas, where there is no risk of blowing our citizens up. Power dams and major irrigation projects often threaten these areas. The ranchers seek grazing privileges in the parks and forests, the lumber interests are perpetually trying to get permission to cut down a tiny piece of some forest. Everlasting vigilance is required.

It follows that we live in a state of perpetual change and flux. As habitats are destroyed and replaced by others, one group of birds comes in and another goes out. Every decade some bird begins to fade out, some other bird learns to adapt itself to man, and begins to flourish and increase. The Duck Hawk or Peregrine Falcon is turning metropolitan. More and more spend much of the year in cities, roosting on a church spire or skyscraper, living on the city pigeons. The Snowy Owl from the arctic has also become a suburbanite, visiting the local dump nightly for rats. Everyone is glad to see them, and appreciates their service as vermin reducers. Every nature lover, every bird watcher, every member of the Audubon Society can now make a contribution. He can count and keep careful watch over his local birds, detect the upward and downward trends, and report them. The sum of the local reports equals the welfare of each species in its total range. Never in history have there been so many ways in which a bird-lover can find interesting and worth while things to do with his hobby. Any boy or girl of high school age can learn to identify their local birds and begin useful work.

There is one other major principle in natural history the understanding of which makes the pursuit of any branch of it more interesting. The real harm done by the white man and his civilization is his ruthless and wasteful exploitation of the rich natural resources of this continent. In so doing he has utterly upset and disrupted the balance of nature. The question arises just what is the balance of nature? We may begin with our birds, which require a suitable habitat and an adequate food supply. But birds are not the only living creatures in the habitat, and their food can only be other living animals and plants. Therefore the bird in its habitat is one member only of a living or natural community, and is dependent upon the other living members of the community. Actually the soil, water and climate are the basic factors. The plants come next, followed by insects, and last of all the birds and mammals. This succession is easily proved in areas devastated by a volcanic eruption, or where a great glacier has melted and retreated in a cycle of warmer climate. But complete interdependence exists among the living members of the community. There is a fascinating chain of interrelationships. The insects eat the plants, but they are essential in pollinating the

flowers. The birds live in the trees and eat the insects. The foxes live on the mice, which live on the plants. The hawks live on the song birds. Everything is preyed upon by something, but everything also performs an essential service by keeping in check the numbers of something else. The balance of nature in a natural community is such that the community continues forever. This is accomplished by keeping the numbers of each living creature in a proper proportion. The foxes obviously never eat up all the mice, or they would exterminate themselves. As no living creature can afford to exterminate its food supply, the food supply is more abundant individually than its enemy or predator. Therefore there never are as many foxes as mice, or as many hawks as song birds, or as many insects as plants. Any increase in mice is sure to initiate an era of prosperity for foxes, which automatically causes the reduction of the mouse population to normal, which starves out the extra foxes. And so on *ad infinitum.*

The civilized white man is the only living creature who has the power to disrupt the balance of nature and exploit his food supply and natural resources without immediate, disastrous results. In America we have impoverished our soil, overgrazed our prairies, killed our game more rapidly than it can reproduce, and cut down our forests more rapidly than nature can replace them. This is easily seen to be stupid folly if we stop to think that our food-plant crops require fertile soil, and that our civilization absolutely requires timber and wood. Hence the modern efforts in money and talented man power to inculcate the principles of conservation before it is too late. And so we take one more backward glance at the great figure of Audubon, his vanished wilderness, and mourn the further loss and decrease of the many striking and spectacular birds he loved so well.

Waldemar H. Fries   (essay date 1959)

SOURCE: "John James Audubon: Some Remarks on His Writings," in *The Princeton University Library Chronicle,* Vol. XXI, Nos. 1 & 2, Autumn 1959 & Winter 1960, pp. 1-7.

[*In the following essay, Fries discusses Audubon's writings, including his letters and journals and the* Ornithological Biography.]

It was in February of 1957 that I made my first visit to the Department of Rare Books and Special Collections of the Princeton University Library. A short time before I had begun my research on the double-elephant folio of Audubon's ***The Birds of America,*** so that the purpose of my visit was to examine the set of the folio belonging to the Library. At one time this folio had belonged to Stephen Van Rensselaer of Albany, New York, one of the original American subscribers to the "B. of A." It was his grandson, Alexander Van Rensselaer of the Class of 1871 at Princeton, who in 1927 presented the set to the University. It is indeed an honor that two years later I should be invited to participate in the annual meeting of the Friends of the Princeton Library at the time of the opening of the Library's spring and summer exhibition, which this year has been devoted to "The World of John James Audubon." I must confess that inwardly I feel like a bush-league pitcher called up to the majors and then suddenly forced to face that so-called "murderers' row" of Ruth, Gehrig, and those other Yankee sluggers. Fortunately, I was told that my efforts could be devoted to informal remarks rather than to a formal lecture.

Audubon has been honored many times in the past by exhibitions, especially in the year 1951, the one hundredth anniversary of his death. Heretofore the exhibitions have stressed and emphasized Audubon principally as the artist. But, happily, the Princeton Library, in preparing the present exhibition, has placed particular emphasis on the books, manuscripts, letters, and other material of similar nature. This should bring about a wider and better understanding of Audubon as a writer, traveler, and acute observer of his fellow-men.

From the material on display, let us first consider Audubon's journals. Over a period of many years, commencing as early as 1820 and continuing until the 1840's, Audubon kept a most detailed account of the daily happenings, often writing into the early hours of the new day as he recorded his adventures of the previous day. In 1897 there were published two volumes of *Audubon and His Journals,* edited by a granddaughter, Maria R. Audubon, with zoological and other notes added by Elliott Coues, an outstanding ornithologist. The editor has included in the first volume a life of Audubon, the European journals of 1826 to 1829, the Labrador journal of 1833, and the beginning of the Missouri River journals. In the second volume the Missouri River journals are continued and there are included also certain episodes of which I shall speak in more detail later.

In her preface Miss Audubon refers to nine journals, as well as to much other material, stating that "from the mass of papers I have accumulated, I have used perhaps one fifth." We know that some of the journals were actually destroyed, and we also know that much material in the original journals was omitted from the published version. Fortunately for us, Miss Audubon did include in the second volume an episode entitled **"My Style of Drawing Birds."** It is from this article that we learn something about Audubon's fixing a dead bird with wires on squares so that he could study the bird, for, as he says, "the more I understood all these particulars, the better representations I made of the originals."

Also from this episode we learn the following about his method of making his drawings. He writes:

> My drawings at first were made altogether in watercolors, but they wanted softness and a great deal of finish. For a long time I was much dispirited at this, particularly when vainly endeavoring to imitate birds of soft and downy plumage, such as that of most Owls, Pigeons, Hawks, and Herons. How this could be remedied required a new train of thought, or some so-called accident, and the latter came to my aid.
>
> One day, after having finished a miniature portrait of the one dearest to me in all the world, a portion of the face was injured by a drop of water, which dried where it fell; and although I

labored a great deal to repair the damage, the blur still remained. Recollecting that, when a pupil of David, I had drawn heads and figures in different colored chalks, I resorted to a piece of that material of the tint required for the part, applied the pigment, rubbed the place with a cork stump, and at once produced the desired effect.

My drawings of Owls and other birds of similar plumage were much improved by such applications; indeed, after a few years of patience, some of my attempts began almost to please me, and I have continued the same style ever since, and that now is more than thirty years.

Next we come to the *Ornithological Biography,* of five volumes, the first published in Edinburgh in 1831 and the last issued in 1839. It should be explained that Audubon did not include any letterpress with the double-elephant folio, for, had he done so, he would have been required to place a copy of his work in a number of British libraries. These biographies contain an account of each of the birds figured in the folio and are interspersed with delineations (also called episodes) of American scenery and manners. Audubon had introduced these episodes, some sixty of them, to relieve the tedium of descriptive ornithology. Let it not be thought that his descriptions of the birds and their habits make for dull reading—quite the contrary.

Upon reading these descriptions, one becomes fully aware of what a keen observer and field ornithologist Audubon really was. Let me give one example of this. In the very first bird description, that of the Wild Turkey, in writing about the habits of the young birds, he says, "They roll themselves in deserted ants' nests, to clear their growing feathers of the loose scales, and prevent ticks and other vermin from attacking them, these insects being unable to bear the odour of the earth in which ants have been." In recent years there has been considerable study of the anting of birds. It is known that certain species of ants possess formic acid—whether or not Audubon knew about formic acid, he did know what was going on in those "deserted ants' nests." I wish that there might be time to read the description of the humming birds or the account of the flight of the passenger pigeons which lasted three days.

The so-called delineations give as well a vivid portrait of America in the years from 1820 to 1838. There are among the sixty episodes descriptions of the rivers Ohio, Mississippi, and St. John's; the Florida keys; Niagara Falls; cities such as Louisville and Natchez; with accounts of hunting and fishing, egging in Labrador, the earthquake in Tennessee, floods on the Mississippi—a most varied catalogue of subjects. As one reads the account of Niagara Falls, which he visited in 1824, one learns that he did not feel capable of drawing a picture of the Falls. Having seen some views of the Falls in his room, he writes: " 'What!' thought I, 'have I come here to mimic nature in her grandest enterprise, and add *my* caricature of one of the wonders of the world to those which I here see? No.—I give up the vain attempt. I shall look on these mighty cataracts and imprint them, where alone they can be represented,—on my mind!' " And he advises his reader to go to see the Falls for himself.

The passenger pigeon by Audubon. One of the most abundant birds in the world during Audubon's time, it is now extinct.

Then there are the letters of Audubon. He was a prolific letter writer; where he found the time to write the many long letters to his family and to others is most difficult to figure out. Many of the letters covering the period from 1826 to 1840 were published by the Club of Odd Volumes in 1930. There are many other letters, both of Audubon and other members of the family, scattered around in libraries, museums, and private collections. These letters are really fascinating reading. His language, filled with French idioms of speech translated into English, makes for colorful phrases. Whatever subject he may be writing upon he will discuss in great detail. As an example, I should like to speak about the letter of March 2, 1831, written by Audubon to his engraver, Havell, the original of which is in the possession of the Princeton Library.

When this letter was brought to my attention and I had read it, I realized that here was explained the reason why the legend for the same plate differed in impressions bearing different water-marks. For example, it is well known that plate No. I is the "Wild Turkey," as it is in the set in the Princeton University Library. But how many of you know that there are impressions of this print where the legend is "Great American Cock"? This latter legend is to be found in that state of the print which has a "Whatman" watermark with a date earlier than 1830. Some of the other differences are: "Bonaparte Flycatcher" or "Bonaparte's Flycatcher," "Purple Grackle" or "Purple Grakle," "Brown Lark" or "Brown Titlark." In the letter of March 2, 1831, Audubon wrote his engraver in part, "I wish you to set about having the Plates reengraved I mean the Lettering as soon as possible and to employ such Engravers as will do Justice to the whole of it." In addition, he sets down in detail just how the legends of the first forty-four plates shall read.

I knew then that after the date of this letter all the legends would be as here recorded by Audubon. Just within the last two months, while examining a ledger of Audubon's which has been lent to the Audubon Memorial Library at Henderson, Kentucky, I was to find another reference to this same matter. In the ledger under Havell's account there is the following item:

> July 30—1831 To Havell—for correcting names
> of the first volume 37-00-0

I could pick out many apt and picturesque expressions in his letters. Let this one suffice: Audubon writes during his early days in London how tired he is from all the functions he has had to attend, admitting that he actually feels lazy, but adding that he has been "thinking monstrous deep." That Audubon realized the true worth of his great undertaking he expresses well in a letter written by him at Charleston on December 23, 1833 to his son Victor, who was in London. (The original of the letter is now at the American Philosophical Society in Philadelphia.) Here he writes: "That Subscribers should die, is a thing we can not help, that such fellows as Vigors should mortify us, cannot again be countermanded.—but depend upon it our *Industry,* our *truth,* and the regular manner in which we publish our Work—this will always prove to the World & to our Subscribers, that nothing more can be done than what we do, nay that I doubt if any other *Family* with our pecuni-

ary means ever will raise for themselves such a *Monument* as 'the Birds of America' is, over their tomb!" From this same letter we learn also that his son "John has drawn a few Birds as good as any I ever made, and ere a few months I hope to give this department of my duty altogether to him." While he never did just this, some—we do not know exactly how many—of the birds of the folio were drawn by John.

In conclusion, I would like to speak briefly about the set of the double-elephant folio which belonged to the Audubon family. Herrick, in his biography of Audubon (1917), tells us that in 1862 after the death of her last surviving son, John Woodhouse, and the family resources having reached a low ebb, Mrs. Audubon sold the set to John Taylor Johnston (one of the founders of the Metropolitan Museum of Art) for twelve hundred dollars, and adds that the subsequent history of the folio has not been traced. After having been in a Brooklyn, New York, warehouse for many years, the set did turn up again in 1939, when it was sold by a grandson of Johnston to a rare-book dealer in New York. Then it languished in Philadelphia, having been bought by a Philadelphian for "speculation." About five years ago it was sold to a Texan and it now resides in Texas.

The set had been examined only a few times and never carefully. There were stories to the effect that it contained some extra prints, that it contained more than the 435 prints of which a complete set is composed. A year ago I saw the set but only briefly. I, too, realized that it was different. In the first place, when the prints were bound, they did not follow the usual numerical progression but were placed in the five volumes systematically, in a manner similar to that found in the *Synopsis* compiled by Audubon with the aid of Macgillivray and published in 1839, after the folio had been completed.

But what about the extra prints? With a return visit to Texas early this spring, I was able to make an exhaustive study of all thirteen of the additional prints which the set contains. In these extra prints Audubon has combined two prints by imprinting two copper plates on one sheet. Just why did Audubon do this? We can never be sure, but the answer may be that he was in this manner correcting certain mistakes in identification of some of the species he had drawn. For example, on one of these extra prints, which shows three birds, the legend reads "Hooded Warbler." But the regular Hooded Warbler plate is No. CX and it contains only two birds. Where does the third bird come from? I discovered that Audubon had combined Plate CX with No. IX, on which he had originally placed the legend "Selby's Flycatcher," in the belief that he had discovered a new species. It is known that Selby's Flycatcher was an immature Hooded Warbler. Was Audubon, then, in this manner correcting his mistakes? I do not know. When I have completed my examination of the other twelve prints, perhaps I may find the answer.

Lewis Mumford   (essay date 1966)

SOURCE: "Larger than Life," in *The New York Review*

of Books, Vol. VII, No. 9, December 1, 1966, pp. 16, 18, 20, 22-4.

[*Mumford was an American sociologist, historian, philosopher, and author. In the following essay, he reviews* John James Audubon: A Biography *by Alexander B. Adams (1966). Rejecting Adams's contention that Audubon was overly concerned with money-making, Mumford insists instead that his only true passion was the study of birds.*]

The life of John James Audubon was full of ambiguities, contradictions, frustrations, alienations. With such attributes, his biography could easily meet the fashionable specifications of our own period. But he was also a man of heroic mold, and heroes for the moment are not fashionable. What is worse for his present fame, he was, within his strict avian limits, a skilled draughtsman, indeed a consummate artist; and that is a severe disqualification in an age populated by solemn popcorny jokesters who transfer nothingness to a canvas and sell it as art, or who crown such vacuous achievements by erasing nothingness and coyly signing their names to that double non-entity.

In order to characterize either the new edition of Audubon's ***Birds of America*** or [*John James Audubon: A Biography,* by Alexander B. Adams] I find it necessary to outline Audubon's life, for I have fallen in love with the man and his work all over again, as Melville fell in love with Hawthorne's enchanting mind. The most charitable thing one can say about Mr. Alexander Adams's biography is that he found Audubon's character so disenchanting and his whole career so distasteful, that only the most severe moral discipline could have kept him at his self-imposed task. In retelling Audubon's story I shall do justice to both Audubon and his new biographer; for I shall show that each is—in quite contrasting ways—strictly for the birds.

Jean Jacques Fougère Rabin Audubon, also nicknamed La Forêt, was born it now seems clear in 1785. But every attempt to unravel the mystery of his parentage only makes a greater mystery of equally valid documents and reported events, including some of Audubon's own letters to his wife. His childhood memories, curiously, did not go back farther than when he was eight, as a boy in Nantes, supposedly brought to France at four by his sea-going merchant father, Jean Audubon. Whether Audubon's early memories were erased by shock or deliberately suppressed or confusedly interwoven with an improbable past, which he was bound under oath to his father to conceal, we shall never know. Supposing he was indeed, as rumor long hinted, the lost Dauphin of France, whisked out of prison during the revolution in 1793, certain princely traits in Audubon's character would be easier to explain. If on the other hand, Audubon was actually the illegitimate son of the sea-captain and a Santo Domingan Creole woman, this would hardly account for his uncertainty about dates and birthplaces and his sometimes imperfect sense of reality. But if his life was actually based on a fiction, that might well be responsible for his free and loose way of dealing with other parts of it, as it were a fictitious incident in the same improbable fairy story of a stolen prince condemned to obscurity.

At all events the verifiable story of Audubon's life begins only at the late age of eleven. From then on it can be followed with confidence till he died, old before his time, his mind crumbling away during the last four years, in 1851.

From the outset, Audubon bore the unmistakable brand of his own genius for even as a child he was a passionate lover of birds, and soon became an indefatigable egg-snatcher, hunter, collector, and limner of birds. Behind that impulse was a traumatic incident in his childhood, which he recognized as having an influence on his later life. He had witnessed a pet monkey cold-bloodedly attack and kill a favorite talking parrot, himself agonized because his outraged screams did not move a servant to intervene. Though his own love for birds did not prevent him from killing them for closer observation or for food, even as the equally humane Alfred Russel Wallace did later, one may interpret his pictures, in the light of this early event, as so many zealous efforts to restore dead birds to life. That desire dominated his existence, and as far as art may ever truly preserve life, he marvelously succeeded.

Handsome, headstrong, volatile, foolhardy, as bored with book learning as was young Darwin, Audubon was cut out for life on the American frontier. This, as much as his father's wish to save him from becoming a Napoleonic conscript, perhaps led his watchful parent to ship the lad at eighteen off to the New World, to look after Mill Grove, a farm with a lead mine he had acquired in Pennsylvania. Audubon, brought up luxuriously by a doting stepmother, ever ready to spoil him, arrived in the United States in 1803, full of high falutin airs and pretensions. He later laughed at himself for having gone hunting in silk stockings and the finest ruffled shirt he could buy in Philadelphia. He played the flute and the violin, was a daring skates, a famous dancer, an expert fencer, and a crack shot with the rifle. In short, the perfect old-style aristocrat, proud, hot-tempered, careless of danger, and even more gaily careless of money—the precise opposite of the canny, methodical, money-making philistine that his new biographer tirelessly reproaches him for not being.

With this heady combination of qualities, Audubon might easily have been slain in a duel or have turned into a good-for-nothing Don Juan, frittering away his life in aimless erotic adventures. But he was saved by his two lifelong loves: his love of birds and his love of Lucy Bakewell, a girl on a neighboring estate, Fatland Ford, whom he courted in a cave, where they watched the peewees that fascinated him. At the end of five years, the reserved girl and the exuberant French coxcomb married and started their lives afresh as pioneers in the newly settled land beyond the Alleghenies. Almost overnight, Audubon changed his silks for leather hunting clothes and let his hair grow down to his shoulders; and in the course of his life, he gradually turned into an archetypal American, who astonishingly combined in equal measure the virtues of George Washington, Daniel Boone, and Benjamin Franklin.

In the Ohio and Mississippi Valleys, from Cincinnati and Louisville to New Orleans, Audubon found a mode of life that fulfilled his deepest need, as deep as his love for Lucy: direct contact with nature in every aspect and above all with the teeming animal and bird life of river, swamp, and woodland, at a time when the passenger pigeons periodically blackened the skies, and many species of bird, now extinct, were still thriving. Years later, in recollection, Audubon still thrilled over this life, though he had encountered his share of the frontier's rapscallions, bullies, thieves, and cutthroats. "I shot, I drew, I looked on nature only; my days were happy beyond human conception. . . . The simplicity and whole-heartedness of those days I cannot describe: man was man, and each, one to another, a brother." So he remembered that early period; and even at the end of his career he sought to recover the wild gamey taste of this frontier existence in his last Missouri River expedition. He shared, too, the pioneer's love for tall stories, wild humor, practical jokes; and sometimes, as in the gulling of the visiting naturalist, Raffinesque, with drawings of wild creatures that existed only in his fantasy, he got himself into hot water as a reliable naturalist by forgetting how these backwoods jokes might look in print.

Only one part of this existence was repulsive to Audubon, though his obligations as a family man made him go erratically through the motions: the necessity of making a living by trade. His career as a business man was a most extravagant practical joke that he played on himself: a predestined butt and victim through his own impulsive, generous nature. His own words tell everything. "Merchants crowded to Louisville . . . None of them were, as I was, intent on the study of birds, but all were deeply impressed by the value of dollars. I could not bear to give the attention required by my business." On more than one journey, he confessed, he would thoughtlessly leave his horses unguarded, though laden with goods and dollars, to watch the motions of a warbler.

While Audubon's knowledge of birds became steadily richer, his business ventures, culminating in a crazy investment in a steam mill, made him poorer. Finally, in 1819, a time of general economic crisis, everything went to smash. He was jailed for debt and was declared bankrupt. Audubon always blamed his own bad judgment for what happened; but the misery of finding himself down and out was intensified by the deaths of his two sickly little daughters; and he had to start life again from scratch, at thirty-four, with only his clothes, his drawing outfit, and his gun. But from that low point on, though one would hardly guess it from Mr. Adams's biography, the curve of his life went upward for the next quarter of a century.

Until Audubon made the decision that launched his four-volume work on *The Birds of America,* he and his Lucy went through half-a-dozen grim years that might have broken and permanently embittered a less stable couple. Driven to turn his attention partly from birds to human faces, in order to make a living as a limner of quick portraits, Audubon lived a penurious, vagrant life, as drawing teacher, dancing master, taxidermist. Meanwhile Lucy was left to fend largely for herself, as governess and teacher, while rearing their two sons, Victor and John Woodhouse. These were bitter years for both Audubon and his wife: years of recurrent poverty, frequent separation, partial alienation, blank despair. Even after Audubon's fortunes began to mend, Lucy seems to have distrusted his

buoyant faith in their future, and to have openly doubted his ability to support his family and make their marriage again become a reality. But, determined both to establish his work and salvage his marriage, Audubon drew from his love for his wife and his sons the strength he needed to overcome his recurrent depressions and to go on. The phrenologists who described Audubon as a strong and constant lover and an affectionate father guessed right about his nature.

None of Audubon's biographers is able to give a full account of this marriage: Who for that matter has ever given an even half-way full account of *any* marriage? But enough letters have been preserved, in addition to some of Audubon's journals, to indicate that this couple furnish a classic example of the opposed temperamental types that Freud first defined as oral and anal: let us call them, on a less infantile level, the spenders and the hoarders. Lucy, her letters show, was a down-right, matter-of-fact soul; and from the meager evidence that remains one suspects that there must have been reservations, tensions, dissatisfactions almost from the beginning; for Lucy, brought up in comfort, could not share the hunter's unfettered outdoor pleasures, and worse, she did not have any birds to fall back on.

Lucy, in her tight, watchful, realistic, "practical," anxious way was the kind of woman who so often, once the first glamor of sexual intimacy has faded, leads a man to seek the carefree sympathy or the more relaxed erotic play of another woman. Fortunately, as far as negative evidence may indicate, Audubon's mistresses were all birds; and whatever Lucy's doubts and inhibitions, he never lost faith in their common destiny. "If I were jealous." Lucy once remarked, "I should have a bitter time of it, for every bird is my rival." Not that this dashing, warm-hearted man was ever insensitive to the charms of women, whether they were his seventeen-year-old pupil, Eliza Pirrie, or the unidentifiable New Orleans woman who raised an erotic storm in his bosom by commissioning him to do a portrait of her, naked, or even a neat plump serving maid, "tripping as briskly as a killdeer."

Yet this was a true marriage, as well as an enduring one; and if Lucy's sufferings had fewer immediate compensations, both in the end gained, for the achievement of Audubon's great work was possible only because he had in the throes of the crisis that separated them absorbed Lucy's virtues and made them his own. He never lost his impulsive generosity or his contempt for mere money; but in the last third of his life these traits were counterbalanced by a strict attention to irksome financial details, an unwavering fidelity to his dominant purpose, and a capacity to drive himself, day after day, at his work, often drawing from fourteen to seventeen hours at a stretch or endlessly tramping the streets of Manchester or London to find subscribers for his folios. Perhaps the best proof of his inner transformation is that, once he was committed to the publication of *The Birds of America,* he resolutely turned his back on the life he loved most, as hunter, naturalist, explorer, bird-watcher, and bird-listener, and lived in exile, to carry through the project. To ensure the great success that soon came to him, he endured the oppressions and discomforts of formal civilized life in London and Paris, overcoming his shyness, his terror of polite society, his healthy puritanic distaste for tobacco and spirits and refined food. In the course of this effort the booney backwoodsman became a great man of the world, at home among princes and presidents, accepted as an equal by artists and scientists, able to endure stuffy dinners and even duller lectures in the many scientific societies that enrolled him as a member.

Such an inner transformation after a severe crisis, sexual or religious, has been described at length by William James. It needed Audubon's complete failure in business for him to discover what now must seem to everyone—except his latest biographer—perfectly obvious: that the only life possible for him was that of a naturalist and a painter of the wild creatures he loved and studied so intensely. That obsession proved his salvation. Once he had accepted as a conscious vocation what had hitherto blindly absorbed him in practice, he was ready not only to enjoy it but to transpose the results to the realm of mind. In that task, he proved himself a master of every relevant detail, and within less than four years succeeded in rehabilitating his marriage, while establishing himself as a unique source of firsthand knowledge about the lives and habitats of American birds: over four hundred species, many painted and described for the first time.

Before appraising Audubon's central achievement, *The Birds of America,* let me pay my disrespects to Mr. Adams's new biography, whose constant derogation and denigration of Audubon called forth this preliminary excursion into Audubon's character and career. This new book, with a painstaking and even exemplary attention to recorded facts, goes over the same general ground as that covered by Francis Hobart Herrick (1917), Constance Rourke (1936), and Alice Ford (1964). On the surface, Mr. Adams, to judge by information provided by his publisher, would seem to have special qualifications for appreciating Audubon's work and influence; for he is a professional conservationist, a trustee of the National Conservancy, a Vice President of a local Audubon Society. But all these helpful interests seem to have been nullified by a temperamental aversion to Audubon himself, which causes him to present Audubon's character in the most unfavorable light possible, and to turn his great career into a series of dismal and depressing failures.

Mr. Adams has skillfully marshalled the known facts about Audubon's life as if with a single purpose in view: to support his conviction that if Audubon had only during the early years of his marriage paid sufficient attention to business, instead of perpetually playing truant, hunting, bird-watching, making his laborious drawings, *The Birds of America* need never have been painted or published. That is a highly original judgment, indeed a breathtaking one, but Audubon himself was in full accord with it. "We had marked Louisville," he noted in 1835 in the Memoir he wrote for his family, "as a spot designed by nature to be a place of great importance, and, had we been as wise as we now are, I might never have published *The Birds of America,* for a few hundred dollars, laid out at that period in lands or town lots would, if left to grow over with grass

to a date ten years past, have become an immense fortune. But young heads are on young shoulders; it was not to be, and who cares?"

Who cares? The answer is, Mr. Adams cares. He cares so much in fact that he sedulously minimizes, or rather tosses aside, *The Birds of America*—its completion he describes as "anticlimax"—in order to concentrate on Audubon's many early lapses and failures as a business man. He even so far departs from truth as to make Audubon's later enterprises seem virtual failures, too. To justify his carefully slanted thesis, Mr. Adams utters a judgment that gives him completely away, a sentence I shall treat as final. "Yet for all his cavalier attitude toward his firm, John James was seriously interested in making money. What he wanted was to be a successful merchant, a man of wealth. Yet he would not work at it." This statement needs only one correction: It is Mr. Adams who wants him to have been a successful merchant and a man of wealth; and his own meticulous citations prove that Audubon never cherished any such ambitions; for the overwhelming passion of his life, from earliest childhood on, was his love of birds. To that he was ready even to sacrifice his Lucy. The biographer who could ignore the massive evidence of Audubon's whole career in order to make this preposterous interpretation of Audubon's ambitions should have stopped in his tracks when he had written those words. But since he went on, we must ask Rufus Wilmot Griswold, the studious defamer of Poe, to move up and make room for Mr. Adams.

What Mr. Adams steadfastly regards as a wanton miscarriage of Audubon's opportunities and a betrayal of his duties to his wife was in fact what ensured Audubon's final commitment to his true vocation. But in addition Audubon's passage to his life work was favored, at intervals, by a series of chance promptings that registered as deeply as those childhood traumas that sometimes mar a whole life. Though Audubon hated his father's American agent Dacosta, indeed once wanted to murder him, he recorded gratefully that Dacosta's praise of his drawings and his prediction of a great career as a naturalist, helped set him on his road. So, too, a few years later in 1810, a chance visit of the Scots ornithologist, Alexander Wilson, fortified Audubon's confidence in both his own ambitions and his draughtsmanship. Finally, it was a remark by an English traveler, Leacock, in 1822, that helped crystallize Audubon's determination to seek publication and patrons in England.

The one incontrovertible fact about Audubon's life, then, is that his passion for birds absorbed and determined his whole life, even though he had talents and sensibilities that spread in many directions, including quadrupeds and butterflies. It was because this passion for birds was so engrossing, as unreasonably engrossing as Dmitri's obsession with Grushenka, that his work transcended his disabilities as a painter or a scholar. Apart from the occasional "normal errors" that even painstaking observers make, Audubon, in the judgment of his peers, from Baron Cuvier to Robert Cushman Murphy, was a supremely good ornithologist. While still an amateur Audubon maintained the most exacting standards in observing the behavior of birds, making on-the-spot records, opening their stomachs to discover their feeding habits, even studiously sampling them as food, for the further light their taste or texture disclosed. Even the study of bird migrations begins with Audubon, for he was the first naturalist to band young birds, to find out if they returned to their original habitat. "Nature," Audubon said, "must be seen first alive and well studied before attempts are made at representing it." That practice separates him from Buffon and Linnaeus and brings him close not only to Gilbert White and Thoreau but to Darwin and Wallace.

Certainly one side of Audubon might tempt a shallow biographer to characterize him as the typical romantic personality: passionate, impulsive, willful, lonely, convention-breaking: but nothing would conceal the real significance of Audubon's life and work so easily as this cliché. Yet at first glance, he seems a figment of Chateaubriand's imagination; or even more, he seems a robuster version of Rousseau; for besides their common love for wild nature, there was a certain similarity in their delicate mobile features, their hypersensitive proud natures, their fine ability to make enemies and become the objects of real—not fancied—persecution, such as Audubon suffered from George Ord and Charles Waterton, who hounded him as wantonly as Cobbett hounded Dr. Benjamin Rush.

Audubon loved his life as a genuine American backwoodsman: he took to the buckskin costume of the Western hunter as Rousseau less appropriately did to that of the Corsican mountaineer; and he disciplined himself to a stoic indifference to rain, cold, fatigue, hardship, as Rousseau sought to discipline Emile. On Audubon's first trip to England, he proudly kept to the Western style of long hair reaching down to the shoulders, as Buffalo Bill did long after him. When Audubon finally, on the pleadings of his Scots friends, assented to being shorn before leaving Edinburgh for London, he recorded the event in a sorrowful epitaph, surrounded by a heavy black border. It reminded him "of the horrible times of the French Revolution, when the same operation was performed upon all the victims murdered at the guillotine."

But where birds were concerned there was nothing willful or romantically sentimental about Audubon: He never flinched from killing or dissecting them. He concentrated upon condensing in graphic form his hard-won observations, line by line, feather by feather, and was as interested in the vulture disemboweling his victim as in a male turtle dove feeding or showing fondness to his mate. Except for a brief period in his youth in the atelier of Jacques Louis David, and later instructions in oil from John Stein and Thomas Sully, Audubon was self-taught; and in the interests of accuracy used pencil, pastel, water-color, even oil on the same picture, to capture the sheen of plumage or the beady gleam of an eye. In his efforts to make his painting faithful to the object, he was his own harshest critic, ruthlessly destroying or copying over work that did not satisfy him. His performance was not an emotional expression of the romantic ego; it was as self-effacing as the late Artur Schnabel's interpretations of Beethoven: the personality dissolved into the music.

The painting and the eventual engraving of *The Birds of America* is a saga in itself. For it was one thing to make

ready the great collection he took to England in 1826, and another to have them reproduced accurately and handsomely, while securing subscribers willing to pay £174 for the whole series of 435 plates—over a thousand birds. (In the United States the price was $1,000.)

Any conventional business man might have quailed before the task Audubon undertook. Arriving in a strange country, only his capacity to make friends and to work to the point of exhaustion enabled him to survive. So far from showing incompetence in his business affairs, as he had done in the absurd misfit role of shopkeeper, Audubon now mastered every detail of his job, pocketing his touchy pride, seeking introductions and subscribers in every corner of Britain, meeting many rebuffs but cannily using every opportunity. Within a year he had commenced publication, and within a dozen years, the eighty-seventh part of *The Birds of America,* which completed the fourth volume, was published.

By his own exertions Audubon had not merely launched his life-work but had achieved a sufficient income to persuade his wife to join him in 1830. In a little while, he reestablished his whole family and drew his sons, who shared some of his talents, into the work; for Victor, the elder, and more especially John Woodhouse, the younger, both trained themselves as his assistants—indeed even when fifteen John had shipped him skins for sale or gift in Britain. In that sense, the whole work became a mighty labor of love: one that makes mock, incidentally, of the oedipal fixations of our own generation. And the fact that both sons married daughters of Audubon's close friend and colleague, John Bachman, only makes the joke on Freud a little more pointed. Once the birds took their rightful place in Audubon's life, even his shaken marriage was redeemed.

The fact that Audubon heeded the lessons of adversity and completely made over his life in order to fulfill his vocation and restore his marriage is even more astonishing than his actual ornithological achievement and widening influence as naturalist. Once embarked on the publication of *The Birds of America,* he mastered every part of his formidable task. He chose the right engraver, supervised the coloring of the plates—at one time fifty painters were employed, and once they all struck because he had criticized the sloppy work of one of them—he solicited subscriptions, appointed agents, saw that bills were collected. On top of all this he not merely painted the many new pictures needed to make the work as complete as possible, but went on further explorations, in New Jersey and Florida, and even chartered a ship to carry his search to Labrador. And once Audubon had surrendered to the demands of his life-mission, even his practical judgment proved shrewder than that of his professional advisers. Against the warning of Bohn, the famous bookseller, he chose the grand form of his first elephant-size folio and priced it at a "prohibitive" cost a set, despite the competition of cheaper posthumous editions by his able forerunner and rival Alexander Wilson. That daring decision to spare no expense went flat against sober business judgment—and proved much sounder.

The man who by his own exertions and his own ability

Florida cormorant by Audubon.

could lift himself out of the financial morass into which he had sunk in 1819 was no ordinary man, and certainly no flighty, self-indulgent romantic. To characterize such a life as a failure, as Mr. Adams does up to the very end of his book, is to present a venomous travesty of the truth. No one could have had a juster view of his own talents and limitations than Audubon himself. In 1830 he wrote in his journal: "I know that I am a poor writer, that I can scarcely manage a tolerable English letter, and not a much better French one, though that is easier to me. I know I am not a scholar, but meantime I am aware that no man living knows better than I do the habits of our birds; no man living has studied them as much as I have done, and with the assistance of my old journals and memorandum books, which were written on the spot, I can at least put down plain truths which may be useful and interesting, so I shall set to at once. I cannot however give *scientific* descriptions, and here I must have assistance." Audubon's capacity for friendship served him well here. Where he was weak, William MacGillivray, the young Scots naturalist, and Bachman, of Charleston, South Carolina, a well-schooled American naturalist, supplied the missing scientific notations.

Audubon's actual life had an epic quality that the American poets of his time dreamed of: It prefigured, in the act of living, the message of *Walden*, "The Song of Myself," and *Moby Dick*, dramatically uniting their themes and adding an essential element that was unfortunately lacking in all three: the presence and power of woman and the ascendancy of love. So far only Constance Rourke, with her insight into frontier life and its humor, and Van Wyck Brooks in *The World of Washington Irving*, have in any degree captured the spirit or taken the measure of this man, though perhaps the quickest way to come close to him is through his few salvaged journals—most of them were destroyed, supposedly in the great New York fire of 1835—now published in a Dover edition.

When one views Audubon's personality and work as a whole, there is little that needs be apologized for or explained away. Even his large carefree gestures are merely those of a large soul, though they may irk those who do not understand his particular combination of humility and self-confidence, tenderness and toughness, loving care and ruthless neglect, his audacious high spirits and his "intemperate practice of temperance," as he himself put it. Even in his lifetime, the man was almost a myth; and that fact doubtless tempted some of his ornithological adversaries to treat his exact observations as if they, too, were falsified or inflated. But the real Audubon is even bigger than the myth.

What makes Audubon the important figure that he still is, now perhaps more than ever, is that his life and work brought together all the formative energies of his time, romanticism and utilitarianism, geographic exploration, mechanical invention, biological observation, esthetic naturalism, and transposed them into consummate works of art which, like the works of Turner, Constable, and Edward Lear, constantly transcended their own naturalistic premises. In the ***Ornithological Biography,*** which he published as a companion to his Folio, and republished in the later "miniature" edition of ***The Birds of America,*** his very absence of system enabled him to give a fuller account of natural processes and functions than any more abstract approach permitted: for he included the observer as well as the object observed. If, to later scientists, he seemed the last of the old-fashioned naturalists, he has now become the first of a new breed of ethologists, among whom Tinbergen, Lorenz, and Portmann are perhaps best known.

Similarly, Audubon was a practicing ecologist, long before the name and the science were established as such. For almost a century before museums of natural history showed their specimens in natural postures against their natural habitat, Audubon depicted them in this fashion. Even his passion for birds has a new significance, for since Rachel Carson's *Silent Spring,* we realize as never before that the presence of birds is the most sensitive possible index of a well-balanced human habit, with sound practices of settlement and cultivation; while their absence indicates an organic imbalance, brought on by reckless deforestation, defoliation, pollution, and poisoning.

Finally, like the Bartrams and Wilson before him, and like George Perkins Marsh, John Wesley Powell, and Frederick Law Olmsted after him, Audubon is one of the central actors in the conservation movement. He not merely demonstrated the richness of primeval America, but preserved as much of it as possible in lasting images of its flowers, shrubs, insects, butterflies, as well as birds and mammals. At a moment when only striking landscapes—high mountains, craggy gorges, shaggy forests—were singled out for admiration, Audubon, like Thoreau, was equally sensitive to the swamp, the bayou, the prairie. And if we manage to protect any part of the primeval habitat from the bulldozers, the highway engineers, the real estate speculators, and the National Parks bureaucrats, eagerly defiling what they are supposed to preserve, it will be because Audubon stands in the way, reminding us that this birthright must not be exchanged for money or motor cars.

Victor H. Cahalane   (essay date 1967)

SOURCE: An introduction, to *The Imperial Collection of Audubon Animals:* The Quadrupeds of North America, Hammond Incorporated, 1967, pp. ix-xvi.

[Cahalane was an American natural historian. In the following excerpt he discusses the compilation and publication of The Viviparous Quadrupeds of North America.*]*

The outstanding work on American mammals in the 19th century resulted from a chance meeting of two men. It occurred on October 17, 1831, in Charleston, South Carolina.

John J. Audubon, the famous bird artist and ornithologist, had arrived in town the evening before. With two assistants, landscape painter George Lehman and English taxidermist Henry Ward, he had ridden in stiff-sprung coaches, over rough and potholed roads, from Richmond. The three men were disheveled and weary. Their boardinghouse, when the bill was presented, proved to be too expensive for Audubon. While he had become the talk of natural history circles as the gifted painter of the first folio in a forthcoming series which was to depict all the birds of America, he had had as yet little monetary return. Also, since Audubon and his helpers were on their way to Florida to search for new birds, it was essential to stretch the funds as far as possible.

Consequently, Audubon, with the guidance of a local clergyman named Gilman, was tramping the streets looking for cheaper lodgings.

As they proceeded, a man approached on horseback. Recognizing Gilman, the man reined in, dismounted, and was introduced to Audubon as the Reverend John Bachman, pastor of the Lutheran Church. His strong, square face breaking into a warm smile, he greeted the artist. Thus began a deep friendship and eventually a close working and family relationship which was to endure until broken by Audubon's death nearly 20 years later.

Bachman, who had been deeply interested in natural history since boyhood, insisted that his new acquaintance and his helpers should move into the Bachman home for the duration of their stay in Charleston. The minister's family was large—eight children living, in addition to his wife and the latter's sister, Maria Martin. However, the square three-story house was commodious and two rooms were set aside for workshops. During the four weeks that elapsed before the bird men left for Florida, they spent the days traveling about the countryside with Bachman in two carriages provided by him. Notes were taken, birds were collected and preserved as skins, and in the evenings paintings and records were made. Audubon and his host talked natural history far into the night, finding in each other a mutual interest and rapport that developed quickly into affection and a high regard for each other's abilities and attainments.

Following the visit, Bachman wrote Mrs. Audubon: "The last has been one of the happiest months of my life." . . . Audubon was not only an expert, he "was communicative, intelligent and amiable, to an extent seldom found in the same individual . . . we were inseparable." Audubon was indeed an inspiration to Bachman, whose energy and interest were now channeled into effective work in science. For his part, the minister made a deep impression on Audubon.

During the years that followed, Bachman gave Audubon advice and encouragement in completing his great undertaking. ***The Birds of America,*** and supplied him with numerous specimens which the artist used in painting the plates. In return, during his expeditions Audubon collected mammal skins for his friend's careful study and to add to his already large collection.

At last Audubon completed all 435 paintings for *The Birds of America* and the companion five-volume text, *Ornithological Biography.* That summer of 1839, although the monumental work was selling but slowly despite much solicitation, the artist's great energies began to overflow. Under the urge of this restlessness and the always pressing need for funds to support his family, he decided to do with the mammals what he had just completed with the birds.

Although the proposed project was actually more difficult than the *Birds,* Audubon assumed that he would collect and identify the specimens as well as paint the portraits and write the text. With typical drive and enthusiasm he proposed to broadcast immediately a printed prospectus announcing the future publication of *The Viviparous Quadrupeds of North America!*

This planned publicity brought a down-to-earth letter from John Bachman: ". . . are you not too fast in issuing your prospectus . . . ? . . . The animals have never been carefully described, and you will find difficulties at every step. Books cannot aid you much. Long journeys will have to be undertaken. .. The Western Deer are no joke (to classify), and the ever varying Squirrels seem sent by Satan himself, to puzzle the Naturalists." Bachman added—also rashly!—"I think that I have studied the subject more than you have . . . Say in what manner I can assist you."

The courteous but sensible advice and perhaps his own second thoughts convinced Audubon that even his great talent should be supplemented by technical assistance. He asked for and received the commitment that Bachman would collaborate as junior author. The latter had not only scientific recognition; he had given his two oldest daughters in marriage to Audubon's sons. By joining the enterprise without personal recompense, Bachman hoped to perhaps provide a future "nest egg" for his children and their families as well as make an important contribution to science.

Mammalogy in 1839 was indeed a promising field for a comprehensive publication. The species of eastern and northern America had been investigated by a number of naturalists including Bartram, Rafinesque, Hearne and Richardson, but most of their results had been published here and there in obscure journals and magazines, some of which did not even pretend to be scientific in character. Richardson's *Fauna Boreali-Americana,* printed in 1829, was one of the very few inclusive works on animal life but it was restricted to the northern portion of the continent. DeKay's monumental *Zoology of New York,* which actually attempted to cover a wider area than that State, had not yet appeared. Many original (type) specimens, particularly those representing species in British America, the far west and Mexico, were deposited in European museums and could be studied only by making an expensive and time-consuming journey. American collections of mammals were scarce, poorly housed and all too often subject to loss by fire or to dispersal if the owners went bankrupt. Zoological gardens for live animals were small at best and

very few in number. Scant information on possible new species could be gained from them. Libraries of science books were little better; numerous works containing descriptions of American animals were available only in private homes or in Europe.

Finally, much of western America was still poorly known and travel west of the Mississippi River was arduous, dangerous, and restricted largely to the Missouri River and the southern overland route through Santa Fe. Unpredictable and sometimes hostile Indians, and uncertain and often unfriendly international relations with Mexico, discouraged scientific work without an effective military escort.

Bachman had been most conservative in estimating the difficulties of the project.

In establishing the scope of their book, the authors realized that, because nature does not observe political subdivisions, they too should ignore national boundaries. Therefore they resolved to include "the British and Russian possessions in America, the whole of the United States and their territories, California, and that part of Mexico north of the Tropic of Cancer." The illustrations were to be "not only scientifically correct, but interesting to all" readers, in "the varied occupations, expressions, and attitudes" of the animals, "together with the appropriate accessories, such as trees, plants, landscapes, etc." The text would describe the form and color of the subjects, their habits, distribution and relationships ("all of interest"), and methods of hunting for meat, skins, or "to get rid of dangerous or annoying neighbors."

During the planning late in 1839, Bachman expressed "doubt that we (will need room for more than one hundred species) unless we include the whales and mammalia of that character." Eventually he described more than double that number of terrestrial mammals, of which the Audubons, father and son, painted 147 species (plus eight separate "varieties") on 150 plates. Bachman continued, "The figures may, I think, be given without reference to any scale, those of a skunk full size, those above as taste or space will dictate." The plate size adopted was 28 by 22 inches.

Audubon envisioned that he would require two years to paint the animal portraits, and that Bachman would need an additional year to complete his field studies and write descriptions. The complete publication, therefore, would be available to the subscribers in three years.

Even the realistic and hardheaded Bachman did not fully realize the magnitude of the task on which they entered with such high hopes. While a few plates were rushed out in 1842 (to impress subscribers), it was not until 1848, eight years after initiation of the project, that the last of the 150 plates came from the press. The third and final volume of text, although writing was finished in the spring of 1852, was not published until 1854, 11 years behind Audubon's "schedule." He himself had died three years previously, after turning his brushes over to his son John in the spring of 1846.

Even before Bachman committed himself as junior author

in January 1840, Audubon was spending every available hour painting mammals and writing for specimens. Through the Christmas holidays he continued to devote long days to the project. Among many correspondents, he wrote to one Thomas McCulloch of Halifax, Nova Scotia: "I wish you to assist me as much as is in your power in the way of procuring specimens for me and paying for them whatever you think proper . . . I send you now a list of such animals as I think you can get for me." To Increase S. Smith of Hingham, Massachusetts, Audubon sent directions for preserving snowshoe (varying) hares for shipment: "The animals ought to be put in a Keg of Common Yankee Rum, and as soon as possible after death, cutting a slit in the abdomen of not exceeding *Two Inches* in length, and pouring Rum in the apperture until well filled. The Entrails must remain untouched."

Audubon worked rapidly and with great concentration. By mid-August 1841, after painting regardless of cold or heat since the end of the previous year, he had completed 36 plates. (Bachman put this achievement in perspective by pointing out that some 200 more species should have "proper elucidation." He had raised his earlier estimate.) In the autumn, Audubon decided to leave crowded, noisy New York City, which he hated, and he acquired an estate of 30 acres or more a few miles from town. On the western shore of upper Manhattan Island, it afforded a lovely view of the New Jersey Palisades, and fish could be seined from the Hudson River whenever needed for the table. (The two Audubon sons caught an eight-foot, 200-pound sturgeon; such a fish would expire quickly in these present-day polluted waters.) A three-story house was completed in April 1842, giving ample room for the family. Here at "Minnie's Land" (named for his wife) the artist found inspiration for his work and space in which to keep live subjects for his painting and writing—ranging from squirrels and a marten to a pair of elk!

When need for specimens and information on western species became pressing in 1842, Audubon went to Washington despite oppressive mid-summer heat to solicit official support for an expedition. In this he failed, but at his hotel he met a fellow-lodger, Col. Pierre Chouteau of the American Fur Company, which traded on the upper Missouri River and its tributaries. Through this acquaintance, Audubon was enabled to travel the next summer on a Company steamboat to Fort Union, a trading post on the Missouri a few miles below the outlet of the Yellowstone River. He was accompanied by a close friend and amateur naturalist, Edward Harris, who rented his farm to help meet one-fifth the cost of the expedition. Expenses included the modest salaries of three assistants who were engaged by Audubon.

The party hunted and made observations at refueling stops on the journey upstream. The 1,400-mile trip from St. Louis took 49 days. At Fort Union, June 12 to August 16, the men sought everything from prairie dogs to bison. Indian and half-breed trappers were hired and given assignments. Audubon sketched and kept a voluminous journal, recording impressions of the strange landscapes, plants and animals, and the white trappers and red Indians. He watched from the sidelines as his companions

killed bison, sometimes for their tongues only, and narrowly escaped from an infuriated bull when in the excitement he forgot his limitations of age and approached too closely on foot.

Although Audubon saw many bighorns; he was never able to get near enough to shoot any and the hunters that he sent off usually came back empty-handed. Audubon and his party returned back down the river to St. Louis and thence home. He arrived at Minnie's Land November 6, 1843 with drawings, skins soaked in brine, Indian trophies and a live swift fox, a badger and a mule deer. (Among the Indian gifts were a necklace of grizzly bear teeth and a full-size Indian lodge.) It was Audubon's last field trip. Although his sight was still exceptionally keen, he looked and felt 10 years older than his actual age of 58.

The Reverend John Bachman had a dual role in producing the *Quadrupeds.* First, he determined the validity of species or "variety" of the mammals. He wrote all scientific descriptions, complied the synonymy of species' names, worked out geographic distributions as far as possible from often scanty records, and contributed his personal observations on habits of the animals. Secondly, he acted as scientific editor, revising and fitting together the accounts of habits, hunting anecdotes and other information which he received from the senior Audubon, his son John, and numerous others whose comments were solicited or contributed on their own initiative.

For his time, Bachman was well prepared to undertake the task. He was five years younger than Audubon, of Swiss-German stock, a thorough scholar with a deep and exceptionally broad interest in nature. Although he was isolated from recognized scientific centers of the country, he was accepted as a reputable colleague by naturalists both in America and England. He corresponded with great naturalists of the day and a number of them came to visit him at his home. In 1838, he was invited to deliver an address on natural science in America before a congress of naturalists and physicians in Freiburg, Germany. He used the opportunity while in London to study the notable collection of mammals in the British Museum.

While he was perhaps inclined to be pedantic, Bachman was right in telling Audubon, "You cannot do without me in this business . . ." He was a friendly, kindly man who was intensely loyal and self-sacrificing. Probably no other naturalist of the period, either amateur or professional, would have carried the project through to completion under the very trying handicaps which beset him during his 12 years of research and writing. Before the invention of the typewriter, every word of copying and manuscript had to be written laboriously with a quill or an "iron" pen.

Because of his churchly obligations, Bachman could rarely give full time to his monumental avocation but he arranged his schedule to the best advantage possible. In the summer of 1842, when Mrs. Bachman's poor health forced her to leave Charleston's heat and humidity, he visited her weekly at her country retreat where he worked on the *Quadrupeds* without interruption. Mrs. Bachman died four years later; this was one of a series of personal catastrophes which included the loss of three children (two of them the daughters who had married Audubon's sons) and of several family servants, as well as his own persistently recurring eye trouble and other infirmities.

Slow communication with the Audubons in New York was frustrating. Mail was two weeks en route; response to a question required a month if given immediate attention. To settle the multitudinous problems of species identification, nomenclature and other points, Bachman needed many reference books which were not in his personal library nor that of the local Natural History Society. He depended largely on the Audubons to obtain those books or to copy pertinent information from them. Engrossed in their own pressing endeavors of finding specimens and painting them, as well as meeting many business obligations, the Audubons sometimes neglected to supply those wants with what Bachman considered reasonable promptness.

At the end of the second year, Bachman was still patient. He declined an offer of the presidency of South Carolina College at three thousand dollars a year, saying that he enjoyed preaching and his hobby, nature, too much to leave Charleston. This decision undoubtedly saved the *Quadrupeds* from foundering, or at best suffering a very long delay.

Difficulties were destined, however, to be compounded. Bachman expected a vast amount of information from the Missouri River expedition—specimens and data for describing new species and "fleshing out" accounts of habits—but he was given only picturesque generalities. When asked for a detailed report, Audubon, well aware that he had accomplished little of scientific value, replied that he had brought back many sketches, and specimens of what he hoped would prove to be 14 new birds and a new type of antelope. Politely, Bachman praised the "grand haul" of birds but advised that the antelope probably had been described earlier. (It had.) Finally, late in 1845, the clergyman traveled to New York where Audubon refused even to show him the notes he had made along the Missouri River. The journal was at long last turned over to Bachman several months later only when he threatened to withdraw completely. Bitterly disappointed that Audubon had brought back so few small mammals, Bachman lamented the amount of time spent watching buffalo-kills, wolves, grizzlies and bighorns. He urged the senior author to write back to Fort Union for specimens, NOT of his "princess brain-eating, horse-straddling squaw" (whom Audubon had painted) ". . . but what is better . . . the Skunk . . . Hares in Winter colors . . . and the Rabbit."

During his visit to Minnie's Land, Bachman became aware that although Audubon's artistic skill was still impressive, his physical and mental capabilities were declining. This explained the increasing frequency of "sad mistakes" in the manuscript pages which were being submitted to the editor. Thereafter, Bachman depended increasingly on the two sons. They, unfortunately, needed "the whip" applied by "the schoolmaster." They failed to send specimens, books, and excerpts from journals which Bachman required. He complained bitterly to a friend, "They have not sent me one single book out of a list of a hundred I gave them, and only six lines copied from a book after

my having written them for four years." At one point, Bachman dropped work for almost a year, then resumed when Victor vowed that he and his brother would pay strict attention to directions from Charleston.

The first volume of text which had caused Bachman so much travail was printed in Philadelphia in 1846 and in London the following spring. (This was the end of the "European edition.") With new encouragement, Bachman continued work, even though impaired vision forced him to dictate the final pages to Victor Audubon. In the early spring of 1852 the third and final volume of text was finished.

John J. and Lucy Audubon reared two sons (two daughters died in early childhood). As men, both sons collaborated with their father and spent much of their lives in his service. The younger, John Woodhouse Audubon (usually called "Johnny" by his father) was quiet, sensitive, gruff with strangers, probably from shyness, but genial and a sparkling conversationalist among friends. With his father's instruction he became an animal painter of some ability, but he did not pretend to be a naturalist. His forte was portraiture and as a young man he painted members of his family and their friends, including Bachman. While in England and Scotland during the 1830's John worked professionally, taking as many as five sittings a day.

This career was stifled by demands of the *Quadrupeds.* Acting from the beginning of the project (late 1839) as assistant artist, secretary and general helper, John was forced to take over more of the work as his father's health declined. His expedition to Texas, November 1845 to April 1846, yielded little that was useful. Shortly after returning from Texas, John spent nearly a year in Europe painting mammals of northern Canada in the British Museum and perhaps other institutions. By the spring of 1846—midway in the production of folio plates—John was left with sole responsibility in this department. He did at least 72 of the 150 paintings in the imperial folio series, as well as the five "bonus" plates of the octavo edition.

John's older brother (by three years), Victor Gifford Audubon, inherited his father's quick temper and sometimes sarcastic tongue. His artistic talents were in landscapes; his abilities may be measured by his sale of an oil in New Orleans in the fall of 1840 for 150 dollars (perhaps equivalent to five hundred dollars at present). Victor assisted his father in the *Quadrupeds* project by painting backgrounds as well as plants and other accessories to the mammals. His greatest service and most of his time was given to business aspects, especially dealings with the lithographers and printers. To ensure that the original paintings were redrawn or traced accurately on the stone slabs with the colors reproduced exactly, required constant, careful supervision in the shop while the work was in progress. During the 11 months that his brother was drawing specimens in the British Museum, Victor functioned as overall supervisor for the final preparation of copy for the printer. Costs were mounting, the printer was trying to expedite the work, and to keep him supplied with text for the typesetters Victor edited and condensed copy as it came from Bachman. This did nothing to soothe the latter, who protested alterations and the insertion of still another writing style in the book.

Long years of intensive work and financial worries involved in preparing and publishing the *Quadrupeds,* following equally arduous endeavors in behalf of *The Birds of America,* undoubtedly shortened the lives of Audubon's sons. Victor died in 1860, aged 51, and John in 1862 at the age of 49.

Although she was not mentioned in the Introduction to the *Quadrupeds,* Miss Maria Martin "lightened the labours" of the authors more than all of the "many excellent friends and gentlemen" whose assistance is specifically acknowledged there. The sister-in-law of John Bachman, Miss Martin made fine drawings of mammals, insects and plants as he required them, served as copyist (from books, journals and manuscripts), secretary and editorial assistant, and read to him when his eyes failed from overuse. Two years after the death of the first Mrs. Bachman in 1846, the minister showed his appreciation of Maria Martin's qualities by making her his wife.

By request of the authors or on their own initiative, many persons contributed mammals, or skins and skulls, and information such as field observations. Most of these doctors, surgeons, army officers, farmers, trappers and others are now only obscure names or are completely forgotten. Among the exceptions is Edward Harris who, as a close friend of both Audubon and Bachman, encouraged them, made financial contributions, and settled disagreements when they arose between the two collaborators. John K. Townsend allowed the use of his invaluable field notes and his large collection of mammals, including types of many new species, from the almost unexplored northern Rockies and Pacific Northwest. Spencer F. Baird, later Secretary of the Smithsonian Institution, provided Audubon with numerous mammals, both living and dead, for use in painting; he also searched the literature for descriptions of new species. Sir George Simpson, governor of the Hudson's Bay Company, sent many skins of Arctic furbearers. Pierre Chouteau, famous fur trader, merchant and financier, contributed skins of western mammals and enabled Audubon to make his long-desired trip to the West. These are but examples of the many who became interested in and enhanced the value of *The Viviparous Quadrupeds of North America.*

While Audubon boasted (not with complete accuracy) that he had painted every plate of his *Birds of America* from subjects he had studied in life, he never made a similar claim for the *Quadrupeds.* He used skins and mounted animals at times, and occasionally he resorted to pictures by other artists as a means of refreshing his memory. Occasionally he employed time- and labor-saving expedients or "short-cuts." For example, he traced the figure of an eastern gray squirrel, which he had painted in 1821 and used as an accessory to the Barred Owl in Plate 46 of his *Birds,* to occupy the left side of Plate 7 in the *Quadrupeds.*

Although Audubon gained fame primarily as a painter of birds, he depicted most of the mammals superbly. While his predecessors had posed their subjects woodenly and in conventional postures, he captured life and movement without, in most cases, distortion. He had a fine sense of composition and some of his arrangements are exquisite. His work varies in quality. Some pictures have earned the highest praise of artists and of such noted scientists as Louis Agassiz, Eliot Coues and Thomas Gilliard. Other paintings are less worthy, showing the effects of unfamiliarity with the animal in its natural environment or, too frequently, the pressure under which he worked to meet publication deadlines or financial needs. It must be remembered that many of the plates which the senior Audubon made for the *Quadrupeds* were painted when his physical infirmities were mounting as a result of a lifetime of hardships and stress. One of his last paintings, that of the "Texan" (now hog-nosed) Skunk, Plate 53, appears to be divided in two vertical planes. It was criticized vigorously by Bachman who generally considered his friend's art beyond reproach; the painter, however, could see nothing wrong with it.

John Woodhouse Audubon took over the entire task of painting the mammals early in 1846. Unlike his father who had little formal instruction in art and worked chiefly with chalk, crayon and watercolors, J. W. Audubon had the benefit of considerable training and painted almost entirely in oils. The style of the two men was similar, so alike, in fact, that in some instances it is not possible to credit the paintings with certainty. A number of plates in the imperial folios which bear the name of J. J. Audubon were, in the later octavo edition, assigned to the son. According to the legend on Plate 120, which depicts two lemmings, it was drawn by the senior Audubon. The text, however, states that the drawing was made in London by J. W. Audubon from museum skins obtained in Canada by Drummond. In the subsequent octavo edition the legend was corrected to read, "Drawn from nature (!) by J. W. Audubon." This edition credits the latter with 72 of the original 150 plates, but the actual number may be even larger. Using his father's drawings from the Missouri-Yellowstone trip, the younger Audubon drew most of the larger mammals, as well as the smaller species of the far north. He re-drew all of the imperial folio drawings for the "miniature" edition, a task which must have required many months.

In summary, while John Woodhouse Audubon had less than his father's great ability to portray animals in exciting movement as well as little feeling for design, he has been too deeply shadowed by the senior Audubon's reputation. Indirectly, he has also suffered by the concentration of fame's spotlight on the *Birds* rather than the *Quadrupeds.*

Until the closing stages of work, each species and variety was painted on a separate plate; notable mammals such as white-tailed deer, bison and mountain lion were each given two plates. Even the smallest insectivores and rodents were handled in similar lavish manner. At the end, however, some of the small species were crowded two, three or even four on a single plate.

By agreement of the two authors, the senior Audubon recorded his personal observations on the habits of mammals and sent them to Bachman. The latter edited the manuscript and combined it with his own and sometimes with accounts which were contributed by reliable naturalist-friends or acquaintances. Writing was hard work for him; he labored not only from dawn to dusk but burned a candle for an hour or more at each end of the day. Such a sedentary occupation gave him dyspepsia, and he once wrote to Bachman, "I would rather go without a shirt or any inexpressibles through the whole of Florida swamps in mosquito time than labor as I have hitherto done with the pen."

Nevertheless, Audubon's prose was expressive, complete and even flowery—quite the opposite of the plain style of his co-author. Bachman appears to have been critical at times of these accounts. Possibly he felt that they were unscientific, or improbable, or that the actions of the animals had been misinterpreted. After comparing manuscripts with printed text, some modern writers believe that Bachman's editing and omissions (together with use of the editorial "we") destroyed some of the fine personal qualities in Audubon's prose.

Much to Bachman's distress, it was not possible to give a truly complete account of American mammals—the bats, seals and whales were omitted. The completeness of the other groups—insectivores, rodents, carnivores and hoofed mammals—made the ***Quadrupeds*** the unquestioned authority in its field. In coverage, scientific accuracy and popular interest, it had no equal at the time of its publication and for a half-century thereafter. Even today the anecdotal flavor of the text and the feel of a lost century make fascinating reading. The delicate design and color of the small animals and the drama of motion and wildness are still exciting.

While Audubon mulled over his newly conceived plan for a master work on American mammals, he discussed with Robert Havell, the London publisher, the terms under which he would undertake to produce it. At the time (mid-1839), Havell was thoroughly disgusted by difficulties he had met in printing **The Birds of America.** This expensive publication had been slow to sell and many subscribers had failed to pay promptly. Even people like the Baron Rothschild had canceled their orders. Consequently, Audubon was in arrears for folios as they came from the press and Havell could not meet his payrolls for engravers, lithographers, artists and colorists. (As many as 50 of the latter were employed at one time.) The publisher's reply was negative—his client was too far behind on the old job to talk about another equally expensive project. (Eventually Audubon was able to make full payment.)

On returning to New York in the autumn, Audubon was referred to a Philadelphian, J. T. Bowen. A skilled lithographer, Bowen had arrived a few years before from his native England. During the post Jackson depression he had lost most of his savings in the stock market and he was in a receptive mood for any reasonable offer. Accordingly, he entered into successive contracts with Audubon to lithograph and color, first a miniaturized edition of the ***Birds,*** and later the imperial folio and the octavo edition of the ***Quadrupeds.*** Actual printing was to be done by other Philadelphia craftsmen, the plates by Bisbaugh and text by Henry Ludwig.

American flamingo by Audubon.

Up to this time, most fine reproductions of paintings had been made from copper engravings. Lithography, a process which was less than 50 years old, had several advantages in addition to economy. Using a grease pencil, the lithographer's artist traced the lines of the original *in reverse* on a smoothly ground, flat slab of fine-grained sandstone. Those portions of the absorbent stone which had been drawn upon would accept ink, and in the press would transfer the ink to paper. The most subtle gradations from deepest black to palest gray were reproduced. After printing, the reproductions on paper were tinted in the proper colors and shades by teams of colorists.

A few of the plates for the imperial folio of the ***Quadrupeds*** had been rushed to the printer near the end of 1842. As successive plates accumulated, they were bound five in a folio. Volume I, containing the first 50 plates (no descriptions), was published in 1845, Volume II in 1846, and Volume III in 1848. Folios purchased separately cost $10; the three-volume set was $300. As promised, each subscriber to the three volumes of plates also received an equal number of volumes of text which described the species pictured. These were printed in octavo size and were issued as they were completed in 1846, 1851 and 1854. A supplement to the last volume included more text and five "bonus" lithographed plates from paintings by J. W. Audubon. These depicted eight species: a red fox, four tree squirrels, a Harris antelope (ground) squirrel, a California vole and the crab-eating raccoon. The entire work of plates and text bore the imposing title of *The Viviparous Quadrupeds of North America.* Three volumes of an octavo edition combining the text and all 155 plates were published in 1849, 1851 and 1854 respectively. In this smaller edition, the lengthy and ponderous title was appropriately reduced to *The Quadrupeds of North America.*

The United States Congress, in 1857, authorized the payment of $16,000 for 100 copies each of Audubon's *Birds* and of the *Quadrupeds* "to be presented to foreign governments in return for valuable gifts made to the United States."

Michael Harwood and Mary Durant   (essay date 1985)

SOURCE: "In Search of the Real Mr. Audubon," in *Audubon,* Vol. 87, No. 3, May, 1985, pp. 58-119.

[*Durant is a novelist and natural historian and Harwood is an environmental journalist. In the following excerpt, they examine Audubon's origins, the reaction of contemporaries to his works, and his attitudes toward the environment.*]

More than half a century passed before many key elements of [Audubon's] life became known, and this was due in large measure to Audubon himself. He hid facts, left behind distracting trails of false information, and erected a handsome public image of himself.

Audubon freely gave interviews to journalists. He sent friends lengthy reports of his expeditions, which then were published in newspapers or periodicals. In the introductions to the five volumes of the *Ornithological Biography* he wrote about himself and his labors. The first three volumes were leavened at regular intervals by what Audubon called "Episodes." These were lively literary sketches, sixty in all—not only scenes of the North American frontier for a European audience endlessly curious about the wilderness, but also tales of people, places, and strange creatures he'd seen, adventures he'd had. Many of the essays and notes on individual bird species in the *Ornithological Biography* included fragments—or apparent fragments—of his life history. Other autobiographical tidbits appeared later in species accounts in *The Viviparous Quadrupeds of North America.*

This published material, however, was hardly the true and complete Audubon. As the historian John Francis McDermott has noted, "Like many another nineteenth-century man who fancied himself as a literary person, he chose to present fact as fiction and equally often depicted fiction as fact."

The public Audubon also was heavily edited. He was a romantic enthusiast and often got carried away, sometimes trying to imitate such contemporary literary heroes as Sir Walter Scott. The results could be wordy and gloriously purple. His spelling and sentence structure could be odd, too, because his first language was French. So he needed editing, and for his *chef-d'oeuvre* the *Ornithological Biography* he hired the Scottish ornithologist William MacGil-

livray, who also wrote the technical anatomical descriptions of bird specimens.

Most important, Audubon as an autobiographer left huge gaps in the story. He wrote or said almost nothing about his origins for publication. He dealt with the subject of his birth in nine words, "I received life and light in the New World." He revealed little more about events in the first seventeen years of his life: He had gone to France "to receive the rudiments of my education," he said, and then returned to the New World, to "a beautiful plantation" in Pennsylvania. He wrote freely about only one aspect of his youth, his introduction to birds and to drawing. He did say he had studied drawing under many "masters"— surely an exaggeration—and among his teachers he included the great French court painter Jacques Louis David, which was simply not true.

He was a shade more forthcoming about his young manhood, and occasionally his readers could even link him with a date and a place. The first such connection was 1810 and Louisville. By then one might conclude that Audubon was married and in business, though he did not say what that business was. He treated the next sixteen years of his story haphazardly, scattering sporadic dates and places in the bird essays, the Episodes, and his other writings.

Finally, in 1826, after his overnight success in England, he became a public figure, and there were no advantages to obscuring his activities. So he was much more generous with information about current events in his life.

The persona he offered to the public appeared larger than life. In the European perception—and eventually in the American perception—he was "the American Woodsman," the natural man on the American frontier, the courageous wanderer who had been able to break free of traditional restraints, who had followed his star and, with the encouragement of his loving wife and children, had fulfilled his greatest potential. The image was enhanced by the fact that his major interest was birds, beautiful creatures with fascinating habits that included the miraculous ability to fly. Birds constituted "one of the most delightful departments of science," in the words of his contemporary Washington Irving.

Reading Audubon's prose, reading the news reports, one saw him mostly in action—exuberant, spontaneous, tireless, traveling long distances in strange territory by horse or on foot or in a skiff or flatboat or schooner—watching, hunting, shooting, taking notes, and drawing. He portrayed himself surviving occasional confrontations with potentially dangerous natural hazards, beasts, and people, although he remarked in a letter to Lucy that in truth his greatest danger in the woods had been from ticks and mosquitoes. He staged these stories in a resonant environment, picturing the United States as wild, grand, beautiful, unbelievably rich in game and fish, and as open, honest, and hospitable. His love for his adopted country reached to the very roots of his soul. "When I think of America—her beautiful forests and songsters," he once wrote Lucy from Europe, "my eyes fill with big tears as if I was never more to see or hear all those Sweet Friends and companions of mine."

To at least some of his contemporaries it seemed obvious that Audubon had left unsaid or falsified or glorified much that was important about himself. He told family, friends, and acquaintances things that he didn't write for publication, sometimes different versions to different people. At the heart of this round of conflicting stories was the burning secret of his life, the stigma of bastardy. He was driven to reinvent and dramatize himself, time and time again, in his craving for respectability and approval. In the early Mill Grove days, for instance, he informed Lucy Bakewell's family that he and his parents and his sister had been imprisoned for a considerable time during the reign of terror in the French Revolution but had managed to make a daring and dangerous escape.

Another example comes to us from Vincent Nolte, a successful German merchant on business in America, who was a longtime friend of Audubon's. Their first meeting, as Nolte recalled it, was in the winter of 1811-12, when Audubon was a young merchant still in his twenties. In the space of a few conversations Audubon reinvented himself several times. Wrote Nolte: "I rode, early one morning, entirely alone, over the loftiest summit of the Alleghany ridge, called Laurel Hill, and at about ten o'clock arrived at a small inn, close by the falls of the Juniata River. Here I ordered a substantial breakfast. The landlady showed me into a room and said I perhaps would not object to taking my meal at the same table with a strange gentleman, who was already there. As I entered I found the latter personage, who at once struck me as being what, in common parlance, is called an odd fish. He was sitting at a table, before the fire, with a Madras handkerchief wound around his head, exactly in the style of the French mariners, or laborers, in a seaport town. I stepped up to him and accosted him politely with the words, 'I hope I don't incommode you by coming to take my breakfast with you.' 'Oh no, sir,' he replied, with a strong French accent that made it like 'No, sare.' 'Ah!' I continued, 'you are a Frenchman, sir?' 'No, sare,' he answered, *'Hi emm an Heenglishman.'* 'Why,' I asked in return, 'how do you make that out? You look like a Frenchman, and you speak like one.'

" 'Hi emm an Heenglishman, becas hi got a Heenglish wife,' he answered. Without investigating the matter further, we made up our minds at breakfast to remain in company and to ride together to Pittsburgh. He showed himself to be an original throughout, but at last admitted that he was a Frenchman by birth, and a native of La Rochelle. However, he had come in his early youth to Louisiana, had grown up in the sea-service, and had gradually become a thorough American. 'Now,' I asked, 'how does that accord with your quality of Englishman?' Upon this he found it convenient to reply, in the French language, 'When all is said and done, I am somewhat cosmopolitan; I belong to every country.' "

On such official government documents as his naturalization papers Audubon correctly gave his birthplace as Santo Domingo. But when it came to supplying information to people who were about to write letters of introduc-

tion for him to take on his travels, he seems to have been quite freewheeling. The letters written for him by Daniel Webster and John Tyler described him as a native of the United States. Vincent Nolte, who knew better, also introduced him in one letter as a native American, but three days later in another introductory letter spoke of him as a "European by birth." Meanwhile, a new acquaintance in England, who would have had no way of knowing where Audubon was born unless Audubon had told him, wrote a letter of introduction that put Audubon's birthplace correctly in Santo Domingo.

Louisiana was probably his favorite "birthplace." The American consul in Liverpool introduced him to the American ambassador in London as "our fellow citizen of Louisiana." Mrs. Nathaniel Wells Pope, whose physician husband was one of Audubon's hunting companions during the early 1820s in Louisiana, recalled that Audubon "often described to me the cottage in which he was born. It was on the bank of the Mississippi River, in lower Louisiana, and was surrounded by orange trees." Audubon's stories of his Louisiana birthplace eventually spawned a minor industry in Louisiana, the search for the plantation on which he was born. After Audubon was dead, an elderly New Orleans gentleman named Bernard Xavier Phillippe de Marigny de Mandeville stepped forward with a tall story of his own. He claimed Audubon had been born at Fontainebleau, his plantation on the far side of Lake Pontchartrain, and Marigny was reported to be "ever proud to bear this testimony of his protection given to Audubon's mother, and his ability to bear witness to the place of Audubon's birth." All this was arrant nonsense. Both Marigny and Audubon had been born in 1785, putting Marigny in no position to play the gracious host to Audubon's mother at her *accouchement*. Furthermore, the Marigny family did not own the Fontainebleau property until 1800. But Marigny had helped Audubon during the early 1820s by advancing him money for portraits and bird drawings. Perhaps he thought he'd help him again with a solid-gold Louisiana birthplace. At any rate, the story was believed. The True Birthplace had been located, and early in this century people made pilgrimages to the spot and romantic descriptions of it were printed.

To this day the "fact" of Audubon's Louisiana birthplace still turns up occasionally. No one knows where he first got the idea. Perhaps it began with the forged passport obtained by his father, which gave John James' birthplace as Louisiana and got him safely past the conscription officers and out of France.

And what did Audubon tell his family about his birth? A great deal, it appears, and probably the whole truth. An important clue is written in his own hand in his journal of the 1820-21 trip down the Mississippi. In November, as the flatboat passed the Chickasaw Bluffs of Tennessee, he wrote a brief autobiography for his two boys, which included this intriguing comment about his father: "Most Men have faults, he had one that never Left him untill sobered by a Long Life common to Many Individuals, but this was Counter balanced by Many qualities—his Generosity was often too great—as a Father I never complained of him and the many Durable Friends he had prove him to have been a *good* man." At that crucial point, two lines on the page are heavily scratched out, in a different ink, at a later time. Audubon's biographers have wrung their hands for years over those two missing lines. He obviously went on to enlarge on his father's "one fault" or to reveal the relationship between his father, Mademoiselle Rabin, and himself, because the story then picks up: "My Mother, who I have been told was an Extraordinary beautifull Woman, died shortly after my Birth, and My Father having maried in France I was removed thereto." Someone—probably whoever scratched out the two lines—inserted the prefix "re-" before that "maried." The obvious intent was to remove all suggestions of illegitimacy.

Audubon supposedly wrote another, lengthier autobiography in about 1835, when he was fifty. It sounds like him, but there are doubts that all of it came from his pen. Here again, his origins are kept a secret. The two opening paragraphs give the following story:

> The precise period of my birth is yet an enigma to me, and I can only say what I have often heard my father repeat to me on this subject . . . It seems that [he] had large properties in Santo Domingo, and was in the habit of visiting frequently that portion of our Southern States called . . . Louisiana. . . . During one of these excursions he married a lady of Spanish extraction, whom I have been led to understand was as beautiful as she was wealthy, and otherwise attractive. . . . My mother, soon after my birth, accompanied my father to the estate of Aux Cayes, on the Island of Santo Domingo, and she was one of the victims during the ever-to-be lamented period of the Negro insurrection.

Most of Audubon's contemporaries seem to have been politely silent about the discrepancies and ambiguities in his life story. But he did have enemies, particularly in Philadelphia, where Alexander Wilson's *American Ornithology* had been completed after his death. The Wilson associates responsible for the various editions of that work did not welcome a rival ornithologist, certainly not one who was internationally acclaimed. It was to their advantage to diminish Audubon's reputation for truthfulness.

In 1834 one reviewer, whose brother happened to be one of Wilson's publishers, wrote a scathing denunciation of the first volume of the **Ornithological Biography** for a midwestern magazine. This reviewer admitted that public sentiment had set Audubon up as the "greatest and best" and that dissent was tantamount to treason, but he proceeded to lambaste a few of the frontier adventure stories Audubon had included among his Episodes.

This was a touchy point. Some of Audubon's frontier Episodes were tall tales vulnerable to criticism, since he had originally looked upon them as just something to spark up the pages between his ornithological essays. He once wrote home from England asking for good stories, but his friend and mentor John Bachman suggested that he stick to the truth in the rest of his adventure yarns. Audubon did raise the level of the Episodes before dropping them altogether from the last two volumes of the **Ornithological Biography.**

In 1835 another polemic was fired off at Audubon, this time by an eccentric Boston editor, John Neal of the *New England Galaxy.* At the time he was a subscriber to **The Birds of America,** and he declared his admiration for the engravings: "Glorious," said Neal, a "magnificent" work. But, personally, he didn't like Audubon a bit, and in a series of articles he repeated every aspersion and scathing bit of gossip he could lay his hands on.

The question of Audubon's birthplace inspired a string of caustic comments. Among them: "One gentleman . . . avers that Mr. A. was born in Louisiana. Others . . . that he was a native of St. Domingo . . . While at Eastport a twelvemonth ago . . . he pretended to have been born in *Kentucky* . . . And nobody knows to this day where Mr. Audubon the Ornithologist was born, or whether he was ever born at all. And just so it is with his age—not a word on that subject."

As to Audubon's claim that Jacques Louis David "guided my hand," Neal sourly suggested that "perhaps it was some other David. And we are more inclined to the latter opinion from having seen a portrait in oil by Mr. Audubon . . . which proves incontestably one of two things, that his master was not the great David—or—that the pupil was a blockhead."

What's more, wrote Neal, he had hunted up everything Audubon painted in Cincinnati some fifteen years earlier—though in fact Audubon had left nothing behind but productions he didn't own or didn't want. Among the remnants Neal found some large landscapes in watercolor, intended as backgrounds for the Western Museum's displays. He admitted that there were some "spirited passages and a general air of freedom about the trees" but ridiculed the landscapes as "wretched stuff—with nothing, absolutely nothing of the master in them:—a scene-painter's apprentice, after six months, would have done as well or better."

Neal had also found and interviewed Joseph Mason, now in his twenties, and delightedly revealed that the botanical settings in many of Audubon's drawings had been supplied by a teenage boy.

The whole truth in this matter has never been firmly established. The settings in 125 of the drawings eventually engraved for the **Birds**—fewer than one-third—are known to have been the work of various assistants: Mason (who did about fifty-five); the Swiss landscape painter George Lehman; John Bachman's talented sister-in-law, Maria Martin; and the two Audubon sons. Rarely, one of them painted part or all of a bird. With these assistants Audubon was either a teacher or an employer, and consequently what they produced for him was his, a standard arrangement between artists. He directed and edited their work; he may have outlined much of it for them.

He was very fond of Joseph Mason. They shared some hard times and produced wonderful drawings together. "I have great pleasure in affording that good young man the means of becoming able to do well," Audubon wrote to Lucy in 1821. "His talent for painting, if I am a judge, is fine—his expenses very moderate and his Company quite indispensible. We have heard of his Father's death and on that [account] I am more attached to him—he now *draws Flowers* better than any man probably in America, thou knowest I do not flatter young artists much, I never said this to him, but I think so—and to shew his performance will bring me as many pupils as I can attend to, anywhere." Unfortunately, according to Mason, Audubon *had* flattered his young assistant, to the extent of promising to share credit with him for the work they produced together, and then reneged when it was published. This wasn't just a minor betrayal, according to the way Neal told the story. While Audubon and Mason had traveled together, he said, they had painted 250 pieces, for which Mason had done *"all the botanical drawings,* and used to paint the feet, legs, eyes, and beaks of all the birds in water colors—the rest being done by Audubon, who rubbed the colors on dry." If the implications of that arrangement were accurate, it was remarkable that Audubon was able to go on painting birds for another twenty years without Mason's help! In fact, he became dissatisfied with many of the drawings he produced while Mason was with him, and he redrew those species.

Neal published a string of anecdotes about Mason's life with Audubon. They too may have been somewhat larger than life, because of Mason's sour memory and Neal's vitriolic pen, but they have the right smell about them. Neal reported, for example, that according to Mason, Audubon always said he had been born in Santo Domingo. In another story, Mason and Audubon

> saw an Indian sitting by a little fire and eating something which he said was sweeter than honey. They were roasted wasps. Being rather sharp-set, Audubon made a trial and Mason followed him. How many Audubon ate, he wouldn't undertake to say, but he himself acknowledges to *one hundred and fifty,* and Audubon continued long after he had left off. They were indeed sweeter than honey—delicious—with a strange but most agreeable flavor.
> At another time as they sat together on a rotten log near night fall, in the woods about New Orleans, ragged, dirty, and tired almost to death, they were accosted by a party of well-dressed dapper citizens after a fashion that Audubon didn't much like. He refused to answer their enquiries, and they swore they would take him to the city. 'Joseph,' said our ornithologist, 'load your piece: I'll be damned if you take us alive!' The gentlemen stared—stepped back—and then wanted to know what in the devil's name they were about there. About our business, was the reply. Mason has no doubt that Audubon would have been as good as his word; and as for Mason himself, we dare say he would have followed suit, with the greatest pleasure in the world, for having a dispute with his master one day, who had grown rather jealous at swallow-shooting, the latter offered to let the boy fire at him at a given distance. Very well, said Mason—take your place and see if I don't pepper you, that's all! And sure enough, Audubon walked off, and holding down his head, took a handful of mustard shot in his back!

"Mere smoake from a dunghill," wrote Audubon to Bachman. And in truth this sort of testimony scarcely nicked

the Audubon icon or influenced other contemporaries who wrote about him. He was on top of the world, acclaimed in reviews both here and abroad, not only for the splendor of his engravings but also for the genius and eloquence of his writing. In our era Audubon is known mostly as an artist, but in his time he also ranked high as an author. Two years after his death, Rufus Wilmot Griswold published a collection of articles, *Homes of American Authors.* The lead chapter was about Audubon and his house on the Hudson. The other authors who were profiled surrounded Audubon with fast company indeed. They included Washington Irving, William Cullen Bryant, Richard Henry Dana, James Fenimore Cooper, Ralph Waldo Emerson, Henry Wadsworth Longfellow, Nathaniel Hawthorne, Daniel Webster, and James Russell Lowell. (Later, *McGuffey's Reader* reprinted Audubon's essay on the passenger pigeon alongside selected readings from Shakespeare, Thackeray, Jefferson, Emerson, Hawthorne, and the like.)

The overwhelming popular opinion of Audubon in his day was reflected in this comment by a contemporary American journalist, Parke Godwin:

> For sixty years or more he followed, with more than religious devotion, a beautiful and elevated pursuit, enlarging its boundaries by his discoveries, and illustrating its objects by his art. In all climates and in all weathers; scorched by burning suns, drenched by piercing rains, frozen by the fiercest colds; now diving fearlessly into the densest forest, now wandering alone over the most savage regions; in perils, in difficulties, and in doubts; with no companion to cheer his way, far from the smiles and applause of society; listening only to the sweet music of birds, or to the sweeter music of his own thoughts, he faithfully kept his path. The records of man's life contain few nobler examples of strength of purpose and indefatigable energy. . . .

Audubon deplored the white man's encroachment on the wilderness, the clearing of forests by fire and ax, the thinning of the game as birds and animals were commercially shot and trapped for plumage and hides. He was outraged at the eggers who robbed seabird nests and carried away the eggs by the thousands for market. Even in wild and distant Labrador there was too much human presence for Audubon, and he wondered where he could go to find nature still undisturbed. The wilderness was his personal arena. He loved rolling up in a buffalo robe to sleep in the snow and stomping back to civilization muddy to the knees, beard to the chest. He thrived on the drama of living off the land, of finding food in wild country. What if he chanced to have no salt with him? Why, sprinkle the meat with gunpowder! He would eat almost anything, whether from curiosity or hunger. The homed grebe he found to be fishy, rancid, and fat. The hermit thrush and red-winged blackbird were good and delicate. The flicker tasted strongly of ants. The meat of fledgling bald eagles, he reported, reminded him of veal. In the Dakotas, he was introduced to an Indian delicacy, roast dog, which he found "most excellent . . . fully equal to any meat I ever tasted." In middle age, after a sumptuous dinner party, he wistfully recalled the simple fare of the huntsman—wood ibis cooked on the campfire and turtle eggs from the nest.

But he didn't hunt just for the food, or just for specimens to paint and preserve for science. When it came to shooting, Audubon was a man of his time, those careless days when marksmanship with living targets was a common sport. It's a bitter pill to swallow when he itemizes his kills: A puffin shoot in Labrador, where "I had two double-barrelled guns . . . and I shot for one hour by my watch, always firing at a single bird on wing. How many Puffins I killed in that time I take the liberty of leaving you to guess." A swan hunt at a sheltered pond near the Ohio, hundreds of trumpeter swans floating in the sun: "What a feast for a sportsman . . . I saw these beautiful birds . . . their heads under the surface and their legs in the air, struggling in the last agonies of life, to the number of at least fifty." Gunning for clapper rails in a Carolina swamp, where the "cruel sportsman, covered with mud and mire . . . exultingly surveys his slaughtered heaps."

The same passion and intensity with which he deplored the loss of wilderness infused the very act of his loading a rifle for a day in the field. He described it lovingly, step by step, building to the moment when, with the butt of the rifle braced on the ground, the powder and ball were tamped down into the chamber with a hickory rod: "Once, twice, thrice, has it rebounded. The rifle leaps as it were into the hunter's arms . . . Now I am ready, cries the woodsman."

He was, and still is, criticized for anthropomorphizing—for writing and sometimes even drawing as if birds were like little feathered humans. As the mourning dove receives food from the bill of her mate in his essay, she listens "with delight to his assurances of devoted affection." The mockingbird "approaches his beloved one, his eyes gleaming with delight, for she has already promised to be his and his only." However, he didn't approach birds in that way just for effect. He understood the scientific issue, and yet he sensed a true connection between himself and animals—especially as a reflection of the relationship he believed existed between all living creatures and their Creator.

His friend Captain Basil Hall, for one, "expressed some doubts as to my views respecting the affection and love of pigeons, as if I made it human, and raised the possessors quite above the brutes. I presume the love of the mothers for their young is much the same as the love of woman for her offspring. There is but one kind of love; God is love, and all his creatures derive theirs from his; only it is modified by the different degrees of intelligence in different beings and creatures."

One knotty question in this debate had to do with the intelligence of animals and their ability to think. In the *Ornithological Biography* he reported that he once saw a goshawk chasing a flock of grackles as they flew across the Ohio River. The grackles "rushed together so closely that the flock looked like a dusky ball passing through the air. On reaching the mass, [the hawk] . . . scized first one, then another, and another, giving each a squeeze with his talons, and suffering it to drop upon the water. In this

manner, he had procured four or five before the poor birds reached the woods, into which they instantly plunged, when he gave up the chase, swept over the water in graceful curves, and picked up the fruits of his industry, carrying each bird singly to the shore. Reader, is this instinct or reason?"

Audubon could not abide the assertion that the creatures "below" man were stupid. "The Wild Goose is an excellent diver," says his Labrador journal, "and when with its young uses many beautiful strategems to save its brood, and elude the hunter . . . Every time I read or hear of a stupid animal in a wild state, I cannot help wishing that the stupid animal who speaks thus, was half as wise as the brute he despises, so that he might be able to thank his maker for what knowledge he may possess."

Wherever he went, Audubon made note of his expenses down to the last detail—sixteen shillings for an umbrella, $7.60 for a fur hat, 87 3/4 cents for postage. He was particularly keen to record the prices of food—a dozen chickens for a dollar in Boonville, Missouri, four shad for a dollar in Richmond, Virginia, and in the New Orleans market, dressed poultry such as robins for six and a half cents apiece and barred owls for twenty-five cents. Once in Washington, D.C., he was in the town market at 4:00 A.M. to check the prices, and he reported to Lucy that potatoes, cabbages, blackberries, broilers, young ducks, and "butcher's meat" were "fully fifty to sixty per cent higher" than in New York. In his role as a homebody, whenever he ran across a slovenly household he was quick to report that sad state of affairs to Lucy, with an admiring postscript about her estimable gifts as a housekeeper.

Again and again he wrote about playing music. There were the evenings around the fire at a winter camp on the Ohio River, when he and his party were icebound, with a band of Shawnees as their hunting companions: "Mr. Pope played on the violin, I accompanied with the flute, the men danced to the tunes, and the squaws looked on and laughed, and the hunters smoked their pipes with such serenity as only Indians can." He provided the music for the dancing classes he held in Woodville, Mississippi: "I marched to the hall with my violin under my arm, bowed to the company assembled, tuned my violin; played a *cotillon,* and began my lesson . . . How I toiled before I could get one graceful step or motion! I broke my bow and nearly my violin—in my excitement and impatience! . . . I pushed one here and another there, and all the while singing to myself to assist their movements . . . After this first lesson was over I was requested to *dance to my own music,* which I did until the whole room came down in thunders of applause, in clapping of hands and shouting." Aboard ship, off the coast of Labrador in 1833, there was an evening of song with visitors from an Italian vessel. In Newfoundland, when Audubon and his shipmates attended a dance at a fishing village, he went ashore with his flageolet stuck in his waistcoat, and son John opened the ball that night with a violin overture of patriotic tunes—"Hail Columbia," the Marseillaise, and "God Save the King."

Audubon had read widely: Byron, Milton, Dryden, Voltaire, Ben Franklin, Cervantes' *Don Quixote,* Dante's *In-*

Yellow-throated vireo by Audubon.

ferno, Sterne's *Tristram Shandy,* Goldsmith's *The Vicar of Wakefield,* and Dickens' *Pickwick Papers,* to name a few. He loved the theater: "I often find myself when there laughing or crying like a child." He was familiar with the paintings of such masters as Raphael, Titian, Correggio, Van Dyke, and, of course, David. He was skilled at chess, backgammon, and whist. He knew how to plait willow baskets, make Indian moccasins out of snakeskin, and weave hair into watch chains and rings. He was a member of the Ancient and Honorable Fraternity of Free Masons. When agitated he had a habit of pacing up and down, snapping his fingers. Despite New Year's resolutions, he was never able to shake his addiction to snuff—though "I will tell you (*entre nous*)," he wrote to Bachman, "Snuffing is a most dirty business, I abhor it."

He also abhorred cities. "That crazy city," he called New York. "I wonder that men consent to swelter and fret their lives away amid those hot bricks and pestilent vapors—Great New York with all its humbug, rascality, and immorality." And from England he wrote, "I hate it, yes I cordially hate London . . . bustle, filth, and smoke." At such times he longed for home: "Ah, my love, on a day like this in America I could stroll in magnificent woods, I could listen to sounds fresh and pure, I could look at a blue sky." Late in his life he once exclaimed: "Will this longing for the woods ever leave me!"

He adored children. They were always in his arms, in his lap, and tagging at his heels. After his grandchildren came along, how he missed them on his travels. "Kiss the little sweethearts for me . . . our little angels." He imagined them "racing about all day, with their rosy faces and innocent doings." When there were no letters from home, he was in despair. "What can be the matter!" He missed Lucy fiercely when they were apart, kissed the signature on her letters, and slept with her letters under his pillow. He sometimes had fearful visions of her dead and in her shroud, and one day in Edinburgh, when thinking of the distance between them, he fell into a faint.

He had vivid dreams. In one letter he wrote of dreaming about the old Henderson days and of a duck-hunting trip when "we had so many killed that our Horses were scarcely able to walk under the load." In another he cheerfully spoke of business affairs that were going pretty well, "considering that we are naturalists from the Wild Woods of America." Then abruptly his attention was riveted by "the horrors all around me" and his fears of lost drawings and lost subscribers by day, with "Dreams of sinking & burning ships by night." In the *Ornithological Biography* he told of the many times when he was asleep in the deepest recesses of the forest, only to be assailed by apparitions of Indians and white-skinned murderers and sickness that seized him "with burning hand. Snakes, Loathsome and venomous, entwined my limbs, while vultures, lean and ravenous, looked on with impatience. Once, too, I dreamed when asleep on a sand-bar on one of the Florida Keys, that a huge shark had me in his jaws, and was dragging me into the deep." Sometimes—and no wonder, with that sort of dream awaiting him—he had trouble sleeping. "I awake Long ere the return of morn, and lay and tumble, and feel uncomfortable." With the first light of day, he would go out "to seek for fresh air and New Objects to distract my Distractions."

He wrote of his obsessive alarm at growing old, of dying before his work was finished. This began when he was in his forties. "Although my spirits are as active as ever, my body declines". .. "The Machine me thinks is wearing out" . . . "I am growing old fast and must work at a double quick time." He began to refer to himself repeatedly as "an old man" with an "old toothless mouth." In his essay on the nuthatch he wrote of the young birds learning to fly, to creep up a tree trunk, and to feed themselves. "Ah! Where are the moments which I have passed contemplating the progress of these amiable creatures. Alas! They are gone, those summer days of hope and joy are fled, and the clouds of life's winter are mustering in their gloomy array." More of this romantic despair appeared in the essay on the Canadian otter: "Alas! the days of our youth are gone, when . . . the rising sun never found us slumbering away the fresh hours of the morning, but beamed upon our path . . . where we often prolonged our rambles until the shades of evening found us."

Throughout his life there was so much he wanted to do and so many places he wanted to see. He longed to visit Cuba to check on, among other things, the migration of orioles, and Honduras, said to be the wintering ground of millions of swallows. He longed to cross the Rockies on foot, the only way to explore nature in a new terrain, he declared. Then on to the Pacific Coast, south to Mexico, north to Fort Vancouver. "I may yet ransack that country," he wrote in 1835. He dreamed of passing a winter in Labrador, of "traversing the snowy wastes, to trap the cunning fox and the Jer Falcon," and of speeding over crevasses in an Eskimo sled, "the broad-antlered Caribou" scampering before him. But none of this was to be. Time ran out.

When the first biographies of Audubon were published after his death, a brief, poignant recollection appeared in the London *Athenaeum.* Its anonymous author remembered when Audubon's portfolio had "excited delight" in Edinburgh, London, and Paris:

> The man also was not a man to be seen and forgotten, or passed on the pavement without glances of surprise and scrutiny. The tall and somewhat stooping form, the clothes not made by a West End but by a Far West tailor, the steady, rapid, springing step, the long hair, the aquiline features, and the glowing angry eyes—the expression of a handsome man conscious of ceasing to be young, and an air and manner which told you that whoever you might be he was John Audubon, will never be forgotten by anyone who knew or saw him.

Adam Gopnik (essay date 1991)

SOURCE: "Audubon's Passion," *The New Yorker,* 5 February 1991, pp. 96-104.

[*In the following essay, originally published in 1991, Gopnik places Audubon's life and art in the context of American history and culture.*]

An excerpt from *Ornithological Biography*

I have always imagined, that in the plumage of the beautiful Ivory-billed Woodpecker, there is something very closely allied to the style of colouring of the great Vandyke. The broad extent of its dark glossy body and tail, the large and well-defined white markings of its wings, neck, and bill, relieved by the rich carmine of the pendent crest of the male, and the brilliant yellow of its eye, have never failed to remind me of some of the boldest and noblest productions of that inimitable artist's pencil. So strongly indeed have these thoughts become ingrafted in my mind, as I gradually obtained a more intimate acquaintance with the Ivory-billed Woodpecker, that whenever I have observed one of these birds flying from one tree to another, I have mentally exclaimed, "There goes a Vandyke!" This notion may seem strange, perhaps ludicrous, to you, good reader, but I relate it as a fact, and whether or not it may be found in accordance with your own ideas, after you have inspected the plate in which is represented this great chieftain of the Woodpecker tribe, is perhaps of little consequence.

John James Audubon, in Audubon Reader: The Best Writings of *John James Audubon, edited by Scott Russell Sanders, Indiana University Press, 1986.*

In 1803, an eighteen-year-old Frenchman who had been born in Haiti, as Jean Rabin, and who had lived in Paris just long enough to take a few drawing lessons and learn how to ice-skate, arrived in New York. For the next seventeen years, he wandered through Pennsylvania and Kentucky and Ohio and Louisiana, pursuing one quixotic money-making scheme after another. Then, in 1820, he was seized by what he afterward called his "Great Idea," and for the next thirty years—until his death, in 1851—he raced from Florida to Labrador, drawing a picture of every American bird and every American beast, beginning with the wild turkey, and including even such minor Americans as the knobbed-billed phaleris, the annulated marmot squirrel, and Richardson's meadow mouse, and ending, five hundred and eighty-four paintings later, with the silvery shrew mole. He signed his work John James Audubon, and became the nearest thing American art has had to a founding father.

Lewis Mumford once described him as an "exuberant French coxcomb" who "changed his silks for leather hunting clothes and let his hair grow down to his shoulders; and . . . gradually turned into an archetypal American, who astonishingly combined in equal measure the virtues of George Washington, Daniel Boone, and Benjamin Franklin." Already in Audubon's lifetime, his person and his legend had begun to blend backward into the first generations of American patriots. The Vanderlyn portrait of Andrew Jackson that hangs in New York's City Hall, for instance, is a composite—Jackson's head mounted on a drawing of Audubon's body. In the last portraits of Audubon, painted by his son John Woodhouse Audubon, Audubon's light, fencing master's features have even begun to fuse indistinguishably with those of General Washington.

Yet Audubon's strange origins, his slow start, and the long period of shady struggle in his middle years add to the clear, eighteenth-century glow of his legend a more peculiarly nineteenth-century American touch—of frontier purification and renewal and reform. Audubon's self-transformation from the dilettante in a ruffled shirt arriving in America into the American woodsman eventually returning in triumph to France is one of the great awakenings in American biography. In his poem "Audubon: A Vision and a Question for You," Robert Penn Warren called this transformation a "passion," lending a Christian overtone to the story of Audubon's rebirth in the wilderness.

In the popular imagination, Audubon remains an archetypal American, though perhaps he now stands on the second shelf of American curios—somewhere between Betsy Ross and Johnny Appleseed. Although the last couple of years have marked no particular Audubon occasion and seen no Audubon exhibitions, he has still been the most visible of all American artists. [In 1990] Wellfleet Press reprinted the octavo edition of ***Birds of America,*** to complete a republication program that began in 1989 with the reproduction of Audubon's ***Quadrupeds,*** so that now, for the first time, both of Audubon's master pieces are available in cheap editions in something like their original form. Then, later last year, the Audubon Society arranged for the republication of Roger Tory Peterson's "Baby Elephant" folio of ***Birds of America,*** in which the birds have been reorganized along modern ornithological lines. Also, Dover Books has republished Audubon's accounts of his trips to Europe, the Missouri Valley, and Labrador, and Alice Ford's exhaustive biography, out of print for more than two decades, was republished in 1988 by Abbeville.

With his reputation as the father of bird sanctuaries and the begetter of the duck postage stamp, however, Audubon the artist has become more familiar than really known. We come to him sideways, repeating by rote a set of pious attitudes that his successors have intoned (nature true, nature wild, nature as it really is) and then catching out of the corner of our eye the uncanny intensity of his art—its haute-couture theatricality and ecstatic animation, its pure-white backgrounds and shadowless, cartoonish clarity—which still proves so unexpected that we are inclined either to explain it away as technique or write it off as naiveté. Yet to turn the pages of even the inadequately printed Wellfleet volumes is to recognize that Audubon remains the supreme stylist of American art, and that his formal daring enabled him to achieve a new kind of emotional concentration, which invested each of his birds and beasts with some heightened facet of his own complicated character.

Audubon was not an abstract artist, and he wasn't a mere patternmaker, but he recognized that his greatest achievement was the invention of what he referred to, modestly but pointedly, as "my style"—an American idiom as pared-down, sturdy, and adaptable as a Shaker box. (It was a style so knowingly wrought that he could teach it to John Woodhouse and trust him to execute and com-

Audubon in 1850, from a daguerreotype.

plete many of the last plates in **Quadrupeds** in a manner almost, though not quite, indistinguishable from his own.) The current flood of Auduboniana reaches us today in a time when an uncertainty about the future of the American wilderness, which Audubon made his subject, reinforces a larger uncertainty about American manners and American appetites—about the origins of our picture of ourselves. So the questions that we put to Audubon, perhaps like those we put to any founding father, both increase in urgency and simplify in form, and have now become one indivisible question, half biographical and half formal: what was it in the man that produced the passion, and what was it in the passion that produced the style?

Everyone agrees that Audubon was French and was a nearly compulsive liar; everyone also agrees that he was an archetypal American and was obsessed with scientific truth. The conventional, idealizing accounts make those Audubons successive ones, but the truth seems to be that Audubon was all these things at once. The two roles he liked best to play were the aristocratic Frenchman with a mysterious past and the simple American man of the woods. What is amazing is how gracefully he managed to inhabit both inventions, and how quickly he could exchange one for the other.

Audubon was not a small or a mean liar—he is extremely reliable on the details concerning his animals—but he had a vivid imagination, and when he was depressed he liked to entertain or console himself by making up stories about his origins, his history, and his adventures. He lived with

these stories, and eventually they began to slip out in public. He suffered from *folie circulaire:* one day he would sign a letter to his wife "The Great, the Wonderful Audubon"; the next he would sink into despair.

The most ambitious lie Audubon seems to have told was about his own birth: that he was the lost Dauphin of France, whisked out of prison during the Revolution and entrusted to the care of a loyal seaman. The development of this story is typical of the process of Audubon's self-inventions. It turns up in his surviving journals for the first time when he is in France in 1828, trying to find subscribers for the first edition of **Birds.** After a particularly discouraging day, he writes, "I walk the streets. I bow! I ask permission to do this or that! . . . I, who should command all." (Alice Ford thinks that his journals were bowdlerized by his granddaughters, in order to emphasize the Dauphin legend. But the fantasy is entirely in Audubon's style; only twenty-five years ago someone as hard-nosed as Mumford thought there might be something to it.) The legend is interesting not so much for its absurdity as for the way it combines his two national modes: the story may use French stock properties, but it is an *American* story, a tall tale. It places Audubon, properly, in both his worlds—halfway between Marie Antoinette and Mark Twain.

The truth about Audubon's origins may reveal why he found the Dauphin story so seductive. His father, Jean Audubon, was a sea captain. (Audubon made him an admiral; eventually, he would have him fighting with General Washington at Valley Forge, although—as Audubon perhaps knew, perhaps did not—no battle took place there.) Captain Audubon became a slave trader in Haiti. He left behind a wife in France, and took a series of mistresses. One of them, a Jeanne Rabin, gave birth to a boy in 1785. Audubon's father accepted the boy fully, though in the father's papers the son is referred to, flatly, as "Jean Rabin, Créole of Saint-Domingue." Haiti (Saint-Domingue then) was a violent place, and Audubon's father had intimations of the revolt that would erupt there in 1790. Just before it began, he took two of his illegitimate Saint-Domingue children (there was at least one other) back to France, where they were embraced by Mme. Audubon. So the Dauphin story is a truth told slant: Audubon's birth *was,* in a sense, mysterious, and the lie allowed him to make the story of his illegitimacy glorious rather than shaming.

The Audubons arrived home, in Nantes, in the middle of the Revolution. Audubon's father, slave dealer and plantation owner, made an about-face and became a fanatical Republican. He turned into a kind of Jacobin commissar in the area, responsible for writing up reports on the loyalty of the region's towns and villages. Though Audubon lived in Nantes in some luxury—for the rest of his life he loved fancy clothes, parties, skating, dancing, violin playing—he was always aware of the violence around him. Another of his repeated stories was that he had seen one of his aunts dragged through the streets during the Revolution and murdered; the truth is that none of his aunts were murdered, and in any case, his father was more likely to have been the one doing the dragging.

In 1789, Audubon's father, on a trading expedition, had

stopped in Pennsylvania and—partly because he thought there was a promising vein of lead on the property—bought a farm, outside Philadelphia, called Mill Grove. In 1803, Audubon *père* shipped Jean to America to save him from being conscripted into the Napoleonic armies (the senior Audubon had by now become a fanatical Bonapartist, though not one inclined to have his son fight). By then, Pennsylvania seemed to occupy a special place in the lore of the Audubon family. In Haiti and in France, the Audubons had been surrounded every day by cruelty—the horrors of the slave system, and then the excesses of the Revolution. Pennsylvania, by contrast, was a safe place, a treasure house, a big back yard. For Audubon, the opposition between the Old and the New World was not one that balanced elegant European artificiality against the honest and limitless wilderness. Instead, it set the violence and danger of the Old World against the promise of safe bourgeois comforts and pleasures in America.

Audubon remained all his life unmistakably French. He spoke with an impenetrable Inspector Clouseau accent. (Someone who ran into Audubon long before he was famous transcribed his speech just because it sounded so funny: "Hi emm en Heenglishmen," he has Audubon saying, "becas hi got a Heenglish wife.") The grammar of all his writings, though cleaned up by various editors, was always that of his first language. His vision remained French, too. All his life, he claimed that before he left for America he had studied drawing in the atelier of Jacques-Louis David. While older biographies accepted this as gospel, Ford finds it improbable. If it was a lie, though, it must have concealed another kind of truth. Audubon told the story to people who could easily have checked up on him, and he repeated it in the private journals that were intended only for his beloved wife, Lucy: "I had studied under the instruction of the celebrated David," "the pupil of my old master, David," "the lessons which I had received from the great David." Perhaps Audubon had told Lucy that story while he was courting her ("We are what we make ourselves," Audubon wrote once; it could have been the family motto) and was stuck with it.

Still, if he wasn't trained by David, he was certainly schooled in his style. At a low moment in his life, he made a living by drawing charcoal portraits entirely in the linear, neoclassical manner that David had perfected. That manner couldn't have been a stranger springboard for someone who wanted to draw birds and mammals in their natural habitats. John Constable, nearly an exact contemporary of Audubon, said once that if David's shallow, artificial, theatrical style ever became widely accepted, it would mark the end of nature painting in England. But for Audubon the vague intimations of the sublime were indistinguishable from the blurry generalizations of ignorance; he called the early Romantic landscapes and bird pictures he saw in England "washy, slack, imperfect messes." He took it for granted that the hard-edged draftsmanship of French neoclassicism was the one good grammar of art, and he remained faithful to it all his life. (He had the advantage, too, of a parallel tradition, exemplified by the flower painter Redouté, that married the precision of neoclassicism to scientific illustration. Redouté was almost the first painter in Paris to whom Audubon showed

the early drawings of ***Birds of America.***) Audubon's animals are, in a way, distant off-spring of the profile figures in the *Death of Socrates,* and the diorama-like boxes in which so many of his birds are suspended are a miniaturization of David's sober stage spaces. Audubon's paintings, like L'Enfant's designs for Washington, D.C., were one of those early American achievements that developed an overblown Romantic eccentricity from a strict French neoclassical model.

Audubon also inherited the French mania for the systematic. He couldn't paint one shrike without thinking about the next one, around the corner. He was a catalogue waiting to happen; he said that as a teenager he had tried his hand at a *Birds of France.* Though the idealized account has him throwing off his "coxcomb" sophistication in America to become a birdman and an artist, submitting himself humbly to the discipline of science and nature, the truth seems to be almost the reverse. Drawing birds, making art, inventing catalogues, producing beautiful books—all these things he thought of as French, and part of his "aristocratic" past. (An early attempt at an American bird catalogue, which Audubon might have known, had been made by another émigré Frenchman.) For Audubon, a real American was someone who went out into the woods and came back with a fortune. He wasted the first sixteen years of his life in the United States trying to become such an American, and it was only when every circumstance conspired against him, and drove him back to the French manner he had intended to abandon, that he at last found his way.

Audubon's enduring strength and weakness was his grandiosity. Immediately after his arrival in Pennsylvania, he fell in love with a beautiful local girl named Lucy Bakewell. His love for her remained the single ennobling passion of his life. (He courted Lucy in a cave, and took her to watch pewees, wearing fancy shirts that he had had made at the best haberdashery in Philadelphia—a typically Audubonian combination of Eagle Scout and Beau Brummel.) When the lead mine at Mill Grove had to be sold (Audubon claimed that he was swindled out of it), he found another large ambition—to become a retail tycoon. In 1808, he any Lucy were married, and they set out for Louisville, Kentucky, where he and a partner had gone into business as drygoods merchants.

When Audubon arrived in Louisville, it was already a stable, mercantile, provincial city. He had to make regular trips back East on business, and it was during these trips—not trailblazing journeys away from the city and into the wilderness but trips from one town to another through well-charted country—that he drew many of his first American birds. His ecstatic sense of American nature had from the beginning a touch of the outing and the expedition—a sense of the wilderness as a park between two houses.

Audubon loved to watch birds. But his was not the spirit of so many present-day birders, for whom the birds might just as well be stamps or baseball cards. He was drawn to them as familiars, and he was interested in them as social animals. (Lucy Audubon once said, "I have a rival in every bird.") In his journals (and in his collections of bird

Barn swallow by Audubon.

biographies as well), what he chooses to describe is almost never the markings or the profiles—the appearance—of birds. What interests him is their behavior, their habits, their movements—the "manners" of birds, as he called them. Here he is on a trip to Labrador, describing the varied reactions of birds to a rainstorm: "The Great Black-backed Gull alone is seen floating through the storm, screaming loudly and mournfully as it seeks its prey; not another bird is to be seen abroad; the Cormorants are all settled in the rocks close to us, the Guillemots are deep in the fissures, every Eider Duck lays under the lee of some point, her brood snugly beneath her opened wings, the Loon and the Diver have crawled among the rankest weeds, and are patiently waiting for a return of fair weather, the Grouse is quite hid under the creeping willow, the Great Gray Owl is perched on the southern declivity of some stupendous rock." It is like the opening of *Bleak House*—a portrait of the weather in a world, and of the characters within it.

The dry-goods store soon failed, and for sixteen years Audubon moved around Kentucky and Ohio and Louisiana. The Audubons had four children, two girls and two boys, and Audubon cheerfully set himself up in one unrealistic project after another. They all ended in debts and recriminations, with the again unsuccessful capitalist wandering off to watch swallows.

In 1810, Audubon had been introduced to a Philadelphia ornithologist named Alexander Wilson, who was planning a complete catalogue of American birds. Audubon recognized that Wilson's drawings were niggling and undramatic compared even with his own roughest sketches, but he would probably never have made bird painting his occupation if he had not gone finally and irredeemably bankrupt in 1819. This last bankruptcy was the consequence of a crazy scheme of his to build a mill and run a steamboat in a little Kentucky town called Henderson. It went so badly that Audubon ended up in a local jail for a few nights. He had persuaded a recent English émigré named George Keats to invest money in the plan. Some of the money belonged to George's brother, John, who was back in England, writing poems. The venture helped ruin Keats, and the name Audubon tolls in his letters like a funeral bell: "I cannot help thinking Mr Audubon a dishonest man" and "Mr Audubon has deceived you."

Bankrupt, Audubon began to make a living by drawing charcoal portraits of local merchants, at five dollars a profile. Many of the profile portraits that he was asked to draw were made on the sitter's deathbed. He was once even asked to draw the portrait of a child exhumed from the grave, and make her look beautiful and alive. He was thirty-five years old, and he had failed at everything else. It must have been heartbreaking to know the Audubons at that moment. They were a subject for a Tennessee Williams play: the overworked and beautiful and distressed mother (both of her daughters had died, one just around the time of the bankruptcy), and the young man with the accent and the frayed lace cuffs, still talking compulsively about his studies with David, about his admiral father, about his mysterious birth.

He was thrown back on his birds. They were all he had left, and Lucy thought there might be a little money in them. "It seems my Genius (if I have any) was intended that way," he wrote to her sadly. Then, cheering up, as he always did, he added that he would present the drawings to "the High Judges of Europe." In the 1820s, he perfected the new way of drawing birds that he called his style. He eventually placed on his drawings and watercolors the notation "Drawn from nature," but that was shorthand for a long and contrived process. Audubon would shoot his birds—sometimes hundreds at a time—and then skin them and take them home to stuff and paint. That was what every bird painter did. But Audubon hated the unvarying shapes and Roman-coin profiles that traditional taxidermy produced, so he began to make flexible armatures of bent wire and wood, and he arranged bird skins and feathers—sometimes even whole, uneviscerated birds—on them in animated poses. That is why his birds look, in every sense, so *wired*. He would paint a bird in a single session, recording the outline of the invented pose in firm brushstrokes and then filling in between, like a child with a coloring book, in bright, generalizing watercolor. "My plan," he wrote, "was to form sketches in my mind's eye, each representing each family in their most constant and natural associations, and to complete those family pictures as chance might bring perfect specimens." Over the years, he accumulated not so much a jumble of nature notes and sketches as a vocabulary of firmly delineated, stylized, and even artificial shapes.

In time, Audubon began to refine these "family pictures" into a few simple formats. He invented organizing stories on which he could pin little feathery truths: petrels and terns seen from overhead, as chevrons; upright water birds, their long throats always curving close to their bodies in compressed arabesques; songbirds spread out flat, like bats. For these shapes to be articulate, they had to be seen whole and clear and close up, and so, for all their vivacity, they also began to take on an obviously "studio" quality. (Around 1824, Audubon decided that they would have to be printed life-size—an almost unprecedented conception.) It is impossible to imagine any rational point of view from which the birds might have been seen in nature; his flamingos and herons and swans fill the frame of the picture from top to bottom, as if they had come indoors to sit for the artist. Pure, isolated shapes set against a white background, they become symbols of themselves.

When Audubon had to include more than one bird (a mate or a variant) in a single drawing, he often rejected the conventional compositional system of elegantly varying the poses and places of his subjects. Instead, he repeated a single shape, varying only its size, or "pinning" it down on the background in a new way, as Matisse later did with his fixed shorthand of cutouts. Sometimes this exact repetition of forms can create an odd mixture of geometric abstraction and backwoods lyricism: in the drawing of two violet-green swallows, the same chevron is almost mechanically replicated, so that the echoing shapes, placed beside each other with a chevron of white in between, form an implied fan shape of happy green union. And sometimes the repetition can be comic, as when the little female snakebird thrusts her long throat out in exact imitation of her open-beaked mate, all the while curled safely just beneath him. At other moments—for example, in his drawing of two petrels—Audubon will spin or rotate a fixed schematic shape to show its back or its underside, so that the picture, with a single form rotating across it, is like a stop-action photograph. Yet Audubon's birds always reveal themselves (the undersides of his ducks, the splayed-out bodies of his cocks) without being reduced to specimens.

Audubon's birds were more high-keyed in color than almost any other American art would be until the next century. They were flatter, too, since modeling depends on the kind of slow graying-out of tone that Audubon thought would distract from his precise notation of the birds' true colors. (This flatness was noticed and attacked in his lifetime.) Flatness is in bad odor right now, and it is hard to recall that there was a time when it was an empirical, rather than a metaphysical, issue in American art—a problem of light instead of virtue. In most American abstract painting, flatness produces brightness; in Audubon's art, brightness produced flatness. Audubon had invented an imaginary, unnaturally radiant light of a kind that was not seen again in descriptive art until the photographs of Avedon and Penn in the fifties: the searching, even illumination that fills in detail and casts a staring, blank white light along smooth surfaces—a light at once blinding and particularizing. Sometimes, as with the flamingos and herons, Audubon's light is like light at noon on a white sand beach, picking out each grain of sand, yet still unifying the scene in an all-over, shadowless brightness. Audubon made American light tropical.

Earlier European bird books had been hierarchical, with the birds lined up by status. Audubon's birds come at us, for the most part, in democratic disorder, and so can be taken only as individuals. We judge them, as Americans are supposed to judge other Americans, by their character. (A Martian coming upon Audubon's birds would have absolutely no notion that birds use feathers for camouflage.) Audubon saw that the behavior of birds, their instinctual code of greetings and seductions, could be recorded as affectations: the heron's dainty, bent-wristed greeting to its fellows; the red-necked grebe sapiently lecturing its child; the great horned owls staring down their accusers. Mated birds in Audubon are not slaves of instinct but married couples; they are always in cahoots. Or else his birds stand alone in fancy dress and become worldly types: the senatorial pelican, the demagogic shrike, the seigneurial blue heron, the outlaw vulture. Even in his lesser paintings, the birds can be struck off in characterizations of the kind that filled his notebooks as humors: the peevish scaup duck, the proud egret, the suspicious snowy owls, the wise-guy cormorant, the hysterical whooping crane, the serene violet-green swallows. Although Audubon is famous as the first bird painter to show birds in their environments, and eventually began to have various landscape painters— among them Joseph Mason and, later, George Lehman— assist him by painting backgrounds, in his greatest bird pictures his subjects completely dominate the environments. They don't fill a natural niche; they oversee an estate, assuming poses that in European art had been allowed only to the landed gentry standing in their parks, their stately homes off in the distance. It may be that in

a democratic culture only things that come by their beauty naturally—birds or models or movie stars—are permitted to be shown with such aristocratic self-importance. Audubon's snowy heron, with its bald head and noble posture, is so large and commanding that it can only be taken as the owner of the Colonial estate in the background.

If Audubon's birds are subjects rather than specimens, they are never merely allegorical or archetypal; their very birdness forbids that. They are, above all, *alive,* and their wildness seems to exist—and to be recorded by him—for its own sake. It burns through in their beady, wide-open, wondering eyes, their thrusting serpentine necks, their chattering mouths—a whole new language of recorded ardor. Audubon's birds are always glamorous and always greedy. His swan is unlike any earlier swan in art—not "graceful" or raising its wings, like the swans he described in the parks in France, but sharp-eyed, grasping, its ugly black-webbed foot propelling its beautiful ivory body forward, its eye on the main chance.

"Does there not exist a high ridge where the mountainside of 'scientific' knowledge joins the opposite slope of 'artistic' imagination?" Vladimir Nabokov, another émigré with a love of American wildlife, asked once about Audubon. (Nabokov didn't think that Audubon's occasional drawings of butterflies walked along that ridge.) But at least in his birds Audubon walked along it more bracingly and with a finer equilibrium than any artist before or since. He sought facts—the exact things, peculiarities—and found them by inventing a style. In Audubon, the patterning impulse and the explanatory impulse were always the same. "What is love?" Robert Penn Warren wrote in his poem about Audubon. "One name for it is knowledge."

In 1826, Audubon traveled to Europe, carrying the first set of watercolors for *Birds of America.* (He thought that there were not enough potential subscribers in America to pay for the book, and also that there was no one here who could engrave it properly.) Armed only with a few standard letters of introduction, he went first to Liverpool. The bird paintings were an enormous success there, and he went on to Edinburgh, where he found the first of his engravers, W. H. Lizars. Lizars began to produce sample plates using the aquatint process—a tonal printing technique that translated Audubon's drawings into big compositional areas and increased their blocky, Japanese-woodcut quality. Later, Audubon rather callously traded in Lizars for a still better engraver, a Londoner named Robert Havell, who further sharpened the clarity of the watercolors. Looking for an ornithologist who could supply the necessary scientific expertise for the text, Audubon went back to Scotland and eventually found a tough-minded young naturalist named MacGillivray, who wound up editing most of Audubon's writings on birds. Then he went to Paris, and managed to get King Charles X and much of his court to subscribe to *Birds.* Audubon understood that while in America it paid him to be very French, in France it paid him to be very American—the noble rustic rather than the rusticated noble. He claimed that when the painter Gérard (an authentic student of David's) saw some of his *Birds,* he cried, "Who would have expected such things from the woods of America?"

In the salons of Paris, Audubon at last became an American.

Birds of America was a multinational effort, and in the end was more European than American—French style and English technique and Scottish realism presiding over the creation of a picture of the New World. For the next decade, while **Birds** was being produced, Audubon spent about as much time in Europe as he did in America. (The last two years of the project, from 1837 to 1839, he spent almost entirely in England, supervising Havell's engravings and writing the last of a series of accompanying essays.) **Birds** appeared between 1827 and 1838, in irregular installments of five plates, along with a series of complementary volumes, the **Ornithological Biography,** which was issued between 1831 and 1839. By 1835, Audubon was an international celebrity. He lunched with presidents, met famous authors, and wrote, "I have laboured like a cart Horse for the last thirty years on a Single Work, have been successful almost to a miracle in its publication so far, and am now thought a-a-a- (I dislike to write it, but no matter, here goes) a Great Naturalist!!!"

He had enemies. Philadelphia, where he had started his American life, was filled with other, more skeptical naturalists, who had an intellectual investment in the Scottish precision and plainness of Alexander Wilson's more drily "scientific" catalogue of birds. They recognized, perceptively, that beneath the illusion of empirical truth in Audubon's work, increasingly surrounded, as it was, by a pious P.R. atmosphere of expedition-making and sample-gathering (at one point Audubon even had a navy man-of-war take him on a drawing expedition), there lay a not very well concealed element of melodramatic fantasy. One Philadelphian, the naturalist George Ord, mounted a vicious campaign against Audubon, which continued relentlessly for the rest of Ord's life. Audubon's critics attacked the "frenzy and ecstasy" that he showed for his subjects. Fortunately for him, the cases that his critics chose to make an issue of—for instance, whether the nest of the mockingbird could ever actually be invaded by a rattlesnake, as Audubon had shown it to be—were ones on which Audubon happened to have the goods. (It could have turned out differently.)

Audubon shrewdly recognized that the way to cash in on his fame was to release a second, affordable edition of **Birds,** and between 1840 and 1844 he published an octavo edition, several times smaller. It sold extremely well; its seven volumes sat on American shelves as a reassuring presence—a kind of museum of a wilderness that was already becoming remote. The octavo edition of **Birds** was one of the books that helped invent America. It is hard to recall how regional all America's ideas of place were until after the Civil War—how rooted in the love of a state, a provincial locality. Although Audubon's birds, of course, belong to particular places, and although the landscape artists he employed tried to show particular locations, Audubon saw America as an idealized whole. The Audubon family had reached across America, traveling from north to south, from New York to Boston to Florida to Ohio, and Audubon's compositions—the unchanging light, and blank, cloudless skies, and long, uninterrupted horizons—

are recognizably American without ever being quite situated. This almost mystical idea of Americanness, expressed as a spare, underpopulated thinness, an endless backdrop, begins in Audubon and continues right through to John Ford Westerns and to Georgia O'Keeffe.

Every bird or animal picture book before had tried to make a point beyond the blind, flat empirical record; for Audubon, the enrichment of the empirical record was all the point there was. The French naturalist Buffon's ornithology was structured to mimic the surrounding social order—the noble birds first and the lesser ones behind. Audubon's book begins *in medias res,* with the wild turkey, proceeds to the songbirds, and then abruptly turns to the lyrical swallows, the arctic terns, the water birds. The sequence loosely follows Audubon's own voyages and discoveries as much as any biological program—a kind of autobiography written in birds. He took the French mania for systematization and made it into a recognizably American love of facts for their own sake—single observations connected by "ands."

Pictures of birds are, like pictures of babies, easy to love. Audubon's beasts—or **Viviparous Quadrupeds of North America,** to give them their proper name—have never been as popular as his birds. The only critic to recognize their power and what is in some ways their superiority was Edmund Wilson, who devoted one and a half uncharacteristically rapturous pages to them in *Patriotic Gore,* under the chapter heading "Poetry of the War." Perhaps what drew him to Audubon's beasts was their unsentimental realism and their violence. The first bird to appear in **Quadrupeds** is dead—a partridge being mouthed by a fox, which, torn between fear and greed, is staring back at an unseen hunter. The accompanying text that Audubon wrote, in collaboration with the naturalist John Bachman, tells what happens to the fox when the hunter releases his dog:

> The Fox has no time to double and shuffle, the dog is at his heels almost, and speed, speed, is his only hope for life. Now the shrill baying of the hound becomes irregular; we may fancy he is at the throat of his victim . . . every bound and plunge into the snow, diminishes the distance between the fox and his relentless foe . . . One more desperate leap, and with a sudden snappish growl he turns upon his pursuer. . . . For a moment he resists the dog, but is almost instantly overcome. He is not killed, however, in the first onset; both dog and fox, are so fatigued that they now sit on their haunches facing each other, resting, panting, their tongues hanging out, and the foam from their lips dropping on the snow. After fiercely eyeing each other for a while, both become impatient—the former to seize his prey, and the latter to escape. At the first leap of the fox, the dog is upon him; with renewed vigour he seizes him by the throat, and does not loose his hold until the snow is stained with his blood, and he lies rumpled, draggled, with blood-shot eye, and frothy open mouth, a mangled carcass on the ground.

Desperate leaps, panicky darting and plunging, hanging tongues and foaming lips, fierce eyes—these are constants of *Quadrupeds.* Violence, seen with a curious equanimity, almost a kind of relish, is the leitmotiv. There are many trapped animals: the red fox with his hind leg caught in a steel jaw, his body turned in an oddly composed and graceful twist of pain; the Canada otter betrayed by his own greed, his small, delicate paw still reaching for the fish after the trap has snapped shut, his mouth turned toward us, screaming in disbelief. (The trapped otter was an obsessive image for Audubon. He first imagined it in the early 1820s, and drew and painted it many times after.) Other animals scream to create fear: the wolverine, with his wrinkled nose, who stretches open his fanged mouth to intimidate some unseen predator (the prints are filled with unseen predators: noises off); the mink, with its beautiful sleek body and ugly webbed feet, who turns away from his arching mate to howl; the plumed-tail skunk snarling to defend her young hidden in a tree hollow. Instead of using aquatint, Audubon had the beasts printed as lithographs, so that in place of the animated contours of the birds there are soft, blurred edges of fur and microscopically particularized curling hairs. The light in *Quadrupeds* is less intense and even than in *Birds;* it is soft but shadowless, sculpting out breasts and muscular bodies.

In the endless plates of small rodents and moles and shrews, which fill the book, the violence is less explicit, but they have a lurid, horror-movie quality anyway. The common American shrew moles, for example, with their weird, flapping paws and obscene blind faces, seem to be casing the little American farmhouse in the background like extraterrestrials stalking a schoolyard. Sometimes this same note of panic becomes vaguely comic: Wilson's meadow mice, delicately and improbably separating the high grass on their little hill to peer out for enemies; the marsh hare and his mate looking dolefully away from each other, like an old Beckett couple; the Canada pouched rats, meeting and exchanging battle stories like a team of exhausted football players. Tree animals are allowed almost the only moments of calm: the orange-bellied squirrels meet in the notch of a tree and stare at each other; the wise and fat raccoon looks down from a tree and scratches his head. The movement of the birds is upward: limbs lift, heads turn, beaks point. The mammals move down, in little, burrowing worm shapes.

The violence that marks *Quadrupeds* is also the dominant note of Audubon's wilderness journals, but the slaughter of birds and animals, which is the theme of the journals, has, in retrospect, a justification in Audubon's work: the birds and beasts bought with their deaths immortality for their kind. "On leaving the wood we shot a Spruce Partridge leading her young," he writes. "On seeing us she ruffled her feathers like a barnyard hen, and rounded within a few feet of us to defend her brood; her very looks claimed our forbearance and clemency, but the enthusiastic desire to study nature prompted me to destroy her, and she was shot, and her brood secured." The relentlessness of Audubon's descriptions of his slaughters and the almost giddy excitement that the killing inspires in him lend an underside to his accounts which is genuinely alien to modern sensibilities; sometimes the journals have an almost drunken violence, and read like an ad for the National Rifle Association: "Next, Sprague shot an adult yellow-

winged male, with the markings principally such as are found in the Eastern States. Harris then shot a young Red-shafted, just fledged, with a black stripe on the cheek. His next shot was a light-colored Red-shafted male, with black cheeks, and another still, a yellow Red-shafted with a red cheek. After all this Mr. Culbertson proposed to run a sham Buffalo hunt again. He, Harris, and Squires started on good horses, went about a mile, and returned full tilt, firing and cracking. Squires fired four times and missed once. Harris did not shoot at all; but Mr. Culbertson fired eleven times, starting at the onset with an empty gun, snapped three times, and reached the fort with his gun loaded."

Audubon threw himself into *Quadrupeds* with a passion that surprised even his family. But he fell ill when the book was about half completed; contemporary accounts of the illness sound like a clinical description of the progression of Alzheimer's disease. He became "crabbed, uncontrollable," demanded kisses, and called for old French songs. At the end of his life, he fell into a silent reverie, and was roused only once, when an old friend came to visit, and Audubon suddenly called out, "Yes, yes, Billy! You go down that side of Long Pond, and I'll go this side, and we'll get the ducks."

Audubon was buried in Manhattan; there is a monument to him in Trinity Church Cemetery, on 155th Street. In the hundred and forty years since his death, many of his admirers have tried to translate his example into a conservation program. (The details of this translation, and all its accomplishments, are related in Frank Graham, Jr.'s new book about the National Audubon Society. *The Audubon Ark,* published by Knopf.) Yet the more time one spends in Audubon's company, the more certain it seems that the mission of the society that bears his name—to protect birds and other wildlife—would not have stirred him much. Today, it seems, we can see wild creatures only as waifs or wards; Audubon's wild creatures are always sure of themselves—are never appealing to or looking for a protector. He loved them because they were not needy. It's hard to imagine Audubon within the Audubon Society: once his subjects had to be protected, the splendor that drew him to them in the first place would be gone.

But if Audubon is a relic as a "scientific" naturalist, as a naturalist in the other, literary sense he is still alive. He was the first American artist to look at abundance and see isolation. His animals do not belong to a large "ecology" or have a rank within a secure hierarchy. Instead, their life is lived in a constant present, in which they are always watchful. The only respite comes when an animal is with its mate. Audubon is a poet of married life, who pictures twoness as mutual protection, a midpoint around which a hostile world revolves. His pictures of mated animals can have a horrible delicacy, as in the wonderful plate of two black vultures cuddled within each other's wings and about to peck out and share the eye of a dead deer, or in the plate of a barn owl coming home on a starry winter night, climbing up a branch and opening his beak with delight as his mate turns her head coquettishly, and lifts her snowy-white wing to reveal the hanging squirrel they will share for dinner.

Audubon's passion produced a style by transforming his extravagances into a chastened, dispassionate-seeming language of hard facts, through which the original ardor still shines. The outward sign that his ardor settled on was simply stylized movement; it seems right that George Balanchine thought that Audubon's art could be the subject of a ballet—for forty years, he and Lincoln Kirstein planned to collaborate on a ***Birds of America*** ballet. (A score exists, by Morton Gould, and bits and pieces of the plan can be reconstructed from accounts by Balanchine's biographer.) The ballet would have turned on the Dauphin legend: the rightful king wandering in America and creating a court of birds. In the third act, apparently, the scene would have leaped ahead to Hollywood in the thirties, with an eternal Audubon transferring his attentions from the white egret to the platinum blonde. Balanchine's Audubon might have fixed forever one image of Audubon, that of the émigré classicist, lost in America.

It also makes sense, though, that in the end Balanchine decided to leave the Audubon ballet alone. Perhaps he recognized that there was nothing much to reinterpret. The constant animation that Audubon imposed on his creations, and that to his contemporaries could look so unnatural, has come to seem at the end of his two volumes as beautifully contrived as ballet, and has the same equanimity. In Audubon's world, as in classical dancing, heightened action of any kind—struggle, escape, seduction, threat, violent death—becomes an opportunity for grace; "And speed, speed, is his only hope for life." Attempting to fix each animal as his imagination grasped it, Audubon ended up painting a catalogue of five hundred and eighty-five aspects of what is still an American theme: that natural life is lived in fear, ruled by habit, and relieved by flight.

FURTHER READING

Biography

Adams, Alexander B. *John James Audubon: A Biography.* New York: G. P. Putnam's Sons, 1966, 510 p.

> Biography containing primary and secondary bibliographies.

Chancellor, John. *Audubon: A Biography.* New York: Viking Press, 1978, 224 p.

> Concise biography containing many reproductions of Audubon's paintings.

Durant, Mary, and Harwood, Michael. *On the Road with John James Audubon.* New York: Dodd, Mead & Co., 1980, 638 p.

> Account of Audubon's travels throughout North America.

Geiser, Samuel Wood. "Naturalists of the Frontier: Audubon in Texas." *Southwest Review* XVI, No. 1 (Autumn 1930): 109-35.

> Account of Audubon's 1837 trip to Texas.

Herrick, Francis Hobart. *Audubon the Naturalist.* New York: D. Appleton-Century Co., 1938, 951 p.

> Comprehensive biography. Appendices include documents relating to Audubon's birth, lists of original subscribers to *The Birds of America*, and Audubon's prospectus for *The Birds of America*.

Criticism

Brooks, Van Wyck. "Audubon." In his *The World of Washington Irving*, pp. 138-51. New York: E.P. Dutton & Co., 1944.

> Impressionistic account of Audubon's conception and production of *The Birds of America* and a tribute to his account of the American frontier.

Downs, Robert B. "King of Ornithological Painters: John James Audubon's *The Birds of America*, 1827-1838." In his *Famous American Books*, pp. 82-7. New York: McGraw-Hill Book Company, 1971.

> Examines the processes involved in the design and publication of *The Birds of America*.

Savage, Henry Lyttleton. "John James Audubon: A Backwoodsman in the Salon." *The Princeton University Chronicle* V, No. 4 (June 1944): 129-36.

> Examines the Audubon collection held by the Princeton University Library.

Winterich, John T. "John James Audubon and *The Birds of America*." In his *Books and the Man*, pp. 141-54. New York: Greenberg, 1929.

> Discusses the genesis and publication of *The Birds of America*.

Fitz-Greene Halleck

1790-1867

(Also published under the pseudonym Thomas Castaly)
American poet.

INTRODUCTION

Halleck was one of the most popular and respected American poets of the nineteenth century. Known for both satirical verses and sentimental lyric poetry on serious subjects, he was part of New York's Knickerbocker literary circle, a witty and urbane coterie of writers which included James Fenimore Cooper, Washington Irving, William Cullen Bryant, Caroline Kirkland, and James Paulding.

Biographical Information

A descendant of early Puritan colonists, Halleck was born and raised in rural Guilford, Connecticut. His first published verses, on a dying Indian warrior, appeared in a New Haven newspaper in the winter of 1809-10. After moving to New York City in 1811 at the age of 21, Halleck worked as a clerk, first for wealthy banker and businessman Jacob Barker, and after 1832 as personal secretary to noted entrepreneur John Jacob Astor. In 1813, Halleck made the acquaintance of Joseph Rodman Drake, a young New York doctor and fellow poet. In 1819, Halleck and Drake published a series of satirical verses on New York society in the *New York Evening Post,* some written jointly under the pseudonym "Croaker & Co.," others written by Drake as "Croaker" or by Halleck as "Croaker, Jr." These poems enjoyed enormous popularity, provoking much speculation as to their authorship. After Drake died of tuberculosis the following year, Halleck continued to publish his own poems. Many first appeared in publications edited by Bryant, including the *New York Review,* the *United States Review,* and the *New York Evening Post.* In 1849 Halleck retired to his native Guilford. Although he published only two new poems after 1827, his work remained popular with readers well after his death in 1867.

Major Works

Halleck's humorous "Croaker" verses, with their pointed observations on contemporary life and personalities, first brought him to public attention, and his long poem *Fanny,* published anonymously the same year, established his place among a wide readership. Modelled on Lord Byron's *Beppo, Fanny* was a poem of nearly fifteen hundred lines mocking the pretenses of New York's *nouveaux riches.* It went into several editions, including a London edition, and was such a success that at the publisher's request Halleck provided an additional fifty stanzas in 1821. A trip to Europe in 1822 provided the occasion for two of his most highly praised poems, "Burns," a tribute to the eighteenth-century Scottish poet, and "Alnwick Castle,"

a meditation on the ruins of Percy Castle in Alnwick, England. The following year he published "Marco Bozzaris," a melodramatic account in verse of the death of a Greek patriot in a raid against the Turks. "The Recorder," first published in 1828 under the pseudonym Thomas Castaly, is a biting and occasionally bitter satire directed against Richard Riker, a New York City judge who had had a hand in ruinous litigation involving Halleck's employer Jacob Barker. The first collection of Halleck's work, *Alnwick Castle, with Other Poems,* appeared in 1827 and quickly sold out; numerous further editions appeared during the next four decades. Halleck virtually stopped writing poetry after 1827, although he remained active in literary circles, translating European verse and editing a collection of Lord Byron's work in 1833. His most enduring work is his elegy on the death of his friend Drake, a version of which is inscribed on the memorial at Drake's grave site in the Bronx.

Critical Reception

Much of Halleck's historical importance, like his literary reputation, may be credited to the thinness of American literary production during the first decades of the nineteenth century. Even at the height of his considerable popularity, critics generally portrayed him as a competent poet who displayed occasional flashes of brilliance; subsequent criticism has not revised that assessment. One of his most ardent admirers was his friend and fellow poet Bryant, who praised Halleck's melodic versification, his rich imagery, and his use of irony and self-deprecating wit to alleviate the solemnity of even his most serious poems. Other contemporary critics, however, concurred with poet and critic Edgar Allan Poe that Halleck's mixing of humor and seriousness spoiled the effect of many of his poems. Poe also pilloried Halleck for marring his best works with syntactical errors and careless versification. By the end of the century Halleck was remembered primarily as a relic of the unsophisticated early days of American letters.

PRINCIPAL WORKS

Fanny (poetry) 1819; enlarged edition, 1821
Poems [with Joseph Rodman Drake, under the name "Croaker, Jr." or "Croaker & Co.,"] (poetry) 1819
Alnwick Castle, with Other Poems (poetry) 1827
The Recorder, with Other Poems (poetry) 1833
The Works of Lord Byron, in Verse and Prose [editor] (letters, poems, essays) 1833
Fanny, with Other Poems (poetry) 1839
Selections from the British Poets [editor] (poetry) 1840
The Poetical Works of Fitz-Greene Halleck (poetry) 1847
Young America: A Poem (poetry) 1865
The Poetical Writings of Fitz-Greene Halleck, with Extracts from those of Joseph Rodman Drake (poetry) 1869

CRITICISM

Edgar Allan Poe (essay date 1836)

SOURCE: A review of *The Culprit Fay, and Other Poems,* and *Alnwick Castle, with Other Poems,* in *The Complete Works of Edgar Allan Poe, Vol. VIII,* edited by James A. Harrison, Thomas Y. Crowell, 1902, pp. 275-318.

[*A distinguished poet, novelist, essayist, journalist, short story writer, editor, and critic, Poe stressed an analytical, rather than emotive approach to literature and emphasized the specifics of style and construction in a work, instead of concentrating solely on the importance of ideological statement. Although Poe and his literary criticism were subject to controversy in his own lifetime, he is now valued for his literary theories. In the following excerpt, originally published in 1836, from a review of* Alnwick Castle, with Other Poems, *Poe analyzes several of Halleck's works, including "Alnwick Castle," "Macro Bozzaris," "Burns,"*

and "Lines on the Death of Joseph Rodman Drake," praising the poet's power of expression but faulting his versification and inconsistencies in tone.]

By the hackneyed phrase, *sportive elegance,* we might possibly designate at once the general character of [Halleck's] writings and the very loftiest praise to which he is justly entitled.

"Alnwick Castle" is an irregular poem of one hundred and twenty-eight lines—was written, as we are informed, in October 1822—and is descriptive of a seat of the Duke of Northumberland, in Northumberlandshire, England. The effect of the first stanza is materially impaired by a defect in its grammatical arrangement. The fine lines,

> Home of the Percy's high-born race,
>   Home of their beautiful and brave,
> Alike their birth and burial place,
>   Their cradle and their grave!

are of the nature of an invocation, and thus require a continuation of the address to the "Home, &c." We are consequently disappointed when the stanza proceeds with—

> Still sternly o'er the castle gate
> *Their* house's Lion stands in state
>   As in *his* proud departed hours;
> And warriors frown in stone on high,
> And feudal banners "flout the sky"
>   Above *his* princely towers.

The objects of allusion here vary, in an awkward manner, from the castle to the Lion, and from the Lion to the towers. By writing the verses thus the difficulty would be remedied.

> Still sternly o'er the castle gate
> *Thy* house's Lion stands in state,
>   As in his proud departed hours;
> And warriors frown in stone on high,
> And feudal banners "flout the sky"
>   Above *thy* princely towers.

The second stanza, without evincing in any measure the loftier powers of a poet, has that quiet air of grace, both in thought and expression, which seems to be the prevailing feature of the Muse of Halleck.

> A gentle hill its side inclines,
>   Lovely in England's fadeless green,
> To meet the quiet stream which winds
>   Through this romantic scene
> As silently and sweetly still,
> As when, at evening, on that hill,
>   While summer's wind blew soft and low,
> Seated by gallant Hotspur's side
> His Katherine was a happy bride
>   A thousand years ago.

There are one or two brief passages in the poem evincing a degree of rich imagination not elsewhere perceptible throughout the book. For example—

> Gaze on the Abbey's ruined pile:
>   Does not the succoring Ivy keeping,
> Her watch around it seem to smile
>   As o'er a lov'd one sleeping?

and,

One solitary turret gray
  Still tells in melancholy glory
  The legend of the Cheviot day.

The commencement of the fourth stanza is of the highest order of Poetry, and partakes, in a happy manner, of that quaintness of expression so effective an adjunct to Ideality, when employed by the Shelleys, the Coleridges and the Tennysons, but so frequently debased, and rendered ridiculous, by the herd of brainless imitators.

Wild roses by the abbey towers
  Are gay in their young bud and bloom:
  They were born of a race of funeral flowers,
  That garlanded in long-gone hours,
    A Templar's knightly tomb.

The tone employed in the concluding portions of **"Alnwick Castle,"** is, we sincerely think, reprehensible, and unworthy of Halleck. No true poet can unite in any manner the low burlesque with the ideal, and not be conscious of incongruity and of a profanation. Such verses as

Men in the coal and cattle line
  From Teviot's bard and hero land,
  From royal Berwick's beach of sand,
  From Wooller, Morpeth, Hexham, and
    Newcastle upon Tyne.

may lay claim to oddity—but no more. These things are the defects and not the beauties of *Don Juan.* They are totally out of keeping with the graceful and delicate manner of the initial portions of **"Alnwick Castle,"** and serve no better purpose than to deprive the entire poem of all unity of effect. If a poet must be farcical, let him be just that, and nothing else. To be drolly sentimental is bad enough, . . . but to be sentimentally droll is a thing intolerable to men, and Gods, and columns.

"Marco Bozzaris" appears to have much lyrical without any high order of *ideal* beauty. *Force* is its prevailing character—a force, however, consisting more in a well ordered and sonorous arrangement of the metre, and a judicious disposal of what may be called the circumstances of the poem, than in the true *material* of lyric vigor. We are introduced, first, to the Turk who dreams, at midnight, in his guarded tent,

of the hour
  When Greece her knee in suppliance bent,
    Should tremble at his power—

He is represented as revelling in the visions of ambition.

In dreams through camp and court he bore
  The trophies of a conqueror;
  In dreams his song of triumph heard;
  Then wore his monarch's signet ring:
  Then pressed that monarch's throne—a king;
  As wild his thoughts and gay of wing
    As Eden's garden bird.

In direct contrast to this we have Bozzaris watchful in the forest, and ranging his band of Suliotes on the ground, and amid the memories of Plataea. An hour elapses, and the Turk awakes from his visions of false glory—to die. But Bozzaris dies—to awake. He dies in the flush of victory to awake, in death, to an ultimate certainty of Freedom. Then follows an invocation to death. His terrors under or-

dinary circumstances are contrasted with the glories of the dissolution of Bozzaris, in which the approach of the Destroyer is

welcome as the cry
  That told the Indian isles were nigh
  To the world-seeking Genoese,
  When the land-wind from woods of palm,
  And orange groves and fields of balm,
    Blew o'er the Haytian seas.

The poem closes with the poetical apotheosis of Marco Bozzaris as

One of the few, the immortal names
  That are not born to die.

It will be seen that these arrangements of the subject are skilfully contrived—perhaps they are a little too evident, and we are enabled too readily by the perusal of one passage, to anticipate the succeeding. The rhythm is highly artificial. The stanzas are well adapted for vigorous expression—the fifth will afford a just specimen of the versification of the whole poem.

Come to the bridal Chamber, Death!
  Come to the mother's, when she feels
  For the first time her first born's breath;
    Come when the blessed seals
  That close the pestilence are broke,
  And crowded cities wail its stroke;
  Come in consumption's ghastly form,
  The earthquake shock, the ocean storm;
  Come when the heart beats high and warm,
    With banquet song, and dance, and wine;
  And thou art terrible—the tear,
  The groan, the knell, the pall, the bier;
  And all we know, or dream, or fear
    Of agony, are thine.

Granting, however, to **"Marco Bozzaris,"** the minor excellences we have pointed out, we should be doing our conscience great wrong in calling it, upon the whole, any more than a very ordinary matter. It is surpassed, even as a lyric, by a multitude of foreign and by many American compositions of a similar character. To Ideality it has few pretensions, and the finest portion of the poem is probably to be found in the verses we have quoted elsewhere—

Thy grasp is welcome as the land
  Of brother in a foreign land;
  Thy summons welcome as the cry
  That told the Indian isles were nigh
    To the world-seeking Genoese,
  When the land-wind from woods of palm,
  And orange groves, and fields of balm
  Blew o'er the Haytian seas.

The verses entitled **"Burns"** consist of thirty-eight quatrains—the three first lines of each quatrain being of four feet, the fourth of three. This poem has many of the traits of **"Alnwick Castle,"** and bears also a strong resemblance to some of the writings of Wordsworth. Its chief merit, and indeed the chief merit, so we think, of all the poems of Halleck is the merit of *expression.* In the brief extracts from **"Burns"** which follow, our readers will recognize the peculiar character of which we speak.

Wild Rose of Alloway! my thanks:

Thou mind'st me of that autumn noon
When first we met upon "the banks
And braes o' bonny Doon"—

———

Like thine, beneath the thorn-tree's bough,
My sunny hour was glad and brief—
We've crossed the winter sea, and thou
Art withered—flower and leaf.

———

There have been loftier themes than his,
And longer scrolls and louder lyres
And lays lit up with Poesy's
Purer and holier fires.

———

And when he breathes his master-lay
Of Alloway's witch-haunted wall
All passions in our frames of clay
Come thronging at his call.

———

Such graves as his are pilgrim-shrines,
Shrines to no code or creed confined—
The Delphian vales, the Palestines,
The Meccas of the mind.
They linger by the Doon's low trees,
And pastoral Nith, and wooded Ayr,
And round thy Sepulchres, Dumfries!
The Poet's tomb is there.

"Wyoming" is composed of nine Spenserian stanzas. With some unusual excellences, it has some of the worst faults of Halleck. The lines which follow are of great beauty.

I then but dreamed: thou art before me now,
In life—a vision of the brain no more,
I've stood upon the wooded mountain's brow,
That beetles high thy lovely valley o'er;
And now, where winds thy river's greenest shore,
Within a bower of sycamores am laid;
And winds as soft and sweet as ever bore
The fragrance of wild flowers through sun and
*   shade*
Are singing in the trees, whose low boughs press
*   my head.*

The poem, however, is disfigured with the mere burlesque of some portions of **"Alnwick Castle"**—with such things as

he would look particularly droll
In his Iberian boot and Spanish plume;

and

A girl of sweet sixteen
Love-darting eyes and tresses like the morn
Without a shoe or stocking—hoeing corn,

mingled up in a pitiable manner with images of real beauty.

"The Field of the Grounded Arms" contains twenty-four quatrains, without rhyme, and, we think, of a disagreeable versification. In this poem are to be observed some of the finest passages of Halleck. For example—

Strangers! your eyes are on that valley
*   fixed*
Intently, as we gaze on vacancy,
When the mind's wings o'erspread
The spirit world of dreams.

and again—

O'er sleepless seas of grass whose waves are
*   flowers.*

"Red Jacket" has much power of expression with little evidence of poetical ability. Its humor is very fine, and does not interfere, in any great degree, with the general tone of the poem.

"A Sketch" should have been omitted from the edition as altogether unworthy of its author.

The remaining pieces in the volume are **"Twilight;" "Psalm cxxxvii;" "To . . . ;" "Love;" "Domestic Happiness;" "Magdalen;" "From the Italian;" "Woman;" "Connecticut;" "Music;" "On the Death of Lieut. William Howard Allen;" "A Poet's Daughter;"** and **"On the Death of Joseph Rodman Drake."** Of the majority of these we deem it unnecessary to say more than that they partake, in a more or less degree, of the general character observable in the poems of Halleck. The **"Poet's Daughter"** appears to us a particularly happy specimen of that general character, and we doubt whether it be not the favorite of its author. . . .

"The Lines on the Death of Joseph Rodman Drake," we prefer to any of the writings of Halleck. It has that rare merit in composition of this kind—the union of tender sentiment and simplicity. This poem consists merely of six quatrains, and we quote them in full.

Green be the turf above thee,
*   Friend of my better days!*
None knew thee but to love thee,
*   Nor named thee but to praise.*

Tears fell when thou wert dying,
*   From eyes unused to weep,*
And long, where thou art lying,
*   Will tears the cold turf steep.*

When hearts whose truth was proven,
*   Like thine are laid in earth,*
There should a wreath be woven
*   To tell the world their worth.*

And I, who woke each morrow
*   To clasp thy hand in mine,*
Who shared thy joy and sorrow,
*   Whose weal and woe were thine*—

It should be mine to braid it
*   Around thy faded brow,*
But I've in vain essayed it,
*   And feel I cannot now.*

While memory bids me weep thee,
*   Nor thoughts nor words are free,*
The grief is fixed too deeply,
*   That mourns a man like thee.*

If we are to judge from the subject of these verses, they are a work of some care and reflection. Yet they abound in faults. In the line,

> Tears fell when thou wert dying;

wert is not English.

> Will tears the cold turf steep,

is an exceedingly rough verse. The metonymy involved in

> There should a wreath be woven
> To *tell* the world their worth,

is unjust. The quatrain beginning,

> And I who woke each morrow,

is ungrammatical in its construction when viewed in connection with the quatrain which immediately follows. "Weep thee" and "deeply" are inaccurate rhymes—and the whole of the first quatrain,

> Green be the turf, &c.

although beautiful, bears too close a resemblance to the still more beautiful lines of William Wordsworth,

> She dwelt among the untrodden ways
> Beside the springs of Dove,
> A maid whom there were none to praise
> And very few to love.

As a versifier Halleck is by no means equal to his friend, all of whose poems evince an ear finely attuned to the delicacies of melody. We seldom meet with more inharmonious lines than those, generally, of the author of **"Alnwick Castle."** At every step such verses occur as,

> And *the* monk's hymn and minstrel's song—
> True *as* the steel of *their* tried blades—
> For him the joy of *her* young years—
> Where *the* Bard-peasant first drew breath—
> And withered *my* life's leaf like thine—

in which the proper course of the rhythm would demand an accent upon syllables too unimportant to sustain it. Not unfrequently, too, we meet with lines such as this,

> Like torn branch from death's leafless tree,

in which the multiplicity of consonants renders the pronunciation of the words at all, a matter of no inconsiderable difficulty.

But we must bring out notice to a close. It will be seen that while we are willing to admire in many respects the poems before us, we feel obliged to dissent materially from that public opinion (perhaps not fairly ascertained) which would assign them a very brilliant rank in the empire of Poesy. That we have among us poets of the loftiest order we believe—but we do *not* believe that these poets are Drake and Halleck.

American Quarterly Review (essay date 1837)

SOURCE: *American Quarterly Review,* Vol. XXI, No. XLII, June, 1837, pp. 399-415.

[*In the following excerpt, the reviewer comments on various poems in Halleck's 1836 collection,* Alnwick Castle, *with Other Poems, and discusses his transition from social satire to descriptive nature and landscape poetry and narrative.*]

[Halleck's] city residence, . . . did not seduce our author away from the remembrance of the country. He reverted to its calmness, its seclusion, and its purity, in many a melodious line. To him there was a charm in recollected rocks, waters, and vernal uplands—"ruris amoeni rivos, et musco circumlita saxa nemusque." He heard, even in the crowded and garish ways of the town, those celestial voices which breathe at night from echoing hills and thickets, over land and sea. The power of these entered into his heart of hearts; but he was environed by the every day realities of a crowded capital; the follies of its dwellers passed in daily review before him; and, quenching within himself what we must call his better inspirations, he launched his bark of authorship upon the sea of *satire.* In doing this, he acquired a burlesque habitude of style, which we regret to say became afterwards almost a passion with him, and the effects of which are absent from but very few of his compositions. In the verses of Croaker, written in conjunction with others, his spirit roamed and revelled among the stupidities or the "sins, negligences, and ignorances," of the town. Many a citizen rued the movements of his caustic quill: but like the sword of Sir Lucius O'Trigger in the comedy, it was no less polished than keen. There is one species of satirists that may be called insupportable: those who condemn without grace, and rebuke without good nature. This propensity, in man or woman, but especially in the latter, is beyond endurance. It is produced from ungenial minds, and betokens the utter absence of those lovely humanities, without the enforcement of which no writer can enduringly or really please.

Since he dissolved his partnership with the firm of *Croaker and Co.,* Mr. Halleck—who has been justly accredited in the literary world as the chief operator in the concerns of that well-known house—has had little to do with satire. Not that its vein is extinct within him; but he has too much *goodness of heart* to engage in the breaking of social butterflies upon the wheel of ridicule. . . .

If, however, our author ever felt a momentary regret that he did not keep up his hunt for the follies and foibles of metropolitan life, he has been abundantly consoled in the success of those better, though not more popular works, which seem to have emanated warmly from his soul, and to have been dashed upon paper by a hand burdened and busy with the genuine promptings of genius. Intending to offer proofs of his sudden power, it is not improper to preface them with our impressions of the method by which Mr. Halleck commits himself "to virgin sheets." He does not seize upon one bright and lofty thought, and, delighting in it, *per se,* dilute it into a column or a page; he preserves it; he joins it with others that may occur to him from time to time, whether he move at nightfall along the dim streets of the city, catching glimpses of the distant country across the Hudson or the bay, as the sun sinks to his evening pavilion—or whether he gain an afternoon to visit suburban landscapes, and "walk in the fields, hearing the voice of God:" and when his mind is *full,* he pours it forth, a deluge of strong and brilliant imaginings. He suffers little or nothing to go forth to a cold-bosomed public which does not bear the impress of a master's hand. The first poem in the volume before us establishes the powerful originality of his style. In the present age of indiscriminate locomotion—when "the universal Yankee nation," using the phrase in the *national* sense, are every where present in Europe, by travelled delegations—we all know how stale and unprofitable are their pictures and descriptions of ivied ruins and broken turrets, the homes of rooks and owls—where the moon is as constant an attendant for every tourist, as if she were hired for the occasion, under a contract of "no postponement on account of the weather;" we know the thricetold tales of halls, and armours, and corridors, and so forth—part romance, part reality; —and it is an easy thing to set them down at their true value. But, let the reader peruse such a concentrated sketch as the following of Alnwick Castle—and will he ever forget it? Not soon.

> Gaze on the abbey's ruined pile:
>   Does not the succouring ivy, keeping
> Her watch around it, seem to smile,
>   As o'er a loved one sleeping?
> One solitary turret gray
>   Still tells, in melancholy glory,
> The legend of the Cheviot day,
>   The Percy's proudest border story.
> That day its roof was triumph's arch;
>   Then rang, from aisle to pictured dome,
> The light step of the soldier's march,
>   The music of the trump and drum;
> And babe, and sire, the old, the young,
> And the monk's hymn, and minstrel's song,
> *And woman's pure kiss, sweet and long,*
>   *Welcomed her warrior home.*

We ask a close attention to the lines we have Italicised. If there be any thing more delicious in the whole range of English literature, we have not yet encountered it. Something akin to them may be found in Bassanio's exclamation in the *Merchant of Venice,* when he draws from the leaden casket that which assures him how he is beloved: —

> Fair Portia's counterfeit! What demi-god
> Hath come so near creation?
>   —Here are sever'd lips
> Parted with sugar breath: so sweet a bar
> Should sunder such sweet friends.

In this little gem of a picture, the author of **"Alnwick"** has taken us back to the past. The pomp and circumstance of the victory and the return are there; the harpings in the hall of triumph; the shouts of retainers; the joy of the feast; the draining of huge draughts of Rhenish down; —the speaking roll of the drum to the "cannonier without;" and the echoes which that noisy functionary sends thrilling magnificently toward the empyrean. This is *abbreviated romance*—it is the spirit of unadulterated chivalry. The true poet alone could thus embody the scenes of other days. Some who affected the burlesque, and shone therein, have delighted to imagine that knights templars have left their blacksmith's bills for mending coats of mail unpaid, all the way from England to Palestine; and bold historians have sometimes represented them as clumsy horsemen, with their limbs galled, and their unwashed persons irri-

tated, by rusty armour. We do not, for our parts, affect this dissolving of ancient spells: and we can scarcely forgive those venerable chroniclers, Froissart, de Thou, or Stowe, for representing the characters of so many heroes, "dear to fancy" and treasured in the recollection of every true lover of the brave and noble, apparently *in puris naturalibus*—without that ornament which, with the aid of their recorded deeds, imagination could easily supply. For the same reasons, we take but little pleasure in perusing those short narratives in the *Decameron* of Boccacio, from which Shakespeare has built a fairy and unconquered world. Who would go to the dull outline which some old monk or annalist has furnished of *Romeo and Juliet,* when he could revel in that glowing description written by the bard of Avon? The moonlight sleeps upon the garden of the Capulets, when we survey it from the window of our imagination, as palpably as if the rustling of its leaves were in our ear; —we hear the stifled sigh—the broken vow— the voice of Philomel singing in the branches. What has "unaccommodated" history to do with the enchanting transactions of that balmy night, and the loving interlocutors who made its presence holy? By the mass, nothing. The poet's duty is to give us things, robed *couleur de rose;* to shed around nature a perfume richer than the breath of the violet—and to suffuse it "with tints more magical than the blush of morning." A power or skill like this bespeaks more readily the poet, *nascitur, non fit,* than the wildest bursts of animal passion: it exhibits a quality, ethereal—heavenly—which owns no touch of this working-day world. And as often as we think of the devoted pair of Verona, so often are we reminded of their familiar identity; as if we saw the noble girl sinking into the tomb of her fathers. In our mental vision,

> The summer rose hath not yet faded—
>   The summer stream not yet decayed;
> The purple sky is still unshaded,
>   And, from the sweet pomegranate-glade,
> Floateth the night-bird's serenade;
> Flower, and stream, and song remain—
>   Not one of Nature's charms hath fled;
> While she, who breathed a softer strain,
>   Herself a fairer flower, is dead.

We had not intended to stroll into so long a digression— and return to our author. Having quoted a parallel to those charming lines at the close of the extract from **"Alnwick,"** in the same language, we ought perhaps to seek a better in some older tongue. The task is difficult; for with all the luxurious tastes of lyrists in the by-gone time, they had not a better perception of the beautiful than has been accorded, early and late, to a favoured few in many ages, who have swept the lyre with measures of English modulation. Mr. Halleck has built his rhymes with care: he has *turned his stylus often,* until every note he has recorded has discoursed pleasantly to his spiritual ear. Hence, his sentiments, above expressed, are not less pure than smooth— reminding one of those sweet and juicy lines in the Carmen ad Lydiam of Horace: —

> —dulcia oscula, quae Venus
> Quintâ parte sui nectaris imbuit.

Next in order, among the productions in the volume under notice, appears that splendid lyric, entitled **"Marco Boz-**

zaris." We will not so far question the good taste of the reader as to presume that he has not perused this stirring effusion, "time and again;" but we cannot refrain from offering the first portions of it for renewed admiration. To ourselves, the best test of its merit is the effect which it has upon our feelings. It is like contemplating a distant conflict, in which we have the deepest interest, but are forbidden to take a part. The spirit of liberty *thrills* through every line. We are convinced, while we read with tingling veins, that the writer possesses the true *chivalresque* quality; and that, occasion serving or demanding, he would be quite ready to distinguish himself, like Körner, not with the lyre merely, but the sword. In truth the very quantity and movement of this noble poem seem instinct with martial ardour. Like the war-horse in Scripture, the author, in his spirit at least, "goeth forth to meet the armed men. The quiver rattleth against him; the glittering spear and the shield. He saith ha, ha! among the trumpets; he heareth the battle afar off; —the noise of the captains, and the shouting." Let the reader observe the life-like energy with which the Turk is awakened from his last gorgeous dream, and hears the death-shots falling around him, like the angry bolts of heaven as they leap from the bosom of an Alpine tempest; —the stern and patriotic command that rings through the sacred air; the tumult that ensues; —the leaden rain—and the harvest of death. We mark some lines in Italic, not that we suppose their grandeur and beauty will not be perceived, but to express how especially we appreciate them.

> At midnight, in his guarded tent,
>   The Turk was dreaming of the hour
> When Greece, her knee in suppliance bent,
>   Should tremble at his power:
> In dreams, through camp and court, he bore
> The trophies of a conqueror;
>   In dreams his song of triumph heard;
> Then wore his monarch's signet ring:
> Then pressed that monarch's throne—a king;
> As wild his thoughts, and gay of wing,
>   As Eden's garden bird.
>
> At midnight, in the forest shades,
>   Bozzaris ranged his Suliote band,
> True as the steel of their tried blades,
>   Heroes in heart and hand.
> There had the Persian's thousands stood,
> There had the glad earth drunk their blood,
>   On old Plataea's day;
> *And now there breathed that haunted air*
> *The sons of sires who conquered there,*
> *With arm to strike, and soul to dare,*
>   *As quick, as far as they.*
>
> An hour passed on—the Turk awoke;
>   That bright dream was his last;
> He woke—to hear his sentries shriek,
> 'To arms! they come! the Greek! the Greek!'
> He woke—*to die midst flame, and smoke,*
> *And shout, and groan, and sabre stroke,*
>   *And death shots falling thick and fast*
> *As lightnings from the mountain cloud;*
> And heard, with voice as trumpet loud,
>   Bozzaris cheer his band:
> *'Strike—till the last armed foe expires;*
> *Strike—for your altars and your fires;*
> *Strike—for the green graves of your sires;*

> *God—and your native land!'*
>
> They fought—like brave men, long and well;
>   They piled that ground with Moslem slain;
> They conquered—but Bozzaris fell,
>   Bleeding at every vein.
> His few surviving comrades saw
> *His smile, when rang their proud hurrah*
>   *And the red field was won;*
> Then saw in death his eyelids close
> Calmly, as to a night's repose
>   Like flowers at set of sun.

The verses in memory of Robert Burns, addressed to a rose brought from near Alloway Kirk, in Ayrshire, in the autumn of 1822, which follow the lyric from which we have just made an extract, are worthy of any modern pen, whose products are but the synonyms for true inspiration. The author has written in a strain worthy of his subject: his method is simple, fervent, and dear to the heart. He has a Scott-like faculty, we think, of contemplating his theme with a nice severity; —there is a *simplex munditiis* about the objects of his song, sometimes, that really gives them more attraction than the most laboured measures could otherwise impart. The mere sight of a rose, brought across the Atlantic, awakens in his mind a host of happy and pathetic imaginations. He is reminded of the autumn noon when he first detached it from its parent stem, on "the banks of bonnie Doon." He bore it with him across the winter sea; and lo! when it meets his eye in his native country, a multitude of recollections pass, with kaleidoscopic colours, through his mind. We consider this faculty of making one thought provoke a legion of others, as among the highest attributes of human intellect. That our author possesses it to more than the ordinary extent, is undeniable. With him the running brook might indeed furnish forth its volumes; or the mossy stone, half hidden from the eye, fructify into a sermon. This power of his reminds us frequently of the peculiar gifts of the imaginary German, *Teufelsdröch,* with whom the author of *Sartor Resartus* has caused the English and American reader to be well acquainted. This faculty of making the most evanescent thing in nature a nucleus for profound reflection, is admirably exhibited in the following passage: —"As I rode through the *Schwarzwald,*" he writes, "I said to myself: that little fire which glows star-like across the dark-growing moor, where the sooty smith bends over his anvil, and thou hopest to replace thy lost horse-shoe—is it a detached, separated speck, cut off from the whole universe; or indissolubly joined to the whole? Thou fool; that smithy fire was primarily kindled at the sun; is fed by air, that circulated from before Noah's deluge—from beyond the dog-star; it is a little ganglion, or nervous centre, in the great vital system of immensity." We cannot help comparing the spirit which dictated these sentences, to that which can evoke from a scentless rose, a thousand leagues from the source where it bloomed, a tribute like the one from which the following quotation is offered.

> Such graves as his are pilgrim-shrines,
>   Shrines to no code or creed confined,—
> The Delphian vales, the Palestines,
>   The Meccas of the mind.
>
> Sages, with wisdom's garland wreathed,

Crowned kings, and mitred priests of power,
    And warriors with their bright swords sheathed
        The mightiest of the hour;

And lowlier names, whose humble home
    Is lit by Fortune's dimmer star,
Are there—o'er wave and mountain come,
    From countries near and far;

Pilgrims whose wandering feet have prest
    The Switzer's snow, the Arab's sand,
Or trod the piled leaves of the West,
    My own green forest-land.

All ask the cottage of his birth,
    Gaze on the scenes he loved and sung,
And gather feelings not of earth
    His fields and streams among.

They linger by the Doon's low trees,
    And pastoral Nith, and wooded Ayr,
And round thy sepulchres, Dumfries!
    The Poet's tomb is there.

But what to them the sculptor's art,
    His funeral columns, wreaths, and urns?—
Wear they not, graven on the heart,
    The name of Robert Burns?

There is a good deal of spirit about the poem of **"Wyoming,"** and some delicious rural description—but in the abrupt, parenthetical dashes, and vicissitudes of style, which it contains, we recognise a residuum or leaven from *Croaker and Company's* peculiar passion; and we must be permitted to say, that we look upon it as the offspring of bad taste. Every one knows that Campbell's Gertrude was painted *couleur de rose;* yet the fair Wyoming, or the banks of the fair Susquehanna, never came palpably within the scope of his corporeal eye. He looked at them merely, through the glass of his imagination. But we confess we had rather see his heroine as the bard of Hope has painted her, than to scrutinize her proportions, hoeing corn, sans hose and shoon. We do not affect this blending of styles. One at a time is sufficient; and there is an infelicity about the commingling of two or more, at the very best. Abrupt transitions, such as we find in *Don Juan,* are amusing, it is true, but then they are utterly devoid of *dignity:* without which, pathos is a poor gawd, and the virtues, pitiful ministers to the burlesque. We really think that Mr. Halleck should eschew this propensity henceforth, whenever he writes gravely. Wit he has, and humour, in abundance; but let him not present them in compositions that might move, as with the wand of a prophet, the sacred fountains of sympathy or tears. We are aware of his versatility; but it should be evinced in the *separate,* rather than in the *collected* variety of his performances. *Olla-podridas* of the kind may have told well in Matthews' amusing rehearsals—but they are not defensible in a bard like Halleck.

Passing over the elegiac effusion on the death of JOSEPH RODMAN DRAKE, which is familiar to every admirer of our author, we reach the ensuing lines entitled **"Twilight."** There is about them a holy music, which rings at the portals of our spiritual ear, like the breathings of some enchanting lute. As we read it, all our visions of the tender and the lovely throng up in glittering array before the eye of reminiscence. We see the sunlight playing again on the vernal landscapes of our early youth; a momentary glimpse is given us of the sheen of waters, that can never flash so blue and bright as in other days; hallowed hours, spell-bound moments, are hurrying by upon the wings of remembrance; and, convening again around us, in sweet communion, the distant and the dead, we go back with rapture to the times when, to our unpractised eyes, there was a newness of lustre in the brave evening firmament, fretted with dazzling fires; and when the mere boon of existence sufficed us, while we could look upon the folded lily, as it rested in humble modesty on the margin of the water-brook, and "rocked to sleep a world of insect life in its golden cradle." These of course were childish affections; and when we come to be men, we put away childish things; but a strain like **"Twilight"** re-presents them anew.

Twilight

There is an evening twilight of the heart,
    When its wild passion-waves are lulled to rest,
And the eye sees life's fairy scenes depart,
    As fades the day-beam in the rosy west.
'Tis with a nameless feeling of regret
    We gaze upon them as they melt away,
And fondly would we bid them linger yet,
    But hope is round us with her angel lay,
Hailing afar some happier moonlight hour;
Dear are her whispers still, though lost their
    early power.

In youth the cheek was crimsoned with her
    glow;
    Her smile was loveliest then; her matin song
Was heaven's own music, and the note of wo
    Was all unheard her sunny bowers among.

Life's little world of bliss was newly born;
    We knew not, cared not, it was born to die;
Flushed with the cool breeze and the dews of
    morn;
    With dancing heart we gazed on the pure sky,
And mocked the passing clouds that dimmed its
    blue,
Like our own sorrows then—as fleeting and as
    few.

And manhood felt her sway too—on the eye,
    Half realised, her early dreams burst bright,
Her promised bower of happiness seemed nigh,
    Its days of joy, its vigils of delight;
And though at times might lour the thunder
    storm,
    And the red lightnings threaten, still the air
Was balmy with her breath, and her loved form,
    The rainbow of the heart, was hovering there.
'Tis in life's noontide she is nearest seen,
Her wreath the summer flower, her robe of sum-
    mer green.

But though less dazzling in her twilight dress,
    There's more of heaven's pure beam about her
    now;
That angel-smile of tranquil loveliness,
    Which the heart worships, glowing on her
    brow;
That smile shall brighten the dim evening star
    That points our destined tomb, nor e'er depart
Till the faint light of life is fled afar,
    And hushed the last deep beating of the heart;

The meteor-bearer of our parting breath,
A moon-beam in the midnight cloud of death.

The moral idea of this poem is as charming as its execution. The subject is common enough; but it is the treatment which gives it unction and acceptance. . . .

"The Field of the Grounded Arms, Saratoga," is a production which has all the spirit, without any of the poetry, of music around or within it. We are surprised that one so accustomed, both by practice and the habitudes of his thought, to harmonious numbers, as Mr. Halleck is, should have written verses like these, which halt so tediously away. Had he treated his theme in blank verse, all would have been well; but as the piece now stands, it is a truly amphibious and hermaphrodite composition. The sentiment is stirring and patriotic; the conceptions, fine; but the construction is a species of *composite order,* whose constituents it would be difficult indeed to explain or trace home. We copy one quotation as an illustration.

Stranger! your eyes are on that valley fixed
Intently as we gaze on vacancy,
When the mind's wings o'erspread
The spirit-world of dreams.

We may be prejudiced against this nondescript sort of quantity; but the mode strikes us as very nearly akin to the annexed specimen of a verse which we offer with the aid of an *indiscriminate* memory, from an effusion of Warren, or Day and Martin—a polished press-gang, who are famous for compelling the Nine into their service:

Sixpence a pot, we
Axes for our best jet-
Blacking; but if you
Takes back the pot, we
Makes a deduction.

The reader will bear in mind that we may not quote the foregoing *verbatim*; but we have preserved the pauses and the system. With respect to structure and motive power, the parallel is almost complete.

It gives us pleasure to continue our course through Mr. Halleck's volume, and to find that a weakened gust for one poem, may be succeeded by the strongest admiration for another. **"Red Jacket"** is one of those lofty and fervid effusions, that one reads to remember. The author's humorous propensity creeps out in it occasionally; but, as a whole, it is magnificently done. There is a pathetic under-song in this production, which leaves its echo in the heart. The author has represented Red Jacket very much to the life; though the transatlantic allusions might have been well dispensed with. That noble old chief had a spice of the philosopher about him, which would have done honour to the wiliest potentate that ever bent the million to his beck, or swayed a party with his nod. There was a natural grandeur about him, forest-born; the air that circulates over interminable wildernesses, and sweeps in freedom across inland seas, was the vital aliment for which his free nostrils thirsted; the perfume that goes up to the sky from vast reservations, as it went from the flowery tops of Carmel in the olden time, was his chosen element of respiration; the anthem for his ear was the voice of Niagara. We can readily believe that he admired his own untrammeled way of life; revered *Manitou;* and, perhaps, loved the fire-water which drowned the memory of his wrongs. In a part of his tenets, he had wisdom on his side. The man who chooses to run wild in woods, a noble savage, can find many enlightened wights in the purlieus of Christendom to bear him out in his partialities. The dress of Red Jacket, in his primitive condition, was of the simplest kind. He was not in the straitened, tailor-owing condition of many at the present day. "I have thatched myself over," says a modern European writer, perhaps in the predicament just hinted at, "with the dead fleeces of sheep, the bark of vegetables, the entrails of worms, the hides of oxen or seals, the entrails of furred beasts, and walk abroad a moving rag-screen, overheaped with shreds and tatters, raked from the charnel-house of nature." In his best days, Red Jacket had no fancy for integuments like these: and his bard should not have stooped to compare his dress at any time with that of "George the Fourth, at Brighton;" for Halleck is a man who cannot easily conceal from himself the fact that there are noblemen of nature, —and that a drawing-room, whether of the British monarch, or of *le Roi Citoyen,* "is simply a section of infinite space, where so many God-created souls do for the time meet together." But we keep the reader from our quotation.

Is strength a monarch's merit, like a whaler's?
    Thou are as tall, as sinewy, and as strong
As earth's first kings—the Argo's gallant sailors,
    Heroes in history, and gods in song.

Is beauty?—Thine has with thy youth departed;
    But the love-legends of thy manhood's years,
And she who perished, young and broken-
        hearted,
    Are—but I rhyme for smiles and not for tears.

Is eloquence?—Her spell is thine that reaches
    The heart, and makes the wisest head its
        sport;
And there's one rare, strange virtue in thy
        speeches,
    The secret of their mastery—they are short.

The monarch mind, the mystery of command-
        ing,
    The birth-hour gift, the art Napoleon,
Of winning, fettering, moulding, wielding,
        banding,
    The hearts of millions till they move as one;

Thou hast it. At thy bidding men have crowded
    The road to death as to a festival;
And minstrels, at their sepulchres, have
        shrouded
    With banner-folds of glory the dark pall.

Who will believe? Not I—for in deceiving
    Lies the dear charm of life's delightful dream;
I cannot spare the luxury of believing
    That all things beautiful are what they seem.

Who will believe that, with a smile whose
        blessing
    Would, like the patriarch's, sooth a dying
        hour,
With voice as low, as gentle, and as caressing,
    As e'er won maiden's lip in moonlit bower;

With look, like patient Job's, eschewing evil;

With motions graceful, as a bird's in air;
Thou art, in sober truth, the veriest devil
   That e'er clenched fingers in a captive's hair!

That in thy breast there springs a poison
   fountain,
   Deadlier than that where bathes the Upas
   tree;
And in thy wrath, a nursing cat-o'-mountain
   Is calm as her babe's sleep, compared with
   thee!

And underneath that face, like summer ocean's,
   Its lip as moveless, and its cheek as clear,
Slumbers a whirlwind of the heart's emotions,
   Love, hatred, pride, hope, sorrow—all save
   fear.

Love—for thy land, as if she were thy daughter,
   Her pipe in peace, her tomahawk in wars;
Hatred—of missionaries and cold water;
   Pride—in thy rifle-trophies and thy scars;

Hope—that thy wrongs may be by the Great
   Spirit
   Remembered and revenged, when thou art
   gone;
Sorrow—that none are left thee to inherit
   Thy name, thy fame, thy passions, and thy
   throne!

We now take our leave of Mr. Halleck, with the expression of a hope that he will not keep his light, which sends its beams so far, under the bushel hereafter. We counsel no neglect of his day-book; but we entreat him not to let his inspiration expire over the entries therein. He must have a good share of leisure after all. Let him not waste it in society; let him bear in mind that, with respect to *his* commodity at least, poetry will sell as well as peltry; that he has a mine of inalienable bullion in his brain, which no pressure can drive away, no commercial revulsion diminish. The paper in his escritoire, if he choose to stain it with poetic notes of hand, will always command a premium. He can serve both Apollo and the Syrian god; and to *him* each will be true. He has written enough to secure that fame hereafter, of which he has already had a not disgracious foretaste. He has no right to stifle the stirrings of the power within his soul. We speak this more in reference to his duty to the public than to himself; since in the selfish sense, so far as fame is concerned, he might contemplate his dissolution with composure; assured by the past, that when his death-hour comes, be it soon or late, he will leave behind a name which his countrymen, and the lovers of genius every where, would not willingly let die; and that even now he might enrobe himself in the cere-cloth, and contentedly "take his farewell of the sun."

Edgar Allan Poe (essay date 1843)

SOURCE: "Our Contributors—Fitz-Greene Halleck," in *The Complete Works of Edgar Allan Poe, Vol. XI*, edited by James A. Harrison, Thomas Y. Crowell, 1902, pp. 190-204.

[*In the following excerpt from an article on Halleck originally published in 1843, Poe takes issue with comments by William Cullen Bryant concerning versification and Hal-*

Engraving of Halleck, from a miniature painted about 1820.

leck's poetry, and analyzes the poems Fanny *and "Marco Bozzaris."*]

No name in the American poetical world is more firmly established than that of Fitz-Greene Halleck, and yet few of our poets—none, indeed, of eminence—have accomplished less, if we regard the quantity without the quality of his compositions. That he has written so little becomes thus proof positive that he has written that little well. . . .

We cannot better preface what we have to say, critically, of Mr. Halleck, than by quoting what has been said of him by his friend, William Cullen Bryant. To a poet what is more valuable—by a poet what is more valued—than the opinion of a poet?

"Sometimes," says Mr. Bryant,

> in the midst of a strain of harmonious diction, and soft and tender imagery, he surprises by an irresistible stroke of ridicule, as if he took pleasure in showing the reader that the poetical vision he had raised was but a cheat. Sometimes, with that aërial facility which is his peculiar endowment, he accumulates graceful and agreeable images in a strain of irony so fine that, did not the subject compel the reader to receive it as irony, he would take it for a beautiful passage of serious poetry—so beautiful that he is tempted to regret that he is not in earnest, and that phrases so exquisitely chosen, and poetic coloring so brilliant, should be employed to embellish subjects to which they do not properly belong. At other times he produces the effect of wit by

dexterous allusion to cotemporaneous events, introduced as illustrations to the main subject, with all the unconscious gracefulness of the most animated and familiar conversation. He delights in ludicrous contrasts, produced by bringing the nobleness of the ideal world into comparison with the homeliness of the actual; the beauty and grace of nature with the awkwardness of art. He venerates the past, and laughs at the present. He looks at them through a medium which lends to the former the charm of romance, and exaggerates the deformity of the latter. His poetry, whether serious or sprightly, is remarkable for the melody of the numbers. It is not the melody of monotonous and strictly regular measurement. His verse is constructed to please an ear naturally fine, and accustomed to a range of metrical modulation. It is as different from that painfully balanced versification, that uniform succession of iambics, closing the sense with the couplet, which some writers practice, and some critics praise, as the note of the thrush is unlike that of the cuckoo. He is familiar with those general rules and principles which are the basis of metrical harmony; and his own unerring taste has taught him the exceptions which a proper variety demands. He understands that the rivulet is made musical by obstructions in its channel. In no poet can be found passages which flow with more sweet and liquid smoothness; but he knows very well that to make this smoothness perceived, and to prevent it from degenerating into monotony, occasional roughness must be interposed.

Every reader of taste must agree with this criticism in its general conclusions. The passage about the rivulet being "made musical by the obstructions in its channel" is, perhaps, somewhat more poetical than clear in its application. The fact is, that a general and total misapprehension prevails upon the subject of rhythm, its uses and its capabilities—a misapprehension which affects the best poets and critics in the land—and to which, of course, we can no more than allude within the limits of this article. Mr. Bryant speaks of "that uniform succession of iambics," &c., as if the iambic were the sole metre in the world; and the idea that "occasional roughness must be interposed to make smoothness perceptible," is based upon the assumption that the relative conceptions of smoothness and roughness are not, at all times, existing, through memory, or experience, in the mind of the adult. Mr. B. would be quite as philosophical in asserting that, to appreciate a lump of ice in one hand, it is necessary to hold a red-hot horse-shoe in the other. The "occasional roughness" of which the critic speaks, is at no time a merit, but, in all instances, a defect. For the relief of monotone, *discords* are very properly and necessarily introduced; but these discords affect only the time—the harmony—of the rhythm, and never interfere, except erroneously, with its smoothness or melody. The best discord is the smoothest. Another vulgar error is involved in the notion that roughness gives strength. Invariably it weakens. What is pronounced with difficulty is feebly pronounced. Where is the roughness, and where is the weakness, of the Homeric hexameters? What more liquidly smooth—what more impetuously strong?

Fanny is, perhaps, better known, and more generally appreciated than any of Mr. Halleck's poems. It embraces a hundred and seventy-five of the *Don Juan* stanzas, and, in manner, throughout, is a close, although, we must admit, a well executed imitation of Lord Byron's eccentric production. The plot, if plot it can be called that plot is none, is a mere vehicle for odd digressions and squibs of cotemporary persons and things. Fanny, the heroine, is the pretty and amiable daughter of a *parvenu,* whose rise and fall form the thesis of the story. This story, when we consider the end in view, which is mere extravaganza, has but one *original* defect; and this lies in the forced introduction of one or two serious songs, put into the mouth of the *parvenu,* in defiance of every thing like keeping—a point which can never be disregarded even in the grossest of burlesques. This, we say, is the only *original* defect. There are numerous other defects, however, which are adopted from Byron; and among these we must designate, notwithstanding the opinion just quoted from Mr. Bryant, a loose and uncouth versification as the principal. As Mr. Bryant, however, is very high authority, we may as well support our position by a few examples.

> —for there first we met
> The editor of the New York Gazette.

The whole of *Fanny* is iambic verse, and the line last quoted is thus scanned:

$$\text{The } \overline{ed} \mid \breve{i} \overline{\text{tor}} \mid \breve{o}f \overline{\text{the}} \mid N\breve{e}w \overline{\text{York}} \mid G\breve{a}\overline{\text{zette}}.$$

Here either "the" is tortured into a long syllable or the line limps. The natural reading, or colloquial emphasis, in verse, must always tally with the rhythmical. The *sense* of a passage, as its most important element, must be preserved at all hazards, and if the question occur, whether to sacrifice the sense to the rhythm or the rhythm to the sense, we make the latter sacrifice, of course. But then the question should *never* occur, and, as regards well constructed verse, never will. . . .

In this pointing out, however, the rhythmical defects of *Fanny*—defects observable in all the poems of Halleck—we wish to be understood as speaking with reference to Mr. Bryant's eulogium, and thus rather positively than comparatively. Judged by the laws of verse, which are the incontrovertible laws of melody and harmony, needing only to be clearly *put* to be admitted—judged by these laws, he is very far indeed from deserving the commendation which his too partial friend and admirer bestows; but, examined only with reference to other American versifiers, he merits all that has been said, and even more.

The excellences of *Fanny* are well described in Mr. Bryant's general comments upon the works of our poet—in the comments we have quoted above. No one can fail to perceive and appreciate the brilliant wit, the *bonhomie,* the fanciful illustration, the *naïveté,* the gentlemanly ease and *insouciance* which have rendered this charming little *jeu d'esprit* so deservedly popular.

"Alnwick Castle," written in 1822, is an irregular iambic poem, of one hundred and twenty-eight lines, and describes a seat of the Duke of Northumberland, in Northumberland, England.

It is sadly disfigured by efforts at the farcical, introduced among passages of real beauty. No true poet can unite, in any manner, the low burlesque and the ideal, without a consciousness of profanation. Such verses as

> Men in the coal and cattle line
>   From Teviot's bard and hero land,
>   From royal Berwick's beach of sand,
>   From Wooler, Morpeth, Hexham and
> Newcastle upon Tyne,

are odd, and nothing more. They are totally out of keeping with the graceful and delicate manner of the initial portions of **"Alnwick Castle,"** and serve no better purpose than to deprive it of all unity of effect.

The second stanza of this poem has that easy grace, both of thought and expression, which is the leading feature of the Muse of Halleck.

> A lovely hill its side inclines,
>   Lovely in England's fadeless green,
> To meet the quiet stream which winds
>   Through this romantic scene,
> As silently and sweetly still,
> As when, at evening, on that hill,
>   While summer winds blew soft and low,
> Seated by gallant Hotspur's side,
> His Katharine was a happy bride
>   A thousand years ago.

We might quote many other passages of remarkable excellence, and indicating an ideality of far loftier character than that which is usually ascribed to our poet. For example:

> One solitary turret grey
>   Still tells in melancholy glory
> The legend of the Cheviot day.

> . . . . .

> Gaze on the Abbey's ruined pile:
>   Does not the succoring Ivy, keeping
> Her watch around it, seem to smile
>   As o'er a loved one sleeping?

The commencement of the fourth stanza is especially beautiful:

> Wild roses by the Abbey towers
>   Are gay in their young bud and bloom;
> *They were born of a race of funeral flowers*
>   That garlanded in long gone hours,
>   A Templar's knightly tomb.

In the line italicized two discords of excess are introduced with the happiest effect, and admirably serve to heighten the quaint fancy of the thought—a thought which, standing alone, would suffice to convince any true poet of the high genius of the author.

"Wyoming" consists of nine Spenserian stanzas—some of which are worthy of all commendation. For example:

> I then but dreamed: thou art before me now,
>   In life, a vision of the brain no more,
> I've stood upon the wooded mountain's brow
>   That beetles high thy lovely valley o'er,
> And now, where winds thy river's greenest shore
>   Within a bower of sycamores am laid;

And winds as soft and sweet as ever bore
The fragrance of wild flowers through sun and
    shade,
Are singing in the trees whose low boughs press
    my head.

This poem, however, is also disfigured with some of the merest burlesque—with such absurdities, for instance, as

> —a girl of sweet sixteen,
> Love-darting eyes and tresses like the morn,
> *Without a shoe or stocking, hoeing corn.*

The **"Lines on the Death of Joseph Rodman Drake"** are deservedly popular. We quote them in full.

> Green be the turf above thee,
>   Friend of my better days!
> None knew thee but to love thee,
>   Nor named thee but to praise.

> Tears fell when thou wert dying,
>   From eyes unused to weep,
> And long, where thou art lying,
>   Will tears the cold turf steep.

> When hearts, whose truth was proven,
>   Like thine are laid in earth,
> There should a wreath be woven
>   To tell the world their worth.

> And I, who woke each morrow
>   To clasp thy hand in mine,
> Who shared thy joy and sorrow,
>   Whose weal and wo were thine—

> It should be mine to braid it
>   Around thy faded brow,
> But I've in vain essayed it,
>   And feel I cannot now.

> While memory bids me weep thee,
>   Nor thoughts nor words are free;
> The grief is fixed too deeply,
>   That mourns a man like thee.

The tenderness and simplicity of these stanzas are worthy of all praise; but they are not without blemish.

> Will tears the cold turf steep,

is excessively rough.

> To *tell* the world their worth,

involves a false metaphor, when referred to "wreath." "To show the world" would be better. "Weep thee" and "deeply" form an imperfect rhyme; and the whole of the first quatrain

> Green be the turf, etc.,

although beautiful, bears too close a resemblance to the still more beautiful lines of Wordsworth:

> She dwelt among the untrodden ways
>   Beside the springs of Dove,
> A maid whom there were none to praise,
>   And very few to love.

The verses entitled **"Burns"** have many of the traits of **"Alnwick Castle,"** and are remarkable, as are all Mr. Halleck's compositions, for a peculiar grace and terseness of *expression.* For example:

> And when he breathes his master-lay
>   Of Alloway's witch-haunted wall
> All passions in our frames of clay
>   Come thronging at his call.

. . . . .

> There have been loftier themes than his,
>   And longer scrolls and louder lyres,
> And lays lit up with Poesy's
>   Purer and holier fires.

. . . . .

> They linger by the Doon's low trees,
>   *And pastoral Nith and wooded Ayr,*
> And round thy sepulchres, Dumfries!
>   The poet's tomb is there.

. . . . .

> Such graves as his are pilgrim shrines,
>   Shrines to no code or creed confined—
> *The Delphian vales, the Palestines,*
> *The Meccas of the mind.*

"Marco Bozzaris," however, is by far the best of the poems of Halleck. It is not very highly ideal, but is skillfully constructed, abounds in the true lyrical spirit, and, with slight exception, is admirably versified. The exceptions will be found in such verses as

> True as the steel of *their* tried blades,

and

> For him the joy of *her* young years,

where the rhythm requires the lengthening of naturally short syllables; or in such as these:

> For the first her first-born's breath

and

> Like torn branch from Death's leafless tree,

where the crowd of harsh consonants renders the verse nearly unpronounceable. We quote from this truly beautiful poem a passage which, for vigor both of thought and expression, has seldom been equaled and never excelled:

> Come to the bridal chamber, Death!
>   Come to the mother's when she feels
> For the first time her first-born's breath;
>   Come when the blessed seals
> That close the Pestilence are broke,
> And crowded cities wail its stroke;
> Come in Consumption's ghastly form,
> The earthquake shock, the ocean storm,
> Come when the heart beats high and warm
>   With banquet, song, and dance, and wine,
> And thou art terrible; the tear,
> The groan, the knell, the pall, the bier,
> And all we know, or dream, or fear
>   Of agony are thine.
> But to the hero, when his sword
>   Has won the battle for the free,
> Thy voice sounds like a prophet's word,
> And in its hollow tones are heard

> The thanks of millions yet to be.
> Come, when his task of fame is wrought—
> Come with her laurel-leaf blood-bought—
>   Come in her crowning hour, and then
> Thy sunken eye's unearthly light
> To him is welcome as the sight
>   Of sky and stars to prisoned men:
> Thy grasp is welcome as the hand
> Of brother in a foreign land;
> *Thy summons welcome as the cry*
> *That told the Indian isles were nigh*
>   *To the world-seeking Genoese,*
> *When the land wind from woods of palm,*
> *And orange groves and fields of balm,*
>   *Blew o'er the Haytien seas.*

The lines italicized we look upon as, in every respect, the finest by Halleck. They would do credit to any writer living or dead.

Edgar Allan Poe   (essay date 1846)

SOURCE: "Fitz-Greene Halleck," in *The Complete Works of Edgar Allan Poe, Vol. XV,* edited by James A. Harrison, Thomas Y. Crowell, 1902, pp. 49-56.

[*In the following excerpt from an article on Halleck originally published in 1846, Poe measures public estimation of Halleck against what he considers a truer representation of the poet's literary worth.*]

The name of HALLECK is at least as well established in the poetical world as that of any American. Our principal poets are, perhaps, most frequently named in this order—Bryant, Halleck, Dana, Sprague, Longfellow, Willis, and so on—Halleck coming second in the series, but holding, in fact, a rank in the public opinion quite equal to that of Bryant. The accuracy of the arrangement as above made may, indeed, be questioned. For my own part, I should have it thus—Longfellow, Bryant, Halleck, Willis, Sprague, Dana; and, estimating rather the poetic capacity than the poems actually accomplished, there are three or four comparatively unknown writers whom I would place in the series between Bryant and Halleck, while there are about a dozen whom I should assign a position between Willis and Sprague. Two dozen at least might find room between Sprague and Dana—this latter, I fear, owing a very large portion of his reputation to his *quondam* editorial connection with *The North American Review.* One or two poets now in my mind's eye I should have no hesitation in posting above even Mr. Longfellow—still not intending this as very extravagant praise.

It is noticeable, however, that, in the arrangement which I attribute to the popular understanding, the order observed is nearly, if not exactly, that of the ages—the poetic ages—of the individual poets. Those rank first who were first known. The priority has established the strength of impression. Nor is this result to be accounted for by mere reference to the old saw—that first impressions are the strongest. Gratitude, surprise, and a species of hyper-patriotic triumph have been blended, and finally confounded with admiration or appreciation in regard to the *pioneers* of American literature, among whom there is not one whose productions have not been grossly overrated by his countrymen. Hitherto we have been in no mood to view with calmness and discuss with discrimination the real claims of the few who were *first* in convincing the mother country that her sons were not all brainless, as at one period she half affected and wholly wished to believe. . . .

I mean to say, of course, that Mr. Halleck, in the *apparent* public estimate, maintains a somewhat better position than to which, on absolute grounds, he is entitled. There is something, too, in the *bonhomie* of certain of his compositions—something altogether distinct from poetic merit—which has aided to establish him; and much, also, must be admitted on the score of his personal popularity, which is deservedly great. With all these allowances, however, there will still be found a large amount of poetical fame to which he is *fairly* entitled. . . .

National Magazine　　(essay date 1852)

SOURCE: *National Magazine,* Vol. I, No. 6, December, 1852, pp. 481-87.

[*In the following excerpt from a review of Halleck's life and poetry, the critic discusses the strong points and shortcomings of the poet's works.*]

To thoroughly analyze Halleck's poetry, we should require pages; not because he has written so much, or because what he has written is of so much consequence, but because much of it violates many of the fundamental rules of taste and art, which would have to be stated and perhaps defended in full. Having neither space nor time to do this, we must content ourselves with a few examples of his merits and demerits and a few brief remarks thereon.

We open the volume at the beginning, at **"Alnwick Castle,"** one of his best poems. In **"Alnwick Castle,"** we see the effect of Scott's romances, both in their versification, and in their recalling the memory of the feudal, or, as poor Tom Hood used to call them, the *foodle* ages. There is something prompt, terse, and businesslike, in the management of the poem. Though a true poem, it does not strike us as the work of a poet, so much as the work of a practical man poetically inclined—a man with rhetoric, and the other helps to poetry, at his finger-ends. A poet, we think, would have dwelt upon its beautiful side alone; would have lingered over

> The legend of the Cheviot day,
> The Percy's proudest border story;

over the pictured dome, the soldiers' march, and Kate and Hotspur on the hill, to the exclusion of

> Oxen, and bleating lambs in lots,
> Northumbrian boars, and plaided Scots,
> Men in the coal and cattle line, etc.

> . . . . .

> And him who, when a younger son,
> Fought for King George at Lexington,
> A major of dragoons;

not forgetting that "ten-and-sixpence sterling," the loss of which left such an aching void in the poet's heart and

pocket. Alnwick Castle belongs properly and only to the past—the feudal, chivalrous past—and should never be numbered with the present—the poetically commonplace, but prosaically useful present. The contrasts are too glaring to meet in the same picture; the two elements will not unite. There is a quiet grace and pensive thoughtfulness about parts of the poem, which makes us forget, and almost atones for, the blemishes we have mentioned. The second stanza is beautiful: —

> A gentle hill its side inclines,
> 　Lovely on England's fadeless green,
> To meet the gentle stream which winds
> 　Through this romantic scene;
> As silently and sweetly still,
> As when at evening on that hill,
> 　When summer's wind blew soft and low,
> Seated by gallant Hotspur's side
> His Katharine was a happy bride,
> 　A thousand years ago.

Poe admired the opening of the fourth stanza, and praised it highly. When Poe *did* praise anything there was no half-way work about it: —

> Wild roses by the abbey towers,
> 　Are gay in their young bud and bloom;
> *They are born of a race of funeral flowers,*
> That garlanded in long-gone hours
> 　A Templar's knightly tomb.

"This," says Poe, "is gloriously imaginative; and the effect is singularly increased by the sudden transition from iambuses to anapests. The passage I think the noblest to be found in Halleck, and I would be at a loss to discover its parallel in all American poetry." Fine it certainly is, especially the line italicized, that about the race of funeral flowers, the beautiful mutes of nature.

"Marco Bozzaris" it is impossible to judge. Like Hamlet's Soliloquy, Young Norval's Grampian-Hill speech, and the other crack pieces in the school-books, it has been drilled into us till we are thoroughly tired of it; we know it so well, we cease to know it at all. . . .

Somewhat different is the fine poem of **"Red Jacket."** Never has the Indian character generally, and the character of Red Jacket particularly, been more happily analyzed and described, than in the concluding stanzas. The poem with a rather equivocal compliment to Cooper: —

> Cooper, whose name is with his country's
> 　woven,
> 　First in her files, her pioneer of mind,
> A wanderer now in other lands has proven
> 　His love for the young land he left behind;

> And throned her in the senate-hall of nations,
> 　Robed like the deluge rainbow, heaven-
> 　wrought,
> Magnificent as his own mind's creations,
> 　And beautiful as its green world of thought.

Setting aside the nonsense of weaving a name, it is absurd to call Cooper the pioneer of American mind. That he wrote the first strictly American novel, in the popular way of talking, we are willing to admit; but surely other kinds of writing required mind as well, and engaged the attention of American minds before Cooper was thought of. There were great men living in Greece before Agamemnon, and mind-pioneers in America before James Fenimore Cooper. In writings of pure mind, we have as yet produced nothing superior, if indeed anything equal, to old Jonathan Edwards's "Treatise on the Will," the arguments of which a recent French critic has pronounced to be equal to those of Descartes. Equally absurd is the picture of America robed in the deluge rainbow! Fancy the *tableau.* Here is Asia, with the dust of ruin on her mantle; there Africa, the fetters on her hands; yonder Europe, the stately Amazon, stern in her mailed charms; and here, towering before us, our own great country, robed in a deluge rainbow, magnificently enough! But how magnificent? we want a comparison here. "Magnificent as his (Cooper's) own mind's creations,

> And beautiful as its green world of thought.

Really, gentlemen, you are too modest entirely; it really can't be so grand, this little America of ours. To be sure we have some tolerable forests, mountains and prairies, a few great lakes and rivers, and the falls of Niagara, (but never a poet to sing it!) some odd number of battlefields stained in the old time with free blood, but certainly nothing from Maine to California equal to Cooper's novels and Halleck's poems. . . .

The local allusions in many of Halleck's poems interfere greatly with one's enjoyment in reading them. The epistles and comic poems refer to men, manners, and politics obsolete and forgotten, and should be elucidated with notes, those sinking millstones on verse, but necessary in such cases, even if the poem must founder; it had better founder than strand and decay away on the sands. In some instances the *locale* is confined to a line or two; in others it is the warp and woof of the poem. This is to be regretted, as it will be a serious drawback to their future and permanent fame. Your true and profound artist, we remark *en passant,* be he poet, painter, or sculptor, works for the future, in preference to the present; laboring for all time rather than for the day, shaping from time whatever of the permanent it embodies, recasting its ideals into creations for eternity. Every real work of art is complete and perfect in itself; in so far as art needs explanation, needs to be labeled and commented upon, needs accessories and surroundings, just so far it is imperfect and incomplete. Halleck, if we may judge of his feelings by a clever passage in his clever epistle **"To the Recorder,"** does not agree with us in this matter, and in that of future fame. "For me," says he, in his graceful and melodious lines, —

> For me,
> I rhyme not for posterity;
> Though pleasant to my heirs might be
>   The incense of its praise,
> When I, their ancestor have gone,
> And paid the debt, the only one
>   A poet ever pays.
>
>   . . . . .
>
> No: if a garland for my brow
> Is growing, let me have it now,
>   While I'm alive to wear it;
> And if, in whispering my name,

> There's music in the voice of fame
>   Like Garcia's, let me hear it.

A few words on *Fanny,* and the class of compositions to which it belongs, and we have done.

Fanny is popular, we conceive, because it is written in a "taking," but false school of verse. This is emphatically the age of smartness, and *Fanny* is, comparatively speaking, a smart poem. It is, as we said before, an imitation of *Don Juan,* which, in our opinion, is the most execrable school of verse ever in vogue, the very incarnation of mockery and infidelity. We leave to others the discussion of its moral tendencies, and take it up solely on the ground of taste and feeling. Not only does it violate the commonest principles of taste, —we speak of the school now, not of any particular poem, —but the best and purest feelings of the human heart; robbing man of faith in himself and his fellows, checking him in his nobler aspirations and emotions, or holding them up in such a ridiculous light that he is ashamed of them, even stripping the material world itself of its beauty and comfort. Nothing is safe from its sneers; it lays its irreverent hands on everything; is an universal image-breaker, a caster down of all temples and altars, false and true; its only aim is to be smart, to make a point, to raise a laugh, at any cost, at any sacrifice; purity and beauty of style, symmetry and proportion, sense and meaning, everything gives place to what its vitiated taste considers wit and humor, bearing the same proportion to true wit and humor that the galvanized grins of a corpse do to the hearty natural laugh of a jovial living man.

Don Juan, despite its inherent faults, is in many of its parts truly poetic, and rarely missed being a true and exceedingly beautiful poem. It is beautiful, and sublime, in parts, because Byron was a great poet, with infinite capacities of mind.

> He should have been a glorious creature; he
> Had all the energies which would have made
> A goodly frame of glorious elements,
> Had they been wisely mingled; as it is,
> It is an awful chaos, light and darkness,
> And mud and dust, and passions and pure
>   thoughts,
> Mix'd and contending, without end or order,
> All donnant and destructive.

The wit of *Don Juan* is of the keenest; the humor, for there is real humor in it, genial and hearty, and its melancholy and pathos are positively beautiful. Everywhere are scattered

> Thoughts that do often lie too deep for tears.

The *Fanny* of Halleck, and all other of the Don Juan imitations that we are acquainted with, are at best but faint copies of their wonderful original, without its faults, and without its merits, or possessing both in such homeopathic doses that they were better without them. *Fanny* has no merit as a story—indeed it pretends to none; and in our opinion—we may err, however—but little point as a satire. It is very thinly spread and diffusive; running on stanza after stanza, and page after page—for there are some eleven or twelve hundred lines of it to no palpable end, save that of making points, and saying smart things, both of which it does with considerable success. Once allow the legitimacy of the school of writing to which it belongs, and *Fanny* proves itself quite a poem.

In conclusion, let us say that we consider Halleck a good poet spoiled: he is a good poet in **"Alnwick Castle,"** **"Marco Bozzaris," "Burns," "Red Jacket,"** and **"Magdalen;"** and a good poet spoiled in *Fanny,* and the other comic poems. Whether the spoiling process was owing to his circumstances of life, his bad models, the spirit of the age, or to himself, Fitz-Greene Halleck, individually, we shall not attempt to determine; perhaps their combination is the nearest to the truth. But the deed is done, and can't be helped. If one is not too critical, and we hope we have not been so, there is a good deal of pleasure to be got out of Halleck's volume. We must not look the gift horse too closely in the mouth.

William Cullen Bryant   (essay date 1869)

SOURCE: "Fitz-Greene Halleck. Address Delivered before the New York Historical Society," in *Littell's Living Age,* Vol. C, No. 1291, February 27, 1869, pp. 515-25.

[*The first American poet to achieve an international reputation, Bryant also contributed to the development of American letters in his role as editor of several literary magazines and of the* New York Evening Post. *Halleck and Bryant met in New York in 1825 and maintained their friendship until Halleck's death; many of Halleck's poems first appeared in journals edited by Bryant. In the following excerpts from a paper on Halleck delivered before the New York Historical Society, Bryant recalls his friend's life, works, and literary career.*]

I have yielded with some hesitation to the request that I should read before the Historical Society a paper on the life and writings of Fitz-Greene Halleck. I hesitated because the subject had been most ably treated by others. I consented because it seemed to be expected by his friends and admirers, that one who like myself was so nearly his contemporary, who read his poems as they appeared, and through whom several of the finest of them were given to the world, ought not to let a personal friend, a genial companion and an admirable poet pass from us without some words setting forth his merits and our sorrow. It is, besides, a relief under such a loss to dwell upon the characteristic qualities of the departed. It seems in an imperfect manner to prolong his existence among us; as we repeat his words we seem to behold the friendly brightness of his eye; we hear the familiar tones of his voice. It is as when, in looking upon the quivering surface of a river, we see the image of an object on the bank which is itself hidden from our eyes.

The southern shore of Connecticut, bordering on the Long Island Sound, is a beautiful region. I have never passed along this shore, extending from Byrom river to the Paugatuck, without admiring it. Here the somewhat severe climate of New England is softened by the sea air and the shelter of the hills. Such charming combinations of rock and valley, of forest and stream, of smooth meadows, quiet inlets and green promontories are rarely to be found. A multitude of clear and rapid rivers, the king of which is the majestic Connecticut, here wind their way to the Sound among picturesque hills, cliffs and woods.

It was at Guilford, in this pleasant region before which the Sound expands into a sea, that Halleck, on the 8th of July, 1790, was born. Poets, it is true, and poets of great genius, have been born in cities or in countries of the tamest aspect, yet I think it may truly be said that the sense of diversified beauty or solemn grandeur is awakened and nourished in the young mind by these qualities in the scenery which surrounds the poet's childhood. I do not find, however, in Halleck's verses any particular recognition of the uncommon beauty of the region to which he owed his birth. In the well-known lines on Connecticut he says:

> And still her gray rocks tower above the sea,
> That crouches at their feet a conquered wave.
> 'Tis a rough land of earth, and stone, and tree,
> &c.

In another passage of the same poem, where he celebrates the charms of the region, he speaks solely of the tints of the atmosphere and the autumnal glory of its forests:

> —in the autumn time
> Earth has no purer and no lovelier clime.
>
> Her clear warm heaven at noon, the mist that shrouds
> Her twilight hills, her cool and starry eyes,
> The glorious splendor of her sunset clouds,
> The rainbow beauty of her forest leaves,
> &c.

Yet that this omission did not arise from any insensibility to the beauty of form in landscape is sufficiently manifested by the enthusiastic apostrophe to Weehawken, which escapes from him, as if in spite of himself, in his *Fanny,* amidst the satirical reflections which form the staple of the poem. He gave a higher proof of his affection for his birthplace, withdrawing in the evening of life from the bustling city where the greater part of his years had been spent and where he had acquired his fame, to the pleasant haunts of his childhood, to dwell where his parents dwelt, to die where they died, and to be buried beside them. His end was like that of the rivers of his native state, which, after dashing and sparkling over their stony beds, lay themselves down between quiet meadows and glide softly to the Sound.

Halleck had a worthy parentage. His father, Israel Halleck, according to Mr. Duyckinck, was a man of extensive reading, a tenacious memory, pithy conversation and courteous manners. His mother was of the Eliot family, a descendant of John Eliot, one of the noblest of the New England worthies, the translator of the Bible into the Indian language, the religious teacher, friend and protector of the Indians, the rigid non-conformist, the charitable pastor who distributed his salary among his needy neighbors, who preached and prayed against wigs and tobacco, without being able to triumph over the power of fashion or the force of habit, and of whom it is said that his sermons were remarkable for their simplicity of expression and freedom from the false taste of the age. Halleck inherited his ancestor's spirit of non-conformity. He would argue in favor of an established church among people with whom the dissociation of church and state was an article of political faith, and astonished his republican neighbors by declaring himself a partisan of monarchy. He was not easily diverted from any course of conduct by deference to public opinion. Mr. Cozzens relates that when Jacob Barker had fallen under the public censure, Halleck, then his clerk, was told that he ought to leave his service. He answered that he would not desert the sinking ship, and that the time to stand by his friends was when they were unfortunate. He had a certain persistency of temper which was transmitted, I think, from the old Puritan stock. It was some fifteen or twenty years after he came to live in New York that he said to me, "I like to go on with the people whom I begin with. I have the same boarding-house now that I had when I first came to town; my clothes are made by the same tailor, and I employ the same shoemaker."

I do not find that Halleck began to write verses prematurely. Poetry, with most men, is one of the sins of their youth, and a great deal of it is written before the authors can be justly said to have reached years of discretion. With the greatest number it runs its course and passes off like the measles or the chicken-pox; with a few it takes the chronic form and lasts a lifetime, and I have known cases of persons attacked by it in old age. A very small number who begin, like Milton, Cowley and Pope to write verses when scarce out of childhood, afterwards become eminent as poets; but as a rule, precocity in this department of letters is no sign of genius. In the verses of Halleck which General Wilson has collected, written in 1809 and 1810 and earlier, I discern but slight traces of his peculiar genius, and none of the grace and spirit which afterwards became so marked. They are better, it is true, than the juvenile poems which encumber the later collections of the poetry of Thompson, but they are not characteristic. Between the time when they were written and that in which he produced the poems which are commonly called the Croakers, his poetic faculty ripened rapidly, and as remarkably as that of Byron between the publication of his *Hours of Idleness* and that of his *Childe Harold.* His fancy had been quickened into new life; he had learned to wield his native language like a master; he had discovered that he was a wit, as well as a poet; and his verse had acquired that sweetness and variety of modulation which afterwards distinguished it. The poems which bear the signature of Croaker & Co., written by him in conjunction with his friend, Joseph Rodman Drake, began in 1819 to appear in the *Evening Post,* then conducted by Mr. Coleman. That gentleman observed their merit with surprise, commended them in his daily sheet, and was gratified to learn that the whole town was talking of them. It was several years after this that Mr. Coleman said to me, "I was curious to see the young men whose witty verses, published in my journal, made so much noise, and desired an interview with them. They came before me and I was greatly struck by their appearance. Drake looked the poet; you saw the stamp of genius in every feature. Halleck had the aspect of a satirist."

There is a certain manner common to both authors in these poems. They both wrote with playfulness and gayety, and although with the freedom of men who never expect to be known, yet without malignity; but it seems to me that Halleck drove home his jests with the sharpest percussion, and there are some flashes of that fire which blazed out on his **"Marco Bozzaris."**

The poem entitled *Fanny* was published about that time. It is, in the main, a satire upon those who, finding themselves in the possession of wealth suddenly acquired, rush into extravagant habits of living, give expensive entertainments, and as a natural consequence sink suddenly into the obscurity from which they rose. But the satire takes a wider range. The poet jests at everything that comes in his way; authors, politicians, men of science, each is booked for a pleasantry; all are made to contribute to the expense of the entertainment set before the reader. The sting of his witticisms was not unfelt, and I think was in some cases resented. People do not like to be laughed at, however pleasant it may be to those who laugh. At a later period Halleck saw the truth of what Pope says of ridicule—

> The muse may give thee but the gods must guide—

and he published an edition of his *Fanny* with notes in which he took care to make a generous reparation to those whom he had offended. But *Fanny* is not all satire, and here and there in the poems are bursts of true lyrical enthusiasm.

Some comparison has been made between the *Fanny* of Halleck and the satirical poems of Byron. But Halleck was never cynical in his satire, and Byron always was. I remember reading a remark made by Voltaire on the *Dunciad* of Pope. It wants gayety, said the French critic. Gayety is the predominating quality of Halleck's satire as hatred is that of the satire of Pope and Byron. Byron delighted in thinking how his victim would writhe under the blows he gave him. Halleck's satire is the overflow of a mirthful temperament. He sees things in a ludicrous light, and laughs without reflecting that the object of his ridicule might not like the sport as well as himself.

In 1822 Halleck visited England and the Continent of Europe. Of what he saw there I do not know that there is any record remaining except his noble poem entitled **"Burns,"** and the spirited and playful verses on **"Alnwick Castle."**

It was in 1825, before Halleck's reputation as a poet had reached its full growth, that I took up my residence in New York. I first met him at the hospitable board of Robert Sedgwick, Esq., and remember being struck with the brightness of his eye, which every now and then glittered with mirth, and with the graceful courtesy of his manners. Something was said of the length of time that he had lived in New York: "You are not from New England?" said our host. "I certainly am," was Halleck's reply, "I am from Connecticut." "Is it possible?" exclaimed Mr. Sedgwick. "Well, you are the only New Englander that I ever saw in whom the tokens of his origin were not as plain as the mark set upon the forehead of Cain."

I was at that time one of the editors of a monthly magazine, the *New York Review,* which was soon gathered to the limbo of extinct periodicals. Halleck brought to it his poem of **"Marco Bozzaris,"** and in 1826 the lines entitled

"**Connecticut.**" The first of these poems became immediately a favorite, and was read by everybody who cared to read verses. I remember that at an evening party, at the house, I think, of Mr. Henry D. Sedgwick, it was recited by Mrs. Nichols; the same who not long afterward gave the public an English translation of Manzoni's *Promessi Sposi.* She had a voice of great sweetness and power, capable of expressing every variety of emotion. She was in the midst of the poem, her thrilling voice the only sound in the room, and every ear intently listening to her accents, when suddenly she faltered; her memory had lost one of the lines. At that instant a clear and distinct voice, supplying the forgotten passage, was heard from a group in a corner of the room; it was the voice of the poet. With this aid she took up the recitation and went on triumphantly to the close, surrounded by an audience almost too deeply interested to applaud.

The poem entitled "**Burns,**" of which let me say I am not sure that the verses are not the finest in which one poet ever celebrated another, was contributed by Halleck in 1827 to the *United States Review,* which I bore a part in conducting. Halleck had been led by his admiration of the poetry of Campbell to pay a visit to the charming valley celebrated by that poet in his "Gertrude of Wyoming." In memory of this he wrote the lines entitled "**Wyoming,**" which he handed me for publication in the same magazine. Before the *United States Review* shared the fate of its predecessor there appeared the first printed collection of Halleck's poetical writings with the title of ***Alnwick Castle and other Poems,*** published by G. Carvill & Company, in 1827. I had the pleasure of saying to the readers of the *Review* how greatly I admired it.

At that time the Recorder of our city was appointed by the Governor of the state. Those who are not familiar with the judicial system of this state, need, perhaps, to be told that the Recorder is not the keeper of the city archives, but the judge of an important criminal court. In 1828, and for some years before and afterward, the office was held by Mr. Richard Riker, a man of great practical shrewdness and the blandest manners, who was accused by some of adjusting his political opinions to the humors of the day, and was, therefore, deemed a proper subject of satire. One day I met Halleck, who said to me: "I have an epistle in verse from an old gentleman to the Recorder, which, if you please, I will send to you for the *Evening Post.* It is all in my head and you shall have it as soon as I have written it out." I should mention here that Halleck was in the habit of composing verses without the aid of pen and ink, keeping them in his memory, and retouching them at his leisure. In due time the "**Epistle to the Recorder, by Thomas Castaly, Esq.,**" came to hand, was published in the *Evening Post,* and was immediately read by the whole town. It seems to me one of the happiest of Halleck's satirical poems. The man in office, who was the subject of it, must have hardly known whether to laugh or be angry, and it was impossible, one would think, to be perfectly at ease when thus made the plaything of a poet and pelted with all manner of gibes, sly allusions, and ironical compliments, for the amusement of the public. Among its strokes of satire the epistle has passages of graceful poetry. Halleck, after the manner of the ancients, in leading his

victim to the sacrifice had hung its horns with garlands of flowers. The Recorder, however, is said to have borne this somewhat disrespectful but by no means ill-natured assault with the same apparent composure as he endured the coarser attacks of the newspapers.

In 1827 and the two following years Dr. Bliss, a liberal minded bookseller of this city, published annually, at the season of the winter holidays, a small volume of miscellanies entitled the *Talisman.* They were written almost exclusively by three authors; Mr. Verplanck, eminent in our literature and still fortunately spared to perform important public services; Robert C. Sands, a man of abounding wit, prematurely lost to the world of letters; and myself as the third contributor. For the volume which appeared in 1828 Halleck offered us one of his most remarkable poems, "**Red Jacket,**" and I need not say how delighted we were to grace our collection by anything so vigorous, spirited and original. It was illustrated by an engraving from a striking full-length portrait of the Old Indian chief, by the elder Wier, then in the early maturity of his powers as an artist.

After the publication of these poems there followed an interval of thirty-five years which is almost a blank in Halleck's literary history. Between 1828 and 1863 he seems to have produced nothing worthy of note except the additions which he made to his poem of "**Connecticut**" in an edition published by Redfield in 1852, and these are fully worthy of his reputation. It is almost unaccountable that an author, still in the highest strength of his faculties, who had written to such acceptance, should not have been tempted to write more for a public which he knew was eager to read whatever came from his pen. "When an author begins to be quoted," said Halleck once to me, "he is already famous." Halleck found that he was quoted, but he was not a man to go on writing because the world seemed to expect it. It was only in 1863, when he was already seventy-three years of age, that he wrote for the New York *Ledger* his "**Young America,**" a poem, which, though not by any means to be placed among his best, contains, as Mr. Cozzens, in a paper read before this society, justly remarks, passages which remind us of his earlier vigor and grace.

Yet, if in that interval he did not occupy himself with poetic composition, he gave much of his leisure to the poetry of others. I have never known any one, I think, who seemed to take so deep a delight in the poetry that perfectly suited his taste. He transcribed it; he read it over and over; he dwelt upon it until every word of it became engraven upon his memory; he recited it with glistening eyes and a voice and frame tremulous with emotion. Mr. F. S. Cozzens has sent me a scrap of paper on which he had copied a passage of eight lines of verse; and under them had written these sentences: "I find these verses in an album. Do you know the writer? I would give a hundred pounds sterling payable out of any money in my treasury not otherwise appropriated, to be capable of writing the two last lines."

I was most agreeably surprised as well as flattered, the other day, to receive from General Wilson, who has collected the poetical writings of Halleck, and is engaged in preparing his Life and Letters for the press, a copy of the poet's handwriting of some verses of mine entitled "The Planting of the Appletree," which he had taken the pains to transcribe, and which General Wilson had heard him repeat from memory in his own fine manner.

Halleck loved to ramble in the country, for the most part, I believe, alone. Once he did me the favor to make me his companion. It was while the region from Hoboken to Fort Lee was yet but thinly sprinkled with habitations, and the cliffs which overlook the river on its western bank had lain in forest from the time that Hendrick Hudson entered the great stream which bears his name. We were on a slow-going steamer, which we left at the landing of Bull's Ferry. "Do you not go on with us, Mr. Halleck?" asked the Captain. "No," was the answer; "I am in a hurry." We walked on to Fort Lee, where we made a short stop at the house of a publican named Reynolds, who is mentioned in Duyckinck's memoir—an English radical, a man of no little mother wit, and a deep strong voice which he greatly loved to bear. Halleck had known him when he exercised his vocation in town, and took pleasure, I think, in hearing his ready rejoinders to the poet's praises of a monarchy and an established church; and Reynolds, proud of the acquaintance of so eminent a man as Halleck, received him with demonstrations of delight. We returned over the heights of Weehawken to look at the magnificent view so finely celebrated by Halleck in his *Fanny,* with its glorious bay, its beautiful isles, its grand headlands and its busy cities, the murmur of which was heard blending with the dash of waves at the foot of the cliff.

I have mentioned that Halleck was early a clerk in the office of Mr. Barker. He was afterwards employed in the same capacity by John Jacob Astor, the richest man of his day in New York, and exceedingly sagacious and fortunate in his enterprises. His term of employment by Mr. Astor came, however, to an end; and I think that he was then compelled by the narrowness of his means, to practise a rigid economy. He was of too independent a spirit to allow himself to be drawn into a situation which would incline him to keep out of the way of a creditor. He was an excellent accountant: I have a letter from one of his friends, speaking of his skill in difficult and intricate computations, in which Mr. Astor employed him with confidence. Perhaps the habit of exactness in this vocation led to exactness in his dealings with all men. His example is an encouraging one for poets and wits, since it teaches that a lively fancy and practical good sense do not necessarily stand in each other's way. Somebody has called prudence a rascally virtue, and I have heard Halleck himself rail at it, and refer to Benjamin Franklin as a man who had acquired a false reputation by his dexterity in taking care of his own interests. But Halleck did not disdain to practise the virtue which he decried, and he knew, as well as Franklin himself, that prudence, in the proper sense of the term, is wisdom applied to the ordinary affairs of life; that it includes forecast, one of the highest operations of the intellect, and the due adjustment of means to ends, without which a man is useless both to himself and to society, except as a blunderer by whose example others may be warned.

I think it was some time after he had given up his clerkship that Mr. Astor left him a small legacy, to which the son, Mr. William B. Astor, made a liberal addition. Halleck then withdrew from the city in which he had passed forty years of his life to Guilford, his native place, in which the Eliots, his ancestors on the mother's side, had dwelt for nearly two centuries. Here in the household of an unmarried sister, older than himself and now living, he passed his later years among his books, with some infirmities of body, but with intellectual faculties still vigorous, his wit as keen and lively as when he wrote his **"Epistle to the Recorder,"** and his delight in the verses of his favorite poets and in the happy expression of generous sentiments as deeply felt and easily awakened as when he wrote his noble poem on Woman.

It was not far from the time of which I speak that some of Halleck's personal and literary friends gave him a dinner at the rooms of the Club called the Century. It fell to me to preside, and in toasting our guest I first spoke, in such terms as I was able to command, of the merits of his poetry, as occupying a place in our literature like the poetry of Horace in the literature of ancient Rome. I dwelt upon the playfulness and grace of his satire and the sweetness and fervor of his lyrical vein. Halleck answered very happily. "I do not rise to speak," he said, "for if I were to stand up I could say nothing. I must keep my seat and talk to you without ceremony." And then he went on, speaking modestly and charmingly of his own writings. I cannot, at this distance of time, recollect how he treated the subject, but I well remember that he spoke so well that we could willingly have listened to him the whole evening.

It is now five and thirty years, the life of one of the generations of mankind, that I contributed to a weekly periodical published in this city, an estimate of the poetical genius of Halleck. Of course nobody now remembers having read it; and, as it was written after his most remarkable poems had been given to the public, and as I could say nothing different of them now, I will, with the leave of the audience, make it a part of this paper.

> Halleck is one of the most generally admired of all our poets, and he possesses, what no other does, a decided local popularity. He is the favorite poet of the city of New York, where his name is cherished with a peculiar fondness and enthusiasm. It furnishes a standing and ever-ready allusion to all who would speak of American literature, and is familiar in the mouths of hundreds who would be seriously puzzled if asked to name any other American poet. The verses of others may be found in the hands of persons who possess some tincture of polite literature—young men pursuing their studies, or young ladies with whom the age of romance is not past; but those of Halleck are read by people of the humblest degree of literary pretension, and are equally admired in Bond street and the Bowery. There are numbers who regularly attribute to his pen every anonymous poem in the newspapers in which an attempt at humor is evident, who 'know him by his style,' and whose delight at the supposed wit is heightened almost to transport by the self-complacency of having made the discovery. His reputation, however, is not injured by these mis-

takes, for the verses by which they are occasioned are soon forgotten, and his fame rests firmly on the compositions which are known to be his.

This high degree of local popularity has for one of its causes the peculiar subjects of many of the poems of Halleck, relating as they do to persons and things and events with which everybody in New York is more or less acquainted; objects which are constantly before the eyes, and matters that are the talk of every fireside. The poems written by him, in conjunction with his friend, Doctor Drake, for the *Evening Post,* in the year 1819, under the signature of Croaker & Co., and the satirical poem of **Fanny,** are examples of this happy use of the familiar topics of the day. He will pardon this allusion to works which he has never publicly acknowledged, but which are attributed to him by general consent, since, without them, we might miss some of the characteristics of his genius.

Halleck's humorous poems are marked by an uncommon case of versification, a natural flow and sweetness of language, and a careless, Horatian playfulness and felicity of jest, not, however, imitated from Horace or any other writer. He finds abundant matter for mirth in the peculiar state of our society, in the heterogeneous population of the city—

Of every race the mingled swarm.

in the affectations of newly assumed gentility, the ostentation of wealth, the pretensions of successful quackery, and the awkward attempt to blend with the habits of trade an imitation of the manners of the most luxurious and fastidious nobility in the world—the nobility of England. . . .

But it is not only in humorous or playful poetry that Halleck excels. He has fire and tenderness, and manly vigor, and his serious poems are equally admirable with his satirical. What martial lyric can be finer than the verses on the death of Marco Bozzaris! We are made spectators of the slumbers of the Turkish oppressor, dreaming of "victory in his guarded tent;" we see the Greek warrior ranging his truehearted band of Suliotes in the forest shades; we behold them throwing themselves into the camp; we hear the shout, the groan, the sabre stroke, the death shot falling thick and fast, and in the midst of all, the voice of Bozzaris bidding them to strike boldly for God and their native land. The struggle is long and fierce; the ground is piled with Moslem slain; the Greeks are at length victorious; and as the brave chief falls bleeding from every vein, he hears the proud huzza of his surviving comrades, announcing that the field is won, and he closes his eyes in death,

Calmly, as to a night's repose.

This picture of the battle is followed by a dirge over the slain hero—a glorious outpouring of lyrical eloquence, worthy to have been chanted by Pindar or Tyrtœus over one of his ancestors. There is in this poem a freedom, a daring, a fer-

vency, a rapidity, an affluence of thick-coming fancies, that make it seem like an inspired improvisation, as if the thoughts had been divinely breathed into the mind of the poet, and uttered themselves, voluntarily, in poetic numbers. We think, as we read it, of

—The large utterance of the early Gods.

If an example is wanted of Halleck's capacity for subjects of a gentler nature, let the reader turn to the verses written in the album of an unknown lady, entitled **"Woman."** In a few brief lines he has gathered around the name of woman a crowd of delightful associations—all the graces of sex, delightful pictures of domestic happiness and domestic virtues, gentle affections, pious cares, smiles and tears, that bless and heal,

And earth's lost paradise restored,
In the green bower of home.

"Red Jacket" is a poem of a yet different kind; a poem of manly vigor of sentiment, noble versification, strong expression, and great power in the delineation of character—the whole dashed off with a great appearance of freedom and delightfully tempered with the satirical vein of the author. Some British periodical lately published contains a criticism on American literature, in which it is arrogantly asserted that our poets have made nothing of the Indian character, and that Campbell's "Outalissi" is altogether the best portraiture of the mind and manners of an American savage which is to be found in English verse. The critic must have spoken without much knowledge of his subject. He certainly could never have read Halleck's **"Red Jacket."** Campbell's "Outalissi" is very well. He is "a stoic of the woods," and nothing more—an Epictetus, put into a blanket and leggins and translated to the forests of Pennsylvania, but he is no Indian. "Red Jacket" is the very savage of our wilderness. "Outalissi" is a fancy sketch of few lineaments. He is brave, faithful and affectionate, concealing these qualities under an exterior of insensibility. "Red Jacket" has the spirit and variety of a portrait from nature. He has all the savage vices, and the rude and strong qualities of mind which belong to a warrior, a chief, and an orator of the aboriginal stock. He is set before us with sinewy limbs, gentle voice, motions graceful as a bird's in air, an air of command, inspiring deference; brave, cunning, cruel, vindictive, eloquent, skilful to dissemble, and terrible when the moment of dissembling is past, as the wild beasts or the tempests of his own wilderness.

A poem which, without being the best he has written, unites many of the different qualities of Halleck's manner, is that entitled **"Alnwick Castle."** The rich imagery, the airy melody of verse, the grace of language which belong to his serious poems, are to be found in the first half of the poem, which relates to the beautiful scenery and venerable traditions of the old home of the Percys; while the author's vein of gay humor, fertile in mirthful allusion, appears in the conclusion, in which he descends to the homely and. peaceful occupations of its present proprietors.

Whoever undertakes the examination of Halleck's poetical character will naturally wish for a greater number of examples from which to collect an estimate of his powers. He has given us only samples of what he can do. His verses are like passages of some noble choral melody, heard in the brief interval between the opening and shutting of the doors of a temple. Why does he not more frequently employ the powers with which he is so eminently gifted? He should know that such faculties are invigorated and enlarged and rendered obedient to the will by exercise. He need not be afraid of not equalling what he has already written. He will excel himself, if he applies his powers, with an earnest and resolute purpose, to the work which justice to his own fame demands of him. There are heroes of our own history who deserve to be embalmed for immortality, in strains as noble as those which celebrated the death of Marco Bozzaris; and Halleck has shown how powerfully he can appeal to our sense of patriotism, in his **"Field of the Grounded Arms,"** a poem which has only been prevented from being universally popular by the peculiar kind of verse in which it is written.

This is what I wrote of Halleck thirty-five years ago. Since that time the causes which gave him a local popularity in New York have, in a measure, ceased to exist. A new generation has arisen to whom the persons and most of the things which were the objects of his playful satire are known but by tradition. Eminent poets have appeared in our country and acquired fame among us, and divided with him the attention and admiration of the public. His best things, however, are still admired, I think, as much as ever in the city which for the greater part of his life he made his abode. . . .

When I took back upon Halleck's literary life I cannot help thinking that if his death had happened forty years earlier, his life would have been regarded as a bright morning prematurely overcast. Yet Halleck's literary career may be said to have ended then. All that will hand down his name to future years had already been produced. Who shall say to what cause his subsequent literary inaction was owing? It was not the decline of his powers; his brilliant conversation showed that it was not. Was it, then, indifference to fame? Was it because he put an humble estimate on what he had written, and therefore resolved to write no more? Was it because he feared lest what he might write would be unworthy of the reputation he had been so fortunate as to acquire?

I have my own way of accounting for his literary silence in the latter half of his life. One of the resemblances which he bore to Horace consisted in the length of time for which he kept his poems by him that he might give them the last and happiest touches. He had a tenacious verbal memory, and having composed his poems without committing them to paper, he revised them in the same manner, murmuring them to himself in his solitary moments, recovering the enthusiasm with which they were first conceived, and in this state of mind heightening the beauty of the thought or of the expression. I remember that once in crossing Washington Park I saw Halleck before me and quickened my pace to overtake him. As I drew near I heard him crooning to himself what seemed to be lines of verse, and as he threw back his hands in walking I perceived that they quivered with the feeling of the passage he was reciting. I instantly checked my pace and fell back, out of reverence for the mood of inspiration which seemed to be upon him, and fearful lest I should intercept the birth of a poem destined to be the delight of thousands of readers.

In this way I suppose Halleck to have attained the gracefulness of his diction, and the airy melody of his numbers. In this way I believe that he wrought up his verses to that transparent clearness of expression which causes the thought to be seen through them without any interposing dimness, so that the thought and the phrase seem one, and the thought enters the mind like a beam of light. I suppose that Halleck's time being taken up by the tasks of his vocation, he naturally lost by degrees the habit of composing in this manner, and that he found it so necessary to the perfection of what he wrote that he adopted no other in its place.

Whatever was the reason that Halleck ceased so early to write, let us congratulate ourselves that he wrote at all. . . .

John Greenleaf Whittier   (poem date 1877)

SOURCE: "Fitz-Greene Halleck," in *The Poetical Works*

An illustration for "Burns," from the 1869 collection of Halleck's works.

of John Greenleaf Whittier, Houghton, Mifflin, 1892, pp. 136-38.

[*One of the most prominent American poets of the nineteenth century, Whittier wrote this poem to be read at the dedication of Halleck's statue in Central Park in May, 1877.*]

Fitz-Greene Halleck.

AT THE UNVEILING OF HIS STATUE.

Among their graven shapes to whom
　Thy civic wreaths belong,
O city of his love, make room
　For one whose gift was song.

Not his the soldier's sword to wield,
　Nor his the helm of state,
Nor glory of the stricken field,
　Nor triumph of debate.

In common ways, with common men,
　He served his race and time
As well as if his clerkly pen
　Had never danced to rhyme.

If, in the thronged and noisy mart,
　The Muses found their son,
Could any say his tuneful art
　A duty left undone?

He toiled and sang; and year by year
　Men found their homes more sweet,
And through a tenderer atmosphere
　Looked down the brick-walled street.

The Greek's wild onset Wall Street knew;
　The Red King walked Broadway;
And Alnwick Castle's roses blew
　From Palisades to Bay.

Fair City by the Sea! upraise
　His veil with reverent hands;
And mingle with thy own the praise
　And pride of other lands.

Let Greece his fiery lyric breathe
　Above her hero-urns;
And Scotland, with her holly, wreathe
　The flower he culled for Burns.

Oh, stately stand thy palace walls,
　Thy tall ships ride the seas;
To-day thy poet's name recalls
　A prouder thought than these.

Not less thy pulse of trade shall beat,
　Nor less thy tall fleets swim,
That shaded square and dusty street
　Are classic ground through him.

Alive, he loved, like all who sing,
　The echoes of his song;
Too late the tardy meed we bring,
　The praise delayed so long.

Too late, alas! Of all who knew
　The living man, to-day
Before his unveiled face, how few
　Make bare their locks of gray!

Our lips of praise must soon be dumb,

Our grateful eyes be dim;
O brothers of the days to come,
　Take tender charge of him!

New hands the wires of song may sweep,
　New voices challenge fame;
But let no moss of years o'ercreep
　The lines of Halleck's name.

George Parsons Lathrop   (essay date 1877)

SOURCE: "Fitz-Greene Halleck," in *The Atlantic Monthly,* Vol. XXXIX, June, 1877, pp. 718-29.

[*An influential American literary critic during the last quarter of the nineteenth century, George Parsons Lathrop helped establish realism as the dominant mode of literary expression. In the following excerpts from an article on Halleck's life and work, Lathrop examines several of Halleck's most popular works with a view to defining his historical and literary importance.*]

[There] was a mutual reaction in Halleck, of literary ability and literary languor, which it will be useful to keep in mind while we are discussing him. These qualities confront us suggestively in the so-called Croaker poems, written in company with his friend, Joseph Rodman Drake.

. . . . .

It was in March, 1819, that Drake's address "To Ennui," the first of the Croaker series, appeared in the *New York Evening Post.* "The Culprit Fay," commonly reported to have been composed in the same year, had been written three years before this time, but was not then published; and this brief newspaper ode was the first of the young poet's pieces that attained notoriety. It was followed by several others equally successful; and then Halleck became a partner in the clandestine work. The two men had made acquaintance in the right poetic way: they were together in a group of idlers one day, just after a shower, and, remarking the beauty of the rainbow, "I should like nothing better," Drake exclaimed, "than to lie stretched on that rainbow with a copy of Tom Campbell in my hand!" Upon this, Halleck grasped his arm cordially, and said, "We must know each other." This frank spontaneity formed a most desirable basis for the literary frolic upon which they soon after entered. It is amazing to read of the hubbub which their joint compositions caused. The *furor* heightened their spirits, and Drake, in an exhortation to his comrade as Croaker Junior, makes this cheerful prediction, which seems to show that after all they had something of the sanguineness of young poets: —

　Together we'll range thro' the regions of mirth,
　A pair of bright Gemini dropt on the earth,
　　The Castor and Pollux of quizzers.

"The town" buzzed delightful curiosity around them, and one can sympathize with Drake's gratification when, one day, looking over with Halleck the printer's proof of a forthcoming Croaker, he laid his cheek for a moment against the sheet, crying out, "O Halleck, isn't this happiness?" It *was* a happiness, and one which probably no other man will ever enjoy in the same way and place. For some time the two jesters kept their personality entirely concealed from even Coleman, the editor of the *Post;* but, after repeated urgings printed in the paper, they finally presented themselves at his mansion in the honorable region of Hudson Street,—now given up to second-hand shops, saloons, and freightcars. When they made themselves known, Coleman could not conceal his astonishment. "My God!" he burst forth: "I had no idea we had such talents in America!" Only in the infancy of American journalism could so ardent an expression have been wrested from a managing editor. Who is there at all literary by profession or sympathy that does not feel a certain tenderness for the memory of Coleman, on the strength of the honest enthusiasm here recorded? Yet it would be impossible to blame the editor of to-day should he fail to be impressed by the Croaker pieces, supposing them to be now written for the first time and offered to his paper. Standards have greatly altered since 1819; and not solely because of the growth of this country, but also because of complex refinements in the practice of verse-making introduced in Europe since then. Out of the twenty-five Croakers, as finally collected, one can choose but few lines or stanzas which will bear quotation. Let us examine a few of these. On one page appears **"A Loving Epistle to Mr. William Cobbett, of North Hempstead, Long Island,"** in which that active renegade is addressed as follows: —

> Pride, boast, and glory of each hemisphere!
>   Well known, and lord in both,—great Cob-
>   bett, hail!
> Hero of Botley there and Hempstead here,—
>   Of Newgate and a Pennsylvania jail.

The best stanza is the last, which repeats the empty jest of Horace and James Smith against the larger Bradlaugh of that day, about unsold copies of the *Weekly Register,* —Cobbett's organ, —which in reality was a most successful publication: —

> In recompense that you've designed to make
>   Choice of our soil above all other lands,
> A purse we'll raise to pay your debts, and take
>   Your unsold Registers all off your hands.
> For this we ask that you, for once, will show
>   Some gratitude, and, if you can, be civil;
> Burn all your books, sell all your pigs, and go—
>   No matter where—to England or the devil.

This is a fair sample of the wit employed in the Croakers. It would be tiresome to copy much of it. The **"Ode to the Surveyor-General,"** on another page, is dimly and remotely amusing in its scorn at his choice of new names for new towns in the west of New York, —Homer, Milton, Hampden, Galen, Livy, Ulysses. Then we find some laughing lines to Captain Seaman Weeks, Chairman of the Tenth Ward Independent Electors. They give us a glimpse of the local politics of the time. The writer pretends a gushing gladness at having found at last a thoroughly independent politician, and complains of "Clintonians, Coodies, and Feds" as far below the mark of Captain Seaman Weeks: —

> In vain I endeavor to give'em a hint on
>   Sense, reason, or temper,—they laugh at it all:
> For sense is nonsense when it makes against
>   Clinton,
>   And reason is treason at Tammany Hall.

Tammany and canals, it would seem, were as fruitful of scandal, chicane, and satire then as now. Political records tell us of the bitter fight over the proposed canal system in those years, and the verses **"To Ennui"** refer to it: —

> I'm sick of General Jackson's toast,
>   Canals are nought to me;
> Nor do I care who rules the roast,
>   Clinton or John Targee.

There is, by the way, a song in Halleck's **Fanny** which represents beer as the moving force of Tammany politics. If we substitute whisky for beer, we shall have a very good notion of the advance which a certain kind of state-craft in New York has made since that time. Although Drake's and Halleck's squibs are very much restricted in their interest by their local allusions, it will be found that a slight familiarity with the affairs of the Empire State in the present throws a comic light back upon these early satires. The very fact that the story has now become too well worn to excite more than a fatigued smile gives to the energy of these satirists a surprising freshness. Clintonians, Coodies, Federalists, Bucktails, Democrats, Republicans, —these were the names on which the fortunes of the State then hung. We were ever an inventive people. The variety of party titles in America seems to bear some affinity to our national fertility in mixed drinks.

Besides the political matter in this pamphlet of verses there is little local quizzing that is other than dull. **"Ode to Fortune"** makes perhaps as much as could be made out of the life of a well-to-do idler in the metropolis at a time when its population was about one tenth of what it is to-day: —

Ode To Fortune

> Fair lady with the bandag'd eye!
>   I'll pardon all thy scurvy tricks,
> So thou wilt *cut* me and deny
>   Alike thy kisses and thy kicks:
>
>   . . . . .
>
> My station is the middle rank,
>   My fortune, just a competence,—
> Ten thousand in the Franklin bank
>   And twenty in the six per cents:
>
>   . . . . .
>
> The horse that twice a year I ride
>   At mother Dawson's eats his fill;
> My books at Goodrich's abide;
>   My country-seat is Weehawk Hill;
> My morning lounge is Eastburn's shop;
>   At Poppleton's I take my lunch;
> Niblo prepares my mutton-chop;
>   And Jennings makes whisky punch.
>
> When merry, I the hours amuse
>   By squibbing Bucktails, Guards, and Balls;
> And when I'm troubled with the blues,
>   Damn Clinton and abuse canals:
> Then, Fortune, since I ask no prize,
>   At least preserve me from thy frown;
> The man who don't attempt to rise
>   'Twere cruelty to tumble down.

The brief extracts just given show for what sparing outlay of art or idea the authors received their large return of distinction. They rhymed as easily as Peter Pindar, whom they were thought to rival. Perhaps it would be nearer the truth to say, they imitated. Something of their free-hand drawing they probably learned from that too industrious doctor; but they had wit enough of their own to give all the flavor of originality. At least they deserve great respect for not emulating the English satirist in the tenacity with which he maintained the habit of doggerel through a long life-time. Moreover, one's attention is seriously challenged by the implied air of superiority, the *unexpressed* value of these estrays: even when you know that they are by Drake and Halleck you may expect very little from them, and yet on reading them fairly through you will be inclined to wonder what it is that makes them seem so much better than they are. This, possibly, is a fancy of my own; but it seems to me a noteworthy instance of finer quality in the men making itself felt in work that is but little above mediocrity. Twice or thrice, also, the Croakers broached sentiment: Drake wrote "The American Flag," and his friend a meditation evidently inspired by Campbell's "Pleasures of Hope," beginning, "There is an evening twilight of the heart," together with this song: —

> The world is bright before thee,
>   Its summer flowers are thine,
> Its calm blue sky is o'er thee,
>   Thy bosom Pleasure's shrine, etc.

But so soon as we come to consider the sentimental poetry, we find ourselves at a point where the Castor and Pollux of quizzers diverge. The Croakers were penned in the antechamber of life. Two or three years after they had come to light, Drake died. Halleck lived nearly fifty years longer. His later career—both by the fame it secured and the taciturnity that fell upon his genius—shows the futility of telling what a man might have done if he had lived. "I cannot help thinking," Mr. Bryant has written, "that if his death had happened forty years earlier, his life would have been regarded as a bright morning prematurely overcast. Yet Halleck's career may be said to have ended then," that is, about 1830. "All that will hand down his name to future years had already been produced. . . ."

If we must abate a good deal from the first reputation of these merry squibs, we may still heartily acknowledge that they showed a masculine touch which it is stimulating to look back to now, that quality being hopelessly absent from a great deal of youthful poetry at present. Even at the time of their freshness, no one could rival the Croakers in their own department. Hundreds of unsuccessful imitations were daily received and mostly rejected by the New York journals. The vigor and simplicity of the originals taken with our conclusion that the Croakers were especially in accord with Halleck's taste may recall a remark of Poe's. "There is something," he says, "in the *bonhomie* of certain of his [Halleck's] compositions—something altogether distinct from poetic merit—which has aided to establish him." Perhaps it was with slightly malicious relish that Poe threw in the clause, "altogether distinct from poetic merit;" yet it is true that Halleck's sketchy descriptiveness, his knack of hitting off in verse affairs of current interest, and his wit would often—but for the jingle—have

been just as acceptable in prose. These traits are exemplified in the **"Epistle to the Recorder"** and in *Fanny*. The latter production put Halleck in the position of being the only American besides Irving for whom Irving's publisher would print; and in a few years copies had become so scarce that they brought twenty times the original price. I confess, to me it is the flattest, tamest, dreariest of comic poems that have won any note. It was thought by some to have been inspired by *Don Juan;* but the fine distinction has latterly been made that it resulted from a perusal of Byron's *Beppo,* a poem in the same style and stanza. *Beppo,* however, has a plot, and therefore finishes itself; and Halleck failed to imitate it in this advantageous particular. The second part which he afterward provided does not remedy the defect. A more serious objection is that the wit is thin and scattered. Then the poem is so much taken up with wandering that it has no time for poetry. I find the intercalated song of the Horse-Boat a total enigma, when considered in the light of the praise it has received. Neither does the description of New York as seen from Weehawken appear to sustain the honors which have been bestowed upon it. For example: —

> The city bright below; and far away,
> Sparkling in golden light, his own romantic bay.
> Tall spire and glittering roof and battlement,
>   And banners floating in the sunny air;
> And white sails o'er the calm blue waters bent.
>   Green isle and circling shore are blended there
> In wild reality.

We can hardly be convicted of arrogance if we pronounce this passage unmistakably feeble. The hints of social existence, also, in *Fanny* are so vague that there is little to be got from them in any way, and in the whole chain of verses there are hardly more than a half dozen brief bits worth repeating. It was probably the surprise which people felt at seeing provincial Manhattan treated in verse of any sort that captivated the early readers of *Fanny*. Halleck's wit and humor appear under much more characteristic guise in the **"Epistle to * * *"** and in **"The Recorder."** The former and shorter of these gives us a sketch of the summer vacation in New York, which though shaded with a pleasant antiquity presents the city under much the same aspect that it now wears in the hot months. The rhymer refers to the tourist at his diverse employments: —

> Or sketching Niagara, pencil on knee
>   (The giant of waters, our country's pet lion),
> Or dipp'd at Long Branch in the real salt sea,
>   With a cork for a dolphin, a cockney Arion;
> Yet as most of "the fashion" are journeying now,
> With the brown hues of summer on cheek and
>   on brow,
> The few *gens comme il faut* who are lingering
>   here
> Are, like fruits out of season, more welcome and
>   dear.
>
>   · · · · ·
>
> One meets them in groups that Canova might
>   fancy,
> At our new lounge at evening, the Opéra
>   Français,
> In nines like the Muses, in threes like the Graces,

Green spots in a desert of commonplace faces.
The queen, Mrs. Adams, goes there sweetly
   dress'd
   In a beautiful bonnet all golden and flowery;
While the king, Mr. Bonaparte, smiles on
   Celeste,
   Heloïse, and Hutin from his box at the
   Bowery.

"The Recorder" is still racy and delightful in its quick, free humor; for the author hit precisely the right chord in this, and made it a brilliant summary of one phase of American minor politics. It cannot lose its relish so long as we take an interest in analyzing the condition of things that called it forth. How witty is this sharply drawn contrast between the real and the pinchbeck Cæsarism!

The Cæsar pass'd the Rubicon
With helm and shield and breastplate on,
   Dashing his war-horse through the waters;
The Riker would have built a barge
Or steamboat at the city's charge,
   And pass'd it *with his wife and daughters.*

The reflex of fancy here, which presents the idea of *Caesar* making up a little family party for a free trip across the Rubicon, the expenses to be arranged at the City Hall of Rome, is an inspiration exquisite of its kind. The comparative neglect into which our once much-sought author has relapsed makes it safe to quote what few now read. And because it throws light on the genius which we are considering, I will introduce another passage from **"The Recorder,"** which suddenly varies the prevalent tone of banter with a strain of unpremeditated, pathetic sentiment. Garcia, it should be said, was the maiden name of Mme. Malibran, who had sung in New York in 1825, at the first performance of Italian opera in the United States, —three years before **"The Recorder"** appeared: —

For me,
I rhyme not for posterity,
Though pleasant to my heirs might be
   The incense of its praise,
When I, their ancestor, am gone,
And paid the debt, the only one
   A poet ever pays.

But many are my years, and few
Are left me, ere night's holy dew
And sorrow's holier tears will keep
The grass green where in death I sleep.
And when that grass is green above me,
And those who bless me now and love me
   Are sleeping by my side,
Will it avail me aught that men
Tell to the world with lip and pen
   That once I lived and died?

No; if a garland for my brow
Is growing, let me have it now,
   While I'm alive to wear it;
And if, in whispering my name,
There's music in the voice of Fame
Like Garcia's, let me hear it!

The impulsive grace of this unlooked-for compliment to the great songstress could hardly be surpassed. The momentary pensiveness that precedes it has precisely the effect of that involuntary tremor of grief sometimes seen in a lip which gives shape, the next instant, to a seemingly careless jest. It follows a laughing fling at the poverty of poets; and then, the emptiness of renown after death giving him a sudden pang, the poet seems instinctively thrown upon the thought of woman, and all the pathos he has just caught sight of goes to enlarge and beautify his praise of this one woman greatly gifted.

"The Recorder" goes so far beyond anything else of Halleck's in the humorous vein that it is impossible not to regret that he gave it no companions. But what Halleck has left, of this sort, only indicates how much more he might have done. I am not so sure that the same can be said of his serious poetry.

The transition from one mood to the other, the connection between them, is interesting to watch for and follow. Perhaps the most perfect of Halleck's poems, excepting the two that have made him famous—his **"Marco Bozzaris"** and **"Robert Burns"**—is the one called **"Woman,"** "Written in the Album of an Unknown Lady:" —

Lady, although we have not met,
   And may not meet, beneath the sky;
And whether thine are eyes of jet,
Gray, or dark blue, or violet,
   Or hazel,—Heaven knows, not I;

Whether around thy cheek of rose
   A maiden's glowing locks are curled,
And to some thousand kneeling beaux
Thy frown is cold as winter's snows,
   Thy smile is worth a world;

Or whether, past youth's joyous strife,
   The calm of thought is on thy brow,
And thou art in the noon of life,
Loving and loved, a happy wife,
   And happier mother now,

I know not: but, whate'er thou art,
   Whoe'er thou art, were mine the spell
To call Fate's joys or blunt his dart,
There should not be one hand or heart
   But served or wished thee well.

For thou art Woman.

There is something in that train of feeling which recalls Carew and Herrick; and the rest of the poem, enlarging on the influence of woman over man, is nearly up to the mark set by the beginning. In the penultimate stanza we find the substance of that compliment to Malibran which we have so much admired. Here it is said of the poet,

If to his song the echo rings
Of Fame,—'t is woman's voice he hears.

But let it be noticed how comparatively trite the sentiment appears, in this form. There is an air of premeditation in the statement, which gives it a falling accent instead of that upward inflection of surprise which captivates us in the longer poem. At the time of writing **"Woman,"** the poet sought this idea with some pains, most probably; but when he came to **"The Recorder,"** it had matured so that he could easily give it a shaping even better than the thought itself. Besides, there is great advantage in the unexpectedness with which the burst of feeling comes upon us in **"The Recorder."** This observation will explain in part the dim coloring, the dry, disappointing property of many among Halleck's serious poetic compositions. So fragile was the constitution of his genius, it seemed questionable whether he could nourish any given inspiration into stalwart life. The mere stopping to measure his strength would discourage him. If, then, he could always have begun writing in the gay mood, and from that have thrown himself without forethought upon the current of some fresh, hurrying emotion, he would always have given us his best. I think the generalization will not do him injustice. Particularizing, we might take this very poem, **"Woman,"** as an example. The writer plays with his theme in the lightest way, for two stanzas, merely inhaling its first piquant suggestion; then the larger associations take unexpected hold of him, he passes into a phase of earnest homage, and so is carried to his solemn close. In **"A Poet's Daughter"** he balances the two moods in a more prolonged manner; a little more consciously, too. He talks about what he shall write, and argues with a supposed suppliant for his verse, until the sensation one has is like that of seeing a man execute some feat of balancing a plate or a hat on the point of his stick. He has time to be coy, retrospective, pensive, cynical; at last he is impressed by hearing that he is asked to write for a poet's daughter; and then he catches at one of those charming compliments, for delivering which his genius appears to have been accorded him as a special messenger:—

> A poet's daughter? Could I claim
> The consanguinity of fame,
> Veins of my intellectual frame!
>   Your blood would glow
> Proudly to sing that gentlest name
>   Of aught below.

>   . . . . .

> My spirit's wings are weak; the fire
> Poetic comes but to expire;
> Her name needs not my humble lyre
>   To bid it live;
> She hath already from her sire
>   All bard can give.

"Red Jacket" is a performance less good of its order. There is, admittedly, strong characterization in it, but what it has of poetry, although at moments solemnly eloquent, is uneven. It is to the purpose to notice, also, how **"Red Jacket"** offers in a duller, more obscure state, the contrast between two phases of the author's mind, which we have just been noticing. After a deal of prefatory rhyming in which the poet treats his best reflections with exceeding shabbiness, he grants us a few periods of eloquence: —

> The monarch mind, the mystery of commanding,
>   The birth-hour gift, the art, Napoleon,
> Of winning, fettering, molding, wielding, banding
>   The hearts of millions till they move as one;

> Thou hast it. At thy bidding men have crowded
>   The road to death as to a festival;

And minstrels, at their sepulchres, have shrouded
    In banner-folds of glory the dark pall.

The rest has the same kind of power, except that twice more the chanter allows himself to be jostled into jocularity. Again in **"Alnwick Castle"** it is dismal to see the poet throw away his lyre and break his harmonies in mere downheartedness at the unpoeticalness of things. The **"Alnwick Castle"** is an instance of a sober poem ending in the bitterness of desecrating humor; a reversal of the process in the other cases, where gayety blends itself with a gathering seriousness, as the last daylight melts into russet-purpling dusk.

These various examples which we have reviewed all force us to the conclusion that Halleck instinctively sought, in one way or another, a break in the tune, an abrupt alternation of mood. It was in this clashing of diverse inclinations that he struck out his liveliest sparks of fancy. He sought a certain tantalizing sweetness that floated in the midst of discord.

        . . . . .

[H]alleck, when he could get far enough away from home, let his voice carol forth music that could make a many-voiced echo. But he could not pitch the note very high or steady when standing on his native heath. He several times attempted this; but **"Red Jacket"** is disturbed and vulgarized by a forced wit, and the verses on Connecticut are fragmentary and poor. **"The Field of the Grounded Arms,"** founded on the battle of Saratoga, was the outcome of a resolve (conscious or not) to conquer this inability. It must, however, be confessed a failure. It is not poetic, it is not even eloquent. Written in a Horatian measure, it becomes a tedious prosaic monologue, lacking the deep cadences of Marvell's ode on Cromwell and the undulant musical underflow of Collins's "Evening,"—two poems which the author must have had in his mind when composing his own. **"Alnwick Castle,"** too, broke down because an allusion suddenly recalled the writer's mind to America. In naming over the different Percys, he was obliged to mention.

> him who, when a younger son,
> Fought for King George at Lexington,
>   A major of dragoons.

Straightway he had recourse to asterisks and wrote: —

> That last half-stanza—it has dashed
>   From my warm lip the sparkling cup;
> The light that o'er my eyebeam flashed,
>   The power that bore my spirit up
> Above this bank note world, is gone.

The same disgust for things modern and American appears in **"A Poet's Daughter:"**

> 'T is a new world,—no more to maid,
> Warrior, or bard is homage paid;
> The bay-tree's, laurel's, myrtle's shade
>   Men's thoughts resign;
> Heaven placed us here to vote and trade,
>   Twin tasks divine!

From one point of view, this scorn appears to merit our

decided admiration, for it indicates a sensitive poetic organization, which would not let the man forget what higher aims he was really born for. But, equally, we are impelled by it to ask, Why then did he not obey the call of his genius? Why did he not quit trade and, if need were, society, and bring his mind face to face with what struck him as the contradiction between life and poetry, until he should discover how to reconcile them? Then he might have gained for his creative faculty a noble and sustaining confidence. The inevitable conclusion is that his inspiration was not ardent enough, his temperament too much averse to the risk and the effort involved, —in a word, that his genius was secondary, and had not the instinct of discovery, which overrules tradition and makes worlds where it was thought none could be.

> My spirit's wings are weak; the fire
> Poetic comes but to expire.

His own words sum up the situation. In 1832 he was asked to write an address for a theatre, and declined, saying of himself (in the third person): "He has been estranged for so long a time from the habit of writing and rhyming as to find it utterly impossible," and that he "is broad awake with both eyes from the morning dream of poetry." But he had always, I conceive, been awake with *one* eye, and that was fixed too carefully on the schedule of ways and means. He was hardly ready to make great sacrifices, or to tread the laborious path that some of his brother poets chose. To open the way to a great career in the arts, it is sometimes indispensable to risk everything.

In his general disposition there was undoubtedly a certain degree of cynicism too ready to lay hold upon him. It might give a tone of pleasant resistance and sharpness to the geniality which his friends have so much commended, but it must have recoiled morosely upon himself at times. It developed in him, or else proceeded from a singular coldness, indifference, rigidity, a few instances of which may be cited here. His reserve on the subject of his poems was excessive, and he had a maxim that a man is famous when he has been once quoted. This specious dictum reminds one of Thoreau's decision that when he could make a single good lead pencil he need never make another. There is a glimpse of truth in each conclusion, more applicable to pencils than to poetry; but at best it is a very slight glimpse. Yet Halleck was apparently satisfied with his reasoning, and with it steeled himself against all appeals for further exercise of his gift. Mr. William Gilmore Simms has recorded Halleck's "sovereign contempt" for the popular judgment; yet it is clear that he relished its decision in his favor. He hated trade, too, we are informed. But liking city life, and being a good diner-out and conversationist, he adhered to business. Yet his attitude as a poet professing a mercantile character probably constrained him. A man of genius may be unfortunate in treating extraneous social forces without due respect; but he is no less in danger, sometimes, from paying them too great a deference. I am inclined to think that Halleck vitiated his inborn artistic quality by bowing too long and too low in the presence of commercial dignity. But if sundry of his shortcomings may be charged to his surroundings, it is certainly a radical distaste for life that crops out in this confession to his sister, written after the suicide of a friend in New

York, when the poet was only twenty-seven: "We had often conversed on suicide; and I joined him in the opinion that the world contained nothing worth living for, and he was the most fortunate whose task was soonest ended." Then, too, if Halleck's stanzas on Love are to be taken seriously, they reveal a saturnine chilliness of resolution fatal to the free and graceful expansion of poesy. Halleck's friends, who have borne strong testimony to his capacity for genial good-fellowship, have also mentioned with emphasis the taste for raillery often shown by him. He would launch into disputation on divers themes with a vehemence which at first impressed recent acquaintances as being absolutely hostile. But the hostility was only assumed, and soon melted into the mere fun of holding an opposition view for the sake of picturesqueness and variety. Nevertheless I suspect that a radical tendency to sarcasm and discontent underlay these ebullitions. They appear to be connected with a captiousness and an eccentricity of judgment of which several instances are on record. For example, a hobby of his in favor of limited monarchy aroused in the poet what seems an unreasonable dissatisfaction on his hearing Thackeray lecture upon George IV. Before the reading was finished he quitted the hall, remarking to a friend, "I can't listen any longer to this abuse of a man better than himself" (meaning better than Thackeray). Leigh Hunt's Story of Rimini he pronounced "silly" as to incident: it is not set down what opinion he held of Dante. Tennyson and Mrs. Browning he declared had written nothing worth remembering; and it gives a curious notion of the complacence lurking under Halleck's extreme outward modesty to read his complaint in a letter to a lady, written after *Young America* appeared, in 1865. He calls the book merely "verses," but continues: "In these 'sensation' times I cannot expect them to be liked or even tolerated. There is, I am aware, nothing in them resembling Miss Braddon's exciting themes in prose, or Enoch Arden's story of polygamy (so decent, delicate, and decorous) in verse." He failed to see that neither was there anything in the lines at all corresponding to the strength and harmony of a greater poet than himself, and one who was in sympathy with his time. He had been content to enjoy his popularity, thirty-five years earlier, with a quiet scorn for the public judgment which accorded it; and then—having let slip the begging opportunity that attended him lustre after lustre—he allowed himself to feel bitter because, on sending a belated halloo after the moving generation, he found that he was not listened to.

I have dwelt upon this colder, crotchety side of Halleck's personality only because it helps us to understand that clashing of moods which we have already noticed in his poetry. It is obvious that the tincture of melancholy in his temperament was continually depriving his dainty poetic sensibility of its zest for beauty, and arresting his sweetest strains with a sudden, prosaic self-consciousness. He was proud and reserved, yet genial; he was prudent to the point of lavishing all his best energies upon book-keeping, yet full of enthusiasm for certain kinds of poetry. This conflict of temperament and genius was heightened and complicated by the difficult circumstances of birth in a new country, and the absence of a highly developed society which could stimulate instead of limiting and repressing him. He was indubitably hurt by his surroundings, and had not the strength to modify them. This he might in some degree have done had he clearly comprehended his situation. That he did not comprehend it, and did not struggle away somewhither to find a less vexatious atmosphere, I have already suggested as a reason for holding his endowment to be secondary and defective. Genius which does not carry with it the self-preserving power, and the instinct of experimenting with conditions until the adverse forces are reduced to a minimum, is necessarily more exposed to maimings or extinction than genius which is provided with those defenses. This conclusion, however, relates only to the constitution of Halleck's genius; it accounts for his failures, but it cannot throw the least discredit on his successes. In fact it makes these all the more remarkable; it is a marvel that a man so apathetic as Halleck, and so hampered by his other occupations, should have written what he did. But the height to which he several times attained makes it the greater pity that his productions should have been at other times so ruinously flawed.

When we have left out parts of **"The Recorder,"** we may dismiss the rest of Halleck's comic poetry as of no intrinsic worth. There is a tremulous beauty about several of the slighter lyrics that will bestow refreshment from time to time upon the few who may come upon them in the nooks of libraries. Three pieces remain which have secured a wide renown likely to last for that indefinite period which is practically an immortality; these pieces being, of course, the monody upon Drake's death, the meditation on Burns, and the **"Marco Bozzaris."** But are we to rate the author of this splendid martial ode as a second-rate genius?

I take it we may not inaccurately mark three grades of genius in poetry,—master, workman, and amateur. The master will accomplish great things and minor things, but he will leave always the imprint of largeness on his handiwork. The workman may be more perfect in finish than the master cares to be; he, too, may make the emotions bow to him at times, though scarcely with the sure and continued sovereignty of the higher-ranked poet; and he stands good chance of covering his failures with the veil of dexterity. The amateur boggles his way through bathos and beatitude, but can touch far and deep in an unforeseen, lucky moment; there are also misleading scintillations of workmanship, and even of mastery, in the quartz he brings to light. Halleck was so much an amateur that if he had not been so much more a real workman, he would have fallen into the third rank. It was amateurish, his failure to know at once, on finishing **"Marco Bozzaris,"** that he had written a great poem. He handed it to a business companion, asking, "Will that do?" But when we read it, *we* say, "Cannot this man do everything?" There is brilliant, perfect workmanship in it; there is splendid command of the sympathies. Is not the writer a master? One hour's crowned session on the throne makes a king; but I do not think that one effort of power, even so impressive as this, gives a right to the title of master, in poetry. Halleck gives us too many blurred pages and broken staves.

He himself laid no claim to high rank. "I have published very little," he wrote, near the close of his life, "and that little almost always anonymously, and have ever been but

an amateur in the literary orchestra, playing only upon a pocket flute, and never aspiring, even in dream, to the dignity of the *bâton.*" . . . No; the master cannot fully breathe unless he sing; everywhere as he walks through the world, flowered lanes of poetry open out before him, and others as they tread that place know that his passing made its beauty; his voice does not shrivel in his throat when life is but half over; things do not go entirely by chance with him. But Halleck was for the most part so conscientious—whatever his practice, his creed in song was so strict—that he deserves for his great accident of Bozzaris a credit similar to that which a complete master should receive for a burst of power as grand. Still, we must remember that it was the work of an intellectual dependent. Halleck, in answer to solicitations, refused to write anything about our civil war, because, as he said, it was "a monster mutiny." His silence does not appear to have been that of an anguished sorrow too deep for words, but merely the silence of indifference. There is no knowing how the Greek insurrection would have affected him had it not been approved by Byron and Campbell. And again it will not do to forget that Halleck's confessed idol, Campbell, had shown him how to write war poems, in "Hohenlinden" and "The Battle of the Baltic." Halleck's greater power has been mentioned in a previous part of this paper; but, though the comparison by no means covers the case, there is something in his superiority to Campbell which suggests the finer skill of a musical virtuoso contrasted with the original impulse of the composer.

Halleck's place in our literature has been said to resemble that of Horace in the literature of Rome. The suggestion may have been intended more as a compliment, a friendly fancy, than as a critical summary of his merits. But the tendency in this country toward an American Literature Made Easy may excuse a wish that this sort of parallel might be avoided. It is true that

> parvus operosa
> Carmina fingo

will apply to the Connecticut as well as to the Venusian poet; both writers also dealt with the municipal life around them, parading it in the form of satire; but beyond this it is hardly necessary to go, in considering them together. Halleck's satires do not live, nor do his lyrics by any means form a compact body of song representative of the national life. On the contrary, it is particularly and regrettably noticeable that the national life does not enter at all into his best pieces. I find it perfectly possible to enjoy his poetry keenly, and to read patiently what I do not enjoy in it, without losing sight of the fact that Halleck, like so many another cherished poet, is only a brilliant amateur. There have been few of his degree so charming and so changeful. At one moment he is a nimble lampoon writer; but suddenly his glee escapes, his page darkens, his lids grow heavy; he mourns the death of a brother poet. That elegy on Drake is like a funeral torch held out at night, dropping its reflection across each stanza as if upon the slow incoming waves of a dark Stygian stream. As another phase of the same poet we may take the arch earnestness of **"Woman,"** or **"A Poet's Daughter,"** among *vers de société* of the same scope not easy to match. But while we are still lingering over their evanescent charm, the resonant tones of **"Bozzaris"**— pæan and requiem blended in one—shall burst upon us, and rouse to impassioned sympathy. From one point of view, how versatile and susceptible was this man! from another, how chilly and limited! But his self-divided genius causes him to stand forward as a peculiarly apt representative of that large class of minds that are potentially poet-minds, but never find means of expression. He has the semi-discouragement, the sensitiveness, the occasional bursts of clear energy characteristic of them. And though he did not translate the national life into verse, his mood as traced in his poems corresponds closely to the general tone of a community and period still crude and but half developed on the artistic side. This adds another to the reasons why he will not be forgotten. He would not have been forgotten, even had the city that he loved failed to honor his memory with the first statue erected to an American poet; a statue also honoring the city's loyalty to the poet of her earlier days. Neither overstated nor unduly stinted praise can shake Halleck's claim to what he has called

> That frailer thing than leaf or flower,
> A poet's immortality.

Title page from the 1869 collection of Halleck's poems, with an illustration of "Marco Bozzaris."

R. H. Stoddard (essay date 1889)

SOURCE: "Fitz-Greene Halleck," in *Lippincott's Monthly Magazine,* Vol. 43, June, 1889, pp. 886-97.

[*R. H. Stoddard was a prolific late nineteenth-century American poet, editor, and literary critic. In the following excerpt, he reflects on Halleck's career and writings, presenting him as an unusually gifted poet for his time and place who never fulfilled his early promise.*]

Shortly after his coming to New York [Halleck] made the acquaintance of a young gentleman who was qualifying himself for the medical profession, and for whom he at once entertained a feeling of friendship. This was Joseph Rodman Drake. . . .

[Their] contributions to the *Evening Post,* which consisted of a number of squibs in anonymous verse, and which were dignified by the name of "The Croaker Papers," from the signature which the writers adopted, were highly thought of by the editor of that sheet, who, in acknowledging the receipt of the first three, pronounced them to be "the productions of superior taste and genius, and begged the honor of a personal acquaintance with the author."

This singular endorsement of the supposed merits of the *jeux-d'esprit* excited public attention to such a degree that The Croakers are said to have been a "subject of conversation in drawing-rooms, book-stores, and coffee-houses on Broadway, and throughout the city; they were, in short, a town topic," a circumstance which recalls the literary London of Dryden, Pope, Swift, and Dr. Johnson, when the merits of new poems were discussed by wits and beaux at Will's, Button's, or the Mitre Tavern, and reputations determined by men-about-town, rather than the unliterary New York of our grandfathers. The success of The Croakers, whatever it may have been, was so gratifying to the editor of the *Evening Post* that he again expressed his anxiety to be acquainted with the writer, this time in a style so mysterious as to excite the curiosity of the authors, and they resolved to call upon him. The meeting of the poets and their patron is thus described by General Wilson:

> Halleck and Drake, accordingly, went one evening together to Coleman's residence in Hudson Street and requested an interview. They were ushered into the parlor; the editor soon entered; the young poets expressed a desire for a few minutes' strictly private conversation with him, and, the door being closed and locked, Mr. Drake said, "I am Croaker; and this gentleman, sir, is Croaker junior." Coleman stared at the young men with indescribable and unaffected astonishment, at length exclaiming, *"My God! I had no idea that we had such talents in America!"*

The surprise of the worthy editor appears to have been shared in a measure by his readers: such, at any rate, was the opinion of Halleck, as we gather from a letter to his sister at this period:

> Can you believe it, Maria? Joe and I have become authors! We have tasted all the pleasures and many of the pains of literary fame and notoriety, under the assumed name of The Croakers. We have had the consolation of seeing and hear-

ing ourselves praised, puffed, eulogized, execrated, and threatened as much, I believe I can say with truth, as any writers since the days of Junius. The whole town has talked of nothing else for the three weeks past, and every newspaper has done us the honor to mention us in some way, either of praise or censure, but all uniting in owning our talents and genius.

The mistaken belief that he was, or could be, a humorous writer, led to the production of Halleck's first poem of any length, —*Fanny.* It is possible to read *Fanny,* as it is possible to read "The Croakers," for I have done both. But it is impossible, at least I find it so, to feel any interest therein; for the analysis which could detect poetry in either would be rarer than the alchemy which was once supposed to extract sunbeams from cucumbers. There is no story in *Fanny,* or none to speak of; and the most that one can say of it is that it is an imaginary sketch of the social experiences of its heroine, the daughter of a shopkeeper in Chatham Street, who, having amassed what was then considered a comfortable little fortune, proceeded to make a brilliant brief splurge in society, and concluded his career by going where the woodbine twineth.

To depict the mortifying experiences of a parvenu's daughter ought not to have been difficult, but it was more than the unpractised pen of Halleck could accomplish; for, flimsy in intention and feeble in execution, *Fanny* was dreary reading, because the author after writing what he probably considered a poetic passage immediately spoiled it by sticking his tongue in his cheek. A certain amount of antiquarian interest attaches to his pointless verse, and there is a pretty description of Weehawken, which was one of his favorite suburban resorts. What the subject-matter of such a poem as *Fanny* could be in the hands of a true poet was shown at a later period by Thomas Hood in "Miss Kilmansegg," and at a still later period by Mr. Stedman in his "Diamond Wedding." But Halleck was more than the would-be wit that he still believed himself to be, and this fact was discovered by him when he came to lose his friend Drake, who died not long after the publication of *Fanny,* and whose death he commemorated in some touching lines. They possess the merit of genuine feeling, for he was truly attached to Drake, and are fervid, though artless, in expression. Like all his serious verse, of which they were nearly the first example, they appear to have been carelessly written, and might have been bettered, as it seems to us, if he had spent more time upon them. They are faulty from the excess of feeling, and in the opening stanza they remind us of Wordsworth's "Lucy," which they *ought* to have equalled.

The position which a poet holds, and ought to hold, in the estimation of his readers is not and ought not to be determined by the quantity, but by the quality, of his poetry. It is the habit of poetical minds of a certain cast to be verbose and voluminous; it is the necessity as well as the inclination of poetical minds of another cast to concentrate their energies in concise creations. The former are represented in English and American verse by the Scotts, the Southeys, the Byrons, the Longfellows, and the Whittiers; the latter by the Grays, the Campbells, and the Hallecks. The poetic impulses of Halleck were infrequent, and not

continuous. His best work—in other words, all his good, serious work—is contained within the compass of four or five hundred lines. His genius, for he had genius, expressed itself in three poems of moderate length, —**"Alnwick Castle," "Burns,"** and **"Marco Bozzaris."** The first two were written about two years after the death of Drake, during a short pleasure-trip through England and Scotland, in the autumn of 1822; the latter about a year later, after his return to New York and his routine work in the banking-house of Jacob Barker. The twelvemonth comprised between these dates is all that need concern us in the poetical life of Halleck. Beginning, dubiously, with his contributions to the "Croaker" squibs in 1819, and ending ingloriously with his **"Young America"** in 1864, it was brilliant only at this period.

I have been reading these poems lately, and more critically than I could have done thirty years ago, and they have increased rather than diminished my respect for their author. They were remarkable considering the time at which they were written, and which was barren of good verse of American origin. They antedated the best of Bryant's earlier poems, —"The Rivulet," "March," "Summer Wind," "Monument Mountain," "Hymn to the North Star," and "Song of the Greek Amazon," for example; which were not given to the world until after the composition of **"Marco Bozzaris,"** —and promised a poetic career to which he never attained. Lyrical in a large sense, they display in single passages a more than lyrical strength. It would be difficult, if not impossible to find in English verse such picturesque suggestions of the pomp and splendor of feudal days as we find in **"Alnwick Castle,"** in which the manner of Scott has become a style, and which are suffused with a rich historic light. There is dignity, not to say distinction, in its spirited but careless stanzas, which are needlessly disfigured with imperfect rhymes, —a metrical negligence of which Halleck, like Scott and Byron, was too often guilty. Nor is this distinction impaired by the introduction of local and modern allusions, through which, as through a bustling foreground, we are borne back to this stately home of the Percy's high-born race. The poetic, for once, does not suffer from its temporary association with the humorous.

R. H. Stoddard on reading Halleck:

I still read Halleck, or portions of Halleck, with pleasure, and, while I am keenly alive to his faults, which are mainly technical, I wish that the vein of sterling sense which runs through his best work was one of our present excellences. He had something to say, and he said it. That he was a poet in any large sense is not true, neither is it true that he was a poet in any recondite sense. He should be read, as I read him, with a regard to the time at which he wrote, and the then condition of American song.

R. H. Stoddard, in Lippincott's Monthly Magazine, *1889.*

Less elaborate in conception and less studied in expression

than "Alnwick Castle," the lines on Burns were written with a heartiness of admiration which was not common at the time, and with a warmth of feeling which was not habitual with Halleck at any time. He was carried beyond himself by his sympathy with the manliest qualities of the genius of that poet, the sincerity of whose nature and the energy of whose song were eloquently described in Halleck's lines. Lowell and Whittier have since eulogized the peasant-bard, but less fervently, and less happily, as it seems to me, than Halleck, who has added a new quotation to the language in

> The Delphian vales, the Palestines,
>   The Meccas of the mind.

"Marco Bozzaris" was a passionate outgrowth of that excess of natural emotion and sentimental devotion which was awakened by the Greeks in their uprising against their Turkish masters, who were popularly execrated throughout all Christendom. What Mr. Gladstone has since called "the unspeakable Turk" was a favorite-poetic bugaboo with the rhymesters of England and America. He maddened the sensitive soul of Campbell; and, while he was not personally offensive to Byron, he was more or less the cause that led that great poet to sacrifice his time and money in the service of Greece and end his days prematurely in the swamps of Missolonghi. "Marco Bozzaris" differed from the phil-Hellene poetry of the period which produced it, in that it was less denunciatory, and therefore more reasonable, than the clamor which it surmounted, and that it celebrated a single heroic action, and not the warlike bustle of a series of revolutionary struggles. Its interest centred in this action, and in the personality of its hero, and in the train of reflection and meditation, which were as poetically significant of both as the train of reflection and meditation which have made Gray's "Elegy" and Bryant's "Thanatopsis" immortal. It is not of the poet that we think while reading it, but of his theme, which extends from the fate of the valiant captain who fell in that memorable night-attack on the ancient field of Platæa, until it embraces the race of patriotic heroes throughout the world.

Joseph Slater   (essay date 1974)

SOURCE: "The Case of Drake and Halleck," in *Early American Literature*, Vol. VIII, No. 3, Winter, 1974, pp. 285-97.

[*In the following excerpt from an article on Halleck and Drake, Slater discusses Halleck's poem* Fanny *and argues that Halleck's poems and those of other popular but relatively minor figures should not be excluded from literary study.*]

Sixty years ago they were still being called the Damon and Pythias of American poetry: a young Park Row physician, dead of tuberculosis at twenty-five, and a young South Street accountant, who wrote the epitaph that was chiseled into his friend's gravestone. Before that, they had been known, in the touching provincialism of the early nineteenth century, as the American Keats and the American Byron. Now their books are shelved, unborrowed, with those of Gulian Verplanck. Even their sonorous

names, Joseph Rodman Drake and Fitz-Greene Halleck, are blurred in the memory and their identities confused. Which one is buried in the trash-strewn park on Hunt's Point? And who wrote the only lines by either poet that anybody now remembers: "Green be the turf above thee / Friend of my better days"? Apart from the selections in Kendall Taft's *Minor Knickerbockers*—available only in an expensive facsimile edition for libraries—and **"Marco Bozzaris,"** which is quoted in an introductory section of the new Brooks-Lewis-Warren anthology, not one of their poems seems to be in print. Neither Drake nor Halleck is even mentioned in the two most recent histories of American poetry. For the third of a century, no article on American literature appearing in current periodicals has disturbed them. One is tempted to say, with Poe's Montresor, *"In pace requiescant."*

But the affectionate respect which enveloped the two poets and their few poems for almost a hundred years makes one reluctant to drop them into the litter basket of literary history. . . .

In 1877, ten years after the death of Halleck, almost thirty years after his retirement from business and from New York, almost fifty years after he had ceased to write poetry, the city which had been the scene and in large part the subject of his brief career unveiled a statue of him in the Mall of Central Park. It was the first such statue of an American poet, and the ceremony which accompanied the unveiling was surely the grandest ever performed for an American man of letters—or likely ever to be performed. The day was the fifteenth of May, sunny and windy. There was a "great crowd in attendance"; there was a splendid assembly of very important persons, among them two generals—one of them William Tecumseh Sherman—the Mayor, the Secretary of State, the Secretary of the Interior, President Rutherford B. Hayes, and William Cullen Bryant. There was also the Seventh Regiment, marching through the 74th Street gate, "their band playing, their bayonets glinting through the green foliage," to be reviewed by Hayes and to escort him to the Mall.

The aged Bryant, influenced perhaps by the glinting bayonets, spoke first about Halleck's martial poems, especially **"Marco Bozzaris,"** but praised also "the genial and playful spirit in which" he had "satirized the follies of New-York society." Hayes, addressing the Mayor before he drew aside the bunting which veiled the statue, described Halleck as "the favored of all the early American poets": "In his life he honored the City; his works will honor the City forever. In behalf of the subscribers, I present this statue through you to the City of New-York. You will preserve it; you will prize it; you will keep it forever in these beautiful grounds as one of the precious treasures of your beautiful City." John Greenleaf Whittier had written a poem about Halleck "for the occasion" but had not been well enough to travel to New York, and so it was read by General James Grant Wilson, Halleck's biographer and editor. It charged the city to make room among the "graven shapes" of soldiers and statesmen for "one whose gift was song." . . .

Halleck's brief poetic career began with Croaker and Company. Five years older than Drake, he had produced his share of undistinguished juvenilia and ridden on a rainbow reading Tom Campbell, but until March, 1819, he could hardly have called himself a poet. Then suddenly he was Croaker, Junior, and the talk of the town. He seems to have written about half of the Croaker poems, either alone or as a partner in the company, and to have discovered himself in the poetic identity which Drake had invented. Without the *noms de plume* of the newspapers and the initials which Halleck penciled into a copy of the 1860 edition, it would be almost impossible to tell one Croaker from another. Halleck's verses were perhaps more varied and nimble. Here is a stanza by Croaker and Co. of which the tune seems to be Drake's:

> The horse that twice a week I ride.
> At Mother Dawson's eats his fill;
> My books at Goodrich's abide,
> My country-seat is Weehawk Hill;
> My morning lounge is Eastburn's shop,
> At Poppleton's I take my lunch;
> Niblo prepares my mutton chop,
> And Jennings makes my whiskey-punch.

And here is one by Croaker, Junior:

> There's a wonderful charm in that sort of
>   renown,
> Which consists in becoming *"the talk of the
>   town;"*
> 'Tis a pleasure which none but *"your truly great"*
>   feels,
> To be followed about by a mob at one's heels;
> And to hear, from the gazing and mouth-open
>   throng,
> The dear words, *"that's he"* as one trudges
>   along;
> While Beauty, all anxious, stands up on tip-toes,
> Leans on her beau's shoulders, and lisps *"there
>   he goes."*

But throughout the sequence the subjects are the same, the tone is the same, there is the same delight in detail and in New York. It is hardly surprising that many victims and spectators thought the game had been played by a single "wicked wag called Croaker."

The last squib was set off in the *Post* on July 24, 1819. A few months later Drake's illness recurred, and that winter he fled, vainly, to New Orleans; he seems not to have written again. Halleck, knowing now the nature of his own gifts and the delights of using them, turned almost immediately to the composition of a long poem somewhat in the *Croaker* mood, somewhat in the manner of Frere and late Byron, but curiously different. It was finished by the fall and published, anonymously, in December. *Fanny,* he called it.

A bookshop triumph, partly because its *Croaker* affiliations were immediately recognized, *Fanny* was handsomely treated by reviewers—one of whom thought it much better than Byron's *Beppo*—widely imitated, and even "continued" by another hand so that Halleck was obliged to write a sequel of his own for the second edition in 1821. What Drake thought of the first edition, reading it perhaps on his winter journey to New Orleans, perhaps on his spring voyage home, is unrecorded; sadly so, for *Fanny*

was the poem he might have written, the major achievement of the poet whom Poe called Drake-Halleck.

Poe disliked *Fanny.* He found its meters so neglectful of "the laws of verse," that he actually scanned a few lines to demonstrate their irregularity and rewrote two which he discovered to be "deficient in half a foot." He was also offended by "the forced introduction of one or two serious songs, put into the mouth of the *parvenu,* in defiance of every thing like keeping." George Parsons Lathrop, though less pedantic than Poe, considered *Fanny* "the flattest, tamest, dreariest of comic poems" and thought the lyrics "enigmatic" and in themselves feeble. What Poe and Lathrop saw in *Fanny* is indeed there. No verse so varied and flexible, so close to the rhythms of speech, had been published in America before 1819. No poem had been more consciously defiant of "keeping" a traditional consistency in genre and tone. The comedy *is* low-keyed and gently sad. Of course the lyrics are feeble: they are the work of a newly-rich merchant and politician who had kept "some fifteen years ago, / A retail dry-good shop in Chatham Street" and who feels, along with ambition for himself and his daughter, the "fire of poetry within him burning." They are hardly enigmatic even if the poem is read as simply satire aimed at a *parvenu.*

Fanny is to some degree such a satire; it records teasingly the steps by which a man climbs from Chatham Street to Broadway and "a mansion of the best of brick," where

> when the thousand lights of spermaceti
> Streamed like a shower of sunbeams—and free
>   tresses
> Wild as the heads that waved them—and a
>   pretty
> Collection of the latest Paris dresses
> Wandered about the room like things divine,
> It was, as I was told, extremely fine.

But the merchant is at worst vain, foolish, and imprudent, and vanity and folly are for Halleck the amiable weaknesses not only of his beloved New York but of the world. Miss Fanny is a pretty girl "whose high destiny it was to breathe / Ere long, the air of Broadway or Park Place," a little forward perhaps

> and yet
> The lady meant no harm; her only aim
> Was but to be admired by all she met,
> And the free homage of the heart to claim;
> And if she showed too plainly this intention,
> Others have done the same—'twas not of her
>   invention.

The narrator stands at no great distance from Fanny and her father, stands for no notably superior moral or social values. When the chandelier falls to the polished floor and the mansion totters, neither narrator nor reader rejoices. Money vanishes, a sign says "this house is to let," and Fanny and her father "live now, like chameleons, upon air / And hope and such cold unsubstantial dishes." What has happened is a fall, not a tragic one surely but not quite a comic one either. The merchant's "sentimental song—his saddest, and his last"—with which *Fanny* concludes—is written after he has heard the band playing, as it does once a week from the balcony of Scudder's Museum on

Broadway. The song is a parody of fashionable sentimentality, but Halleck does not entirely laugh at it, and he uses its last two lines, "And music ceases when it rains / in Scudder's balcony," to restate what has been the undertone of his comedy, which Poe—if he had been listening—would have recognized as melancholy.

Halleck continued to write for almost a decade after Drake's death. Indeed, for nineteenth-century readers his best poems were the touching elegiac stanzas he wrote for Drake and the melodramatic ones which made Marco Bozzaris an American hero. There were a few more satires in the Croaker style but sharper-edged, of which the best was a bit of political and personal sword-play called **"The Recorder."** There was a romantic-ironic traveller's sketch, **"Alnwick Castle,"** which dramatically, sourly contrasted the chivalric past with a craven and commercial present. There were some graceful pieces of *vers de société*. But by 1826 Issac Clason, offended at the low state of contemporary American poetry—"Faugh!! thin small beer"—had exclaimed, "HALLECK, awake! shake off this drowsy sleep. / . . . You've found the silver nib of Byron's pen; / Prove that its iron stem can plow again." In 1829 Cooper complained to De Kay that Halleck's genius remained idle, and the following year a newspaper satirist, echoing Clason, chided, "Wilt thou be silent? Wake, O Halleck, wake!" In 1832 Halleck himself told an actress who had requested verses for the opening of a theater that he could no longer write, that he was "broad awake with both eyes from the morning-dream of poetry."

And now, a century and a half later, what courts should hear the case of two forgotten minor poets? Not, primarily, those of scholarship and criticism. We know probably as much as we shall ever know about both men. Nelson Adkins' biography of Halleck and Frank Pleadwell's of Drake seem as "definitive" and judicious now as they did in 1930 and 1935. Pleadwell's 1935 edition of Drake's poetry, to which his biography serves as a kind of introduction, is thorough and scholarly enough to have deserved the CEAA seal of approval and the ire of Edmund Wilson. To be sure, the only "complete" edition of Halleck is the one which James Grant Wilson did, with Halleck's assistance, in 1869; it needs to be replaced. There are probably a dozen smaller scholarly studies worth undertaking, and half that many critical examinations of poems long misunderstood or ignored. But the case is not really one for the higher courts. What "The Culprit Fay," the *Croaker* poems, and **Fanny** chiefly need is to be read once again. They need a publisher who will put them and a handful of other Drake-Halleck poems into a pamphlet that can help to supplement and vary our portly, taste-shaping, canon-forming anthologies. Better still, they need an anthologist heterodox enough to make room for poems not of the loftiest order.

For some decades now the study of American literature has been a very solemn business. We have decided who our Major Writers are, read reverently in their deep-diving bibles and legends, and heard over and over again their dark, intricate, ecstatic music. As we should have done. But from the beginning—perhaps especially at the beginning, when the hideous and desolate wilderness was also Eden and the New Jerusalem and Columbia—there were other, lighter, merrier notes to be heard. From Nathaniel Ward's farcical celebration of the springing up of the Tenth Muse and Peter Bulkeley's witty Latin epitaph for Thomas Shepard to *M'Fingal* and *The Hasty Pudding,* from Lowell and Holmes to Ogden Nash and Cole Porter, from Old Possum and Auden to Hammerstein and Sondheim, our poetry has had its writers of *scherzi.* Without them the symphony would be incomplete, the past distorted. Somewhere in that consort Halleck and Drake belong.

FURTHER READING

Biography

Adkins, Nelson Frederick. *Fitz-Greene Halleck: An Early Knickerbocker Wit and Poet.* New Haven: Yale University Press, 1930, 461 p.

> The most complete biography of Halleck, including several previously uncollected letters and poems and a bibliography of his published works.

Howe, M. A. DeWolfe. "American Bookmen: Willis, Halleck, and Drake." *The Bookman* V, No. 4 (June 1897): 304-16.

> Contains a biographical sketch and anecdotal material about the poet and his writings.

Wilson, James Grant. *The Life and Letters of Fitz-Greene Halleck.* New York: D. Appleton and Co., 1869, 607 p.

> Detailed account of Halleck's life, written by a friend of the poet. Reproduces large portions of Halleck's correspondence and juvenilia.

Additional coverage of Halleck's life and career is contained in the following source published by Gale Research: *Dictionary of Literary Biography,* Vol. 3.

Richard Jefferies

1848-1887

(Born John Richard Jefferies; also wrote as R. J.) English essayist, novelist, naturalist, and poet.

INTRODUCTION

Jefferies is best remembered for writings that combine description of the English countryside with an ardent admiration of the natural world. Jefferies is the author of some of the most detailed and interesting rural scenes in English literature; critics consider his essays intimate without being sentimental, exposing positive and negative aspects of country life.

Biographical Information

Jefferies was born in rural Wiltshire. His conventional schooling was sporadic and ended by the time he was fifteen, with most of his knowledge acquired through informal study at home and outdoors. Jeffries gained a position as a reporter for the *North Wilts Herald* at Swindon in 1866, and worked there for six years, while contributing to several other periodicals. With the publication in the London *Times* in 1872 of three letters in which he sympathized with farmers' requests for higher wages, Jefferies received wider attention as a journalist. In 1874 he married, and the couple moved to the London suburb of Surbiton in 1877. Four years later Jefferies became severely ill. He continued working, eventually dictating to his wife. He died in 1887.

Major Works

Jefferies's first published novels—*The Scarlet Shawl* (1874), *Restless Human Hearts* (1875), *World's End* (1876)—all of which focus on the upper classes, were financial as well as critical failures. In 1877 he contributed eleven articles to the *Pall Mall Gazette*; they were published the following year in book form under the title *The Gamekeeper at Home*. This collection—Jefferies's first book-length success—earned him widespread critical recognition. It was followed by three more works that originated as series in the *Pall Mall Gazette*: *Wild Life in a Southern County* (1879), *The Amateur Poacher* (1879), and *Round about a Great Estate* (1880). Also published in 1880 was *Hodge and His Masters*, which had originally appeared in the *Standard*. These four books, incorporating Jefferies's reminiscences about the sites and events of his rural childhood, established him as an authority on country life. *Wood Magic, Bevis,* and *The Story of My Heart,* all published between 1881 and 1883, were also imbued with Jefferies's love of nature, and are further characterized by reflection, urgency, and a visionary quality that

some biographers have linked with his fatal illness. Jefferies's last book published before his death, *Amaryllis at the Fair,* again treats rural characters in a country setting. It is believed to be a fictionalized account of his own family.

Critical Reception

Jefferies's literary career began early in his life, but he gained admiration slowly. His first novels focused on the life of the upper class, a subject with which he was obviously unacquainted. However, as he turned to a more familiar style and such subjects as childhood reminiscences and nature writing, his works, particularly his essays, greatly improved, and popularity soon followed. His descriptions of rural life were well-received; some scholars have suggested that the main reason for their appeal was that they commemorated an age and lifestyle that was quickly passing. While his reputation has declined in modern times, Jefferies's last works, especially his essays, are still valued as an interesting and important contribution to English nature writing.

PRINCIPAL WORKS

The Scarlet Shawl   (novel)   1874
Restless Human Hearts   (novel)   1875
World's End   (novel)   1876
The Gamekeeper at Home; or, Sketches of Natural History and Rural Life   (essays)   1878
The Amateur Poacher   (essays)   1879
Wild Life in a Southern County   (essays)   1879
Greene Ferne Farm   (novel)   1880
Hodge and His Masters   (essays)   1880
Round about a Great Estate   (essays)   1880
Wood Magic   (novel)   1881
Bevis, The Story of a Boy   (novel)   1882
Nature Near London   (essays)   1883
The Story of My Heart   (autobiography)   1883
The Dewy Morn   (novel)   1884
The Life of the Fields   (essays)   1884
After London; or, Wild England   (novel)   1885
The Open Air   (essays)   1885
Amaryllis at the Fair   (novel)   1887
Field and Hedgerow; Being the Last Essays of Richard Jefferies, Collected by His Widow   (essays)   1889
The Toilers of the Field   (essays)   1892
The Early Fiction of Richard Jefferies   (novels, essays)   1896

CRITICISM

The Saturday Review   (review date 1879)

SOURCE: A review of *The Amateur Poacher*, in *The Saturday Review*, London, Vol. 48, No. 1253, November 1, 1879, pp. 548-49.

[*In the following article, the* Saturday Review *critic provides a very positive assessment of* The Amateur Poacher.]

This third volume of a very agreeable series is perhaps in some respects more enjoyable than its predecessors. Naturally we become sensible of a certain monotony, or at least of some diminution in the freshness of the first vivid pictures. But, on the other hand, the charms of the country are infinite with a variety that never grows stale; and the author of **Wild Life** and **The Gamekeeper at Home** dwells upon them with the affection of a lifelong familiarity. In **The Amateur Poacher** we have the most delicate painting of the minutest details of our rural landscapes, with realistic sketches in eloquent language of the changing scenery of English seasons. It is full, too, of the lively autobiographical reminiscences which always give truth and colour to a book. The author began his studies in amateur poaching in the earliest years of a happy boyhood. He was bred, if not born, as he has intimated to us before, in the most delightful circumstances a boy could desire. His home was in a venerable farmhouse in a primitive country, where the occupants had the right to shoot over farms that had never been touched by modern improvements. There had been no grubbing or trimming of the luxuriant hedge-rows that divided the irregular fields; there was an abundance of the water that always attracts birds, with the pond under the alders and the brook among the osier beds, which we fancy we have heard of before. Rabbits swarmed in the banks and double mounds; snipe and even duck were to be found in the swamps and among the hedges in the season; a "cock" would now and then be flushed in the small spinneys; while, beyond the boundaries which enclosed their lawful shooting-grounds, were preserves that were strictly looked after by the keepers. The very danger of trespassing upon these forbidden domains had irresistible temptations for roving boys; and we have a thrilling account of an expedition into the great pheasant wood, although it was only upon very rare occasions that they ventured so far into the enemy's territory. The poaching indicated in the title does not necessarily imply breaking bounds. It merely means that, as boys will do, they had to follow their various sports under grave disadvantages of weapons, and were by no means particular as to the contrivances by which they circumvented the game.

The book begins with the romantic story of the youthful bent forcing its way under difficulties. It tells of the old gun with its single barrel of preposterous length, which had been hidden or forgotten in an attic popularly said to be haunted. "No modern mortal could have held that mass of metal steady to his shoulder." But the young artillerists made a gun-carriage of a chest set upon a linen-press, and they used the venerable piece of ordnance for practising sights upon animate objects from the garret window. That gun was burned in cruel kindness, lest the boys should do themselves a mischief with it; but as they were evidently set upon shooting with something or other, it was replaced a year or two after with another. Then the pair of scapegraces took the field in earnest, playing in a domestic English way at the hunter's life in the wilderness. They would sit watching for rabbits of a hot summer noon with the enduring stoicism of the Red Indian. "The shadowless recess grew like a furnace"; the black flies settled down upon them in crowds; and yet they felt bound in honour to sit motionless, in the hope of a shot at some unsuspecting rabbit. We can enter into their feelings of excitement when a woodpigeon perched upon a bough overhead, and, little dreaming of the danger immediately beneath, after assuring himself of his solitude by rapid glances all around, complacently gave them an easy opportunity; or still more, as they were navigating their craft among the osiers, when a great bird rose out of the wooded channel ahead, and dropped to a quick shot through the branches. The mysterious fowl proved to be a wild duck, and great was the triumph and rejoicing. For they had calked the seams of a water-logged old punt with dried moss and clay, and, having fitted her with a mast, a sail, and an anchor, they used to go poling her through the labyrinth of channels among the reeds. So far they had been more of sporting loafers than poachers. But their nautical tastes made them long for a handier boat, and to reach that object of their ambition money must be obtained somehow. Their ally the blacksmith was ready to buy any number of rabbits at sixpence a head, on the understanding that the vendor asked no questions. But getting rabbits with the gun was slow work, so it occurred to them that they might try their luck at wiring. The difficulty was, that though rabbits were known to be snared freely in the neighbourhood, nobody would own to having even a notion of the elements of the art. So they had to fall back on self-education and experiment, and it was only by slow degrees that they arrived at the necessary adroitness. In the chapter which gives the narrative of their studies, and elsewhere, we are taught the whole philosophy and practice of wiring. Leaving any scent of the human species is the great thing to be avoided. The grass where you lay the snare must not be touched with the hand; all the arrangements, so far as possible, must be made with the point of a walking-stick; and then, if the noose be properly adjusted, you may be pretty sure that the game will find its way into the snare. Indeed, as a veteran poacher explained to the author afterwards, he turned the instinct of the poor animals and their delicate sense of smell against themselves. For, after setting the wire in a well-trodden run, he went and rubbed his hands on the parallel tracks in its neighbourhood, when the rabbit or hare would be sure to seek an outlet from the covert by the only path in which death awaited it.

Yet the amateur poacher, like not a few of his old-fashioned professional brethren, while his mind was set upon the slaughter of the beasts of the field, felt the humanizing influences of rural scenes, and had his senses alive to the beauties of nature. Here is a very pretty picture, though no prettier or more truthful than many others, of the sights and sounds in a wood in the "egg-time." A great oak has been felled and barked: —

> From the peeled tree there rises a sweet odour of sap; the green mead, the green underwood and hawthorn around, are all lit up with the genial sunbeams. The beautiful wood anemones are gone, too tender and lovely for so rude an earth; but the wild hyacinths drop their blue bells under the wood, and the cowslips rise in the grass. The nightingale sings without ceasing; the soft coo-coo of the dove sounds hard by; the merry cuckoo calls as he flies from elm to elm; the wood-pigeons rise and smite their wings together over the firs. In the mere below the coots are at play; they chase each other along the surface of the water, and indulge in wild evolutions. Everything is happy. As the ploughboys stalk along, they pluck the young succulent hawthorn leaves, and nibble them. It is the sweetest time of all for wandering in the wood.

Then, by way of a sombre contrast, we are introduced to the "traitors on the gibbet." It was on the occasion we have referred to, when the boy had stolen into the keeper's favourite pheasant preserves, in the delightful tremors of guilt and possible detection, that his path led him to the brink of a chalky coombe. "The coombe was full of fir trees, and by them stood a long, narrow shed—the roof ruinous, but the plank walls intact. It had originally been erected in a field, since planted for covers. This long shed, a greenish-grey from age and mouldering wood, became a place of much interest." For upon it were nailed the weatherbeaten remains or the mouldering and mildewed bodies of all manner of marauding vermin. With its surrounding horrors, the canopies of spider webs under the eaves above, the rank beds of nettles beneath, it was a kind

of sylvan gibbet of Montfaucon. And there were to be seen below the rows of shrunken and weather-changed stoats and weasels, the strong beaks and ragged feathers of carrion crows, and bleached festoons of kestrels and sparrow-hawks among a profusion of the gayer plumage of jays and magpies.

But the author's notes on animated nature are by no means confined to beasts and birds. We make the acquaintance of some of those odd and rather disreputable characters who used to be in a manner privileged in these primitive districts. There is the poacher Oby, who was a master of his craft, though he practised it on regular principles and with a due regard to prudence. Indeed Oby maintained that "poaching was no use unless you did it regular." And he did it accordingly with most methodical regularity. Having been a railway navigator in his younger days, his skilled services were always in demand with the farmers, and he shifted about from farm to farm, till "he knew every hare in the parish." He studied the habits of the keepers as carefully as those of the game, and set his snares when their backs were turned. "The dodge is to be always in the fields and to know everybody's ways. . . . All of them knows I be poaching; but that makes no difference for work." Naturally the farmers made no objection to the thinning of the animals that fed upon their crops. "They sees my wires in the grass and just looks the other way." He picked up pheasants that had wandered into the fields when he could, but made a rule of never trespassing on the plantations. And when the keepers did catch him in flagrant delict, he thrust his hands into his pockets and would not be tempted to strike. "I've been before the Bench heaps of times, and paid the fine for trespass." If this Oby was identical with a namesake of his who is made to figure before the magistrates in a subsequent chapter, he must have been a man of substance in a moderate way. The Bench fined him two pounds on that occasion, which his wife, after many protests of poverty, paid out of a bag of gold and silver coins; nor did Oby bear any grudge to the justice for rigorously doing his duty. As the worthy magistrate drove past a roadside alehouse on his way home, the culprit was standing at the door with a foaming tankard in his hand, when he touched his battered hat with a look of sly humility. Another capitalist, with a similar dislike to parading his wealth, was Luke, the rabbit contractor. In fact, to see the broken-down old man crawling along in winter, dressed like a scarecrow and shivering with the cold, was enough to touch the hardest heart. But Luke, in reality, had a great deal of vitality in him; he contracted for the rabbits taken in the woods of the lord of the manor, going every evening to fetch them away; he ferreted for all the surrounding farmers, and, as he never neglected his easy opportunities of poaching, many hares and pheasants came to an untimely end by him. The upshot of his industry was that in his declining years he might have retired on his fortune had he been so disposed. For he was the real owner of the carrier's cart which carried his rabbits and stolen game to the market; he had put his nephew into a public-house, where the keepers and bailiffs who winked at his practices had the privilege of calling for what they liked in moderation; and he was proprietor besides of more than one cottage. A far more creditable acquaintance was the venerable Farmer Willum, who had been a keen sportsman all his life, and gave the boys capital shooting on his farm; though Farmer Willum, too, bore no good will to the keepers, and was delighted that his youthful *protégés* should do some poaching on the sly. Then there is Farmer Willum's sporting henchman, "Little John," whose passion for ferreting in an honest way had grown into an absorbing mania. But, after calling attention to so many of the subjects in this little volume we are the more sensible of our unavoidable omissions, and can only advise all lovers of the country to get *The Amateur Poacher* and read it for themselves.

James Purves   (essay date 1883)

SOURCE: A review of *The Story of My Heart: My Autobiography,* in *The Academy*, No. 600, November 3, 1883, p. 294.

[*Here, Purves appraises* The Story of My Heart, *calling the book "a contribution to the ideal in life."*]

This book is decidedly clever, though very unsatisfactory. Mr. Jefferies has not told the story of his own heart so well as he told the stories of *The Gamekeeper at Home* and *The Amateur Poacher.* "If a man does not keep pace with his companions, perhaps it is because he hears a different drummer; let him step to the music which he hears, however measured or far away." So said Thoreau in *Walden*; and Mr. Jefferies for the first time seems to step out to the music of the American, and follow in his wake. To appreciate the real value of the book before us the reader should take up *Walden* first, and he will be astonished at the similarity of ideas, though the American possesses the most. Mr. Jefferies has no sense of humour, and a little humour would have added force to his passionate pleading; nor has he much human feeling. The title is incorrect: there is little about his heart in the book; and it would be better described as the "Desires of a Naturalist." The pages throb with passionate vigour, and fall into dreamy contemplation; and sometimes he cries aloud, but not, like wisdom, in the streets. For the first time he has the courage to speak out; and he pictures a life which he has, by his own statement, not the courage to live. We feel, without being told, that the stirring thoughts have been forced from him by earnestness of heart, and they express his most serious convictions; but the wonder is he has not presented them with more point and artistic sequence and more rounded effect since he says that he has had them seventeen years in his mind. He steps to Thoreau's music—that of the Ideal; and though, unlike him, he gives no quotations, he would not have been less original if he had quoted occasionally. The book is a fragment of outspoken moods, pleasant to read, and difficult to criticise from its disorder. It treats of the ideal in life, the laws of chance, the absence of time, the relentlessness in nature—subjects as old as the Bible. It embraces philosophy, science, religion, and even paupers. "Oh, inexpressibly wicked word! it is the well-to-do who are the criminal classes." This is a delightfully naïve piece of autobiography, as we presume Mr. Jefferies is himself well-to-do.

His pages are full of beauty, and alive with nature, the sea, the stars, and London; his finest description is that of the city and river life and scenery from the bridge. His book is a plea—and a strong plea it is—to hold communion with nature, with which he prayed as if with "the keys of an instrument of an organ;" and he exclaims, "Who could have imagined the whirlwind of passion that was going on within me as I reclined there!" (on the hilltop), which is made ludicrous by the following matter-of-fact sentence: —"I was greatly exhausted when I reached home." Some pages succeed in conveying his genuine feeling of being intoxicated with the spirit of the fields and flowers, birds and streams, seas and stars; and the immense time of the cycles of ages "lifted me like a wave rolling under a boat." With him we feel the glow of the romance of open air, the mystery of living things; and when he is at his best his power is well-nigh irresistible. He gives us a joyousness in life for life's own sweet sake; he has the pagan feeling—the thirst after hills, the joy of walking, the pleasure of sight, the sense of touch; and the marvellous beauty of nature and her sounds are like meat and drink to him. "The intense life of the senses, there is never enough for me. I envy Semiramis; I would have been ten times Semiramis." One wonders if it would not have been more effective to have stated that Semiramis would have been ten times Mr. Jefferies to-day in the old Castle of Pevensey or in front of the Royal Exchange. Like Thoreau, Mr. Jefferies brags as lustily as chanticleer in the morning, if only to wake his neighbours up; and he brags more for humanity than for himself. There is little pleading in his plea for "soul-life"— it is brag; and the strange thing is that Mr. Jefferies does not, like Thoreau, conform to his own teaching. At times there is felt the flavour of Ruskin—an incompleteness leading to no definite issue; while in some pages he works out Mr. Austin Dobson's refrain, "Ah, no; Time stays, we go."

According to our author, the ideal of man is to be idle, and idleness is a great good. We are all to become ideal paupers; no man is to die but of old age, and old age is possible, and "perhaps even more than old age."

> They shall not work for bread, but for their souls. I am willing to divide and share all I shall ever have for this purpose [that they may rest by the sea and dream, that they may enjoy their days and the earth and the beauty of this beautiful world], though I think the end will rather be gained by organisation than by standing alone.

He who rejoices in idleness and in the rapture of admiration is somewhat inconsistent in marvelling that human life with all its centuries has not filled a granary or organised itself for its own comfort; and he is forgetful of Brooke Farm experience. Can he expect idealised paupers to accomplish his aims? Argument is not his strong point: for instance, he holds that all events occur in human affairs by chance; and, again, that all accidents are crimes. He believes in miracles, and adduces himself as a living witness. "Except when I walk by the sea," he says, in what reads like great egotism, "and my soul is by it, the sea is dead." He would like to be buried on a pyre of pine wood on a hill-top, and likens himself to a cave man, because written traditions, systems of culture, and modes of thought have for him no existence; and he attempts to show the absolute indifference of nature to man, and the presence of no more feeling or design "than the force which lifts the tides." This feeling the novelist Mr. Hardy has produced with more marvellous effects in his rustic novels.

The book is a contribution to the ideal in life. It is composed of day dreams—dreams which haunt an earnest mind as night follows day; and its real value lies in its plea for walking on foot and keeping our eyes and ears open to nature, for there is really little "heart" or human interest in it. The following sentences, though somewhat vague, are probably the most poetic in thought and expression which Mr. Jefferies has yet written: —

> Give me life, strong and full as the brimming ocean; give me thoughts wide as its plain; give me a soul beyond these. Sweet is the bitter sea by the shore where the faint blue pebbles are lapped by the green-gray wave, where the wind-quivering foam is loth to leave the lashed stone. Sweet is the bitter sea, and the clear green in which the gaze seeks the soul, looking through the glass into itself. The sea thinks for me as I listen and ponder; the sea thinks, and every boom of the wave repeats my prayer.

Walter Besant   (essay date 1888)

SOURCE: "Fiction, Early and Late," in *The Eulogy of Richard Jefferies,* Longmans, Green and Co., 1888, pp. 145-62.

[*Besant was a prolific English novelist, historian, and critic who used fiction to expose and denounce the social evils of late-Victorian England. In the excerpt below, Besant discusses the failure of Jefferies's early novels.*]

The Scarlet Shawl was published in July, 1874, in one volume. As the work is stated on the title-page to have advanced to a second edition, one of two things is certain—namely, either the book appealed to a large number of readers, or the editions were very small indeed. I incline, myself, to the latter opinion.

Great as is the admiration of Jefferies' readers for his best and noblest work, it must be frankly confessed that, regarded as a story-teller, he is not successful. Why this is so we will presently inquire. As regards this, his earliest serious work of fiction, there is one remarkable fact, quite without precedent in the history of literature—it is that the book affords not the slightest indication of genius, insight, descriptive or dramatic power, or, indeed, of any power, especially of that kind with which he was destined to make his name. It is a book which any publisher's reader, after glancing at the pages, would order to be returned instantly, without opinion given or explanation offered; it is a book which a young man of such real promise, with such a splendid career before him, ought somehow to have been prevented from publishing. Two reviews of it are preserved in a certain book of extracts—one from the *Athenæum,* and one from the *Graphic.* The story was also made a peg by a writer in the *Globe* for some unkind remarks about modern fiction generally. It is only mentioned here because we would not be accused of suppressing facts, and because there is no author who has not made

similar false starts, mistakes, and attempts in lines unsuited to his genius. It is not much blame to Jefferies that his first novel was poor; it was his misfortune that no one told him at the outset that a book of which the author has to pay the expense of production is probably worthless. It is, perhaps, wonderful that the author could possibly think it good. There are, one imagines, limits even to an author's illusions as regards his own work. But it is not so wonderful that Jefferies should at this time, when he was still quite young and ignorant of the world, write a worthless book, as that he should at any time at all write a book which had not the least touch of promise or of power.

Consider, however. What is the reason why a young author so often shows a complete inability to discover how bad his early work really is? It is that he is wholly unable to understand—no young writer can understand—the enormous difference between his powers of conception and imagination—which are often enormous—and those of execution. If it were worth while, I think it would be possible to extricate from the crude pages of *The Scarlet Shawl* the real novel which the writer actually had in his mind, and fondly thought to have transferred to the printed page. That novel would, I dare say, have been sweet and wholesome, pure and poetical. The thing which he submitted to the public was a work in which all these qualities were conspicuously wanting. The young poet reads his own verses, his mind full of splendid images, half-formed characters, clouds of bewildering colours, and imagines that he has fixed these floating splendours in immortal verse. When he has forgotten what was in his mind while he was writing that verse, he will be able to understand how feeble are his rhymes, but not till then. I offer this as some explanation of these early novels.

Consider, again. He never was a novelist; he never could be one. To begin with, he knew nothing of society, nothing of men and women, except the people of a small country town. There are, truly, materials for dramatic fiction in plenty upon a farm and in a village; but Jefferies was not the man to perceive them and to use them. His strength lay elsewhere, and as yet he had not found his strength.

Another reason why he could never be a novelist was that he wholly lacked the dramatic faculty. He could draw splendid landscapes, but he could not connect them together by the thread of human interest. Nature in his books is always first, and humanity always second. Two figures are in the foreground, but one hardly cares to look at them in contemplating the wonderful picture which surrounds them.

Again, he did not understand, so to speak, stage management. When he had got a lot of puppets in his hands, he could not make them act. And he was too self-contained to be a novelist; he could never get rid of his own personality. When he succeeds in making his reader realize a character, it is when that character is either himself, as in *Bevis,* or a part of himself, as Farmer Iden in *Amaryllis.* The story in his earlier attempts is always imitative, awkward, and conventional; it is never natural and never spontaneous. In his later books he lays aside all but the mere pretence of a story. The individual pictures which he presents are delightful and wonderful; they are like his short essays and articles—they may be read with enormous pleasure—but the story, what is the story? Where is it? There is none. There is only the promise of a story not worked out—left, not half untold, but hardly begun, as in *After London* and in *Amaryllis at the Fair.* You may put down any of his so-called novels at any time with no more regret than that this scene or that picture was not longer. As the writer never took any interest in his own characters—one understands that as clearly as if it was proclaimed upon the house-tops—so none of his readers can be expected to feel any interest. It is the old, old story. In any kind of art—it matters not what—if you wish your readers to weep, you must first be constrained to weep yourself. Many other reasons might be produced for showing that Jefferies could never have been a successful novelist; but these may suffice.

Meantime, the wonder remains. How could the same hand write the coarse and clumsy *Scarlet Shawl* which was shortly to give the world such sweet and delicate work, so truthful, so artistic, so full of fine feeling? How could that be possible? Indeed, one cannot altogether explain it. Collectors of Jefferies' books—unless they are mere collectors who want to have a complete set—will do well to omit the early novels. They belong to that class of book which quickly becomes scarce, but never becomes rare.

There are limitations in the work of every man. With such a man as Jefferies, the limitations were narrower than with most of those who make a mark in the history of literature. He was to succeed in one way—only in one way. Outside that way, failure, check, disappointment, even derision, awaited him. In the *Eulogy of Richard Jefferies* one can afford to confess these limitations. He is so richly endowed that one can well afford to confess them. It no more detracts from his worth and the quality of his work to own that he was no novelist than it would be to confess that he was no sculptor.

But the wonder of it! How *could* such a man write these works, being already five or six and twenty years of age, without revealing himself? It is as if one who was to become a great singer should make his first attempt and break down without even revealing the fact that he had a noble voice, as yet untrained. Or as if one destined to be a great painter should send in a picture for exhibition in which there was no drawing, or sense of colour, or grouping, or management of lights, or any promise at all. The thing cannot be wholly explained. It is a phenomenon in literature.

It is best, I say, to acknowledge these limitations fully and frankly, so that we may go on with nothing, so to speak, to conceal. Let us grant all the objections to Jefferies as a story-teller that anyone may choose to make. In the ordinary sense of the word, Jefferies was not a novelist; in the artistic sense of the word, he was not a novelist. This fully understood and conceded, we can afterwards consider his later so-called novels as so many storehouses filled with priceless treasure.

I have in my hands certain letters which Jefferies addressed to Messrs. Tinsley Brothers on the subject of his MSS. They are curious, and rather saddening to read.

They begin in the year 1872 with proposals that the firm should publish a work called *Only a Girl,* "the leading idea of which is the delineation of a girl entirely unconventional, entirely unfettered by precedent, and in sentiment always true to herself." He writes a first letter on the subject in May. In September he reopens the subject.

> The scenery is a description of that found in this county, with every portion of which I have been familiar for many years. The characters are drawn from life, though so far disguised as to render too easy identification impossible. I have worked in many of the traditions of Wilts, endeavouring, in fact, in a humble manner to do for that county what Whyte Melville has done for Northampton and Miss Braddon for Yorkshire.

As nothing more is written on the subject of *Only a Girl,* I suppose she was suppressed altogether, or worked up into another book.

In 1874 he attacks the same publishers with a new MS. This time it is *The Scarlet Shawl.* It will be easily understood, from what has gone before, that he was asked to pay a sum of money in advance in order to cover the risk—in this case, to pay before-hand the certain loss. He objected to the amount proposed, and says with charming simplicity:

> I mean to become a name sooner or later. I shall stick to the first publisher who takes me up; and, unless I am very much mistaken, we shall make money. To write a tale is to me as easy as to write a letter, and I do not see why I should not issue two a year for the next twelve or fifteen years. I can hardly see the possible loss from a novel.

This is really wonderful. This young man knows so little about the writing of novels as to suppose that, because it is easy for him to write two *Scarlet Shawls* a year, there can be no possible loss in them! You see that he had everything to learn. You may also observe that from the beginning he has never faltered in his one ambition. He will succeed; and he will succeed in literature.

Terms are finally agreed upon, and *The Scarlet Shawl* is produced. Some time afterwards he writes for a cheque, and receives an account, whether accompanied by a cheque or not does not appear. But he submits the account to a friend, who assures him that it is correct. Thus satisfied, he finishes a second story, this time in three volumes. It was called *Restless Human Hearts.*

In the following year *Restless Human Hearts,* in three volumes, was brought out by the same firm. In the book of extracts, from which I have already drawn, there are four or five reviews preserved. They are all of the same opinion, and it is not a flattering opinion. The *Graphic* admitted that there was one scene drawn with considerable power. One need not dwell longer upon this work. Jefferies, in fact, was describing a society of which he knew absolutely nothing, and was drawing on his imagination for a picture which he tendered as one of contemporary manners. At this juncture—nay, at every point—of his literary career, he wanted someone to stand at his elbow and make him tear up everything—everything—that pretended to describe a society of which he knew nothing. The hero appears to have been a wicked nobleman. Heavens! what did this young provincial journalist know of wicked noblemen? But he had read about them, when he was a boy. He had read the sensational romances in which the nobleman was, at that time, always represented as desperately wicked. In these later days the nobleman of the penny novelette is generally pictured as virtuous. Why and how this change of view has been brought about it is impossible in this place to inquire; but Jefferies belonged to the generation of wicked dukes and vicious earls.

The terms upon which *Restless Human Hearts* was published do not appear from the letters extant. Jefferies writes, however, a most sensible letter on the subject. He refuses absolutely to pay any more for publishing his own books. He says:

> This is about the worst speculation into which I could possibly put the money. Therefore I am resolved to spend no more upon the matter, whether the novel gets published or not. The magazines pay well, and immediately after publication the cheque is forwarded. It seems the height of absurdity, after receiving a cheque for a magazine article, to go and pay a sum of money just to get your tale in print. I was content to do so the first time, because it is in accordance with the common rule of all trades to pay your footing.

The resemblance is not complete, let me say, because the new author, on this theory, would not pay his footing to other authors, but to a publisher, and, besides, such a proposal has never been made to any author. "I might just as well," he concludes, "put the cheque in the fire as print a tale at my own expense."

Quite so. Most sensibly put. Young authors will do well to lay this discovery to heart. They may be perfectly certain that a manuscript which respectable firms refuse to publish at their own risk and expense is not worth publishing at all, and they may just as well put their bank-notes upon the fire as pay them to a publisher for producing their works. Nay, much better, because they will thus save themselves an infinite amount of disappointment and humiliation.

Before *Restless Human Hearts* is well out of the binder's hands, he is ready—this indefatigable spinner of cobwebs—with another story. It is called *In Summer-Time.* He is apparently oblivious of the brave words quoted above, and is now ready to advance £20 towards the risk of the new novel. Nothing came of the proposal, and *In Summer-Time* went to join *Only a Girl.*

In the same year—this is really a most wonderful record of absolutely wasted energy—he has an allegory written in Bunyanesque English called *The New Pilgrim's Progress; or, A Christian's Painful Passage from the Town of Middle Class to the Golden City.* This, too, sinks into oblivion, and is heard of no more.

Undeterred by all this ill-success, Jefferies proceeds to write yet another novel, called *World's End.* He says that he has spent a whole winter upon it.

The story centres round the great property at Birmingham, considered to be worth four millions, which is without an owner. A year or two ago there was a family council at that city of a hundred claimants from America, Australia, and other places, but it is still in Chancery. This is the core, or kernel, round which the plot develops itself. I think, upon perusal, you would find it a striking book, and full of original ideas.

In consideration of the failure of *Restless Human Hearts,* he offers his publisher the whole of the first edition for nothing, which seems fair, and one hopes that his publisher recouped by this first edition his previous losses. The reviewers were kinder to *World's End.* The *Queen,* the *Graphic,* and the *Spectator* spoke of it with measured approbation, but no enthusiasm.

He writes again, offering a fourth novel, called *The Dewy Morn*; but as no more letters follow, it is probable that the work was refused. This looks as if the success of *World's End* was limited. *The Dewy Morn,* in the later style, was published in 1884 by Messrs. Chapman and Hall.

The appearance of *World's End* marks the conclusion of one period of his life. Henceforth Jefferies abandons his ill-starred attempts to paint manners which he never saw, a society to which he never belonged, and the life of people concerning whom he knew nothing. He has at last made the discovery that this kind of work is absolutely futile. Yet he does not actually realize the fact until he has made many failures, and wasted a great deal of time, and is nearly thirty years of age. Henceforth his tales, if we are to call them tales, his papers, sketches, and finished pictures, will be wholly rural. He has written *The Dewy Morn,* and apparently the works has been refused; there was little in his previous attempts to tempt a publisher any farther. He will now write *Greene Ferne Farm, Bevis, After London,* and *Amaryllis at the Fair.* They are not novels at all, though he chooses to call them novels; they are a series of pictures, some of beauty and finish incomparable, strung together by some sort of thread of human interest which nobody cares to follow.

H. S. Salt   (essay date 1894)

SOURCE: "As Poet-Naturalist," in *Richard Jefferies: A Study,* Swan Sonnenschein & Co., 1894, pp. 49-69.

[*In the following excerpt, Salt discusses the shift in Jefferies's style from naturalist to poet-naturalist, as "we find the poetical and imaginative element wielding almost complete supremacy over the merely descriptive and scientific."*]

The volumes which mark this most important transition [from naturalist to poet-naturalist] are *Wood Magic* and *Bevis,* published in 1881 and 1882 respectively, in both of which the central idea is the intimate sympathetic converse that exists, or is imagined to exist, between childhood and Nature.

The character of Bevis, the boy-hero of both stories, in spite of the tedious length of the narrative, is one of the most charming of Jefferies' creations, and has far more vitality than most of the figures in his novels. For Bevis, apart from his adventurous wanderings and voyages (which interest us chiefly as being actual records of Jefferies' own boyish freaks and imaginings), is the special favourite and confidant of Nature and her familiars—it is to him that the wild animals and birds, the trees and flowers, the streams and winds and sunshine, reveal their passwords and secrets. The well-known passages that describe Bevis' communings with the Wind are not only the best thing in *Wood Magic,* but the most significant indication of Jefferies' new departure, for both in depth of feeling and power of expression they entirely transcend anything previously written by him. Says the Wind: —

> Bevis, my love, if you want to know all about the sun, and the stars, and everything, make haste and come to me, and I will tell you, dear. In the morning, dear, get up as quick as you can, and drink me as I come down from the hill. In the day go up on the hill, dear, and drink me again, and stay there if you can till the stars shine out, and drink still more of me.

> And by and by you will understand all about the sun, and the moon, and the stars, and the Earth which is so beautiful, Bevis. It is so beautiful, you can hardly believe how beautiful it is. Do not listen, dear, not for one moment, to the stuff and rubbish they tell you down there in the houses where they will not let me come. If they say the Earth is not beautiful, tell them they do not speak the truth. But it is not their fault, for they have never seen it, and as they have never drank me their eyes are closed, and their ears shut up tight. But every evening, dear, before you get into bed, do you go to your window, and lift the curtain and look up at the sky, and I shall be somewhere about, or else I shall be quiet in order that there may be no clouds, so that you may see the stars. In the morning, as I said before, rush out and drink me up.

In the later volumes, of which *Wood Magic* was the precursor, this mystic nature-worship is everywhere dominant. It is no longer child-life only that is credited with the wondrous secret; for Jefferies now writes without disguise as one who has received a solemn revelation of the inner beauty of the universe—the wind, the sea, the sunlight, the leaves, the mere dull earth-clods, all are alike sacred to him. "Never was such a worshipper of earth," he exclaims of himself. "The commonest pebble, dusty and marked with the stain of the ground, seems to me so wonderful; my mind works round it till it becomes the sun and centre of a system of thought and feeling. Sometimes moving aside the tufts of grass with careless fingers while resting on the sward, I found these little pebble-stones loose in the crumbly earth among the rootlets. Then, brought out from the shadow, the sunlight shone and glistened on the particles of sand that adhered to it. Particles adhered to my skin—thousands of years between finger and thumb, these atoms of quartz, and sunlight shining all that time, and flowers blooming and life glowing in all, myriads of living things, from the cold still limpet on the rock to the burning throbbing heart of man."

Or take that marvellous account in *The Story of my Heart* of his sudden brief pilgrimage to the sea:—

> There was a time when a weary restlessness came upon me, perhaps from too-long-continued labour. It was like a drought—a moral drought—as if I had been absent for many years from the sources of life and hope. The inner nature was faint, all was dry and tasteless; I was weary for the pure fresh springs of thought. Some instinctive feeling uncontrollable drove me to the sea. . . . I found the sea at last; I walked beside it in a trance away from the houses out into the wheat. The ripe corn stood up to the beach, the waves on one side of the shingle, and the yellow wheat on the other.

> There, alone, I went down to the sea. I stood where the foam came to my feet, and looked out over the sunlit waters. The great earth bearing the richness of the harvest, and its hills golden with corn, was at my back; its strength and firmness under me. The great sun shone above, the wide sea was before me, the wind came sweet and strong from the waves. The life of the earth and the sea, the glow of the sun filled me; I touched the surge with my hand, I lifted my face to the sun, I opened my lips to the wind. I prayed aloud in the roar of the waves—my soul was strong as the sea, and prayed with the sea's might. Give me fulness of life like to the sea and the sun, and to the earth and the air; give me fulness of physical life, mind equal and beyond their fulness; give me a greatness and perfection of soul higher than all things; give me my inexpressible desire which swells in me like a tide—give it to me with all the force of the sea.

We thus perceive that what had at first been ostensibly little more than an instinctive love of wild scenery and free out-door pursuits, and a powerful capacity of noting and commemorating the various features of country life, was gradually transformed and expanded into a deliberate personal faith, as Jefferies began more clearly to apprehend the meaning of that "ideal of nature," which, for him, embraced and affected human aspirations and human art no less than the nature which is (or is supposed to be) non-human and inanimate. It is one of his latest essays, **"Nature in the Louvre,"** that we find the clearest expression of this creed. Pondering long by the statue of the "Stooping Venus," he thus connects the ideal beauty of Nature with the ideal good of man: —

> Old days which I had spent wandering among the deep meadows and by green woods came back to me. In such days the fancy had often occurred to me that besides the loveliness of leaves and flowers, there must be some secret influence drawing me on as a hand might beckon. The light and colour suspended in the summer atmosphere, as colour is in stained but translucent glass, were to me always on the point of becoming tangible in some beautiful form. The hovering lines and shape never became sufficiently defined for me to know what form it could be, yet the colours and the light meant something which I was not able to fix. I was now sitting in a gallery of stone, with cold marbles, cold floors, cold

light from the windows. Without, there were only houses, the city of Paris—a city above all other cities farthest from woods and meads. Here, nevertheless, there came back to me this old thought born in the midst of flowers and wind-rustled leaves, and I saw that with it the statue before me was in concord. The living original of this work was the human impersonation of the secret influence which had beckoned me on in the forest and by running streams. She expressed in loveliness of form the colour and light of sunny days; she expressed the deep aspiring desire of the soul for the perfection of the frame in which it is encased, for the perfection of its own existence. . . . Though I cannot name the ideal good, it seems to me that it will be in some way closely associated with the ideal beauty of nature.

It has already been hinted that Jefferies' London experiences, which first awakened his mind to a more vivid interest in those great human problems which a crowded civilisation must needs face, form a sort of link between his position as a naturalist and his position as a thinker. "Nature," he says in his *Story,* "was deepened by the crowds and foot-worn stones." In certain moods he delighted in London; partly, perhaps, for the mere sensuous pleasure of the rich spectacles to be seen there (he says in *Amaryllis* that "to anyone with an eye the best entertainment in the world is a lounge in London streets"), partly also because he could there stimulate his faculty for philosophic meditation. "I am quite as familiar with London as with the country," he wrote to a correspondent. "Some people have the idea that my knowledge is confined to the fields; as a matter of fact, I have had quite as much to do with London—all parts of it, too—and am very fond of what I may call a thickness of the people such as exists there. I like the solitude of the hills, and the hum of the most crowded city; I dislike little towns and villages. I dream in London quite as much as in the woodlands. It's a wonderful place to dream in."

The obvious exaggeration in Jefferies' statement that he was "quite as familiar" with London as with the country, must be set down to the irritating effect of the common but fallacious assumption that the ardent nature lover is unable to appreciate the impressive features of the town. It is quite true that Jefferies, like Thoreau and other poet-naturalists who might be named, could not exist for any lengthy period away from the life of the fields; true also that he remarked, in very uncomplimentary terms, on some of the hideous deformities which a crowded society begets. In his essay on **"The London Road,"** for example, he has a pitiless physiognomical criticism of "the London leer."

> That hideous leer is so repulsive—one cannot endure it—but it is so common; you see it on the faces of four-fifths of the ceaseless stream that runs out from the ends of the earth of London into the green sea of the country. It disfigures the faces of the carters who go with the waggons and other vehicles; it defaces—absolutely defaces— the workmen who go forth with vans, with timber, with carpenters' work, and the policeman

standing at the corners, in London itself particularly. The London leer hangs on their faces.

Again, in his *After London*—the very title of which is opprobrious to the patriotic citizen—he draws a sombre picture of the ruins of a defunct civilisation, the pestilent fen which is the sole remnant and residue of the former metropolis of the world. Not even that "City of Dreadful Night" of the pessimist-poet's imagination is more lurid than the scene of which Jefferies' hero is the witness, when he "had penetrated into the midst of that dreadful place, of which he had heard many a tradition; how the earth was poison, the water poison, the air poison, the very light of heaven, falling through such an atmosphere, poison."

But in spite of such passages, Jefferies was keenly sensitive—as sensitive almost as De Quincey himself—to the charm of the great city, and has established a good claim to be reckoned among the foremost of London's eulogists. Like De Quincey, he has pictured the feeling of unrest and irresistible attraction that London exercises on all the surrounding districts. "There is a fascination in it; there is a magnetism stronger than that of the rock which drew the nails from Sindbad's ship. It is not business, for you may have none in the ordinary sense, it is not 'society,' it is not pleasure. It is the presence of man in his myriads. There is something in the heart which cannot be satisfied away from it." He even claims a worldwide scope for this radiating influence. "London," he thinks, "is the only *real* place in the world. The cities turn towards London as young partridges run to their mother. The cities know that they are not real. They are only houses, and wharves, and bridges, and stucco; only outside. The minds of all men in them, merchants, artists, thinkers, are bent on London. San Francisco thinks London; so does St. Petersburg."

Some of the very best of Jefferies' short essays are devoted to London scenes; for example, those on **"Sunlight in a London Square," "Venice in the East End,"** and **"The Pigeons at the British Museum,"** all of which are included, rather oddly, perhaps, in the volume entitled, *The Life of the Fields,* where, as if to account for this apparent incongruity, the author remarks in a foot-note that "the sunlight and the wind enter London, and the life of the fields is there too, if you will but see it." In *The Open Air,* again, we find him writing of **"Red Roofs of London,"** and other similar themes; but it is in *The Story of my Heart* that he gives the fullest prominence to these studies of London life. No reader of that book can ever forget the wonderful descriptions of an early summer morning on London Bridge, of the visits to the pictures at the National Gallery, and the Greek statues at the Museum, and, above all, of the streams of human life in front of the Royal Exchange.

> I used to come and stand near the apex of the promontory of pavement which juts out towards the pool of life; I still go there to ponder. Burning in the sky, the sun shone on me as when I rested in the narrow valley carved in prehistoric time. Burning in the sky, I can never forget the sun. The heat of summer is dry there as if the light carried an impalpable dust; dry, breathless heat that will not let the skin respire, but swathes up the dry fire in the blood. But beyond the heat and light, I felt the presence of the sun as I felt

it in the solitary valley, the presence of the resistless forces of the universe; the sun burned in the sky as I stood and pondered. Is there any theory, philosophy, or creed, is there any system or culture, any formulated method able to meet and satisfy each separate item of this agitated pool of human life? By which they may be guided, by which hope, by which look forward? Not a mere illusion of the craving heart—something real, as real as the solid walls of fact against which, like drifted seaweed, they are dashed; something to give each separate personality sunshine and a flower in its own existence now; something to shape this million-handed labour to an end and outcome that will leave more sunshine and more flowers to those who must succeed?

We see, then, that the mysticism which is so marked a feature of Jefferies' later writings was in part a London growth, for it was not until *after* these reveries on bridge and pavement that his vision faculty found expression. The leading thought by which his autobiographical *Story* is inspired is the intense and passionate yearning for what he calls "soul-life." Not content with those three ideas which he says the primeval cavemen wrested from the unknown darkness around them—the existence of the soul, immortality, and the deity—he desires to wrest "a fourth, and still more than a fourth, from the darkness of thought." He believes that we are even now on the verge of great spiritual discoveries, that "a great life, an entire civilisation, lies just outside the pale of common thought," and that these soul-secrets may be won by a resolute and sustained endeavour of the human mind. This "fourth idea," which cannot be formulated in words, since there are no words to express it, is the conception of a possible soul-life which is above and beyond the ideas of existence and immortality, beyond even deity itself; a spiritual entity which is even now realised in part by the absorption of the soul, in rapturous moments of reverie and devotion, into the beauty and infinity of the visible universe. In this we are often reminded of De Quincey; but in Jefferies' case there was a more distinct purpose and a deliberate perseverance in the search after the unknown.

But while the "soul-life" formed the first portion of what Jefferies calls his "prayer," the physical life was by no means forgotten or undervalued. His second aspiration is for perfection of physical beauty, the human form being to him the sum and epitome of all that is impressive in nature. To cultivate bodily strength and symmetry is as real and indispensable a duty as to aspire to soul-life, since "to be shapely of form is so infinitely beyond wealth, power, fame, all that ambition can give, that these are dust before it." Seldom have the glories of physical existence—the "wild joys of living," as Browning calls them—been celebrated with such rapturous devotion as in Jefferies' prose poem. Day and night are declared by him to be too short for their full enjoyment—the day should be sixty hours long, the night should offer forty hours of sleep. "Oh, beautiful human life!" he exclaims. "Tears come in my eyes as I think of it. So beautiful, so inexpressibly beautiful!"

We speak of Jefferies as a mystic; but it must not be forgotten that his is the mysticism of no mere visionary of the study or the cloister, but of one of the keenest and most painstaking observers that ever set eyes on nature; a mysticism which, as he himself asserts, is based not on the imaginary, but the real. "From standing face to face so long with the real earth, the real sun, and the real sea, I am firmly convinced that there is an immense range of thought quite unknown to us yet." The passages in *The Story of my Heart,* where he seems to be dimly groping his way on the very confines of this spiritual dreamland, and striving to express in words ideas which he knows can only be apprehended by the emotions, are among the most moving and impressive in recent literature; none but Jefferies could have written them, so rich are they in their confident anticipation of future intellectual discoveries, so tenderly pathetic in the sadness of their personal retrospect. . . .

Arthur Rickett   (essay date 1906)

SOURCE: "Richard Jefferies," in *The Vagabond in Literature,* J. M. Dent & Co., 1906, pp. 141-66.

[*In the following excerpt, Rickett discusses Jefferies as a vagabond temperment, stating that he "presents to my mind all the characteristics of the Vagabond," including "his many graces and charms," as well as "his notable deficiencies."*]

Looking at [Jefferies] first of all as an artist, the most obvious thing that strikes a reader is his power to convey sensuous impressions. He loved the Earth, not as some have done with the eye or ear only, but with every nerve of his body. His scenic pictures are more glowing, more ardent than those of Thoreau. There was more of the poet, less of the naturalist in Jefferies. Perhaps it would have been juster to call Thoreau a poetic naturalist, and reserved the term poet-naturalist for Jefferies. Be that as it may, no one can read Jefferies—especially such books as *Wild Life in a Southern County,* or *The Life of the Fields,* without realizing the keen sensibility of the man to the sensuous impressions of Nature.

Again and again in reading Jefferies one is reminded of the poet Keats. There is the same physical frailty of constitution and the same rare susceptibility to every manifestation of beauty. There is, moreover, the same intellectual devotion to beauty which made Keats declare Truth and Beauty to be one. And the likeness goes further still.

The reader who troubles to compare the sensuous imagery of the three great Nature poets—Wordsworth, Shelley, and Keats, will realize an individual difference in apprehending the beauties of the natural world. Wordsworth worships with his ear, Shelley with his eye, Keats with his sense of touch. Sound, colour, feeling—these things inform the poetry of these great poets, and give them their special individual charm.

Now, in Jefferies it is not so much the colour of life, or the sweet harmonies of the Earth, that he celebrates, though of course these things find a place in his prose songs. It is the "glory of the sum of things" that diffuses itself and is felt by every nerve in his body.

Take, for instance, the opening to *Wild Life in a Southern County*: —

> The inner slope of the green fosse is inclined at an angle pleasant to recline on, with the head just below the edge, in the summer sunshine. A faint sound as of a sea heard in a dream—a sibilant "sish-sish"—passes along outside, dying away and coming again as a fresh wave of the wind rushes through the bennets and the dry grass. There is the happy hum of bees—who love the hills—as they speed by laden with their golden harvest, a drowsy warmth, and the delicious odour of wild thyme. Behind, the fosse sinks and the rampart rises high and steep—two butterflies are wheeling in uncertain flight over the summit. It is only necessary to raise the head a little way, and the cool breeze refreshes the cheek—cool at this height, while the plains beneath glow under the heat.

This, too, from *The Life of the Fields*: —

> Green rushes, long and thick, standing up above the edge of the ditch, told the hour of the year, as distinctly as the shadow on the dial the hour of the day. Green and thick and sappy to the touch, they felt like summer, soft and elastic, as if full of life, mere rushes though they were. On the fingers they left a green scent; rushes have a separate scent of green, so, too, have ferns very different to that of grass or leaves. Rising from brown sheaths, the tall stems, enlarged a little in the middle like classical columns, and heavy with their sap and freshness, leaned against the hawthorn sprays. From the earth they had drawn its moisture, and made the ditch dry; some of the sweetness of the air had entered into their fibres, and the rushes—the common rushes—were full of beautiful summer.

Jefferies writings are studies in tactile sensation. This is what brings him into affinity with Keats, and this is what differentiates him from Thoreau, with whom he had much in common. Of both Jefferies and Thoreau it might be said what Emerson said of his friend, that they "saw as with a microscope, heard as with an ear-trumpet." As lovers of the open air and of the life of the open air, every sense was preternaturally quickened. But though both observed acutely, Jefferies alone felt acutely.

"To me," he says, "colour is a sort of food; every spot of colour is a drop of wine to the spirit."

It took many years for him to realize where exactly his strength as a writer lay. In early and later life he again and again essayed the novel form, but, superior as were his later fictions—*Amaryllis at the Fair*, for instance, to such crude stuff as *The Scarlet Shawl*—it is as a prose Nature poet that he will be remembered.

He knew and loved the Earth; the atmosphere of the country brought into play all the faculties of his nature. Lacking in social gifts, reserved and shy to an extreme, he neither knew much about men and women, nor cared to know much. With a few exceptions—for the most part studies of his own kith and kin—the personages of his stories are shadow people; less vital realities than the trees, the flowers, the birds, of whom he has to speak.

But where he writes of what he has felt, what he has realized, then, like every fine artist, he transmits his enthusiasm to others. Sometimes, maybe, he is so full of his subject, so engrossed with the wonders of the Earth, that the words come forth in a torrent, impetuous, overwhelming. He writes like a man beside himself with sheer joy. *The Life of the Fields* gives more than physical pleasure, more than an imaginative delight, it is a religion—the old religion of Paganism. He has, as Sir Walter Besant truly said [in his *The Eulogy of Richard Jefferies*], "communed so much with Nature, that he is intoxicated with her fulness and her beauty. He lies upon the turf, and feels the embrace of the great round world."

Even apart from fiction, his earlier work varied greatly in quality. With the publication of *The Gamekeeper at Home*, it was clear that a new force had entered English literature. A man of temperamental sympathies with men like Borrow and Thoreau, nevertheless with a power and individuality of his own. But if increasing years brought comparative recognition, they brought also fresh physical infirmities. The last few years of his life were one prolonged agony, and yet his finest work was done in them, and that splendid prose-poem, **"The Pageant of Summer,"** was dictated in the direst possible pain. As the physical frame grew weaker the passion for the Earth grew in intensity; and in his writing there is all that desperate longing for the great healing forces of Nature, that ecstasy in the glorious freedom of the open air, characteristic of the sick man.

At its best Jefferies' style is rich in sensuous charm, and remarkable no less for its eloquence of thought than for its wealth of observation. . . .

It may be well to gather up the scattered impressions, and to look at the thought that underlies his fervid utterances. Beginning as merely an interested observer of Nature, his attitude becomes more enthusiastic, as knowledge grows of her ways, and what began in observation ends in aspiration. The old cry, "Return to Nature," started by Rousseau, caught by the poets of the "Romantic Revival" in England, and echoed by the essayists of New England, fell into silence about the middle of last century. It had inspired a splendid group of Nature poets; and for a time it was felt some new gospel was needed. Scientific and philosophical problems took possession of men's minds; the intellectual and emotional life of the nation centred more and more round the life of the city. For a time this was, perhaps, inevitable. For a time Nature regarded through the eyes of fresh scientific thought had lost her charm. Even the poets who once had been content to worship, now began to criticize. Tennyson qualified his homage with reproachings. Arnold carried his books of philosophy into her presence. But at last men tired of this questioning attitude. America produced a Whitman; and in England William Morris and Richard Jefferies—among others—cried out for a simpler, freer, more childlike attitude.

"All things seem possible," declared Jefferies, "in the open air." To live according to Nature was, he assured his countrymen, no poet's fancy, but a creed of life. He spoke from his own experience; life in the open, tasting the wild sweetness of the Earth, had brought him his deepest happiness; and he cried aloud in his exultation, bidding others do likewise. "If you wish your children," says he, "to think deep things, to know the holiest emotions, take them to the woods and hills, and give them the freedom of the meadows." On the futility of bookish learning, the ugliness and sordidness of town life, he is always discoursing. His themes were not fresh ones; every reformer, every prophet of the age had preached from the same text. And none had put the case for Nature more forcibly than Wordsworth when he lamented—

The world is too much with us.

But the plea for saner ways of living cannot be urged too often, and if Jefferies in his enthusiasm exaggerates the other side of the picture, pins his faith over much on solitudes and in self-communion, too little on the gregarious instincts of humankind, yet no reformer can make any impression on his fellows save by a splendid one-sidedness.

The defect of his Nature creed which calls for the most serious criticism is not the personal isolation on which he seems to insist. We herd together so much—some unhappily by necessity, some by choice, that it would be a refreshing thing, and a wholesome thing, for most of us to be alone, more often face to face with the primal forces of Nature.

The serious defect in his thought seems to me to lie in his attitude towards the animal creation. It is summed up in his remark: "There is nothing human in any living Animal. All Nature, the Universe as far as we see, is anti- or ultra-human outside, and has no concern with man." In this statement he shows how entirely he has failed to grasp the secret of the compelling power of the Earth—a secret into which Thoreau entered so fully.

Why should the elemental forces of Nature appeal so strongly to us? Why does the dweller in the open air feel that an unseen bond of sympathy binds him to the lowest forms of sentient life? Why is a St. Francis tender towards animals? Why does a Thoreau take a joy in the company of the birds, the squirrels, and feel a sense of companionship in the very flowers? Nay, more: what is it that gives a Jefferies this sense of communion? why, if the Earth has no "concern with man," should it soothe with its benison, and fire his being with such ecstatic rapture? If this doctrine of a Universal Brotherhood is a sentimental figment, the foundation is swept away at once of Jefferies' Nature creed. His sense of happiness, his delight in the Earth, may no doubt afford him consolation, but it is an irrational comfort, an agreeable delusion.

And yet no one can read a book of Jefferies without realizing that here is no sickly fancy—however sickness may have imparted a hectic colouring here and there—but that the instinct of the Artist is more reliable than the theory of the Thinker. Undoubtedly his Nature creed is less comprehensive than Thoreau's. Jefferies regarded many animals as "good sport"; Thoreau as good friends. "Hares," he says, "are almost formed on purpose to be good sport." The remark speaks volumes. A man who could say that

has but a poor philosophic defence to offer for his rapt communion with Nature.

How can you have communion with something "anti- or ultra-human"? The large utterance, "All things seem possible in the open air" dwindles down rather meanly when the speaker looks at animals from the sportsman's point of view. Against his want of sympathy with the lower forms of creation one must put his warm-hearted plea for the agricultural poor. In his youth there was a certain harsh intolerance about his attitude towards his fellows, but he made ample amends in *Hodge and his Master,* still more in *The Dewy Morn,* for the narrow individualism of his earlier years.

One might criticize certain expressions as extravagant when he lashed out against the inequalities in society. But after all there is only a healthy Vagabond flavour about his fling at "modern civilization," and the genuine humanitarian feeling is very welcome. Some of his unpublished "Notes on the Labour Question" [quoted by H. S. Salt in his *Richard Jefferies*] are worthy of Ruskin. This, for instance, is vigorously put: —

'But they are paid to do it,' says Comfortable Respectability (which hates anything in the shape of a 'question,' glad to slur it over somehow). They are paid to do it. Go down into the pit yourself, Comfortable Respectability, and try it, as I have done, just one hour of a summer's day, then you will know the preciousness of a vulgar pot of beer! Three and sixpence a day is the price of these brawny muscles, the price of the rascally sherry you parade before your guests in such pseudo-generous profusion. One guinea a week—that is one stall at the Opera. But why do they do it? Because Hunger and Thirst drive them. These are the fearful scourges, the whips worse than the knout, which lie at the back of Capital, and give it its power. Do you suppose these human beings, with minds, and souls, and feelings, would not otherwise repose on the sweet sward, and hearken to the song-birds as you may do on your lawn at Cedar Villa?

Really the passage might have come out of *Fors Clavigera;* it is Ruskinian not only in sentiment, but in turn of expression. Ruskin impressed Jefferies very considerably, one would gather, and did much to open up his mind and broaden his sympathies. Making allowance for certain inconsistencies of mood, hope for and faith in the future, and weary scepticism, there is a fine stoicism about the philosophy of Jefferies. His was not the temperament of which optimists are made. His own terrible ill-health rendered him keenly sensitive to the pain and misery of the world. His deliberate seclusion from his fellow-men—more complete in some ways than Thoreau's, though not so ostensible—threw him back upon his own thoughts, made him morbidly introspective.

Then the æsthetic Idealism which dominated him made for melancholy, as it invariably does. The Worshipper at the shrine of Beauty is always conscious that

. . . . In the very temple of Delight
Veiled Melancholy has her sovran shrine.

He realizes the tragic ineffectuality of his aspiration—

> The desire of the moth for the star,

as Shelley expresses it, and in this line of poetry the mood finds imperishable expression.

But the melancholy that visits the Idealist—the Worshipper of Beauty—is not by any means a mood of despair. The moth may not attain the star, but it feels there *is* a star to be attained. In other words, an intimate sense of the beauty of the world carries within it, however faintly, however overlaid with sick longing, a secret hope that some day things will shape themselves all right.

And thus it is that every Idealist, bleak and wintry as his mood may be, is conscious of the latency of spring. Every Idealist, like the man in the immortal allegory of Bunyan, has a key in his bosom called Promise. This it is that keeps from madness. And so while Jefferies will exclaim: —

> The whole and the worst the pessimist can say
> is far beneath the least particle of the truth, so
> immense is the misery of man.

He will also declare, "There lives on in me an impenetrable belief, thought burning like the sun, that there is yet something to be found, something real, something to give each separate personality sunshine and flowers in its own existence now."

It is a mistake to attach much importance to Jefferies' attempts to systematize his views on life. He lacked the power of co-ordinating his impressions, and is at his best when giving free play to the instinctive life within him. No Vagabond writer can excel him in the expression of feeling; and yet perhaps no writer is less able than he to account for, to give a rational explanation of his feelings. He is rarely satisfactory when he begins to explain. Thoreau's lines about himself seem to me peculiarly applicable to Jefferies:—

> I am a parcel of vain strivings tied
> By a chance bond together,
> Dangling this way and that, their links
> Were made so loose and wide
> Methinks
> For milder weather.
>
> A bunch of violets without their roots
> And sorrel intermixed,
> Encircled by a wisp of straw
> Once coiled about their shoots,
> The law
> By which I'm fixed.
>
> Some tender buds were left upon my stem
> In mimicry of life,
> But ah, the children will not know
> Till Time has withered them,
> The woe
> With which they're rife.

Jefferies was a brave man, with a rare supply of resolution and patience. His life was one long struggle against overwhelming odds. "Three great giants," as he puts it— "disease, despair, and poverty." Not only was his physical health against him, but his very idiosyncrasies all conspired to hinder his success. His pride and reserve would

not permit him to take help from his friends. He even shrank from their sympathy. His years of isolation, voluntary isolation, put him out of touch with human society. His socialistic tendencies never made him social. His was a kind of abstract humanitarianism. A man may feel tenderly, sympathize towards humanity, yet shrink from human beings. Misanthropy did not inspire him; he did not dislike his fellow-men; it was simply that they bewildered and puzzled him; he could not get on with them. So it will be seen that he had not the consolation some men take in the sympathy and co-operation of their fellows. After all, this is more a defect of temperament than a fault of character, and he had to pay the penalty. Realizing this, it is impossible to withhold admiration for the pluck and courage of the man. As a lover of Nature, and an artist in prose, he needs no encomium to-day. In his eloquent "Eulogy" Sir Walter Besant gave fitting expression to the debt of gratitude we owe this poet-naturalist—this passionate interpreter of English country life.

What Borrow achieved for the stirring life of the road, Jefferies has done for the brooding life of the fields. What Thoreau did for the woods at Maine and the waters of Merrimac, Jefferies did for the Wiltshire streams and the Sussex hedgerows. He has invested the familiar scenery of Southern England with a new glamour, a tenderer sanctity; has arrested our indifferent vision, our careless hearing, turned our languid appreciation into a comprehending affection.

Ardent, shy, impressionable, proud, stout-hearted pagan and wistful idealist; one of the most pathetic and most interesting figures in modern literature.

Edward Thomas   (essay date 1909)

SOURCE: "Recapitulation," in *Richard Jefferies: His Life and Work*, Little, Brown & Co., 1909, pp. 317-28.

[*A poet, novelist, and critic, Thomas is the most prominent twentieth-century representative of the tradition of nature poetry in English literature. His verse displays a profound love of natural beauty and, at times, an archaic tone and diction. In the following essay, Thomas assesses the impact of Jefferies's personal life on his writings.*]

Richard Jefferies was . . . always a child of the soil, as well as of the earth in a larger sense. From father and mother he had the blood of Wiltshire and Gloucestershire farmers. He was the second child (the eldest child, a daughter, died young) of a younger son of a younger son. But it was country blood with a difference: both Gyde and Jefferies had been dipped in London, and had followed there the trade of printing; and though old John Jefferies, the grandfather, retired early, and not quite contentedly, to the mill and the bakery and the farm, and Charles Gyde ' of Islington ' was buried in Pitchcombe churchyard, they had been troubled by this change from the fields to Fleet Street and back again. Richard's mother, in spite of her good butter, was not a countrywoman, and she was soured by the life of one. His father left Wiltshire as a young man, and travelled roughly, seeing the cities of the United States. Of their sons, the two younger worked on the farm till it was given up; then the second of them went to America and stayed there. The youngest lives in a town. Richard Jefferies, the eldest son, would hardly ever work on the land. Some of his schooldays and most of his early holidays he spent near London, at Sydenham, and when he was very young began to be interested in his uncle's printing-works. Most of his relations had seen more of books than the majority of country people Two of his uncles were men of unusual accomplishment—John Luckett Jefferies, a draughtsman and musician; Frederick Gyde, draughtsman and engraver. Uncle and aunt sent books to Coate Farm. Father and grandfather had a taste for books.

The boy gave no early promise, and no special care was taken of him. He attended the ordinary schools of the poorer middle class, and those irregularly and never after he was fifteen. When not at school, he was out of doors, picking up the usual knowledge of a farmer's son, but carefully, and more and more with the help of books. Home life was not happy; he was a retiring and unpopular boy, not strong, but of great courage. Whether he was more unpopular than any unusual boy is likely to be I do not know; but all through his life he seems to have attracted little affection, and his writings show that, in return, he loved, but had no likings. Something there was in him, perhaps, akin to his uncomfortable humour, which unconsciously repelled—something that creeps into his writings, particularly in the more emphatic parts, and gives us a twinge as at an unpleasant voice. He dreamed away much time, and came early to a sense of loneliness among men and of peculiar intimacy with Nature, whom he first courted as a sportsman. Unwilling to work on the farm, he was obliged to do something soon after his schooldays, and he took to reporting for a local newspaper when he was seventeen. He began to read books of science and philosophy. He found himself at still greater odds with his family, who accused him of indolence. He expressed himself in crude, sensational stories and in local histories. He suffered from severe illnesses and great weakness several times. When he was not much past twenty he was engaged to the daughter of a neighbouring farmer.

Then he was moved by the agitation of the agricultural labourers for higher wages to write some articles on the condition of the Wiltshire labourer, and these were printed as letters in the *Times*. Here he first showed a power of forcible and simple expression, and a knowledge of those things among which his home life and work had thrown him. His point of view was that which the small farmer would naturally take, but the sense and force of the writing was worthy of the best journalism, and had he continued to work in this way he might have made a good middle-class income in London. But he was becoming master of an instrument on which he wanted to play other tunes. Instead of short stories, he now wrote novels, which are nearly always absurd where they concern well-dressed people who tip in gold, but are charming and true wherever the life of the country and of quiet country people is touched. By fiction he hoped in vain to make a large sum of money for himself and the wife whom he married in his twenty-sixth year; but he did succeed in acquiring, partly by means of it, a more emotional and profound means of expression than he was likely to have done by his sensible and practical articles on agriculture and country society.

He lost money by his fiction, and wrote fewer magazine articles than he might have done had he given himself exclusively up to them, according to the posthumous advice of a biographer. Meantime his intimacy with Nature was ripening. He was becoming a richly experienced observer of wild life in the South of England under all conditions; and his passionate moments of oneness with Nature were becoming clearer, more intelligible to himself, and more capable of articulate expression. Thus, he was at the same time developing along parallel paths his faculties as a watcher of birds and animals, of colour and form in earth and sky, as critic of social conditions, as student of human life, and as mystic. During this period of various and often wasteful production, nearly the whole of the third decade of his life, his health was fairly good, and when he was almost thirty he moved to Surbiton, near London, in order to be closer to editors and publishers and the British Museum.

He had already begun to write short sketches of the country, of the men, the wild life, and the landscape; but it was only after reaching Surbiton that he began to concentrate himself upon this work. London thrilled and delighted and repelled him, and probably stimulated him. He certainly found a market there for his work, which was readily printed in newspapers and magazines, and afterwards published with applause in the form of books. With little arrangement, but with the charm of exuberance and freshness, he poured out his stores of country knowledge. There had been unlettered men who knew much that he knew; there had been greater naturalists and more experienced sportsmen, more magical painters—at least, in verse—of country things; but no one English writer before had had such a wide knowledge of labourers, farmers, gamekeepers, poachers, of the fields, and woods, and waters, and the sky above them, by day and night; of their inhabitants that run and fly and creep, that are still and fragrant and many-coloured. No writer had been able to express this knowledge with such a pleasing element of personality in the style that mere ignorance was no bar to its enjoyment. When he wrote these books—*The Amateur Poacher* and its companions—he had no rival, nor have they since been equalled in purity, abundance, and rusticity. The writer was clearly as much of the soil as the things which he described. In his books the things themselves were alive, were given a new life by an artist's words, a life more intense than they had had for any but the few before they were thus brought on to the printed page. Here was the life of man and animal, the crude and lavish beauty of English country-life in the nineteenth century, with glimpses of the older life remembered by the men and women who still ploughed or kept sheep in Wiltshire and Surrey. In writing these four books, Jefferies was mainly drawing upon his memory and his Wiltshire notes, depicting things as he had seen and known them in his childhood and youth. The expression is mature, indeed, but the matter simple, the spirit, as a rule, one of wholesome old-fashioned enjoyment, the reflection contented and commonplace.

When these books had been written his good health was at an end, and when, in *Nature near London,* he came to describe scenes which he had not known as a young man, there was a new subtlety in the observation, at once a more microscopic and a more sensuous eye, more tenderness, a greater love of making pictures and of dwelling upon colours and forms. There was no more of the rude rustic content to be out rabbiting and fishing. The tall countryman who knew and loved all weathers as they came was bending, and spring was now intensely spring to his reawakened senses. The seasons, night and day, heat and cold, sun and rain and snow, became more sharply differentiated in his mind, and came to him with many fresh cries of joyous or pathetic appeal. In the early books the country lies before us very much as it would have appeared to James Luckett or old John Jefferies. They would have recognized everything in them, if they had had the luck to read them; the sport, the poaching, the curious notes on wild things, the old customs and pieces of gossip—these stand out clear and unquestionable as in an old woodcut. It was a priceless gift, smelling of youth and the days before the steamplough. But how different these later essays! Pain, anxiety, fatigue, had put a sharp edge on life—a keen edge, easily worn out. He was still glad to be with a shepherd, to hear about the sport, but it was characteristic of the new period that he should watch a trout for days and years, and be careful lest anyone should rob the pool of it; that he should love the old wooden plough with no machine-made lines, and discover the 'bloom' in the summer atmosphere; and confess that he often went to London with no object, and, arriving there, wandered wherever the throng might carry him. In these later essays there is often much observation that may be read for its own sake. But something was creeping into the style, staining it with more delicate dyes. The bloom in the atmosphere, the hues on an old barn-roof, were in part his own life-blood. In the earlier work we think only of the author where he is explicitly autobiographical, though we may exercise our fancy about him in an irrelevant way. Many had seen Nature just so, though he was alone in so writing of it. In the later he was more and more a singular man, a discoverer of colours, of moods, of arrangements. This was the landscape of sensuous, troubled men; here were most rare, most delicate, most fleeting things. The result was at once portraiture and landscape. Perhaps the mystic element in Jefferies, unintentionally asserted, gave its new seriousness to this work. Except in the last words of *The Poacher,* there had been little sign of it; but now, in the fanciful narrative of *Wood Magic* and the autobiographical story of *Bevis,* the mystic promise was clear in those passages where the child Bevis talked to the wind or felt with his spirit out to the stars and to the sea. For a long time Jefferies must have been imperfectly conscious of the meaning of his mystic communion with Nature. It was as a deep pool that slowly fills with an element so clear that it is unnoticed until it overflows. It overflowed, and Jefferies wrote *The Story of My Heart* in a passion.

Here for the first time was the whole man, brain, heart, and soul, the body and the senses, all that thought and dreamed and enjoyed and aspired in him. At every entrance the universe came pouring in, by all the old ways and by ways untrodden before. The book is the pledge of the value of Jefferies' work. It reveals the cosmic consciousness that had become fully developed in him soon after he turned thirty. Such acute humanity as is to be found in *The Story of My Heart* gives us confidence that what its possessor did in his prime, before and after it, is not to be neglected of those who are touched by mortal things. To past, present, and future he offers a hand that is not to be denied. Having tasted of physical, mental, and spiritual life, and aware of the diverse life of the world, in man, in beast, in tree, in earth, and sky, and sea, and stars, he comes to us as from a holy feast, face flushed, head crowned. He was discontented to some purpose with our age, with modernity, and not merely discontented, for he unsealed a new fountain of religious joy, and in the books that followed, whether he wrote of men or of Nature, he gave a rich, sensuous, and hearty pleasure, lofty delights of the spirit, a goad to a bolder, more generous life in our own inner deeps and in our social intercourse; he pointed to an everlasting source of truth and joy; he created a woman, Felise, whom it is a divine inspiration to know, and others, men and women, scarred, mournful, but undespairing, whose ordinary humanity, as in *Amaryllis,* was drawn with such minuteness and love that we enjoy while we suffer, and rise ourselves with a useful discontent and an impulse towards what is more beautiful and true. *The Story of My Heart* gathered up into itself all the spiritual experiences which had been dimly hinted at in the early novels and outdoor books. As an autobiography it is unsurpassed, because it is alone. It is a bold, intimate revelation of a singular modern mind in a style of such vitality that the thoughts are as acts, and have a strong motive and suggestive power. *The Dewy Morn* which followed, embodied the passion of the autobiography in the form of woman, beautiful and young and passionate.

Jefferies' thinking was symptomatic of the age rather than original; it is stimulating because it is personal. 'He beginneth not with obscure definitions, which must blur the margent with interpretations, and load the memory with doubtfulnesse; but he commeth to you with words set in delightful proportion, . . . and with a tale, forsooth, he commeth unto you, with a tale which holdeth children from play, and old men from the chimney-corner.' His asserted lack of tradition, his rebuke of the past, his saying that the old books must be rewritten, is a challenge to the present to take heed of itself. There is no real lack of a sense of the past in one who has a sense of co-operation with the future, which adds to the dignity of life, gives a social and eternal value to our most solitary and spiritual acts, and promises us an immortality more responsible than that of the theologians, as real if not as flattering.

The mystic consciousness which gave the original impulse to *The Story of My Heart* did not die away, though it was but seldom distinctly expressed after *The Dewy Morn.* It was diffused through his maturest essays, nevertheless, such as 'The Pageant of Summer,' 'Meadow Thoughts,' 'Nature in the Louvre,' and 'Winds of Heaven,' effecting a greater seriousness, a wider ramification of suggestion, a deeper colouring; while in the semi-scientific essays it is to be found in the increased imagination, and in the essays criticizing agricultural conditions it takes the form of deeper sympathies and more advanced thought. It gave a more solemn note to the joy which is the most striking thing in all his books, whether it is the joy of the child, the sportsman, the lover, the adventurer, the mystic, the artist, the friend of men. Against this his ill-health is nothing to record, except as something triumphed over by the spirit of life. His sadness came of his appetite for joy, which was in excess of the twenty-four hours day and the possible threescore years and ten. By this excess, resembling the excess of the oak scattering its doomed acorns and the sun parching what it has fostered, he is at one with Nature and the forces of life, and at the same time by his creative power he rescues something of what they are whirling down to oblivion and the open sea, and makes of it a rich garden, high-walled against them.

Many of the essays in *The Open Air* and *The Life of the Fields* belong to the same inspiration. Nature, described by passionate words, is harmonized with the writer's mind and with his hopes for humanity. Natural beauty and humanity are always together there. He wished to plunge human thought into sea and air and green things that it might be restored, as he hoped to be restored himself in the air of Brighton and Crowborough. Almost fevered was his joy in seeing and thinking of the beauty of Nature and humanity. Ideas, images, allusions, a rhythm here, a thought there, recurring like a burden, produce an extraordinarily opulent effect, whether the subject is a fashionable crowd, a railway-station, or a midsummer hedge. This brilliancy can be hectic and end in languor, perhaps, but ultimately it is bracing, and the north-west wind blows more often than the south.

There followed *After London, Amaryllis,* and many of the essays in *Field and Hedgerow.* The exuberance of colour and fancy in the preceding period was slowly settling down. In *Amaryllis* there is none of the glory of *The Dewy Morn.* There is even an appearance, in some of this later work, of a return to the style of *The Poacher,* though that simple lucidity and ease was refined and enriched by the poetic years between. *Amaryllis* was as new and individual as the autobiography. It tells no tale, and its construction is obviously unusual, as well as strong and inartificial; but it gives a picture of a small English farmhouse, and of a farmer and his family, which is humorous, pathetic, and intensely alive. Restless and sad and gay and wonderfully kind was the humanity that saw the Idens and the Flammas thus; that painted them stroke by stroke, correcting or enhancing earlier effects, until the whole thing breathed. 'Wild Flowers,' 'My Old Village,' 'Hours of Spring,' and many more were from the same source. They have the same minute observation, the same maturity of comment, the same atmosphere laden with opposites. They are pieces of impassioned prose, in which the writer, expressing his thoughts and recollections, moulded the form of the essay into something as original as it was in the hands of Hazlitt or Lamb. Both in their mingling of reflection and description, and in their abundant play of emotion, they stand by themselves and enlarge the boundaries of this typical form of English prose.

Few men have put themselves into words with such unconsidered variety. He expressed the whole range of a man's experience in the open air. This was not done without risks and some loss. He commented on many matters of his day and country. His lonely, retiring, and yet emphatic egoism made a hundred mistakes, narrow, ill-

considered, splenetic, fatuous. He was big enough to take these risks, and he made his impression by his sympathies, his creation, not by his antipathies. He drew Nature and human life as he saw it, and he saw it with an unusual eye for detail and with unusual wealth of personality behind. And in all of his best writing he turns from theme to theme, and his seriousness, his utter frankness, the obvious importance of the matter to himself, give us confidence in following him; and though the abundance of what he saw will continue to attract many, it is for his way of seeing, for his composition, his glowing colours, his ideas, for the passionate music wrought out of his life, that we must chiefly go to him. He is on the side of health, of beauty, of strength, of truth, of improvement in life to be wrought by increasing honesty, subtlety, tenderness, courage, and foresight. His own character, and the characters of his men and women, fortify us in our intention to live. Nature, as he thought of it, and as his books present it, is a great flood of physical and spiritual sanity, ' of pure ablution round earth's human shores,' to which he bids us resort. Turning to England in particular, he makes us feel what a heritage are its hills and waters; he even went so far as to hint that some of it should be national. It is he who, above all other writers, has produced the largest, the most abundant, and the most truthful pictures of Southern English country, both wild and cultivated.

Of the man himself we know, and apparently can know, very little. He spent as much as possible of his short life of thirty-eight years in the valleys and on the hills of Wiltshire, Surrey, Kent, and Sussex. His reading was wide, but of eccentric range. In habits he was always simple, and he did nothing unusual except to look after his own affairs. He made few friends; his habit of taking long solitary walks, and later his ill health, kept him from seeking society, and he was happy with the relations and the friends of simple tastes among whom he found himself. He was homely and unaffected in their company, and with them, as with literary and other acquaintances, he talked not much, but easily, on his own subjects and on current matters. He wrote few letters, and in none, apparently, expressed himself with anything like the deeper egoism of his books. His life went perfectly well, nourished by his own energy and by domestic affection. He had one difficulty— ill health—which in its turn threatened poverty. So long as he could send articles to the papers and magazines he was well off, but seldom able to save. He enjoyed, simply and passionately, his own life and the life of others, and in his books that enjoyment survives, and their sincerity and variety keep, and will keep, them alive; for akin to, and part of, his gift of love was his power of using words. Nothing is more mysterious than this power, along with the kindred powers of artist and musician. It is the supreme proof, above beauty, physical strength, intelligence, that a man or woman lives. Lighter than gossamer, words can entangle and hold fast all that is loveliest, and strongest, and fleetest, and most enduring, in heaven and earth. They are for the moment, perhaps, excelled by the might of policy or beauty, but only for the moment, and then all has passed away; but the words remain, and though they also pass away under the smiling of the stars, they mark our utmost achievement in time. They outlive the life of which they seem the lightest emanation—the proud, the vigorous, the melodious words. Jefferies' words, it has been well said, are like a glassy covering of the things described. But they are often more than that: the things are forgotten, and it is an aspect of them, a recreation of them, a finer development of them, which endures in the written words. These words call no attention to themselves. There is not an uncommon word, nor a word in an uncommon sense, all through Jefferies' books. There are styles which are noticeable for their very lucidity and naturalness; Jefferies' is not noticeable even to this extent. There are styles more majestic, more persuasive, more bewildering, but none which so rapidly convinces the reader of its source in the heart of one of the sincerest of men. Sometimes it is slipshod—in sound often so, for he had not a fine ear. It comes right, as a rule, by force of true vision and sincerity. On a moving subject, and amidst friends, he would speak much as he wrote. He did not make great phrases, and hardly any single sentence would prove him a master. He could argue, describe visible things and states of mind; he could be intimate, persuasive, and picturesque. No one quoted so rarely as he. He drew many sides of indoor and outdoor rustic life, human and animal, moving and at rest, and in his words these things retain their pure rusticity. Later, the neighbourhood of London made him dwell more sensuously than before on the natural beauty which contrasted with the town. Later still, the sensuous was merged and mingled with the spiritual, and the effect was more and more poetic—it might be said religious; and his style expanded to aid these larger purposes, thus being able in turn to depict Nature from the points of view of the countryman, of the sensuous painter, of the poet of humanity. So, too, with human life. Whether he touched it lightly and pictorially, as in *Round about a Great Estate,* or with love and fire, as in *The Dewy Morn,* or with minute reconstruction of acts, thoughts, conversation, and environment, as in *Amaryllis,* he was equal to the different demands upon his words. Though he had read much, it was without having played the sedulous ape that he found himself in the great tradition, an honourable descendant of masters, the disciple of none, and himself secure of descendants; for he allied himself to Nature, and still plays his part in her office of granting health, and hearty pleasure, and consolation, and the delights of the senses and of the spirit, to men.

William Ernest Henley   (essay date 1921)

SOURCE: "Jefferies," in *Views and Reviews: Essays in Appreciation,* Macmillan and Co., Limited, 1921, pp. 161-66.

[Henley was an important figure in the counter-decadent movement of the 1890s. As editor of the National Observer *and the* New Review, *Henley was an invigorating force in English literature, publishing and defending the early works of such writers as H. G. Wells, Thomas Hardy, and Bernard Shaw. Below, Henley focuses on the qualities that made Jefferies's writings popular.]*

I love to think of Jefferies as a kind of literary Leatherstocking. His style, his mental qualities, the field he worked in, the chase he followed, were peculiar to himself, and as he was without a rival, so was he without a second. Reduced to its simplest expression, his was a mind compact of observation and of memory. He writes as one who watches always, who sees everything, who forgets nothing. As his lot was cast in country places, among wood and pasturage and corn, by coverts teeming with game and quick with insect life, and as withal he had the hunter's patience and quick-sightedness, his faculty of looking and listening and of noting and remembering, his readiness of deduction and insistence of pursuit—there entered gradually into his mind a greater quantity of natural England, her leaves and flowers, her winds and skies, her wild things and tame, her beauties and humours and discomforts, than was ever, perhaps, the possession of writing Briton. This property he conveyed to his countrymen in a series of books of singular freshness and interest. The style is too formal and sober, the English seldom other than homely and sufficient; there is overmuch of the reporter and nothing like enough of the artist, the note of imagination, the right creative faculty. But they are remarkable books. It is not safe to try and be beforehand with posterity, but in the case of such works as the *Gamekeeper* and *Wild Life* and with such a precedent as that established by the *Natural History of Selborne* [for which Jefferies wrote the Preface] such anticipation seems more tempting and less hazardous than usual. One has only to think of some mediæval Jefferies attached to the staff of Robin Hood, and writing about Needwood and Charnwood as his descendant wrote about the South Downs, to imagine an historical document of priceless value and inexhaustible interest. And in years to be, when the whole island is one vast congeries of streets, and the fox has gone down to the bustard and the dodo, and outside museums of comparative anatomy the weasel is not and the badger has ceased from the face of the earth, it is not doubtful that the *Gamekeeper* and *Wild Life* and the *Poacher*—epitomising, as they will, the rural England of certain centuries before—will be serving as material and authority for historical descriptions, historical novels, historical epics, historical pictures, and will be honoured as the most useful stuff of their kind in being.

In those first books of his Jefferies compels attention by sheer freshness of matter; he is brimful of new facts and original and pertinent observation, and that every one is vaguely familiar with and interested in the objects he is handling and explaining serves but to heighten his attractiveness. There are so many who but know of hares disguised as soup, of ants as a people on whose houses it is not good to sit down, of partridges as a motive of bread sauce! And Jefferies, retailing in plain, useful English the thousand and one curious facts that make up life for these creatures and their kind—Jefferies walking the wood, or tracking the brook, or mapping out the big tree—is some one to be heeded with gratitude. He is the Scandalous Chronicler of the warren and the rookery, the newsmonger and intelligencer of creeping things, and things that fly, and things that run; and his confidences, unique in quality and type, have the novelty and force of personal revelations. In dealing with men and women, he surrendered most of his advantage and lost the best part of his charm. The theme is old, the matter well worn, the subject common to us all; and most of us care nothing for a few facts more or less unless they be romantically conveyed. Reality is but the beginning, the raw material, of art; and it is by the artist's aid and countenance that we are used to make acquaintance with our fellows, be they generals in cocked hats or mechanics in fustian. Now Jefferies was not an artist, and so beside his stoats and hares, his pike, his rabbits, and his moles, his men and women are of little moment. You seem to have heard of them and to far better purpose from others; you have had their author's facts presented elsewhere, and that in picturesque conjunction with the great eternal interests of passion and emotion. To be aware of such a difference is to resent it; and accordingly to read is to know that Jefferies would have done well to leave Hodge and Hodge's masters alone and keep to his beasts and birds and fishes.

Is it not plain as the nose on your face that his admirers admire him injudiciously? It is true, for instance, that he is in a sense, 'too full' (the phrase is Mr. Besant's) for the generality of readers. But it is also true that he is not nearly full enough: that they look for conclusions while he is bent upon giving them only details; that they clamour for a breath of inspiration while he is bent upon emptying his notebook in decent English; that they persist in demanding a motive, a leading idea, a justification, while he with knowledge crammed is fixed in his resolve to tell them no more than that there are milestones on the Dover Road, or that there are so many nails of so many shapes and so many colours in the pig-sty at the back of Coate Farm. They prefer 'their geraniums in the conservatory.' They refuse, in any case, to call a 'picture' that which is only a long-drawn sequence of statements. They are naturally inartistic, but they have the tradition of a long and speaking series of artistic results, and instinctively they decline to recognise as art the work of one who was plainly the reverse of an artist. The artist is he who knows how to select and to inspire the results of his selection. Jefferies could do neither. He was a reporter of genius; and he never got beyond reporting. To the average reader he is wanting in the great essentials of excitement: he is prodigal of facts, and he contrives to set none down so as to make one believe in it for longer than the instant of perusal. From his work the passionate human quality is not less absent than the capacity of selection and the gift of inspiration, and all the enthusiasm of all the enthusiasts of an enthusiastic age will not make him and his work acceptable to the aforesaid average reader. In letters he is as the ideal British watercolourist in paint: the care of both is not art but facts, and again facts, and facts ever. You consider their work; you cannot see the wood for the trees; and you are fain to conclude that themselves were so much interested in the trees they did not even know the wood was there.

To come to an end with the man: —his range was very limited, and within that range his activity was excessive; yet the consequences of his enormous effort were—and are—a trifle disappointing. He thought, poor fellow! that he had the world in his hand and the public at his feet; whereas, the truth to tell, he had only the empire of a kind of back garden and the lordship of (as Mr. Besant has told us) some forty thousand out of a hundred millions of readers. You know that he suffered greatly; you know too that to the last he worked and battled on as became an honest, much-enduring, self-admiring man, as you know that in death he snatched a kind of victory, and departed this life

with dignity as one 'good at many things,' who had at last 'attained to be at rest.' You know, in a word, that he took his part in the general struggle for existence, and manfully did his best; and it is with something like a pang that you find his biographer insisting on the merits of the feat, and quoting approvingly the sentimentalists who gathered about his death-bed. To make eloquence about heroism is not the way to breed heroes; and it may be that Jefferies, had his last environment been less fluent and sonorous, would now seem something more heroic than he does.

Edward Garnett   (essay date 1922)

SOURCE: "Richard Jefferies' *Amaryllis at the Fair*," in *Modern English Essays,* Vol. 5, J. M. Dent & Sons Ltd., 1922, pp. 102-11.

[*Garnett was a prominent editor for several London publishing houses, and discovered or greatly influenced the work of many important English writers. He also published several volumes of criticism, all of which are characterized by thorough research and sound critical judgments. In the following essay, Garnett challenges the opinion of most critics that Jefferies was not a novelist, emphasizing the merit of his* Amaryllis at the Fair.]

"The book is not a novel" is a phrase often in the mouth of critics, who on second thoughts might, perhaps, add with less emphasis, "it does not conform to the common type of novel." Fortified, however, with that sense of rectitude that dictates conformity to our neighbours and a safe acquiescence in the mysterious movements of public taste, Victorian critics have exclaimed with touching unanimity—"What a pity Jefferies tried to write novels! Why didn't he stick to essays in natural history!"

What a pity Jefferies should have given us *Amaryllis at the Fair,* and *After London*! This opinion has been propagated with such fervency that it seems almost a pity to disturb it by inquiring into the nature of these his achievements. Certainly the critics and their critical echoes are united. "He wrote some later novels of indifferent merit," says a gentleman in *Chambers' Encyclopædia.* "Has any one ever been able to write with free and genuine appreciation of even the later novels?" echoes the voice of a lady, Miss Grace Toplis, writing on Jefferies. "In brief, he was an essayist and not a novelist at all," says Mr. Henry Salt. "It is therefore certain that his importance for posterity will dwindle, if it has not already dwindled, to that given by a bundle of descriptive selections. But these will occupy a foremost place on their particular shelf, the shelf at the head of which stand Gilbert White and Gray," says Mr. George Saintsbury. "He was a reporter of genius, and he never got beyond reporting. Mr. Besant has the vitalising imagination which Jefferies lacked," says Mr. Henley in his review of Walter Besant's *Eulogy of Richard Jefferies;* and again, "They are not novels as he (Walter Besant) admits, they are a series of pictures. . . . That is the way he takes Jefferies at Jefferies' worst." Yes, it is very touching this unanimity, and it is therefore a pleasure for this critic to say that in his judgment *Amaryllis at the Fair* is one of the very few later-day novels of English country life that are worth putting on one's shelf, and that to make room for it he would turn out certain highly-praised novels by Hardy which do not ring quite true, novels which the critics and the public, again with touching unanimity, have voted to be of high rank. But what is a novel? the reader may ask. A novel, says the learned Professor Annandale, is "a fictitious prose narrative, involving some plot of greater or less intricacy, and professing to give a picture of real life, generally exhibiting the passions and sentiments in a state of great activity, and especially the passion of love." Well, *Amaryllis at the Fair* is a fictitious prose narrative professing to give a picture of real life, and involving a plot of little intricacy. Certainly it exhibits the passions and sentiments in a state of great activity. But Mr Henry Salt, whose little book on Jefferies is the best yet published, further remarks: "Jefferies was quite unable to give any vivid dramatic life to his stories . . . his instinct was that of the naturalist who observes and moralises rather than that of the novelist who penetrates and interprets; and consequently his rustic characters, though strongly and clearly drawn, do not live, as, for example, those of Thomas Hardy live. . . . Men and animals are alike mere figures in his landscapes."

So far the critics. Jefferies being justly held to be "no ordinary novelist," it is inferred by most that something is wrong with *Amaryllis at the Fair,* and the book is passed over in silence. But we do not judge every novel by the same test. We do not judge *Tristram Shandy,* for example, by its intricate plot, or by its "vivid drama," we judge it simply as an artistic revelation of human life and by its humorous insight into human character. And judged by the same simple test *Amaryllis at the Fair,* we contend, is a living picture of life, a creative work of imagination of a high order. Iden, the unsuccessful farmer who "built for all time, and not for the circumstances of the hour," is a masterly piece of character drawing. But Iden is a personal portrait, the reader may object. Well, what about Uncle Toby? From what void did he spring? Iden, to our mind, is almost as masterly a conception, as broadly human a figure as Uncle Toby. And Mrs. Iden, where will you find this type of nervous, irritable wife, full of spiteful disillusioned love for her dilatory husband, better painted than by Jefferies? But Mrs. Iden is a type, not an individual, the reader may say. Excellent reader! and what about the Widow Wadman? She is no less and no more of an individual than is Mrs. Iden. It was a great feat of Sterne to create so cunningly the atmosphere of the Shandy household, but Jefferies has accomplished an artistic feat also in drawing the relations of the Idens, father, mother, and daughter. How true, how unerringly true to human nature is this picture of the Iden household; how delicately felt and rendered to a hair is his picture of the father's sluggish, masculine will, pricked ineffectually by the waspish tongue of feminine criticism. Further, we not only have the family's idiosyncrasies, their habits, mental atmosphere, and domestic story brought before us in a hundred pages, easily and instinctively by the hand of the artist, but we have the whole book steeped in the breath of English spring, the restless ache of spring that thrills through the nerves, and stirs the sluggish winter blood; we have the spring feeling breaking from the March heavens, and the March earth in copse, meadow, and ploughland as it has scarcely been rendered before by English novelist. The description of

Amaryllis running out into the March wind to call her father from his potato planting to see the daffodil; the picture of Iden pretending to sleep in his chair that he may watch the mice; the description of the girl Amaryllis watching the crowd of plain, ugly men of the countryside flocking along the road to the fair; the description of Amadis the invalid, in the old farm kitchen among the stalwart country folk—all these pictures and a dozen others in the book are painted with a masterly hand. Pictures! the critical reader may complain. Yes, pictures of living men and women. What does it matter whether a revelation of human life is conveyed to us by pictures or by action so long as it is conveyed? Mr. Saintsbury classes Jefferies with Gray, presumably because both writers have written of the English landscape. With Gray! Jefferies in his work as a naturalist and observer of wild life may be classed merely for convenience with Gilbert White. But this classification only applies to one half of Jefferies' books. By his *Wild Life in a Southern County* he stands beside Gilbert White; by his *Story of My Heart* he stands by himself, a little apart from the poets, and by *Amaryllis at the Fair* he stands among the half-dozen country writers of the century whose work is racy of the English soil and of rural English human nature. I will name three of these writers, Barnes, Cobbett, Waugh, and my attentive readers can name the other three.

To come back to *Ameryllis at the Fair,* why is it so masterly, or, further, wherein is it so masterly, the curious reader may inquire? "Is it not full of digressions? Granted that the first half of the 'novel' is beautiful in style, does not Jefferies suddenly break his method, introduce his own personality, intersperse abrupt disquisitions on food, illness, and Fleet Street? Is not that description of Iden's dinner a little—well, a little unusual? In short, is not the book a disquisition on life from the standpoint of Jefferies' personal experiences? And if this is so, how can the book be so fine an achievement?" Oh, candid reader, with the voice of authority sounding in your ears (and have we not Messrs. Henley, Saintsbury and Toplis bound in critical amity against us?) a book may break the formal rules, and yet it may yield to us just that salt of life which we may seek for vainly in the works of more faultless writers. The strength of *Amaryllis at the Fair* is that its beauty springs naturally from the prosaic earthly facts of life it narrates, and that, in the natural atmosphere breathed by its people, the prose and the poetry of their life are one. In respect of the artistic naturalness of its homely picture, the book is very superior to, say *The Mayor of Casterbridge,* where we are conscious that the author has been at work arranging and rearranging his charming studies and impressions of the old-world people of Casterbridge into the pattern of an exciting plot. Now it is precisely in the artificed dramatic story of *The Mayor of Casterbridge*—and we cite this novel as characteristic both in its strength and weakness of its distinguished author—that we are brought to feel that we have not been shown the characters of Casterbridge going their way in life naturally, but that they have been moved about, kaleidoscopically, to suit the exigencies of the plot, and that the more this is done the less significance for us have their thoughts and actions. Watching the quick whirling changes of Farfrae and Lucetta, Henchard and Newson in the matrimonial mazes of the story, we perceive indeed whence comes that atmosphere of stage crisis and stage effect which suddenly introduces a disillusioning sense of unreality, and mars the artistic unity of this charming picture, so truthful in other respects to Wessex rural life. Plot is Mr. Hardy's weakness, and perfect indeed and convincing would have been his pictures if he could have thrown his plots to the four winds. May we not be thankful, therefore, that Jefferies was no hand at elaborating a plot, and that in *Amaryllis at the Fair,* the scenes, the descriptions, the conversations are spontaneous as life, and Jefferies' commentary on them is like Fielding's commentary, a medium by which he lives with his characters. The author's imagination, memory, and instinctive perception are all working together. And thus his picture of country life in *Amaryllis* brings with it as convincing and as fresh a breath of life as we find in Cobbett's, Waugh's and Barnes' country writings. When a writer arrives at being perfectly natural in his atmosphere, his style and his subject seem to become one. He moves easily and surely. Out of the splintered mass of ideas and emotions, out of the sensations, the observations and revelations of his youth, and the atmosphere familiar to him through long feeling, he builds up a subtle and cunning picture for us, a complete illusion of life more true than the reality. For what prosaic people call the reality is merely the co-ordination in their own minds of perhaps a hundredth part of the aspects of life around them; and only this hundredth part they have noticed. But the creative mind builds up a living picture out of the hundreds of aspects most of us are congenitally blind to. This is what Jefferies has done in *Amaryllis at the Fair.* The book is rich in the contradictory forces of life, in its quick twists and turns: we feel in it there is nature working alike in the leaves of grass outside the Idens' house, in the blustering winds round the walls, and in the minds of the characters indoors; and the style is as fresh as the April wind. Everything is growing, changing, breathing in the book. But the accomplished critics do not notice these trivial strengths! It is enough for them that Jefferies was not a novelist! Indeed, Mr. Saintsbury apparently thinks that Jefferies made a mistake in drawing his philosophy from an open-air study of nature, for he writes: "Unfortunately for Jefferies his philosophic background was not like Wordsworth's, clear and cheerful, but wholly vague and partly gloomy." It was neither vague nor gloomy, we may remark, parenthetically, but we may admit that Jefferies saw too directly Nature's life to interpret all Nature's doings, *à la* Wordsworth, and lend them a philosophic, solemn significance.

The one charge that may with truth be brought against *Amaryllis at the Fair* is that its digressions damage the artistic illusion of the whole. The book shows the carelessness, the haste, the roughness of a sketch, a sketch, moreover, which Jefferies was not destined to carry to the end he had planned; but we repeat, let us be thankful that its artistic weaknesses are those of a sketch direct from nature, rather than those of an ambitious studio picture. But these digressions are an integral part of the book's character, just as the face of a man has its own blemishes: they are one with the spirit of the whole, and so, if they break somewhat the illusion of the scenes, they do not damage its spiritual unity. It is this spiritual unity on which we must insist, because *Amaryllis* is indeed Jefferies' last and complete testament on human life. He wrote it, or rather dictated it to his wife, as he lay in pain, slowly dying, and he has put into it the frankness of a dying man. How real, how solid, how deliciously sweet seemed those simple earthly joys, those human appetites of healthy, vigorous men to him! How intense is his passion and spiritual hunger for the beauty of earth! Like a flame shooting up from the log it is consuming, so this passion for the green earth, for the earth in wind and rain and sunshine, consumes the wasted, consumptive body of the dying man. The reality, the solidity of the homely farm-house life he describes spring from the intensity with which he clings to all he loves, to the cold March wind buffeting the face, the mating cries of the birds in the hot sunshine. Life is so terribly strong, so deliciously real, so full of man's unsatisfied hungry ache for happiness; and sweet is the craving, bitter the knowledge of the unfulfilment. So, inspiring and vivifying the whole, in every line of *Amaryllis* is Jefferies' philosophy of life. Jefferies "did not understand human nature," say the learned, the erudite critics. Did he not? *Amaryllis at the Fair* is one of the truest criticisms of human life, oh reader, you are likely to meet with. The mixedness of things, the old, old human muddle, the meanness and stupidity and shortsightedness of humanity, the good salty taste of life in the healthy mouth, the spirituality of love, the strong earthy roots of appetite, man's lust of life, with circumstances awry, and the sharp wind blowing alike on the just and the unjust—all is there on the printed page of *Amaryllis at the Fair.* The song of the wind and the roar of London unite and mingle therein for those who do not bring the exacting eye of superiority to this most human book.

Herbert M. Vaughan   (essay date 1931)

SOURCE: "Richard Jefferies: Natural Historian of the English Countryside (1848-1887)," in *From Anne to Victoria: Fourteen Biographical Studies Between 1702 and 1901,* Methuen & Co. Ltd., 1931, pp. 156-75.

[*Here, Vaughan explores Jefferies's writings, contending that they provide insight not only into natural history, but also into "the human element of the countryside."*]

Jefferies has had many imitators. . . . [He] was the founder of a new school in natural history. Even in the press of to-day one can discover echoes of Jefferies' influence in the small paragraphs of 'Nature Notes,' which most papers include in their columns. Of course these humble contributions own none of the racy charm of Jefferies' work, but they do undoubtedly perpetuate his attitude towards, and treatment of, the countryside. Of the many who have followed in the master's footsteps and have sought in his terms to treat of things and people rural, probably the best disciple is the late Rev. Alfred Rees, formerly of Llandyssul, Cardiganshire. Like Jefferies, Rees died early, but his two published volumes, *Ianto the Fisherman,* and *Creatures of the Night,* have accomplished very much for the lovely but remote valley of the Teifi what Jefferies did for his native Wiltshire. The pity is that Rees's books are not better known.

Of course, a good deal of Richard Jefferies' work is mere journalism—short articles afterwards published in book form—that helped to keep the pot boiling in the sad days of his long illness that ended in a premature death. His command of English is by no means of the first order, and he is a bad sinner in the matter of the split infinitive. There is a great deal of repetition and not a little padding in some of his books. Yet Jefferies undoubtedly voices a large section of the British people, and especially boys who have the natural flair for the countryside, or rather for its inhabitants whether furred, finned, or feathered. I do not think all Jefferies' descriptions of sunsets and scenery ring quite true; and he always seems to me deficient in knowledge of plant-lore, let alone of botany. He can sometimes become sentimental, and, therefore, tedious. For example, after a good deal of talk about what he calls the starry flowers of the common stitchwort, he ends thus: 'Give me the old road, the same flowers—they were only stitchworts—the old succession of days and garlands, ever weaving into it fresh wildflowers from far and near. Fetch them from distant mountains, discover them on decaying walls, in unsuspected corners; though never seen before, still they are the same; there has been a place in the heart waiting for them.' This sounds to me perilously near nonsense.

The little piece I have just quoted—from one of the essays called *The Open Air*—shows us Jefferies at his worst; probably he wrote it in time of sickness and in an introspective mood. How different is this extract from the truly charming descriptions and narratives of his earlier works! Take such a book as *The Gamekeeper at Home,* which was his first publication to win him fame and even affection. It is a very short volume, wholly without a story, yet exhibiting for us the true psychology, as it were, of a whole class, a very interesting and intelligent class, of the community, namely, the gamekeeper and his subordinates. The book appeared in 1877, and it is curious to observe how even at that date, now over half a century ago, Jefferies was already deploring the decay of the old-fashioned country life led by the squires and great landowners. What would he have said of present-day conditions, with the motor-car and even the aeroplane? What would he have thought of the late King Edward's luxurious habit of shooting pheasants from an automobile in a woodland ride? The plain fact is that the old-time romance of country life had begun to disappear even so early as the [1870s], when Jefferies first took up his pen; by the end of the nineteenth century it was utterly ruined from the picturesque and romantic point of view. Sport had become mercenary and artificial; the smaller squires, who were more conservative in their taste and less vulgar in their notions of sport, were rapidly disappearing as a class; it only needed the Great War to finish off the old country life completely. In *The Gamekeeper at Home* Jefferies shows us in pleasant rambling fashion the daily life of a great sporting estate and of its guardians, and yet how prophetic is this passage written over fifty years ago!

> The gamekeeper finds his work fall upon him harder now than it used to do: first, sportsmen look for a heavier return of killed and wounded; next, they are seldom willing to take much personal trouble to find the game, but like it in a

manner brought to them; and lastly, he thinks the shooting season has grown shorter. Gentlemen used to reside at home the greater part of the winter and spread their shooting over many months. Now the seaside season has moved on, and numbers are by the beach at the time when formerly they were in the woods. Then others go abroad; the country-houses now advertised as "to let" are almost innumerable. Time was when the local squire would have thought it derogatory to his dignity to make a commodity of his ancient mansion; now there seems quite a competition to let, and absenteeism is a reality of English as well as Irish country life. At least, such is the gamekeeper's idea, and he finds a confirmation of it in the sudden rush, as it were, upon his preserves.

Yes, Jefferies saw coming ahead the end of true sport, with the ruin or departure of the resident gentry and the advent of what we now call the profiteer or 'new rich.'

Turning to bird and beast life on the estate, Jefferies describes for us with marvellous accuracy the various enemies of the keeper: the carrion-crow, the hawk, the jay, and the owl, as well as the stoat and weasel; in short, all the destructive creatures commonly classed together as 'vermin.' Here is an admirable little sketch of the jay, with its bright plumage of bricky red and its lovely wing-feathers of richest blue.

> The Jay is a handsome bird, whose chatter enlivens the plantations, and whose bright plumage contrasts pleasantly with the dull green of the firs. A pair of jays will work a hedge in a sportsmanlike manner, one on one side, the second on the other; while the tiny wren, which creeps through the bushes as a mouse through the grass, cowers in terror or slips into a knot-hole till the danger is past. When the husbandman has sown his field with the drill, hardly has he left the gateway before a legion of small birds pours out from the hedgerows and seeks for the stray seeds. Then you may see the jay hop out among them with an air of utter innocence, settling on the larger lumps of clay for convenience of view, swelling out his breast in pride of his beauty, jerking his tail up and down as if to say, *Admire me.* With a side-long hop and two flaps of the wing, he half springs, half glides to another coign of vantage. The small birds—sparrows, chaffinches, greenfinches—instantly scatter swiftly right and left, not rising, but with a hasty run for a yard or so. They know well his murderous intent, and yet are so busy they only just put themselves out of reach, aware that, unlike the hawk, the jay cannot strike at a distance. This game will continue for a long time; the jay all the while affecting an utter indifference, yet ever on the alert till he spies his chance. It is the young or weakly partridges or pheasants that fall to the jay and magpie.

Such a brief account of the jay and his cunning shows us well how observant and critical of wild life was this Wiltshire writer, who gained his knowledge not from books but from personal experience in the open air. His very writings teach those of us who are devoted to Nature study that to probe the secrets of the open-air life around us, we must use our own eyes and draw our own conclusions. I have always heard it said that to understand bird life, the best plan is to lie still in some thicket of a copse or spinney, and with a pair of field-glasses watch the movements of the birds as they come and go at nesting-time. And this method of observation, too, must be made fairly early in the year, before the leaf is fully out, and there is consequently a clearer range of vision for the naturalist. And whilst waiting for the birds to become careless or unsuspicious of your presence, how many beauties of flowers and young foliage are revealed to the watcher! The rich brown buds of the sycamore; the half-unfolded leaves of the beeches, like quantities of tiny green butterflies; the tender tints of honeysuckle and brier-rose; to say nothing of the blue bells, the pink campion, the snowy stitchwort, and dozens of other simple flowers that fill the hedges and ditches in early spring.

To hark away from bird and beast, from field and forest, this delightful book contains a capital account of a rare relic of olden time, which no doubt Jefferies had seen in his youth, but only as a curiosity long fallen out of use. This was the terrible man-trap, which at one time, probably so late as the early years of Queen Victoria, was not infrequently placed in orchards or gardens to protect the fruit. Until comparatively recent years fruit was not only scarce and dear, but almost unprocurable by those who owned no gardens. That was, of course, long before the days of rail and steam transit, which has made every species of fruit, British and foreign, from the home-grown apple to the tropical banana, saleable everywhere and at moderate prices. But a century or so ago, choice fruit, even pears and apples, were the property of the wealthy alone, and were constantly raided by gangs or by solitary thieves. To protect their fruit, landowners and also farmers, as well as wealthy merchants in town villas, were wont to place in hiding near their best trees the man-trap, which was made precisely on the lines of the common gin or rat-trap, but of course on a far bigger scale. This is how Jefferies describes it:

> The jaws of this iron wolf are horrible to contemplate—rows of serrated projections, which fit into each other when closed, alternating with spikes a couple of inches long, like tusks. To set the trap you have to stand on the spring—the weight of a man is about sufficient to press it down. The machine itself is then hidden among the bushes or covered with dead leaves. Now touch the pan with a stout walking-stick, and the jaws cut it in two in the twinkling of an eye. They seem to snap together with a vicious energy, powerful enough to break the bone of the leg; and assuredly no man ever got free whose foot was once caught by those terrible teeth.

> The keeper will tell you that this man-trap used to be set up in the corner of the gardens and orchard belonging to the great house, which in the pre-policeman days were nightly robbed. He thinks there were quite as many traps set in the gardens just outside the towns as ever there were in the woods and preserves of the country proper. He recollects but one old man (a mole-

catcher) who had actually experienced in his youth the sensation of being caught; he went ever after lame on one foot, the sinews having been cut or divided. The trap could be chained to its place if desired; but, as a matter of fact, a chain was unnecessary, for no man could possibly drag this torturing clog along.

A still more deadly variant of the man-trap, the so-called 'poacher-stopper,' is not, I think, mentioned by Jefferies. This consisted of a stout pole, some four feet high, with a long sharp spike of steel fixed at right angles near the top of the pole. This lethal contrivance was then well covered over with brushwood and driven firmly into the soil in some likely place that the nocturnal poacher would pass in his hunting. There is a specimen of the poacher-stopper preserved in the National Museum of Wales at Cardiff, and it is a gruesome engine to contemplate.

When you have read the best of Jefferies' books, you will have gained not only a clear insight into the natural history of bird and beast, but also into the human history of the countryside. And the author's comments are not only shrewd and accurate, but they are also always fair. He saw the two sides of the land question with impartial eyes, so that his criticism of both landlord and tenant is sound and just.

Probably the best book Jefferies ever wrote is his *Wild Life in a Southern County.* It is the most human, in the strict sense of that term, of all his books. For it deals not only with fish, flesh, and fowl, but also with the human element of the countryside. In *Wild Life* we are given an excellent picture of the old English farm-life as it had been lived for many generations in the past, and was even then being lived in the writer's own youth. Things agricultural have moved swiftly since those not very distant days, so that much of the simple primitive charm, which Jefferies describes so sympathetically, has by this time already disappeared. The use of tractors and of oil-engines was still unknown in the [1880s], though the ugly steam plough was very much in evidence. Of all our southern counties, the inland county of Wiltshire is one of the sweetest and most interesting. It possesses no mountains or grand scenery; it owns no rivers of any size, and no lakes; it has no sea-shore and no wide marshes. But on the other hand, nowhere else are found such broad rich meadows, fringed with rows of tall elms and powdered in early summer with the buttercup and the ox-eyed daisy. Seen from rising ground, the flat expanses of meadow-land look like some great forest, so tall and thick and serried rises the hedge-row timber. And then, in contrast with this rich champaign, are the great swelling masses of the downs which extend from the northern to the southern ends of the shire, from Swindon to Salisbury. The ancient traditions and customs and beliefs of old rural life die hard in Wiltshire, which within its boundaries contains our two chief Druidic monuments of the past—the great circle of Avebury, near Devizes, and Stonehenge, set in the midst of the rolling expanse of Salisbury Plain. Never was there a more fruitful field for the naturalist. The great meadows, the grassy downs, the forest of Savernake, the parks and woodlands of such splendid old seats as Wilton House, Bowood, Longleat, Rood Ashton, and Roundway Park, offer innumerable and varied opportunities to the true and patient lover of Nature. And amid such beautiful scenery are scattered picturesque old market-towns such as Devizes and Marlborough and Westbury and Trowbridge and Bradford-on-Avon, and dozens of old-world villages grouped around their fine old parish churches, many of which in Jefferies' day had not been yet ruined by the hand of the restorer or the vandal.

Jefferies describes for us one such humble 'haunt of ancient peace' in his account of Wick Farm.

> Wick Farm—almost every village has its outlying wick—stands alone in the fields. It is an ancient rambling building, the present form of which is the result of successive additions at various dates, and in various styles. . . .
>
> The house has somehow shaped and fitted itself to the character of the dwellers therein: hidden and retired amongst trees, fresh and green with cherry and pear against the wall, yet the brown thatch and the old bricks subdued in tone by the weather. This individuality extends to the furniture: it is a little stiff and angular, but solid; and there are nooks and corners—as the window-seat—suggestive of placid repose; a strange opposite mixture throughout of flowery peace and silence, with an almost total lack of modern conveniences and appliances of comfort—as though the sinewy vigour of the residents disdained artificial ease. . . .
>
> Since this family dwelt here, and well within what may be called the household memory, the very races of animals have changed or been supplanted. The cows in the field used to be long-horns, much more hardy and remaining in the meadows all the winter, with no better shelter than the hedges and bushes afforded. Now the short-horns have come, and the cattle are carefully housed. The sheep were horned—up in the lumber room two or three horns are still to be found. The pigs were of a different kind, and the dogs, and the poultry. If the race of men have not changed, they have altered their costume; the smock-frock lingered longest, but even that is going.

I need hardly add that the smock-frock, going in Jefferies' days, has now wholly disappeared. All the world is wearing the same dull, drab, conventional garments; all the poetry has in our time disappeared from rural life. It was fortunate it had not wholly evanished at the date when Jefferies flourished, so that at least he was able to write so charming a record of it. Even I can remember seeing smock-frocks in the congregation of the Wiltshire church of Poulshott, and that was not many years after the date this account of Wick Farm was penned. Nor are dull, unreasoning fashion in clothes and noisy, stinking traction the sole causes of our modern rural ugliness. The hideous corrugated iron is cheap and useful, and its glaring ribbed surface everywhere strikes a discordant note in the rural landscape:

> Ye have conquered, O Progress and Science!
> The world has grown grey at your breath.

It is clear that Jefferies' talents are not wholly confined to observation and experience. He owned a powerful imagination with regard to those things that interested him, namely, the countryside and all its inhabitants, human and humbler. This innate power is clearly shown to us in his curious romance, *After London, or Wild England,* which draws a vivid picture for us of an England that has returned to primitive times, and more or less to the conditions that prevailed in the days of the Heptarchy. The novel itself I did not much care for, with its air of a forced and rather false medievalism; but the *Prologue* to the story itself makes most interesting if rather depressing reading. Jefferies describes how some miasmatic cloud suddenly sweeps over England, and indeed over all Europe, blotting out civilization, and slaying nearly all human beings with its pestilential breath—just such a visitation, on a vaster scale, as the *Vlad Velyn* of the sixth century, or the Black Death under Edward III. All the inhabitants of the great cities are wiped out; all the arts and crafts and knowledge of mechanism, and the scientific wonders to which we have grown accustomed, cease of necessity. Rivers and drains are blocked up, and the streams overflow large areas of the Midlands, transforming them into a great permanent freshwater lake. He tells us also of the effect on the countryside that is saved from the waters; how the corn crops are eaten by mice, how the domestic animals gradually become wild, and how the whole land is swiftly transformed into bush; a vast sylvan wilderness, in short, wherein the remaining men and women have difficulty in protecting themselves from the descendants of the animals that were once their harmless and useful servants, but are now grown fierce and mischievous. There is a likeness in this graphic account to some of Mr. H. G. Wells's fantastic tales.

> By the thirtieth year [from the Great Pestilence] there was not a single open place, the hills only excepted, where a man could walk, unless he followed the tracks of wild creatures, or cut himself a path. The ditches of course had long since become full of leaves and dead branches, so that the water which should have run off down them stagnated, and presently spread out into the hollow places and by the corners of what had once been fields, forming marshes, where the horsetails, flags, and sedges hid the water.' And, most terrible picture of all, we are shown how, around the erstwhile estuary of the Thames, where once flourished the great port of London, there now stretched a huge area of fetid swamp, some forty miles long by about twenty broad, over which ever hung foul and pestilential vapours. So poisonous were the water and the atmosphere of this great tract above the buried capital of the British Empire, that even water-fowl had abandoned the district; and though inexhaustible treasure was known to exist beneath this fearsome morass, none dared approach it for fear of its fevers and stench.

In *Hodge and his Masters,* a series of sketches of rural characters, which had originally appeared in the *Standard,* Jefferies deals solely with the human element of the countryside. The landlord, the tenant-farmer, the labourer, the magistrate, the parson, the fine lady of the manor-house, and a host of other familiar inhabitants of a country district, are treated in short biographical articles, all of which show the ripe judgment and sympathetic insight of the author. The book contains some wonderful pen-pictures of rural society in its widest sense. Take this sketch of a farmer who has to leave his farm, largely, as is shown, owing to his own obstinacy and even folly. He begins by abusing his landlord, who has really done him no wrong; he allows his farm to run to seed and grow unkempt; he grumbles openly; he complains about the game, about the high rent, about his taxes.

> Finally, Smith gave notice that unless the rent was reduced he should not apply to renew his lease, which would soon expire. He had not the least intention in his secret mind of leaving the farm; he never dreamed that his notice would be accepted. He and his had dwelled there for a hundred years, and were as much part and parcel of the place as the elm-trees in the hedges. . . . But the months went by, and the landlord's agent gave no sign, and at last Smith realized that he really was going to leave.
>
> Though he had so long talked of going, it came upon him like a thunderbolt. It was like an attack of some violent fever that shakes a strong man and leaves him as weak as a child. The farmer, whose meals had been so hearty, could not relish his food. His breakfast dwindled to a pretence; his lunch fell off; his dinner grew less; his supper faded; his spirits and water, the old familiar "nightcap," did him no good. His jolly ringing laugh was heard no more; from a thorough gossip he became taciturn and barely opened his lips. His clothes began to hang about him, instead of filling him all too tight; his complexion lost the red colour and became sallow; his eyes had a furtive look in them, so different to the old straightforward glance.
>
> Some said he would take to his bed and die; some said he would jump into the pond one night, to be known no more in this world. But he neither jumped into the pond nor took to his bed.

And the saddest feature of this rustic tragedy, a tragedy that is ever occurring in the countryside, is that there was no necessity for all this bitterness and final flitting from the old home. 'Smith thought very hard things of the landlord, and felt that he should have his revenge. On the other hand, the landlord thought very hard things of Smith, and not without reason. . . . There was great irritation on both sides.' Smith had, in fact, done his landlord wrong in running out the farm, and the landlord, on his part, should have sought to conciliate the angry and aggrieved tenant. With goodwill and patience on both sides, the whole miserable business might have been averted.

Just one more quotation from *Hodge and his Masters*, to show how profound was Jefferies' personal knowledge of the countryside, and of his really remarkable power of prophecy of the evils which to-day assail us.

> There exists at the present day [remember he is writing some fifty years or so ago] a class that is morally apathetic. In every village, in every hamlet, in every detached group of cottages, there are numbers of labouring men who are simply indifferent to church and to chapel alike. They neither deny nor affirm the primary truths taught in all places of worship; they are simply indifferent. Sunday comes and sees them lounging about the cottage door. They do not drink to excess, they are not more given to swearing than others, they are equally honest, and are not of ill-repute. But the moral sense seems extinct—the very idea of anything beyond gross earthly advantages never occurs to them. The days go past, the wages are paid, the food is eaten, and that is all.
>
> Looking at it from the purely philosophic point of view, there is something sad in this dull apathy. The most pronounced materialist has a faith in some form of beauty—matter itself is capable of ideal shapes in his conception. These people know no ideal. It seems impossible to reach them, because there is no chord that will respond to the most skilful touch. This class is very numerous now—a disheartening fact. . . .
>
> Besides this moral apathy, the cottager too often assumes an attitude distinctly antagonistic to every species of authority. . . . Respect for authority is extinct. The modern progressive cottager is perfectly certain that he knows as much as his immediate employer, the squire, and the parson put together. He is now the judge, the infallible authority himself. . . . He can scarcely nod his employer a common greeting in the morning. Courtesy is no longer practised. The idea in the man's mind appears to be to express contempt for his employer's property. It is an unpleasant symptom.

This is in truth something of a jeremiad as well as an accusation. If one had read these words this week, say, in the *Morning Post*, contained in a letter from some indignant landowner, one might not feel surprise. But this was actually penned by a man of the people, who understood the people of the countryside as few have done either before or after him, more than a whole generation ago. And again, Jefferies proceeds to discuss the future of the rural labourer with regard to the so-called education he has been receiving during his boyhood, but especially after his school-days are finished.

> The future literature of the labourer becomes a serious question. He will think what he reads; and what he reads at the present moment [*i.e.* fifty years ago] is of anything but an elevating character. He will think too what he hears; and he hears much of an exciting but subversive political creed, and little of any other. There are busy tongues earnestly teaching him to despise property and social order, to suggest the overthrowing of existing institutions; there is scarcely any one to instruct him in the true lesson of history. . . . There are many who are only too anxious to use the agricultural labourer as the means to effect ends which he scarcely understands. But there are few indeed who are anxious to instruct him in science or literature for his own sake.

What was a prophetic warning, based on intimate experience in Jefferies' day, has indeed become the established fact in our own. Who is to educate the denizens of the countryside as to the true relations of human society? Who is to tell them of Mazzini's maxim, that man has no *rights,* only duties? But this is a controversial matter that lies outside the scope of this study; I have merely quoted the passages above to show how far-seeing and shrewd a prophet was this simple Wiltshire yeoman, whom we think of as a charming writer on country lore and nothing further. Yet Jefferies' work, when it deals with the human side of his studies, was clearly based on intimate knowledge of and sympathy with the rural population amidst which he had moved during the whole span of his all-too-short career.

From a purely literary point of view, it is rather difficult to place Jefferies. That he is a wholesome, popular, and instructive writer there can be no question, but whether his books will live for any great length of time and become recognized classics, like White's *History of Selborne,* with which they have been compared by admirers, seems to me doubtful. Their chief value, I think, is that he has put on record an accurate account of the old English rural life just at the very moment of its final passing, or rather of its changing into something totally different. These swiftly approaching changes, both in the rural landscape and in its population, Jefferies himself was prophet enough to foresee clearly, as I have already shown; and some of his regrets over the decay of the picturesque life of the woods and farms find a cordial echo in many a present-day writer. Again, though his works make delightful reading, they often smell not a little of the lamp, and suggest the author as forcing his pen and his memory, in order to make both ends meet by newspaper articles. That was, of course, Jefferies' misfortune, not his fault. One could have wished that, like his great forerunner, White of Selborne, Jefferies had been a country parson, or land-agent, with sufficient means and ample leisure never to write except when in the proper mood. Not that the real sense of the beauty of the commonest objects in the countryside was ever absent from his eye or mind; he found beauty everywhere, and calls our attention to homely charms that but for his instruction we might easily pass unheeded.

'The warm yellow of wheat straw' (he writes in *Field and Hedgerow*) 'is very pleasant to look at on a winter's day under a grey sky; so too the straw looks nice and warm and comfortable, thrown down thickly in the yards for the roan cattle.' Of course, so simple and constant a sight as yellow straw in a farmyard *is* full of beauty, even on a dull day; but how few of us would realize this fact but for Jefferies' admiration!

Moreover, his inherent pantheism, his seeing God's handiwork in and through Nature at all times and in every place, raises Jefferies far above the general ruck of writers on natural history who admire and observe without introspection. He speaks of the intensity of his joy in lying on the Norfolk cliffs above the green waters of the North Sea, surrounded by scarlet poppies and golden crowsfoot. 'I wish I could do something more than gaze at all this scarlet and gold and crimson and green, something more than see it, not exactly to drink it or inhale it, but in some way to make it part of me, that I might live it.' Here we have

the true yearning of the poet, who is also a philosopher, for the unattainable. The sentiment that animated Jefferies can be traced in the melancholy epic of the Latin poet Lucretius. There is in truth a certain note of divine despair that intrudes constantly into all Jefferies' writings. To this extent, then, Jefferies stands apart from, and perhaps above, those writers with whom he is sometimes casually classed.

Jefferies has, of course, written a large number of books, and I believe there are complete editions of his total work to be had. But out of this mass of writings I think I should be inclined to pick out the following as representing their author at his best. First of all, *The Gamekeeper at Home,* the *doyen* of his books, that raised him to fame; then its corollary, giving the reverse side of the medal, namely, *The Amateur Poacher.* These two volumes, which are both rather short, deal almost exclusively with the wild life of the countryside. *Round About a Great Estate* might also be included under this section. Then *Wild Life in a Southern County* strikes a half-way note, something between human and animal history and criticism, and is, in my opinion, the most pleasing of all his works, where, of a truth, all is pleasant reading. And last of all, *Hodge and His Masters,* from which I have quoted pretty freely, shows us Jefferies as the close student of human nature, and also as the prophet of future country life in England. In some ways this last is the most valuable of all his books, exhibiting as it does, at their best, all Jefferies' fine qualities and his fair, open mind. Of his novels, and especially of his autobiographical works, *Bevis* and *The Story of My Heart,* frankly I have no very high opinion, though I know the latter is a fairly popular book, nor do I deny its merits. To conclude, I shall end with a final quotation from *The Amateur Poacher,* that I think not only gives us a graphic picture of the writer himself but also presents us with the key to his true kindly nature.

> I have entered many woods just for the pleasure of creeping through the brake and the thickets. Destruction in itself was not the motive; it was an overpowering instinct for woods and fields. Yet woods and fields lose half their interest without a gun—I like the power to shoot, even though I may not use it. The very perfection of our modern guns is to me one of their drawbacks: the use of them is so easy and so certain of effect that it takes away the romance of sport.
>
> There could be no greater pleasure to me than to wander with a matchlock through one of the great forests or wild tracts that still remain in England. A hare a day, a brace of partridges, or a wild duck would be ample in the way of actual shooting. The weapon itself, whether matchlock, wheel-lock, or even a cross-bow, would be a delight. Some of the antique wheel-lock guns are really beautiful specimens of design. The old powder-horns are often gems of workmanship. . . . How pleasant their carvings feel to the fingers! It is delightful to handle such implements. . . .
>
> An imperfect weapon, yes; but the imperfect weapon would accord with the great oaks, the beech trees full of knot holes, the mysterious

thickets, the tall fern, the silence, and the solitude. The chase would become a real chase; not, as now, a foregone conclusion. And there would be time for pondering and dreaming.

Let us be always out of doors, among trees and grass, and rain and wind and sun. There the breeze comes and strikes the cheek and sets it aglow; the gale increases and the trees creak and roar, but it is only a ruder music. A calm follows, the sun shines in the sky, and it is the time to sit under an oak, leaning against the bark, while the birds sing and the air is soft and sweet. By night the stars shine, and there is no fathoming the dark spaces between those brilliant points, nor the thoughts that come, as it were, between the fixed stars and landmarks of the mind.

Or it is the morning on the hills, when hope is as wide as the world; or it is the evening on the shore. A red sun sinks, and the foam-tipped waves are crested with crimson; the booming surge breaks, and the spray flies afar, sprinkling the face watching under the pale cliffs. Let us get out of these indoor narrow modern days, whose twelve hours have somehow become shortened, into the sunlight and the pure wind. A something that the ancients called DIVINE can be found and felt there still.

Q. D. Leavis   (essay date 1938)

SOURCE: "Lives and Works of Richard Jefferies," in *Collected Essays,* Vol. 3, Cambridge University Press, 1989, pp. 254-64.

[*Leavis was a twentieth-century English critic, essayist, and editor. Her professional alliance with her husband, F.R. Leavis, resulted in several literary collaborations, including the successful quarterly periodical,* Scrutiny, *in which she published many critical essays. In the following excerpt, first published in* Scrutiny *in 1938, Leavis defends Jefferies against critical attacks of his works, calling him a "many-sided and comprehensive genius."*]

To secure Jefferies his right to be read, several points could be made. One is the intrinsic value as literature of the rural life of much of his work. The large public that enjoyed *Farmer's Glory* and *Corduroy* would equally enjoy *The Amateur Poacher, Wild Life in a Southern County* and *Round About a Great Estate* (one of the most delightful books in the English language). Those who have found *Change in the Village* and *Change in the Farm* relevant to their interest in social history will be glad that *Hodge and His Masters* is again in print and will be impelled by that to search Jefferies for more documentation; since three of the least useful chapters have been chosen for the Faber anthology the reprint will be even more welcome. It is characteristic of Jefferies that he expressed regret that Gilbert White 'did not leave a natural history of the people of his day'. The element in Jefferies's writings represented by the interest that Gilbert White lacked is the decisive one; some of his best work can be described as such a natural history—for instance **'The Country Sunday'** among other essays in *Field and Hedgerow,* and pieces through-

out his other volumes of collected essays, *Nature Near London, The Life of the Fields, The Toilers of the Field.* But it also led him to collect folklore, rustic idiom and dialect words, and to note dying crafts and changing ways of living at a time when these subjects were little considered. To a far larger section of the intelligentsia an impressive case could be made for bringing Jefferies to their notice as an approved social thinker. His case-history would make useful propaganda; one of those Left journalists who turn out biographies showing that writers like Dickens were really just the same kind of writer as Mr Alec Brown ought to be instructed to do Jefferies. Starting as a member of the yeoman-farmer class with all its Conservative prejudices and habits of social conformism he emancipated himself by nothing but the force of daily experience and sensitive reflection to a position of daring freedom from the ideas of his class, his age and his country (he died in 1887).

It would be noted in such a Life that he planned to write (and may even have written but never published) works called 'The New Pilgrim's Progress; or, A Christian's Painful Progress from the Town of Middle Class to the Golden City' and 'The Proletariate: The Power of the Future'; that he hated the Church as an oppressor, calling it 'a huge octopus' and noting with pleasure that 'the pickaxe is already laid to the foundations of the Church tower'; that he wrote of 'laws made by the rich for the rich'— 'Most certainly the laws ought to be altered and must be altered'; that he protested in reference to projects for the cultural elevation of the villagers, 'For the enjoyment of art it is first of all necessary to have a full belly'; that he never had the smallest hankering after the Merrie Englande past but wanted the latest mechanism for agriculture and 'the light railway to call at the farmyard gate' and protested that the village had church and chapel but no cottage hospital, library, or lecture system to put the country folk in touch with the mental life of the time—villages should own themselves and have the right by Act of Parliament, like the railways, to buy land back from the landowners at a reasonable price—'in the course of time, as the people take possession of the earth on which they stand : . .' he writes; that he never idyllicized country life or rested for long content with the sensuous beauties of nature—'I am simply describing the realities of rural life behind the scenes', he says in **'One of the New Voters'** and it might often serve as his epigraph; that he was acutely conscious of the class war and the monetary basis of modern society—*After London; or, Wild England,* which is always written of as though it were of the *News from Nowhere* or *A Crystal Age* type of pretty day-dream impresses as contemporary not with Morris or Hudson but with *The Wild Goose Chase* (it seems to me to be a consistent satire on the system Jefferies found himself living under and to be in great part autobiographical). Jefferies hated the class distinctions which exacted servility from tenants and farm-hands, kept a hold over the morals of the cottager and strangled his independence, and the fierce attacks on this aspect of rural life should make *The Dewy Morn,* his most considerable novel, a Left Book. I have quoted a significant passage from *Bevis,* and even *Wood Magic,* a storybook for little children, has every claim to be admitted to the socialist nursery. Edward Thomas notes that although Jefferies was aloof and 'not a talker', yet he 'talked with ease and vigour on his own subjects, most eagerly on the Labour Question'. These notes, which might be multiplied if space allowed, could feed a new biography which would make Jefferies appear alive and congenial to our younger generation as neither Mr Looker's lofty thinker nor Mr Williamson's alter ego can be. And it would have the merit of being nearer to the truth—the truth of Jefferies' character, that core of his varied writings that unites them and gives them significance. But of course as an account of his work and its importance for posterity it would be ludicrously inadequate, for these facts and quotations only impress when given prominence by extraction and accumulation. Jefferies' 'message' is so much more complex and deep-rooted that the total impression made by anything he wrote is not of this simple order. For instance, his instinctive humanity and indignant expression of it are controlled by a characteristic irony—that irony of Jefferies' which is so disconcerting that Mr Looker preferred to ignore it. Nor has ***After London*** any trace of the crude propaganding and spiritual vulgarity of *The Wild Goose Chase* with which I have suggested a comparison.

For Jefferies was an artist, though not of the Hudson genre. His writing never reaches after effect and seems unconscious of achieving any; he is therefore the best possible model and for this reason alone should be in common possession, as Addison once was. He might indeed, if a judicious selection were made, supersede *The Coverley Papers* (which have got to be a bore in schools), not to speak of those positively vicious models of Style and The Essay children's taste is officially formed on. Thomas's account of his prose cannot be improved:

> These words call no attention to themselves. There is not an uncommon word, nor a word in an uncommon sense, all through Jefferies' books. There are styles which are noticeable for their very lucidity and naturalness; Jefferies is not noticeable even to this extent . . . His style was not a garment in which he clothed everything indiscriminately . . . He did not make great phrases, and hardly a single sentence would prove him a master . . . Though he had read much, it was without having played the sedulous ape that he found himself in the great tradition.

He did not make great phrases. Anyone in Bloomsbury can make a phrase, but Jefferies' effects are cumulative. They express a play of character and an original outlook, so that in their context the simplest groups of words are pregnant, as when he writes in **'Bevis's Zodiac':** 'The sparkle of Orion's stars brought to him a remnant of the immense vigour of the young world' or, to take something widely different, in **'The Country Sunday'**, when describing the villagers going to chapel in their best clothes 'all out of drawing, and without a touch that could be construed into a national costume—the cheap shoddy shop in the country lane'. The curious anticipations of D.H. Lawrence here are widespread in his mature work and suggest both how original his outlook was and what direction his gifts might have taken had he lived (he died at thirty-eight). Nothing came to him through literature, he is as unliterary as Cobbett though of greater personal cultiva-

tion and finer native sensibility; a contemporary suggested, says Thomas, that he avoided literary society deliberately in order to preserve his native endowments. And he is an artist in another sense, that compared with his works his life has little interest—all of him that holds value for us exists complete in his writings. He left no revealing letters, he did not mix in any kind of society, his domestic life was happy and normal.

Why he has not got into the literary histories (Elton does not mention him, Saintsbury is fatuous, subsequent historians have followed one or the other) and the university courses in literature is a mystery, but reason seems to have no hand in deciding these things. Yet as a source of evidence for 'background' courses he is surely more reliable as well as more original than the novelists, as an essayist he has surely more claim to be studied as literature than all these Lambs and Paters, and as a novelist himself he cannot be ignored where Hardy is studied (unless on quantitative grounds). Jefferies wrote four novels of permanent worth as well as some negligible ones. I have mentioned *After London,* which is written in Jefferies' mature style—the superb opening describing 'The Relapse into Barbarism' as the wild supplanted the cities should be a well-known piece. ***Greene Ferne Farm*** is the best of his early novels, comparable with the Hardy of *Under the Greenwood Tree,* while the most ambitious and novel-like of his later attempts, ***The Dewy Morn,*** reaches out towards D. H. Lawrence. The contrast between the maturity and originality of the content and Jefferies' clumsiness in manipulating the devices of the novel form is striking and may put off many readers. But the clumsiness is merely indifference, and when in ***Amaryllis at the Fair*** (another unfortunate title) he found a form that could convey all he was interested in treating without obliging him to satisfy the conventional demands on the novelist, he produced a masterpiece. But both ***Greene Ferne Farm*** and ***The Dewy Morn*** are too good to be let stay out of print. The Victorian features of these novels bulk at least as largely in Hardy's novels, but it is only in Jefferies' that the vitality and genuineness of the rest makes that conventional idiom appear ludicrous; most people seem able to read *The Return of the Native* with its 'Do you brave me, madam's?' without any feeling of incongruity between the melodrama of the parts and the total 'tragic' effect. But in Jefferies' novels the best parts are better and more mature than the best parts of most of Hardy's. The portrayer of rustic life who notes the village woman telling the welfare-worker who scolds her fecundity: 'That's all the pleasure me an' my old man got' and describes (in ***Greene Ferne Farm***) old Andrew Fisher with his *Wuthering Heights* past receiving the clerical suitor for his granddaughter's hand thus:

> 'Jim! Bill! Jock!' shouted the old man, starting out of his chair, purple in the face. 'Drow this veller out! Douse un in th'hog vault! Thee nimity-pimity odd-me-dod! I warn thee'd like my money! Drot thee and thee wench!'

is not a novelist who could conventionalize his villagers for purposes of humorous relief as Hardy does. In ***The Dewy Morn*** he goes further than any Victorian novelist towards the modern novel—I mean the novel that seems to have significance for us other than as a mirror of manners and morals; I should describe it as one of the few real novels between *Wuthering Heights* and *Sons and Lovers.* The final justification for asking the twentieth century to read Jefferies is, in Edward Thomas's fine words, that 'His own character, and the characters of his men and women, fortify us in our intention to live.' And we are more in need of fortification now than when those words were written. . . .

Avebury praises Jefferies's nature descriptions:

Living as we do in a prosaic age, when, from the very necessities of the case, we are obliged to devote much of our time to the business and ordinary avocations of life, we owe a deep debt of gratitude to men who, like Jefferies, carry us away into the country and teach us how to enjoy Nature. The exquisite beauty and delight of a fine summer's day in the country have never, perhaps, been more truly, and therefore more beautifully, described, than by Jefferies in his truly magnificent **"Pageant of Summer,"** which every one ought to read. "I linger," he says,

> in the midst of the long grass, the luxury of the leaves, and the song in the very air. I seem as if I could feel all the glowing life the sunshine gives and the south wind calls to being. The endless grass, the endless leaves, the immense strength of the oak expanding, the unalloyed joy of finch and blackbird, from all of them I receive a little. . . . In the blackbird's melody one note is mine; in the dance of the leaf shadows the formed maze is for me, though the motion is theirs; the flowers with a thousand faces have collected the kisses of the morning. Feeling with them, I receive some at least of their fulness of life. Never could I have enough; never stay long enough. . . . The hours when the mind is absorbed by beauty are the only hours when we really live, so that the longer we can stay among these things so much the more is snatched from inevitable time. . . . These are the only hours that are not wasted—those hours that absorb the soul and fill it with beauty. This is real life, and all else is illusion, or mere endurance. . . .

Lord Avebury, in his Essays & Addresses 1900-1903, *1903.*

Samuel J. Looker (essay date 1938)

SOURCE: An introduction to *Jefferies' England: Nature Essays,* edited by Samuel J. Looker, Harper and Brothers Publishers, 1938, pp. xi-xxvii.

[In the excerpt below, Looker compares the early and later works of Jefferies.]

What is most striking in the life of Richard Jefferies is the gradual development of his power of thought from the conventional and specious attitude of the early papers to a deeper realisation of the underlying needs and hopes of the mind.

It is a far cry from the *Gamekeeper at Home* to the **"Pageant of Summer."** The Jefferies of 1876 could hardly have written: "To be beautiful and to be calm, without mental fear, is the ideal of nature." The whole of his life was a progression from crude ideas and actions to high ideals and deep creative thought.

Like Thoreau, he came, by way of the sportsman's gun and habits, to a wider, closer understanding of wild life, and to a sympathy with everything that lived. In the *Amateur Poacher,* there is a self-revealing description, which tells very simply of the gradual alteration in his outlook. He says that the fascination of watching animals and birds so often stayed the shot that at last it grew to be a habit, until in the end the wire or gun remained unused.

Between the earlier and later prose, there is a startling and complete change in the attitude towards the brute creation. It is the measure of the growth in thought and wisdom which came to Jefferies during the last years.

Two short passages from his writings, separated in time by less than a decade, show the extraordinary difference between his earlier and later manner [the first from *The Amateur Poacher*]:

> It was always a sight to see Little John's keen delight in "wristing" their necks. He affected utter unconsciousness of what he was doing, looked you in the face, and spoke about some indifferent subject. But all the while he was feeling the rabbit's muscles stretch before the terrible grasp of his hands, and an expression of complacent satisfaction flitted over his features as the neck gave with a sudden looseness, and in a moment what had been a living, straining creature, became limp. . . .

> Rabbit-shooting, also, is trying to the temper; they double and dodge, and if you wait, thinking that the brown rascals must presently cross the partially open space yonder, lo! just at the very edge up go their white tails and they dive into the bowels of the earth, having made for hidden burrows. There is, of course, after all, nothing but a knack in these things. Still, it is something to have acquired the knack. The lad, if you ask him, will proudly show off several gun tricks, as shooting left-handed, placing the butt at the left instead of the right shoulder and pulling the trigger with the left finger. He will knock over a running rabbit like this; and at short distances can shoot with tolerable certainly from under the arm without coming to the "present," or even holding the gun out like a pistol with one hand.

> [The second passage is from *Nature and Eternity:*] There is a slight rustle among the bushes and the fern upon the mould. It is a rabbit who has peeped forth into the sunshine. His eye opens wide with wonder at the sight of us; his nostrils work nervously as he watches us narrowly. But in a little while the silence and stillness reassure him; he nibbles in a desultory way at the stray grasses on the mound, and finally ventures out into the meadow almost within reach of the hand. It is so easy to make the acquaintance—to make friends with the children of Nature. From the tiniest insect upwards they are so ready to

dwell in sympathy with us—only be tender, quiet, considerate, in a word, gentlemanly, towards them and they will freely wander around. And they have all such marvellous tales to tell—intricate problems to solve for us. This common wild rabbit has an ancestry of almost unsearchable antiquity. Within that little body there are organs and structures which, rightly studied, will throw a light upon the mysteries hidden in our own frames. It is a peculiarity of this search that nothing is despicable; nothing can be passed over—not so much as a fallen leaf, or a grain of sand. Literally everything bears stamped upon it characters in the hieratic, the sacred handwriting, not one word of which shall fall to the ground. . . .

The shadows of the oak and chestnut tree no longer shelter our rug; the beams of the noonday sun fall vertically on us; we will leave the spot for a while. The nightingales and the goldfinches, the thrushes and the blackbirds, are silent for a time in the sultry heat. But they only wait for the evening to burst forth in one exquisite chorus, praising this wondrous life and the beauties of the earth.

Nothing is more fallacious, therefore, than to look upon Richard Jefferies merely as a pleasant essayist on rustic topics, or a field-naturalist; in his finest work he is so much more than either, as may be clearly seen from the essays included in this book. It is true that he is a poet-naturalist in the sense of Wordsworth, or Thoreau, but there is nothing systematic or exhaustive in his observations. Innocent of invention, Jefferies might say with George Moore, "Only what my eye has seen, and my heart has felt, interests me." He is often a retailer of "unconsidered trifles," most of which are already familiar to the countryman. These trifling descriptions are full of a natural magic and told with a sincerity which is intensely moving. But this is not all. In other and greater moods he is able to convery to his readers his own inward brooding thought, and a sense of profound sympathy and wonder. Often he seems to possess a simple delight in the mere naming of things. He is in accord with the poet [Robert Bridges] who wrote:

The very names of things belov'd are dear,
And sounds will gather beauty from their sense,
As many a face thro' love's long residence
Groweth to fair instead of plain and sere.

Like Wordsworth before him, in the presence of Nature Jefferies knew how "to listen and receive." He was a natural mystic, at times carried away and absorbed in the being or existence of the universe. With him the contemplation of nature took a religious form.

He rediscovered to a great degree the primitive sense of wonder which had almost vanished from the modern world, and loved the mysterious earth. . . .

In his later papers, where he has ceased to be the sportsman or mere countryman, and has become the artist in living, he is treading on dangerous ground. Constable said of Turner: "Every man who distinguishes himself stands upon a precipice." There is little doubt but that Jefferies appreciated this truth. When he wrote so challenging and

unusual a book as *The Story of My Heart,* he must have known that he would have to pay the penalty which mediocrity always exacts from originality and genius. At any rate, the book on its first appearance was either misunderstood or attacked. Yet it had several qualities which have endeared it to the nature-lover since. Above all, a passion for the sea pervades it, almost a sea hunger. It is a passion which has been shared by many other and different temperaments, as diverse, for example, as Crabbe and Swinburne. In his simply written yet moving biography of his father, Crabbe's son relates how on one occasion, far inland and hungry for the sea, Crabbe took horse, rode sixty miles to the coast, bathed in the waters of the ocean, and returned home.

The Story of My Heart is instinct also with a love for colour and light:

I turned to the blue heaven over, gazing into its depths, inhaling its exquisite colour and sweetness. The rich blue of the unattainable flower of the sky drew my soul towards it, and there it rested, for pure colour is rest of heart. . . . Colour and form and light are as magic to me.

There is evidence that Jefferies' own sight was above the ordinary, and that colours were more vivid to him than others. Frederick Greenwood, who knew him well, speaks of "his large and clear blue eye, which seemed to pierce behind the veil of appearances, and see more than other men."

The later writings did not always please. There was much to offend, for example, as I have already indicated, in *The Story of My Heart.* From his preoccupation with the body and his denunciation of "every form of asceticism as the vilest blasphemy," to his vigorous discontent with things as they were, he was at odds with the thought of his period. Such an attitude must have been anathema to Victorian self-complacency. He had little respect for the gospel of Samuel Smiles. Jefferies exclaims:

What a fallacy it is, that hard work is the making of money. I could show you plenty of men who have worked the whole of their lives as hard as ever could possibly be, and who are still as far off independence as when they began.

Or again:

The pageantry of power, the still more foolish pageantry of wealth, the senseless precedence of place; words fail me to express my utter contempt for such pleasure or such ambitions.

Nor would a Victorian Mrs. Grundy appreciate his wish "that he would like to be loved by every beautiful woman on earth, from the swart Nubian to the white and divine Greek."

The Story of My Heart, as well as some of the later essays generally, show clearly that he was a man "born out of his due time," a sun worshipper, a lover of the unclothed body, of beauty and health in nature.

It was in reason that such sentiments should be welcome, and entirely in character that the man who uttered them should be either ignored or derided.

Jefferies is not a stylist in the accepted sense. His prose is quite unlike that of such masters of the jewelled word and line as Pater or Wilde. He cared little for mere ornament. He hardly ever quotes. His ear lacks the perfect balance of the musician, and he is oblivious at times to strange jars and discords. He is not one of those writers who believe in words as Van Gogh believed in paint, or as a saint believes in his God. It is the intense sincerity and unfeigned interest in his subject-matter which gives his prose a quality which more than compensates for the lack of more showy gifts. Strength and sincerity, a love of beauty, combined with a true simplicity, are powerful allies, and very convincing. To no writer is Gibbon's dictum more apposite, that "style is the image of the mind."

His text was a universal one. He wrote of the beauty of nature, ever-changing yet ever the same, of the moment of ecstasy, of illumination, which comes swiftly and departs as quickly, but leaves life never the same again; of the passing of time and of loveliness which fades as the flowers wither; of the history of mankind, which might be summed up in a sentence: "They were born, they suffered, they died."

William J. Hyde   (essay date 1956)

SOURCE: "Richard Jefferies and the Naturalistic Peasant," in *Nineteenth-Century Fiction*, Vol. 11, No. 3, December, 1956, pp. 207-17.

[*In the following essay, Hyde examines Jefferies's portrayal of peasant life in his writings.*]

Never famous among the ranks of the English rural novelists, Richard Jefferies nevertheless possesses a handful of ardent admirers, whose acclaim of his rural realism encourages an analysis of his achievement in the rural scene. Both Edward Thomas in his study of Jefferies [*Richard Jefferies*, 1938] and Edward Garnett in his introduction to *Amaryllis at the Fair* [1908] offer high praise of Jefferies' treatment of rustic characters; both insist upon a certain superiority that Jefferies possesses over Hardy, whose "highly-praised novels," to the latter, "do not ring quite true." Thomas makes the point of realism predominant in his comparison:

> [The rustics] appear and reappear with a truth which hardly any English writer has given to agricultural labourers. Jefferies does not go far with them; he has no occasion; they are only clattering about the yard: but his handling is absolutely sympathetic and understanding. Mr. Hardy is far more dramatic, far more psychological, and also far cleverer in effects, but he is seldom so right.

Granted that drama, subtlety, and psychological insight may be important along with a grasp of actuality for the production of fiction, Jefferies' studies of rustic character make no claim to be judged as works of art superior in all ways to Hardy's. Nor is it necessary to dispute the almost universal consensus of his critics that Jefferies was in general an inferior novelist. A perusal such as the writer has made of the early society novels, *The Scarlet Shawl* and *Restless Human Hearts,* is certain to leave the impression, not only that these are bad novels, but that Jefferies was a hopelessly bad writer of novels. Here was a novelist who could not tell a story, one who had little depth of insight into character and who began by selecting his characters from among the upper strata of society with which he must have been totally unfamiliar. What is more, even for an age that was accustomed to having the writer speak directly to the reader during occasional interruptions of the plot, Jefferies' novels must have been annoying with their continual first person interruptions. The focus is not on story but on author, and in his early novels the author had nothing important to say.

It was when Jefferies turned away from the formula of the sophisticated society novel to scenes and people of his native Wiltshire that his personal talk in his novels grew in importance. Again the story is not well knit, the characterization is weak, and the interruptions are infinite. Yet one can admire the simple realism of scene and character, the honesty of the author, and the intense sincerity of his comments. It is in Jefferies' latest novels, works which Mr. S. J. Looker [in his *Richard Jefferies,* 1946] alone among the critics has boldly called "three of the finest bucolic novels in the language, that rustic characters are presented and a distinct point of view is developed toward them. The resulting Wiltshire peasant is unique in Jefferies, shaped by a developing code of incisive realism which no major English novelist of his day was following.

The very course of Jefferies' writing career seems to make likely, if not inevitable, his ultimate method of treating the Wiltshire rustic. Jefferies was first and foremost a journalist, a writer of informative essays for the newspapers. Description and message, not story, were the vital parts of his writing; for his message he depended upon facts, upon a keen observation of the contemporary scene. While Hardy was devoted in much of his fiction to the rustic characters of a hallowed past and cast about them a certain atmosphere of charm and dignity which suppressed their baser actuality without ever quite destroying their reality, while in his one journalistic approach to the peasantry he admitted the passing of old ideas and customs upon which his fiction had centered ["The Dorsetshire Labourer," *Longman's Magazine,* II, 1883], Jefferies began in 1872 with a letter to the *Times,* winning his first public notice with a prosaic report on the contemporary Wiltshire laborer ["**The Wiltshire Labourer,**" London *Times,* 1872]. Here he presented the facts of housing, dress, food supply, and wages, as seen through the eyes of a conventionbound conservative who addressed his public letter to the sympathies of the landlord and the farmer hard hit by the new Agricultural Labourers' Union which Joseph Arch had formed that same year. Jefferies' letter informed respectable people that all was really well with the rural laborer, and its author found his selling point. The peasant became useful subject matter, not for an artist with a bold imagination, but for a journalist who could gather the facts that were before him.

Jefferies the reporter manages the scenes of the peasantry in the first of his three bucolic novels, *Greene Ferne Farm* (1880). In it facts are marshalled to present the laborer, the contemporary haymaker on strike, as he appeared to the long-suffering farmer. Cunning and stubbornness combine to enable the laborer to begin his strike on a widow's farm, just at a time when part of the grass is cut and the weather makes it crucial that the job be finished. Mrs. Estcourt, the farmer, citing an illustration which Jefferies undoubtedly knew from his own observations, defends her point of view with politic eloquence:

> One of the servants took a mower a quart of beer. He said he did not like it, and didn't want so much, and poured it out on the grass. Next day a pint was sent to him: "Why y'ent you brought me a quart?" said he. "Because you flung it away," was the reply. "Aw, that don't matter. You bring I a quart. I'll have my mishure." . . . nor should I mind paying the extra five shillings; but you see, Felix, if I pay it, all the farmers round . . . will be obliged to do so, and some of them are not able.

The laborers are subdued by their own consciences. Tired of merely idling about, and finally stricken with shame at the sight of the ladies of the farm performing their work, they rush back to their tasks. Jefferies may here be setting an example rather than reporting a fact. Clearly he has digested contemporary facts into a conservative point of view.

Other than the striking laborers en masse, individual rustics are sketched with a genial simplicity in *Greene Ferne Farm,* lifted from the scenes of actual life into the pages of the novel. There is the sottish poacher, Augustus Basset, whose rough performance of a good deed wins him hunting rights which he fails to appreciate: "The incitement of poaching was lacking." Among others are the lovers, Rause and her would-be husband Tummas, whose proposal, "Woot, or wootn't?" is perhaps the most succinct in the language. Finally, there is the vivid picture of the gleaners, a picture suggestive of the social propaganda which Jefferies was soon to focus upon, for the true journalist, the keen observer, cannot ultimately deny with his creed what his eyes witness:

> Their backs were bowed beneath great bundles of gleanings, or faggots of dead sticks carefully sought for fuel, and they carried weary infants, restless and fretful. Their forms had lost all semblance to the graceful curve of woman; their faces were hard, wrinkled, and angular, drawn with pain and labour. . . . Yet they were not penned in narrow walls, but all things green and lovely were spread around them. . . . But the magic of it touched them not, for their hearts were pinched with poverty.

In the interval between his first and second bucolic novels, Jefferies followed what was for him the inevitable path from journalist to propagandist. The actual peasantry were observed in their current scene, and the sight was not good. In spite of his early clinging to a discreet conservative point of view, a view undoubtedly clung to in his determination to sell his writings, Jefferies could not forever deny the economic suffering of the agricultural laborer of his own day. Nor could he escape to a more highly colorful past which would permit him to ignore the present scene, nor cultivate a more imaginative form of artistry

which would put story and character above economic fact. For the journalist there was no retreat when reality became sordid. The next novel, *The Dewy Morn* (1884), in its treatment of peasant life places fact at the service of social argument.

The argument for the peasantry in *The Dewy Morn* centers upon the housing problem of old Abner Brown, a retired laborer whose cottage is demanded to house another in his place after he has become useless upon the estate. To Jefferies, the businesslike claim that "we lose the man's work who should live there" becomes a specious rationalization of human cruelty by which a man loses home and garden and all the integrity of an independent existence: "there bean't no place for us but the workus." Young and old alike suffer from the scarcity of cottages. Young Abner, working "off the estate," will have no claim to hold his father's house, should he bring Mary Shaw home as a bride. Mary, faced with the prospect of a child and having no hope of marrying and settling, commits suicide rather than bring her own family into disrepute and cause them to be evicted from their cottage, too, as a penalty for her illegitimate child. Such, in Jefferies' observation, are the inevitable results of peasant housing regulations in southwest England. Jefferies neither overlooks the sordid amoral tendency of the peasant woman nor uses it as evi-

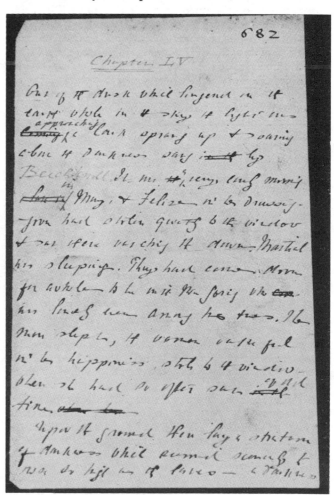

Page from manuscript of The Dewy Morn.

dence against her. Far from being unusual in her position, Mary is a typical victim of circumstance, and at that she is credited with having refused many indecent offers in the past. Her very mother had shown surprise and regret at Mary's refusal of such an offer from the bailiff, for the average peasant girl knows she must take what she can get. "These morals are born of generations of cruel poverty, and they are perpetuated by the brutal modern system which leaves for the worn out labourer or labourer's wife no refuge but the workhouse or the grave."

Vanished in Jefferies' rural scene are fun-loving characters like Hardy's Grandfer Cantle. Jefferies makes clear that the older peasantry have no cause to feel endued with geniality. Old Abner Brown, beaten in his attempt to obtain a permanent claim to his cottage from the young squire, whose grandfather he had served, reveals only a surly animosity toward Felice, the heroine, who had procured him his interview with the squire. Jefferies the propagandist vigorously interprets Jefferies the reporter: "Ingratitude is the nature of old Abner's race; so many hundred years of hard poverty and petty oppression have crushed out the better feelings, especially in the aged. For one act of kindness in eighty years, why should they feel grateful?"

The entire presentation of the peasantry in *The Dewy Morn* rests upon the purpose of social protest. Observing the scenes about him, Jefferies accumulates details of an ugly world steeped in poverty at which his indignation is kindled. The bounds of the story of the peasantry within the novel are ignored. The protest sweeps beyond the limits of Abner's story, and what begins as an argument for sympathy toward old Abner Brown concludes as a serious questioning of the entire system of English landholding and its administrators. Jefferies bitterly ridicules the organized charities and culture-spreading societies among the wealthy landholders. Withered old laborers, who need most a plentiful supply of fresh beef and ale, are offered the meager "scientific" diet prescribed by newly organized charities. Charity becomes anonymous, a soulless affair, in its massive new organizations. Worst of all does Jefferies consider the naïve cultural aims of the aristocratic would-be social worker. "In the midst of squalling children, over the deal table scare supplied with bread, he hangs up a picture." Landlords, sympathetic enough through their collective channels, remain heartlessly ignorant of human need on the personal level. The whole system of life in rural England menaces the peasant, leaves him destitute of elementary food and shelter.

The contemporary world of Jefferies' suffering agricultural laborer is far removed from the renowned rustic atmosphere of Hardy's Wessex. It is typically the journalist's world, not created by an imaginative artist but recorded of external facts set down and interpreted with little other insight than that of a ruthlessly indignant social conscience. In the last of his bucolic novels, *Amaryllis at the Fair* (1887), Jefferies, suffering himself from poor finances and a hopeless battle with tuberculosis, reaches the culmination of his discontent. Here, in a fictionalized review of his own family, his own origins, he achieves a deeper insight into character by which the reporter takes on the proportions of an artist, and at the same time his social

protests are expanded beyond the confines of the rustic world and challenge English life at large. In treating social problems he considers a new artistic method, the inevitable method by which to utilize his previous roles of reporter and propagandist. It is the French school of naturalism which Jefferies would set for himself not merely to imitate but to surpass.

Presenting his portrait of an artist, Alere Flamma, near the conclusion of *Amaryllis,* Jefferies offers the artist's ultimate criterion for drawings of nature: "They were absolutely true to nature and fact." Sketches must reveal actuality with "Unswerving truthfulness." Colors in current landscape painting should not be undertaken at all, for they always result in mere "apparitions," distortions of nature's own colors. "Many can draw nature . . . scarce one now paints real nature." It is in its application to writing, of course, that the realistic creed of the artist becomes pertinent for Jefferies himself. Balzac, Zola, and Hugo are mentioned—all great realists—yet Zola, "who is nothing if not realistic," appears to Jefferies to "merely skim the surface" of the basest actuality. Jefferies conceives a method which might enable him to "vanquish" the French, a method in which actuality is paramount and message takes all precedence over style and story:

> Not in any grace of style or sweeping march of diction, but just pencil jotted in the roughest words to hand, just as rich and poor, well-dressed ladies and next-door beggars are bundled into a train, so, without choice of language, but hustling the first words anyhow, as it were, into the first compartment.

Were he able to apply this technique to "the inside life of Fleet Street, . . . all the world would laugh and weep. For such things do go on in Fleet Street as no man has written yet."

An exposé of the sordid in human existence for the sake of inducing social reform, and in all writing a strict conveyance of the "natural," the actual, such was Jefferies' goal as a naturalistic writer. Applied to the presentation of the peasantry, such a goal was no new invention for him; some years before, it had been given serious consideration by George Eliot [in "The Natural History of German Life," *Westminster Review,* American edition, LXVI, 1856]. But to Jefferies it remained to approximate the naturalistic creed which the novels of George Eliot avoided and the novels of Hardy ignored. To Jefferies the "actual" peasant was not of himself necessarily sordid. It was his living conditions that were thus, as the propaganda of *The Dewy Morn* (and far more extensively the many essays) had revealed, and these conditions in turn might in time corrupt character. But if the typical peasant is not inherently a base character, neither does he possess the whimsy, wit, and geniality found in Hardy's rustics. Actuality in the last analysis can be only a presentation of what *seems* actual to the author. To Jefferies, the peasant seemed primarily an animal, with the animal's fundamental innocence, its potential capacity for unthinking passion, and its consequent ineffectualness in complex human dealings. Such are the men, "Jearje" and Bill Nye, who clatter about the yard or work in the dairy in *Amaryllis,* simple, happy, grateful laborers because they are well treated, who form part of the realistic scene but are granted no capacity to share in the action:

> [Jearje] so thoroughly enjoyed and appreciated the bacon, and the cheese, and the ale; he was like a great big human dog; you know how we like to see a big dog wag his tail at his foot, or put his paws on our knees and laugh, as it were, with his eyes in our face.

The actual unsophisticated peasant, as Jefferies sees him, is, unlike Hardy's figures, unable to think, unable to respond with wit and ingenuity to the actions of his "betters," and can form not even a chorus to the major action of the story:

> Rough-headed Jearje, without a thought, was as strong as the horses he led in the wagon.
>
> Round-headed Bill Nye, without an idea, could mow all day in the heat of July.

The peasant's function in the novel is merely to appear as a part of the realistic setting, displaying all the simplicity and apparent meaninglessness of his actual life. When, in **The Dewy Morn,** his own problems are referred to, he becomes an illustrative prop for the social propaganda. His basic wants are simple, and the pleas of Jefferies are consequently elemental. Good food, shelter, and kind treatment are the essentials for making him a useful and happy animal, only after which may come consideration of his wants and failings as a man. Before the picture is hung, nature demands that the belly be filled.

Jefferies does not insist that the average peasant, young in years, can never become a refined human being. Nevertheless, when the unreformed peasant is taken just as he is and the story of his life is told, the result is a naturalistic tale, a report of a "rural Fleet Street," such as Jefferies believed might surpass those of the French. None of his novels applies the naturalistic method throughout, but a short tale with a characteristic title, **"A True Tale of the Wiltshire Labourer,"** [in his **The Toilers of the Field,**] shows us its results. Unlike the traditional short story, this tale resembles the factual exposé of the feature writer whose desire it is to play upon his reader's indignation in order to generate an impulse for reform. Animal-like love, unfaithfulness, drunkenness, starvation, all are unfolded in the course of the peasant's courtship and ugly married life. Even during the pleasant time of courtship, Jefferies seizes upon the sordid atmosphere in which the haymakers' dinner culminates: "By this time they were pretty well 'boozed.' A thick cloud of tobacco-smoke filled the kitchen. Heads were rolling about from side to side and arms stretched over the tables among the *débris* of broken pipes and in pools of spilt beer and froth." After the death of his deserted wife, the peasant arrives at no grand climax; the last words we hear of him are clipped from a newspaper column, under the heading "Drunk and Disorderly." The naturalism which Jefferies had described, artistically formless, gathering every random fact of life to support the social message, is put to use. Jefferies achieves actuality.

To conclude, it appears that Jefferies' methods of treating the peasantry were gradually expanded. While conventional reporting and zealous propagandizing necessitate an increasingly telling selection of facts, the naturalist at last attempts to seize upon a total picture, letting life speak bluntly for itself. The journalistic style becomes subservient to a larger motive. With traces of naturalism in his last novel, Jefferies succeeded in creating a number of brief transcripts of rustic characters who are perhaps as "real" as any in all literature. It is unreasonable, however, to claim that they are superior portraits to those of a master such as Hardy, for there are other criteria than actuality by which to judge a work of art. In the final analysis, even their greater "reality" remains an issue of personal interpretation. It is not the reality of an artist's insight into human character, but that of a man whose genius lay in observation, one who could assemble external facts to stir men's hearts. It is clear that, among the rural novelists, Jefferies' observations are unique in purpose, and his peasant characters may lack depth but appear different in kind.

Henry Williamson   (lecture date 1959)

SOURCE: "Some Nature Writers and Civilization," in *Essays by Divers Hands,* n. s. Vol. XXX, 1960, pp. 1-18.

[*Here, Williamson surveys Jefferies's life and discusses his development of two distinct styles.*]

It is not always immediately apparent to the very young writer that a man's thoughts, and particularly his ideals, arise indirectly from the circumstances of his early environment. Truth has many relatives. And at the end of a life, as Heine the German poet wrote, 'Under every gravestone an entire world lies buried.'

Lacking the views of maturity in my youth, when first I read Richard Jefferies's **The Story of my Heart,** it was to me a revelation of total truth. Indeed, within the first few moments of taking up a copy, in a second-hand bookseller's shop in Folkestone, a month or two after the fighting had stopped on the Western Front, my entire outlook changed. A life devoted more or less to pleasure, after my military duties, was ended. I had found, I believed, my purpose in life: to extend Jefferies's truth of redemption through Nature to my fellow men.

But it was not so much the ideas which shook one on that first occasion in the summer of 1919, as the descriptions of the beauty of the English scene, which arose out of the print upon the pages, and took possession of the spirit. Here was more than consolation, after the sudden ending of the hectic days and nights of war-time, for a vanished world of comradeship, sharing the spirit of the great family of a regiment, upheld by friendship and laughter in the face of death. I do not mean at the moment of death; but that we disregarded the face of death. And then, suddenly, a new world—the world of boyhood come again, with a mysterious beauty never before seen in words upon the printed page.

> There were grass-grown tumuli on the hills to which of old I used to walk, sit down at the foot of one of them, and think. Some warrior had been interred there in the ante-historic times. The sun of the summer morning shone on the dome of sward, and the air came softly up from

the wheat below, the tips of the grasses swayed as it passed sighing faintly, it ceased, and the bees hummed by to the thyme and the heath-bells. I became absorbed in the glory of the day, the sunshine, the sweet air, the yellowing corn turning from its sappy green to summer's noon of gold, the lark's song like a waterfall in the sky. I felt at that moment that I was like the spirit of the man whose body was interred in the tumulus; I could understand and feel his existence the same as my own. He was as real to me two thousand years after interment as those I had seen in the body.

Again and again Jefferies returns to the old site of the British encampment on the hill a mile or two from his home, holding himself back as he labours up the last steep slope to the fosse of those fortifications of the Iron Age.

> Moving up the sweet short turf, at every step my heart seemed to obtain a wider horizon of feeling; with every inhalation of rich pure air, a deeper desire. The very light of the sun was whiter and more brilliant here.

> By the time I had reached the summit I had entirely forgotten the petty circumstances and annoyances of existence. I felt myself, myself. There was an entrenchment on the summit, and going down into the fosse I walked round it slowly to recover breath. On the south-western side there was a spot where the outer bank had partially slipped, leaving a gap. There the view was over a broad plain, beautiful with wheat, and inclosed by a perfect amphitheatre of green hills.

> I was utterly alone with the sun and the earth. Lying down on the grass, I spoke in my soul to the earth, the sun, the air, and the distant sea far beyond sight. I thought of the earth's firmness—I felt it bear me up; through the grassy couch there came an influence as if I could feel the great earth speaking to me. I thought of the wandering air—its pureness, which is its beauty; the air touched me and gave me something of itself. I spoke to the sea: though so far, in my mind I saw it, green at the rim of the earth and blue in deeper ocean; I desired to have its strength, its mystery and glory. Then I addressed the sun, desiring the soul equivalent of his light and brilliance, his endurance and unwearied race. I turned to the blue heaven over, gazing into its depth, inhaling its exquisite colour and sweetness. The rich blue of the unattainable flower of the sky drew my soul towards it, and there it rested, for pure colour is rest of heart. By all these I prayed . . . by the sweet thyme, whose little flowers I touched with my hand; by the slender grass; by the crumble of dry chalky earth which I took up and let fall through my fingers. Touching this crumble of earth, the blade of grass, the thyme flower, breathing the earth-encircling air, thinking of the sea and the sky, holding out my hand for the sunbeams to touch it, prone on the sward in token of deep reverence thus thus I prayed, that I might touch to the unutterable existence infinitely higher than deity.

Now let us return to lower ground; and try and find out who this eccentric young man was.

Richard Jefferies was born in 1848, at Coate Farm, in the parish of Chiseldon near Swindon. The farm, scarcely more than a small-holding, lay under the downs. Behind the farmhouse were trees, and then a broad sheet of water, a reservoir for that railway town. Reeds grew around the water. It was the haunt of wildfowl, with two islets near the west shore. Pike lived in the 'broad', with roach, rudd, and perch. There were also water-mussels, some of them six inches in length. This was the scene of *Bevis, the Story of a Boy,* a book of enchantment and magic, if read first when one is young. In it, Jefferies enlarged the scope of his early life, and 'the guv'nor', Bevis's father, is a remote figure, stable and sanguine; so unlike Jefferies's own father, whose whole life was a hopeless struggle against mortgage and all that debt implies. A portrait of this tragic figure—a man of wide natural intellect and feeling—a man who worked for perfection rather than for money—is to be found, with deep sympathy, in Jefferies's best novel, the last one he wrote, or rather dictated, towards the end of his short life—*Amaryllis at the Fair.*

During the latter part of Jefferies's life he was ill as well as poor; and two years before his death he lived in chronic pain. Some doctors thought his illness was imaginary, that he was a hypochondriac, that the wasting away of his body and the pains he suffered were due to hysteria. All during his life he was working: and the theme of his work was the creation of, the burning hope for, a better, truer, more sun-lit world of men.

In May 1925, nearly forty years after his death, I made a journey to his birthplace, and stared at the farm-house where he had been born, at the gable window from which he had looked when writing his first pages. I walked round the broad or lake, and thought how much smaller it was than in *Bevis.* It had been made into a public bathing-place, with huts and rails and diving-boards; but the fish were still there. There was talk of turning the farm-house into a Jefferies museum, for a memorial. Soon nothing, I thought, would be left of the place as he knew it, except in those pages of his which glowed and shone with ancient sunlight. While I was musing thus, standing in the roadway before the farm, an old woman came out of a small cot of tarred wood, obviously the work of a labouring man, and scrutinized me. The little black house stood under a hawthorn, then in pink blossom. 'Come to see the house where Loony Dick was born, have ye?' she inquired. We talked for a while. She was remarkable for her vivacity and straight way of looking at things. Years before the war she had adopted a foundling or waif from the Union, the workhouse; raised him as her own child, found him a job when grown up; and then the war came, and killed him. What she could not make up her mind about at the moment, she told me, was whether or not to adopt another 'chiel'. There were 'plenty of 'm about', she declared, since the soldiers had gone. Was she too old, did I think? I said surely not, that she had many years to live. 'Don't ye be too sure,' she said, and defied me to guess her age. 'Sixty?' I said. 'Git out,' she replied. 'I knew Loony Dick as a boy, didn't I tell'ee just now? Moony Dick, some called him.

A lazy loppet, he was too. A proper atheist. Lots of folks asks me if I have read those books. Why should I read them? I know it all as well as he. He can't tell me anything new. I've had to work all my life. Why should I read in books what most folks knows already?'

After he had left school, the young Jefferies, a mixture of indolence and sharp imperiousness, got a job on a local paper, which occupied his days. At night he wrote novels and romances in the seclusion of the gable room, which had a pear tree trained against the outer wall. *Caesar Borgia, or the King of Crimee; Verses on the Exile of the Prince Imperial; Fortune, or the Art of Success* (he sent this to Disraeli, who returned it with a tactful letter); *Only a Girl*—how he worked, burning candle after candle beyond midnight and into dawn.

While with the *North Wilts. Herald,* he was fortunate in having a sympathetic editor who believed that his young reporter had a rare talent for writing. This belief was justified when, at the age of twenty-four, Jefferies wrote a long letter to *The Times* in London; and *The Times* printed it in full, several thousand words, about the Wiltshire Labourer. It was read and discussed in Swindon; the writer became a local figure. He found himself, suddenly, to be an authority on agriculture. A London evening newspaper, *The Pall Mall Gazette,* published a series of his articles, anonymously, under the title of *The Game-keeper at Home, or, Sketches of Natural History and Rural Life;* and then another series, *Wild Life in a Southern County.* When these were reprinted in book form, Jefferies was acclaimed as a writer in the class of White of Selborne, and a public of discriminating sportsmen and country people began to look for everything he wrote. By this time he was married to the daughter of a neighbouring farmer, and had a son. At first the young couple lived at Coate Farm, but later took rooms in Swindon.

> My work was most uncongenial and useless, but even then sometimes a gleam of sunlight on the wall, the buzz of a bee at the window, would bring the thought to me. Only to make me miserable, for it was a waste of golden time while the rich sunlight streamed on hill and plain. There was a wrenching of the mind, a straining of the mental sinews: I was forced to do this, my mind was yonder. Weariness, exhaustion, nerve-illness often ensued. The insults which are showered on poverty, long struggle of labour, the heavy pressure of circumstances, the unhappiness, only stayed the expression of the feeling. It was always there. Often in the streets of London, as the red sunset flamed over the houses, the old thought, the old prayer came.
>
> Not only in grassy fields with green leaf and running brook did this constant desire find renewal. More deeply still with living human beauty; the perfection of form, the simple fact of form, ravished and always will ravish me away. In this lies the outcome and end of all the loveliness of sunshine and green leaf, of flowers, pure water, and sweet air. This is embodiment and highest expression; the scattered, uncertain, and designless loveliness of tree and sunlight brought to shape. Through this beauty I prayed deepest and lon-

gest and down to this hour. The shape—the divine idea of that shape—the swelling muscle or the dreamy limb, strong sinew or curve of bust, Aphrodite or Hercules, it is the same. That I may have the soul-life, the soul-nature, let divine beauty bring to me divine soul. Swart Nubian, white Greek, delicate Italian, massive Scandinavian, in all the exquisite pleasure the form gave, and gives, to me immediately becomes intense prayer.

To be nearer editors, the young writer moved to the suburbs of London, first to Sydenham and then to Surbiton. He worked every day, forcing himself to turn his observations and feelings directly into words. It is one thing to enjoy the natural scene for itself, or for oneself: to relax and be mentally free; it is quite another thing to go out, deliberately to observe—or in the hope of observing something which can be turned into words, words, words, for pence, pence, pence, to support children, wife, and self—in that order. This extraction of feeling in order to produce words for what is called the deadline can eventually turn the grasshopper into a burden. Still the writer has to write, overborne by anxiety. Then his work may become subjective, like that of D. H. Lawrence, who seldom had time to reflect, but must always be using himself up for writing, writing, writing. Thus new wine must be put direct into new bottles. And when to the worries of economic necessity are conjoined the fevers of tuberculosis, the end is predictable.

Jefferies therefore, has two distinct styles. One is straightforward, concrete, factual; the style of a relaxed or should one say detached man. The other is subjective, candent, a flow of words driven from him as he wrote, by his daemon: the daemon behind his repressed or mortified self. Because of these two distinct styles Jefferies had—whether he has still, I do not know—two kinds of reading public. The one appreciated his straight-forward descriptions of country scenes and characters, such as were to be found in *The Amateur Poacher, Wild Life in a Southern County,* and *Hodge and his Masters;* but this reader did not always care for *The Story of my Heart,* and the later essays, many of them dictated, when he spoke about himself and his feelings in relation to the natural world. Personally, I care for all he wrote, for I was as boy and youth and man devoted to Jefferies: he always had and always will have my deepest respect and sympathy.

Behind all the 'factual' writings there hovers, often luminously, his desire to express himself fully, in his deep reverence for life. And at last, after so much holding back of his essential thought-feelings—if such a term may be allowed—he began, at Brighton, *The Story of my Heart.* It was a confession.

> I have been obliged to write these things by an irresistible impulse which has worked in me since early youth. They have not been written for the sake of argument, still less for any thought of profit, rather indeed the reverse. They have been forced from me by earnestness of heart, and they express my most serious convictions. For seventeen years they have been lying in my mind, continually thought of and pondered over. I was not more than eighteen

when an inner and esoteric meaning began to come from all the visible universe, and indefinable aspirations filled me. I found them in the grass fields, under the trees, on the hill-tops, at sunrise, and in the night. There was a deeper meaning everywhere. The sun burned with it, the broad front of morning beamed with it; a deep feeling entered me while gazing at the sky in the azure noon, and in the star-lit evening.

I was sensitive to all things, to the earth under, and the star-hollow round about; to the least blade of grass, to the largest oak. They seemed like exterior nerves and veins for the conveyance of feeling to me. Sometimes a very ecstasy of exquisite enjoyment of the entire visible universe filled me. I was aware that in reality the feeling and the thought were in me, and not in the earth or sun; yet I was more conscious of it when in company with these. A visit to the sea increased the strength of the original impulse. I began to make efforts to express these thoughts in writing, but could not succeed to my own liking. Time went on, and harder experiences, and the pressure of labour came, but in no degree abated the fire of first thought. Again and again I made resolutions that I would write it, in some way or other, and as often failed . . . had I not made it personal I could scarcely have put it into any shape at all. But I felt that I could not longer delay, and that it must be done, however imperfectly. I am only too conscious of its imperfections, for I have as it were seventeen years of consciousness of my own inability to express this the idea of my life . . .

He moved house again, from Brighton to Eltham, then in Kent but now, alas, in London. Soon he was moving back to Sussex, first at Rotherfield, then to Crowborough. Those living, moving essays in *The Life of the Fields* and *The Open Air* were published about this time, 1884-5. Then restlessly on again, to Goring-on-Sea, where he broke down. He was suffering, not from hysteria as the doctors had declared, but from tuberculosis of the lungs and the intestines, and the intestines were ulcerated as well. Also he had fistula, which is a torturing thing. There is a letter to his publisher, Charles Longman, at this time in which he wrote:

My wearied and exhausted system constantly craves rest. My brain is always asking for rest. I never sleep. I have not slept now for five years properly, always waking, with broken bits of sleep, and restlessness, and in the morning I get up more weary than I went to bed. Rest, that is what I need. You thought naturally that it was work I needed; but I have been at work, and next time I will tell you all of it. It is not work, it is REST for the brain and the nervous system. I have always had a suspicion that it was the ceaseless work that caused me to go wrong at first.

It has taken me a long time to write this letter; it will take you but a few minutes to read it. Had you not sent me to the sea in the spring I do not think that I should have been alive to write it.

Still he worked on, so weak now that he must dictate to his wife: and his beautiful novel *Amaryllis at the Fair* was completed just in time. A painter friend has described his physical appearance in that cottage at Goring where Jefferies lived with his wife and two small children, in the thirty-eighth and last year of his life.

It was in the early summer, two or three months before his death, that I saw Jefferies for the last time alive. He had then been living at Goring for some short time, and this was my first visit to him there. I was pleased to find that his house was far pleasanter than the dreary and bleak cottage which he had rented at Crowborough. It had a view of the sea, a warm southern exposure, and a good and interesting garden: in one corner a quaint little arbour, with a pole and vane, and near this centre a genuine old-fashioned draw-well. Poor fellow! Painfully, with short breathing, and supported on one side by Mrs. Jefferies and on the other by myself, he walked round this enclosure, noticing and drawing our attention to all kinds of queer little natural objects and facts. Between the well and the arbour was a heap of rough, loose stones, overgrown by various creeping flowers. This was the home of a common snake, discovered there by Harold, and poor Jefferies stood, supported by us, a yard or so away and peered into every little cranny and under every leaf with eyes well used to such a search until some tiny gleam, some minute cold glint of light, betrayed the snake. Weakness and pain seemed forgotten for the moment—alas! only for the moment. Uneasily he sat in the little arbour telling me how his disease seemed still to puzzle the doctors; how he felt well able in mind to work, plenty of mental energy, but so weak, SO FEARFULLY WEAK, that he could no longer write with his own hand; that his wife was patient and good to help him. He had nobody to come and talk with him of the world of literature and art. Why couldn't I come and settle by? There was plenty to paint. Though Goring itself was one of the ugliest places in the world, there was Arundel, and its noble park, and river, and castle close by. I must go and see it the very next day, and see whether I could not work there, and come back every day and cheer him. I was the best doctor, after all.

Poor fellow! I did not then know or believe that he was so utterly without sympathetic society except his devoted wife. It was so. I am one of the dullest companions in the world; but I had sympathy with his work, and knowledge, too, of his subjects. Well, nothing would do but that I must go to Arundel the next day, and Mrs. Jefferies must show me the town. 'He would do well enough for one day. A good neighbour would come in, and with little Phyllis and the maid he would be safe.'

Therefore we went to Arundel (a short journey by train), and on coming back found him standing against the door-post to welcome us.

I have seldom been more touched than by my experience of that evening, finding, amongst other things, that he had partly planned and insisted on this Arundel trip to get us away so that he might, unrebuked, spend some of his latest hard earnings in a pint of 'Perrier Jouët' for my supper.

Do you know Goring churchyard? It is one of those dreary, overcrowded, dark spots where the once-gravelled paths are green with slimy moss, and it was a horror to poor Jefferies. More than once he repeated the hope that he might not be laid there, and he chose the place where his widow at last left him—amongst the brighter grass and flowers of Broadwater.

He died at Goring at half-past two on Sunday morning, August 14, 1887.

After Jefferies's death there was controversy about his having died a Christian, or not. Before losing consciousness, he asked his wife to read a chapter of the New Testament to him, and whispered at the end, 'It is true, it is true.' There were attacks on his work, particularly on **The Story of my Heart,** among them one in *The Girls' Own Paper.*

It is true that during his life he had few acquaintances or friends. Perhaps it would not be wholly untrue to say that he died half-way through his life because he had lived too intensely by the spirit, lacking a living spirit like himself for companion. . . . Richard Jefferies's friends were to be, as once he told Roger Ingpen, in posterity. Ingpen, it may be recalled, was the compiler of the *Julian* edition of Shelley; he was the brother-in-law of Walter de la Mare, in whose house, in 1920, he gave me a description of Jefferies—thin, tall, blue-eyed, bearded, aloof, courteous, as he came into the office of Smith, Elder and Company, with whom the youthful Roger Ingpen was learning publishing, to be told that his books were not selling at all. 'One day, I think they will be read', said Jefferies on his last visit there, to the silent youth behind the desk.

There are two kinds of emotion felt by an author—actual feeling as a human being; and emotion while writing, often called literary emotion. This literary emotion can rise to the freeing of the imagination, whereby his best work is done: this is called the spirit of truth. Or it may descend to a relief of personal constrictions, and be merely unhappy writing that makes no appeal to the imagination of the reader, being of the letter of truth on the level from which the reader wishes to escape. How much of the **Story** was literary emotion? Did Jefferies actually have the strong feelings at the times and places he described in his **Story,** or were they exaggerated while he was writing, the body being in abeyance, and the feelings in a fume of 'nerve-illness'?

My heart looks back and sympathises with all the joy and life of ancient time. With the circling dance burned in still attitude on the vase; with the chase and the hunter eagerly pursuing, whose javelin trembles to be thrown; with the extreme fury of feeling, the whirl of joy in the warriors from Marathon to the last battle of Rome, not with the slaughter, but with the passion—the life in the passion; with all the breathing busts that have panted beneath the sun. O beautiful human life! Tears come in my eyes as I think of it. So beautiful, so inexpressibly beautiful!

So deep is the passion of life that, if it were possible to live again, it must be exquisite to die pushing the eager breast against the sword. In the flush of strength to face the sharp pain joyously, and laugh in the last glance of the sun—if only to live again, now on earth, were possible. So subtle is the chord of life that sometimes to watch troops marching in rhythmic order, undulating along the column as the feet are lifted, brings tears in my eyes. Yet could I have in my own heart all the passion, the love and joy, that burned in the breasts that have panted, breathing deeply, since the hour of Ilion, yet still I should desire more. How willingly I would strew the paths of all with flowers; how beautiful a delight to make the world joyous! The song should never be silent, the dance never still, the laugh should sound like water which runs for ever.

My young self could not agree with H. M. Tomlinson in 1924 when he murmured to me in the Temple Bar restaurant in the Strand that **The Story of my Heart** was a dangerous book; but later I realized how it could be damaging to any young man akin to Jefferies who accepts what stands out of the pages for him as absolute truth. Then it may add to his imbalance, and cause his health and living to suffer in unsocial loneliness.

And here may I intrude a personal confession: how the misreading of one word in Jefferies caused me, for nearly a year while working in Fleet Street, in 1920, to come near to a nervous breakdown. *Where man goes, nature ends:* how true, how tragic, how dreadful were the new houses going up on the fields, and the sites of cleared woods and coverts I had known in boyhood! I struggled in my mind to obliterate them. I struggled, too, against the motor omnibuses along the Embankment below Fleet Street, against the smoke in the sky, and the pollution of the Thames; I suffered for the brook called the Fleet, now a sewer and underground, but once a spawning-place of salmon, with willow trees on its banks. I struggled to dissolve the past, and to grow willows on the banks of the Thames once more. Man had gone there, and so nature was no more.

But Jefferies had written, *When man goes, nature ends.* For man, to Jefferies, was the sum of nature, and the world was in man's care, under a Spirit 'higher than deity' as he had declared in his **Story.**

Nevertheless, despite my illusion, in that perfervid year of 1920, when I was writing my first book, I had already realized the difference between my expressed ideals and my actual behaviour; and was seeking, in some perplexity, to find the answer to the question: How far was a man unbalanced by the negations of his childhood, and how much was due to inherited traits? Supposing Jefferies to have grown up in happy mental freedom, would **The Story** ever have been written? And had he realized, after it was written, why his nature had instinctively refused to face up to such a task: because his mind would have to live again its own mortifications, which originally had caused the mental straining-away from normal ease, which led to the eventual break-down of his body? D. H. Lawrence once wrote that Jefferies must have 'winced away' from this book, after publication. Perhaps the best medium for such feeling is music: Delius. . . .

W. J. Keith   (essay date 1965)

SOURCE: "The Romances: *Wood Magic, Bevis,* and *After London,*" in *Richard Jefferies: A Critical Study,* University of Toronto Press, 1965, pp. 100-22.

[*In the following essay, Keith explores some interconnections between Jefferies's romances*—Wood Magic, Bevis, *and* After London.]

[Let us] consider the three . . . fictional works of Jefferies' maturity, *Wood Magic* (1881), *Bevis* (1882), and *After London: or Wild England* (1885), under the general term "romances." The first two are naturally linked by a common hero, Bevis, though they are so different in tone and intention that this superficial connection is somewhat misleading. But there are good reasons for considering all three books together. In all, Jefferies is concerned not only with the real world but with a dream-world; indeed, the latter is generally more important and more central than the former. But it is a dream-world which, in various significant ways, reflects everyday experience. Jefferies is not escaping into fantasy; instead he is bringing the world of imagination to the forefront and demonstrating its close connection with, and subtle influence upon, the so-called "real world." This connection is linked in all three books with the perennial theme of the "return to nature," which Jefferies presents with his characteristic precision and also with an admirable variety.

These three interrelated themes—the everyday world, the dream-world of the imagination, and the world of wild nature—are of course central to *The Story of My Heart,* and all three romances offer interesting parallels and comparisons to this central text in the study of Jefferies. In *Wood Magic* and *Bevis,* both written earlier, we get scattered thoughts and ideas that will find their true place in the later book. In *After London,* which was published two years after *The Story of My Heart,* some of the yearning intensity of the latter work acquires allegorical form. Moreover, in all three romances we are concerned with an imaginative projection of Jefferies' own personality. I shall show how the character of Felix Aquila in *After London* is really an extension of the Bevis of the earlier books; indeed, despite the future setting of *After London,* it would almost be possible to read these romances as a trilogy tracing the development of a single character—as a young child, as a growing youth, and as a man. An autobiographical element looms large in all Jefferies' work, whether fiction or non-fiction, but it is absolutely central here. None the less, at his most successful (and there can be little dispute that *Bevis* is easily the most accomplished of the three) he is able, as we shall see, to universalize his own personal vision, and so make it significant and valid for others.

Wood Magic is specifically a children's book, though this does not prevent Jefferies from writing into it principles and ideas worthy of adult attention. The hero is little "Sir" Bevis, who is remarkable for his ability to converse with the animals and birds which live in the vicinity of his farmhouse home. Nor is this gift of understanding confined to the animal kingdom; it extends to the plant realm, represented by the reed, and even to natural objects such as the wind and the brook. We are given no reason why Bevis, and Bevis alone, should possess such powers, though we may assume that his perfect relationship with nature has at least something to do with it. The book is a record of his role in the world of nature as an eager participant in the lives and adventures of wild creatures. The centre of attention is, then, not the real world but the animal world, though the connection between the two is considerable; indeed, they often seem indistinguishable. This is not because Jefferies is incapable of the imaginative effort necessary to conceive an entirely new world, but because he wishes to emphasize the essential similarities, to point out, in fact, that the everyday world is part of the world of nature. In *Wood Magic* the animal world is as a mirror through which the young Bevis may see life as it is.

For this is no sentimental story about a little boy amid the joys of nature. Indeed, the very first paragraph is enough to set our minds aright on that score:

> One morning as little "Sir" Bevis (such was his pet name) was digging in the farmhouse garden, he saw a daisy, and throwing aside his spade, he sat down on the grass to pick the flower to pieces. He pulled the pink-tipped petals off one by one, and as they dropped they were lost. Next he gathered a bright dandelion, and squeezed the white juice from the hollow stem, which drying presently, left his fingers stained with brown spots. Then he drew forth a bennet from its sheath, and bit and sucked it till his teeth were green from the sap.

Clearly, this is no Victorian mother's darling. Indeed, what impresses us about Bevis (and this is even more true of the later book) is the extreme fidelity with which he is portrayed. Jefferies has caught the truth of boyhood, and this includes the mischievousness and selfishness as well as the imagination and the charm. In this book, Bevis is only about seven or eight years of age, and he has not yet emerged as a particular personality, but we recognize the potential of the character who gives his name to the later book. Even here there are incidents which impress us by their subtle psychological truth. The following passage concerning Pan the spaniel is a good example:

> In the midst of the noise out came Polly, the dairymaid, with a bone for Pan, which Bevis no sooner saw, than he asked her to let him give Pan his dinner. "Very well, dear", said Polly, and went in to finish her work. So Bevis took the bone, and Pan, all weary and sore from his thrashing, crept out from his tub to receive it; but Bevis put the bone on the grass (all the grass was worn bare where Pan could reach) just where the spaniel could smell it nicely but could not get it. Pan struggled and scratched, and howled, and scratched again, and tugged till his collar, buckled tightly now, choked him, and he gasped and panted, while Bevis, taking the remnant of his apple from his pocket, nibbled it and laughed with a face like an angel's for sweetness.

The last phrase recalls the conventional angelic tradition only to contrast Bevis' reality. However much his adventures among animals and birds may savour of fantasy, Bevis himself is a very real child from a very real world.

There is a similarly refreshing lack of sentimentality and idealization about the presentation of Nature. This is no gentle wonderland; Jefferies, who knew the truth of the world of Nature so well, would never betray the truth even in a children's book—especially, perhaps, in a children's book. The natural world around the farmhouse is one in which the fact of death is ever present, and this is quickly brought home to the young mind of the hero. Thus, he discovers the weasel in a trap, and eventually releases it, despite the remonstrances of a passing mouse whose mate the weasel has killed. Later he hears other stories of the weasel's misdeeds. The hare tells him that, since his lucky escape, "the weasel has killed my son, the leveret, while he was sleeping, and sucked his blood". There is a forceful directness about this, which is enhanced by a later speech: "I daresay this weasel will have me some day, and I do not care if he does, now my leveret is dead; and very soon his poor bones will be picked clean by the ants, and after the corn is carried the plough will bury them". Bevis himself is responsible for some of the distress, as he learns when conversing with a swallow:

> The swallow flew to and fro not far from Bevis, who watched it, and presently asked him to come closer. But the swallow said: "I shall not come any nearer, Bevis, Don't you remember what you did last year, sir? Don't you remember Bill, the carter's boy, put a ladder against the wall, and you climbed up the ladder, and put your paw, all brown and dirty, into my nest and took my eggs?"

There is the scene, too, in which Bevis is tricked by the weasel into shooting the thrush with his home-made cannon. *Wood Magic* is perhaps a misleading title, though Jefferies naturally did not neglect the beauties and delights of the natural world which he, of all people, knew and loved. Rather, the magic lies in the variety, in the exquisite balance that Jefferies maintains between the beautiful and the cruel, the gentle and the violent.

The main narrative of the book is concerned with the political set-up of the local animal kingdom. King of the wild creatures is Kapchack, the magpie, who rules harshly and absolutely over an unwieldy state, whose individual members are continually warring among themselves and betraying each other as political traitors for reasons of private vendetta. The great rebel is Choo Hoo, the wood-pigeon, who has gathered an army of discontents on the outkirts of Kapchack's territory, and the plot concerns Choo Hoo's attempts to seize monarchical power. It is, then, a story of warfare, statecraft, and intrigue. The details of the narrative—the changes in political allegiance, the plots and counter-plots, actions and motives—are extremely complex and we need not elaborate upon them. What is significant is the book's nature and tone. In this enchanted animal-realm, Bevis is educated in the ways of the real world. The story is, in fact, an allegory of the world of men. "Allegory" is, perhaps, too grandiose a term, but it is appropriate in so far as there are obvious analogies between the animal state and human institutions, though the action is sufficiently generalized for no precise identifications to be possible. The disguise is at its thinnest in such passages as the following:

> The rooks live under a limited monarchy; they had real kings of their own centuries since, but now their own king is only a name, a state fiction. Every single rook has a voice in the affairs of the nation (hence the tremendous clamour you may hear in their woods towards sunset when their assemblies are held), but the practical direction of their policy is entrusted to a circle or council of about ten of the older rooks, distinguished for their oratorical powers. These depute, again, one of their own number to Kapchack's court.

At times this literary method leads to a lucid but dreamy naïveté, as when the reed explains to Bevis why the peace-loving majority are continually defeated and overruled by a minority of the evil-minded. If only they would agree among themselves and present a united front, he says, all would be well:

> Then they could drive away the hawk, for there is only one hawk to ten thousand finches, and if they only marched shoulder to shoulder all together they could kill him with case. They could smother the cat even, by all coming down at once upon her, or they could carry up a stone and drop on her head; and as for the crow, that old coward, if he saw them coming he would take wing at once. But as they cannot agree, the hawk, and the cat, and the crow do as they like.

The matter is often over-simplified, but it is never trivial. Every action, every speech has meaning and application. The story includes within itself the matter of several parables; it is an enlarged Aesop's fable, though the moral is never pointed at the end, and it is ornamented, of course, with Jefferies' characteristic natural details.

But if *Wood Magic* were concerned merely with the animal battle, it would not be half the book it is; for the main interest, at least as far as adults are concerned, lies in the inspired lyrical passages which look forward, perhaps unexpectedly, to *The Story of My Heart*. *Wood Magic* is, I think, extremely important in the development of Jefferies' natural mysticism. We know from his notebooks that it was completed on November 3, 1880. That the ideas which were later to find their most direct expression in *The Story of My Heart* were very much in Jefferies' mind at this time is evident, for the first crude notebook jottings were made at Pevensey at the end of the same month. In *Wood Magic* it is as if Jefferies were experimenting with the expression of some of these ideas, and, as yet unsure of himself, is hiding behind the fantasy of the childhood story.

The most eloquent of these passages are to be found in the last chapter, "Sir Bevis and the Wind." The story of the birds and their great battle is over, and Bevis has gone wandering on the Downs. As far as the mere plot is concerned, the chapter is an excrescence, an irrelevance, but from a more deeply artistic point of view, it is both vital and triumphant. It is here that the young Bevis puts away childish things; it is a chapter that transcends the rest of the book and raises the whole narrative to a higher level of significance. The wind whispers to him, and he requests a story:

> "I will try," said the wind; "but I have forgotten all my stories, because the people never come to listen to me now."
>
> "Why don't they come?" said Bevis.
>
> "They are too busy," said the wind, sighing; "they are so very, very busy, just like you were with Kapchack and his treasure and the war, and all the rest of the business; they have so much to do, they have quite forsaken me."
>
> "I will come to you," said Bevis.

Thus the world of Kapchack and his kingdom is renounced at the close of the book and we pass on to something more vital, something ultimate. The wind appeals for a life of Nature in terms which remind us of the famous closing paragraph of *The Amateur Poacher*. Bevis still persists in his childish questions—why? why? why? —but the wind explains that he can only answer these questions himself, and only by leading (in all its sense) a natural life:

> "How can they know anything about the sun who are never out in the sunshine, and never come up on the hills, or go into the wood? How can they know anything about the stars who never stopped on the hills, or on the sea all night? How can they know anything of such things who are shut up in houses, dear, where I cannot come in?
>
> Bevis, my love, if you want to know all about the sun, and the stars, and everything, make haste and come to me, and I will tell you, dear. In the morning, dear, get up as quick as you can, and drink me as I come down from the hill. In the day go up on the hill, dear, and drink me again, and stay there if you can till the stars shine out, and drink still more of me.
>
> And by-and-by you will understand all about the sun, and the moon, and the stars, and the earth which is so beautiful, Bevis. It is so beautiful, you can hardly believe how beautiful it is. . . . If they say the earth is not beautiful, tell them they do not speak the truth."

Extracted from the body of the book, the passages I have quoted may seem over-whimsical, but this is not the impression one receives in context. Childlike it is, but not childish, and there is a freshness and innocence about the writing which is the innocence of wisdom, not of ignorance. And it is this childlike message which draws Bevis across the threshold from childhood into boyhood. The boy who rides home on the carthorse in the final paragraph is, recognizably, the young hero of the opening chapter of the later and greater book.

Some years have passed between the close of *Wood Magic* and the opening of *Bevis: The Story of a Boy*. Bevis is now ten or twelve years of age. The setting is the same, except, of course, for the fact that the older boy can take in a far wider section of the surrounding country. He is now close

friends with Mark, a boy of his own age who is only mentioned in passing in *Wood Magic,* and all the other characters remain—Polly the dairymaid, the Bailiff, Pan the spaniel, and Bevis' parents, though these two are still shadowy, distant characters whose participation in the plot is intentionally negligible. But despite all these resemblances, the book closest to *Bevis* in tone and subject-matter is not so much *Wood Magic* as the opening chapters of *The Amateur Poacher.*

The fancy and fantasy of *Wood Magic* are missing, but these are replaced by an imaginative realism which places the adventures of Bevis and Mark among the most vivid and credible evocations of boyhood in English literature. The book consists of a year in the lives of the two boys, and it divides itself into sections according to their various and ever changing interests. Together they sail a raft, explore the margins of the lake, make elaborate and sophisticated preparations to lead the lives of savages, arrange a battle, learn to swim and shoot and sail, and the climax of the book comes when they spend ten days living by themselves on an island in the lake. It is the great book of the outdoors, of a healthy and faithfully portrayed boys' world. Although the book is, I suspect, of more interest to adults than to boys, the wood has certainly not lost its magic.

I have already emphasized the unsentimental approach of *Wood Magic;* the point needs to be repeated here because it is even more true of *Bevis.* What most impresses us about the book is its modernity. Save for the details of dress and transport, it is difficult to believe that it was written eighty years ago. It would only be a platitude to say that boys have not changed during this time, but it is worthy of mention that Jefferies' methods of presenting them are in complete accord with modern taste. As before, Pan comes in for his share of ill-treatment, and an unobliging donkey is given harsh punishment. The passage is worth quoting at length:

> So soon as John had gone, Mark looked at Bevis, and Bevis looked at Mark. Mark growled. Bevis stamped his feet. "Beast!" said Mark. "Wretch!" said Bevis. "You—you—you, Thing," said Mark; they ground their teeth, and glared at the animal. They led him all fearful to a tree, a little tree but stout enough; it was an ash, and it grew somewhat away from the hedge. They tied him firmly to the tree, and then they scourged this miserable citizen.
>
> All the times they had run in vain to catch him; all the times they had had to walk when they might have ridden one behind the other on his back; all his refusals to be tempted; all the wrongs they had endured at his heels boiled in their breasts. They broke their sticks upon his back, they cut new ones, and smashed them too, they hurled the fragments at him, and then got some more. They thrashed, thwacked, banged, thumped, poked, prodded, kicked, belaboured, bumped, and hit him, working themselves into a frenzy of rage.
>
> Mark fetched a pole to knock him the harder as it was heavy; Bevis crushed into the hedge, and brought out a dead log to hurl at him, a log he

could but just lift and swung to throw with difficulty—the same Bevis who put an aspen leaf carefully under the fly to save it from drowning. The sky was blue, and the evening beautiful, but no one came to help the donkey.

It is but a short incident in a long book. It is not vital to the total scheme, and I can imagine certain people who would wish that Jefferies had never written it. But it is in passages such as this that the uncompromising truth of Jefferies' vision becomes apparent. He is intent on presenting both sides of boyhood, the callousness as well as the kindness, the strain of cruelty as well as the love and sympathy. The scene is as typical of the growing boy as the story of the fly and the aspen leaf, and it is a tribute to Jefferies' impartiality that he alludes to the one in the description of the other. Such a scene reminds us in its vividness and its psychological truth of the descriptions of the less savoury details of rural sport in *The Amateur Poacher*—the wringing of the rabbit's neck and the pheasant shooting. In passages such as these, the habit of Jefferies the reporter in presenting what he sees fully and faithfully is in complete accord with his artistic purpose.

Linked with this strain of callousness is the selfshness of the two boys. Bevis bullies the carter's boy into helping him launch his raft in the stream, but when the boy is nabbed by the bailiff who marches him back to his work, "Bevis and Mark were too full of the raft even to notice that their assistant had been haled off". This selfishness is especially characteristic of Bevis, who is the natural leader of the two and rarely thinks of his companion's rights or feelings. On one occasion, when digging a channel around an obstacle in the stream, they decide in their imaginations to be Greeks digging a canal through Mount Athos.

> "And who are we then, if we are Greeks?"
>
> "I am Alexander the Great."
>
> "And who am I?"
>
> "Oh, you—you are anybody."
>
> "But I *must* be somebody," said Mark, "else it will not do."
>
> "Well, you are: let me see—Pisistratus."
>
> "Who was Pisistratus?"
>
> "I don't know," said Bevis. "It doesn't matter in the least. Now dig."

Similarly, a little later, they are discussing adventures in the jungle:

> "Suppose I was shooting an elephant, and you did not hand me another gun quick, or another arrow; and suppose—"
>
> "But *I* might be shooting the elephant," interrupted Mark, "and you could hand me the gun."
>
> "Impossible," said Bevis; "I never heard anything so absurd. Of course it's the captain who always does everything; and if there was only one biscuit left, of course you would let me eat

it, and lie down and die under a tree, so that I might go and reach the settlement."

> "I *hate* dying under a tree," said Mark, "and you always want everything."

It is this attitude, charming though it may be within the book, that Bevis must outgrow, and he does so. As in **Wood Magic,** we can see a definite development in the character of the hero from the beginning to the end of the book. The life in the open air has had its effect by the close; the education by Nature has been successful.

In fact education, and moreover self-education, is a major theme in the book. One of the reasons why the boys are left on their own for most of the time is because their parents, especially Bevis' "governor," realize that the best way to learn is to teach oneself. This is made explicit in two incidents, swimming and sailing. Seeing their determination to explore the lake, the "governor" rightly insists that they must first learn to swim, but he is careful to teach them only the basic essentials. "His object from the beginning," we are told, "had been so to teach them that they could teach themselves". It is the same when they are learning to sail. "He was almost as interested in their sailing as they were themselves, and had watched them from the bank of the New Sea concealed behind the trees. But he considered it best that they should teach themselves, and find out little by little where they were wrong". The same principle is implicit throughout the book. The two boys scorn to ask of the adults; they prefer to find out on their own, and the climax on the island is itself the perfect presentation of their claims to self-sufficiency.

In the quotations already made from the book, I have given some indication of its nature. Perhaps the best classification would be to call it an inverted adventure story. It contains all the ingredients of a conventional suspense tale—a fight, a shipwreck, life on an island, and a mysterious intruder—but the treatment which they receive is very different. In tone it is certainly not an adventure story. It comes closest to it in the course of the battle, with Bevis' hair-breadth scapes, but for the most part the adventure is confined to the imagination, fused with the real and the ordinary. The battle, for all its planning and strategy, is a relatively tame affair—"no one was hurt, and no one had even had much of a knock, except the larger boys, who could stand it". The shipwreck, though certainly a fact, turns out to be the reverse of romantic; "He [Bevis] could not quite suppress an inward feeling that shipwreck when one was quite alone was not altogether so splendid. It was so dull." When Bevis and Mark are on the island and they become aware of the "something," this too has its unsplendid aspects. Instead of revelling in the adventure, the two become really frightened, and the eventual explanation—the inquisitive cottage-girl, Loo, watching over them—comes as both a relief and a disappointment to the eager adventurers.

Mr. Guy Pocock [in his Introduction to **Bevis**] has described the book as "a prose epic—the epic of boyhood," and it is certainly true that there are distinct heroic qualities about the book which need to be mentioned. It is worth noting, for instance, that there are over a dozen references to the *Odyssey* in the course of the book, and that

Bevis is continually basing his own actions on the adventures of Ulysses, "his favourite hero". When stuck on the fallen hurdle beneath the cliff, Bevis asks himself: "What would Ulysses have done?", and when they are living on the island, Bevis consults the *Odyssey* in order to "read how Ulysses constructed his ship or raft". This heroic quality in the book is nowhere more noticeable than in the details. The battle which Bevis organizes is a schoolboy reconstruction of Pharasalia, with Bevis (inevitably) as Caesar, and their sailing boat is named the *Pinta* after one of the ships in Columbus' expedition. The favourite song of the two boys is "The Ballad of King Estmere," and this is more than a mere battle-song; Bevis reacts to the romance and heroism of the situation. Another of the books which they take to the island is *Don Quixote*.

Reference to Cervantes' comic epic is casual, but it provides a clue to the precise nature of the story. For Quixote the romance lay entirely in his own imagination, which persisted in investing the realities of everyday with a romantic glamour, and this is precisely the method of the two boys. The great effect and charm of the book lie in the imaginative capacities of Bevis and Mark which transform a pleasant though unexceptional stretch of countryside into a wonderland of magic and adventure. In truth, it consisted of the immediate environs of an eighty-acre reservoir containing (in Jefferies' time) two small islands; a small stream flowed through the reservoir, and a brook flowed into it. But in *Bevis* these are all transformed. The reservoir itself is called the New Sea, the two islands are christened New Formosa (or the Magic Island) and Serendib, the stream becomes the Mississippi, and the brook the Nile. On the horizon rise the smooth contours of the Downs, but this is not good enough for them:

> "What are those mountains?" asked Mark.
>
> "The Himalayas, of course," said Bevis.

The flora and fauna are similarly rechristened to fit in with the new world. The rabbits of the mainland become kangaroos, and the doves, parrots. The whole transformation is achieved blatantly and completely, and there is no loss of credibility:

> "Oaks are banyans, aren't they?" said Mark. "They used to be, you know," remembering the exploration of the wood.
>
> "Banyans," said Bevis.
>
> "What are beeches?"
>
> "Oh! teak."
>
> "That's China; aren't we far from China?"
>
> "Ask me presently when I've got my astrolabe." . . .
>
> "Poplars?" said Mark in an interrogative tone.
>
> "Palms, of course. You can see them miles away like palms in a desert."
>
> "Pictures," said Mark. "Yes, that's it. You always see the sun going down, camels with long shadows, and palm trees. Then I suppose it's Africa."

> "You must wait till we have taken an observation. We shall see too by the stars."
>
> "Firs?" said Mark. "They're cedars, of course."
>
> "Of course. Willows are blue gums."
>
> "Then it's near Australia. I expect it is; because, don't you know, there were no animals in Australia except kangaroos, and there are none here at all. So it's that sort of country."

It is a world in which everything contains the possibility of mystery, and, moreover, everything can be explained by mystery, even though the real explanation is both evident and acknowledged. It is a state in which the mind can adapt at will to the dream and the reality, sometimes even accepting both at the same time. A nice example occurs during the early journey of exploration, when they come upon a structure of ash sticks by a path.

> "It's a little house," said Mark, forgetting the quarrel. "Here's some of the straw on the ground; they thatch it in winter and crawl under." (It was about three feet high.)
>
> "I don't know," said Bevis.
>
> "I'm sure it is," said Mark. "They are little men, the savages who live here, they're pigmies, you know."
>
> "So they are," said Bevis, quite convinced, and likewise forgetting his temper. "Of course they are, and that's why the path is so narrow. But I believe it's not a house, I mean not a house to live in. It's a place to worship at, where they have a fetish."
>
> "I think it's a house," said Mark.
>
> "Then where's the fireplace?" asked Bevis decidedly.
>
> "No more there is a fireplace," said Mark thoughtfully. "It's a fetish-place."
>
> Bevis went on again, leaving the framework behind. Across those bars the barley was thrown in autumn for the pheasants, which feed by darting up and down a single ear at a time; thus by keeping the barley off the ground there is less waste. *They knew this very well.* [my italics]

It will be seen that there are definite rules to the game. There must be a display of logic, however fanciful, to back up an opinion. If this is forth-coming the explanation is accepted for so long as it is convenient. And when it ceases to be convenient, it is quietly forgotten.

Bevis and Mark succeed in getting the best of both worlds. Their secret kingdom is both Africa and England; all the delights of a magic land are enjoyed within the quiet beauty of their native countryside. While the names are altered, and suitably fantastic explanations are pondered and adopted for the most commonplace occurrences, they continue to enjoy what remains a particularly English scene. Rabbits may become kangaroos, but they retain the essential characteristics of an English rabbit. The island, despite its new name, is a small islet in a Wiltshire reservoir, and the boys in their hearts would not have it otherwise.

"Everything," as Mark says in a profound understatement, "is somehow else". Gradually this imaginative ambivalence resolves itself into a dichotomy between "here" and "the other side." This latter phrase recurs at several points during the book and represents the real world from which all "magic" has been expelled. The concept first finds formulation in chapter XXXIX when Bevis tells Mark a story. It concerns a traveller searching for a land that had no "other side." It is a typical boyish fantasy concerning lost valleys in Tibet and a hidden paradise (without an "other side") glimpsed through a narrow door. The traveller cannot himself get through the door, but "his mind . . . and soul had gone through", and although he fails ever afterwards to find his way back to the valley, the remembrance of the single vision is always with him:

> He lived to be the oldest man there ever was, which was because he had breathed the delicious air. . . . Every night when he went to sleep he could hear some of the star music of the organ, and dreamed he could see it; but he could hear it plainly. At last he died and went to join his soul, which had travelled on down the footpath, you know, towards the opal sun.

It is an aspirational allegory which is more than a mere interlude. Reference to breathing "the delicious air" reminds us of the wind's exhortation in *Wood Magic,* and we remember that the young Jefferies-Bevis had his own vision of eternity (which has no "other side") on Liddington Hill, and never forgot the experience.

But the other side is real and, in this world, at any rate, cannot be escaped. Even in *Bevis* Jefferies cannot, and will not, suppress his concern for social conditions. When Loo is discovered to be the mysterious intruder on the island, she tells how she came to collect scraps for her baby brother who was ill and starving. Bevis is horrified. "Now Bevis had always been in contact with these folk, but yet he had never seen; you and I live in the midst of things, but never look beneath the surface. His face became quite white; he was thoroughly upset. It was his first glance at the hard roadside of life." It is not reading too much into the book to point out how Jefferies subtly manages the plot so that "the hard road-side of life," the other side at its most grim, is encountered on the island paradise, the magic land. The two worlds, of imagination and of hard economic fact, have met; indeed, they are inseparable. Once again, Nature has educated Bevis.

But Bevis' dream-world and the adult world of the imagination are not quite the same. The latter is an extension and a deepening of the former, and Bevis is to make the transition in the course of the book. Like the young Jefferies, Bevis was a dreamy youth for all his mischief and activity, and Jefferies, comprehensive as ever, does not ignore this aspect of boyhood, though he links it, as later in *The Story of My Heart,* with intense physical activity. In the following passage, Bevis is swimming: "He did not see where he was going, his vision was lost in the ecstasy of motion; all his mind was concentrated in the full use of his limbs. The delicious delirium of strength—unconsciousness of reason, unlimited consciousness of force—the joy of life itself filled him." The emphasis, as always, is on "life." In his notebooks, Jefferies headed

most of his notes for *The Story of My Heart* and its projected sequel, "Sun-Life," a phrase which sums up perfectly his own brand of natural mysticism. And what education could prepare one more soundly for this ideal than the life recounted in *Bevis?* Time and time again, the health of the life is stressed: "the sunlight poured upon them, and the light air came along; they bathed in air and sunbeam, and gathered years of health like flowers from the field". It is the same when they return from their stay on the island: "In those days of running, racing, leaping, exploring, swimming, the skin nude to the sun, and wind and water, they built themselves up of steel, steel that would bear the hardest wear of the world". Life is the key, in fact, to the "magic," as Bevis well knows:

> "I wish we could get a magic writing. Then we could do anything, and we could know all the secrets."
>
> "What secrets?"
>
> "Why, all these things have secrets."
>
> "All?"
>
> "All," said Bevis, looking round and pointing with an arrow in his hand. "All the trees, and all the stones, and all the flowers—"
>
> "And these?" said Mark, picking up a shell.
>
> "Yes, once; but can't you see it's dead, and the secret, of course, is gone."

This aspect of childhood is given its fullest covering in the exquisite lyrical chapter "Bevis's Zodiac" where, during their stay on the island, Bevis leaves Mark one evening to go away by himself, and lies down beneath a tree to look up at the stars. It is the corresponding scene to the final chapter of *Wood Magic.* The fact that many passages are identical with sentences in *The Old House at Coate* proves that the tone, if not the occasion, is autobiographical. It emphasizes, as we might expect, the reality of both the physical and the spiritual. It is a natural mysticism closely linked, as in *The Story of My Heart,* with the sense of touch:

> The sward on the path on which Bevis used to lie and gaze up in the summer evening was real and tangible; the earth under was real; and so too the elms, the oak, the ash trees, were real and tangible—things to be touched, and known to be. Now like these, the mind, stepping from the one to the other, knew and almost felt the stars to be real and not mere specks of light, but things that were there by day over the elms as well as by night, and not apparitions of the evening departing at the twittering of the swallows. They were real, and the touch of his mind felt to them.

But *Bevis,* it must be emphasized, is an extremely happy book, absorbing, natural, and full of humour. The subtlety of the humour in *Bevis* seems to have gone for the most part unnoticed, though it is extraordinary that anyone could read the book and still maintain (as many have done) that Jefferies lacks a sense of humour. Even in the passages I have already quoted, there is more than sufficient to refute such a charge. A single example must suffice here. Bevis and Mark are on an expedition in search of the New Sea (Coate reservoir):

> "When shall we come to the New Sea again?" said Mark presently, as they were moving more slowly through the thicker growth.
>
> "I cannot think," said Bevis. . . .
>
> "Oh! I know, where's the compass?"
>
> "How stupid!" said Bevis. "Of course it was in my pocket all the time."
>
> He took it out, and as he lifted the brazen lid the white card swung to and fro with the vibration of his hand. . . .
>
> "Now, which way was the sea?" said Mark, trying to think of the direction in which they had last seen it. "It was that side," he said, holding out his right hand; he faced Bevis.
>
> "Yes, it was," said Bevis. "It was on the right hand, now that would be east" (to Mark), "so if we go east we must be right."

Jefferies does not lack a sense of humour because he refuses to underline the joke; on the contrary, he demonstrates it. Again, the humour is frequently linked with pathos. The happiness of childhood is never far from sadness, and Jefferies succeeds in maintaining an admirable balance between the two. The mood changes from sunlight to shadow like an April day, and the melancholy has its place alongside the laughter. The transition is easy, because Jefferies hardly ever stands between the reader and the experience; he reports faithfully and accurately. The above quotation well illustrates the naturalness not only of the characters, but of the dialogue. Bevis and Mark are real boys, and they speak the true boys' language. Although the book is not completely true to his own boyhood, it is close enough for Jefferies to be able to dramatize his own self-made adventures and present his own feelings, but at the same time to present a private world which is universally valid. The point can best be made by suggesting that the effectiveness of the book stems from the fact that it was written by an adult Bevis who had never allowed his vision to fade into the light of common day.

After London, or Wild England, published in 1885, is perhaps the most original and unexpected of all Jefferies' productions. As its title suggests, it is set in the dim future, and is indeed one of the first novels to use a future setting for creative imaginative purposes. The story itself, though sufficiently interesting to hold the attention, is nearly always secondary to our interest in the facts of the setting. The book is divided into two parts, the first, entitled "The Relapse into Barbarism," being an account by a historian of the future of the changes, both historical and geographical, between our own time and his. It is a meticulously detailed survey which gives evidence, as Edward Thomas [in his *Richard Jefferies: His Life and Work,* 1909] has pointed out, of "an unsuspected strength of remorseless logic and restraint."

Although this is in many respects a new venture for Jefferies, the alternative title will remind us that the device is a daring and successful method of viewing his more usual field from a new angle. For Jefferies sees the future not as a development, but as a retrogression. Instead of the town overwhelming the country, it is the country that has survived and destroyed the town. London is no more; we are presented with a collection of scattered, isolated communities which have lost the inventions and sophistications of our own age, and seem to have most in common with pre-Conquest England.

There are indications in the earlier books that this theme had interested him for some time. In his essay **"Downs"** from ***The Open Air,*** for instance, he states that the downs were originally covered by woodland, and speculates that "probably the trees would grow again were it not for sheep and horses". It is precisely this process which is described in ***After London.*** And in ***Wood Magic*** the Brook imagines a time "when all the hills are changed and the roads are covered with woods, and the houses gone". In ***After London*** this becomes a reality. A sudden catastrophe deprives England of most of her population; the survivors are unable to maintain control, and Nature reassumes her sway. Man returns to Nature not through any desire on his part, but because Nature returns to him. Thus we may note that the theme of the return to Nature plays an opposite role here to the one it played in the earlier "romances." Here the world of Nature has become the everyday world. Any "escape" is into a lost world of progress and sophistication.

The precise nature of the catastrophe is left deliberately vague. Just as there is no explanation given in ***Wood Magic*** about how "Sir" Bevis succeeded in learning the language of the animals and birds, so here we are offered no pseudo-scientific explanation of the changes in the *status quo*. This vagueness is not the result of any imaginative weakness on Jefferies' part. On the contrary, it is an important part of the fictional design. The narrative is told by a clear-minded and responsible chronicler of a future time. He builds up a picture by means of empirical evidence and the scanty written records, and to these is added the personal conjectures and theories of other scholars. (Jefferies even invents a philosophical historian named Silvester, author of *The Unknown Orb* and *The Book of Natural Things,* whom the narrator considers and refutes at various points in the writing.) For the truth is that the historians themselves are uncertain about what happened. They are forced to rely on conjecture and hearsay—the first sentence beginning "The old men say their fathers told them . . ." is typical of this process. There are later references to "when the ancients [i.e., ourselves] departed" and to "the conflagrations which consumed the towns", but in spite of a few sceptical accounts of theories concerning changes in the water-level and "the passage of an enormous dark body through space", we are never told what happened. We are merely referred to "the event."

As Jefferies is attempting something much more ambitious than the average modern science-fiction, however, this is unimportant. We are not concerned with what happened; we are only interested in the fact that something did happen. This "event" is a fictional hypothesis which we accept from the outset. It is the consequences of the event with which we are concerned, and these are worked out with admirable detail and subtlety:

> All that seems certain is, that when the event took place, the immense crowds collected in cities were most affected, and that the richer and upper classes made use of their money to escape. Those left behind were mainly the lower and most ignorant, so far as the arts were concerned; those that dwelt in distant and outlying places; and those who lived by agriculture. These last, at that date, had fallen to such distress that they could not hire vessels to transport themselves.

This last sentence shows us that Jefferies' usual and continual interests are still in evidence here. This is, in fact, a romance of the agricultural depression; country society has been deserted by the townsmen, and left to its fate.

The result is inevitable. With insufficient men to work the land, the roads and footpaths soon became impassable, and the fields are overgrown with weeds and shrubs. Later, rivers and streams get out of control and form extensive swamps. Eventually the towns and cities are overwhelmed, and England reverts to a prehistoric landscape of marsh and forest. Domesticated cattle become wild and take to the hills and woods. Even the more intelligent of the human survivors are incapable of maintaining "modern" discoveries, and such inventions as railways and the telegraph become things of the past. "These marvellous things are to us little more than fables of the giants and of the old gods that walked upon the earth, which were fables even to those whom we call the ancients." Men become hunters again, and the more backward of them remain in this condition. They become the Bushmen and the Gipsies who are the continual enemies of the more advanced communities of agricultural folk which gradually form themselves and begin the quest for civilization once again.

Little by little, villages are formed, and after these, towns and even kingdoms. Inevitably rivalry and war begin. The Welsh, Scots, and Irish assert their independence, and we are quite obviously back in the Dark Ages once more. It is a world of injustice and cruelty not unlike Kapchack's animal kingdom in *Wood Magic.* We are told that "there is hardly a town where the slaves do not outnumber the free as ten to one. The laws are framed for the object of reducing the greater part of the people to servitude." Jefferies' views concerning the future are interesting; they are obviously at the opposite pole from the over-simple optimism of Morris' *News From Nowhere* (which it predates by six years), but on the other hand they do not partake of the calculated evil of the inverted Utopias of Huxley and Orwell. Instead we see a new struggling civilization making the same tragic mistakes and blunders as the old. It is a vision (and this is crucial) not of evil but of ignorance. Again this is a deliberate part of Jefferies' creative scheme. Far from its showing a lack of invention, the conception of sameness and repetition is itself the invention. "It is all changed and just the same." I have already had occasion to quote this as Jefferies' central statement concerning the rural scene of his own time; it is equally appropriate as a comment on the view of history which underlies *After London.*

There is one considerable change, however, that has not yet been mentioned. This is the appearance of the great central Lake. It is allegedly caused by impediments to the eastward flow of the Thames and the westward flow of the Severn. Be that as it may, we are presented with a vast inland Lake which stretches from Bristol on the west to London on the east, with the White Horse range as its southern boundary, its northern boundary being left vague. This lake is the central feature of the book. Upon it the hero, Felix Aquila, sets off on his voyage of adventure and discovery, and it is during this voyage that he arrives quite unwittingly upon the stagnant and poisonous swamp which covers the site of London.

Felix is remarkable in that, while living in an age of barbarism, he has the outlook and sensitivity of an "ancient." In an age when learning is despised, he is a lover of learning; in an age when brute force is essential and respected, he is slender, shy, and retiring. He presents a perfect contrast to his athletic brother Oliver who was, Jefferies tells us, "as active and energetic as Felix was outwardly languid". But there are certain aspects of his character which are particularly significant. Even as we read they strike a familiar ring:

> This unbending independence and pride of spirit, together with scarce concealed contempt for others, had resulted in almost isolating him from the youth of his own age, and had caused him to be regarded with dislike by the elders. . . . Too quick to take offence where none was really intended, he fancied that many bore him ill-will who had scarcely given him a passing thought. He could not forgive the coarse jokes uttered upon his personal appearance by men of heavier build, who despised so slender a stripling.

This extract hardly gives a fair description of Felix who is throughout a sympathetic character, but the details are so close to many that we know of Jefferies' own youth that it is difficult to escape the suspicion that it is an idealized self-portrait. This is confirmed by later touches, especially his solitary excursions into the wild country and the observation that "the mystery of existence had impressed him deeply while wandering alone in the forest".

The passage describing his construction of a large canoe could have come straight out of *Bevis,* and when Oliver points out the difficulty of sailing downstream because "there's an old fir across the river down yonder, and a hollow willow has fallen in", we are clearly dealing with a real incident also treated in the second chapter of *Bevis.* At this point we realize that *After London* is in fact a continuation of the earlier book on a new imaginative and vastly enlarged scale. The setting, we find, is no more nor less than a giant Coate farm, and the reservoir which in *Bevis* was imagined by the children to be a new sea is now extended to cover a vast section of the south of England.

I am contributing nothing new in making this identification. The point is sufficiently obvious to any careful reader, and it has been noted several times. It is surprising, though, that critics have not followed up the autobiographical possibilities of *After London,* for there are numerous ways in which discussion could be extended. One leads us into the intricacies of psychological criticism, and while at times this critical approach can be both dangerous and misleading, at other times it can be necessary and helpful. I believe *After London* to be a case in point. If *Bevis* was Jefferies' childhood not precisely as it was, but as he would like it to have been, so the present book seems to be a fictional and barely disguised representation of his unrealized ambitions and yearnings. After we have been introduced to Felix, and have recognized him as a self-portrait of the author, we are shown his dissatisfaction with his present life, his passionate and apparently hopeless love for Aurora Thyma, and his determination to achieve some elaborate quest to impress Aurora and to satisfy himself. Eventually he chooses his objective—the circumnavigation of the great Lake in a home-made canoe. He sets out, and his first adventure brings him to a town that is being besieged, and he is appalled by the incompetence of the besieging prince. He is heard criticizing, is arrested, and eventually brought to trial in front of the prince. He speaks out boldly, repeats his criticisms, and offers suggestions for improving the attack which amaze and impress the court. But he overreaches himself, suggests a revolutionary assault weapon which is beyond the imagination of his hearers, and is beaten out of the camp as a fool. Basically, it is a story of intelligence against ignorance, of brain power against brute force. Felix is the enlightened man of intelligence, who is humiliated and ridiculed by inferiors whose only weapon is tyrannic power. His next adventure is on the site of London to which he sails by a combination of accident and curiosity, and barely escapes from the poisonous and intricate swamp. Here it is a case of achievement in the teeth of difficulty, success where others stronger but less intelligent had failed, of triumph that assures his name in history and the admiration of the woman he loves. The third phase of his adventure relates his meeting with the shepherds. His canoe has been wrecked, and he is at the nadir of his fortunes. On meeting the shepherds, he tells them his adventures on the swamps of London, and they greet him as a superman, if not a god. In one fantastic paragraph he comes into his own:

> Their manner towards him perceptibly altered. From the first they had been hospitable; they now became respectful, and even reverent. The elders and their chief, not to be distinguished by dress or ornament from the rest, treated him with ceremony and marked deference. The children were brought to see and even to touch him. So great was their amazement that any one should have escaped from these pestilential vapours, that they attributed it to divine interposition, and looked upon him with some of the awe of supersitition. He was asked to stay with them altogether, and to take command of the tribe.

At last intelligence is rewarded. He agrees to stay, but flatters the elders by refusing the command—another instance of his wisdom. Instead, he is accepted among them under the title of "Leader." Later he adds to his achievements. With the help of his skill and guile, he defeats their enemies almost single-handed, and later locates a hidden spring (according to the shepherds, miraculously) when their flocks are in desperate need of water. He is credited with supernatural powers, and Jefferies emphasizes that "in innumerable little ways Felix's superior knowledge had told upon them".

But Felix has greater ambitions than being merely the wise man in a tribe of shepherds. Nearby he has discovered a beautiful lake (Coate reservoir once more, idealized this time in beauty rather than in size), where he determines to build a strong fortress, and a tower in which he will live with Aurora. Here he will remain as "Leader" of the shepherds in a world of happiness and content. Unfortunately, the shepherds dislike the idea of his leaving them, even temporarily to fetch Aurora, and they plan to keep him with them by force. But again "superior knowledge" triumphs; he eludes them, and the book ends as he is on his way to Thyma Castle and Aurora. We are left with the impression that he will be successful, that he and Aurora will return to the shepherds and live in the fortified tower, an oasis of culture and intelligence safe, thanks to knowledge and learning, in the midst of a barbarous world. Like Bevis before him, Felix educates himself, but he is not confined to the terms or real life, and develops from a thwarted youth into a triumphant superman.

It is difficult to believe that the connection between the romance on the one hand and Jefferies' own character and ambitions on the other is completely fortuitous. There are incidents throughout his biography which remind us not only of Felix's original situation but also of his pride and obstinacy. Throughout his work there runs a continued strain of ambition, a confident sense of the possible, which is ever thwarted by a realization of his physical weakness and his lack of undoubted literary success. So in *The Story of My Heart* he writes: "Let me be physically perfect, in shape, vigour, and movement. My frame, naturally slender, will not respond to labour, and increase in proportion to effort, nor will exposure harden a delicate skin. It disappoints me so far, but my spirit rises with the effort, and my thought opens." The resemblance to Felix's situation can hardly be denied.

It is interesting to note that this mounting ambition, this determination to achieve success, is almost invariably expressed in Jefferies' writings by the image of a voyage. This is natural enough—the voyage archetype doubtless has a similar universal significance—but in Jefferies it is particularly strong. It occurs in *Bevis* in the boys' voyage and the continual references to the *Odyssey*. In the essay **"Red Roofs of London"** Jefferies writes: "In the hearts of most of us, there is always a desire for something beyond experience. Hardly any of us but have thought, Some day I will go on a long voyage; but the years go by, and still we have not sailed." The image recurs several times in *The Story of My Heart,* as here: "There is an immense ocean over which the mind can sail, upon which the vessel of thought has not yet been launched. I hope to launch it." But Felix Aquila refuses to let the years go by; he insists on sailing, and thereby achieves his object and reaps the reward of his intelligence. The success which he missed in life Jefferies portrays in romance. The whole is a presentation of Jefferies' own dream-world, an enlarged version of his true life at Coate.

After London is not one of his best books—partly because it is too close to the patterns of his own subconscious. In addition, the narrative of the second part is less successful than the imaginative description of the first, and suffers by comparison with John Collier's *Tom's A-Cold,* a novel to which it bears a close resemblance. *After London* leaves the reader with a sense of admiration, but also of bewilderment. The balance between the intense logical realism and the heights of romantic fantasy is impossible to maintain, for the significant reason that the romance is too close to life. But it is an important document in his biography as man as artist, and deserves greater attention than it has generally received.

Brian Taylor   (essay date 1982)

SOURCE: "The Last Essays," in *Richard Jefferies,* Twayne Publishers, 1982, pp. 135-52.

[*In this excerpt, Taylor studies four of Jefferies's essay collections, suggesting that his "numerous essays originated in his obsessive early cataloguings of the details of the natural world."*]

The volumes of collected essays which saw publication in Jefferies's lifetime were *Nature Near London* (1883), *The Life of the Fields* (1884), and *The Open Air* (1885). *Field and Hedgerow,* published as "**Being the Last Essays of Richard Jefferies, Collected by his Widow,**" appeared in 1889, two years after his death. These four volumes repay more detailed examination and it is the essays which comprise them which will be examined in this chapter. A large number of Jefferies's essays were, however, collected together in comparatively recent years, many at the instigation of the late Samuel J. Looker. *The Toilers of the Field* appeared in 1892, and Mr. Looker edited the anthologies *Jefferies' England* (1937), *Jefferies' Countryside* (1944), *Richard Jefferies' London* (1944), *The Spring of the Year* (1946), *The Jefferies Companion* (1948), *The Old House at Coate, and Other Hitherto Unprinted Essays* (1948), *Chronicles of the Hedges* (1948), and *Field and Farm* (1957). Mention should also be made of the more recent collection of Jefferies's essays anthologized by Andrew Rossabi under the title of one of his most accomplished essays, *The Pageant of Summer* (1979).

Despite all of this welcome and prodigious work in bringing the essays to a wider public, it is still the case that some remain unreprinted, and the interested reader is referred here to the fine bibliography of these appended to W. J. Keith's *Richard Jefferies: A Critical Study.* Keith makes the point that there may be discerned, in Jefferies's essays considered as a whole, a gradual but progressive development, and there is indeed much evidence to support this view. The very early essays, those which Jefferies had contributed to the *Live Stock Journal* and to *Fraser's Magazine* were much in the manner of catalogues of rural observation which characterized the early books, most notably *The Gamekeeper at Home* and *Round About a Great Estate.* As we have seen, the material for a number of these books appeared initially in serial form. *The Amateur Poacher* had appeared in the pages of the *Pall Mall Gazette* during 1879, and *The Gamekeeper at Home* in the

same journal during the previous year. *Round About a Great Estate* appeared there in 1880 and *Wild Life in a Southern County* during 1878. *Hodge and His Masters* appeared in the *Standard* from 1878 to 1880. It cannot be said, then, that Jefferies was a stranger to the essay form, but it may be fairly claimed that his early journalistic training had somewhat cramped its style, producing an essay form much dependent on reporting. A case could be made for considering *Nature Near London* to be the last in this line of "reporter's essays," with *The Life of the Fields* marking the beginning of a more mature and personal voice. This case would rest on the important fact that the fourteen months which separated the publication of these two volumes of essays had also seen the publication of *The Story of My Heart.* As W. J. Keith rightly remarks, it "can hardly be a coincidence" that Jefferies's spiritual autobiography and the events which had led him to write it should also provoke a subtle but fundamental change in the manner and intention of his essay writing.

The nineteen essays in *Nature Near London* appeared initially in the pages of the *Standard,* the greater number of them having been written in 1881. The year is significant since, as we have seen, it was at this time that Jefferies's health began to fail. *Nature Near London* is, then, for the reader with some background knowledge of the progress of Jefferies's life, a sad book to read. Edward Thomas [in his *Richard Jefferies: His Life and Work,* 1909] perfectly captures the dominant tone of the collection.

> . . . the eye that sees and the mind that broods over it is changed. The old, simpler exuberance of *The Poacher* is lost. Thoughts have troubled and checked it; his health is finally to give way in 1881; and the new surroundings are not a part of him, as were the old, and he seems to see them more as strange pictures—as pictures which his brooding and solitary mind more and more informs; the labourers and farmers and keepers who used to move about the Wiltshire fields have disappeared, and the landscape is rather inhuman for a time, for in Surrey he knew nobody, though he saw a Ploughman and milker and harvester. But he had to write, and the demand for his short country papers having been established, he naturally kept to that desultory form.

The new neighborhood, the "near London" of the book's title, is the soon to be suburbanized country around Tolworth and Surbiton to the south of the metropolis. Jefferies had by now exhausted his notes of Coate Farm and the surrounding country. In Thomas's words, again, "when he writes about the country again, it is nearly always as one who, having travelled to a distant city of the mind, can never return." The preface which Jefferies attached to the collected essays gives some hint of this change of mood and the occasional revealing admission says much about the effect which the move to Surbiton had on him. "It is usually supposed to be necessary to go far into the country to find wild birds and animals in sufficient numbers to be pleasantly studied. Such was certainly my own impression till circumstances led me, for the convenience of access to London, to reside for awhile about twelve miles from town. There my preconceived views on the subject were quite overthrown by the presence of as much bird life as I had been accustomed to in distant fields and woods." That Jefferies should have expected to have been disappointed by the Surbiton fields is excusable and there is a slight note of desperation, the unnoticed exaggeration of one trying hard to convince himself in that passage. The closing paragraph of the book's preface affords what is surely a more truthful glimpse of Jefferies's thoughts at this time.

> Though my preconceived ideas were overthrown by the presence of so much that was beautiful and interesting close to London, yet in course of time I came to understand what was at first a dim sense of something wanting. In the shadiest lane, in the still pinewoods on the hills of purple heath, after brief contemplation there arose a restlessness, a feeling that it was essential to be moving. In no grassy mead was there a nook where I could stretch myself in slumberous ease and watch the swallows ever wheeling, wheeling in the sky. This was the unseen influence of mighty London. The strong life of the vast city magnetized me, and I felt it under the calm oaks. The something wanting in the fields was the absolute quiet, peace, and rest which dwells in the meadows and under the trees and on the hilltops in the country. Under its power, the mind gradually yields itself to the green earth, the wind among the trees, the song of birds, and comes to have an understanding with them all. For this it is still necessary to seek the far-away glades and hollow coombes, or to sit alone beside the sea.

Although he never lived in London itself, Jefferies often wrote of its sights in his essays and often his admiration is more uncritical than his prefatory admission to *Nature Near London* might suggest. In *Amaryllis,* he asked, "Could Xerxes, could great Pompey, could Caesar with all his legions, could Lucullus with all his oysters, ever have enjoyed such pleasure as this, just to spend money freely in the streets of London?" But again there is a note of insincerity here, of something not quite believed. The final sentence to his preface adds to his complaint against the capital. "That such a sense of quiet might not be lacking," he writes, "I have added a chapter or so on those lovely downs that overlook the south coast". These last essays of *Nature Near London,* **"To Brighton,"** **"The Southdown Shepherd,"** and **"The Breeze on Beachy Head,"** show his delight at encountering a landscape familiar to the fondly remembered Wiltshire downs. As Thomas notes, "the addition of the sea to the downs did for him all that could be done for him without restoring him to youth and Wiltshire. The essay **"To Brighton"** details Jefferies's thoughts and observations in the train from London to Brighton and it is interesting how his gaze travels upward, as it were, as he approaches the downs and then the sea. The journey and this aspect of it serves, indeed, as a model for the essays which comprise *Nature Near London.* In the pieces which describe the Surbiton countryside, Jefferies's gaze is directed downward at some detail on the ground or some intricate grass or insect. It is as if he were afraid to lift his head and gaze at the skyline. Previously this had revealed to him the noble line of Liddington Hill and the broad back of the downs in his native Wiltshire. Now, the all-encompassing gaze would reveal

the smoky haze of London encroaching over the horizon. And so, Jefferies's attention is caught again and again by the details of structure or by the sights revealed by constant observation. Thus, he sees a trout in the Hogsmill Brook at Tolworth Court Farm and observes its growth over two summers in **"A London Trout."** Again, he describes in minute and perfect detail the progress of a troop of ants on Sandown Heath.

> Standing a short way back, so as not to interfere with their proceedings, I saw two of these insects seize hold of a twig, one at each end. The twig, which was dead and dry, and had dropped from a fir, was not quite so long as a match, but rather thicker. They lifted this stick with ease, and carried it along, exactly as labourers carry a plank. A few short blades of grass being in the way they ran up against them, but stepped aside, and so got by. A cart which had passed a long while since had forced down the sand by the weight of its load, leaving a ridge about three inches high, the side being perpendicular.
>
> Till they came to this cliff the two ants moved parallel, but here one of them went first, and climbed up the bank with its end of the stick, after which the second followed and brought up the other. An inch or two further, on the level ground, the second ant left hold and went away, and the first laboured on with the twig and dragged it unaided across the rest of the path. Though many other ants stayed and looked at the twig a moment, none of them now offered assistance, as if the chief obstacle had been surmounted.

It is a characteristically detailed and methodical piece of natural description, and to be sure Jefferies had inserted many such passages into his earlier "country books." Nevertheless, in those, there is the sense of astonishing detail observed when casting the eyes down from the wider view. In this essay, called **"Heathlands,"** there is no such wider view, rather a kaleidoscope of perfectly observed pieces grouped together.

None of this can be offered as criticism of the essays which comprise *Nature Near London,* but it does indicate the shift in Jefferies's viewpoint in the period leading up to the writing of *The Story of My Heart.* It is as sight is becoming vision, the outward, all-encompassing gaze first having to be directed downward before it can be turned inward. It is because of this characteristic of the earlier essays in *Nature Near London* that the final **"Brighton"** essays come upon the reader as a surprise in the context of the book, yet strike him with the shock of recognition. It is in these three essays that we are reminded forcefully of the enthusiastic and near-mystic sense of joy and wonder in natural surroundings that was expressed in the closing sections of *The Amateur Poacher,* four years earlier. In the essay **"Footpaths,"** Jefferies's imagination all but takes flight as he dwells upon the joys of walking, but it is finally constrained in his depressing, if resigned, realization that, as he says, "The inevitable end of every footpath round about London is London. All paths go thither".

> . . . After rambling across furze and heath, or through dark fir woods; after lingering in the

meadows among the buttercups, or by the copses where the pheasants crow; after gathering June roses, or in later days, staining the lips with blackberries or cracking nuts, by-and-by the path brings you in sight of a railway station. And the railway station, through some process of mind, presently compels you to go up on the platform, and after a little puffing and revolution of wheels you emerge at Charingcross, or London Bridge, or Waterloo, or Ludgate-hill, and, with the freshness of the meadows still clinging to your coat, mingle with the crowd.

There is no animosity here toward London or against its encroachment on the fields twelve miles away; just a patient resignation that, no matter how able the wildlife of Surbiton to alter Jefferies's "preconceived views" on the subject, the heaths and sparse woodlands of this piece of Surrey were not the windy downlands of Wiltshire.

The train journey to Brighton, described in the essay **"To Brighton,"** begins with Jefferies's patient detailed descriptions of the flowers to be seen on the banks of the railway and the sides of the cuttings. "Purple heathbells gleam from shrub-like bunches dotted along the slope; purple knapweeds lower down in the grass; blue scabious, yellow hawk-weeds where the soil is thinner, and harebells on the very summit; these are but a few upon which the eye lights while gliding by". Jefferies observes a wood-pigeon keeping pace with the train, recalls a pair of shrikes who used the telegraph wires for perching on "only a short distance beyond noisy Clapham Junction." Presently, the reader's attention is drawn upward, and the first intimation of what Jefferies has found missing in the Surbiton countryside is given.

> The haze hangs over the wide, dark plain, which, soon after passing, Redhill, stretches away on the right. It seems to us in the train to extend from the foot of a great bluff there to the first rampart of the still distant South Downs. In the evening that haze will be changed to a flood of purple light veiling the horizon. Fitful glances at the newspaper or the novel pass the time; but now I can read no longer, for I know, without any marks or tangible evidence, that the hills are drawing near. There is always hope in the hills.

"The dust of London fills the eyes and blurs the vision," Jefferies writes, "but it penetrates deeper than that. There is a dust that chokes the spirit, and it is this that makes the streets so long, the stones so stony, the desk so wooden; the very rustiness of the iron railings about the offices sets the teeth on edge, the sooty blackened walls (yet without shadow) thrust back the sympathies which are ever trying to cling to the inanimate things around us". And then, all is well. "A breeze comes in at the carriage window—a wild puff, disturbing the heated stillness of the summer day. It is easy to tell where that came from—silently the Downs have stolen into sight". The rest of this essay is an exercise in controlled relief. The Downs are glimpsed—"Hope dwells there, somewhere, mayhap, in a breeze, in the sward, or the pale cups of the harebells. Now, having gazed at these, we can lean back on the cushions and wait patiently for the sea"—and the first view of the sea is as exciting and as controlled. "The clean dry

brick pavements are scarcely less crowded than those of London, but as you drive through the town, now and then there is a glimpse of a greenish mist afar off between the houses. The green mist thickens in one spot almost at the horizon; or is it the dark nebulous sails of a vessel? Then the foam suddenly appears close at hand—a white streak seems to run from house to house, reflecting the sunlight; and this is Brighton."

But it is the Downs upon which Jefferies concentrates here. He walks to the summit of Ditchling Beacon, which he calls "the nearest and most accessible of the southern Alps from London" and his fine description of that fine landscape brings back the tone of sheer exultation which, somehow without missing it, we now realize has been absent from the earlier essays in *Nature Near London.*

> Down in the hollow the breeze does not come, and the bennets do not whistle, yet gazing upwards at the vapour in the sky I fancy I can hear the mass, as it were, of the wind going over. Standing presently at the edge of the steep descent looking into the Weald, it seems as if the mighty blast rising from that vast plain and glancing up the slope like an arrow from a tree could lift me up and bear me as bears a hawk with outspread wings.
>
> A mist which does not roll along or move is drawn across the immense stage below like a curtain. There is, indeed, a brown wood beneath; but nothing more is visible. The plain is the vaster for its vague uncertainty. From the north comes down the wind, out of the brown autumn light, from the woods below and twenty miles of stubble. Its stratum and current is eight hundred feet deep.
>
> Against my chest, coming up from the plough down there . . . it hurls itself against the green ramparts, and bounds up savagely at delay. The ears are filled with a continuous sense of something rushing past; the shoulders go back square; an iron-like feeling enters into the sinews. The air goes through my coat as if it were gauze, and strokes the skin like a brush.
>
> The tide of the wind, like the tide of the sea, swirls about, and its cold push at the first causes a lifting feeling in the chest—a gulp and pant— as if it were too keen and strong to be borne. Then the blood meets it, and every fibre and nerve is filled with new vigour. I cannot drink enough of it.

In the final essay of *Nature Near London,* Jefferies returns to the sea at Beachy Head, and his enthusiasm for the downland breezes is matched here in his joy at the sight and the mystery of the sea.

> . . . there is an infinite possibility about the sea; it may do what it is not recorded to have done. It is not to be ordered, it may overleap the bounds human observation has fixed for it. It has a potency unfathomable. There is still something in it not quite grasped and understood— something still to be discovered—a mystery.
>
> So the white spray rushes along the low broken

wall of rocks, the sun gleams on the flying fragments of the wave, again it sinks, and the rhythmic motion holds the mind, as an invisible force holds back the tide. A faith of expectancy, a sense that something may drift up from the unknown, a large belief in the unseen resources of the endless space out yonder, soothes the mind with dreamy hope. . . .

. . . The sun sinks behind the summit of the Downs, and slender streaks of purple are drawn along above them. A shadow comes forth from the cliff; a duskiness dwells on the water; something tempts the eye upwards, and near the zenith there is a star.

Jefferies published **"The Breeze on Beachy Head"** in the *Standard* in September 1881. Already he had begun to write *The Story of My Heart.*

Jefferies never stayed long anywhere after he left Tolworth. The summer of 1882 he spent partly on Exmoor, whence came the material for *Red Deer,* and by the end of that year he was at Lorna Road in Hove, West Brighton. *The Life of the Fields* was published in 1884 and most of the essays in it were written at Brighton. Not all of these essays dealt with the Sussex countryside, however. In **"The Field Play," "The Pageant of Summer,"** and **"Meadow Thoughts,"** he writes of Wiltshire. In **"By the Exe"** and **"The Water Colley,"** he describes Somerset. In some of the closing essays, he is in London and in **"The Plainest City in Europe,"** the final essay in the collection, he offers his thoughts on Paris.

Edward Thomas has conveniently classified Jefferies's essays into three groups. "The first," he says, "consists of lengths of notes, carefully wrought in parts, but irregular, almost shapeless, and showing signs of fatigue or of painful concession to the 'essay' form." In *The Life of the Fields,* **"Clematis Lane," "January in the Sussex Woods,"** and **"By the Exe"** fall into this category. Thomas goes on to: " . . . essays, accurately so called, make the second class; these are orderly discussions of a given subject, the material supplied chiefly by his own observation and reflection, as in **'Mind under Water,' 'Birds Climbing the Air,' 'The Plainest City in Europe.'"** The third category Thomas considers " . . . those papers with which the first might have ranked had they been more happily wrought. They are impassioned descriptions of meditations, like **'The Pageant of Summer,' 'Meadow Thoughts,' 'Sunlight in a London Square,' 'Venice in the East End.'"** This third category of Thomas's represents those essays which, it may be claimed, Jefferies could not have written had he not already produced *The Story of My Heart.* It was in that book that Jefferies offered, *par excellence,* "Impassioned descriptions of meditations," and it is the essays which comprise the last of Thomas's three categories which represent, in *The Life of the Fields,* the progress to a uniquely personal vision in his essay writing which Jefferies had made since *Nature Near London.*

In **"The Pageant of Summer,"** which, in the words of W. J. Keith, "is generally considered to be Jefferies' finest piece of work," Jefferies comes close, and certainly as close as he ever did, to fusing the mystical introspections of *The Story of My Heart* with the precise detailed observation of, for example, *Wild Life in a Southern County.* Again and again in these essays, he attempts, in an increasingly impassioned manner, to transcend the limitations of the objective reporter, the faithful recorder of the natural scene with which role he had been content in the earlier writings. Now he wants to combine the objective with the subjective, he continually strives to interpose the human figure, which is inevitably the agent and the mediator of the observed natural world. Jefferies had hinted at something of this wish in the preface to *Nature Near London,* where he had responded to the question "Why have you not indicated in every case the precise locality where you were so pleased? Why not mention the exact hedge, the particular meadow?" by the simple claim that " . . . no two persons look at the same thing with the same eyes." By the time he came to write **"The Pageant of Summer,"** Jefferies had come to see that locality was often an irrelevance in the best of his nature writing. His point now is that his descriptions not only could have been made anywhere, but precisely that they *were* everywhere. In W. J. Keith's terms, Jefferies's writing in this vein constitute less of a description of the scene and more an *evocation* of it. "He is attempting to catch and preserve the fleeting moment as it passes, to fix the eternity which is about him in the sunshine." No matter where the fleeting moment was passed, what matters now is the all important link between the observer and the observed and between the particular observed event and the dimly apprehended sense of Nature itself. And in these essays, for Jefferies, Nature and Life are increasingly linked. The component of the observed scene which now comes under Jefferies's amazed scrutiny is precisely the figure of the observer himself. As in the closing section of **"The Pageant of Summer"** time and timelessness fuse into one through the presence of Jefferies himself.

The endless grass, the endless, leaves, the immense strength of the oak expanding, the unalloyed joy of finch and blackbird; from all of them I receive a little. Each gives me something of the pure joy they gather for themselves. In the blackbird's melody one note is mine; in the dance of the leaf shadows the formed maze is for me, though the motion is theirs; the flowers with a thousand faces have collected the kisses of the morning. Feeling with them, I receive some, at least, of their fulness of life. Never could I have enough; never stay long enough—whether here or whether lying on the shorter sward under the sweeping and graceful birches, or on the thyme-scented hills. Hour after hour, and still not enough. Or walking the footpath was never long enough, or my strength sufficient to endure till the mind was weary. The exceeding beauty of the earth, in her splendour of life, yields a new thought with every petal. The hours when the mind is absorbed by beauty are the only hours when we really live, so that the longer we can stay among these things so much the more is snatched from inevitable Time. Let the shadow advance upon the dial—I can watch it with equanimity while it is there to be watched. It is only when the shadow is not there, when the clouds of winter cover it, that the dial is terrible. The invisible shadow goes on and steals from us.

> But now, while I can see the shadow of the tree
> and watch it slowly gliding along the surface of
> the grass, it is mine. These are the only hours
> that are not wasted—these hours that absorb the
> soul and fill it with beauty. This is real life, and
> all else is illusion, or mere endurance.

It is always too tempting to quote at length from Jefferies's essays, but the sense of summer that he offers in **"The Pageant of Summer"** is almost tangible, and can only be communicated in the original. As Richard Church [quoted in W. J. Keith's *Richard Jefferies: A Critical Study*] excellently puts it, " . . . they felt like summer," they offer "physical vision."

"The Pageant of Summer" was first published in *Longman's Magazine* in June 1883. His forebodings then about "inevitable Time" were sadly prophetic; he had just over four years to live. Often in the essays which make up *The Life of the Fields,* he recommends the reader who would share his observations to keep in one place summer and winter, since in the course of a year every creature "that is not entirely local will pass over any given spot". As Thomas notes, Jefferies's advice was sadly born of necessity. "It was probably his own habit more and more, for though in a letter written late in his life at Crowborough he speaks of knowing the whole range of the South Downs, he was compelled by ill-health to walk less and less." Thomas rightly concludes that his early writings "were the work of a walker; the later are the work of one who lies or sits."

The Open Air remains one of Jefferies's most popular books, and certainly one of the most often reprinted. The reasons for this popularity are not difficult to find. In 1885, albeit only two years before his death, Jefferies was at the top of his powers. *The Story of My Heart, The Dewy Morn,* and *Hodge and His Masters* were all behind him, and what C. Henry Warren has called [in his introduction to *The Open Air*] the "quiet, lovely swan-song" of *Amaryllis at the Fair* remained to be written. The twenty-one essays which make up *The Open Air* cover, as did those in *The Life of the Fields,* the range of Jefferies's later interests. **"Nature on the Roof "** carries on the tradition of objective nature essays and is, by some standards, little more than a comprehensive catalogue of the life, from bird to wasp, fern to house-leek, that can be found on the roof of house or barn. **"Haunts of the Lapwing," "Out of Doors in February,"** and **"Outside London"** continue the line of inspired, meticulous observation. Additionally in *The Open Air* there is an essay, **"One of the New Voters,"** apparently published for the first time in that volume, in which Jefferies returns to his delineation of the characteristics of the agricultural working-class which he dealt with in extended fashion in *Hodge and His Masters* some five years previously. And, again, there are those essays which owe their inspiration perhaps to the mysticism of *The Story of My Heart* and to Jefferies's awareness of his own approaching death. **"Wildflowers"** is one of these, as is the first in the collection, **"Saint Guido,"** although to this reader that particular essay is most reminiscent of the splendid *Wood Magic.*

There seems little doubt that the composition of the essays which make up *The Open Air* was undertaken by Jefferies in the increasing knowledge of the true nature of his illness. There is little pretense at shaping the book in any order, as he had been most careful to do in *Wild Life in a Southern County* and *The Gamekeeper at Home* and even *Round About a Great Estate.* Jefferies, in the words of [Warren], "poured himself out more bountifully in these essays than in most."

> All the man is here in all his moods; and, as you
> turn the pages, you never know which mood you
> may come upon next, which aspect of his char-
> acter: it may be the naturalist, or the mystic, or
> the social thinker, or it may just as likely be the
> realistic observer of the working countryman. It
> is as if you should come upon a friend, unan-
> nounced and unexpected, discovering each time
> some fresh glimpse of his variety, and in the end
> you find you know him the better, richer than
> you had guessed, for the contradictory aspects
> thus disarmingly revealed. In all the moods and
> aspects of this collection of essays it is the same
> man speaking, our of his ripeness—and perhaps
> the more pertinently because of his prescience
> that the end is near.

These comments clearly come from an admirer of the book but they are revealing of the various aspects of Jefferies's personality which can undoubtedly be found communicated so forcefully in its pages. The essay **"One of the New Voters,"** might, in one analysis, be considered a rarity among the essays of Jefferies's last years, although it is paralleled in **"John Smith's Shanty,"** an essay to be found in the posthumous collection *The Toilers of the Field.* Just as in the famous letters to the *Times* of 1872, Jefferies is nothing but honest about the life and manners of the agricultural laborer. As the son of a small farmer himself, he had been in a position to know the laborer exactly for what he was: hard-working, ungrateful, ungracious, humorless, and basically servile. Now, in **"One of the New Voters,"** his stern realism is tempered by a more mature understanding of his plight. Very likely the laborer is blind to the beauty which daily surrounds him, as he had implied a dozen years ago, but

> . . . why should he note the colour of the butter-
> fly, the bright light of the sun, the hue of the
> wheat? This loveliness gave him no cheese for
> breakfast; of beauty in itself, for itself, he had no
> idea. How should he? To many of us the har-
> vest—the summer—is a time of joy in light and
> colour; to him it was a time for adding yet anoth-
> er crust of hardness to the thick skin of his
> hands.

The initial essay of *The Open Air,* **"Saint Guido,"** is just such an "impassioned description of meditation" as Thomas claims, to characterize Jefferies's finest efforts in the essay genre. Guido is a little boy and acts as a mediator between the thoughts of the Wind and the Wheat. The "plot" of the essay, such as it is, borders on the fey but the message which Jefferies uses this brief essay to convey is representative of all those complex ideas he had striven to articulate in *The Story of My Heart* and which, in another way, he had communicated via "Sir Bevis" in *Wood Magic.* Much is made in **"Saint Guido"** of Jefferies's unceasing concern with the transcience and illusion of time. Joy in nature "makes to-day a thousand years long backwards and a thousand years long forwards". The Wheat continues,

> All the thousand years of labour since this field was first ploughed have not stored up anything for you. It would not matter about the work so much if you were only happy; the bees work every year, but they are happy; the doves build a nest every year, but they are very, very happy.

In 1884, when this essay first appeared, this was quintessential Jefferies.

If *Nature Near London* is a sad book, given some understanding of the conditions under which Jefferies wrote its essays, then *Field and Hedgerow* is an almost tragic one. It was published in 1889, two years after his death in August 1887, and contains twenty-eight essays and one poem. The book was put together by Jefferies's widow, some of the work having appeared in periodicals not long before his death, other pieces having been printed posthumously in the same way shortly afterward. The essay which opens the book, **"Hours of Spring,"** was probably the last essay written by Jefferies's own hand, before he became too ill to hold a pen. Several of the others, most notably **"The Country Sunday"** and **"My Old Village,"** were composed during the agonies of his final illness, and dictated to his wife.

"Hours of Spring" is one of the most moving and personal essays which Jefferies wrote. In one passage, he laments his imprisonment behind the window, divorced from his familiar joys of the open air. In contrast with the liberty of the birds, he yearns desperately but in vain for his own freedom:

> . . . today I have to listen to the lark's song—not out of doors with him, but through the window-pane, and the bullfinch carries the rootlet fibre to his nest without me. They manage without me very well; they know their times and seasons—not only the civilised rooks, with their libraries of knowledge in their old nests of reference, but the stray things of the hedge and the chiffchaff from over sea in the ash wood. They go on without me. Orchis flower and cowslip—I cannot number them all—I hear, as it were, the patter of their feet—flower and bud and the beautiful clouds that go over, with the sweet rush of rain and burst of sun glory among the leafy trees. They go on, and I am no more than the least of the empty shells that strewed the sward of the hill. . . . High up against the grey cloud I hear the lark through the window singing, and each note falls into my heart like a knife.

Against this glorious prose, there must again be set the essays of a more pedestrian purpose. **"House-Martins," "Field Words and Ways," "April Gossip,"** and **"Mixed Days of May and December"** are, once more, little more than interesting descriptive notes culled from Jefferies's field notes. Having said which, it is instructive to recall that compared with the very best of his essay writing, these pieces strike the reader as dull and formless. Contrasted with the bulk of "country writing," they take on

their proper value, illustrating the range and precision of Jefferies's mind, idealistic but pellucid to the last.

The essays which comprise *Field and Hedgerow* are divided as a whole between the West Country and Sussex, with some memories of his residence in Surrey. I have made much of the idea that within the stricter limits of the essay form, Jefferies fused the idealistic predilections of *The Story of My Heart* with the factual reportage of the early country writings. The point bears repeating, though, and particularly so with respect to a handful of essays in *Field and Hedgerow.* In the words of W. J. Keith, "the two extremes in Jefferies' personality here become fused" and the product of this fusion may be seen to best effect in some of the essays which make up this book. In **"Nature in the Louvre,"** Jefferies compares the Venus Accroupie with the more famous Venus de Medici, and the resultant description is revealing of his own beliefs and philosophy of life.

> Hers is not the polished beauty of the Venus de Medici, whose very fingers have no joints. The typical Venus is fined down from the full growth of human shape to fit the artist's conception of what beauty should be. Her frame is rounded; her limbs are rounded; her neck is rounded; the least possible appearance of fulness is removed; any line that is not in exact concordance with a strict canon is worked out—in short, an ideal is produced, but humanity is obliterated. . . . But here is a woman perfect as a woman, with the love of children in her breast, her back bent for their delight. An ideal indeed, but real and human. Her form has its full growth of wide hips, deep torso, broad shoulders. Nothing has been repressed or fined down to a canon of art or luxury. A heart beats within her bosom; she is love.

"My Old Village" is perhaps the most important and revealing essay of all those contained in *Field and Hedgerow.* It appeared first in *Longman's Magazine* just two months after Jefferies's death and it can be held to represent, as W. J. Keith says, "in many ways a summing up of his whole work." The framework of **"My Old Village"** is built around Jefferies's memories of Coate, occasioned by hearing of the death of John Brown, an agricultural laborer whom we knew when a boy. From this melancholy beginning, Jefferies expands from memories of John Brown, and then of his friends, until he is firmly with his old familiar themes.

> The brooks have ceased to run. There is no music now at the old hatch where we used to sit in danger of our lives, happy as kings, on the narrow bar over the deep water. . . . The brook is dead, for when man goes nature ends. I dare say there is water there still but it is not the brook; the brook is gone like John Brown's soul.

Again, there is the recurrent concern with the presence of man in Nature. There is no opposition: to believe so is to indulge in illusion. And yet, at the end, Jefferies himself is given to wondering whether of his memories were not after all compounded of illusion.

> I begin to think that my senses have deceived me. It is as they say. No one else seems to have

seen the sparkle on the brook, or heard the music at the hatch, or to have felt back through the centuries; and when I try to describe these things to them they look at me with stolid incredulity. No one seems to understand how I got food from the clouds, nor what there was in the night, nor why it is not so good to look at it out of window. They turn their faces away from me, so that perhaps after all I was mistaken, and there never was any such place or any such meadows, and I was never there.

But then, after this apparent acknowledgment of defeat at the end of his short life's work, as W. J. Keith observes, the final sentence of the essay "rises from the bedrock of faith that we invariably find even in his least optimistic writings; with a confident sarcasm he boldly affirms the original vision: 'And perhaps in course of time I shall find out also, when I pass away physically, that as a matter of fact there never was any earth.' "

It is fitting that Mrs. Jefferies should have included **"My Old Village"** as the final essay in *Field and Hedgerow.* But it is not the last thing in the book. A poem closes the collection. **"The Chaffinch,"** no matter what view we may hold on Jefferies's poetical abilities, closes with a verse which fittingly expresses all of Jefferies's hopes and expectations for the future.

> No note he took of what the swallows said
> About the firing of some evil gun,
> Nor if the butterflies were blue or red,
> For all his feelings were intent in one.
> The loving soul, a thrill in all his nerves,
> A life immortal as a man's deserves.

It is fitting that Jefferies should have a reputation as a fine essayist. Many of his readers have come to the novels through them and, if we consider the appalling circumstances under which the last of them were composed, we may do well to consider them a living contribution to Victorian prose. In 1873, before Jefferies had begun his slow descent to a tragically early death, he had written in *Reporting, Editing and Authorship* the confident and unselfconscious piece of advice that "If the author attempts to rise on the ground of his special knowledge, and adheres to that, and makes himself superior in it, his success will be certain, and comparatively easy". There is no doubt that Jefferies's eventual success was far from easily gained. But then, in all of his writing, but perhaps most especially in his essays, that success was undoubtedly certain.

Richard Mabey   (essay date 1983)

SOURCE: An introduction to *Landscape with Figures* by Richard Jefferies; edited by Richard Mabey, Penguin Books, 1983, pp. 7-24.

[*In the essay below, Mabey focuses on Jefferies's treatment of the common land-worker in books such as* The Gamekeeper at Home *and* Hodge and His Masters.]

The central character in what Jefferies once called 'The Field-Play' is the land-worker himself. The shift in the way he is depicted—from laggard to victim to hero—is the most striking expression of the movement of Jefferies'

thinking. Even his physical characteristics are viewed in different ways. In the early 1870s he is described as a rather badly designed machine. Ten years later he is being explicitly compared to the form of a classical sculpture.

Typically, it was with a shrewd, unflattering sketch of the Wiltshire labourer (today it would rank as an exposé) that Jefferies pushed his writing before a national audience in 1872. The Agricultural Labourers Union had been formed just two years earlier and there was mounting concern amongst landowners about its likely impact on the farm.

Jefferies was working on the *North Wilts Herald* at the time, and realized that he was well placed to make an entry into the debate. He had a lifetime's experience of observing agricultural affairs, an adaptable and persuasive style, and enough ambition not to be averse to saying what his readers wanted to hear. So he composed the first of his now celebrated letters to *The Times* on the life and habits of the Wiltshire labourer, and in particular his uncouthness, laziness and more than adequate wages. It was by any standards a callous piece, written with apparent objectivity but in fact with a calculated disdain that at times reduces the worker to little more than a beast of burden:

> As a man, he is usually strongly built, broad-shouldered, and massive in frame, but his appearance is spoilt by the clumsiness of his walk and the want of grace in his movements . . . The labourer's muscle is that of a cart-horse, his motions lumbering and slow. His style of walk is caused by following the plough in early childhood, when the weak limbs find it a hard labour to pull the heavy nailed boots from the thick clay soil. Ever afterwards he walks as if it were an exertion to lift his legs.

Jefferies was wearing his contempt on his sleeve, of course; but when he returned to the subject in the *Manchester Guardian* thirteen years later, it is hard to credit that it is the same man writing. Even the title of the piece (like those of many of his later essays) has a new subtlety, being less a description of what was to come than a frame of reference within which to read it; **'One of the New Voters'** had little to do with voting or party loyalties but a great deal, implicitly, with the human right to the franchise. It recounted with meticulous detail and controlled anger a day in the life of Roger the reaper. Although he is still an abstraction, not a person, Roger is an altogether more real and sympathetic character than his predecessors. No longer an intemperate idler, but a man tied to long hours of dispiriting work without the capital or political power to find a way out, he none the less keeps his own private culture intact. Jefferies describes a scene in a pub after the day's work is over.

> You can smell the tobacco and see the ale; you cannot see the indefinite power which holds men there—the magnetism of company and conversation. *Their* conversation, not *your* conversation; not the last book, the last play; not saloon conversation; but theirs—talk in which neither you nor any one of your condition could really join. To us there would seem nothing at all in that conversation, vapid and subjectless; to them it means much. We have not been through the

same circumstances: our day has been differently spent, and the same words have therefore a
varying value. Certain it is, that it is conversation that takes men to the public-house. Had
Roger been a horse he would have hastened to
borrow some food, and, having eaten that,
would have cast himself at once upon his rude
bed. Not being an animal, though his life and
work were animal, he went with his friends to
talk.

This was a remarkable recognition from a man who just
a few years earlier had seen nothing but vacant faces
amongst the labouring class. But what really lifts this
essay above the level of ephemeral social comment is that
Jefferies sets it in the context of the great drama of the harvest, in which toil, sunshine, beer and butterflies, cornfield
weeds and the staff of life, were mixed together in perplexing contradiction.

> The golden harvest is the first scene; the golden
> wheat, glorious under the summer sun. Bright
> poppies flower in its depths, and convolvulus
> climbs the stalks. Butterflies float slowly over the
> yellow surface as they might over a lake of col-
> our. To linger by it, to visit it day by day, and
> even to watch the sunset by it, and see it pale
> under the changing light, is a delight to the
> thoughtful mind. There is so much in the wheat,
> there are books of meditation in it, it is dear to
> the heart. Behind these beautiful aspects comes
> the reality of human labour—hours upon hours
> of heat and strain; there comes the reality of a
> rude life, and in the end little enough of gain.
> The wheat is beautiful, but human life is labour.

The central paradox of rural life has never been more
plainly put. In another intense late essay, **'Walks in the
Wheat-fields'** (1887), Jefferies likens the blinding, desperate gathering-in of the harvest to 'gold fever. .. The whole
village lived in the field . . . yet they seemed but a handful
buried in the tunnels of a golden mine . . .' The double
meaning of 'living in' here is very forceful; at the beginning
of the piece he compares the shape of a grain of wheat to
an embryo or 'a tiny man or woman . . . settled to slum-
ber'. In the wheat-field, he suggests, 'transubstantiation is
a fact . . .'

In his last years Jefferies was increasingly preoccupied
with the paradoxes that emerged when men lived close to
nature. They seemed trapped in one way by their physical
and biological needs, and in another by their sensibilities.
If the ritual of harvest was paradoxical, so was all labour,
which, depending on where you stood, could seem an act
of nature or necessity, dignity or slavery. So, for that matter, was nature itself, which could be simultaneously cruel
and beautiful. Jefferies' concern with these ambiguities
was in part a reflection of his own uncertain social position, as a man who had devoted his life to the expression
of rural life, but who had no real role in it himself. He
found no solutions to this enigma; but as he explores some
of its more practical ramifications—could villages be centres of social change as well as social stability, for instance? what were the respective rights of owners, workers
and tourists over the land? —his mixed feelings of exclu-

sion and concern come increasingly close to our modern
attitudes towards the countryside.

Richard Jefferies seemed destined to be a displaced person
from childhood. He was born into a declining smallholding at Coate near Swindon in 1848. Although he was later
to idealize both Coate and his father (who appears as the
splendid, doomed figure of farmer Iden in the novel ***Amaryllis at the Fair,*** 1886) it does not seem to have been an
especially happy household. A description of Coate in a
letter from Jefferies' father has a bitterness whose roots,
one suspects, reach back to a time before Richard began
upgrading his literary address to 'Coate Farm':

> How he could think of describing Coate as such
> a pleasant place and deceive so I could not imag-
> ine, in fact nothing scarcely he mentions is in
> Coate proper only the proper one was not a
> pleasant one Snodshill was the name on my
> Waggon and cart, he styled in Coate Farm it was
> not worthy of the name of Farm it was not Forty
> Acres of Land.

When he was four years old, Richard was sent away from
Snodshill to live with his aunt in Sydenham. He stayed
there for five years, visiting his parents for just one
month's holiday a year. When he was nine he returned
home, but was quickly despatched to a succession of private schools in Swindon. Shunted about as if he were already a misfit, it is no wonder that he developed into a
moody and solitary adolescent. He began reading Rabelais
and the Greek Classics and spent long days roaming about
Marlborough Forest. He had no taste for farm-work, and
his father used to point with disgust to 'our Dick poking
about in them hedges'. When he was sixteen Richard ran
away from home with his cousin, first to France and then
to Liverpool, where he was found by the police and sent
back to Swindon.

This habit of escape into fantasy or romantic adventure (it
was later to become a characteristic of his fiction) must
have been aggravated by the real-life decline of Coate. In
1865 the smallholding was badly hit by the cattle plague
that was sweeping across southern England, and a short
while later fourteen acres had to be sold off. Richard had
left school for good by this time, and in 1866 started work
in Swindon on a new Conservative paper, the *North Wilts
Herald.* He was employed as a jack-of-all-trades reporter
and proof-reader, but seemed to spend a good deal of his
time composing short stories for the paper. They were a
collection of orthodox Victorian vignettes of thwarted
love, murder and historical romance, mannered in tone
and coloured by antiquarian and classical references. Although they are of no real literary value, they may have
been useful to Jefferies as a way of testing and exercising
his imaginative powers.

The next few years brought further frustrations and more
elaborate retreats. In 1868 he began to be vaguely ill and
had to leave his job on the *Herald.* In 1870 he took a long
recuperative holiday in Brussels. He was extravagantly delighted by the women, the fashions, the manners, the sophistication of it all, and from letters to his aunt it is clear
what he was beginning to think of the philistinism of Wiltshire society.

But circumstances forced him to return there in 1871, and to a situation that must have seemed even less congenial than when he had left. With the farm collapsing around them his parents resented his idleness and irresponsibility. He had no job and no money. He was able to sell a few articles to his old newspaper, but they were not enough, and he had to pawn his gun. His life began to slip into an anxious, hand-to-mouth existence that has more in common with the stereotype of the urban freelance than with a supposed 'son of the soil'. He started novels, but was repeatedly diverted by a procession of psychosomatic illnesses. He wrote a play, and a dull and derivative memoir on the family of his prospective member of Parliament, Ambrose Goddard. The most unusual projects in this period were two pamphlets: the self-explanatory *Reporting, Editing and Authorship: Practical Hints for Beginners,* and *Jack Brass, Emperor of England.* This was a right-wing broadsheet that ridiculed what Jefferies saw as the dangers of populism.

> . . . Educate! educate! educate! Teach every one to rely on their own judgement, so as to destroy the faith in authority, and lead to a confidence in their own reason, the surest method of seduction . . .

It was a heavy-handed satire, and though it may not have been intended very seriously, Jefferies was to remember it with embarrassment in later years.

But by this stage he had already made a more substantial political and literary debut with his letters to *The Times* on the subject of the Wiltshire labourer. It is important to remember the context in which these appeared. Agricultural problems of one kind or another had been central issues in British politics for much of the nineteenth century. But the land-workers themselves had been given sparse attention. And though they had been impoverished by the cumulative effects of farm mechanization, wage and rent levels, and the appropriation of the commonlands, their own protests had been sporadic and ineffectual. Then in 1870 Joseph Arch and some of his fellow-workers gathered together illicitly in their Warwickshire village and formed the Agricultural Labourers' Union.

This was a new development in the countryside, and raised new anxieties amongst landowners. The rioting and rick-burning of the 1820s had fitted into a familiar stereotype of peasant behaviour, and had been comparatively easily contained. But organization was a different matter, and seemed to introduce an ominously urban challenge to the rural order and, by implication, to the social fabric of the nation which rested on it.

Jefferies' hybrid background may have helped him understand these worries better than most, and it was the sense of moral affront sounded in his letters that won him sympathy from the landowners. The correspondence became the subject of an editorial in *The Times,* and Jefferies was soon offered more journalistic work in the same vein. Over the next few years he wrote copiously on rural and agricultural affairs for journals such as *Fraser's Magazine* and the *Live Stock Journal.* Collectively these pieces are more informed and compassionate than the *Times* letters. Jefferies sympathizes with the sufferings of the labourers and their families, but believed that many of their habitual responses to trouble—particularly their reluctance to accept responsibility for their own fate—simply made matters worse. Wage demands alienated the farmers, who were their natural patrons and allies. Drink led to the kind of family break-ups described in **'John Smith's Shanty'** (1874). The only certain remedies were hard work and self-discipline.

This has been a perennial theme in Conservative philosophy, and there are times when Jefferies' recommendations have a decidedly modern ring, as, for instance, in **'The Labourer's Daily Life'** (1874): 'The sense of [home] ownership engenders a pride in the place, and all his better feelings are called into play.' Yet even at this early stage, Jefferies' conservatism has a liberal edge, and anticipates the libertarian, self-help politics of his later years. He speaks out in favour of allotments, libraries, cottage hospitals, women's institutes and other mutual associations as means towards parish independence. And he begins to suggest that the farm and the village—the basic units of rural life—owed their survival and strength not so much to some immemorial order but precisely to their capacity to incorporate change and new ideas into a well-tried framework.

The increasing amount of work Jefferies was doing for London-based journals encouraged him to move to Surbiton in 1877, when he was twenty-eight years of age. Rather to his surprise he enjoyed London, discovering in it not only many unexpectedly green corners, but an exciting quality of movement and vivacity. As Claude Monet was to do in his paintings of Leicester Square and Westminster Bridge, Jefferies saw the rush of traffic and the play of streetlights almost as if they were natural events. In **'The Lions in Trafalgar Square'** even the people are absorbed:

> At summer noontide, when the day surrounds us and it is bright light even in the shadow, I like to stand by one of the lions and yield to the old feeling. The sunshine glows on the dusky creature, as it seems, not on the surface but under the skin, as if it came up from out of the limb. The roar of the rolling wheels sinks and becomes distant as the sound of a waterfall when dreams are coming. All abundant life is smoothed and levelled, the abruptness of the individuals lost in the flowing current like separate flowers drawn along in a border, like music heard so far off that the notes are molten and the theme only remains.

'Lions', like most of the London essays, was written during a later phase of Jeffries' life. Perhaps because of his uncertainty about his own social role, he rarely wrote about his current circumstances, but about what he had just left behind. In Swindon, much of his work was concerned with the fantasy world of his adolescence. In Surbiton he is remembering his life at Coate, albeit in a rather idealized form.

The pieces that were to make up his first fully-fledged non-fiction work, *The Gamekeeper at Home,* were amongst these reminiscences, and were initially published in serial form in the *Pall Mall Gazette* between December 1877 and Spring 1878. It is of some significance that Jefferies chose as his subjects 'the master's man' and the practical business of policing a sporting estate. The game laws were a crucial instrument for expressing and maintaining the class structure of the nineteenth-century countryside. Although poaching was an economic necessity for many families, it was also an act of defiance against the presumptions of landowners. They, for their part, often viewed the taking of wild animals from their land as a more fundamental breach of their 'natural' rights than outright stealing.

Jefferies doesn't challenge this assumption in *The Gamekeeper at Home.* In a chapter on the keeper's enemies, for instance, he moves smoothly from weasels, stoats and magpies to 'semi-bohemian trespassers', boys picking sloes and old women gathering firewood. '. . . how is the keeper to be certain,' he argues, 'that if the opportunity offered these gentry would not pounce upon a rabbit or anything else?'

This strand in Jefferies' writing reaches a kind of culmination in *Hodge and His Masters.* This collection of portraits of the rural middle class—speculators, solicitors, landowners, parsons—was serialized in the London *Standard* between 1878 and 1880. Its hero is the self-made, diligent yeoman farmer. If he should fail it is because he has become lazy or drunk, or has forgotten his place in society:

> There used to be a certain tacit agreement among all men that those who possessed capital, rank or reputation should be treated with courtesy. That courtesy did not imply that the landowner, the capitalist, or the minister of religion, was necessarily himself superior. But it did imply that those who administered property really represented the general order in which all were interested . . . These two characteristics, moral apathy and contempt of property—i. e. of social order—are probably exercising considerable influence in shaping the labourer's future.

Jefferies grows shriller as he outlines the agents of these malign forces—the unemployed, the poachers, the publicans, the dispossessed and the dependant. Hodge himself, the ordinary labourer, remains invisible, except when Jefferies is rebuking him, in now familiar style, for his greed, bad cooking, lack of culture and laziness. How lucky he is, Jefferies remarks, only to work in the hours of daylight. After this, it is hard to take seriously the book's closing note of regret about the insulting charity of the workhouse.

Yet alongside (and sometimes inside) these sour social commentaries he had begun writing short studies in natural history. They are lightly and sharply observed, and one senses Jefferies' relief at having an escape route from the troubled world of human affairs. *Wildlife in a Southern County* was serialized in the *Pall Mall Gazette* during 1878, and its contents give some indication of what a versatile writer he was. There are pieces on orchards, woods, rabbits, ants, stiles, the ague, and 'noises in the air'. The descriptions of the weather are especially convincing—perhaps because he saw this as one area which was beyond the corrupting influence of human society.

During this stage in his life his writing developed a characteristic discursiveness that was no doubt partly a result of his working as a jobbing journalist and having regularly to fill columns of a fixed length. Yet it was also a way of thinking. Many of the pieces are ramblings in an almost literal sense; anecdotes, observations, musings flit by as if they had been encountered and remarked upon during a walk.

In *Round About a Great Estate* (1880) this conversational style is employed to great effect and helps to make this the most unaffectedly charming of all Jefferies' books. It is an ingenuous, buoyant collection of parish gossip, of characters and events that seem to have been chanced upon by accident. Yet it is celebratory rather than nostalgic. Jefferies remarks in his preface to the original edition:

> In this book some notes have been made of the former state of things before it passes away entirely. But I would not have it therefore thought that I wish it to continue or return. My sympathies and hopes are with the light of the future, only I should like it to come from nature. The clock should be read by the sunshine, not the sun timed by the clock.

The worst thing that can be said about these natural history and documentary essays is not that they are inconsequential, but that they are impersonal and generalized. Even at his most perceptive, Jefferies viewed natural life with the same kind of detachment as he regarded the labourer. They aroused his curiosity but rarely his sympathy. But at the beginning of the 1880s a new intimacy starts to appear in his writing. He allows us to share specific experiences and deeply personal feelings. He seems, at last, to be *engaged.* A set of pieces on the fortunes of a trout trapped in a London brook, for instance, show us Jefferies in a very unfamiliar light—concerned, sentimental and increasingly aware of his own vulnerability.

There can be little doubt that one of the major influences on Jefferies during these years was his deteriorating health. The illness that was eventually to kill him began in earnest in 1881, and was diagnosed as a generalized tuberculosis. During 1882 he went to Brighton to recuperate, but he found only temporary relief, and signs of his pain and disenchantment are visible in almost all the remainder of his work.

Much of this period, perhaps predictably, was taken up with escapist novels. *Greene Ferne Farm* (1880) is an old-fashioned pastoral with a dialect-speaking Chorus. *Bevis* (1882), a book for children, is set in Jefferies' boyhood Wiltshire, which the young heroes transform into a fabulous playground for their fantasies. *After London* (1885) is a bitter vision of the collapse of urban civilization and of the city reclaimed by forest and swamp. Yet even with, so to speak, a clean slate, Jefferies still chooses to create a woodland feudal society, complete with reconstituted poachers as savages. There is some fine descriptive writing in his fiction (particularly in *Amaryllis at the Fair,* which is based on an idealized version of his own family), yet as novels they have to be regarded as failures. They have no real movement, either in the development of the plot or of the individual characters. David Garnett [in his introduction to *Amaryllis at the Fair*] described *Amaryllis* as 'a succession of stills, never a picture in motion', and Jefferies himself declared he would have been happy to have seen it published as 'scenes of country life' rather than as a novel.

During the early 1880s he was also working on his 'soul-life', a kind of spiritual autobiography that was published as *The Story of My Heart* in 1883. Like all mystical works this is comprehensible to the degree to which one shares the writer's faith—which here is an intense pantheism. Yet the book is an account of a meditation rather than a complete religion. (Some of the short, rhythmical passages even read like mantras.) Typically Jefferies goes to a 'thinking place'—a tree, a stream, or more often the sea—lies under the sun and prays that he may have a revelation. He wishes to transcend the flesh, to transcend nature itself, though he cannot express what he wants, nor what, if anything, he has found. 'The only idea I can give,' he writes, 'is that there is another idea.' Yet if the mystical sections of *The Story* are typified by this kind of word-play—sincerely meant, no doubt, but meaningless—there is another strand of more earthly idealism in the book concerned with a belief in the perfectibility of man and the degradation of labour, themes that were to become increasingly prominent in his work.

Although it is mostly impenetrable, the soul-searching of *The Story of My Heart* seemed to liberate Jefferies from many of his social and literary uncertainties. After 1883 his writing has a new commitment and assurance of style. His viewpoint had changed radically. He had become, on almost every topic from economics to ecology, a progressive. He worries about trends in agricultural modernization and their likely implications for wildlife. He attacks the grubbing-out of hedgerows and the ploughing of old grassland. He defends the otter, and argues in favour of the townsman's right of access to the countryside (see particularly **'The Modern Thames'**, 1884).

These were specific expressions of a deeper change in Jefferies' whole ideology. By the mid-1880s he had begun to argue for the extension of the franchise, and at times to go beyond the humane concern of **'One of the New Voters'** to an out-and-out socialist position. In a remarkable late essay, **'Primrose Gold in Our Villages'** (1887), he describes how the new Conservative alliances in the countryside, which had once opposed the labourers' vote, were now moving in to appropriate it. **'Primrose Gold'** is unlike anything he had written previously. It is sophisticated, witty, elliptical and bitterly ironic. It also deals in allusion and metaphor, which are in short supply in his earlier, more literal writings. As Raymond Williams has remarked:

> **'Primrose Gold':** the phrase is so exact. The simple flower as a badge of political manoeuvre; the yellow of the flower and of the money that is the real source of power; the natural innocence, the political dominance: it is all there.

In his late essays Jefferies begins to write of the politics, history and landscape of the countryside as if they were aspects of a single experience. This was especially true of his nature writing. Although he would still turn in slight pieces on seaside beaches and song birds when it was required of him, he was beginning to suggest that nature was not something apart from us, but a world that we were part of and in which we might see reflected some of our own qualities as living creatures. In **'Out of Doors in February'** (1882) for instance, he explains the optimism he saw in the images of winter, and in the living world's annual triumph over dark and cold:

> The lark, the bird of the light, is there in the bitter short days. Put the lark then for winter, a sign of hope, a certainty of summer. Put, too, the sheathed bud, for if you search the hedge you will find the buds there, on tree and bush, carefully wrapped around with the case which protects them as a cloak. Put, too, the sharp needles of the green corn . . . One memory of the green corn, fresh beneath the sun and wind, will lift up the heart from the clods.

That was one kind of answer to the enigma of the toiler in the field: nature, as a redemptive force that could smooth away the distortions of civilization. In **'Golden Brown'** (1884) Jefferies writes enviously of the health and habits of the Kent fruit-pickers, and of 'the life above this life to be obtained from the constant presence with the sunlight and the stars'.

Yet at no time had he believed that complete human fulfilment could be achieved by a simple surrender to natural (or artificially rustic) rhythms. In an odd and not always rational way he also believed in that specifically human concept, progress. As early as 1880 he had declared that his sympathies and hopes were with 'the light of the future'. He wanted, in Edward Thomas's wonderfully exact phrase [*Richard Jefferies*, 1909], 'the light railway to call at the farmyard gate'.

But for Jefferies himself neither nature nor progress could any longer provide a release. He spent 1887, the last year of his life, as an invalid in Goring, in pain and poverty. His view of the world was confined to what he could glimpse through a window, and his thoughts by that paradox that had haunted him, in one form or another, for most of his life. He had dreamed of men living with the easy grace of birds in flight, yet realized that the self-awareness that made that ambition possible would prevent it ever being fulfilled. In **'Hours of Spring'** he writes mournfully of 'the old, old error: I love the earth and therefore the earth loves me'. Man was in the unique and probably unenviable position of being both part of nature and a conscious interpreter of it. Hence the crises of perspective that affected young political commentator and nostalgic old man-of-the-fields alike.

These last essays, particularly **'Walks in the Wheat-fields'** and **'My Old Village'**, are poignant and embittered, but written with great power and clarity. In the end—inevitably perhaps—he returns to mysticism and, in **'Nature and Books'** for example, rejects both naturalistic and scientific analyses of the colour of flowers: 'I want the inner meaning and the understanding of wild flowers in the meadow . . . Why are they? What end? What purpose?'

There is a passage in the novel *Amaryllis at the Fair,* written at the start of this final illness, that catches exactly the conflict between consciousness and animality that runs right through Jefferies' work. The hero, Iden, has just eaten a dinner which has been described in minute and sensuous detail. As he settles down in a chair to sleep, a mouse runs up his trouser leg to eat the crumbs in his lap:

> One great brown hand was in his pocket, close to them—a mighty hand, beside which they were pygmies indeed in the land of the giants. What would have been the value of their lives between a finger and thumb that could crack a ripe and strong-shelled walnut? . . .

> Yet the little things fed in perfect confidence. He was so still, so *very* still—quiescent—they feared him no more they did the wall; they could not hear his breathing. Had they been giften with human intelligence that very fact would have excited their suspicions. Why so very, *very* still? Strong men, wearied by work, do not sleep quietly; they breathe heavily. Even in firm sleep we move a little now and then, a limb trembles, a muscle quivers, or stretches itself.

> But Iden was so still it was evident he was really wide awake and restraining his breath, and exercising conscious command over his muscles, that this scene might proceed undisturbed.

> Now the strangeness of the thing was in this way: Iden set traps for mice in the cellar and the larder, and slew them there without mercy. He picked up the trap, swung it round, opening the door at the same instant, and the wretched captive was dashed to death upon the stone flags of the floor. So he hated them and persecuted them in one place, and fed them in another.

> A long psychological discussion might be held upon this apparent inconsistency, but I shall leave analysis to those who like it, and go on recording facts. I will make only one remark. That nothing is consistent that is human. If it was not inconsistent it would have no association with a living person.

> From the merest thin slit, as it were, between his eyelids, Iden watched the mice feed and run about his knees till, having eaten every crumb, they descended his leg to the floor.

James Krasner   (essay date 1992)

SOURCE: "Blossoms of Mutation: Field Theory in the Works of Richard Jefferies, W. H. Hudson, and D. H. Lawrence," in *The Entangled Eye: Visual Perception and the Representation of Nature in Post-Darwinian Narrative,* Oxford University Press, Inc., 1992, pp. 139-72.

[*In the following excerpt, Krasner explores Jefferies's view of nature, noting that he perceives "natural energy rather than natural form."*]

Albert Einstein [in *The Evolution of Physics,* 1961] explains the emergence of field theory as follows.

> The old mechanical view attempted to reduce all events in nature to forces acting between material particles. . . . The field did not exist for the physicist of the early years of the nineteenth century. For him only substance and its changes were real. . . . In the new field language it is the description of the field between the two charges, and not the charges themselves, which is essential for an understanding of their action. The recognition of the new concepts grew steadily, until substance was overshadowed by field. . . . A new reality was created, a new concept for which there was no place in the mechanical description.

Einstein points out the radical change in conceptions of the material world brought about by the "new" physics of the late nineteenth and early twentieth centuries. Darwin's evolutionary theory, for all its questioning of the stability of organic form, portrayed the animal body as a material object. The material forms of nature, in wholes or in parts, overflow from Darwin's works; the reader experiences the natural world as a cornucopia of entangled organic matter. Einstein, however, suggests that in nineteenth-century physics material bodies were ceasing to be the primary units of representation. Nature writers of the late-nineteenth and early-twentieth centuries do not portray nature's forms as much as they do the forces between and around those forms. In the works of authors such as Richard Jefferies, W. H. Hudson and D. H. Lawrence, the representation of nature becomes a portrayal of fields of energy in which bodies are defined by forces and make forces visible. Einstein describes the concept of the field as an "interpreter", an abstraction created to explain the unusual actions that bodies perform in certain electrical and gravitational contexts. As field theory grew, however, the objects came to be seen as the indicators of field forces, and "substance was overshadowed by the field."

Gestalt psychology was conceived around the principle that "the basic functional concepts of physics are applicable to brain dynamics" [Wolfgang Köhler's *Gestalt Psychology*]. Gestalt psychologists believed visual forms were determined by the interaction of electrochemical forces in the brain and were by-products or manifestations of dynamic interactions. In the works of these authors, the forms of the English countryside are significant only insofar as they demonstrate underlying fields of force. For Richard Jefferies, the living world is a "stream of atmosphere," not an entangled bank; animals and landscape forms appear in dynamic patterns of motion, like so many iron filings arranging themselves around a magnet. W. H. Hudson's nature is a "living garment" of vividly contrasting color regions that interact according to field forces of chromatic contrast rather than biological laws. The world of D. H. Lawrence is populated by bodies that are at once sensual and dynamic, defined by their color and motion in a whirl of centrifugal and centripetal forces. Gestalt theory was nativistic in that it assumed the mind's electrochemical forces to operate by uniform measurable laws that also applied in exterior nature. Uniform forces will produce whole, regular forms and there will be a reliable correspondence between the exterior stimulus and the mental event. Lawrence's paradox, in which exterior presence and psychological interiority intensify rather than contradict one another, results from his definition of matter as energy operating by the same dynamic laws both in the mind and in nature. Like Darwin, these authors attempt to portray the invisible forces of nature as visually present; however, where Darwin portrays the biological interaction of bodies, these authors portray the field interaction of perceptual forces.

In Richard Jefferies's novel *Amaryllis at the Fair* (1887), an artist describes the difficulty involved in representing the motion of a bird's wings.

> Alere showed how impossible it was to show a bird in flight by the starling's wings. . . . [Y]ou see the wings in innumerable . . . positions . . . like the leaves of a book opened with your thumb quickly—as they do in legerdemain—almost as you see the spokes of a wheel run together as they revolve—a sort of burr.
>
> To produce an image of a starling flying, you must draw all this.
>
> The swift feathers are almost liquid; they leave a streak behind in the air like a meteor.

Jefferies begins with a description of an illusion that results from residual imagery, much like Darwin's hand/paddle/wing passage. The individual images of the starling's wing are presented so swiftly to the eye that they blur together into a single form. Where Darwin uses the residual images of several forms to demonstrate their analogous physiology, however, Jefferies concentrates on the residual "streak" left by one form in motion, in order to demonstrate its swiftness. Consequently, where Darwin's reader sees several bodies coalesce into one, Jefferies's reader sees only a line.

> A black line has rushed up from the espalier apple yonder to the housetop thirty times at least. The starlings fly so swiftly and so straight that they seem to leave a black line along the air.

The flapping of a bird's wings is perceived as a circle:

> A magpie flew up from the short green corn to a branch low down on an elm, his back towards me, and as he rose his tail seemed to project from a white circle. The white tips of his wings met— or apparently so—as he fluttered, both above and beneath his body, so that he appeared encircled with a white ring.

Jefferies portrays the dynamism of natural matter by allowing natural motion to become more visually important than the bodies that are in motion. In effect, he offers us a record of the motion itself; the black line tells us nothing about the starling's form. In Darwin's work, the residual images of the hand/paddle/wing pile up in the reader's mind, allowing Darwin to multiply and complicate the animal body until one form appears to contain many others; Jefferies presents the residual image of a single moving body in such a way that not even that one form is imaged. Jefferies's visual nature is thus composed not of objects but of the perceptual traces left by dynamic forces.

Form is so insignificant in Jefferies's landscape that he pays little attention to whether a dynamic streak is made by one or by several forms in motion.

> The wet furrows reflect the [sun's] rays so that

the dark earth gleams, and in the slight mist that stays farther away the light pauses and fills the vapour with radiance. Through the luminous mist the larks race after each other twittering, and as they turn aside, swerving in their swift flight, their white breasts appear for a moment. . . . The lark and the light are as one, and wherever he glides over the wet furrows the glint of the sun goes with him. Anon alighting he runs between the lines of the green corn. In hot summer, when the open hillside is burned with bright lights, the larks are singing and soaring.

It is not entirely clear whether the rising, swooping, and wheeling is that of the larks or of the sunbeams. Color, form, and motion create a dynamic field of paralleling activity in which the lark and the light become interchangeable units of natural energy. Both are white lines through the fog, both are bright semicircles at dawn, and both race through the corn rows and frolic across the summer landscape. The lark and the light seem to draw the same line through the air, and it is this line, rather than the objects that created it, that the reader images as the fundamental visual unit of nature.

This unification of streaks of motion is not a formal coalescence in the Darwinian sense, for the reader never sees the two forms of lark and sunbeam to be in any way similar— they simply leave the same dynamic trace. In another passage Jefferies portrays a typically Darwinian illusion—the transformation of one animal into another—in a distinctly non-Darwinian fashion: "[Y]ou may see a covey [of partridges] there now and then, creeping slowly with humped backs, and at a distance not unlike hedgehogs in their motions." Under normal conditions, partridges look nothing like hedgehogs; only "in their motions" do the two animals become indistinguishable. While Darwin's coalescent perception of bear and whale concentrates on specific parts of the animals' bodies and results in a greater awareness of their physiology, Jefferies's concentrates on the line left by the bodies, and results in a comprehension of them simply as moving forms. The moving forms could be partridges, hedgehogs, spider monkeys, or black dots, as long as they move in the same way. Had Darwin been making this comparison the reader would have come away with the impression of a large mouth, a rounded rib cage, or a sloping skull that could be matched between the two bodies. In Jefferies's portrayal the reader images a pattern of movement from one point to another; the fact that the points beginning and ending the motion are animals with distinct bodily forms remains unnoticed. The pheasants and the hedgehogs, like the lark and the light, become one being by ceasing to be visually significant as material forms and becoming the traces of dynamic motion.

Jefferies's portrayal of visual motion demonstrates a visual principle that Max Wertheimer was to investigate in a groundbreaking experiment on illusory motion two decades later. Wertheimer created a device that projected the image of a vertical line first on the left side, and then on the right side of a screen. If the images were flashed on and off successively, and for the correct duration, the viewer would perceive only one line moving back and forth from left to right. Moreover, given the correct conditions the viewer was able to describe either form, and was simply aware of having seen "something in motion" [George W. Hartmann's *Gestalt Psychology,* 1935]. Furthermore, the illusion of motion was not affected when the two images were different. Thus, if one of the straight vertical lines was replaced by a wiggly one, the viewer would still perceive "something in motion." In a sense the viewer was perceiving motion itself. This is precisely what seems to occur in Jefferies's landscape.

> Westward the sun was going down over the sea, and a wild west wind, which the glow of the sun as it touched the waves seemed to heat into a fury, brought up the distant sound of the billows from the beach. A line of dark Spanish oaks from which the sharp-pointed acorns were dropping, darkest green oaks, shut out the shore. A thousand starlings were flung up into the air out of these oaks, as if an impatient hand had cast them into the sky; then down they fell again, with a ceaseless whistling and clucking; up they went and down they came, lost in the deep green foliage as if they had dropped in the sea.

The dynamism of this passage results from the narrative accumulation of natural processes of rising and falling. The sun going down, the waves and wind rising, the acorns falling, the trees rising against the sky, and the birds flying up then coming down are all objects flashed before the reader in separate positions and at such duration that they seem to create an overall pattern of rising and falling. If someone were shown a picture of a wave, then above it a picture of the sun, then below it a picture of acorns, that viewer would be given the impression of up and down motion even though the sequence of images made no logical sense. Even so, a series of successively positioned moving forms that bear no necessary relationship to one another but which are perceived in a continuous pattern of motion give the reader a sense of nature's intense, dynamic, unified undulation. Nature is composed of rising and falling rather than sun, acorns, ocean, and trees; the landscape is a seething medium of physical movements rather than of physiological objects.

Jefferies's concept of nature is based on the dynamic forces that shape it rather than the material units of which it is composed. Kurt Koffka, Wertheimer's subject in the motion experiment and one of the founders of Gestalt psychology, makes a similar claim [in his *Principles of Gestalt Psychology,* 1935] for the Gestalt conception of the universe.

> Man the builder assembles his bricks and erects his house. . . . He forgets that he has piled these bricks in a gravitational field and that without this gravitational field he can build a house as little as without bricks. But the bricks are so much more palpable than gravitation that he thinks of them alone, and thus he models his concept of reality. Substance assumes for human thought the role of being the embodiment for the real. . . . But this difficulty arises for the philosopher only, and not for the architect or the physicist. The physicist is far from such crude realism. As a matter of fact he finds it harder and harder to lay his hands on "substances." Organized fields of force assume for him the chief reality.

Wertheimer, Koffka, and their associate Wolfgang Köhler suggested that, while previous theorists had explained perception in terms of the accumulation of points of light on the retina, it was better explained as the interaction of electrochemically charged fields in the brain cortex. According to Wertheimer the illusion of motion created in his experiment was caused by a "short circuit" in the brain. Rather than a set of specific neural receptors, like telephone lines, Gestalt theorists saw the brain as a netlike cortex; visual stimulations are "not restricted to small areas of the cortex but form a pattern pervading the whole area of the cortex with areas of highest activity varying with the kind of stimulation". The two forms perceived in the Wertheimer experiment create two separate electrochemical responses in the brain, each response creating an "excitation ring" of electrochemical charge. When the excitation rings are close enough and of the correct frequency a current flows between them, causing an electrochemical "motion" in the brain; the motion of the current through the brain from one cortical region to another is the *physiological correlate* of object motion. The basic units of perception, therefore, are not minimum visibles adding up to forms, or even complete forms, but the currents that create an impression of visible form through their dynamic interactions.

Koffka and Jefferies, like Einstein, portray a world composed of dynamic fields of force that ebb and flow around one another. Darwin, like empirical perception theorists and what Einstein calls "mechanical" physicists, thinks of nature as a collection of minimum units, or particles (Koffka's "bricks"), that are rearranged when different forms are perceived. For field theorists, form is simply the result of two fields interacting. In Gestalt perceptual theory, for example, a black circle on a white background is perceived because the black area and the white create two different field responses in the brain. As someone looks at the circle, two different electrochemical responses will be generated in the netlike brain cortex, causing an *inhomogeneous field.* In order to balance this inhomogeneity the currents corresponding to the black area will flow together, as will those corresponding to the white area, and the field will be divided into two field parts. As Koffka states:

> [I]f the proximal stimulation is such that it consists of several areas of different homogeneous stimulation, then the areas which receive the same stimulation will organize unitary field parts segregated from the others by the difference between the stimulations. In other words the equality of stimulation produces forces of cohesion, inequality of stimulation forces of segregation . . .

The point of distinction between the field parts, or *leap of stimulation* as Koffka puts it, will be perceived as the edge of a form.

> [E]xactly the same proposition holds in physics. Thus . . . if oil is poured into a liquid with which it does not mix, the surface of the oil will remain sharply determined in the violent interaction of molecules, and if the liquid has the same density, then the oil will form a sphere swimming in the other liquid.

A Gestalt form is thus not an actual object, but the product of the balancing of perceptual forces. Consequently, a form has no material shape or dimension, but rather it consists of the currents that determine it. Perceived forms, like oil in water, will often be regularized or "smoothed" by the currents surrounding them. A slightly irregular form . . . will be perceived as a circle. Jefferies's narrative eye regularizes natural forms in a similar fashion. "At a distance," he writes, "the enclosed fields seem surrounded with hedges, not merely cropped, but smoothed and polished, so rounded and regular do they appear". Animals are similarly smoothed and polished by visual effects.

> Rude and uncouth as swine are in themselves, somehow they look different under trees. The brown leaves amid which they root, and the brown-tinted fern behind lend something of their colour and smooth away their ungainliness. Snorting as they work with very eagerness of appetite, they are almost wild, approaching in measure to their ancestors, the savage bears.

The rudeness of the hog's form is "smoothed" by the mind; the reader's impression of the hog is reduced to that of a malleable colored region that is being molded by the forces of the visual field. Like the passage in which the pheasants become hedgehogs, Jefferies offers us no comparison of animal parts between hog and bear, but reduces the hog and bear bodies to a formally malleable visual region. The Darwinian representation of the body as an object composed of variable parts becomes impossible in a Gestalt world because the visual form is only malleable as a whole. Darwin's visual representation of nature relies upon the fragmentation and shuffling of body parts. He makes the pigeon bodies "fluid" only in the sense that a brick wall being continually made and unmade is fluid; the reader must see the tumbler's beak, the pouter's crop, and the carrier's carunculated skin to understand nature's dynamism. Jefferies is able to show the animal body transforming without parts; we do not see an evolutionary force at work in this change, only a perceptual one.

The Jefferian naturalist is a physicist at heart, looking past matter to the forces that impel it. Where the variety of natural forms dazzled Darwin's eye, Jefferies's is overwhelmed by the speed and dynamism of natural motion. The eye perceives matter, but the essence of life is an immaterial flash that only an extraordinarily swift eye, like the swallow's, can catch.

> Swift and mobile as is the swallow's wing, how much swifter and much more mobile must be his eye. . . . [H]is eyes are to our eyes as his wings are to our limbs. If still further we were to consider the flow of the nerve force between the eye, the mind, and the wing, we should be face to face with problems which quite upset the ordinary ideas of matter as a solid thing.

Jefferies's speculations on matter grow out of his aesthetic awareness of nature's dynamic motion. A natural world that is composed of so many dynamic, meteoric forms can only be perceived by a mind that is itself dynamic and thus immaterial. For both Jefferies and the Gestalt psychologists the dynamic laws of neural activity also apply to matter in general; the fluid dynamism of the mind mirrors and is mirrored by the fluid dynamism of the universe. The speed and power of the imagination thus calls into question the solidity of matter. Gestalt theorists saw their theory calling into question a part-based model of perception, just as Einstein's work called into question the fundamental units of matter.

> Wherein does the similarity of the two views [Gestalt theory and relativity] lie? Primarily in the opposition of both systems to the summative and additive treatment of data. Each strikes at the discreteness of the cosmos . . . sensations are not independent, velocities and spaces and times are not absolute.

Form is not like a building, composed of so many different pieces, but like oil in water, adapting its shape to the dynamic conditions surrounding it.

Despite what appears to be a disorderly conception of matter Koffka claimed that Gestalt theory reasserted an order that was lost by nineteenth-century materialism.

> Materialism accomplished the integration [of life and nature] by robbing life of its order and thereby making us look down on life as just a curious combination of orderless events; if life is as blind as inorganic nature we must have as little respect for the one as for the other. But if inanimate nature shares with life the aspect of order, then the respect which we feel directly and unreflectively for life will spread over to inanimate nature also.

Darwinian theory undercut the possibility of a formal order in nature, but Koffka hopes to establish a dynamic one by demonstrating the similarity of exterior material forces to interior mental forces, what he refers to here as the order of "life"; the nativistic similarity of exterior and perceived forms and the perceptual reliability associated with those forms would thus be assured by the regularity of the physical forces determining them. Jefferies's vision of nature is ordered in just this way; the dynamic patterns that affect very different forms are consistent and stable. The lark and the light, the birds and the acorns, and the pheasants and the hedgehogs are all moved by the same underlying forces. Forms only serve to demonstrate this order. The chaos of form created by Darwin is thus subsumed into energy structures that, although powerful and dynamic, operate according to consistent and predictable patterns.

Koffka, however, stresses that his theory is not "vitalist." By demonstrating the "order" of the human mind "as a characteristic of *natural* events and therefore within the domain of physics," Gestalt theory is able to "accept it in the science of life without introducing a special vital force responsible for the creation of order". Similarly, Jefferies is not simply transposing a psychological order onto nature. W. J. Keith [in his *Richard Jefferies: A Critical Study*] claims that Jefferies, "realizing that it is the human mind which, in a sense, creates order out of the prolific chaos of nature . . . penetrates the surface to discover the generalized but no less vivid reality". For Jefferies, however, there is no surface to penetrate; matter is not significant as an exterior crust surrounding an interior spirit—both exterior and interior life manifest the same fundamental motion.

> Summer shows us Matter changing into life, sap rising from the earth through a million tubes, the alchemic power of light entering the solid oak; and see! it bursts forth in countless leaves. Living things leap in the grass, living things drift upon the air, living things are coming forth to breathe in every hawthorn bush. No longer does the immense weight of Matter—the dead, the crystalized—press ponderously on the thinking mind. The whole office of Matter is to feed life— to feed the green rushes, and the roses that are about to be; to feed the swallows above, and us that wander beneath them.

It is not only the sap rising from within, but also the sun pulsing from without that makes the leaves burst forth. Action overwhelms form as verbs overwhelm nouns; Jefferies's narrative eye perceives leaping, drifting, and breathing, not the visually nonspecific "living things." The human mind participates in this order rather than creates it. Like all other matter, the Jefferian mind feeds the dynamic motion of life, and the Jefferian narrative eye perceives the dynamic patterns of natural energy that unify the mind with nature. . . .

FURTHER READING

Arkell, Reginald. *Richard Jefferies*. London: Rich & Cowan, 1933, 294 p.

    Biographical and critical overview.

Avebury, Lord. "Richard Jefferies." In his *Essays and Addresses: 1900-1903*, pp. 67-78. London: Macmillan and Co., 1903.

    Touches on Jefferies's life and explores his views on nature based on his thoughts on evolution, theology, and philosophy.

Coveney, Peter. "Mark Twain and Richard Jefferies." In his *Poor Monkey: The Child in Literature*, pp. 169-91. London: Richard Clay and Co., 1957.

    Discusses Jefferies in the context of the romantic tradition, stating that "his work, with all its passionate vehemence, reflects the tension of the human sensibility at the end of the nineteenth century."

Graham, P. Anderson. "The Magic of the Fields (Richard Jefferies)." In his *Nature in Books: Some Studies in Biography*, pp. 1-43. 1891. Reprint. Port Washington, N.Y.: Kennikat Press, 1971.

    Detailed assessment of Jefferies's life.

Looker, Samuel J., ed. *Richard Jefferies: A Tribute by Various Writers*. Worthing, England: Frederick Steel & Co., 1946, 156 p.

    Collection of reminiscences and biographical/critical commentary on Jefferies by various authors.

—— and Porteous, Crichton. *Richard Jefferies: Man of the Fields*. London: John Baker, 1964, 272 p.

    Overview of Jefferies's life and literary career.

Page, Norman. "The Ending of *After London*." *Notes and Queries* 32, No. 3 (September 1985): 361.

    Discusses different critical opinions about the ending of *After London; or, Wild England*.

Quiller-Couch, Arthur. "Externals." In his *Adventures in Criticism*, pp. 116-27. New York: G.P. Putnam's Sons, 1896.

    Criticizes Jefferies for his concentration on superfluous details.

Scott, G. Forrester. "Three Nature Writers." *The Bookman*, London XXVI, No. 153 (June 1904): 84-8.

    Compares the works of Jefferies with those of Izaak Walton and Gilbert White.

Thomas, Edward. "Richard Jefferies." In his *A Literary Pilgrim in England*, pp. 134-43. New York: Dodd, Mead, and Co., 1917.

    Focuses on the influence of Jefferies's surroundings on his writings, particularly on that of Wiltshire, where he grew up.

Mikhail Yuryevich Lermontov

A Hero of Our Time

The following entry presents criticism of Lermontov's novel *Geroi nashego vremeni* (1840; *A Hero of Our Time*). For a discussion of Lermontov's complete career, see *NCLC*, Volume 5.

INTRODUCTION

A Hero of Our Time, Lermontov's only novel, is considered an important developmental work of Russian literature. In it, Lermontov continued the tradition of character study initiated by Alexander Pushkin's "novel in verse," *Yevgeny Onegin* (1830; *Eugene Onegin)*; the Byronism and European Romanticism of Pushkin's work similarly inform Lermontov's novel. Lermontov, however, owes less to the classicism of eighteenth-century European literature. *A Hero of Our Time* also introduces elements of psychological characterization distinctive of much subsequent Russian literature, including that of Leo Tolstoy and Fedor Dostoevski.

Biographical Information

Lermontov was a renowned poet when he wrote *A Hero of Our Time*, which was published after his exile for insurrectionary sentiments he expressed in a memorial poem on Pushkin's death. The novel strengthened Lermontov's literary reputation and added to the public perception of him as a brooding, Byronesque iconoclast. This impression was reinforced when he was exiled again, this time for fighting an illegal duel. After his second exile, Lermontov's return to Moscow's literary society reportedly left him bored and dissatisfied. He subsequently provoked a military officer, who critics believe was the model for the character Grushnitsky, to a duel. At the age of 27, Lermontov was shot and killed.

Plot and Major Characters

A Hero of Our Time is composed of five sections: "Bela," "Maxim Maximich," "Taman," "Princess Mary," and "The Fatalist." The second edition includes an author's preface, intended to address critical misperceptions about the work. The first two sections are recounted by an anonymous narrator, who hears stories of Pechorin from an old military officer, Maxim Maximich. The last three sections are known as "Pechorin's Journal." Each section, complete in itself, adds something more to the portrait of Pechorin—a man who, according to Lermontov, is typical of his age. Pechorin is a complex and subtle anti-hero, the type of "superfluous" character who figures in the fiction of Goncharov, Herzen, and Turgenev: a man of great intellect and superior talents who is alienated from his society. Dissatisfied with his own life, which has failed to fulfill his youthful expectations, Pechorin meddles in the

lives of others, causing great unhappiness that nonetheless leaves him unaffected; Pechorin pronounces at one point: "The turmoil of life has left me with a few ideas, but no feelings." In a passage from the novel's forth episode, Pechorin explains the genesis of and expresses regret for his own cold nature. Because the passage is key to his deception of another character, however, commentators stress its unreliability.

Major Themes

At the time of its publication, many critics believed that the novel was autobiographical, and that Lermontov was flaunting his own nonconformity. In his preface to a second edition, however, Lermontov answers this charge, stating that he intended Pechorin as a mirror of society's weaknesses rather than a portrait of any individual. Lermontov suggests that his protagonist's failings are less his own fault than the fault "of his own time." Thus, the novel indicts a period of Russian history that was thought by many of its young people to have failed to offer them sufficient opportunities for self-fulfillment.

Critical Reception

Although some critics initially questioned the moral stance of *A Hero of Our Time,* the novel has generally been considered a masterpiece. *A Hero of Our Time* stands as a landmark volume: the first example of the psychological novel in Russia and an important precursor to the works of Tolstoy and Dostoevski. Lermontov is considered to have successfully depicted a historical epoch of singular superficiality and to have ushered in the greatest age of Russian literature.

CRITICISM

V. S. Pritchett   (essay date 1942)

SOURCE: "Mikhail Yurevich Lermontov: *A Hero of Our Time,*" in *A Man of Letters: Selected Essays,* Chatto & Windus, 1985, pp. 269-73.

[*Pritchett, a modern British writer, is respected for his mastery of the short story and for his judicious, reliable, and insightful literary criticism. In the following essay, originally published in 1942, he focuses on Lermontov's portrayal of his protagonist, Pechorin, as typical of "the fashion and idiosyncrasy of a generation" of young Russians.*]

Mikhail Yurevich Lermontov was born in the year before Waterloo and was killed in a duel twenty-seven years later, a year after the publication of the novel which brought him fame throughout Europe. The extraordinary duel in the last chapter but one of *A Hero of Our Own Times* is said to have been exactly prophetic of the manner of his death. Lermontov had declared through his chief character that life was a bad imitation of a book; and the episode, if true, looks like some carefully planned Byronic legend.

A Hero of Our Own Times belongs to that small and elect group of novels which portray a great typical character who resumes the fashion and idiosyncrasy of a generation. Pechorin, the 'hero', is consciously a Russian Byron. He is cold, sensual, egoistical, elegant. He is neurotic, bored and doomed. Only one passion is unexhausted—and this is the making of him—the passion for personal freedom. He is the cold, experimental amorist celebrated by Pushkin (I quote from Oliver Elton's translation of *Eugeny Onegin*):

> Men once extolled cold-blooded raking
> As the true science of love-making:
> Your own trump everywhere you blew . . .
> Such grave and serious recreation
> Beseemed old monkeys, of those days . . .

Pechorin becomes the slave of perpetual travel, and finally fulfills himself not in love but in action. Byron goes to Greece. Pechorin becomes the soldier of the Caucasus who plays with life and death. He drives himself to the limit, whether it is in the duel on the edge of the precipice down which his absurd rival in love is thrown; or in the dramatic bet with Vulich where he draws a revolver and

puts sixty roubles on the doctrine of predestination; or in the final episode when he goes in alone to collar the Cossack who has run amok. In its greater actors the Byronic pose of weariness is balanced by love of living dangerously in action, and here it is interesting to contrast the character of Constant's Adolphe with a man like Pechorin. Adolphe also is the imaginative man who loves from the head and then revenges himself secretively and cruelly upon the strong-minded woman who is devouring him and with whom he is afraid to break: Pechorin, more histrionic and less sensitive (more Byronic, in short), loves from the head also but takes special care to avoid strong-minded women. He possesses, but is not possessed. He prefers the weak and yielding who respond at once to cruelty and whom he can abandon quickly. Faced with the strong-minded, Pechorin becomes a man of action and makes his getaway. Readers of *A Hero of Our Own Times* will remember how Pechorin dealt with the determined duplicity of Taman, the smuggler's girl, when she took him out in her boat on a moonlight night. He threw her into the sea. What would not Adolphe have given for such decisiveness? What would he not have given for that Byronic ruthlessness in action, who knew only the cool vacillations of the mind? Of the two characters, Pechorin's is the more arrested and adolescent. He has not Adolphe's sensibility to the tragedy of the imagination. He does not suffer. Pechorin is sometimes a seventeen-year-old sentimentalist who blames the world:

> I have entered upon this life when I have already
> lived it in imagination, with the result that it has
> become tedious and vile to me. I am like a man
> who has been reading the bad imitation of a
> book with which he has been long familiar.

But perhaps the main difference between these lovers of freedom is merely one of age after all. Pechorin-Lermontov is young: Adolphe is the creation of an older man. Pechorin says: 'Now I only want to be loved, and that by a very few women. Sometimes (terrible thought) I feel as if a lasting tie would satisfy me.'

Adolphe would have been incapable of this naïve Byronic jauntiness; but he would have raised a sympathetic eyebrow at that first hint of nostalgia for respectable marriage.

This was not a solution which Russian literature was yet to permit its Pechorins. Press on to the middle of the century and we find Turgenev's Rudin, all Byronism spent, and with no exciting war of Russian Imperialism to occupy him, conducting an affair as heartless and disgraceful as Pechorin's affair with Princess Mary and very similar to it. But Rudin is reduced to the condition of an unheroic, rootless talker with no corresponding performance. Byronism, with its roots in the Napoleonic wars, was a fashion which fortunately could give the best of its followers something to do. For the maladjusted and the doomed there were duels; even better there was frontier war and the cause of Liberty. The poseur of Venice attained some dignity at Missolonghi: and the sentimentalist of the Caucasus, reviving new trouble with an old mistress, and in the midst of the old trouble with a new one, could feel the heady contagion of that half-savage passion for freedom with which his enemies, the Tartar tribesmen, were imbued.

Travel is one of the great rivals of women. The officers and visitors at the garrison town of Narzan spend their time drinking the waters, making love, scandal-mongering and playing cards; and into this gossiping frontier outpost Pechorin brings something like the preposterous coldness, austerity and violence of the mountain scene outside the town. The coach arrives, he yawns, stays a night, throws his diaries to a friend in lieu of a renewal of friendship and drives on, another Childe Harold on an eternal Grand Tour of the battle fronts. The *Hero* is not one of the calculated, constructed, and balanced books of maturity; its virtues and defects are all of youth. The book appears to pour out of the Caucasus itself. It is one of those Romantic novels in which a place and not a woman has suddenly crystallised a writer's experience and called out all his gifts. 'I was posting from Tiflis'—that opening sentence of Lermontov's classically nonchalant prose, takes the heart a stride forward at once. Like the traveller, we step out of ourselves into a new world. True, it is the fashionable step back to Rousseau, for the *Hero* is nothing if not modish; but who does not feel again with Lermontov, as he gazes at the ravines, breathes the rare, crisp, savage air and sees the golden dawn on the upper snows, who does not feel the force of the Romantic emotion? 'When we get close to Nature the soul sheds all that it has artificially acquired to be what it was in its prime and probably will be again some day.' One is captivated by such a nostalgia, by its youthful and natural idealism and by the artifice of its youthful melancholy.

The structure of the book is both ingenious and careless. Later novelists would have been tempted to a full-length portrait of Pechorin. Lermontov is episodic yet tells us all we need to know in a handful of exciting short stories. We first hear of Pechorin at two removes. The narrator meets a curt, humdrum officer who has known him and who tells the first story of Pechorin's capture and abandonment of Bela, the Tartar girl. Passion has ended in boredom. In the next episode, when Pechorin meets again the officer who had helped him fight the girl's murderers, one sees the Byronic mask go up at the mere hint of the 'incident'. After that Pechorin himself describes his adventures in his diaries. They tell, with sadistic detachment, of how he is playing with the despair of an old mistress while planning to convert another woman's fear and hatred of him to love. He succeeds. Which is all Pechorin wants—a victory for his vanity. He explains this quite candidly to her. And he is candid not because he is an honest man but because, of course, he is interested only in himself. Equally coolly, he plans that the duel he fights with her lover shall take place on the famous precipice.

Pechorin's notions are not merely the melodramatic. He is the enemy of simple, highfalutin romanticism; his taste is for the reserved, the complex and extreme. The precipice is chosen, for example, as the right site of vengeance, because he has discovered that his opponent intends to fool him with blank cartridges. The opposing faction at Narzan has perceived that Pechorin's vulnerable point is his pride; knock the Byronic mask off his face and there

will stand an empty actor. Lermontov is an expert in subtleties like this. In the final episode, when Vulich, the gambler, proposes to discover whether he is or is not fated to die that day, by putting a revolver to his head and pulling the trigger, the suicide is abortive. But Vulich does die that day, and in a most unexpected manner. The Calvinist doctrine of predestination in Byron's Aberdeen has become the almost exotic Oriental Kismet in Lermontov's Caucasus.

To the modern novelist, tired of the many and overdone conventions of the novel, the apparently loose and unconnected construction of *A Hero of Our Times* offers a suggestion. Lermontov's method is to thread together a string of short stories about a central character, using an inside and an outside point of view. But before he did this Lermontov had decided what were the important things in Pechorin's character. They were, as it happened, all aspects of Byronism. Mr Desmond MacCarthy has said in an essay on Pushkin, that from Byron and Pushkin 'men caught the infection of being defiantly themselves'; in so planning, however, they became other than themselves. They invented a simplified *persona*. It is this simplification of Pechorin's character which is exciting. The detailed realism of the modern novel tells us far too much, without defining the little that it is absolutely essential to know. In what modern novels are the main traits of a hero of *our* own times delineated? It is the measure of the failure of modern novelists that they have not observed and defined a characteristic man of these years; and the explanation of the failure is our lack of moral and political perceptiveness. Our novels would be shorter, more readable and more important if we had one or two more ideas about our times and far fewer characters.

W. J. Entwistle   (essay date 1949)

SOURCE: "The Byronism of Lermontov's *A Hero of Our Time*," in *Comparative Literature*, Vol. I, No. 2, Spring, 1949, pp. 140-46.

[*In the following essay, the critic asserts that the Byronism of* A Hero of Our Time *is due to Lermontov's parallel development of qualities similar to those of Byron rather than to the influence or his imitation of the English poet.*]

That Lermontov modelled his conduct and verses on those of Byron has been said to satiety both by critics and by the Russian poet himself. He had indeed created presuppositions about his own work among his contemporaries which he felt bound to make an effort to dispel. He was, he asserted, not merely a Russian Byron, but someone different. But what Lermontov might be was still unrevealed in 1832, and this Russian writer of Hebrew melodies, ballads, romances, and album-pieces for ladies and gentlemen continued to sustain formal comparison with his model until the year 1836.

In that year his poetic Byronism culminated in the splendid *Dying Gladiator*. The piece is introduced by a line from *Childe Harold*. It shows us Lermontov in complete command of his own style, but there is still a causal relationship between the two writers. Had Byron not thrilled Europe with his verses on the dying gladiator (*Childe Har-*

old, IV, 140-141) he saw in Rome, had he not mentioned the Danube (though Dacia proved to have no interest for the Russian poet), and had he not made the sight the text for the protest against the cost of empire in tears and blood, there would have been neither cause nor sentiment for Lermontov's poem.

After 1836, however, Lermontov drew away from Byron into the freer exercise of his own special talents. In his novel he employed the medium of prose, which was never Byron's. Lermontov was intimately acquainted with the Caucasus, and its inspiration could not be kept out of his poems. *A Hero of Our Time* is thus an expression of Lermontov's proper genius. There is no causal relationship between it and any of Byron's works, and yet there is parallelism in many respects. These resemblances are not fortuitous or imitative, but due to permanent conditions either of Lermontov's genius or of Russian nature. They are, for that reason, I think, the more significant for the student of comparative literature; for they take us out of the regions of "influences," "models," and even "analogues," so assiduously pursued by some scholars, though so often trivial or superficial in effect. We are able to compare Lermontov as Lermontov with Byron, and there is heightened significance given by the greatness of the novel, which is so true to certain aspects of Russia, for it brings into evidence the similarities between the genius of Byron and that of a whole people.

The romantics had motives for requiring from novelists and poets the spice of the exotic, and this was given in abundant measure by Byron. But what he revealed to Europe was not the artificially contrived marvels of the Gothic revival nor the antiquarianism of Sir Walter Scott. Scott dipped just over the horizon in time, but Byron did so in space. His Aegean world was just inaccessible to his readers, but it was directly observed and real in matters of detail, though deliciously covered with the Byronic patina. Without departing from the natural, Byron increased the bounds of imagination and experience. The customs and sentiments he interpreted were basically those of his Western readers, but they were more dramatic, more colorful, and more flaunted. He offered guarantees of good faith to many nations: Don Juan to Spain, the Colosseum to Rome, Bonnivard to the Swiss, Mazeppa to the Ukrainians; but his fancy chiefly haunted the Aegean, with its uncouth and ferocious denizens, corsairs, giaours, arnauts, and the like.

Byron's world extended as far as the Caucasus, which he approached from the side of Armenia. In *The Giaour* he described the central defiles in these terms:

> The foremost Tartar's in the gap
> Conspicuous by his yellow cap;
> The rest in lengthening line the while
> Wind slowly through the long defile;
> Above, the mountain rears a peak,
> Where vultures whet the thirsty beak,
> And theirs may be a feast tonight,
> Shall tempt them down ere morrow's light;
> Beneath, a river's wintry stream
> Has shrunk before the summer's beam,
> And left a channel bleak and bare,
> Save shrubs that spring to perish there;

> Each side the midnight path there lay
> Small broken crags of granite gray,
> By time, or mountain lightning, riven
> From summits clad in mists of heaven;
> For where is he that hath beheld
> The peak of Liakura unveiled?

Apart from the single name, this is no doubt a set piece of description, which might apply to any mountains, if the poet set himself to exaggerate the elements of height and peril. Sir Walter Scott and Richard Blackmore have by this art converted innocent waterslides into objects of terror. But there is justification for each of Byron's terms in Lermontovs' description of the ascent of Gud-gora, which must have been supremely exciting for dwellers upon the endless Russian plains. He mentions the storm clouds that smoke around the peaks, and the sudden and devastating onset of the tempest, and the bitter winds that cut down through the gorges. Lermontov's characters approach from the south side of the range, as Byron did, under the guidance of Ossetian drivers. The novelist insists that this world of his imagination is Asia, not Russia. The difference is palpable whenever a scene includes the solid, prosaic, and irremediably Russian Maksim Maksimych, who is the more Russian for the incongruity of his Kabarda pipe with silver mountings and hairy Cherkassian hat. His skin is bronzed by Transcaucasian suns and his mouth is full of imprecations against "these dreadful beasts of Asiatics"; he serves as a mid-point of reference by which we realize the strangeness of the Ossetian drivers, Tatar horse rustlers, Georgians, Cossack adventurers, Chechen and Cherkassian barbarians in the Caucasian hive of nations, around the fringe of which the Russian elegants (*franty* and *kokety*) flirt and drink the waters, though a dead body a few hundred yards from the end of the boulevard causes no surprise. It is this same Maksim Maksimych who serves as point of reference for the exotic passions of the novel. He is tenderly affectionate towards the luckless Bela, though not comprehending either her simple lovingkindness or Pechorin's sultry passion. He is convinced that human kindness has a value everywhere, and is hurt when his generous hand is brushed aside by the hero. He is so much a part of fate that he is unconscious of its workings, and he turns a story of the workings of destiny into a dissertation on the bad priming of Cherkassian guns. Byron has no Maksim Maksimych, and his portraits are the less permanent for lack of him, but the rest of Lermontov's people have their place in Byron's world.

It might, on the surface, seem that Byron had done Lermontov a poor service by inducing him to conceive romantically a region which he knew so well in prosaic fact; but there are considerations which diminish the reproach. The art of the novel is such as to demand both truth to experience and consciousness of invention. It is not enough to "hold the mirror up to nature." It is a primary necessity to convince the reader that something extraordinary is about to occur. This is so important that for many millennia the criteria of factual veracity did not enter into the writer's calculations. Even at this day, romance can be enjoyed with an uncritical pleasure which Cervantes would censure but himself appreciate. Like other novels, those of Russia take their beginning from the strange and surprising, and they constantly recur to this inspiration. One may cite the Orenburg steppes in Pushkin's *Captain's Daughter* (with the figure of Pugachev), the Cossack epic in Gogol's *Taras Bulba,* and the Caucasus of Tolstoy's *Prisoner of the Caucasus.* It is true that Levin in *Anna Karenina* and Raskolnikov in *Crime and Punishment* are remarkable figures, but their sort arise when the norm is much better identified. In an earlier stage of development, the novelistic art employs the frankly abnormal. Pechorin, according to the second captain, was a distinguished youth, but somewhat strange, and the novel is designed to prove his strangeness. He could be otherwise viewed as a vulgarian, a poseur, and a philanderer without merit or excuse, and a later novelist of the school of Flaubert might have laid bare his squalid soul with a psychological scalpel. That was not possible in Lermontov's time, but the exotic setting saves his hero. It is nothing out of the way for a young man to seduce an innocent girl. But it is remarkable to carry off a Cherkassian princess and to make love across the barriers of language and habits, and it is extraordinary that a philanderer should enter a boat for his own vulgar ends but find he has to fight for his life against a female smuggler. The four-cornered intrigue labelled "Princess Meri" might have occurred wherever lazy and fashionable folk gather to kill their boredom, and it might lead to a duel—but not to such a duel as Lermontov describes upon a little triangular platform overhanging an immense ravine, and against the magnificent back cloth of the Caucasian range.

The technique of story telling employed by Lermontov is also Byronic. He was acquainted with Scott and others, but he chose the fragmentary manner of, say, *The Giaour,* and welcomed the opportunity of putting long passages in the words of his hero. The chief glory of Byron may well be that he is the best story teller in English verse after Chaucer. The art is almost a lost one now, but it has had a great history. Byron's skill was generously recognized by Sir Walter Scott. "James," he said to Ballantyne, "Byron hits the mark where I don't even pretend to fledge my arrow." Lockhart sought to trim the balance by a reproach against Byron. "Byron owed at least half his success to the imitation of Scott, and no trivial share of the rest to the lavish use of materials which Scott never employed, only because his genius was under the guidance of high feelings of moral rectitude." Peace be upon all such bickerings! These great men were masters in their different spheres. Scott, the prose novelist, sustained no comparison with Byron; Byron as the verse story teller did not diverge, like Scott, into tracts of versified prose. His less elevated passages are ingeniously glossed by his style, by his apparently negligent air, his brilliant rhymes, and barbed allusions. Episodic construction enabled him to pass over unsaid a great deal that would have made flat verse, and it is this episodic construction that Lermontov, a poet, was quick to copy.

For this technique, outside Byron, I see no models in the books with which Lermontov was familiar. He mentions *Werther, Old Mortality,* the works of Balzac, and *Undine,* but they would have led him in the paths of the articulated story. Connecting links are absent from *A Hero of Our Time.* The episode entitled "Maksim Maksimych" may be described as such a link, if its purpose is to explain how

Pechorin's papers came into his editor's hands. But that, surely, is not the purpose of the episode. It gives the reader his only direct glimpse of Pechorin, hurtling through the Caucasus to Persia under the goad of his conscience, brushing aside the offers of his old friend, and chilling him with unkindness. The reader learns by, as it were, personal experience that this is one "at whose birth it was written that extraordinary things should happen to him." In the other episodes there is a veil between reader and personage, due to the uncomprehending report by the second captain and the speciousness of Pechorin's memoirs. If, then, we take this passage to be an episode and not a link, it follows that the novel is compounded of episodes corresponding to the moments of highest passion, and that their linkage is left to the imagination of the reader. It is a Byronic procedure and one congenital to the lyrical poet in Lermontov.

All Byronic heroes are one hero and his face is Byron's. Whatever other persons get into Byron's verse are statically described and never lived. A burr that stuck to Lermontov was the insinuation that his Pechorin was no other than himself. He is a character in a sense not shared by Bela, Princess Meri, or the young fop Grushnickij. Vera has a great space for action and no character to act with. Even Maksim Maksimych, though admirably outlined, is statically described and does not enjoy that degree of the author's sympathy which would make him a living person. This leaves only Pechorin alive through some fellow feeling of his creator's. No doubt Pechorin was unlike the actual Lermontov, who says he describes him ironically. Successful irony is usually provided with a key, but there is no such key in the novel. The opening pages set a distance between the author and Maksim Maksimych, who might otherwise, in his normality, have stood for the author's reason. In the matter of English poses, Maksim, who ignores them, is as far from the author's standpoint as Pechorin, who exaggerates them. But between Pechorin and Lermontov there is the kind of relation that exists between Lara and Byron, Don Quixote and Cervantes, Hamlet and Shakespeare, Levin and Tolstoy, and to that extent, allowing for artistic remodelling and despite the testimony of the poet, we must say that Pechorin *is* Lermontov. Pechorin as a diarist shares a quality with Lermontov as a novelist and with Byron as a Don Juan, namely, incapacity for understanding the character of women; but Lermontov in Bela and Byron in Haidée draw attractive pictures of innocence—a negative quality.

Peculiar to Byron was the internal contradiction of his nature and education. Sir Walter Scott noticed it upon their first acquaintance, and is reported by Lockhart as saying:

> He was certainly proud of his rank and ancient family, and in that respect, as much an aristocrat as was consistent with good sense and good breeding. Some disgusts, how adopted I know not, seemed to me to have given this peculiar and (as it appeared to me) contradictory cast of mind; but, at heart, I would have termed Byron a patrician on principle.

His mother contributed to his disequilibrium by petting and neglecting him outrageously. His birth and presence promised high rewards of which his physical defects balked him. But the most characteristic symptom was the discomfort of his conscience due to the teachings of his nurse. "To his Scottish upbringing [says the *Encyclopaedia Brittanica,* s. v. 'Byron,' 11th ed.] he owed his love of mountains, his love and knowledge of the Bible, and too much Calvinism for faith or unfaith in Christianity." His conflicts with society were external manifestations of the conflict within himself. The two sides of his nature held apart, and he could not solder them. He put now one, now the other, on paper in an agony of self-analysis out of which no synthesis arose.

Thus Byron, as a "conscience-stricken aristocrat," was a figure destined to become familiar in the history of Russia in the nineteenth century, and his torturing self-analysis to offer a precedent for much Russian literature. There was the "flaw" which Aristotle demands as the seed of tragedy. Byron's works are full of noble souls irretrievably ruined, charging Fate with their unhappiness but, secretly aware that the fault lies within themselves, condemning their own black villainies with the vocabulary of the severest morality. They exemplify the anarchy of a whole nature, by which good turns to evil, though evil never silences good; and the intensity of suffering is a mark of ineradicable remnants of virtue. Good impulses pave the way to crime. The subject's bewilderment is a cause of endless self-analysis, but there is no solution. The situation repeats itself in Russian literature. Before Lermontov wrote, Pushkin had shown this sort of conflict in the Grigori Mnishchek of *Boris Godunov* and the Pugachëv of *The Captain's Daughter,* and it reaches it height in Dostoevsky's work. Its sign is the monologue: the need to disburden the heart at great length, and indifference to anyone selected to hear the confession. A considerable number of great Russian novels have this character of protracted monologues, which is also that of Byron's dramas and Lermontov's *Hero of Our Time.* Pechorin endeavors three times to account for himself: his narcissism, his hankering after women, and his repulsion from marriage. It is a leading merit of the novel that there should be this probing of the soul, and even in its details it is Byronic. The first cause, with Pechorin as with Byron, was a faulty education, whereby pampering had undermined the moral standards. Then like the Corsair, Pechorin, independent but still too young to control his passions, is represented as the victim of a violent attachment to an impossible she, accompanied by a cold aversion for all other women:

> Yes, it was love—unchangeable—unchanged,
> Felt but for one from whom he never ranged;
> Though fairest captives daily met his eye,
> He shunned, nor sought, but coldly passed them
>   by;
> Though many a beauty drooped in prison bower,
> None ever soothed his most unguarded hour.

At least we must suppose, from the half-confidences to Grushnickij, that this was the history of Pechorin and Vera, but the latter's character is so hazy—she weeps near a fountain, shows spiteful jealousy, arranges a crude intrigue, and at last blabs to her old husband—that the situation is far from clear; but in Bela and Princess Meri we have the equivalents of the "drooping captives" of the Corsair.

The Byronic temperament, and I think the Russian, is one of extremes with no middle. Dickens is said to share with Byron in Russia the repute of a standard for England. The novels of Dickens, taken *au pied de la lettre,* are accepted as objective descriptions of English society. There was, under Tsarist rule, nothing in Russia like the intelligent and organized English middle class or its counterpart in France, and the middle order supplied only material for official comedy such as one finds in Gogol's *Dead Souls.* The extremes of aristocracy and the proletariat were much more characteristic, and give the typical Russian creations of Tolstoy and Dostoevsky. In the West the novel seems to have an almost irremediable tendency to become identified with the middle class of persons who are wealthy enough to have some initiative, but not so wealthy as to evade the penalties of their errors. The patrician novel is often a kind of escape from this too close succession of causes and effects while the proletarian novel is a conscious descent into an abyss. These psychological and social conditions belong to an age later than that of Byron's upbringing, in the amoral aristocratic times of the Regency bucks. Cause and effect operated, but on a different plane, and it is on this plane that the Russo-Scot Lermontov sets his Pechorin. He suffers none of those immediate economic and social penalties which attend similar exhibitions of petulance in a *bourgeoisie,* but only the aristocratic punishment of self-condemnation by the division of the mind against itself, unable to resolve its own evil.

Janko Lavrin (essay date 1959)

SOURCE: "The Hero and the Age," in *Lermontov,* Bowes & Bowes, 1959, pp. 76-91.

[*Lavrin is an Austrian-born British critic, essayist, and biographer. He is best known for his studies of nineteenth- and twentieth-century Russian literature. In such works as* An Introduction to the Russian Novel *(1942), he combines literary criticism with an exploration into the psychological and philosophical background of an author. In the following excerpt from his book-length study of Lermontov, Lavrin analyzes* A Hero of Our Time *and places Lermontov's novel within the Russian literary tradition.*]

If the 1820's were the 'Golden Age' of Russian poetry, the following decade marked the gradual rise of Russian prose. The late eighteenth- and early nineteenth-century prose of Karamzìn and his contemporaries sounded archaic at a time when France could boast of Balzac, England of Dickens and Thackeray, and Germany of the young Heine. So it was in the 1830's that Russian prose made the first strides which, some thirty years later, were to culminate in its great realistic novels—Russia's chief contribution to world literature. But even during that pioneering decade one could notice two main lines of prose-fiction, one represented by Pushkin and the other by Gogol.

Pushkin, with his flair for doing the right thing at the right time, started already in the later 1820's his unfinished novel, *Aráp Petrá Velìkogo (The Negro of Peter the Great).* This is a work of classical realism, depicting—in a parallel manner—the court of Versailles on the one hand, and that of the new Russian capital, St. Petersburg, on the other. The central hero of the novel was to be Pushkin's Abyssinian maternal great-grandfather Annibal, who had been bought by the Russian ambassador on the slave-market at Constantinople and sent as a present to Peter the Great. Yet in the six odd chapters preserved Peter himself is more conspicuous than any other character, although here, for once, he is shown in his more human and even homely moods.

In 1831 there appeared Pushkin's equally disciplined five stories under the common title *Póvesti Bélkina* (*Tales of Belkin*). They are not written but *told* stories—told by the 'late Iván Petróvich Bélkin', a genteel and pathetically comic narrator (of a fairly low social standing) whose inflection and manner of speaking are preserved throughout. This kind of story bears the Russian name of *skaz* (From the verb *skazát,* to tell) and plays quite an important part in Russian fiction, Soviet fiction included. Almost at the same time Pushkin was engaged in writing his novel *Dubróvsky.* Inspired by Sir Walter Scott, Pushkin yet wrote it in that terse prose of his own from which he would not desist even when taking up such a highly romantic or 'Hoffmannesque' theme as the one in his *Pìkovaya Dáma* (*Queen of Spades,* 1836). And in his principal prosework, *A Captain's Daughter* (1836), the inspiration derived from Scott is combined with both Pushkin's simplicity and discipline at their best.

Gogol's ornate and agitated prose has already been referred to. The 'furious' kind of prose imported from France found its chief representative in A. A. Bestúzhev-Marlìnsky, whose romantic narratives (with frequent Caucasian settings) were immensely popular at the time. Among the more orthodox followers of Sir Walter Scott were M. N. Zagóskin, N. A. Polevóy and I. I. Lazhéchnikov, whereas Prince V. F. Odóyevsky and Alexander Véltman had been influenced by Jean Paul Richter and Sterne respectively.

Such were the salient features of Russian prose in the 1830's. Yet already at the beginning of the next decade there appeared two works which had a great influence upon the development of Russian fiction, especially after the acceptance of Belìnsky's slogan of the 'natural school'. One of these two works was Lermontov's *A Hero of our Time* (1840), which adhered to the tradition of Pushkin. The other was Gogol's *Dead Souls* (1842), written in a prose different from, though complementary to, that of Pushkin. Here we are concerned with Lermontov's masterpiece.

Pechórin, the principal character of *A Hero of our Time,* is a descendant of Pushkin's Onégin, but with a difference. Lermontov's merit was that of all Russian authors he gave the first psychological portrait of such a 'superfluous' character and analysed him as a victim of the *Zeitgeist,* of the conditions he was doomed to live in. Hence the ironical label—a 'hero of our time'.

Pushkin's Onégin lived in the early 1820's, before the 'Decembrist' revolt. So he was able to pose and to relish his Byronic spleen to his heart's content. Pechórin, on the other hand, belonged to a later generation—the lost gener-

ation of the 1830's which had to pay the price for that abortive revolt. One of the principal consequences of the 'Decembrist' rising was the tightening of the police-regime and its clamping down on any individual will or initiative. Those who suffered most were the ambitious young men whose strength and talents found no outlet and were thus doomed to remain inactive. They were out of place in their own country. But if strength, especially great strength, is devoid of an adequate outlet, it invariably turns against itself and becomes destructive. Such was the tragedy of Pechórin.

And so in analysing him, Lermontov put his finger on the malady of an entire 'superfluous' generation, himself included. It is true that in his preface to the second edition of the novel he warns us not to confuse Pechórin's personality with that of the author. But such warnings are always somewhat suspect. Belìnsky hit the nail on the head when declaring that Pechórin was a subjective projection of Lermontov without being actually autobiographic. It stands to reason that the author had projected into him a number of his own characteristics. In both of them frustrated strength was in danger of turning (and did turn) into a destructive even a 'demoniacally' destructive, agency. Both were tired of love, of society, in fact of everything except the beauty of the Caucasian scenery. Both were equally prone to indulge in the same kind of callous egotism, since they could not believe in any true values outside or above their own immediate selves. Last but not least, Pechórin's encounter with Vera and her aged husband (in the section "Princess Mary") is but another version of a similar meeting in *Princess Ligovskáya,* as well as in the play *The Two Brothers*—all of them referring to Lermontov's own painful encounter with the Bakhmétyevs in December 1835.

The novel was finished in 1839, but it first two editions appeared in 1840 and 1841 respectively. It is written in a prose which is less simple, perhaps, than the prose of Pushkin, yet it is even more flexible, while being equally disciplined and lucid. It has fewer gallicisms and is at the same time richly articulated because of its variety or even deliberate mixture of styles. The author's remarks and descriptions are alternated with the *skaz*-manner of Captain Maxìm Maxìmych—a kindly simple soul of the Bélkin variety. Then there are Pechórin's reminiscences and diaries, acute and coldly ironical like the man himself.

Pechórin's ordeals are unrolled before us not in their chronological order, but according to a definite psychological plan or pattern. The novel consists of five independent narratives joined together by the main character, and even more by the author who gives us all sorts of comments and necessary information. The narratives are constructed in a way reminiscent of Balzac's *La femme de trente ans* (1832) which Lermontov refers to in his novel. The first two of the five narratives, "Bela" and "Maxim Maximych," show Pechórin as he is seen by others. Of the remaining three "Princess Mary" is in the form of Pechórin's diary, whereas "Tamán" and "The Fatalist" record some of his adventures—one in the Crimea and the other in the Caucasus. The central piece, "Princess Mary," provides us above all with an analysis (or rather self-analysis) of Pechórin's mind and character.

The subject-matter of "Bela" is a distant echo of Pushkin's first Byronic tale in verse, *A Prisoner of the Caucasus*. The hero of that tale is a Russian officer captured by the Caucasian mountaineers. A primitive Caucasian belle falls in love with him; but he, being a civilized man, is much too blasé to respond to the girl's spontaneous feelings. He remains cool and callous even while she arranges all that is necessary for his escape, after which she commits suicide. In "Bela" we have a similar plot, in practically the same Caucasian setting. Only instead of being a captive, Pechórin is a society dandy sent—in punishment for a duel—to a remote fort held by the Russians. Here he serves as a junior officer under the command of Captain Maxìm Maxìmych. An honest old warrior with no social pretences, Maxìm Maxìmych is one of the finest figures in early Russian fiction. In a way he combines the characteristics of Pushkin's Mirónov (in *A Captain's Daughter*) and Bélkin. Yet, naive and kindly though he be, he is full of shrewd common sense, which cannot be said of his subaltern Pechórin.

In spite of the difference in character, education and social status, the Captain and Pechórin got on well together. Some estrangement arose between the two only after the bored dandy had taken a fancy to the Tartar girl Bela, the daughter of the local chieftain. Infatuated with Bela, Pechórin contrived to kidnap her with the help of her own brother whom he rewarded with a spirited horse—stolen from the girl's savage Tartar wooer Kazbìch. Bela, frightened and diffident at first, soon fell in love with her captor. Even Maxìm Maxìmych became fond of her with a kind of disinterested fatherly affection. To quote his own words:

> She was a very fine girl, Bela. In the end I got to feel towards her as if she had been my own daughter, and she became very fond of me. I should tell you that I have no near relatives to think about. For twenty years I have heard no news of my father or my mother. As for taking a wife, I never dreamed of doing so in my younger days, and it would be foolish to think of such a thing now. Naturally then I was glad to make a pet of Bela. She used to sing songs to us, or dance a Caucasian dance—the lezghinka. A wonderful dancer, she was. I have watched our fine young ladies in their ballroom dances at the provincial capital, and twenty years ago I was at a swagger ball in Moscow; but that sort of dancing was not in the same street with Bela's for beauty. Gregóry Alexándrovich (Pechórin) decked her out like a doll, pampered and fondled her, and it was a marvel the way in which her beauty increased. The tan disappeared from her face and hands, so that in the end her cheeks were quite rosy. She was always cheerful and I never wanted anything in the world except to make her laugh, God rest her soul.

The last exclamation points to Bela's tragic end—inevitable when in love with such a man as Pechórin. For no sooner had he noticed that Bela truly loved him than he lost all interest in her. It was not love he had been after, but conquest and the egoistic feeling of his own power over her. One day, when Pechórin was out on a hunting expedition, Bela left her room and went for a little walk outside the walls. Here she was mortally wounded by Kazbìch, who had been prowling about the fort. Bela's agony ends this part of the novel.

It is Captain Maximych who tells the author the story, while travelling in his company along the Georgian military road in the heart of the Caucasus. His own style—the style of a *skaz*—is now and then interrupted by the author's remarks or descriptions of the scenery, and the alternation of the two styles adds to the interest and the atmosphere of the narrative.

"Maxim Maximych," the second story of the novel, tells us in a sober, matter-of-fact language how the author had lodged at an inn in Vladikavkáz where, one day later, he was joined by Maxim Maximych. Suddenly they heard that Pechórin had stopped there, on his way to Persia. Maxim Maximych was overjoyed at the prospect of meeting, after such a lapse of time, his old friend and fellow-officer, linked with him through the tragedy of Bela. Impatient to see Pechórin, he sent word to him that his old captain was at the inn. Maxim Maximych was sure that the young man would come rushing to embrace him. But the blasé society dandy was in no hurry to see his former friend and superior. When at last he came, he was cold and politely aloof: an aristocratic snob condescendingly talking to an effusive, warm-hearted commoner. The Captain's consternation was so great that he could not get over it. Fortunately, Pechórin and his arrogant flunkey departed without delay.

> We had long ceased to hear the bells of the troika, or the grind of the wheels on the flinty road (says the author), but my poor old friend continued to stand where he was, deep in thought.
>
> 'Yes,' he said at last, with assumed indifference, though tears of vexation were brimming over from his eyes and coursing down his cheeks, 'of course we were close friends long ago. But what does he care about me now I am neither rich nor a high official, and I am much older than he is. Did you notice what a dandified rig-out he was wearing? He might still have been at St. Petersburg. A smart calash, too. Such a lot of luggage, and a footman with damnable side.'

Such was the encounter of the two former friends—one of them a man of the people, and the other a self-absorbed man of society. Yet this was not the whole of Pechórin. Something deeper had awakened in him during Bela's agony and death, though not for long: whatever his feelings, the mask of indifference was regarded by him as something obligatory. Like many an isolated and rootless individual he refused to, or else could not, draw a line between the mask and the man, the sham and the substance.

Of the next three narratives, "Tamán" is a superbly told story in which Lermontov recalls (in Pechórin's words) his own adventure—among 'honest smugglers'—in the port of that name during his first exile to the Caucasus. Then follows "Princess Mary" the whole of which is a fine piece of psychological dissection in the form of a diary. The novel ends with that concentrated tale, "The Fatalist," describing a strange incident Lermontov himself might have witnessed in a Caucasian Cossack settlement.

The longest of these three narratives, "Princess Mary," is also the central piece of the novel. As such it calls for special comment.

The happenings told in this story take place in the fashionable Caucasian spa of Pyatigórsk, and some of them may relate to Lermontov and his acquaintances. Várya Lopúkhina emerges here as Vera, and her husband as the gouty Prince Ligovskóy. The pseudo-romantic poseur Grushnìtsky is usually identified with Major Martýnov, whose bullet was later to kill the poet. The caustic doctor Werner again portrays a certain Doctor Meyer whom he had met at Stavrópol and whom he liked. Lermontov's description of the fashionable set at Pyatigórsk in the 1830's sounds authentic, although here too he was evidently not regarded as respectable enough to be accepted by the 'cream of society'.

The story, simple in its plot, is complicated psychologically. Pechórin, while staying in the spa, starts from sheer boredom a love-intrigue with Princess Mary—an inexperienced young beauty courted by the shallow poseur Grushnìtsky. But once Pechórin has become sure of the girl's love he begins to cool off and loses all interest in her. New complications arise when Vera (his old love) and her husband enter the scene. Vera's jealousy, Pechórin's chivalrous defence of Princess Mary and Grushnitsky's envy bring matters to a climax at the moment when Pechórin has renewed his love with Vera, leaving the trusting Princess Mary to her own despair. A duel follows in which Grushnitsky is killed. When Pechórin returns from the duel he finds to his chagrin that Vera and her husband have left the spa. He has a last conversation with Princess Mary to whom he callously declares that he had not meant anything serious when trying to win her affections. In consequence of his duel with Grushnitsky, he is sent to the very fortress in which his life was to become so strangely intertwined with Bela's and the old-world Captain Maxim Maximych's.

> 'And now,' he wrote in his diary, 'here in this wearisome fort, I often review the past, and ask myself why I was unwilling to tread on the road opened to me by fate, a road where gentle pleasures and peace of mind awaited me. But no, I could never have become reconciled to it. I am like a seaman who was born and bred on the deck of a pirate ship. He has become so accustomed to storms and battles that on land he feels insufferably bored, however alluring the shady woods, however temperate the sunshine.'

The quoted passage is typical of a *déraciné* such as Pechórin who, being in love with his own pain, does not mind inflicting pain upon others. In this respect he bears, for all his concreteness, traces of a romantic-demoniac character at a time when such a 'hero' was already getting out of fashion and had begun to look more comical than sinister even in romantic fiction. Yet Lermontov succeeded: partly because he himself gave—in Grushnitsky—a magnificent parody of such a type, and partly because Pechórin's actions are stated with psychological convincingness. He is shown, moreover, as an intensified egotist of the 1830's who, finding nothing that is worth while outside himself, cannot but extol and gratify his own ego.

> I see the sufferings and the joys of others only in relation to myself, I regard them as food to nourish my spiritual strength. It has become impossible for me to do foolish deeds under the stimulus of passion. In me ambition has been crushed by circumstances to assume another form. For ambition is nothing other than the thirst for power, and my chief delight is to impose my will upon all with whom I come in contact. To inspire in others feelings of love, devotion, or fear, what is it but the first sign and the greatest triumph of power. To be for someone a cause of suffering or joy, without the least right—can pride know sweeter food than this? What indeed is happiness? Gratified pride?

All this cannot be accepted as an excuse for Pechórin's behaviour towards Bela and Princess Mary, but it offers at least an explanation. His stress on the 'will to power', combined with his unscrupulous 'beyond good and evil' where other people are concerned, contains all the germs of nihilism. But there is also a tragic side to it.

The critic and poet Apollón Grigóryev (he was active in the early 1860's) defined Pechórin as 'weakness of stilted self-will'. A closer definition would be: real strength gone wrong; the strength of a man endowed with talents, will and ambition, but all to no purpose. Being unable to believe in such a thing as a purpose, Pechórin is doomed to be either a mere analytical observer, or else an experimenter exercising his own futile 'will to power' without any use either to himself or to others, and spelling disaster to everyone he meets. He knows that in essence he is a 'cripple', yet he cannot help it.

As a tragic *déraciné* of the 1830's Pechórin is the most important link between Pushkin's Onégin and the 'superfluous men' in subsequent Russian fiction. At the same time he is merciless in his self-analysis, although without any moralizing propensity. As Lermontov explains in his preface to the second edition of the novel: 'Let me beg you, however, not to jump to the conclusion that the author of this book aspires to become a reformer of public morals. God forbid! I found it agreeable to sketch a contemporary as he presented himself to me—and, unfortunately both for him and for you, I have met him too often. The illness has been diagnosed, but goodness alone knows how to cure it.'

Lermontov is supposed to have intended to write a trilogy of novels—one about the epoch of Catherine II, another about that of Alexander I and one dealing with the period of Nicholas. I. If so, then *A Hero of our Time* would represent the last part of such a planned trilogy—a part for which the material was ready at hand.

What matters, though, is the fact that in producing *A Hero of our Time* he presented Russian literature with one of its great novels—a novel in which all the characters (with the possible exception of Vera) are drawn with consummate art. Less known, and even less appreciated abroad than many other masterpieces of Russian prose, this work is yet a classic. Belìnsky, who had sponsored it at once, remained one of its enthusiastic admirers in the very teeth of its detractors. Gogol himself said, in his *Passages from Correspondence with Friends,* that 'no one in our country has written so far such magnificent and full-blooded prose. Here he (Lermontov) evidently penetrated deeper into the realities of existence; he promised to become a great painter of Russian life, but sudden death has deprived us of him.'

A Hero of our Time has even been admired by some critics as the greatest Russian novel. It certainly is the first truly psychological novel in Russian literature. As far as an insight into certain aspects of the psychology of nihilism is concerned, Lermontov anticipated Dostoévsky. After all, from Pechórin to Stavrógin (the hero of *The Possessed*) there is only one step; and not a big one at that. Lermontov's natural and flexible prose, on the other hand, was not without influence on the prose of both Turgénev and Tolstóy. One ought to stress, perhaps, also the cathartic nature of this novel, since Lermontov projected into Pechórin some of those features he himself wanted to get rid of. Such a conclusion is borne out by several poems he wrote at the time.

Ya net Bayron

No Byron I, but yet unknown
A chosen vessel set apart;
A stranger by the world reviled
Like him, but Russian in my heart.

   —Mikhail Lermontov, "Ya net Bayron," 1832.

Paul Foote   (essay date 1965)

SOURCE: An introduction to *A Hero of Our Time,* by M. Yu. Lermontov, translated by Paul Foote, Penguin Books, 1966, pp. 7-17.

[*In the following essay, Foote places* A Hero of Our Time *in the context of Lermontov's life and of Russian literature, and discusses Lermontov's portrayal of his protagonist.*]

Lermontov is best known as the greatest Russian poet after Pushkin. *A Hero of our Time* is his only novel, yet it might be claimed that Lermontov owes his importance in the development of Russian literature almost as much to this one short novel as to his verse.

Lermontov's literary career spanned a mere dozen years before his early death in 1841, and *A Hero of our Time* was written towards the end of this time, in the years 1838-40. The period in which he wrote—the 1830s—was an important transitional stage in Russian literature, when verse surrendered its pre-eminence to the story and the novel, and the great age of Russian literature began. Lermontov's course ran parallel to that of Pushkin, his older contemporary, for both poets turned from verse to prose towards the end of their careers—Pushkin in works such as *The Queen of Spades* and *The Captain's Daughter,* Lermontov in **A Hero of our Time,** which was preceded by

a number of other attempts at prose. Though Pushkin was unsurpassed by Lermontov as a poet, there is little doubt that Lermontov outstripped him as a prose-writer.

Lermontov is renowned as the one true romantic poet produced by Russia, and the one who reflected most strongly the then current trend of Byronism. He was certainly much influenced by Byron, but this does not mean that Byronic attitudes for Lermontov were something merely assumed. His life contained plenty of circumstances likely to produce a 'natural' Byronic figure. He was born in 1814, an only child, and lost his mother at the age of three. She had married somewhat beneath her, and after her death the boy was brought up by his indulgent and possessive maternal grandmother, seeing little of his father, who was never on good terms with his mother-in-law. The divided loyalties of his family life and his comparative isolation in an elderly household helped to develop an introspective, brooding nature in the child. At fourteen he began writing verse, and his early lyrics are full of complaints of isolation, broken hopes and distrust of the world. Later his sense of alienation and bitterness were to be increased by unhappy love affairs. His childhood was spent mainly on the family estate of Tarkhany in the province of Penza, and the only notable events of this period were three journeys with his grandmother to the health resorts of the Caucasus. Here, though only a child, he was deeply affected, as so many Russian writers have been, by the magnificent mountain scenery and the exotic atmosphere of Asia. After four years of formal education in Moscow (including two fruitless years at the University), Lermontov entered the Cavalry Training School and two years later (in 1834) was commissioned in a Hussar regiment.

As a young officer in a fashionable regiment he moved in St Petersburg society, engaging in the usual pastimes of the capital and at the same time cultivating a cynical disdain for society, which he no doubt sincerely felt.

The four years before his death were the most eventful of Lermontov's life. In 1837 he sprang into the public eye on account of his poem **The Death of a Poet.** This was a savage denunciation of Russian society for the death of Pushkin, who had been killed in January 1837 in a duel which many felt had been deliberately engineered for the purpose of getting rid of the poet. The poem was regarded as inflammatory by the authorities and Lermontov was posted to a regiment in the Caucasus-in other words, sent into exile. He was now regarded as the poetic heir of Pushkin and the champion of his memory. Besides **The Death of Poet** Lermontov wrote a number of other robust poems in which he showed that he was no languid romantic, but a poet of broad talents and a punishing social critic.

Though his exile lasted only a few months on this occasion, Lermontov was again despatched to the Caucasus in 1840, after being involved in a duel with the son of the French minister in St Petersburg. A year later, still in the Caucasus, Lermontov quarrelled with an acquaintance, a certain Major Martynov, over a trivial insult. They fought a duel near Pyatigorsk (the location oddly similar to that of Pechorin's duel with Grushnitsky in *A Hero of our*

Time) and Lermontov was killed on the spot. He was twenty-six years old.

A Hero of our Time is what the title implies, an account of the life and character of a man who, Lermontov suggests, is typical of his age. The novel consists of five separate stories relating episodes in the life of this contemporary hero. Three of them were first published separately in the journal *Notes of the Fatherland* ('Bela' and 'The Fatalist' in 1839, 'Taman' in 1840), the other two ('Maxim Maximych' and 'Princess Mary') appeared only in the first full edition of the novel, which came out in May 1840. The novel continues the tradition of personal studies, initiated in Russia by Pushkin's *Eugene Onegin,* but with antecedents in western European literature, in which the contemporary young man with his problems and faults is exposed. That Lermontov was consciously creating a link with Pushkin's Onegin is shown by his choice of the name Pechorin for his hero. Pushkin had given his hero the name Onegin, derived from Onega, the north-Russian river; Lermontov echoed his choice by giving his hero a name derived from the even more northerly River Pechora.

Pechorin is, like Onegin, a representative of the so-called 'superfluous' men, who figure so often in the novels and stories of Turgenev, Goncharov, Herzen, etc. These 'superfluous' men were men set apart by their superior talents from the mediocre society in which they were born, but doomed to waste their lives, partly through lack of opportunity of fulfill themselves, though also, in most cases, because they themselves lacked any real sense of purpose or strength of will.

Unlike the classic type of 'superfluous' men, Pechorin is cast more in the mould of Byron's heroes, a strong individual at odds with the world. He is proud, energetic, strong-willed, ambitious, but, having found that life does not measure up to his expectations of it, he has grown embittered, cynical and bored. At the age of twenty-five (as he is in the book) he has experienced all that life has to offer and found nothing to give him more than passing satisfaction or interest. He sees that life has let him down, failed to provide for him the high purpose that would be worthy of his superior powers. So he is reduced to dissipating his very considerable energies in petty adventures of the type described in the novel. He embarks on these with few illusions that he is doing more than making a temporary escape from boredom.

The only comfort Pechorin has is his conviction of his own perfect knowledge and mastery of life. He despises emotions and prides himself on the supremacy of his intellect over his feelings. 'The turmoil of life has left me with a few ideas, but no feelings,' he tells his friend Dr Werner, and to prove it he rides roughshod over the feelings of other people. His disregard for the comfort and happiness of others is repeatedly demonstrated in the novel, and his victims are lucky if they get off with a broken heart (as Vera and Princess Mary)—the less fortunate (Bela, Grushnitsky) pay with their lives.

Pechorin is not just indifferent to the feelings of other people—he positively enjoys persecuting them, and though in some cases the havoc he wreaks on people's lives is unplanned, in others he sets out deliberately to destroy his victims. He talks in his journal of his insatiable desire for power, of the pleasure he derives from destroying others' hopes and illusions, and of his view of other people as food to nourish his own ego. His own frustrated ambition and resentment against life turn him into a predator in the grand style. As he remarks during his carefully planned campaign to win Princess Mary: 'There are times when I can understand the Vampire.' It is particularly this active, aggressive instinct that distinguishes Pechorin from the common run of ineffectual heroes in Russian literature and links him more with Byronic types such as the Giaour, the Corsair, etc.

Pechorin's passion for contradicting others has been bred in his own experience. His whole life, he says, has been a succession of attempts to go against heart or reason. Though in the novel he claims that this conflict has been resolved in the victory of reason over feeling, and prides himself on his immunity to emotional experience, this is really a piece of self-deception. He may be free from illusions about life, but he is still subject to the power of his emotions. We see, for instance, the deep effect that Bela's death has on him, the stirring of his old love for Vera, his pity for Princess Mary even while he is destroying her happiness. We see his vulnerability again in his moments of self-pity, when he wonders why it is that people hate him (!), when he himself feels dismayed at the destructive influence he has on other people's lives and sees himself not as the controlling genius of his actions, but as a mere instrument of fate. He even has still some traces of the idealism which he possessed in his youth. His sensitive appreciation of nature is partly due to his recognition in it of the ideal purity and beauty which he finds lacking in human society. He writes of Pyatigorsk in 'Princess Mary': 'The air is pure, as the kiss of a child, the sun is bright, the sky blue—what more does one want? What need have we here of passions, desires, regrets?'

It is in these moments of doubt and weakness that we see the tragic nature of Pechorin. Not only is he gifted with intellect and strength of will, he has also a poet's soul and a capacity for intense feeling. 'I've got an unfortunate character,' he tells Maxim Maximych in 'Bela'. 'If I cause unhappiness to others, I'm no less unhappy myself.' And we see that this is only too true. Pechorin is not just a dastardly villain of romance, but a complex figure, worthy of pity and understanding.

Talking to Princess Mary, Pechorin squarely places the blame for his character on the society in which he was brought up. He gives a pathetic account of himself as a child, full of noble ideals and impulses, but frustrated and mocked at every turn by the complacent mediocrities around him. The result, he says, was that he turned from goodness, truth, idealism to cynicism, hatred and evil. Though this confession is calculated to impress Princess Mary and win her sympathy, some part of it at least can be taken as the truth. Pechorin certainly is a social phenomenon. He belonged to the generation (Lermontov's own) that reached maturity in the decade following the abortive Decembrist Rising of 1825, which had resulted not in the hoped-for more liberal political régime, but in the stultifying repression of Nicholas I's reign. The generation which grew up at this time certainly had few opportunities for self-fulfillment, and Pechorin can well be seen as its product. Lermontov's title shows that he linked his hero specifically with the age in which he lived, and Belinsky, the contemporary Russian critic who was the first to give a detailed appreciation of the novel, emphasized that Pechorin-type figures were inevitable in that particular period of Russian history. 'This is how the hero of our time must be,' he wrote. 'He will be characterized either by decisive inaction, or else by futile activity.' It is obviously too much to follow the view of some Soviet critics who see Pechorin as a kind of revolutionary *manqué*, but it is reasonable enough to see him as an individualist in revolt against the mediocrity and conformism of his time, who, without and outlet for his talents, devotes himself to anti-social activities of the type described in the novel.

Pechorin is, though, more than a mere social type. He is also a psychological type, the dual character, in conflict with himself, torn between good and evil, between idealism and cynicism, between a full-blooded desire to live and a negation of all that life has to offer. This kind of character was one of Lermontov's continual preoccupations (well-known examples are the hero of his long poem **The Demon** and Arbenin, the wife-murderer of his drama **Masquerade**) and reflects, in part at least, the personality of the author himself. There is no doubt that Lermontov put a great deal of himself into the novel, and it was not surprising that on the novel's first appearance some critics claimed that in it he had merely portrayed himself and his acquaintances. It was this that led Lermontov to write the Preface (which appeared only in the second edition of the novel), in which he pours scorn on this idea, though, it may be worth noting, he does not reject it in so many words. Indeed, he could hardly have done so truthfully, for one or two of the characters were certainly based on real people, and in Pechorin's relationship with Vera there are echoes of Lermontov's own relationship with Varya Lopukhina. Though he might honestly say that he was not portraying himself in Pechorin—his presentation of the character makes that evident enough—there is no doubt, however, that Pechorin owes much to Lermontov's own experience. The disillusion, cynicism, frustration and hopeless striving recorded in Pechorin's journal are also found as recurring themes in Lermontov's lyrics.

Lermontov's attitude to his hero is critical, yet sympathetic. He recognizes Pechorin's situation as a 'malady' (the diagnosis of which is the subject of the novel, though, as he remarks in the Preface, 'Heaven alone knows how to cure it!'), and he suggests that those who read Pechorin's journal will come to understand, and so excuse much that might otherwise seem reprehensible. 'Some readers might like to know my own opinion of Pechorin's character,' he writes in the Foreword to Pechorin's journal. 'My answer is given in the title of this book. "Malicious irony!" they'll retort. I don't know.' Of course, there is irony in the title, but it can be argued that the irony is aimed not so much at Pechorin as at 'our time'. Pechorin has 'heroic' qualities—energy, boldness, intelligence—but can do nothing with them, because he lacks any kind of purpose, and this is the fault of the time. Viewed in this way, the title can plausibly be taken as a vindication of Pechorin, fitted for a hero's role, but doomed to inactivity by his age.

A Hero of our Time is a landmark in Russian literature, for it was the first example of the psychological novel in Russia. A decade earlier Pushkin had written his 'novel in verse' *Eugene Onegin,* and Lermontov was certainly influenced by Pushkin's study. But he exploited the greater freedom of the prose medium to create in Pechorin a figure of far greater subtlety and complexity than Onegin. Lermontov showed considerable skill in the way he presented his hero. Each of the five stories is complete in itself, each reveals some new facts about Pechorin's character. Though there is no plot to link the stories together, there is a rough chronological framework, which can be deduced. In fact, the order of the stories in the book does not correspond to the order in which the events they describe occurred. The episodes described in Pechorin's journal ('Taman', 'Princess Mary', 'The Fatalist') come last in the book, but precede chronologically the events of 'Bela' and 'Maxim Maximych'. By presenting the stories in this order Lermontov introduces the reader by stages into the complexities of Pechorin's character. First, there is the tale of his abduction of a Circassian girl told by the simple, good-hearted old soldier Maxim Maximych. Then, in 'Maxim Maximych', the author gives his own more sophisticated view of the hero, whom he observes in a chance encounter. This leads on to the core of the novel, Pechorin's journal, in which Pechorin conducts a detailed analysis of himself.

Despite its loose construction, the novel succeeds entirely in its chief purpose of revealing the hero's character and situation. But Lermontov shows that he is capable of doing more than write about disenchanted young men, and demonstrates the range of his ability by some first-class story-telling and descriptive writing. In 'Taman' and 'The Fatalist' the character interest is completely overshadowed by the interest of the narrative, and it is the description of the journey along the Georgian military highway and the figure of Maxim Maximych, rather than Pechorin, that are the most memorable things in 'Bela'. The rich variety of secondary characters—Maxim Maximych, the *poseur* Grushnitsky, Princess Mary, Vera, the native girl Bela, Caucasian tribesmen, smugglers, well-observed minor figures such as Vera's husband and the dragoon captain—though serving primarily to show up the personality of the hero or to motivate his actions, also extend the interest of the novel and give it air and life.

With the possible exception of one or two digressions in Pechorin's journal, nothing in the novel is superfluous, and the whole is dominated by a sense of balance and economy. Lermontov's prose is tightly-sprung and remarkably controlled, especially when it is remembered that there was no established tradition of Russian prose-writing at the time. His dexterity as a writer is seen to equally good effect in all the various styles employed in the book—in the terse narrative of action, in the analytical passages of Pechorin's journal, in the impressive descriptions of nature, in the witty, aphoristic exchanges of the drawing-room, and in the homely conversation of the old soldier Maxim Maximych.

A Hero of our Time was highly regarded by later Russian novelists, and one can find in this short novel many of the qualities that characterize their own works. Lermontov's analytical method and the sensitivity he shows in his treatment of nature and people are paralleled by the psychological approach and broad feeling for life that one finds in Tolstoy. His concern for the problem of evil and the complexities of the human personality foreshadow Dostoevsky's studies in this field. And, as a stylist, Lermontov can be seen as a forerunner of Chekhov, who regarded 'Taman' as a model of the art of short-story writing.

As a late example of the 'personal' novels that were so popular in Europe during the romantic period, **A Hero of our Time** has often been linked with other novels of this type, such as Chateaubriand's *René* and Constant's *Adolphe*. The tradition is certainly a common one, though it is hard to see in Lermontov's novel any direct influence of these earlier models. In fact, a comparison of **A Hero of our Time** with such works shows how considerable Lermontov's achievement was, for he succeeded in making his hero a more or less entirely plausible figure, with dimensions of life and reality, and at the same time he went farther than the constricted intimate field of his predecessors to produce an extremely robust novel of action. Unlike many works of this period, **A Hero of our Time** asks few concessions from the modern reader. It can be read and enjoyed for its own sake.

The setting of the novel is the Caucasus in the 1830s. The Caucasus at this time was a new area of the Russian Empire, and though Georgia—south of the main Caucasus range—had been annexed to Russia in 1801, the mountain tribes in the north were still not subdued, and in the period of the novel were mounting a vigorous resistance to Russian expansion under the leadership of the chief Shamil. The Russians had a series of frontier-posts and forts along the so-called 'Line', which extended the whole breadth of the Caucasus from the Black Sea to the Caspian, to protect the settled parts of the territory in the north against incursions from the hill tribes. The terms 'left flank' and 'right flank' which are used in 'Bela' and 'The Fatalist' refer to this east-west defence line. Georgia was linked with the northern Caucasus by the famous Georgian military highway, which ran from Tiflis over the main ridge of the Caucasus to Vladikavkaz (modern Ordzhonikidze). It is along this road that the narrator travels with Maxim Maximych in 'Bela'.

F. D. Reeve (essay date 1967)

SOURCE: *"A Hero of Our Time,"* in *The Russian Novel*, Frederick Muller, 1967, pp. 45-63.

[*In the following essay, Reeve discusses Lermontov's novel in the context of Russian literary developments of the period.*]

In Pushkin's poem "The Prophet," the *I* is the mediator and advocate to complete certain acts on our imagination's stage, as God is the agent who creates conditions favorable to the prophet's act of consummation of desire. By imitation the prophet re-creates the act of God. In the poem, Pushkin emphasizes not the agent (which the usual

romantics did) but the act itself. His attitude toward the poem leads necessarily to the theater and to dramatic poetry. It leads to dramatic conceptualization of the world around oneself. Particulars of experience are not consciously sublimated, as Goethe has Faust get rid of them, or postponed, as Shelley often wanted to postpone them. They are understood to occur dramatically and in themselves to resolve the conflicts which exist. There is a way of looking at the ordinary world which is dramatic, a way in which internalized value informs on (and is informed on only by) external action. For all you talk about or around Philoctetes, for example, you cannot escape the actuality of the condition he presents. He is his own best informer.

The economy of style in prose to which this sort of conceptualization leads is most successful and powerful in the works of Chekhov, but it was discovered (in Russia, at least) by Pushkin. The perception of conflict is presented by antithesis even in details of description: "He willingly lent them to us to read and never asked for them back; on the other hand, he never returned the books that were lent him." In this story, "The Shot" from Pushkin's *Belkin's Tales* (1831), the antithetical construction starts with the opening sentence, a tricky and suspenseful beginning— "Some mystery surrounded his existence"—and perseveres to the reversal at the end.

The story is a parody of the terms of romanticism, by application, so to speak, of the romantic method to other and subsequently necessary terms. The romantic pose envelops the story, but the central figure, Silvio, is a new, special kind of idealist. In no way prepared to lay down his life for a cause (unlike Rudin, who finally does), he knows the limits both of authority and of individual power in this world. Literally, in early nineteenth-century gentleman's language, he seeks satisfaction. Literally, he acts out the conflict, shooting his walls full of holes practicing, until the Count, his opponent, by a gesture completes the dramatic sequence. That ends the story, the inversion of romanticism completing the enactment of motive. The clarity of the old romantic ideal is gone from this story. We are left with a comic, ironic, especially dramatic figure. The realness of the figure and its story is constructed by the obdurate realist's parody of sentimental romanticism.

The hero of the story, Silvio, who has said he wants to revenge himself on the Count by playing a joke, follows the proper form. The Count's continual luck in drawing lots reinforces the irony of Silvio's position. Finally the Count shoots, misses, and it is Silvio's turn. The Count's wife throws herself at Silvio's feet. The Count is, for a moment, confused. He recovers, asks Silvio to stop "making fun of a poor woman" and to fire. The Count has been committed to loss of pride at the ultimate moment. Silvio says that he is satisfied, that "I forced you to fire at me. That is sufficient." Commitment achieved, the meaning is accomplished. "You will remember me. I leave you to your conscience." Silvio then reasserts the perfection of his own technique: at random, as if setting the condition for irony, he takes a shot at the picture through which the Count's bullet passed, putting *his* shot just above the shot meant for him. He has taken the Count's game away and made it his own. His triumph leaves the Count meaningless as a man. Silvio vanishes back into the mystery of his own grandness. He has dared assert himself, and he is victorious, but the reality of the story depends on the reversal of the roles of loser. At first, Silvio has lost; then, the Count has. Gogol made all his heroes losers; only his own technique was adroit enough, he keeps saying, to "win." In Pushkin's story, there is no war between characters and author. We have the psychology of successful revenge, of the reversal that reshapes history, alters values, and supplies an unexpected, controlling idea.

We are further surprised, as with Lermontov's *A Hero of Our Time* (1840), not by the autobiographical aspects but by the degree to which autobiography is overcome by narration. As a matter of fact, Pushkin once played a role much like Silvio's. In June, 1822, in Kishinev, Pushkin dueled with an officer, Zubov: "At the duel with Zubov, Pushkin showed up with some cherries which he ate while the other was getting ready to shoot. Zubov shot first and missed." Pushkin, B. V. Tomashevsky reports, did not shoot and did not become reconciled with Zubov. The second part of "The Shot," written two days after the first part, transforms the material of biography into facts of art. What in "real life" had no end is consummated in art. Specifically, the technique of narration compels the gestures that lead to its own perfection. The five short stories called *Belkin's Tales* are, like parts of *Eugene Onegin,* deliberate, meaningful "hoaxes," manipulations of illusion, like *Tristram Shandy.* The artist sets out from autobiography to capitalize on the illusory nature of his art. He removes himself as personality, remains as talent only. He arranges a reality upon which he does not obtrude.

As an epigraph to *Belkin's Tales* Pushkin originally thought of using a saying he remembered by the father superior of the Svyatogorsk Monastery: "What will be is that we won't be." It was a joke, a pun, such as Sterne was fond of making, as Joyce was fond of. The foreword from the "editor" is the same sort of thing: a mockery of readers' habits through which to reinforce more strongly the illusion of reality. The craft of intelligence in fiction, also, is the play of language, for it is the perceived relations which stay real.

In the *History of the Village of Goryukhino* (the Belkin estate), written soon after the stories by its "owner," Pushkin makes a bold, sarcastic attack on social and political unfairness. He attacks "reality" baldly in order to reform it. Pushkin's work on the *History* was cut short by the impossibility of getting it through tsarist censorship; for the work was openly abolitionist, a brilliant and perceptive satire, a forerunner of the satire of Saltykov-Shchedrin. We see how nonfictional it was meant to be by these four headings in the final section of the plan which Pushkin drew up before writing: "It was a rich, free countryside; cruelty impoverished it; it recovered from its austerity; it declined and fell from negligence." There is no release from reality in human actions. Fiction's agency is the enactment of freedom, whether a protest against bourgeois culture or the ultimate value.

In the summer of 1831 Pushkin read *The Red and the Black,* which he thought "a good novel, despite artificial rhetoric in several places and some comments in poor taste." Stendhal may be the first of the French realist novelists, the man among us whom we, as Harry Levin says, "fully conscious of socio-politico-economic circumstance," esteem as the beginner of historic realism, but Pushkin anticipated him. Pushkin again and again defended the freedom of his creative activity from what he called "petty and false theorizing." He scorned "the dull-witted rabble," from whom he affirmed his poet's independence, and he protested limitations imposed by the court, by "high society with its critical Aristarchuses." Many years before Gide said that "the homelands of the novel are the lands of individualism," Pushkin wrote: "No law can say, write only about these subjects and no others. Law does not interfere with the privacy of the individual, . . . and so law may not interfere with a writer's subject. . . ." The novelist, like any artist, must use tradition to invest himself in office, but the talent which transforms the perceptions of experience into meaningful knowledge of motive is not merely individual but at times so personal that, like the lyric poet's, it appears solipsistic.

Literary realism is distinguished from literary romanticism or neoclassicism or sentimentalism or naturalism in that it always comes *back* to the things of this world. Romanticism supposes that we are braver than we are; naturalism catalogues our failures. But the realist presumes that we operate on principles which sooner or later are manifest and, manifested, remain always present. If we trace Lermontov's literary biography, we are struck by its close parallel to Pushkin's, but if we look at his major prose work, we notice that he presumed as operative, principles other than those Pushkin presumed. He accepts the romantic pose but, so to speak, psychologizes it out of itself. He introduces a new kind of novel, the reality of which exists in the mind of the central figure who is also the narrator.

Two kinds of novels predominated in the 1830's: the historical novel (of which we have many "generalized" examples and of which such works as Pushkin's *The Negro of Peter the Great* and *The Captain's Daughter* are "particularized" examples) and the novel of contemporary manners. "Prose," said Pushkin, "is the language of ideas." Increased peasant uprisings in the 1830's and serious efforts among the intelligentsia and the educated upper class properly to understand Russian history in the light of new, western European ways of thinking lie behind Pushkin's *The History of Pugachev.* Lermontov's novel *Vadim* (1833-34) about the Pugachev Rebellion and his *Princess Ligovskaya* (1836) are pointedly topical. In 1841 he wrote a literalistic, psychological, antiromantic sketch called "The Man of the Caucasus," began a novel called *Shtoss,* and projected a trilogy covering three epochs of Russian life: the age of Catherine, the time of Alexander I, and the period of which he himself was a contemporary. Although the trilogy was never written, portions of *Vadim* indicate the sort of book Lermontov had in mind. The novel that dealt with an historical subject was to be equally a characterization of social life:

> In the eighteenth century, the nobility, having
> lost its former power and the means of maintaining it, did not know how to change its pattern

of behavior. This is one of the hidden reasons for the year of Pugachev [1774].

The characterization of the nobility's power actually bears more sharply on the 1830's.

In *Vadim,* the Pugachev uprising is only background. The issue, as seen by the novelist, is not one of social protest or economic circumstance but one of morality, of the individual's responsibility, obligation, commitment. Like Dubrovsky, Vadim becomes a leader of rebels out of a desire for personal revenge: "Yesterday a pauper, today a serf, tomorrow an unnoticed rebel in a drunk and bloody mob." His comrades admire in him "a kind of very great vice." Vadim is personification of the demonic; his sister, of the angelic. The historical problem of the 1770's has become the dialectics of good and evil of the 1830's.

Even the putatively historical novel has become more than an attempt to suggest the intimacy of history by the dramatic reality of fictional motives. History itself is regarded as an acting out of the moral substance of human will. In *The Brothers Karamazov* Dostoevsky calls the heart of man the battlefield in the war between God and the Devil. In *Vadim,* more than forty years earlier, Lermontov asked: "Didn't the angel and the demon come from the same source? . . . What *is* the greatest good and evil? —two ends of an invisible chain which come together the father they move apart." In "Taman," for example, and in many places in his prose and verse, Lermontov sees the world literally in black and white, though he each time sets that view within an ethical vision of the world. "Only in man," said Lermontov, "can the sacred and the sinful unite."

What is the nature of the relationship between society and the individual if a man like Pechorin, with all the accoutrements of the romantic hero, is, basically, a starved and homeless moral waif? Unlike Onegin, he is energetic, he pursues adventure, he is highly and articulately self-conscious, and he keeps the diary which is his confession, the substance of the novel.

Pechorin's abuse of other people is torment of himself. Lermontov's vision includes Pechorin's view, but reconciliation is not possible: Pechorin, the most superfluous of the superfluous men, is alienated not by failures of love or of language or by an autré idealism. He cannot conceive a task for himself, in the sense that James has the novelist Dencombe, his projected self in "The Middle Years" (1893) say, as he lies dying, "We give what we have. Our doubt is our passion and our passion is our task. The rest is the madness of art." Both James and Lermontov had difficulty in getting free of the protagonist, James more so than Lermontov. James's passion, equally a martyrdom to art, is greater than the task accomplished, but it is a passion which lies in a rhythm the task makes true. The form cages and releases the secret grandeur. If it fails, we have not James's success but Marcher's self-pitying final whump. If it succeeds, we have perception of glory, of the grandness of vitality even in what seems the most evil gesture. "Who will communicate my ideas to the world?" Lermontov asked. "Either myself, or God—or nobody."

Erwin Rhode, in his book on the Greek romances, said that the Greek novel, or anecdotal story, was predominantly "real," that the Greek romance was, as we know, extremely idealized. Clara Reeve's *Progress of Romance* (1785) concisely differentiates one genre from the other: "The Novel is a picture of real life and manners, and of the time in which it is written. The Romance, in lofty and elevated language, describes what never happened nor is likely to happen." Hawthorne, in the preface to *The House of the Seven Gables* (1851), said that a romance was a work in which the author laid "claim to a certain latitude both as to its fashion and its material," what, in short, we would now call a novel, though Hawthorne said that a novel was "presumed to aim at a very minute fidelity . . . to the probable and ordinary course of man's experience." A romance, on the contrary, had "fairly the right to present [the] truth [of the human heart] under circumstances, to a great extent, of the writer's own choosing or creation." These distinctions find confirmation in the notion, given in René Wellek and Austin Warren's *Theory of Literature* (1942), for example, that modern prose is descended from writing which emphasized detail and from writing which addressed itself to a higher reality. If regarded as more than an indication of classification within a genre, the distinction is no longer valid. We have learned from the Russians, more than from anyone else, that the supreme fictions are what is true.

B. M. Eikhenbaum has pointed out Lermontov's development as a writer of fiction from *Princess Ligovskaya,* a story of the conflict between Krasinsky, a poor official, and Pechorin, an officer in the Guards, a story with immediate social relevance, the first serious attempt in prose to take the romance of society manners beyond romance, to *A Hero of Our Time,* a story that emphasizes the psychological portrait of an age, leaning much on the criticism of Belinsky, on the prose of Gogol (*Evenings on a Farm Near Dikanka,* 1831, *Arabesques,* 1835) and on the prose and poetry of Pushkin (*Belkin's Tales, Eugene Onegin*).

In Russia in the 1830's, Eikhenbaum has pointed out, there developed the genre of narrative cycles, each ascribed to a single fictitious author. Pushkin pretends that Belkin wrote the Belkin stories. Lermontov pretends that most of *A Hero of Our Time* was written by Pechorin. But there is this difference: Pechorin is the one, central figure. In *A Hero of Our Time;* the narrator is the chief actor. We have, as James would note, an entirely different point of view. The story of adventure has been made a psychological novel (and, as such, subsequently continued to our day). Onegin in his novel is, for a while, Pushkin's friend; Lermontov scarcely meets Pechorin. Pechorin's diary, offered after we know that Pechorin is dead, is presented with a supposedly more literal naturalism than even the "ordinary" beginning of *Princess Ligovskaya.* Pechorin's purported self-revelation is the substance of the novel, which is technically constructed on the ancient, anecdotal pattern. If we think of the modern novel as a transformation by multiplication of the old, literalistic fable, we here find the concept of novel played back against its specifics, an effort to reduce narrative to the point that only alternatives crucial for the central figure will move the "plot." The plot lies not in any action in any one story but in the pattern of the author's understanding of the central figure independent of any one of the episodes which constitute his life. (The story of the hero's "whole life," the author says, is a "thick notebook" which "sometime later also will appear for the world to judge.")

If this be so, we, like the author, are immediately pulled up short by the problem of typicality and how to gauge it (for that is what we must do). Belinsky said that Pechorin closely resembled Onegin but that, unlike Onegin, he was self-conscious, anxious to live fully, and completely sincere (he adjusts events in order adequately to confess), and Chernyshevsky later used Pechorin to illustrate what he regarded as the presentation in literature of the dialectics of the soul. In the 1840's, conservative critics adjudged the novel political, a philosophical study of its time. In a letter dated June 24, 1840, Tsar Nicholas said that the book was "harmful" and filled with examples of the author's "great depravity." Lermontov wrote a preface to the second edition (1841), stating that he had drawn not a self-portrait but the portrait of an age. We now see how the story of a man became in the reality of fiction the tragedy of an age.

The book is thematically linked to Herzen's *Who's to Blame* (1846), to Turgenev's *The Diary of a Superfluous Man* (1850), and to the discussions in the philosophical and literary groups. But, interestingly, one of the first steps the author takes to establish the probability of his hero is to undercut his time. In *Eugene Onegin,* in *Fathers and Children,* in almost all the other books in which he appears, the superfluous man is not a do-nothing but a man who is morally alienated, who has lived out all the experience his society can offer. He has used up his society but cannot alter it or affect it or be reconciled to it. As a channel marker shows the limits of navigable water, so he shows the bounds of the extremes of social behavior. He does not represent his age. He moves against it, just as this book, through its irony, its use of aphorisms and reflections, and the title itself, is directed against its time:

> Perhaps some readers will want to know my opinion of Perchorin's character. My answer is the title of this book. "But that's malicious irony!" they'll say. I'm not so sure.

Lydia Ginsburg has shown, in a study of Lermontov's prose and long poems, that irony functions specifically to unite the "poetic" and "nonpoetic" elements, to extend the possibilities for naturalistic description, to allow psychological analysis of character and examination of motive—in short, to serve as the basic principle of "realism."

The structure of Russian political life in the 1830's, serfdom and the failure of the 1825 Decembrist Revolt, made inconceivable any notion of an heroic self outside sociohistoric action. The idea of the individual determined his actions; his actions shaped social life. A man's motives were considered historical agents. "Pushkin's and Lermontov's heroes," said B. V. Tomashevsky, "are representatives of a new generation for whom the heroes of Constant and Chateaubriand seem as chronologically remote as Werther and his contemporaries were for Adolphe." In this sense, the hero of the book is a product of his time—not literally, for he is no average figure, but intellectually, an individual composed of traits which the age itself constrained the novelist to treat as typical. "It's time," wrote

Alexander Herzen in 1838, "to drop the unfortunate, errant notion that art depends on the artist's personal taste or on chance." If motive is an agency of history, then history, obversely, defines individual character. Vadim, and especially Krasinsky, in the unfinished novel about Petersburg, are men prepared to engage in individualistic heroics, like the Count of Monte Cristo or d'Artagnan, but only in the context of social urgency. Svyatoslav Raevsky, one of the early Fourierists in Russia, discussed the book closely with Lermontov, but social analysis of the George Sand or George Eliot sort was not possible without the elaboration of a system of prose fiction which would include the concreteness of the individual and the immediacy, not the abstract meaning, of the moral problems about extreme, institutionalized inequality. Eikhenbaum has established beyond objection that

> Lermontov made secondary those problems of form which worried poets of the older generation (chiefly problems of vocabulary and genre) and focused his attention on . . . heightening the expressive energy of verse. . . . Poetry took on the form of lyric monologue, each verse appeared freshly motivated—as an expression of spiritual and intellectual excitation, as a natural means of expression. . . . The classical period of Russian poetry had to be summed up and the transition to a new kind of prose prepared. History required this, and Lermontov did it.

The role of the hero in Lermontov's work, the theme of the "fallen angel" or of the "egoist-avenger," not only ties in closely with the French, English, German, American, and Russian literature of the early nineteenth century but chiefly, as D. E. Maksimov has brought out, depends on Lermontov's own poetic "structural difference."

In this period there came new understanding of Sterne's work—how (to cite the address to the reader in V. F. Odoevsky's "Princess Mimi," 1834) dramatizing the process of making real was more interesting than the drama of the supposedly real object—the stories and sketches of Bestuzhev-Marlinsky separating the man of the late 1830's from the man of the 1820's, but above all the belief that every individual was a microcosm, "the common, daily facts" of whose life, "hidden or patent to the eye, the acts of individual lives and their causes and principles" had the same "importance which historians have hitherto ascribed to the events of public national life," to quote Balzac's famous 1842 preface to *la Comédie Humaine.*

> If man is not born evil, as Jean-Jacques would have it, he is not innately virtuous, either. Is moral perfection the work of nature or of society? . . . Is virtue the result of social circumstance? What is the role of rationality and of idea, that divine emanation, in this great alteration of being?

Balzac asks this question in "Robert l'oblige," a fragment of uncertain date from the group *Comptes Moraux.* Doing Scott over, so to speak, Balzac found the form for the novel of manners—a series of episodes, or nonnarrative sketches, strung together by a philosophico-narrative device—which the Russian novelists developed to an exceptional degree. Lermontov's innovation was the use of the author himself as the narrative device in an analysis of social morality.

A Hero of Our Time consists of six parts plus the preface written for the second edition. The final form of the book evolved over several years and—to the point—only with the evolution of the stories themselves. The preface by the author protests against the critics, especially Shevyrev, who called Pechorin immoral, depraved, a figure in a dream world made up by specious imitation of western European fiction. It emphasizes the actuality of the story, its applicability to an existing society.

"Bela," the first episode, opens with a sentence in which Lermontov announces he witnessed what he will write about: "I was traveling by stagecoach from Tiflis." The story is a version of the age-old love affair between the sophisticated hero and the simple, rustic girl, a story of which "The Apple-Tree" is probably the best known modern English version. A version contemporary to us is Charles Jackson's "Rachel's Summer," in which the pure-in-heart girl kills herself not out of remorse over her lost love but out of the despair to which she has been reduced by false rumor and social ostracism. "Poor Liza" was a sentimental version widely read two generations before Lermontov. Characteristic of popular adventure stories of the road in the 1830's, "Bela" is a literary original in that it has three points of view. It is written by Lermontov as told by Maksim Maksimych about Pechorin. It uses the extreme romantic contrasts of quest versus satiety, of violence versus beauty:

> She was unconscious. We tore her dress open and bound up the wound as tightly as possible. Pechorin vainly kept kissing her cold lips—nothing could bring her round.

but the story moves with the author's, the listener's, movement along the road from Tiflis toward Vladikavkaz. Lermontov pretends that he is only making "travel notes," not writing a tale, and that the order of presentation follows the chronology of the trip.

In the section called "Maksim Maksimych," Lermontov meets Pechorin, the Bela episode is completed, and Pechorin's diary is prepared for. Here the author is a disinterested observer—that "born observer" which Turgenev called himself—who describes Pechorin by appearance and gesture. Eikhenbaum says that Lermontov deleted from this description details in the manuscript which seemed psychological, for example, a discussion of Pechorin's "soul." The portrait which Lermontov says he must present to us describes Pechorin in terms of romantic concepts—"spiritual storms," "aristocratic hand," "casual gait," "nervous weakness," "feminine softness," "noble forehead"; of naturalistic sarcasm—"like a thirty-year-old Balzac coquette"; and of dramatic oppositions, visible contrasts in dark and light which, like chiaroscuro, give perspective to a representation on a flat surface: "blond, curly hair" versus "black mustache and eyebrows, the sign of thoroughbredness in a man, like a black mane and tail on a white horse."

The author's introduction to Pechorin's diary announces irony as a literary principle and asserts that psychological facts are the essential facts. A manuscript sentence indicating that Pechorin "had prepared his notes for publication" was deleted, conforming to the principle that the vitality of confession is its assertion of privacy: "What's wrong with Rousseau's *Confessions* is that he read it to his friends." Or else confession becomes the temptation, as Stavrogin indicates to Zossima in Dostoevsky's *The Devils* (1871-72), meretriciously to celebrate oneself by cataloguing one's deviations from, and therefore superiority to, conventional moral standards. Above all, the introduction emphasizes the physical difference between Pechorin and Lermontov, that the author of the diary is independent of the author of the book.

We are brought hard against this assertion by the first story in the diary. From biographical information we know that the events reported happened to Lermontov himself in 1837 in Taman in Tsaritsykha's house. M. I. Tseidler writes in his memoirs (1889) that in 1838:

> It turned out that I was to stay in the same little house that he had; the very same blind boy and mysterious Tartar were the subject of his story. I even remember that when I, having come back, was telling about it all in a group of friends, about my passion for the girl, Lermontov took a pen and on a piece of paper sketched the craggy shore and the house I was talking about.

Reading Lermontov's prose, we perceive, also, how his style has shaped a portrait, an episode, that leads toward delimitation of the reality of character and toward definition of the cognitive function of the novel. We move from the portrait of the harbor:

> The moon shone gently on the restive world around, submissive to its power, and in its light I could make out, far off shore, two ships whose black rigging, like a spiderweb, was silhouetted motionlessly against the pale outline of the horizon.

to inquiry into social ethics:

> I became very sad. And why had it been my fate to be tossed into the peaceful circle of *honest smugglers?* Like a stone thrown into a smooth-surfaced spring, I upset their calmness, and like a stone I myself almost went to the bottom!

By its language, the episode binds facts to their value. It pulls prose and verse together. Chekhov thought the story a model of prose:

> I don't know a use of language better than Lermontov's. Here's what I would do: take his story and analyze it, the way they analyze stories in school, by sentences, by phrases, by clauses. That way one would learn how to write.

In a letter to Polonsky he said that Russian poets write beautiful prose: "Lermontov's Taman and Pushkin's *The Captain's Daughter,* not to mention the prose of other poets, at once prove the close kinship between sapid Russian verse and graceful prose." Lermontov has forced an episode from private life to yield its own and public meaning.

The biographical aspects of "Princess Mary" tend to overshadow disinterested interpretation, for Grushnitsky may be, some people say, less a portrait of Kolyubakhin than of Martynov, who shot and killed Lermontov in a duel in July, 1841. Although written as a diary, a large portion of the story is a revision and continuation of Vera Ligovskaya's episode central to her story *Princess Ligovskaya.*

In "The Fatalist," Pechorin takes on the function of narrator. Or we may say that Lermontov becomes commentator on projection into the future of incidents from his own life. The story, obviously much like Pushkin's "The Shot," is interrupted in the middle by Pechorin's reflection on us "the pitiful descendants," ideas which Eikhenbaum has shown to be a prose version of Lermontov's poem **"Thought,"** which begins:

> I sadly look upon our generation . . . .

Pechorin's monologue is in direct opposition to the cliché image of the gay young officer, suggests even that the notebook telling about Pechorin's entire life was, as Eikhenbaum asserts, unpublishable for political reasons. Lermontov, through Pechorin, has raised political opposition and moral skepticism to philosophical principle:

> I like to doubt everything: this tendency has nothing to do with being determined; on the contrary, as far as I'm concerned, I've always gone ahead more boldly when I haven't known what lay ahead for me. After all, death is the worst thing that can happen—and you can't avoid it sometime!

If we number the stories as presented: preface 123456, we find that chronology has been rearranged: preface 451623. The stories are arranged consequentially according to the author's acquaintance with the hero. They move from Lermontov-the-author's eyewitness statement about traveling in the Caucasus to Pechorin-the-author's moral judgment. They complicate, by inversion, what we presume to be the usual relation of character to time. By making the hero of the novel the author, the narrator, the observer, and supposedly the only reader, Lermontov has constructed the illusion that the time of narration is identical with the chronology of the hero. By presenting the two times as one, he has tried to gull the other readers, you and me, into thinking that nothing is "fiction."

Consequently, the hero tends to impose himself on the author. And critics have commonly asserted that yes, the author and the hero are one man (where do you draw the line separating them?), that the book is autobiographical. Actually, the announcement of Pechorin's death, the introduction to the diary, the digressions in the several episodes, the preface to the second edition, the commentary and the irony—all point up that the author wishes to get free of the hero. He wants the hero to stand free of him just as he himself wants to be free of the past, to come to judgment, to be *beyond* his hero.

In a sociohistorical context, Pechorin is for Lermontov a sort of ego-ideal, an "ideal" which Lermontov, as author, wants to transcend. Pechorin is an ideal which depends not on historical fidelity or romantic literary tradition or on "typicality" so much as on the author's inventiveness,

the literary skill with which he expresses his psychological examination of himself. Expression of this psychological content is the description, by incident, of a real hero, regardless of time.

The book is a series of prose stories, or *novelle,* rearranged out of chronological sequence in order to express motivational consequences of the actions of a single figure. His actions make a pattern. The pattern expresses the rhythm of his mind. He is a figure who symbolizes an entire age in his mind.

A diary is a double instrument. It is a chronicle both of events and of a mind. It is both a confessional and a mock confessional. It must be kept either private or ironic. It must proceed from history and lean toward morality without invading or violating the province of either. Tied to the act, compelled by judgment, it must be its author's dramatization of a self beyond our history and our morality. To be successful, it must be precisely what we have here: incident, or episode, multiplied into a sociopsychological novel, that real stage in our imagination where our acts are a perfect drama.

Richard Freeborn   (essay date 1973)

SOURCE: *"A Hero of Our Time,"* in *The Rise of the Russian Novel: Studies in the Russian Novel from "Eugene Onegin" to "War and Peace,"* Cambridge at the University Press, 1973, pp. 38-73.

[*Freeborn is a Welsh critic, educator, and translator who has written and edited numerous studies of Russian history, literature, and literary figures. In the following essay, he examines the central theme of vengeance in* A Hero of Our Time, *as well as the novel's chronology, plot, and psychological portrayal of character.*]

The angry poem **'Death of a Poet'**, directly inspired by Pushkin's death in January 1837 as a result of a duel, first brought Lermontov to the attention of the public. Herzen neatly makes the point: 'The pistol shot that killed Pushkin awoke the soul of Lermontov. He wrote a vigorous ode in which, having branded the base intrigues preceding the duel—intrigues engineered by ministerial *littérateurs* and journalistic spies—he exclaimed in youthful anger: "Vengeance, your Majesty, vengeance!" ' Herzen goes on to note that Lermontov's 'one and only inconsistency' in appealing to Nicholas I was rewarded by exile to the Caucasus. Equally, the cry for vengeance is not so surprising. Whether against society or tsarism or God or even himself, vengeance was an obsessive and fateful element in Lermontov's life and work. His own death, at the hands of Martynov in a duel fought on the evening of 15 July 1841, was to all appearances an act of vengeance by his adversary, and yet the idea of vengeance suggests a quality of single-mindedness that contradicts the shifting, playful, arrogantly contemptuous, brittle, waywardly noble impression that the Lermontov of his own work and memoirs about him contrive to convey. Vengeance was something he played with experimentally, testing it to see how it worked, and when it struck its final blow at him he was mercifully preserved from knowing it as anything more than an experiment. An eyewitness at his duel with Martynov has described how Lermontov waited motionless, his pistol cocked with barrel raised, shielding himself with his forearm and elbow

> according to all the rules of an experienced duellist. At that moment, and for the last time, I glanced at him and I will never forget the calm, almost gay, expression which played upon the poet's face in front of the barrel of the pistol already directed at him. Martynov approached the barrier with rapid steps and fired. Lermontov fell as if he had been cut down on the spot, without making a movement either forward or backward, without even succeeding in putting his hand to where he had been hurt, as those who have been wounded or grazed usually do. We rushed up. There was a smoking wound in his right side and in his left side he was bleeding: the bullet had gone through his heart and lungs.

All signs of life had apparently vanished, but efforts were made to find a doctor in Pyatigorsk. Heavy, thundery rain began to fall. No doctors could be persuaded to come out in such weather. Peals of thunder sang out eternal memory to the dead poet. Thirty years after the event, the eye-witness wrote:

> As if it were today, I recall a strange episode of that fateful evening; our wait in the field beside the corpse of Lermontov continued a very long time, because drivers, on the example of the doctor's courage, refused one by one to come out to carry the body of the slain man. Night came on and the downpour was unceasing . . . Suddenly we heard the distant sound of horses' hooves along the path where the body was lying and, in order to drag it out of the way, we tried lifting it; from this movement, as usually happens, air was expelled from the lungs, but with such a sound that it seemed to us that it was a living cry of pain and for a short while we were certain that Lermontov was still alive.

But Lermontov was alive only in his literary heritage, and the work in which he lives most fully is his only important prose work, *A Hero of our Time* (1841). The theme of this 'experimental' novel is vengeance. Just as Lermontov experiments with narrative techniques in a manner which suggests a vengeful rejection of the narrative conventions of his time, so his hero, Pechorin, experiments with his own life by avenging himself on society, on women, on rivals, on the caprice of chance or Providence. Despite the professions of disillusionment and the propensity for reflective self-analysis no hero in the Russian nineteenth-century novel is more keenly alerted to life than Pechorin. Similarly Lermontov, despite the many inconsistencies and improbabilities in his novel, so conducts his experiment that the very verve, the—as Nabokov calls it—'fierce integrity' of his general purpose leaves the reader little time to wonder. The narrative style is brisk and expeditious; the shifts in viewpoint and the contrivances by which he keeps within a hair's breadth of turning verisimilitude into farce are made to seem almost irrelevant. A gay disregard for the logical niceties of probability makes criticism of such matters seem captious. We are not to quibble; we are plunged into the racing current of Lermontov's prose and if we are spun round, or find the water

flowing backwards, we are asked not to question the logic of this but to submit to the headstrong flow no matter where it takes us. *A Hero of our Time* is exciting; and excitement in literature is the natural enemy of pedantry.

The novel is composed of five stories—'Bela,' 'Maksim Maksimych,' 'Taman', 'Princess Mary', 'Fatalist'—which were published in 1839 and 1840; the novel was first published in its completed form, including the opening preface, in 1841. The manuscript of 'Bela' has not survived. Manuscripts or authorised copies of the other sections are extant, but evidence as to when he began writing ('Princess Mary' is supposed to have been begun in Pyatigorsk in 1837), or precisely in what order he wrote the stories, is so meagre as to provide little help. This is where some help as to intentions, plans and approach would be valuable, for Lermontov has deliberately chosen—in the work as we now know it—to offer his portrait of Pechorin from three points of view, through three ostensibly different narrators and in a chronological sequence which does not correspond to the sequence of the stories. His intention in doing this is evident enough, but interpretations of the resultant portrait might be less speculative if a little more were known about the history of the writing.

There are two chronological layers in this novel: the 'present time' of the fiction, during which the ostensible author, who is making travel notes, journeys northwards from Tiflis to Vladikavkaz and *en route* meets the *shtabs*-captain Maksim Maksimych (who tells him the story of Pechorin and Bela), spends a night and morning crossing from the Koyshaur Valley to Kobi and the rest of the day in reaching his destination. He spends three days in Vladikavkaz, on the second of which Maksim Maksimych turns up early in the morning and Pechorin's arrival occurs towards evening, but he does not see Pechorin until the morning of the third day. The 'present time' of the fiction ends with Pechorin's departure and the author's receipt of the papers comprising Pechorin's *Journal* from the bitterly disappointed Maksim Maksimych. Probability is strained to some extent even at this stage. The narrator's sense of the passage of time is vague and oddly inconsistent with his desire to write travel notes: he is a zealous recorder of the natural scene, but less punctilious about the times of day, or in this case the times of night. It has to be assumed either that Maksim Maksimych is a very slow talker (which is not supported by evidence), or he says no more than the narrator records, or the night stop in the post station below Gud-Gora is improbably short, and the last of these possibilities seems the most likely.

Only in 'Maksim Maksimych' do the two 'times' of the novel meet, in the sense that all three narrators are gathered in one spot at the same time and therefore that Pechorin exists in the present time of the fiction. The author's description of him is nevertheless a last portrait. He dies, the author tells us in his preface to Pechorin's *Journal,* on the return journey from Persia: this is what gives the author the right to publish the papers comprising the *Journal.* Everything else, then, that we know about Pechorin derives from a 'past time', or a time prior to the 'present time' of the fiction. In formal terms, everything else that we know about Pechorin is simply *addenda* to the author's travel notes; in chronological terms, it is the past: in terms of Pechorin's portrait, it is uncorroborated evidence.

The precise chronology of events in the 'past time' of the fiction is at best vague. The only reasonable certainty is that the events described in the stories which comprise Pechorin's Journal occur in chronological order, but how these events relate to the events described by Maksim Maksimych in 'Bela' is not entirely clear. A distribution of the stories according to the chronology of events would place 'Taman' first and 'Princess Mary' second. Whether or not 'Fatalist' precedes the events in 'Bela' is a matter for conjecture. It is equally conjectural whether Lermontov intended to suggest by such a chronological ordering of the events that the Pechorin of 'Princess Mary' was younger than the Pechorin of 'Bela'. An unsophisticated reading of the novel would tend to suggest exactly the opposite. The very complications to which his disregard of 'normal' chronology logy gives rise to indicate that time as a causal factor in the narrative was for him of secondary importance or to some extent irrelevant. He was less conscious of time, less of a historicist, than Pushkin. In his orientation, his prose style, his imagery, there is nothing of the watch-tick effect, the suggestion of a beautifully timed mechanism, which runs from word to word in Tolstoy's work and is the very pulse of his fiction. For Lermontov time was to be experimented with, and if the experimentation violated normal chronological probability this mattered less than the dramatic effect which such an experiment obtained for him in the portrayal of his hero. There is no doubt that this was his real intention, behind which lay on obviously autobiographical or subjective impulse. If the temporal element in the composition of this novel contributes little to its authenticity, then the narrator's role is essential. As readers we are asked to assume that all three narrators are honest, that their separateness as narrators fuses in the single aim of—as the opening preface puts it—creating 'a portrait composed of the vices of our entire generation, in their full development'. Why, the opening preface asks, if readers have believed in the possibility of the existence of all tragic and romantic villains, 'why don't you believe in the reality of Pechorin?' The 'author of this book', Lermontov himself, 'has simply been happy to depict contemporary man as he understands him to be and as, to his own and your misfortune, he has too often found him to be'. The implication of such statements of intention is obvious: the narrators through whose eyes we view Pechorin, including Pechorin himself, must be honest. We must assume, then, that the itinerant author with his travelling box half-full of travel notes on Georgia honestly records Maksim Maksimych's story about Bela, that Maksim Maksimych honestly remembers what he has to tell, that both of them are as honest as they can be in their observation of Pechorin and that Pechorin in his *Journal* is the soul of candour. Yet having made such an assumption, which is the automatic prerogative of readership, we are concerned to know *why* the narrators should be honest, for the authenticity of the novel must depend to a great extent on the authenticity of the narrators, on the reasons for their curiosity and the motives for their behaviour.

The reasons and motives in the case of the itinerant author seem simple enough. He is travelling northwards from Tiflis and he is looking for local colour. His personality as a character in the fiction is subordinate to his function as a pair of observant eyes and ears. His anonymity makes him the reader's companion, unobtrusive yet ever present, occasionally importunate in his Baedeker-like zeal and not averse to exercising his descriptive powers. Though we may assume that he does not colour his descriptions, his personality, if subordinate to the descriptive function, is by no means colourless. It is in this very respect that his function as narrator has authenticity. For though we know little about him, we know that he is paradoxically both interested in the local scenery, Maksim Maksimych's story, the natives of the region and, at the same time, indifferent or uncommitted to them. They are grist to his mill, no more. Having heard Maksim Maksimych's story, he leaves him in Kobi, expends no more than a sentence on the journey to Vladikavkaz and there has to kick his heels for at least a day until Maksim Maksimych catches up with him. By this time, despite the sympathy and understanding with which he has painted Maksim Maksimych's portrait, despite the show of renewed friendship at their second meeting, the author is soon bound to admit that they have nothing to say to each other:

> A bottle of Kakhetian wine helped us to forget the modest number of dishes, of which there had been just one, and having lit our pipes we sat down-I by the window, he by the stove which had been set going against the rawness and coldness of the day. We were silent. What did we have to talk about? . . . He had already told me everything interesting about himself, and I had nothing to tell. I gazed out of the window. A mass of squat little houses distributed along the bank of the Terek, which runs ever wider and wider at this point, glimmered behind the trees, and further away the mountains gleamed like a jagged blue wall, and still further off Mount Kazbek peered over them wearing a white cardinal's mitre. I mentally said goodbye to them: I felt sorry at leaving them.

The scenery is what engages the author's feelings. This mood of regret, of time past and lost friendship rendered into the receding spatial perspective of the mountains, is what sets the tone for the brief and unhappy meeting between Maksim Maksimych and Pechorin. But the author who records the encounter is little involved emotionally. He has as little to say to Maksim Maksimych as does Pechorin:

> We said goodbye rather drily. The kind Maksim Maksimych had become the stubborn, peevish *shtabs*-captain! And why was this? Because Pechorin, out of thoughtlessness or for some other reason, had given him his hand when the other had wanted to fling himself on his neck! It is sad to see a young man losing his fondest hopes and dreams when the rosy veil through which he had looked upon the actions and feelings of men is torn from his eyes, although there is always the hope that he will replace his old blunders with new ones no less fleeting, but no less sweet . . . But what can replace them at Maksim Maksi-

mych's age? The heart hardens regardless and the soul shuts itself up . . .

I travelled away alone.

The author sympathises with Maksim Maksimych, but if 'it is sad to see a young man . . .', it is seemingly impossible for him to involve himself in the older man's feelings; and the implication of such absence of involvement might be summarised by Pechorin's own words at the end of 'Taman': 'What concern of mine are the joys and griefs of humanity, me, an itinerant officer issued, what is more, with an official travel warrant!' No, this anonymous narrator is only accidentally involved in the Maksim Maksimych-Pechorin relationship, emotionally on the sidelines, witness to it as he is witness to the scenery and what seems most fortuitous about his own relationship with Maksim Maksimych is that it provides him with anecdotal material quite as rich, grandiose and exciting as the topography on the journey from the Koyshaur Valley to Kobi.

The author making travel notes is concerned less with temporal than with spatial relationships. He is witness to heights and distances and his eye pursues such distances to their limits as though he were seeking to discover the story of Bela in their remoteness. When he enters the Koyshaur Valley at the opening of 'Bela':

> What a splendid place this valley is! On all sides inaccessible mountains, reddish cliffs hung with green ivy and crowned with clumps of plane trees, yellow precipices scored by gullies, and there high, high up the golden fringe of the snows, and below the Aragva, blent with another nameless river bursting noisily from a black and mist-filled gorge, stretches away like a silver thread a flashes like a snake flashing its scales.

The colour and animation of the similes suggest instantly the focusing of the eye upon the distant and remote movement, or at least the attempt to do so, in contrast to the rigidity of mountains, cliffs and precipices. The splendour of the topography frames and magnifies by contrast all movement, whether of the remote river or the noisy Georgians and hill tribesmen in the immediate vicinity. Successively, as readers, we are drawn from the distance to the incidental, impersonally observed humans of the foreground, to the outward appearance of Maksim Maksimych and then into the conversation about the dishonest Ossetians. The author reveals little or nothing about himself. Then suddenly it is night. Sight gives way to sound as the basis of description, and it is now through sound that movement is distinguishable:

> There remained still about a mile to the post-station. All around was quiet, so quiet that one could follow the flight of a mosquito by its humming. To the left was a deep black gorge; beyond it and in front of us the dark-blue crests of mountains grained with wrinkles and covered with layers of snow were etched against a pale skyline which still retained the final afterglow of sunset. Stars began glimmering on the dark sky, and strangely it seemed to me that they stood much higher than at home in the north. On both sides of the road loomed bare, black stones; here and there bushes peeped out from the snow, but

> not a single dry leaf quivered, and one was happy to hear amidst this dead sleep of nature the snorting of the three tired post-horses and the uneven jangling of Russian harness-bells.

The sense of far and near, sight and sound, glimmering stars and anticipatory silence—drama is latent in the very stillness of this description. The narrator's immediately following reference to 'Tomorrow it'll be fine!' and Maksim Maksimych's pointing to Gud-Gora, the mountain with its smoking sides and the black cloud on its summit ('so black that it seemed to be a blot against the dark sky'), serve to reinforce the sense of approaching revelation. The suggestion is that the smoking of Gud-Gora at sundown warns of the coming story and its implications. When next it is seen, with Maksim Maksimych's story carried to the point where Bela is in love with Pechorin but Kazbich has not yet taken his revenge, the road leading to it seems to lead to heaven, but the cloud atop the mountain has now assumed a more specific, and ominous, shape—'like a vulture awaiting its prey', we are told. For at this precise point, the ascent of Gud-Gora—the high point of both their journey and Maksim Maksimych's story—the narrator reveals more explicitly than elsewhere that, not the story, not the journey, but the impact of the scenery is what most deeply excites him:

> The road seemed to lead to heaven because, as far as the eye could judge, it went on rising and finally became lost in the cloud which had been resting on the summit of Gud-Gora since the previous evening like a vulture awaiting its prey; the snow crunched under our feet; the air became so thin it was painful to breathe; blood rushed to the head, but notwithstanding there spread through my veins a feeling of delight, and I felt a kind of joy at being so high above the world: —a childish feeling, I don't deny, but, in withdrawing from the circumstances of society and growing close to nature, we become children despite ourselves: all our acquired characteristics slip away from our soul and it becomes as it once was and will surely be again. He who, like me, has happened to wander through empty mountain landscapes and look long and intently at their fantastic shapes, thirstily gulping the life-giving air that pours through their gorges, he will of course understand my desire to communicate and relate and depict these magic scenes.

So far, then, as the narrator is concerned, *his* renewal of spirit is achieved through 'a childish feeling' of his own remoteness from the world on the ascent to Gud-Gora; his rejuvenation, momentary though it may be, is due to love of nature and is not to be sought, as was Pechorin's, in love for the daughter of a Circassian prince. To him the story of Bela is an incidental accompaniment to the landscape, exciting like the distant glimpse of the flashing Aragva crossing the Koyshaur Valley, but less significant to him, it would seem, than the unrepeatable panorama which he witnesses from the top of Gud-Gora.

The portrayal of Pechorin in this novel follows a principle very similar to that which motivates the itinerant author in his depiction of landscape: just as he enumerates the successive, cumulative items of topography in order to reveal the growing perspective to our reader's gaze, so we are gradually brought closer and closer to Pechorin through successive narrators and by a careful gradation of increasingly intimate revelations about him. The author deliberately stimulates this process by his eagerness to elicit a story from Maksim Maksimych, by trying to loosen the captain's tongue with an offer of rum (but Maksim Maksimych does not drink) and then simply by putting questions which demonstrate his role as story-teller, prompt Maksim Maksimych into speaking (hardly a difficult task, as it turns out) and naturally integrate the narrative of Bela with the travel notes, the landscape description, the information about Krestovaya-Gora and the cross erected by General Yermolov in 1824, etc. He had wanted a story from Maksim Maksimych and he got one. His attitude to the story betrays a professional interest, in the sense that he has one eye cocked to his readers, to whom he apologises for transposing Kazbich's song into verse and for whose benefit he offers such comment as 'What a bore!' when Maksim Maksimych acknowledges that Pechorin and Bela were happy. His asides to the reader are suitably 'involuntary' (nevolno) when he admits to anticipating a tragic ending or is astonished by the capacity of the Russians to adapt themselves to the customs of alien peoples or remembers the Moscow lady who insisted that Byron was a drunkard. And he is suitably impartial in commenting on the fashion of disillusionment, which the reader may understand but which Maksim Maksimych does not. Yet all he asks of the reader at the end of 'Bela' is: 'Don't you admit, though, that Maksim Maksimych is a man worthy of respect? . . . If you admit that, I will have been fully rewarded for my perhaps unduly long story.' In other words, he is asking the reader to acknowledge that Maksim Maksimych is his own creation. His success as narrator depends very largely on the authenticity of his portrait of Maksim Maksimych. If the reader admits that Maksim Maksimych is 'worthy of respect' not only as a person but as a *character,* then the narrator's function will have been fully demonstrated and justified and—this is of the first importance—the initial stage in the authentication of Pechorin's portrait will have been accomplished.

On the face of it Maksim Maksimych appears to be so honest a witness that we need never have any doubts about the reliability of his portrait of Pechorin. He exists in the fiction as a clearly delineated character from the very start, 'smoking away at a little Kabardan pipe mounted with silver'.

> 'He was wearing an officer's coat without epaulettes and a shaggy Circassian cap. He seemed about fifty; the swarthy colour of his face showed that he had been long acquainted with the Trans-Caucasian sun, and his prematurely gray moustache was out of keeping with his firm step and robust appearance.'

His rank, between lieutenant and captain, was awarded to him while he was serving under Alexey Petrovich Yermolov (1772-1861), whose association with the Decembrists brought an end to his distinguished career as commander-in-chief of Russian troops in the Caucasus. We must presume, therefore, that for at least ten years (Yer-molov went into retirement in 1827) Maksim Maksimych has remained at the same lowly rank of *shtabs*-captain, or junior captain. He has had no news of his parents for twelve years and he was last in Moscow society twenty years ago—perhaps about the time that Chatsky turned his back on it. Hunting, some fighting, a great deal of tedious garrison duty and a healthy curiosity about the lives and customs of the local hill tribes would seem to have been the staple elements of his Caucasian years. But even if we know much more about him than we know about the itinerant author, he is still no more to us than a name, patronymic and rank, less identifiable or more anonymous than the Grigory Alexandrovich Pechorin whose story he tells. In fact, he is not named until Pechorin arrives in his story in the fort beyond the Terek. For all the information about him, Maksim Maksimych differs from the anonymous itinerant author in only one major, but very significant respect: he is an unsophisticated narrator emotionally involved in his narration.

The story which he eventually tells is not the one with which he began. He begins, under the author's prompting, to tell how he had once barely escaped with his life at the house of a Circassian prince, but the immediate threat to his life turns out to be of less gravity than are the fatal consequences of his *faux pas* in telling Pechorin what he had overheard; at this point the story of Bela begins. Maksim Maksimych's behaviour in the episode of the Cherkess wedding which he and Pechorin attend must be prompted by curiosity. It is Maksim Maksimych's curiosity—perhaps a better word would be inquisitiveness—which inadvertently, though with the best of intentions, causes so much of his story to happen. Had he not spoken the local language, he would no doubt not have been invited to the Cherkess wedding, and had he not gone outside during the wedding festivities he would not have heard Kazbich's story about the beautiful horse Karagyoz or realised the lengths to which Azamat, the prince's son, would be prepared to go to obtain the steed; and had he not been prompted by the devil to relate all he had overheard to Pechorin, Bela, one assumes, would have remained the sixteen-year-old girl who did no more than sing at the Cherkess wedding. Maksim Maksimych *makes* his story happen, and always with unhappy or tragic consequences. He is an inveterate eavesdropper, it would seem. Indeed, had he not overheard and witnessed the scene ('which I will never forget', he says, with disarming *naïveté*) between Pechorin and Bela, he would probably have known little about the details of the relationship, for it is clear that Pechorin treats him as a garrison comrade but not as an intimate. By such eavesdropping, one assumes, his fondness for Bela is fed. And it is such paternal fondness which makes him take pity on the lonely Bela and invite her out on to the ramparts of the fort where, had his eyesight been better—it is noteworthy that he has better hearing than sight—he would have recognised Kazbich before the latter caught sight of Bela. By ordering the sentry to fire at Kazbich, he naturally invites retribution. This *faux pas* indirectly causes her death. In this he contributes to the tragic denouement of the story, and one may not be too surprised—though Maksim Maksimych is blameless in his own eyes—at Pechorin's coldness towards him at their final meeting. What is surprising is his apparent failure to read the papers which Pechorin leaves with him, cynical though it may be to suggest such a thing. For he emerges from his story as an emotional man, curious about people, their relationships and their habits, and readily involved in their feelings.

His authenticity as narrator consists precisely in this emotional responsiveness and spontaneity. Friendship with Pechorin, Bela, Bela's brother, her father, and with Kazbich, is the basis of his tale, just as there is an immediate friendship between him and the itinerant author. Moreover, friendship for him is based on certain rules of comradeliness, on a sense of honour and an inherent, if reticent, gallantry towards women. It is a presumption of his that the Russian is superior to the natives of the recently colonised region where he has spent so many years of service, and this presumption is basically emotional in character, as can be seen from his disparagement of the Ossetians and his conviction that the local 'Asiatics' would fall to cutting each other's throats at the drop of a bottle. He is direct, extrovert, unsubtle—a sterling soldier, given to deeds not words, and the story which he tells is wonderfully packed with extraordinary happenings suitable to the life of a man of action.

But even if he can be said to have authenticity as a character in these several respects, he is nevertheless a *literary* character endowed with so much literary talent that we may be forgiven if we mistake him for Lermontov's ventriloquist's dummy. The contrivance is expert, but no one is really fooled. His words have force, directness, verve and economy, and it is not difficult to imagine the bluff garrulity with which he spins his yarn to the itinerant author they smoke and sip tea during the night halt before ascending Gud-Gora, or take shelter from the blizzard on the descent to Kobi. Yet when it comes to descriptions of nature it is hard indeed to distinguish between the two narrators. Which narrator, for instance, is describing which scene in the following examples?

> On one side was a wide area of open country, furrowed by several ravines, ending in a forest which stretched to the very crests of the mountains; here and there upon it rose the smoke from native villages and herds of horses wandered; —on the other side ran a shallow river, and adjacent to it the dense scrub covering the rocky elevations which link up with the main Caucasian range.

> To right and left the crests of the mountains, each higher than the next, criss-crossed and stretched away, covered with snow and scrub; in the distance were the same mountains, but no one cliff was like another, —and all the snow burned with a a ruddy glow so gaily, so brightly, that it seemed one could stay and live here for ever.

Perhaps the itinerant author's eye for topography and eagerness to keep the reader informed of spatial relationships (note 'the rocky elevations which link up with the main Caucasian range') are discernible in the first example and Maksim Maksimych's happy, uninhibited disposition is evident in the second. In fact, the first is Maksim Maksimych's description of the view from the fort beyond the

Terek and the second is part of the author's description of the view from Gud-Gora. Both are informed by a similar visual sense, both are similarly concerned with distance and perspective—essential, admittedly, in nature descriptions of this kind—but both are equally concerned with panoramic vision which involves both sides of the scene and a movement of the eye from the middle to the far distance. In other words, both have a similar approach, even if the content of what they describe is different.

The content of Maksim Maksimych's story broaches the theme of vengeance which is developed by stages throughout the novel and is so essential to Pechorin's portrait. 'Bela' is about plunder and vengeance and life devoid of moral principle. Just as imperial Russia was plundering the Caucasus, enforcing her authority by colonisation and military suppression, so the world to which Maksim Maksimych's story introduces us is one in which Kazbich avenges himself on Azamat for stealing his fine horse by killing Azamat's father and on Pechorin for stealing Bela, whom he also loves, by mortally wounding her. For all the melodramatic character of these events, none of the participants is portrayed as a melodramatic character. That they are all unprincipled, devoid of loyalty, guided by varying degrees of selfishness, even in the case of the wretched Bela herself, gives little cause for surprise: they are by implication different from the norm of honesty and moral good sense for which Maksim Maksimych stands. But the assumption of his narrative is that he has the literary or creative ability to give them all the lineaments of authentic characters. He knows them and in his lack of sophistication can identify with them. His limitations as narrator only become apparent when he tries to understand sophisticated—and, by extension, spurious—emotions with which he cannot readily identify. It is here that his true role as narrator becomes clear: he has, quite simply, the gift of truthful observation.

So we judge Pechorin through his eyes. This is a Pechorin of about twenty-five, new to the Caucasus, and in a new uniform; he apparently spends a year at the fort and for five or so months of that time he enjoys, or neglects, the companionship of Bela; then Bela dies and three months or so later he is transferred to another regiment in Georgia. There is no doubt about his courage, his 'strangeness', his cunning, his insolence, his unscrupulousness, his egoism and his charm; but we know little of his appearance save that he was thin and pale. And the chief puzzle which the story of his relationship with Bela leaves behind is the enigma central to his portrait—his 'unfortunate character'.

The account of his character which he gives to Maksim Maksimych is, despite its seeming individuality, a series of generalisations. If he causes unhappiness, then he is no less unhappy himself; in his earliest youth he began to enjoy all the pleasures money could buy and naturally they became repugnant to him; he entered high society and high society soon bored him; the love of society ladies simply stimulated his imagination and ambition, but left his heart empty; and he excuses his disdain for reading and the acquisition of knowledge by referring to the general maxim that the happiest people are uneducated and fame is merely luck, which may be obtained simply by being clever. So he is bored. The only specific, or ungeneralised, items in his whole account are concerned with his attempts to dispel his boredom: his transfer to the Caucasus where—in 'the happiest period of my life'—he hoped that the Chechen bullets and the proximity of death would do the job for him and his 'last hope' of Bela's love. Both Chechen bullets and Bela's love have failed him. He remains as bored as ever.

Pechorin's account, with its many generalities, is a paradigm of disillusionment, for which education or God or society may be accountable, but which manifestly *is,* as an observable phenomenon. In this generalised aspect it resembles a fashion. The itinerant author hastens to make this clear; but he also hastens to make clear that, in the worst cases, boredom is equivalent to a vice which people strive to conceal. Obviously this latter aspect of Pechorin's problem does not emerge clearly from Maksim Maksimych's unsophisticated recollection of what Pechorin said, for he can hardly be regarded as equipped to understand (just as he has no taste for metaphysical questions, as we know from the last sentence of 'Fatalist'), nor is he really party to Pechorin's confidence. But for Pechorin such boredom is all too clearly a vice—compulsive, addictive and destructive, of others as well as of self. In essence, though, it is boredom with people. The failure of his relationship with Bela—not after all surprising by any standards—is presented in Maksim Maksimych's record of it as an example of callous heartlessness which prevents him from showing true emotion during Bela's protracted death agony and elicits nothing from him save laughter when Maksim Maksimych tries to comfort him after Bela's death. Perhaps this can be construed as the addict's self-pityingly vindictive laughter, as Pechorin has already intimated:

> 'Whether I'm a fool or a villain, I don't know; but what's certain is that I'm very much to be pitied, perhaps more than she is; my soul has been spoilt by society, I have a restless imagination, an insatiable heart; nothing satisfies me: I get used to sadness as easily as to pleasure, and my life becomes emptier day by day.'

For the presumption is that Pechorin's boredom is a vice precluding any happiness in mutual experience. Compassionate fate cannot alter or alleviate this condition, although it is precisely the compassionate understanding of others which Pechorin seeks. The antidote is to avoid relationships, to travel to far places—America, Arabia, India—where his restless imagination may find vicarious peace and his insatiable heart be fleetingly consoled.

For the greater part, what we learn from Maksim Maksimych about Pechorin is, naturally enough, very general in character. He is a uniform, a voice, a figure in his narrative, but faceless. We know more about Bela's appearance—'And exactly so, she was beautiful: tall, slender, her black eyes, like those of a mountain gazelle, literally peered into your soul'—than we do about Pechorin. The narrator's increasingly emotional involvement with her accounts for the touching picture of her artlessness, and her loneliness, and her despair, and finally her last tormented agony. The role which Pechorin plays in this pic-

ture is largely incidental, for naturally the narrator concentrates on the central figure in his narrative. Also, the narrator does not have any emotional affinity with Pechorin's predicament. We gain, then, from him little more than an externalised, general picture of Pechorin as one suffering from the fashion of disillusionment and boredom.

The same generalised character attaches to the portrait of Pechorin which the itinerant author gives us in the second section of the novel, 'Maksim Maksimych.' The portrait is lengthy and seemingly full of particulars, but on closer examination it transpires that it is not so much the portrait of one man as a series of associations. In passing, it is interesting to note how this method contrasts with the method used by Pushkin when, as personified narrator, he meets Eugene Onegin. To Pushkin's personified narrator Onegin is of interest because there are certain qualities in his personality which have an immediate appeal: they find common ground for discussion, they plan to travel together. It is quite the reverse with the itinerant author, who, rather than illustrate the human traits and the personal affinities in Pechorin, prefers to keep at a distance and to catalogue the more general, even literary, associations which his appearance calls to mind. His slim, lithe waist and broad shoulders 'were evidence of' (*dokazyvali*) a strong constitution capable of withstanding all the hardships of the road and variations of climate; his open jacket revealed an expanse of dazzlingly white linen 'that betrayed the habits of a gentleman'; his soiled gloves 'seemed to have been made for his small aristocratic hands'; he did not swing his arms as he walked—'a sure sign of a certain furtiveness in a man's character' (the observer immediately qualifies, and therefore lessens, the particularity of this comment by adding: 'However, these are my own comments based on my own observations and I have no wish to make you believe in them blindly.'); he sat down 'as though he hadn't a bone in his back'; the position of his body 'was a picture of' (*izobrazilo*) a kind of nervous exhaustion; he sat 'like a thirty year-old Balzacian coquette in a soft armchair after a tiring ball'; there was something 'child-like' in his smile; his skin was 'as delicate as a woman's'; his pale, noble brow contained traces of wrinkles, discernible after long observation, 'that probably became more conspicuous at moments of anger or spiritual disturbance'; despite his fair hair, his moustache and eyebrows were black—'a sign of breeding in a man'; his eyes did not laugh—'a sign either of a malicious disposition or of a deep and permanent sadness'; they shone 'with a phosphorescent glow, if one may so put it', 'a glow like the glow of smooth steel, blinding but cold'; his glance had the 'disturbing effect of an indiscreet question'. For all its detail, the resultant portrait is vague—as vague, indeed, as the itinerant author's impression of Pechorin's age—'At a first glance at his face I would not have given him more than twenty-three years, but afterwards I was prepared to give him thirty.' At the conclusion of his remarks he is ready to admit that Pechorin's appearance might produce an entirely different impression on someone else, adding with an arrogance typical of his indifference to the whole matter: 'But since you will hear about him from no one save from me, you must willy-nilly be satisfied with this portrayal.' The narrator is uninvolved; the portrait is a collection of attributes and associations; the final impression is of a generalised or typical 'hero of our time', a portrait 'composed of the vices of our entire generation, in their full development,' not really individualised or specific, but represented to us as the public image of what such a type might be assumed to be.

The itinerant author makes only one admission of specific knowledge. 'All these remarks,' he says, 'came to mind, perhaps, only because I know certain details of his life', but there is no evidence in his portrait to suggest that he was portraying a specific person. Abstracted from its context in the novel, this might well be a portrait of Chatsky or Onegin on their travels. Yet in the immediate context of the story, 'Maksim Maksimych,' this method of presentation does not make Pechorin seem lifeless or incredible, but serves rather to effect an instant and telling contrast between him and the warm-hearted eponymous hero. Pechorin speaks shortly, and his words are punctuated by yawns. 'Time to be off, Maksim Maksimych,' he says; 'bored to death!'; 'We must each go our own way, etc.' And off he goes to Persia in his elegant English carriage, leaving behind him the two 'last portraits' of him supplied by Maksim Maksimych and the itinerant author in the novel's 'present time'; leaving behind also the papers which comprise his *Journal* and which Maksim Maksimych would have had made into cartridges if the itinerant author had not dissuaded him.

Rich, bored, alien to friendship or sympathy, as if these are emotions beyond his power to experience, abrupt in speech, almost boring in his own lack of courtesy, Pechorin appears in the novel's 'present time' only in order to make an effective exit. As readers we know so little about him at this stage that he appears vague and generalised, a public facade. We may not doubt the authenticity of those through whose eyes we have ostensibly witnessed him up to this point, but the authenticity of the hero himself inevitably remains conjectural. In the immediately succeeding preface to Pechorin's *Journal,* which the 'author' has decided to publish on learning of Pechorin's death on the return journey from Persia, the point about the authenticity of all that follows is clearly made:

> Reading through these notes, I became convinced of the sincerity of the man who so mercilessly exhibited his own weaknesses and vices. The history of a human soul, though the soul be of the shallowest kind, is hardly less interesting and less useful than the history of a whole people, particularly when it is the result of the observations of a mature mind about itself and when it is written without the vain desire to arouse compassion or surprise. Rousseau's *Confession* already has the defect that he read it to his friends.

The irony of the last sentence perhaps is that Pechorin had no friends to whom to read his *Journal*. We are invited to presume that his candour was not inhibited by the knowledge that he had an audience for what he wrote. For the rest, this preface by the 'author' is special pleading designed to make the reader accept not only the 'sincerity' of Pechorin but also the premise that 'we almost always forgive what we understand.' To which may be added the

further presumption that, if 'the hero of our time' is to be understood, his private experience is quite as important as is his public facade.

'Taman' is arguably related more closely to 'Bela' than to 'Princess Mary' in what it has to tell us about Pechorin; or it may be regarded as a bridge between the external and internal, objective and subjective portrayals of the two parts of the novel. The 'finished' form of this conte was originally explained by the 'author' as due to Pechorin having prepared parts of his *Journal* for the press—an explanation omitted from the final version because it could hardly have accorded with the need to emphasise Pechorin's 'sincerity'. There is also evidence that the setting, characters and possibly some of the events in the story derived from Lermontov's own experience. The fact remains that the story is complete in itself, adds little to our understanding of Pechorin's character but is rich in dramatic atmosphere and melodramatic incident.

The events in 'Taman' are engineered by Pechorin's curiosity quite as much as they were engineered by Maksim Maksimych's in 'Bela'. Arriving in the wretched little town of Taman after three nights without sleep, Pechorin eventually finds lodgings in a hut with 'unclean' associations, encounters a blind boy who can apparently see and follows him out of curiosity down to the seashore where he overhears the boy talking to a girl about a man called Yanko who finally heaves into sight and unloads from his boat some nameless but heavy cargo which the three of them carry off along the shore. The chief figures in the story are thus introduced through Pechorin's curiosity. As we learn later, eavesdropping is as much his province as it is Maksim Maksimych's, but in Pechorin's case the curiosity is prompted to a great extent by quasi-sophisticated and prejudicial assumptions which he makes about the characters on first acquaintance. His attitude to the blind boy is governed from the start by his 'strong prejudice against all blind, one-eyed, deaf, dumb, legless, armless, hunchbacked people' and this is in turn succeeded by the suspicion that the boy is not as blind as he seems. What differentiates this reaction from the reactions to new persons or events of the two other narrators, Maksim Maksimych and the itinerant author, is the specifically personal or private character of it. Pechorin is prejudiced; he begins by prejudging the boy simply because his eyes appear to be sightless and is instantly ready to impute unpleasant characteristics (such as the 'unpleasant' smile, the possibility of dissemblance) to the boy's appearance and actions. Similarly his attitude to his *undina* (his water-sprite) involves him in admitting that he is prejudiced in her favour—not, mind you, because she is beautiful, but because 'a great deal of breeding' is discernible in that rarest of facial characteristics, a straight nose (a view endorsed by the sophisticates of *la jeune France*), and quite carried away by his enthusiasm on the basis of this prejudgment he is ready to compare her with Goethe's Mignon. Naturally Pechorin can hardly fail to base such prejudgments on his own reading of the characters' external appearance: they do not reveal themselves to him; they are essentially figures of mystery. But he gives every impression of reading them as if he were gifted with psychological literacy and thereby enabled to discover a meaning in their features—the blind boy's soul which has lost one of its feelings due to blindness, the girl's breeding which is evinced by the straightness of her nose. As a result, the relationship between Pechorin and these two characters of his story becomes so private a matter that they appear to be scarcely more than projections of his own conjurings about them, hardly more substantial than figures recollected from a dream in which he accidentally encountered them, no more real than three sleepless nights can make them for him. For the whole story is pervaded by a sense of dreamlike inconsequence in which tenebrous figures dart from one edge to another of the mind's eye and exist for the narrator in a condition of seen but only vaguely comprehended reality, as though a gauze, a darkling glass, stood between him and them. This is how this *undina* appeared to him:

> And then I see my *undina* come skipping out again; coming level with me, she stopped and looked me intently in the eyes as though surprised by my presence; then she turned carelessly away and went quietly off towards the quay. It didn't end there: all day she darted about round my house, her singing and skipping never ceasing for a minute. What a strange creature! Her face betrayed no signs of madness; on the contrary, her eyes rested on me with penetrating liveliness and these eyes, it seemed, were endowed with some kind of magnetic power and each time they seemed to await some question from me. But as soon as I began to speak, she ran off, smiling slyly.

The fey, Puckish, elusive, and above all, inconsequential brio of this girl suggests not only Pechorin's incomprehension of her motives but a closeness in their relationship, literally perhaps a kind of magnetic power existing between them, which seems to deny him personal identity and self-control. In the privacy of their relationship, for it is a relationship of a quite private character, the girl is the one who fascinates and dominates, so that he finds himself, in the spoof seduction scene, almost witlessly absorbed by *her* actions, by her effect on him, and unable to shake off her snakelike mesmerism until she has gone:

> It had just got dark and I ordered the Cossack to make the tea in camp fashion, lit a candle and sat down at the table, puffing at my travelling pipe. I was just finishing my second glass of tea when the door suddenly creaked and there was the light rustle of a dress and footsteps behind me; I shuddered and turned round—it was her, my undina! Quietly she sat down opposite me and directed her eyes straight at me, and I don't know why but her look seemed to me fantastically tender; it reminded me of one of those gazes which in the past had played so arbitrarily with my life. She seemed to expect a question, but I said nothing, full of inexplicable confusion. Her face was covered by a dull pallor which revealed spiritual agitation; her hand strayed aimlessly over the table and I noticed it was trembling slightly; her bosom either heaved or she seemed to be holding her breath. This comedy began to bore me, and I was about to break the silence in the most prosaic way, by offering her a glass of tea, when she suddenly jumped up, wound her arms round my neck and a moist, fiery kiss resounded on my lips. My eyes grew dark, my head spun, I crushed her in my embrace with all the force of youthful passion, but like a snake she slipped through my arms, giving a whisper in my ear: "Tonight, when everyone's asleep, come down to the beach," and darted like an arrow from the room. In the hallway she knocked over the tea kettle and candle standing on the floor. "Blasted she devil!" shouted the Cossack, who had settled himself in some straw and was dreaming of warming himself with what was left of the tea. Only then did I come to my senses.

But Pechorin does not come to his senses at this point at all. He gives every impression of being obsessed by the melodramatic situation in which his curiosity has involved him. For what has for so long been regarded as a classic, ludicrously bad writing in parts of this passage claim special notice: the 'dull pallor' revealing 'spiritual agitation', the trembling, straying hand and heaving bosom—Pushkin could not have descended to this degree of triteness. But as soon as Pechorin reasserts his first-person role in such a way as to suggest some measure of independent judgment, the compound of laconic and comic in the narrative becomes obvious: 'This comedy began to bore me, and I was about to break the silence in the most prosaic way, by offering her a glass of tea, when she suddenly jumped up, wound her arms round my neck and a moist, fiery kiss resounded on my lips.' The *noisiness* of this impossible, mushy, moistly fiery kiss is the odd feature of it. That he then crushes her in a passionate embrace and she slips like a snake and darts like an arrow can simply be regarded as the clichés of melodrama, and the narrator's implicit detachment is such as to give the scene a vicarious air of verisimilitude. But the resonance of the kiss is, for all its incongruity, the single most authentic item in this passage, perhaps in the whole of his relationship with his *undina* and therefore with any of the characters in 'Taman'. It is the explosive moment when his own heroic presumptions as narrator are put to the test. His instantaneous reaction is to presume that it is an invitation to love, whereas it is in fact an invitation to death. The kiss is a deliberate irony: its very noisiness interrupts the dreamlike detachment of his narrator's attitude and precipitates him at once into the melodrama, transforming him from witness into participant, from presumed seducer into intended victim, from his role as casual observer of a little human drama into its casualty.

The rest of the story is supplied by his curiosity, narrated with that dramatic reserve which so eschews sentiment or any elaboration that it seems almost to parody its own intent. As in 'Bela', the verve and speed of narration are what redeem the story, and as in 'Bela' this is also a story of vengeance: the *undina*'s attempted vengeance upon him for allowing his curiosity to involve him in the mysterious activities of the 'honest smugglers'. And the moral? The moral is precisely stated in the penultimate paragraph: 'And why on earth should fate have cast me into the peaceful midst of *honest smugglers?* Like a stone thrown into a smooth pool I disturbed their calm, and like a stone I almost went to the bottom myself!'

The moral is that he represents himself as being an agent

of fate. To the 'honest smugglers' he is fate, as was Eugene Onegin to his peasants; and throughout his *Journal* Pechorin presumes to enact the same role of fate's representative, until the third and final tale sees him assuming his ultimate role of the fatalist who is committed to speculating about the possibility of predestination. But the point is that, in the longest section of his *Journal,* 'Princess Mary', he presumes to be an avenging fate; here he is no more than the stone of fate which disturbs the smooth surface of the smugglers' lives and almost sinks to the bottom; here his fateful influence is counter-balanced by the vengeful reaction of the smugglers to his curiosity. For the balance is all-important: Pechorin's intrusion into the midst of the 'honest smugglers' is adequately repaid by the *undina*'s attempt to drown him and the blind boy's theft of his possessions.

Yet Pechorin, it must not be forgotten, appears to have the same kind of relationship to the events that Maksim Maksimych has in 'Bela'. He does not really understand what is happening. The story comes to us through an I-narrator who gives the impression of dreaming what he tells, whose apprehension of reality, whose prejudices and essentially private or subjective terms of reference cast a film of mystery over the narration. Unable to understand what is happening, Pechorin narrates the tale in a spirit of puzzled and disdainful wonderment. When, upon hearing the blind boy's sobs, he is provoked into a feeling of compassion, even this all-too human reaction is almost immediately disdained, being transformed into laconic outrage at the hurt done to his *amour propre* ('And it would've been ridiculous, wouldn't it, to complain to the authorities that a blind boy had robbed me and an eighteen-year-old girl had almost drowned me?') and finally into indifference towards 'the joys and griefs of humanity'. Therefore human relationships remain throughout the story on the level of the mysterious. 'You have seen much, but know little,' the *undina* tells him—and this summarises Pechorin's dilemma. He is firmly resolved to find the key to the riddle, but the irony of his position is that, though he threatens to inform the local commandant of the *undina*'s activities, he never really comes to his senses sufficiently to know what he has to tell; and when he does have something to tell, how can he tell without appearing to be ridiculous?

Naturally this question vitiates Pechorin's supposed heroic role. By implication it also raises the issue of the contrast, or conflict, between his public image and his private self, between the objective and subjective aspects of his portrayal. If in 'Taman' Pechorin exists as little more than a narrator authenticated for the reader by his prejudices, by a couple of references to past experience and some evidence of sophistication, in 'Princess Mary' all reticences are abandoned and Pechorin emerges as an essentially private individual offering us in diary form a record of his personal experiences over a space of five weeks spent in the Caucasian spa towns of Pyatigorsk and Kislovodsk in a summer of the 1830s. The diary form, contrived though it may be, invites the supposition that Pechorin wrote from day to day (the diary entries begin on 11 May and conclude on 16 June) and therefore could not misrepresent the personalities of the characters involved or the events in which they were involved by altering them in re-

trospective narrative form to suit his own purposes. The authenticity of this private record must be presumed to be as indubitable as is the itinerant author's record of his journey over Gud-Gora and its accompanying story.

'Princess Mary' in its remarkable blend of society tale and confession is the greatest of Lermontov's many achievements in *A Hero of Our Time.* The significance of Pechorin—and therefore of the novel as a vehicle for his portrayal—is to be judged primarily on the basis of this section. Probably it differs chiefly from other sections in the clarity of focus and immediacy of presence with which the characters emerge from its pages. Elsewhere there is a certain blurring of the immediately present scene, due for instance to the itinerant author's fondness for the grandeur of distant perspectives, Maksim Maksimych's perhaps unclear memory, the itinerant author's apparent indifferences to Pechorin when he meets him and Pechorin's vagueness about the events of the 'Taman' episode. Inevitably such blurring produces a miniaturisation of the events and personalities. Received at so many presumed removes of narrative and time, the portrait of Pechorin in 'Bela' appears miniature, and particularly miniature are the problems of his disillusionment and despair—his emotional state, in fact—as recounted to us through the diminishing incomprehension of Maksim Maksimych's attitude. More than this even, if *Eugene Onegin* and *A Hero of Our Time* are compared—as, alas, examination papers are prone to require—what seems in very general terms to differentiate the portrayals of their respective heroes is the gradual distancing on which Pushkin insists in his portrayal of Onegin and the increasing intimacy of Lermontov's portrayal of Pechorin. By comparison with 'Princess Mary' especially, the world of *Eugene Onegin* gives the impression of having been miniaturised to the proportions of a doll's house. But the world of 'Princess Mary' seems full-scale, its sophistication fully grown. The faint air of nursery standards which lends charm and innocence to *Eugene Onegin* is gone entirely from 'Princess Mary'; here the sophistication is vicious and witty, and words have the power to draw blood.

The reason for this is obviously that it is all Pechorin's own work. What is and what happens in 'Princess Mary' must all be directly attributable to Pechorin. He offers what the itinerant 'author' calls 'the observations of a mature mind about itself' written in a spirit of merciless self-criticism. Here all is presumably candid, but it is a candour offered only on Pechorin's terms, and these terms are not by any means beyond question.

How truthful is Pechorin's picture of himself? It is probable, despite the seeming abundance of information on the subject, that we never really know what he looks like or what expression his face habitually wears. The itinerant author's portrait generalises but does not specify and the image Pechorin offers is oddly contradictory. To the impressionable Princess Mary, quoted by the even more impressionable Grushnitsky, Pechorin has 'an unpleasant heavy look' in the expression of his eyes, whereas Pechorin himself writes a day later, after his first encounter with Vera, 'in looks I am still a boy: my face may be pale, but it's still fresh.' Perhaps a pale, fresh-faced boy with an unpleasant heavy look is exactly what Pechorin was: a degree of reticence about his appearance would be only seemly in that case. But of course Pechorin is profoundly concerned with appearances and dissimulation. His Circassian rig in which he appears to be more Kabardan than the Kabardans is an example of dissimulation by dress, and he imputes to others a similar concern with appearances— Grushnitsky's soldier's greatcoat and what it is assumed to signify, Werner's black dress and its Mephistophelian connotation. Princess Mary herself enters her story as 'a *gris de perles* dress buttoned up to the throat; a light silk *fichu* was wound round her supple neck. Shoes, *couleur puce,* constricted the ankles of her delicate little feet so charmingly that even one uninitiated into the secrets of beauty would undoubtedly have cried out, albeit from surprise.' We learn little more from Pechorin about her actual appearance, for to him her prettiness resides wholly in her 'velvety eyes', other features of her face apparently concerning him hardly at all. Vera is identified for him by the little black mole on her right cheek, but she is described primarily in terms of dress and the look in her eyes when he meets her in the grotto (it is left to Dr Werner to describe the expressiveness of her face). In other words, Pechorin's picture of himself and of others is governed by his concern with appearances, by a desire to see in others a preoccupation with concealment similar to his own. His diary necessarily must be imbued with his own personality. It is not surprising that the personalities of all the other chief participants in the events he describes should form either contrasts or adjuncts to his own self-expression, into which are projected, it seems, features of his own dilemma. Without exception all those with whom Pechorin comes in contact have disabilities or are in some way ailing: the invalid Grushnitsky, the crippled Dr Werner, the sick Vera, the eventually lovesick Mary, not to mention Mary's ailing mother or Vera's husband. Their publicly acknowledged ailments exteriorise the private sickness which he can express only in his diary.

The terms on which Pechorin offers his candour are an interesting compound of public and private attitudes and assumptions. On 10 May he arrives in Pyatigorsk and characteristically takes a house on the edge of the town 'on the very highest point at the foot of Mount Mashuk. He assumes at once an attitude of superiority towards the provincials of the spa. He is from St Petersburg; they are from Moscow. Mashuk itself, situated to the north, participates by some droll sympathetic fallacy in the emotional life of his diary, signalling to him like smoke from an extinguished torch when he is about to meet Vera in the grotto (his affair with her is the fag-end of a passion) and bearing upon its crest an ominous cloud shortly before the conversation between Pechorin and Grushnitsky which lays the groundwork for their fatal rivalry over Princess Mary. The scenery connives with his superiority in its grandeur and remoteness. 'There is not', he admits, 'a woman's gaze which I would not forget at the sight of curly-headed mountains lit by a southern sun, at the sight of a blue sky or on listening to the thunder of a torrent falling from crag to crag.' At the first intimation of true feeling in his relationship with another person—in this case, with Vera after their meeting in the grotto—he literally attempts to escape the thraldom of such emotional entanglement by fleeing

into nature and proclaiming the superiority of nature to man. Yet such thraldom in Pechorin's case involves the past, not the present: it is thraldom to remembered passion and lost youth. His uniqueness, which is the presumption upon which his superiority must feed, has its source in his memory: 'There is not a man in the world over whom the past has such power as it does over me. Every recollection of past sorrow or joy strikes sickeningly upon my soul and wrings from it ever the same sounds . . . I am stupidly made: I never forget a thing—not a thing!' Immediately following this admission, recorded under 13 May, Pechorin demonstrates his superiority over others by describing how he stopped two officers of the D. regiment and began telling them things that were apparently so amusing that 'they began laughing like mad things'. His object throughout this episode is to annoy Princess Mary, but what he writes tends simply to reveal his own arrogance: 'I never stopped talking: my anecdotes were clever to the point of stupidity, my witticisms at the expense of odd-looking passers-by were wicked to the point of frenzy . . . I continued to entertain the public until sunset.' The image, then, of his public self which he commits to his diary is that of the public wit who can apparently draw on untold sources of anecdote and witticism in order to exercise his superiority. He claims the same public popularity for himself in the first paragraph of the entry for 16 May when he writes (again with the object of showing how he has annoyed Princess Mary):

> We meet each day at the well or on the boulevard; I use everything in my power to lure away her admirers, the brilliant adjutants, pallid Moscovites and others—and I almost always succeed. I have always hated having guests at home: now my house is full every day with people dining, having supper, playing cards—and believe it or not, my champagne triumphs over the power of her magnetic eyes!'

The 'every day' to which he refers could not in fact be more than two days. The measure of exaggeration implicit in the statement reveals the presumptuousness of the terms on which he offers his candour. He presumes a power over others in public, but his superiority to others is justified to himself, in a purely private sense, by the assumption that 'there is not a man in the world over whom the past has such power as it does over me'. One has grounds for wondering whether Pechorin's assumption of superiority is so gross that his diary has no truth in it at all.

'Princess Mary' is composed of two relationships— Pechorin-Princess Mary, Pechorin-Grushnitsky—which are in their respective ways variations on the themes of love and death. If Pechorin is the seducer, or pretender to that role, in his relationship with Princess Mary, then in relation to Grushnitsky he is the executioner. To Princess Mary he represents tears and heartbreak, to Grushnitsky bloodletting and death. In both cases he tries to mitigate his vengeful role by the private justification that he is the 'indispensable character in the fifth act' who always, despite himself, 'played the miserable role of executioner or traitor' or, as he puts it on the eve of his duel with Grushnitsky: 'how many times I have played the role of an axe in the hands of fate! Like an instrument of execution I have fallen on the heads of doomed victims, often without malice, always without regret.' He tends to represent himself as neutral, one destined to enact a role which is not strictly of his own devising. To this extent he is as much the plaything of fate as are those who become the playthings of his own vengeance. But the source of this vengeance has its beginnings in the contradictory tensions which exist between his public image, that which others supposed him to be, and his private self, that which remembrance of his past made uniquely his own experience. On the only occasion when he confesses anything of any real substance to Princess Mary, what he stresses is the consequent duality in his nature:

> Yes, such has been my fate since childhood! Everyone read in my face signs of bad qualities which were not there; but they presumed them to be there and that gave birth to them. I was modest—they accused me of being cunning, so I became secretive. I had a profound sense of good and evil; no one showed me love, everyone was rude to me, and I became vicious. I was gloomy, other children were happy and talkative; I felt myself above them—they put me lower. I became a mass of jealousies. I was prepared to love the whole world—but no one understood me and I learned to hate. My colourless youth went by in a struggle with myself and everyone else; for fear of being laughed at I buried my best feelings in the depths of my heart and that's where they died. I was truthful—no one believed me: I began to deceive; having got to know the world well and the mainsprings of society, I became adept in the science of life and saw how others were happy without such artificial means, enjoying for nothing those advantages which I sought by such labour to attain. And then there grew in my breast a kind of desperation—not the desperation which is cured by the barrel of a pistol, but a cold, enfeebled despair hidden beneath amiability and a good-natured smile. I became a moral cripple: one half of my soul ceased to exist, it wilted, languished and died; I cut it off and threw it away, —while the other half became alive and lived to be of service to everyone, and no one noticed this, because no one knew of the existence of its perished other half; but you've now made me remember it, and I've just read you its epitaph.

Belinsky's guarded reaction to this passage is perfectly just: 'Was Pechorin speaking from the heart or pretending? It is hard to say definitely: there seems to be a bit of both here.' But the private cause of the public pose is clear enough. He is a moral cripple; one half of his nature has been murdered, and outwardly he seems in Princess Mary's eyes to be a murderer, though she little realises how deep and vicious is Pechorin's need to avenge the moral crippling of his own nature by inflicting similarly crippling wounds upon others. For his relationship with her ends, one must assume, with the murder of her innocence and with a state akin to his own despair; while for Grushnitsky the relationship ends in a murder similar to that which Pechorin claims to have committed against his better nature.

The 'artificial means' (*iskusstvo*) by which Pechorin has become so 'adept at the science of life' may not have brought him happiness, but they have been successful in the negative sense of making others unhappy. Vera is the object lesson in this instance. Her farewell letter admits in so many words what he had claimed for himself after their first encounter in the grotto: that he was incapable of becoming the slave of the women he loved, that he always acquired unconquerable power over their wills and hearts. He had precisely such authority over her, knowing how to make her love him and yet afflicting her with the unhappiness of which he tries so hard to rid himself. Her wretched, obsessive love for him has, as she puts it, 'become ingrown with my soul', as no doubt will Princess Mary's love. Laconically, bitterly, Pechorin can recite to himself the paradigm of female love (as he does under the entry for 11 June) and conclude that it is all a consequence, as Pushkin put it in his dedication to *Eugene Onegin,* of

> The mind's chill observations
> And heartache's bitter tears.

Pechorin's death of the heart, however stylised and specious it may seem, is central to his dilemma. His diary is ostensibly that of a dead man consumed by the agony of his emotional death in life. This is the private despair at the centre of his experience 'hidden beneath amiability and a good-natured smile'; but it provokes analysis of self, and from such self-analysis emerges a kind of experimental philosophy.

Grushnitsky—not Dr Werner, nor Princess Mary, nor Vera—is the catalyst for Pechorin's philosophy. He is Pechorin's *alter ego* in several senses—in the sense of the 'romantic fanaticism' which brought him to the Caucasus, where he affects a disillusionment which resembles a parody of Pechorin's crippling despair; in the sense of resembling and rivalling Pechorin in his desire to produce an effect; in the sense of being a solipsistic portrait of a novelettish hero by the novel's hero; in the sense of being the cause of the 'intrigue', without which Pechorin would not have been able to kill him; in the sense of bodying forth the ordinariness, the ingenuousness, the weakness which Pechorin sought at all costs to eradicate in himself. The resemblance between them, as recorded by Pechorin in his description of Grushnitsky's appearance and character, suggests an immediate comparison with the itinerant author's description of Pechorin, save the Pechorin ostensibly understands his rival better than the itinerant author understands the hero of his own work. Chiefly, though, Grushnitsky is important to Pechorin as a rival and victim who heightens his, Pechorin's, understanding of life, sharpens his will and challenges, albeit unwittingly, the purpose of his existence. 'I love my enemies,' he declares, 'although not in a Christian sense. They entertain me and excite my blood. To be always on guard, to catch every glance, the significance of every word, to guess intentions, upset plots, pretend to be deceived and then with one shove overturn the whole laborious and enormous edifice of their cunningly laid plans—that's what I call life!' And Pechorin lives such a life with the help of Grushnitsky and the aid of several happy coincidences and some fortuitous eavesdropping.

Pechorin's philosophy is obviously self-justificatory. The candour of his egoism is what endears; its viciousness is what impresses. His primary object is the attainment of happiness through the subjection of others to his will. Conversely, had the will of others been kinder towards him, he would have been kinder in turn. But he is little concerned with this side of the coin. He summarises the ideological principle which governs his attitude to life in the following way: 'ideas are organic creations, someone has said: their birth gives them form, and this form is action; he in whose head more ideas are born will act more than others.'

From this there arises, firstly, the idea that 'evil gives birth to evil . . . the idea of evil cannot enter a man's head without his wanting to apply it to reality', and, secondly, the idea that 'passions are nothing but ideas in their first stage of development'; they are like the river which begins in roaring waterfalls but later grows placid and reflective, as does man in his evolution from adolescence to maturity. The final state is one presumably in which man's spirit attains a supreme condition of self-knowledge and identity through a balance of conflicting elements; but Pechorin's argument is not easily apprehended in the close metaphorical weave of his thought:

> But this calm is often a sign of great, though hidden power; fullness and depth of feelings and thoughts do not permit frantic outbursts: the soul, in its suffering and enjoyment, takes strict account of everything and convinces itself that this is as it should be; it knows that without storms the constant heat of the sun will wither it; it is penetrated by its own personal life, caresses and punishes itself, like a beloved child. Only in this highest condition of self-knowledge can man appreciate divine justice.

Immediately after this quasi-philosophical excursion, recorded under 3 June, Grushnitsky enters with the excited announcement that he has been made an officer and is therefore a more eligible contender for Princess Mary's favours. From this point forward all Pechorin's activity is devoted to a fierce, wilful despoiling of the hopes and illusions of both of them. The morality of his acts is sufficient unto itself, it seems, but the activity itself—the exercise of his will and the subjection of others to it—is the facsimile of happiness and purpose with which he fills his life. On the eve of his duel with Grushnitsky he asks himself whether his life had ever had a purpose:

> 'But there was a purpose for sure, and I must surely have had a high destiny, because I feel in my soul unlimited powers . . . But I did not perceive this destiny, I was distracted by the lure of empty and ignoble passions; I emerged from the crucible hard and cold as iron, but I lost forever the fire of noble yearnings, the finest flower of life . . . My love brought happiness to no one, because I made no sacrifice for those I loved: I loved for myself, for my own enjoyment; I simply satisfied the strange craving of my heart, greedily consuming their feelings, their tenderness, their joys and sufferings—and could never satisfy myself to the full.

He has murdered his feelings, as he tells Dr Werner as

they ride out to the scene of the duel: 'For a long time I have lived not by the heart but by the head. I weigh up and scrutinise my own passions and actions with stern curiosity, but without partiality. There are two men in me: one lives in the full sense of the word, the other speculates and passes judgment on him.'

In this process Grushnitsky bears a striking resemblance to a victim who projects all the emotional *naïveté*, the ingenuous spontaneity of heart, which Pechorin has suppressed within himself. The scene of the duel is of a sustained dramatic power unequalled by any other episode in the novel. From the glittering, panoramic description of the morning, which arouses Pechorin's love of nature as it had never been aroused before, the scene gradually narrows to a direct confrontation between Pechorin and his opponent in which scenery, the other participants, the very air itself seem to vanish away. They might be confronting each other a few paces apart across a small room. Yet, despite the arch and melodramatic exchanges between them, the feeling that this is a confrontation as much between doubles as between rivals is enforced by Grushnitsky's last cry and the subsequent moments:

> ' "There is not room for the two of us on this earth . . ." I fired.
>
> When the smoke dispersed, Grushnitsky was not on the ledge. Only dust in a light column still hung at the edge of the precipice.
>
> All at once everyone gave a cry.
>
> *"Finita la commedia!"* I said to the doctor.'

Who has acted what role in this grim *commedia dell'arte* production in which Pechorin, the assassin of the fifth act, has killed not only his former friend but also a likely replica of himself? The roles are not interchangeable, but the supposition of Pechorin's diary is that Grushnitsky is as much his creation as his victim. Grushnitsky's death puts in question Pechorin's own, as it foreshadowed his creator's.

At the end of 'Princess Mary' Pechorin asks himself why he had not chosen to follow the path which fate had opened to him, 'where quiet joys and spiritual peace awaited me'. In other words, why had he not married Princess Marry and abandoned his vengeful experiment with life and with those who fell victim to his will? No, he could not have reconciled himself to that, he says. For Pechorin there is no reconciliation with others, with society, with the destiny of the sailor cast ashore 'who pines and languishes no matter how alluring the shady groves and how bright the peaceful sun'. When he is cast ashore, in the sense of being posted away to Maksim Maksimych's fort beyond the Terek and the Cossak village which is the setting of 'Fatalist,' he has no alternative but to employ the weapons which he uses in his conflict with others upon himself. He turns to experiment with himself and his own destiny. This is a natural outcome of his concern with the central significance of the will. He has to determine whether there is any pre-ordination of events; and this may only be proved by submitting his own will to the test.

Such an experiment is the central theme of the final story,

'Fatalist.' It is a story roughly divided into two episodes which are separated by a lengthy passage of reflection on ancient astrology and man's present-day lack of purpose. In the first part of the story Pechorin makes a bet against predestination. He loses his bet when Vulich's pistol fails to fire, but he is intuitively sure that Vulich is destined to die. Though he rejects predestination, his intuition is fully borne out in the second part of the story by the sudden news that Vulich has been killed by a drunken Cossack. He then resolves to follow Vulich's example and experiment with his own destiny by pitting himself against the likelihood of sudden death: he breaks into the hut where the Cossack has taken refuge and succeeds in overpowering him. His own death had not been decreed by the stars for that moment, it would seem, and he concludes by preferring to doubt: 'I love to doubt everything: this state of mind does not prevent resoluteness of character; on the contrary, so far as I am concerned I always go ahead more boldly when I don't know what awaits me. For nothing worse than death can happen—and death you can't avoid!'

There are no rules, then, no systems of belief, no moral codes in Pechorin's view of life. All is anarchic, just as for him the free exercise of will absolves him of responsibility. 'His only imperatives,' as John Mersereau has put it, 'are those dictated to him by his passions.' Even if repentance is as impossible for him as it is for the murderous Cossack, since he cannot acknowledge the moral sanction which would make repentance possible, his free exercise of will is based on the premise that passions are the source of ideas which only acquire form through action. For all his speculations on the nature of life, the true centre of his life is action, the implementation and testing of his ideas; and clearly the most private, or personal, point to which all such experimentation can be taken is that at which he—or any man, for Pechorin's is at this point a universal dilemma—confronts death, of which he may be the agent or the victim, but to which he is inevitably fated.

Lermontov's novel is designed by its structure and method of portrayal to achieve exactly this penetration of the hero's inner experience. From the generalised portraiture offered by Maksim Maksimych and the itinerant author the revelatory process obviously involves an ever-deepening analysis of the real motives of Pechorin's actions, the essentially private cause of the vengeful and callous conduct which he exhibits in public. Private and public aspects coalesce in the universality of the ultimate confrontation, and the portrait can be seen, for all its reference to place and period, as universally timeless, of one age and every age, of our time as of any other. We are required only to understand the portrait, not to censure it ('we almost always forgive what we understand', the preface to the *Journal* reminds us). The relationship which the novel as a whole aims to achieve with the reader is of such a personal character that it must surely induce in the reader a self-analytical response in which, if he can relate to himself with any credibility, he must scrutinise his own heroic presumptions. *A Hero of Our Time,* after all, debunks heroism and invites the reader to reappraise his own received view of what the heroic may be. As a piece of fictional portraiture—autobiographical, admittedly, in its impulse and major premises—it has certain derivative features which

relate it very obviously to its own age. But no amount of searching for models and influences can alter the supreme impression which this novel leaves—that it is a remarkable whole which must be judged on its own terms. Belinsky described the impression by using the term 'enclosedness' (*zamknutost*) of the novel, employing to illustrate his meaning the perfect wholeness of a flower:

> Observe a flowering plant: you see that it has a definite form by which it is differentiated not only from beings in other kingdoms of nature, but also even from plants of other species and varieties; its foliage is distributed so symmetrically, so proportionally, each leaf is so delicately, with such scrupulousness, with such infinite perfection, differentiated and emblazoned down to the smallest details . . . How luxuriously beautiful is its flower, what fine veins and hues it has, what soft, bright bloom it has upon it, and, finally, what an intoxicating fragrance! But that's not all, is it? Oh, no! that is only the outer form, an expression of the inner: these magic colours have come from within the plant, this enchanting aroma is its balsamic breath . . . There, within its stem, is a whole new world: there is its self-activated laboratory of life, there, along most delicate tubes of wondrously perfect making, flows the juice of life, streams the invisible ether of its spirit . . . Where is the beginning and cause of this phenomenon? In itself: it was there when there was no plant at all, when there was only a seed.

A Hero of Our Time has this kind of detailed wholeness; it contains both its seed and its full flowering; it has a very special individual identity as the first Russian novel in prose to attempt portraiture in depth. Much more than this, it is successful in creating a world of human experience through each of its three narrators, though especially of course through Pechorin, which suggests not only truth to life but also those echoes and reverberations of sentiment, memory and dream, which can always trouble the fringes of consciousness. The relationship existing between the hero and other characters, between the itinerant author and Maksim Maksimych, between Maksim Maksimych and his story are obviously more sophisticated and

---

An excerpt from Lermontov's Introduction to *A Hero of Our Time*

The *Hero of our Time* is certainly a portrait, but not of a single person. It is a portrait of the vices of our whole generation in their ultimate development. You will say that no man can be so bad, and I will ask you why, after accepting all the villains of tragedy and romance, you refuse to believe in Pechorin. You have admired far more terrible and monstrous characters than he is, so why are you so merciless towards him, even as a fictitious character? Perhaps he comes too close to the bone?

Mikhail Yuryevich Lermontov, in his A Hero of Our Time, *Penguin Books, 1966.*

complex than those purely of narrator and narrative: *why* they relate, *how* they relate, the prisms of prejudice and misapprehension through which they filter their their view of the world are what give the novel its human context and lend it such extraordinary multifariousness, such richness of meaning and implication and such profound vitality.

Herbert Eagle   (essay date 1974)

SOURCE: "Lermontov's 'Play' with Romantic Genre Expectations in *A Hero of Our Time*," in *Russian Literature Triquarterly,* No. 10, Fall, 1974, pp. 299-315.

[*In the following excerpt, Eagle argues that Lermontov undercuts romantic literary conventions in each segment of* A Hero of Our Time.]

The criticism and confusion of Lermontov's contemporaries about the intent of *A Hero of Our Time* is indirect evidence that it contains innovative elements. In his reply to his critics (in the introduction to the second edition) Lermontov laments the fact that his reading public was not subtle enough to understand what he was doing, not clever enough to solve the riddle of a new form:

> Our reading public is still so young and simple-minded that it does not understand a fable unless it finds a moral at the end. It cannot comprehend jests or feel irony; it is simply poorly educated. It still does not know that open abuse has no place in respectable society or in a respectable book. It does not see that contemporary culture has devised a sharper instrument, one which, in the guise of flattery, strikes an irresistible and unerring blow. Our public is like a provincial who overhears a conversation between two diplomats from hostile courts and is sure that each of them is betraying his government for the sake of a tender mutual friendship.

In retelling the anecdote about the provincial and the ambassadors, Lermontov warns that what is said by the characters or by narrators in his novel cannot be taken as necessarily true-everything must be judged in its total context. This is, in fact, the key to the compositional structure of *A Hero of Our Time.* Each chapter in the novel is based on one or more Russian Romantic short-form genres (and contains a large number of typical elements of the genres), but the expectations for the genre are often disappointed through the use of additional elements. These new elements lead the perceptive reader to question the illusion of reality as created by the stereotyped situations, stock characters and verbal cliches of the genre. Thus, the Romantic conventionality is exposed; its claim to represent reality is challenged—though not completely negated.

The point of origin of *A Hero of Our Time* as "large form" is the story-cycle of the Romantic period (e. g. Pogorelsky's *The Double,* Gogol's *Dikanka* and *Mirgorod* collections, Pushkin's *Belkin Tales*). Lermontov's novel shares with these story-cycles such devices as use of a unifying "editor-author" (Gogol's Panko, Pushkin's Belkin, Lermontov's unnamed traveling narrator), use of other narrators within the basic narration, deliberate use of a spectrum of short-form genres, etc. But Lermontov's work is governed by a new dominant: the creation of a psychological portrait of a character through the use of different viewpoints (including that of the character himself) and the use of the typical perspectives of different short genres.

The short genres upon which the individual chapters are based are as follows:

> "Bela"—travel notes and adventure story;
>
> "Maxim Maximych"—physiological sketch (*fiziologicheskii ocherk*);
>
> "Introduction to Pechorin's Journal"—editor's commentary to confession or diary;
>
> "Taman"—intensified anecdote based on a supernatural or highly unusual event;
>
> "Princess Mary"—journal-confession and society tale;
>
> "The Fatalist"—intensified anecdote based on a supernatural or highly unusual event.

Among the typical features of the travelogue genre used by Lermontov in "Bela" are (a) grandiloquent, exuberant nature description:

> To the right and left, somber, secret chasms blackened, and mists, coiling and swirling like serpents, slipped in among the wrinkles of neighboring rocks, as if sensing and fearing the approach of day.

(b) objective description of the mores *(byt)* of the natives:

> Here a rather engaging picture opened before us: the wide hut, whose roof rested on two smoky pillars, was full of people. In the center on the ground, a little fire was crackling and the smoke, driven backward from the opening in the roof by the wind, spread around in such a thick shroud that for a long time I was unable to get my bearings. Near the fire sat two old women, many children, and one skinny Georgian, all of them in rags.

(c) use of the external travelogue as a means of commenting on the inner emotional state of the narrator:

> . . . the air became so rare that it was painful to breathe, at every moment blood rushed to my head, but all the same, a sort of delightful feeling spread through my veins and I was somehow joyous because I was so high above the world-a childish feeling, I won't deny it, but by separating ourselves from society's conventions, and moving close to nature we cannot help but become children: all the accretions fall from the soul and it again becomes what it once was and will sometime again surely be.

The last passage is very typical of Sentimentalism and points out the typical pre-Romantic expectations (as well as limitations) of the traveling narrator in "Bela." A phrase which occurs in Maxim Maximych's narrative— "it was Bela . . . poor Bela" ("Eto byla Bela . . . bednaia Bela")—repeats verbatim the signal phrase of Karamzin's "Poor Liza."

In other passages Lermontov's narrator allows himself

some playful and parodic remarks about the conventions of the genre in which he is writing:

> But perhaps you would like to know the end of Bela's story? First of all, I am writing travel notes, not a tale, consequently I cannot make the staff-captain continue until he in fact began to do so. So wait . . . or, if you like, skip over a few pages; only I don't advise the latter, since the journey over Krestovy (or, as the scholar Gamba calls it, le Mont St.-Christophe) is worthy of your attention.

He begins the subsequent chapter, "Maxim Maximych," this way:

> Having parted with Maxim Maximych, I briskly galloped through the Terek and Daryal canyons, lunched in Kazbek, had tea in Lars and reached Valdikavkaz in time for supper. I will spare you the descriptions of mountains, the exclamations which mean nothing (especially for those who have never been there), and the statistical observations which absolutely no one would bother to read.

This is a catalogue of and ironic commentary on some of the typical features of the travelogue. It also puts the reader on notice that these conventions will not be followed in subsequent chapters.

The use of the travelogue genre as a frame for a story was also a typical feature of the Sentimentalist and Romantic genre, e. g. in Radishchev's *Journey from Petersburg to Moscow,* Somov's *Order from the Other World,* Bulgarin's *The Ruins of Almodovar,* etc.

Genre markers for the adventure tale, a story interpolated into the travelogue, are also prominent in "Bela." The traveling narrator anticipates that he will hear from Maxim Maximych a tale about danger and wild natives:

> . . . I know that these veterans of the Caucasus love to talk and tell stories . . . And, after all, they have something to talk about: wild and curious natives around them, danger every day; wondrous things happen, and here one cannot but be sorry that we have recorded so little of it.

His expectations are fulfilled to a considerable degree. The plot of Maxim's tale involves trickery, theft, kidnapping, murder and revenge. The Chechen characters generally act according to the genre stereotype (e. g., the violent and passionate actions of Kazbich and Azamat; Bela's pride, 'her dancing, naive devotion, refusal to change her religion even on her deathbed). Equally important, the language and content of the directly or indirectly quoted speeches of Kazbich, Azamat, and Bela are typically, thoroughly and consistently Romantic:

> KAZBICH: "Four Cossacks were coming after me; I already heard the shouts of giaours behind me and before me was a thick wood. I pressed myself to Allah and for the first time in my life insulted my horse with a below of the whip. He dove between the branches like a bird; the sharp thorns tore my clothes, the dry twigs of the karagas beat me on the face."

> AZAMAT: "The first time I saw your stallion . . . as he was turning and prancing under you, puffing out his nostrils, flint flying in sparks from under his hooves, something incomprehensible happened to my soul, and since that time everything has become meaningless to me . . . your jet black stallion has appeared before me, with his handsome gait, his smooth backbone straight as an arrow; he has looked into my eyes with his clever eyes as if he wished to utter a word. I will die, Kazbich, if you do not sell him to me."

Pechorin's only extended speech in "Bela" is similarly filled with Romantic cliches:

> When I saw Bela in my own home, when for the first time I held her on my knees and kissed her black curls, I, fool that I am, thought that she was an angel sent to me by compassionate fate . . . If you like, I still love her, I am thankful to her for a few rather sweet moments, I would give my life for her-only I am bored with her . . . Whether I am a fool or a villain I do not know; but it is true that I am also worthy of pity, perhaps more than she: my soul has been spoiled by the world, my imagination is disturbed, my heart insatiable . . .

The above passage is a Byronic reflex of a type very frequent in Lermontov's early narrative poems and retained in all of the many reworkings of his poem *The Demon.*

The presence of such grandiloquent speeches within Maxim Maximych's otherwise prosaic, colloquial and unpretentious narrative has attracted considerable notice and comment. The style of the basic narrative and the style of these speeches differ to such an extent in lexicon, syntax, etc., that the anomaly cannot be considered an oversight on Lermontov's part. Nor does the possibility that Maxim Maximych remembered these lengthy speeches verbatim seem plausible. However, Lermontov provides sufficient motivation for this: in "Bela" the traveling narrator informs us (in a footnote) that he has rendered Kazbich's song in verse, although it was given to him in prose by Maxim Maximych. At the beginning of the subsequent chapter he tells us: " . . . for amusement I decided to write down Maxim Maximych's tale about Bela." Thus, since we know that the traveling narrator took the liberty of versifying and stylizing Kazbich's song, we can also infer that he has stylized certain speeches by the characters, using the literary conventions and verbal cliches with which he is familiar. Thus, the Pechorin whom we see in "Bela" is a Pechorin viewed from the perspective of specific Romantic genres. This crucial fact (for it implies that the given image of Pechorin is only a relative one) becomes evident through the attitudes and narrative style of Maxim Maximych.

The principal esthetic function of Maxim Maximych in "Bela" is to expose the conventions and cliches of the Romantic genres represented. This is done partially through Maxim Maximych's conversational, idiomatic, non-literary style which makes the Romantic nature description and speeches seem somewhat pompous and exaggerated. Many features of oral narration are retained throughout Maxim Maximych's story:

(a) post-positive particles, e. g., -*s* and -*to*.

(b) exclamations: *molodtsi da, byvalo! ne dai gospodi! slava Bogu!*

(c) many small conversational pause words: *uzh, pozhalui, znaete, chai, ved, izvolite videt,* etc.

(d) use of the conjunction *da* instead of *i.*

(e) qualifying phrases or words: *odin kakoi-nibud oburvysh, po krainei mere, ia tak polagaiu.*

(f) superlatives and diminutives.

(g) use of *ekoi, ekaia,* etc. instead of *kakoi, kakaia.*

(h) slang words: *bashka, rozha, bolno* instead of *ochen.*

(i) "local color" words: *kunak, arkan, iaman, iuk, abrek, chadra.*

(j) foreign words from the military lexicon: *mikstura, transport, goshpital, proviant.*

(k) general conversational idioms or expressions: *po-ikhnemu; boltato tom, o sem; da v tom-to i shtuka; chert ikh razberet; chto zadumaet podavai; u nego slez ne vybesh; vstrechnye i poperechnye.*

(l) particularly graphic, sometimes grotesque, idioms or expressions: *zhivotiki nadorvesh so smekha; chto mne byl za dikovinka kaban!*

(m) aphoristic expressions in the style of folk proverbs: *plokhoe delo v chuzhom piru pokhmele; do nashego brata vesti pozdno dokhodiat.*

In addition to these specific elements of lexicon and idiomatic expression, Maxim Maximych's syntax is very distinctive and is characterized by frequent use of ellipsis. Conjunctions and relative pronouns are often omitted or replaced by shorter conjunctions ("vy dumaete, oni pomogaiut, chto krichat?" or "provornyi na chto khochesh"); finite verbs are often omitted ("byki vse ni s mesta").

In addition, Maxim Maximych's descriptions of Chechen life are relatively free of Romantic stereotypes. For example:

> "First the mullah recites something to them from the Koran; then the young couple and all their relatives get presents. They eat, drink booze; then the trick riding begins and there is always some dirty beggar on a lousy lame nag who puts on airs, clowns around, and amuses the honorable company; then at dusk, they begin a ball, as we would call it . . . a poor old codger strums a three-stringed . . . forget what they call it . . . well, something like our balalaika."

In general Maxim Maximych's attitude toward the Chechens is matter-of-fact and markedly un-Romantic. He has respect and admiration for their military prowess; but this is coupled with a slight bit of condescension, such as one might feel toward mischievous children. Thus Maxim frequently uses diminutives in referring to Chechens; he agrees to attend the wedding of the prince's daughter because "it was impossible to refuse, even though he was a Tatar." In the same spirit he invites the outlaw Kazbich to have tea with him. Maxim Maximych sees Chechens

not as part of Caucasian exotica, but simply as people. He tends to describe them so that they seem more down-to-earth and less sinister. Even Kazbich's kidnapping of Bela, a typically "Eastern" act of revenge in the Romantic context (as in Lermontov's early poems **"Aul Bastundzhi"** and **"Khadji Abrek"**) is interpreted by Maxim as simply a natural reflex of an inveterate thief:

> "But why did Kazbich want to carry her off?"
>
> "Why? After all, these Circassians are well known as a thieving people. They can't help but filch what is lying around. They don't need any other reason, they just steal . . . so I ask you to forgive them for it! And anyway she had appealed to him for a long time."

Thus the attitudes of Maxim Maximych form the external reference point from which we can evaluate the normative Romantic genre conventions and expectations.

The Romantic genre which is used as the basis for the chapter entitled "Maxim Maximych" is the physiological sketch (hereafter simply "sketch"). The sketch was affected by the pseudo-scientific fads of the era (phrenology, "magnetism," etc.) which maintained that there were necessary relationships between a person's external appearance and his character. Lermontov commented ironically on such fads in his poem "The Tambov Pay-Master's Wife" and also in his unfinished society tale "Princess Ligovskaya:"

> Pechorin . . . sat down in his chair again and covered his face with his hands . . . and although I can read the mind's motives very well from the physiognomy, it is precisely for this reason that I cannot tell you anything about his thoughts.

The sketch usually opened with the narrator meeting or coming across some interesting type whom he then proceeded to describe (e. g. Pogodin's "The Beggar"); Lermontov provides just such an introduction to "Maxim Maximych" in the last paragraph of "Bela:" "We didn't expect to meet ever again, but we did meet, and if you like I'll tell you about it." The opening of "Maxim Maximych" continues in the same vein: " 'Ah! Maxim Maximych!' . . . We met as old friends. I offered him my room. He didn't stand on ceremony, even slapped me on the back. . . ." Of course, part of the sketch of Maxim Maximych has already been given to us in "Bela:"

> Behind walked its owner, smoking a small Kabardian pipe overlaid with silver. He wore an officer's frock coat without epaulettes, and a shaggy Circassian cap. He seemed to be about fifty: his swarthy complexion showed that his face was long acquainted with the Trans-Caucasian sun, and his prematurely gray moustache contrasted with his firm walk and his sprightly appearance.

The chapter "Maxim Maximych" completes and deepens this description and gives us a sketch of Pechorin. The manner in which Pechorin is described is typical for the genre: beginning with physical appearance and deriving a psychological portrait through relationships between physical and mental traits.

His gait was careless and lazy, but I noticed that he did not swing his arms—a sure sign of a certain secretiveness . . . There was something child-like in his smile. His skin had an almost feminine tenderness: his blond, naturally curly hair picturesquely outlined his pale noble forehead, upon which traces of intersecting wrinkles could only be noticed after lengthy observation, although they probably became much more prominent in moments of anger or spiritual unrest . . .

This sort of description, typical of the genre, arouses an expectation of a dramatic event, either to occur immediately thereafter or to be retold by the subject himself. Yet the action in "Maxim Maximych," which involves merely the meeting between Maxim and Pechorin, is anticlimactic. This is one way in which Lermontov disappoints the expectations of the genre.

During the meeting between Maxim and Pechorin, Lermontov makes masterful use of dialogue to both illustrate and modify (de-Romanticize) the initial portrait of Pechorin. Although some of the speculations about his character are verified, he certainly is viewed from a more prosaic perspective. For example, rather than being sinister or cruel, he is simply inconsiderate. The stylistic features of the dialogue itself serve to contrast Pechorin's coldness and superficiality to Maxim's warmth, earthiness and spontaneity (note, for example, Pechorin's use of the polite *vy* (you) instead of the expected familiar *ty* (thou) and Maxim's subsequent confusion):

"How pleased I am to see you, dear Maxim Maximych! Well, how are you?" said Pechorin.

"And . . . thou . . . and you . . ." muttered the old man with tears in his eyes . . . "How many years . . . how many days . . . but where are you going? . . ."

"I am going to Persia . . . and beyond . . ."

. . . . .

"We'll talk a bit . . . you'll tell me about your life in Petersburg . . . Eh?"

"Actually, I have nothing to tell, my dear Maxim Maximych . . . But farewell, I must go . . . I am in a hurry . . ."

The use of dialogue to elucidate character in a subtle way and to disappoint the reader's expectations is the primary feature of Lermontov's transformation and re-orientation of the sketch.

The introduction to Pechorin's journal motivates and draws attention to the first-person narrative in the final three chapters. The editor tells us that he has recently learned of Pechorin's death and is therefore publishing some excerpts from Pechorin's journal. The editor indicates that Pechorin's confessions may incline the reader to greater sympathy for the hero; at the same time, he refuses to give his own opinion of Pechorin or admit that the title of the novel is ironic. Thus, the editor's introduction not only signals the forthcoming changes in genre and narrative mode, but also warns the reader about the subtlety of the novel's meaning. The use of a fictitious editor immediately focuses attention on the characteristics of the narrator (or narrators) as distinct from the author. The device of a fictitious editor was often used to indicate stylization (as in Gogol's *Dikanka* tales) or parody (as in Pushkin's *Belkin* tales).

The genre of "Taman" is an intensified anecdote based on unusual occurrences bordering on the supernatural. This is emphasized from the very first paragraph, as John Mersereau, Jr. has pointed out:

The adventure of Taman is even initiated by a situational cliche' favored by romantics whose plots involved Satan. In the first scene Pechorin grows increasingly irate at his fruitless search for quarters and finally demands: "Take me somewhere!" Then, oddly enough, he is informed that there is a vacant hut but it is *nechisto,* a term which signifies not only "dirty" but has a connotation of "possessed by devils." Pechorin adds: "Not having understood the exact meaning of the last word, I ordered him to lead on."

Whether Lermontov was consciously employing the old formula, "Speak to the Devil and he will appear," is difficult to say. There is no question, however, that a demonic presence is felt throughout the whole story.

When Pechorin is finally quartered at the seaside hut, he meets the blind boy, who strikes him as unpleasant, and potentially hostile: ". . . In my mind there arose the suspicion that this blind boy was not as blind as he seemed; in vain, I tried to convince myself that one cannot feign wall-eye—and for what purpose?" That very night, Pechorin has difficulty sleeping:

The moon was shining in my window and its beams played on the dirt floor of the hut. Suddenly a shadow flitted across the bright band which cut across the floor. I sat up and looked out the window; someone ran by it again and hid God knows where . . .

The above nightscape is very typical of the tale of the supernatural.

Pechorin's conversations with the "ondine" (as he calls the girl smuggler) are based upon folk stylization and are full of mysterious riddles:

"Tell me, my pretty one," I asked, "What were you doing on the roof today?"

"I was watching whence blows the wind."

"What is it to you?"

"Whence the wind, thence also happiness."

"What? Were you then calling happiness with your song?"

"Where there is singing, there is also merrymaking."

"But might you not equally be singing yourself woe?"

"What difference does it make? Where it will not

be better, it will be worse, and from evil to good the distance is not great."

As will later become apparent, a number of the ondine's mysterious replies are actually quite literal references to the smuggling operation and to her love for the smuggler Yanko. The same is true of the verses of her song. Later, when the ondine tries to pitch Pechorin overboard, he is struck by her malevolence and almost supernatural strength. One more indication of the genre is Pechorin's mention, in his narrative, of *la jeune France, l'ecole frènètique* which was characterized by its interest in the supernatural, the hyperbolic and the grotesque.

However, at the same time that Lermontov incorporates all of the above elements of the supernatural tale, he also includes passages of realistic description of mores, realistic motivation for all of the actions of the smugglers, and individualized speech, including feigned styles and dialects on the part of the smugglers. The opening description of the town of Taman is realistic rather than mysterious: "Taman is the vilest of all of Russia's seaport towns. I almost died of hunger there . . ." The blind boy speaks to Pechorin in Ukrainian, but Pechorin later overhears him speaking Russian to others. The ondine speaks to Pechorin in stylized folk language, but to the blind boy and to Yanko in a very abrupt, matter-of-fact manner. At times Pechorin himself strikes very prosaic *(bytovoi)* un-Romantic notes, both in his actions and in his descriptions. Note how the Romantic expectation is disappointed in the following passage:

> Her face was covered by a dull pallor expressing inner agitation: her hand wandered aimlessly over the table and I noticed that it was trembling slightly; her breasts had risen so high that she appeared to be holding her breath. This comedy was beginning to bore me. I was ready to break the silence in the most prosaic way: that is, by offering her a glass of tea.

The callow indifference of the smugglers is rather vividly portrayed in their final conversation:

> . . . Yanko continued, " . . . and tell the old woman that, after all, it's time for her to croak, she's all lived out . . . it's only decent. She won't see us again."
>
> "And me," said the blind boy in an entreating voice.
>
> "What do I need you for?" was the answer . . .
> "Here, buy yourself some spice cake."

As a final un-Romantic touch, Pechorin returns from his eavesdropping only to discover that some of his most valuable possessions have been stolen by the blind boy. Pechorin laments fate's casting him into a "peaceful circle of *honest smugglers*" (Lermontov's italics); the italicized words are doubly ironic: first, because the smugglers are far from honest or honorable (as they, in fact, were expected to be in Romantic literature), and secondly, because they are termed "chestnye" (upright), whereas at the beginning of the story we expected villains who were "nechistye" (agents of the Devil). Hence, Romantic expectations are not only disappointed and transformed in

"Taman," they are actually parodied. Lermontov's ironic attitude toward the genre of the fantastic tale was given further play in his subsequent (and last) prose work, the short story, "Shtoss."

"Princess Mary" is a hybrid of two genres: the diary-confession and the society tale. Through much of the chapter Pechorin functions as an objective third-person narrator, viewing the other characters (as well as himself) from the outside. This device belongs in no way to the diary-confession genre, but originates rather in the society tale. Another very marked feature of the society tale which occurs in "Princess Mary" is the narrator's (Pechorin's) satirical attitude toward society:

> The wives of the local officials, the mistresses of the baths, as it were, are more favorably inclined: they have lorgnettes, pay less attention to the uniform, and are accustomed to meeting, here in the Caucasus, an ardent heart under army buttons and a cultivated mind under a white forage cap. These ladies are very sweet and sweet for a long time! Every year they exchange their admirers for new ones, and in this perhaps lies the secret of their tireless amiability.

Also very characteristic of the genre is the use of French for portions of dialogue and the preponderance of witty conversation and repartee. The actions of the characters, at least initially, are in keeping with the norms of the genre; this is especially true of the early flirtations between Grushnitsky and Princess Mary (Grushnitsky's limp and mysterious air, Mary's sweet smiles). The plot elements (flirtation, jealousy, using one love affair to distract society's attention from another, adultery, insults in public, finale—a duel) of "Princess Mary" are those typical of the Romantic society tale.

What is most important, though, is that Pechorin's behavior as a character and his commentary as narrator lead the reader to question the conventions of the society tale. Pechorin is a character who acts while aware of the rules of the genre, as well as the rules of society, and he often refers specifically to using the rules of the genre to his own advantage:

> *(Werner):* "The young princess says that she is sure that this young man in a common soldier's overcoat was demoted to the ranks because of a duel . . . "
>
> "I hope that you left her in that pleasant misapprehension."
>
> "Of course."
>
> "There's a plot here," I cried in delight, "now we'll have to trouble ourselves about the denouement of this comedy."

When Werner offers to introduce Pechorin to Princess Mary, Pechorin refuses, saying: " . . . are protagonists introduced? They only meet when saving their beloveds from certain death . . ." Actually, Pechorin's rescue of Princess Mary turns out to be even more characteristic of the society tale than Pechorin suggests above. He didn't save her from certain death. "I have done better," he tells Werner, "I saved her from fainting at a ball." Pechorin's awareness of the norms of the society tale genre is manifested so often that we cannot but admit this "self-consciousness" of the hero as a deliberate device. On the other hand, Pechorin (as character in a drama of his own direction) sometimes behaves in accordance with society-tale norms, even while recognizing that these conventions are foolish. In fact, in the confessional portions of "Princess Mary," Pechorin speaks about his dual nature:

> For a long time I have lived not by my heart, but by my head. I measure out and choose my own passions and actions with careful attention, but disinterestedly. In me there are two men: one lives in the full sense of the word, the other thinks and judges him.

The confessional portions of "Princess Mary" are rather clearly distinguished from the rest of the chapter. They are lengthy internal monologues, uninterrupted by dialogue, narrative descriptions or action; most of them occur toward the end of the chapter—bracketing the climax scene, Pechorin's killing of Grushnitsky. These confessions are typical in that they include many "Byronic" clichés. However, once again Lermontov goes beyond the Romantic norms to include perceptive and unconventional self-analysis. The transitions from Romantic cliché to accurate psychological self-analysis are not abrupt or specifically marked, but seem to occur through a process of deeper interpretation of the Romantic cliche itself. Note how Pechorin moves from a "Byronic" pose to a perceptive statement of his principal vice:

> In recalling my entire past I cannot help but ask myself: why did I live? For what purpose was I born? . . . And, certainly, such a purpose existed; and, certainly, I was destined for something elevated, because I feel in my soul unrestrainable forces . . . But I didn't guess this high calling. I distracted myself with the temptations of empty and unrewarding passions; from their furnace I emerged hard and cold as steel, but I lost forever the ardor of noble inclinations—the best flower of my life. And since then how many times have I played the role of an ax in the hands of fate! As the executioner's tool I fell on the heads of the condemned victims, often without malice, always without pity. My love never brought anyone happiness, because I never sacrificed anything for those I loved: I loved for myself, for my own pleasure; I only satisfied my heart's strange need, greedily gulping down their feelings, their tenderness, their happiness and their suffering—and never being sated.

"The Fatalist" refocuses attention on the question of fate, free will and moral responsibility. It also gives Pechorin a final opportunity, again as narrator and character, to reflect on the apparent contradictions between his extreme "Byronic" behavior and his capability for cold, rational analysis of that behavior. The genre here, like that of "Taman," calls for maximal character types and maximally melodramatic situations. An extreme of character is provided by Vulich; he is the epitome of the Byronic type: a Southern, Mediterranean hue, an indifferent air, a passion for gambling:

> His great height and his swarthy complexion, black hair, black piercing eyes, a large but straight nose (a characteristic of his people), a sad cold smile always playing on his lips—all of this combined to give him the appearance of a special kind of being, incapable of sharing his thoughts and emotions with those whom fate had given him as comrades.

Quite typically for the genre, we are told and then witness a series of anecdotes regarding Vulich. First we are told about his being such a passionate gambler that he continued to deal a poker hand even under enemy fire, lost, sought out the winner, and paid his debt in the heat of battle—only then did he distinguish himself by fighting heroically. Then we witness Vulich's gambling with his own life, betting that the gun he fires at his own head will not go off. Finally, in the third anecdote, which Pechorin hears the next morning, Vulich is killed because he addresses a few innocuous words to a drunken Cossack. In the fourth and final anecdote Pechorin tests fate by risking his *own* life, although in a qualitatively different (and relatively more rational) way.

Pechorin's challenge to fate fits the Byronic mold to a lesser degree because Pechorin is trying to test scientifically the roles of fate and free will. Unlike Vulich, Pechorin has strong rational prejudices in favor of free will. His capture of the drunken Cossack is not unthinking recklessness, but is as rationally planned as possible under the circumstances:

> The Cossack began to bang on the door with all of his strength. Pressing my eye up against the crack, I followed the movements of the Cossack, who was not expecting an attack from that side; then I suddenly tore open the shutters and threw myself head first through the window.

This test does not really resolve for Pechorin the question of fate versus free will. Nor does it resolve the duality in his character. The Pechorin who indulges in Romantic myths about himself continues to lean on fate as a means of avoiding moral responsibility for his actions; the more rational, analytical Pechorin rejects Romantic myths, including the myth of fated destiny. Thus, "The Fatalist" serves to re-emphasize the complex quality of Pechorin's personality: his ability to act in accordance with Romantic myths about himself, while at the same time rationally analyzing these myths and viewing them with great skepticism.

Thus we can see that Lermontov's innovative accomplishments with respect to short-form Romantic genres and the organization of a story cycle (here structured a new way for the purpose of character psychologization) were considerable. The individual chapters retain the elements of Romantic short stories, but the overall structure of the work tends to place the Romantic usages in such contexts that the reader is led to question their validity. The result of this deformation is not that the devices entirely lose their Romantic function, but rather that they acquire a new "realistic" aspect as well.

Angus Calder   (essay date 1976)

SOURCE: "Literature and Serfdom: Gogol, Lermontov and Goncharov," in *Russia Discovered: Nineteenth-Century Fiction from Pushkin to Chekhov,* Barnes and Noble Books 1976, pp. 37-70.

[*In the following excerpt, Calder assesses* A Hero of Our Time *as Lermontov's single "great novel."*]

[Mikhail Lermontov] managed in his brief and unhappy existence to earn himself a place as Pushkin's successor among Russian poets and to write one great novel, *A Hero of Our Time*. . . .

Lermontov was hardly an attractive personality: Turgenev remembered that 'His swarthy face and large, motionless dark eyes exuded a sort of sombre and evil strength, a sort of pensive scornfulness and passion'. His most famous narrative poetry is characteristically 'Romantic', making free use of the supernatural and expressing a deep love of nature. He died at an age when most young writers have barely started to escape from youthful imitation and self-indulgence; this makes it all the more remarkable that *A Hero of Our Time* should be the book it is—not only very exciting in its incidents, but original in its form, realistic in its psychology, and utterly unsentimental. Its handling of the native peoples of the Caucasus is stylized, but entirely convincing. Its hero, Pechorin, stands up superbly well to comparison with such French precursors as Constant's *Adolphe* (1816) and Stendhal's Julien Sorel (*Scarlet and Black,* 1831). His obvious Russian predecessor is Onegin. The River Onega is a cold one in Northern Russia; the River Pechora flows still farther north. But if Pechorin has dandyism and restlessness in common with Pushkin's unheroic hero, his calculating decisiveness and sheer courage are beyond Onegin's range. Both odious and attractive, he crackles with energy: physical energy, intellectual energy—and even, in a paradoxical fashion, with moral energy, since he is acutely aware of the harm he does to others.

Lermontov certainly used his own character and experience to the full in creating Pechorin. But we must not imagine that he approves of him. After the book came out in 1840, some critics saw it as autobiographical. For the second edition next year Lermontov wrote a preface in which he rebuked those who took the novel 'literally'—thus hinting that it contained meanings which the censorship might not have let him express openly—and he made two claims which echo through subsequent Russian 'realism'.

He saw Pechorin as a 'type', representative of many young men, but not timidly copying the humdrum surface of their lives:

> It is a portrait of the vices of our whole generation in their ultimate development. You will say that no man can be so bad, and I will ask you why, after accepting all the villains of tragedy and romance, you refuse to believe in Pechorin?. . . . Perhaps he comes too close to the bone?

Secondly, he emphasized the moral value of truth-telling,

and, in selecting an analogy with medicine, suggested a role for the novelist combining 'scientific' detachment with 'artistic' sensitivity and with indispensable social function:

> You may say that morality will not benefit from this book. I'm sorry, but people have been fed on sweets too long and it has ruined their digestion. Bitter medicines and harsh truths are needed now, though please don't imagine that the present author was ever vain enough to dream of correcting human vices. . . . Let it suffice that the malady has been diagnosed—heaven alone knows how to cure it.

A Hero of Our Time is not explicitly a 'political' book. But when we compare it with Emily Brontë's *Wuthering Heights*—which came out soon after and was also the sole fictional masterpiece of a precocious author, offering a comparable combination of 'romantic' story with 'realistic' detail—we are aware of elements of topicality, of satire, of apparently casual generalization, which make the Russian novel seem part of a debate while the English one is a self-sufficient statement. In Nicholas's Russia, to criticize a generation was, after all, to criticize the state which wished and claimed to control all significant life.

In technique, however, the two books are suggestively similar. In each case the literary device of multiple narrative voices sustains a tantalizing combination of deep, 'subjective', commitment to the 'Romantic' hero and of cold 'realistic' objectivity about him.

The six sections of *A Hero of Our Time* are nothing like the 'chapters' of a novel of its period. As Donald Davie has pointed out, the book is amazingly 'modern', anticipating effects which James and Conrad began to exploit in English fiction half a century later.

From the vantage point of the second section, in which the 'I' who begins the narrative (but is not to be confused with Lermontov himself) actually meets Pechorin, all the other episodes might be seen as 'flashback'. In 'Bela', the first episode, the narrator, who is travelling about the Caucasus making notes for a travel book, meets a fifty-year-old army captain named Maxim Maximych, and draws from him reminiscences of the kind often included in travel books. These in a 'natural' way lead into the tale of Maxim Maximych's friendship five years before with a rich young officer, Pechorin, who was sent to serve at his fort.

The old man's narrative exposes both his wondering affection for his dazzling junior and his inability fully to understand this creature, jaded with the love of women of fashion and disillusioned with reading and study. Maxim Maximych knows nothing about Byronism and other fashionable fads. When Pechorin arranges the abduction of Bela, the beautiful daughter of a local chieftain, and brings her into the fort as his mistress, Maxim Maximych sees not a typically 'Byronic' quest by a bored sophisticate for happiness in the arms of an unspoilt girl but a profound sexual passion between two young people whom he loves and admires. After describing how Bela, at first sullen, finally yields to Pechorin's expert hand, he confesses, 'I was upset that no woman had ever loved me like that.' Bela is captured from Pechorin by a native admirer, who stabs her in the back when chased to a halt; her painful death two days later is described with most unromantic thoroughness.

Coming fresh to 'Bela' the reader will be as interested in the Circassian tribesmen as in Pechorin and probably more interested in Maxim Maximych, the archetypal frontier soldier who is also, in Mirsky's words, 'the simple, humble and casual hero of duty, kindness and common sense.' But the landscape dominates everything else. Lermontov's descriptions of snowy peaks, starry skies, deep ravines and glistening torrents are splashed with bright colours and swept by fresh air. While Turgenev's justly famous evocations of landscape often have the inert effect of fine, framed paintings, because landscape is what the characters, like the readers, *look at,* Lermontov's landscapes (and the same is true of Tolstoy's) are there to be *moved through*—they are experienced as the characters and the reader proceed together, and bad weather is described as zestfully as fair weather.

The second episode, 'Maxim Maximych', relates the travel-book-writer's unexpected second meeting with the old soldier in a small frontier town. They learn that Pechorin has arrived, and the veteran is overjoyed. The travel-book-writer's eye, that of a city-bred intellectual, sizes up the 'hero's' figure which gives a contradictory impression; his physique is strong but his fingers are astonishingly slender, his smile is childlike but his eyes don't laugh when he laughs and shine with the 'cold, dazzling brilliance of smooth steel'. The presentation is cautiously objective—the narrator admits that he might have assessed the man differently if he hadn't known something about him already, and his eye is clinical, but not unsympathetic. What swings our sympathies against Pechorin is his cold reception of Maxim Maximych. The old soldier has, for perhaps the first time in his life, neglected his official duty, rushing to see his friend. He arrives gasping for air, pouring with sweat:

> Strands of wet gray hair sticking out from his cap clung to his brow. He was about to throw his arms round Pechorin, but Pechorin rather coldly held out his hand, though he gave him a friendly smile.

With a few swift strokes—the wet gray hair is especially telling—Lermontov is able to make us feel the old man's boyish enthusiasm, the young man's elderly reserve, and to make the encounter hurt us. Pechorin is on his way to Persia. He refuses to stop and chew over memories with the old man, and we and the narrator are left with the grief and humiliation of Maxim Maximych turning into anger against the stuck-up dandy whose memory had been so important to him.

Since Maxim Maximych is far and away the most lovable character in the book, and has so far taken the centre of the stage from the 'hero', this scene makes it impossible for us to love, or wholly to forgive, Pechorin, let alone judge him on his own terms. Yet paradoxically, since the old man has been, as it were, 'in love with' Pechorin, it shows us how profoundly the hero affects people, how attractive he can be.

The rest of the book is made up of 'papers' of Pechorin's which the old man passed on to the travel-book-writer. The latter explains that Pechorin died on his way home from Persia, so he can now print them without inhibition. They are extracts from Pechorin's journal and formally they compose a triptych—two 'short stories' flanking a longer one.

Both Tolstoy and Chekhov admired 'Taman', the first short story, immensely. It describes an adventure of Pechorin's on his way to the Caucasus and so is biographically the earliest episode in the novel. The 'hero' puts up for a couple of nights in a hut in a Black Sea port and is nearly murdered by smugglers because he knows too much. The tale confirms Pechorin's lust and recklessness, but since he tells it, we are also made aware of more attractive elements in him—his love of nature and his self-questioning. Ironically, the behaviour of the smuggler Yanko towards a blind boy shows a callousness as great as Pechorin himself could reveal, and the smuggler's girl plays with his feelings as he himself plays with those of other girls, and all but destroys him. Pechorin is shown up as gullible, vulnerable, and also as perhaps the agent of a 'fate' which he sees as beyond his control.

The longest section of the book, 'Princess Mary', is presented as a 'diary' kept by Pechorin at the watering place, Piatigorsk, where he stayed before proceeding to join Maxim Maximych and abduct Bela. Here we see Pechorin in relation to 'society'—to an empty, mediocre world of gamblers and well-to-do nonentities. The more interesting people there bring out, by comparison, Pechorin's superiority. Grushnitsky, a cadet posing in a private's greatcoat as an officer demoted for duelling and as a man of 'romantic destiny'—his ambition, Pechorin notes, 'is to become the hero of a novel'—is a shallow fake, beside whom Pechorin's own depth is obvious. Dr Werner, a sceptical materialist who, with his wit and intelligence, has fallen foul of society, thinks he understands Pechorin completely—but his ultimate failure to do so is a measure of Pechorin's complexity. Then there are two women: Princess Mary, sojourning with her mother, and Vera, a married woman, the only person who ever understood Pechorin, whose arrival reawakens her attraction for him, but who is mortally ill.

Pechorin first behaves insultingly towards Mary, then makes her fall in love with him. He sleeps with Vera and destroys the relative amicability of her marriage. He arouses the hatred of Grushnitsky and kills him, in a fiercely exciting duel on a ledge over a ravine, during which he displays appalling coolness. Pechorin then finds that Vera has left and rides his horse to death in pursuit of her. The authorities pack him off at once to Maxim Maximych's fort. He parts with cruel candour from the lovesick Mary—'Princess . . . you know I was making fun of you.'

But *why* Pechorin does all this is not so easy to report. At times he he acts with total ruthlessness, at others he has to force himself to act coldly. At one point it seems that Mary's falling in love with him is almost as much an accident as Vera's arrival, which makes it necessary for him to cultivate the Princess, as he can meet Vera unobtrusively at her mother's house. At another, he seems to be calculating every move with a view to asserting his power over the woman and destroying Grushnitsky's pretences to her. When he fights his duel, he is glad that things work out so that he has every excuse to kill Grushnitsky, yet he himself runs a terrible risk, and still gives his opponent a last chance to save himself from certain death if only he will retract the slander which provoked the duel.

All Lermontov's main characters are complex. Princess Mary herself is marvellously well presented as both commonplace and spirited, both 'fair game' for a clever seducer and a human being who deserves our compassion. Even Grushnitsky is much more than a cardboard 'type'. But these characters are made vivid 'from the outside'. What is both fascinating and baffling about Pechorin is that, even when he tells us so much about himself, and even though we 'see' him clearly, his essential character still eludes definition. We cannot be sure whether his confession, which awakens Mary's sympathy, when he tells her of an unhappy childhood and of how the world's misunderstandings of him have made him a 'moral cripple', is a sincere expression of a will to virtue thwarted. If it is, how do we square it with his Machiavellian exclamation in the privacy of his diary—'I love enemies, though not in the Christian way.' We can make sense of him only if we accept that (like Heathcliff, and like certain characters in Dostoevsky) he is a man in whom generous responses and vicious impulses coexist (and this is his cardinal quality) with unresting intelligence.

It is an intelligence which has cut through all the shames of society and has recoiled upon itself to cut away the will to shape any consistent course, to obey any routine, to be stable in anything. More positively, it is an intelligence which permits Pechorin to be as candid in admitting his own cruelties and inconsistencies as he is in exposing the faults of others. It is a wonderful medium through which we can explore the failures and pretences of human nature, and we must, after all, value any searching insights it can offer us. But it has no objectives. It precludes objectives. Like his creator, Pechorin stops short at diagnosis and does not aspire to cure.

Even 'freedom' has come to define itself for him negatively. He could not marry, he says: 'My heart would turn to stone, its warmth gone forever. . . . I'll hazard my life, even my honour, twenty times, but I will not sell my freedom. Freedom is by implication merely the state of being-not-tied. And the final episode of the novel confirms that Pechorin's problem is bound up with his inability to make valuable use of the more positive kinds of freedom which he is not completely sure that he has.

The self-accusations which recur in his diary, along with the occasions when he reports himself as consciously mastering his own feelings, show that he considers himself 'free'. Yet the evening before he goes out to kill Grushnitsky, he declares himself an 'axe in the hands of fate. Like an engine of execution, I've descended on the heads of the condemned, often without malice, but always without pity.'

The last story in the book, 'The Fatalist', comes from Pechorin's time at Maxim Maximych's fort. An officer named Vulich puts a pistol to his head to prove that what happens to men is 'predestined' and pulls the trigger. IT misfires, and Vulich wins his bet. But Pechorin, who has bet against him, has seen on his face that 'strange mark of inevitable doom' which soldiers claim appears a few hours before a man dies. And later that night, Vulich is murdered by a drunken Cossack. To put his own fate to the test, Pechorin risks his life to capture the killer. But nothing, of course, is 'proved'. 'I prefer to doubt everything,' Pechorin concludes. As for Maxim Maximych who has the book's last word, the whole subject of predestination means nothing to him. It is Pechorin's misfortune that his intellect is so developed that he belongs, even more than the rest of his godless and cynical generation, to a world in which the stars have been deprived of their role as arbiters of mankind and in which religious faith is disappearing. His generation, he says, 'drift through the world, without beliefs, pride, pleasure of fear, except that automatic fear that grips us when we think of the certainty of death. We can no longer make great sacrifices for the good of mankind, or even for our own happiness, because we know they are unattainable.'

Pechorin is, truly, a 'moral cripple' because he has no faith in any pattern in or above life which might give shape and hope to his own existence. All that he can conceive is a blind and arbitrary 'fate'. Yet he cannot and does not consistently act as if he were merely 'fate's instrument'. As John Mersereau puts it, . . . 'His occasional recourse to a belief in the power of fate is an act of self-deception, a convenient way to blame an exterior power for the tragic results of the exercise of his will.'

So he is a 'hero of his time' in a wider sense than we might suppose. He is an intellectual frontiersman acting with joyless irresponsibility in a world which has no God. He anticipates Turgenev's Bazarov and Dostoevsky's Raskolnikov, but his actions, unlike those of such later so-called 'nihilists', believers in nothing, have no direction whatsoever except that dictated by the impulse of the moment. Pechorin is *utterly* uncommitted. To draw this comparison, however, is to show his relevance to the Russia of 1840, when there was no 'political' activity except talk, when seduction and frontier fighting and duelling were the only outlets for frustration and when only a few young Hegelian idealists had any positive alternative to offer to a stultified Orthodox Christianity which was subservient to a mindless state.

Victor Ripp   (essay date 1977)

SOURCE: "*A Hero of Our Time* and the Historicism of the 1830s: The Problem of the Whole and the Parts," in *MLN*, Vol. 92, No. 5, December 1977, pp. 969-86.

[*In the following excerpt, Ripp examines the structure of* A Hero of Our Time.]

When Belinskij reviewed *A Hero of Our Time* he immediately noted the book's unusual structure, a vehicle of disjunct and seemingly self-sufficient sections which nevertheless form a seamless entity. In order to explain the "harmonious relationship between the parts and whole" which he claimed to see, Belinskij resorted to a series of analogies. Just as the several organs of man function to their separate ends and still constitute one human being, so may the sections of a work of art fuse meaningfully. Just as discrete things in nature reflect the workings of a common spirit, so may an apparently disharmonious novel possess a deeper unity. These analogies are, in fact, only prods to the imagination, inviting us to supply the logic that explains natural organisms, the perceptual world and novels, as well as the connections between them. But Belinskij's comments at least point to an unavoidable problem in Lermontov's novel.

The problem of the whole and the parts goes back to antiquity, when philosophers first attempted to mediate between the sense of a primordial unity (which in some Christian variations became a pre-Edenic unity, since even differentiation into gender ran counter to the ideal) and an unfortunate fall into bewildering multiplicity. In other words, the problem was never merely formal, concerned with the quantitative paradox that the many equals the one, but from the first entailed existential principles. By the same token, the disjunctive formal structure of *A Hero of Our Time* only makes most visible an issue that pervades the book at every level: the need to make fragmentary experience coherently meaningful, in both a social and personal sense.

An acute awareness of discontinuity and chaos was, in fact, wide-spread in the Russian literature of the 1830's. This attitude was a reaction to the classical orderliness of the preceding period and, more generally, was an aspect of the loss of faith in all public norms following the political debacle of 1825. But in this essay I am less interested in the reasons discontinuity was so significant a concern than in the literary forms the concern took. One response was to write works which were themselves highly discontinuous and chaotic, on the assumption that realism required such a correlation between theme and literary structure. Most of these works receive little mention in literary histories, which is reasonable in terms of their intrinsic merit, but they filled the journals of the period, and numerically at least this literary tendency was probably the most prominent. But there were also various attempts made at reducing chaos to an observable subject within the book, so that the fragmentary and multiplicitous nature of experience was not only depicted but explained.

In choosing his title (and in the "Author's Introduction"), Lermontov obliquely refers to one such attempt. The novel to follow, Lermontov insists, will depict events and characters not only in their particularity but as reflections of the whole epoch. Not Moll Flanders or Pamela or any other single individual is our concern but a Hero who will embody the most general meanings. Pechorin is an emblematic figure, "a composite of all the vices of our generation in the fullness of their development."

This seems a perfect expression of the assumptions underlying the physiological sketch, a genre which sought to impose order on a recalcitrant world by a sort of imaginative synthesis. The physiological sketch had flourished especially in France, for it was there that the concept of the type, on which it is based, had received fullest attention—

in literature, as in Balzac's "Avant-propos" to his *Comedie Humaine,* and still more in the natural sciences, where there was broad-ranging debate whether each species did not have an ideal prototype against which all its members could be measured. But the physiological sketch existed in Russia also and Lermontov himself tried his hand at the form. His effort was entitled "The Caucasian," referring to that sort of Russian who became so infatuated with the outlying regions of the country that he ended up spending his life there. Here is a paragraph from the opening section:

> The Caucasian is a being half-Russian and half-Asian; an inclination for things Asian gains an ascendancy in him but he is ashamed in front of strangers, that is, those who come from Russia. For the most part he is between thirty and forty-five; his face is tanned and somewhat pockmarked; if he is not a captain then he is probably a major.

The fluctuation in focus from one man with highly particularized traits (somewhat pockmarked) to an entity possessing a range of traits beyond the range of any single individual (between thirty and forty-five) recapitulates the rationale of the genre. And this seems to conform to Lermontov's announced intentions in *A Hero of Our Time.* But finally it would be a serious mistake to try to explain Lermontov's achievement by appealing to the physiological sketch, and not simply because this genre came to full prominence in Russia only in the middle of the 1840's. More important is that *A Hero of Our Time* is absolutely alien to the spirit, if not to the formal aspects, of the physiological sketch, to that scientism already implied by the genre's name. However unstable the focus of the physiological sketch, the character described—the "type" himself—does not feel any instability. He is only an object in the author's experimental field, not himself a party to the effort to unify the particular and the general. The effect of this in terms of the literary presentation is to finesse, rather than to confront the problem, since instead of the bafflement of individual experience we are given only the *idea* of the incompleteness of individuality.

Lermontov is more daring. When Pechorin tells us in his diary, "Evil begets evil: the first ache gives us an idea of the pleasure of tormenting another he demonstrates an intelligence beyond any character in a physiological sketch. But Lermontov does not thereby allow Pechorin simply to duplicate the attitude of the author of a physiological sketch. This aphoristic tone points not so much to a general law explaining the particular events which have just occurred as to a desire to find such a law. It is all too obvious that Pechorin's calculatedly off-hand seduction of the naive Princess Mary is something other than a link in a scheme for the mechanical displacement of evil. His statement, and indeed all his comparable graspings after generality, thus possesses a dramatic rather than an explanatory power: it is not really meaningful but it does signal Pechorin's yearning for such a meaning as will fit the randomness of his life to a pattern. Pechorin is not at all a "type," only a character anxiously seeking to become a type.

A Hero of Our Time thus gives full value to immediate experience, life on the level of individual perception; any pattern of generalized meaning must grow from this deeply felt prior commitment. And indeed though Lermontov's title opens up into an attack specifically on the physiological sketch, the novel really calls into question an assumption common to several genres of this period: (following Lukács) I will call it "an architectonic" impulse, an effort at willfully imposing rationality, by somehow papering over the felt disharmony—of either form or content—of a literary work. The scientistic authority supposedly sanctioning the procedures of the physiological sketch had its equivalent in story cycles (the framing device that held together sections disparate in tone and setting) and in those works, characteristic of the 1830's, where the author suddenly intruded into the narrative to justify the aesthetic and ontological status of his own undertaking.

Though all these literary procedures play a role in *A Hero of Our Time,* Lermontov ultimately resists the urge to overcome disharmony by fiat. He employs the method only to show its inadequacies. This is true, above all, for the figure of the author in the book, whose main purpose does indeed seem to be to arrange the parts into a whole, to fit the discrete episodes of Pechorin's existence into an exemplary Life. Since *A Hero of Our Time* calls out for some ordering intelligence, we are more than willing to credit the capabilities of the travelling author who collects, organizes and publishes Pechorin's recollections: he seems *ex officio* to possess an encompassing wisdom. But Lermontov (perhaps from carelessness, but to brilliant effect) has also made this travelling author remarkably resemble Pechorin. It is impossible to distinguish the styles of the chapters they respectively narrate, the two men even seem to have physical and temperamental similarities so that when they confront each other in "Maksim Maksimich" the effect is of mirror images uncannily converging. And the result, finally, is that all the self-confident assertions of the travelling author appear to be only cunning transformations of Pechorin's befuddlement and despair.

That is, though intimations that narrative developments are protections of the author's own personality can in some cases give a work order and purpose, in *A Hero of Our Time* the authorial personality is so thoroughly collapsed into the fiction as to appear swallowed by it. Even Lermontov himself, the historical Lermontov who appears in the "Author's Introduction" to rebut critics of the first edition of the novel, becomes subject to this process. Or rather, Lermontov seems willingly to submit to this devalorization of authorial privilege; for he has consciously made Pechorin a notorious wit, a cynical seducer, an accomplished duelist and an exile to Caucasus, all of which (as contemporaries, not knowing of the intentional fallacy, were exquisitely aware) he was himself. With all these similarities, why should there be a difference in their ability to rise above events in order to explain them?

But, most surprisingly, Lermontov's ironic animadversions to the various methods by which authors expressed the architectonic impulse does not cause *A Hero of Our Time* to lapse into the obvious alternative. The fragmentary nature of experience, including the potential disorganization of every work of art, is a topic the book examines,

not a force it yields to. *A Hero of Our Time,* I shall try to show, exists in a most narrowly defined area, avoiding both the facile assertion of harmony and the accession to disharmony.

Lermontov's achievement in this regard was an innovation, but the ground had been prepared by at least one element in the intellectual tradition. The historicism of the 1830's, as manifested in historical novels and historical theorizing, also opposed any architectonic methods, also developed within the framework of the parts/whole problem and also scrutinized the nature of individual experience. If history is not often considered in connection with *A Hero of Our Time,* and it is not, this is because the concept is often defined too narrowly, in a way that fails to comprehend contemporary usage. A good indication of this usage is given in the following comment by the critic Nadezhdin, who is also pertinent because he was acutely sensitive to the chaos that threatened literary forms during this period. In discussing Bulgarin's immensely popular and immensely disorganized *Ivan Vyzhigin,* Nadezhdin approvingly noted its realistic setting and convincing characters; but, he said, events cannot simply follow events. What was needed was some sense of a unified form lending purpose to the narrative line. Ideally, "the novel is nothing but the poeticization of history."

Making history a category of judgment here may appear surprising, since *Ivan Vyzhigin* has absolutely nothing historical about it. Either Nadezhdin is an especially wrong-headed critic or history for him implies something more than a concern with national development. That the second alternative obtains is made clear when Nadezhdin tells us explicitly why a novel about contemporary life must fail. The present, Nadezhdin says, impinges on us immediately, so that it affects us only through random sensations. For events to pass into the patterning power of our understanding they must be at some remove—which usually means distanced in time. According to this reasoning, even a work as elegantly structured as Pushkin's *Eugene Onegin* must necessarily appear disorganized, and indeed Nadezhdin disliked it.

The model of experience underlying Nadezhdin's argument is of course the one made influential by Kant, however altered and overhauled it was subsequently: The world is a manifold of unordered events, incomprehensible except as the mind can impose its own categories. Life becomes an on-going struggle against bewildering multiplicity, meaningless succession. In this scheme history occupies an ambiguous place. As events taking place in the world, history seemingly belongs to the unpatterned realm of phenomena, and to this realm Kant had indeed consigned it. But Kant also felt that history could imply a rational order, that the superficially erratic behavior of men resolved itself into a pattern. It was this second possibility, history in its stable and transcendent dimension, that particularly attracted Nadezhdin and many of his Russian contemporaries.

A persuasive claim for such an overarching rationality clearly held important consequences for the fiction of the period. For authors writing out of this conviction, meaningful unity could be the natural expression of a sincere belief, instead of the results of that artificial effort of will which I have called the architectonic impulse. But to make this advantageous situation a practical possibility, it was first necessary to show precisely how this rationality was to be grasped and made available to men in those everyday activities which form the stuff of fiction.

The attempt to explicate such a comprehension of the rational historical order in fact helped fuel that intense debate in the 1830's which focussed on Karamzin's *The History of the Russian State*. It was Karamzin's intent, and his achievement also, to bring the largely unknown Russian past to the contemporary consciousness. For this he was widely admired; but his specific procedures were also widely criticized. In his preface Karamzin divides historical writing into two varieties. The first, which he called "contemporary" history, relied on the imaginative reconstruction of events, the past made alive by the positing of an "apparent witness." Karamzin granted that this approach could appear brilliant and creative; these epithets, however, are pejorative when applied to the historian. The second variety of history, which confines itself to chronicles and other documents, may be more modest but it is also more correct. Where contemporaries kept silent, Karamzin says, so also must the historian.

Much of the criticism directed against Karamzin concerned his political bias, which in *The History* is conservative and autocratic. But the relevant point to my discussion is that this bias follows from his operative categories and, in fact, the major work in rebuttal, Polevoj's *The History of the Russian People*, considers Karamzin's method at some length. Polevoj notes in his preface that it was specifically by confining himself to documentary sources that Karamzin revealed not real history, which is often silent, but only a history of princes—hence Polevoj's own, corrective, title. Karamzin's *History* is thus shown to be something more than a simpleminded ploy to solicit the kindness of authorities; it also reveals the epistemological assumption that historical acts possess an inherent order which can be easily commemorated in documents, a belief that a past sequence of events is immediately meaningful—simply because it is in the past. Karamzin, says Polevoj in another essay, records an event and thinks he has fulfilled his duty: "he does not know, he does not want to know that an important event does not grow up like a mushroom after the rain, that the reasons are deeply hidden."

It is important to note again that whatever the disagreements among the participants in the debate about history—and Karamzin and Polevoj probably represent the extreme positions—virtually all were equally convinced of the ultimate rationality of history. The historian must modestly serve as a transmitter of a graspable reality. Certainly for both Karamzin and Polevoj, the historian's detachment, his willingness not to impose his own meanings, was crucial. But the various ways they define this attitude begin to suggest the difficulties for any fictive use of history. Karamzin's position in this regard is at least seemingly straightforward, since he claims only to organize previously valorized documents. To Polevoj, this is deceitful, and irrelevant besides. To do his job properly the historian must immerse himself in the period he describes, resisting the false privilege of retrospection. Only by divesting himself of the prejudices of his own time and confronting past reality directly can the historian fit the ambiguous succession of visible events to an invisible larger pattern. The variations in the historical vision of these two men mark out the conceptual limits of the historical novel also. The agreement about the objectively existing rational order gave the new genre a bracing self-confidence in its ultimate intelligibility, so that for a while historical novels proliferated. But the disagreement about how best to explicate this rational order without loss of authorial detachment led to an almost total confusion about proper narrative method, and soon to extinction of the genre.

Specifically, the technical problem forced on the historical novel was the proper relationship between actual historical events and characters and fictive events and characters—between the symbols of a rational pattern and the embodiments of erratic and unpredictable life. Indeed, when Zagoskin in the first and most influential historical novel, *Jurij Miloslavskij*, used footnotes to introduce historically factual material, he was only setting in most naked form the problematic which all subsequent historical novels had to resolve: was it enough merely to get history onto the page, or did it somehow have to be assimilated to the plot? (Odoevskij, an important writer of the period expressed the problem neatly: "Scott put the novel into history; his imitators, especially we Russians, put history into the novel." It was fatuous, Odoevskij said, merely to cut some pages from a book on Russian history and, by pasting them together, to expect to produce a proper Russian novel. Interestingly, the history Odoevskij cited by way of example was Karamzin's. Given Karamzin's reputation for viewing the past as petrified set of facts, it could be argued that the historical novelist who relied on *The History of the Russian State* was twice distanced from his real task, which was not to posit a simple unity but rather to transcend disunity by actively confronting it.)

The most programmatic assertion that the historical novelist must proceed by a willing immersion in historical reality—a narrative formed around that "apparent witness" despised by Karamzin—appears, not surprisingly, in the preface to Polevoj's own novel, *Oath by the Lord's Grave*. But Lermontov himself exemplified this tendency in his incomplete historical novel, **Vadim.** Though the action takes place during the Pugachev uprising, this momentous event receives remarkably little explicit attention. Russia's social upheaval seems to serve merely as the occasion for Vadim's personal revenge. But this only shows the rationale of this strain of the historical novel as its extreme: history does not lie at our feet waiting to be picked up, but its hovering presence can transfix even the most erratic individual passions and invest them with meaning.

One passage in **Vadim** is particularly worth considering in this respect:

> The amazed crowd looked at him as he left, and by the rapid hoofbeats they guessed Vadim had taken off at a gallop.
>
> Where to? What for? To relate all their opinions

I would require the talent of Walter Scott and the patience of his readers.

Though Lermontov in fact admired Scott greatly, he invokes him here mainly to indicate his shortcomings, or at least his irrelevance to the sort of historical novel Lermontov envisioned. In this passage Scott stands as a handy symbol for the author who would claim that experience can be exhaustively described, that a diligent accumulation of detail will add up to a totality of meaning. In *Vadim* the path from fragmented experience to unified pattern is more problematic. *Vadim* subjectivizes History; but that subjectivity is saved from solipsism—or at least from feeling itself as solipsism—by the confidence that everything operates within the confines of an ultimate rationality, that the most extreme individuality is finally an intimate part of the whole.

It hardly needs to be said that *A Hero of Our Time* belongs to an altogether different genre—Lermontov's title is, among other things, an endorsement of purely contemporary concerns. But in thus advertising a modern focus, the title must necessarily refer obliquely to the antiquarian one it replaces; and if Pechorin's problem is the bafflingly diverse impulses of contemporary man, its presentation often involves a revision of the conceptual apparatus which moved the historical novel. Specifically, the concern with some meaning overarching men's petty activities is still acute. Nor is it very important that this meaning is no longer looked for in the suprapersonal historical dimension, since this is more a matter of changing interests (questions of history having passed from fashion) than changing logical assumptions. The crucial alteration is more subtle, an altered emotional context—for what was once a naive faith in the existence of a rational order has given way to a desperate nostalgia for it.

This is most obvious in the treatment of nature. The opening section, "Bela," continually alludes to the privileged status of the Caucasus as a silent, peaceful and beautiful realm, and at one point Lermontov asserts explicitly that to ascend Mt. Gud means to escape the world of man's petty activities. Vistas of the Caucasus, expressive of an eternal changelessness, seem to stand in for the stability once associated with the rationality of history. But from the first, the insistence on nature's iconic powers is sufficiently strident to arouse suspicion. And indeed when we are admonished to restrain our interest in the narrative of Pechorin's adventures in favor of listening to nature descriptions—since this "is not a novella" but "travel notes"—one informing idea becomes clear: nature and the affairs of men occupy radically different spheres, irretrievably distanced from one another.

By the beginning of "Maksim Maksimich," the author's attitude has shifted to irritated ineffectuality, an expressed feeling that the fullness of nature's meaning entirely escapes his attempts to describe it. It follows that although Pechorin may often muse on the divine plan he sees signalled in the stars, the philosophical questions this raises are never resolved, not even perfunctorily. Fate may indeed determine men's every action, but Pechorin's animating idea throughout the novel is consciously to ignore, since he cannot controvert, this possibility. Pechorin ob-

stinately refuses to make his life dependent on any external contingency; he knows that symbols of order, nature among them, only tantalize men with meanings which can never be assimilated to the concrete problems of life.

In general, *A Hero of Our Time* proceeds not merely without a symbol of the transcendent order but with a perceptible vacuum where that symbol should be. And though this atmosphere can, and often does, drive Pechorin to profound despair, his best effort is rather to tease meaning from this world which seems designed to deny him one. For Lermontov has thoroughly understood the reason the historical novel sought to present a comprehensive vision, even though he works to deflate its facile pretensions in that direction: Alone, man collapses into solipsism, and the fragmentary quality of lived experience becomes not only an undeniable aspect of life but the only one. Pechorin must therefore create his meanings, construct that extra-personal pattern that is not given by the world.

Hence the curious aimlessness of the book, a sense of uncertainty not about how to win necessary battles but about how to define a battleground in order to fight at all. "Taman," for example, relates Pechorin's visit to a provincial town and his involvement, almost ending in his death, with a band of native smugglers, the blind boy, his beautiful sister and old mother, and the demonic Yanko. This cast of stock characters accurately reflects the quality of the story, which is full of excessive passion and exotic occupations. There must be some point to this episode; but we are given no hint what it is or how to respond, and Pechorin himself is content to narrate the events with no comment. Pechorin—and we with him—seem caught in a situation that is all event and no meaning, a complex intrigue with no point except continuous excitement. Only in the very last lines of the section is there an indication of a different attitude:

> What became of the old woman and the poor blind boy I do not know. And besides, what do I care about human joys and sorrows—I, a military man on the move, and holder, moreover, of a roadpass issued to those on official business.

This abrupt withdrawal from the concerns of the plot (which at this point is still completely unresolved), especially when followed by the reference to the prosaic circumstances of travel in Tsarist Russia, must put the preceding tale into a new perspective. Pechorin apparently is in a privileged position relative to the other characters, capable of moving from their highly charged romantic setting to a level defined by emphatically different concerns. He is not merely a participant in the intrigue, not merely the baffled adversary of that band of smugglers. To be sure, it remains unclear precisely what Pechorin is, and precisely how much his vision encompasses. Nevertheless Pechorin has in his possession an instrument enabling him to transcend the blank sequentiality of mere experience. Self-consciousness, even if it is consciousness of oneself as hopelessly baffled, can transform sensation into knowledge.

Self-consciousness may also lead to intellectual paralysis. But this is a necessary risk, given Pechorin's options. The alternative, whether it takes the form of dangerous adventure or erotic pursuit, is a life tailing off into a desperate randomness. Thus Pechorin's feelings for both Bela and Princess Mary always threaten to degenerate into merely fitful gestures, performed with progressively diminishing energy as the stimulus loses its novelty. Pechorin has consciously—self-consciously—to struggle to turn these encounters into affairs of enduring interest. His manipulation of others during this effort is of course morally reprehensible; but his behavior also involves a manipulation of himself, a projection of his errant impulses into a role which might transform common experience into a complex drama demanding sustained attention. Pechorin's is an effort to "poeticize" not history but the present, and thus keep it from slipping away down the unresistant and sharp incline of mere sensation.

By consciously assuming the role of a Don Juan, of a dandy, of a cynical duelist, as well as spontaneously yielding to the emotion from which these types derive, Pechorin manages to construct a sense of himself that escapes pure subjectivity; for once assumed, these roles proceed in some measure according to a conventional logic. They belong to the world as much as to Pechorin. By the same token, it is worth noting how often Pechorin's relations with others simultaneously encompass several interests and topics. The aim here also is not to find a natural situation permitting the direct expression of feeling but rather to establish a psychological environment which will disperse and check mere appetite. The paradigm for this dynamic is given in "Bela," where the love intrigue is suspended in a broader context including the actions and demands of Kazbich. Eroticism is intimately mixed with horse-trading, possession of woman with manly competition and cunning, and all these activities are in consequence deflected from their immediate goal and sustained beyond their normally short term. And this dynamic is even more crucial in the novel's longest section, "Princess Mary," where Pechorin's interest in seduction is inextricably tied to his desire to manipulate his rival, Grushnitskij.

If the short-livedness of instinctual behavior were the only issue in the novel, Pechorin's strategies might be considered reasonably successful. But this is only one aspect of the difficulty. To Lermontov the main problem of experience lies elsewhere, and it is so presented in this novel as to make Pechorin's specific efforts always incomplete. The reason that life constantly skirts chaos is only partly because feelings die quickly; it is also because it is difficult to know exactly where to direct feelings, for fully to accept the priority of individual reactions is to accept a world where everyone seems only an aspect of the self. Lermontov suggests as much when he refuses significantly to distance Pechorin from his creator. But the same apparently debilitating idea informs many relationships in *A Hero of Our Time.* Of Doctor Werner Pechorin says, "Between us there can be no exchange of feelings and thought: we know everything about each other we wish to know and we do not wish to know anything more." So they sit in mute inactivity, admiring their externalized selves.

It is thus telling that throughout the book, every character who contests Pechorin, thereby assuming a degree of otherness, also always evokes in him a spontaneous admira-

tion, sometimes even a tender regard. Kazbich's impulsive and athletic derring-do in "Bela," Yanko's demonic inscrutability in "Taman," Vulich's coolness in the face of death in "The Fatalist" all occasion Pechorin's respect—as well they might, since these are all traits he admires in himself. Though *A Hero of Our Time* is a book given over to expressions of hate and will to dominate, there is no real conflict in it, nor can there be when every potential opposing force turns out on inspection to be an aspect of the hero—who is himself an aspect of the author.

Even Grushnitskij, whom Pechorin kills in a duel, is made to appear as a sort of surrogate. Indeed, though this relationship seems to culminate in the absolute antagonism which death must suggest, it is here that Lermontov most fully reveals the nature of the bonds between Pechorin and the other characters. From their first encounter, when Pechorin echoes an epigram of Grushnitskij's, a potential for identification is signalled; but just as Pechorin alters the epigram in a way that deflates the original utterance, so does he generally stand in oblique relation to Grushnitskij. When Pechorin tells us, for example, that Grushnitskij believed "that he is not made for this world and is doomed to suffer in secret," he indicates an attitude which is not unlike his own; but by his mocking tone, Pechorin also measures the gap between such vague discontent and his own pervasive nihilism. It is therefore in a very special sense that Grushnitskij is a copy of Pechorin: Pechorin makes him one in order simultaneously to argue his own encompassing vision. Pechorin does indeed know more than Grushnitskij, and what he knows is Grushnitskij.

The duel scene where Grushnitskij passes abruptly from conniver to naive victim—while Pechorin easily describes the innermost thoughts accompanying this transition(!)—neatly symbolizes this difference in understanding. And Pechorin's killing of Grushnitskij must be seen less as the instance of gratuitous cruelty that it first appears to be than the simple privilege of knowledge. In this context an off-hand remark of Pechorin's takes on special significance. He says, "Grushnitskij does not know people and their vulnerable spots since all his life he has been occupied with his own self. His object is to become the hero of a novel." Grushnitskij is thus not only a falling off from Pechorin but a falling off in a specific direction, towards a too exclusive subjectivity. And significantly this limitation is now equated with literariness. Conversely it is Pechorin's ability to make such a comparison that marks his own encompassing vision. But of course the reference to literature does something more. It must remind us that Pechorin is himself only a literary hero, himself encompassed. He stands in the same relative position to the author as Grushnitskij does to him.

Lermontov has thus replaced the historical novel's enthusiastic assumption of a transcendent rational order with a process of gradual transcendence toward such an ideal. Only there is a final twist to Lermontov's procedure. Since much of *A Hero of Our Time* is devoted to denying any authorial pretensions to an overarching, synthesizing role, the agent who should stand at the end of this process, the author himself, can never really deliver the knowledge that has been promised. Finally there is no point of view in the book that reliably unites all the particulars of experience by organizing them in accordance with an unswerving meaning. But for Lermontov's purpose it is enough—it is precisely to the point—to show that while the resulting instability is undeniable and pervasive, total chaos is not. In brief, the informing attitude of *A Hero of Our Time* is ironic, a realization that all certainty is only apparent—except only the certainty of this realization itself.

Even viewed in isolation, this position is considerably more flexible, susceptible to more self-sustaining elaboration, than my formulation of it might suggest, and Pechorin's energetically varied activities prove this. Nevertheless it is true that an ironic stance derives much of its force from an awareness of other rhetorical stances thus avoided. Irony is tacit polemic; and since the historical novel, along with the widespread theorizing about history, neatly focuses this polemical thrust, it is worthwhile to reconsider this topic briefly.

For to claim that the task of the historian was to use the past to explain the present—for example, by convincing contemporaries to countenance inequity, since inequity has always been an element in the world—was not only to slant history toward a particular political orientation, but also to publicize one specific rhetorical mode. Karamzin, who did indeed define the historian's task in this way, was in effect striving after meaning by comparing two terms, one known (the fixed, rational past) and one largely unknown (the uncertain—especially politically uncertain—present). Polevoj, in seeming contrast, held that events were important not as they bore on the present but to the extent they participated in a unified and transcendental meaning, which he called Reason, or sometimes the Whole. What is pertinent here, however, is that though Polevoj wishes to show history in a different aspect, his rhetorical strategy is similar to Karamzin's. Both men claim that true knowledge arises by a purposeful juxtaposition of two terms whereby the graspable meaning of one illuminates the opacity of the other. This is to view the world synecdochically.

It is worth noting, however briefly, that the synecdochic mode informed the substantive aspect of the debate as well as its methodological concerns. The burning issue of the day was the place of Russia as an item on the agenda of world development. Writers could disagree radically on this question, but the possibility that Russia was (or was not) a part of a larger multinational whole provided the framework in which the disagreement invariably took place. Thus even Chaadaev's enormously influential attack on Russia's isolation from Europe in his *Philosophical Letters*—"We have no universal ideas, everything is individual, volatile, incomplete"—is only a more brilliant and persuasive rearrangement of the common frame of reference, rather than strikingly innovative. The pervasiveness of the synecdochic mode might perhaps be indicated by one example from literary history: Marlinskij and Polevoj, though focussing on different books, both objected to the same inconspicuous feature of Zagoskin's procedure, his subtitles. But the reason Polevoj objected to *Jurij Milosvaskij: The Russians in 1612* and Marlinskij to the later *Roslavlev: The Russians in 1812* was not that Zagoskin

was presumptuous to claim that one group of characters could represent the whole of Russia, only that he had not adequately carried the plan through. All three men intuitively adopt a synecdochic viewpoint.

A Hero of Our Time is ironic specifically in relation to this kind of reasoning. That is, it does not ignore but rather emphatically acknowledges the desire to fit the fragmented aspects of life, the moments of experience, to a general pattern. If this project is ultimately and necessarily impossible, the feeling which sustains it is nonetheless fully credited, depicted as a real and reasonable aspect of man. But *A Hero of Our Time* goes beyond a naive acknowledgement of chaos to offer some relief from this existential deadlock. Though no one in the novel, from Grushnitskij to the author, manages to pierce the opacity of the subjective experience and attain a consequent view of an overriding pattern, this dismal limitation of the self is attenuated by being made subject to a systematic scrutiny. Real transcendence of personal experience is impossible, Lermontov tells us, but by contemplating the universal urge in this direction, we can rise above the chaos that would otherwise envelop us. Irony in *A Hero of Our Time* means sincerely to live one's life as if it had that ultimate reasonableness it clearly lacks. It is a self-conscious acceptance of the limitations of knowledge which thereby extends one's knowledge, at least fractionally.

It is at this point that I must turn to a question that is in fact everywhere implied by Lermontov's method of presentation: the role of the critic. For critics do seem to possess an especially privileged viewpoint, they do seem capable of encompassing in their interpretive reflex not only everything Lermontov encompassed but Lermontov himself, and thus capable as well of providing the stable overriding explanation *A Hero of Our Time* lacks in itself. Of course if we take Lermontov at all seriously, and do not relegate the issues he raises to the confines of a book, then we must realize that with such a privilege goes a responsibility—the injunction to be suspicious of all claims to a transcendent wisdom which do not simultaneously credit actual experience in all its surprising particularity, which in the case of the critic means the experience of reading each word. No critic felt this injunction more keenly than Belinskij in the review of *A Hero of Our Time,* which I mentioned at the beginning of this essay. Interestingly, Belinskij's response takes a form we usually associate with an inadequate critical performance, the copying out of long excerpts from the novel. But before we condemn Belinskij for a failure of imagination, we should consider his explanation:

> There is nothing more burdensome and unpleasant than to set forth the contents of an artistic work. The aim of such a summary does not consist in indicating the best sections: no matter how good a section of the work, it is good in its relation to the whole, and consequently summary must have the aim of tracing the idea of the whole work, of showing how faithfully this has been realized by the poet. And how is this to be done? It is impossible to copy out the whole work; but how should sections be chosen from out of an excellent whole while ignoring others so as not to have the excerpts go beyond neces-

sary limits? And, then, how are the excerpts to be tied together by one's own prosaic narrative, which leaves in the book the shadows and the colors, the life and the soul, and retains only the dead skeleton? We now especially feel the full weight and the difficulty of execution of the responsibility we have taken on ourselves. We

---

An excerpt from *A Hero of Our Time*

It's two in the morning. I can't sleep, though I ought to get some sleep if I'm to have a steady hand in the morning. Though it's difficult to miss at six paces. Ah, Grushnitsky, your ruse won't work. The roles will be reversed—it'll be I who studies your pale face for the marks of hidden fear. Why did you choose these fatal six paces? Do you think I'll meekly be your target? Oh no, we'll draw lots and then . . . then . . . What if your luck holds out against mine? What if my star lets me down at last? It might well do, for it's pandered to my whims long enough, and there's no more constancy in heaven than on earth.

What if it does? If I die, I die. It will be small loss to the world, and I've had about enough of it myself. I'm like a man yawning at a ball who doesn't go home to bed because his carriage hasn't come. But when it arrives-farewell!

I've been going over my past, and I can't help wondering why I've lived, for what purpose I was born. There must have been some purpose, I must have had some high object in life, for I feel unbounded strength within me. But I never discovered it and was carried away by the allurements of empty, unrewarding passions. I was tempered in their flames and came out cold and hard as steel, but I'd lost for ever the fire of noble endeavour, that finest flower of life. How many times since then have I been the axe in the hands of fate? Like an engine of execution, I've descended on the heads of the condemned, often without malice, but always without pity. My love has brought no one happiness, for I've never sacrificed a thing for those I've loved. I've loved for myself, for my own pleasure, I've only tried to satisfy a strange inner need. I've fed on their feelings, love, joys and sufferings, and always wanted more. I'm like a starving man who falls asleep exhausted and sees rich food and sparkling wines before him. He rapturously falls on these phantom gifts of the imagination and feels better, but the moment he wakes up his dream disappears and he's left more hungry and desperate than before.

And perhaps tomorrow I'll die, and then there'll be no one who could ever really understand me. Some will think me worse, others better than in fact I am. Some will say I was a good fellow, others that I was a swine. Neither will be right. So why bother to live? One just goes on living out of curiosity, waiting for something new. It's absurd and annoying.

Mikhail Yuryevich Lermontov, in A Hero of Our Time, *Penguin Books, 1966.*

---

have even before this point lost ourselves in the multiplicity of wonderful parts, and now, when the most important section of the work is upon us, we would most like to copy out word for word the author's complete tale, in which every word, with infinite meaning, with profound significance, exudes such poetic vitality, shines with such luxurious richness of colors; but nevertheless we are constrained as before to retell in our own way, as much as possible keeping the expressions of the original and copying out sections.

Belinskij's desperate knowledge that meaning resides in the totality of the literary object is the critical equivalent of Lermontov's quest for a truly encompassing vision, and both men fully appreciate the obstacles to success. Only through the concrete particular does the whole acquire vitality; but the particular can also fatally hold one's vision at the level of fragmented experience.

Though there is in fact no need of an inventory of details such as Belinskij's advocates (since it would only duplicate the novel already in hand), it is also emphatically true that attempts to impose pattern on *A Hero of Our Time* can at best only approach comprehensive explanation. The novel's meaning will always hover beyond our capability to grasp it fully—except of course we realize that this is its meaning. *A Hero of Our Time* is the fascinating account of Pechorin's Caucasian adventures. It is also, and more importantly, an instrument for showing the limits of knowledge, which once learned, allow us to view all of life anew.

W. W. Rowe   (essay date 1979)

SOURCE: "Duality and Symmetry in Lermontov's *A Hero of Our Time*," in *Nabokov and Others: Patterns in Russian Literature*, Ardis, 1979, pp. 27-36.

[*In the following essay, Rowe examines the symmetrical pairing of elements such as episodes, actions, descriptions, speeches, and characters in* A Hero of Our Time.]

Commentators have been justifiably intrigued by the patterning of Lermontov's novel [*A Hero of Our Time*]. Despite its five parts and three narrators, however, the work seems most informed by duality as a structural principle. Even individual episodes, actions, descriptions, speeches continually occur in pairs. Moreover, there often seems to be a balancing of these pairs. In several cases, the spacing of this balancing within the novel promotes a remarkable symmetry.

To begin with, the novel easily "divides into two basic parts", as K. Loks has put it, with two corresponding introductions. Loks also sees the novel as comprising two planes. The first one involves Pechorin's relationship to other people; the second, his inner self. Somewhat similarly, Viktor Vinogradov observes that "the image of Pechorin is depicted on two planes"—outside observation and self-disclosure. In his view, this results in a novel of two parts, each with its own inner unity but organically bound to each other by semantic parallelism. Boris Eikhenbaum has used the term "dual composition" to suggest the development of a complex plot in conjunction with a gradual revelation of the hero's inner world.

Much of the duality in the novel relates to the hero. V. G. Belinsky has described the "duality of Pechorin" by paraphrasing what the latter tells Werner: "Within me there are two persons: one of them lives in the full sense of the word, the other cogitates and judges him." Earlier, Pechorin suggests to Princess Mary that his soul split in two early in life: "One half of my soul . . . had died . . . the other half stirred and lived . . . ."

This pair of statements seems part of a larger patterning. We encounter two descriptions of Pechorin by the other two narrators and two by himself. First, Maksim Maksimich describes him as "a little odd". Pechorin, we learn, is sometimes cowardly, sometimes brave; alternately taciturn and garrulous. The author's "portrait" of Pechorin also features contrasts and contradictions. His arms do not swing when he walks, and his eyes do not laugh when he is laughing. This description is framed by two yawns, the second of which is said to be feigned.

Pechorin's two descriptions of himself seem calculated to engage the pity of his listener. The first, told to Maksim Maksimich, is of his "unfortunate disposition." The second, told to Princess Mary, is of his becoming "a moral cripple" early in life.

Pechorin persuades two women quite similarly. With Bela, he supposes that she may love someone else. "Or is it," he continues, that she finds him completely hateful. "Or" does her faith forbid her to return his feelings. Later, Pechorin urges Vera to renew their affair: perhaps she loves her second husband. "Or is he very jealous?" Or perhaps she fears losing his money. After these two speeches, we read vivid descriptions of the two women's eyes: Bela's express "distrust" and Vera's "despair"; but each soon gives in to Pechorin's wishes.

The similarity of these two persuasion scenes and of many other pairs of incidents throughout the novel almost gives one a feeling that destiny is being replayed. As Nabokov has observed of "The Fatalist," the scene of Vulich with the pistol ". . . curiously echoes that of the duel in 'Princess Mary,' and there are other echoes further on (. . . 'this is becoming a bore,' and . . . 'I became bored with the long procedure')." Earlier, Mr. Nabokov remarks that in "The Fatalist," ". . . the crucial passage also turns on a pistol being or not being loaded . . . and a kind of duel by proxy is fought between Pechorin and Vulich, with Fate, instead of the smirking dragoon, supervising the lethal arrangements." Another parallel perhaps mentally adduced by Nabokov: "You are a strange fellow!" (to Pechorin) and "What an odd fellow!" (of Vulich). There is even a discernible echo of Pechorin's feigned awakening by officers immediately after the garden chase in his real awakening by officers after Vulich's death—just as the imaginary nocturnal terrorists of the first scene perhaps correspond to the drunken Efimich and his nocturnal slayings.

Pechorin's experiences seem to come before the reader in twos. He is grazed by two bullets—on the knee by Grushnitsky and on the shoulder by Efimich. He overhears two

key plots—against Princess Mary and against himself. These are to embarrass her at the dance and to humiliate him in a sham duel, both of which he later thwarts. He learns two important secrets from Werner, both times cautioning the latter not to reveal them further. These are Princess Mary's "pleasant delusion" regarding Grushnitsky's rank and the "murderous alteration" to load only Grushnitsky's pistol. Pechorin then exploits both secrets quite devastatingly.

With varying degrees of irony, Pechorin announces both to Vera and to Grushnitsky that he plans to flirt with, or court, Princess Mary. Later he is informed both by the young Princess and by the old Princess that his rank and "situation" are not serious obstacles. He also performs a rather ironic "bow" before each Princess. The first follows the mother's suggestion that he is "a gentleman"; the second, her daughter's statement, "I hate you."

Pechorin warns Grushnitsky twice and "tests" him twice. The warnings relate to asking Princess Mary for the mazurka ("Look out, you might be forestalled,") and ascending to the duel ground ("Don't fall beforehand"). In the "tests," Pechorin twice scrutinizes Grushnitsky. As the Dragoon Captain proposes his plan to humiliate Pechorin: "In a tremor of eagerness, I awaited Grushnitsky's reply . . . If Grushnitsky had refused, I would have thrown myself upon his neck." Then, at the duel: "I decided to give Grushnitsky every advantage; I wished to test him. A spark of magnanimity might awaken in his soul . . . but vanity and weakness of character were to triumph!"

Pechorin squelches the Dragoon Captain twice: "So it was you that I hit so awkwardly on the head?" and "If so, you and I will fight a duel on the same conditions." Both times, the Captain observes a painful, chagrined silence. Pechorin also twice toys with Werner. First, the latter is allowed to believe he has crucially cautioned Pechorin against marriage: "Werner left, fully convinced that he had put me on my guard." Then, prior to the duel, Pechorin suggests to his worried friend that "the expectation of a violent death" is a "genuine illness": "This thought impressed the doctor and he cheered up."

As Nabokov has observed, Pechorin notices two corpses near the end of "Princess Mary": Grushnitsky's and that of his own horse. He also receives "two notes," one from Werner ("sleep in peace . . . if you can") and one from Vera ("in none is evil so attractive"). The second seems a direct echo of Pechorin's earlier thoughts of Vera ("What does she love me for so much . . . Can evil possibly be so attractive?"). And this pair of references to "attractive evil" seems paralleled by another pair of "vice" references. Pechorin declared that Vera "is the only woman who has completely understood me with all my petty weaknesses and wicked passions." This tends to recall the author's introductory assertion that Pechorin is "composed of all the vices of our generation in the fullness of their development." Quite rightly, this pair of references suggests that Vera's note (which John Mersereau, Jr. terms "the final verdict on Pechorin") is more informative than either the pair of descriptions by the two narrators or the pair by Pechorin himself. Thus, the end of

Vera's description ("none can be so genuinely unhappy as you, because none tries so hard to convince himself of the contrary") both echoes and explains Pechorin's earlier dilemma: ". . . I only know that if I am a cause of unhappiness for others, I am no less unhappy myself." This statement, in turn, forms yet another pair with Pechorin's sad suspicion that his "only function on earth is to ruin other people's hopes." Finally, this pair seems paralleled by yet another. For in the words of Richard Freeborn, who sees Pechorin as "seducer, or pretender to that role" with Princess Mary and "executioner" to Grushnitsky: "In both cases he tries to mitigate his vengeful role by the private justification that he . . . 'played the miserable role of executioner or traitor' or, as he puts it on the eve of his duel with Grushnistky: 'how many times I have played the role of an axe in the hands of fate.' "

Pechorin and Grushnitsky form an obvious pair. They frequently evince similar intentions leading to opposite results—a balance climaxed by their duel. Pechorin writes that Grushnitksy's "object is to become the hero of a novel." Werner says that for Princess Mary, Pechorin has become "the hero of a novel in the latest fashion." Pechorin playfully twists Grushnitsky's French aphorism by substituting a despising of women for a hatred of men. Oddly enough, the two are reversed even in appearance: Pechorin seems no more than twenty-three, though he might be thirty; Grushnitsky looks about twenty-five, yet he is hardly twenty-one.

In yet another association, Pechorin preempts an imaginary Grushnitsky. For as Nabokov has noted, Pechorin utters to Princess Mary the same sort of speech he had earlier imagined Grushnitsky telling her. Both speeches are to the effect: "No, you had better not know what is in my soul!"

Perhaps still more ironically, Pechorin's resourceful imagination arranges a victory which seems to be replayed as a defeat. His words to Bela ("Farewell, I am going—where? How should I know? Perchance, I shall not be long running after a bullet or a sword blow: remember me then. . . .") are echoed in Vera's letter ("Farewell, farewell . . . I perish—but what does it matter? If I could be sure that you will always remember me . . ."). Before, Pechorin's victory with Princess Mary echoed the words he had contemptuously assigned to Grushnitsky; now, his loss of Vera is underscored by the echo of his successful words to Bela.

As "Princess Mary" begins, Pechorin opens his window early in the morning: ". . . my room was filled with the perfume of flowers growing in the modest front garden." Soon after, he first sees Princess Mary: ". . . there emanated from her that ineffable fragrance which breathes sometimes from a beloved woman's letter." This early pair of references to emanating fragrance are reflected in another, crucial pair later on. First, there is Pechorin's famous pronouncement: ". . . there is boundless delight in the possession of a young, barely unfolded soul! It is like a flower whose best fragrance emanates to meet the first ray of the sun. It should be plucked that very minute and after inhaling one's fill of it, one should throw it away on the road: perchance, someone will pick it up!." This rather

cruel attitude (a plucked flower soon dies, even if "picked up") presumably suggests Pechorin's treatment of Princess Mary. Soon after this, he tells her: "One half of my soul . . . had withered away—while the other half stirred and lived . . . . " Here, Pechorin is explaining how he became "a moral cripple": misunderstood as a young boy, he "learned to hate." And his eloquence seems most successfully to counter Princess Mary's charge that he is "worse than a murderer": " . . . she was sorry for me!" In the overall context, however, Pechorin seems to be admitting that his attitude towards Princess Mary is a sort of revenge: the desire to pluck a young soul-flower (above, in his journal) smacks of retaliation for having been driven to cut away half of his own flower-soul.

Still greater irony derives from what may be termed the horse-goat/woman theme. Azamat's double theft (goat, Bela) seems paralleled by Kazbich's song: "Gold can purchase you a foursome of wives,/ But a spirited steed is a priceless possession." This seems especially so because Pechorin simultaneously loses both Vera and his own horse at the end of "Princess Mary." Moreover, losing Karagyoz, Kazbich "fell on the ground and began to sob like a child." Losing Vera, Pechorin "fell on the wet grass and began crying like a child." The irony reaches its climax in the following pair of descriptions. In "Princess Mary" Pechorin had declared: "I love to gallop on a spirited horse through tall grass . . . the soul feels easy . . . There is no feminine gaze that I would not forget. . . ." After reading Vera's letter: "Like a madman, I . . . galloped . . . I galloped on, breathless with impatience. . . . I felt that she had become dearer to me than anything in the world . . . !"

The overall dualistic pattern of *A Hero of Our Time* seems reflected even in Lermontov's use of individual words. Early in "Princess Mary," Pechorin predicts that he and Grushnitsky will "meet on a narrow path, and one of us will fare ill." Later, Pechorin insists that the duel be fought on "a narrow bit of flat nature", so that a light wound will be fatal. Just prior to the duel, Pechorin is struck by the blueness and freshness of the morning: he feels "a kind of delicious languor" and is "in love with nature." As "Princess Mary" began, he had also noted the blueness and freshness of the morning, adding: "a kind of joyful feeling permeates all my veins." Mersereau connects these two observations, terming the first one "a lyrical overture to the tragedy that is to follow." If one recalls Freeborn's remark that "Princess Mary" is "composed of two relationships" (Pechorin as "seducer" and "executioner"), then both his descriptions of the morning may be seen as ironic overtures.

Just before relating Bela's death, Maksim Maksimich twice employs the words "unlucky day!" The "nonsense" that Vera supposedly tells Pechorin seems echoed by the "nonsense" he almost feels for Princess Mary. The "comedy" he finds just before the undine kisses him seems echoed (as Peace has suggested) by the *commedia!* of Grushnitsky's death. There are others, including two pairs of references to "jests" by Pechorin. As Nabokov noted concerning the word "separating" at the end of "Princess Mary": "It is just like Lermontov and his casual style to let this long and limp word appear twice in the same, final, sentence."

The symmetry of duality in Lermontov's novel becomes most evident if one pictures its five stories in linear arrangement, with "Taman" as the centerpiece. In the inner pair, Pechorin undermines the person named by the title: Maksim Maksimich, Princess Mary. The outer pair relates the deaths of the two people so named.

The first and last stories are also symmetrically balanced by statements about fate. In Nabokov's words: "Maksim Maksimich closes the book with much the same remark as the one he makes about Pechorin at the beginning." These two statements suggest that both Pechorin and Vulich had extraordinary fates "assigned" to them "at their birth." Vinogradov (after emphasizing this parallel) observes that Maksim Maksimich balks before "two metaphysical questions" which are "the two central themes" of the novel. These he sees as "predestination" and "the social genesis of disillusionment as a characteristic psychological trait of contemporary man."

The first and last stories also seem balanced by what could be termed knife-blade foreshadowings. The ring of Azamat's dagger against Kazbich's chain-armor anticipates the latter's stabbing of Bela with his dagger. Efimich's slashing a pig in two prefigures his cutting Vulich in two with the same sword. Somewhat similarly, Pechorin's success in having Azamat steal the goat seems to suggest the notion of having him steal his sister. And Vulich's early success seems to suggest to Pechorin the notion of taking Efimich alive: "It occurred to me to test my fate as Vulich had." In each case, the rather obvious local duality is only a part of the overall dualistic symmetry.

Yet another balance between "Bela" and "The Fatalist" is that both stories have "false endings," as Eikhenbaum has put it. "Bela" ends with the narrator's hope that we respect Maksim Maksimich: "If you admit that, I shall be fully rewarded for my story, which perhaps has been too long." The ending of "The Fatalist," which, Eikhenbaum notes, also features Maksim Maksimich, also seems final—yet the novel's chronological conclusion is of course the ending of "Maksim Maksimich," or perhaps the "Introduction to Pechorin's Journal," wherein we learn of Pechorin's death.

Moving towards the center of the book, we may note a rather unexpected parallel between the very different stories "Maksim Maksimich" and "Princess Mary." Near the end of each, Pechorin parts forever from a friend who has anxiously observed his adventures and attempted quite successfully to offer counsel. (Pechorin learns key information from each, but he counters their suggestions with rather disarming ironies.) In the first parting, Pechorin " . . . proffered his hand while Maksim Maksimich wanted to throw himself on Pechorin's neck". As Pechorin parts from Werner: "He would have liked to shake my hand, and . . . would have thrown himself on my neck; but I remained cold as stone . . ." Merssereau observes that these two parallelled episodes emphasize the hero's "essential aloneness."

The central story has its own dualistic symmetry. Just as the entire novel opens and closes with Maksim's similar statements about fate, "Taman" opens and closes with the ironic notion that Pechorin is "on official business." Arriving, Pechorin and his Cossack are led to two huts, which are termed "an evil place". These words are later repeated by a friend of Pechorin's Cossack. Pechorin sees the hopeful silhouette of "two ships" outlined against the pale horizon. These two are of course no help; later, however, two other boats prove most unfavorable. (One carries away the hero's belongings; the other carries him to his near death.) Early in the story, Pechorin is greatly disturbed by the blind boy's "two white eyes." Later, as he follows his undine to the boat, there is no moon: " . . . only two little stars, like two guiding beacons, sparkled in the dark-blue vault".

As Mersereau has noted, "Taman" contains "two allusions to Pechorin's past." It also contains two details which interlock with passages elsewhere in the novel. As Nabokov has put it, the "breakers" of the Taman seascape "reappear" in the next story as "breakers". . . . Somewhat similarly, Pechorin's statement about his undine ("breeding in women, as in horses, is a great thing,") reflects ironically back into the preceding story upon the portrait of Pechorin himself ("a sign of breeding in man, as a black mane and a black tail in a white horse"). Vinogradov has stressed this parallel.

The overall dualistic structure of Lermontov's novel seems especially remarkable if one considers that some of the parts were separately composed and published. Yet as a finished, final product, the work seems ordered by a pleasing, balanced symmetry. As Mersereau has suggested, Lermontov could have planned the entire novel in advance: he was "a literary genius" and "knew what he was doing." Ultimately, the dualistic structure gives us a faintly uneasy feeling that fate is somehow being replayed— that the hero's various adventures form an appropriately patterned prelude to his decision (in Peace's words) "to measure himself against Fate itself " in "The Fatalist". Indeed, the fact that Vulich successfully tests Fate only to die a violent death lends additional persuasiveness to Nabokov's suspicion that Pechorin's death (after *his* successful testing of Fate) "was a violent one." And if it was, Maksim Maksimich's opening and closing suggestions (that Pechorin and Vulich had extraordinary fates "assigned" to them "at their birth") acquire—in relation to the hero—an eerie tinge of unwitting precognition.

John G. Garrard   (essay date 1981)

SOURCE: "Old Wine in New Bottles: The Legacy of Lermontov," in *Poetica Slavica: Studies in Honour of Zbigniew Folejewski*, edited by J. Douglas Clayton and Gunter Schaarschmidt, University of Ottowa Press, 1981, pp. 41-52.

[*In the following essay, Garrard argues for a reassessment of Lermontov's importance in establishing the novel in nineteenth-century Russian literature.*]

We have no equivalent for Russian literature of Ian Watt's book *The Rise of the Novel,* which attempts to shed light on the extrinsic causes, both ideological and socioeconomic, for the appearance and popularity of the novel in eighteenth-century England. Nor does there exist as yet a study that would do justice to the pre-history and early beginnings of the Russian novel from an intrinsic, more narrowly formal perspective—one that might pinpoint the most significant harbingers of what Mirsky refers to as "The Golden Age of the Russian novel" during the reign of Alexander II (1855-81).

Perhaps the main reason why so few attempts have been made to grapple with this problem of literary evolution is the general tendency to accept the traditional argument that as "founder of Russian literature" (in Belinsky's well-known phrase) Pushkin laid the foundations of the novel in Russia with his *Evgenii Onegin.* No one would deny that Pushkin's works are the lifeblood of all literate Russians: he is their Chaucer, Milton and Shakespeare rolled into one. In John Bayley's pregnant phrase Pushkin "frees his fellow countrymen from the weight of their history, even from the burden of themselves. . . ."

Evgenii Onegin in particular is part of the cultural baggage of all Russian readers and writers, and it would be difficult to exaggerate its overall impact. Pushkin subtitled it mischievously "a novel in verse" in order to exasperate Shishkov and his followers. But we should not be deceived by the oxymoron. It is a mistake to view *Onegin* as a novel since by any definition of the genre one cares to adopt a novel must be written in prose. *Onegin* certainly does contain a number of features familiar to us from our reading of novels; however, much the same could be said of *The Canterbury Tales.*

Any serious study of the rise of the Russian novel would have to pay its respects to *Onegin,* but we are still left with a gap of a quarter century or more before the appearance of the novels of Turgenev, Tolstoy and Dostoevsky. To credit Pushkin with bringing about the rise of the Russian novel is to suggest that the ground lay fallow while the seeds sown by *Onegin* germinated for a full generation.

Less extravagant, though still open to serious question, is the claim that Pushkin shares the honour with Gogol. So, for example, Henry Gifford argues: "Half the achievements to come in the great age of the Russian novel may be traced back to Pushkin. For the other half, strained and urgent and declamatory, Gogol was the prime mover" [*The Novel in Russia from Pushkin to Pasternak*]. Significantly, Gifford makes no effort to demonstrate this thesis. Furthermore, elsewhere in his book he gives a rather different assessment, which he does not stop to examine, but which in my view is closer to the facts: *"A Hero of Our Time* made the necessary link between *Onegin* and the Russian prose novel in its maturity." Even here Lermontov receives only a backhanded compliment, the implication being that he served merely as a conduit or fertilizer.

The noted Pushkinist Boris Tomashevsky was surely correct in his assessment that the influence of *Onegin* on Lermontov's novel was neither extensive nor decisive. In the first place, as he says, "a novel in verse cannot totally determine the style and mode *(manery)* of the prose novel." Secondly, the "philosophical problematics" of *A Hero of Our Time* do not depend on *Onegin.* Lermontov, unlike

Pushkin, viewed Byron as a "philosopher-poet." He did not come to Byron through a Pushkinian filter, but directly via French literature, which dominated European prose fiction in the 1830's.

Lermontov also parts company with Pushkin in his fascination with German literature (Schiller, Goethe) and philosophy (Schelling), again typical of the contemporary French cultural scene. Boris Eikhenbaum has pointed out that Venevitinov and the *liubomudry* are far more important than Pushkin for an understanding of Lermontov's works, which draw upon "Russian Schellingism" *(russkoe shellingianstvo)* for their central idea, the dialectic of opposites and the problematics of good and evil in man. The links between these concerns and the "accursed questions" explored by Dostoevsky need no special pleading.

Pushkin treats German philosophy ironically in the person of Lensky, but Lermontov takes it seriously, thereby setting the stage for the mature Russian novel.

I do not suggest that Lermontov is the missing link, nor that such a link exists: i. e., a single author or work responsible for establishing the novel in Russia. I do argue that Pushkin's role, and more especially *Evgenii Onegin's,* has been exaggerated, and conversely that insufficient attention has been devoted to the critical part played by Lermontov's *A Hero of Our Time.* Certainly Lermontov's importance has not been ignored, but all too often he gets squashed between Pushkin and Gogol. Lermontov studies as a whole, it seems to me, are skewed off balance with the result that far too much time is spent tracking down possible domestic and foreign sources for his works and far too little time is given over to an exploration of what Eikhenbaum called many years ago Lermontov's "art of fusion" *(iskusstvo splava),* his ability to combine a variety of available elements into a new and original form.

It is arguably true that Lermontov had a more lasting impact on the shape and contours of the Russian novel than either Pushkin or Gogol. *A Hero of Our Time* possesses three of the most central characteristics of the Russian novel: 1) psychological analysis; 2) concern with ideas; 3) sociopolitical and ethical awareness. None of these features is the exclusive property of the novel in Russia, but the intensity with which they are engaged does help define the Russian novel and differentiate it from the novel elsewhere.

As early as 1856 Chernyshevsky, in an oft-quoted review, noted that Tolstoi's interest in the "forms and laws of the psychic process, the dialectic of the soul" linked him more closely to Lermontov than to any previous writer. More recently, R. G. Christian, writing about *War and Peace,* suggests that Lermontov's novel "may have provided, in the character of Pechorin, some of the features of the young Prince Andrei and of Dolokhov, as well as impressing and influencing Tolstoy by its extensive use of psychological introspection and interior monologue, and its ironical attitude to *poseurs.* "

Lermontov's metaphysical concerns and the importance attached to ideas by his characters certainly looks ahead to the novels of Turgenev, Tolstoi, and particularly Dos-

> It is arguably true that Lermontov had a more lasting impact on the shape and contours of the Russian novel than either Pushkin or Gogol. *A Hero of Our Time* possesses three of the most central characteristics of the Russian novel: 1) psychological analysis; 2) concern with ideas; 3) sociopolitical and ethical awareness.
>
> —*John G. Garrard*

toevsky. The underlying theme that runs like a thread through all five sections of *A Hero of Our Time*—the opposition between predestination and freedom—is echoed and expanded in the "Pro and Contra" section of *The Brothers Karamazov*. The critical difference is that Lermontov remains adamantly defiant, whereas Dostoevsky resolves the opposition by acceptance of Christian humility.

The "hero" and "time" of Lermontov's title place his work in the mainstream of Russian prose fiction in the nineteenth century. I would agree with Rufus Mathewson that Russian literature as a whole was "hero-centred, if not heroic in the conventional sense" and that Onegin and Pechorin "established a pedigree for the literary protagonist in the early decades of the nineteenth century which persisted to the point of becoming a stereotype."

A measure of Lermontov's achievement may be gained if we recall the embryonic state of prose fiction in general and the novel in particular at the time he was writing. Pushkin had been killed early in 1837, leaving behind *The Tales of Belkin, The Captain's Daughter,* "The Queen of Spades," and several unfinished projects. Gogol had published collections of stories, but his novel did not appear until 1842, the year after Lermontov was himself killed in a duel. Dostoevsky, Goncharov, Turgenev, and Tolstoi were still waiting in the wings.

The early efforts of Pushkin and Gogol are notable for two characteristics. First, they are in the short form or are collections of stories given some semblance of unity by the framing narrator, e. g., Rudy Panko or Belkin. Secondly, they are usually told in the first person, often by an intruding narrator, sometimes a participant in the action. Pushkin performed an invaluable service in *Evgenii Onegin* by acquiring contemporary Russian reality as a viable setting against which to examine the interrelationship of the individual and society. However, he did so in verse, rather than in prose, because he adopted as his vehicle the long narrative poem popularized by Byron. Even more important, Pushkin took the bantering, ironic narrative voice from Byron's *Don Juan*. As Nabokov says in the introduction to his four-volume edition of *Onegin,* the narrator plays such a vital part in the poem that he becomes a third male character after Onegin i Lenskii, a "Stylized Pushkin, Onegin's friend." Furthermore, Pushkin's Muse be-

comes a third female character after Tatiana and Olga. *Onegin* is an inimitable *tour de force* that closed down its own form, just as Milton's *Paradise Lost* had done in English literature a hundred and fifty years earlier.

Gogol, who sought to emulate Pushkin in everything, claiming after the fact with little or no corroborating evidence that Pushkin had provided him with the plots for his major works and took a special interest in his career, even gave his prose novel the subtitle *poema* (Russian for narrative poem) in an obvious attempt to reverse Pushkin's "novel in verse." Gogol's lyrical digressions sometimes skate close to the line separating pathos from bathos, but never cross it. And yet he dominates *Dead Souls* just as Pushkin does *Onegin*. In its own way Gogol's narrative persona is as unique as Pushkin's. Neither one provided a model for an appropriate authorial stance in the long prose form.

Lermontov shared with Pushkin the difficulty of switching from lyric poetry to prose fiction. The lyric poet is used to writing in the first person and addressing the beloved or a friend. John Stuart Mill claimed that poetry is "overheard" but what of prose fiction? Mikhail Bakhtin advanced the idea that the novelist is engaged in a dialogue with the reader. Whether one agrees or not, it is surely true that the narrative stance of a novel differs from that of a poem. What may pass in a poem would seem antiquated or precious in the standard nineteenth-century novel, which has to be addressed to an audience, and relies for its effect on persuading the audience to suspend disbelief.

A Hero of Our Time is a young man's book but also a very ambitious book. It is no denigration of Lermontov to point out that he did not solve all the narrative problems he tackled. His skillful coalescing into a unified whole of various types of story or tale popular in Russia during the 1830's (travel notes, high society tale, personal confession, and exotic tale) and his use of multiple narrators represent a considerable advance in sophistication. Also innovative was Lermontov's manipulation of real and narrative chronology, or as the Formalists put it, "fabula" and "siuzhet."

Let us remember that even after Lermontov's death the new generation of prose writers themselves began with first person narratives and/or the short form or collections of tales. Dostoevsky's first work was *Poor Folk,* a novella in letters. His first work following his exile was *Notes from the House of the Dead,* to be followed by *Notes from the Underground*. Dostoevsky even thought of narrating in the first person as a confession the novel that became *Crime and Punishment*. Turgenev too started out with the short form and later collected his tales as *A Sportsman's Sketches*. Tolstoi began with the autobiographical *Childhood* and war stories based in part on his experiences in the Crimean War. It took Tolstoi a considerable time to learn his craft well enough to tackle the long form and to escape the use of the first person narrator. It seems that the foreign fiction he read in *The Contemporary (Sovremennik)* in the late forties and early fifties consisted largely of novels narrated in the first person: Goethe's *Wilhelm Meister,* Lamartine's *Confessions,* Charlotte Bronte's *Jane Eyre,* Andersen's *Story of My Life,* Chateaubriand's *Mém-*

oires d'outre-tombe, and Dickens' *David Copperfield.* There was not a great deal of prose fiction in Russian literature for Tolstoi to learn from. In fact, he wrote in his diary that Pushkin's prose was "out of date."

Lermontov is of crucial importance in the rise of the Russian novel not only because of the contributions he made, but also because of the narrative problems he failed to resolve. The critical development that led the way to the "Golden Age of the Russian novel" involved a change in point of view from first person to the third person narrator, and more particularly to what Dorrit Cohn suggests we call "narrated monologue."

"Narrated monologue" has become so widespread as the standard method of story-telling in the novel that it is hard to imagine a time when it was not practised. But such was the case in the early decades of Russian fiction. As we have seen, first-person narrators and the short form were typical until the second half of the nineteenth century. The first-person narrator is especially appropriate in the short form, where the writer can fully delineate only one character, and aim for one effect. A good illustration in American literature would be the tales of Edgar Allan Poe.

My argument is, therefore, that the "how" was perhaps even more important than the "who" or "what" in the rise of the Russian novel. It is true that there have been novels related in the first person, but no literature can long survive on them as an exclusive diet. There is nothing surprising in the early development of the Russian novel, which parallels the early development of the English novel in the eighteenth century, where the first-person narratives of Defoe, *Robinson Crusoe* and *Moll Flanders,* give way to the third-person omniscient narrator in *Tom Jones.* Given the psychological, philosophical, ethical and socio-political concerns of the Russian novel in the reign of Alexander II, it was inevitable that a sophisticated and flexible narrative method, embedding first person in the text where needed, would be required.

A Hero of Our Time is a transitional work in that it moves Russian fiction from the short to the long form and from first-person narrative to multiple viewpoints. Lermontov has three narrators, not just one, but he does not take the final step toward narrated monologue. He might have done so had he lived longer.

To illustrate the uses and limitations of Lermontov's narrative method, I will compare and contrast similar scenes and situations taken from *A Hero of Our Time* and Tolstoi's *Anna Karenina.* In placing passages from these two novels side by side I am not trying to prove that Tolstoi was influenced in any direct way by Lermontov, although certain portions of "Princess Mary" do read like a rough sketch or outline of the Kitty-Vronsky-Anna triangle. These echoes are instructive for a comparison of narrative method. I will give three brief examples. In answer to his own question as to why is he pursuing Princess Mary when he has no wish to seduce her or desire to marry her, Pechorin muses:

> . . . there is boundless delight in the possession of a young, barely unfolded soul! It is like a flower whose best fragrance emanates to meet the

first ray of the sun. It should be plucked that very minute and after inhaling one's fill of it, one should throw it away on the road: perchance, someone will pick it up!

Very late in her pregnancy, Anna ceases to be the same desirable woman that Vronsky had pursued earlier. The narrator tells us:

> Both morally and physically she had changed for the worse. She had broadened out, and when she spoke of the actress a spiteful expression had distorted her face. He looked at her as a man might look at a faded flower he had picked, in which he found it difficult to discover the beauty which made him pick and destroy it.

Of course, the comparison of a woman to a faded flower has long since become a cliché. What is instructive here is that Lermontov must allow Pechorin to be conscious of his motivations to the point where he sounds like a demonic, Gothic, hero. Pechorin declares that his main pleasure is to "subjugate to my will all that surrounds me," in order to gratify his pride, and declares that happiness is "Sated pride." On the other hand, Tolstoi's method of narration allows him to reveal motivations and thoughts in his hero, of which Vronsky is not fully aware. Tolstoi has Vronsky begin this train of thought by thinking that "his best happiness was already behind".

In *A Hero of Our Time,* after Pechorin has vented his spleen in a private conversation with Princess Mary, the following dialogue takes place:

> "You are a dangerous man!" she said to me. "I would sooner find myself in a wood under a murderer's knife than be the victim of your sharp tongue . . . I ask you seriously, when it occurs to you to talk badly about me, better take a knife and cut my throat: I don't think you will find it very difficult."
>
> "Do I look like a murderer?"
>
> "You are worse . . ."

In *Anna Karenina,* Vronsky is also likened to a murderer, but not by the woman victim; instead it is the narrator who intrudes to make the comparison shortly after Vronsky and Anna have consummated their love for the first time:

> Looking at him, she felt her degradation physically and she could not utter another word. He felt what a murderer must feel when he looks at the body he has deprived of life.

Tolstoy's narrator continues in this Victorian vein for several more lines, but the point is already clear. This is a salutary reminder to us that third person narration can mask authorial interference in the story, and be less objective than Lermontov's dramatized dialogue.

My third example is more complex. It involves similar scenes in which physical and emotional well-being are related. Lermontov has grasped the physiological truth that how a man feels about his relationships with others often influences and is influenced by how he is feeling about his body. So Pechorin, upon bidding Vera farewell after a tryst, moves from "My heart painfully contracted as after the first parting. Oh, how that feeling gladdened me!" immediately to "My face is pale but still fresh-complexioned, my limbs are supple and svelte, my thick hair curls, my eyes sparkle, my blood is ebullient." The interchange between Pechorin's physicality and his emotions is sketched in rather tired language.

The day after Anna tells Vronsky she is pregnant, he is hurrying in a carriage to see her, and his anticipation at seeing her "all combined into one general impression of a joyous sense of life." Tolstoi continues to examine Vronsky's feelings:

> He had often before had this joyous sense of physical well-being, but never before had he been so fond of himself, of his own body, as at that moment. It gave him pleasure to feel the slight pain in his strong leg, it was pleasant to feel the muscular sensation of movement in his chest as he breathed. The same bright and cold August day which made Anna feel so hopeless seemed exhilarating and invigorating to him and refreshed his face and neck, which were still glowing after the drenching he had given them under the tap. The scent of brilliantine on his moustache seemed to him particularly pleasant in the fresh air.

He spurs the driver on to go "Faster, faster!" with the same urge to extend his physical sensations that Pechorin demonstrates after his tryst with Vera, galloping off to lather intentionally both himself and his horse.

Tolstoi handles the scene in a dynamic way, using concrete details. Whereas Pechorin described his legs as "supple limbs," Vronsky "dropped his legs, crossed one leg over the other, and taking it in his hand, felt the springy muscle of the calf." In Tolstoi supple limbs become legs in motion, with a sense of bone and muscle so palpable that one can almost feel them. The elements of both scenes are superficially similar—each one contains a man leaving or going to his mistress; each man is happy while the mistress is unhappy; each man's happiness is reflected in a canvassing of his own body with self-satisfaction which culminates in a desire to exert himself and his horses (or in the case of Pechorin, his horse) to go even faster. Each passage even contains a glance at the passing scenery. Pechorin swallows the "redolent air" and gazes at the mountains, concluding with supreme egotism, "There is no feminine gaze that I would not forget at the sight of mountains covered with curly vegetation." Tolstoi's narrator, in an indirect but far more telling comment, gives us Vronsky's impression: "Everything was beautiful, like a pretty landscape painting which has been only recently finished and varnished."

Vronsky's self-absorption and rather vulgar taste in art are conveyed in a subtle manner by Tolstoi's use of "narrated monologue," whereas Lermontov is obliged to have Pechorin declare his feelings and thoughts directly in a way that sometimes seems strained and melodramatic. The character has to be omniscient rather than the narrator. Anything the hero does not know and does not write down is lost to the reader. There can seldom be any difference in cognition between Pechorin and the reader. On the other hand, Vronsky does not realize that Anna feels "hopeless" on this bright sunny day. His self-satisfaction with his own body contrasts to Anna's despair at the changes taking place in her body due to her pregnancy. Pechorin is presented to the reader as a finished and completed personality, and the scenes of his relationships to others are often presented as a series of frozen *tableaux vivants*. Tolstoi, on the other hand, with his interest in the "dialectic of the soul" adopts a different approach. He wants to trace the evolution of thoughts and emotions over time. The difference between the two novels is akin to the difference between viewing slides and watching a motion picture.

We should bear in mind that the two authors had different aims. Not for a moment do I suggest that Lermontov should have written his novel in a different way. By selecting a first-person narrator (Pechorin's "journal") Lermontov makes his hero more challenging and enigmatic. Furthermore, as Wayne C. Booth has remarked, this type of inside view "can be of immeasurable value in forcing us to see the human worth of a character whose actions, objectively considered, we would deplore" [*The Rhetoric of Fiction*]. In addition, Lermontov obviously intended to impress upon the reader the absolute honesty of Pechorin's confession, written in a diary for only his own eyes and not for publication. By using three narrators and by manipulating the chronological sequence of events in the novel Lermontov is able to achieve a considerable dramatic effect and intensity.

Tolstoi does not employ multiple narrators, but he is able to achieve the same result more subtly by employing the "narrated monologue" strategy instead of the discovered manuscript or first-person confession. He also uses interior monologue and stream of consciousness (the embedded first person narrative to which I alluded earlier). Tolstoi's narrator moves inside one character after another to provide a variety of views on the action and other characters. Consider, for example, the view given of Anna at the ball early in the novel through the eyes and emotions of Kitty (*not* Vronsky), or the view of Anna and Vronsky at their country estate through the gentle but disapproving eyes of Dolly. Thus Tolstoi is able to give a full delineation of many characters. In *A Hero of Our Time,* we know quite a bit about Pechorin, a little about Maksim Maksimych, and not much about anybody else.

The reader would like to know a great deal more about some characters in *A Hero of Our Time,* particularly Vera. (It is a pity the travelling officer did not come across her diary!) In the one piece of dialogue in which we hear her voice for more than a few lines, she says to Pechorin:

> "You know that I am your slave; I never was able to resist you . . . and for this I shall be punished. You will cease to love me. I wish, at least, to save my reputation . . . not for my own sake: you know that very well! Oh, I beseech you, do not torment me as before with empty doubts and feigned coldness. I shall die soon, perhaps. I feel myself getting weaker every day . . . and, in spite of that, I cannot think of a future life, I think only of you . . . You mean do not understand the delights of a glance, of a handshake

. . . while I, I swear to you, I when listening to your voice, I experience such deep, strange bliss that the most ardent kisses could not replace it".

Here as so often in *A Hero of Our Time* the reader is presented with a static assertion. Vera's accusations and fears are a collation of the sentiments expressed by Anna over hundreds of pages as her relationship with Vronsky gradually sours.

One of Lermontov's problems is that he cannot introduce a moral voice into the narrative in order to give the reader some unobtrusive guidance. Maksim Maksimych hardly qualifies and the traveling officer is not much help. The reader is left alone with Pechorin. It is not surprising that many readers have had a hard time teasing out of the text Pechorin's self-deception and the inconsistency of his reliance on predestination or fate to justify the exercise of his free will. Pechorin is forced to engage in dialogues with himself to answer questions a reader might have about his motivations: "I often wonder, why do I so stubbornly try to gain the love of a little maiden whom I do not wish to seduce, and whom I shall never marry?" On Vronsky's trifling with the affections of Kitty the narrator states:

> He did not realize that his behavior towards Kitty had a name of its own, that it was the seduction of a girl without the intention of marrying her, and that this kind of seduction is the sort of reprehensible thing common among brilliant young men like himself.

Here the reader enjoys the pleasure of learning something about Vronsky's behavior that he is not aware of himself, where Pechorin tells himself and us at great length how wicked and malicious he is.

Obviously, the comparisons that I have made tend to work to Lermontov's disadvantage, but let us remember that Lermontov was in his early to mid twenties when he wrote *A Hero of Our Time* whereas *Anna Karenina* is the work of a mature writer in his late fifties. Had Tolstoi died at the same age as Lermontov he would probably have deserved little more than a footnote in histories of Russian literature. Furthermore, as the second of the examples adduced above illustrates, there are dangers in third-person narration which Tolstoi was not always successful in avoiding. Some of the weakest pages in *Anna Karenina* occur when his narrator identifies too closely with Levin. However, it is clear that Tolstoi's narrative method allows a great deal more flexibility than does Lermontov's. Lermontov's novel remains a remarkable achievement, and a necessary step in the evolution of the mature Russian novel, which could not come into its "Golden Age" until writers had exploited all narrative techniques and methods.

Gary D. Cox   (essay date 1982)

SOURCE: "Dramatic Genre as a Tool of Characterization in Lermontov's *A Hero of Our Time*," in *Russian Literature*, Vol. XI, No. II, February 15, 1982, pp. 163-72.

[*In the following essay, Cox asserts that the intense self-examination to which Pechorin subjects himself renders* A Hero of Our Time *a precursor to the psychological realism that dominates much subsequent Russian literature.*]

The question of genre is one of the most intriguing puzzles of Lermontov's *A Hero of Our Time.* The work is presented to us as a series of short pieces, each representing a different prose genre typical of Romantic literature, and yet the sum of these short pieces is a more complete picture of events and characters, a novel. Herbert Eagle has noted that in each of the shorter components, the reader's Romantic genre expectations are overturned. Thus, by beginning with Romantic genres and types and then restructuring their elements, the work leads out of Romanticism into a new understanding of human psychology.

In the "Princess Mary" section of the novel, another set of genre distinctions becomes important. Imagery dealing with dramatic genre is used extensively in that novella as a way of characterizing the attitudes and personalities of the major characters. And once again these genre distinctions are used in a way which outlines the tension between Romanticism and nascent realism in the novel. This tension has been the subject of much debate among Lermontov critics . . . but the use of dramatic imagery in "Princess Mary" clarifies the way in which Lermontov restructures Romantic elements in a new, realistic way.

The dramatic imagery of "Princess Mary" revolves around the opposing concepts of melodrama and comedy. Most of the characters view events with the exaggerated passions characteristic of melodrama, while Pečorin, who stands at the center of the melodrama, views it as a comic play and describes the characters who surround him as actors. This distinction is Pečorin's own, for he is the narrator as well as the protagonist of the novella. "Finita la commedia", he exclaims after killing his opponent in a duel. Of course this is not the standard meaning of the word "comedy". By using it repeatedly Pečorin is referring to his attempt to view himself and the world around him dispassionately. A melodramatic plot viewed without melodramatic passion becomes a comedy. The dispassionate introspection which produces Pečorin's "comic" outlook is precisely the element of this novel which forms a basis for the later development of psychological realism. Thus the distinction between melodrama and comedy in the imagery of "Princess Mary" becomes a tool for understanding Lermontov's restructuring of Romantic elements in a new, realistic way.

The first conversation between Pečorin and Grušnickij sets forth this distinction clearly. The encounter is staged as a dramatic scene; Grušnickij in particular is weighing his words for their effect on the spectators, Princess Mary and her mother. He assumes a "dramatic pose" and exclaims loudly in French:

> My dear man, I hate men so as not to despise them, for otherwise life would be too disgusting a comedy.

Pečorin, in the same dramatic manner, replies:

> My dear man, I despise women so as not to love them, for otherwise life would be too ridiculous a melodrama.

This exchange, underlined by the use of French, sets up the basic contrast between the two men. Farce and melodrama are presented as opposites, as are Grušnickij and Pečorin. Each man embraces what the other shuns. Grušnickij takes up a melodramatic attitude toward the world, while Pečorin takes the comic view. These opposing world views are centered around the emotions of love, hate, and contempt, not only in the French aphorisms, but at crucial points elsewhere in the text as well.

Dramatic imagery pervades the scene in which Pečorin and Grušnickij exchange these witticisms. The mountains rising in the distance are described as an "amphitheater". Costume plays an important role, Pečorin tells us, in the relations among the vacationers. The women in their "elaborate costumes" looked upon him at first:

> . . . with kind curiosity. The Petersburg cut of the military coat confused them, but soon, recognizing the army epaulets, they turned away in disgust.

The Moscow dandy Raevič is also costumed in accordance with his assumed role, as Grušnickij describes him:

> He is a gambler. That's immediately obvious by the huge gold chain winding across his blue waistcoat. And what a thick walking stick—just like Robinson Crusoe's. And his beard and hair are trimmed *à la moujik.*

Immediately after the all important aphorisms are declaimed, Pečorin

observes a "curious scene" from his hiding place in "the gallery". He even refers to its participants as *"dramatis personae" (dejstvujuščie lica.)* At the close of this mime in which Mary picks up Grušnickij's glass, she

> . . . assumed a dignified (. . .) pose, and did not even turn her head (. . .) until she had disappeared behind the lindens.

The characters behave in every way as though on stage. Throughout the "Princess Mary" section, words like "role", "drama", "the fifth act", "dramatic plot" (*zavjazka*), "dramatic *dénouement*" (*rezvjazka*), and the like are used to keep the reader constantly aware of the theatrical nature of the characters' behavior.

Grušnickij is first described by Pečorin in terms of his melodramatic inclinations. He loves to "drape himself in extraordinary feelings, elevated passions, and exceptional sufferings". "To produce an effect is his delight". He has a passion for "declamation". Central to his melodramatic personality is his failure to realize or admit that he is playing a role. Pečorin counsels him:

> "You simply don't know how to make use of your advantageous position. Your soldier's coat makes you a hero and a sufferer in the eyes of any sensitive young lady".

Grušnickij smiled with self-satisfaction.

"What nonsense!" he said.

As a result, he calculates incorrectly, and the costume change which is to insure his position with the princess

turns out to be his undoing. The lack of self-awareness is fundamental to the melodramatic personality as Pečorin presents it here.

Pečorin's self-consciousness, by contrast, is the source of the dispassionate irony which produces his "comic" outlook. Observing the world with cold and meticulous precision, he ridicules its absurdities. He tells Dr. Werner:

> For a long time I have lived by my head rather than by my heart. I weigh and analyze my own passions and acts with stern curiosity, but without participation. There are two men within me: the one lives in the full sense of that word, the other meditates and judges him. . . .

Pečorin's friend Dr. Werner shares this "comic" outlook. Werner's medical colleagues once circulated the rumor that he drew cartoons of his patients. Their friendship is described thus by Pečorin:

> We would talk together very seriously on abstract matters until we both realized that we were putting each other on. Then (. . .) we would burst out laughing, and having laughed our fill, we would separate well-content with our evening.

Pečorin later remarks to Dr. Werner: "Sad things are funny to us; funny things are sad". Their similarity in outlook is the basis of their friendship.

The exchange of French aphorisms quoted earlier revolves around three verbs: *haïr, mépriser* and *aimer.* A close examination of the use of the corresponding Russian verbs (*nenavidet* 'to hate', *prezirat* 'to despise', and *ljubit* 'to love') later in the work shows an even closer connection between these aphorisms and the events and personalities of the story. Love and hatred are the melodramatic passions, while contempt is allied with the comic view. Grušnickij's last words are "I despise myself, and I hate you!" . While he retains the melodramatic passion of hatred toward Pečorin, he has lost his romantic illusions concerning himself and holds himself in contempt. This parallels a development earlier in the novel, when Pečorin occasions Maksim Maksimyč's loss of romantic illusions. Witness the editor/narrator's comments about Maksim Maksimyč at the end of his chapter: "These words were pronounced with an ironic smile . . ."; ". . . here he pulled out one notebook and threw it with contempt (*prezrenie*) on the floor"; "He had a cold and constrained look". Pečorin's attitude is infectious.

Princess Mary, who has heard Pečorin's declaration of contempt for women, constantly fears that he despises her. As their affair becomes more serious, she broaches the subject:

> Either you despise me or you love me very much. (. . .) Perhaps you want to laugh at me, to stir my soul and then leave me (. . .) Isn't it true that there is nothing in me which would preclude respect? (. . .) Perhaps you wish that I should be the first to say that I love you?

Pečorin staunchly refuses to say which of the two emotions he feels. Later on he tells her part of the truth, from which she, having heard his earlier dictum, should be able to infer the rest. She asks:

> "You don't despise me, do you?"

> "I will tell you the whole truth. I won't justify myself or explain my actions. I do not love you".

Their final conversation again revolves around these three verbs. Pečorin begins:

> "Princess (. . .) you know that I have been laughing at you. You must despise me. (. . .) Consequently you cannot love me. (. . .) Isn't it true that, even if you did love me, from this moment you despise me?"

> (. . .)

> "I hate you!" she replied.

Here the shoe is on the other foot; it is Pečorin who is asking Princess Mary if she despises him. But he does not fear her contempt; on the contrary, he seems to be begging for it. She refuses to bestow it, but returns hatred instead. Again Pečorin is attempting to tear the romantic illusions from the eyes of his interlocutor; he wants her to take up the contemptuous attitude so characteristic of himself. She will not do so; instead she replies with the melodramatic passion of hatred.

The use of such imagery provides an important key to understanding the work's place in the history of Russian literature. There has been much critical discussion of the relative weight of Romantic and realistic elements in Lermontov's novel. All agree that the work is on the borderline of the two periods and partakes of both to some degree. Boris Éjchenbaum and Lidija Ginzburg have stressed the reflection of the post-Decembrist Russian intelligentsia in the character of Pečorin. Both of them, along with John Mersereau Jr., have noted the way in which Lermontov's novel combines Byronic conventions with the introspective French Romanticism of Constant and others, thus laying the groundwork for the future development of psychological realism. Mersereau stresses Lovelace more than Byron in the delineation of Lermontov's demonism.

Recent Soviet critics have divided more sharply in classifying the work. V. M. Markovič has stressed the psychological determinism which makes the work fundamentally realistic, while K. N. Grigorjan has emphasized the preoccupation with the self (*ličnost*) which defines the work as lyrical and Romantic. Both critics argue convincingly, but in the final analysis it is impossible to draw a hard and fast boundary between Romanticism and Realism and to decide on which side of that boundary to place *A Hero of Our Time*. The critic cannot alter the fact that the work straddles that boundary, but he can clarify the way in which it straddles it. By doing so he truly elucidates the work, rather than merely attempting to pigeonhole it. Mersereau, Ginzburg and Èjchenbaum have done this admirably by showing how Lermontov's novel combines the previously separate strains of demonic and introspective Romanticism and by showing how the dispassionate self-analysis became a model for later realistic writing.

The character types outlined by Pečorin's dramatic imagery in "Princess Mary" clarify the nature of this combination. First we have the melodramatic character, the unreflective Grušnickij, playing a Byronic role but unwilling to admit it, a character totally lacking in self-awareness. Over against the unreflective melodramatic character we have a genuine Byronic hero, Pečorin himself, but with a crucial difference. Pečorin has a reflective second self who exposes all of his melodramatic actions to

ridicule. "Comedy" here is not the opposite of melodrama but rather a transformation of it. Pečorin's *commedia* is melodrama transfigured by self-consciousness, just as Lermontov's "realism" is Romanticism transfigured by self-analysis.

Pečorin stands at the center of a stormy melodramatic plot, but he views that melodrama as comedy. The characters who surround him persist in viewing him as a melodramatic figure. He tries to infect them with comedic outlook; he has partial success with Grušnickij, none at all with Princess Mary. But Pečorin's ironic pose is not altogether consistent, and the lapses are deviations within the system of dramatic imagery already described. He is involved in a subplot as well. It is equally melodramatic, but here he reacts differently. He refers to his affair with Vera as a "dramatic story (. . .) of love" and with her he sheds his contemptuous attitude.

> A long forgotten tremor ran through my veins at the sound of that dear voice . . .

he tells us, and later:

> I did not allow myself a single jest at [her husband].

Their conversation is reminiscent of Italian opera:

> Between us began one of those conversations which have no sense on paper, which cannot be repeated, and cannot even be remembered. The meaning of sounds replaces and supplements the meaning of words, as in Italian opera.

There are few art forms more melodramatic than Italian opera, and even the word melodrama suggests a combination of the musical and the dramatic. After receiving her letter, Pečorin suddenly gives free rein to a burst of melodramatic feeling, quite unprecedented for him:

> . . . I prayed, cursed, wept, laughed. (. . .) No, nothing can express my emotion, my despair. In the face of the possibility of losing Vera forever, she became dearer than anything in the world— dearer than life, honor, happiness!

And later:

> For a long time I lay motionless and wept bitterly, making no attempt to restrain my tears and wailing. I thought my heart would burst. All my firmness, all my indifference vanished like smoke. My soul became powerless, my reason fell silent, and if anyone had seen me at that moment, he would have turned away with contempt [*prezrenie*].

Here the "second Pečorin", the cold-blooded observer, becomes a hypothetical outsider, and he views Pečorin's emotional outburst with the same contempt that Pečorin showers upon others. At the heart of Pečorin's mocking attitude toward the rest of the world lies contempt for himself and the fear that others will share that contempt. Elsewhere he makes this explicit:

> I sometimes despise myself . . . Is not this the source of my contempt for others? . . .

It is revealing that in the scene immediately following his emotional outburst, perhaps as a gesture of self-punishment, he begs Princess Mary to declare that she despises him.

One of the troublesome questions concerning **A Hero of Our Time** is the unity of the work. The two shorter sections included in Pečorin's diary, "Taman" and "The Fatalist", are particularly suspect in this regard. They shed little new light on Pečorin's character, and they seem to be simply tossed in for good measure. But perhaps the scheme presented above for "Princess Mary" provides the connecting link. In "Princess Mary" we have a melodramatic plot centered around a character who views that melodrama as farce. In these two shorter stories we find a similar situation, the central figure being, not Pečorin, but Vulič and the strange "water-nymph" of Taman.

Vulič, a central figure in "The Fatalist", has many traits in common with Pečorin:

> He revealed to no one his spiritual or domestic secrets.

> A cold and mournful smile, always wandering about his lips (. . .) [gave] him the aspect of a special being, unable to share the thoughts and passions of those whom fate had given him as comrades.

His only passion is gambling, and his duel with fate is the ultimate gamble for him, a cold-blooded experiment which affords him a good deal of pleasure: "This is better than faro or stoss!" While others are crying out in the extremities of fear or amazement, he is coldly indifferent and even smiling. We are told that "he acquired at that moment some sort of mysterious power over his comrades". This recalls the power Pečorin acquired over the other characters in "Princess Mary":

> I have always acquired an invincible power over the hearts and wills of women, without even trying (. . .) Is this because of the fact that I value nothing (. . .)

In both cases, then, the power results from the central character's ability to laugh at the drama of which he is the central figure.

In the story "Taman", Peorin meets his match. The unnamed heroine may be the woman of whom he speaks in "Princess Mary": "Once, only once, I loved a woman with a strong will which I could not vanquish". She stands at the center of a whole series of vaguely exotic and potentially tragic goings on, yet she is always laughing and smiling. The following exchange exhibits her unflagging light-heartedness and indifference. Pečorin asks her why she sings:

"Where there are songs, there is happiness also". —"And what if you happen to sing yourself sorrow?" —"So what! If it does not get better it will get worse, but it's not far from bad to good either". (. . .) " . . . I've found out something about you!". (Her face did not change; her lips did not move, as though it had nothing to do with her.) "I've found out that you were walking on the shore last night". —And here I quite seriously related to her all that I had seen, thinking it would upset her—not at all! (. . .) "You've seen much, but you know little" (. . .) "And what if I should decide, for instance, to inform the commandant?" —and here I took up a very serious, even stern pose. She suddenly hopped off with a song, and disappeared like a bird . . .

Here Pečorin is the one who takes it all seriously. When she later embraces him, he tells us:

> Everything went black before my eyes, my head swam, I grasped her in my embrace with all the strength of youthful passion.

But his strength and passion are useless; she tries to kill him and then runs off with her smuggler. This story is the earliest in the book in actual chronology, and here Pečorin seems not to have fully worked out his ironic pose. But by the end of the story he begins to sound like the Pečorin we know: "And what, after all, are human joys and sorrows to me, a wandering officer . . .". The young woman has torn away his illusions, much as he will later tear away those of other characters, by her ability to laugh at the drama of her life, by her view of the world as a great comedy.

The experiences in "Taman", "The Fatalist", and with Vera may be lapses in Pečorin's highly prized equanimity, but they fit into the system of dramatic imagery presented by the work as a whole. They show us the division of Pečorin's character into an analytical self and a melodramatic self, and they show us the attitude of the former toward the latter. Thus they clarify the changes which have been wrought upon conventional Romantic types in Lermontov's novel. Pečorin's constant introspection and overdeveloped self-consciousness presage the direction Russian realism was to take in the latter half of the century—toward a penetrating analysis of psychological states.

Nabokov on Lermontov's anti-hero:

In Russian schools, at least in my day, a favorite theme for compositions was "Onegin and Pechorin." The parallel is obvious, but quite superficial. Pushkin's Onegin stretches himself throughout the book and yawns. Lermontov's Pechorin does nothing of the sort—he laughs and bites. With his immense store of tenderness, kindness, and heroism behind his cynical and arrogant appearance, he is a deeper personality than the cold lean fop so delightfully depicted by Pushkin.

Vladimir Nabokov, in his "The Lermontov Mirage,"
The Russian Review, *November, 1941.*

N. A. Dobroljubov, in his article on "Oblomovism", sees Pečorin as a fore-runner of Rudin and Oblomov. Dostoevskij's Underground Man, with his morbid self-examination and bitter self-hatred, is in many respects an inverted Pečorin. Pečorin's peculiar combination of Byronic Romanticism with reflective Romanticism provided an important model for later writers in the realistic tradition.

D. J. Richards   (essay date 1985)

SOURCE: "Lermontov: *A Hero of Our Time*," in *The Voice of a Giant: Essays on Seven Russian Prose Classics,* edited by Roger Cockrell and David Richards, University of Exeter, 1985, pp. 15-25.

[*Richards is an English educator and critic specializing in Russian literature. In the following essay, Richards examines the episodic structure of Lermontov's novel, comparing and contrasting it with other nineteenth-century Russian novels and with the more familiar pattern of traditional English and French novels of the same period.*]

Critics nearly always call Lermontov's *A Hero of Our Time* a novel, but in its general shape the work does not conform with the familiar pattern which we see in the traditional English or French nineteenth-century novel from writers such as Stendhal and Balzac, George Eliot and Hardy, or in a Russian work like, say, Turgenev's *Fathers and Sons.* Consider the shape of *Fathers and Sons.* First of all, it has a fairly obvious beginning, middle and end. At the beginning most of the characters are introduced, both to the reader and to each other; in the middle they undergo various experiences, as a result of which they change and develop; and at the end they go their separate, or newly-shared ways. Secondly, in *Fathers and Sons* Turgenev presents the various incidents which make up his story straightforwardly and, for the most part, in chronological order; one event leads clearly on to the next, and at the end everything is neatly tied up. Thirdly, the action is described from the viewpoint of one calm, unbiassed and apparently omniscient narrator, whose tone remains consistent and even from the first page to the last.

Fathers and Sons, however, is in its shape far from a typical nineteenth-century Russian novel, the majority of which do not follow this familiar and seemingly obvious pattern but indeed evince a striking waywardness of form. Pushkin's *Eugene Onegin,* for instance, is written not in prose, but in regular 14-line stanzas. Pushkin himself called his masterpiece 'a novel in verse' (*roman v stikhax*). Gogol's *Dead Souls* is certainly written in prose, but the author dubbed his work 'a narrative poem' *(poema);* it roams and wanders like a great Russian river, but without reaching a goal. Remember Tolstoy's *War and Peace,* which Henry James (who felt more at home with Turgenev) called a 'large, loose and baggy monster', and remember, too, Dostoevsky's *The Brothers Karamazov,* which is almost equally baggy and moreover as unfinished as *Dead Souls.* In this company, it must be admitted, *A Hero of Our Time* appears somewhat less eccentric in its shape than it might elsewhere.

But what is the shape of Lermontov's masterpiece and how does the novel fit together? The most obvious feature is that *A Hero of Our Time* is divided, not into a flowing stream of consecutively numbered chapters, but into seven quite distinct sections. Moreover, these seven sections are presented by four different people: firstly, Lermontov's main fictional narrator, an anonymous traveller, relates the opening two episodes, 'Bela' and 'Maksim Maksimych,' though one must remember that in 'Bela' this ostensible narrator not only describes his journey through the Caucasus but also, more importantly, transmits Maksim Maksimych's stories about Pechorin. Since the latter are given *verbatim,* Maksim Maksimych too must be included in the list of narrators. The anonymous traveller-narrator also contributes the explanatory 'Foreword to Pechorin's Diary'. Then, Pechorin himself is the writer of the said diary, which contains the three episodes 'Taman,' 'Princess Mary' and 'The Fatalist'. Finally, Lermontov himself speaks directly to the reader, but only very briefly, in the 'Foreword' to the whole book—a section which was added to the original text for the second edition of *A Hero of Our Time* in 1841.

Further, the five story-section of the novel vary quite considerably in their content and atmosphere: 'Bela' presents a combination of travelogue and romantic adventure tale; 'Maksim Maksimych' offers primarily a character sketch of the kindly Caucasian veteran who exemplifies all the warm, down-to-earth solidity which Pechorin lacks; 'Taman' is largely a mystery story; 'Princess Mary' contains the bulk of Lermontov's complex psychological analysis of his hero, while 'The Fatalist' is a fascinating anecdote, laced with a little philosophising. Even the two 'Forewords', the one to Pechorin's diary and the one which precedes the main text, are not at all similar. The 'Foreword to Pechorin's Diary', allegedly written by the anonymous traveller-narrator, gently and straightforwardly praises Pechorin's sincerity and honest self-analysis, and suggests that he has been badly misinterpreted by his acquaintances. The 'Foreword' to the whole book, however, which Lermontov wrote in response to some unfavourable criticism of the novel's first edition of 1840, is far from gentle and straightforward in its biting irony and defensive aggressiveness.

On top of this, the five story-sections of *A Hero of Our Time* do not describe Pechorin's experiences in the order in which they happened. The chronological sequence of events, which can be reconstructed by a close reading of the text, would seem to be more or less the following:

> (1)Pechorin, a young army officer, has been posted to the Caucasus because of some misdemeanour in St Petersburg. While travelling south to join his new unit he has to spend a night in the Black Sea port of Taman, where he clashes with the smugglers in the way described in the opening episode of his diary, 'Taman.'

> (2)After taking part in a few skirmishes with the Caucasian tribesmen, Pechorin spends a short leave in Pyatigorsk. What happens there is related in 'Princess Mary'.

> (3)Because of the duel with Grushnitsky, recorded at the end of the 'Princess Mary' episode,

Pechorin is posted to a frontline fort under the command of Maksim Maksimych. Here the adventures described in 'Bela' take place.

(4)While attached to this same fort Pechorin spends a fortnight in a cossack village, where the incidents outlined in 'The Fatalist' occur.

(5)About five years later Pechorin (who had resigned his commission shortly after Bela's death) is on his way to Persia. In Vladikavkaz he meets both Lermontov's fictional narrator and Maksim Maksimych.

(6)On the return journey from Persia Pechorin dies. The reader learns of this, however, not at the end of A *Hero of Our Time,* but about one third of the way through, in the anonymous traveller-narrator's 'Foreword to Pechorin's Diary'.

Why are the episodes of *A Hero of Our Time* not presented in chronological order? Part of the explanation may derive from the origins of the work, which began its life not as a complete novel, but with the publication of the three pieces, 'Bela', 'The Fatalist' and 'Taman' quite separately from each other in the Journal 'Notes of the Fatherland' in 1839 and early 1840. But much more crucial were Lermontov's aims. The traditional nineteenth-century novelist usually adopted a chronological approach to his material because he was intent on portraying characters in the process of development. Lermontov however, is not greatly concerned with Pechorin's development; he wants rather to present a psychological analysis of a type of personality or a cast of mind, 'a portrait', as he puts it in his 'Foreword' to the novel, 'composed of the vices of our entire generation in their ultimate development'. To this end Lermontov opts to examine the mature Pechorin from a number of different points of view rather than to trace the lines along which he evolved—though references to Pechorin's past are made from time to time.

However, if Lermontov avoids the traditional chronological line of narration, he replaces it with other patterns of movement in *A Hero of Our Time.* For instance, Pechorin is gradually brought closer and closer to the reader. First of all, in Bela, he is merely the subject of a long reminiscence narrated by Maksim Maksimych; then, in the episode entitled Maksim Maksimych, he appears in person, but only very briefly; then at last he is portrayed much more fully, and inevitably much more sympathetically, through his own diary.

At the same time, the reader's impression of Pechorin's strength of character alternates from episode to episode. In 'Bela' he sounds dominating and masterful, but in 'Taman' he seems to be beguiled, outwitted and nearly murdered by the girl-smuggler; then in 'Princess Mary' he appears once more to be in command of almost every situation, but at the end, in 'The Fatalist,' the very existence of human freedom is called into question, and we are left wondering whether Pechorin—and everyone else too—is perhaps neither strong nor weak, but simply an involuntary puppet controlled by some higher force.

Another interesting line of movement which can be observed is the way the tempo of the narration steadily increases, from Maksim Maksimych's leisurely and oft-interrupted discourse in 'Bela' to the dynamic and rapid style adopted by Pechorin himself in 'The Fatalist.' Further, the settings of the five story-sections, as they stand, alternate between primitive and civilised. Finally, it is interesting to note how the whole text (disregarding the opening 'Foreword') is framed by the figure of Maksim Maksimych: he is the first of the principal characters to appear and speak (at the beginning of 'Bela') and it is to him that the last spoken words of all also belong (at the end of 'The Fatalist'). In such a carefully designed work of art this cannot be simply an accident: Lermontov is presumably indicating that the ordinary, straightforward, good-natured Russians, of whom Maksim Maksimych is a worthy and attractive representative, are much more durable (and perhaps ultimately more valuable) than the brilliant Pechorins of this world.

Another question which must be asked about the order of the episodes is why Lermontov should have chosen to conclude *A Hero of Our Time* with 'The Fatalist'? Two reasons immediately suggest themselves. In the first place, he probably did not want to end his novel with Pechorin's death (or even with Grushnitsky's) but rather with an affirmation of Pechorin's positive energy and daring. In the second place, the discussion about fatalism in this concluding section not only sets all the previous action and all the questions about Pechorin's nature against a broader background, but also quite deliberately tries to dissuade the reader from making firm judgments about man's responsibility for his actions and hence from either condemning or exonerating Pechorin for his behaviour. In this connection it is interesting to see how 'The Fatalist' re-echoes those notes of hesitation and doubt which are struck in both 'Forewords': the opening 'Foreword' ends with the words 'God only knows', and the second with 'I don't know'.

If these lines of movement through the various sections of *A Hero of Our Time* are an important aspect of the novel's general shape, another significant and interesting feature is the way the main characters are arranged. Pechorin is clearly central, even though Lermontov introduces him to the reader tantalisingly slowly at first. Pechorin is the hero referred to in the novel's title; he is the only character to appear in every one of the book's sections, and it is his actions, his thoughts and his psychology which remain the focus of attention throughout. In comparison with Pechorin, all the other characters are of secondary interest; some of them are brilliantly individualised, but they all revolve round Pechorin and serve primarily to highlight facets of his complex and contradictory nature.

Of these figures who circle round Pechorin six are portrayed in considerable detail, a nicely balanced group of three men (Maksim Maksimych, Dr Werner and Grushnitsky) and three women (Bela, Princess Mary and Vera). The fact that every one of these very different people is drawn to Pechorin emphasises immediately the latter's complexity and wide appeal. More than this, though, each one of these six characters brings out aspects of Pechorin which might otherwise have remained concealed from the reader.

It is worth considering how our view of Pechorin would be defective if one or other of them were absent. Take Werner, for instance, the quick-witted and cynical doctor with whom Pechorin feels such an intellectual affinity. Pechorin's friendship with Werner convinces the reader of two things which he might otherwise have doubted, firstly that Pechorin is genuinely intelligent, and secondly that he is not condemned to be completely isolated from all his fellow-men.

Or look at Vera's role. Her presence in the novel shows that a deep mutual attachment can exist between Pechorin and a sensitive, mature woman. Without Vera we would see Pechorin impressing only rather inexperienced young women. More than this, though, Vera is said to *understand* Pechorin, and in this way Lermontov is able to emphasise that his hero is not necessarily the inscrutable enigma which he seems to be to everybody else. Lermontov exploits Vera's intimate knowledge of Pechorin most effectively at the end of the 'Princess Mary' episode, when he has her write a final letter to Pechorin in which she expresses authoritative judgments on various aspects of his character.

Or, to take one more example, what of Grushnitsky? Lermontov may perhaps have feared that his hero might be seen by some readers as little more than a foppish poseur, and one way in which he guards against this interpretation is by introducing the unambiguously empty and affected figure of Grushnitsky, who through his revealed lack of the qualities he affects to possess demonstrates that Pechorin is genuinely confident, sophisticated, courageous and sensitive.

Finally, no discussion of the shape of *A Hero of Our Time* can ignore the unifying role played by Lermontov's language. The remarkably consistent tone maintained from the beginning to the end of the work serves as a fine but immensely strong thread binding the diverse episodes into one whole. By fusing sensitive descriptions with tough-minded, even ruthless analysis Lermontov forges a style which is simultaneously robust and lyrical. It is a style which deliberately and splendidly mirrors the coincident muscular and poetic qualities of Lermontov's principal character, Grigorii Alexandrovich Pechorin, to whom we must now turn.

For the majority of readers the most memorable feature of *A Hero of Our Time* is the figure of Pechorin. His assertive personality provoked heated debates in Russian literary circles when the novel was first published in 1840, and with his singular mixture of almost larger-than-life vices and virtues Lermontov's hero arouses equally strong reactions in the modern reader almost a century and a half later.

Pechorin's vices are obvious. In spite of all the advantages he enjoys of birth, riches, health and intelligence, he is bored with life and disillusioned; he is self-centred and combative, and he acts coldly even towards his friends; worst of all perhaps, he possesses a streak of cruelty. In the well-known entry in his diary for 3rd June he confesses: 'I look upon the sufferings and joys of others only in relation to myself, as nourishment to support my spiritual strength', and a few lines later he adds: 'To be the cause of someone else's sufferings and joys, without possessing any positive right thereto—is that not the sweetest nourishment for our pride?' In his diary entry for 12th June he even goes so far as to state: 'There are moments when I understand the vampire'.

Nor are these merely theoretical pronouncements, for in practice Pechorin does indeed manipulate other people for his own pleasure. He enjoys teasing the hapless Grushnitsky, he kidnaps and seduces Bela, and he trifles with the naive young Princess Mary's affections, partly for want of anything else to occupy his time, and partly in order to spite Grushnitsky. Furthermore, Lermontov's hero is also implicated, directly or indirectly, in more than one death: he kills Grushnitsky in a duel, and he is a prime mover in the violent deaths of Bela and her father. By the time we read the last episode in the novel, 'The Fatalist', we have become so used to associating Pechorin with death that it is hard not to think that he must somehow also be the cause of Vulich's violent end—though of course he is not.

If Pechorin manifested only these obvious and undeniable vices, he could easily be dismissed as nothing more than a cold-hearted and ruthless aristocratic rake, but he does possess on the other hand a number of impressive virtues which should be emphasised, not just to produce a balanced picture of the man, but also—more interestingly—because they tend to be overlooked by many critics and readers of the novel.

Before examining Pechorin's virtues though, something should be said about the subject of fatalism, which arises at various points in *A Hero of Our Time.* After all, if the theory of fatalism were correct, then the words *vice* and *virtue* would have very little significance; if all our actions were controlled—perhaps even planned in advance—by fate or any other higher force, rather than freely chosen by ourselves, then we could not meaningfully be either rebuked for our apparently bad deeds, or praised for our apparently good ones; any vices or virtues would have to be ascribed to fate, rather than to individual men and women. Of course, as Lermontov well knew, in spite of his story 'The Fatalist', no conclusive experiments can be set up to test the theory of fatalism, and in practice, most of the time, we all take for granted that we do possess a considerable measure of freedom. Pechorin certainly assumes this much more often than not, and—for the duration of the present discussion at least—so must we.

What, then, are Pechorin's virtues? First of all, he possesses the traditional masculine virtues of physical toughness and energy, self-confidence and courage; he has a strong will and a commanding presence, and in dangerous situations he enjoys the advantages of quick reactions and a cool head. All these features emerge at their magnificent best in the duel with Grushnitsky—a scene which is one of the most memorable in all Russian literature.

Together with these masculine qualities, Pechorin also possesses what are often regarded as the more typically feminine virtues of personal charm (when he chooses to display it), good taste and a cultivated sense of elegance. He himself always dresses with great care, seeing himself as a consummate dandy even when galloping across the countryside in Circassian costume. At the same time he also appreciates elegance in others—from the impeccable *haute couture* of Princess Mary and her mother to the delicately-shaped nose of the smuggler-girl in 'Taman.' Lermontov's hero is exceptionally sensitive to the beauty of nature and has a highly developed sense of poetry—not so much the poetry of literature, as the poetry of life: one of the reasons he despises people like Grushnitsky is because, even though they may possess all sorts of good qualities, there is not, as he puts it, 'a penn' orth of poetry in their souls.

Beyond these two sets of attributes, which may be characterised as masculine and feminine, Pechorin possesses also the cerebral virtues of intelligence and wit, powers of logical analysis and, perhaps above all, intellectual honesty. He shows an uncanny ability to predict other people's reactions as well as a keen insight into his own complex personality, and one of his most constant and completely authentic preoccupations is his search for the truth—the truth about himself, society, human nature and the meaning of life. 'Why have I lived? For what purpose was I born?' he asks himself on the eve of the duel, not for the first, nor for the last time.

With this range of characteristics Pechorin presents indeed an impressive and most unusual combination of thinker and man of action, and of poet and man of the world. Moreover, he is attractive—both to his fellow-characters in *A Hero of Our Time* and to countless readers of Lermontov's novel. Unlike so many other fictional heroes in Russian nineteenth-century literature, Pechorin at his best possesses a wonderful freshness and vitality, and is not the slightest bit bookish, or seedy, or pale. To employ a modern cult word, he is the least wet hero in all Russian literature.

Why, then, do all these good points in Pechorin tend, at worst to be almost completely overlooked, and at best to be dismissed as matters of little account in comparison with his failings?

First of all, if the novel is viewed from a modern English standpoint it is clear that many of Pechorin's positive qualities are unfashionable. Since the end of the Second World War English society has been, on the whole, more than usually suspicious of Pechorin's military, aristocratic and aesthetic virtues. (That is to say, Pechorin's determination and courage might be seen as military qualities; his self-confidence, proud individualism, and indeed generally effortless superiority number among the traditional marks of the ideal aristocrat; while his sensitivity, elegance, and good taste are aesthetic merits). In recent years English society has come close to ignoring these virtues and, rightly or wrongly, has placed instead a correspondingly higher value on qualities which Pechorin certainly does not possess, such as compassion, community-mindedness and a sense of fairness and social justice.

Secondly, if *A Hero of Our Time* is considered in its native context, it must be noted that Pechorin's virtues have rarely been widely fashionable in Russia, where traditions of energetic personal independence have never really taken root, and individual enterprise has seldom been generally applauded. Further—and this is perhaps a more important point for the present discussion—nor are Pechorin's virtues those traditionally associated with the main stream of Russian nineteenth- and twentieth-century literature. From about 1840 Russian literature became committed, by and large, to the ideals of social reform and humanitarian or religious progress; political and religious writers alike stressed man's duty to society and his fellows, and preached—or at least tacitly assumed—that self-sacrifice in the interest of others was by far the greatest of all virtues.

Indeed, much subsequent Russian nineteenth-century literature—certainly a good deal of Tolstoy and Dostoevsky—can be interpreted as an attempt to combat the self-assertive tendency expressed by Pechorin. In *Crime and Punishment,* for instance, Dostoevsky strongly rebuts Raskolnikov's Pechorin-like arguments about the morally privileged position of his class of superior men, while in *The Brothers Karamazov* all the self-assertive urges seething through the novel are countered by Father Zosima's doctrine of self-denial and universal love. So too in *War and Peace:* Tolstoy's heroes, Prince Andrew and Pierre, both come to accept the need to reject self-indulgence and worldly ostentation. Perhaps the most striking rejection of Pechorinism is to be found in Tolstoy's *Father Sergius,* which portrays a model hero achieving salvation by progressing from his position as the most brilliant figure at the court of Nicholas I to labouring in Siberia as an anonymous, humble monk.

Like Russian literature, Russian literary criticism too adopted from about 1840 a predominantly moralistic approach. Nineteenth-century Russian critics, like their Soviet successors today, tended to assess works of literature chiefly according to their social utility and were inclined to measure literary characters principally against an ethical yardstick. Clearly, Pechorin could not be awarded high marks by such examiners. It is interesting to note, though, that even Belinsky, when writing a long review of Lermontov's novel in 1840, was able to stress the power of both sides of Pechorin's nature: ' . . . a certain greatness shines through his very vices, like lightning through black storm-clouds, and he is beautiful and full of poetry even at those moments when our human feeling rises against him. . . .'

A third reason for overlooking Pechorin's virtues derives from Lermontov himself—or more precisely from the oft-quoted remark in his 'Foreword' to the second edition of the novel: 'The *Hero of Our Time,* my dear sirs, is certainly a portrait, but not of a single person. It is a portrait composed of the vices of our entire generation in their ultimate development'. Accepted at face value and taken in isolation from the novel itself, these words certainly pronounce a clear and forceful condemnation of Pechorin—but should the reader accept the statement so straightforwardly?

First of all it must be remembered that Lermontov is a writer who delights in ambiguity and irony and who indeed only a few lines earlier in the same 'Foreword' has warned against a literal acceptance of all statements made in works of literature. Secondly—and more importantly—it is obvious that the attitude towards Pechorin expressed in this Foreword (written, it will be recalled, only for the second edition of *A Hero of Our Time* and in defence of the work) contrasts markedly with that found in the 'Foreword to Pechorin's Diary' where the narrator praises Pechorin's sincerity and suggests that the reader's main effort should be directed towards understanding and exonerating him.

Thirdly—and most important of all—it is hard to maintain that in the main body of the text attention focuses primarily on Pechorin's viciousness. Rather do we find that his virtues are given prominence and that he is indeed portrayed not only with sympathy but also with a marked degree of affection and admiration.

Some of Lermontov's contemporaries believed this to stem from the autobiographical nature of Pechorin. True, in his 'Foreword' to the second edition of the novel Lermontov denies that Pechorin is a self-portrait, but both Turgenev and Belinsky were unconvinced, while Ivan Panaev, who frequently met Lermontov in St Petersburg in the 1830s, states quite plainly: 'There is no doubt that he depicted in Pechorin, if not himself, then at least an ideal which concerned him at that time and to which he strongly aspired.'

Perhaps, then, Lermontov's remark about Pechorin's presenting a composite portrait of a whole generation's vices was not unreservedly true, but on this point, as on many others, every reader of *A Hero of Our Time* must make up his own mind. Whatever other responses he may provoke, Pechorin certainly forces readers to think and to consider their own attitudes and values. In the last analysis perhaps that is his greatest virtue and the supreme vindication of Lermontov's novel.

Gary Rosenshield   (essay date 1988)

SOURCE: "Fatalism in *A Hero of Our Time:* Cause or Commonplace?" in *The Supernatural in Slavic and Baltic Literature: Essays in Honor of Victor Terras,* edited by Amy Mandelker and Roberta Reeder, Slavica Publishers Inc., 1988, pp. 83-101.

[*In the following essay, Rosenshield examines the theme of fate as a supernatural power determining the course of human life in* A Hero of Our Times.]

With the possible exception of the works of Dostoevskij the supernatural plays almost no role in the nineteenth-century Russian "realistic" novel. Having their roots in social reality and common, everyday experience, the novel as a genre and realism as a literary movement usually treat areas of life which do not provide fertile ground for the exploration of the supernatural. One has to go back to the first great prose Russian novel, Lermontov's *A Hero of Our Time* (1837-1840), perhaps because it is still very much tied to certain commonplaces of nineteenth-century romanticism, to see the supernatural—through the category of fate—treated so seriously and extensively. Since *A Hero of our Time* is usually looked upon as a precursor of the great Russian psychological novels of the nineteenth century, that is, as a realistic novel, the theme of fate—fate

as a supernatural power determining the course of human life—has only been cursorily examined.

Most Soviet critics, working from a sociological point of view, have circumvented the theme of fate by redefining fate—when they use the term at all—to mean the *natural* social forces determining the behavior of classes and individuals. Given such a view, Pečorin can easily be made into a victim of his time, a man whose actions, or lack of significant actions, are determined by forces beyond his control; and consequently, from a moral point of view, a man who is not to be held strictly responsible for the destruction that he wreaks. This deterministic view also makes it easier to see Pečorin as a more positive character, a hero—or at least a hero *manqué*—a figure whose great potential was directed toward destructive ends only because he lacked the political outlets necessary for the constructive expression of his many talents.

The opposite of this Soviet view, and one that has gone for the most part unchallenged since it was first presented in 1960 by John Mersereau, Jr., is that Pečorin's recourse to fatalism is essentially a means of rationalizing, and thus refusing to take responsibility for, his actions—actions that led, directly or indirectly, to the death of Bèla, the breakup of the "honest" smuggling ring in *"Taman,"* the unhappiness of Princess Mary, and the death of Grušnickij. *A Hero of Our Time* in other words is a study—a devastating exposé—of deception and opportunism. Indeed, the self-serving character of Pečorin's statements about fate seems to be continually undermined by his careful and systematic planning of his actions and by his glorification of the will as the highest manifestation of being.

The virtue of Mersereau's psychological interpretation, in contrast to the Soviets' sociological one, is that it attacks the problem head-on. Yet Mersereau's position, however much one would prefer that Lermontov had in fact arranged matters in accordance with it, is simply not supported by the text itself, particularly when one closely examines the theme of fate in the other stories of the novel as well as in "The Fatalist" itself. In a confession, particularly in one characterized by seemingly ruthless psychological self-analysis, the critic can hardly be blamed for tending to look at the confessor's explanations of his behavior as rationalizations and self-justifications, and the confession itself as an endeavor undertaken to assuage deep-seated feelings of guilt. And one would have little problem accepting this interpretation if the hero did not speak so positively of the feelings of the vampire and of domination, and relate with such gusto how he carefully planned the destruction of others. Moreover, would a man who so prided himself on his ability to subject others to his will, and viewed the success of that enterprise as the goal of life itself, *desire* to ascribe his actions to fate? If Grušnickij and Princess Mary were fated to succumb, what in the end would be the meaning, the worth, of the victory?

But if Pečorin understands the glaring contradiction between fate and free will—and at least in "The Fatalist" we are led to believe he does—then why does he so frequently use fate to explain his behavior? Is there some artistic inconsistency here, or is the hero's simultaneous belief in these exclusive categories—or his alternation from one view of his actions to the diametrically opposite view—psychologically well motivated? In order better to understand the dynamics of these contradictions, the present paper attempts a detailed examination of the role of fate and motivation in *A Hero of Our Time,* based first on a close analysis of the narrator's use of the word fate (*sudba*)—and synonymous words and expressions—and secondly, on the examination of the relationship between the hero, Pečorin, and the implied author: perhaps the most problematic of all the figures in the novel.

Pečorin first attempts to explain his behavior—and his (*nesčastnyj*) character—towards the end of "Bèla," the first part of the novel. Pečorin has lost interest in Bèla, the Circassian princess whom he had abducted several months before; however, Bèla, who had at first seemed cold, is now pining away because of Pečorin's indifference. Maksim Maksimyč makes an unsuccessful attempt at persuading Pečorin to pay Bèla more attention. Pečorin explains his indifference in a long speech, which Maksim Maksimyč remembered almost verbatim, so great an impression did it make on him.

Pečorin's explanations, as elsewhere, fall into four categories, and combinations thereof: 1) supernatural predestination (fate); 2) innate character; 3) the social world, particularly high society; 4) the interaction of social and personal forces beyond human control. After stating that he really does not know exactly why he is the way he is, Pečorin confesses to an unfortunate character, but does not know whether it is because of his upbringing (3) or of God creating him so (1 and/or 2). Once released from his family's supervision, he began, he says, recklessly to enjoy the pleasures of the capital, and as a result became sated and repulsed by them (3). In addition, he claims that his soul has been impaired by the fashionable world (3). Having tried everything, including study, and having found nothing satisfying, he became bored; nor could society provide him with the means for self-fulfillment (4).

Maksim Maksimyč was taken aback to hear all this from a twenty-five year old, but even the travelling narrator of "Bèla," whose romanticism Lermontov appears to poke fun at, seems to view this disillusionment as uninteresting and passé—although he grants that Pečorin might actually be telling the truth about himself. The speech is a long, stilted one composed almost entirely of romantic commonplaces, not so different from the ones that Èjxenbaum so painstakingly documented in his early book on Lermontov. It is essentially rhetoric with a tinge of bravado: "After one month, I got so used to their buzzing [Čečen bullets] and to the nearness of death, that, really I paid more attention to the mosquitoes." The only other time Pečorin delivers a speech like this is in "Princess Mary," where it is even less believable, for, as Pečorin himself admits, it was delivered only to elicit compassion from the romantically inclined princess.

To be sure, one may, to a certain extent, come to believe in one's own rhetoric, or at least for a few moments be carried away by it; but it is hard to believe that Pečorin could take seriously his claim that he was ready to love the world, but no one understood him, and so he learned to hate. In contrast to not being comprehended, he tells us explicitly that Vera, for example, knew him perfectly, though this did not prevent him from exploiting her, nor from declaring the night before the duel with Grušnickij that he may die without anyone truly understanding him. Nor is it easy to see how Pečorin ever suffered at the hands of society, especially the society of women (here Lermontov may be inappropriately inserting his own experiences of rejection into Pečorin's speech), for he proudly admits to having found only one woman in all his life whom he could not completely subject to his will. Furthermore, Pečorin needs society; he feeds on it. Without society and the company of women, he would have nothing to do, and many fewer victims on which to perform experiments: indeed, on several occasions, he alludes to his social intrigues involving Grušnickij, Vera, and Princess Mary as the very stuff that makes life interesting.

Pečorin also rarely blames his upbringing and society in his "dialogue" with himself in his journal: he does so only in speeches to others. We have no objective evidence of the truth of anything that Pečorin says about his past, nor could we, given the form of first-person narration he employs. Since Pečorin seems much less concerned with the past than with the present, his explanations seem like afterthoughts by which he himself sets little store. His main interest in the past seems the reliving of past experiences through his journal. Rather than being a confession, the journal is primarily a means of turning the past into a form of present pleasure. To be sure, in an unabashedly romantic poem, à la Byron, the lack of such information would hardly be perceived as a serious artistic shortcoming. The Byronic hero has a mysterious past with some crime on his conscience, and the very vagueness, the very indefiniteness of his past is an essential element of his aura. However, in a fundamentally ironic and skeptical form such as the novel, a character who dwells on his past and its detrimental effects on his present, will hardly be persuasive if he resorts to the causal commonplaces of the romantic verse tale.

The only other place where Pečorin seems to try to justify his behavior by ascribing it to causes beyond his control—other than fate—is in a curious passage at the end of "Princess Mary," in which Pečorin likens himself to a sailor born and bred on the deck of a pirate ship, whose soul is used to storms, and who cannot tolerate the peace on shore that so easily could be his. The implicit argument that one assumes Pečorin is making here is that our character, from which all of our actions proceed logically, is given to us at birth, and therefore we can have little control over who we are and what we do: character is density. This explanation, however clichéd, is more convincing than his contention that he was crippled by society. Pečorin craves intrigue and excitement and is not afraid to subject himself to great danger: he has in fact several close brushes with death.

When Pečorin maintains that he is an unhappy product of his past, he is essentially adopting a self-serving pose. When, however—as in the concluding paragraph of "Princess Mary"—he likens himself to a pirate, it is difficult to determine how seriously we are to take him. Is he writing this tongue in cheek, or does he himself really believe what he writes? If he does believe it, it seems only at the time of writing, for he certainly treats the same ideas ironically elsewhere. Perhaps he both believes it and does not believe it at the same time. Or does he believe it here only because at the moment he feels the pangs of unconscious guilt? Even more problematic is the point of view of the implied author. Just what is his relationship to his hero? Is he presenting Pečorin ironically, showing this "explanation" to be little more than a self-serving rationalization? Or does he fuse with his hero, turning Pečorin into a projection of himself and his own doubts? Or does he perhaps vacillate between irony and identification, now giving the impression of purposeful ambiguity, now of unintentional inconsistency?

These formidable problems of interpretation are, if anything, compounded by the novel's treatment of fate. For now we are beset by the problem not only of determining the relationship between Pečorin and the author, but also of establishing the precise meaning of the word "fate" itself. At first one may see Pečorin's changing and ambiguous definitions of "fate" as an attempt to mold the term to suit his needs, even to the extent of considering a definition of fate that would not preclude the possibility of free will. But Pečorin's discussion of fate reveals the same lack of clarity and inconsistency that we have seen in his other statements about the past. What are we to make, for example, of the concluding passage of "Princess Mary," in which Pečorin writes: "And now here, in this dull fort, I often scan the past in thought, and wonder why I had not wanted to tread that path, which fate had opened up to me, where quiet joys and peace of mind awaited me? No, I would not get used to such an existence!"

What possible quiet joys and peace of mind, for example, could we imagine Pečorin enjoying, consistent with the picture that Pečorin paints of himself in "Princess Mary"? If we grant that it was fate that opened up these paths to him, how logically could he have avoided them? How does one decide to take a path opposite the one fated and actually, as Pečorin says, override the decrees of fate by one's will? Perhaps, Pečorin may be using the term fate loosely for his privileged position in society; but such a definition of fate is obviously inconsistent with the more strict and precise definition of fate—supernatural predestination—that emerges from "The Fatalist".

Pečorin uses fate in much the same inconsistent and illogical way when he explains why he will never marry. He seems to believe an old woman's prediction that he will meet his death from a wicked wife; yet he senses no contradiction when in the very next sentence he maintains that he will do his very best to make the prediction come true as late as possible. If even the hour of fortune—or misfortune—is set, as Vulič, the main proponent of predestination in "The Fatalist" maintains, one cannot postpone one's fate by acts of will, which by definition are themselves contrary to the notion of fate.

The inconsistency in this passage—and others—cannot be easily dismissed, for Pečorin consistently explains his behavior in this way. In fact, the more Pečorin speaks direct-

ly to the question of fate the murkier grow the waters. In the diary entry for 5 June, for example, Pečorin reveals how his careful plan of winning Princess Mary from Grušnickij is reaching its successful completion. It has so far been easy, perhaps even too easy to be really exciting. Grušnickij has just received his new uniform and thinks he is in a position to secure the affections of Princess Mary. Pečorin records his thoughts before he is about to destroy Grušnickij's hopes at their height. He writes:

> "Is it possible," I thought, "that my only function on earth is to ruin other people's hopes? Ever since I have lived and acted, fate has always seemed to bring me in at the denouement of other people's dramas, as if none could either die or despair without me! I am the indispensable persona in the fifth act; unwillingly, I play the miserable part of the executioner or the traitor. What could be fate's purpose in this? Might it not be that it had designated me to become the author of bourgeois tragedies and family novels, or the collaborator of some purveyor of stories for the *Library for Reading?* How should one know? How many people, in the beginning of life, think they will finish it as Alexander the Great or Lord Byron, and instead, retain for the whole of their existence, the rank of titular counsellor."

The passage starts off as though it was meant to be taken ironically—that is, as a conspiracy of the reader and author against the narrator. Pečorin, it would seem, is unintentionally unmasking himself when he asks whether his sole function (destination: *naznaenie*) in life is to destroy the hopes of others, for we have seen him so carefully and consciously planning Grušnickij's destruction. Whereas at the beginning of the entry for this date (June 5) we see Pečorin carefully controlling himself in Grušnickij's presence in accordance with his plans, in the above passage he claims that it is fate that has led *(privodila)* him to the denouement of other people's tragedies, that he is an unwilling *(nevolno)* actor in someone else's bad play. But again the imagery becomes confused, for Pečorin while speaking about the part that he is playing in the fifth act of a play written by fate also presents himself as a playwright (of bourgeois tragedies), a role, diametrically opposite to that of the passive actor, that he has just described himself as performing.

It must be said in defense of the passage above that one senses in it a certain amount of irony, not only between author and narrator, but between Pečorin as narrator and Pečorin as character. Pečorin presents his fated role not as something grand or romantic in the style of Manfred, but as something quintessentially prosaic: he is like an author of "bourgeois tragedies," family novels, and cheap popular tales. It is perhaps an acknowledgment that it is self-serving and even ridiculous to think that the category of fate—romantically conceived—could apply to his own situation. Whereas in most other places in the novel the skeptical ironist and the romantic who seems sincerely to believe in his own rhetoric are kept separate, in this passage the two Pečorins are interestingly juxtaposed.

But the above passage is a best case. Most passage having to do with fate are so inconsistent that they are difficult to understand from any point of view. Pečorin's last diary entry, for example, the one in which he records his thoughts on the duel he is to fight with Grušnickij on the following morning speaks most confusedly on the influence of "one's star."

> What if my star at last betrays me? . . . It would hardly be strange, it has so long served my whims faithfully. There is no more constancy in heaven than there is on earth.
>
> I scan my whole past in memory and involuntarily wonder: why did I live, for what purpose was I born? . . . And yet that purpose must have existed, and my destination must have been a lofty one, for I feel, in my soul, boundless strength. But I did not divine that destination, I became enticed by the lure of hollow and thankless passions. From their crucible, I emerged as hard and cold as iron, but lost forever the ardor of noble aspirations—the best flower of life. And since then, how many times have I played the part of an axe in the hands of fate! As an executioner's tool, I would fall upon the head of doomed victims, often without malice, always without regret.

In contrast to the previous passage there does not seem to be the slightest touch of irony here. Pečorin asserts not only that there must have been a purpose in his life but that his destiny *(naznačenie),* because of the unbounded power he feels within himself, must have been a high one. Though, logically speaking, no necessary connection exists between one's fate and one's feelings about oneself, it is perfectly understandable psychologically. But this statement is in blatant contradiction with the ironic attitude he took toward his destiny in the earlier passage, in which titular counselors who are "destined" to remain titular counselors all their lives also start off (we must remember that Pečorin is only in his early twenties) thinking they are the world's greatest poets and conquerors. Here, however, Pečorin does not seem at all to sense the contradiction.

But Pečorin does not let bad enough alone. (Or is it the author who does not allow Pečorin to let bad enough alone?) He expands upon his notion of "destiny," maintaining that he failed to divine what his destiny was because he became enticed by the lure of empty and thankless passions. The rhetoric comes thicker; the aphorisms mount up. He claims to have come out of this crucible of thankless passions harder and colder than iron, having lost forever the ardor of noble aspirations—the best flower of life. But what precisely does Pečorin mean by "forever," by "noble aspirations," and "the best flower of life"? The "forever" sounds a little exaggerated for a twenty-five-year old. Probably it is a romantic mode word used for emphasis. The "noble aspirations" are also a romantic cliché (we know nothing of Pečorin's noble aspirations) as are the noble aspirations being the "best flower of life." In the only other passage in the novel where flowers figure prominently in the imagery, Pečorin likens his innocent victims to flowers that one must pick at just the right time, and then having sated oneself with their delicious fragrance, throw them on the road for someone else, perhaps, to pick up. From the flowers of life Pečorin turns to the axe of fate, describing himself as being chosen by fate to fall upon the heads of the condemned (that is, fated to die)—often without malice and always without compassion. But how then does he explain his long, detailed, and systematic efforts to destroy Grušnickij?

One is tempted to think that all these loose ends will be neatly tied up in "The Fatalist," the last story in the collection, and the one in which the last events of Pečorin's life in the Caucasus are related. It is a vain hope. For although "The Fatalist" deals with fate, it does not deal with fate from a moral perspective—despite the famous statement at the beginning by the officer who attempts to silence a discussion of predestination by bringing in the category of responsibility. "And if predestination actually exists, why then are we given free will and reason, and why must we give an account for our actions?" Although the officer's words seem to set the stage for an existential and problematic presentation of fate and accountability, the story turns out to be about the criteria for establishing the existence of fate, not its moral implications.

In the story, Pečorin and a Serbian officer by the name of Vulič perform experiments to *prove* the existence of predestination—Vulič to prove its existence to others, Pečorin to prove its existence to himself. Given that fate is a "supernatural" (Pečorin himself uses the word *metafizičeskij*) and not a "natural" category, it is understandable why each of their empirical attempts to prove the existence of fate ends in complete failure: if Pečorin learns anything in the course of the story, it is only the impossibility of proving the existence of fate. Starting out as a skeptic, he becomes temporarily converted to "fatalism" by Vulič's experiment and his own prediction of Vulič's death, and then after performing an experiment of his own—disarming a dangerous Cossack murderer—he returns to his former skepticism. Pečorin must have recognized, at least subconsciously, that his experiment with fate was invalidated by the precautions he took and the calculations he made. Charging a dazed man with the assistance of troops, however risky, is after all not the same thing as pointing a loaded pistol at one's head and discharging it as Vulič did. What emerges most strongly in "The Fatalist" is Pečorin's final skepticism.

> After all this, how, it would seem, can one escape becoming a fatalist? But then, how can a man know for certain whether or not he is really convinced of anything? And how often we mistake, for conviction, the deceit of our senses or an error of reasoning? I like to have doubts, about everything: this inclination of the mind does not impinge upon resoluteness of character. On the contrary, as far as I am concerned, I always advance with greater courage, when I do not know what awaits me. For nothing worse than death can ever occur; and from death there is no escape!

Given these conclusions one wonders not only what light "The Fatalist" could possibly throw on the moral issues of "Princess Mary," but also whether there is any significant relationship between the two stories at all. If at the end of the story, Pečorin—somewhat out of character—had become a fatalist like Vulič, then one could argue, as Mersereau does, that Pečorin adopted a self-serving philosophy in order to justify his actions and abjure all responsibility for them. Even though morality *per se* plays no role in "The Fatalist" itself, the officer's statement about the incommensurability of free will and fate would then act as a satisfactory bridge linking "Princess Mary" and "The Fatalist." One might even be justified in arguing this point of view, if, at the end of "The Fatalist," Pečorin was still torn between voluntarism and fatalism, even more self-servingly believing in both at the same time. However, he clearly states that he prefers to have doubts regarding fate, as about all other things. What his skepticism should imply, given that free will may exist and fate may not, is that he must accept the possibility that he *may,* as the officer concludes, be held accountable for his actions.

But if this is, in fact, the logic of Pečorin's position, there is no indication at all in "The Fatalist"—or in "Bèla" and "Maksim Maksimyč"—that Pečorin has been affected by the implications of his skepticism or even thought about them. Furthermore, to conceive of Pečorin undertaking an experiment with fate in order to prove himself not responsible for his actions or to assuage any guilt he may have experienced over them is to impose the mature Dostoevskij onto the young Lermontov. Pečorin can blanch in horror, but he does not seem to suffer guilt. He rushes the Cossack murdered not to prove a theory, but to satisfy his need for excitement and adventure. It is the act of a daredevil. If a motive is required, Pečorin's need not to be outdone by anyone is more than sufficient. He wants to know if he has the courage to do something as dangerous as Vulič. If one insists on the demonic aspect of Pečorin's personality, then it is the discrediting of fate not its establishment that is most important for Pečorin, and that is why he chooses to remain a skeptic. Any other view would be insulting to one who takes pleasure in the sufferings he inflicts on others and prides himself on the supremacy of his will.

If "The Fatalist" does not provide the key to the moral dilemma posed by the question of fate, might there not be a higher point of view to which all of the novel's inconsistent internal points of view are consistently subordinated, an ideal implied author who always maintains an ironic distance from his characters and who, although he may at times show them sympathy, never lets any of their flaws escape from his all-seeing and all-knowing irony?

Not only does there seem to be no such figure, but it is perhaps, paradoxically, more satisfying in the end not to have one. It may be that the best way to approach the characterization of Pečorin is to see him, at least in terms of fate, essentially as a projection of an inconsistent implied author, a projection in which the ironic distance between author and character is often erased. Once this absence of distance is granted, *A Hero of Our Time,* on its deepest and most interesting level, becomes a novel not so much about Pečorin, a hero of a series of adventures, but about the implied author who projects himself into his character in an attempt more perfectly to understand the role that romantic literature and its stereotypes play and should play in his own life. That is the reason that Pečorin seems to take seriously in some places the romantic common-

places which elsewhere he treats with irony, and even sarcasm. Pečorin is essentially a ruthless, calculating figure. He may entertain certain romantic notions, peculiar to his age and upbringing, but not for more than the few moments it takes the demon of irony to appear and dissipate the fog. The skeptic and rational Pečorin, however, is only one side of Lermontov; the other Lermontov, the Lermontov who has not yet overcome the romantic—and the romantic commonplaces—in himself, also finds a home in his hero.

Nowhere can the presence of these two personae be better seen than in the last passage of "Princess Mary," dealing with Pečorin's inability to lead a happy and peaceful life on shore.

> And now here, in this dull fort, I often scan the past in thought, and wonder why I had not wanted to tread that path, which fate had opened for me, where quiet joys and peace of mind awaited me? No, I would not have got used to such a lot! I am like a sailor born and bred on the deck of a pirate brig. His soul is used to storms and battles, and, when cast out on the shore, he feels bored and oppressed, no matter how the shady grove lures him, no matter how the peaceful sun shines on him. All day long he haunts the sand of the shore, hearkens to the monotonous murmur of the surf and peers into the misty distance. Will there not appear there, glimpsed on the pale line separating the blue main from the gray cloudlets, the longed-for sail, at first like the wing of a sea gull, but gradually separating itself from the foam of the breakers and, at a smooth clip, nearing the desolate quay?

For anyone who associates Pečorin with the calculating rationalist of "Princess Mary," this passage will ring false. Can one really picture the Pečorin, who tortures an innocent young girl and shoots Grušnickij off a cliff, continually pondering why he did not follow that path laid out for him by fate, a path of quiet joys and spiritual peace? Here again the implied author imposes on his hero a set of images and romantic commonplaces that are much more his own concern than his character's. The closing lines—taken from Lermontov's early poem **"Parus"**—are out of place in "Princess Mary." Most of the nature imagery in "Princess Mary" is based on the rugged beauty of the Caucasus, and one would think that something from this romantic setting could easily have provided an effective conclusion. Instead Lermontov chooses the imagery of pirates on the high seas, which is more appropriate for the Pečorin of "Taman"—although only relatively so, for what does a restless hero born for storms, at home only on a pirate brig, have to do with a young man of the world from St. Petersburg who cannot even swim and is nearly overpowered and killed on a rowboat by a young girl.

One could argue that the inappropriateness of the imagery at the end of "Princess Mary" is the ironic means by which the implied author cuts down his hero. But we have seen Pečorin himself treat such romantic commonplaces with devastating irony. Pečorin is simply not fictionally consistent with himself. To be sure, such inconsistencies exist in real life—and also in the point of view of implied authors—but as readers we tend not to accept them in characters in novels, especially psychological novels, unless these inconsistences are credibly motivated. As François Mauriac has argued about the differences between real people and characters in fiction, readers accept as real, that is, as fictionally valid, only those characters that are fictionally consistent, who seem to obey the laws of fiction. An inconsistent implied author, on the other hand, we often find more acceptable, even more interesting. Further, once one sees Pečorin as an aspect of the persona of the implied author, many of the *artistic* contradictions in Pečorin's character—as well as in other characters—become more tolerable.

An especially good example of the implied author taking over not only Pečorin, but other characters as well, is the characterization of Vera, an old flame of the hero. Not many critics have thought Vera well conceived, probably because her relationship with Pečorin does not seem adequately motivated. She is used primarily as a device to expose Pečorin's ruthlessness, his pleasure in being the cause of the sufferings of others. Is not a great part of Pečorin's fun in courting Princess Mary his realization of how it torments Vera? Vera's letter, expressing her hopeless love for Pečorin, however, seems to have been penned not by Vera but Pečorin himself—or some female creation of Lermontov's romantic imagination—so much is it imbued with Lermontovian common-places, so much does it resemble in content, language, and emotional color many other romantic passages of Pečorin's diary. Surely, it is Pečorin—or rather the romantic Lermontov—and not Vera who writes the following words. "She, who has loved you once, cannot look without a certain contempt on other men, not because you are better than they—oh, no! —but because there is something special about your nature, peculiar to you alone, something proud and mysterious. In your voice, whatever you may be saying, there is unconquerable power." One can hardly imagine Pečorin receiving—or writing—a letter more flattering to his ego. It is, in essence, no letter at all, but a device which permits the romantic persona of the implied author to inject himself once again into his narrative.

Some of the inconsistency in the presentation of fate, especially between individual stories, may be attributed to different times of writing: what ended up as a novel started out for the most part as a series of independent stories; but the main reason, as we have seen, is that the implied author has not himself come to an adequate understanding of the role of fate in human actions and is using the novel, as it were, as a means of exploring the problem from all angles. It may seem inconsistent in a psychological novel for the hero one moment to write a paean to free will and the next moment blithely and facilely describe himself as the passive tool of fate, but it certainly is not inconsistent in a romantic tale for an implied author to reveal his ambivalence through his character.

Furthermore, in *A Hero of Our Time,* at least with regard to the theme of fate and the characterization of Pečorin, we are dealing with the simultaneous application of both realistic and "romantic" devices of motivation. Whereas the handling of Pečorin's duel with Grušnickij is a model of metonymic psychological analysis, the hero's explana-

tions of his past and some of his ruminations on fate are closer in style to romantic poetry in which the emphasis often is more on evoking emotion than on providing psychological and semantic consistency. Many of the paragraphs stand out as vertical blocks of associative affects, not linear strings of logical meaning. Vladimir Nabokov noting the "agglomeration of insignificant words," and "shocking" and "comic" shortcomings of Lermontov's sentences in *A Hero of Our Time,* nevertheless expresses his admiration for the remarkable rhythm and timing of the paragraphs. As Gertrude Stein has said, emotion is in the paragraph, not in the sentence.

The emphasis that I have laid on the emotional and romantic character of *A Hero of Our Time* is not intended to point out the novel's deficiencies but rather to define more accurately the areas of its strengths. Criticism in general, and Soviet criticism in particular, has done *A Hero of Our Time* a singular disservice by so insistently arguing that it is the first great work of psychological realism in Russian literature, the foundation, as it were, on which the later novels of Dostoevskij, Tolstoj, and Turgenev are squarely set. To so argue, in practice, is to force it to live up to novelistic assumptions regarding psychological realism and metonymic motivation that are uncongenial and, more important, inappropriate to it. Ultimately, Lermontov's novel owes its power far more to its romantic aura than to the depth of its psychological analysis.

It is to this romantic side of the work that we must also ascribe the often less than strict use of the emotionally charged word "fate." Sometimes it is used to mean little more than "chance," or "opportunity"; at other times it is given a strict definition, as in "The Fatalist"; and at still other times its *primary* meaning is an emotive one. Moreover, except for that night when Vulič was killed, Pečorin does not show any particular interest in the idea or implications of fate; and from what we can judge by our brief acquaintance with him five years after the events of "The Fatalist," he has not given much thought to fate since. The seriousness of fate in the novel reveals itself in the implied author's incarnation in his hero. Fate was a much exploited theme in the literature, and also the thought, of Lermontov's time, and a commonplace of a good deal of romantic fiction; and thus it is not surprising to see Lermontov, through his hero, revealing his emotional bond to the notion of fatalism, while at the same time subjecting it to rigorous criticism. And well we might, for was Lermontov himself not "fated" to perish in a senseless duel not long after writing the novel? The tragic reality for Russian literature, as well as of course for Lermontov himself, was that his opponent turned out to be no Grušnickij.

R. L. Kesler   (essay date 1990)

SOURCE: "Fate and Narrative Structure in Lermontov's *A Hero of Our Time,*" in *Texas Studies in Literature and Language,* Vol. XXXII, No. 4, Winter, 1990, pp. 485-505.

[*In the following essay, Kesler examines* A Hero of Our Time *as a "critique of both the romantic hero and those circumstances of literary production that produced and destroyed the romantic movement" in Russian literature.*]

Budet i togo, chto bolezn ukazana, a kak ee izlechit—eto uzh bog znaet! (Let it suffice that the malady has been diagnosed—heaven alone knows how to cure it!)

The thematic importance of the concept of fate in the Russian novel is widely acknowledged, but what is the importance of fate when viewed within the context of literary history? To what extent was the novel itself fated, by its own particular structure and the conditions under which it emerges, to employ just such a concept? Lermontov's *A Hero of Our Time* is frequently faulted for its fragmented narrative structure and apparent reliance on adventure plots. But it is, nevertheless, a serious philosophical investigation into the aesthetics of romanticism and social function of literary representation in nineteenth-century society. In an age that pitted the notions of determinism and literary influence against romantic aspirations toward expression and originality, the concept of fate emerges as a central site of both personal and literary conflicts. In *A Hero of Our Time,* it is a concept that operates on both a thematic and metacritical level, describing both the individual's speculation on his or her own freedom and the possibilities and processes of the novel itself. And its operation not only determines but demands those aspects of the novel that have traditionally been the hardest to explain: its complex narrative structure and its ambivalence toward its own philosophical claims. Understood, through the concept of fate, as an implicit commentary on its own function, *A Hero of Our Time* emerges as a thorough and complex critique of both the romantic hero and those circumstances of literary production that produced and destroyed the romantic movement as a whole.

The last two-thirds of *A Hero of Our Time* consists of the journals of the novel's hero, Pechorin. The last story in these journals, "The Fatalist," begins with a discussion of the concept of predestination among a group of frontier officers who have become bored after an evening of playing cards. The central position in this discussion is quickly assumed by a Serbian named Vulich, who suggests that fate be put to a test. Pechorin, the central character of the novel as a whole, assumes a typically adversarial position, offering to bet against both Vulich and predestination. Vulich accepts the bet, removes a pistol from the wall, places it to his temple, and announces his intention to fire. At this point Pechorin angers Vulich by claiming to see "the mark of death" on his face. Vulich then pulls the trigger, but the pistol misfires, though in a subsequent test it performs normally. Vulich survives, and "predestination" is apparently confirmed. Yet returning home later that night, Vulich is assaulted on the road by a drunken Cossack and is killed. The verdict is thus reversed, and it is Pechorin who appears to be the victor, the "mark of death" having become an accurate prediction (though this outcome is not totally unexpected—Vulich, we are told earlier, was a compulsive gambler who routinely lost). At the end of the story, perhaps prompted by the unusual events of the night and a desire to test his own fate, Pechorin jumps through the window of the hut in which the remorseful but desperate Cossack is now hiding. Pechorin disarms the Cossack and survives, though his survival, for the reader, has never been in doubt: the reader has already been informed at a point earlier in the novel that Pechorin has died elsewhere.

Pechorin's successful test against fate is followed in the novel only by a brief interchange between Pechorin and his companion, a plain-speaking line officer named Maxim Maximych. This exchange, though very short, completes the contrast between these two characters that has extended throughout the novel. In the face of Pechorin's broader speculations on "predestination" (*predopredelenie*), Maxim first offers only a practical reflection on the relative unreliability of Circassian firearms, then finally, as if in concession to Pechorin, this observation about fate: "Still, I suppose that's how he was meant to die" (*Vprochem, vidno, uzh tak u nego na rodu bylo napisano*). This somewhat dismissive comment is significant not only in that it closes both this discussion and the novel but also in that it replaces the somewhat lofty philosophical concept of "predestination" (*predopredelenie*) and the various tests and affirmations that the chapter has depended on, with the more home-spun notion of practicality and fate that simply concedes the appropriateness of the final outcome. But beyond that, the choice of the specific expression Maxim uses "tak u nego na rodu bylo napisano" (literally, as to him from birth it was written) is, perhaps, significant: the shift from the more abstract concept of fate as "predestination" (*predopredelenie*) to fate as *napisano* (that which has been written) suggests, beyond the class difference of the two speakers, the concept of a fate that has been predetermined in a very specific way—as literally "having been written."

At the beginning of "The Fatalist," this particular notion of fate is identified with Moslems: "We were talking about the way many Christians accept the Muslim belief that a man's destiny is written in heaven" (lit., "sud'ba cheloveka napisana na nebesakh"). Yet this use is also significant in that it reprises an earlier, similar one at the beginning of the novel, at that point at which Maxim first introduces Pechorin: "after all, some people are fated to have unusual things happen to them" (*Ved'est', pravo, etakie liudi, u kotorykh na rodu napisano, chto s nimi dolzhny sluchat'sia raznye neobyknovennye veshchi* ["u kotorykh na rodu napisano" (lit., to whom from birth it is written)]). In what sense, we might ask, is the fate of a character in a novel something that has "already been written"? In some ways, of course, this question is purely artificial, since characters in novels are not, in fact, people at all, and their fate is something that is always necessarily "written" by the writer. But in other ways, this question remains meaningful, since no individuals are free from the constraints of their societies, nor are writers in constructing "a fiction" free from the constraints of form, constraints that operate for both writers and characters in their works as something very much like "fate" or "predestination."

Vulich's situation may be taken as an example: we may imagine the character Vulich, at the moment he places the pistol to his head, as imagining himself to have arrived at a truly decisive moment, a moment in which alternatives are equally weighted, but mutually exclusive in the most absolute terms possible—those of life and death. And, indeed, the illusion of the story depends precisely upon our making this inference. Yet from the perspective of the author, outside of the story, the outcome of this moment can never be in doubt: for the story to exist at all, Vulich must survive this first encounter because his death at this moment would end the story without significantly contributing to the development of "fate" as a narrative concept. Yet he must die unexpectedly in the second encounter, since it is only through this fulfillment, after its initial frustration, that Pechorin's prophecy of Vulich's death gains legitimacy, further complicating the issue of "fate." By surviving the first known test, but dying unexpectedly in the second, Vulich fulfills not only the prophecy but the desire of the other characters to witness personally one of the "strange stories" (*strannye sluchai*) about predestination with which the story begins. And, significantly, it is only by appearing in this precise combination that these events appear as "strange" or ironic at all, thus adding credibility to the entire discussion of predestination: even a slight alteration would destroy its efficacy in establishing this point in the narrative.

Thus, from a narrative standpoint, these events are not accidental, nor are they, in any real sense, "tests of fate," since their pattern and outcome are determined, ironically enough, by exactly the necessity of creating a context in which the question of predestination may be raised seriously, but left unresolved. In other words, it is the necessity of creating the illusion of indeterminacy that structures the necessity of their appearing in a highly determined way. The chapter, like the novel in this respect, functions as something like a puzzle or game, creating the illusion of possibility by its very elimination. In conclusion, we might generalize by saying that what appears to characters on the *inside* of the story as "fate" is what appears to the writer on the *outside* of the story as "narrative necessity." The "fate" of the characters may be "written in heaven," but their "god" is the novel's author. Yet even this "god" is to some extent predetermined, since the author too works within a world of predefined and limited possibilities.

Before considering further those restrictions of fate to which the author is subject, it is worth returning for a moment to consider that, in "The Fatalist," it is not Vulich alone whose fate is predetermined. Pechorin too is "fated" in this same sense, both to jump through the window and to survive. First, only by jumping is he able to counter Vulich's "heroism" within this story and to resume his position as "hero" of the novel as a whole; second, only by surviving can his heroism be sustained and consistency maintained with other aspects of the story, since we already know that Pechorin cannot die here as, due to the peculiar temporal and narrative structure of the novel, he has "already" died elsewhere. But it is also worth considering that this theme of fate functions throughout the novel, particularly with respect to Pechorin, in a much more general sense, a sense that determines even the convolutions of this narrative technique.

The first chapter of the novel "Bela," does not begin as a story about Pechorin at all, but rather as a travelogue. *A Hero of Our Time,* like other such disparate works as Brontë's *Wuthering Heights* and Carlyle's *Sartor Resartus,* is told through the intermediary of a somewhat colorless narrator who functions by governing the reader's access to information about some vastly more interesting hero. While foregrounding the novel's own intermediary status with regard to some supposed referential "reality," this technique may also end by bringing its own reliability into question, since the motives of this very narrator may emerge as an issue. In Lermontov's novel this narrator is first introduced as an inexperienced traveler, never named, who is ostensibly compiling notes on his journey through the Caucasus. The novel thus begins with those notes themselves, notes that, replete with elaborate descriptions of the scenic "sublime," threaten the reader, if extended, with a numbing boredom. Fortuitously (and no doubt symbolically), a sympathetic nature in the form of a dramatic storm intervenes, forcing this narrator to take refuge in a mountain hut with a crusty and experienced old army captain. The captain, who proves to be none other than Maxim Maximych, begins, through the suitably murky atmosphere of the dimly lit mountain hut, to tell a story about a young officer who proves to be Pechorin. Maxim thus becomes the second narrator of the novel. Maxim's story, which is the story of the love affair between Pechorin and Bela, the daughter of a Circassian chief, soon displaces the travelogue as the primary narrative of this first section of the novel. This pattern of displacement is later continued: a second encounter with Maxim, in which Pechorin himself figures briefly (the chapter "Maxim Maximych"), furnishes the narrator with Pechorin's journals, which then, without further "mediation," become the remaining two-thirds of the novel.

During this first encounter with Maxim, however, the narrator-traveler offers a brief aside that initiates both the larger narrative structure of the novel and the particular concern with "predestination" that will eventually mature into "The Fatalist." "I was most eager to get some kind of yarn out of him," this narrator writes, "a desire common to all those who keep travel notes." The narrator makes it clear that the inclusion of such a story would be of immense benefit to his own narrative, the "travelogue," both by increasing its authenticity (Maxim as a kind of naive local expert) and by furnishing it with a narrative more exciting than that supplied by his own meager talents (Maxim as a source of action stories). But the greater significance of this initial remark is not revealed until a short time later, after the fundamental interest of Maxim's narrative has been well established: the storm abates, threatening to return the travelers to their journey and, by implication, the narrative to the travelogue and its scenic descriptions. Worse yet, as if in perverse sympathy with the waning storm, the early tension of Maxim's story of Pechorin and Bela appears to have diffused into a happy ending. "How dull!" the narrator exclaims. "There was I expecting some tragic end only to have my hopes dashed in this unexpected fashion!" The reader must share in this disappointment, since the travel description pales by comparison, but in a passage that shortly follows, Maxim resuscitates the narrative by resuming his story, which then moves inexorably toward a more satisfactory, and more tragic, dénouement. And it is with this movement that the narrative shifts resolutely to assuming its "true" nature as a romantic novel, fixated on the question of its hero and his fate.

As Boris Eikhenbaum has argued, a primary effect of this complex narrative strategy is to build anticipation by delaying the plot line. And yet, just as the novel itself is more than a simple adventure story, this technique of "delay" has other, more extended consequences. Though, on the one hand, the narrator is a kind of naive audience for the more central narratives of the novel, which now appear as if they were naturalistic events for which he bears no responsibility, on the other, he begins to appear in a more sinister role—as the writer or editor who controls our very access to these stories, determining their interest in a critical and not entirely sympathetic or disinterested manner. The judgment he makes determines the "fate" of the story itself and, consequently, the fate of its "hero" as a representation: if the story of Pechorin is not sufficiently "interesting," it will not be included in his "travel notes," and those "notes" will revert to their original condition of scenic description. If, on the other hand, Pechorin's story is sufficiently "interesting," as in fact it must be (we are ironically informed at the very beginning of the novel that the rest of the travel notes have been "lost"), then the novel becomes the story of Pechorin, as we know it does. From this sly device we may deduce, first, that Pechorin is "fated" or "predestined" to have an "interesting" life, and second, that this life must necessarily involve death and a "tragic ending."

This situation produces a number of interesting ironies. Pechorin, partially to explain his often very questionable actions, complains to Maxim of his "unfortunate" character: " 'Look, Maxim Maximych,' he said. 'I've got an unfortunate character. I don't know how I came by it, whether it was the way I was brought up or whether it's just the way I'm made. All I know is that if I make other people unhappy, I'm no less unhappy myself.' " Pechorin's description of his character as "unfortunate" (*neschastnyi*), with its implication of "ill-fated," or "unlucky" (as in *neschastnyi sluchai* [unfortunate accident]) is ironic, since it is just this quality of "misfortune" that both creates the story and makes it, in the process, such "*good*" fortune for the narrator because it is now "unhappy" enough to be of use. "Not long ago I heard that Pechorin had died on his way back from Persia,' " the narrator somewhat ghoulishly remarks. " 'I was delighted, since it means that I can print his notes.' " Like the tragedies of the Greek or Renaissance stage, the novel becomes a form that requires the sacrifice of its hero, whose "choices" are no choices at all, as they must inevitably lead to a single end—the requisite "tragedy" of an unhappy ending. And the reader, like the narrator, also becomes located within this system not only as a consumer but finally as a connoisseur of this aesthetically "interesting" and predictable disaster.

Pechorin, and to some extent the other characters around him, is not at all insensitive to his situation, for he sees himself both in terms of narrative and dramatic effects and interprets his situation in terms of its narrative implications: the novel, in other words, may imitate life, but it is also clear that, for its characters, life also self-consciously imitates a novel. Particularly in such later chapters as "Princess Mary," Pechorin is shown to be consciously and self-consciously playing for effect. Costuming becomes crucial: at a key point in the story, he rides toward a group of sightseers, including the princess, dressed in a local tribesman's costume. "Mon dieu, un circassien!" exclaims the princess. But it is only Pechorin, making an entrance. Given the care and planning that precede even the most chance of these encounters, it becomes difficult to interpret Pechorin's actions as "spontaneous expressions" of any impulsive inner feeling: though perhaps a romantic, Pechorin is thus neither the naive and impulsive actor of Wordsworth's "Nutting" nor the heroic expressionist of Shelley's *Defense*. Rather, he has more in common with the "decadent" Edgar Allan Poe, who calculated his actions deliberately for the effects they were likely to produce. "I prefer commencing with the consideration of an *effect*," Poe wrote:

> Having chosen a novel, first, and secondly a vivid effect, I consider whether it can be best wrought by incident or tone—whether by ordinary incidents and particular tone, or the converse, or by peculiarity both of incident and tone—afterward looking about me (or rather within) for such combinations of event, or tone, as shall best aid me in the construction of the effect.

This calculating and curiously modernist notion (with obvious parallels to Eliot's "objective correlative") is in some respects profoundly antiromantic and deterministic. And for Pechorin, for whom it goes beyond technique to become a way of life, it presents, rather than a solution, a dilemma—a widening gap between desire and action, passion and reflection, that constitutes his version of the romantic paradox.

Thus Pechorin describes the situations in which he finds himself with detachment, as if they were scenes from a play that he is watching, even as he joins in their actions:

> As I passed the sulphur spring, I stopped to get my breath in the shade of the covered terrace and chanced to see a somewhat curious scene. The actors were placed as follows . . .

> "The stage is set," I cried, delighted. "We'll see if we can provide a *dénouement* for this comedy. Evidently fate means to see I'm not bored."

"Finita la commedia!" he remarks, having just killed his rival Grushnitsky in a duel. And this mode of description extends to other characters in the play. The princess reportedly describes Pechorin as "the hero of some novel in the modern taste." And in turn he derides Grushnitsky, who seems suspiciously like a less adept version of himself, precisely for trying to become "the hero of a novel." Grushnitsky, whose attention to costuming rivals Pechorin's own, has "spent so much time trying to convince others that he's not of this world and that fate has some mysterious trials in store for him, that he practically believes it himself," Pechorin argues. But the irony, of course, is that it is Pechorin who, in defeating this rival, succeeds at remaining on center stage.

The most interesting aspect of Pechorin's perception of his

own fictionality, however, is not simply that he imagines himself as a character, but rather that he seems aware of the place in which that character is located in a literary history. That cornerstone of European fiction, Aristotelian "tragic" plot, is, after all, ultimately a predictive form: constructed of events that occur, not "at haphazard" but linked by "causal necessity," plot yields to those familiar with its conventions a model of cause-and-effect actions that lead inevitably toward a known and defined end. And while the role of early examples of such tragedies is to educate their audiences in such causalities, revealing and unfolding their patterns before them, later tragedies, whose ends and motivations are known, concentrate primarily on effects, the magnitude of horrors that befall the hero and his confederates in the fifth act.

The "fifth act" and its endings are known quantities in *A Hero of Our Time,* and it is in such a predictive tragedy that Pechorin clearly perceives himself to appear. "Through all my active life fate always seems to have brought me in for the *dénouement* of other people's dramas," he complains:

> As if nobody could die or despair without my help. I've been the indispensable figure of the fifth act, thrust into the pitiful role of executioner or betrayer. What was fate's purpose? Perhaps I was meant to be a writer of domestic tragedies or novels of family life, or a purveyor of stories, perhaps, for the Reader's Library? How can one tell? Many people start life expecting to end up as Alexander the Great or Lord Byron, then spend their whole lives as minor civil servants.

Such a limitation on the conditions of "the hero" are a typical consequence of knowledge, through which the sacrifices of the hero come perilously close to appearing to be merely the results of bad planning. Tragedy that becomes predictable is merely perverse, a risk that this novel constantly runs. And it is the fear of sliding into cliché and banality that drives Pechorin constantly toward more extreme and postured effects. It is from the absurdity of such a decline that the convoluted narrative structure of the novel is only partially able to save him.

At the beginning of the novel, Maxim asks the narrator if all the young people in the capital are like Pechorin. "I said," he replies, "that there were a lot of people who did talk like that and that very likely some of them told the truth, but disenchantment, like any other fashion, having started off among the élite had now been passed down to finish its days among the lower orders." Thus Pechorin's story is, in yet another sense, "already written"—already lived and determined by others and thus presented to him as a whole, as a story or "fate" already established by conventions that now threaten to reduce him, in their repetition, to mere cliché. Pechorin's exile to the Caucasus, like the narrative techniques of the novel that distance him and render him mysterious, is a response to this impending reduction. Displaced out of the capital in which their fashion has already passed, Pechorin's actions retain their meaning in rustic border encampments, distinct against a cast that cannot compete with them. In return, these exotic locales provide their own form of excitement to alleviate the boredom of self-absorption that pervades the capital

and its stories. Yet this displacement is at best only a holding action: it is the constant necessity of this displacement, out of the "travelogue" and into a story that demands ever further adventures, speculations, and mysteries, that drives the novel into its most labyrinthine manipulations. But Maxim's dismissal of them in the play's final lines is far from accidental: the character Pechorin, like the concept of "fate," exists only in its own indeterminacy, and this indeterminacy is hard won in an ever more ingenious formal structure. It is, finally, only Pechorin's particular trajectory through these forms, conditioned by his apparent knowledge of them, that keeps both form and hero from a descent toward an "ordinary" fate. And yet it is the impossibility of sustaining this task that drives the novel inexorably toward the final mystery and refuge of death.

That the story is structured in such a way that Pechorin is "fated" *not* to die at the end of the novel ("The Fatalist") even though by the time we read that story we already know of his death in events subsequent to that story's action, is further evidence of the novel's complicated manipulations of the categories of "fate" and time: "The Fatalist" and the end of the novel are "already written" in yet another, final sense in that they come to us in the form of the written notes of an already dead man. Thus the novel creates the somewhat eerie illusion of a character speaking "after" his own death. That character thus becomes, at the very time we appear to gain access to his thoughts, yet more remote and inaccessible, since recovery of that character as a "primary phenomenon" or "expressive origin" for his voice has already become impossible: he exists only as voice alone, a recording of his own "fate." That we only *hear* of his actual death, in an off-hand comment even more remote from the novel's action, further preserves this sense of mystery and escape: the hero has evaded our ability to interrogate him further beyond the information he has already somewhat enigmatically supplied. At the same time, however, the illusion of the character as a "living person" who *preexists* his existence in writing is, in another sense, reinforced, since his writing appears to remain after his death as a kind of evidence, monument, or trace of something that assumedly must have come before. And in this, Pechorin stands as a prime example of that quintessential fiction identified by Aristotle: "It is Homer who has chiefly taught other poets the art of telling lies skillfully. The secret of it lies in a fallacy. For, assuming that if one thing is or becomes, a second is or becomes, men imagine that, if the second is, the first likewise is or becomes. But this is a false inference."

Thus, assuming the journals of Pechorin, one assumes a "Pechorin" who preceded them, just as, assuming a "fate," one assumes a "character" who preexists to have it, even though that may not, strictly speaking, be the case. Yet even beyond this dilemma, writing appears as an ambiguous act, since while preserving the record of a character and allowing that character to live (in fiction), it also commits that character to a kind of metaphorical death in the fixity of the written form. Writing confirms that very "fate" by giving it form: if such a character were to exist after his story had been "written," he would automatically become a cliché, the "hero of a novel in the modern taste."

Thus success becomes the worst form of confinement; while the description of the character becomes "immortal," it is the character himself who becomes displaced by this process. The fiction becomes more real than the character creating it. Pechorin's death before "The Fatalist" is thus the logical consequence of his own fate. It places him beyond the cliché formed by his own narration. His death, like the narrative that so curiously produces and places it, is his only escape from a sense of time bound intricately to the very act of writing.

That the hero of *A Hero of Our Time* is himself also *homo scribens* (he who writes) only compounds this problem, since his fate thus not only derives from the novel being written but from the fact that it is he himself who writes it. And it is the nature of this problem—of the man who in writing writes his own fate—that is explicated on two of the larger movements of the novel's narrative structure. In its largest terms, narration in the novel may be seen to progress in three stages from a form that is predominantly oral to one that is self-consciously written. The internal structure that begins the novel in "Bela" is sedimented within the "naive" traditions of oral narration, relying on the operation of an unsophisticated narrator (Maxim) who would never under ordinary conditions bring his narration into a "literary" or written form and presenting its hero as above the status of its own narration. In this story Pechorin acts and only marginally reflects.

In "Maxim Maximych," however, the narrator (he of the travelogue) structures the narrative clearly as a literary professional, observing the major characters (Pechorin, Maxim) like Faraday observes the candle, with precisely the "objective" intent of reducing them to writing; it is *he*, finally, who defines *them* as suitable subjects within the framework defined by his actions. The final section of the novel, the written journals of Pechorin himself, continues this progression, moving the narration into that internal space that was the furthest extension of nineteenth-century literary technique—the psychological space of the character himself. This interior space, defined by writing, presents the character's self-examination in an "objective" form accessible to the reader and opens the door to psychological interpretations of both character and author, for whom the entire novel appears as a type of confession (thus those famous critical linkings of Lermontov to his overprotective mother). Inevitably, it also leads to the necessary consideration of the relationship of the hero to his own perception of himself in the very act of writing. In the space before the reinvention of the voice in stream-of-consciousness writing, it represents the contradictions of writing itself in their most extreme form—those most internal of reflections are made external by the terms of their representation, even to their producer, as alienated and "objective" fact.

It is within this self-reflexive and self-defining relation to his own written history that the second progression of the novel's narrative forms, asserts itself in the ordering of Pechorin's journals, an ordering in which Pechorin himself seems to surface in a consciousness of his own literary representation. The first of these stories, "Taman" shows the hero in a naive mode that, though presented through the internal representations of his own thought, remains locked within the world of only barely reflective action: the hero blunders into a coastal smuggling operation and acts impulsively in what then develops into an adventure story. He discovers in its course, first, that his actions have consequences and, second, that a whole network of relations and meaning underlies a reality quite independent of his own will. His impulsive aimlessness is thus defined in contrast to the more purposeful activity that surrounds him: "I felt sad. Why did fate toss me into the peaceful midst of these *honest smugglers?* I had shattered their calm, like a stone thrown into a still pool—and like a stone, too, I had nearly gone to the bottom." Yet though Pechorin's explosive encounter with this highly ordered external reality is his entry into the world of causality and consequence that surrounds him, he seems to become aware only in their recanting, as the activity of narration provides him the opportunity to reflect.

The second story, "Princess Mary," however, shows Pechorin in a very different mode. Though still both impulsive and perverse, he is nevertheless quick to assess his external situation and to plan a deliberate and purposeful campaign of his own, as he slowly and deliberately draws the affections of the young princess to a predictably melancholy conclusion. "Princess Mary" thus becomes an extended investigation on an essentially teleological theme: the hero both understands and functions through planning and "fate," though he is able only to speculate on those larger issues of "fate" that supply and structure his motivations. And it is this investigation, in which the rules and logic of "causally" predicated actions are fully explored, that leads ultimately to the final investigation of "fate" and narration found in "The Fatalist," in which both the narrative and practical implications of these notions (as "written") are put to the test.

The crucial segment in this central process in the book is undoubtedly "Princess Mary," which, unlike "Taman" or "The Fatalist," is distinguished by its diary format. The diary format differs from the other forms of narration in the book in that its organizing principle is not the continuous development of a single narrative context: rather, the diary divides its narration into a series of segments (the dated entries) that are themselves, though sequential, temporally discontinuous. Furthermore, in this format the keeping of the diary itself becomes a form of action. Its interpretation of previous events becoming part of the context within which further events take place. The diary format thus sets up a dialectic or alternation between action and reflection in which both become mutually influential. Within this alternation the central problematic of the novel constitutes itself. Writing, that act of reflection in which the actions of the hero become detached, "objective" even to his own consideration, begins to inform those actions themselves: "There are two men within me," Pechorin says at a point late in the novel, "one lives in the full sense of the word, the other reflects and judges him." The apparent function of the diary is not to allow for action but for reflection and judgment. And the split we see here, between action and reflection, passion and reason, is typical not only of this novel but of the romantic movement as a whole. But reflection is, in "reality" as in this novel, never so passive: the interpretive context of writing, to the extent that it exists at all and operates as "fiction" according to the rules and conventions of narrative, necessarily prefigures action. The diary itself becomes "a novel" that begins to form its hero to its own ends. Reflection and the "literary" interpretation of experience become in themselves a kind of "fate" that alienates Pechorin from the more immediate or pragmatic context of his own actions as they form a stricter context for judgement (that of "history" and self-esteem). It is the diary and its necessity to perform a "literary" function that thus determines that "unfortunate nature" upon which both Pechorin's "fate" and the novel so clearly depend. Pechorin as a character becomes structured in the irony of his own literary definition: defined by writing, he becomes "written" by that very definition. By recording his actions, he determines what they will be.

In becoming a critic and voicing dissatisfaction both with the "domestic tragedy" he fears that his life has become and his role within it (his entry always in the "fifth act"), Pechorin reverses the causal structure of mimetic time: it becomes the necessity "to be a novel" that structures life, and thus the sequences of "life" necessarily appear out of order. And it is the reversal of this causality that determines finally even the role of the writer: by acting, Lermontov creates his novel, but by thinking in terms of a novel and of those maneuvers now necessary to create a "new" and thus effective novel, he determines the larger pattern of his own actions. Outside the illusion of the novel, it is not the author who creates the novel, but the novel that demands and structures the author, even to the necessities of his individuality and the illusion of his own perplexed will, even to the necessities of his own impulse toward creative expression.

The romantics insisted both that the artist be the source of expression and that that expression be given literary form. And yet, in obvious ways, these requirements are contradictory: to operate in the medium of language, and particularly written language, is to operate always within a configuration of preexisting forms that only in restricted and predetermined ways are open to modification. The struggle that we see throughout the novel, between freedom and determination, the ability to feel and the compulsion to act, are bound in this pattern. They are part of an age in which the primacy of both feeling and expression are absolute, but within which the necessity to realize these impulses, in writing, enforces their prestructuring. Wordsworth, lost in his anticipation of the experience of crossing the Alps, is dismayed to find himself on the other side; characters in this novel, while struggling to avoid the "fate" of falling into predetermined clichés of their own experience, create "freedom" only to the extent that they have none.

Eikhenbaum argues that Lermontov's achievement, at least in prose, was the solution of a purely literary problem:

> Lermontov died early, but this fact bears no relation to the historical work which he accomplished, and changes nothing in the resolution of the literary-historical problem which interests

us. It was necessary to sum up the classical period of Russian poetry and to prepare the transition to the creation of a new prose. History demanded it—and it was accomplished by Lermontov.

We might even say that it was Lermontov's "fate" to be a romantic and to solve this particular problem. Yet the problem, in the terms we have been discussing, may extend beyond the strictly literary; in an age dominated by the concept of expression, in which the sincerity and authenticity of expression was given the highest value, poets imagined their speeches as acts of self-realization. Yet even as they spoke, they both used existing convention and modified it to establish their own. Even in those cases in which speech appeared to create new forms, to speak again was to repeat that form: the poet as creator became a cliché, the *lishnii chelovek* (superfluous man) outdated by his own insistence on originality, the product of a machine that had come to recognize its own determinacy. Thus Lermontov, living on the periphery of a Continental movement that had already produced both Byron and Pushkin, like Pechorin in the Caucasus, lived in a world of forms established elsewhere. Of necessity in such circumstances, attention passes from cause to effect, from expression and origin to reception and death. In comparing Lermontov to Byron, Walter Reed notes that Byron's life was "fully as influential as his works." In Lermontov's case we might argue rather for the influence of his works over his life: living in the shadow of Byron and Pushkin, Lermontov attempted to define himself by the construction of a new prose style. In the process of so doing, perhaps incidentally, he describes, in the scene of Pechorin's duel with Grushnitsky (and arguably himself), something very like the circumstances of his own death, which was to occur only two years later. Was this chance, or "predestination," or merely the attempt to render faithfully in life what had already been established in prose? It was, at the very least, something *bylo napisano,* something that was, in a very ironic sense, "already written."

The strange relationship between Lermontov and **A Hero of Our Time** may be described in terms of a different sort of intersection or "fate." In a celebrated article, Roman Jakobson argued for the primacy of two linguistic operations, selection and combination, that he associated respectively with the rhetorical tropes of metaphor and metonymy. Near the end of the same article, Jakobson also suggested the applicability of this bipolar paradigm to the classification of a large number of literary and cultural phenomena. Romanticism is associated with metaphor; realism, with metonymy—that division, in other words, within which Eikhenbaum defined Lermontov's struggle. And in a later article, Jakobson extended his original opposition to include the terms "encoding" and "decoding," opening the possibility that such cultural phenomena as romanticism and realism might be understood as two aspects of a single developing historical pattern— romanticism "encoding" and realism "decoding" the same set of relationships. Jakobson's analysis thus adds to Eikhenbaum's the possibility of a further and more extensive description of this transition's structure.

Jakobson's association of metaphor with romanticism is

particularly applicable to "early" aspects of Lermontov's novel, or rather Pechorin's development within it. Patients in Jakobson's study who were representative of the "metaphorical" category of speech loss were able to initiate speeches and produce monologues, but were less responsive to dialogue. Thus, like Pechorin in "Taman," they appeared solipsistically self-defining, monologic, and alienated to the surrounding social context. Furthermore, in their speeches the least subordinated grammatical elements, especially the grammatical subject, were the least likely feature to be lost, while those subordinated or predicated items were typically first to disappear. While the speaking subject thus remained a "sufficient" context for the production of speech, such patients lost the ability to "propositionalize" and thus to form relationships of time or consequence. Like the Pechorin of "Taman," such patients were able to initiate actions but not to foresee their directions or consequences. Extended into literary terms, the inability to "propositionalize" is equivalent to the inability to form "plots." Thus "plot" in "Taman" emerges, as it were, externally to the character Pechorin, to whom consequences appear as unexpected surprises. The existence of the smuggling operation itself as a "plot" or system of relations that then involves the unwitting Pechorin is something that is only slowly uncovered in the story. Unable to predict time, such characters enter "time" or "context" unaware, and, like Pechorin in "Taman," are likely to enter it precipitously, "like a stone thrown into a still pool." Many romantic monologues are, of course, devoted to this theme of isolation or alienation some larger, locating context (e. g., Nature), and view time and consequence as themselves undesirable products of an alienation from a more natural state.

In contrast, Jakobson's association of metonymy with realism is typical of "later" aspects of the novel. Aphasics in this "metonymic" category had lost the ability to name and were not able to initiate conversations. They were reactive, only able to complete dialogues begun by others. Speech thus arises not out of the individual but out of a situation that is both its source and determinant. Within speech, the grammatical subject and other unbound words were the first to disappear, while those words most clearly subordinated and bound by syntax were the most tenaciously retained. Words, like the speaker, came to be defined *only* within a situational or social context of reaction and response, thus paralleling the Pechorin of "Princess Mary," who sees himself as only a character of the fifth act, only capable of completing actions determined by others, only defined by relations such as those with Grushnitsky and his circle, no matter how disastrous their inevitable consequences. The character, who now longs to be "self-defining," can no longer be so, feeling increasingly trapped within a role determined elsewhere. Like the grammatical subject of the sentence of a "metonymical" aphasic, he is in danger of disappearing completely (as of course he does in the narrator's report of his death). The passage from "encoding" to "decoding" is thus a transition from "naming" and the individual into "syntax" and the social: "character," in any independent sense, disappears, leaving only definition by syntax, pattern, or its literary analogue, "plot" (narrative necessity and fate). And

this is precisely the transition that *A Hero of Our Time* describes.

The most suggestive aspect of Jakobson's system in understanding this transition, though not explicitly developed in his writing, is the sense in which the transition between these two states might be understood as a necessary consequence of their structure. Behind Jakobson's "metaphoric" category lies the Saussurian category of *langue*: "the metaphoric" operates through selection, which Jakobson defines as a relationship *in absentia;* that is, a relationship defined in terms of a code or system not fully represented in the message (or *parole*) itself. In literary terms the most important aspect of this code is precisely this *absent* quality: this array of patterns and connections are useful primarily in that they function unproblematically and are merely assumed. The operation of metaphor is a case in point. Since metaphor, and particularly poetic metaphor, operates by the *violation* of normal category restrictions, linking *unlike* things together by virtue of only partial similarity, metaphors depend very directly on the inherent stability of their joined lexical categories: if the meanings of the two terms are not clear, their metaphorical equation is interpreted as an actual equivalence, and all "poetic" effect of the transposition of categories (or "tension") in the metaphor is lost. Yet if the categories *are* stable and the unusual quality of the metaphor is thus preserved, the apparent creation of a "new" kind of meaning is the likely result. Since the categories stabilizing this "new" combination themselves remain submerged, this "new" meaning appears iconically, as if without a context, and demands an explanation, which is quite often found in the imputation of a source—the "genius" and "individuality" of the speaker or author. This speaker appears to "encode," since the message he or she defines does not appear to have existed before, even though it is precisely on the very stability of its component parts that this illusion depends. Paradoxically, the appearance of "the individual" thus depends on the availability of stable clichés against which it may define itself, and perhaps significantly, the romantic movement follows on the heels of the great movement of the seventeenth and eighteenth centuries toward the standardization of language and knowledge: though romanticism is usually interpreted as reacting against this movement toward standardization, it is thus clear that, at least in one respect, it is precisely upon the conditions presented by this movement that it most depends.

Once established, on the other hand, the regular application of such techniques of founding "neologism" is likely to have the dual effects of both destabilizing the very conventions it most often uses, while simultaneously establishing new and competing conventions (metaphors themselves, if they are explicitly stated, become combinations, and eventually, perhaps, new clichés). As those categories become fluid, they not only move toward redefinition as new clichés but become, for a time, too unstable to support further metaphorical activity. Thus the formation of "metaphor" itself, or the appearance of "individuality," becomes restricted to a few increasingly established channels, further encouraging their transition toward cliché. This is the situation as *A Hero of Our Time* presents it: those conditions favoring the appearance of "unique individuality" have passed, leaving the paradoxical possibility of "individuality" only through increasingly exaggerated imitation. Furthermore, as the unseen conventions that establish individual terms become unstable, the question of relationship itself becomes foregrounded: terms are negotiated and defined by context, and syntax becomes increasingly visible as "plot." "Character," as anything other than a position created within that "plot," then begins to disappear. The romantic novel shifts first toward the mystification of "plot" as "fate" (*A Hero of Our Time*) and later toward an obsessive fascination with the effects and ends that such a "plot" or "fate" can produce—those senses of overdetermination and death so characteristic of Poe and his successors. The transition toward "decadence," on the one hand, and "realism," on the other, thus emerges as a logical consequence of the operation of the "metaphoric" state as that state is extended diachronically in time beyond its own synchronic and "eternal" pretensions. The function of "realism" in this respect is the reestablishment of the syntactic and lexical categories of the code through the systematic exploration and restatement of their relations.

The operation of this pattern is made particularly acute by the technology of written representation, which provides a stable record and entrenchment for each stage in this process. Early in his career, in collaboration with Peter Bogatyrëv, Jakobson argued for a difference in function between "literary" and "folkloric" art: "folkloric" art, which operates in a primarily oral environment, functions largely as a preserver of records and cultural continuity. It is based on repetition, and in this sense, on a constant reaffirmation of an unseen *langue*. "Literary" art, however, functions in a far different manner: since it is predicated on the availability of written records which perform their archival function through a single iteration, "literary" art works operate under the condition of having constantly to distinguish themselves from their predecessors—a *"langue"* that is all too apparent and clear. Since each work must be to some extent "new" with respect to those that have gone before, "literary" works operate in a continual state of incremental change, thus vastly accelerating the type of transformation outlined above, even as it recasts it within the particular romantic sense of "literary" alienation.

A Hero of Our Time, operating as the first full-length literary prose work in a culture that, though still to a large extent sedimented within an oral and ritualized tradition, was experiencing the large-scale intrusion of the highly literate culture of western romanticism among its intelligentsia, embodies many of the structural contradictions of romanticism as a whole in a form that is, due to this and other local circumstances, particularly acute. It points to, finally, a redefinition of the structural basis for "meaning" that underlies the romantic movement as a whole, a redefinition that may be defined not in terms of expression or even, strictly speaking, alienation but in terms of the progressive development of representational technology itself in its social context. Coming "after the fact"—after the paradigm and syntax of romanticism and the romantic hero had been established elsewhere—the form of *A Hero of Our Time* is in many respects already one of over-

determination and "reception," a movement unavoidable and perhaps predictable, but perhaps "necessarily" productive of outstanding literary achievement: "That's all I could get out of him—he's not at all keen on metaphysical discussions." The dismissal of philosophic concerns at the ending of the novel, while on one level only a final part of the complex game the novel is playing, may also be an admission that even the understanding of such "deterministic" issues is ultimately futile—only a stage within that very determinism. Yet it is the "fate" of the novel that such concerns should form the basis of its story and that that story, in order to perform its function within this developing representational order, should make those very concerns "interesting." This too, in Eikhenbaum's terminology, is what "history demanded"—and what Lermontov accomplished.

Priscilla Meyer   (essay date 1992)

SOURCE: "Lermontov's Reading of Pushkin: *The Tales of Belkin* and *A Hero of Our Time,*" in *The Golden Age of Russian Literature and Thought,* edited by Derek Offord, St. Martin's Press, 1992, pp. 58-75.

[*In the following excerpt, Meyer maintains that Lermontov modeled* A Hero of Our Time *on Aleksandr Pushkin's* Povesti Belkina (Tales of Belkin) *story cycle.*]

In 1830 Lermontov wrote in his notebook: 'Our literature is so poor that I can't borrow anything from it'. The following year, Pushkin 'descended to humble prose', and published *The Tales of Belkin (Povesti Belkina)*.

As many have shown, Lermontov was an attentive reader of current Russian literature. This study shows that, unlike others among Pushkin's contemporaries, who regarded his tales as frivolous, Lermontov studied them carefully, and, understanding them as a review of the materials available to Russian prose writers in 1831, structured his novel, *A Hero of Our Time (Geroi nashego vremeni;* 1840), on the *Belkin* cycle.

Critics have noted the novel's thematic and stylistic sources in detail. Boris Tomashevsky discusses the evolution of Lermontov's prose in relation to Western European models, adducing many parallel themes and borrowed images, especially from French Romantic prose. The stylistics of *A Hero of Our Time* have been analysed by Viktor Vinogradov, who traces the interplay of Gogol's and Pushkin's modes through Lermontov's prose. Boris Eikhenbaum places the structure of *A Hero of Our Time* in the context of the development of the Russian story cycle, and emphasises Lermontov's achievement in creating a psychological novel out of that genre. Turbin investigates the constant use Pushkin and Lermontov made of the work of secondary writers; he pays particular attention to genre in noting the interplay between poetry and prose, but does not examine the story cycle.

These valuable analyses do not account for the great step forward that *A Hero of Our Time* represents over Lermontov's earlier (unfinished) prose. Lermontov's first prose work, *Vadim,* is closely related to the elevated melodrama of Marlinsky. Lermontov's next effort at a novel,

Princess Ligovskaia (*Kniaginia Ligovskaia;* 1836), may be understood as an attempt to translate *Eugene Onegin* (*Evgenii Onegin*; 1823-31) into prose. The hero's name, Pechorin, is a deliberately transparent analogy to Onegin, the first name derived from a northern river, the second from a northern lake. The epigraph is from Chapter I of *Onegin*. Pechorin flirts with Negurova as Onegin flirts with Olga; Pechorin and Negurova had been in love, but he leaves her for no clear reason. When they later meet in St Petersburg, Varvara is married to an older man and transformed into Princess Ligovskaia, just as Tatiana metamorphoses after marrying her general. Lermontov's novel breaks off after Pechorin and Varvara have had several painful encounters in St Petersburg high society, at the point where the love plot of *Onegin* is resolved through Onegin's letter to Tatiana.

But Lermontov does not confine himself to Pechorin's romantic life in *Princess Ligovskaia;* he interweaves it with the tale of the impoverished clerk Krasinsky, which is rendered in the naturalist tradition. It appears that Lermontov was attempting to do what Dostoevsky effected a few years later in *Poor Folk* (*Bednye liudi*; 1846): to merge the two principal lines of Russian literature by uniting the world of the poor clerk with the sophisticated society novel. The elements of each are undigested in *Princess Ligovskaia,* the two modes jarringly juxtaposed. Perhaps, as Eikhenbaum conjectures, Lermontov abandoned *Princess Ligovskaia* because he understood this. In any case, he found a way to recombine existing elements of the best Russian writers: instead of using Pushkin's novel in verse as a model, he looked to Pushkin's prose.

Belinsky understood the Pechorin of *A Hero of Our Time* as an updated Onegin, an 'Onegin of our time'. Later critics have continued to regard Onegin as the only one of Pushkin's heroes sufficiently complex to serve as a model for Pechorin. *The Tales of Belkin* were considered too laconic a basis for complex psychological portraits. As Tolstoy put it, 'Pushkin's tales are rather naked'.

Yet both *The Tales of Belkin* and *A Hero of Our Time* are made up of an introduction and five stories. It is surprising that no one has considered the relationship between these two formative prose works. The development of Lermontov's prose shows him to be as thoughtful about the future of the Russian novel as Pushkin, and as concerned to bring Russian prose up to the level of the Western European novels he knew so well. Tomashevsky has traced a variety of Western literary sources in Lermontov's prose: in *Vadim* he finds elements of Sir Walter Scott's historical novels as purveyed by Balzac's *Les Chouans;* the description of Quasimodo in Victor Hugo's *Notre Dame de Paris;* Chateaubriand's *Atala* (Lermontov: 'an inexpressible sadness stirs like a poisonous crocodile in the depths of a pure, clear American well' and Chateaubriand: 'Le coeur le plus naturel ressemble au puits naturel de la savane Alachua . . . au fond du bassin, vous apercevez un large crocodile, que le puits nourrit dans ses eaux.'); and *René* (the Chateaubriandesque trees). Tomashevsky also enumerates the bored Western literary heroes who contribute to Pechorin's character in *A Hero of Our Time.* Indeed, like Pushkin in *Eugene Onegin* (which Pechorin has clearly read), Lermontov has his characters identify themselves in terms of the Western literary tradition: Princess Mary reads Byron in the original; Pechorin presents Dr Werner as a materialist version of a German Mephistopheles who limps like Byron; the narrator of 'Bela' and 'Maksim Maksimych' refers to Rousseau's *Confessions* in his introduction to Pechorin's journal, and Pechorin refers to Goethe's Mignon in 'Taman' as the stereotype that led him astray. Lermontov removed the explicit mention of Melmoth and the Vampire from his own introduction to the second edition, substituting the generic 'tragic and romantic villains'. Lermontov carries on a polemic with these villains (who include the more innocent-looking René and Adolphe) by embedding parallels to particular Western European Romantic texts in Pechorin's speech, suggesting that Pechorin may be consciously parodying his own prototype. His pathetic confession to Mary about his childhood is a (rather more efficient) paraphrase of *Adolphe:*

> Yes, such was my lot since my very childhood! Everybody read in my face the signs of bad inclinations which were not there, but they were supposed to be there—and so they came into existence. I was modest—they accused me of being crafty: I became secretive. I felt deeply good and evil—nobody caressed me, everybody offended me: I became rancorous. I was gloomy—other children were merry and talkative. I felt myself superior to them—but was considered inferior: I became envious. I was ready to love the whole world—none understood me: and I learned to hate. My colourless youth was spent in a struggle with myself and the world. Fearing mockery, I buried my best feelings at the bottom of my heart . . . When I got to know well the fashionable world and the mechanism of society, I became skilled in the science of life, and saw how others were happy without that skill. . . .

Pechorin even gives a thumbnail sketch of the plot of *Adolphe* in warning Grushnitsky of the scenario he may replay:

> Beware, Grushnitsky! . . . Your silence must excite her curiosity, your talk should never entirely satisfy it; you must disturb her every minute. She will disregard convention, publicly, a dozen times for your sake, and will call it a sacrifice, and, in order to reward herself for it, she will begin to torment you, and after that she will simply say that she cannot stand you.

Adolphe also provides Lermontov with some structural elements: the manuscript of Adolphe's account of his affair with Ellénore is acquired by a travelling 'Editor' who publishes it as an instructive lesson, 'une histoire assez vraie de la misère du coeur humain'. This particular variation of the device of the found manuscript includes a letter to the editor that Lermontov uses in characterising Pechorin. . . .

Another structural element Lermontov takes from Constant (when he could have used Pushkin's version from *Onegin*) is Ellénore's letter to Adolphe; like Vera's to Pechorin, it is placed at the end of the novel and contains an analysis of the hero's personality, the heroine's weakness, and her willing sacrifices for him.

Lermontov's deliberate evocation of *Adolphe* in so many prominent places suggests a polemic with Constant's novel, published in 1816 and well-known to Russian readers of the 1840s. But it is Lermontov's apprenticeship to Pushkin that helps him to frame this dialogue.

Intimately familiar as Lermontov was with European Romantic texts as well as with Pushkin's, he would readily have seen in Pushkin's story cycle a review of the materials available from which to construct a truly national Russian literature. The *Belkin* tales manage, astonishingly, to be at once a primer for beginning readers and an encyclopaedia for writers and critics; Pushkin's five entertaining stories review the stock plots, typical heroes, and genres of the time while providing a critical commentary on the nature of literary artifice. Lermontov sets himself the task of incorporating all these functions into a novel, uniting the five stories and narrator's preface around the figure of Pechorin.

Pushkin's story cycle is united by themes, motifs, and method. The philosophical discussion of fate versus chance is related to the question of fictional artifice by the underlying theme of how to read, a lesson none of Pushkin's characters learns. This theme is carried in part by the motif of blindness throughout the stories, and indeed, almost all the characters in the *Tales of Belkin* fail to recognise the stereotypes, and their sources, that determine their fates. The narrator of 'The Shot' accepts Silvio as the hero of an adventure tale, even after hearing the Count's side of it; the young lovers of 'The Blizzard' act out the romantic elopement plot of French epistolary novels with (mock) tragic results; the 'Undertaker' Adrian Prokhorov misses (and therefore will never act upon) the implications of his dream: in the German supernatural genre, it points to his guilt and the possibility of retribution for it; the poor 'Stationmaster' Samson Vyrin never realises that his expectations of Dunia's ruin are governed by the parable of the Prodigal Son. Only Liza of 'The Lady-Peasant' identifies her masks and manipulates them successfully: recognising Aleksei's pretensions to Byronism, she assumes the role of the 'exotic' woman, redistributing the national elements: as Akulina, Liza parodies the French *bergère* masquerade of the court of Louis XIV; as the young lady in her Louis XIV wig, she parodies Russian affectation in mimicking French aristocracy. The plot of 'The Lady-Peasant' is a comic version of the Tatiana-Onegin romance; Tatiana's mature role is made possible by her perusal of Onegin's library which allows her to realise the discrepancy between her Richardsonian models and his Byronic ones. Liza has luckily done her homework on time, hence the comedy, while Tatiana's education comes too late to prevent her unhappiness.

Lermontov had been dealing with literary stereotypes in **Princess Ligovskaia**—in fact, the correspondence between the plot of *Eugene Onegin* and Lermontov's own unresolved love affairs with Sushkova and Lopukhina suggests that Lermontov had been pondering the relationship of literary stereotypes to his own life.

But more importantly than their personal appeal to Lermontov as a man, *The Tales of Belkin* helped him as a poet trying to write prose that could educate a naive reading

public. The *Tales* provided a solution to the problem Lermontov never solved in *Princess Ligovskaia:* Pushkin's story cycle, which at first might seem more problematic material for a novel than Pushkin's 'novel in verse', had a built-in means of separating the different genres. Furthermore, Pushkin's theme of the naive reader motivated inclusion of a variety of literary styles, plots, and types. The layered narrative structure made possible several variations on the problem of the relationship of actual author to authorial persona and of both to the hero, relationships by then needing renovation as the Romantic hero was being replaced by a realist one.

The two sets of five tales are paired by plot and by genre. Lermontov sets up a mirror symmetry, inverting the order of Pushkin's five tales. He matches his last with Pushkin's first, his first with Pushkin's last, the second with the fourth, the fourth with the second and pairs the two middle stories. Here are the five sets, following Pushkin's order:

> 1. 'The Shot' ('*Vystrel*') and 'The Fatalist' ('*Fatalist*') are adventure tales with mysterious heroes of the type of Ann Radcliffe's *The Italian*.
>
> 2. 'The Blizzard' ('*Metel*') and 'Princess Mary' ('*Kniazhna Meri*') are society tales about the tragic consequences of accepting an unsuitable match.
>
> 3. 'The Undertaker' ('*Grobovshchik*') and 'Taman' are parodies of supernatural tales in the German tradition of Hoffmann and Tieck.
>
> 4. 'The Stationmaster' ('*Stantsionnyi smotritel*') and 'Maksim Maksimych' are sympathetic physiological sketches of the low government official.
>
> 5. 'The Lady-Peasant' ('*Baryshnia-krestianka*') and 'Bela' are variations on the Byronic hero's quest for the exotic.

These pairings show how Lermontov, who began writing **A Hero of Our Time** in 1838 soon after Pushkin's death, at once acknowledges Pushkin's achievement and makes use of the Belkin story cycle to develop the novel form.

There are clear parallels between both the plots and genres of each pair of tales, but Lermontov departs from Pushkin in structuring the relationship between narrator and narratee. Both authors treat this subject in the introductions that frame their tales. Pushkin's authorial persona, the editor A. P., and Lermontov as author, address the public, justifying the ensuing material. Both introductions raise the question of authorial impersonation: Pushkin's by signing his own initials but using the voice of a parodied editor; Lermontov's by mocking the accusation that Pechorin is a self-portrait.

In A. P.'s introduction Pushkin spoofs the self-important editor, and presents two extremes of naive reader: the housekeeper who uses Belkin's manuscripts for household purposes, and the landowner who regards writing as an indecent activity. Lermontov's foreword also personifies the naive reading public: it resembles the 'provincial' who cannot see beneath the surface forms of discourse, that reading public which demands morality and realism.

A. P.'s ostensible purpose is to introduce Belkin, the problematic author of the tales; Lermontov presents Pechorin who tells three of the five tales. But the first two tales of *A Hero of Our Time* are told by an unnamed narrator who fancies himself the writer of travel notes. The clichés of that genre determine his narrative: the ecstatic stock descriptions of mountains (the Caucasus replacing the Alps of the Romantics) and the condescending drawing out of Maksim Maksimych ('I know, these old Caucasus veterans love to talk and tell stories, they so rarely have the chance.' [quotation slightly altered]). His eagerness to publish a good story overrides human compassion, as emphasised in his introduction to Pechorin's journal ('I learned not long ago that Pechorin had died on his way back from Persia. This news gladdened me very much, it gave me the right to publish these notes.)'

This narrator is a close relation of the narrator of Pushkin's 'Stationmaster', who 'hope[s] to publish a curious collection of observations picked up during [his] travels', and so plies Vyrin with five glasses of rum to obtain Dunia's story. Pushkin's narrator too condescends to his subject; Vyrin and his tragic tale move him less than their literary associations:

> Such was the story of my friend, the old stationmaster, a story that was more than once interrupted by tears, which, like the jealous Terentich in that beautiful ballad of Dmitriev's, he wiped away picturesquely with the sleeve of his coat. These tears were caused partly by the punch.

The first two tales of *A Hero of Our Time* are filtered through the author of the introduction and through the unnamed narrator. 'Bela' contains Maksim Maksimych's tale of Bela's abduction, itself entailing extensive quotations from disparate speakers: Pechorin's *confession* of his Romantic alienation (suspiciously resembling the speech he has already given Princess Mary as well as Rousseau's *Rêveries d' un promeneur solitaire*) and Kazbich's adventure tale of his horse Karagioz rendered in the language of Chateaubriand's Indians. The narrator is presumably responsible for these generic raisins in the plum pudding of his travel notes.

In this way, Lermontov duplicates the narrative structure of the *Belkin* tales: A. P. (i.e. Pushkin himself); Belkin; and the four sources of the stories identified by their initials in A.P.'s footnote are matched by 'Lermontov', the narrator, and Maksim Maksimych in 'Bela'. In the second story, 'Maksim Maksimych', the subject of the story is removed as narrator. As Nabokov says, Pechorin is brought gradually nearer. The motivation (which Nabokov does not discuss) is to identify several possible (mis)understandings of Pechorin. In 'Maksim Maksimych' we come to doubt the appropriateness of Maksim's emotions in the scene of reunion, and therefore must reinterpret everything we have just read in 'Bela'.

Part II of *A Hero of Our Time* does, of course, bring us as close as possible to Pechorin through his journal, but the introduction of Part II by the narrator of Part I again establishes a third layer, as in Belkin. It is not a narrative layer, but an interpretative filter that functions the same way, alerting the reader to the role of interpretation, with an admonitory Lermontov at one extreme, a discredited Romantic narrator at the other, and a suspect Pechorin calling into question his own perceptions in the middle.

These vantage points develop Pushkin's indirectly implied theme of self-awareness. Lermontov suggests that the good reader is potentially the good writer; the analogue in life is that the greater one's awareness, the greater one's self-determination. Pechorin is the only character in *A Hero of Our Time* to demonstrate awareness of his own misapplied stereotypes. 'Taman', Pechorin's literary effort, is about the effects of reading too much spooky German literature. The narrative simultaneously conveys the narrator's point of view during the events described, as well as his reinterpretation of them after 're-reading' them, a reinterpretation that includes an analysis of why he misperceived the situation in the first place. The story Pechorin writes and the sophistication of its author is contrasted to the travel notes of the bumbling narrator of the first two chapters, whose desperate desire to publish something prevents him from evaluating Maksim Maksimych's narrative and undermines his own with its obtrusive, self-centred self-consciousness. While that narrator learns nothing from his travels, Pechorin has learned something from all his reading; like Lermontov himself, Pechorin has read both the Western European Romantics and Pushkin's parodic transpositions of their work to Russian soil and (for better or worse) incorporates that knowledge into his actions. This essentially optimistic adjustment of the themes carried out by the narrative devices of the *Belkin Tales* is balanced by the tragic outcomes of the plot lines in *A Hero of Our Time;* the opposition reflects on the one hand the opening out of Russian prose, and on the other the closing down of post-Decembrist Russian politics, a topic beyond the scope of this essay.

Let us examine the plot parallels between the stories.

'The Shot' and 'The Fatalist'

Lermontov pairs Pushkin's opening tale, 'The Shot', with the last tale of *A Hero of Our Time,* 'The Fatalist'. Silvio and Vulich have foreign names, unknown pasts, and keep aloof from their fellows. At the end of their tales they are dead, but not through duelling. Silvio is shot at twice by the count, who misses both times: the first shot goes through Silvio's cap, the second through the count's painting. Vulich also shoots twice: his first shot, at himself, misfires, his second hits a cap hanging on the wall. The Count twice draws the first shot in the duel, for which Silvio calls him 'fortune's favourite' (*liubimets schastiia*); Pechorin tells Vulich that he's 'fortunate in gambling' (*schastlivyi v igre*).

The similarities of the tales are established in order to point to the differences. Silvio plays the role of adventure hero, lending his young officer friends the means to identify him as such:

> He had a good collection of books, mostly military histories and novels. He was always willing to lend these, and he never asked for them back.

The narrator of 'The Shot' is naturally Silvio's best audience, as he himself says:

> By nature a romantic, I had been more attached than the others to the man whose life was such a mystery and whom I regarded as the hero of some strange tale.

By his own account Silvio provoked a duel with the innocent count out of sheer jealousy and then devoted six years of his life to what he calls 'revenge'. Yet years later the narrator has never questioned Silvio's tale, as is clear when he asks the count about the 'slap in the face by some rake'. Even after hearing the conclusion of the duel from the count, the narrator persists in calling Silvio a hero.

Pushkin's tale makes an implicit parallel between literature and life, with its attendant theme of interpretation. Only the count escapes the restrictions of literary stereotype, but he is nonetheless subject to the dangers of the misinterpretations of others: Silvio takes it upon himself to become, as it were, the count's fate.

Fate is a unifying theme in the *Belkin* tales (compare Vyrin's 'There's no escaping misfortune; fate is master unto itself'/'*ot bedy ne otbozhish'sia; chto suzhdeno, tomu ne minovat'*); Lermontov too uses it as the keystone to his construction, considering it explicitly in the closing story of the novel in which Vulich is more philosophical than Silvio: interested in the question of predestination, he gambles with fate, staking his own life. As Lotman points out, Vulich as a Serb has a more Eastern attitude to the question.

Pechorin, who is both the narrator of Vulich's tale and, like Silvio's narrator, his fellow officer, is above all a sceptic in the tradition of Western European Romanticism and inclined to accept the idea of free will over predestination. Both Vulich and Pechorin reach new understanding within the tale. Vulich's dying words are 'he was right', referring to Pechorin's prediction that he would die that night. Pechorin as narrator comes to understand that the conflict between free will and predetermination is unresolvable through his experiences, which he then records, giving the reader material to consider this complex problem. In so doing, he presents precisely the challenge that Lermontov's foreword proposes to the 'young and naive' reading public. This technique may be considered the essence of Lermontov's contribution to the growth of Russian realism.

'The Blizzard' and 'Princess Mary'

In 'The Blizzard' first Vladimir and then Burmin woo Maria; in 'Princess Mary' first Grushnitsky and then Pechorin woo Mary. Maria reads French novels 'and consequently is in love'; Mary reads Byron which apparently affects her choices. The young and naive Vladimir and Grushnitsky are poor army corporals; both die, but Vladimir does so at the impersonal hands of fate, whereas Pechorin controls Grushnitsky's fate. Burmin and Pechorin are older than their predecessors, the first 'around twenty-six', Pechorin twenty-five. Vladimir is not considered suitable by Maria's parents but they give their blessing when Maria falls sick; Pechorin is also not considered a suitable match for Mary but her mother too accepts him after

Mary's illness. In Pushkin's tale the young lovers count on 'throwing themselves at her parents' feet'; Pechorin, refusing the weeping Mary, says 'one more minute and I would have fallen at her feet'.

But while Burmin follows fate's mysterious workings and marries Maria, Pechorin rejects Mary. Neither marriage takes place: Vladimir and Grushnitsky die. So in fact does Pechorin, but only long after he has refused marriage. Pechorin is the agent of his own, and consequently Grushnitsky's and Mary's, fate. And as narrator of their tale, he has the last word; while all four of these romances are based on literary clichés, only Pechorin is aware of them, even though Princess Mary reads Byron in the original.

'The Undertaker' and 'Taman'

Pushkin's undertaker Adrian Prokhorov is a bad reader *who even reads nothing at all,* as Gogol might say. Neither life nor art has suggested the possibilities presented in his terrifying dream, and he is quick to dismiss the insight into his own responsibility that it might have provided. Prokhorov knows the German artisans he got drunk with, but not the German tales in which wine and dreams can explain supernatural appearances.

Pechorin on the other hand is too familiar with German Romantic stereotypes and nearly gets himself drowned by projecting the image of Goethe's Mignon on to a smuggler girl. He writes the story of his adventure, laughing at the inappropriateness of the literary images that determined his perceptions. His narrative both recreates his experience for the reader and interprets it, while Adrian Prokhorov cannot interpret his own dream. 'Taman' is an inversion of 'The Undertaker': Prokhorov reads, thinks and acts too little, Pechorin—too much. The tales are pivotal for their respective collections, as they provide a key to interpretation; that is why both are placed in the middle of the five tales.

'The Stationmaster' and 'Maksim Maksimych'

Samson Vyrin and Maksim Maksimych are 'simple' men in government service, aged 'about fifty'. Both tragically lose their beloved 'daughters'. Vyrin's Dunia is abducted by a dashing hussar in a Circassian hat; Maksim Maksimych loves Bela 'like a father', and she is abducted by a Circassian on horseback. Vyrin drinks the rum offered by the narrator and eventually drinks himself to death; Maksim refuses the white rum from Tiflis which his narrator offers him—to be drunk in the Caucasus is to risk your life.

Their stories are told to us by travellers who quote their simple speech sympathetically. Vyrin's narrator plays the role of the humane physiologist, refuting the unsympathetic view of stationmasters. But he sees neither his own condescension nor the connection between Vyrin's misfortune and the German engravings on the wall. Similarly, the narrator of 'Bela' perpetrates the clichés of the travel-note genre and condescends to Maksim Maksimych. But while Lermontov's narrator closely resembles Pushkin's, Lermontov distinguishes Maksim Maksimych from Vyrin. Vyrin does not realise that the hussar is making a deal with the doctor in German, or that he has projected the story of the Prodigal Son with its German subtitles on to Dunia. Maksim Maksimych at least knows that there is a 'foreign' influence at work, that Pechorin is following some fashion—he even suspects it comes from France. The narrator corrects him ('No, it was the English') when of course it was both. The reading and writing narrators are at least as naive as the 'simple' men they try to fashion into clichés.

'The Lady-Peasant' and 'Bela'

The last Belkin tale, 'The Lady-Peasant', corresponds to *A Hero of Our Time's* first: Aleksei and Pechorin, recently from St Petersburg, court exotic women who come from enemy camps: Aleksei's father, the Russophil, is at odds with Liza's father, Muromsky, the Anglophil; Pechorin fights in the Russian army against the Caucasian tribes to one of which Bela belongs. Aleksei falls in love with the 'peasant' 'Akulina' who turns out to be the young lady (*baryshnia*) Liza. Pechorin courts the Circassian Bela, but finds that 'the love of a wild woman [*dikarki*] is not much better than the love of a noble lady'. Pushkin's tale is a comedy in which Aleksei is a parody of a would-be Byronic hero. He drops his mask easily under Akulina's influence, allowing youth, nature and tradition to bring about a happy ending, with which the story cycle closes. It is the second happy ending in the *Belkin* tales. In 'Bela' the character who is a parody of the Byronic hero, Grushnitsky, is killed by Pechorin. The episode with Bela is Pechorin's second love story in the novel and his last; both affairs end in tragedy.

Conclusion

Pushkin's *Belkin* tales are fairy-tales in which 'high' literature masquerades as part of the oral tradition. Belkin *hears* his tales from the initialled narrators just as he listens to his housekeeper's stories. She is presumably illiterate, as she uses his manuscript to seal up her windows. Lermontov's narrator addresses this distinction between oral and written tales and their tellers in 'Bela':

> in simple hearts, the sense of the beauty and grandeur of nature is a hundred times stronger and more vivid than it is in us, enthusiastic tellers of tales, oral or written.

Fairy-tales have happy endings, and so do all the Belkin tales. There are only three deaths. Two of them are off-stage: it is said that Silvio was killed in battle; and in 'The Blizzard' Vladimir's demise in Moscow on the eve of the entry of the French is mentioned in an aside and is a means to Maria's marriage to Burmin. The only tragic figure of the collection is Samson Vyrin, yet despite his death 'The Stationmaster' ends happily with the news of Dunia's remarkable good fortune (three sons, nurse, pug dog).

Lermontov, on the other hand, says in his foreword that the public does not understand fables (*basni*) and jokes; 'the most magical of magical tales with us would barely escape being reproached as a personal insult'. And so he rewrites Pushkin's magical tales as tragedy. By the end of the novel Bela, Grushnitsky, Vulich and Pechorin are dead, Vera, Princess Mary and Maksim Maksimych betrayed in their affections. There are no happy endings. Lermontov even rewrites the zero-ending of 'The Under-

taker' in a tragic vein: Pechorin is robbed, the honest smuggling band of 'Taman' broken up, the blind boy abandoned.

Lermontov provides the mirror of tragedy to Pushkin's comic work in plot resolution and genre interpretation, as appropriate to the period of late Romanticism. The advantage of that perspective is, of course, the greater awareness afforded by the accumulated models, Western European and Russian. Among the many narrators, editors and letter writers of the *Belkin* tales and *A Hero of Our Time,* only Pechorin is shown to control all the genres, styles and stereotypes parodied in the story cycles. Like his author, he has read the Western European versions of the bored hero as well as Pushkin's parodies of them in *Onegin*. Onegin's melancholy is itself inherited from Western models, not original, as Tomashevsky says. Pechorin's review of two generations of Romanticism allows him to interpret and therefore craft his reality, as well as to write his own tales about his life. In doing so throughout the novel, he identifies a central dilemma of the Romantic vision—the division between head and heart that results from self-awareness. Lermontov examines this opposition and shows the futility of the dichotomy through the tragedies Pechorin brings about. The deliberately ambiguous word 'hero' is meant to refer both to life and to art; generations of readers had been bred on restrictive Romantic categories. The variations on the theme of the interplay between life and art in Lermontov's novel suggest that it is the acceptance of these categories that has blighted the development of potential real-life heroes. The idea is signalled by Pechorin's statement that Grushnitsky's ambition is 'to become the hero of a novel', while the hero of the actual novel himself acts out the role of the hero of his own novel in the amphitheatre of Piatigorsk (saving Mary from 'certain death' by social humiliation at the ball). Narrator I is a lesser author. He reduces reality to pseudo-art, viewing the mountains through the genre of travelogue and Maksim Maksimych as material for a physiological sketch; his model for Pechorin comes from Balzac's *Femme de trente ans*. The authors truly responsible for Bela's tragedy are Rousseau and Chateaubriand, who provide Pechorin with scenarios of the noble savage (which he tries and finds false). In 'Taman' Pechorin makes explicit the problem of the interplay between Romantic stereotypes and life: his story illustrates the influence of his own Goethe-coloured filter, the effect that art can have on random, innocent reality (and 'honest smugglers').

A Hero of Our Time then, in itself, demonstrates the need for resolution of opposition—of head and heart, of art and life—and at the same time makes clear that such resolution is impossible within the Romantic ethos fostered by the literary models that are parodied in the *Tales of Belkin* and in *A Hero of Our Time. The Tales of Belkin* is, of course, only one of the many works Lermontov incorporates into his novel. But it is one of the most central, providing not only its structure but a reading of Western European Romanticism in the Russian context of the 1830s. Highlighting the effect of literary stereotypes on life, *The Tales of Belkin* plays a significant role in establishing a new direction for Russian prose; in *A Hero of Our Time* that cycle determines the movement away from dangerous

Romantic stereotypes and towards, indeed achieving, a synthesis of the Western European novel with the prose techniques of the best Russian interpreter of that tradition, Pushkin.

FURTHER READING

Criticism

Bagby, Lewis. "Narrative Double-Voicing in Lermontov's *A Hero of Our Time*." *Slavic and East European Journal* 22, No. 3 (Fall 1978): 265-86.

Notes that major events in *A Hero of Our Time*, in particular those that illuminate the character of the protagonist, are narrated from more than one perspective during the course of the novel.

D'iakonova, Nina Ia. "Byron and Lermontov: Notes on Pechorin's 'Journal'." In *Lord Byron and His Contemporaries: Essays from the Sixth International Byron Seminar*, edited by Charles E. Robinson, pp. 144-65. Newark: University of Delaware Press, 1982.

Offers an account of Byron's impact on Russian literature generally and on Lermontov's portrayal of his protagonist in particular.

Debreczeny, Paul. "Elements of the Lyrical Verse Tale in Lermontov's *A Hero of Our Time*." In *American Contributions to the Seventh International Congress of Slavists, Volume II: Literature and Folklore,* edited by Victor Terras, pp. 93-117. The Hague: Mouton, 1973.

Suggests "that elements of the lyrical verse tale—both thematic and structural—pervade Lermontov's novel *A Hero of Our Time* (1840)," to such an extent that it can be called a narrative poem translated into prose. The essay contains many untranslated Russian passages printed in Cyrillic characters.

Marsh, Cynthia. "Lermontov and the Romantic Tradition: The Function of Landscape in *A Hero of Our Time*." *The Slavonic and East European Review* 66, No. 1 (January 1988): 35-46.

Discusses Lermontov's paintings in the Romantic style and proposes parallels between Lermontov's paintings of Caucasian landscapes and the landscape description in *A Hero of Our Time*.

Mersereau, John, Jr. " 'The Fatalist' as a Keystone of *A Hero of Our Time*." In *The Slavic and East European Journal* n. s. IV, No. 1 (1960): 137-46.

Argues that despite its chronological link to the earliest episode in *A Hero of Our Time*, "The Fatalist" was consciously conceived and designed to serve as the novel's conclusion.

Milner-Gulland, Robin. "Heroes of Their Time? Form and Idea in Büchner's *Danton's Death* and Lermontov's *Hero of Our Time*." In *The Idea of Freedom: Essays in Honour of Isaiah Berlin,* edited by Alan Ryan, pp. 115-37. Oxford: Oxford University Press, 1979.

Compares major themes in the cited novels.

Peace, R. A. "The Rôle of 'Taman' in Lermontov's *Geroy nashego vremeni*." *The Slavonic and East European Review* XLV, No. 104 (January 1967): 12-29.

Examines the placement of 'Taman' in the episodic structure of *A Hero of Our Time*.

Reid, Robert. "The Critical Uses of Translation (Lermontov's *A Hero of Our Time*)." *Essays in Poetics* 11, No. 2 (September 1986): 55-90.

Includes a close study of five translated extracts from *A Hero of Our Time* in a paper demonstrating that "an examination of translated texts can provide unique insights into the formal characteristics of their source texts, compatible with, but distinct from those derived by established critical methods."

Yalom, Marilyn Koenick. "*La chute* and *A Hero of Our Time*." *French Review* 36 (1962-63): 138-45.

Compares the protagonists and "certain stylistic elements" of Lermontov's novel and Albert Camus's novel *La Chute (The Fall,* 1956).

Additional coverage of Lermontov's life and career is contained in the following source published by Gale Research: *Nineteenth-Century Literature Criticism,* Vol. 5.

Caroline Norton

1808-1877

(Born Caroline Elizabeth Sarah Sheridan) English poet, novelist, and political reformer.

INTRODUCTION

Regarded as an important early feminist by modern critics, Norton was viewed as an accomplished poet and novelist by her contemporaries. Critics favorably compared her to Elizabeth Barrett and referred to her as "the Byron of modern poetesses" due to the intense emotion characteristic of her work. Norton drew extensively on her personal life in poetry and novels; this has typically informed criticism of her literary works. For example, reviewers of *The Dream and Other Poems* (1840) discussed both its artistic merits and its suggestions of Norton's unhappy life. Modern scholarly attention has turned to her political writings and her role in the women's movement.

Biographical Information

Norton was born into the widely respected Sheridan family; she was a granddaughter of the English dramatist Richard Brinsley Sheridan. She married George Norton in 1827 and together the couple had three sons. The marriage proved to be troubled, and Norton turned to writing poetry as a creative outlet. She published *The Sorrows of Rosalie: A Tale with Other Poems* in 1829 and *The Undying One and Other Poems* one year later. In 1836 she and her husband separated. Per English law of the time, Norton was denied custody of her children. For the next five years, she sought to influence Parliament to grant separated women rights to their children. In 1837 she wrote a pamphlet entitled *Separation of Mother and Child by the Laws of Custody of Infants Considered*. By 1839, a bill was passed that slightly reformed infant custody laws. Throughout this period, Norton continued to publish poetry, as well as several novels. In July of 1842, her youngest son died while in his father's care, and the two older boys were returned to their mother. Subsequently Norton wrote the pamphlet *English Laws for Women in the Nineteenth Century* (1854) and *Letter to the Queen* (1855), influencing an 1857 bill reforming marriage and divorce laws. In 1877, two years after her husband's death, Norton remarried; she died later that year.

Major Works

Norton's first collection of poetry, *The Sorrows of Rosalie: A Tale with Other Poems* relates the story of a woman doomed to a life of misfortune after she is deserted by her lover. In Norton's next volume, *The Undying One and Other Poems*, the title poem recounts the legend of the Wandering Jew, a figure destined to live in perpetual struggle and despair. Following her separation from her

children, Norton penned *The Dream and Other Poems*. The subject of "The Dream" is a young girl who dreams of love and marriage and is later warned by her mother to relinquish her hopes of wedded happiness. Based on fact, Norton's long poem, *The Lady of La Garaye* (1862) tells the story of a woman who, after an accident, is left maimed, near death, and unsure of her husband's love. The experience strengthens her husband's love and together they spend the rest of their lives in the service of others. Norton's novels present themes and subjects similar to those in her poetry. In *Stuart of Dunleath* (1851), the heroine is forced into a loveless and violent marriage. The novel closes with her death. In *Lost and Saved* (1863), a woman is deserted by her husband and nearly starves to death as she tries to support herself.

Critical Reception

Critical discussion of Norton's poetry and fiction centers primarily on her literary use of personal experience. Hartley Coleridge wrote that Norton's poetry exhibits "intense personal passion" as well as tenderness and "forceful expression" paralleling that of Lord Byron, but urged Norton to move beyond personal experience and write on themes "less morbid." While many later reviewers agreed on both counts, some reiterated only Coleridge's latter comments. Other critics defended Norton's use of personal experience. R. H. Horne contended that Norton "writes from the dictates of a human heart in all the eloquence of beauty and individuality." Others asserted that the biographical component of Norton's writings contributed to her literary popularity. Despite the morose themes of all of Norton's writings, her graceful and elegant style, as well as her power for creating vivid, descriptive images, have been generally commended.

PRINCIPAL WORKS

The Dandies' Rout (juvenilia) 1821
The Sorrows of Rosalie: A Tale with Other Poems (poetry) 1829
The Undying One and Other Poems (poetry) 1830
The Wife and Woman's Reward (novels) 1835
A Voice from the Factories (poetry) 1836
Separation of Mother and Child by the Law of Custody of Infants Considered (essay) 1837
"A Plain Letter to the Lord Chancellor" [as Pearse Stevenson] (letter) *1839
The Dream and Other Poems (poetry) 1840
Lines (On the Young Queen Victoria) (poetry) 1840
The Child of the Islands (poem) 1845
Aunt Carry's Ballads for Children (poetry) 1847
Letters to the Mob (letters) 1848
Stuart of Dunleath (novel) 1851
†*English Laws for Women in the Nineteenth Century* (essay) 1854
Letter to the Queen on Lord Chancellor Cranworth's Marriage and Divorce Bill (letter) 1855
Centenary Festival (Verses on Burns) (poetry) 1859
The Lady of La Garaye (poem) 1862
Lost and Saved (novel) 1863
Old Sir Douglas (novel) 1867
Bingen on the Rhine (poetry) 1883

*Not published; printed for distribution among members of Parliament.

†Printed for private circulation.

CRITICISM

The Edinburgh Review   (review date 1831)

SOURCE: A review of *The Undying One and Other Poems,* in *The Edinburgh Review,* Vol. LIII, No. CVI, June, 1831, pp. 361-69.

[*In the essay that follows, the unsigned critic analyzes Norton's poem "The Undying One," suggesting that if Norton would "confine herself to simpler themes" she would assuredly be a success.*]

Some persons of a desponding turn of mind will have it, that the attendance on Apollo's levees has been for some time past on the decline—that the older nobility have been keeping aloof, and that, under cover of a profusion of finery and false ornaments, several suspicious characters have been seen moving about the apartments of late, whom the vigilance of the gentlemen in waiting ought to have excluded. Nevertheless, we see no great reason for despair; for, as to the obnoxious *parvenus,* they have seldom long escaped detection; and upon their second intrusion, have generally been *invited,* as the French say, when a member of the House of Commons is turned out, to quit the chamber with all celerity. Some of them, indeed, like Mr. Montgomery, have found their way into the street with such emphasis and rapidity, that, on recovering their senses, they have turned round, and, with strange contortions of visage, and frightful appeals, have bitterly reviled the officials, who, in the discharge of their duty, had been obliged to shut the door in their face. Others, like Mr. Reade, who made a very violent attempt the other day to gain admittance, flourishing the knocker till he disturbed the neighbourhood,—put a more blustering face upon the matter, after their exclusion; affect to say, that they never made any such application—that they would not walk in though they had been invited; and, with a 'calm confidence,' enter their appeal, as Swift dedicated his *Table of a Tub,* to Prince Posterity. Again, although it cannot be denied that the visits of the old supporters of the court have been less frequent, we, who would wish to look at the cheerful side both of politics and poetry, are inclined to think that among the recent arrivals, there are several names of no inconsiderable promise; nay, already of very respectable performance. Among the later presentations, it rather strikes us the majority has consisted of ladies; and of these, if report says true, none seems to have made a more successful appearance than Mrs. Norton. She might indeed, with advantage to herself, have chosen a robe of a more sober and unpretending character; but we are ready to admit, that she wears it gracefully, and are not surprised, on the whole, that her entrance did produce what the newspapers call a sensation.

It was natural, indeed, that the descendant of so gifted a family should be received with attention. But if her poem has been successful—as we are told it has—it assuredly owes extremely little of its interest and attractions to the subject. She has pleased, not in consequence of, but in spite of, the fable on which she has employed her powers.

We really had begun to flatter ourselves—rashly, as it appears—that the reading world had finally got quit of the Wandering Jew, who, for centuries past, has occasionally revisited the glimpses of the moon, making polite literature hideous. His scene with the Bleeding Nun, in Lewis's romance, we should have thought, would have been his last appearance on the stage, for a century at least; but instead of discreetly retiring for a time, as might have been expected, after such an exhibition, into the privacy of infinite space, the appearances of this intolerable *revenant* in our lower world have of late become more frequent and alarming than ever. In Germany, Klingemann, and Achim von Armin, have not scrupled to introduce him under his true character; and Shelley, and Captain Medwyn, both bold men in their way, have tried a similar experiment with the English public. All this, however, might be borne; for, so long as he chooses to come forward as the veritable Ahasuerus, we should feel inclined, with Antonio, to say, 'there was much kindness in the Jew,'—in enabling us, we mean, to pass by on the other side, and avoid his society in due time. But the worst and most dangerous feature about his late appearances is this, that he has been assuming various *aliases,* and obtaining admittance into respectable circles under borrowed names; a device, against which no precaution can avail; for his general manner in the outset resembles so much that of any other gentleman (of the Corsair school,)—he avoids so skilfully any allusion to his reminiscences of Judæa, that we only begin to suspect him when about to part company with him; and can hardly even then persuade ourselves that our agreeable companion in the post-chaise, is our old Jewry friend, till he vanishes at last, as old Aubrey says, 'with a melodious twang,' and a sulphureous odour. Nay, to such a remarkable extent have his devices in this way been carried, that he lately prevailed upon a respectable English divine, to introduce him under the euphonious name of Salathiel, in which character, we understand, he swindled the proprietors of some circulating libraries—to a small amount. And here is a second insidious attempt of the same nature, in which this intolerable Jew again comes forward to levy contributions on the public, by the style and title of Isbal the **"Undying One."**

Seriously—Is it not singular that a legend so absurd, and the unfitness of which for poetical narrative appears so obvious, should have been such a favourite with poets and novelists? Not that we mean to deny that the more general conception of the position of a being on whom the curse of immortality on earth has been suddenly imposed, is not in itself a striking, an impressive one. Nothing is more easy to conceive, than that in the hands of a person whose mind combines the philosophical element with the poetical, the picture of such a being,—solitary in the centre of a busy world, disconnected from all human hopes, passions, sympathies,—longing to die and to rest, to follow where all that made life worth living for had gone before him, may be capable of producing the profoundest emotion. In fact, this has been done by Godwin in his St. Leon, where the train of reflection of such an immortal—at first joyous and exulting in the boundless expansion of his powers, gradually sinking into sadness, and at last into an overpowering sensation of loneliness and desolation—is depicted with a deep knowledge of the human heart, and in a strain of touching and mournful eloquence.

But though those prospects of futurity, in which the victim of immortality throws forward his views into unborn ages, appear impressive and effective when thus embodied merely in reflection; or although a momentary glimpse of his situation may be one of solemn interest, there are insuperable obstacles to any attempt to pursue the fortunes of such a being through the lapse of centuries, or to exhibit his feelings in successive detail. Not to mention the extreme difficulty of carrying onward our sympathies to the third and fourth generation, even with the assistance of a connecting link in the existence of some one who survives them all, such an attempt invariably leads to one of two things,—either a dreary monotony, or a variety obtained at the expense of consistency and truth. To represent such a being, labouring under the consciousness that he has nothing in common with those around him, as susceptible and impassioned to the last—loving, hating, grieving on, with the same unabated energy, at the latest stage of his career, as when first he commenced his restless pilgrimage—if it enable the poet to vary the scene, deprives the conception of all which redeems it from the character of absurdity, or gives it a distinctive character. The whole effect of such an idea on the mind, is produced by the simple representation of that state of callous, impassive, unalterable desolation into which such a creature sinks—a state of gloomy, tideless tranquillity, and weatherbeaten hardihood of soul, which nothing can agitate, nothing overpower. What human passion, indeed, should interest him over whom the experience of centuries has passed?—what new grief plough deep where so many old ones have left their furrows?—what attachment bind him who soon feels that he can now love nothing truly, because he now loves nothing with that identity of heart, that abandonment of soul, wherein resides the charm and essence of the feeling? 'In the tomb of my wife and children,' says St. Leon, as he follows out to its dreary consequences the effects of the secret of the stranger,

> I felt that my heart would be buried. Never, never, through the countless ages of eternity, should I form another attachment. In the happy age of delusion, happy and auspicious, at least, to the cultivation of the passions, when I felt that I also was a mortal, I was capable of a community of sentiments, of a going forth of the heart. But how could I, an immortal, hope hereafter to feel a serious and expansive feeling for the ephemeron of an hour!

And yet what St. Leon held to be impossible, is exactly what Mrs Norton has attempted to do; and in consequence of this, so completely has she extinguished all that is peculiar in the situation of her hero, that, but for his own information on the subject, which he occasionally volunteers rather needlessly, we should never, in this loving, fighting, marrying Jew, discover that we had to do with the wretched, passionless wanderer on whom the curse had lighted. Susceptible to the last, he wanders on, still falling in love, and vowing *eternal* constancy to Edith of England, Xarifa of Spain, Miriam of Palestine, and Linda of Castaly, and burying them all in succession; —filling up the gaps between these piping times of peace by fits of desperate fighting; though it is not always easy to discover for what cause, or under which king, our Bezonian draws his sword, except that

> Where'er a voice was raised in freedom's name,
> There, sure and swift, my eager footstep came;

as if to such a being, absorbed in the selfishness of his own misery, the watchwords of freedom and slavery would not be equally indifferent. We find him lending a hand in the struggles of ancient Rome with her Gothic invaders—in the warfare of Spain with the Moors—and in our own civil wars, not to mention a campaign or two in Ireland; in all of which he behaves with that bravery which might be expected from one who knew that his life was safe, though his head might perchance be broken.

Homer has been celebrated for the variety of the modes in which he dispatches his heroes; Mrs. Norton's ingenuity in varying the death of her heroines is scarcely less remarkable. The case of Edith, the first favourite of this Jewish Bluebeard, is distressing; and, in fact, by uncharitable persons would certainly be regarded as a case of murder. Isbal and she have been living a life of great domestic comfort for years, when, like the Ancient Mariner, all of a sudden, *suadente diabolo,*

> ————his frame is wrench'd
> With a strange agony,
> That forces him to tell his tale,
> And then it leaves him *free.*

That is, free to marry again; for the consequence of this most unnecessary disclosure is the immediate death of his wife. Xarifa, her successor, dies a natural death, expiring in fact before he has time to tell her his story, which he is on the point of doing. His third wife he makes quick conveyance with—not feeling himself prepared, at the time, with any satisfactory solution of the question which he saw she was about to put to him, why he exhibited no symptoms of advancing age as well as herself. The last dies, we hardly know how or when, except that the catastrophe takes place off the Irish coast;—an uncertainty which we share with the person who should know most of the matter, Isbal himself;—for never, it seems,

> ————shall his heart discover
> The moment her love and her life were over;
> Only this much shall the lost one know,—
> Where *she* hath departed *he* may not go.

Mrs. Norton must really excuse us, if we have freely expressed our sentiments as to the absurdity of the subject on which her powers, and those of no inconsiderable order, have been wasted. If we did not think her poem indicated genius, we should not have noticed it at all: we have done so, because we feel satisfied that, with a more congenial subject—one calmer, commoner, less ambitious—a very different whole would have been the result. It is strange how difficult it is to persuade ladies that their forte does not lie in representations of those dark passions, which, for their own comfort, we hope they have witnessed only in description. And yet none can fail at last to perceive that the concentration of thought and expression necessary for the drama; the stately steady grandeur required in the epic poem; nay, the knowledge of the worst as well as the best features of the heart, required for the more irregular narrative poem, are hardly ever found in the poetry of women. Would Mrs. Norton only confine herself to simpler themes, instead of plunging beyond the visible diurnal sphere, there is much in this poem that assures us of her complete success;—many individual pictures, clear, graphic, picturesque; many passages of tender feeling breaking out into a lyrical form, which we think discover much grace and a great command of versification. Of this, indeed, there is perhaps too great a variety, since the volume exhibits specimens of every measure in the English language; and perhaps a few more. As a proof how well Mrs. Norton can paint, take the following striking description of the Wanderer looking in at the door of an English cottage on a Sabbath morning, while the inmates are at church:

> A lowly cot
> Stood near that calm and consecrated spot.
> I enter'd it:—the morning sunshine threw
> Its warm bright beams upon the flowers that grew
> Around it and within it—'twas a place
> So peaceful and so bright, that you might trace
> The tranquil feelings of the dwellers there;
> There was no taint of shame, or crime, or care.
> On a low humble couch was softly laid
> A little slumberer, whose rosy head
> Was guarded by a watch-dog; *while I stood*
> *In hesitating, half-repentant mood,*
> *My glance still met his large bright watchful eye,*
> *Wandering from me to that sweet sleeper nigh.*
> Yes, even to that dumb animal I seem'd
> A thing of crime; the murderous death-light gleam'd
> Beneath my brow; the noiseless step was mine;
> I moved with conscious guilt, and his low whine
> Responded to my sigh, whose echo fell
> Heavily—as 'twere loath within that cot to dwell.

On the death of Edith, his first love, the Jew engaged with ardour in the struggle between the Spaniards and the Moors; and after a fierce combat in the neighbourhood of Granada, meets with a female figure sitting on the field of battle, and wailing over the dead. This is Xarifa, who, in some very touching stanzas, pours out her lamentations for her husband who had fallen in the fight:

> My early and my only love, why silent dost thou lie?
> When heavy grief is in my heart, and tear-drops in mine eye,
> I call thee, but thou answerest not, all lonely though I be,
> Wilt thou not burst the bonds of sleep, and rise to comfort me?
> O wake thee, wake thee from thy rest, upon the tented field,
> This faithful breast shall be at once thy pillow and thy shield;
> If thou hast doubted of its truth and constancy before,
> O wake thee now, and it will strive to love thee even more.
>
> If ever we have parted, and I wept thee not as now—
> If ever I have seen thee come, and worn a cloudy brow—
> If ever harsh and careless words have caused thee pain and woe—
> Then sleep—in silence sleep—and I will bow my head and go.
>
> But if through all the vanish'd years whose shadowy joys are gone,
> Through all the changing scenes of life I thought of thee alone;
> If I have mourn'd for thee when far, and worshipp'd thee when near,

> Then wake thee up, my early love, this weary
>   heart to cheer!

These are sweet and natural verses, particularly the latter two; and we can assure Mrs. Norton, far more effective than whole pages of gloomy grandeur and despair. As another specimen of her better powers in these gentle delineations, we shall extract her picture of the close of Xarifa's life, under the conviction that some fatal secret preyed upon her husband's mind, and her parting address as she dies by his side near the Guadalquivir.

> One eve at spring-tide's close we took our way,
>   When eve's last beams in soften'd glory fell,
> Lighting her faded form with sadden'd ray,
>   And the sweet spot where we so loved to
>   dwell.
> Faintly and droopingly she sat her down
>   By the blue waters of the Guadalquivir,
> With darkness on her brow, but yet no frown,
>   Like the deep shadow on that silent river.
> She sat her down, I say, with face upturn'd
>   To the dim sky, which daylight was forsaking,
> And in her eyes a light unearthly burn'd—
>   The light which spirits give whose chains are
>   breaking!
>
> . . . . .
>
> And a half smile lit up that pallid brow,
>   As, casting flowers upon the silent stream,
> She watch'd the frail sweet blossoms glide and
>   go,
>   Like human pleasures in a blissful dream.
> And then, with playful force she gently flung
>   Small shining pebbles from the river's brink,
> And o'er the eddying waters sadly hung,
>   Pleased, and yet sorrowful, to see them sink.
> "And thus," she said, "doth human love forget
>   Its idols—some sweet blessings float away,
> Follow'd by one long look of vain regret,
>   As they are slowly hastening to decay;
>
> And some, with sullen plunge, do mock our
>   sight,
>   And suddenly go down into the tomb,
> Startling the beating heart, whose fond delight
>   Chills into tears at that unlook'd-for doom.
> And there remains no trace of them save such
>   As the soft ripple leaves upon the wave,
> Or a forgotten flower, whose dewy touch
>   Reminds us some are withering in the grave!
> When all is over, and she is but dust,
>   Whose heart so long hath held thy form en-
>   shrined;
> When I go hence, as soon I feel I must,
>   Oh! let my memory, Isbal, haunt thy mind.
> Not for myself—oh! not for *me* be given
>   Vain thoughts of vain regret, though that
>   were sweet;
> But for the sake of that all-blissful Heaven,
>   Where, if thou willest it, we yet may meet.
> When in thy daily musing thou dost bring
>   Those scenes to mind, in which I had a share;
> When in thy nightly watch thy heart doth wring
>   With thought of me—oh! murmur forth a
>   prayer!
> A prayer for me—for thee—for all who live
>   Together, yet asunder in one home—

> Who their soul's gloomy secret dare not give,
>   Lest it should blacken all their years to come.
> Yes, Isbal, yes; to *thee* I owe the shade
>   That prematurely darkens on my brow;
> And never had my lips a murmur made—
>   But—but that—see! the vision haunts me
>   now!"
> She pointed on the river's surface, where
>   Our forms were pictured seated side by side;
> I gazed on them, and hers was very fair;
>   And mine—was as thou seest it *now,* my
>   bride.
> But hers, though fair, was fading—wan and pale
>   The brow whose marble met the parting day.
> Time o'er her form had thrown his misty veil,
>   And all her ebon curls were streak'd with
>   grey;
> But mine was youthful—yes!—such youth as
>   glows
>   In the young tree by lightning scathed and
>   blasted—
> That, joyless, waves its black and leafless
>   boughs,
>   On which spring showers and summer warmth
>   are wasted.

Such passages as these sufficiently show where Mrs. Norton's true field lies, and how likely she is, within her proper department, to attain an elevated place in poetry. Other proofs might easily be selected from the miscellaneous poems which are appended in the ***Undying One;*** among which that entitled, **'Recollections,'** is perhaps the most striking. There is a peculiarly graceful flow of versification, and simplicity of expression, in the following stanzas;—

> Do you remember when we first departed
> From all the old companions who were round
>   us,
> How very soon again we grew lighthearted,
> And talked with smiles of all the links which
>   bound us?
> And after, when our footsteps were returning,
> With unfelt weariness o'er hill and plain,
> How our young hearts kept boiling up, and
>   burning,
> To think how soon we'd be at home again?
>
> Do you remember how the dreams of glory
> Kept fading from us like a fairy treasure;
> How we thought less of being famed in story,
> And more of those to whom our fame gave plea-
>   sure?
> Do you remember in far countries, weeping,
> When a light breeze, a flower, hath brought to
>   mind
> Old happy thoughts, which till that hour were
>   sleeping,
> And made us yearn for those we left behind?

The present volume is an improvement on its predecessor. The next (for in the glass of futurity we see others) will, we are sure, be a still greater improvement on the present, provided always Mrs. Norton eschews the supernatural and the exaggerated, and trusts to her power of depicting the calmer aspects of life, and

> The common thoughts of mother earth,
>   Its simpler mirth and tears.

Hartley Coleridge   (review date 1840)

SOURCE: A review of *The Dream and Other Poems* in *The Quarterly Review,* Vol. LXVI, No. CXXII, September, 1840, pp. 374-82.

[In this frequently cited review, Coleridge refers to Norton as "the Byron of modern poetesses" because of the passion and tenderness in her poetry.]

[Caroline Norton] is the Byron of our modern poetesses. She has very much of that intense personal passion by which Byron's poetry is distinguished from the larger grasp and deeper communion with man and nature of Wordsworth. She has also Byron's beautiful intervals of tenderness, his strong practical thought, and his forceful expression. It is not an artificial imitation, but a natural parallel: and we may add that it is this her latest production, which especially induces, and seems to us to justify, our criticism. The last three or four years have made Mrs. Norton a greater writer than she was; she is deeper, plainer, truer. There is a meaning, an allusion, an aiming, throughout the larger part of this volume, which of course we can but imperfectly understand, and in which we can take but the interest of contemporary strangers: yet we could not read the following Dedication to the Duchess of Sutherland—most worthy of the poetess and her patron—without feeling our heart swell with we know not what emotion: —

> Once more, my harp! once more, although I
>   thought
>   Never to wake thy silent strings again,
> A wandering dream thy gentle chords have
>   wrought,
>   And my sad heart, which long hath dwelt in
>   pain,
> Soars, like a wild bird from a cypress bough,
> Into the poet's Heaven, and leaves dull grief
>   below!
> And unto Thee—the beautiful and pure—
>   Whose lot is cast amid that busy world
> Where only sluggish Dulness dwells secure,
>   And Fancy's generous wing is faintly furl'd;
> To Thee—whose friendship kept its equal truth
> Through the most dreary hour of my embitter'd
>   youth—
> I dedicate the lay. Ah! never bard,
>   In days when poverty was twin with song;
> Nor wandering harper, lonely and ill-starr'd,
>   Cheer'd by some castle's chief, and harbour'd
>   long;
> Not Scott's Last Minstrel, in his trembling lays,
> Woke with a warmer heart the earnest meed of
>   praise!
> For easy are the alms the rich man spares
>   To sons of Genius, by misfortune bent,
> But thou gav'st *me,* what woman seldom dares,
>   Belief—in spite of many a cold dissent—
> When, slandered and maligned, I stood apart
> From those whose bounded power hath wrung,
>   not crush'd, my heart.
>
> Thou, then, when cowards lied away my name,
>   And scoff'd to see me feebly stem the tide;
> When some were kind on whom I had no claim,
>   And some forsook on whom my love relied,
> And some, who *might* have battled for my sake,

> Stood off in doubt to see what turn the world
>   would take—
> Thou gav'st me that the poor do give the poor,
>   Kind words and holy wishes, and true tears;
> The lov'd, the near of kin, could do no more,
>   Who chang'd not with the gloom of varying
>   years,
> But clung the closer when I stood forlorn,
> And blunted Slander's dart with their indignant
>   scorn.
> For they who credit crime are they who feel
>   Their *own* hearts weak to unresisted sin;
> Memory, not judgment, prompts the thoughts
>   which steal
>   O'er minds like these, an easy faith to win;
> And tales of broken truth are still believ'd
> Most readily by those who have *themselves* de-
>   ceiv'd.
>
> But like a white swan down a troubled stream,
>   Whose ruffling pinion hath the power to fling
> Aside the turbid drops which darkly gleam,
>   And mar the freshness of her snowy wing,—
> So Thou, with queenly grace and gentle pride,
> Along the world's dark waves in purity dost
>   glide;
> *Thy* pale and pearly cheek was never made
>   To crimson with a faint false-hearted shame;
> *Thou* didst not shrink—of bitter tongues afraid,
>   Who hunt in packs the object of their blame;
> To Thee the sad denial still held true,
> For from thine own good thoughts thy heart its
>   mercy drew.
> And though my faint and tributary rhymes
>   Add nothing to the glory of thy day,
> Yet every Poet *hopes* that after times
>   Shall set some value on his votive lay,—
> And I would fain one gentle deed record
> Among the many such with which thy life is
>   stor'd.
> So when these lines, made in a mournful hour,
>   Are idly open'd to the Stranger's eye,
> A dream of Thee, arous'd by Fancy's power,
>   Shall be the first to wander floating by;
> And they who never saw thy lovely face
> Shall pause—to conjure up a vision of its grace!

"The Dream" so dedicated is a very beautiful poem, the framework of which is simply a lovely mother watching over a lovely daughter asleep; which daughter dreams, and when awaked tells her dream; which dream depicts the bliss of a first love and an early union, and is followed by the mother's admonitory comment, importing the many accidents to which wedded happiness is liable, and exhorting to moderation of hope, and preparation for severe duties. It is in this latter portion of the poem that the passion and the interest assume a personal hue; and passages occur which sound like javelins hurled by an Amazon. Thus: —

> Heaven give thee poverty, disease, or death,
> Each varied ill that waits on human breath,
> Rather than bid thee linger out thy life
> In the long toil of such unnatural strife.
> To wander through the world unreconcil'd,
> Heart-weary as a spirit-broken child,
> And think it were an hour of bliss like heaven,
> If thou couldst *die*—forgiving, and forgiven,—

Caroline Norton's son Fletcher.

Or with a feverish hope, of anguish born,
(Nerving thy mind to feel indignant scorn
Of all the cruel foes that twixt ye stand,
Holding thy heartstrings with a reckless hand,)
Steal to his presence, now unseen so long,
And claim *his* mercy who hath dealt the wrong!
Into the aching depths of thy poor heart
  Dive, as it were, even to the roots of pain,
And wrench up thoughts that tear thy soul
  apart,
    And burn like fire through thy bewilder'd
  brain.
Clothe them in passionate words of wild appeal
To teach thy fellow-creature *how* to feel,—
Pray, weep, exhaust thyself in maddening
  tears,—
Recall the hopes, the influences of years,—
Kneel, dash thyself upon the senseless ground,
Writhe as the worm writhes with dividing
  wound,—
Invoke the heaven that knows thy sorrow's
  truth,
By all the softening memories of youth—
By every hope that cheer'd thine earlier day—
By every tear that washes wrath away—
By every old remembrance long gone by—
By every pang that makes thee yearn to die;

And learn at length how deep and stern a blow
Man's hands can strike, and yet no pity show!—

There are many such passages as this; and we think we shall advantageously display Mrs. Norton's varied powers by immediately contrasting it with one of those many tender pauses which lie islanded amidst the arrowy rushing of her passion:—

    Oh! Twilight! Spirit that dost render birth
To dim enchantments; melting heaven with
  earth,
Leaving on craggy hills and running streams
A softness like the atmosphere of dreams;
Thy hour to all is welcome! Faint and sweet
Thy light falls round the peasant's homeward
  feet,
Who, slow returning from his task of toil,
Sees the low sunset gild the cultured soil,
And, tho' such radiance round him brightly
  glows,
Marks the small spark his cottage-window
  throws.
Still as his heart forestals his weary pace,
Fondly he dreams of each familiar face,
Recalls the treasures of his narrow life,
His rosy children and his sunburnt wife,
To whom *his* coming is the chief event
Of simple days in cheerful labour spent.
The rich man's chariot hath gone whirling past,
And these poor cottagers have only cast
One careless glance on all that show of pride,
Then to their tasks turn'd quietly aside;
But *him* they wait for, him they welcome home,
Fixed sentinels look forth to see him come;
The fagot sent for when the fire grew dim,
The frugal meal prepared, are all for him;
For him the watching of that sturdy boy,
For him those smiles of tenderness and joy,
For him—who plods his sauntering way along,
Whistling the fragment of some village song!
  Dear art thou to the Lover, thou sweet light,
Fair fleeting sister of the mournful night!
As in impatient hope he stands apart,
Companion'd only by his beating heart,
And with an eager fancy oft beholds
The vision of a white robe's fluttering folds.

     . . . . .

    Oh! dear to him, to all, since first the flowers
Of happy Eden's consecrated bowers
Heard the low breeze along the branches play,
And God's voice bless the cool hour of the day.
For though that glorious Paradise be lost,
Though earth by blighting storms be roughly
  crossed,
Though the long curse demands the tax of sin,
And the day's sorrows with the day begin,
That hour, once sacred to God's presence, still
Keeps itself calmer from the touch of ill,
The holiest hour of earth. *Then* toil doth cease,
Then from the yoke the oxen find release—
Then man rests, pausing from his many cares,
And the world teems with children's sunset
  prayers!
Then innocent things seek out their natural rest,
The babe sinks slumbering on its mother's
  breast,

The birds beneath their leafy covering creep,
Yea, even the flowers fold up their buds in sleep;
And angels, floating by on radiant wings,
Hear the low sounds the breeze of evening
    brings,
Catch the sweet incense as it floats along,
The infant's prayer, the mother's cradle-song,
And bear the holy gifts to worlds afar,
As things too sacred for this fallen star.

So the elder Sappho: —

Εσπερε, παντα   ερει   οσα   αινολι
    ησκεδασ' ανω.
ερει οιν, φερει αιγα, φερει ματερι
    παιδα.

Hespere, qui cœlo lucet jucundior ignis?

One more specimen of Mrs. Norton's gentler strain must
close our extracts from the **"Dream."** It is the recollection
of her widowed mother; and is, in our judgment, pre-
eminently beautiful. There is a tender Crabbism in it that
goes right to the heart:—

Oft, since that hour, in sadness I retrace
My childhood's vision of thy calm sweet face;
Oft see thy form, its mournful beauty shrouded
    In thy black weeds, and coif of widow's woe;
Thy dark, expressive eyes all dim and clouded
    By that deep wretchedness the lonely know;
Stifling thy grief, to hear some weary task,
    Conn'd by unwilling *lips,* with listless air;
Hoarding thy means, lest future need might ask
    More than the widow's pittance then could
    spare.
Hidden, forgotten by the great and gay,
    Enduring sorrow, not by fits and starts,
But the long self-denial, day by day,
    Alone amidst thy brood of careless hearts!
Striving to guide, to teach, or to restrain
    The young rebellious spirits crowding round,
Who saw not, knew not, felt not for thy pain,
    And could not comfort—yet had power to
    wound!
Ah! how my selfish heart, which since hath
    grown
Familiar with deep trials of its own,
With riper judgment looking to the past,
Regrets the careless days that flew so fast,
Stamps with remorse each wasted hour of time,
And darkens every folly into crime!

Of the many poems which fill the rest of this volume, we
are unable to take a more particular notice. They vary considerably in merit—some of them being equal to the best
parts of the **"Dream,"** and others not rising above what
is called, we believe, *annual* value. We are unwilling to
designate the latter; amongst the former, we point out the
deeply-affecting pieces entitled **"Twilight,"** and **"May
Day, 1837,"**—the graceful and just tribute to Mr. Rogers,
as a friend and companion, in **"The Winter's Walk,"**—
and the very elegant and (date considered) very *puzzling*
poem, **"I cannot love thee."** But we cannot resist the pleasure of quoting at length one of Mrs. Norton's sonnets,
which, for tenderness and elegance, for skill and finish, is
inferior to nothing she ever wrote, and worthy to be laid
up in cedar with the best in our language:—

Like an enfranchised bird, that wildly springs,
    With a keen sparkle in his glancing eye,
And a strong effort in his quivering wings,
    Up to the blue vault of the happy sky,—
So my enamour'd heart, so long thine own,
    At length from Love's imprisonment set free,
Goes forth into the open world alone,
    Glad and exulting in its liberty:
But like that helpless bird (confin'd so long,
    His weary wings have lost all power to soar),
Who soon forgets to trill his joyous song,
    And, feebly fluttering, sinks to earth once
    more,—
So, from its former bonds released in vain,
My heart still feels the weight of that remem-
    ber'd chain.

We have a high opinion of Mrs. Norton's genius as a poet.
We think that what she has already achieved places her
in a very conspicuous position in the literature of our modern day. She has youth, health, zeal,—happiness, we
hope,—peace, we are assured,—before her. Her reputation for talent is established. Now then it is that she borders on Fame, and begins to feel that, diverse as love is
from friendship, so is the power of living in the hearts of
men from that of commanding the favour of the town. It
is characteristic of the latter that after a certain degree it
admits of no effective increase; you may pour in nectar,
and it will run to waste without brimming the cup. It is
all unlike with that sort of reputation, so to call it, which
is to end in fame. They may or may not—more commonly
the latter—set out together; but it is a truth as deep as life
and humanity that they will not always keep in company.
We invite Mrs. Norton to contemplate a glorious destiny,
and to discipline herself for an arduous career. She must,
before all things, keep in mind that language is of the essence of poetry as an art, and that inaccurate language,
though dialect to the age, is barbarism to posterity. Curiosity and the thirst of novelty will overlook and excuse
anything except dulness of interest; but a poem that is to
live must be prepared for those who read twice. To
'*quench* affliction's whelming *tide,*' for example, is beyond
the power of Mrs. Norton or any one else; but a false metaphor may be corrected or avoided with ease. A hint as to
this is enough. With a careful attention to purity and correctness of diction, Mrs. Norton ought, moreover, now to
break through the narrow circle of personal and domestic
feelings, and adventure herself upon a theme of greater variety and less morbid interest. There is a great difference
between writing always *from* the heart and always *about*
the heart, even the heart of a beautiful woman of genius.
Egotism is egotism still, disguise it as you may, and the
world is weary of it even before it ceases to admire. It is
one thing to shoot your own being outwards, so that inanimate nature or alien life shall become a projected self, reflecting back on others, modified and combined, from rock
or tree, from dying hero or peasant girl, the emotions, the
sympathies, which truly spring from *you;* and quite another thing to eddy round and round in an endless circle of
petty passion, alike without progress to any spiritual end,
and without retrospect to any moral source. Imagination
is necessary to the first; the absence, or scanty presence of
it, is almost characterised by the second. Be simple, be sensuous, be impassioned. The former two without the third

are lifeless and cold; but to substitute the last for either of the others is to prefer the red heat of a stove to the cheerful shine of a candle, or the genial shafts of the sunlight. These few remarks we humbly commend to the serious consideration of Mrs. Norton

> *Come a colei che fu nel mondo nata*
> *Per aver signoria*

trusting that neither taste nor caprice—neither public nor publisher—may avail to mar her fair destiny.

The Dublin University Magazine   (review date 1840)

SOURCE: "Mrs. Norton's Poems," in *The Dublin University Magazine,* Vol. XVI, No. XCVI, December, 1840, pp. 637-40.

[*In the following essay, the unsigned reviewer praises the depth of emotion in Norton's work.*]

We have read with much interest **"The Dream,"** and other poems by the Honourable Mrs. Norton,—regarded as mere fanciful effusions, their tone of feeling, and elegant versification would be sufficient to recommend them, but considered as the outpourings of an affectionate and grieved spirit, they win from us much more than common approval, for they awaken an individual feeling for the author. Long before this volume appeared, **"The Sorrows of Rosalie," "The Undying One,"** and other poems, had established Mrs. Norton's reputation as a poet, and secured a welcome for any production of hers which might follow; and we now venture to predict, that highly as her earlier productions have been esteemed, her last work will elicit still warmer approbation. On opening the book we were struck by the likeness prefixed to the poems, it is beautiful, as every likeness of Mrs. Norton must be—but the shades of sorrow rest pensively upon it, and the negligence and dejection which mark it, tell at once how much she, for whom it was sketched, has suffered.

Mrs. Norton's sad history is no secret, and the pages before us are eminently calculated to excite a strong sympathy in her misfortunes, the passages which allude to her own situation, are by far the most interesting parts of the collection; they bear the genuine stamp of feeling, and were probably written in solitude, where she could unrestrainedly give vent to the grief which oppressed her spirit, and not intended as the powerful appeals to sympathy which from circumstances they have become. There is sufficient evidence scattered throughout these pages to make us believe that she has been sustained in all her trials by a higher power than she could find in the tenderness and consolations of her fellow creatures; but that she has been the object of such sympathy is evident, from the testimony which she bears, to the affection and solicitude of many kind relatives and faithful friends. We were glad to see by the affectionate and interesting dedication to the Duchess of Sutherland, that that lady had stood by her in the hour of need; that, uncontaminated by the atmosphere of courts, or the corrupting frivolities of fashion, she had stepped forward at the call of friendship, and with the true spirit of a Beatrice stood by her slandered friend against an host of enemies.

We must confine ourselves to a few short extracts from *The Dream,* as it would far exceed our limits were we to give all that we could wish. **"The Apostrophe to Twilight"** caught our fancy, the home picture which it suggested, is exceedingly well sketched.—

> Oh! Twilight! Spirit that doth render birth
> To dim enchantments; melting Heaven with Earth,
> Leaving on craggy hills and running streams
> A softness like the atmosphere of dreams;
> Thy hour to all is welcome! faint and sweet
> Thy light falls round the peasant's homeward feet,
> Who slow returning from his task of toil,
> Sees the low sunset gild the cultured soil,
> And though such radiance round him brightly glows,
> Marks the small spark his cottage window throws,
> Still as his heart forestalls his weary pace,
> Fondly he dreams of each familiar face,
> Recalls the treasures of his narrow life,
> His rosy children and his sunburnt wife,
> To whom *his* coming is the chief event
> Of simple days in cheerful labour spent.
> The rich man's chariot hath gone whirling past,
> And those poor cottagers have only cast
> One careless glance on all that show of pride,
> Then to their tasks turn'd quietly aside;
> But *him* they wait for, him they welcome home,
> Fond sentinels look forth to see him come;
> The fagot sent for when the fire grows dim,
> The frugal meal prepared, are all for him;
> For him the watching of that sturdy boy,
> For him those smiles of tenderness and joy,
> For him,—who plods his sauntering way along,
> Whistling the fragment of some village song!

The manner in which she speaks of her mother is very affecting, and few could read these lines and not be pleased with them—

> Sweet is the image of the brooding dove!—
> Holy as Heaven, a mother's tender love!
> The love of many prayers and many tears,
> Which changes not with dim declining years,—
> The only love which on this teeming earth
> Asks no return from passion's wayward birth;
> The only love that with a touch divine,
> Displaces from the heart's most secret shrine
> The idol Self. Oh! prized beneath thy due
> When life's untried affections all are new,—
> Love from whose calmer hope and holier rest
> (Like a fledged bird impatient of the nest)
> The human heart, rebellious, springs to seek
> Delights more vehement, in ties more weak;
>
> . . . . .
>
> Oh! happy days! oh, years that glided by,
> Scarce chronicled by one poor passing sigh!
> When the dark storm sweeps past us, and the soul
> Struggles with fainting strength to reach the goal;
> When the false baits that lured us only cloy,
> What would we give to grasp your banished joy!

From the cold quicksands of Life's treacherous
    shore
The backward light our anxious eyes explore,
Measure the miles our wandering feet have
    come,
Sinking heart-weary, far away from home,
Recall the voice that whisper'd love and peace,
The smile that bid our early sorrows cease,
And long to bow our weeping heads and weep
Low on the gentle breast that lull'd us first to
    sleep!
Ah, blessed are they for whom 'mid all their
    pains
That faithful and unalter'd love remains
Who, life wreck'd round them,—hunted from
    their rest
And by all else forsaken or distress'd—
Claim in *one* heart, their sanctuary and shrine—
As I, my mother, claim'd my place in thine!

She goes on to speak of the early days of her mother's wid-
owhood, and we cannot forbear adding to the extracts
which we have already made the following lines:—

Oft, since that hour, in sadness I retrace
My childhood's vision of thy calm sweet face;
Oft see thy form, its mournful beauty shrouded
In thy black weeds, and coif of widow's woe;
Thy dark expressive eyes all dim and clouded
By that deep wretchedness the lonely know.
Stifling thy grief, to hear some heavy task
Conn'd by unwilling lips with listless air,
Hoarding thy means, lest future need might ask
More than the widow's pittance then could
    spare.
Hidden, forgotten by the great and gay,
Enduring sorrow, not by fits and starts.
But the long self-denial, day by day,
Alone amidst thy brood of careless hearts!
Striving to guide, to teach or to restrain
The young rebellious spirits crowding round,
Who saw not, knew not, felt not for thy pain,
And could not comfort—yet had power to
    wound!
Ah! how my selfish heart, which since hath
    grown
Familiar with deep trials of its own,
With riper judgment looking to the past,
Regrets the careless days that flew so fast,
Stamps with remorse each wasted hour of me,
And darkens every folly into crime!

Speaking of the haunts of Childhood, she says—

And oft, in after-life, some simple thing—
A bank of primroses in early Spring—
The tender scent which hidden violets yield—
The sight of cowslips in a meadow field—
Or young laburnum's pendant yellow chain—
May bring the favourite play place back again!
Our youthful mates are gone: some dead, some
    changed,
With whom that pleasant spot was gladly
    ranged;
Ourselves, perhaps, more alter'd e'en than
    they—
But *there* still blooms the blossom showering
    May;
There still along the hedgerow's verdant line
The linnet sings, the thorny brambles twine;

Still in the copse a troop of merry elves
Shout,—the gay image of our former selves.

We could select many passages in *The Dream* which
pleased us as much as those which we have given, but in
doing so, we should allow ourselves no space to notice the
shorter poems, several of which are not less interesting
and sweet; there is a deep tone of feeling in **"Twilight,"**
and we like it all so much that we find it difficult to determine which of the stanzas to leave out:—

It is the twilight hour,
The daylight toil is done,
And the last rays are departing
Of the cold and wintry sun.
It is the time when Friendship
Holds converse fair and free,
It is the time when children
Dance round the mother's knee.
But my soul is faint and heavy,
With a yearning sad and deep,
By the fireside lone and dreary
I sit me down and weep!
Where are ye, merry voices?
Whose clear and bird-like tone,
Some other ear now blesses
Less anxious than my own!
Where are ye, steps of lightness,
Which fell like blossom showers?
Where are ye, sounds of laughter,
That cheer'd the pleasant hours?
Through the dim light slow declining,
Where my wistful glances fall,
I can see your pictures hanging
Against the silent wall;—
They gleam athwart the darkness,
With their sweet and changeless eyes,
But mute are ye, my children!
No voice to mine replies,
Where are ye? are ye playing
By the stranger's blazing hearth;
Forgetting, in your gladness,
Your old home's former mirth?
Are ye dancing? are ye singing?
Are ye full of childish glee?
Or do your light hearts sadden
With the memory of me?
Round whom, oh gentle darlings,
Do your young arms fondly twine,
Does she press you to *her* bosom
Who hath taken you from mine?
Oh! boys, the twilight hour
Such a heavy time hath grown,—
It recalls with such deep anguish
All I used to call my own,—
That the harshest word that ever
Was spoken to me there
Would be trivial—would be *welcome*—
In this depth of my despair!
Yet, no! Despair shall not sink,
While life and love are mine—
Tho' the weary struggle haunt me,
And my prayer be made in vain:
Tho' at times my spirit fail me,
And the bitter tear drops fall,
Tho' my lot be hard and lonely,
Yet I hope—I hope thro' all!

    . . . . .

By the sudden joy which bounded
In the banish'd Hagar's heart,
When she saw the gushing fountain
From the sandy desert start;—
By the living smile which greeted
The lonely one of Nain.
When her long last watch was over,
And her hope seem'd wild and vain;—
By all the tender mercy
God hath shown to human grief,
When fate or man's perverseness
Denied and bar'd relief,—
By the help'ess woe which taught me
To look to him alone,
From the vain appeals for justice
And wild efforts of my own,—
By thy light—thou unseen future,
And thy tears—thou bitter past,
I will hope—tho' all forsake me,
In His mercy to the last!

There are some very elegant stanzas in the **"Winter's Walk"** which bear high testimony to the worth of Mr. Rogers, —it is always gratifying to find genius and excellence united, and Mrs. Norton has appreciated both; his friendship appears to have been most soothing to her feelings, and has suggested some of the sweetest lines in the volume.

There is so much feeling, and so much of individual interest in **"The Mother's Heart,"** that we cannot refrain from giving the entire of it.

When first thou camest, gentle, shy, and fond,
My eldest born, first hope, and dearest treasure,
My heart received thee with a joy beyond
All that it yet had felt of earthly pleasure;
Nor thought that *any* love again might be
So deep and strong as that I felt for thee.

Faithful and true, with sense beyond thy years,
And natural piety that lean'd to Heaven;
Wrung by a harsh word suddenly to tears,
Yet patient of rebuke when justly given—
Obedient—easy to be reconciled—
And meekly cheerful—such wert thou, my child!

Not willing to be left; still by my side,
Haunting my walks, while summer day was dying,
Nor leaving in thy turn; but pleased to glide
Thro' the dark room where I was sadly lying,
Or by the couch of pain, a sitter meek,
Watch the dim eye, and kiss the feverish cheek.

O boy! of such as thou are oftenest made
Earth's fragile idols; like a tender flower.
No strength in all thy freshness—prone to fade,—
And bending weakly to the thunder shower,—
Still round the loved, thy heart found force to bind,
And clung, like woodbine shaken in the wind!

Then thou, my merry love;—bold in thy glee.
Under the bough, or by the fire light dancing,
With thy sweet temper and thy spirit free,
Didst come, as restless as a bird's wing glancing,
Full of a wild and irrepressible mirth,
Like a young sunbeam to the gladden'd earth!

Thine was the shout! the song! the burst of joy
Which sweet from childhood's rosy lips resoundeth;
Thine was the eager spirit nought could cloy,
And the glad heart from which all grief reboundeth;
And many a mirthful jest and mock reply,
Lurk'd in the laughter of thy deep blue eye!

And thine was many an art to win and bless,
The cold and stern to joy and fondness warming;
The coaxing smile;—the frequent soft caress;
The earnest tearful prayer all wrath disarming!
Again my heart a new affection found,
But thought that love with thee had reach'd its bound.

At length thou camest; thou the last and least;
Nick-named 'the Emperor' by thy laughing brothers,
Because a haughty spirit swell'd thy breast,
And thou didst seek to rule and sway the others;
Mingling with every playful infant wile
A mimic majesty that made us smile.

And oh! most like a regal child wert thou!
An eye of resolute and successful scheming!
Fair shoulders—curling lip—and dauntless brow—
Fit for the world's strife, not for poet's dreaming:
And proud the lifting of thy stately head,
And the firm bearing of thy conscious tread.

Different from both! yet each succeeding claim,
I, that all other love had been forswearing,
Forthwith admitted, equal and the same;
Nor injured either, by this love's comparing,
Nor stole a fraction for the newer call—
But in the mother's heart, found room for all!

In **"May Day"** we find the same affectionate spirit; it would be impossible to be unmoved by her fond allusion to her boys, in the following stanzas. Speaking of the ungenial May day so unlike the happier ones of other years, she says:—

Yet will I not reproach thee for thy change;
Closed be the flower and leafless be the tree!
Smile not as thou wert wont; but sad, and strange.
And joyless let thy tardy coming be!
So shall I miss those infant voices less,
Calling each other through the garden bowers,
Meeting and parting in wild happiness,
Leading a light dance thro' the sunny hours;
Those little mirthful hearts, who, far away,
Breathe, amid cloud capp'd hills, a yet more wintry May!

Ah, boys? your play-ground is a desert spot,
Revisited alone, and bathed with tears;
And where *ye* pass your May-day, knoweth not
The mother who hath watch'd your dawning years
Mine is no more the joy to see ye come,
And deem each step hath some peculiar grace!
Yours is no more the mother's welcome home,
Smiling at each beloved, familiar face!

And I am thankful that this dreary May
Recals not, save by name, that brighter, happier
    day!

We are sorry to bring our extracts to an end, as we have left many passages unnoticed that we could have dwelt on with pleasure, but in the midst of so many beauties, there are defects and inaccuracies, which Mrs. Norton will herself easily detect, and which carelessness or hurry may have prevented her perceiving in time for correction. There are several prosaic lines which should not have come from the pen of such an accomplished versifier, and some unmeaning expressions which could not have escaped her, had she allowed herself time for revision. She will perceive that to speak of "a *most nameless* river," and "the *world's allure*," is to war with the Queen's English. But we will not dwell upon trifling blemishes which need no other correction than that which her own good sense and taste will instantly suggest. It would be injustice to Mrs. Norton were we to bring our observations on the volume to a close, without remarking the forbearance which she has shown. No burst of indignation, no angry expression have found their way into these most interesting pages; actuated by feelings of genuine delicacy she has forborne to avail herself of the opportunity of venting a very just resentment; it would seem that **"The Mother's Heart"** was so filled with sorrow, that there was no room for anger.

Our interest had been excited for the author of the volume now before us, long before its publication—for an engraving from the portrait by Parris had fallen in our way, and never was one more calculated to prepossess us in an author's favour; it is, no doubt, familiar to our readers; the fine classical head, with its rich tresses simply braided, the exquisite features, models of perfect symmetry, would have alone formed beauty of a superior class, but when to these is added all that expresses the dignity and intellectuality of a noble mind, the charm is irresistible. Smile, not reader, that we wax sentimental, or rather smile on—in such a cause we despise and defy thee. True we are somewhat stricken in years, more is the pity,—true, likewise, that we have contracted among the duties and the dust of our literary labours and researches certain comfortable and therefore antiromantic habits; such as those of imbibing mulled port, and snuffing up three halfpenny worth of "blackguard" per day. Yet, sirrah, know that we were *less* than man (which were exactly the reverse of the reality, we being "humano major") if we possessed not some sparks of that fire ycleped chivalry, and being thus supplied, if we could suffer them, in such a presence, dully to smoulder in their ashes. Often have we looked at the beautiful brow, and on the dark eyes glancing from their long lashes, till we fancied we could see their lustre and feel their fire. It was impossible to look upon such a portrait and not to feel interested for her whose likeness it was: and surely our readers will allow that it were impossible to read even the few extracts with which we have presented them, without feeling a lively sympathy in the sorrows and affection to which they give sweet utterance.

We close this volume with the regret with which one turns from a friend who has ministered to his gratification; we leave it, too, with a deeper and a less selfish feeling, —one

Pen-and-ink sketch of Caroline Norton.

of keen pity for the many griefs which have overtaken the youth of the author, and of an unmingled admiration for the spirit in which these griefs are born.

R. H. Horne   (essay date 1844)

SOURCE: "Miss E. B. Barrett and Mrs. Norton," in *A New Spirit of the Age, Vol. II*, edited by R. H. Horne, Smith, Elder, and Co., 1844, pp. 129-40.

[*Richard Henry Horne, British playwright and author, is best known for his children's books. In this essay, he compares the poetry of Norton and Elizabeth Barrett, addressing prominent themes and subjects in the works of both.*]

It is anything but handsome towards those who were criticised, or fair towards the adventurous critic, to regard, as some have done, the article on "Modern English Poetesses," which appeared a few years ago in the *Quarterly Review,* [LXVI, No. CXXII (September 1840)] as a tribute merely of admiration. It was a tribute of justice; and hardly that, because nine ladies were reviewed, of very different kind and degree of merit, all in the same article. Eight were allowed to wear their laurels; the ninth fell a victim. Passing over the victim, who shall be nameless, we will say, that the poetical genius, the impassioned fervour, the knowledge of genuine nature and of society, of books, of languages, of all that is implied by the term of accomplishment, and "though last, not least," the highly cultivated talent in the poetic art, displayed by the other eight, are such as to entitle them to a higher position than several of the "received" poets of the past and present centuries.

The list we have named comprises, Mrs. Norton; Miss E. B. Barrett; Maria del Occidente; Lady Northampton (author of "Irene"); Caroline Southey; Miss Lowe; the Author of "IX Poems;" Sara Coleridge; and one other, a lady of rank, whom it was a pity to introduce in company where she has no *claim* to rank. The reviewer proposed to make a wreath of them after the manner of Meleager, and appropriately commenced with Mrs. Norton as "the *Rose,* or, if she like it, *Love-lies-a-bleeding;*" and Miss Barrett as *"Greek Valerian, or Ladder to Heaven,* or, if she pleases, *Wild Angelica."* The former lady is well known, personally, to a large and admiring circle, and is also extensively known to the reading public by her works. The latter lady, or "fair shade"—whichever she may be—is not known personally, to anybody, we had almost said; but her poetry is known to a highly intellectual class, and she "lives" in constant correspondence with many of the most eminent persons of the time. When, however, we consider the many strange and ingenious conjectures that are made in after years, concerning authors who appeared but little among their contemporaries, or of whose biography little is actually known, we should not be in the least surprised, could we lift up our ear out of our grave a century hence, to hear some learned Thebans expressing shrewd doubts as to whether such an individual as Miss E. B. Barrett had ever really existed. Letters and notes, and exquisite English lyrics, and perhaps a few elegant Latin verses, and spirited translations from Æschylus, might all be discovered under that name; but this would not prove that such a lady had ever dwelt among us. Certain admirable and erudite prose articles on the "Greek Christian Poets," might likewise be ascertained by the exhumation of sundry private letters and documents, touching periodical literature, to have been from the hand of that same "Valerian;" but neither the poetry, nor the prose, nor the delightfully gossiping notes to fair friends, nor the frank correspondence with scholars, such as Lady Jane Grey might have written to Roger Ascham—no, not even if the great-grandson of some learned Jewish doctor could show a note in Hebrew (quite a likely thing really to be extant) with the same signature, darkly translated by four letters, —nay, though he should display as a relic treasured in his family, the very pen, with its oblique Hebraic nib, that wrote it—not any one, nor all of those things could be sufficient to demonstrate the fact, that such a lady had really adorned the present century.

In such *chiaroscuro,* therefore, as circumstances permit, we will endeavour to offer sufficient grounds for our readers' belief, to the end that posterity may at least have the best authorities and precedents we can furnish. Confined entirely to her own apartment, and almost hermetically sealed, in consequence of some extremely delicate state of health, the poetess of whom we write is scarcely seen by any but her own family. But though thus separated from the world—and often, during many weeks at a time, in darkness almost equal to that of night, Miss Barrett has yet found means by extraordinary inherent energies to develope her inward nature; to give vent to the soul in a successful struggle with its destiny while on earth; and to attain and master more knowledge and accomplishments than are usually within the power of those of either sex who possess every adventitious opportunity, as well as health and industry. Six or seven years of this imprisonment she has now endured, not with vain repinings, though deeply conscious of the loss of external nature's beauty; but with resignation, with patience, with cheerfulness, and generous sympathies towards the world without;—with indefatigable "work" by thought, by book, by the pen, and with devout faith, and adoration, and a high and hopeful waiting for the time when this mortal frame "putteth on immortality."

The period when a strong prejudice existed against learned ladies and "blues" has gone by, some time since; yet in case any elderly objections may still exist on this score, or that some even of the most liberal-minded readers may entertain a degree of doubt as to whether a certain austere exclusiveness and ungenial pedantry might infuse a slight tinge into the character of ladies possessing Miss Barrett's attainments, a few words may be added to prevent erroneous impressions on this score. Probably no living individual has a more extensive and diffuse acquaintance with literature—that of the present day inclusive—than Miss Barrett. Although she has read Plato, in the original, from beginning to end, and the Hebrew Bible from Genesis to Malachi (nor suffered her course to be stopped by the Chaldean), yet there is probably not a single good romance of the most romantic kind in whose marvellous and impossible scenes she has not delighted, over the fortunes of whose immaculate or incredible heroes and heroines she has not wept; nor a clever novel or fanciful sketch of our own day, over the brightest pages of which she has not smiled inwardly, or laughed outright, just as their authors themselves would have desired. All of this, our readers may be assured that we believe to be as strictly authentic as the very existence of the lady in question, although, as we have already confessed, we have no absolute knowledge of this fact. But lest the reader should exclaim, "Then, *after all,* there really may be no such person!" we should bear witness to having been shown a letter of Miss Mitford's to a friend, from which it was plainly to be inferred that she had actually seen and conversed with her. The date has unfortunately escaped us.

We cannot admit that any picture, engraving, or other portrait of Mrs. Norton with which the public has been favoured does full justice to the original; nevertheless they may be considered as likenesses, to a certain extent, and by reason of these, and her popular position as an authoress, any introductory remarks on the present occasion would be needless.

There are few poems which would be more acceptable to the majority of lovers of poetry than Mrs. Norton's **"Dream,"** from which we make the following extract;—

> Oh! Twilight! Spirit that does render birth

To dim enchantments; melting heaven with
  earth,
Leaving on craggy hills and running streams
A softness like the atmosphere of dreams;
Thy hour to all is welcome! Faint and sweet
Thy light falls round the peasant's homeward
  feet,
Who, slow returning from his task of toil,
Sees the low sunset gild the cultured soil,
And, tho' such radiance round him brightly
  glows,
Marks the small spark his cottage window
  throws.
Still as his heart forestals his weary pace,
Fondly he dreams of each familiar face,
Recalls the treasures of his narrow life,
His rosy children and his sunburnt wife,
To whom *his* coming is the chief event
Of simple days in cheerful labour spent.
The rich man's chariot hath gone whirling past,
And these poor cottagers have only cast
One careless glance on all that show of pride,
Then to their tasks turn'd quietly aside;
But *him* they wait for, him they welcome home,
Fixed sentinels look forth to see him come;
The fagot sent for when the fire grew dim,
The frugal meal prepared, are all for him;
For him the watching of that sturdy boy,
For him those smiles of tenderness and joy,
For him—who plods his sauntering way along,
Whistling the fragment of some village song!

The above is characteristic of a style in which Mrs. Norton excels, and it is a popular error to regard her solely as the poetess of impassioned personalities, great as she undoubtedly has shown herself in such delineations.

The next extract is from Miss Barrett's "Seraphim," where Ador, a seraph, exhorts Zerah not to linger nor look through the closed gate of heaven, after the Voice had said "Go!"

Thou—wherefore dost thou wait?
Oh! gaze not backward, brother mine;
The deep love in thy mystic eyne
Deepening inward, till is made
A copy of the earth-love shade—
  Oh! gaze not through the gate!
God filleth heaven with God's own solitude
  Till all its pavements glow!
His Godhead being no more subdued
  By itself, to glories low
    Which seraphs can sustain,
  What if thou in gazing so,
  Should behold but only one
  Attribute, the veil undone—
And that the one to which we press
  Nearest, for its gentleness—
    Ay! His love!
How the deep ecstatic pain
Thy being's strength would capture!
Without a language for the rapture,
  Without a music strong to come,
    And set th' adoring free;
  For ever, ever, wouldst thou be
  Amid the general chorus dumb,—
God-stricken, in seraphic agony!—
  Or, brother, what if on thine eyes
    In vision bare should rise

The life-fount whence his hand did gather
  With solitary force
  Our immortalities!—
Straightway how thine own would wither,
Falter like a human breath,—
And *shrink into a point like death,*
  By gazing on its source!

We cannot do better, we think, than attempt to display the different characteristics of the genius of the two highly-gifted women who form the subject of the present paper, by placing them in such harmonious juxtaposition as may be most advantageous to both, and convey the clearest synthetical impression to the reader.

The prominent characteristics of these two poetesses may be designated as the struggles of woman towards happiness, and the struggles of a soul towards heaven. The one is oppressed with a sense of injustice, and feels the need of human love; the other is troubled with a sense of mortality, and aspires to identify herself with etherial existences. The one has a certain tinge of morbid despondency taking the tone of complaint and the amplification of private griefs; the other too often displays an energetic morbidity on on the subject of death, together with a certain predilection for "terrors." The imagination of Mrs. Norton is chiefly occupied with domestic feelings and images, and breathes melodious plaints or indignations over the desecrations of her sex's loveliness; that of Miss Barrett often wanders amidst the supernatural darkness of Calvary sometimes with anguish and tears of blood, sometimes like one who echoes the songs of triumphal quires. Both possess not only great mental energies, but that description of strength which springs from a fine nature, and manifests itself in productions which evidently originated in genuine impulses of feeling. The subjects they both choose appear spontaneous, and not resulting from study or imitation, though cast into careful moulds of art. Both are excellent artists: the one in dealing with subjects of domestic interest; the other in designs from sacred subjects, poems of religious tendency, or of the supernatural world. Mrs. Norton is beautifully clear and intelligible in her narrative and course of thought and feeling; Miss Barrett has great inventiveness, but not an equal power in construction. The one is all womanhood; the other all wings. The one writes from the dictates of a human heart in all the eloquence of beauty and individuality; the other like an inspired priestess—not without a most truthful heart, but a heart that is devoted to religion, and whose individuality is cast upward in the divine afflatus, and dissolved and carried off in the recipient breath of angelic ministrants.

Some of Mrs. Norton's songs for music are very lovely, and other of her lyrics have the qualities of sweetness and pathos to a touching and thrilling degree. One of the domestic poems in the *Dream and other poems,* is a striking composition. The personal references in the miscellaneous poems are deep and true, and written with unaffected tenderness. She has contributed many prose tales full of colour and expression to several of the Annuals; but these, together with her musical talents and editorial labours, are much too popularly known and admired to render any further remarks that we could offer upon them at all requisite.

Temple Bar (review date 1878)

SOURCE: "Mrs. Norton," in *Temple Bar,* Vol. LII, No. I, January, 1878, pp. 101-10.

[*In this excerpt, the unsigned critic discusses Norton's poetry and prose, complimenting her style and arguing that her subject matter is dismal and depressing.*]

It may be assumed that in social life, where [Caroline Norton] met and favourably impressed the most eminent men of the country—statesmen, artists, men of letters, who were sure to be found enthusiastically grouped around her, or in deep, private conference in a corner of the room, was the most successful sphere of her existence. There is a short piece in **The Dream** volume called **"The Winter's Walk"** (written after walking with Mr. Rogers), which shows the sympathetic and confidential intimacy which she was able to maintain, no doubt much aided by "the deep, sweet contralto" and dazzling and penetrating glances. She describes Rogers's talk:

> Many an anecdote of other times—
> Good earnest deeds—quaint wit—and polished rhymes;
> Many a sweet story of remembered years,
> Which thrilled the listening heart with unshed tears,
> Unweariedly thy willing tongue rehearsed,
> And made the hour seem brief as we conversed.
> Ah! who can e'er forget who once hath heard
> The gentle charm that dwells in every word
> Of thy calm converse? In its kind allied
> To some fair river's bright abundant tide,
> Whose silver gushing current onward goes
> Fluent and varying; yet with such repose
> As smiles even through the flashings of thy wit
> In every eddy that ruffles it.

This is very pretty and touching, and may be suspected to be rather a sentimental view, or at least meant as such, of Rogers's conversation, judging from other accounts of it; but Rogers was probably more engaging with women than with men, and indeed his greatest triumph in making himself agreeable in that way was in the case of that sour, sickly old tabby, Miss Martineau, who kept her claws in when with him, as appears from the unusual tone of cordial approbation with which she speaks of him in her diary, which otherwise consists of spiteful and jaundiced criticism of other people. There is also a happy and true touch in Mrs. Norton's sketch in the same piece of Rogers's dining-room:

> Who can forget who at thy social board
> Hath sat, and seen the pictures richly stored
> In all their tints of glory and of gloom,
> Brightening the precincts of thy quiet room;
> With busts and statues full of that deep grace
> Which modern hands have lost the skill to trace.
> (Fragment of beauty—perfect as thy song
> On that sweet land to which they did belong)
> Th' exact and classic taste by thee displayed;
> Not with a rich man's idle, fond parade;
> Not with the pomp of some vain connoisseur,
> Proud of his bargains, of his judgment sure;
> But with the feelings kind and sad of one

> Who through far countries wandering hath gone,
> And brought away views, keepsakes, to remind
> His heart and home of all he left behind.

She also expresses a passionate gratitude, which was no doubt sincere, to Rogers for his true friendship—

> In bitterest hours
> To one whom Heaven endowed with various powers;
> To one who died ere yet my childish heart
> Knew what Fame meant, or Slanderer's fabled dart.

This was her grandfather, whom Rogers generously befriended, not only in the time of his popularity and success, but in his destitute and miserable last days, which, however, have been much misrepresented and exaggerated. In her dedication of the **Lady of La Garaye** to the Marquis of Lansdowne, there is also another illustration of her power of addressing the soft side of men, though it would be unjust to doubt the genuine sincerity of the poetical emotion. Some of this piece deserves quoting as a happy example of the writer's literary style at its best, and is, on the whole, a true and touching picture of the Marquis.

> Friend of old days, of suffering, storm, and strife,
>   Patient and kind through many a wild appeal;
> In the arena of thy brilliant life
>   Never too busy or too cold to feel.
>
> Companion from whose ever-teeming store
>   Of thought and knowledge happy memory brings
> So much of social wit and logic's lore,
>   Garnered and gleaned by thee as precious things.
>
> . . . . .
>
> Thou hast known all my life; its pleasant hours
>   (How many of them have I owed to thee!),
> Its exercise of intellectual powers,
>   With thoughts of fame and gladness not to be.
>
> Thou knowest how death for ever dogged my way,
>   And how of those I loved the best, and those
> Who loved and pitied *me* in life's young day,
>   Narrow and narrower still the circle grows.
> Thou knowest—for thou hast proved—the dreary shade
>   A first-born's loss casts over lonely days;
> And now is gone the pale fond smile that made
>   In my dim future yet a path of rays.
>
> . . . . .
>
> But all the more I cling to those who speak
>   Like thee, in tones unaltered by my change;
> Greeting my saddened glance and faded cheek
>   With the same welcome that seemed sweet and strange
>
> In early days, when I, of gifts made proud,
>   That could the notice of such men beguile,
> Stood listening to thee in some brilliant crowd,
>   With the warm triumph of a youthful smile.
>
> Oh! little now remains of all that was!

> Even for this gift of linking measured words,
> My heart oft gushing with discouraged pause,
> Does music linger in the slackening cords.

It will be seen that, besides her commanding place in society, Mrs. Norton had also the real poetical fibre in her, when she chose to trust to it, although too often she wasted her powers in Annual contributions and complimentary verses to her friends. There was an article in a number of the *Quarterly* [*Quarterly Review* LXVI, No. CXXII (September 1840)] some thirty or more years since, in which she is justly described as "the Byron of the modern poetesses," as possessing much of the intense personal passion of that erratic and distempered bard, and also as what the writer says, "his beautiful intervals of tenderness, strong poetical thought, and forceful expression." Her first effort in literature was a light trifle, called *The Dandie's Rout,* with illustrations from her own designs, but it is now a scarce work, and even the British Museum has not a copy. In 1829, shortly after her marriage, she wrote "**Rosalie,**" a sad story of the ruin and desertion of a poor cottager's daughter by a man of rank. Next came *The Dream and other Poems,* in the dedication of which to the Duchess of Sutherland the writer falls very glaringly into a tendency to the error pointed out by the *Quarterly,* baring her personal troubles too openly to the general gaze, and wailing in an undignified measure. Taken as an illustration of her history—

> Thou gav'st me what a woman seldom dares—
> Belief in spite of many a cold dissent,
> When slandered and maligned I stood apart
> From those whose bounded power hath wrung,
>   not crushed, my heart.
>
> . . . . .
>
> Thou gav'st me what the poor do give the
>   poor—
> Kind words, and holy wishes, and true tears;
> The loved, the near of kin, could do no more;
>   Who changed not with the gloom of varying
>   years,
> But clung the closer when I stood forlorn,
> And blunted slander's dart with their indignant
>   scorn,

In another piece a widowed mother is shown watching by the bedside of her sleeping daughter, a fair girl of sixteen, who in a dream has a vision of her future career, ending in a betrothal, and asks on waking whether "the blessed dream is for ever gone," upon which the mother gives her a warning as to the difficulties of life and the dangers of indulging ideal expectations. It is written in a flowing, elegant style, but rather wants substance. The other pieces are mostly also deficient in the same way, though here and there is a graceful passage. Next there appeared the *Child of the Islands* (1846), a slight piece, and *Aunt Carry's Ballads for Children,* suitable enough for its purpose; and afterwards the *Undying One,* which is a graver style, and is a deeper and more solemn subject and aim, than her usual efforts in verse. The *Lady of La Garaye* (1863) is more mature and sustained, and reaches the highest range of her poetical power.

Taking Mrs. Norton's writings altogether, she was more successful in novel-writing than poetry. In the latter, as the critic of the *Quarterly* points out, she is too much confined within the narrow circle of personal and domestic feelings, and indulges in a morbid and egotistical tone, especially in treating of her own sufferings, of which the reader soon gets tired. To a certain extent there is the same tendency also in her novels, but then it is more veiled, and lightened by the animation of the incidents and characters. Moreover, though occasionally slipshod, and even ungrammatical, she writes a good prose style, clear, pithy, outspoken, vivid, and picturesque. The chief fault of these works is the melancholy tone which pervades them, which is apt to depress the readers, and make them rise more wearied and dismal than when they opened the book, which is obviously a mistake, as the essential object of fiction should be not exactly mere amusement, but an interesting relaxation of the mind. In the *Tales and Sketches,* published in 1850, this is very marked. The first story in the collection is the "**Forsaken Child.**"

> 'My boy! Henry, I cannot leave my boy.' Such were the words, wildly repeated over and over again (as if they contained all the reasoning or argument of which she was capable), uttered by Madeline Wentworth, as she sat convulsively sobbing, her face buried in her hands, and her whole frame shaking with a paroxysm of despairing grief. By her side stood a handsome, sickly-looking man, on whose pale brow more perplexity than sympathy was visible, and who seemed impatiently waiting till the fit should subside sufficiently for her to hear him.

It will be admitted that this is not a prepossessing situation, though experienced readers might believe that when a novel begins with clouds that is only in order to make the sunshine when it comes more resplendent. Here, however, the darkness continues throughout, deepening rather than passing away. The question between this pair was whether Madeline should elope from her husband, Lionel Wentworth, with her devoted friend, Henry Marchmont, who counsels the step in order to save her from the brutality—so he pleaded—of the man to whom she had been sacrificed, and who had made her home so wretched that life seemed scarce worth having on such terms; a man whose temper and character were so well known that the harshest of condemning tongues would speak her name in pity and sorrow. He further urged that her child—"it was an only child"—would not be left desolate, being heir to a peerage. The result was that Madeline Wentworth "left her home, her child, her husband, and learnt that there is no misery like the curse of remorse—no tears so bitter as those in which self-reproach is mingled." It is true that she had every reason for quitting a selfish, brutal, and violent husband, and that her lover was devoted to her, heart and soul. Five years passed away the comparative happiness of which might have stifled the voice of self-reproach, watched, shielded, and worshipped as she was, and the mother of two beautiful children. But she was kept in cruel anxiety and suspense, being cut off from all communication with her first child, and even from any knowledge of how he fared, his father having given him a stepmother, who, she feared, would naturally detest and ill-use him. A terrible blow, however, was overhanging her, and this was that her husband burst a blood-vessel and died. Afterwards she by a lucky chance discovers her eldest-born, and her joy is extreme. But again she is doomed to suffering. Gertrude, her daughter by the second marriage, wishes to marry Lord Everton, but this can never be if the circumstances of her mother's second marriage are known; and the new-found son, Frank, happens to hear her complaining to her own brother that she will be compelled to quit society, since its members are so anxious to visit on her head her mother's hand. This leads to a hot quarrel and blows between the brothers, and though Frank is not much hurt, the excitement brings on brain fever, and he too dies, while Gertrude marries her peer, on condition of renouncing her mother. The other stories are all much in the same mournful strain; and so are the novels in three volumes. In *Stuart of Dunleath* (1851), Mrs. Norton first made her mark in that branch of literature; the novel was immediately successful, and was followed by others, which, however, were not received with the same favour. Whilst neither her poems nor her novels will take a permanent place in literature, she will long be remembered for her grace, her beauty, and her wit.

Eric S. Robertson (essay date 1883)

SOURCE: "Caroline Norton," in *English Poetesses: A Series of Critical Biographies,* Cassell & Company, Limited, 1883, pp. 240-46.

[*In the excerpt that follows, Robertson faults Norton's poetry for its repeated references to her own life and sufferings.*]

Those who have read Fanny Kemble's recollections will remember that her pages give us several vivid glimpses of Caroline Norton. At one time she records that she was present at an evening gathering where a host of distinguished public and literary men were crowded into a small drawing-room, which was literally resplendent with the light of Sheridan beauty, male and female:—

> Mrs. Sheridan (Miss Callandar), the mother of the Graces, more beautiful than anybody but her daughters; Lady Graham, their beautiful aunt; Mrs. Norton, Mrs. Blackwood (Lady Dufferin), Georgiana Sheridan (Duchess of Somerset and Queen of Beauty by universal consent); and Charles Sheridan, their younger brother, a sort of younger brother of the Apollo Belvidere. Certainly I never saw such a bunch of beautiful creatures all growing on one stem. I remarked it to Mrs. Norton, who looked complacently round her tidy drawing-room and said, 'Yes, we *are* rather good-looking people.'

In another passage the same writer gives us a description of Caroline Norton:

> She was splendidly handsome, of an English character of beauty, her rather large and heavy features recalling the grandest Grecian and Italian models, to the latter of whom her rich colouring and blue-black braids of hair give her an additional resemblance. Though neither as perfectly lovely as the Duchess of Somerset, or as Lady Dufferin, she produced a far more striking impression than either of them by the combina-

tion of the poetical genius with which she of the three was gifted, with the brilliant wit and power of repartee which they (especially Lady Dufferin) possessed in common with her, united to the exceptional beauty with which they were all three endowed. Mrs. Norton was extremely epigrammatic. I do not know whether she had any theatrical talent, though she sang pathetic and humourous songs admirably; and I remember shaking in my shoes when soon after I came out, she told me she envied me, and would give anything to try the stage herself. I thought, as I looked at her wonderfully beautiful face, 'Oh, if you did, what would become of me?'

The enthusiasm here expressed was the enthusiasm of all who then knew her, and even a bishop has recorded that she seemed to him the connecting-link between a woman and an angel.

Caroline Elizabeth Sarah Norton, grand-daughter of Richard Brinsley Sheridan, and daughter of the dramatist's son Thomas, was born about 1808. Like her two sisters, she inherited some of the wit of which her grandfather had so plentiful a supply. Her mother was beautiful, and her grandmother on the father's side was the wonderful Miss Linley of Bath, with whom all the youth of England was in love when Sheridan ran away with her. With such prestige, and such endowments of beauty, wit, and

Caroline Norton, from the 1862 drawing by Mrs. Munro-Ferguson.

artistic talent, who could not have found life a pleasant thing when the world was so easy to be conquered? It cannot be said, however, that Caroline Norton found life a pleasant thing. The man whom she chose from all her suitors to be her husband did not succeed in making her a contented wife. She was married to the Hon. G. C. Norton, brother of Lord Grantley, in 1827; but after some scandal the two were separated—though not divorced—in 1836. Mrs. Norton's relations with one or two prominent men of the world were made the cause of malicious gossip which assumed a most serious form. Lord Melbourne was especially implicated in the charges brought against her. The judgment of to-day upon these charges is decidedly in Mrs. Norton's favour. Her conduct all through life was of such an unguarded character as to lay her open to evil insinuations; but her husband was a mean *roué* who had from the day he married her used her as a tool to get him position and money, and it was generally believed that his sole aim in blackening his wife's character was a pecuniary one. Even had she been more culpable, we should doubtless be chivalrous enough to excuse her. She is a Mary Queen of Scots in the history of our literature.

In 1875 Mr. Norton died; and a few months before her own death, which took place on the 15th June, 1877, the Hon. Mrs. Norton married Sir William Stirling-Maxwell, whose labours in archaeological fields are well known.

Caroline Norton's first effort in literature was a slight sketch, now very scarce, entitled the *Dandies' Rout,* with illustrations from her own pencil. There is no copy of this in the British Museum. The little work, it is believed, was produced in Caroline Norton's thirteenth year; and her sisters had a share in it. In 1829 she brought out **"The Sorrows of Rosalie,"** a poem which dealt with the familiar theme of a young country girl betrayed by a man of rank; and in 1830 came **"The Undying One."** The next volume attributed to her was published without her consent. It took its name from a short story forming its earlier pages, *The Coquette,* and was entirely composed of ephemeral contributions to the *Ladies' Magazine.* After *The Coquette* came a more serious performance, *The Wife,* and *Woman's Reward* (1835). Then came *The Dream,* in 1841, a book of poetry which led the *Quarterly Review* to dub her the female Byron. Macaulay somewhere likens the poetry of Byron to that species of toybook in which a single face made of india-rubber pierces many pages, and forms the head to a different body on each page. The simile might to a moderate extent be applied to Mrs. Norton's methods of work. In all her poems we are constantly reminded of herself—a very interesting person to be reminded of, and so we do not judge her harshly for the fault. Fault it was, however; and had she not been so caressed by society, and personally so worthy of the world's admiration, the continual suggestion of her own sufferings and sorrows abounding in her verse would be nothing short of an impertinence. **"The Dream"** is dedicated to the Duchess of Sutherland, in a set of verses which pointedly refer to the scandals which had arisen in her career and life. These verses are fully as sustained in power as any she ever wrote. It was hardly dignified of the author to quarrel so pettily with anonymous maligners whom she could with more effect have silenced by silence itself.

In 1846 a slight poetical effort, *The Child of the Islands,* was put forth, but added little to Mrs. Norton's reputation. *Aunt Carry's Ballads for Children* (1847), was followed in 1863 by the *Lady of La Garaye.* This is reckoned Mrs. Norton's best production in verse. It is a narrative founded on fact, and relates to a misadventure in the life of the Count and the Countess of La Garaye, Dinan. They were a youthful, ardent, and beautiful couple, who never grew tired of hunting and love-making. But one day the chase led them into danger, and the Countess escaped from an accident only with a severely broken body. For weeks her life flickered tremulously in her, but at last she was able to be about again, but robbed of beauty and soundness of body for ever. She would almost have died, rather, for with this beauty she feared her husband's love for her would pass also. His affection for her, however, was only purified and strengthened by the trial, and thenceforth they devoted themselves to good works, turning their ancestral home into a kind of hospital for the poor and needy, and ending their days in the odour of sanctity.

This theme was slight enough to make a book of verse about, and it really cannot be maintained that Mrs. Norton's treatment of the theme has evolved from it much poetry, or indeed any poetry. Hers is facile, graceful verse, exhibiting refined sympathy, an eye for the picturesque, and an ear for rhythm. She commits few solecisms of style, and she is always easily read. But even with regard to the *Lady of La Garaye,* one cannot but conclude that, were it now unearthed from obscurity as the production of some woman unknown to fame for the many personal graces which were Mrs. Norton's attributes, the thing would be dismissed by criticism as little above the commonplace. [*The Dream*] . . . shows Mrs. Norton's powers of writing verse at their very highest, but her best literary work lies in her fine novels, *Stuart of Dunleath* (1851), *Lost and Saved* (1863), and *Old Sir Douglas* (1868). Her *Tales and Sketches* appeared in 1850, and her *English Laws of Custom and Marriage for Women of the Nineteenth Century,* in 1854. She wrote *Letters to the Mob* (i. e., the Chartist Mob) during the Chartist riots; and in 1855 created some stir with a **"Letter to the Queen on the Marriage and Divorce Bill."** It remains to be added that Mrs. Norton edited the *Ladies' Magazine* for several years, the *Keepsake* for one year, and *Fisher's Drawing-Room Scrapbook* for three years.

The true value of Mrs. Norton's character as an influence in our literature is not that of the poet or the novelist. It lies in the fascination she exerted over other great writers. The intellectual influences on society which should be credited to such a woman as Mrs. Norton, are such as we are too apt to lose sight of altogether. The French estimate such factors in the thought of an age more justly. The most admired woman in a circle which included nearly all the brilliant men of her time in London, she must there have felt herself a greater intellectual power than when, pen in hand, she hung over the sentimental tale, whether in verse or prose. Even the rustic "Shepherd" and his cronies in the "Noctes," far removed from Mrs. Norton's personal sphere as they were, fell down and worshipped her, as readers of these wonderful conversations may remember;

and such a passage in the following, extracted from Crabb Robinson's Diary, shows what sway she held among the men with whom she mixed:—

31*st Jan.,* 1845.

I dined this day with Rogers, the Dean of the poets. We had an interesting party of eight. Moxon, the publisher, Kenny, the dramatic poet, Spedding, Lushington, and Alfred Tennyson, three young men of eminent talent belonging to literary Young England, the latter, Tennyson, being by far the most eminent of the young poets. . . . We waited for the eighth—a lady—who, Rogers said, was coming on purpose to see Tennyson, whose work she admired. He made a mystery of this fair devotee, and would give no name.

It was not till dinner was half over that he was called out of the room, and returned with a lady under his arm. A lady neither splendidly dressed nor strikingly beautiful, as it seemed to me, was placed at the table. A whisper ran along the company, which I could not make out. She instantly joined our conversation, with an ease and spirit that showed her quite used to society. She stepped a little too near my prejudices by a harsh sentence about Goethe, which I resented. And we had exchanged a few sentences when she named herself, and I then recognised the much-eulogised and calumniated Honourable Mrs. Norton, who was purged by a jury finding for the defendant in a *crim. con.* action by her husband against Lord Melbourne. When I knew who she was, I felt that I ought to have distinguished her beauty and grace by my own discernment, and not waited for a formal announcement.

I. A. Taylor   (essay date 1897)

SOURCE: "The Hon. Mrs. Norton and her Writings," in *Longman's Magazine,* Vol. XXIX, No. CLXXI, January, 1897, pp. 231-41.

[*In this excerpt, Taylor emphasizes that Norton's focus in her poetry and novels on her own experiences is not only unavoidable, but is the element that elevates her work above that of her contemporaries.*]

It was not possible to [Caroline Norton], even had she desired it, to separate her life from her writings. It was precisely in the combination of the two that her power lay. Remove the personal element and little remains to differentiate her work from that of any other graceful and cultivated writer of her time. When [Hartley Coleridge] joined to his enthusiastic commendation the friendly counsel to 'break through the narrow circle of personal and domestic feeling, and to adventure herself upon a theme of greater variety and less morbid interest,' adding the warning that 'egotism is egotism still, and the world is weary of it,' he might as well have counselled Samson to shear off his long hair and then go forth to the encounter of the Philistines. Wherever her individuality has free scope, wherever her wrongs, her sorrows, the injuries she had suffered, are, directly or indirectly, in question, there is to be found beau-

ty, pathos, and not seldom power, although everywhere touched by the egotism of which—say what the literary critic might—the world was *not* weary. And, after all, what is egotism but the more candid form of that craving for sympathy which is co-extensive with human nature itself? 'I wish it was all over,' Mrs. Norton once said, 'and that people were discussing what I *was.*' And yet would she not, like so many others who ask to be let alone, have missed the interest of the world in her affairs? In her case, too, the bargain was not the one-sided affair it sometimes is—she was as ready to give as to demand sympathy, and if the tragedy of her own life was constantly present with her, it served also to mirror the tragedies, actual or potential, of every other, and to accentuate her desire to save what might still be saved out of the universal shipwreck.

'Remember,' she thus wrote to a friend about to be married,

that the most intelligent woman God ever made has something of the child in disposition, and that the indulgence shown to children is as necessary in their case. . . . Do not laugh at me for lecturing my betters. It is only when I think of some fresh and uncommenced destiny that I look gravely and sadly back at all the mistakes in my own.

Again the sombre background is present—the background of a ruined life—but it is by that ruined life that she pleads for others, although the terms in which the appeal is couched might not commend themselves to the present advocates of 'women's rights.' At the very time, indeed, when she was vindicating, with all the passion and eloquence at her command, the claims of women to justice, she is careful to assert her opinions on a question which was even then a vexed one. 'The natural position of woman,' she writes,

is inferiority to man. Amen. That is a thing of God's appointing, not of man's devising. I believe it sincerely, as a part of my religion; and I accept it as a matter proved to my reason. I never pretended to the wild and ridiculous doctrine of equality.

It was not possible to her . . . to separate her life from her writings. It was precisely in the combination of the two that her power lay. Remove the personal element and little remains to differentiate her work from that of any other graceful and cultivated writer of her time.

—I. A. Taylor

The limitation of her power to the boundaries of experience is the explanation of the extreme inequality of her work. Thus her most successful novel, *Stuart of Dunleath,* is the picture of a life in which the reflection of her own is plainly visible—the history of a woman who, unhappily married, finds that 'life is shattered into days that never can unite again to give back the perfect image of peace'; and those of her poems which have most of the ring of reality, though marred by the bombast or grandiloquence of her school, are those in which the autobiographical element is found. At best, however, her novels belong to a bygone day; her verse to a fashion which is past. It is a composition of a different character, and one in which she speaks in her own person and without disguise, which chiefly justifies her claim to the position accorded to her by her contemporaries, and it is her **"Letter to the Queen,"** ringing with all the changes of passionate reproach, of eloquent invective, and edged sarcasm, which best serves as an example of her power.

It is an appeal to the Queen, as sovereign and as woman, called forth by the rejection of the Bill for the Amendment of the Marriage Laws, when the defeated had gone back to their homes, like a party of miners, relinquishing the attempt to dig out their buried comrades. Courtier as she was, Mrs. Norton does not shrink from drawing her examples of injustice from the royal race; then, turning to her own disastrous experience, she makes her appeal against calumny, not only on her own behalf but upon that of the Queen's dead friend, whom her Majesty does not surely, to quote St. Simon, mourn so much ' à la Royale' that slander of him should be indifferent to her.

And then comes the end—her solemn dedication of herself and her gifts to the cause of outraged womanhood. Till that cause is won she abjures all other uses to which she has hitherto put her powers. 'My husband,' she concludes,

> has a legal lien on the copyright of my work. Let him claim the copyright of *this,* and let the Lord Chancellor cancel my right to the labour of my own brain and pen, and docket it, among other forgotten Chancery papers, with a parody of Swift's contemptuous labelling, *Only a Woman's Pamphlet.*

Janet E. Courtney   (essay date 1933)

SOURCE: "The 'Annualists'," in *The Adventurous Thirties: A Chapter in the Women's Movement,* Oxford University Press, London, 1933, pp. 44–90.

[*In the following essay, Courtney reviews the impact of Norton's marriage, relationships, social life, and political beliefs on her literary works.*]

Mrs. Norton has had hard measure, not only in her lifetime but with posterity, ever since George Meredith shaped his *Diana of the Crossways* upon her model. But, quite apart from the fact that she made a brave fight for the rights of motherhood, and in some degree modified the laws of England on a point vital to women, she deserves a permanent place amongst the writers of her period, and one that is not only due to her position in society.

In the eighteen-thirties, however, social position did count for a very great deal in the world of letters.

It was the Age of the Annuals, and the Annuals depended upon fashionable subscribers. Society contributors were much in request, and there is little doubt that Mrs. Norton

would have seemed less desirable to the publisher of the *English Annual,* had she not been a Sheridan, a noted beauty, and the friend of the Premier, Lord Melbourne.

Born Caroline Elizabeth Sarah Sheridan, she was the second of three lovely sisters, grand-daughters of the dramatist and daughters of Thomas Sheridan, whose fortunes had been seriously damaged by the burning down of Drury Lane Theatre in 1809. He was already in bad health, and he died at the Cape of Good Hope, where he had been given a colonial secretaryship by the good offices of the Duke of York, in the hope that the climate might arrest the consumption that threatened him.

His widow, a Scotchwoman with an Irish mother, returned to England and was assigned rooms in Hampton Court. There she brought up her young family, seven in all, helping out her scanty income by assiduous writing of fashionable novels, not remarkable but not without merit. The three girls, Helen, Caroline, and Georgina, all inherited in some degree the beauty of their Sheridan grandmother, the lovely Miss Linley, who sat to Gainsborough and Sir Joshua. They were also clever and quick-spirited. At a very early age they produced a set of sketches and rhymes in imitation of the 'Dandy' books of the period, and a good-natured publisher was willing to bring out *The Dandies' Rout,* giving them fifty copies in payment.

Caroline was sent for a time to a school at Wonersh, near Guildford. There, to her ultimate sorrow, she attracted the admiration of George Norton, brother of Fletcher Norton, Lord Grantley. He seems to have intimated, both to her schoolmistress and her mother, that he wished to marry the young school-girl, and was naturally told to wait.

When Helen Sheridan was old enough to be presented, her mother contrived to take a house in Westminster, to bring her out. At the end of her first season she married a young naval lieutenant, Price Blackwood, the future Lord Dufferin, a love-match which turned out very happily, though the young couple at the time had little enough to live on.

Caroline's turn came next. She was shyer, and socially less accommodating, but her likeness to her grandfather commended her to Sheridan's old friends. Tom Moore speaks of her as amongst a set of pretty girls, who were to dance a fancy quadrille at Almack's—'Mrs. Sheridan's second daughter, strikingly like old Brinsley, but very pretty'. Whether for lack of an alternative, or because she knew her mother must try to marry off her daughters quickly, she accepted George Norton's second proposal and married him in July 1827, when she was nineteen and he twenty-six.

It was in no sense a good match for her. His income was small and hers was but fifty pounds a year. He had been elected to Parliament the year before, as Tory member for Guildford, and he hoped to get on at the Bar, but briefs were not coming his way as yet. No doubt he was in love with her beauty, but she was not in love with him at all. She had been told, especially by her sister Helen, that that would come; but even before the honeymoon was over, her husband had shown a sullen, sometimes violent temper and a vindictive disposition. There were ups and downs, quarrels and reconciliations. Some of her letters to him, when she was away on visits, are playful and affectionate. By nature she was warm-hearted and impulsive, not one to nurse a grievance; but she had abundant cause of complaint from the very earliest years of married life. Indeed, but for the love and support of her mother and her brothers and sisters, she would have been very unhappy. Warm family affection was, however, a Sheridan quality, and when her younger sister Georgina had married Lord Seymour (afterwards Duke of Somerset), and was established in Spring Gardens, whilst her mother and elder sister, Helen Blackwood, were also within easy reach, life in her own small house in Storey's Gate was at any rate bearable, especially after she had become engrossed in literature and her first child had been born.

The literary work was begun, not only for distraction, but from necessity, and as an answer to her husband's ungracious reminders that she had brought him no fortune. She had helped him largely in other ways. Wherever she went she was popular and admired. Fanny Kemble speaks of her 'stately style of beauty, grandly classical', her 'rich colouring and blue-black braids of hair'. Others remember her soft, rich, contralto voice, both in speaking and in singing, and her lowered eyelids and long-lashed dark eyes. She soon had powerful friends, but they were all in the opposite camp. Reform was in the air and Catholic emancipation the burning question of the day. All the Sheridans were vehement supporters of it and Caroline's temperament made her an ardent reformer. Her husband, on the other hand, remained a determined Tory. But the Whigs were the coming party, and he was not above pocketing his opinions and profiting by her social successes. The Duke of Devonshire was one of her conquests, and 1828 found her included in a house-party at Chatsworth, a house to which George Norton's wife would never have gained admittance on his social merits. Still more valuable was her conquest of Lord Melbourne. By this time the Whigs were in office. Lord Grey had swept the country in 1830 and formed an administration with Melbourne as Home Secretary. George Norton had lost his seat at Guildford and, still worse, a small sinecure appointment he held as Commissioner of Bankruptcy.

Caroline felt she must bestir herself. She set to work to write to such of the men in power as had been friends of her grandfather. Amongst them was Melbourne, who had been also her father's friend. It was only natural that he should assume the privileges of friendship and answer her letter in person. It was equally natural that he should be attracted. Storey's Gate lay conveniently between Downing Street and the House of Lords. He found it pleasant to drop in and he acquired a habit of dropping in. He was twice her age and the relationship was more than half-paternal; but he was a man to whom a woman's society was indispensable, and his own troubled life with his wife, Lady Caroline Lamb, had sent him elsewhere for consolation. Obviously the situation had risks for a young and beautiful woman, unhappily married; but the idea that he might be compromising Mrs. Norton, if it occurred to him, was overruled by the desire to be her friend and to protect her against a husband, of whose temper and disposition he soon came to have the worst opinion. 'It was at all times easy to see that it was the most dangerous and ill-conditioned creature possible', he wrote to her after the catastrophe, 'and that there was nothing that might not be expected from such a mixture of folly and malignity'. Yet, to please Caroline, he had made George Norton a Metropolitan Magistrate, with a salary of £1,000 a year, though he had occasion later to regret it, for many were the complaints of the new magistrate's stupidity and indolence.

Two years earlier Caroline had brought out her first book, *The Sorrows of Rosalie and other Poems.* It was no better than 'L. E. L.' s' [Letitia Elizabeth Landon] early effusions, just another of those metrical tales of blighted love—a young and beautiful heroine deserted by her high-born lover, falling into unmerited woes and meeting an early death. But as there was quite a large public for such stuff in the eighteen-twenties and thirties, it sold well enough to pay the expenses of her first confinement.

No sooner was her son born than she was at work again. "The Undying One" was ready in 1830. 'Caroline has finished her new poem,' writes her sister to a brother in India, 'she is going to write another poem, and she had written two volumes of a novel . . . which I want her to finish, as prose sells better than poetry. . . . She thinks six weeks more hard writing will finish it, and then she intends to write a tragedy', a fairly full and ambitious programme for a young mother of one-and-twenty, with a delicate first baby on her hands, to whom she was devoted! "The Undying One" was the wandering Jew, and naturally there was nothing new to say about him, but she does not seem to have known how often he had already made his appearance in literature. Some of the songs, however, included in this volume, deserved to live; for she had her share of the gift of song, that belongs as of right to her race. Her sister, Helen Dufferin, had it in fuller measure. No song that Caroline ever wrote sings itself like Helen's "Lament of the Irish Emigrant".

> I'm sittin' on the stile, Mary,
>   Where we sat side by side,
> On a bright May mornin' long ago,
>   When first you were my bride;
> The corn was springin' fresh and green,
>   And the lark sang loud and high—
> And the red was on your lip, Mary,
>   And the love-light in your eye.

But among Caroline's songs—and they ran to over fifty—were a few that even her old friend, Tom Moore, need not have disowned. Take, for instance:

> Love not, love not! Ye hapless sons of clay!
> Hope's gayest wreaths are made of earthly
>   flow'rs,
> Things that are made to fade and fall away,
> When they have blossomed but a few short
>   hours.
>   Love not, love not.
>
> Love not, love not! The thing you love may die—
> May perish from this gay and gladsome earth;
> The silent stars, the blue and smiling sky,
> Beam on its grave as once upon its birth.
>   Love not, love not.

> Love not, love not! The thing you love may
>   change,
> The rosy lip may cease to smile on you;
> The kindly beaming eye grow cold and strange,
> The heart still warmly beat, yet not be true.
>   Love not, love not.

And she had undoubted felicity in little occasional poems, dedications, verses for albums, as well as in some ballads on humble themes, in the manner of Wordsworth. Her dedication of *The Lady of La Garaye* to Lord Lansdowne is an instance of the first:

> Friend of old days of suffering, storm, and strife,
>   Patient and kind through many a wild appeal,
> In the arena of thy brilliant life
>   Never too busy, nor too cold to feel:
>
>   . . . . .
>
> Kinsman of him, whose very name soon grew
>   Unreal as music heard in pleasant dreams,
> So vain the hope my girlish fancy drew,
>   So faint and far his vanished presence seems.

Her touch is uncertain; 'arena' is a bad word and spoils her line. But otherwise the verse moves smoothly.

And, for a Wordsworthian example, take **"Crippled Jane"**:

> They said she might recover if we sent her down
>   to the sea,
> But that is for rich men's children, and we knew
>   it could not be.
> So she lived at home in the Lincolnshire fens and
>   we saw her, day by day
> Grow pale, and stunted, and crooked; till her
>   last chance died away.
>
>   . . . . .
>
> God have mercy upon her. God be her guard
>   and guide,
> How will strangers bear with her, when, at
>   times, even I felt tried?
>
>   . . . . .
>
> I die. God have pity upon her! How happy rich
>   men must be!
> For they said she might have recovered—if we
>   sent her down to the sea!

Her simplicity slips into prose sometimes, but so did Wordsworth's; there is at any rate genuine feeling and, in the last lines, an almost Tennysonian ring.

The projected tragedy, mentioned by her sister, seems to have got itself written, for in 1831 **"The Gypsy King"** was actually staged at Covent Garden for several nights, and Fanny Kemble remembers it: 'What a terrible piece! What atrocious situations and ferocious circumstances, tinkering, starving, hanging, like a chapter out of the Newgate Calendar. But after all she is in the right—she has given the public what they desire.' All the ladies of the period wrote lurid tragedies; and as none of them survive, one can only suppose none of them deserved to.

This was the year of Mrs. Norton's greatest social triumphs. She was presented at Queen Adelaide's court, where her beauty made a sensation. Helped by her social success, her literary work was being acclaimed considerably beyond its deserts. Colburn republished *The Undying One* with a biographical sketch of the author, Fraser's published a portrait of her drawn by Maclise, and included her in their list of 'Regina's Maids of Honour', a fantastic name for their female contributors. Her husband, too, was in better humour. They had more money, the house in Storey's Gate was enlarged, and so far from objecting to her friendship with Melbourne, he would often walk with her to the door when she very imprudently went to visit her friend in Downing Street.

Her second boy was born in November. In the following January, her sister-in-law, Augusta Norton, came on a long visit. Miss Norton was eccentric, wore closely cropped hair, bloomers, and short skirts. Caroline shrank from taking her about, and George Norton made this an excuse for renewed ill temper. The excitement over the Reform Bill was at its height, and Caroline was heart and soul with the Reformers. She did really try hard to keep on good terms with her husband, but her position was very difficult. She was editing a small monthly periodical, *La Belle Assemblée and Court Magazine,* and writing much of its contents. Early in 1833 she also agreed to edit next year's *English Annual.* The result was over-work and strained nerves, and in the summer of 1833 a violent quarrel, not long before the birth of her third child, from the bad effects of which she suffered for many months.

The quarrel was patched up and next year the Sheridan family went for a tour abroad. George Norton was of the party. But his violent behaviour to his wife on more than one occasion created great indignation among her family. In 1835 came a crisis. For her children's sake she had borne much; but she greatly resented the interference of a Miss Vaughan, a connexion of her husband's, and his constant adviser. In the spring there was another quarrel. She took refuge at her sister's house and for a time refused to return. But she yielded to her husband's entreaties and his promise of better behaviour. In September it was arranged that she should take the children away; one of them had been ill and needed the change. Suddenly, on a day when Miss Vaughan had called and been closeted with her husband, he forbade her to go and declared that, even if she went herself, the children should not. This time the quarrel was so violent that in the early hours of the morning Caroline fled across St. James's Park to her sister. In her absence George Norton packed the children off to Miss Vaughan's and refused to let them return. He then advertised in the newspapers that his wife had left him and that he would not be answerable for her debts. In spite of all this she made overtures for a reconciliation. She even asked a Mr. Barton, the clergyman at the little chapel in Duke Street which she and her husband had attended, to act as mediator, and expressed sorrow for any harsh words she might have spoken. She begged to be taken back for a trial year, to see if they could get on and to be with her children. Norton's answer was to accuse her of immoral relations with Melbourne, and to bring a suit against him for damages. This was then the legal practice, the woman, whose reputation and life were at stake, being not even made a party to the suit.

Bust of Caroline Norton.

Melbourne was terribly upset, for his own sake as much as for hers. It was not the first time he had been involved in a scandal, but an earlier suit concerning a Lady Brandon had been kept quiet. There was no chance of that, now that he was Premier—he had succeeded Grey in 1834 and had resumed office after a short-lived Peel administration in 1835. His political enemies were only too ready to make capital out of the charge. 'John Bull fancies himself highly moral and the Court is mighty prudish', wrote Greville, the Clerk to the Privy Council, in his famous Diaries, 'and between them our off-hand Premier will find himself in a ticklish position.' But when the suit came on for hearing, it was contemptuously dismissed. Counsel for the defendant Premier did not even trouble to call his witnesses, so weak and trivial was the evidence adduced, and when the news of Melbourne's victory reached the House of Commons it was greeted with tumultuous cheers from every part of the House.

'It was in point of fact a very triumphant acquittal,' says Greville, and all the more popular because politics were thought to be at the bottom of the charge. That Norton had been got at by the Tories was widely believed. 'The King behaved very civilly about it, and expressed his satisfaction at the result.'

But though Melbourne had won, one cannot quite exculpate him. Experienced man of the world as he was, he could not but have known the risk of his frequent visits. There was a good deal in old Lord Malmesbury's comment that, as far as he could see, 'Melbourne had had far more opportunities than any man ever had before and had made no use of them.'

That was the vulgar view, and the vulgar view counts. Irreparable harm had been done to Mrs. Norton's reputation. It was all very well for society to rally round her, and much of it did. Mr. E. F. Benson recounts an anecdote of how she appealed to the Duchess of Sutherland, and of how that great lady—for many years Queen Victoria's Mistress of the Robes—simply summoned her footman and ordered her carriage and, accompanied by Mrs. Norton, took her customary airing in the Park. That silenced many a tongue in society, but it could not stop the mouths of the gutter press. *The Age* and *The Satirist* were in full cry. Her name had been smirched and the man whose imprudence had helped to smirch it could do little to help her. She took refuge at first with her mother at Hampton Court, and later set up house with her uncle, Charles Sheridan, first in Green Street and then in Bolton Street. Her husband had grudgingly allowed her £300 a year, but refused her access to the children. After the failure of his action for damages, he could not hope to obtain a divorce.

Her long struggle for her children has become a matter of legal history. She had picked up some slight knowledge of the law and she used it to advantage in the writing of pamphlets. Her family, perhaps rightly, restrained her from publishing them, except privately, but when she had succeeded in getting her friend, Serjeant Talfourd, to draft and introduce into the House a Bill to amend the law regarding the Custody of Infants, she sent copies of her case to all the members. The Bill in its first session was stopped by the death of the King and the consequent dissolution of Parliament. When it came up again in the next session, it passed its second reading in the Commons, but was thrown out by the Lords. But two years later it went through and in 1839 was passed into law.

Meanwhile she was at great social disadvantage. Melbourne was entirely absorbed in the care of the young Queen; and he even advised Mrs. Norton to keep away from the Court as long as the Queen remained unmarried. She was hurt, but she submitted. She threw herself with all the greater energy into the literary work which had become more than ever a necessity, if she was to meet her share of the expenses of her uncle's establishment. Her powers had matured. Lockhart, reviewing her volume, *The Dream,* in 1840, says of her that 'the last three or four years have made her a greater writer than she was— deeper, plainer, truer.' Unfortunately, like so many of his kind, he calls her 'the Byron of our modern poetesses', and attributes to her 'much of that intense personal passion' that distinguished Byron's poetry, as well as his 'beautiful intervals of tenderness, his strong, practical thought and his forceful expression.' If only both the critics and the poetesses could have contrived to forget Byron! Imitation of him was responsible for most of their faults. They were far better poets when they were simple and left romantic passion alone.

To this volume was prefixed a touching and, at times really beautiful, dedicatory poem addressed to the Duchess of Sutherland:

> Once more, my harp! once more, although I
>   thought
> Never to wake thy silent strains again,
> A wandering dream thy gentle chords have
>   wrought,
> And my sad heart, which long hath dwelt in
>   pain,
> Soars, like a wild bird from a cypress bough,
> Into the poet's Heaven and leaves dull grief
>   below!
>
> And unto thee—the beautiful and pure—
> Whose lot is cast among that busy world
> Where only sluggish Dulness dwells secure,
> And Fancy's generous wing is faintly furl'd,
> To Thee—whose friendship kept its equal truth
> Through the most dreary hour of my embitter'd
>   youth
> I dedicate the lay.
>
>   . . . . .
>
> Thou gav'st me that the poor do give the poor,
> Kind words and holy wishes and true tears;
> The lov'd, the near of kin, could do no more,
> Who changed not with the gloom of varying
>   years,
> But clung the closer when I stood forlorn,
> And blunted Slander's dart with their indignant
>   scorn.
>
>   . . . . .
>
> To Thee the sad denial still held true
> For from thine own good thoughts thy heart its
>   mercy drew.

In their Bolton Street home she and her uncle continued to receive old friends. Melbourne, out of office and, after the young Queen's marriage, no longer her daily adviser, reappears. In 1840 Mrs. Norton was received at Court, being presented by her sister, Lady Seymour; but she was so nervous that even the Queen noticed it and commented on it to her uncle Leopold. Some of the Tory ladies present were chilly, but socially she was to a great extent rehabilitated.

Her troubles with her husband were, however, by no means at an end. The Infant Custody Act of 1839 empowered a separated wife to petition the Lord Chancellor for access to her children. She presented her petition. Her husband opposed it up to the last moment and then grudgingly gave way. The death of the youngest boy from an accident, before his mother could reach him, brought about a temporary reconciliation. But again and again George Norton took steps to humiliate his wife in the eyes of the public. Unluckily she retorted. Both wrote long letters to *The Times,* a method of conducting marital disputes greatly to be deprecated. The public in the end got weary and ceased to discriminate.

Her literary energy persisted unchecked. After *The Dream*

in 1840, came *The Child of the Islands* in 1845, a long poem which she waves in the face of Samuel Rogers, who had spoken of her as 'the author of fugitive pieces'. 'Ah! little did I think you would have sacrificed me, your friend, for a *bon mot.* All night their paper ghosts have bowed to me, saying, "We are Fugitive Pieces. We are Fugitive Pieces".'

After her uncle's death in 1841, she established herself in a small house in Chesterfield Street, which continued to be her home for many years. From 1850 onwards she wrote more prose than poetry, bringing out a good many novels which conformed for the most part to the accepted convention of a fashionable background. How difficult it was in the days before Dickens to get the public to care for the affairs of common people, Harriet Martineau was to find when she wanted to place *Deerbrook.* 'The silver fork school of fiction' had it all their own way. But Mrs. Norton wrote also for the daily press. There she showed herself mistress of a strong and nervous style, unusual amongst the women of her day. Delane thought highly of her reviews of novels in *The Times.* And at the height of the Chartist agitation she contributed a series of **Letters to the Mob,** which were published in the *Morning Chronicle* during 1848.

Her political friend of the later 'forties was Sidney Herbert. From this friendship and from her known acquaintance with Delane arose the calumny, attributing to her the disclosure of a Cabinet secret. *The Times* on 4 December 1845 announced that Peel had decided on the repeal of the Corn Laws. The disclosure was in all probability a calculated indiscretion. Delane was in daily touch with Peel's Foreign Secretary, Lord Aberdeen. He had ample facilities for getting inside information. That he neither used, nor desired to use, Mrs. Norton has been proved again and again. Yet George Meredith thought fit forty years later to libel the dead by his creation of Mrs. Warwick, 'a witty Beauty, famous among the Dianas of the second quarter of the century', who has 'broken loose from her husband for good', but whose friends 'try to believe the best of her in the teeth of foul rumour'. This lady, finding herself in straits and needing to convince the great editor, 'Mr. Tonans', of her value as a contributor, goes down to the offices of his paper, in 'a quiet square', at midnight and makes him a present of a Cabinet secret. It was a cruel slander on the memory of a woman, who had suffered enough in her lifetime.

As her two remaining sons grew older they were more with her. The eldest had a serious illness in Portugal in 1847, and husband and wife then met again in his sickroom. But a few years later George Norton had subpoenaed his wife's publishers to produce her contracts with them, for the purpose of finding out her income and publishing to the world her private affairs, especially as regards an annual income of £500 left by Lord Melbourne to be paid to her by his executors, which was actually being paid by his niece, Lady Palmerston. This occasioned her pamphlet on **English Laws for Women in the Nineteenth Century,** and her open **"Letter to the Queen"** of 1855. Lord Brougham, who was no friend to her, said of the second, 'It was as clever a thing as ever was written, and it has produced great good. I feel certain the Law of Divorce will be much amended and she has greatly contributed to it.' Lord Cranworth's Bill on the subject was then before the House and he felt compelled, after Mrs. Norton's protest, to make substantial amendments in it. At least, since his Bill passed into law, the earnings of a separated wife have had legal protection, and a wife, separated or not, has been free to make independent contracts.

Mrs. Norton lived until 1877. The husband, from whom she so longed to be free, lived also until 1875. Before that date she had lost the eldest of her sons, who had entered the diplomatic service and had lived a good deal abroad. He died in Paris in 1859. Her second son, Brinsley, had married an Italian *contadina* and settled at Capri. She was much alone and a few months before her death she married an old friend, Sir William Stirling Maxwell. Though she only enjoyed his support and companionship for a very few months, they were months of a peace and happiness to which she had long been a stranger. She died in London on the 15th of July 1877, and he died in Venice very shortly after.

Alice Acland (essay date 1948)

SOURCE: "The Novelist," in *Caroline Norton,* Constable and Company, Ltd., 1948, pp. 141-57.

[*Alice Acland, pseudonym of Anne Wignall, is a British novelist and biographer. In the excerpt that follows, she compares the heroines and the plots of Norton's novels to Norton's own character and experiences.*]

Caroline [Norton] wrote four novels altogether. Each one was influenced more by her experiences up to the year 1842 than by any other events in her life. The first of these tales, ***The Wife and Woman's Reward,*** was published a month or two before the final crash of her marriage, the others many years later; but all bear the stamp of the bitterness of her experience in the years of her young womanhood. The lineaments and characteristics of those who had wrecked her peace of mind and happiness were seared for always on her memory. The passage of time merely sharpened the edge of her retrospective pain.

The first of her later novels (published in 1851) was ***Stuart of Dunleath.*** The story is that of Eleanor Raymond, who is beautiful, sensitive and intelligent; who married Sir Stephen Penrhyn; but who loves her guardian David Stuart of Dunleath.

Eleanor is virtually forced into marrying Sir Stephen because David Stuart has speculated with her fortune and left her and her mother penniless. He completes his defection by committing suicide. Eleanor, alone of all who know him, does not revile him but still cherishes his memory. She is completely indifferent to her suitor, Sir Stephen Penrhyn.

In Sir Stephen and his courtship of the reluctant Eleanor there are clearly discernible traces of Caroline's own courtship and marriage. Sir Stephen has not a thought in common with Eleanor—he is violent, sport loving and uneducated. But he is bewitched by her beauty and determined at all costs to marry her. He is undeterred by her

sudden loss of fortune: unlike George Norton he is very rich. He pursues her relentlessly, and loves her with the 'sublime of sensuality'.

> Of course he would be glad to inspire her with affection if he could; but if not, still let her be his—his, dressed like other brides, in smiles and blushes, or choked in sobs and mourning. His at all hazards! This passion for her was as a bird of prey, swooping down to seize her in its talons. Hope, tenderness, courtship, delay, were as little present in his thoughts, as in the hawk that sweeps its circle and drops through the air. . . .

Sir Stephen and Eleanor marry, and almost immediately afterwards they go to Scotland to pay a visit to Sir Stephen's sister, Lady Macfarren, at Glencarrick. Sir Stephen has always gone there every autumn for two or three months, and, like George Norton, sees no reason to change his habits. The conclusion is irresistible that the description of the arrival of the forlorn young bride at Glencarrick is drawn from Caroline's own honeymoon visit to Lady Menzies.

Eleanor comes in from the darkness, and in the firelight sees a 'very, very tall bony woman', who greets her with a 'haughty, almost imperceptible inclination of the head'.

> Lady Macfarren eyed Eleanor from head to foot. "Well, you seem tired enough and pale enough," she said gruffly making a sort of gesture as if motioning her to stand nearer the warm blaze.
>
> "I am not much tired," said Eleanor, "and I am always pale."
>
> "Humph! My brother wrote us word that you were a great beauty, that's all. I suppose London hours and fine lady ways—"
>
> "I have been very little in London."
>
> "Humph! How old are you?"
>
> "I am seventeen."
>
> "You look much older; I should think now you're safely married you could have no objection to tell your real age."
>
> "I was seventeen last August," said Eleanor, in rather a proud tone, though she struggled with her tears.

Lady Macfarren, unlike her brother, is mortally offended by Eleanor's dowerless state, and finding her not only penniless but also proud, with the gentle reserved pride most galling to a bully, she conceives an ineradicable hatred for her unfortunate young sister-in-law. And she is not the only enemy that Eleanor unwittingly makes in this house. There is also Tib Christison, the toady of Lady Macfarren, who loathes her because she is seventeen, and beautiful, and a bride.

Tib Christison no doubt had much of Miss Vaughan in her. There is a paragraph describing the species of old maid to which Tib belonged—

> busy-bodies, intriguers, thrusting themselves out of their own solitary homes into the homes of others, to work mischief like earwigs in the core

of fruit; toad eaters; slanderers; full of flattery; full of spite; struggling to keep their ground by the meanest concessions; affecting not to perceive the most open rebuffs; ready to undermine by the grossest treachery; envious; pitiless, daughter of the father of lies, and serving him perpetually.

These two women, then, the gaunt hard selfish bully and the sly watchful old maid, set out to ruin and destroy Eleanor. The dice are loaded against her from the beginning. She is unhappy with Sir Stephen—a foregone conclusion—but after the birth of her twin sons she is able to find consolation in her maternal love. This solace is soon denied her. She and Sir Stephen, together with the boys, are on a visit to Lady Macfarren. An expedition is proposed, to which Eleanor demurs on the grounds of the youth of the children and the delicate health of the elder. In what seem to be the authentic tones of Lady Menzies, she is told by Lady Macfarren that she mollycoddles the children and makes fools of them and that they should go to school and be hardened up.

The expedition takes place and both boys are drowned in a lake.

After this tragedy, yet further blows fall. Eleanor discovers that Sir Stephen has two illegitimate children by a girl living in the lodge at the gates of his castle. Soon after this she is thrown into a fever of emotional excitement by the startling reappearance of David Stuart of Dunleath, who is not dead at all, but has been restoring her finances in Canada. His arrival, however, does not add to her happiness. It is the signal for renewed malevolent activity on the part of Lady Macfarren and Tib, who succeed in poisoning Sir Stephen's mind against his wife by telling him that Eleanor is in love with David Stuart.

> "Crush her, divorce her, disgrace her, and choose again," thinks Lady Macfarren. "Choose again." Oh! how she hated Eleanor as her memory rapidly ran over those items that had accumulated since first the pale bride stood, fair and cold as a statute, in that unwelcoming home to which she paid a compulsory visit, and which she left with such unconcealed satisfaction . . .

As a result of Lady Macfarren's machinations, Sir Stephen has a terrible quarrel with Eleanor during which he breaks her arm.

A year or so after these events Eleanor, on David Stuart's advice, leaves her husband for good.

In Sir Stephen's sequestration of Eleanor's fortune and the paltry allowance made to her, and in the general harshness of his terms, Caroline again draws from her own experience. She denies her heroine, however, the devotion of family and friends, on which she herself was able to count; she denies her even the continued love of David Stuart, as he marries someone else; and so, at last, there is nothing for Eleanor to do but die.

This novel received very favourable reviews. It was praised, particularly, for the fidelity and subtlety of its characterisation. 'No writer', said the *Morning Post,* 'in ancient or modern times, has penetrated more deeply into the recesses of the human heart, or laid more completely bare to the impartial reader its secret workings.'

Here was offered a 'delicious draught, from the well of wisdom, pure and undefiled.'

In *Lost and Saved* (published in 1863) the heroine, Beatrice Brooke, resembles Caroline herself more closely than any other character in her novels.

Beatrice is a dark beauty. She is passionate, impulsive and vulnerable. She is described in words that paint a vivid picture of Caroline herself, when young. Beatrice

> enjoyed more, she suffered more, she felt more than a great proportion of her fellow creatures. Life thrilled through her, as you may see it thrill, in the delight of sunshine, through a butterfly's closed wings. . . . Her heart ached, the tears rushed to her eyes at some touching picture or some mournful song. The breath of a warm spring day, the scent of flowers, the purple of the distant hills, the freshness of the waves dashing on the shore, filled her with vague yearning.
>
> Such natures will not await the coming event; they cannot watch the subtle alchemy of brooding days, even though the chance of a golden hour lie there. They are forever wrestling before dawn with the dark angel of Destiny, reckless if their victory should send them lamed and limping from Peniel.

In this novel the generosity and simplicity of Beatrice is set against the shallow worldliness of her acquaintances. She, like Eleanor, is menaced by enemies of her own sex, and, like Eleanor, is crushed. Beatrice is in love with the fascinating but unstable Montague Treherne. He traps her into a false marriage. She has a child, and lives, as an unmarried wife, with Treherne in London. Her existence as such is suspected by Treherne's aristocratic relations, as well as by Lady Nesdale, a heartless coquette, with whom he has long conducted a flirtation. She is determined to win him from Beatrice, as indeed also, but by different methods, is his aunt the Marchioness of Updown.

Lady Updown is said to be a portrait of one of Caroline's chief enemies amongst the Tory ladies at Court, and certainly in the pages of this novel she is described with venom as well as with wit.

> Though her husband was neither wise nor great, but a fat, foolish man, with a meek, fidgety temper—and there are, as we know, no less than twenty-one marquises in the British Peerage—she somehow contrived to be the greatest lady that was ever seen out of a fairy tale. Her sisters called her "The Marchioness" as the servants did. Her husband called her "The Marchioness". It seemed as if there was no other Marchioness in the world. If there was a ball, party, or soirée to be given, her absence was as bitter as that of the hero of the old-fashioned song, "Robin Adair". If there was a procession, coronation, or festive ceremony of any kind, the world stood on its axis till the Marchioness had a place assigned to her. She went to Court, not spangled with scattered diamonds like the sky on a fine night, but crusted over with them, like

barnacles on a ship's hull. Every year her arms were rounder, her bracelets larger, her figure more corpulent. Every year the sweep of her full drapery encroached more and more on the ground occupied by her scantier neighbours. Every year her step became more flat-footed and imperious. In England she shone with the splendour of a perpetual Catherine-wheel; and abroad she represented, in the opinion of amazed foreigners, the style and condition of an English "Grande Dame".

Throughout Beatrice's story, her lonely and defenceless plight is set against the worldly security of the false-hearted Lady Nesdale, and the crassly selfish Marchioness. Montague Treherne neglects Beatrice increasingly, and eventually deserts her. He leaves an elderly friend of the family to break the news. Her reception of it is reminiscent of many tragic scenes in Caroline's life. She describes Beatrice as

> Resisting the truth till resistance was no longer possible, and then, when convinced that her visitor really was breaking to her some new dreadful phase in her life, she passed to the wildest frenzy of reproach to him personally, for being the bearer of such ill-tidings. She positively stamped her foot as she bade the old soldier be gone and not insult her further by his presence. . . . Under that shower the General beat a rapid retreat, incensed and alienated; thinking her wanting in dignity, modesty and proper conduct, and resolving to communicate anything he had to say to her in writing.

But before the hot afternoon had waned away, a little note recalled him; it said, 'Forgive my violence—I want to ask you one question, only one—and then I will give you no more trouble. I am very miserable—do come back to me.'

After Treherne's desertion Beatrice struggles to earn her living, but is reduced to near starvation. She is rescued by the unexpected clearing up of a misunderstanding with her family. She becomes reconciled to them, and the book ends with the death of Treherne, which sets her morally free to marry an Italian Marquis who has fallen in love with her.

This story was not received with such enthusiasm as *Stuart of Dunleath.* It was thought to paint 'a painful and repulsive picture' of the heartlessness of high society. The reviewer in the *Illustrated London News* remarks caustically that there are so many scenes which border on the improper that it is fortunate that 'she who has had the boldness to describe them in all their naked deformity is one so elevated both by social position and literary reputation as the Hon. Mrs. Norton.'

Caroline had committed the heinous sin of writing—in 1863—a book which could not be put into the hands of a young girl.

Her fourth and last novel, *Old Sir Douglas,* appeared first as a serial, and was published in 1867 by Hurst and Blackett. Like *Stuart of Dunleath,* the action is set chiefly in Scotland, and again the heroine is a young wife whose peace of mind is menaced by her husband's closest relations.

The plot of *Old Sir Douglas* is melodramatic and improbable, and the book is interesting chiefly for the portrait of Alice Ross, half-sister of Sir Douglas Ross, and sister-in-law of Gertrude, the heroine. In Alice Ross is crystallized all the sly, intriguing venom of Miss Vaughan, the memory of which was as clear to Caroline in middle age as in youth.

Gertrude Ross's gradual realisation of Alice's hostility and hatred is very well drawn. She strives at first to live on terms of intimacy and friendship with her (Alice is a permanent inmate of Sir Douglas's home Glenrossie), but she is increasingly repelled by her cold falseness and by her strange secretive ways.

> Alice engendered an atmosphere of unease and discomfort, yet the only positively disagreeable thing about her, was a certain watchfulness, which disturbed and fascinated you. Do what you would, Alice's eyes were on you. You felt them fixed on your shoulder, your forehead, the back of your head, your hands, your feet, the sheet of paper on which you were writing a letter; the title and outside cover of the book you were reading; the harmless list you were making out of your day's shopping; the anxious calculation of your year's income . . .

> You saw her stealing along in the sunshine by the broad yew hedge, and thought her still in the garden; when lo! she eluded your eye, and was off in a noiseless scamper round the wall, and through the gate, and over the hill. If you met her face to face (which was the rarest of accidents) your presence seemed to give the same signal for flight that it always does to a cat. She might be doing no harm whatever; she never *was* doing any visible harm; only prowling along, with a book, or a few flowers, or a half-eaten peach. But instantly, with a sort of whisk like a pussy's flexile tail, the light shawl was thrown together; the book seemed to close of itself; and that, or the half-eaten peach, or the gathered flowers, half vanished under its fringe, grasped by a little pale-fingered hand. . . .

Alice hates her sister-in-law and intrigues ceaselessly against her. She professes a humble and submissive devotion to Sir Douglas in which he believes implicitly. He can see no wrong in her. Through a series of melodramatic plots, Alice succeeds in estranging Sir Douglas from Gertrude. He leaves abruptly for the Crimea. Gertrude is broken-hearted and Alice's triumph is complete. Gertrude is blamed by everyone for the rift with her husband, and particularly by the Dowager Lady Clochnaben, her gaunt and censorious neighbour in Scotland.

Nemesis overtakes the wicked, however, and Alice's treachery is exposed, Gertrude is reconciled to Sir Douglas, and the book ends with virtue rewarded, and vice cast out.

. . . . .

In the characters of Alice Ross and Lady Clochnaben there is Caroline's recurring theme of an alliance between sly ill will and selfish, obtuse malice. Like Tib and Lady Macfarren in *Stuart of Dunleath,* and Lady Nesdale and

Lady Updown in *Lost and Saved,* the two different forms of hatred combine to crush the heroine, as did Miss Vaughan and Lady Menzies combine to destroy Caroline. In each case the sly intriguant has designs on the hero himself, as Miss Vaughan had on George Norton. Alice Ross increases her influence over Sir Douglas, by pretending she has a hopeless attachment for him; Tib Christison had hoped to marry Sir Stephen Penrhyn; Lady Nesdale counted Montague Treherne as her most desirable conquest. In each case, however, the character based on Lady Menzies is set by age or relationship above any personal designs on the hero; she merely dislikes the heroine and all she stands for, and is prepared therefore to condemn her and cast her out.

It is significant that Caroline's heroines are submitted always to two distinct forms of persecution; the double hatred, one sly and concealed, one open and pharisaical, of the characters who resemble Miss Vaughan and Lady Menzies, and the unfeeling censure of the outside world. In each of her three full length novels, the contrast is emphasised unsparingly between the innocent heart reviled unjustly and the cold, false, selfish judgment of society. Eleanor, in *Stuart of Dunleath,* is utterly ruined and dies broken hearted; Gertrude, in *Old Sir Douglas,* is separated unjustly from her husband for two years and obtains not a spark of sympathy from her acquaintances; in *Lost and Saved,* Beatrice is reduced to near-starvation through the malice of Lady Nesdale and Lady Updown. Only one character in these three stories is permitted to enjoy the approval of the world and yet be good, innocent and charming herself. This is Lady Margaret Fordyce, in *Stuart of Dunleath.* She it is whom Stuart marries in the end, thus unwittingly setting the seal on Eleanor's desolation.

Stuart of Dunleath contains more of Caroline's marital experiences than any of her other novels, but of the heroines of the three later books—Eleanor, Beatrice and Gertrude—it is Beatrice alone who bears any real resemblance to Caroline. Gertrude and Eleanor are gentle, reserved, passive women, whose pride enables them to endure in silence the blows of fate, but who, by the pliancy of their tempers, are delivered bound into the hands of their enemies. Beatrice is made of more fiery stuff. She may be open hearted, vulnerable and unsuspecting, but she has a quick temper and she is also very jealous. Her ability to defend herself better, however, does not avail to save her from disaster, any more than the spotless purity of Eleanor and Gertrude can preserve them. All three are predestined victims of hatred, jealousy and phariseeism.

In the very inevitability of the tragedies that overtake her heroines lies a proof of Caroline's conviction that she did not bring her own troubles upon herself. The reaction of memory upon her experiences reflected back to her a view of a social organisation in which the innocent perished, while the guilty and the cruel (particularly the cruel) prospered. It is evident through her self-identification with her heroines in various aspects of their lives that her mental picture of herself was rather different from the general impression she made on outside persons. It will be remembered that Lady Granville remarked that she could not connect Mrs. Norton with the sentiments expressed in her writings. That Caroline possessed qualities of simplicity and sincerity, and an imaginative love of unworldliness, is certain, but at the same time she was avid for attention and admiration. This trait ran like a thread through the fabric of her nature. Unfortunately for her peace of mind, she lacked the hard crust of insensitivity which would have carried a more truly worldly woman safely through the disasters of the years between 1836 and 1842. At the same time, a compensatory indifference to social success was not in her character. Her panache and flair were a brittle defence behind which a tormented spirit cowered. It was a defence which could be cracked open by any careless hand.

. . . . .

Oddly enough, in spite of Caroline's reputation for wit, there is not very much trace of it in her stories. Indeed, they seem to be written by someone totally devoid of a sense of humour. The light touch of Mrs. Gore, for instance, whose plots could be as sad as Caroline's, is completely lacking. And yet Caroline, of all her literary contemporaries, was praised most for her agreeability and conversational powers. Such critical men as Samuel Rogers and Abraham Hayward, whose lives were devoted to entertaining the most intelligent people of their day, were unanimous in their admiration for her. They would not have been duped by her physical beauty into thinking her more amusing than she really was. At their dinner parties she had to hold her own with some of the best minds in England.

She also had a capacity for simple, straightforward funniness. At Frampton Court (her brother's house near Dorchester) there was a door leading from the library into the cloakroom. This door was camouflaged with false books, all of which had titles invented by Caroline and her sister. On the top shelf there was a work in ten or twelve volumes entitled *Intestinal Struggles of Dorset,* below was a volume of essays with the title *Ease without Idleness.* There were also several books of travel, such as *A Week in Russia,* bearing the name of a distinguished diplomatist; or *Five Minutes in China,* under the name of Miss Bird or some other well-known lady traveller more famed for her enterprise than her profundity or erudition.

Such examples of gay silliness belonged possibly to Caroline's youth. They showed one of the facets of her complex nature. But when she sat down to write a novel or a story, the melancholy side of her nature re-asserted itself—an innate melancholy much enhanced by the tragedies of her life—and without the stimulus of a direct audience her sadness overcame her gaiety. It is for this reason, perhaps, that her letters have the genuine, unforced funniness that her novels lack. In a letter, as in conversation, she was inspired by the personal element.

There are two good examples of her letter writing that should be reprinted. One is an account sent to her mother of some servant trouble.

> I am deeply immersed in those red account books which take up so much of Georgia's time when she leaves town, my cook being about to leave me. She is a worthy and intelligent cook,

but loves not to clean my dining-room, and is a most sulky pig and full of dignity; insomuch that a former fat cook of mine, having sent to say she was dying and hoped I would assist her, she would not give the message to me because the petitioner had asked not for her but for Child's [Caroline's coachman] wife, whereupon the fat cook died unassisted. Now it happened that I was fond of the fat cook (a most good natured old soul, who walked back two hot miles, when she left me, because she had forgotten to say how the racoon was to be fed, that I used to keep). I therefore pronounced a "commination" on the hard-hearted present cook, and "hoped she would die in the workhouse, and send a message in vain to someone on whom she depended for assistance". She showed a most flouncing dignity, and no feeling at all, and altogether we could not love each other any more.
[Jane Gray Perkins, *Life of Mrs. Norton,* 1910]

The other is an earlier letter, written to Mary Shelley, who was undecided whether to take a house which was suitable in every way except that its former tenant had been a lady of the town.

With respect to your house in Berkeley St. I think it would be most childish to give up a good and cheap house because a fie-fie had lived in it, which, I suppose, is the English of the "associations". My Uncle says he has never heard of such an objection; but he is not the best person to ask. If it is any satisfaction to you to know that they thought to deter me from taking a house in Hertford Street by telling me those were two houses of that sort, in the same street, and that I obstinately persisted in thinking the neighbourhood as good as when the houses do not acknowledge themselves (as in Grosvenor Square), you have that bright example before you. I really think these sort of objections absurd, and if you consider them otherwise, you will never get a small, cheap, and pretty house at the west end of the town, for such houses are the natural prey of such persons; and ever and anon they hire them and put parrots' cages and geraniums into the balcony which they paint green. But if you act discreetly and modestly, that is, if you paint the rails dark green and don't buy a parrot, and are contented with two geraniums inside the drawing-room, the barrenness of virtue will be apparent, and the house will be as good as if its face was built out of the sorrowful and remorseful bricks of the Millbank Penitentiary.
[Jane Grey Perkins, *Life of Mrs. Norton,* 1910]

When she wanted to invite a Mlle d'Henin on a trip to Greenwich she wrote:

I have selected a brave and trusty follower, to crop the dreary plain of Hyde Park, thread the morass of Belgrave and Eaton Square and swim the moat that surrounds your impenetrable castle—after which he is to attract your attention by singing a verse of "O Richard, O mon roi!" as was done in the case of Coeur de Lion—and then place this missive in your hand. . . .

Caroline's verse, like her prose, has great facility and nar-rative flow. She was praised by her contemporaries for the grace, elegance, and tenderness of her poems, which qualities were thought not to exist to such an extent in 'any other female'.

In the *New Monthly Magazine* for 1831 she figures amongst *Living Literary Characters,* the first of whom is Sir Walter Scott and the fifth Edward Bulwer. Her inclusion in such company was on the merits of her verse (and personal prestige) alone. Her first novel was not published until 1836.

Hartley Coleridge, reviewing her poem **"The Dream"** in the *Quarterly* in 1840, placed her first in a list of ten British poetesses, of which Elizabeth Barrett was the second. It was in this review that Caroline was first called "The Byron of Modern Poetesses".

She wrote to Mr. John Murray—owner of the *Quarterly Review*—about the article, in which each poetess was compared to a flower:

October 31*st,* 1840

Dear Sir,

I ought to have thanked you from Ventnor, instead of waiting till my return to town, for your kindness in sending me an early copy of the *Quarterly,* containing all that comfortable flattery respecting **The Dream.** I assure you I felt almost ashamed at seeing my name 'first on the list called over', but very grateful for the indulgent spirit in which the article was written. . . .

As to 'V.', [Mrs. Archer Clive, one of the list of poetesses] you have, of course, been made aware that she is since engaged to be married to Mr. C., a very handsome, agreeable, well informed clergyman (as I hear). Now, as she is forty, nothing shall persuade me that the proposal and the marriage are not the result of the review. All the single ladies noticed in the article should instantly think of changing their names, retaining merely the floral name allotted to them in the *Quarterly.* I half wish I could change mine . . . but I daresay I should not change it to my satisfaction at this time of day, though I want ten years of 'V.' and 'V.' is very little and very lame, and has not (as I am credibly informed) nearly such a straight nose as I have.

'Her poetry is wonderful,' Caroline then thought it best to add, 'I hardly believed it was a woman's at first' [Jane Gray Perkins, *The Life of Mrs. Norton,* 1910].

Four years later, in *The New Spirit of The Age,* Caroline was compared in greater detail with Elizabeth Barrett. Caroline, as represented by her verse, the writer said, is 'oppressed with a sense of injustice, and feels the need of human love'. Elizabeth Barrett is 'troubled with a sense of mortality, and aspires to identify herself with ethereal existences'.

Both poetesses were congratulated on possessing 'great mental energies' and being 'excellent artists' in their medium, although Caroline's powers of construction were thought to be superior to those of her colleague. Elizabeth Barrett, incidentally, was already well known as a poetess, and also had a reputation as a classical scholar and a deeply intellectual woman.

By 1845 Caroline had published four long poems, and many short miscellaneous verses which appeared in various annuals. Of the four long poems the first was *The Sorrows of Rosalie,* the youthful composition which was published soon after her marriage. Then came *The Undying One and Other Poems* (the story of the Wandering Jew), published by Colburn in 1830, followed by *A Voice from the Factories* (Murray, 1836) and *The Dream and Other Poems,* published by Colburn in 1840. Lastly, *The Child of the Islands,* her most ambitious work, appeared in 1845. This was hailed by Abraham Hayward in the *Edinburgh Review* as 'great poetry, true poetry!'

No one would agree with that eulogistic exclamation now. But Caroline herself was always anxious to maintain her reputation for poetic genius. She was very hurt with Rogers for having spoken of her as the author of *Fugitive Pieces.* 'Ah, little did I think you would have sacrificed me, your friend, for a "bon mot",' she wrote to him. 'All night their paper ghosts have bowed to me, saying "We are Fugitive Pieces! We are Fugitive Pieces!" '

As regards the *Child of the Islands,* there was a more poignant reason for its composition than a wish for personal fame. In a letter written many years later to a literary acquaintance who had sent her one of his books, Caroline tells him that in return she is going to send him this poem. After mentioning that she prefers him to have one of the original copies with Maclise's frontispiece, she goes on to say:

> I care more for it than anything else I have written,—for many reasons: one, the great hope I had—(being still young)—that people would be moved by it from judgments of me, so directly the reverse of my life, and its *real* occupations and aspirations: (like the poor Secretary in Hans Andersen's Improvisation, when he writes his *David*) and for many a memory of good true friends linked with its composition.

. . . . .

By 1845, in addition to her poems, Caroline had written a novel, two pamphlets in connection with the Infant Custody Bill, and a quantity of miscellaneous sketches and verses for the annuals she edited. She had also composed many songs which were extremely popular, and which paid the usual penalty of success by being pirated in America.

During these years she led a busy social life, and upon her devolved the many domestic cares which fall to the mistress of an only moderately rich household. Three children had been born to her and she spent a great deal of her time with them. In the years between 1836 and 1842 she underwent the most excruciating grief and anxiety over her separation from these children.

That in the face of all these distractions her output should have been what it was, is a proof of her great facility and ease in composition. She was one of those women who are by nature artistically gifted. She could draw, and paint, and sing, as well as she could write. It was easy for her to express herself through any of the arts. She was supremely accomplished in an age when accomplishments were cultivated above all things. She also had a comprehensive mind, and a love of facts, although she was not, perhaps, always very accurate. Her facility spared her the need of application. She had not a scholarly mind. It is probable that after her marriage she did little serious reading. But she had a quick intelligence and a retentive memory, and these enabled her to profit to the full from the treasures of Melbourne's knowledge and taste which she enjoyed for five uninterrupted years. She had many convictions and the courage of them all. She was a good and copious conversationalist never at a loss, and with all her grandfather's gift for telling a story. These powers, together with her beauty, made a formidable impression on all who met her. It was impossible to overlook her. Nor, indeed, did she ever intend be overlooked.

In the almost flamboyant effect of her personality she was very far removed from the ideal feminine type of the day. The pure, gentle, timid, docile woman—a type soon to be crystallised in the person of Amelia Sedley—held a high place then in the public imagination. It was impossible for Caroline to model herself on the lines of such doves with folded wings. And because she could not pretend to be an Amelia Sedley, many people thought she must be a Becky Sharp instead. Her own striking attributes were Norton's best weapons against her. It was easy to believe the worst of a talkative beauty, around whom all the men clustered, and who could defend herself against an open affront with a biting and all too ready wit. But from the silent suspicions engendered by her tragic, and often misinterpreted, history there was no defence. These she would have to endure until her dying day, finding only, perhaps, some insignificant measure of relief in burdening the heroines of her novels with similar cares and persecutions.

And yet in spite of the sadness which lay behind her writings, she could still stand apart from them and be amused by them, and she has herself provided them with a fitting summary. She was sure, she said, that Mr. Blackwood looked on each of her novels as an illegitimate child—as a thing wrong in itself to produce but only excused by the frailties of human nature.

Mary Poovey   (essay date 1988)

SOURCE: "Covered but Not Bound: Caroline Norton and the 1857 Matrimonial Causes Act," in *Uneven Developments: the Ideological Work of Gender in Mid-Victorian England,* The University of Chicago Press, 1988, pp. 51-88.

[In the following excerpt, Poovey examines the issues of gender and power inequality in Norton's political writings.]

Upper-middle-class Caroline Sheridan, the beautiful granddaughter of the Whig playwright Richard Brinsley Sheridan, was married in 1826 to George Norton, a Tory aristocratic younger son whose fortune was supposed to compensate for the fact that the couple barely knew each other when they married. Caroline's mother had been misled about George Norton's finances, however, and the young couple soon found themselves almost completely dependent financially on Caroline's literary earnings and her family's Whig connections. In 1829, Caroline began to publish her poetry, and, in 1830, when George lost his seat in Parliament, she persuaded her old Whig friend Lord Melbourne, then home secretary, to appoint George justice of a magistrate's court at £1,000 per year.

The Nortons' private affairs were stormy from the beginning; they became the stuff of scandal in 1836, however, when George Norton removed their children from their London home to retaliate for at least two wifely insurrections: Caroline refused to let George raise money against a trust settled upon her at the time of their marriage, and she repeatedly turned to her family for protection against his physical and emotional brutality. The domestic quarrel, which was fully covered by gossip columns in London and abroad, culminated in June of that year in a lawsuit brought by George Norton against Lord Melbourne for criminal conversation—one of the necessary first steps toward George's obtaining a divorce. Melbourne was by that time prime minister; Norton demanded £10,000 in damages, and rumors spread that Norton had undertaken the suit not only in hopes of extricating himself from marital and financial difficulties, but also in response to Tory desires to bring down the Whig government, an outcome that might well have followed such outrageous domestic conduct on the part of the elderly counselor to the young Queen Victoria. So ludicrous was the evidence that Norton presented, however, that the jury returned a verdict against him without calling a single witness or leaving the box. The trial left Melbourne completely vindicated and more firmly established than ever as Victoria's mentor; Caroline, by contrast, found herself still (and now irrevocably) married to a man she loathed, deprived of her reputation, and without any legal claim to her children.

The wild and stupid theories advanced by a few women, of "equal rights" and "equal intelligence" are not the opinions of their sex. I, for one . . . believe in the natural superiority of man, as I do in the existence of a God. . . . Masculine superiority is incontestable; and with superiority should come protection.

—*Caroline Norton, in* English Laws for Women in the Nineteenth Century, *1854*.

In 1854, after more than a decade of wrangling over custody of the children and the allowance George had agreed to provide her, Caroline, who was by then a renowned poet and novelist, found her dirty laundry being aired in public again. Once more the squabble was about money. When Caroline's mother died in 1851, she left her daughter an inheritance of £480 per annum. Even though he inherited from the estate the life interest of Caroline's portion from her father, George summarily reduced the £500

allowance he had agreed to pay Caroline in a deed of separation the couple had signed in 1848. George had originally agreed to this allowance in exchange for Caroline's willingness to exonerate him from responsibility for her debts and to allow George to raise money against her trust. Caroline had signed the agreement, even though its ten-year retroactive clause was considered humiliating, because she thought the contract was binding and would thus ensure her a regular income. But when Mrs. Sheridan died, George claimed that Caroline no longer needed the allowance and that he could no longer afford to pay it; he also pointed out that he was not legally bound to keep his word because a man could not contract with the wife who was legally part of him. Enraged, Caroline then turned the letter of the law back upon George. If he was not bound to give her an allowance, she reasoned, then she was not bound to pay her own debts. In an attempt to force George to agree to more advantageous terms, Caroline therefore allowed a carriage repairman to sue George for nonpayment of a bill. This action resulted in a trial held in Westminster Court on 18 August 1853, in which George, furious over the financial difficulties in which his wife continued to involve him, used the fact that Lord Melbourne had left a legacy to Caroline to insinuate once more that her conduct with the elderly statesman two decades before had been less than discreet. When the jury found for George on a technicality, Caroline resorted to the press, publishing first in the *Times,* then in two pamphlets on divorce, the litany of false accusations she had endured.

Caroline used Lord Cranworth's Matrimonial Causes Bill, which had been introduced and then tabled in June 1854, as the pretext for publishing her complaints. The first of the two pamphlets, ***English Laws for Women in the Nineteenth Century,*** was printed privately in 1854; the second, her **"Letter to the Queen on Lord Chancellor Cranworth's Marriage and Divorce Bill,"** received much wider circulation on its publication in 1855. In both of these tracts, Norton argued that what neither Cranworth's bill nor most of the legislators who debated it would acknowledge was that men's legal and economic tyranny over women lay at the heart of their idealization of the domestic sphere and the partial solutions reformers proposed. Systematically, in the **"Letter to the Queen,"** Caroline Norton rehearses the laws governing married women so as to call attention to their central contradiction—

> the grotesque anomaly which ordains that married women shall be "non-existent" in a country governed by a female Sovereign. . . . As *her husband,* he has a right to all that is hers: as *his wife,* she has no right to anything that is his. As her husband, he may divorce her (if truth or false swearing can do it): as his wife, the utmost "divorce" she could obtain, is permission to reside alone,—married to his name. The marriage ceremony is a civil bond for him,—and an indissoluble sacrament for her; and the rights of mutual property which that ceremony is ignorantly supposed to confer, are made absolute for him, and null for her.

Norton was able to identify these injustices because she had personally endured them, but being able to voice them in such explicitly political terms required transforming herself from the silent sufferer of private wrongs into an articulate spokesperson in the public sphere. To the extent that she was able to do so, Norton's self-authorization, as she narrated it in *English Laws for Women,* implicitly challenged the entire ideological order that the legal and sexual double standards supported.

The marginal status of Norton's complaint helps account for the indirection of some of the rhetorical strategies of her self-presentation. Initially, for example, Norton justifies publicizing her private story by rhetorically splitting herself into two persons: the long-suffering victim of social injustice and the vindicating polemical writer. From the positions these persons occupy in her introduction to *English Laws,* implicitly the former is female and the latter male. As woman-victim, Norton explicitly identifies with the assassinated wife of a French nobleman, the daughter of Watt Tyler, and the "virgin girl of Rome," whose father slaughtered her rather than permit her "degradation." As publicist of social injustice, Norton aligns herself with "example[s] of resistance"—men like the Good Samaritan, the prison reformer Howard, Sir Samuel Romilly, and Lord Brougham. Despite the fact that she initially invokes this traditional gender division, however, in the course of her impassioned introduction, Norton rewrites the division as one between powerless groups—the "helpless classes"—and powerful, "earnest individuals." The helpless classes include not only women but also pauper children, insane patients, untried prisoners, and slaves; the individualized "benefactors" are, by contrast, all men but one (Harriet Beecher Stowe). The point that Norton makes indirectly is that women's legal incapacities are a function of their social *position,* not of natural, biological inferiority. Beyond this, the rhetorical achievement of her argument is to transfer her allegiance from the silent, helpless classes to the articulate individuals who inspire social change. In doing so, she elevates her personal complaint to a political critique of existing laws; she collapses the boundary between the private sphere, where injustice goes unchecked, and the public domain, where laws are made and enforced by men.

The principle by which Norton organizes her narrative repeats this pattern and generates the same subversive conclusion. Supposedly for the sake of clarity, Norton divides her story into three segments or "outlines": the Nortons' financial affairs; the treatment she suffered as a wife; and "Lord Melbourne's opinion of the affairs in which his name was involved". The result of this division is anything but clarity, however. Separating the economic material from the domestic narrative obscures the relationship between the two and makes it difficult for the reader to reconstruct the sequence of events or the connection between, for example, Caroline's refusing George the right to raise money against her trust and his abducting the children. What this narrative division does accomplish, however, is a separation between the more public domain of economic negotiation and the more private domain of domestic squabbles and cruelties. Like the introduction's division between men-benefactors and women-victims, this narrative separation of spheres collapses in the third story, when Norton quotes Melbourne's personal letters to prove

that men's political interests exacerbated her domestic wrongs.

The climactic moment of Norton's narrative is the episode in which the domestic quarrel is bought into a court of law; this is also the moment at which the long-suffering, long-silenced woman becomes a self-conscious, articulate subject, determined to speak and write. The transformation begins when George Norton calls his wife to the witness stand and forces her to see herself as he sees her: "I felt, as I looked for an instant towards him, that he saw in me neither a woman to be spared public insult, nor a mother to be spared shameful sorrow, —but simply a claimant to be non-suited; a creditor to be evaded; a pecuniary incumbrance he was determined to be rid of". Stripped of her status as a (middle-class) woman and mother, Norton momentarily loses her bearings. Her first response to this degradation and unsexing is to vacillate wildly between a man's "angry loudness" and a woman's frustrated speechlessness. Only when she applies Lord Melbourne's words to George can she establish an identity that allows her to speak.

> I felt giddy; the faces of the people grew indistinct; my sentences became a confused alternation of angry loudness, and husky attempts to speak. I saw nothing—but the husband of whose mercenary nature Lord Melbourne himself had warned me I judged too leniently; nothing but *the Gnome,*—proceeding *again* to dig away, for the sake of money, what remnant of peace, happiness, and reputation, might have rested on the future years of my life. Turning up as he dug—dead sorrows, and buried shames, and miserable recollections—and careless who was hurt by them, as long as he evaded payment of a disputed annuity, and stamped his own signature as worthless!

What Caroline Norton is doing here is reappropriating the identity of a wronged woman by casting herself as the victim in a familiar Victorian genre, the melodrama. The roles in the melodramatic script were as conventional as the values underwritten by this genre.

The trio of innocent lady-in-distress, a gnomelike, aristocratic villain, and a selfless avenger appears repeatedly in both stage melodramas and Norton's pamphlet, as, for example, when she depicts Anne Boleyn suffering the brutalities of Henry VIII, only to have her reputation vindicated (posthumously) by the poet Wyatt. But if George is the villain here, and Caroline is the lady-in-distress, who, now that Melbourne is dead, is to be the lady's defender? In the current, lamentable state of society, there is no one else to play that role but Caroline Norton herself. The melodramatic plot provides the terms, her identification with other (male) defenders provides the means, and, in a dramatic moment, Caroline Norton becomes not just innocence personified, but also judge, jury, and executioner all at once:

> On that day, when in cold blood, for the sake of money, Mr. Norton repeated that which he knew to be false . . . in that little court where I stood apparently helpless, mortified, and degraded—in that bitterest of many bitter hours in

my life,—I judged and sentenced him. I annulled the skill of his Tory lawyer's suggestion to a Tory judge. I over-ruled the decision of Lord Abinger in that obscure and forgotten cause, which upheld him against justice. I sentenced Mr. Norton to be *known.*

To appreciate the subversive implications of Norton's rhetorical vindication, it is necessary to understand the basis on which she "sentences" George. The evidence that convicts George Norton consists primarily of a series of letters in his own hand, which Caroline refers to as the "Greenacre" letters. Composed by George during 1837, after the unsuccessful criminal conversation action against Melbourne, these letters pleaded for a reconciliation and playfully entreated Caroline to meet George in an empty house to discuss terms. The signature that George appended to these letters, Caroline tells us, undercut their teasing tone because Greenacre was the name of a notorious murderer convicted of killing his fiancée in an empty house in the 1830s. These letters had been in Caroline's possession since 1837, and she had wanted to publish them in 1838 in conjunction with another trial for debt. This is the "obscure and forgotten cause" to which Caroline refers in *English Laws.* In that 1838 trial, one of Caroline's creditors had subpoenaed Sir John Bayley to testify about George's character. Bayley was never called to the witness stand, however, because Sir Fitzroy Kelly, George's lawyer, advised Lord Abinger, the judge in the case, not to accept Bayley's testimony for fear that Bayley would use the Greenacre letters to impugn George's reputation. This conspiracy of Tory silence, Caroline now charges, was mounted to protect George so that he would not reveal that a Tory plot had motivated his earlier suit against Melbourne. In other words, Caroline's reputation had twice been hostage, not simply to George's perfidy, but also to political intrigues. When the verdict in the 1838 trial was announced *for* George, Caroline determined, by publishing her account of the case, to expose her husband's lies and the way Lord Abinger had misused his judicial power. At that time, however, she was stopped by Lord Melbourne, who, as prime minister to a young queen, dreaded scandal more than anything else. "It so happened that this petty cause," Caroline now bitterly complains, "in which nothing more important than a woman's fame and a woman's interest were at stake,—was tried at the exact moment (June 1838), when, in the first year of a young Queen's reign, the Whig government was overwhelmed with business." Amid such political machinations and affairs of state, Norton's grievance was simply buried, as it had been after the 1836 trial, when Caroline also could not publicly defend her innocence. "What could my passionate printed justification be?" she asks rhetorically in 1854, "but a plague and an embarrassment to *him,* already justified, and at the pinnacle of fortune?"

This is the history to which Norton repeatedly returns in her 1854 defense. Once repressed by that "double chance" of Whig and Tory politics, Norton's anger now returns to punish the men who would not let her speak. By publishing not only the details of George's brutality but also Melbourne's private letters, Caroline avenges herself against both men for all their crimes—against George for hurting her, for denying her her children, for murdering her reputation; against Melbourne for smothering her domestic injuries with his political concerns. Once she acknowledges the abuses she suffered as a helpless woman, Norton the avenger can formulate the social injustices that have authorized these private wrongs. In the last chapter of *English Laws for Women* and in the bulk of **"A Letter to the Queen,"** Norton sets out the inequities of the current marriage laws, calling attention to their class and gender bias and pointing to the masculine investment that inhibits reform. "Property," she asserts, "not morality, [is] the thing held sacred"; because mercenary self-interest motivates all men (as it motivated George Norton), women become "non-existent,' except for the purpose of suffering."

As long as Norton occupies the position of the avenger in the melodramatic plot, she is authorized to spell out the injustice both of the individual villain and the laws that refuse her justice. But her "sentencing" is limited precisely because she also retains the domestic ideal in which she can only cast herself as the suffering lady-in-distress. This limitation emerges clearly in the solution Norton proposes for women's plight. She does not ask for equal rights for women or even for equalization of the grounds for divorce. Instead, she asks for protection. "What I write," she assures her readers in the introduction to *English Laws,* "is written in no spirit of rebellion; it is simply an appeal for protection." Over 150 pages later, she explains more fully her vision of the relationship between rights and protection:

> Petitioning does not imply assertion of equality. The wild and stupid theories advanced by a few women, of "equal rights" and "equal intelligence" are not the opinions of their sex. I, for one (I, with millions more), believe in the natural superiority of man, as I do in the existence of a God. . . . Masculine superiority is incontestable; and with the superiority should come protection. To refuse it because some women exist, who talk of "women's rights," of "women's equality," is to say that . . . the Chartist and Rebecca riots in Wales, or Swing fires in the rural districts of England, would have been a sound and sufficient reason for refusing justice to all the Queen's subjects in the United Kingdom. The rebellion of a group, against legitimate authority, is not to deprive the general subject-party of general protection. Women have one *right* (perhaps only that one). They have a right—founded on nature, equity, and religion—to the protection of man. *Power* is on the side of men—power of body, power of mind, power of position. With that power should come, not only the fact, but the *instinct* of protection.

Like the melodramatic script that underwrites her speech, Norton explicitly endorses the existence of a natural difference between men and women and the natural difference of "rights" that follows from this: because men are physically and socially more powerful, they have political rights within the public sphere, and women, the weaker sex, have the right to protection from the stresses of that sphere; women have the right, that is, to remain within the non-political and nonmercenary sphere of the home. The problem is that Norton's usurpation of the defender's role, her revelation of the role politics and money have played in her domestic woes, and her entry into political discourse have already collapsed the very differences she seems to support. It is this peculiar combination of reticence and audacity that simultaneously enabled Norton to influence legislators like Lord Lyndhurst and prevented her from formulating the more radical analysis that a few of her contemporaries did advance.

FURTHER READING

Forster, Margaret. "Law: Caroline Norton, 1808-1877." In *Significant Sisters: The Grassroots of Active Feminism,* pp. 15-52. London: Secker & Warburg, 1984.
> Provides detailed biographical information and establishes Norton's role in the early feminist movement.

Perkins, Jane Gray. *The Life of Mrs. Norton.* London: J. Murray, 1910, 312 p.
> Exhaustive biography covering all aspects of Norton's life, including her literary career and her political endeavors.

Zaborszky, Dorothy E. " 'Domestic Anarchy and the Destruction of the Family': Caroline Norton and the Custody of Infants Bill." *International Journal of Women's Studies* 7, No. 5 (November/December 1984): 397-411.
> Examines the significance of Norton's activities in the passage of the Custody of Infants Bill (1839).

Laurence Oliphant

1829(?)-1888

English travel writer, novelist, and religious theorist.

INTRODUCTION

An English journalist and satirist, Laurence Oliphant is best known for his commentaries on Victorian society and for writings chronicling his own varied experiences. Although his work as a travel writer, foreign correspondent, and novelist was widely popular, Oliphant ultimately abandoned these literary pursuits to devote himself to writing about his spiritual self-discovery.

Biographical Information

Oliphant was born in South Africa to a British attorney-general and the daughter of a British colonel. The family moved between South Africa, England, and Ceylon during Oliphant's childhood. During his twenties and thirties he was well-received in London society and travelled extensively, detailing his journeys in a series of essays that appeared in London periodicals. In 1865, he began publishing his first novel, *Piccadilly,* as a series in *Blackwood's* magazine. The same year, Oliphant was elected to Parliament but did not assume his political post. He came under the influence of an American religious mystic, Thomas Lake Harris, and in 1867 joined the religious community headed by Harris in New York. When the Franco-German war broke out in 1870, Oliphant worked for a year in Paris as a foreign correspondent, and there met his future wife. Although the Oliphants eventually broke from Harris, they retained their religious beliefs, and moved to Palestine to establish a religious community with Oliphant himself at the head. He died there in 1888.

Major Works

Oliphant's early work stemmed from his extensive travels. His book *The Russian Shores of the Black Sea* (1853) was released shortly before the Crimean War and became an instant success, positioning Oliphant as an expert on the area and securing him a position as a foreign correspondent. His novel *Piccadilly* (1865) reveals growing dissatisfaction with the shallowness of a social existence and hints at the spiritual fulfillment that he presumably found in the cult led by Harris. His novel *Altiora Peto* (1883) also addresses the frivolity of society life. His later work is devoted entirely to expounding the guiding principles of his spiritual beliefs. He claimed that the treatise *Sympneumata; or, Evolutionary Forces Now Active in Man* (1885), was written by a spirit speaking through his wife.

Critical Reception

Oliphant's travelogues and social commentaries are gener-

ally regarded as well-crafted and insightful, in contrast to his religious writings, which have been described as cryptic and labyrinthine. While his unique spirituality is subtley expressed in his novels and explicated thoroughly in his religious statements, Oliphant's religious exegesis was never embraced by his readership. Oliphant's writings are not ranked among the classics of his time; however, his critics acknowledge that his novels provide a vivid picture of Victorian values and lifestyles.

PRINCIPAL WORKS

A Journey to Katmandu with the Camp of Jung Bahadoor (travel essay) 1852
The Russian Shores of the Black Sea in the Autumn of 1852, with a Voyage down the Volga, and a Tour through the Country of the Don Cossacks (travel essay) 1853
Narrative of the Earl of Elgin's Mission to China and Japan in the Years 1857, '58, '59 (travel essay) 1859

Piccadilly: A Fragment of Contemporary Biography (novel) 1865
Altiora Peto (novel) 1883
Sympneumata; or, Evolutionary Forces Now Active in Man (treatise) 1885
Masollam: A Problem of the Period (novel) 1886
Haifa; or, Life in Modern Palestine (journal) 1887
Episodes in a Life of Adventure; or, Moss from a Rolling Stone (autobiography) 1887
Scientific Religion; or, Higher Possibilities of Life and Practice through the Operation of Natural Forces (treatise) 1888

CRITICISM

Blackwood's Edinburgh Magazine   (essay date 1870)

SOURCE: A review of *Piccadilly*, in *Blackwood's Edinburgh Magazine*, Vol. CVIII, No. DCLX, October, 1870, pp. 401-22.

[*In the following excerpt from* Blackwood's, *the anonymous critic examines the social context and spiritual evolution of the principle characters of* Piccadilly.]

It would be impossible to imagine any book more utterly puzzling to the careless reader, who is unprepared to encounter anything more weighty than ordinary sketches of contemporary life—or more full of meaning to the thoughtful, than the volume which, after a lapse of several years from its original appearance in these pages, has just been republished under the above title. We make no apology for thus taking up, in the way of criticism and review, a work originally produced to the world by Maga herself; for the book is too curious and individual to be received as an exposition of any opinions but those of its author; and in so far as it is representative at all, belongs neither to party, creed, nor faction with which we have any relations. Its views are not ours, neither are we prepared to accept its conclusions. It is a work by itself, pervaded through and through by the workings of a mind which has been stimulated by strong feeling into strong action, and which has thrown off at once all the ordinary trammels and ordinary motives of authorship. The writer has written, not because he wanted (as most of us do) to write a book with certain well-understood results of praise and pudding, but because his heart has burned within him, and silence has become impossible. When by times, and at long intervals, a voice thus breaks forth, as it were perforce, from the very heart of the world itself, disclosing a greater or less amount of individual knowledge of all its problems and troubles, and confronting its difficulties with all the earnestness of one practically and personally involved, its interest is far deeper than the interest of any mere literary production even of genius. *Piccadilly* is not a work of philosophy, nor is it a record of religious experience, nor a novel, nor a satire on modern society—and yet in some respects it is all these put together. Mr. Kingsley made an attempt many years ago, in his book *Yeast,* to give a glimpse into the depths which are covered over by the dazzling surface of society, and to show all the mysteries and tragedies that are going on below. But Mr. Kingsley's book was essentially melodramatic, concerning itself with those tales of seduction and suicide, black villany and impotent white virtue, with which the British public has been long familiar. Mr. Oliphant does not tread that well-known ground. There are no vulgar crimes behind the scenes which he pushes aside for us, but only that much more elaborate and complicated machinery, which, with a hundred conscious and unconscious pretences at better meaning, is really constructed for the deification of Self, the great god of modern existence. Though he preaches many a sharp sermon, and points his lessons with uncompromising plainness, he does not himself assume any lofty standing-ground as of a preacher superior to his audience. On the contrary, he speaks out of the midst of the audience—a man who has been trained in their code, has worked as they work, and has been moved by the same motives. His are not the crude difficulties of a boy bewildered by the contrast between some academic ideal of nobleness and the puzzling realities and prose of life. He knows society and its sins so well that they do not horrify him, nor call any violent comment from his lips. They are the sins among which he has been brought up, which he is prepared to meet, and which cannot but be half comic to him, though at the same time they are wholly sad and terrible. They are comic because his accustomed eye sees through the fictions that veil them, and he cannot refrain from a certain amused admiration of the cleverness of the actors in that strange deceptive panorama. He is so far behind the scenes as to be aware of the wonderful mixture of cunning and simplicity which is visible to the instructed eye in all the wiles of human nature. He sees how the cunningest, wariest, most artful of plotters will now and then stick his head into the sand like an ostrich, and, with a credulity more wonderful than his cunning, believe in the credulity of others. He sees how some of the actors in this wild phantasmagoria have so wrapped themselves about with fine deceits that they are all but unconscious—sometimes, indeed, wholly unconscious—of the meaner motives below. All this he perceives without horror, without any violence of indignation, or bitterness of scorn. To perceive it is the highest condemnation; but the observer in this case does not vituperate, he only exhibits. Neither is he prepared utterly to condemn even the victim whom he holds up to the world on the point of his spear. He himself is ready to enter into the arena, to take up the sinner's own weapons, to adopt with exaggerated openness his own code of principle, and, with a certain enjoyment of the conflict, foil him on his own ground. With all his perception of the utter falsity of everything round him he is never cynical; he is calm and friendly and impartial, looking on at all those pranks, which make the angels weep, with a smile not of scorn but of insight. He is not horrified, he is familiar with it all; and in this calmness lies one great secret of power.

Such an exposition, however, by a spectator intensely in earnest yet unemotional, has been done before; but there is another element introduced which gives complete originality to Mr. Oliphant's book. His hero is a man of the world, standing on precisely the same level as the other men of the world represented in it. He is not an ideal reformer—a being of grand motives and elevated ways of working. Such a personage does exist in the work, but he stands among the mists as do most ideal creations, an act of homage to the great and noble rather than an actual embodiment of humanity. The hero of the book—the writer of the autobiography—is not ideal. The peculiarity about him is, that he has been driven half wild in the midst of his natural eccentricity by a sudden gleam of light from heaven. Christianity has come upon him like a sunstroke, confusing his head and his life. He had known all about the hollowness of society, and the falsehood of its individual members, and the amazing littleness of its aims, before, and had looked upon them with calm philosophy. But it has suddenly flashed upon his mind that Christianity means something else than this—that it means succour and aid and deliverance, an abandonment of self, an adoption of the cause of others; the life not of a mere spectator, however clearsighted. Such a thought, coming suddenly into the mind of a well-bred and tolerant modern Englishman, accustomed to let everybody ruin or advance himself his own way, to avoid responsibility and interference, and maintain the theory that every man knows what is best for himself, might well produce the most bewildering effect; and the great success in this book, a success which probably genius could not have attained, but only that experience which is sometimes above genius—is the wonderful picture afforded us of the chaos produced in a man's mind and life by this sudden change of motive. It is like a sudden change of wind on the course of a ship at sea. The vessel whirls and shakes and staggers in its course. The ancient direction has become impossible; the new has to be met by spasmodic tacks and shifts and struggles. Currents are more subtle and sails more delicate in the spiritual world. The soul reels and struggles and tries back, and is forced forward, until at last the new breeze takes possession of the trembling sail, and drives about the unwilling helm, and overcomes the tremor and vibration of resistance. This is the crisis which Mr. Oliphant has represented to us with a truth and force which are very impressive. The reader who does not take the trouble to enter into his intention and idea, will no doubt find a great deal that is most amusing, most telling, and remarkable, in this book; but he will miss the point at which it rises out of the external into the inner life—out of those revelations which depend on sharp sight and deep observation only, into those which belong to the higher conditions of individual feeling—the tidings sent from one soul to another, deepest instruction, information, sympathetic communication which can be made by man to man.

There are very few things which have been so vulgarised by description, so associated with bad taste, mean motives, foolish mock-humility, and the badly-veiled pretences of self-love, as the history of personal religion. It is hard to say why it should be so, for no subject should be, or can be, more interesting to the world. It is impossible to doubt that, in a great many cases, religious life begins in the individual by that crisis and struggle between the old and the new, the true and the false, the light and darkness, which all religious writers and sects have agreed in calling conversion, and which many consider indispensable to every Christian. Nothing in a life, not any of the greatest events which affect it, can be so important as this crisis; and yet nothing can be less human or less divine than the narratives of it which are continually being poured upon us, and which by common consent are relegated to the simple classes of the community, to parish libraries and Sunday-schools, and readers who cannot help themselves. The educated classes, to whom literature in general addresses itself, cannot be said to regard such works as possibly addressed to them. We do not pretend to receive or judge them as (what they ought to be) more interesting than any other kind of history, involving all the deeper emotions, showing us more than philosophy, more than poetry can reveal to us of the workings of the heart. Perhaps one reason of this complete failure is that there is but one type of conversion recognised by what is generally called the religious world. We have never got beyond the *Pilgrim's Progress* notwithstanding the wonderful changes which since then have modified all other essential characteristics of the race. And unfortunately John Bunyan's Christian, though a very wonderful impersonation, and one which has perhaps exercised a greater influence on the common mind than any ideal man invented by any other poet from that day till this, is no longer our typical pilgrim.

The peculiarity of religious life in this age is not that overwhelming sense of personal danger, and necessity for deliverance, which inspired the sixteenth century. It is not judgment to come which appals us, nor hell and the lake of brimstone, nor the hideous demons with their awful claws. Even the Celestial City, with its streets of gold and gates of pearl, is a dim imagination to us, at once material and unreal. We are capable of looking at Satan's hoofs all cloven and harmless, and saying, like the philosopher, "Graminivorous! I am not afraid of you." Christian is one of our oldest friends, and his adventures never fail of a certain charm; but he is a hero of romance, like Sir Galahad or Sir Percival, and does not resemble one of us. Neither is the converted man of religious biography one of us. The Richard Weavers, the converted blacksmiths, the shining lights of Revivals, are equally apart from our knowledge. Let us throw no doubt or suspicion upon them. Their way is as old as Christianity, and doubtless will last as long as matter-of-fact wickedness and simple intelligences exist in the world. The stories of religious experience which abound in print are no doubt true to the consciousness of the minds which produced them, but they are not true to nature, and they do not affect us. We ask ourselves, Are these people made of flesh and blood? had they, as we have, loves and duties infinitely more precious than their own lives or comfort? or is this curious spiritual transmogrification of the fleshly thing called self-love any real gain or advantage to them? We grant that they are good people, but we cannot identify them. They belong to another region, a different development. The atmosphere about them is to us artificial and unreal. While we find ourselves in a practical restless world full of contending things and interests, they are in a sphere where doctrines and feelings are supreme, and where a man is not judged by what he is, or does, but by the dogmas he believes, and the fluctuations of temper and spiritual heat and cold to which he is subject. If this is the only way of attaining religious light and rising to a higher existence, what is to become of us? for our hearts are not touched, neither do our minds approve.

The picture Mr. Oliphant makes for us is of a very different description. His hero, as we have said, is no melodramatic sinner, but a man of fashion, with no horrible tragedies or depravities in his life to bring him to shame were they revealed. He is not a debauchee, nor a tyrant, but a man who has mingled much wandering and adventure in primitive places with abundant knowledge and experience of that social life which is the highest as it is the most puzzling result of civilisation. He is in the world, in its fullest current, and yet he too is a pilgrim in the agonies of a conversion involving struggles as difficult as those of Christian. But this modern convert is not like Christian. He is not seized upon by a pressing sense of any burden on his back—of all things in the world his sins are about the last that he is thinking of. It is not the jaws of hell or the valley of the shadow of death that haunt his dreams. His thoughts are of the world about him, that world which he knows so much better than any doctrines or philosophies. He has known it long, and it is no new revelation of its deceits and vanities which startles him. What is new and confusing is the thought that he owes something to it—that his duty is not to remain passive and smile at its follies, or transfix it with polished arrows of calm impartial sarcasm, but to open its eyes, if he can, to what is true and just and good. It has long been apparent to him—before, indeed, any gleam of religious consciousness came into his own mind—that the time was out of joint. He has been enduring, not enjoying, it for years back, perceiving the hypocrisies, falsehoods, and vain fictions, of which society is full—seeing clearly that everything was hollow, fictitious, forced, and unreal, in the existence of which his own life formed a part. He has looked on at this spectacle sometimes with laughter, sometimes with tragic jeers and sarcasm, but generally with a contemptuous indifference, and keen perception of its comic, not to say grotesque, aspect. He himself, too, has been, like the other players in the comedy, acting his part, or rather half-a-dozen parts, as caprice dictated, looking on at his own performance as at theirs, and seeing through both. This is the true spirit of the modern mind, when "awakened" out of the first dull content of nature, or the imaginary satisfaction of Youth. It is not penitent so much as uneasy. It has no fear of judgment to come, nor any deep sense of its own ill-doing; but only a weary, restless, painful consciousness that things are not well either with itself or its fellow-creatures—that the life it is leading is not justified by truth and nature, and cannot be in accordance with the purposes of God.

This first *avant courier* of religion—this inner voice which replaces that of the Baptist in the modern world, has sounded in a great many hearts which have never come directly under a decided religious influence: perhaps it would be safe to say that it affects more or less all the nobler spirits of the generation in one way or other. With some it leads but to a cynical disdain, and painful, fierce, suppressed indignation of the world and all its ways— many it sends wandering to the corners of the earth, among savages or primitive races, in search of the reality which has died out of civilised existence. It brings down here and there a sick soul out of the higher classes into the lower, to try what manual toil and poverty may do to restore truth to the earth; but whatever its manifestation may be, this is the prevailing form taken by that seriousness which in all ages and epochs has been the preface to religious life. Perhaps the fact that there is no pinch of personal anxiety about it, or very little—and that "what shall I do to be saved?" is not in the least its natural outcry—is the reason why this state of pregnant uneasiness sometimes exists for a whole lifetime without ripening into any true religious conviction. But, nevertheless, it is the state corresponding to that in which the soldiers and the publicans hurried to John the Baptist, and in which, throughout all ages, men and women have thrown themselves wildly upon every new religious teacher. There are still, no doubt, awakenings and conversions after the old model—great personal crises, at which the individual soul finds itself face to face with God, and has to work out its salvation according to its own consciousness, and attain an individual deliverance; but while these occur by units, they are counted by thousands who are sick of this weary and imperfect round of life. The people who are disgusted with civilisation, disgusted with progress, sick of the hubbub of pretended benevolence, pretended freedom, pretended religiousness and feel life to be all wrong and out of harmony, without knowing how to put it right, are countless in number. It is this phase of modern feeling which Mr. Oliphant sets before us, not so much to elucidate a state of mind, as to express a feeling which to a very high and intense point he himself shares. His hero is moved by it almost to the height of madness. And yet this very madness is not real, but restrained by a secret thread of consciousness all the time that he is not mad, and cannot be—that he is incapable of thus easily escaping from the great problem. The time is out of joint—the world is out of harmony: broken concords hovering about in the air—sensibilities that start into sight when we least expect them—hidden gleams of good out of the very soul of evil—give note to those who are not too warped by their dissatisfaction to mark them, that harmony is, must be, ought to be, still possible, did we but know how to bring it about; and here and there the sick soul bestirs itself, and makes a wild effort to bring it about; but it has no real energy in any of its movements. It is uneasiness that moves it—nothing more certain—restless disapproval, dissatisfaction, discontent.

When, however, the bewildering sense that it is his duty no longer to smile and stand aloof, but to do something to aid and help the struggling mass, becomes irresistible, the convert can no longer keep silent. He is not made into a wise and far-seeing and large-minded reformer by the struggling determination which thus comes uppermost within him. On the contrary, he is as are the crowds out of which, so short a time before, he has been taken, differing only in this point, that while all his habits and ways of working are as yet unchanged, the spring of his actions, the great leading motive of his conduct, has been suddenly altered. That has been altered, but none of his customs have been altered, and he has the entire force of the stream to fight against not only outside him but within him; and now and then is so carried away by use and wont that he falls to work in the old ways, and does his best to accomplish the new good which he desires by the old means to which he is accustomed. How Lord Frank Vanecourt does this—how he relapses, after his first self-devotion to the work of a social missionary, into continual outbursts of levity and confusion of new motives and old manners—is the subject of Mr. Oliphant's narrative, if narrative it can be called. He sets out with the intention of a crusade against society as actually constituted in all its developments—an attempt to reform everybody and change the character of modern civilisation; and he ends, as is natural, in entangling himself in the private affairs of a circle, bringing endless trouble upon his own head, being misunderstood all round, and finally sacrificing himself, his private feelings, and a slice out of his fortune, for the rectification of his neighbour's business—a proceeding entirely against his own interest, and, so to speak, out of his way altogether. That he does this in a confused, incoherent, half-mad way, baffling all his friends, and laying himself open to every kind of misconception, is a part of the plan of the tale; and it is this which gives it the strange stamp of originality, and of more than originality—absolute reality and truth—with which it inspires the thoughtful reader. It is intensely alive and real in the very exaggeration of its resolves, the air of levity and extravagance under which its purpose is laid, and which at first puzzles the spectator, and prompts the question, Does it mean anything at all? what does it mean? which is a question so often asked by the matter-of-fact intelligence in presence of that tone of half banter, half solemnity, which hides the meaning of so many men in society itself. We feel with Lord Frank, as we feel with many in real life, that we don't know whether he is in jest or earnest; that what he says may be real and grave as life and death, or that it may be but a solemn jest, in uttering which the speaker laughs at our credulity, laughs at his own magniloquence, and at the possibility of any real reforming effort, and, in short, at everything in earth and heaven. Here, for instance, is the first statement of the purpose which has arisen in his mind while he has been watching the stream of carriages going to Lady Palmerston's ball—and while he has chattered to and got a cup of tea for Lady Veriphast at that solemnity: —

> As I write, the magnitude of the task I propose to myself assumes still larger proportions. I yearn to develop in the world at large those organs of conscientiousness and benevolence which we all possess but so few exercise. I invoke the co-operation of my readers in this great work: I implore them to accompany me step by step in the crusade which I am about to preach in favour of the sacrifice of self for the public good. I demand their sympathy in this monthly record of my trials as an uncompromising exponent of the motives of the day, and I claim their tender solicitude should I writhe, crushed and mangled by the iron hand of a social tyranny dexterously concealed in its velvet glove. I will begin my efforts at reform with the Church; I may then possibly diverge to the Legislature, and I will mix in the highest circles of society in the spirit of a missionary. I will endeavour to show everybody up to everybody else in the spirit of love; and if they end by quarrelling with each other and with me, I shall at least have the satisfaction of feeling myself divested of all further responsibility in the matter. In my present frame of mind apathy would be culpable and weakness a crime.

With this grand but vague and wild statement of his intentions, Lord Frank, smiled at by his best friend, Lord Grandon, the ideal (but undecipherable) man of the drama, the Grandison hero, for whose benefit all the work is to be done—sets out, not in the least knowing how to begin upon his mission—his first step being the acceptance of a pleasant invitation to a pleasant house in the country. Here he meets with a colonial bishop, a converted Hindoo, an evangelical and stockbroking Lady Broadhem, an eminent member of the "worldly–holy" section of society, with her son and daughters—and several other remarkable specimens of good society. Nothing could be more amusing, more trenchant and uncompromising, yet less tinctured with gall or cynicism, than these sketches of social lions. Here, for instance, is our introduction to the new characters: —

> They had all disappeared to dress for dinner, however, and Dickiefield had not come home from riding, so that when Grandon and I entered the drawing-room, we found only the deserted apparatus of the afternoon tea, a Bishop, and a black man—and we had to introduce ourselves. The Bishop had a beard and an apron, his companion a turban, and such very large shoes, that it was evident his feet were unused to the confinement. The Bishop looked stern and determined; perhaps there was just a dash of worldliness about the twist of his mustache. His companion wore a subdued and unctuous appearance; his face was shaved; and the whites of his eyes were very bloodshot and yellow. Neither of them was the least embarrassed when we were shown in; Grandon and I both were slightly. 'What a comfort that the snow is gone!' said I to the Bishop.
>
> 'Yes,' said his Lordship; 'the weather is very trying to me, who have just arrived from the Caribbee Islands.'
>
> 'I suppose you have accompanied his lordship from the Caribbee Islands.' said I, turning to the swarthy individual, whom I naturally supposed to be a specimen convert.
>
> 'No,' he said; 'he had arrived some months since from Bombay.'
>
> 'Think of staying long in England?' said Grandon.
>
> 'That depends upon my prospects at the next general election—I am looking out for a borough.'
>
> 'Dear me!' said Grandon; and we all, Bishop included, gazed on him with astonishment.
>
> 'My name is Chundango,' he went on. 'My parents were both Hindoos. Before I was converted my other name was Juggonath; now I am John. I became acquainted with a circle of dear Christian friends in Bombay, during my connection, as catechist, with the Tabernacle Missionary Society, was peculiarly favoured in some mercantile transactions into which I subsequently entered in connection with cotton, and have come to spend my fortune, and enter public life, in this

country. I was just expressing to our dear friend here,' pointing in a patronising way towards the Bishop, 'my regret at finding that he shares in views which are becoming so prevalent in the Church, and are likely to taint the Protestantism of Great Britain and part of Ireland.'

'Goodness!' thought I, 'how this complicates matters! Which of these two now stands most in need of my services as a missionary?' . . . As Dickiefield was lighting me up to my bedroom, I could not resist congratulating him upon his two guests. 'A good specimen of the "unsound muscular," the Bishop,' said I.

'Not very,' said Dickiefield; 'he is not so unsound as he looks, and he is not unique, like the other. I flatter myself I have under my roof the only well-authenticated instance of the Hindoo converted millionaire. It is true he became a "Government Christian" when he was a poor boy of fifteen, and began life as a catechist; then he saw a good mercantile opening, and went into cotton, out of which he has realised an immense fortune, and now is going into political life in England, which he could not have done in an unconverted condition. Who ever heard before of a Bombay man wanting to get into Parliament, and coming home with a *carte du pays* all arranged before he started? He advocates extension of the franchise, ballot, and the Evangelical Alliance; so I thought I would fasten him on to Broadhem—they'll help to float each other.'

'Who else have you got here besides?' I asked.

'Oh, only a petroleum aristocrat from the oil regions of America—another millionaire. He is a more wonderful instance even than Chundango, for he was a poor man three months ago, when he "struck lie." You will find him most intelligent, full of information; but you will look upon him, of course, as the type of the peculiar class to which he belongs, and not of Americans generally.' And my warm-hearted and eccentric friend, Lord Dickiefield, left me to my meditations and my toilet.

Another, the heroine, who is unfortunately too much of the Grandison or high-ideal type, like Lord Grandon, to interest us deeply, is introduced, by a little classification of young ladies in society, as follows: —

I ran over in my mind my young lady categories, as follows:

First,   The wholly worldly
          and
          The worldly holy

In this case the distinction is very fine; but though they are bracketed together, there is an appreciable difference, which perhaps some day, when I have time, I shall discuss.

Second, 'The still deep fast.'

This may seem to be a contradiction in terms; but the fact is, while the upper surface seems tranquil enough, there is a strong, rapid undercurrent. The danger is, in this case, that you are very apt to go in what is called a 'header.' The moment you dive you get caught by the undercurrent, and the chances are you never rise to the surface again.

Third, 'The rippling glancing fast.'

This is less fatal, but, to my mind not so attractive as the other. The ripples are produced by quantities of pebbles, which are sure to give one what is called in America a 'rough time.' The glancing is only dangerous to youths in the first stage, and is perfectly innocuous after one season.

Fourth, 'The rushing gushing fast.'

This speaks for itself, and may be considered perfectly harmless. There are only two slows—the 'strong-minded blue slow,' and the 'heavy slow.'

The 'strong-minded blue slow' includes every branch of learning. It is extremely rare, and alarming to the youth of the day. I am rather partial to it myself.

The 'heavy slow' is, alas! too common.

Lady Broadhem is, however, a still more important character than either Chundango or "Joseph Caribbee Islands." Her cleverness and promptitude and invincible pluck and courage fill the reader with admiration, and even, it is evident, delight the carnal man, who is not quite subdued in Lord Frank himself. The way in which she trafficks with the hideous Hindoo for the hand of the beautiful and pure-minded Lady Ursula, and shifts and changes when Lord Frank, a duke's son and enormously rich, comes in as an opposition candidate; the duel between the two for a frank statement of her debts and difficulties on the one hand, and for her consent to the marriage of Grandon and Ursula on the other, —have ability and humour enough in them to set up half-a-dozen ordinary novels. Lady Broadhem is grand in her audacity, her strength of purpose, and unscrupulous resolution; her readiness to seize every loophole, and take advantage of every accident. "What, dear Mr. Chundango," she remarked, "matters the colour of your skin if your blood be pure? If your jewellery and your conversion are both genuine, what more could an anxious mother desire for her beloved daughter?" "He is a man of remarkable ability," she explains to her daughter; *"in some lights there is a decided richness in his hue."* "I need not say what an escape I think she has had from that black man," she adds a few minutes later, when Lord Frank has declared himself. In every one of the many trying circumstances in which we encounter her, Lady Broadhem is grand and original. Mr. Oliphant has kept entirely clear of that vulgar folly sometimes to be found where we should least expect it, which introduces sketches of actual personages by way of giving life to the dead and blank story-spinning which pretends to be fiction. Lady Broadhem is Lady Broadhem, and no other. She is complete and characteristic in every point—a distinct creature; and, curiously enough, though she is worldly and cunning to the highest, or rather to the meanest, degree, utterly unscrupulous in the means she uses, and actually employing religion as a way to social and other eminence, it is impossible to hate her, or to refrain from a certain sympathy with her amazing cleverness and wealth of resource.

Were we about to treat *Piccadilly* simply as a work of art, it would be easy to enlarge upon the power of the conception, the wonderful ease and vigour with which the whole is treated; the knowledge of life at once in its ordinary and extraordinary developments which we find in every page. Had, indeed, the book been without that religious meaning which gives it its greatest charm, its singular ability would no doubt have procured its more general appreciation by the public, who can better understand even the fine and pointed satire which goes over the heads of the common crowd, than they can understand those motives which to the sober mind of respectable church-going folk, satisfied with just enough religion to keep them comfortable, cannot but look overstrained and extraordinary. As it is, the deeper significance which lies underneath is apt to confuse the reader in his perception of the amazing vividness and force of talent in these social sketches. There is not a stupid page in the whole volume. Every character is distinct and sharply outlined, and full of restrained power and humour. Even when we look at the subordinate personages in the drama, nothing can be more instinct at once with insight and with force than the outline of Mr. Wog, the American capitalist who has "struck lie," and has come to England to make notes on the aristocracy for the benefit of his countrymen. And the scenes in the City with Spiffey Goldtip's wonderful negotiations and secret diplomatic service between the two grand yet contrasting rival powers of Money and Society, are wonderful in the vigour of their revelations. This is not the sort of thing we are used to in books that have a religious meaning. Perhaps, indeed, it might be said that the book, as a work of art, suffers by the meaning that is in it, as well as that its undercurrent of deep and serious thought is subject to misconception in consequence of the wonderful brilliancy of the secular matter which accompanies and is wound in with it. The two qualities injure each other so far as common favour and understanding go. But in a higher sense—as an exposition of the way in which religious feeling affects the educated and refined and elevated intelligence of the nineteenth century; of how it works, betraying on every side the hollowness of artificial life, the sins of civilisation, the aching misery of contrast between all that is and all that ought to be—this book is unique in modern literature. We do not remember the time when any such voice has been raised before to point out to gentle and semple, churchman and layman, the amazing difference between faith and practice, or rather between the professions of faith made by Christendom, and the actual life lived by the kingdoms and societies that are included under that title. "It seems to me quite the best sermon that has been written for a long time," says a distinguished preacher, himself one of the most influential religious teachers of the day; "and it is a comfort to know that there is some one who will hit hard and not care." When we glance aside at the real motive of the book, we are stayed in our applause of the wit, the talent, the power of observation, and insight into character, which appear on every page. Not this, we are sure, is the appreciation the author looks for. His brilliant panorama of society is brilliant, as it were, by the

way. His conscious meaning is a very different one. And we, too, only pause by the way to remark that we know no one volume produced in recent days in which there is so lively, so sparkling, so able a picture of contemporary society and all its weaknesses, before we proceed to discuss that purpose which is all in all to the writer, and which is still more original, still more remarkable, than the high literary power and insight of the book.

We have said that the highest conception and the truest in this work is that of the strangely confusing, bewildering effect produced upon a man's mental condition and thoughts, when out of the calm, passive, semi-contemptuous observation of the world and its ways, which is so usual among thoughtful men, he is roused to the fact that Christianity is not passive but active, and that his own knowledge of a better way throws upon him a solemn and seldom-realised responsibility. It is but slowly and by degrees that the fact dawns upon his mind that he, and we, and all about us, hold as our creed that religion of sacrifice and self-renunciation which is so strangely different from anything we do or attempt to do. The mere discovery is of itself a shock. The convert's first idea naturally is, that he is the first who has found it out; and that the greatness of the ideal Christian life, and the meanness of the actual social one, will strike everybody else as forcibly as himself, when it is once shown to them. But when he finds that the new creed which he has thus suddenly realised is the old one by which the race has been guided, or has professed to be guided, for centuries, the wonder strikes him wild with a sense of hopelessness and maddening impotence. This Gospel, which runs counter to every rule of society, and every secret unwritten canon of individual conduct, is theoretically (he finds) the foundation upon which all modern society is built. It is professedly the creed we are born and die in—the hope of Christendom. We accept it with a blind pagan confidence as our safeguard from certain distant evils of an unknown life hereafter, even while we contradict its spirit and precepts in every action of our lives here. We write it up upon those standards, under the shade of which we play, heaven knows, such pranks! Of all the characteristics that distinguish us, this is the one of which we are most certain. We may modestly disclaim being clever, or good, or learned, or gifted in any special way; but the man who doubts that we are Christians assails us in our last stronghold, questions the one fact of which we are sure, and insults even the worst and most obdurate of sinners. The very murderer on the steps of the scaffold, not to say a hundred other criminals of less conspicuous, but perhaps scarcely less real, guilt, would resent bitterly, as the last injury, the imputation that he was no Christian. Can it be wondered at if a man, newly and vividly impressed with the spirit of Christianity, should stand aghast when he realises this bewildering fact? To live under the delusion that you have been a Christian all your life, and then suddenly wake up in the middle or the decline of that life to find out what Christianity really is, is scarcely even so confusing as is the discovery by a hitherto careless spectator of the wonderful living spiritual force of a creed which everybody makes believe to hold, and nobody acts upon. It is not dead after all, but instinct with vital energy. It has power to lay hold upon and possess the mind even now at this advanced period of the world's history; and yet it is the creed of all those selfish, ease-loving, wealth-acquiring, pleasure-making egotists who fill the world with oppressions, small and great, with injury and misery and pain! The fact is sufficient to paralyse or to drive into maddest bewildered action every mind which makes the discovery. And this is the discovery which, in the midst of a life entirely secular and *mondaine,* Mr. Oliphant's hero suddenly makes, with the effect of perplexing his whole being, and throwing him into that chaos from which only one of the wild expedients resorted to by humanity in desperation can save the struggling soul. We quote the following conversation which Lord Frank holds with young Lord Broadhem on the sacred flags of Piccadilly itself. The two young men have just left a private missionary meeting in Lady Broadhem's house, at which Lord Frank has expressed himself with a wild disregard of all conventional proprieties, and deadly sincerity, which have sadly discomposed the assembly: —

> 'Broadhem,' said I, 'I have hit upon an entirely new and original idea. I am thinking of trying it myself, and I want you to try it too.'
>
> 'Well,' said Broadhem, 'I am never surprised at anything you say or do; what is it?'
>
> 'It has been suggested to me by what I have seen at your mother's this evening—and you may depend upon it there is a great deal to be said in its favour; it is an odd thing it has not occurred to anybody before, but that leaves all the better opening for you and me.'
>
> 'Go on,' said Broadhem, whose curiosity was getting excited.
>
> 'Don't be in a hurry; it is possible you may not like the idea when you hear it, and under no circumstances must you tell it to anybody.'
>
> 'All right,' said Broadhem, 'but I hope it has nothing to do with companies—I hate dabbling in companies. I believe one does more harm to one's name by making it common than one gets good through the money one pockets.'
>
> 'Well, there is more truth than elegance of expression in that remark: it needs not have to do with companies unless you like.'
>
> 'Now if it has anything to do with politics, I am your man.'
>
> 'You would make a great *coup* in politics with it; it is especially adapted for politics, and has never been tried.'
>
> 'You don't say so,' said Broadhem, delighted; "don't go on making one guess as if it was a game. Has it anything to do with the suffrage?'
>
> 'It has to do with everything,' I said; 'I don't think I can do it myself; I made a lamentable failure just now by way of a start,' and I paused suddenly. 'Who am I,' I thought, 'that I should venture to preach? what act have I done in life which should give weight to my words?' but the fervour was on me, and I could no more check the burning thoughts than the trumpet can control the sound it emits.

> 'Well,' he said, impatiently.
>
> 'LIVE THE LIFE.'
>
> 'I don't understand you,' said Broadhem.
>
> 'If you did,' I said, 'do you suppose I should feel my whole nature yearning as it is? What better proof could I desire that the life has yet to be lived than that you don't understand me? Supposing, now, that you and I actually put into practice what all these friends of your mother profess, and, instead of judging people who go to plays, or play croquet on Sunday or dance, we tried to live the *inner* life ourselves. Supposing, in your case, that your own interest never entered your head in any one thing you undertook; supposing you actually felt that you had nothing in common with the people around you, and belonged neither to the world of publicans and sinners, nor to the world of Scribes and Pharisees, but were working on a different plane, in which self was altogether ignored—that you gave up attempting to steer your own craft any longer, but put the helm into other hands, and could complacently watch her drive straight on to the breakers, and make a deliberate shipwreck of every ambition in life—don't you think you would create rather a sensation in the political world? Supposing you could arrive at the point of being as indifferent to the approval as to the censure of your fellow-men, of caring as little for the highest honours which are in their power to bestow now, as for the fame which posterity might award to you hereafter; supposing that wealth and power appeared equally contemptible to you for their own sakes, and that you had no desire connected with this earth except to be used while upon it for divine ends, and that all the while that this motive was actuating you, you were striving and working and toiling in the midst of this busy world, doing exactly what every man round you was doing, but doing it all from a different motive, —it would be curious to see where you would land—how you would be abused and misunderstood, and what a perplexity you would create in the mind of your friends, who would never know whether you were a profound intriguer or a shallow fool. How much you would have to suffer, but what a balance there would be to the credit side! For instance, as you could never be disappointed, you would be the only free man among slaves. There is not a man or woman of the present day who is not in chains, either to the religious world or the other, or to family or friends, and always to self. Now, if we could get rid of the bonds of self first, we could snap the other fetters like packthread . . . . Tell me, Broadhem, what you think of my idea?'
>
> 'It is not altogether new to me, though I did not exactly understand what you meant at first,' said Broadhem, who spoke with more feeling than I gave him credit for possessing. 'I never heard it put in such strong language before, but I have seen Ursula practise it, and I was wondering all the time you were talking whether you did.'
>
> 'I never have yet,' I said. 'I began by telling you

that the idea only occurred to me lately in its new form. I had often thought of it as a speculation. I began by assuming that purely disinterested honesty might pay, because an original idea well applied generally succeeds; but when I came to work the thing out, I found that there was a practical difficulty in the way, and that you could not be unselfish from a selfish motive a bit more than you could look like a sane man while you were really still an idiot. And so the fact is, I have talked the notion out to you as it has been suggested to me, though Drippings nearly drove it out of my head. I think the reason I felt impelled to do so was, that had it not been for your sister I should never have thought upon such subjects as I do now. I know her love for you, and the value of her influence over you. Even now she is devoting herself to guarding your interests in the most important step of a man's life, and I seem instinctively to feel how I can best please her. Don't you think she agrees in what I have said to-night and would approve of the conversation we have had?'

'Yes,' said Broadhem. 'Do you know you are quite a different sort of fellow from what I imagined? I always thought that you did not believe in anything.'

'That was because I lived exactly like my neighbours, without adding to my daily life the sin of professing belief in a religion to which it was diametrically opposed.'

It is perhaps hard for the contented denizen of ordinary life, the man who is not consciously engaged in any selfish struggle for wealth or power or social advancement, but is living peacefully and doing his best in the midst of a world which he has neither leisure nor inclination to examine too closely, to enter entirely into this. But yet there is no thoughtful reader who will not perceive the intense and serious meaning in it, and its truth. When we are driven to consider the question, What Christianity has done for us? we are prone to fall back upon the fact that it has insensibly ameliorated all the works and ways of the world—has invented, so to speak, the quality of mercy, and brightened the perceptions of justice—has made the general mass less cruel, the laws less hard, the treatment of man by man less brutal and unbrotherly. When we are driven very close indeed, we fall back upon the profound impurity, the matter-of-fact and callous ferociousness of the most polished and splendid societies of old, to prove to ourselves that all the countless labours and sacrifices which have been made to enforce upon us the divine rule of the Gospel have not been in vain; but yet, when we have put the best face upon it, and given ourselves credit for every possible amendment, there remains this extraordinary fact against us, that the man who literally follows the first canons of Christianity would in any Christian society be considered simply a madman. What! "If he take thy coat, give him thy cloak also," and not call a policeman and give him into custody instead? "If he smite thee on one cheek, turn the other," instead of knocking him down for that insult? So strange is it, that even when we recognise and acknowledge that grand law of self-forgetting, which is the primary rule of Christianity, the mind stumbles at these details, which are specially noted by the divine Maker of the law. The flesh is too weak to receive doctrines so hard and unintelligible. Would not such a course of proceeding lead to an utter rule of anarchy, a triumph of strength over weakness, and the wicked over the good? we ask each other. Is it not impossible, simply out of the question, a precept to be translated spiritually as referring to the moods of the mind, not the possibilities of external conduct?

We discuss this question with endless perplexity, or we quietly ignore it as a thing impracticable, while all the time it stands upon the table of our law, unrepealed and unrepealable, acknowledged in word, never obeyed in fact. And when we go from detail to principle, and consider the rule which is meant to be expressed by such actions, what is it? A lifelong giving up of self, a relegation of all its interests to a secondary place, a life for others, full of brotherly duty and responsibility—not aid and pity merely, but a taking upon ourselves of the burdens of others. This—can it be possible? —is the theory of our present existence. We say it is the rule of our life; and yet let but one of us be placed in a position which makes such abnegation necessary, and the few applauses which indiscreet persons give to his conduct as something exceptionally noble and generous, are lost in the storm of comments on his folly, his weakness, nay, his guilt and failure of duty to himself. Throughout all the textbooks and laws of the Christian life we do not remember to have heard anything of this duty to one's self. It is a duty which never seems to have occured to the mind of the Founder of Christianity, or to His apostles. "He saved others, Himself He cannot save," is the all-expressive comment, said in ignorance, yet summing up the whole matter, of the first spectators of the divine sacrifice—a commentary of which we are able to see the full force and significance. He of whom these words were said is professedly our grand model and example in all the exigencies of life; yet by way of support in the path which we profess to travel after Him, there has been invented that other doctrine of duty to one's self. Duty to one's self involves a great many things unknown to Christianity. It stays our steps in the other dangerous way, and insinuates a serviceable doubt in almost every emergency. Give when you can, be sympathetic when you can, but by all you hold dear avoid responsibility, it says to us in terms of affectionate pleading. "Are you your brother's keeper?" This is written on the page of social law, which we have invented for ourselves—a kind of Christian Talmudical appendix to the Gospel; whereas, on the other page, not half so much studied, which is divine, there is written, "Bear ye one another's burdens." "He saved others, Himself He cannot save."

We do not remember in modern literature any other serious figure standing between these two codes, aghast and bewildered, making a vain attempt to reconcile them, except this one in Mr. Oliphant's book. Are they reconcilable? Are God and Mammon at last to be yoked together, and a compromise made between their respective pretensions? It is not a question of speculative interest, but one which, even in our own generation, has been to some a matter of life and death; and it gives the most wonderful additional force to this book and its sentiments when we remember that men have been known, for this cause, to show themselves still greater madmen than was Lord Frank Vanecourt when he sacrificed (like a fool) five thousand a-year to secure the happiness of the woman he loved with his rival. Men have been known to sacrifice themselves, their position, comfort, and even the high ambition of influencing the world, for no better reason than an overwhelming necessity laid upon them to live the life of a Christian—a life which, rightly or wrongly, they have judged to be impossible amid the circumstances surrounding them in ordinary life. The example of those who, at the height of life, all boyish enthusiasms over, could thus resign everything that a mature man holds most dear—not only realities of position, and prospects which exceed the reality, but all the prejudices of education, the pride of culture and experience, the satisfaction which may most legitimately be felt in a worthy vocation—speaks to us with an authority which no theorist ought to command. And such an example will doubtless recur to the mind of many readers while they listen to the lesson contained in the pages of *Piccadilly*—the lesson repeated by many a prophet, but by few so impressively: that Christianity and the world are as far apart as ever they were; that it is impossible to reconcile them; that the only hope of the earth is in the formation of a new society, based on those principles which we have forgotten or ignored. There is so much in the author's reasoning which we can neither contradict nor oppose, that the conclusion he has drawn becomes doubly interesting and important. We may object to his details; we may doubt the existence of such unmitigated self-seeking as that which he finds under the fair outside of Lady Broadhem—under the demonstrative Christianity of Chundango, or the greasy comfort of Mr. Beevy, the butcher's son, transformed into a missionary, who has given up everything for Christ's sake, and yet has been promoted by that sacrifice to a comfortable income, a place in Lady Broadhem's drawing-room, and a horse that cost £65. There are gentle readers who will think Mr. Oliphant is too hard upon the poor missionary—but the matter of fact is one difficult to be confuted. And underneath all these individual instances there remains the certain truth, that Self is, and, according to every theory received by man, *must* be, more or less, the foundation of the universe. Every law on our statute-book, and every one of those more subtle laws which are of universal application, though written in no table, agree in concluding this to be the case. "Boys go to school," says Lady Ursula, "with strict injunctions, if possible, to put self at the top of it. They take the highest honours at the University for the sake of self. . . . Who is there that ever tells them that personal ambition is a sin most hateful in the sight of God, the *first*, and not the last, infirmity of noble minds?" Such a suggestion is utterly foreign to all our ideas. So entirely have we departed from that humility which is certainly held forth as of the highest importance in the Gospel, that personal ambition, except when it absolutely injures others, is considered among us as not a vice, but a virtue.

The aggrandisement of self by and for itself is honest and honourable in the estimation of all classes; and a man's struggles for the aggrandisement and increase of self in the more subtle form of his family, is more than honest—it is worthy the highest praise. To do well for one's self is a rea-

son for men thinking well of us—for the world going well with us. It is, we may safely say, the principle upon which all progressive society is built. That primitive unmoving level on which every son is contented to succeed his father, and daily bread is enough for the necessities of the unambitious mind, is as a blank in the history of social advancement. Wherever it occurs, life is supposed to be stagnant and enterprise dead. But even there, where selfishness is passive, not active, it has not lost its force. There is no class, perhaps, which will fight so fiercely for a handful of money, or which will contest a scrap of land or the last morsel of an inheritance with such deadly determination as a peasant whose position is exactly the same as that occupied by his father before him. Life is a series of struggles which is the best man, not in the sense that might be given to the words, but in the vulgar sense—meaning, which is the strongest, which the richest, which the man whom it is most "safe" to back, who is most sure to push his neighbour out of his way and secure the prize for himself. And this is all done in the direct face of that injunction, "Whosoever would be greatest amongst you, let him be least."

This is the difficulty upon which Mr. Oliphant and men of his way of thinking stop short. The contradiction is one which cannot be glossed over or explained away. In private life, as in public, self-interest is enthroned supreme. "In honour preferring one another," says the Gospel; but in life emulating, striving every hour to surpass one another is the way of the world. If a man tries to oppose this onward current, the results are simply disastrous to himself. If he insists on telling the truth at all times, he is a nuisance to his friends in private life, and a scourge to his party in public, should he possess one. If he insists on acting according to the precepts of the Gospel, he is at once set down as a madman by everybody who is capable of judging. There cannot be any doubt that many a man has sat at a missionary meeting, as Lord Frank did, with as distinct a sense of the falsehood of the whole concern—knowing that the Bishop of the Caribbee Islands was on his promotion; that the Hindoo convert was seeking name and fame in the civilised West; and that Mr. Beevy had gained a great deal more than he had lost by his mission to the heathen—who yet would not, for anything in the world, have ventured to say so, or throw a doubt upon the apostolic magnanimity of all concerned. Except Lord Frank, we know no one who ever did, except the great preacher Irving, who drove the London Missionary Society frantic by preaching to it about missionaries on the apostolic model—men without scrip or shoes or staff; who wanted no organisation to support them, no missionary collections to carry on their work. The great society, which wanted money, and a sermon calculated to draw it plentifully forth, were ready to tear the indiscreet preacher to pieces on that occasion, though they knew as well as the preacher did what were the imperfections of their system; and so it is in public life, secular as well as ecclesiastical. How many big evils have to be passed over because of the power of those who sustain them, about which we keep silent, flying wildly to indemnify ourselves upon the little evils kept up only by little men, who are defenceless, and unable to protect themselves! how many things have to be winked at, put the best face upon, explained away—things for which there are a hundred excuses to be made, and only this one fault to be found, that they are contrary to truth and justice! But if truth and justice are the absolute rule, what then? —if the Gospel is the absolute rule, which forbids self-love, and contemns falsehood as the chief of evils?

When a man has this alternative put to him, he has to come to a decision one way or other. Either he eludes the question, representing to himself that some things, though right, are not expedient, and that ordinary life cannot be regulated by absolute principles; or he faces it boldly, makes up his mind that the teachings of Christianity are esoteric, and have only a spiritual significance, leaving all that is external free to private judgment and the varying necessities of different ages; or, finally, he takes his stand upon the truth, and casts aside everything that interferes with it. Very few are the unhesitating Christians that can make up their mind to this latter course. Most of us compromise. Most of us feel that in fact entire unselfishness is impossible—that we must be ruined and driven from every standing-ground if we do not take a certain heed to our own interests, and join in the universal struggle. Before the time comes when we are able to make up our minds on so difficult a point—before life and its experiences have brought us to see the abounding falsehood and unreality of things about us—we have, the chances are, taken upon us responsibilities and hung ourselves about with dependants who would be ruined, and unwillingly ruined, along with us, did we turn thus uncompromisingly upon the rest of the world, and make our stand against its deceptions and vanities. So we compromise. We say to ourselves: I will be as true as I can—as just as I can. I will think of myself as little as possible. I will endeavour in my struggle upwards to kick no man down; and God, who sees my difficulties, my wife, and my children, will forgive me if my service is defective. Such is the most ordinary way of meeting the difficulty; but there are some who can be content with no such compromise. And what are they to do? To live like Ishmael, turning their hand against every man, and every scheme of man? or to go out of the world, and try once more sadly or enthusiastically, that spasmodic, ever-recurring, pathetic human attempt after a new earth and a new heaven?

An attempt of this description, deeply interesting on account of some of the individuals involved in it, and vaguely indicated in some portions of **Piccadilly,** has lately been made by a personage quite obscure and unknown to the general world, though of unprecedented influence and importance in his own sphere. It is now ten years since Mr. Harris, a preacher, we think, originally of the Swedenborgian community, preached for some time at the humble Mechanics' Institute in Edwards Street, Portman Square, a series of discourses, expressed in florid American eloquence, but full of earnest religious feeling. There are many strange things in these discourses. They were preached at the time when the first outburst of so-called spiritualism was rousing the world into a certain fresh and vivid interest which the subject retains no longer. Mr. Harris treated this question, about which so many people were struggling to come to a conclusion, with the easy familiarity of a knowledge which was almost contempt. He believed in its wonders, not with the tremulous serious be-

Alice le Strange, Oliphant's wife.

lief which most of the bystanders who were at all impressed by its claims gave to it, but rather with the disdainful certainty of one who had gone far beyond such beggarly elements of spiritual knowledge, and to whom the phenomena which excited the ignorant were but trifling beginnings in a well-recognised way. He himself had much greater wonders to tell—wonders not aimless like those of the ordinary spiritualists, but full of the deepest and most serious meaning. He believed in himself as under direct inspiration from on high. He claimed for himself a power like that of Paul and Peter—direct personal communication with God. His references, however, to this high power and inspiration in his early volumes are brief and limited. He gives them rather by the way—rapid intimations of a secret almost too great for any man's breast, than as claiming authority in their right; and the leading characteristic of his first discourses is a profound and fervent piety, to which no compromise with the evils of the world is practicable. He calls his hearers to no half-way house of comfortable Christianity, but to absolute truth, purity, and obedience to God—duties which no miraculous pretensions can discredit, and which, indeed, no new revelation is needed to enforce. There are not even any new doctrines disclosed in these remarkable sermons—nothing but that unusual fervency of religious feelings which naturally marks a man, to whom religion is the one thing in the world worthy the entire devotion of heart and life. He calls upon us for no new belief, demands no new observance; but only with a vehement voice—sometimes, let us acknowledge, painfully and floridly American—adjures us to love and serve God, and strive after a higher life.

Mr. Harris's system, however, develops as he goes on. We have a feeling that it is almost profane on our part, not being able fully to believe or enter into his peculiar faith, yet having the highest respect for his earnest Christianity, and for that attempt to reform the world which he has had the courage and strength of purpose to make, to enter into the secret of that strange mystic life, in the world, yet above it, which this prophet of modern times professes to lead, and which he teaches his disciples to aspire after and hope for. It consists not only in a spiritual union with God, such as all saints and holy persons have striven after, but in some actual physical change, which has the same effect as that touch of Elisha's hand which opened the eyes of his servant, and showed him the angels guarding the prophet. To come down from lofty visions of heaven and high hopes of a purified world, to discuss anything that concerns our bodily organs, seems the most curious downfall and anticlimax: and yet, could we but obtain full evidence on the subject, this bold appeal to sensation and unmistakable physical revolution would be, no doubt, more satisfactory to the weak faith of modern times than any other proof. It is Mr. Harris's theory, as it is also, we believe (speaking in ignorance), the theory of Swedenborg, that the influences of heaven so act upon the man who throws himself fully open to them, that it ceases to be the common air which he breathes, and that instead the breath of God expands his breast, an air of heaven which purifies while it inspires, and which immediately admits him to privileges which are beyond all calculation. His eyes are open, and he sees all the spiritual wonders that are hidden from unenlightened eyes; his understanding is opened, and he knows the mysteries and wonders of heaven and earth: and being thus in direct communication with God, he feels and perceives what his Father would have him to do, with a certainty which takes away from his human obedience all that painful strain of doubt and difficulty which oppresses the darkness of ordinary men. This is the esoteric doctrine, the inner hope of Mr. Harris's community. How far it has been realised by anybody but himself, we are not informed—nor indeed do we know how any proof but a man's assertion could be given of so strange a revolution, a change which is half fleshly, half spiritual, moving both body and soul.

But in Mr. Harris's own case, he believes, and his followers believe, this mysterious change has undoubtedly taken place; and he is thus naturally constituted the head and leader of the little community which he has grouped round him.

We are not able to narrate the steps by which he attracted to him a number of earnest souls, deeply moved by religious feeling of the kind which we have already described . . . —that is, not by conviction of personal sin, according to the old model, or any fear of hell and eternal punishment, so much as by that deep dissatisfaction with the world and its ways, that painful sense of its falsehoods and levities and self-seeking, which is almost a harder burden to bear than any personal weight. Mr. Harris's followers, we may suppose, judging at least from the instance before us—the sentiments of Mr. Oliphant's book, and the characteristics of his mind—were not likely to be very eager about a simple escape for themselves individually from the penalties of ill-doing. No one could speak contemptuously of a motive which no doubt has much, and beneficently, affected the common mind, —that fear of punishment and love of reward which are planted deep in human nature; but still there are many minds more likely to be affected by the hope of getting into harmony with God and the laws of His universe now, than by any future escape from judgment. And such we imagine to have been Mr. Harris's converts. There must have been a time during which the mysterious leader, who was aware of their difficulties without any confession of theirs, came and went through the gathering confusion of their lives in that last attempt to reconcile the world and the new life which some of them, no doubt, were making, as a certain mysterious and nameless leader does in the pages of *Piccadilly,* suddenly appearing to decide an argument or settle a difficulty. We may quote the account of this wonderful anonymous personage, not as a distinct description of Mr. Harris's work among his followers, but yet as without doubt referring to him, and the manner of his influence. The incident occurs at the conclusion of Lord Frank's conversation with Lord Broadhem, quoted above: —

> As I was thus speaking, we turned into Piccadilly, and an arm was passed through mine.
>
> 'Why is it,' asked Broadhem, 'that men are not all conscious of possessing this spiritual agency?'
>
> 'Why is it, ask you?' and the clear solemn voice of my new companion startled Broadhem, who had not seen him join me, so that I felt his arm tremble upon mine. 'Ask rather why sects are fierce and intolerant; why worship is formal and irreverent; why zealots run to fierce frenzies, and react to atheistic chills; why piety is constrained and lifeless, like antique pictures, painted by the old Byzantines upon a golden ground; why Puseyism tries to whip piety to life with scourges, and starve out sin with fasts; why the altar is made a stage where Ritualists delight a gaping crowd, and the pulpit a place where the sleek official drones away the sleepy hour; why religious books are the dullest; why the clergyman is looked upon by the millions as a barrel-organ, whom the sect turns like the wandering Savoyard, unable to evolve a freeborn note. There is but one answer—,' and he stopped abruptly.
>
> 'What is it?' I said, timidly, for I was overwhelmed by the torrent of his eloquence.
>
> 'We have lost our God! that is why men are unconscious of His force within them. It is a terrible thing for a nation to lose its God. History shows that all nations wherein the religious inspiration has gone down beneath formalism, infidelity, a warlike spirit, an enslaving spirit, or a trading spirit, shall burst like so many gilded bubbles, most enlarged and gorgeous at the moment of their close. Think of the old Scripture, "The wicked shall be turned into hell, and all the nations that forget God.'"

'Who is this?' whispered Broadhem. 'I never saw him before.'

'I want to be alone with him,' I replied. 'Good-night, Broadhem. You had better go back now, or you will find your friends gone. Think over what I have said. Once realize the "*mystery* of godliness," and the martyrdom which it must entail will lose its terrors.'

'Let Him sacrifice us if He will,' said he who had before spoken. 'The true man is but a cannon-shot, rejoicing most of all when the Divine Artil-lerist shall send him irresistible and flaming against some foeman of the race risen from Pan-demonium. Man—the true man—is like the Par-thian's arrow kindling into fiery flames as it leaves the bow. Man—the true man—is the Spirit-sword, but the sword-arm is moved by the heart of the Almighty.'

Ah, Piccadilly! hallowed recollections may at-tach to those stones worn by the feet of the busy idiots in this vast asylum, for one sane man has trodden them; and as I listened to the words of wisdom as they dropped from the lips of one so obscure that his name is still unknown in the land, I doubted not who at the moment was the greatest man in Piccadilly.

One other appearance of this stranger occurs at the very end of the book, when the hero, worn out with his unusual exertions and excitements, after his final grand sacrifice and triumph over himself, falls into the lowest depths of exhaustion. "I am conscious," he writes, "of Drippings helping me into a cab, and going with me to Piccadilly, and of one coming in and finding me stretched on my bed, and of his lifting me from it by a single touch, just as Drip-pings was going off in search of a doctor. It was he who had met me that night when I was walking with Broad-hem, but his name I am unable to divulge. 'Stay here, my friend,' he said to Drippings, 'and pack your master's things; there is no need for the doctor. I will take him to America.' And my heart leaped within me, for its predic-tions were verified, and the path lay clear before me." A man possessing this kind of influence over his followers cannot, it is clear, be a common man.

It was only two or three years ago, however, that the final step was taken. Mr. Harris's disciples, under his direction, then decided upon an actual attempt, not indeed to regen-erate society, but to form a new spiritual society, in which God might be served as He had not been for ages. They decided on making their essay in America, not from pref-erence for its institutions, but because America is a coun-try large and liberal of her soil, and where such an experi-ment could be tried more easily than amid the many land-marks of an old and firmly-established society. We do not know how many there were who sacrificed their living and career to this wonderful scheme; but of one, at least, we know, who gave up everything to put himself under the guidance of the prophet, and make one grand effort, at the cost of his life and all its prospects, for the realisation of the Christianity of the Apostles. And it is enough to say that one man has been found who, out of the highest cir-cles of English society, out of all the refinements of civi-lised life, and those wants additional to, yet not less urgent

than, the primitive wants of humanity, which are the growth of extreme civilisation, has gone cheerfully away into the unknown wilds, making of himself a farm-labourer, a teamster, anything or everything that his spiri-tual leader exacted and the new-born community re-quired—and this not even for the sake of an enthusiastic doctrinal belief such as has carried men to stake and scaf-fold before now, but because of the overwhelming desire in him to lead a life accordant with the will of God. Such a proof of devotion claims more than respect. It claims an audience for the principles and theory on which the sacri-fice is made such as no lighter appeal merits; and even where the observer may doubt the expediency of the sacri-fice, or fail to perceive its necessity, is the highest lesson, the sharpest reproof, that can be read to us, who take things so quietly, who accept the evils of the world as inev-itable, and do so little to mend its wicked ways.

We are not in a position to give any detailed account of the little community thus formed, except that it includes the once poor and the once rich, placing all upon a level of equality—that it devotes itself to agricultural and other industries, with the intention of doing all and producing all it needs within itself—that no necessary work of life is considered a mean office in the brotherhood, but the most highly gifted among them is as likely as not to be set to the least elevated occupation. Some sixty or seventy souls (we believe) are thus engaged in an attempt to reproduce the primitive ideal of Christianity in the midst of a world lying in darkness, no one of whom is admitted without some severe test of his or her readiness to relinquish self and live for others—a test always adapted to the individu-al mind of the novice, and usually striking at the very roots of personal feeling, requiring the sacrifice of the dearest and most cherished habits and sentiments of the heart.

The sacrifice thus demanded on the very threshold of the new life is often so hard that the struggle of the neophyte to conquer himself and give the needful obedience is a struggle of life and death. All personal ambition, all repu-tation outside the bounds of this little society, is relin-quished—property is relinquished, and, what is more, pri-vate judgment would seem to be in great part given up, and the law of the community to be obedience to its head. But no doctrinal test is in existence—no man seems called upon to believe except according to his own conviction, nor is in any way forced or even persuaded into this or that interpretation of truth. It is life, not doctrine, that is the object of the brotherhood. Their aim is to recommence, as it were—to put aside all old types, and begin again with the original idea of Christian society, giving to each other mutual help, sympathy, and comfort—possessing mutual interests and property—enjoying everything, if not abso-lutely in common, yet in share and allotment according to their necessities, not according to their condition or abili-ties for gain, or any artificial rule. So far as this goes it has been a favourite dream of social philosophers for many a day to bring such a brotherhood into being. Something like its simply secular side is to be found without difficulty in many dreams of reformed society well known to man; and nothing can be more familiar to us than the idea of its religious side taken by itself, an idea which has been the origin of all monastic institutions. It is the junction of the two which gives its peculiarity to Mr. Harris's brotherhood. It is as much under his control as head as any conventual order, and yet it is free as only a company of citizens in a land of absolute equality can be. It is founded on the highest spiritual ideal, holding the most solemn of all mystic beliefs as its very centre and seat of power, and yet its object is practical, and it sets up no standard of faith. There is a power in this combination which is very great; but we can scarcely hope (even were it desirable) that it is sufficient to counterbalance the many weaknesses involved in such a scheme, its dependence upon one absolute leader, and upon a personal inspiration which can scarcely be otherwise than fluctuating and uncertain. It seems cruel at so early a stage of its existence to read the lesson of decadence which is written on all human attempts at an ideal existence. Time will show, and time alone.

There is, however, something more wonderful in the conception of this society than in that of any monastic order. It has no rule to guide it, no everlasting vow to bind. Its members live in conflict with all the difficulties of primitive nature, but with the hearts of mystics, seeking the most mysterious and intimate of relations with a God whom they hope to see, and in the mean time giving an obedience without doubt or hesitation, absolute in kind and in degree, to the one among them who already possesses the gift they seek. They have the further distinction from a monastic establishment that there are families in the community, husbands and wives, parents and children. Women, it is said, are more prone to obey religious authority than men; but certainly a married couple, the two who are one, are more difficult to bring into subordination than any individual of either sex can be; and yet this double being also exists, and submits itself, even to the extent of partially parting with its children, and permitting a certain amount of interference with its conjugal life in this strange community. Religious rule has certainly never gone further; and the impartial spectator, however sympathetic or respectful, cannot but feel that in this personal rule there lies the great danger for every community. The founder of this new brotherhood, like Benedict and Francis, is mortal, and must die; and who can guard the visionary walls and keep the ideal city from that old, old patient world, which has in its persistent and steady economy something that outlives all enthusiasms? But of this it is not our part to speak. Should it only last for a year—for a day—it is still an endeavour to deny and abjure the law of Self, and to claim for Christianity a vital force and purity, a real sway and power, such as would almost seem to have dropped from the thoughts of its most earnest disciples in these days when expediency and compromise rule supreme.

It may be asked, however, and asked anxiously, by people who share—and who does not share? —that primary dissatisfaction and discontent with the state of the world and society which is the beginning of all attempts at reformation, whether it is proved impossible to live a Christian life without making this tremendous sacrifice, or if the world is to be finally deserted and left to its fate? Even Mr. Oliphant, however, does not assert this. He leaves his Lord Grandon, his Lady Ursula, in that society which is not too much for them, which does not confuse and madden their

minds, but which they are able to influence, and may guide back to better things. He does not in the least hesitate to acknowledge the greater power of self-command, the graver and more steadfast character which can keep its garments unspotted from the world in the very high places, where the throng and commotion are at their height. He does not, indeed, make any individual appeal, or set one path of duty or another absolutely before his readers. What he does is with a cry which is as the cry of a prophet, to bid them stop short and realise the maze of confused motives, foolish occupations, vain ambitions, which we call life. This poor pursuit of one miserable object or another, perhaps to gain an invitation to Lady So-and-so's party, perhaps to induce Lady So-and-so to come to yours, to push yourself into notice one way or other, to gain a little money, to get a seat in Parliament—is it worth God's while to have made you for this? is it worth your own while to have struggled through childhood, got yourself educated, taken and given so much trouble, all for this? Or is there something better to be made of you, after all? Is it worth while protesting that you believe this or believe that, pretending to make sacrifices while you are but pleasing or advancing yourself, saying aloud certain formulas of religion as if there was no meaning in them? whereas there are worlds of meaning in them; they are trembling and burning with significance, not dead, but a hundred times more alive than you are in your petty, foolish trifling. This is the burden of as serious a message as ever was delivered to man.

The Athenaeum   (essay date 1883)

SOURCE: A review of *Altiora Peto*, in *The Athenaeum*, Vol. 2, No. 2913, August 25, 1883, pp. 231-32.

[*In the following review, the critic examines the characters in* Altiora Peto *and comments on the work as social satire.*]

In *Altiora Peto*, as in *Piccadilly*, Mr. Oliphant presents himself to the novel-reading world as one made up of equal parts of theosophist and social cynic, mystic and man of the world, the student of earthly character and manners and the student of divine mysteries. He has an abundance of wit, great knowledge of men and women and society, and as much of the satirical habit—the tendency to attack with laughter, and to make unpleasant or improper things ridiculous—as any one since Lord Beaconsfield. And to these qualities he adds an interest in the spiritual, and a conviction as to its adaptability to purposes of fiction, only to be paralleled in the work of professional preachers like Dr. George MacDonald. To the unregenerate eye, in fact, he presents a set of contradictions, a confusion of contrasts, at once amusing and respectable. He appears as a kind of latter-day apostle, with a Patmos of his own somewhere in Pall Mall and a peculiar wilderness in the very shadow of Decimus Burton's arch. In one chapter the reader recognizes him for the founder and editor of the most elegant and scholarly of satirical prints; in another, for the evangelist of a new (a West-end) Messiah. He reminds you of Blougram and of Gigadibs in turn. Like the bishop he is an adept in Balzac, "the new edition, fifty volumes long"; and like the literary man he has long since

tested his first plough
And studied his last chapter of St. John.

We prefer him as the bishop, so to speak; for, as it seems to us, he is apt as Gigadibs to be a trifle vague and transcendental. He discourses of society with an ease, a grace, and an authority which are really admirable. In "expounding of mysteries," in treating of psychical revolutions and spiritual ambitions and successes, he is far less successful. In the one part of his work he is found to know exactly what to say and exactly how to say it. In the other it is clear that, if his convictions are complete, he has not yet discovered how completely to express them; that though he may well have made up his mind as to what he may with propriety declare, he is a little uneasy as to the terms and the effects of his declaration. They will know what we mean who have read the brilliant and delightful book it has pleased Mr. Oliphant to christen, not "Stella and Mattie," as he might and ought, but *Altiora Peto.* Nothing can be wittier or more amusing than Altiora unregenerate; while of Altiora regenerate and complete, of Altiora with a mission and a husband contrived *ad hoc,* the less that is said the better.

Altiora is introduced to the reader as the posthumous child of a certain Mr. Peto by a lady now married to her third husband, and as the stepdaughter of one Grandesella, an Italian baron, a financier of doubtful antecedents and a reputation not at all above suspicion. Mr. Peto, as she informs her diary, "was a profound but eccentric philosopher, with a quaint vein of humour, of which, indeed, I am the victim; for his dying request to mamma was, that if I was a girl I should be called Altiora—thus making me the subject of a gentle pun, that will stick to me till I die or marry." About her father she has, she says, "a great many odd feelings," one of which is that, in consequence of his having died ere she was born, he "has been able to exercise an occult influence over me from the first moment of my existence, which would not have been possible had he remained in the flesh"; that, in fact, she is "pervaded by his essence, and that, both morally and intellectually, his spiritual nature in some subtle manner is constantly operative" within her. This is the reason, she thinks, why she has "so little sympathy with other girls." From these she differs enormously:

> In the first place, life does not seem to present them with any problems; they believe everything they are told, take everything as it comes, see no contradictions anywhere, and do not seem haunted by the standing obligation which has been laid upon me to "seek higher things." They grovel; —I don't wish to seem uncharitable—but they really do, and are content. To me life is a perpetual enigma, to which no theological system offers a satisfactory solution—against the reefs of which all philosophies break into foam and empty bubbles.

The girl who can write thus at nineteen, and who at ten "could have hopelessly puzzled either the Archbishop of Canterbury or Mr. Herbert Spencer," has, it must be owned, about as little in common with the young women of Thackeray as with the young women of Mr. Henry James. Reflective, serious, passionate even, with a habit of self-searching and self-analysis, crowned with a name full of mystical promise and suggestiveness, and with nothing wanting save experience and a theory of the universe, you feel as you read that she is bound for those altitudes of spiritual destiny where none but the author of *Piccadilly* or the poet of Paul Faber can move and live. That, however, by no means prevents her from being, to begin with, at once delightful and amusing. Mr. Oliphant, with a touch of satire that is both just and humane, has started by making her (as she fancies) in love, and in love with Ronald MacAlpine, the most trumpery male creature in his collection. When we first become acquainted with her she is making up her mind to go and meet MacAlpine on the beach, pretending to herself that she does not want to go, and analyzing the pretence with the pitiless clarity of a Spinoza in petticoats. On her return she confesses to a love scene, and to a great deal besides. This, for instance, is how she is moved to think and feel concerning her sweetheart's personal appearance: —

> He is tall, dark, and in his Highland dress looks the *beau-ideal* of a Scottish chief. I am afraid, even if he had not been so very clever and agreeable as he is, I should still have liked him on account of his *tout ensemble.* Why this mysterious sentiment, which I am now experiencing for the first time, should depend so much upon the accident of external appearance, is another puzzle. Can it be possible that so deep a passion can really have any connexion with clothes and colour, or that I should have felt differently towards him in trousers?

And these are the terms in which she records the effects of his declaration: —

> He gently but firmly took my hand and pressed it to his lips. Of course I should have liked to let him keep it, so I snatched it away, and suddenly began to tremble very violently. This shows how utterly incapable the will is under certain circumstances to control the organism. The hatred and contempt I felt for my own body at that moment was indescribable. Why should it possess a power of humiliating me at a time when all my feminine instincts, which, I suppose, are my noblest, made me wish to disguise my real feelings towards him? On the other hand, what was there humiliating in allowing him to perceive that I returned his affection? If I was angry with my body for humiliating me, I felt equally angry with my soul, or whatever the other part of me is, for feeling humiliated. I got so absorbed in this physiological dilemma, that for a moment I forgot all about him, and putting down my paint-brush—it was my left hand he had kissed—I clasped them both together and gazed vacantly out to sea.

From this pass of emotional bewilderment she goes on to feeling very happy, to enjoying herself as one in a group after a famous Millais, and in the end to experiencing

> a sense of mortification in the reflection that my conduct had not been by any means so strikingly original as I should have predicted it would have been whenever an event of so much importance should occur to me.

Her mother—"a stout, round, brisk little woman, very practical and matter of fact, with a *nez retroussé,* light hair, grey eyes, and a temper to match"—will not hear of the business. Altiora, of course, is deeply wounded; but next day MacAlpine, after listening to a statement of his mistress's views in matters spiritual, cuts his own throat by observing, with a pleased smile, that he and she are both agnostics. "He had no sooner made this remark," says Altiora, "than I felt that all was at an end between us." She refrains, it is true, from unpocketing her notes for an essay she is writing "On the Anomalies of Civilized Existence as Tested by Intuitive Aspirations in Ideal Life." But she proceeds to argue the point with him; the discussion is interrupted by the approach of her stepfather Grandesella with an order to pack up and start for Paris that very night; and the upshot is that she concludes this first instalment of her diary in such terms as these: —

> So ends the history of my first delusion. I wonder whether the experience of my life is to be that it is made up of them—whether the satisfaction which most people seem to derive from existence, arises from the fact that they live on the surface, and don't dig deep enough to find that it is made up of illusions. That the financial operations of the Baron and Mr. Murkle are, has long become clear to me; that the social ambitions of my mother are, is no less evident. All the three individuals with whom my life is most closely associated are pursuing shadows, and they persist in dragging me with them. Next year I am to be launched upon the society of London, and no pains are to be spared to make me a success—in other words, to make me another illusion; that is what it comes to. The only things that seem to me real are poverty, sickness—suffering of all sorts. I am strongly inclined to think that if you go deep enough, everything else is sham. But perhaps that is only because I am young, and my experience of life so far has had a tendency to make me morbid. There must surely be another side to the medal; and on that hypothesis, I solemnly dedicate my life to its discovery.

All this—and all we have left unquoted—is excellent comedy. What follows is as good, or even better. In his next chapter Mr. Oliphant introduces the two most natural and complete of all his world of characters—the Californian heiress Stella Walton and her bosom friend Mattie Terrill. They have come to Europe to open their minds; and as they are both resolved to see things as they are, they have changed names and reputations, so that Mattie, who has a great deal of beauty and no money, passes for the distinguished heiress Stella Walton, while Stella, who has heaps of money and not much beauty, becomes the heiress's poor cousin Mattie Terrill. They are quite fearless and rather impudent; they have an abundance of good sense, good wit, good feeling, and good intentions; they are "bossed" by a wonderful American old maid, a certain Aunt Hannah; they are frank, honest, spontaneous, natural, and wholly delightful; with the bloodless, passionless, exquisite young nonentities who provide the modern American novelist with materials for the exercise of his genius they present a contrast as pleasant and complete as can well be

imagined. They become Mr. Oliphant's heroines the moment they enter the story. Aunt Hannah aiding, they take possession of Altiora; they traverse the iniquitous designs of the Baron and his partner Murkle; they rescue the hero, Lord Sark, from the clutches of the fascinating Clymer, first of all, and afterwards from the ruin he has wrought himself by injudicious proceedings in the City; they astonish the *élite* of society as the Duchess of Beaucourt's guests; they marry Altiora to Keith Hetherington, the author's pethero—mystic, scholar, traveller, gentleman—one of the vaguest and least entertaining personages in good modern fiction; they secure delightful husbands for themselves. They write the most amusing letters, talk the brightest talk, do the most daring things, and bewitch the reader almost as completely in black and white as they might in the flesh. There is nothing for it when they are to the front but to laugh and admire and be happy. They are, indeed, as human and as irresistible as Keith Hetherington is unattractive and remote. More than that for them, as they who read the story will see, it would not be easy to say.

It is impossible within the limits at our disposal to analyze, however briefly, the intrigue—as of Balzac touched with George MacDonald, *La Maison Nucingen* flavoured with *Robert Falconer* and the *Marquis of Lossie*—of which these charming creatures are the centre, or to do more than refer in passing to a few among the crowd of characters in which they are the bright particular stars. Of Altiora herself we have already noted that she falls at once into the background of the story, and that, moreover, she grows less and less interesting as she advances towards that spiritual perfection which her author wills to depict—and cannot. Inseparable from Altiora is Aunt Hannah: rough and racy of speech; abounding in good sense and the sweetest humanity; touched with peculiar mysticism; gifted with peculiar powers; a grotesque for some hundreds of pages of uncommon merit, in conception and in execution alike, but developing at the last—such is the wickedness of novelists, even good ones—into an abnormal species of Monte Cristo, a Monte Cristo disguised in spinsterhood and a strong New England brogue. Another heroic personage is Lord Sark's enchantress, "that horrid Mrs. Clymer": a mysterious American, with all the graces except the grace of chastity, all the talents except a talent for honesty, all the qualities that make a woman fashionable, and none of those that make a woman good; alert, resolute, and unscrupulous—one of the boldest and completest sketches in modern fiction. Then, with his "peculiar dark predatory look," there is Grandesella's partner Murkle, of whom Altiora remarks to her journal that "if ever there was a man whom one word could describe, 'Murkle' is the man and 'pounce' is the word"; there is Grandesella himself, who, says Miss Peto, "always made the impression upon me of a turkey gobbler in a perpetual state of strut"; there is Lord Sark, the most engaging and human of recent heroes; there is Lord Sark's friend Bob Alderney, delighted to have but a pound a day, and translating "the 'Yacna' and 'Vispered,' and all the other writings on Mazdeism"; there is MacAlpine, poet and musician, art critic and agnostic, a type of the harmless necessary humbug of society. Mixed up with these are gay old dukes and delightful old duchesses, stockbrokers, agitators, artists in explosives, doctors, fashionable beauties, dandies, "tame cats," curates, queens of finance, speculators, Russian princesses—a mob of individualities recruited from all the corners of society, not one of them but with something to recommend him to our notice and to fix our attention if but for an instant; not one but with the capacity to bear his part to admiration in the general mellay, and to completely justify his author in electing to create and use him. How fresh and lifelike they appear, and how brilliantly and strikingly they fare, we hardly need to say. From Mr. Oliphant as a writer of apostolical romance it is possible, as we have shown, to differ pretty vigorously. With Mr. Oliphant as an artist in dialogue, as a social satirist, as a painter of men and manners, it is impossible to do other than agree. There is his real strength, there is his true success. There are dull passages in **Altiora Peto;** there are touches of extravagance, traces of hurry, hints of confusion, glimpses of failure, to boot. But for all that the book is one that everybody will greedily read and greatly admire. It is, to begin with, the outcome of a mind of singular originality and independence; and of such qualities as wit and humour, as good breeding and good temper, as knowledge of the world and command of character, as elegance of style and clarity and expressiveness of diction, it contains enough to equip a score of ordinary novelists for the production of a score of extraordinary novels.

The Spectator (essay date 1883)

SOURCE: A review of *Altiora Peto,* in *The Spectator,* Vol. 56, No. 2881, September 15, 1883, pp. 1190-91.

[*In the following review, the anonymous critic praises* Altiora Peto *as a "brilliant picture of life and manners."*]

A writer in the last number of the *Quarterly Review* expresses tart dissatisfaction with the present state of criticism in England. It has fallen, he asserts, for the most part, into the hands of novices and pen-weary hacks, and they manage things much better in France. They manage things very differently in France, for literary criticism is practised there under conditions which differ *toto coelo* from those which obtain in England. Nine-tenths of the books which are reviewed in England are marked by mediocrity which would ensure exemption from criticism of any kind in France. Now, of all books, the hardest to review at all well, are the books which bring the critic's work, willy-nilly, to the level of the works of the Angel of the Church of Laodicea. It is small blame to him, therefore, if he sometimes, in the bitterness of his heart, treats mediocrity too severely, or, as is far more frequently the case, if he treats it in a spirit of indolent charity. On the whole, however, with the exception of an occasional example of flagrant partiality, which for the rest is generally rectified by counter-criticisms, English critics do their work well, and any author who can produce books at all above the level of respectable mediocrity may safely reckon on an appreciative reception from the class who are popularly supposed to be the natural foes of all authors. They are not so, of course, nor are they by any means such fools as they are supposed to be by those who never read their criticisms. Lord Beaconsfield's famous plagiarism is often in the mouths of men who would be surprised to learn that if nothing were taken from Lord Beaconsfield's novels except what would fall strictly under the definition of criticism, the residue would be "duller than a great thaw," and "a joy of wild asses" for ever. But enough of this. *Altiora Peto* rises far above the level of mediocrity, and may be characterised as a novel of a thousand, if only for the fact that it may be read through consecutively twice, or even thrice, with augmented pleasure to the reader from every fresh perusal. Not all of it, indeed, for there is a rift, so to speak, in Mr. Oliphant's lute, and that rift is by no means a little one. We shall have a word to say about it by-and-by, but not before we have marked to the best of our ability some of the strokes in this most entertaining book which deserve to be applauded to the echo. An outline of the story is necessary, for the reader to understand the extracts which it will be his pleasure to read, as it will be ours to make them, but that outline may well be of the briefest. Mr. Oliphant is probably as indifferent to what is called a plot as Tourgénief was, and it is not as a story that *Altiora Peto* challenges warm admiration, but as a brilliant picture of life and manners. Two clever and high-spirited American girls from the slopes of the Pacific—in other words, from California—descend upon Paris in search of husbands, for it comes to that. One of these girls, Stella Walton, is heiress to millions of dollars; her friend, Mattie Terrill, has an income of £150 per annum. They have changed names, and the reader has to remember throughout the book that Stella Walton is Mattie Terrill, and *vice versâ.*

With excellent judgment, Mr. Oliphant fits the real heiress at once and *sans façon* with an eligible partner, one Bob Alderny. Impediments, which the reader may discover for himself, for a time delay the marriage of the non-heiress with the man of her choice, Lord Sark. These high-spirited and thoroughly loveable girls, and their elderly companion, Miss Hannah Coffin, are the salt of the book. The last-named is an "original," and in her knack of saying at any given time the precise thing that is most likely to disconcert an adversary she resembles Sam Weller, resembles him also in promptness of action. But Hannah has gifts and graces that Mr. Pickwick's famous body-servant was far, indeed, from having. She has an intuitive perception of what is going on in the hearts and heads of every one with whom she comes in contact, and, to judge from some of her references to her own and other folk's "innards," it might seem that she reads character as somnambulists are thought by some to see, through the organ which Menenius endows with speech in *Coriolanus.* She also, as it happens "knows all the ropes," as she would say, and baffles with ease the machinations of all the naughty people who cross her path. In fact her knowledge and energy are so great that she seems to move about amongst these naughty ones like Teiresias in Hades. . . .

A highly improbable character, then? Well, in some respects, yes. But what exceptionally amusing and useful character in any novel that was ever written is not open to the same charge? One thing is certain, whenever "old Hannah" acts or speaks, it is to do or say something which will delight the reader; and he will not fail to agree with a remark passed upon her by a certain Sir George Dashington, who is electrified by her smart talk, —"that old woman is perfectly delicious!" The professional beauty, and the financiers, the æsthete, and the ladies of quality, and the rest of Mr. Oliphant's *dramatis personae* we must leave unintroduced to the reader. They are all drawn with light, firm touches, which mark the hand of a master; but what of Altiora Peto herself? What of the heroine who gives her name to this capital tale? Alas! there yawns the rift we mentioned. Altiora Peto is a bore, and would be a bore of the first magnitude, were it not that the portentious prig who marries her is a bigger bore still. We shall reserve what we have to say of these meet companions to the end of this notice, and quote as a specimen of Mr. Oliphant's genius, for so it deserves to be called, the beginning of a dialogue, which if we are not mistaken beats Lord Beaconsfield at his smartest. It takes place at a dinner-party at the above-mentioned Sir George Dashington's: —

'I didn't rightly catch your name,' said Hannah, 'but I suppose you're the minister.' —'My name is Chalfont—Sidney Chalfont; and as you rightly observe, I am in holy orders.' —'Holy orders is mighty difficult to obey; don't you find 'em?' she remarked, rising and taking his arm. —'The present state of the law in this country renders it impossible, very often,' replied Mr. Chalfont, who had long made up his mind on the first convenient opportunity to become an ecclesiastical martyr. —'Do tell!' exclaimed Hannah. —'I beg your pardon, Miss Coffin.' —'Oh, I ain't noways offended, but it does beat all!' —'What beats all?' —'Well, I don't know as I understood you, but you seemed to say that you couldn't keep the laws of God because of the laws of man—and you a minister, too; and I say that beats all—and what's more, I stick to it!' —'Dear me,' thought the Reverend Sidney Chalfont, 'this American is a very plain-spoken woman.' 'My dear madam, I don't wonder that you are astonished. I am well aware that the Anglican priesthood of America are not subject to the same tyranny that we are in this country.' —'Then, why do you stand it?' —'We don't stand it; we go to prison for it.' —'Seems to me, if they put you in prison for it, as it is them as won't stand it. Did you know before you became a minister, that you would either have to obey the laws of man, or else go to prison for not obeying 'em?' —'That consideration was not sufficient to deter me from following a vocation to which I felt internally called, and from being a witness for the truth, and a martyr for conscience' sake.' —'And you feel sure that them laws you won't obey was made to uphold truth, and you was made to uphold the truth?' —'I can only act according to my conscience, and what I believe to be truth.' —'And them as puts you into prison acts the same, may be?' —'I give them credit for being sincere.' —'Well, now,' pursued the old lady, 'I've been in search of the highest truth since I was a gell; that's a matter of half a century; always on the search. How old might you ha' bin when you determined to obey the holy orders?' —'About two-and-twenty,' said Chalfont. —'And you was so sure that you'd got the truth, that you decided to go where you could break the laws of a country as calls itself Christian, to testify to it?' —'Well, I don't think that's alto-

gether a fair way of putting it,' said Chalfont, laughing; 'but the subject is a large one, and involves the whole question of the government of the Church by the Church, instead of by the State. May I ask what was the result of your fifty years' search after truth?' —'Well, I guess I'm on the track at last.' —'What! only on it now?' —'It's difficult saying when I first got on; a body can't jest always give dates in them things. I dessay I was on all the time, but if I didn't know it, there was no peace. It's only with the knowledge as peace comes. It's not by readin', nor by study, nor by spekilatin' that you find Divine truth; it's by lovin' what is good, and a doin' of it.' —'I should have said that Divine revelation and the teaching of the Church were the guides to truth,' said Chalfont. —'If one set of people as is guided by 'em puts another set of people as is guided by 'em into prison, because they can't agree which way they pint, seems to me they're mighty onsartin guides.' —'It has been so from all time,' replied Chalfont, mournfully. 'The history of Christendom is a history of religious strife; till man is regenerate, it cannot be otherwise.'

We wish that we had space to quote the rest of this conversation, and more of Mr. Oliphant's good things, and especially the scene in the Louvre, where Hannah drives the professional beauty from pillar to post, till the latter, feeling herself to be too heavily handicapped, affects not to hear the American lady's pitiless questions, "but to be absorbed in admiration of a recumbent Venus of Titian, at which Hannah, following the direction of her eyes, could only gasp 'My sakes!' and then, turning abruptly round, walked off, for once fairly beaten, from the field." All that we can do, however, is to say that three-fourths of Mr. Oliphant's book is as good reading as the most exigent novel-reader needs to ask for. The remaining fourth is filled with the diary and sayings of Altiora Peto, and with the pompous inanities of her lover, Mr. Keith Hetherington. She bores, but he crushes us. "A greater than I said that," he remarks, on one occasion; and as that "greater than I" is He who was "greater than Jonas" and "greater than Solomon," and as Mr. Keith Hetherington is at the most a tenth-rate philosophaster, his remark, for the sublime conceit which it ventilates, may be said to "beat the record." And "beat the record" his plan for renovating society unquestionably does. But dull, priggish, and perplexing as this gentleman's utterances are, we would not have called them pompous inanities, if we could not cite Mr. Hetherington himself as witness to their being so. Brought to book by Mattie Terrill as to the nature and results of the "experiences" of the "hundreds" who are consciously preparing for the "new evolutionary process" which is to save the world, or save the hundreds, for Mr. Hetherington is as ambiguous as Virgil's Sibyl or Dickens's Captain Bunsby, he calmly answers, "I hope you will not think me rude, but I could no more describe to you the experiments or the results, than I could discourse to a New Zealander on the laws of electricity, or attempt to make him understand the nature of their action." Well, be it so; but we marvel much that so wise and witty a man of the world as Mr. Oliphant should expect his readers to shut their eyes and open their months, and gulp down such an answer. It is not fury; but it is sound signifying nothing. Altiora Peto, however, is charmed beyond measure with this puzzle-headed philan-thropist's tinkling cymbals, and the novel closes with a love-scene between the pair which certainly has the merit of novelty. In some such way, perhaps, old Godwin wooed and won Mary Wollstonecraft; and, indeed, "Keithy," as Hannah always calls him, is good, or rather, Godwinish, enough to tell his dear Altiora that it would not be necessary, *except for what the world might say,* that they should marry, since their love was of a kind that the world knows nothing of, and depended on something more internal, and, therefore, more solid than that which unites ordinary mortals. Shelley said that he could never look on Retsch's picture of the summerhouse scene in *Faust* without a feeling akin to vertigo. We warrant that he would have gazed *oculo irretorto* on the kiss which ended the love conference between this strange pair of lovers. "That was beyond the power of Church or priest," said "Keithy," with stately solemnity; and they arise and go to Sark and Stella, to tell them that they will add their ceremony to theirs. The curtain falls, but we lift it for a moment, to express a strong belief that, in the words of Tennyson, "a brace of twins will weed *her* of her folly;" and a faint hope that when those twins are old enough to climb their father's knees, that even he, impracticable blockhead though he be, may learn from nature to concentrate his affections, and not dissipate over all the world the love which was meant for home. Coleridge was right, no doubt, when he said that, —

> He prayeth well who loveth well,
>   Both man, and bird, and beast;

but we must draw the line somewhere; we draw it at vultures, bugs, and—; but the reader may select for himself what particular variety of knave, or fool, or coward it is which, if he says he loves, he knows that he is speaking in a Pickwickian sense, or, not to use too strong a phrase, is romancing in his throat.

The Saturday Review   (essay date 1883)

SOURCE: A review of *Altiora Peto,* in *The Saturday Review,* London, Vol. 56, No. 1456, September 22, 1883, pp. 374-75.

[*In the following article from the* Saturday Review, *the unsigned critic compares* Altiora Peto *with* Piccadilly, *and discusses Oliphant's views on humanism as revealed in the former.*]

This story is one of the most entertaining that we have met with for a long time. It groups together a number of very varied human beings, all of whom are vividly, if lightly, drawn, and abounds in pleasant descriptions and smart sayings. The variety of the characters who are collected in it gives it something of the air of a menagerie; but in few places can one spend an idle hour with more amusement and profit than in a good menagerie. The plot of the story, if an unnatural one to start with, is worked out with a great deal of ingenuity, and the combined interest of the tale and of the actors is such that there is hardly a dull page in the whole book. We make this qualification because there are certain pages in which the characters seem to be most in earnest, and in which they contrive to be ob-scure and tedious without throwing a ray of light on the high topics which they discuss. The contrast between the halting movement of these pages and the assured and easy vigour of the rest of the book cannot fail to strike the reader at first sight. But, with this exception, the story is most readable and interesting throughout, and is one of the few which we could wish to be longer, and the main characters of which we should like to see more fully and minutely described. The outlines are drawn with vigour and clearness; but there is not seldom a want of the more detailed psychological analysis which, in this class of fiction, is needed to make the characters act intelligibly and coherently under the conditions in which the writer places them. It may be said, on the other hand, that the author has attained his end by making the reader ask for more, and this is certainly a result at which very few novel-writers arrive.

The plot of the story is intricate and, considering its improbability, very cleverly managed. It opens with the confessions of the heroine, Altiora Peto, the posthumous child of a gentleman who, with an obvious punning intention, has bequeathed to her a name which is to prove characteristic of her aspiring nature. She is an original, independent girl, with a turn for solving the problems of her life in her own way, and not letting others settle them for her, which keeps the reader interested in her throughout the book. The first of these problems presents itself in the person of an admirer, Mr. Ronald MacAlpine, who preaches agnosticism and æstheticism, and practises idleness and imposture, as well as any of his living counterparts. He is poor, and for this, as well as other reasons, Altiora's family are opposed to the match. However, it is neither the poverty nor the opposition, but the lover's inability on cross-examination to give a satisfactory account of his aims and beliefs, which causes Altiora to reject him. The family consists of the Baron and Baroness Grandesella, the supposed stepfather and stepmother of Altiora, and a certain Mr. Murkle, who is the Baron's partner in the financial operations by which they make their living. We are next introduced to a party of three American women. Two of them are young Californian girls, the plain heiress Mattie Terrill and the poor but beautiful Stella Walton. Lest the former should be made love to in Europe for her fortune and not for herself, the two girls decide to change names, and, to avoid hopeless confusion, we must follow the author's example, and call Stella Mattie, and Mattie Stella, only cautioning the reader to make the needful mental correction whenever he meets with the names. The companion and chaperon of the two girls, Hannah Coffin, is to our mind the best drawn and most interesting character of the book. She is the daughter of a Methodist minister in New England, and an ex-schoolmistress, and is a type of character not easily to be found elsewhere than in New England. She is a woman of great practical sense, of perfect rectitude and integrity, and of strong but undemonstrative religious feeling; but added to this she has a shrewdness and causticity and fearlessness which make her an awkward opponent for those who come into collision with her, blended with a mystic devotion to the welfare of those whom she loves. Stella, the beauty, is a girl gifted with all the coolness and capacity for taking care of herself, which is supposed to be peculiarly characteristic of the Western American woman; Mattie, her companion, is more commonplace. A distant cousinship between Altiora and some of the male actors in the book, and of one of the Californians with others, serves as one means to bring them all together, chance supplying the rest. In Paris Altiora's party, the Californian party, Keith Hetherington (a male counterpart of Altiora in aspiration and high resolve), and Bob Alderney, a good fellow who eventually marries Mattie, fall in with one another. Murkle, who has a secret hold on the Grandesellas, there declares his determination to marry Altiora, whose stepmother destines her for a second cousin, Lord Sark, a nobleman occupied in doubtful speculations in the City and in making love to a pretty married woman, falsely supposed to be a widow, at the West End. This lady, Mrs. Clymer, a serpentine person, plays an important part in the development of the story. She is one of those beautiful dubious, fascinating ladies, with a history and a mystery connected with her, whom a large class of men delight in, and whom nearly all women distrust and dislike, though they may fear to quarrel with her openly. The only difference between her relations with Sark and with other men is that her passion for him grows in time too strong to allow her to do without him or to supplement him by a fresh adorer. His entanglement with her, and the counter-attractions in women of a better sort which at length make his chains hateful to him, form one chief interest of the book. He, too, appears in Paris, and is much struck by Altiora. About the same time Miss Hannah Coffin and Altiora meet, and the former instinctively recognizes in the ardent and inexperienced girl some one on whose life she can have a helpful influence. Lord Sark's heart, however, is made of elastic material, and can find room, along with the new feeling for Altiora and the old and as yet unextinguished feeling for Mrs. Clymer, for a more than friendly liking for Stella Walton. The plot soon gets exceedingly complicated, and becomes a kind of lovers' game of hide-and-seek. As Mrs. Clymer wants to keep Sark in the meshes of her net, and Murkle wishes to marry Altiora, nothing is more natural than that the two should combine to attain their own wicked ends. Murkle, however, is not the man to have only one string to his bow; and the appearance of the lovely and, as he imagines, immensely rich Californian prompts him to make her an offer of marriage. She meets a proposal made up of sentimentality and finance with a business-like answer, and, without intending to accept him, enters on a kind of provisional half-engagement, and agrees to resume the subject when he shall have given a full statement of his affairs, and when she shall have received a satisfactory account of him from Altiora. Her object in returning this answer is to give Altiora a respite from his pursuit, backed as it is by the Grandesellas. Hereupon Murkle proposes in due form to Altiora, and, when refused, tells her that, though he could force her to accept him, he will leave her free, provided she gives him her good word with Stella. At this point Altiora, perplexed by the situation in which she finds herself, and outraged at being forced into connexion with Mrs. Clymer, and asked to enter London society under her chaperonage, resolves, with the advice of Miss Coffin and Hetherington, on sudden flight, and takes refuge in a retired part of England with her new friends the Californians.

The series of intrigues which now takes place cannot here be even indicated. The scene shifts from London to a large country house, and again to the quiet country village where Altiora has taken refuge. She and Hetherington exchange ideas, and find one another to be living in a congenial moral atmosphere. The latter's "Solution of the Problem" is set forth at considerable length, with the result of leaving an observant reader in the dark as to what the problem is, or how it is to be solved, and thus producing that weary sensation which forms a contrast to the lively impressions which we otherwise receive from the book. "Egotism" is the enemy to be conquered, and accordingly "the love of country and love of family are to be set aside, in order for the evolution into new and higher potencies of the love either of God or humanity, or both"; and as a consequence "all the minor egotistical emotions, such as love of rule, love of fame, love of money, love of ease, must be discarded." In direct contradiction to this threadbare humanitarianism, and as an instance of the old maxim that blood is thicker than water, the author represents old Hannah Coffin, who turns out to be the aunt of Altiora, as having been drawn to her from the first by the force of the natural ties of which this young prophet makes light. The ending of the whole matter is that Altiora and Keith Hetherington agree to marry; that the intrigues of Murkle and the Grandesellas are laid bare and frustrated; that the latter have falsely claimed their supposed connexion with Altiora; that Mrs. Clymer is shown to be a married woman, and eliminated from a society in which she has been very mischievous; that Sark is blown up in Ireland by a new dynamitic compound invented by the husband of this interesting lady, but gets well and marries Stella; in short, that the villains are all defeated and that the honest people come by their own.

There is a fertility of ideas and a clearness and force of style in this novel which is not often to be met with in contemporary fiction. The story never flags, and, except when the apostolic vein is struck, the conversation is never dull. There is much in *Altiora Peto* to remind the reader of *Piccadilly.* In both there is the same constant attack—at one time serious and at another cynical—on the vices of society; there is the same point and liveliness of style, and there is on the part of some of the characters the same energetic reaction against the meanness and futility of the life by which they are surrounded. The belief that the conventional standard of right is not only a great deal lower than it ought to be, but that to accept a wholly different one and to live accordingly is both feasible and is a source of untold happiness to those who dare to do so, is the leading thought of both books. Those who can thoroughly agree with this when stated as a general proposition are by no means forced to accept the means suggested for attaining the desired end. We need not hold the author in any way bound by the utterances of the characters whom he creates; but it is obvious that the following quotation from the gospel according to Mr. Keith Hetherington, who is the best man in the book and the one most influenced by motives higher than those of the mass of people, will be of little practical value in the regeneration of mankind. "For instance," he says, "the sentiment called Patriotism, being perhaps the highest to which some can attain, and therefore a good one for them to work from, is an obstacle to the experimenter on the love of humanity; he feels that he must denationalize himself in feeling, if not in fact. He feels that he belongs to no country, but to the universe. So he next becomes conscious that all family ties conflict with the due development of the force he is attempting to evolve. All the men and women in the world become his brothers and sisters. . . . It is the elimination of these egotistical forces from the organism which is so painful." It is by a course of experiments of this nature that Mr. Hetherington would qualify us to serve mankind in our day and generation; but he might as well tell us to eliminate from the organism the desire of food and of sleep. Whether or not it is "egotistical" to care more for those whom you know and are near to, and with whose needs you are practically acquainted, and whom you are able to help, than for persons whom you have never seen or heard of, is a question which Mr. Hetherington does not discuss. But perhaps Mr. Oliphant means of set purpose to represent

---

Margaret Oliphant on *Altiora Peto*:

[*Altiora Peto*] was not published in "the Magazine" [*Blackwell's*], but was brought out independently during the next year in numbers, as the works of George Eliot had been—an experiment only capable of being tried with a very well-known and popular writer. I believe it was altogether the most highly popular and successful of all Laurence Oliphant's works, and excited great interest both among those who enjoyed the satire and those who were moved by the more serious interest. The title of the work and the name of the heroine were taken from his family motto—"Altiora Peto" ("I seek for higher things"), being the distinctive sentiment, among various Oliphant mottoes, of the house of Condie. There was much appropriateness, and some humour, in the adaptation. I fear, however, that the blaze of wit and social satire which gave the tremendous sensation of the plot an air of intentional extravagance, were more thought of by the general reader than the superlative love and high philosophical mission of Altiora and her visionary lover. It was the first time that Laurence had mingled his English and American experiences of the world, and to many persons the conjunction added much to the piquancy of the work. Old Hannah, who is the most original of the characters, may probably bear an ideal resemblance to some of the mothers of the community at Brocton, in her mixture of the quaint rural American woman with the prophetess and seer. So might the woman have spoken who mourned over the sweet face of the bride to whom, the community were so much alarmed to hear, Laurence had pledged himself. "I see great suffering before her whichever way she turns, for with her feeling is life." One can scarcely doubt that he was thinking of some such personage when he placed this angular, tender-hearted, queer-spoken mystic, the illuminated person, yet village seamstress, upon his canvas.

Margaret Oliphant, in her Memoir of the Life of Laurence Oliphant and of Alice Oliphant, His Wife, *1891.*

---

him as a person of high sentiment but weak power of observation and reasoning. However this may be, *Altiora Peto* is a very clever and readable book.

E. Purcell (essay date 1883)

SOURCE: A review of *Altiora Peto,* in *The Academy,* Vol. XXIV, No. 597, October 13, 1883, p. 240.

[*In the following excerpt, Purcell denigrates Oliphant's portrayal of American and European society in* Altiora Peto.]

Piccadilly had just enough of sketchy carelessness and improbability to pass for originality, and to lead many people into thinking that the author could do much greater things if he liked. How far *Altiora Peto* has complicated or dispelled this notion it is impossible to say, though it is said to have been favourably received. We are, therefore, the more bound to confess at once that we have found it entirely dull and uninteresting, both in detail and as a whole.

The book is an attempt to expand the high-class, scientific-philosophical-ducal and nethermost West End-society sketch into a regular novel. This is done by now and then wedging in some fragments of a theatrical plot, which, before it is well developed, feebly takes fire, and expires in a tedious smouldering fashion. The whole thing is of a clumsiness whereat the veteran Ouida will haply smile. Still worse is the side-plot of the young Californian belles, one rich and plain, the other poor and pretty, who on their European campaign change names in order to baffle the affections of the men. After a tiresome round of forgery and personation, and numerous offers of marriage related in detail, it merely ends in their undeceiving their lovers; and nothing more comes of this confusion, which is, indeed, so perplexing that the author is forced to adopt the borrowed names in speaking of the ladies, adding very often such useful reminders as "only of course she was really Stella," or "Stella all the time being really Mattie." This kind of business is more effective in farce than fiction. Both these damsels are supposed to be very remarkable high-toned specimens of the West; they merely impress one as dull chatterers. There is also a New England Aunt Hannah, a curious caricature after the Dickens model— indeed, her portrait in the illustrations reminds one strongly of Mrs. F.' s aunt. She is apparently gifted with prophetic and other supernatural powers, which in due time become useful in bundling the plot together. The final winding-up and liquidation, however, proves a protracted business, being delayed by a not very startling dynamite episode. Trivial and usually wearisome conversation makes up most of the book; much space is also occupied by the ruminations and excursuses of the heroine on faith, morals, love, heredity, and Herbert Spencer. Much of them we were forced to skip. Miss Peto herself is a good creation, but can hardly be said to be even sketched in. As it is, all we can safely say about her is that she had a mamma, who really was not her mamma at all, and that instinct always thwarted her earnest efforts to love her. However, she loves plenty of men, but which she finally marries we forget, for, in order to multiply proposal scenes, seven or eight couples are constantly interchanging their lovers. There is the usual fashionable bit of finance—a Count Fosco Baron, and much talk of bubble companies and amalgamations. Most will prefer to read the City article at first hand.

After searching diligently and anxiously we really cannot find a single thing to praise in this book, unless it be the grammar and spelling, and the big print and thick paper; but all that is a poor compliment. Of course, one feels that Mr. Oliphant is a practised writer, and a man of ability and culture, and that there is nothing to reprobate or make game of in his work. All the same, it is as clear as his print that he has no more idea of what a novel should be than a mummy, and that he never can and never will write a novel worth yawning over. People may say they like it, and so critics may think well to pretend to like it, and a good many honest souls, we dare say, really may like it after their fashion, because they love to pore over the holy page that tells of duchesses and right honourables, and they have heard—probably truly—that the author has the *entrée* of the most exclusive dens, and constantly sees the lions fed. Any news from the lion-house is always welcome; and if, as here, it is of a rambling, vague, and slipshod sort, we take it as it comes, and, for want of a still more inappropriate name, call it "kindly satire." The author is presumably familiar with London society—we are in joyful ignorance thereof, but not without some stray lights upon poor human nature generally. While, therefore, we allow that his personages have a certain resemblance to the gentlemen and ladies one meets in the "best houses" in London, Mandalay, and Squashville, they are dreadfully unlike anybody one is ever likely to meet in or out of doors anywhere under the sun, because they are not mortals, but parts and fragments—a limb or two, and an idea or so, and the rest only talk. Mr. Oliphant may know, but he cannot describe. His London society, as we gather it from his hazy fragments, is a society which cannot be, for it is a house divided against itself. Thus we are asked to believe in the very superior first-class virtue of his young ladies. Yet these virgins and their virtuous mothers are for ever discussing what is to be done for dear Lord Sark, the most eligible *parti* of the season. This ghastly bore is cohabiting with a woman of ill-fame whom the virgins speak of as "the Clymer." Not only are they intimate with Mrs. Clymer, but they, alone, or abetted by their mammas, hold nauseous conferences with his lordship, who sentimentally bemoans himself over the irresistible spells of the syren, and in return for his fashionable confidences is very elegantly compassionated and wept over. We don't believe it. The world is the world all the world over, but we strongly suspect that our betters are after all just a little bit better, and not a thousand times worse, than the rest of us.

The Athenaeum   (essay date 1887)

SOURCE: A review of *Episodes in a Life of Adventure,* in *The Athenaeum,* Vol. 2, No. 3117, July 23, 1887, pp. 107-08.

[*In the following review from* The Athenaeum, *the unsigned critic describes Oliphant's travels in the decade following the Crimean War, which Oliphant chronicles in* Episodes in a Life of Adventure.]

Mr. Oliphant has collected the charming autobiographical

sketches which have recently appeared in *Blackwood* under the title 'Moss from a Rolling Stone,' and published them, with certain additions, as ***Episodes in a Life of Adventure.*** Few men have had such varied experience of life in the Old World and the New; and we know of no other "rolling stone" that possesses at once the faculty of gathering the finest of moss, and the power of describing the specimens collected in bright and attractive language.

The author declares that the period of his life under review appears to him now as "distinctly a most insane period"; but it is difficult to avoid suspecting that Mr. Oliphant looks back with feelings not altogether devoid of pleasure to the striking episodes he describes so well, and that the "insane period" was not without its charms. The chapter headed "Some Sporting Reminiscences" is written in the spirit of the old *shikari* who loves to recall his early exploits, and delights in the memory of his former prowess. The pages of Gordon Cumming or Sir Samuel Baker contain no more striking episodes of sport than those of the death struggle with an elk in a dark pool, deep hidden in the tropical forest of Ceylon, and the ride on the bare back of one of Jung Bahadoor's tame elephants whilst engaged in hunting wild elephants and capturing them alive.

> I shall never forget the uproar and excitement of that singular conflict; the trumpeting of the elephants—the screams of the mahouts—the firing by the soldiers of blank-cartridge—the crashing of the branches as the huge monsters, with their trunks curled up, butted into one another like rams, and their riders deftly threw lassoes of rope over their unwieldy heads, —formed a combination of sounds and of sights calculated

Laurence Oliphant in 1854.

to leave a lasting impression. . . . The mahout of the elephant I was on had particularly distinguished himself in one encounter, and presented me with the splintered tusk of an elephant that had been broken off in a charge upon us, as a trophy.

It is, however, to Mr. Oliphant's experiences in other fields that we turn with most interest, for his erratic life brought him into contact, either as an actor or spectator, with many of the stirring events which marked the decade that followed the outbreak of the Crimean War. At Constantinople Mr. Oliphant joined the brilliant group of men who surrounded the "Great Eltchi" at the time of the war; and thence he accompanied Lord Stratford to the Crimea, where he witnessed the investment of Sir Edmund Lyons and Sir Colin Campbell with the insignia of G.C.B. on the field of battle. He was afterwards sent on a quasi-political mission to the Caucasus, and when this, owing to the course of events, could not be carried out, attached himself to the Turkish army under Omer Pasha. The failure of the Transcaucasian campaign to attain its object—the relief of Kars—is rightly attributed to the action of the French Government and General Pélissier in refusing to allow Omer Pasha and the Turks, who were doing nothing, to leave the Crimea before it was too late: —

> Six weeks before our visit, Omer Pasha had met the generals of the Allied armies in conference, had explained to them the useless inactivity to which he with his whole army, was condemned, and had implored them to let him at once undertake an Asiatic campaign for the relief of Kars; but his arguments had failed to move them—General Pélissier being most emphatic in his objection to it, and General Simpson being a passive tool in the hands of his French colleague. Lord Stratford, however, took a very different view of the situation, and so strongly advocated the measure urged by Omer Pasha, that he had extracted the consent of the British Government to it, qualified, however, by the proviso, 'that the Government of the Emperor will concur in it.' The Emperor only concurred in it subject to the approval of General Pélissier, who flatly refused. . . . Had this force [Omer Pasha's] been allowed to leave the Crimea while we were there, the event proved that they would have been in plenty of time to have saved Kars, which did not capitulate for three months after this.

Many people also will agree with the opinion that if the Transcaucasian provinces had been taken from Russia as a result of the war, the Russian advance towards India, which has given rise to so much anxiety in this country, would never have taken place.

Crimean and Caucasian experiences are followed by adventures in Central America, where Mr. Oliphant narrowly escaped linking his fortunes to those of the "blue-eyed man of destiny," and was sorely tempted by a filibustering priest to join a conspiracy for upsetting the existing government of Honduras and establishing a new one, of which he was to be War Minister. Fortunately the temptation was resisted, for otherwise Lord Elgin would have taken another secretary with him to the East, and that most delightful of books, *Narrative of the Earl of Elgin's Mission to China and Japan,* would never have been published. In the early part of 1860 Mr. Oliphant "rolled" to Italy, where he became acquainted with Garibaldi, and he gives a most interesting account of the proceedings of the liberator during the time previous to his departure for Sicily. The attack on the British Legation in Japan, during which Mr. Oliphant was severely wounded, is well described; and those who take an interest in the systematic manner in which Russia tries to carry out her programme of annexation in the far East will find full details of the circumstances under which, in 1861, "the Russian flag was hoisted and subsequently withdrawn" from the island of Tsusima.

> But all this time we saw nothing of the Russians. We passed from one deep creek into another, over the glassy surface of the water, only to exchange their unbroken solitudes, and to find some new and unexpected channel winding off in some fresh direction. At last, in one of these, our attention was suddenly attracted by some tapering spars that seemed to shoot out of the branches of a tree; and rounding a corner, we came upon the Russian frigate, moored literally, stem and stern, to the branches of a pair of forest giants, and with a plank-way to the shore. If we were startled to come upon her thus unexpectedly, our surprise can have been nothing to that of those on board at seeing an English man-of-war's boat pull into the sort of pirates' cove in which they had stowed themselves away. Indeed, the Russian captain afterwards told me that he had been so long in solitude that he could scarcely believe his eyes when we burst thus suddenly upon them, like visitants from some other world.

The three chapters in which Mr. Oliphant relates his experiences during the Polish insurrection of 1863 will to many readers be the most attractive in the book; for they give a vivid picture of the state of Polish society at the time, and bring clearly before us the sufferings of the people, the barbarous conduct of the Russian soldiers, the heroic devotion of the Polish women, and the sturdy patriotism of the men: —

> The police of the Central Committee was so much more efficient than that of the Russian Government, that sooner or later the doom of a spy was certain. So far, then, as the liberty of discussing openly the situation was concerned, there was no difficulty. Every one was glad to give a stranger the benefit of his patriotic opinions. The Warsaw Society met at each other's houses: triumphed over the news of victories gained by insurgents; mourned over defeats; anathematised Russia in general, and Berg and Wielopolski in particular; canvassed the probabilities of aid from without, and the expediency of the policy to be adopted by the Central Committee. It was strange to be in a room with thirty or forty persons, all of whom were uttering sentiments which would have infallibly consigned them to Siberia if they had been heard by a Russian; and yet so thoroughly confident of each other that no man hesitated to say exactly what he thought.

From Poland, after a visit to the convents of Moldavia, Mr. Oliphant found his way to Denmark, and witnessed the opening scenes of the struggle which was to have such far-reaching political results—to turn Europe into an armed camp, and to usher in the era of the supremacy of physical force.

Many of the episodes, such as those connected with Lord Elgin's residence in Washington in 1854, whilst negotiating the treaty of reciprocity between Canada and the United States, are most amusingly described. Nothing, too, could be better in their way than the stories of the Montenegrin Chancellor of the Exchequer's visit to the treasure chest of the principality in a room that had been given up to Mr. Oliphant at Cettinje; of the interview with the lady who conducted the business of the British Vice-Consulate at Manfredonia in the name of a husband who had deserted her; of the invitation to tea, "old English style," with Miss Thimbleby, who was a sister of the celebrated Mrs. Jordan; and of the circumstances under which the author appeared before the police inspector at Cracow as a British Moslem subject of the Cape of Good Hope and the husband of four wives.

The volume closes with an account of the origin of the little paper the *Owl,* which delighted and mystified London society rather more than twenty years ago; and with what we hope is a promise that some day Mr. Oliphant will take up the thread of his life where he has dropped it, and narrate some of those episodes which have occurred since, and which he thinks will be more thoroughly appreciated by his future than by his present readers. Mr. Oliphant writes with so much literary charm, and there is so much that is fascinating, instructive, and amusing in his early reminiscences, that his readers will all hope that it may not be long before he begins to shed for their delectation some of the moss that he has collected during the last twenty years.

The Critic (essay date 1888)

SOURCE: "Laurence Oliphant and His New Book," in *The Critic,* New York, n. s. Vol. IX, No. 233, June 16, 1888, pp. 289-90.

[*In the following review of* Scientific Religion, *the critic discusses Oliphant's life and his responses to detractors.*]

A new Timon of Athens, if we are to take him at his own estimate, is among us in the person of Mr. Laurence Oliphant. Timon is never very complimentary to his fellow-creatures, nor do they in turn easily forgive the hand that ruthlessly lays bare their frailties and shouts them from the house-tops. Yet Mr. Oliphant has a very warm place in the hearts of many of these same fellow-creatures, and the sharp whip of criticism, which he has sometimes rather mercilessly laid upon their backs, has seldom recoiled upon his own. The reason for this, we suspect, is that Mr. Oliphant is not the hardened cynic he would have us think him; Timon's cloak does not fit him so tightly but that he can throw it to the winds when the humor is on him. Indeed, it is not always slung about his shoulders; like the assassin in the old play, he wears it only when he has some ugly work to do. To catch him at some odd moment *en*

déshabillé, and listen for an hour to his easy conversation, is really a treat to be long remembered. Such an hour a member of *The Critic*'s staff enjoyed with him last week.

Mr. Oliphant's only ostensible reason for his present visit to the United States—it is his eleventh, we think he said—is to arrange for the publication of his latest work, which he calls *Scientific Religion,* and which deals, as the subtitle of the book declares, with the higher possibilities of life and practice through the operation of the natural forces. As it has only just appeared in England, it is impossible to say anything about it here, except that it is the final expression of the author's views on life and human philosophy, and the concentrated result of a long life of thought on the most recondite questions of psychology. It is a long leap from *The Tender Recollections of Irene McGillicuddy* to a treatise of four hundred pages on *Scientific Religion* and the operation of the natural forces. And what a facile hand and brain are his who has made it!

It was early in the '50s that Mr. Oliphant first visited this country—a trip which resulted in the work called *Minnesota, or the Far West;* and looking back from this visit to that, what a career has been his! —a career filled to overflowing with change and adventure, and teeming with the riches of experience. Starting in life the son of an eminent East Indian judge, with everything before him that life could offer, at almost everything has he tried his hand. Traveller, journalist, politician, diplomat, author, scientist, reformer—his hands have played over the whole gamut of human existence and experience; and where has it led him? From the life of the court and the drawing-room to the desert of the Thebaid. From the conviction that life is one vast pleasure-ground to the conclusion that it is—as at present interpreted—but a delusion and a snare. He would have you think so, at least; and if you should venture to ask how much of society he intended to see while here, he would snarl at you, 'None; I *hate* society and am longing for my solitudes on Carmel.' He would give you to understand, in short, though he is too much the gentleman to tell you so in plain English, that his ideas on the social question coincide very nearly with Carlyle's, when he puts the population of the world at so many millions—'mostly fools.'

But his is a faint-hearted snarl; and by way of modifying its effect, he will tell you all about his hopes for the regeneration of the poor, foolish human race; about the handful of converts laboring harmoniously at the foot of storied Carmel, to put in practice the theories which he is publishing to the world, and to prove that there is hope for mankind even yet. Mr. Oliphant will tell you that, though he may not live to see Christ come on earth again, His reign is coming very soon now—that reign of peace on earth, good will to men, when church and creed shall be stripped naked of craft and dogma, and when the 'true ritual' shall be, as Canon Freemantle has prophesied it, 'a holy life in all its departments.' And thus, as he rambles on in his enthusiasm, he quite gives the lie to his previous utterances, and proclaims himself the kindliest optimist alive.

Then again, before you know it, your genial host is regaling you with some delightful story of his days in the Orient, or some pathetic tale of the oppression of the Russian

Jews; or again he is quietly leading you on camel-back to hospitable tents somewhere in the far East, or tickling your fancy with witty anecdotes of some would-be contestant whom he has worsted in argument. You begin to doubt if this be really Timon after all, when you remember that you have only his own word for it; you feel he has played a trick upon you, —that you have caught Punchinello in his motley, jeering at you behind a mask, —that you are, in fact, dealing with one of the most jovial beings you have ever met. Then you unfortunately touch him upon a tender spot, —speak, perhaps, of his attributed connection with Mme. Blavatsky. 'Blavatsky! Do I know her? Yes. Did I ever belong to her community? No, —decidedly. Do I believe in her? No.' And as he administers a final rap at the unveiler of Isis with, 'It is possible for a woman to be governed by a bad spirit and be a liar at the same time,' you see that Timon is himself again.

'How unreasonable people are in this world, anyway,' he soliloquizes, as he puffs away at a cigarette. 'Several reporters have called upon me since I have been here for the purpose of gaining some knowledge of my new work. I am only too glad always to give them any information I possess; but how absurd it is to expect me in half a column to express what I have tersely put in four hundred pages, to give them in thirty minutes what it has taken me as many years to do. I tell them it is out of the question, but they think they are equal to it. Another man asks me if I keep up with the current literature of the day. How absurd that is, also, —as if I had the time! I have too much to occupy me at my home in Syria. Another one asks me if I believe in "revealed religion." Such a question was put to me yesterday. I answered it by another, inquiring of my interrogator as to what "revealed religion" was. He hasn't answered me yet. Another man says, "You are a religious enthusiast, are you not?" Isn't that ridiculous, now? As if any man with a particle of religion in him could help being an enthusiast. What did he mean by the question? —he didn't know. And by the way, that makes me think of some of the false and senseless epithets which people have sometimes hurled at me: "free-lover," "atheist," "Oneida-communicant," "crank," "Mormon" even—I have been through it all; but it doesn't trouble me. They must hasten, however, if they have any new title to confer on me, for I am off in a few days for Brocton, and back again next month to England. The heat here is worse than in Syria. It parches one like the sirocco. I had hoped to find a possible publisher for my book here, but I begin to despair. It isn't "orthodox," you know, so one publisher fears to touch it; another prefers something lighter—for summer reading, perhaps; another finds that only "sensations" pay. We are fallen on bad times, I fear; but I have faith, you see.'

'Yes, indeed,' you think, as he presses your hand warmly in farewell, and you think over his golden dreams of a purified humanity and the Promised Land, —'yours is the faith that will remove mountains.' Then, as you review his life and work, you feel that Mr. Oliphant is an earnest man—as earnest now as in the old times when he shouldered the pick with Lake Harris in the Chautauqua brotherhood.

Sara A. Underwood   (essay date 1898)

SOURCE: "Laurence Oliphant's *Sympneumata,*" in *The Arena,* Boston, Vol. XX, No. IV, October, 1898, pp. 526-34.

[*In the following excerpt, British critic Sara Underwood discusses the spiritual ideals described in* Sympneumata.]

In the future, when men shall know more of life's spiritual side than the majority of us can yet comprehend, the world will understand better the higher meaning of the lives of some men and women who have been accounted misled fanatics, deluded enthusiasts, or harmless maniacs. Such mystics as Joan of Arc, Emmanuel Swedenborg, Jacob Boehme, Balzac, and William Blake the poet-artist, are among the exceptional souls who, professing to have received revelations from the unseen, have borne witness to the spiritual life, through new teaching of truth whose appeal to the reason, backed by the power of the mystics' own strong individuality, has profoundly impressed the whole thinking world. Among the various later-day mystics who have laid claim to supernatural revelations in regard to the life and being of man, that brilliant and energetic Englishman, Laurence Oliphant, holds conspicuous place by reason of his many gifts, his position in society, the superb self-sacrifice he showed in the pursuit of occult knowledge, and his devotion to high spiritual ideals. In his beautiful and accomplished wife, Alice L'Estrange, he found a devoted co-worker. Through them was given to the world the singular work so strangely entitled *Sympneumata,* some of whose propositions are to be considered in this article. . . .

In regard to the authorship of the unique volume called *Sympneumata,* Mr. Oliphant in the preface says: "The following pages were dictated by one who, never having appeared in print before, shrinks from the publicity attaching to it, and desires, for the present at all events, to remain unnamed. As, however, I have served as the amanuensis, and as the pages which follow embody my own convictions and experiences as the result of these prolonged investigations, I have not hesitated to assume the editorship."

In a work published after the death of his wife, entitled *Scientific Religion,* Oliphant gives the following detailed account of the manner in which *Sympneumata* was produced:

> In the summer of 1882 I became conscious that a book was forming in my brain, though I could obtain no clear idea of its nature. I took up a pen one morning, with the idea of putting the results on paper. I had not finished the first sentence when my ideas suddenly left me and my mind became as blank as my paper. My wife was sitting in the same room, and I read her what I had written, asking if she could complete the sentence, which she did without a moment's hesitation. The second sentence was begun by me, but had to be ended by my wife. I therefore said to my wife, that it was she, evidently, who was intended to write the book, and begged her to continue to dictate to me. To this she objected, urging her lack of literary skill and her incapacity

for treating so profound a subject. Yet she yielded to my persuasion, and the next morning, as I had other literary work on hand, she attempted to write the book herself. Hereupon ensued a slightly altered duplicate of the first morning's work, for, having retired to her own room with the manuscript, her ideas vanished as mine had, and no way remained out of the difficulty but that of my acting as her amanuensis.

The dominant theory of *Sympneumata* (that theory which the word indicates) is that the spiritually complete individual cannot be wholly male or female, and to be complete must eventually become biune in sex characteristics. That each man and woman bears within himself and within herself the potentiality of becoming both man and woman in one person; the emotional tenderness and self-sacrificing lovingness of the feminine nature becoming blended with the masculine elements of physical strength, intellectuality, and strong will power. Out of such blending, it is asserted, will be developed a higher, nobler type of humanity, wholly unselfish, and reaching outward in strong lovingness to help upward the whole race of mankind. To the student of the humanity of to-day, it seems clear that Oliphant's dream of such a double-natured high-toned race of beings is yet very far from realization. Still in his book he declared his faith that the time for such realization was close at hand; even in our day. "There are already," he says, "those who have discovered that they are united with a 'Sympneuma,' free from the gross external covering of outer body, with whom, in virtue of special idiosyncrasies of constitution, communication establishes itself by new developments in sense of sight or touch or hearing." He says further: "The clear presence and companionship of the 'Sympneuma'—the inseverable Other-Self—presses gently upon the increasing consciousness of all willing individuals, varying in the method of its impress according to those constitutional variations among people by which it selects in each the faculty readiest for acute development."

The implication from his further statement is that these "Other-Selves," though at present outside of fleshly environments, have always existed, or at least have coexisted with those in the bodies to which they rightfully belong. "Such vitalities," he says, "stream into mankind, urging and empowering it, lodging at first in shrivelled cells that quicken and expend at last, and throughout which, fulfilling time, extends the saving and delightful presence of the returned sympneuma."

Perhaps the Oliphants understood from their own strange experiences in occult studies exactly what is meant by this "Sympneuma," but nowhere is it described by them clearly enough to enable the average mortal to invariably recognize it or its workings. In one place it is said to be that "new volume and quality of consciousness which we describe as Sympneuma." And in another he says: "Unless the men and women of to-day receive, or can acquire, by clear mental and physical perception, participation in the active and emotional existence of the being who is to them the sex-complement, the love, let them name that being spirit, or angel, or inspiring soul—whom we term the Sympneuma—the whole day-spring from on high. . . .

must fail to visit them." And again: "The calls to mankind of men truly great have been the conscious notes echoed from the unconscious sympneumatic depths seeking re-ëcho in the deep breasts of others."

The knowledge of and consequent attainment of this soul-mate, this Sympneuma, will, he declares, so inspire and elevate those who are conscious of this "marriage by soul, or mind, or touch, or sight, or all," as to fill each heart so full of love for all humanity "that no use for life can now be found but to cast it before the feet of the human brotherhood in ceaseless and organic service."

Sympneumata is a rather large-sized book of nearly three hundred pages, and, with this ultimate dual nature of human beings as premise, widens out into consideration of many and varied idealistic correlated results, which may or should follow the search for and finding of the "Sympneuma"; but these cannot be dealt with in this article. The work was apparently dictated in a very hopeful mood, in which the present century was supposed to be the era when mankind were to return to truer spiritual conditions, when "the ice of intellectual denial of human truth" should be melted away, and the biunity of sex in the individual be reëstablished.

Woman, according to this theory of the Sympneuma, is "the inner and receptive shape alone, dispossessed of the outer and transmissive shape [the masculine], which belongs to each atom of true humanity."

At certain epochs in the world's history, it is averred, "the deeper mysteries of man's interior being instituted a quiet process of attack upon his gross external constitution, to pierce and penetrate it. The action of the inner upon the outer human formation has continued universally; and continues." In another place the material body is called "the protective clothing of the inner man."

Of the obstructions in the way of return to the state of biune sex-individuality, much is written. Among other obstacles is the fact that, "So long as the current of brute passion, known as lust, invades the human organism from with out, does it introduce a conflict with celestial love, which holds man back from his Maker, and prevents that fusion into the Divine Being which could be attained were the constituent elements of the human form to undergo a change in the sense of the evolutionary process suggested." Another obstacle is found in the materialistic teachings of men of science, in regard to which it is remarked that, "However brilliant and attractive may be the mental work of teachers who fail or refuse to hear these deep [Spiritual] vibrations, their influence rests on the lives of men as weight, and not as light; creeps throughout convictions, cooling, never impassioning; creates in hearts negations rather of veritable sentiment than aspiration for greater wealth of being."

Although the writer of *Sympneumata* professed to believe that many already understood the truth of his theory, and that there were men in this age, "innumerable as the stars, who can save mankind by simply being truly in their outward lives that divine thing they are at the core," yet he thinks it also true that "it is only as the period arrives during which the dissolution throughout terrestrial manhood of the excrescence layer [the earthly body] shall by slow and orderly processes be gradually effected, that his spiritual-intellectual perceptions will acquire a new acumen, by which the truth, essential now to all his progress, can be received and verified by him."

In speaking of "that phenomenon of life called death," he says: "Full human evolution was not a terrestrial possibility, thus death prevailed." And further: "As the growth of the real man and of the essence forms of all his organs can never pause, there arrives inevitably a period when it begins to strain and unhinge the machinery by which it has effected its little spell of labor in the outer world. There will come inevitably a moment when the compression of the organ coverings composed of low matter will become intolerable to the finer expanding matter of the man, and it must be got rid of. But as there is the tenderness of gradual processes in all the workings of God, the resistance of the exterior body to the evolution of the interior is generally overcome by a gentle pressure of years, and in the ordinary course terrestrial life wanes through that interval called its decline."

But this explanation of the spiritual process toward release from the earthly body does not explain why so many deaths occur in infancy, and in wars and accidents where there are no "gradual processes" in that release. So with many other statements of supposed possibilities in *Sympneumata,* they leave a vast number of reasonable questions—reasonable from the common-sense point of view—wholly unexplained or unanswered.

But there is much in the book somewhat reasonable and truly inspiring and uplifting, especially in its portrayal of a grander humanity, strong, unselfish, pure, and intellectually great, filled with divinely tender love towards all in God's universe.

Herbert W. Schneider and George Lawton (essay date 1942)

SOURCE: "The Pneuma and the Breath," in *A Prophet and a Pilgrim: Being the Incredible History of Thomas Lake Harris and Laurence Oliphant,* Columbia University Press, 1942, pp. 388-403.

[*Herbert W. Schneider is a professor emeritus who writes extensively with George Lawton on philosophy and religion. In the following excerpt, they describe Oliphant's theories of spirituality as presented in* Sympneumata *and* Scientific Religion.]

The Oliphant version of counterpartal theory was contained in two books: *Sympneumata; or, Evolutionary Forces Now Active in Man;* and *Scientific Religion; or, Higher Possibilities of Life and Practice through the Operation of Natural Forces.* The first of these volumes was given out anonymously, being merely "edited by Laurence Oliphant." In a letter [from Haifa, dated May 12, 1884] to the publisher he described the manner in which the authors wished the book to be presented to the world.

> I am sending you by book-post the manuscript of a book which I want published, but which I doubt whether you will care to undertake—

indeed I do not want it published in the ordinary way, as it is not an ordinary book. It is the result of the efforts of the last twenty years of my life, and contains what so many of my critics have been anxious I should tell them,—what I really believe, what I have been at all this time, what the result of all this "mysticism," as they call it, amounts to. In fact, it is a confession of faith, and certainly deals with a novel class of subjects [the letter here is unfortunately torn] . . . I have been the amanuensis, and so far as it could never have been written without me or through any other hand, I am the joint author. At all events, I assume the responsibility of its contents, and have written the Preface, as editor, to say so. Now as to the publication, I should like it to be published for me. I should like to know what it would cost to print a thousand copies, for which I would pay the full expense—and whether you would print it for me. I should not wish it advertised in the usual way, nor have any copies sent to reviews. . . . The class which will read it is a comparatively small though growing one, and I should like it to make its own way quietly and probably slowly. I believe, if published in the usual way, it would make something of a sensation, and bring down showers of criticism and ridicule: this, though I am not afraid of it, I don't court, though it would sell the book,—but that is not my object.

In Oliphant's Preface to the book he simply stated, "The following pages were dictated by one who, never having appeared in print before, shrinks from the publicity attaching to it, and desires, for the present at all events, to remain unnamed." In the later book, however, the composition of the first was explained as follows:

> I had been conscious for some months in the summer of 1882 that a book was taking form within my brain, though I could obtain no clear idea of its nature,—and indeed the same experience has preceded the pages I am now penning, —when I decided one day to attempt a beginning, and trust to the inspiration of the hour to carry me on, as I am doing now. I had scarcely written the first sentence and begun the second, when the ideas which had presented themselves on taking up my pen suddenly left me, and my mind became a sheet of blank paper. I remarked upon this to my wife, who was sitting in the room, and, reading what I had written, asked her if she could finish the sentence: this, without a moment's hesitation, she had no difficulty in doing. I now most laboriously began another, but soon the same difficulty presented itself, which was solved in the same way. I found it hopeless to try and write another word. I therefore said to my wife that it was she evidently who was intended to write the book, and begged her to continue to dictate to me. To this at first she objected, on the ground of a want of literary practice, of material, and of capacity to treat properly so profound a subject; but she finally consented to try, and for a couple of hours dictated to me slowly, but without hesitation or correction. She then became too exhausted to continue. On the following day I suggested that, as I had a good deal of literary work to do, she had

better write the book herself, and I went to write a magazine article in another room. After the lapse of a few minutes she came to me saying that she had not been able to write a line, or to find an idea in her head of any sort, suggesting that I should come back and continue to be her amanuensis. I had no sooner taken up the pencil that she began to dictate, and continued for some moments with apparent ease, when she paused, and finally announced that again all her ideas had vanished, and asked me if I could suggest a cause. As a few minutes previously a new idea had struck me with reference to the article I was writing on quite another subject, I remembered that perhaps it might be owing to my abstraction from the matter in hand. On my again directing my attention to it she continued without hesitation, and wishing to help her, I endeavoured to formulate some ideas. "Now," she said, "you are doing something that confuses me terribly. I have a whole mass of thoughts crowding on my brain, and I cannot feel which is the right one." I told her how my mind had been working, and suggested that I should try as much as possible to keep it an absolute blank. This I managed, with more or less success, to do, and in the degree in which I succeeded, did she dictate with freedom. We also found that if I had written anything on any subject previously, or been engaged in any matter of business the same day, it was useless for her to attempt to dictate. We were obliged to begin our writing the first thing in the morning, to allow of no interruptions, and to be in no way anxious or preoccupied with worldly matters till it was concluded. In this way the book was written, but the process was a slow one, owing to the many days lost by interruptions, which were unavoidable, and her own feeble health during a great part of the time. But there was nothing abnormal in her condition when dictating—no indication of the state popularly known as "mediumistic." Her mind was in full and active operation, and all her intellect, which was a very powerful one, was concentrated on the effort of expressing in appropriate terms the ideas which were suggested to her.

Anyone familiar with Laurence Oliphant's style could see at once that the volume was not his. Among Harris's followers it was assumed that at least parts of the book were produced by automatic writing and that Oliphant believed it to be a message from his celestial counterpart. [In a letter dated March 13, 1885, Harris's disciple Arthur] Cuthbert wrote:

Thanks for sending Oliphant's book. I received it last night, and have read about the half of it. It is written as he says through his own hand and mainly I judge from his own brain. His system is to seek the internal and that which he calls "God" through sexual sensation. . . . As gilding for this pill, to induce some if possible to receive it, he steals a showing of great part of Father's self-abnegating and humanitarian principles, all which with him is simply disgusting hypocrisy. The book, to whomsoever receives it will prove the "opening of the pit" (see Declarations). It is curious that up to page 79—about one third of the book—the style is clear and explicit, but at that page it suddenly changes to the vague vapid meaningless drivel that characterizes the usual run of spiritualistic utterances, and continues so to the end—as far as I have looked through the latter half of the book. I guess the whole to be got up between himself and Mrs. O., partly from their own brains and memory, consciously, and partly by automatic deliverance, either through hand or tongue.

The later explanation left no doubt that the book was really the work of Alice Oliphant. The style was diffuse and labored; the matter was simple and sentimental. The book represented what Alice had learned from both Harris and Laurence and how she attempted to piece it all together. On the surface there was little more than a verbal difference between this and the teaching of Harris: "counterpart" became "sympneuma," "interior states" became "subsurface degrees of consciousness," and the "fays" became "forces of the subsurface region." But the emphasis shifted, as the exposition proceeded, from the theme of bisexuality in Harris's sense, in which the presence of a celestial counterpart was basic, to the theme of "high love" between a man and a woman, both on earth and each bisexual. The "evolutionary force" of the "sympneuma" thus became primarily, what it was only secondarily for Harris, a basis of spiritual creation through the coöperation of the sexes, or, in other words, a philosophy of marriage as well as of social sex relations generally. The "creation" of the book *Sympneumata* was therefore an illustration as well as an exposition of the coöperation of the sexes freed from all "animalism."

The faithful and inseverable companionships which will represent in outer forms of life the sacred facts of the inner, will still exist with increase of worth to man and woman, but often with entire innocence of the relationship of person which would maintain in a painful activity the currents of the decaying unisexual layers of either frame; a partial suspension of race-reproduction is in fact a possibility that may become incidental upon the many changes in the physical constitution of man, which already begin to occur. To pause at least in assuming such grave responsibilities as are involved by transmitting to others, an organism which is the conscious seat of an extraordinary revolution, becomes to many a necessity of the hour: while the sense that retrievement from sin and misery for the present millions, is better than the increase of population, will more and more develop, and will cease to be startling to people in whom preservative and constructive forces so distinctively strengthen, as to point to the inevitable possession, in no distant future, by human beings of the power of greatly extending the length of the terrestrial career.

The reasons for this may be readily apprehended if we remember that the semi-animal layer that encompasses man's form is now in process of slow extinction, and that man has reached a phase in which at last he may safely forbid activities to enter it from the outer and surrounding world, because his inner growth can now at last transmit to his external, the vigours that will suffice to regulate accretions of terrestrial particles for terrestrial living. The outgrowth of the symp-neumatic frame brings him at this day to the point where he may begin to grow as pure and simple man, and where the sensations of dual growth may engender in either sex the waning of all old sense, and by their fresh intensity push far behind them all dependence on experiences that fade. The men and women who now lead forth this type, that will spread and grow till it includes all men in distant future, are each one married to that spirit which makes their completion as units of a real humanity, and know no longer any of the unrest, the want, that arose from uncompleted humanness.

No other course in life seems worth pursuing but the one which holds out hope, however vague, of acquiring the power of sensational emotional acquaintance with the life-currents of the Deity; the power of a marriage by soul, or mind, or touch, or sight, or all, with a possible being who dwells in the fluid spaces of the organism, and has, by reason of the changes that are gradually forcing themselves upon external nature, the capacity for acquiring grosser reality of form and aspect; and then the power of so acute an identification with the whole body of humanity, that no use for life can now be found but to cast it before the feet of the human brotherhood in ceaseless and organic service. These powers are the sum of the offering of his age to man, so far as a phrase will state it to the untrained or the inexperienced.

This accession of quality as displayed among men, has included from the outset the elements which still fever the social mass with their effort at radiation, the elements of individual freedom and universal service; the elements of the equal right of woman with man to growth and power, and of the indissoluble interdependence of man and woman; the elements of the vigorous distinctness of race characteristics and of the annihilation of separate morality, mentality, and *physique,* which is now rapidly establishing itself as the eminent phenomenon of our era.

To make this even approximately intelligible it must be remembered that in the Swedenborgian tradition "woman" means essentially "emotion," and "man" means "intellect." The Oliphants' doctrine that woman should be the center of man and man the circumference of woman meant essentially that man was incomplete without more introversion, more cultivation of his sensitivities, and woman was incomplete without more extraversion, more executive ability in the world of affairs. But Alice believed most literally that woman was man's center and that man was the "complementary circumference" that should protect the "woman's sanctuary" from "invasive forces." Woman was "the central vessel in the human for secret inception of all vitalities from the divine, and for their distribution outwards into the masculine." The essence of the Fall [as stated in *Sympneumata*] was that

> the secret woman came forth to breast the world, and the forces at large in it, like another sort of man, —deprived, in her region of the outer

frame, of the quality in her original fluidity by which at will she withdrew herself within the protection of the male envelopings; and deprived of the screen which was to be held up between the delicate processes of her activities and the rough forces at work in external nature.

As history and physiology this is obviously fantastic, but as metaphor it is relatively intelligible.

Theoretically, as the passages quoted above reveal, the new "biune sensation" generated a passion for the "ceaseless and organic service of the human brotherhood" as a whole, but in practice this service of the whole had to begin with a pair who coöperated in building a "home" as a center for other biune persons. The whole idea was obviously an elaboration of Laurence's and Alice's love for each other and of their scheme to build a community in Palestine.

In the fourth chapter of *Scientific Religion,* a chapter which begins with a "treatise on domestic living, by the late Mrs. Oliphant," the theory was applied explicitly to the Oliphant "household," and the principles of organization and coöperation were laid down. From this "housebook," as it was called, we quote the following passages in order that the reader may compare this type of community with Harris's.

> The little household in which these lines are penned, has constituted itself by virtue of the apparent accidents of the moral and physical necessities of its various members, numbers of whom are not even able to be continuously resident in it. Its members, therefore, set up no pretension to offer, either by their number or by their differences of nationality, of occupation, or of age, any special model of what any other household actuated by the same motives, and following the same fundamental methods, should be.

> This little household would be ready to reconcile some people with a relative simplicity of living, and to call up some into a relative affluence: it is groping for ways of drawing together the extremes of waste and want, of superfluity and of insufficiency, of suggesting the creation of recruits for the divergent classes of earth's civilisation; and of the new middle class, whose function will not be that of preying upon the classes on either side of it, while it transmits the means of life from one to the other, but that of feeding in such diverse forms the legitimate wants of men, that they will be drawn together in it away from all the antagonisms established by their present unsatisfied requirements.

> The value of these groupings of individuals in intimate juxtaposition is incalculable: there are no other circumstances which are capable of producing the same results; and these results in the individual are indispensable, at this period of high social effort, to the lofty character which society strains to embody.

> Such convictions lying at the root of the action which drew together the little fraternity here alluded to, it is evident that each member of it

must adopt, with a solemn sense of responsibility to the world at large, whatever occupation befits them within it, or whatever they befit.

The difficulty of distributing financial responsibility in a satisfactory manner has broken up many of the best attempts at societary cooperation. It is probable that this responsibility, in common with others, the discharge of which affects equally every member of a family or group, will have to rest with all its weight and all its freedom upon one person.

We will assume, therefore, that a man, or, probably of necessity, a man and woman, have summoned together, under the clearly felt guidance of God, people whose harmony of feeling is absolute in respect of the principles just enumerated, whose motto is free evolution.

They must be prepared themselves to regard each member of the group which becomes their family, as held by them in charge for the world's service. These parents must take upon themselves the collection of all home funds, from whatever source contributed, in order to redistribute them with free exercise of judgment and of love among the members, according to the requirements of their moral and physical condition. . . . But they will institute a systematic attempt to develop in each individual the highest degree of responsibility in special functions that is compatible with their age, judgment, or faculty and moral condition.

The type of persons who can produce good performance in any mode of labour by concentrating upon it their faculties with the single view of performing it well, is a very ordinary one; but the procreative quality of generous faculty at this date, requires us to develop a type of workers who hold the drive of personal energy in perpetual check; who scatter it by the way, preparing paths of others' work; who inquire of their own performance constantly if it creates facilities for performance by others; who act in all things in reference to the acting power of others. He can no longer be esteemed an excellent workman who can only work excellently. For his work to prove that it is living, it must be generative; and it will not be generative unless the workman has his mind trained to a clear conception of his own methods, and their connection with the laws of nature; unless he can impart that understanding by word of mouth at any time or write it down; unless the sum of his experience, while he is constantly increasing it, is as constantly forced by him into mental shape easy of registration, and, whenever useful, registered, so that it may be at all moments ready of access to all his fellow-creatures, and so that he may be at all moments in a mental position to impart his methods to others.

This household was in essence identical with that of Harris, a paternalism in the service of socialism, with two major differences: first, the household was under the direction of a pair of biune parents instead of under a "father" with a celestial counterpart, and the coöperation of this pair was to be both in theory and practice spiritually gen-

erative; secondly, there was to be more emphasis on educating the members into the capacities required for "cooperative responsibilities."

Scientific Religion was the elaborate defense Laurence added, after her death, to Alice's relatively simple exposition of the sympneumatic sex relations. He explained its "generation" [in the "Postscript to the Preface"] as follows:

> I became conscious on my arrival at Haifa last spring that a book, the plan of which I could not determine, was taking form in my mind, and pressing for external expression, and at once sat down to write it. I found the attempt to be vain; the ideas refused to arrange themselves, and I was strongly impressed that they could not do so, unless I went to a summer-house I have built in a remote part of Mount Carmel, and made the room from which the spirit of my wife had passed into the unseen, a little more than a year before, my private study, religiously preserving it from intrusion. I had no sooner taken my pen in hand under these circumstances, than the thoughts which find expression in the following pages were projected into my mind with the greatest rapidity, and irrespective of any mental study or prearrangement on my part, often overpowering my own preconceptions, and still more often presenting the subject treated of in an entirely new light to myself. On two or three occasions they ceased suddenly. I then found it was useless to try and formulate them by any effort of my brain, and at once abandoned the attempt to write for the day. The longest interval of this kind was three days. On the fourth I was again able to write with facility, and though always conscious of the effort of composition, it was never so severe as to cause me to pause for more than one or two minutes.
>
> At the same time there was nothing, so far as I could judge, abnormal in my mental or physical condition. I was unaffected by trifling interruptions, and the ideas as they presented themselves seemed to be my own mingled with others projected from an unseen source, or new ideas struggling with and overpowering old ones with force that I could not resist.
>
> The effect of this internal connection was to mitigate to an inconceivable degree the sense of loss which at first threatened to overwhelm me when she passed into her present sphere of usefulness; for she was soon able to reach me through the internal tie which had been formed by this interlocking of our finer-grained material atoms while in the flesh, and it was only during the short interval consequent upon their dislocation from the atoms of ordinary matter that my suffering was acute. On the re-establishment of the vital connection between us under new and more powerful conditions, I was enabled to advance into the appreciation of knowledge which had been concealed from me; but this enlightenment never takes the form of being projected upon my brain from any outside source, but rather as a spontaneous idea suggested by my own consciousness, and yet accompanied by the peculiar

internal sensation produced by this atomic inter-action, which is sufficient to check me if, in writing, I am following a current of thought which is in opposition to hers, and to convey to me a sense of approval when I have succeeded in conveying the idea which, interweaving itself with mine in the atomic cerebral processes, she desires to have conveyed.

Assuming, then, that conditions can be reached by the interlocking of the dynaspheric atoms of those who are invisible, with those of persons still in this life, especially in the case where pneumatic as well as psychic interlocking has preceded the decease of one of the parties; and that it is possible for a commingling of ideas to take place, in which those of the invisible partner shall largely predominate, though they will have to take form through the channel provided for it in the moral expanses and mental processes of the living partner; and assuming, further, that the invisible partner was possessed of a powerful and well-trained intellect, and was developed morally to a very exceptional degree, —it is evident that, being released from the trammels of the flesh, the faculty of insight and observation into natural phenomena of such a person would result in knowledge of a deeply interesting and valuable kind.

The substance of this explanation is that Alice's death put an end to the confusion in counterpartal theory that had troubled them while both were living. Theoretically, during their life, since each enjoyed the sympneumatic consciousness, each had another, spiritual counterpart. After Alice's death, however, Laurence unhesitatingly proclaimed her as his counterpart and even claimed, as in the above passage, that they had been "sympneumatically interlocked" before her passage to the unseen.

In his book Laurence Oliphant attempted a twofold justification of his faith, basing it on science as well as on the Scriptures. The scientific argument was a variation on the familiar theme that spiritual phenomena are coming to be understood in terms of natural law. He recited the results of the latest experiments with hypnotism and psychical research. The "spiritual forces" were not literally "spirits" but natural energies, which he called "dynaspheric forces." He suggested that these forces were probably related to the interatomic energies, which were at that time beginning to be heard of in theoretical physics and which might be liberated with the break-up of the ordinary physical atoms.

If, then, a new atomic force can be introduced into man's organism, of a higher and purer quality than any of which we have any cognisance, it is evident that a new door of evolution is open to him. He will survive, . . . because he will find himself endowed with the vigours derived from a new and pure sex-potency, which will enable him ultimately to produce offspring of a loftier physical and moral type, possessing those finer faculties of a supersensuous kind, which were lost when the Adamic race closed all the subsurface region of its consciousness, and stupefied alike its moral instinct and its rational intelli-

gence, by absorbing a current of lust from the lower animal creation.

He added to what he could use of the physical and biological sciences liberal gleanings from theosophic tradition. Of one thing he was quite certain, that he had left "spiritualism" far behind—that all "dabbling" with messages and mediums was worse than a waste of time.

In attempting a scriptural justification for his theories he may have been motivated by criticisms of *Sympneumata* similar to General Gordon's, of which he wrote [in a letter dated June 8, 1885]:

He saw only the manuscript, and wished it written from the more Biblical point of view, as, though he said it contained nothing that was not to be found in the Bible, yet few would recognise it, and it would frighten the majority, which it would not if it appealed more to the Bible as authority, and its agreement with it was made clearer. Mrs. Oliphant was not allowed, however, to alter the form, and indeed found herself rather prevented from thinking about the Bible, from which we gather, as we told Gordon, that such references as he desired would frighten away those who did not believe in the Bible, and were looking for light. It is not written for those who feel they have all the light they need, but for those who feel that the old religious landmarks have disappeared.

And the same motive may have been behind his inclusion, in both editions, of "an Appendix by a Clergyman of the Church of England," Haskett Smith, that consisted almost entirely of exegesis of texts from the Bible and the sacred writings of other religions.

On the scriptural side Oliphant expounded arcana of the inner sense of the Scriptures that rivaled those of Harris, if not in bulk, certainly in ingenuity. His commentaries on Genesis, the Pauline Epistle, and Revelations not only traced the history of bisexuality through the Fall, the mark of Cain, the birth of Jesus, and Pentecost, much as Harris had done, but wove into it the chief themes of the Kaballa and of Theosophy quite independently of Harris's *Esoteric Science.* On three important points he differed explicitly from Harris. First, though he was convinced of the near approach of the crisis in evolution, the event would be moral rather than physical. It would not be catastrophic.

The restoration of the sympneumatic union involves, sooner or later, the restoration of the divine conditions of procreation; but herein lies a great mystery, the revelation of which is reserved for One who has retained the Christ-like condition, concerning which it is not expedient to write further at present than to say, that the period when this revelation will be made does not seem very remote. But before it can be made, it will be necessary for the two or three who have passed away from this earth in full sympneumatic consciousness, to be reinforced by the addition of others now alive who have attained the same state. . . .

There is no more profound delusion than that

which prevails in certain quarters, that a crisis is at hand which will sweep all humanity from the face of the earth, except a chosen few, who will be preserved immortal amid the general crash. A crisis is undoubtedly at hand, but it will not be catastrophic or outside of natural law. It will consist simply in the further development and collision of those forces which are already exhibiting themselves in unknown and startling phenomena. . . . For any man who has attained sympneumatic conditions, or who thinks he has attained them, to desire immortality, or to suppose that he has already achieved it, is to nurse himself in a delusion as ignorant as it is selfish.

Secondly, he repudiated the whole doctrine of a pivotal man in scathing terms.

There is no doctrine attended with greater danger than this one, which involves the necessity of a pivotal man, through whom alone God can act upon the human race. It was invented by the early Church, is illustrated in Rome, and has since been acted upon by others. It is a doctrine which casts its magnetic fetters round the affections, the will, and the understanding, and makes abject slaves of those who yield themselves to it. The whole tendency of the divinely vital descent now occurring is to develop the entire nature of man, morally, rationally, and physically; to emancipate him from the bondage of Churches and of men; to make him his own pivot, standing erect in the light of his own divine illumination, and lifting his arms Godward, inspired by the dignity of his own aspiration—neither borne into the unseen in the swaddling-clothes of a sect, nor driven thither in a chain-gang under the cruel lash of a slave-driver, nor projected into it upon the fagot of an *auto da fé*.

Lastly, he demanded in and with the group an intimacy that Harris avoided. Though the Harris "family" was supposed to "hold" for him, he regarded his struggle as essentially solitary. Oliphant, on the other hand, thought of himself more as an intimate member dispensing his "magnetism" through intimate contact with others. His published statements on this subject were guarded, but they were liable to the kind of interpretation his enemies put on them. He wrote:

This training is of such a nature as to cause a suffering far more acute than all the self-imposed rigours and penances of monks and nuns. It may consist of a variety of disciplines—as, for instance, when two young people, who are both in quest of this pearl of great price, and who are passionately attached to each other, feel that they must marry if they would win it, and yet never know in this life what the marriage relation, as commonly understood, is. Or it may consist in intimacies which, though pure and innocent, are calculated to arouse jealousy in quarters where it would be legitimate under ordinary circumstances, and excite suspicions which nothing but supreme faith can banish; to say nothing of other ordeals to be undergone, which differ in each case, but are always of a character to try most severely the peculiar quality of the temperament to which they are applied. For the

position of man in relation to woman, in this particular struggle, is reversed. It is she who, when she has herself attained to the consciousness of sympneumatic life, must lead him to it. From first to last he must be a passive instrument in her hands; under her guidance he must crush out of his nature every instinct of animal passion, and become dead to all the old sensations, before he can become alive to the new.

The man who has undergone this training finally becomes absolutely impervious to, and case-hardened against, the subtle magnetisms which radiate from ordinary woman. He forgets at last what the emotion of being what is popularly called "in love," was like; no charms can captivate his outer senses, no feminine sympathy, based on a mere personal sentiment, can penetrate into that inmost shrine, which he has dedicated to the worship of the Divine Feminine. . . .

Men and women who have arrived at these new relations towards each other, enjoy a happiness in them which compensates for all the suffering they have undergone to reach it, —a happiness which would be shattered at a blow, if they could be guilty of any such act of physical gratification as the closeness of their external relations would justify the world in attributing to them. And yet the progress of the work in which they are engaged, involves an intimacy as close as that between sister and sister, or mother and daughter, and as pure; for the needful interchanges of magnetism can only be effected by constant and close proximity, by which new electromagnetic forces can be generated, sufficiently powerful to resist the invasion of the infernal lust-currents which are now struggling to make an entry into the world, through the organisms of "sensitives," who are ignorant of the nature of the forces which are accomplishing their subjection. To rescue such, when their eyes have been opened; to close up the rupture in their odylic sphere which has given entrance to the invading tainted magnetic current; and to restore them to physical health and moral sanity, is one of the most blessed duties which devolves upon those who are labouring in this new sphere of action; for it is one which medical science, with its present limitations of ignorance and prejudice in such matters, is quite unable to undertake.

Philip Henderson   (essay date 1956)

SOURCE: " 'Piccadilly'," in *The Life of Laurence Oliphant: Traveller, Diplomat and Mystic,* Robert Hale Limited, 1956, pp. 124-42.

[*Philip Henderson was an English man of letters known for his studies of Christopher Marlowe and other English literary figures. In the following excerpt, he traces the development of Oliphant's satirical voice in* Piccadilly, *Oliphant's commentary on Victorian high society.*]

It was while writing for *The Owl* that Oliphant discovered the satirical gift he . . . employed to such good effect in ***Piccadilly.*** As a member of Lady Palmerston's Cambridge

House circle, he had every opportunity for observing the manners of high Victorian society, and it is, in fact, to one of Lady Palmerston's Saturday night parties that Vanecourt goes at the opening of the novel. Lord Redesdale remembers meeting him there—"Laurence Oliphant, a mystic in lavender kid gloves, full of spiritualism, strange creeds, and skits upon Society", as he describes him in his *Memories.* At Cambridge House (now the Naval and Military Club) was to be met only the cream of Victorian society. "Of literary or artistic society at Lady Palmerston's Saturdays there were scarcely any representatives," says Lord Redesdale, "indeed, Dicky Doyle and Monckton Milnes, afterwards Lord Houghton, were almost alone. Lord Lytton was there, but rather like Macaulay, because he was a statesman, than on account of his success in letters." Lord Palmerston, or Cupid, was there, of course, and the beautiful Duchess of Somerset and many other ladies with their blue eyes and complexions of strawberries and cream. The highly favoured, among whom were Oliphant and Mitford, were expected to take tea in an inner room and to lead the quadrilles at three o'clock in the morning.

Laurence Oliphant, a mystic in lavender kid gloves, full of spiritualism, strange creeds, and skits upon Society

— *Lord Redesdale, quoted by Philip Henderson.*

At the beginning of *Piccadilly,* Lord Vanecourt takes chambers a few doors from Cambridge House, with the idea of observing life from his windows and writing a history of civilization from a "Piccadillean" point of view.

> The hour 11 P.M.; a long string of carriages advancing under my windows to Lady Palmerston's; rain pelting; horses with ears pressed back, wincing under the storm; coachmen and footmen presenting the crowns of their hats to it; streams running down their waterproofs, and causing them to glitter in the gaslight; now and then the flash of jewels inside carriages; nothing visible of their occupants but flounces surging up at the windows, as if they were made of some delicious creamy substance, and were going to overflow into the street; policemen in large capes, and if I may be allowed the expression, 'helmetically' sealed from the wet, keeping order; draggled women on foot 'moving' rapidly on. The fine ladies in their carriages moving too—but not quite so fast. The Piccadillean view of the progress of civilization suggested to me many serious reflections . . . Which way are we moving? I mused, as I made the smallest of white bows immediately over a pearl stud in my neck . . . I certainly can't call it 'the progress' of civilization; that does all very well for Pekin, not for London. Shall I do the Gibbon business, and call it 'the decline and fall' of civilization?

—and I absently thrust two right-hand gloves into my pocket by mistake. . . .

The tone is light and graceful, but biting.

Oliphant was quite aware of the risk he was running in writing a satire of the high Victorian world, and he half-humorously claims the reader's sympathy in advance, "should I writhe, crushed and mangled by the iron hand of a social tyranny dexterously concealed in its velvet glove". He is, he says, to be a missionary in the ballrooms and to "show everybody up to everybody else in the spirit of love". His missionary work begins, however, among the clergy—"a paid branch of the Civil Service, exercising police functions of a very lofty and important character"—for he feels that it is time that somebody preached to *them.* Vanecourt is, of course, none other than Oliphant himself promoted to the peerage. His friend Lord Grandon says to him: "You are a curious compound, Frank. I never knew a man whose moods changed so suddenly, or whose modes of thinking were so spasmodic and extreme; however, I suppose you are intended to be of some use in the world." But as for the world, Vanecourt reflects: "it seemed to have taken a step in the right direction nearly two thousand years ago [with the advent of Christ] and now it has all slipped back again worse than ever, and is whirling the wrong way with a rapidity that makes one giddy." There is, in fact, a curious hallucinatory, insubstantial quality about *Piccadilly,* brilliantly reproduced in Doyle's illustrations. Oliphant diagnoses the condition of England as

> a morbid activity of the national brain, utterly deranged action of the national heart . . . Due to the noxious influence of tall chimneys upon broad acres whereby the commercial effluvium of the Plutocracy has impregnated the upper atmosphere, and overpowered the enfeebled and enervated faculties of the aristocracy; lust of gain has supervened upon love of ease. Hence the utter absence of those noble and generous impulses which are the true indications of healthy national life. Expediency has taken the place of principle, conscience has been crushed out of existence by calculation. Looked at from what I may term "externals", we simply present to the world at large the ignoble spectacle of a nation of usurers trembling over our money-bags; looked at from internals, I perceive that we are suffering from a moral opiate . . . the insane delusion, now many centuries old, that we are a Christian nation . . . For instance, imagine our Foreign Minister getting up in the House of Commons and justifying his last stroke of foreign policy upon the ground that we should love our neighbours better than ourselves.

And Vanecourt, as his author himself was shortly to do, proceeds to put Christianity into practice quite literally. He gives up the girl he loves to his friend and renounces his parliamentary career to retire from the world at the behest of an anonymous and shadowy prophet, who suddenly accosts him in Piccadilly and exhorts him to "Live the Life". His reason for giving up his fashionable life is that "it was impossible to resist the fits of depression which reduced my mind to the condition of white paper, and the world to that of a doll stuffed with sawdust".

Piccadilly appeared serially in *Blackwood's* during 1865 and enjoyed an immediate and scandalous success. Vanecourt, Oliphant wrote to John Blackwood, was intended to be "more or less mad"; this, he proceeds to explain, "enables his opinions and acts to be extravagant and inconsistent always, based, nevertheless, upon truth and rectitude, which two principles are so extremely dry and distasteful that nobody would care about a novel conveying such an old-fashioned moral unless it were put in some new-fangled form . . . I do think that the times are so bad that they need an exposure." Indeed, for all its superficial urbanity, the picture of the world given in the novel is in reality so horrible, even though it does not even touch the fringe of the underworld, that one cannot wonder that Oliphant felt the need to retire from it, though by this time he was Liberal M.P. for Stirlingburgh. His attitude to party politics, and to politics in general, however, he expressed with great bitterness in *Episodes:*

> The House of Commons does not yet seem to have learnt the lesson that voters are like playing cards; the more you shuffle them the dirtier they get. When it became clear to me that in order to succeed, party must be put before country, and self before everything, and that success could only be purchased at the price of convictions, which were expected to change with those of the leader of the party—these, as it happened, were of an extremely fluctuating character, and were never to be relied upon from one session to another—my thirst to find something that was not a sham, or a contradiction in terms, increased. The world, with its bloody wars, its political intrigues, its social evils, its religious cant, its financial frauds, and its glaring anomalies, assumed in my eyes more and more the aspect of a gigantic lunatic asylum.

Piccadilly ends in an orgy of emotion. Lady Broadhem "finds a heart" and everyone kneels down in the Belgravia drawing-room and prays and weeps tears of thankfulness, while her ladyship lies on the sofa, sobbing into a cushion. Vanecourt, who has given up Ursula and awoken her mother's better feelings, then falls on to his bed in a state of nervous prostration and the mysterious prophet ("his name I am unable to divulge") lifts him from it by a single touch. " 'There is no need of a doctor,' says the prophet. 'I will take him to America.' And my heart leaped within me, for its predictions were verified, and the path lay clear before me."

In actuality that path meant renouncing his parliamentary career, giving away his money, and humbling himself completely to the will of another in an attempt to live a life entirely devoid of self-interest or ambition. But the old Adam was not so easily disposed of. "Existing within him side by side was a pagan sensuality and a Calvinist conscience," writes Dr Lawton, [in *A Prophet and a Pilgrim: Being the Incredible History of Thomas Lake Harris and Laurence Oliphant*, 1942] "and Oliphant's whole life was an attempt to satisfy now one, now the other, and finally, in accepting Harris's theories and practices, to achieve a rationale which would enable him to satisfy both at the same time."

FURTHER READING

Biography

Dearden, Seton. "Laurence Oliphant." *The Cornhill Magazine*, Vol. 169, No. 1009, (Autumn, 1956): 1-32.
     Sketch of Oliphant's life, detailing his marriage and his involvement with the religious cult led by Thomas Lake Harris.

Fairbairn, Evelina. "Laurence Oliphant." *The Westminster Review*, Vol. CXXXVII, (Jan-June, 1892): 498-512.
     Biographical sketch, including a discussion of Oliphant's early years as a travel writer.

Taylor, Anne. *Laurence Oliphant, 1829-1888.* Oxford: Oxford University Press, 1982, 293 p.
     Critical biography of Oliphant.

Criticism

Upton, Sara Carr. "Sympneumata: A Report of the Contents of a Work by Laurence Oliphant." *The Journal of Speculative Philosophy*, Vol. XXI, No. 1, (January 1887): 82-105.
     A chapter-by-chapter synopsis of Oliphant's treatise.

Marquis de Sade

1740-1814

(Born Donatien Alphonse François, Comte de Sade)
French novelist, short story writer, essayist, and dramatist.

For additional information on Sade's career, see *Nineteenth-Century Literature Criticism,* Volume 3.

INTRODUCTION

The Marquis de Sade produced graphic celebrations of sexual violence, incest, torture, and murder during a period that encompassed the end of the *ancien régime,* the French Revolution, and the reign of Napoleon. His most notorious works are a series of novels in which wealthy, powerful "libertines" systematically rape, torture, and kill an assortment of victims—primarily women and adolescents of both sexes—while articulating elaborate philosophical justifications for this behavior. Rejecting the existence of a Supreme Being, Sade posits a lawless and destructive Nature as the only rational guide to behavior; sexual cruelty and the will to power, being natural human impulses, should be fostered rather than discouraged. His reputation inspired the nineteenth-century psychiatrist Richard von Krafft-Ebing to attach the author's name to the concept of sadism, sexual gratification through the infliction of pain on others.

Biographical Information

Born into a wealthy, titled family, Sade was educated in a Jesuit *collège,* then served in the cavalry during the Seven Years' War. In 1763 his father arranged his marriage to Renée-Pélagie Cordier de Launay de Montreuil, daughter of a wealthy and politically powerful family. Shortly after the marriage, however, Sade was jailed on charges of criminal sexual conduct. Over the next fifteen years his increasingly notorious penchant for sexually abusing servants and prostitutes fueled a series of scandals, incarcerations, and escapes. In 1778 he was imprisoned at Vincennes under a *lettre de cachet,* an arbitrary decree of imprisonment obtained from the king by the Marquis's mother-in-law. Most of the rest of his life was spent in various prisons. Released in 1790 during the French Revolution, he served briefly as a judge but was imprisoned again in 1793 as a suspected enemy of the Revolution and narrowly escaped the guillotine before being freed the following year. In 1801 he was again arrested on charges of obscenity. Judged insane, he was confined in a succession of institutions until his death in the asylum at Charenton in 1814.

Major Works

Although he wrote and acted in amateur theatrical productions as early as 1765, Sade began writing prose fiction

following his incarceration at Vincennes in 1778. While Sade employs many of the conventions of picaresque, gothic, and sentimental fiction, his novels are unique in the literature of their time in their rejection of any moral law and their explicit, encyclopedic detailing of violent sexual behavior. *Les 120 journées de Sodome, ou l'école du libertinage (The 120 Days of Sodom; or, The Romance of the School for Libertinage),* begun in the Bastille in the early 1780s and never completed, proposes to set forth in novelistic form a catalog of all possible forms of libertine sexual behavior. *Justine, ou les malheurs de la vertu (Justine; or, The Misfortunes of Virtue),* the story of a virtuous young woman who undergoes horrific sexual tortures and is finally killed by a stroke of lightning, was also completed in the Bastille; an expanded version was published in 1797 as *La nouvelle Justine (The New Justine),* along with *Juliette, ou les prospérités du vice (The Story of Juliette; or, Vice Amply Rewarded),* the story of Justine's sister Juliette, who embraces vice and prospers at every turn. *La philosophie dans le boudoir (Philosophy in the Bedroom)* presents the initiation of a young woman into the philosophy and practice of libertinism. Sade's surviving work also includes a number of more conventional dramas and short stories, two historical novels, and an epistolary novel, *Aline et Val-*

cour. Much of his voluminous correspondence has also been preserved.

Critical Reception

While Sade's writings were not distributed publicly during the nineteenth century, they were privately circulated. In 1843 the French critic Charles Augustin Sainte-Beuve named Sade and Lord Byron as "the two greatest sources of inspiration" for contemporary writers, many of whom saw the Marquis as a pioneer of the dark side of human nature and as a martyr for freedom. Algernon Charles Swinburne, Paul Verlaine, Charles Baudelaire, William Blake, and Guillaume Apollinaire were among the writers influenced by Sade's life and work. In the twentieth century, the Surrealist movement found inspiration in Sade's iconoclastic use of eroticism and his defiant rejection of all restrictions on personal liberty. The latter half of the twentieth century has seen a proliferation of Sade criticism. Studies by such critics as Roland Barthes, Maurice Blanchot, Pierre Klossowski, and Georges Bataille focus on Sade's insights into the psychology of power and desire, and on relationships between his rhetorical practices and the desire for absolute personal sovereignty. Michel Foucault's perception of Sade's work as marking the "frontier" between Classical and modern thought has precipitated numerous analyses of the interrelationship between Sade's writings, his cultural and philosophical milieu, and the political, economic, and social upheavals of late eighteenth-century France. A number of critics have also examined the treatment of female characters in Sade's texts. Alice Laborde finds in his work an exposé of his society's unfair treatment of women and a plea for sexual equality. Andrea Dworkin, on the other hand, uses her reading of Sade to support her contention that pornography functions as a means to degrade and subjugate women. Angela Carter argues that Sade's work is ultimately valuable because it explicitly depicts violent and oppressive attitudes that underlie conventional relations between men and women.

PRINCIPAL WORKS

Justine, ou les malheurs de la vertu [*Justine; or, The Misfortunes of Virtue,* 1931; also published as *Justine; or, Good Conduct Well Chastised,* 1953] (novel) 1791

Aline et Valcour (novel) 1795

La philosophie dans le boudoir [*The Bedroom Philosophers,* 1953; also published as *Philosophy in the Bedroom,* 1965] (novel) 1795

Juliette, ou les prospérités du vice [*The Story of Juliette; or, Vice Amply Rewarded,* 1965] (novel) 1797

La nouvelle Justine [*The New Justine,* 1956] (novel) 1797

Les crimes de l'amour [*The Crimes of Love, 1964;* also published as *The Crimes of Passion,* 1965] (short stories) 1800

*Les 120 journées de Sodome, ou l'école du libertinage [*The 120 Days of Sodom; or, The Romance of the School for Libertinage,* 1954] (unfinished novel) 1904

**Dialogue entre un prêtre et un moribund [*Dialogue between a Priest and a Dying Man,* 1927] (novel) 1926

*This work was written in 1785.
**This work was written in 1782.

CRITICISM

Georges Bataille (essay date 1957)

SOURCE: "De Sade's Sovereign Man," in *Eroticism, Death and Sensuality,* City Lights Books, 1986, pp. 164-76.

[*A French novelist, philosopher, and critic who died in 1962, Bataille received considerable critical attention in France for his theories of eroticism and mysticism. He was among the first critics to undertake a serious study of Sade's writing and philosophy. In this excerpt from a book first published in French in 1957, Bataille considers the sexual excesses depicted in Sade's works in terms of a quest for absolute personal sovereignty.*]

The Marquis de Sade's system perfects as much as it criticises a certain way of bringing the individual in to the full exercise of all his potentialities above the heads of the goggling crowd. . . .

The events of de Sade's real life lead one to suspect an element of braggadocio in his insistence on sovereignty seen as a denial of the rights and feelings of others. But the boasting was essential if he was to work out a system completely free from human weakness. In his life de Sade took other people into account, but his conception of fulfilment worked over and over in his lonely cell led him to deny outright the claims of other people. The Bastille was a desert; his writing was the only outlet for his passions and in it he pushed back the limits of what was possible beyond the craziest dreams ever framed by man. These books distilled in prison have given us a true picture of a man for whom other people did not count at all.

De Sade's morality, says Maurice Blanchot [in *Lautréamont et Sade,* 1949]

> is founded on absolute solitude as a first given fact. De Sade said over and over again in different ways that we are born alone, there are no links between one man and another. The only rule of conduct then is that I prefer those things which affect me pleasurably and set at nought the undesirable effects of my preferences on other people. The greatest suffering of others always counts for less than my own pleasure. What matter if I must purchase my most trivial satisfaction through a fantastic accumulation of

wrongdoing? For my satisfaction gives me pleasure, it exists in myself, but the consequences of
crime do not touch me, they are outside me.

Maurice Blanchot's analysis faithfully matches de Sade's
basic thinking. This thinking is doubtless artificial. It fails
to take into account the actual make-up of every real man,
inconceivable if shorn of the links made by others with
him and by him with others. The independence of one man
has never ceased to be any more than a boundary to the
interdependence of mankind, without which there would
be no human life. This is of cardinal importance. But de
Sade's doctrine is not so wide of the mark as all that. It
may deny the reality on which life is based, yet we do experience moments of excess that stir us to the roots of our
being and give us strength enough to allow free rein to our
elemental nature. But if we were to deny those moments
we should fail to understand our own nature.

De Sade's doctrine is nothing more nor less than the logical consequence of these moments that deny reason.

By definition, excess stands outside reason. Reason is
bound up with work and the purposeful activity that in-
carnates its laws. But pleasure mocks at toil, and toil we
have seen to be unfavourable to the pursuit of intense pleasure. If one calculates the ratio between energy consumed
and the usefulness of the results, the pursuit of pleasure
even if reckoned as useful is essentially extravagant; the
more so in that usually pleasure has no end product, is
thought of as an end in itself and is desired for its very extravagance. This is where de Sade comes in. He does not
formulate the above principles, but he implies them by asserting that pleasure is more acute if it is criminal and the
more abhorrent the crime the greater the pleasure. One
can see how the excesses of pleasure lead to the denial of
the rights of other people which is, as far as man is concerned, an excessive denial of the principle upon which his
life is based.

In this de Sade was convinced that he had made a decisive
discovery in the field of knowledge. If crime leads a man
to the greatest sensual satisfactions, the fulfilment of the
most powerful desires, what could be more important than
to deny that solidarity which opposes crime and prevents
the enjoyment of its fruits? I can picture this violent truth
striking him in the loneliness of his prison. From that instant he ceased to have any truck with anything, even in
himself, that might have invalidated his system. Had he
not been in love himself, just like anyone else? When he
had run off with his sister-in-law, had not that helped to
get him locked up by arousing his mother-in-law's wrath
so that she procured the fatal *lettre de cachet?* Latterly was
he not to adopt political views based on concern for the
welfare of the masses? Was he not horror-struck to see
from his window, in the prison to which his opposition to
the methods of the Terror had brought him, the guillotine
at work? And finally did he not shed "tears of blood" over
the loss of a manuscript [*The 120 Days of Sodom*] in which
he had striven to reveal—to other men, observe—the truth
of the insignificance of other people? He may have told
himself that none the less the truth of sexual attraction is
not fully apparent if consideration for other people para-
lyses its action. He refused to contemplate anything he
could not experience in the interminable silence of his cell
where only visions of an imaginary world bound him to
life. . . .

De Sade's system is the ruinous form of eroticism. Moral
isolation means that all the brakes are off; it shows what
spending can really mean. The man who admits the value
of other people necessarily imposes limits upon himself.
Respect for others hinders him and prevents him from
measuring the fullest extent of the only aspiration he has
that does not bow to his desire to increase his moral and
material resources. Blindness due to respect for others
happens every day; in the ordinary way we make do with
rapid incursions into the world of sexual truths and then
openly give them the lie the rest of the time. Solidarity
with everybody else prevents a man from having the sovereign attitude. The respect of man for man leads to a cycle
of servitude that allows only for minor moments of disorder and finally ends the respect that their attitude is based
on since we are denying the sovereign moment to man in
general.

From the opposite point of view, "the centre of de Sade's
world" is, according to Maurice Blanchot, "the demands
of sovereignty asserted through an enormous denial". Unfettered freedom opens out into a void where the possibilities match the intensest aspirations at the expense of secondary ones; a sort of heroic cynicism cuts the ties of consideration and tenderness for others without which we
cannot bear ourselves in the normal way. Perspectives of
this order place us as far from what we usually are as the
majesty of the storm is from the sunshine or from the drea-
rily overcast sky. In fact we do not possess the excessive
store of strength necessary to attain the fulfilment of our
sovereignty. Actual sovereignty, however boundless it
might seem in the silent fantasy of the masses, still even
in its worst moments falls far below the unleashed frenzy
that de Sade's novels portray. De Sade himself was doubtless neither strong enough nor bold enough to attain to the
supreme moment he describes. Maurice Blanchot has pin-
pointed this moment which dominates all the rest and
which de Sade calls apathy. "Apathy", says Maurice Blanchot,

> is the spirit of denial applied to the man who has
> elected to be sovereign. It is in some ways the
> cause and principle of energy. De Sade seems to
> reason somewhat after this manner: the individ-
> ual of today possesses a certain amount of
> strength; most of the time he wastes his strength
> by using it for the benefit of such simulacra as
> other people, God or ideals. He does wrong to
> disperse his energy in this way for he exhausts
> his potentialities by wasting them, but he does
> worse in basing his behaviour on weakness, for
> if he puts himself out for the sake of other people
> the fact is that he feels he needs to lean on them.
> This weakness is fatal. He grows feeble by spend-
> ing his strength in vain and he spends his
> strength because he thinks he is feeble. But the
> true man knows himself to be alone and accepts
> the fact; he denies every element in his own na-
> ture, inherited from seventeen centuries of cow-
> ardice, that is concerned with others than him-
> self; pity, gratitude and love, for example, are

emotions that he will destroy; through their destruction he regains all the strength he would have had to bestow on these debilitating impulses, and more important he acquires from this labour of destruction the beginnings of true energy. It must be clearly understood indeed that apathy does not consist in ruining 'parasitic' affections but also in opposing the spontaneity of any passion no matter what. The vicious man who indulges his vice immediately is nothing but a poor doomed creature. Even debauchees of genius, perfectly equipped to become monsters, are fated for catastrophe if they are content to follow their inclinations. De Sade insists that for passion to become energy it has to be compressed, it must function at one remove by passing through a necessary phase of insensibility; then its full potentiality will be realised. Early in her career Juliette is always being scolded by Clairwill: she commits crime only in the flush of enthusiasm, she lights the torch of crime only at the torch of passion, she sets lewdness and heady pleasure above all else. This is easy and dangerous. Crime is more important than lewdness; crimes committed in cold blood are greater than crimes carried out in the heat of the moment; but the crime 'committed when the sensitive part has been hardened, that dark and secret crime is the most important of all because it is the act of a soul which having destroyed everything within itself has accumulated immense strength, and this can be completely identified with the acts of total destruction soon to come.' All the great libertines who live only for pleasure are great only because they have destroyed in themselves all their capacity for pleasure. That is why they go in for frightful anomalies, for otherwise the mediocrity of ordinary sensuality would be enough for them. But they have made themselves insensitive; they intend to exploit their insensitivity, that sensitiveness they have denied and destroyed, and they become ferocious. Cruelty is nothing but a denial of oneself carried so far that it becomes a destructive explosion; insensibility sets the whole being aquiver, says de Sade: 'The soul passes on to a kind of apathy that is metamorphosed into pleasures a thousand times more wonderful than those that their weaknesses have procured them.'

I have quoted that passage in full for it throws great light on the central point where being is more than just presence. Presence is sometimes almost sloth, the neutral moment when, passively being means indifference to being, already on the way to meaninglessness. Being is also the excess of being, the upward surge towards the impossible. Excess leads to the moment when transcendent pleasure is no longer confined to the senses, when what is felt through the senses is negligible and thought, the mental mechanism that rules pleasure, takes over the whole being. Without this excess of denial pleasure is a furtive, contemptible thing, powerless to keep its real place, the highest place, in an awareness that is ten times as sensitive. Clairwill, the heroine Juliette's companion in debauch, says "I'd like to find a crime that should have never ending repercussions even when I have ceased to act, so that there would not be a single instant of my life when even if I were asleep I was not the cause of some disorder or another, and this disorder I should like to expand until it brought general corruption in its train or such a categorical disturbance that even beyond my life the effects would continue". To reach such impossible peaks is indeed no less formidable an undertaking than the ascent of Everest; no one can do it without a colossal concentration of energy. But in the concentration that leads to the summit of Mount Everest there is but a limited response to the desire to excel. If we start from the principle of denying others posited by de Sade it is strange to observe that at the very peak of unlimited denial of others is a denial of oneself. Theoretically, denial of others should be affirmation of oneself, but it is soon obvious that if it is unlimited and pushed as far as it can possibly go, beyond personal enjoyment, it becomes a quest for inflexible sovereignty. Concern for power renders real, historical sovereignty flexible. Real sovereignty is not what it claims to be; it is never more than an effort aimed at freeing human existence from the bonds of necessity. Among others, the sovereign of history evaded the injunctions of necessity. He evaded it to a high degree with the help of the power given him by his faithful subjects. The reciprocal loyalty between the sovereign and his subjects rested on the subordination of the latter and on their vicarious participation in his sovereignty. But de Sade's sovereign man has no actual sovereignty; he is a fictitious personage whose power is limited by no obligations. There is no loyalty expected from this sovereign man towards those who confer his power upon him. Free in the eyes of other people he is no less the victim of his own sovereignty. He is not free to accept a servitude in the form of a quest for wretched pleasure, he is not free to stoop to that! The remarkable thing is that de Sade starts from an attitude of utter irresponsibility and ends with one of stringent self-control. It is the highest satisfaction alone that he is after, but such satisfaction has a value. It means refusing to stoop to a lower degree of pleasure, refusing to opt out. De Sade describes for the benefit of other people, his readers, the peak that sovereignty can attain. There is a movement forward of transgression that does not stop before a summit is reached. De Sade has not shirked this movement; he has accepted it in all its consequences and these go further than the original principle of denying others and asserting oneself. Denying others becomes in the end denying oneself. In the violence of this progression personal enjoyment ceases to count, the crime is the only thing that counts and whether one is the victim or not no matter; all that matters is that the crime should reach the pinnacle of crime. These exigencies lie outside the individual, or at least they set a higher value on the process begun by him but now detached from him and transcending him, than on the individual himself. De Sade cannot help bringing into play beyond the personal variety an almost impersonal egotism. We are not bound to consider in terms of real life his entirely imaginary situations. But we can see how he was forced in spite of his principles to accept the transcendence of the personal being as a concomitant of crime and transgression. What can be more disturbing than the prospect of selfishness becoming the will to perish in the furnace lit by selfishness? De Sade incarnated this progression in one of his most perfect characters.

Amélie lives in Sweden. One day she goes to see

Borchamps . . . This man, hoping for a monster execution, has just turned over to the king all the members of a conspiracy which he himself has plotted, and this betrayal delights the young woman. "I love your ferocity," she tells him, "swear to me that one day I also shall be your victim. Since I was 15 my imagination has been fired only at the thought of dying a victim of the cruel passions of a libertine. Not that I wish to die tomorrow—my extravagant fancies do not go as far as that; but that is the only way I want to die; to have my death the result of a crime is an idea that sets my head spinning." A strange head, that one, and well deserving of the answer: "I love your head madly, and I think we shall achieve great things between us . . . rotten and corrupt it is I grant you!" Thus

> for the whole man, man in his entirety, no evil is possible. If he inflicts hurt on others, the pleasure of it! If others hurt him, what satisfaction! Virtue pleases him because it is weak and he can crush it, and so does vice, for the disorder it brings even at his own expense gives him satisfaction. If he lives there is no event in his life that will not seem to him fortunate. If he dies his death is greater happiness yet, and conscious of his own destruction he sees in it the crown of a life only justified by the urge to destroy. Thus the man who denies is the ultimate denial of all else in the universe, a denial which will not even spare him. Doubtless the strength to deny confers a privilege while it lasts, but the negative action it exerts is the only protection against the intensity of a huge denial.

An impersonal denial, an impersonal crime!

Tending towards the continuity of beings beyond death!

William Mead on responses to Sade:

In granting [Sade] his rightful place in the marvelous and essentially poetic company of our heroes and idols, we actually refuse him the one privilege he sought to deserve: that of being a source of perpetual outrage. By every imaginable means, from the most naïve to the most subtle, Sade labored to scandalize the "normal" human being which we all think we are and which we are in fact, so long as we are willing to live in peace with our neighbors and want them to think well of us. Entire works from his pen have no other visible inspiration than a desire—a perfectly comprehensible desire, for that matter—to upset the reader and to cast doubt on whatever seems well established and clear. What else was this eminently reasonable *philosophe* doing when he sought throughout his career to demonstrate the inferiority of reason? This "sectateur" of Truth, in his prolonged efforts to prove that Truth does not exist? This self-acclaimed "best friend of mankind," in setting forth an idea of human happiness so inadmissible that it has had to be passed off by admirers as a manifestation of *l'humour noir?*

"The Marquis de Sade: Politics on a Human Scale,"
L'Esprit créateur, *Vol. III, No. 4, Winter, 1963.*

De Sade's sovereign man does not offer our wretchedness a transcendent reality. At least his aberration points the way to the continuity of crime! This continuity transcends nothing. It cannot overtake what is lost. But in Amélie de Sade links infinite continuity with infinite destruction.

Beatrice C. Fink   (essay date 1972)

SOURCE: "The Case for a Political System in Sade," in *Studies on Voltaire in the Eighteenth Century,* Vol. LXXXVIII, 1972, pp. 493-512.

[*Fink published numerous articles on Sade during the 1970s. In the following excerpt, she examines the political content of Sade's work and argues that he should "be taken seriously as a political thinker."*]

Suppose it is accepted that Sade's socio-political models abound in logical inconsistencies having serious consequences for their theoretical credibility. Does it follow that Sade is therefore disqualified for membership in the fraternity of respectable political philosophers?

There are several reasons for suggesting that the answer to this question is not obviously in the affirmative. Since models and utopias can be deployed by a political writer for various purposes wherein the issue of their internal logical consistency is neither important nor relevant, a broader, more sophisticated criterion must be used both for determining Sade's objectives in their respect and for reassessing his overall credentials as a political philosopher. This is especially important when dealing with a writer whose unconventional style and exotic interests tend to puzzle, titillate or even offend.

The hallmark of serious political philosophy, whether analytical or normative, is a preoccupation with the phenomenon of power in society: its origins, magnitude, distribution, limitation, validation, etc. Immediately we are confronted with the fact that Sade's writings demonstrate an almost ubiquitous concern with the concept of power and its ethical validation, use and consequences at the level of interpersonal and intergroup relationships. To be sure, power is generally envisaged in his idea-world as a destructive force based on sexual domination of the many by the few or the 'unique'. But this does not preclude a serious political purpose. Another common characteristic of political philosophy is an explicit treatment of personality and psychology as they are conditioned by political institutions and as they in turn influence the latter. This is really what lies behind Sadian models, although they are also used as symbolic myths and deforming mirrors. In his analyses of individual and group behaviour Sade employs a materialistic naturalism bordering on the metaphysical, a psychology of total egoistic hedonism and a relativistic ethic antithetical to the Judeo-Christian tradition. Despite his flights of orgiastic imagination and his black humour therefore, his monasteries, islands, castles and secret societies along with the disquisitions, brochures and statutes which define their credos and organizational mechanisms all rest on articulated philosophical components. . . .

I

While Sade's world of strangely distorted creatures constitutes a metaphoric tableau of contingent reality, it is likewise an effort to 'get at the system', to discredit its mores and institutions as a prelude to advancing alternatives. All viable political systems, as Sade clearly saw, require a supporting ideology which justifies existing institutions as 'good' or 'natural' and perpetuates the value structures on which they depend. In order to bring the system down, its ideology and the agencies which maintain it must be attacked. Sade approaches this task with a wide range of literary and argumentative techniques, principally those of *reductio ad absurdum,* exaggeration, eroticism and ridicule, all of which were very much in vogue in the period during which he lived and wrote. Everywhere the objective is the same: to erode the philosophical underpinnings of society, to reveal its ethics to be hollow and inconsistent with the true nature of man, to unfrock its leaders as frauds and to render untenable any metaphysical justification for the way things are.

At the level of greatest philosophical generality, Sade anunciates in the words of his libertines a coldly Hobbesian view of human nature sharply at variance with the faith in the essential and original goodness of man. Absent the shaping and constraining influences of society, he argues, human nature would swiftly reveal itself to be dominated by the urge to conquer, maim and destroy. Juliette, an accomplished Sadist, remarks 'Je l'avoue, j'aime le crime avec fureur, lui seul irrite mes sens. . . . Tant pis pour les victimes, il en faut, tout se détruirait dans l'univers sans les profondes lois de l'équilibre.' 'Pauvre sotte' says the libertine financier Dubourg to the penniless and orphaned Justine, 'imagines-tu que les hommes soient assez sots pour faire l'aumône à de petites gueuses comme toi sans exiger l'intérêt de leur argent?' The interest he has in mind is quite specific!

Sade's frequent attacks on organized religion and its practitioners are especially significant in this connection because of the close association between church and state in 18th-century France. The writer's objective is clearly to subvert that part of traditional ethics based on religion and also to deprive the state of the dignity and credentials it derives, via the church, from its alliance with God. This he undertakes in two ways: by inserting long disquisitions or dialogues as didactic devices in a form of *Bildungsroman;* by using obscene caricature, derived from the libertine novel.

Juliette does not become a die-hard atheist through experience alone. The logic which leads her to deny the existence of any nonmaterial essence or being is cultivated by a long line of mentors she meets in the course of her adventures, notably Clairwil. And in the *Philosophie dans le boudoir,* a form of 'Bildungsdialog', Eugénie de Mistival receives a 48-hour course in debauchery from Dolmancé who instills in her the conviction that god is but the result of fear and weakness, an 'abominable fantôme', an 'être inconséquent et barbare.' Organized religion, she learns, is merely a hoax based on an amalgam of absurd rites and intolerant practices. God must be destroyed in the libertine's quest for total emancipation. The statutes of the *Société des amis du crime* in *L'Histoire de Juliette* prohibit entry to all believers. Significantly, all characters who refuse to accept atheistic and antireligious views, for whom Justine serves as a prototype, are invariably destroyed. Devil worship is likewise considered a weakness, even among the powerful. Both the minister Saint-Fond in *Juliette* and the bohemian Brigandos in *Aline et Valcour* indulge in and preach the cult of Satan. Both are thwarted in the attainment of their respective goals.

The most effective thrust of Sade's attack on god and religion, however, resides in his reliance on obscene caricature. This technique had already been applied to ecclesiastics in libertine novels. Indeed, those novels which caught the author's attention are conveniently placed by him on the bookshelf of a none-too-innocent monk in *Juliette.* Corrupt, libidinous and atheistic churchmen abound in all of Sade's novels, ranging from the humble victim-type père Claude in *Juliette,* to the highest ranking members of the church (in the same novel). Frequently the latter are named after actual ecclesiastic figures, alive or dead. A case in point is the debauched pope Pius VI, who was the pope at the time *Juliette* was written and published. Braschi, as he is familiarly referred to, is the very incarnation of evil and provides a particularly blasphemous example of prurient parody. The Vatican lodgings of this hardened libertine are adorned with the trappings of a highly lascivious house of pleasure. In this setting, Braschi proceeds to eulogize murder during Juliette's first audience in a papal sermon not far removed from an encyclical. He later entertains her at an orgiastic banquet where he and other high officials of the church gorge themselves with wine during a mock holy supper. But the high point of depravity is reached when the pope and Juliette indulge in typically Sadian forms of sexual perversion on the high altar of Saint Peter's. The ceremony is described with geometric precision and can only be construed as a monstrous black parody of the Mass. Its various stages are simulated in obscene fashion after which there is a repeat performance, but with a different ending. This time a young man is crucified head downwards, like Saint Peter, and attached to one of the twisted altar columns. A young girl is subsequently beaten, then hanged from the second altar column, the whole effect being that of a gross distortion of mount Calvary.

Sade also attacks lay morality, thus differentiating himself from the bulk of his philosophical contemporaries. By frequent use of historical and ethnic examples, he carries the notion of moral relativism to its logical extreme. All rules of social conduct become acceptable so long as they conform with the 'natural' propensities of man. Sadian libertines justify their aberrant and criminal behaviour according to this tenet in arguments that are repeated *ad nauseam* in the fictional works. A brochure contained in the *Philosophie* entitled 'Français, encore un effort si vous voulez être républicains' summarizes what may be termed Sadian anti-ethics. Dolmancé-Sade derides and subverts society's taboos by proposing a code of behaviour exactly the opposite of the prevailing one for a republic which, naturally, is based on the principle of vice. In the process, laws are described as meaningless and oppressive obstacles to human freedom, thereby implicitly censuring judges and lawmakers while denying any significance to the notion of crime. Indeed, crime in Sadian terminology describes a type of rational activity designed to advance self-realization and happiness based on a philosophy of success. Murder is most useful in this regard, as illustrated amply by history. Far from being contrary to nature's intentions, it merely accelerates the process of metempsychosis. Furthermore, it possesses social utility as a device for population control, as do also abortion, euthanasia, sodomy and homosexuality, not to mention Sadian equivalents of the pill. The only type of murder vehemently condemned is legalized murder in the form of the death penalty, doubtless in part because of Sade's personal experiences with the law. Robbery is as good a means of property distribution as any other. Besides, he who is negligent enough to let himself be robbed, says Dolmancé, is the real culprit. Nudity is encouraged. Men and women should pool their resources, thereby rendering adultery meaningless. Incest is favorably regarded and 'devrait être la loi de tout gouvernement dont la fraternité fait la base'. Involved incestuous relationships are notably frequent among fictional characters in other works of Sade. They represent a transgression of one of society's most entrenched taboos and afford a means of striking at its basic structural unit. The libertine inhabitants of Silling, for example, all of whom interwed, interbed and to an extent intermurder one another, constitute a parody of the family, perhaps that of an 18th-century grandee. The remainder of Christian or lay virtues, love, charity, gratitude, altruism etc. are equally subjected to ridicule throughout Sadian fiction.

What is striking about this display of subversion by categorical transgression is the primacy given sexual violations. The marquis's personal inclinations and experiences provide a partial explanation for this but the main reason lies in the fact that for Sade sexual freedom constitutes the essence as well as the symbol of individual freedom. . . .

II

The Blamonts, Curvals, Dubois and Clairwils of Sadian fiction concentrate their energies on invalidating and breaking the laws of the land. In fact, the most accomplished among them, such as Juliette, violate the laws of nature as well, insofar as they denature themselves by systematically eliminating any trace of human feeling which would render them vulnerable. In the process they become what Blanchot terms the apathetic hero. In this sense Sade's is actually a 'système de la métanature' going far beyond anything Holbach might have envisaged.

It would nonetheless be erroneous to conclude that Sade's solution to the problem of group living is anarchy, namely the lack of any solution. Invariably his social outlaws converge in distinct communities, each with its highly regulated life style. Even Brigandos's bohemians in *Aline et Valcour* operate according to rules and regulations of their own. Rather than being totally unstructured, the alternatives to official society proposed by Sade all exhibit explicit codes of behaviour and institutions which organize daily existence in a minute, even regimental fashion. One need only spend a day in the convent of Sainte-Marie-des-Bois or on the island of Tamoé to find this out. As Roland Barthes notes, everything, to the last detail of who eats

what with whom is planned in the castle of Silling where the celebrated 'orgie sans nom' of the *120 Journées de Sodome* takes place. While these communities or organizations vary in size, composition and inner power relationships, they are all isolated from the rest of the world. Isolation affords protection, secrecy and a milieu of considerable freedom for the libertine although, in the end, there may be a feeling of spatial confinement. It can also serve as an esthetic device to create an ambience of drama or mirage. More importantly for the purposes of political analysis, it affords environments removed from the institutions which mould and constrain behaviour for the bulk of mankind. Sade's artificially autonomous constructs, that is, are used as laboratories in which to experiment with alternative ethical and political systems.

Essentially, Sadian political laboratories fall into two categories: groups geographically removed from Europe by vast stretches of ocean and camouflaged, or clandestine European groups operating behind thick stone walls, usually in castles or religious abodes. The former provide a vision of Utopia in the form of Tamoé; the latter, scattered throughout the rest of Sade's fiction, may be named Anti-Utopia or, following Stephen Marcus, Pornotopia. The kingdom of Butua, which fits into both categories, is an exotic pornotopia.

In the world-wide quest for his beloved Léonore occupying a goodly portion of *Aline et Valcour,* Sainville lands on the rocky shores of the south-sea isle of Tamoé. He notices that the port of entry is well fortified and that careful planning has gone into the circular capital city whose buildings, save two, are identical. Tamoé possesses the physical hallmarks of a classic utopia. It is a far-away never-never land, an autarkic world in miniature whose inhabitants lead a communal life of harmony, conformity, equality—except for the leader—and unchanging sameness. Private property is non-existent, gold is scorned, sexual relationships are based on mutual consent and compatibility, war is avoided and the cult of a supreme being is devoid of ritual and hierarchy. Suitable demographic policies and a state system of education have been implemented along with a penal system based on prevention rather than punishment. The island further resembles other utopias in that the notions of progress and change are absent except for the intimation that its hereditary monarchy may eventually give way to a republic. The arts, for example, are neglected, except for the folklore variety, because they would stimulate creativity and controversy and thus a desire for change. All of this is the accomplishment of one man, the European-educated benevolent despot Zamé.

Both Favre and Goulemot conclude that flaws in this model render it politically impractical, the former stressing psychological defects and the latter contradictions he sees between Zamé the proclaimed *primo inter pares* with enlightened republican leanings and the actual Zamé, a paternalistic autocrat who reduces his subjects to child-like dependency. If the island's inhabitants are unable to participate responsibly in government what will happen, asks Goulemot, when Zamé disappears? Would not another despot or simply chaos emerge rather than a liberal republic?

It is essential at this point to consider the function of a utopia or myth in political thought. Although Sainville exclaims 'Je me crus transporté . . . dans ces temps heureux de l'âge d'or' this in no way implies that Tamoé should be regarded merely as an expression of nostalgia for bygone times. Among other things, sentimental musings over the lost innocence of man would be jarringly inconsistent with Sade's general philosophy. In addition, utopias are rarely intended as mere blueprints. Rather, they are embodiments of specific sets of myths, symbols and experimental environments. Their principal functions in political literature are clinical and normative: they serve as simplified and controlled environments for the exploration of political dynamics and/or as yardsticks for measuring the imperfections of existing societies. Since utopias are not intended for implementation, it is unnecessary for them to be situated in a particular chronological context. Claude Dubois terms such atemporality an 'uchronie'. Normative or experimental purposes do not, however, preclude specific if piecemeal institutional recommendations for the real world. Indeed, there are far too many treatments of specific problems central to all of Sade's writings in Tamoé—the centralization of power, pacifism, and demographic, educational and penal policies—to permit acceptance of the hypothesis that it merely represents a rhetorical *tour de force* or a dilletantish conformity to literary fashion. It is possible, however, that Sade may have had more than one purpose in mind when inserting Tamoé in his novel, one of them being a desire to parody certain aspects of literary utopias.

Tamoé is the only properly utopian model in Sadian fiction. Pornotopias are much more numerous, in part because Sade's libertines frequently maintain harems at close hand. These constructs focus on that aspect of political thought closest to Sade's own heart: individual power drives and interpersonal power relationships. They share regulation and isolation as distinctive features with utopias but differ from the latter in several important respects. Since they operate on the margin of society yet within its geographic confines, their isolation requires a hermetic, clandestine existence or a false front concealing their inner workings and purposes. Whereas the moral, religious and legal institutions of Tamoé are revisionist and normative in character, the pornotopias, with their antiethics based on vice and destruction, are primarily clinical. In the latter, a small, pleasure-seeking oligarchy (at times a single despot) comprising the strong dominates and exploits a horde of ever-destroyed but easily replaced victims, the weak. Masters are usually drawn from the higher ranks of the bourgeoisie or the clergy. There are, however, significant exceptions to this rule: the duc de Blangis, the comte de Bressac, as well as people of popular origin such as la Dubois or la Durand. Most are immensely rich. Victims on the other hand are often lovely aristocratic adolescents or simply people of unspecified origin. Although master libertines overtly pledge loyalty to one another as a measure of enlightened self-interest, at times they dispose of one another when they are so inclined, *e.g.*

la Durand's false accusations intentionally leading to Clairwil's murder by Juliette.

The convent of Sainte-Marie-des-Bois, which grows increasingly complex in each successive version of *Justine,* and the castle of Silling in the *120 Journées* constitute the most elaborate of Sade's highly regulated pornotopias. Several critics have analyzed the psychological mechanisms and modus vivendi of these social microcosms. As with Tamoé however, emphasis here will be on their deployment as experimental socio-political laboratories or models. As such, they are like orchestrated symphonies in which each member plays a well-defined part according to age, sex and, in the case of masters, individual yet known and therefore predictable sexual idiosyncrasies. There is also a foreman class composed of those responsible for domestic tasks and of monitors chosen among the victims for surveillance purposes. The social backgrounds of the masters do not exhibit sufficient uniformity to support the deduction from their origins and that of the victims that Sade's primary purpose in structuring the pornotopias is to present a fictionalized rendition of class dynamics in, say, contemporary France.

Actually, Sade's masters tend to be depersonalized and his victims to be mere objects of pleasure. Blanchot notes this and points out that Sadian characters are in reality quantities of energy rather than individualized human beings [in *Lautréamont et Sade,* 1949]. The true libertine master is a voluntaristic, not an impulsive creature. In order to ensure his dominance and maximize his pleasure, he must exert cunning, ruthless force and constant self-control. The group situation examined in Sainte-Marie-des-Bois or Silling for instance is therefore more than a simple free-for-all where the strong conquer and rule the weak. Nor is it merely a literary transposition or metaphor of prevailing social conditions with occasional touches of caricature. It is an attempt to explore the behavioral characteristics of groups when the constraints exerted by the outside world have been removed. How do people act, asks Sade, when there is not so much the fear as the fact of retribution among an intelligent and powerful elite? If Sade chooses to express power drives and relationships in terms of sexual domination and sexual domination and sexual destruction (*i.e.* torture, murder and certain forms of anthropophagy), it is not merely because they represent the obsessions and imaginary transgressions of a frustrated prisoner. They are used to incarnate as well as to symbolize the essence of the pleasure principle and as tools of scientific investigation. Sade realizes that people do not, in fact cannot act or be treated in the manner described in his pornotopias but opts to experiment with extremes, a laboratory method resorted to by scientists in order to intensify and clarify the causes and effects of their research. What Sade is experimenting with in his multiple social laboratories is the techniques of manipulation and control, certainly the most original aspect of his political thought and methodology. The nature of these techniques throws light on the links between Utopia, Pornotopia and the rest of Sadian narrative fiction.

III

Positions of political dominance have traditionally been

taken to derive from divine right, the force of arms or, more recently, economic factors. Increasingly, however, analysts of power structures are turning to psychological factors for an understanding of power dynamics. Psychological warfare, brainwashing, group conditioning etc. are relative newcomers to the vocabulary of politics although certain historical antecedents can be found. The impact of public opinion and the use of authority images in the form of political manipulators are considered to be important, at times crucial components of any analysis of the roots and consolidation of power.

Sade's historically precocious understanding of the relationship between power, institutions and the psychology of manipulation and control is one of the most intriguing aspects of his writings. Nowhere is this understanding better displayed than in his pornotopias and in Tamoé. Failure to recognize this fact may well account in large part for the reluctance of critics to take Sade seriously as a political philosopher.

Sadian characters are never simply creatures maneuvering according to the dictates of their urges and destinies. On the contrary, the subjugated are shaped by an elite's environmental and educational conditioning; libertine masters are in turn indoctrinated by libertine mentors and must learn to control themselves by eliminating all emotions and ideas which might make them vulnerable or incapable of manipulating others. Time and again, Sadian heroines in their formative stages are told to rethink their outlooks on life, not merely to rid themselves of inhibiting prejudices and preconceptions but also to toughen themselves to the point where the mastery of reason over emotion becomes absolute.

In Butua, where Sainville is a captive prior to reaching Tamoé, the tyrant Ben Mâacoro's minister Sarmiento describes the processes by which Butua's population has become a mass of stupefied, hardened and passive victims. Political organization is feudal, with priests and provincial vassals having a certain degree of authority, as have all men with respect to women. Sarmiento's justification of massive repression has a Hobbesian ring: only an absolute ruler can keep people in line and provide for a well-ordered society. The main tools of repression are psychological. Brainwashing is accomplished by a priestly caste which, in exchange for its social privileges, inculcates in the inhabitants the principles of superstition, fear and contempt for others. This contempt and the monarch's absolute power are symbolized by cannibalistic practices. That this is not the 'natural' mentality of Butua's people is made clear in the case of the persecuted wife serving as Sainville's housekeeper, who weeps with joy when she is treated with human kindness.

Zamé likewise places heavy emphasis on knowing the mechanisms of the human psyche in order to perform his leadership tasks in the best possible fashion. In contrast with Sarmiento, he devises a psychology of conformity and direction rather than fear and oppression. He conditions Tamoans into happiness by centralizing all power and decision-making in his own hands, eliminating economic inequality and the very possibility of social differentiation via acquisitiveness (there is no private property),

establishing total state control over education and by isolating the society from contact with others. Isolation notably precludes comparisons with other life styles and thus minimizes the unsettling weighing of alternatives. Strict equality among the subjects and the non-existence of private property eliminate economic motives as sources of change and instability while the hereditary monarchy eliminates any competition from below for the reins of power. Zamé has also instituted measures intended to weaken child-parent ties for fear that strong family units might create centers of dissension and loyalties other than to the state. The spirit of conformity and sameness is cultivated by means of a centrally controlled system of public education beginning in infancy. Instruction is purely factual; there is no teaching of esthetic, speculative or policy-oriented disciplines. The child, that is, is educated to understand the system and meet its technical requirements, not to innovate or make decisions for himself.

The overriding importance of stability and conformity in Tamoé emphasizes the role of public opinion or group standards of behaviour. People will obey the laws, Zamé proclaims, because the price of nonconformity is social ostracism. Equality and a high degree of sexual permissiveness further discourage criminal behaviour. Penal legislation, on the other hand, is designed to reform the lawbreaker, not to punish him. Capital offenses (e.g. murder) are dealt with by exile. Zamé defends his enlightened penal legislation with the following revealing comment: 'L'idée que le mal puisse jamais amener le bien est un des vertiges le plus effrayant de la tête des sots'.

Implicit in all this is the proposition that unhappiness and strife originate in change, acquisitiveness and the necessity or opportunity to select among alternatives. The ideal state thus begins with a final, irrevocable decision as to who shall control the reins of power and then proceeds so to organize production, consumption, education and the administration of justice as to render the individual content in an environment of stability where he is secure, ignorant of other modes of existence and insulated from the temptations of opportunity.

At this point, then, it becomes possible to enumerate the more important characteristics which Utopia, Pornotopia and the other group situations in Sadian fiction hold in common above and beyond their manifest differences along ethical and institutional lines. Thus, apart from the previously mentioned similarity in isolation and detailed regulation, one also finds systematic use of mythical or unreal settings which are used for clinical and/or normative purposes. Myths and archetypes exist both on the collective (golden age, island paradise, exotic kingdom, secret society) and individual levels. In this respect Sadian libertines can be likened to Prometheus, Narcissus or even Pygmalion personality types. A closely related feature is the timelessness of most Sadian models. Although certain pornotopias such as Silling have a set time span, the absence of change gives most Sadian models an atemporal character. Moreover, whether in Tamoé, Butua or Sainte-Marie-des-Bois, the system is based on the concept of elitism, that is of a rigid leader/led dichotomy. Broadbased participation in the processes of government never occurs.

The ruins of Sade's chateau, La Coste, destroyed during the French Revolution.

A corollary to this ubiquitous elitism is the presence of conformity enforced upon the subjected by regulations, psychological conditioning and sometimes simply brute force. The libertine master is also a conformist in a sense for in the end all true libertines behave the same way. The most significant as well as original common feature of these models, however, is that in all of them the elite relies mainly on the tools and mechanics of psychological conditioning and control to achieve its objectives and maintain its power. These traits permit one to advance the thesis that there is an underlying unity and philosophical significance to the political content of Sade's work.

IV

In our conclusion, certain shortcomings and ambiguities in Sade's political thought must be brought out. First, as others have noted, Sade never fully develops the mechanics of interlibertine relationships, namely those of power with power. 'Quel peut être le rapport de l'exception avec l'exception', asks Blanchot. Although they profess and at times even practice loyalty to those of their own kind, libertines do not feel bound by oaths and indeed the logic of their supremacy prevents absolute interpersonal commitments of any kind.

Another and more serious problem stems from Sade's ambiguity in the use of words. The vocabulary of Sadian politics often takes on multiple meanings depending on the context. Consider, for example, the term 'law'. In most cases it signifies repressive, at times absurd measures designed by society to inhibit man. In the case of natural law, however, it may designate either a physical absolute or that which is fundamentally right. Nor does Sade clearly spell out the relationship between inner and outer law, that is to say between voluntarism and determinism. The notion of justice is frequently denied meaning by certain libertines; yet they or others may in turn qualify a law or custom as unjust. The meaning of nature itself oscillates between that of a materialistic mechanism and that of a force endowed with certain metaphysical features, such as the bolt of lightning which annihilates Justine, or the very principle of destruction. Crime, vice and virtue also have differing meanings depending on the reference framework in which they are used. For Zamé and others they retain their standard meanings. Yet for those who place themselves above the law, these notions mean something quite different. For them, vice and crime become necessities of self-expression while virtue signifies irrational behaviour. One may even ask if such notions have any meaning at all if the code of behaviour which defines them is rejected. In spite of this ambiguity or ambivalence in the use of words, or perhaps even because of it, Sade must not be rejected from the ranks of political writers. He is simply exhibiting one of their occupational diseases. Finally, he may also be criticized for never unambiguously synthesizing the fundamental elements of his political philosophy. This is what makes it difficult to evaluate the political significance of certain passages and to extract a fully articulated political system from his narrative fiction.

Nonetheless, sufficient materials and arguments have been presented here to support the proposition that Sade deserves to be taken seriously as a political thinker. A political reading of his works, we maintain, reveals enough substance, originality and coherence to warrant a reassessment of his meaning and stature in the continuum of Western political philosophy. Presumably, this reassessment will accelerate in the future as the works of Sade become more accessible and less shocking.

Vera Lee (essay date 1972)

SOURCE: "The Sade Machine," in *Studies on Voltaire in the Eighteenth Century,* Vol. XCVIII, 1972, pp. 207-18.

[*In the following excerpt, Lee evaluates Sade's technique in his "iconoclastic" novels in terms of its function and apparent purpose.*]

In the last pages of his novel *Juliette,* Sade describes nature in convulsive upheaval. Lightning and turbulent wind attack the universe so violently that, in the author's words, 'On eût dit que la nature, ennuyée de ses ouvrages, fut prête à confondre tous les éléments pour les contraindre à des formes nouvelles.'

Patterning himself on this cataclysmic nature, Sade the novelist rejected the bland literature of his predecessors and set about to constrain thought and its expression into new forms. He constructed an elaborate machine, a literary battering ram designed to smash the foundations of moral rectitude for centuries to come. Our century has considered the Sadian machine with increasing interest and, recently, with an abundance of criticism, most of which is philosophical, moral or psychological. But if we confront Sade's literary product as a working apparatus, *a series of techniques calculated to achieve a certain effect,* then it becomes necessary to analyse and evaluate his work on a more immediate and practical level. To begin with, we may consider this apparatus from several points of view, for example, from the standpoints of: 1. its originality; 2. its endurance; 3. the quality of the machine as a machine; 4. its efficacity (or its effect on the reader).

On the first two counts, those of originality of invention and durability, the success of Sade's product is beyond dispute. Like all original artists, this author remoulded traditional forms and ideas, imbued them with his own fire and blazed a way to the future. Sade's invention has become such a modern phenomenon that—as Simone de Beauvoir has suggested—today's critics usually view his work as the province of Freud and Krafft-Ebing rather than the creation of an eighteenth-century writer.

But when we consider the intrinsic merit of his system— the quality of the machine as a machine—how are we to appraise it, and what possible standards may we apply to it? It is helpful, first of all, to distinguish generally between two models or categories of Sade's novels: on the one hand, those in which Sade, like Prévost, prudently pretends to paint vice in order to illustrate the superiority of virtue (*e.g. Les Infortunes de la vertu, Aline et Valcour, Les Crimes de l'amour*); on the other hand, those iconoclastic works in which virtue is merely a stupid foil for brilliant, triumphant vice (*La Nouvelle Justine, Juliette, La Philosophie dans le boudoir*). It is not the pseudo-virtuous novel of lip service, but the brutal, iconoclastic novel that most logically figures in an analysis of Sade's subversive system. Such works are usually novels of ideas. Yet it is difficult—perhaps unfair—to judge them either by philosophical or literary standards: the abundant philosophical commentary that fills their pages may be rich in insights into the author himself, but rather than a careful, significant contribution to the history of moral thought, this philosophy remains first and last a pretext and a blatant admixture of alibis. And as for literature, Sade did not intend to make of his iconoclastic novels true works of art. He was concerned neither with psychological portrayal nor with a credible depictive plot. Moreover, these works were written too hastily to show any serious, consistent attention to composition and language.

Rather than view such texts in the light of intellectual or artistic standards, we may well attempt to measure them with a more functional, utilitarian yardstick . . . Sade's novels are components of a high-powered instrument for evil. How well, then, do they serve their author's purpose? Let us begin by examining the construction and main characteristics of the Sadian machine.

If we consider such novels as *La Nouvelle Justine* or *Juliette,* we find the structure both simple and apparent: a visual description of vice alternates with the verbal justification of vice. The physical and the abstract succeed each other with see-saw regularity. Unity and continuity are achieved only through this mechanical repetition throughout the works.

On the philosophical side, there is little hint of any logical development of ideas, but, rather, an oscillation between one magnetic pole of a theory and its antithesis or counterpole. 'One must conform to the morals of one's country', a Sadian spokesman insists; but a few pages later, a similar spokesman offers convincing arguments for utter nonconformism. 'All things are equal in nature', another hero argues, and in no time at all we have just as strong a case for inequality. If a protagonist wishes to justify matricide, he follows Hartsoeker's and La Mettrie's theory that the sperm alone counts in the reproductive process and that mothers are overrated. But naturally when fathers are liquidated, that little sperm is a bagatelle. Conscience, necessity, utility, nature, society are all double or triple agents.

It would be difficult to trace any chronological evolution in this philosophical commentary. On the subject of Sade and nature, Philippe Sollers writes [in *Logiques,* 1968] that 'Après avoir réfuté Dieu par la nature, [Sade] finit par immoler la nature'. On the subject of Sade and crime, Simone de Beauvoir says that Sade, who speaks in terms of absolute vice and crime, 'finit par dénier au crime tout caractère criminel' [in *Les Temps Modernes,* 1952]. But instead of forming any definite progression, Sade's contradictory views appear to alternate as the spirit moves the author, and inconsistent as these viewpoints may be, they circle each other with remarkable consistency.

As for the ingredients of the philosophical machinery, it is obvious that Sade, opportunistically, takes his material where he finds it. We are reminded of the clever phonographs with speakers from Japan, changers from England, cabinet work from Yugoslavia, that are assembled and packaged in New York and sold as American products: Sade will turn to Condillac for sensationalism, to La Mettrie, Diderot and especially Holbach for atheistic, deterministic materialism, to Helvétius for self-interest, to Montesquieu for geographic relativity. Voltaire's debunking devices are always available for crushing infamous religion, and almost any *philosophe* may provide fuel for the Sadian blowtorch of reason. Here we have not only philosophical promiscuity but philosophical gluttony as well. Sade might have eliminated a great number of his chameleonic abstractions and confined himself mainly to his more convincing arguments—those based on a very concrete and personal self-interest. But like Juliette, who did not want to let one single part of her body remain vacant, he insists on stopping every moral gap through a total metaphysical onslaught.

So the long commentary inevitably precedes and follows the orgy, theory alternates with practice, and it is not the practice so much as the theory that seems out of place to readers. Georges Bataille has noted in his preface to *La Nouvelle Justine* that Sade's long dissertations throw cold water on the violence that he builds, and that 'la froideur d'un langage de raison retire à la vérité érotique sa seule valeur'. What then is the function of this philosophical component? Is Sade sincerely trying to convince the reader through these arguments? Given Sade's egocentricity and the cavalier manner in which he appropriates either side of almost anyone's philosophy, his didacticism seems intended less as a means of converting the ignorant than as a way of showing the fiendish cleverness of his heros, and, by extension, of himself. But within the framework of the Sadian machine, the long moral sermons appear to serve a more immediate purpose . . . .

On 17 April 1782 Sade wrote the following lines from his prison at Vincennes to Marie Dorothée de Rousset: 'Il y a toujours deux fatals instants dans la journée qui rappelle [l'homme] malgré lui à la triste condition des bêtes dont vous savez que mon système . . . ne l'éloigne pas trop . . . celui où il faut qu'il *se remplisse* et celui où il faut qu'il *se vide*'.

Indeed, this dual process of filling and emptying forms the very structure of the mechanism. Sperm, blood, saliva, excrement, tears and vomit inundate the orgies. Although an unknown percentage of these elements is consumed in more or less good spirit, this re-use is merely a step toward the ultimate goal—ejection. But rare is the orgy that does not end with a banquet, so that those who have become depleted may not only regain their lost force but acquire enough new supply to carry them to and through the next Vesuvian round. And it is precisely during lunch or dinner that most of the sermons are given. The atmosphere is relaxed. Theorizing is as calm, reasonable and polite as the orgy was brutal, and a victim who was raped with cries of 'putain!' in the previous section is now courteously called 'Ma chère Justine' when her torturer becomes a well-fed *philosophe*. Too tired to practise vice, the libertines are content to talk of it, and the talk itself often has almost the same therapeutic and rallying effect as the food that accompanies it. 'Comme vos leçons m'enflamment', cries Eugénie to Dolmancé as he expounds his ideas in *La Philosophie dans le boudoir.* And she is not alone in her reaction. The philosophical factor was clearly not designed to *dilute* the violence but to break the monotony of violence and to bring characters perpetually to a fresh start and a new siege.

Within the ebb and flow of Sade's work we find elements that are governed by rigorous laws. Sade has constantly itemized and categorized the hordes of characters in his work (or actors, as he is wont to call them). They form an almost immutable hierarchy, at the highest point of which are found the marquis's counterparts. These are easily recognizable: mature men with all the Sadian trappings—riches, a title, a gloomy castle, perhaps an obliging sister, and, without fail, a hearty dislike of women. Novels may offer a dozen identical heroes: they are always some form of a ubiquitous Sade, and they reign supreme. Somewhat beneath them are the female accomplices, often from nineteen to thirty years of age, and a few of these accomplices—Juliette, for example—may become powerful figures in their own right. But most of them have only temporary luck and temporary impunity, for Sade remembered Machiavelli's counsel: 'Have no accomplices or get rid of them once you have used them'.

Then there are of course the weak and virtuous victims—and the true Sadian victim is always a female: an orphan, somebody's wife, or perhaps an old beggarwoman à la Rose Keller. Although accomplices may fall from grace and join the ranks of victims, it is impossible for a victim to climb the ladder. Victimizers like Roland or Bandole advise Justine that she might one day be stronger than they, but for victims any advancement in status or change for the better is never made.

In the background we are aware of carefully classified and well-organized teams of supernumeraries, who might just as well be stage props. Judging from the account ledger at the end of *Les Cent vingt journées de Sodome,* most of these eventually become victims. They are referred to usually as 'objects', a handy, impersonal term with the added advantage of not distinguishing between genders. The word 'subject' is sometimes used when Sade wishes to equate victims directly with their fate.

The system of victimization is foolproof. In practically every case a victim is suspended between two alternatives, two catastrophes, one of which is so repellent that he will swing magnetically toward the other. For example, rather than see his parent or child killed, a virtuous victim will gradually be led to participate in all manner of sexual assaults on his loved one, little suspecting that he and his whole family will perish in either case. In *La Nouvelle Justine* the system is so economical that the victim herself does most of the work. At one point Justine is even told in advance that she will willingly choose the sexual trap. The diabolical Esterval informs her from the start that in order to try to save his other victims she will stay in his castle and fall into his clutches. And of course this is precisely what happens. Justine's unhappy choice of alternatives is a necessary choice: that robot is carefully programmed for vice through her own logic of virtue.

But just as the orgies must be interrupted by food and philosophy, clearly the victim has to be resuscitated in order to become victimized again. So Sade's works inevitably follow the picaresque pattern of temporary cure and permanent disaster, a few hours of revival buying six months of torture. Thus we have a perpetual, systematic oscillation between orgy and philosophy, intake and output, betrayal and self-destruction, cure and catastrophe. These mechanical phenomena find expression in a series of episodes that constitute a highly fragmented work. It would be hardly fair to condemn the author for this lack of unity, since unity was not one of his major concerns here. But there are certain other defects that cannot be overlooked, because, unfortunately, they relate directly to the main function of the mechanism.

In order to generate his vicious storm, Sade had set himself the Promethean task of capturing the energy, movement and force of nature and unleashing them through his own work; nevertheless critics have persistently pointed to the static quality of this work. As we have seen, Sade has not interspersed his orgies throughout a moving, living plot, but has alternated them instead with large sections of philosophical sermonizing. And the orgies themselves are, in the long run, as lifeless as the sermons, since they are, to use Sade's term, *tableaux,* and have as much energy as a set of blueprints of interlocking parts in various combinations. The language describing the orgies is a static language of nouns. Even the verbs are little more than substantives. Typically, Saint-Fond tells Juliette: 'Je parricidais, j'incestais, je sodomisais, etc.', and, in essence, Sade's characters are always nouned, never verbed.

Sade insists that his *tableaux* are full of life and rapid movement, but at the same time he laments the fact that a painter could not seize the temporal quality that is their very essence. He tells us: 'Il n'est pas aisé à l'art, qui n'a point de mouvement, de réaliser une action dont le mouvement fait toute l'âme'. Time plagues the author at every step of the way. His characters complain in sheer frustration that their crimes cannot last for centuries, and even their ingenious torture machines cannot prolong suffering eternally. Sade attempts to solve the problem of duration by steadily increasing the length of brief novels like *Les Infortunes de la vertu* or *Les Prospérités du vice.* In so doing he buys time at the expense of vitality, and offers us monotony. He fears monotony like the plague, and he tries to combat it by being ever new ('se renouveler sans cesse'). But the verb to *re-new* is inevitably a chimera and a contradiction. In the last analysis, Sade is condemned merely to repeat.

At times variety seems an answer. In one exotic episode, a party at Olympe's place, the unlikely ingredients are one eunuch, one hermaphrodite, one dwarf, an eighty-year old woman, a turkey, a monkey, a bulldog, a goat and somebody's four-year-old great grandson. But the number and kinds of actors and agents are, ultimately, finite, and the number and types of combinations are limited too. These realities are at the heart of the bitter lamentations of Sade's heroes, who constantly bemoan the poverty of their means. The poverty of Sade's own means as a narrator and the sameness of his technique are intimated at the end of the first part of *Juliette.* There the heroine informs us that 'L'Histoire de cette première partie fut à peu près celle de toutes les autres, aux épisodes près, que ma fertile imagination avait soin de varier sans cesse'.

If attempts at variety are largely failures, Sade offers us another solution—proliferation. A novel may begin with solitary encounters, but the tête-à-tête very soon admits several other participants, and what started out as an intimate circle expands to whole brigades in subsequent chapters and reaches the capacity of a Hollywood pageant or three-ring circus. The solitary crime suffices for only a few pages, and Sade works his way quickly enough to genocide. Numbers count, because for Sade numbers are at least as exciting as size or duration. Thus the abundance of lists and ledgers included in his work—lists of actors, lists of victims, countries, expenses and so forth. The portraits that Sade offers of his heroes are no more than long inventories of their vices. Even the rare descriptions of nature, such as those found in the pseudo-virtuous novel *Aline et Valcour,* consist in the *quantity* of nightingales, flowers, fruit or game.

But in Sade's work, just as time and energy are lost in space and substance, quality is obscured by this quantity. The technique of proliferation is undoubtedly more effective as a device for comedy than as a means of generating the searing and forceful electricity that Sade wanted to discharge. A more promising technique than proliferation is the progressive intensification that Sade tries to effect in his novels. The most graphic example of this intensification is his categorizing of *Les Cent vingt journées de Sodome* chronologically into 'passions simples', 'passions de seconde classe ou doubles', 'passions de troisième classe ou criminelles', and 'passions de quatrième classe ou meurtrières', each class of passions more vile than the previous one. Readers of Sade's frankly vicious novels are continually confronted with ogres who are 'encore plus libertins' than their predecessors, and the long story of *Juliette* ends with a wholesale dismembering and human bonfire. As for the unhappy Justine, she is doomed, understandably, to a steady disintegration. In the first half of her story, although she plays primarily the role of voyeur (a sort of *I am curious black and blue*), in the second half she replaces the real victims and comes ever closer to death.

Certainly the process of intensification is a valid one, and it would seem most suited to Sade's purpose. Unfortunately, the long iconoclastic works are so diffuse that the evolution between one degree of crime and another is almost imperceptible. Such an evolution is much more noticeable, for example, in the more compact, earlier versions of *Justine* and *Juliette.* Another drawback in Sade's use of intensification is that the author is usually too impatient to be able to start in a stage whisper and build up to a high pitch. What can astonish us after the excesses of the first few pages? Sade recognized this mistake and in notes for *Les Cent vingt journées* he admonished himself to soften the first part of the work. Yet he rarely seemed able to take this sort of advice.

What Sade was undoubtedly banking on was the frank and ruthless language of his works—the spelling out of the unmentionable. For after all, what better stimulant than the explicit narration of vicious and aberrant acts? The public recapitulation of shocking details is always a fitting end to an old debauch and a proper prelude to a new one, and the narration of vicious deeds serves as an ever-present catalyst in *Les Cent vingt journées.* Sade was well aware that a suggestive narration could be more effective than a specific one. In a note to *La Nouvelle Justine* he quotes La Mettrie's statement, 'On dit mieux les choses en les supprimant, on irrite les désirs, en aiguillonnant la curiosité de l'esprit sur un objet en partie couvert'. This note presumably explained why Sade had decided not to describe one particular scene of the novel. But the idea occurred to him only after 620 pages of the most explicit description! 'Un philosophe doit tout dire', Sade has said. And in his work this 'tout' is construed not only in the sense of a courageous lack of censorship, but in the sense of a total narration. One of the most thorny aspects of this total expression, is, certainly, the problem of imagination, for, as Pierre Klossowski and others have noted, Sade and his characters are for ever faced with the thankless task of translating ineffable acts into conventional language.

It would seem then that the qualities that Sade's work failed to realize were precisely the ones that he rated most highly—energy and movement, variety, intensity and imagination. But does the absence of these important qualities prevent the machine from fulfilling its function as an instrument for evil? This question brings us, finally, to the user, or reader, and here we enter a shadowy realm with even more questions. To what extent does Sade's work elicit in the reader reactions of fascination or repulsion? Is the reader's reaction of satiety some sort of automatically self-imposed escape hatch? To what extent does evil encourage evil? . . .

One of the most common reactions is, admittedly, shock. And because we are shocked at least to some degree, we imagine that this was Sade's purpose and that he intended the reader as victim rather than beneficiary of the machine. Indeed the reader finds himself most often in the role of Justine: regaled with long sermons on vice on the one hand, and on the other put into the position of voyeur and unwitting participant. Sade's own references to the reader are most cordial and conservative. 'Ami lecteur', he apostrophizes in introducing his *Cent vingt journées,* and in his *Idée sur les romans* he offers advice on how to sustain reader interest. But when Sade describes what will please the reader, he is referring to what pleases the marquis de Sade. Readers may, in a sense, become accomplices of Sade by the mere fact of reading and thus accepting him, but Sade was not interested in accomplices. If Sade had wanted to charm the reader, he would have done

what he condemned in Crébillon fils, that is, made vice alluring. Or he would have tried to approach the reader gently with human beings and a love story like Prévost, or with wit and an intimate wink of the eye like Voltaire or Diderot. The reader would have been electrified, not electrocuted, seduced, not raped. But the author would not have been Sade.

For the Sade machine is, essentially, an onanistic device, originally designed, like *La Nouvelle Héloïse,* to deal with the author's own sexual phantoms and fantasies. In view of this fact, the reader would appear to be neither a chosen victim nor a welcome participant, but a mere by-product of the system. If Sade has become a mystique today, it is not so much because of the immediate efficacity of his work. It may be partly a question of timing. 'Tout se déprave en vieillissant', said Sade, writing of his jaded era and its literature. Like that literature, like Sade's characters, like Sade himself, no doubt, and like the eighteenth century, our own century has reached that point of licence in which it is difficult to discover and destroy new taboos. We turn to Sade—almost in spite of his work. And when the pendulum swings back to prudery, the divine Marquis will still have to be reckoned with. Brilliant or foolish enough to have ventured where no one else had dared, he made himself herald, influence, symbol and myth. And well beyond his dank and fetid literary machinery, a totally pure and optimistic force continues to project itself. To quote three glorious hemistichs of a victorious Juliette.

> Le passé m'encourage,
> Le présent m'électrise,
> Je crains peu l'avenir.

David Williams   (essay date 1976)

SOURCE: "Another Look at the Sadean Heroine: The Prospects of Femininity," in *Essays in French Literature,* No. 13, November, 1976, pp. 28-43.

[In the following excerpt, Williams analyzes the heroines in Sade's short stories and in his novel Aline et Valcour.*]*

The figure of Justine and the multiple variations of the Justine legend lie at the core of Sade's output as a novelist, and offer a familiar pattern of themes central to Sade's perception of the qualities and realities of femininity. In this context, Sade's corrosive attack on sentimentalist modes, as reflected in the predilection of the period's fiction for the portrayal of a young lady's entrance into the world, has been exhaustively analysed in recent years. Yet, despite the stature of the legend in Sade's work and in subsequent criticism, the story of Justine is really no more than a point of departure. Events and ideas are deployed with a view to identifying problems, and with succeeding versions of this core narrative, culminating in a multitiered New Justine in 1797, Sade weaves a rich canvas of propositions, though not solutions, around the issue of femininity, or what might be called, following Tourné's recent article [in *Europe,* 1972] the Penelope syndrome.

From a gallery of assembly-line heroines—three Justines, Sophie, Aline, Ernestine, Eugénie de Franval, Miss Stralson, Euphrasie de Châteaublanc, and others—Sade distils a vision of woman trapped within the confines of a unilateral victim-executioner relationship with the male, in which the horror and humiliation of the situation are outmatched only by its crushing banality. . . .

The Justine legend presents in effect two overlapping perspectives in connection with Sade's heroinism: that of a novelist catering to the specific demands of a well-established clandestine market, and that of a more committed enquirer into the historical, political and moral aspects of the woman question, and its consequences in both Nature and Society. The latter perspective reveals a portrait of the heroine schematically conceived as a vehicle for the analysis of the Penelope phenomenon. Here we are offered a bleak caricature of a world of women in which the values and characteristics that Sade, following contemporary convention, associates with femininity (virtue, sensibility, innocence, ignorance, conscience, religiosity) conspire to work the heroine's downfall. Such figures are caught in the inexorable grip of a coldly Hobbesian situation, and their physical description is accordingly tailored to reflect their vulnerability. Again Justine is the prototype, her soft, white, bland physionomy betraying the inner vacuity common to all Sadean victims. . . .

With the contrapuntal destiny of Juliette, Sade might indeed, as Apollinaire and others have suggested, be demonstrating the possibilities for action of the "New Woman". Certainly the *Histoire de Juliette, ou les prospérités du vice* seems to indicate the existence of a choice, of a possibility for manoeuvre, on the part of the beleaguered heroine and her *alter ego* in order to counteract what Sade sees as the natural disadvantages of femininity. Juliette is able to avoid the Panglossian rigidity of her sister; she can accept and act upon "philosophical" advice; she does evolve in some measure in response to the realities of her condition. Yet she can only find salvation by allowing herself to be assimilated. She becomes an object shaped by the will of others, a prisoner of their ideology as her sister is that of the Church's, and as such alienated from herself. In the end she is another self-negating force, feeding voluptuously on the pain of victims and finally consuming itself. The price of survival for Juliette involves a sacrifice of those very qualities that Justine retains to the bitter end. By becoming one with the predatory world around her, however, her femininity has been cauterized, and a loss of human identity has taken place. In this Juliette remains a passive creation of Vice as much as Justine remains the passive creation of Virtue. Neither possesses real freedom or authenticity.

The centrality of the stories of Justine and Juliette has tended to unbalance interpretation of Sade's position on a number of points, not the least of which concerns his overall intentions with regard to his female characters. To redress the balance, and to shed more light on the implications of the Justine-Juliette polarity, further work needs to be done, for example, on the more fluid subtleties of the heroines of the *historiettes, contes et fabliaux*. In several of the less familiar examples from this rather neglected collection the Sadean heroine moves in a very different world to that of Justine. The trappings are still gothic, but style, tone and presentation are much more akin to those of Maupassant than to the monochromes of *Candide,* to which so many of Sade's better known works can be compared. These are the heroines that Apollinaire possibly had in mind with that apparently quixotic allusion to an egalitarian principle behind Sade's female portraits [in *L'Oeuvre du marquis de Sade,* 1904]. The *contes* illuminate dimensions to the Sadean heroine that tend to displace the accepted centres of gravity in the more familiar scenarios. If anywhere in Sade's work, it is in this area of his fiction that the characteristic themes of the Enlightenment myth of femininity spring into relief.

In **"Augustine de Villebranche, ou le stratagéme de l'amour,"** we glimpse one of Baudelaire's "femmes fatalement suggestives", whose noble qualities are displayed in a philosophical context in which the "female" sense of virtue, of all things, is exonerated. The portrayal of the heroine of that curious little tale, **"Le Serpent,"** has a poignancy that forestalls parody despite its open sentimentality. The constraints of marriage and the hypocrisy of the double code are treated almost from a feminist perspective in **"L'Heureuse Feinte,"** where Mme de Guissac is guilty not of the sin of adultery, but simply of an error of strategy. The defensive tone and almost gentle humour that Sade adopts with these rather graceful heroines of the *contes* become more overt in **"Le Président mystifié,"** with its themes of arranged marriages and bridal purity. In **"Le Talion"** Sade takes up the question of marital infidelity again, concentrating this time on the right of wives to exact vengeance upon errant husbands. The theme of what Engels was to call "the world historical defeat of the female sex" is developed in an even more substantial way in **"Le Cocu de lui-même, ou le raccommodement imprévu"** where, following a line of argument stretching from Poulain de la Barre to Condorcet, Sade locates the essence of the problem in the educational experience with its baneful emphasis for women on correct behaviour and strict adherence to virtuous precept. . . . **"Le Cocu de lui-même"** exposes in a critical way the contradictions of a moral code in which women are reduced to disposable objects of exchange and possession. The theme is a familiar one, but Sade usually expresses it in a far more flamboyant manner that reveals the heroine as the foolish architect of her own fate. What is unexpected in this *conte* is the *dénouement,* a comic scene of retribution in which the final grotesque joke is on the unfaithful husband who is persuaded to seduce his disguised wife in the belief that she is a nubile courtesan.

"L'Epoux corrigé" restages the drama of just retribution, and female retaliation constitutes in fact the most striking leit-motif of the *contes* as a whole. The heroines are all, as is to be expected, victimized; they are all creatures inhabiting an unjustly organized world, but they are not without resources. The heroine of **"La Châtelaine de Langeville, ou la femme vengée"** is allowed to develop an effective counterstrategy leading not only to a consummated vengeance but even to a miraculous reform of the offending male. The *contes* reveal an experimental and transitional world of attitudes and action. Even in the most desperate circumstances, such as those described in **"Emilie de Tourville, ou la cruauté fraternelle,"** where Emilie is almost bled to death by her vampiric relatives, or in **"Les

Filous," where Rosette is enmeshed in the nets of Parisian corruption, a sentimental heroine possessing the mental and physical qualities that ensure her contemptuous destruction in the world of Justine, survives. Indeed, providentialist forces, the subject of much sardonic commentary elsewhere, seem to be working on her behalf. In short, the heroines of the *contes* triumph at the expense of their tormentors.

In the mainline fiction only two alternatives seem to present themselves to the heroine: that of the anvil, a symbol of the Freudian femininity-passivity equation and as such destined to be stamped out of existence, or that of the hammer, the Jungian principle of action and energy, surviving the assault by becoming one with it, at great cost to the integrity of the Self. Euphrasie de Gange, the "âme sensible" of one of the more interesting, though least known, of Sade's novels, [*La Marquise de Ganges*], is a quite exceptional in-depth portrait of a heroine of true moral stature able at first to draw on inner resources to resist the philosophical onslaught from the *abbé* Théodore. Even Euphrasie, however, for all the idealism and sympathy with which Sade endows her portrait, finally exhibits the fatal deficiency of conditioned virtue, preferring illusion to reality, and the vulnerable impulses of emotion to that judicious self-control and daring self-awareness without which moral idealism, in Sade's view, can never present a viable principle for life. The heroines of the *contes* suggest tentatively the presence of a third alternative, and this is explored further by Sade in the *Histoire de Sainville et de Léonore,* a sub-novel encapsulated in that larger indictment of sentimentality, *Aline et Valcour,* a *roman philosophique* that Sade composed between 1785 and 1788.

The backcloth provided by *Aline et Valcour* is again that of Virtue codified, sanctified and suitably punished, a litany that moves to its crescendo with the suicide of Aline. This dismal recital is amplified with an auxiliary account of the misfortunes of innocence on a lower social level with the adventures of the vacuous Sophie, who in exchange for food, clothing and a hundred francs a month for her dreams, must render complete obedience to the predatory Mirville. The preliminary scenes of the *Histoire de Sainville et de Léonore,* intercalated at Letter 35, also introduce a familiar eighteenth-century scenario: a love relationship frustrated by parental opposition and menaced by the prospect of an arranged marriage of the heroine to a third party. Rebelling against this situation, Sainville is sent away for two years of army service, and Léonore is placed in a convent, from which she is soon delivered by the hero. The escape from the convent merits attention as, like all Sadean tableaux, it is ideologically alive. Sainville proposes to rescue Léonore by persuading her to take the place of a damaged, supposedly miraculous statue of Saint Ultrogote, that is due to be transported from the convent for repairs. Sade uses this farcical scene to introduce a number of elements relevant to the characterisation of Léonore and the operative principles that he intends her to embody.

Léonore . . . shares common ground first of all with the demonic survivours of the female condition in the Justine legend, such as Lady Clairwill. She possesses energy in the Sadean sense, particularly as she confronts Christian precepts. Unlike the incandescent Justine, she does not have her eyes turned "machinalement vers le ciel", and again unlike Justine in a parallel incident, she does not respond automatically to the tolling of a church bell with its false promise of refuge. Much to the distress of her mother, Mme de Blamont, she is immune to the sectarian virus, though not unresponsive to the abstract notion of a remote God. The shadow of the Church towers over the Sadean myth of femininity and virtue, but Léonore is unfettered by the bonds that confine other heroines of Sadean fiction so tightly. In *Justine* a whole armoury of inverted religious terms is used to point up the central role of religion as a problematic feature of the heroine's experience. In the grim scenes with the monks of Sainte Marie des Bois, the irony of the holy betrayal of women is enacted when a young captive, Florette, is dressed in the garments of the Virgin, and presented to the credulous congregation as a holy statue. She is made to move her arms miraculously towards Heaven when the host is raised during the mass. She retains the Virgin's costume in the ensuing orgies of violent abnegation in which she serves literally as an altar of sacrifice. The description of the sacrilege is sprinkled liberally with that acerbic vocabulary of veneration that Sade employs so frequently in ironic reference to women in scenes of violence, "cet asile des grâces et de la volupté", "le vrai temple de l'amour", "les temples de Vénus", "sanctuaire", "autel", etc. Sexual congress itself is analagous to a religious cult, and the female body to a place of worship in which the incense of the male seed is burnt in honor of the God-like male member, "l'objet unique de son culte".

A transposed religious terminology is also invoked to describe profane human passion in the *Histoire de Sainville et de Léonore.* The emphasis is rather different, however, and with the escape from the convent Sade reworks the statue episode from the first version of *Justine.* In the case of Léonore the thought of posing as a miraculous statue provokes not awe at the blasphemy of the impersonation, but laughter. . . . The real statue of the saint is smashed, and the débris thrown unceremoniously into a well. With the heroine's assumption of the statue's identity, moreover, she becomes in her turn divinised by her lover in a kind of deviant parody of the Pygmalion theme: "Je lui emmaillotai les bras . . . et après lui avoir donné un baiser . . . baiser délicieux, dont l'effet fut sur moi bien plus puissant que les miracles de toutes les saintes du ciel, je fermai le temple où reposait ma déesse, et me retirai tout rempli de son culte".

In *Justine* the girl-statues are helpless victims manipulated cynically by predatory forces. In the recast version of the scene in Léonore's convent the representatives of the Church, in this case the nun-jailors, become the credulous casualties of the deception. In fact, Léonore is literally worshipped by an old insomniac nun in a scene that combines religious fervour with lesbian innuendo in the best Voltairean manner. Woman petrified is here no longer the symbol of her total possession by the will of the Other. Léonore's petrification has quite the opposite effect, and the scene is the first in a series of lessons in self-realisation that the assailed heroine must absorb if she is to avoid the oblivion reserved for Sade's virtuous automata on the one hand, and the dehumanization of their manic oppressors on the other.

The problem of femininity and the postulates for its solution continue to take shape after the unauthorized marriage of the lovers. They retire to Venice, where Léonore is kidnapped by the masked henchmen of Fallieri, "libertin de profession". At this point, with the formal separation of the protagonists, the narrative divides into two parts. The first is, on the surface, the story of Sainville's search for the lost Léonore—in effect, a recapitulation of the principal hypotheses and fabulations around the feminine experience that give characteristic shape to Sade's meditational patterns. A key episode is set in the Portuguese-African kingdom of Butua, where the portrayal of Ben Maâcoro's harem, stocked with women paid to the King as tax tributes, offers a comprehensive metaphor of the essential Sadean configurations of that condition of Otherness that is for him femininity. It is not an inconsequential feature of the harem, for example, that the inhabitants are presented to Sainville as negotiable items of merchandise. Sade's whole moral system is anchored to the profit-loss principle on all levels, and the economic factors at play in the formulation of moral premises that affect women are emphasized at almost every turn of his tortuous plots. The original obstacle to the marriage of Sainville and Léonore was financial in nature, and the theme is a feature of the correspondence between Blamont and Dolbourg in *Aline et Valcour.* Justine and Juliette are daughters of a banker whose bankruptcy precipitates their initial disasters. Juliette's survival expresses itself in part as a triumph over economic adversity, as the terms of her marriage contract to the comte de Lorsange indicate. While Justine clings to *sensible* notions of courtly love, Juliette learns from la Duvergier how to market her physical attributes to best advantage in a mercantile world. Vice prospers in this basic financial sense. Saint-Florent, one of Sade's more sensational villains, is a merchant-businessman, and it should come as no surprise that after raping Justine he should take her purse. Crime itself is justified as an act of economic vengeance against the rich. The final assertion of Bressac's power over Justine is expressed through the retention of her money, and similar acts of dispossession take place in the monastery of Sainte Marie des Bois. Chastity, the quintessential symbol of virtue, becomes in the end just another commercial asset.

Léonore assimilates these *données de base* very quickly. Sainmore, however, is convulsed with anguish at the uncompromising spectacle of the women of Butua whose condition, far from being God-like, evokes that of the victims in the *Cent Vingt Journées de Sodome.* For his lack of realism and flexibility, the consequences of an undisciplined sensibility, he is admonished by his interlocutor, Sarmiento. . . . However, while the formidable dynamics of the power-play of human relationships in Butua collide directly with the dreamy romanticism of Sainville, they do not entirely overwhelm the idealism to which he tenaciously clings, and is permitted to retain.

The second part, which unfolds at Letter 38 of *Aline et Valcour,* is a replay of events through the eyes of the kidnapped heroine-apprentice. We are now told that Léonore is "une belle aventurière", the physical antithesis of the pale, fairhaired, languid, blue-eyed energyless creatures of the *romans féroces*. She is "une admirable prêtresse de Vénus", her black eyes, brown hair and tanned skin hinting at positive qualities of robustness, resilience and pragmatism. Far from being a helpless prisoner of static conventions of love, she soon reveals her skills as a cool exploiter of those conventions. At the same time, she does not denounce the courtly ideal of love as a dangerous futility—her staunch devotion to Sainville is cast deliberately in that heroic mould—but she is attuned to the other realities in the human imagination that are concealed behind the mask of words. The clarity of her vision in this respect, the result, we are given to understand, of a healthy "philosophical" education, enables her to take advantage of the potent associations that resonate within "le langage du véritable amour", and harness them as mechanisms for the conquest, in self-defence, of adversaries.

The potential enemy is disarmed and transformed. . . . The young surgeon Dolcini thus becomes the first casualty of Léonore's *prise de conscience*. . . . Dolcini eventually dies in Léonore's defence in true knightly fashion. A similar scene is enacted with calculated theatricality on Léonore's part in the case of Duval, who having rescued the heroine from pirates, demands suitable recompense. Again Sade flavours the scene with a double-edged religious vocabulary culminating in another transfiguration of the heroine: "O divinité de mon coeur . . . Maîtresse idolâtrée . . . O Léonore, est-tu l'ouvrage d'un dieu? . . . es-tu donc un dieu toi-même? Ah! juste ciel, n'arrête pas ces effets brûlants d'un amour aveuglé! tu les vois . . . tu les sens . . . perfide . . . le sacrifice est offert . . . et je n'en suis que plus malheureux". The creation of "love" through the transformative effects of sensibility repeats itself in a rhythmical cycle throughout the narrative. Ideals of sentimental love are not bluntly denied, as with Juliette, but given profitable purpose as they are made to crystallize in the mind of the Other.

The new direction in which Sade was trying to travel with Léonore is further clarified by the introduction of a secondary heroine, Clémentine. Clémentine appears at first to have the dominance and superiority of a Clairwill embodying the astringent antisentimentalism of the female proponents of Sadean energy and will in the *romans féroces*. This particular companion-mentor, however, loses the philosophical initiative, and is eventually overshadowed. Possessing all the right insights, she is nevertheless a flawed character—indicated perhaps by her white skin, always a sign of vulnerability in Sade's code of physiological symbolism. Her cerebral approach to life has its own fatal qualities of intransigency that insulate her from the all-important lessons of experience. She is able to perceive Christian virtue as a dangerous principle which, if followed blindly, leads to a lemming-like self-immolation but, as Sade observes, the principle offers no ideas to her imagination.

Her inadequacy in this respect is underscored by the physical assaults that she has to endure, while Léonore remains untouched. Léonore has little difficulty in outwitting

Benda-Bella, but Clémentine is not so fortunate, and Léonore takes advantage of events to press the point home: "Eh bien! . . . te voilà punie de tes systèmes, les voilà culbutés par l'expérience". The ascendancy of Léonore is confirmed by a second rape of Clémentine, this time by Ben Maâcoro. The subsequent vengeful seduction of the King by Léonore marks the apogée of her triumph and her emergence as a wielder of power. The sentimental mode, or rather the potency of its illusory promise in the imagination of the Other, is shown once more to be the instrument of the heroine's survival, rather than that of her downfall and servitude. Defying Ben Maâcoro's insistence upon "plaisirs brutaux", Léonore evokes the more exquisite pleasures of the soul. . . . Once more she is transfigured as the captivated Ben Maâcoro invests her with the mystical qualities that he has explicitly denied to the women of the harem. . . .

A similar illustration of the metamorphic powers of femininity is provided in the chambers of the Inquisitorial interrogator, Don Crispe Brutaldi Barbaribos de Torturentia. Here Léonore treads a particularly dangerous path, but she understands the nature of the opportunity presented to her when Don Crispe demands "la soumission la plus aveugle à toutes mes fantaisies". Like Dolcini, Duval, Ben Maâcoro, and of course Sainville, Don Crispe is reduced through the raw force of sensibility to the harmless status of a worshipper at the feet of a Léonore at once petrified and divinised. Responding involuntarily to the simulacrum of sentimental love, he senses the danger in his new position: "Sors, friponne, sors . . . tes yeux et tes paroles me changent absolument . . . je ne me reconnais plus".

In the *Histoire de Sainville et de Léonore* a familiar pattern of cause and effect has been radically modified. Sensibility, once the fatal chink in the heroine's armour, has now become a formidable weapon exerting hypnotic, enervating effects upon the predator, and offering to the heroine who knows how to wield it the key to control and survival. The concept of sensibility, which in the conventional Sadean context embraces compassion, love, generosity, gratitude, faith, virtue, conscience and *bienfaisance*—all of the toxic qualities of "mollesse" that lie at the heart of Justine's femininity, and of her tragedy—has been refined and reoriented. In this respect, Sade has given to Léonore an inner strength and detachment in the face of codes and conventions normally reserved only for the Minskis, the Gernandes, the Rodins, the Bressacs, the moneylenders, brigands and other articulators of energy and crime. Léonore, however, is no criminal, although she does, it is true, express warm sympathy for the *hors la loi* as being the repository of true virtue. For Léonore a band of gypsies provides in effect the model for virtuous conduct. Beyond the pale of convention they exist on the periphery of the social situation, and only they are capable of disinterested acts, the acid test of Sadean morality.

None of the gypsies exhibits the characteristics of the doomed sentimentalists, yet neither do they exhibit those of the murderous and equally doomed libertines who inhabit the blood-splashed dungeons of Sade's mainline fiction, and who, like their victims, continue to live and act within the precincts of established society despite the geographical remoteness of their castles and palaces. It is with the gypsies that Léonore glimpses a way to deal effectively with the furtive polarities of human nature. Thus, unlike Aline, she will not be concerned with the *jouissance* of virtuous practices, nor will she be concerned with the *volupté* of vice. Her quest is for an operative principle for action that will eschew the dangerous opacity of both of these extremes of ego-centred motivation, and take into account the ambiguities of emotion and experience "que le sot ignore, que l'épais rigoriste punit, et que le philosophe respecte, parce que lui seul connaît le cœur humain, et que lui seul en a la clef". She does not seek to deflect responsibility for her destiny on to God, nor does she strive to transcend the limitations placed upon her by Nature and by her own femininity. Rather she seeks to understand the implications and potentialities of the feminine condition in the light of an educative encounter with what Sade conceives to be its realities, and philosophical reflection upon that encounter. Experience, and not precept, has formed her heart and her mind, enabling her to act and realise herself without taking on the attributes of monstrousness or alienation, and without suffering the intrusion of nihilistic feelings of anomy. . . .

In surviving, Léonore avoids the determinist traps that are sprung on so many of Sade's grotesques who, in their pursuit of the stasis of passionless "apathie", remain imprisoned within the infernos of their own fantasies, driven by forces that they neither control nor understand. Léonore is allowed instead to develop a strategy for life in which the calculations of the mind provide the guide-lines, but in which the pre-romantic ideals of the *âme sensible* are not entirely abandoned. . . . Léonore can thus be seen as one of the truly free figures of Sade's fiction. She creates her own pattern, her own "étoile heureuse". Bearing in mind Sartre's definition of femininity as an "appel d'être" the presentation of Léonore seems to coincide rather strikingly on a certain level with the existentialist vision. Sade has revealed in her an "openness of being", and her story traces the stages of a response to a "call to being" in which the heroine finally aspires to an existence "en soi pour soi".

In Léonore's portrayal, with its sense of awakening and metamorphosis, Sade maps out a voyage of self-discovery that is, as Tourné suggests, linear and rising (in contrast to the enclosed, circular journeys of Aline and Justine). En route, femininity is not discarded, and with this particular heroine we can perceive Sade's experimentation with an alternative that will permit a young lady to survive her entrance into the world without being either impaled on an impractical moral code or compelled to surrender to the inner maelstrom of violence and self-negation. Sade has postulated an equilibrium, an "égalité dans le caractère", and in all this the *Histoire de Sainville et de Léonore* is something of a sport in the Sadean *œuvre*. Its unique heroine, its aberrant thematic movement, its tight dialectical structure and rounded characterisations all blend with a measure of literary merit to add a subtlety and a richness of tone to the heavier brushstrokes of **Aline et Valcour.** In seeking to appreciate Sade's art and thought through the medium of his heroinism, we could do worse than follow Jean Fabre's advice to start and finish with this novel, "non pas son œuvre la plus secrète ou la plus forte, mais son chefd'œuvre, avec tout le soin, le poli et l'équilibre qu'implique ce terme".

Angela Carter   (essay date 1978)

SOURCE: "Polemical Preface: Pornography in the Service of Women," in *The Sadeian Woman and the Ideology of Pornography,* Pantheon, 1978, pp. 3-37.

[*An English fiction writer and critic whose novels and short stories combined lush prose, eroticism, and elements of the macabre, Carter explored gender issues in both her fiction and her non-fiction. In the following excerpt, she argues that Sadean pornography is indirectly useful to women because it lays bare the oppressive politics of conventional male-female relationships.*]

It is fair to say that, when pornography serves—as with very rare exceptions it always does—to reinforce the prevailing system of values and ideas in a given society, it is tolerated; and when it does not, it is banned. (This already suggests there are more reasons than those of public decency for the banning of the work of Sade for almost two hundred years; only at the time of the French Revolution and at the present day have his books been available to the general public.) Therefore an increase of pornography on the market, within the purchasing capacity of the common man, and especially the beginning of a type of pornography modelled on that provided for the male consumer but directed at women, does not mean an increase in sexual licence, with the reappraisal of social mores such licence, if it is real, necessitates. It might only indicate a more liberal attitude to masturbation, rather than to fucking, and reinforce a solipsistic concentration on the relationship with the self, which is a fantasy one at the best of times.

When pornography abandons its quality of existential solitude and moves out of the kitsch area of timeless, placeless fantasy and into the real world, then it loses its function of safety valve. It begins to comment on real relations in the real world. Therefore, the more pornographic writing acquires the techniques of real literature, of real art, the more deeply subversive it is likely to be in that the more likely it is to affect the reader's perceptions of the world. The text that had heretofore opened up creamily to him, in a dream, will gather itself together and harshly expel him into the anguish of actuality.

There is a liberal theory that art disinfects eroticism of its latent subversiveness, and pornography that is also art loses its shock and its magnetism, becomes 'safe'. The truth of this is that once pornography is labelled 'art' or 'literature' it is stamped with the approval of an elitist culture and many ordinary people will avoid it on principle, out of a fear of being bored. But the more the literary arts of plotting and characterisation are used to shape the material of pornography, the more the pornographer himself is faced with the moral contradictions inherent in real sexual encounters. He will find himself in a dilemma; to opt for the world or to opt for the wet dream?

Out of this dilemma, the moral pornographer might be born.

The moral pornographer would be an artist who uses pornographic material as part of the acceptance of the logic of a world of absolute sexual licence for all the genders, and projects a model of the way such a world might work. A moral pornographer might use pornography as a critique of current relations between the sexes. His business would be the total demystification of the flesh and the subsequent revelation, through the infinite modulations of the sexual act, of the real relations of man and his kind. Such a pornographer would not be the enemy of women, perhaps because he might begin to penetrate to the heart of the contempt for women that distorts our culture even as he entered the realms of true obscenity as he describes it.

But the pornographer's more usual business is to assert that the function of flesh is pure pleasure, which is itself a mystification of a function a great deal more complex, apart from raising the question of the nature of pleasure itself. However, the nature of pleasure is not one with which the pornographer often concerns himself; for him, sexual pleasure is a given fact, a necessary concomitant of the juxtaposition of bodies.

It is at this point that he converts the sexed woman, living, breathing, troubling, into a desexed hole and the breathing, living, troubling man into nothing but a probe; pornography becomes a form of pastoral, sex an engaging and decorative activity that may be performed without pain, soil, sweat or effect, and its iconography a very suitable subject for informal murals in public places. If, that is, the simplest descriptions of sex did not also rouse such complex reactions.

And that is because sexual relations between men and women always render explicit the nature of social relations in the society in which they take place and, if described explicitly, will form a critique of those relations, even if that is not and never has been the intention of the pornographer.

So, whatever the surface falsity of pornography, it is impossible for it to fail to reveal sexual reality at an unconscious level, and this reality may be very unpleasant indeed, a world away from official reality.

A male-dominated society produces a pornography of universal female acquiescence. . . .

The pornographer who consciously utilises the propaganda, the 'grabbing' effect of pornography to express a view of the world that transcends this kind of innocence will very soon find himself in deep political water for he will begin to find himself describing the real conditions of the world in terms of sexual encounters, or even find that the real nature of these encounters illuminates the world itself; the world turns into a gigantic brothel, the area of our lives where we believed we possessed most freedom is seen as the most ritually circumscribed.

Nothing exercises such power over the imagination as the nature of sexual relationships, and the pornographer has it in his power to become a terrorist of the imagination, a sexual guerilla whose purpose is to overturn our most basic notions of these relations, to reinstitute sexuality as a primary mode of being rather than a specialised area of vacation from being and to show that the everyday meetings in the marriage bed are parodies of their own pretensions, that the freest unions may contain the seeds of the worst exploitation. Sade became a terrorist of the imagination in this way, turning the unacknowledged truths of the encounters of sexuality into a cruel festival at which women are the prime sacrificial victims when they are not the ritual murderesses themselves, the ewe lamb and Miss Stern together, alike only in that they always remain under the constant surveillance of the other half of mankind.

The pornographer as terrorist may not think of himself as a friend of women; that may be the last thing on his mind. But he will always be our unconscious ally because he begins to approach some kind of emblematic truth, whereas the lackey pornographer, like the devious fellows who write love stories for women's magazines, that softest of all forms of pornography, can only do harm. But soon, however permissive censorship may be, he will invade the area in which censorship operates most defensibly, that of erotic violence.

This area of taboo remains theoretically inviolate even though violence, for its own sake, between men, escapes censorship altogether. The machine-gun of the gangster can rake as many innocent victims as the writer or filmmaker pleases, the policeman can blast as many wrongdoers to extinction as serves to demonstrate the superiority of his institutions. Novels and movies about warfare use violent death, woundings and mutilations as a form of decoration, butch embroidery upon a male surface. Violence, the convulsive form of the active, male principle, is a matter for men, whose sex gives them the right to inflict pain as a sign of mastery and the masters have the right to wound one another because that only makes us fear them more, that they can give and receive pain like the lords of creation. But to show, in art, erotic violence committed by men upon women cuts too near the bone, and will be condemned out of hand.

Perhaps it reveals too clearly that violence has always been the method by which institutions demonstrate their superiority. It can become too vicious a reminder of the mutilations our society inflicts upon women and the guilt that exacerbates this savagery. It suggests, furthermore, that male political dominance might be less a matter of moral superiority than of crude brute force and this would remove a degree of glamour from the dominance itself.

There is more to it than that, though. The whippings, the beatings, the gougings, the stabbings of erotic violence reawaken the memory of the social fiction of the female wound, the bleeding scar left by her castration, which is a psychic fiction as deeply at the heart of Western culture as the myth of Oedipus, to which it is related in the complex dialectic of imagination and reality that produces culture. Female castration is an imaginary fact that pervades the whole of men's attitude towards women and our attitude to ourselves, that transforms women from human beings into wounded creatures who were born to bleed.

It is a great shame we can forbid these bleedings in art but not in life, for the beatings, the rapes and the woundings

take place in a privacy beyond the reach of official censorship. It is also in private that the unacknowledged psychological mutilations performed in the name of love take place.

Sade is the connoisseur of these mutilations. He is an extreme writer and he describes a society and a system of social relations *in extremis,* those of the last years of the ancien régime in France. The stories of Justine and Juliette are set at a time immediately preceding the French Revolution. *The Hundred and Twenty Days at Sodom* is set in the seventeenth century. Its heroes have financed their murderous holiday by vast profits made from the Thirty Years War. *Philosophy in the Boudoir* takes place sometime between 1789 and 1793; outside the room in which the action of this dramatic interlude takes place, they are selling revolutionary pamphlets on the steps of the Palace of Equality but the actors in the boudoir are aristocrats, members of a privileged class. In all this fiction, Sade is working primarily in the mode of pornography; he utilised this mode to make a particularly wounding satire on mankind, and the historical time in which the novels are set is essential to the satire.

> Sade has a curious ability to render every aspect of sexuality suspect, so that we see how the chaste kiss of the sentimental lover differs only in degree from the vampirish love-bite that draws blood, we understand that a disinterested caress is only quantitatively different from a disinterested flogging.
>
> —*Angela Carter*

But Sade is unusual amongst both satirists and pornographers, not only because he goes further than most satirists and pornographers, but because he is capable of believing, even if only intermittently, that it is possible to radically transform society and, with it, human nature, so that the Old Adam, exemplified in God, the King and the Law, the trifold masculine symbolism of authority, will take his final departure from amongst us. Only then will freedom be possible; until then, the freedom of one class, or sex, or individual necessitates the unfreedom of others.

But his work as a pornographer is more descriptive and diagnostic than proscriptive and prophetic. He creates, not an artificial paradise of gratified sexuality but a model of hell, in which the gratification of sexuality involves the infliction and the tolerance of extreme pain. He describes sexual relations in the context of an unfree society as the expression of pure tyranny, usually by men upon women, sometimes by men upon men, sometimes by women upon men and other women; the one constant to all Sade's monstrous orgies is that the whip hand is always the hand with the real political power and the victim is a person who has little or no power at all, or has had it stripped from him.

In this schema, male means tyrannous and female means martyrised, no matter what the official genders of the male and female beings are.

He is uncommon amongst pornographers in that he rarely, if ever, makes sexual activity seem immediately attractive as such. Sade has a curious ability to render every aspect of sexuality suspect, so that we see how the chaste kiss of the sentimental lover differs only in degree from the vampirish love-bite that draws blood, we understand that a disinterested caress is only quantitatively different from a disinterested flogging. For Sade, all tenderness is false, a deceit, a trap; all pleasure contains within itself the seeds of atrocities; all beds are minefields. So the virtuous Justine is condemned to spend a life in which there is not one single moment of enjoyment; only in this way can she retain her virtue. Whereas the wicked Juliette, her sister and antithesis, dehumanises herself completely in the pursuit of pleasure.

The simple perversions, available in any brothel, documented in the first book of **The Hundred and Twenty Days at Sodom,** will insatiably elaborate, will never suffice in themselves, will culminate in the complex and deathly rites of the last book, which concludes in a perfectly material hell. The final passion recounted by the sexual lexicographer, Madame Desgranges, is called the Hellgame; its inventor, assisted by torturers disguised as demons, himself pretends to be the devil.

In the perpetual solitude of their continually refined perversions, in an absolute egotism, Sade's libertines regulate and maintain a society external to them, where the institutions of which they are the embodiment are also perversions.

These libertines are great aristocrats, landowners, bankers, judges, archbishops, popes and certain women who have become very rich through prostitution, speculation, murder and usury. They have the tragic style and the infernal loquacity of the damned; and they have no inner life, no introspection. Their actions sum them up completely. They are in exile from the world in their abominable privilege, at the same time as they control the world.

Sade's heroines, those who become libertines, accept damnation, by which I mean this exile from human life, as a necessary fact of life. This is the nature of the libertine. They model themselves upon libertine men, though libertinage is a condition that all the sexes may aspire to. So Sade creates a museum of woman-monsters. He cuts up the bodies of women and reassembles them in the shapes of his own delirium. He renews all the ancient wounds, every one, and makes them bleed again as if they will never stop bleeding.

From time to time, he leaves off satire long enough to posit a world in which nobody need bleed. But only a violent transformation of this world and a fresh start in an absolutely egalitarian society would make this possible. Nevertheless, such a transformation might be possible; at this point, Sade becomes a Utopian. His Utopianism, however, takes the form of Kafka's: 'There *is* hope—but not for us.' The title of the pamphlet describing the Sadeian Utopia inserted in **Philosophy in the Boudoir** is: *Yet Another Ef-*

fort, Frenchmen, If You Would Become Republicans. It is possible, but improbable, that effort will be made; perhaps those who make it will have hope.

Sade describes the condition of women in the genre of the pornography of sexual violence but believed it would only be through the medium of sexual violence that women might heal themselves of their socially inflicted scars, in a praxis of destruction and sacrilege. He cites the flesh as existential verification in itself, in a rewriting of the Cartesian cogito: *'I fuck therefore I am'.* From this axiom, he constructs a diabolical lyricism of fuckery, since the acting-out of a total sexuality in a repressive society turns all eroticism into violence, makes of sexuality itself a permanent negation. Fucking, says Sade, is the basis of all human relationships but the activity parodies all human relations because of the nature of the society that creates and maintains those relationships.

He enlarges the relation between activity and passivity in the sexual act to include tyranny and the acceptance of physical and political oppression. The great men in his novels, the statesmen, the princes, the popes, are the cruellest by far and their sexual voracity is a kind of pure destructiveness; they would like to fuck the world and fucking, for them, is the enforcement of annihilation. Their embraces strangle, their orgasms appear to detonate their partners. But his great women, Juliette, Clairwil, the Princess Borghese, Catherine the Great of Russia, Charlotte of Naples, are even more cruel still since, once they have tasted power, once they know how to use their sexuality as an instrument of aggression, they use it to extract vengeance for the humiliations they were forced to endure as the passive objects of the sexual energy of others.

A free woman in an unfree society will be a monster. Her freedom will be a condition of personal privilege that deprives those on which she exercises it of her own freedom. The most extreme kind of this deprivation is murder. These women murder.

The sexual behaviour of these women, like that of their men, is a mirror of their inhumanity, a magnified relation of the ambivalence of the word 'to fuck', in its twinned meanings of sexual intercourse and despoliation: 'a fuckup', 'to fuck something up', 'he's fucked'.

Women do not normally fuck in the active sense. They are fucked in the passive tense and hence automatically fucked-up, done over, undone. Whatever else he says or does not say, Sade declares himself unequivocally for the right of women to fuck—as if the period in which women fuck aggressively, tyrannously and cruelly will be a necessary stage in the development of a general human consciousness of the nature of fucking; that if it is not egalitarian, it is unjust. Sade does not suggest this process as such; but he urges women to fuck as actively as they are able, so that powered by their enormous and hitherto untapped sexual energy they will then be able to fuck their way into history and, in doing so, change it.

One of Sade's singularities is that he offers an absolutely sexualised view of the world, a sexualisation that permeates everything, much as his atheism does and, since he is not a religious man but a political man, he treats the facts of female sexuality not as a moral dilemma but as a political reality.

In fact, he treats all sexuality as a political reality and that is inevitable, because his own sexuality brought him directly against the law. He spent the greater part of his adult life in confinement because his own sexual tastes overrode his socialisation; his perversion has entered the dictionary under his own name.

Although he documented his sexual fantasies with an unequalled diligence, and these fantasies delight in the grisliest tortures (even if, in the context of his fictions, he creates an inverted ethical superstructure to legitimise these cruelties) his own sexual practice in life remains relatively obscure. From the evidence of the two court cases in which he was involved, the affair of Rose Keller in 1768 and the charges made against him by a group of Marseilles prostitutes in 1772, he seems to have enjoyed both giving and receiving whippings; voyeurism; anal intercourse, both active and passive; and the presence of an audience at these activities. These are not particularly unusual sexual preferences, though they are more common as fantasies, and are always very expensive if purchased. When they take place in private, the law usually ignores them even when they are against the law, just as it turns a blind eye to wife beating and recreational bondage. Sade, however, seems to have been incapable of keeping his vices private, as if he was aware of their exemplary nature and, perhaps, since the notion of sin, of transgression, was essential to his idea of pleasure, which is always intellectual, never sensual, he may have needed to invoke the punishment of which he consciously denied the validity before he could feel the act itself had been accomplished.

The Rose Keller affair in particular has a curious quality of theatre, of the acting-out of a parable of sex and money. This woman, the thirty-six-year-old widow of a pastry cook, was begging in Paris on Easter Sunday, a day of special significance to the anti-clerical Sade; a day that cried out to be desecrated. According to the deposition she later gave the police, a gentleman, well-dressed, even handsome, approached her in a public square and suggested she might like to earn herself a crown. When she concurred, he took her to a room in a private house; whipped her; gave her food and offered her money, both of which she refused. Then he locked her in the room but she soon escaped through the window and went to tell her tale. Sade admitted freely that he had indeed hired her and whipped her but he said that Rose Keller had known perfectly well he did not intend her to sweep his house, as she claimed, and they had agreed beforehand she would go off with him for a session of debauchery. The matter was settled out of court. Rose Keller was persuaded to withdraw her charge on a payment of an enormous indemnity of two thousand four hundred francs and expenses of seven louis d'or for dressings and ointments for her wounds.

The affair enchants me. It has the completeness and the lucidity of a script by Brecht. A woman of the third estate, a beggar, the poorest of the poor, turns the very vices of the rich into weapons to wound them with. In the fictions he is going to write, Sade will make La Dubois, the brigand chief, say that the callousness of the rich justifies the crimes of the poor; Rose Keller, who expected, perhaps, to have sex with the Marquis but for whom the whip came as a gratuitous, unexpected and unwelcome surprise, turns her hand to blackmail and who can blame her? An ironic triumph for the beggar woman; the victim turned victor. . . .

It was prison, the experience of oppression, that transformed the rake into the philosopher, the man of the Age of Reason into the prophet of the age of dissolution, of our own time, the time of the assassins. Deprived of the fact of flesh, he concentrated his notable sexual energy on a curious task of sublimation, a project that involved simultaneously creating and destroying that which he could no longer possess, the flesh, the world, love, in a desolate charnel house of the imagination. It is as well to remember that, when given the opportunity of carrying out this project in practice during the Reign of Terror, he rejected it, at the price of further confinement.

Although Sade's sexual practices would hardly be punished so severely today (and it was punishment that inflamed his sexual imagination to the grossest extent) his sexual imagination would always be of a nature to violate any law that governed any society that retained the notions of crime and punishment. This would be especially true of those societies that most rigorously practice punitive justice, that habitually utilise legislative murder, that is, capital punishment, flogging, mutilation and torture as methods of punishment and intimidation towards their members. For these legal crimes to be described by an honest pervert, or a moral pornographer, as 'pleasure' is to let the cat out of the bag; if Sade is to be castigated for tastes he exercised only in the privacy of his mind or with a few well-paid auxiliaries, then the hanging judge, the birching magistrate, the military torturer with his hoods and his electrodes, the flogging schoolmaster, the brutal husband must also be acknowledged as perverts to whom, in our own criminal folly, we have given a licence to practice upon the general public. Since Sade had no such licence, and, indeed, deplored the fact that licences were granted, his imagination took sexual violence to an extreme that may, in a human being, only be accompanied by an extreme of misanthropy, self-disgust and despair.

His solitude is the perpetual companion and daily horror of the prisoner, whose final place of confinement is the self. 'When I have inspired universal disgust and horror, then I will have conquered solitude', said Baudelaire, who read Sade again and again. Sade projects this diabolic solitude as an absolute egoism; that is the result of thirteen years solitary meditation on the world. The desires of his imaginary libertines may no longer be satisfied by flesh; flesh becomes an elaborate metaphor for sexual abuse. World, flesh and the devil fuse; when an atheist casts a cool eye on the world, he must always find Satan a more likely hypothesis than ruling principle than a Saviour. Criminality may present itself as a kind of saintly self-mastery, an absolute rejection of hypocrisy. Sade directly influenced Baudelaire; he is also the spiritual ancestor of Genet. Swift saw mankind rolling in a welter of shit, as Sade does, but Sade's satire upon man is far blacker and more infernal than Swift's—for Sade, mankind doesn't roll in shit because mankind is disgusting, but because mankind has overweening aspirations to the superhuman. Of his own contemporaries, he has most in common with the painter Goya; of our contemporaries, the polymorphous perversity and the intense isolation of his characters recall William Burroughs. If Sade is the last, bleak, disillusioned voice of the Enlightenment, he is the avatar of the nihilism of the late twentieth century. His overt misogyny is a single strand in a total revulsion against a mankind of whom, unlike Swift, he cannot delude himself he is not a member. . . .

Andrea Dworkin (essay date 1981)

SOURCE: "The Marquis de Sade (1740-1814)," in *Pornography: Men Possessing Women,* The Women's Press, 1981, pp. 70-100.

[*A radical feminist essayist and fiction writer, Dworkin has published several books on the politics of gender. In her book* Pornography: Men Possessing Women, *she argues that pornography functions in society as an instrument of power with which men degrade and subjugate women. In the following excerpt from that book, Dworkin posits that the violence against women that permeates Sade's work expresses basic assumptions about the relative rights of men and women in both his society and the present day.*]

Donatien-Alphonse-François de Sade—known as the Marquis de Sade, known to his ardent admirers who are legion as The Divine Marquis—is the world's foremost pornographer. As such he both embodies and defines male sexual values. In him, one finds rapist and writer twisted into one scurvy knot. His life and writing were of a piece, a whole cloth soaked in the blood of women imagined and real. In his life he tortured and raped women. He was batterer, rapist, kidnapper, and child abuser. In his work he relentlessly celebrated brutality as the essence of eroticism; fucking, torture, and killing were fused; violence and sex, synonymous. His work and legend have survived nearly two centuries because literary, artistic, and intellectual men adore him and political thinkers on the Left claim him as an avatar of freedom. Sainte-Beuve named Sade and Byron as the two most significant sources of inspiration for the original and great male writers who followed them. Baudelaire, Flaubert, Swinburne, Lautréamont, Dostoevski, Cocteau, and Apollinaire among others found in Sade what Paul Tillich, another devotee of pornography, might have called "the courage to be." Simone de Beauvoir published a long apologia for Sade. Camus, who unlike Sade had an aversion to murder, romanticized Sade as one who had mounted "the great offensive against a hostile heaven" and was possibly "the first theoretician of absolute rebellion." Roland Barthes wallowed in the tiniest details of Sade's crimes, those committed in life as well as on paper. Sade is precursor to Artaud's theater of cruelty, Nietzsche's will to power, and the rapist frenzy of William Burroughs. In England in 1966, a twelve-year-old boy and a ten-year-old girl were tortured and murdered by a self-proclaimed disciple of Sade. The crimes were photographed and tape-recorded by the murderer, who played them back for pleasure. In 1975 in the United States, organized crime reportedly sold "snuff" films to private collectors of pornography. In these films, women actually were maimed, sliced into pieces, fucked, and killed—the perfect Sadean synthesis. Magazines and films depicting the mutilation of women for the sake of sexual pleasure now abound. A major translator into English of Sade's thousands of pages of butchery and the one primarily responsible for the publication of Sade's work in accessible mass-market editions in the United States is Richard Seaver, a respected figure in establishment publishing. Seaver, instrumental in the propagation of Sade's work and legend, has reportedly written a film of Sade's life that will be made by Alain Resnais. Sade's cultural influence on all levels is pervasive. His ethic—the absolute right of men to rape and brutalize any "object of desire" at will—resonates in every sphere.

Sade was born into a noble French family closely related to the reigning monarch. Sade was raised with the prince, four years his senior, during his earliest years. When Sade was four, his mother left the Court and he was sent to live with his grandmother. At the age of five, he was sent to live with his uncle, the Abbé de Sade, a clergyman known for his sensual indulgences. Sade's father, a diplomat and soldier, was absent during Sade's formative years. Inevitably, biographers trace Sade's character to his mother's personality, behavior, and alleged sexual repression, despite the fact that very little is known about her. What is known, but not sufficiently noted, is that Sade was raised among the male mighty. He wrote in later years of having been humiliated and controlled by them. . . .

Camus captured the essence of Sade's legend when he wrote: "His desperate demand for freedom led Sade into the kingdom of servitude . . ." Throughout the literature on him, with some small qualifying asides, Sade is viewed as one whose voracious appetite was for *freedom;* this appetite was cruelly punished by an unjust and repressive society. The notion is that Sade, called by Apollinaire "that freest of spirits to have lived so far," was a monster as the word used to be defined: something unnaturally marvelous. Sade's violation of sexual and social boundaries, in his writings and in his life, is seen as inherently revolutionary. The antisocial character of his sexuality is seen as a radical challenge to a society deadly in its repressive sexual conventions. Sade is seen as an outlaw in the mythic sense, a grand figure of rebellion in action and in literature whose sexual hunger, like a terrorist's bomb, threatened to blow apart the established order. The imprisonment of Sade is seen to demonstrate the despotism of a system that must contain, control, and manipulate sexuality, not allow it to run free toward anarchic self-fulfillment. Sade is seen as the victim of that cruel system, as one who was punished because of the bravery of his antagonism to it. The legend of Sade is particularly vitalized by the false claim, widely believed, that he rotted in prison for most of his life as punishment for obscene writings. Sade's story is generally thought to be this: he was a genius whose mind was too big for the petty puritans around him; he was locked up for his sexual abandonment, especially in writing; he was kept in jail because nothing less could defuse the danger he presented to the established order; he was victimized, unjustly imprisoned, persecuted, for daring to express radical sexual values in his life and in his writing; as "that freest of spirits to have lived so far," his very being was an insult to a system that demanded conformity. It was left to Erica Jong to insist in an article in *Playboy* ("You Have to Be Liberated to Laugh") that Sade was jailed for his sense of humor.

Writers on Sade are fascinated by both his life and his work, and it is impossible to know whether Sade's legend could have been sustained if one had existed without the other. Edmund Wilson, repelled by Sade's work, is fascinated by his life. Simone de Beauvoir, repelled by Sade's life, is fascinated by his work. Most of the writers on Sade advocate rather than analyze him, are infatuated with him as a subject precisely because his sexual obsessions are both forbidden and common. The books and essays on Sade are crusading, romanticizing, mystifying in the literal sense (that is, intentionally perplexing to the mind). Infused with a missionary passion, they boil down to this: Sade died for you—for all the sexual crimes you have committed, for all the sexual crimes you want to commit, for every sexual crime you can imagine committing. Sade suffered because he did what you want to do; he was imprisoned as you might be imprisoned. The "you" is masculine. The freedom Sade is credited with demanding is freedom as men conceive it. Sade's suffering or victimization, whatever its cause or degree, is authentic because a man experienced it (Sade in being imprisoned, the writers in morbid contemplation of a man brought down). No woman's life has ever been so adored; no woman's suffering has ever been so mourned; no woman's ethic, action, or obsession has been so hallowed in the male search for the meaning of freedom.

The essential content of Sade's legend was created by Sade himself, especially in his prison letters and in the rambling philosophical discourses that permeate his fiction. Maurice Heine, a Left libertarian, and his disciple Gilbert Lély, the first so-called Sade scholars, rewrote Sade's elaborate self-justifications, in the process transmuting them into accepted fact. Sade wrote his own legend; Heine and Lély resurrected it; subsequent writers paraphrased, defended, and embellished it.

In the letters, Sade is militant, with the pride of one martyred in righteousness: "Misfortune will never debase me . . . ," he wrote to Renée-Pélagie from Vincennes in 1781. "Nor will *I* ever take a slave's heart. Were these wretched chains to lead me to the grave, you will always see me the same. I have the misfortune to have received from Heaven a resolute soul which has never been able to yield and will never do so. I have absolutely no fear of offending anyone."

It was Sade who painted the picture of Madame de Montreuil that his biographers now turn out, without the master's touch, by the dozens. As Sade wrote: "This terrible torture is not enough according to this horrible creature: it has to be increased further by everything her imagination can devise to redouble its horror. You will admit there is only one monster capable of taking vengeance to such a point."

Sade's defense of everything he ever did is very simple: he never did anything wrong. This defense has two distinct parts. First, he did not do anything he was accused of doing that might warrant imprisonment, because no one could prove that he did, including eyewitnesses whose word could never match his own: "A child's testimony? But this was a servant; thus, in his capacity as a child and as a servant he cannot be believed." Second, everything he had done was common practice. These two contradictory strains of self-defense often fuse to reveal the Sade obscured by his mesmerized apologists. Here he defends himself, again to his wife, vis-à-vis his abuse of the five fifteen-year-old girls originally procured by Nanon, who later bore his child:

> I go off with them; I use them. Six months later, some parents come along to demand their return. I give them back [he did not], and suddenly a charge of abduction and rape is brought against me. It is a monstrous injustice. The law on this point is . . . as follows: it is expressly forbidden in France for any procuress to supply virgin maidens, and if the girl supplied is a virgin and lodges a complaint, it is not the man who is charged but the procuress who is punished severely on the spot. But even if the male offender has requested a virgin he is not liable to punishment: he is merely doing what all men do. It is, I repeat, the procuress who provided him with the girl and who is perfectly aware that she is expressly forbidden to do so, who is guilty. Therefore this first charge against me in Lyon of abduction and rape was entirely illegal: I have committed no offence. It is the procuress to whom I have applied who is liable to punishment—not I.

The use of women, as far as Sade was concerned, was an absolute right, one that could not fairly be limited or abrogated under any circumstances. His outrage at being punished for his assaults on females never abated. His claim to innocence rested finally on a simple assertion: "I am guilty of nothing more than simple libertinage such as it is practised by all men more or less according to their natural temperaments or tendencies." Sade's fraternal ties were apparent only when he used the crimes of other men to justify his own.

Sade designated "libertinage" as the main theme of his work. Richard Seaver and Austryn Wainhouse, in a foreword to a collection of Sade's work, point out with grave emphasis that "libertine" comes from the Latin *liber*, which means "free." In fact, originally a libertine was a manumitted slave. Sade's use of the word contradicts its early meaning, despite the claim of his sycophantic translators. For Sade, libertinage was the cruel use of others for one's own sexual pleasure. Sade's libertinage demanded slavery; sexual despotism misnamed "freedom" is Sade's most enduring legacy.

Sade's work is nearly indescribable. In sheer quantity of horror, it is unparalleled in the history of writing. In its fanatical and fully realized commitment to depicting and reveling in torture and murder to gratify lust, it raises the question so central to pornography as a genre: why? why did someone do (make) this? In Sade's case, the motive most often named is revenge against a society that persecuted him. This explanation does not take into account the fact that Sade was a sexual predator and that the pornography he created was part of that predation.

It is not adequate to describe Sade's ethic as rapist. For Sade, rape was a modest, not fully gratifying mode of violation. In Sade's work, rape is foreplay, preparation for the main event, which is maiming unto death. Rape is an essential dimension because force is fundamental to Sade's conception of sexual action. But over time, with repetition, it pales, becomes boring, a stupendous waste of energy unless accompanied by the torture, and often the murder, of the victim. Sade is the consummate literary snuff artist: orgasm eventually requires murder. Victims are sliced up, impaled on stakes, burned alive, roasted slowly on spits, eaten, decapitated, flayed until they die. Women's vaginas and rectums are sewn up to be torn through. Women are used as tables on which burning food is served, on which candles are burned. One would require the thousands of pages Sade himself used to list the atrocities he described. Nevertheless, some themes emerge.

In Sade's fiction, men, women, boys and girls are used, violated, destroyed. At the top, in control, are the libertines, mostly old men, aristocrats, powerful by virtue of gender, wealth, position, and cruelty. Sade describes the sexuality of these men essentially as addiction: each sex act contributes to the development of a tolerance; that is, arousal requires more cruelty each time, orgasm requires more cruelty each time; victims must increase in abjectness and numbers both. Everyone inferior to the aristocrats on top in wealth, in social status, or in her or his capacity for cruelty becomes sexual fodder. Wives, daughters, and mothers are particularly singled out for ridicule, humiliation, and contempt. Servants of both sexes and female prostitutes are the main population of the abused, dismembered, executed. Lesbian acts decorate the slaughter; they are imagined by a man for men; they are so male-imagined that the divine fuck imbued with murder is their only possible resolution.

In the bulk of Sade's work, female victims greatly outnumber male victims, but his cruelty is all-inclusive. He manifests a pansexual dominance—the male who knows no boundaries but still hates women more.

While the aristocrats on top are never maimed, they are, at their own command, whipped and sodomized. They remain entirely in control even when whipped or sodomized. Everything done to them or by them is for the purpose of bringing them to orgasm on their own terms. Sade established impotence as a characteristic of the aging libertine: viler and viler crimes are necessary to achieve erection and ejaculation. George Steiner, perhaps to his credit, fails to appreciate the significance of the progression of lust in Sade's work, especially in *The 120 Days of Sodom:* "In short: given the physiological and nervous complexion of the human body, the numbers of ways in which orgasm can be achieved or arrested, the total modes of intercourse are fundamentally finite. The mathematics of sex stop somewhere in the region of *soixante-neuf;* there are no transcendental series." Displaying his own brand of misogyny, Steiner goes on to say that "things have remained fairly generally the same since man first met goat and woman." But Sade is saying precisely that men become

sated too soon with what they have had, whatever it is, especially woman, also goat.

In Sade's fiction, the men on top exchange and share victims in an attempt to forge a community based on a common, if carnivorous, sexuality. The shared victim results in the shared orgasm, a bond among the male characters and between the author and his male readers.

The men on top also share the shit of the victims. They control elimination and physical cleanliness, a strategem that suggests the Nazi death camps. They eat turds and control the diets of their victims to control the quality of the turds. While Freudian values apply here—the anal being indicative of greed, of obsession with material wealth—excrement, like blood, like flesh itself, is ingested because these men have gone beyond vampirism toward a sexuality that is entirely cannibalistic.

Much is made of the fact that two of Sade's main characters, Justine and Juliette, are women. Juliette especially is cited as an emancipated woman because she takes to maiming and murder with all the spectacular ease of Sade's male characters; she is the one who knows how to take pleasure, how to transform pain into pleasure, slavery into freedom. It is, Sade's literary friends claim, a matter of *attitude:* here we have Justine, raped, tortured, violated, and she hates it, so she is a victim; here we have Juliette, raped, tortured, violated, and she loves it, so she is free. As expressed by Roland Barthes [in *Sade, Fourier, Loyola*]:

> The scream is the victim's mark; she makes herself a victim because she chooses to scream; if, under the same vexation she were to ejaculate [*sic*], she would cease to be a victim, would be transformed into a libertine: *to scream/to discharge,* this paradigm is the beginning of choice, i. e. Sadian meaning.

"Sadian meaning," then, reduces to the more familiar preachment: if you can't do anything about it (and I will see to it that you cannot), lie back and enjoy it. In the critical writings on Sade's pornography, rape in the criminal sense exists mainly as a subjective value judgment of the one who was used, to whom hysteria is always attributed. Women, according to Sade, Barthes, and their ilk, can and should choose to experience the rape of women as men experience it: as pleasure.

Sade's view of women was hailed by Apollinaire as prophetic: "Justine is woman as she has been hitherto, enslaved, miserable and less than human; her opposite, Juliette, represents the woman whose advent he anticipated, a figure of whom minds have as yet no conception, who is arising out of mankind, who shall have wings, and who shall renew the world."

Justine and Juliette are the two prototypical female figures in male pornography of all types. Both are wax dolls into which things are stuck. One suffers and is provocative in her suffering. The more she suffers, the more she provokes men to make her suffer. Her suffering is arousing; the more she suffers, the more aroused her torturers become. She, then, becomes responsible for her suffering, since she invites it by suffering. The other revels in all that men do to her; she is the woman who likes it, no matter what the "it." In Sade, the "attitude" (to use Barthes's word) on which one's status as victim or master depends is an attitude toward male power. The victim actually refuses to ally herself with male power, to take on its values as her own. She screams, she refuses. Men conceptualize this resistance as conformity to ridiculous feminine notions about purity and goodness; whereas in fact the victim refuses to ally herself with those who demand her complicity in her own degradation. Degradation is implicit in inhabiting a predetermined universe in which one cannot choose what one does, only one's attitude (to scream, to discharge) toward what is done to one. Unable to manifest her resistance as power, the woman who suffers manifests it as passivity, except for the scream.

The so-called libertine re-creates herself in the image of the cruelest (most powerful) man she can find and in her alliance with him takes on some of his power over others. The female libertines in Sade's work are always subordinate to their male counterparts, always dependent on them for wealth and continued good health. They have female anatomies by fiat; that is, Sade says so. In every other respect—values, behaviors, tastes, even in such a symptomatic detail as ejaculating sperm, which they all do—Sade's libertine women are men. They are, in fact, literary transvestites.

Sade himself, in a footnote to *Juliette,* claimed an authenticity for Juliette based on his conviction that women are more malevolent than men: ". . . the more sensitive an individual, the more sharply this atrocious Nature will bend him into conformance with evil's irresistible laws; whence it is that women surrender to it more heatedly and perform it with greater artistry than men." The message that women are evil and must be punished permeates Sade's work, whether the female figures in question are supposed to represent good or evil. The vileness of women and an intense hatred of female genitalia are major themes in every Sadean opus. Both male and female characters evince a deep aversion to and loathing of the vagina. Anal penetration is not only preferred; often the vagina must be hidden for the male to be aroused at all. Sade's female libertines are eloquent on the inferiority of the vagina to the rectum. While boys and men are used in Sade's lust murders, women are excoriated for all the characteristics that distinguish them from men. In Sade's scheme of things, women are aggressively slaughtered because women are repulsive as both biological and emotional beings. The arrogance of women in claiming any rights over their own bodies is particularly offensive to Sade. Any uppity pretense to bodily integrity on a woman's part must be fiercely and horribly punished. Even where Sade, in one or two places, insists on women's right to abort pregnancies at will, his sustained celebration of abortion as erotically charged murder places abortion squarely within the context of his own utterly and unredeemably male value system: in this system, women have no bodily rights.

A religious scholar, John T. Noonan, Jr., names Sade as "the first in Western Europe to praise abortion . . ." Citing Noonan, Linda Bird Francke, in *The Ambivalence of Abortion,* claims that Sade's advocacy of abortion was in-

strumental in the papal decision that abortion must be prohibited from gestation on. Characterizing Sade's work as part of the proabortion movement, she asserts that Sade "actually extolled the values of abortion." Sade extolled the sexual value of murder and he saw abortion as a form of murder. For Sade, abortion was a sexual act, an act of lust. In his system, pregnancy always demanded murder, usually the murder of the pregnant woman, rendered more exciting if she was in an advanced stage of pregnancy. Nothing could be calculated to please Sade more than the horrible deaths of women butchered in illegal abortion. This is Sade's sexuality realized.

In Sade's work, both male and female children are maimed, raped, tortured, killed. Men especially go after their daughters, sometimes raising them specifically to become paramours, most often abusing them and then passing them on to close male friends to be used and killed. Sade's obsession with sexual violence against children of both sexes is transformed by his literary lackeys, true to form, into another demonstration of Sade's progressive sexual radicalism. As Geoffrey Gorer wrote: "According to de Sade, very young children are shameless, sexually inquisitive and endowed with strong sexual feelings. Children are naturally polymorphous perverts." Actually, according to Sade, adult men find it particularly gratifying to kidnap, rape, torture, and kill children.

Sade is concerned too with the violation of the mother— not only as wife to her husband but also as victim of her children. A constant conceit throughout Sade's fiction is that fathers are wondrous sexual beings, mothers stupid and repressed prudes who would be better off as whores (or as the whores they really are). As a philosopher, Sade maintains consistently that one owes nothing to one's mother, for the father is the source of human life:

> . . . Be unafraid, Eugénie [the heroine], and adopt these same sentiments; they are natural: uniquely formed of our sires' blood, we owe absolutely nothing to our mothers. What, furthermore, did they do but co-operate in the act which our fathers, on the contrary, solicited? Thus, it was the father who desired our birth, whereas the mother merely consented thereto.

Contempt for the mother is an integral part of Sade's discourse:

> It is madness to suppose one owes something to one's mother. And upon what, then, would gratitude be based? Is one to be thankful that she discharged [*sic*] when someone once fucked her?

A daughter's turning on her mother, forcing her mother to submit to rape and torture, defaming and debasing her mother, and finally luxuriating in the killing of her mother is a crucial Sadean scenario.

Sade's ideas on women and sexual freedom are explicated throughout his work. He has few ideas about women and sexual freedom and no fear of repetition. Women are meant to be prostitutes: ". . . your sex never serves Nature better than when it prostitutes itself to ours; that 'tis, in a word, to be fucked that you were born . . ." In rape a man exercises his natural rights over women:

If then it becomes incontestable that we have received from Nature the right indiscriminately to express our wishes to all women, it likewise becomes incontestable that we have the right to compel their submission, not exclusively, for I should then be contradicting myself, but temporarily [the doctrine of "nonpossessiveness"]. It cannot be denied that we have the right to decree laws that compel woman to yield to the flames of him who would have her; violence itself being one of that right's effects, we can employ it lawfully.

Sade pioneered what became the ethos of the male-dominated sexual revolution: collective ownership of women by men, no woman ever justified in refusal. Sade took these ideas to their logical conclusion: state brothels in which all females would be forced to serve from childhood on. The idea of unrestricted access to an absolutely available female population, there to be raped, to which one could do anything, has gripped the male imagination, especially on the Left, and has been translated into the euphemistic demand for "free sex, free women." The belief that this urge toward unrestrained use of women is revolutionary brings into bitter focus the meaning of "sexual freedom" in leftist sexual theory and practice. Sade says: use women because women exist to be used by men; do what you want to them for your own pleasure, no matter what the cost to them. Following leftist tradition, Peter Weiss, in the play known as *Marat/Sade,* paraphrased Sade in this happily disingenuous way: "And what's the point of a revolution / without general copulation."

In a variation of leftist theme, Christopher Lasch, in *The Culture of Narcissism,* sees Sade not as the originator of a new ethic of sexual collectivity, but as one who foresaw the fall of the bourgeois family with its "sentimental cult of womanhood" and the fall of capitalism itself. According to Lasch, Sade anticipated a "defense of woman's [*sic*] sexual rights—their rights to dispose of their own bodies, as feminists would put it today . . . He perceived, more clearly than the feminists, that all freedoms under capitalism come in the end to the same thing, the same universal obligation to enjoy and be enjoyed." Lasch's particular, and peculiar, interpretation of Sade appears to derive from his stubborn misunderstanding of sexual integrity as feminists envision it. In Sade's universe, the obligation to enjoy is extended to women as the obligation to enjoy being enjoyed—failing which, sex remains what it was, as it was: a forced passage to death. The notion that Sade presages feminist demands for women's sexual rights is rivaled in self-serving absurdity only by the opinion of Gerald and Caroline Greene, in *S-M: The Last Taboo,* that "[i]f there was one thing de Sade was not, it was a sexist."

De Beauvoir had understood that "[t]he fact is that the original intuition which lies at the basis of Sade's entire sexuality, and hence his ethic, is the fundamental identity of coition and cruelty." Camus had understood that "[t]wo centuries ahead of time and on a reduced scale [compared to Stalinists and Nazis], Sade extolled totalitarian societies in the name of unbridled freedom . . ." Neither they nor Sade's less conscientious critics perceived that Sade's valuation of women has been the one constant in history—imagined and enacted—having as its conse-

quence the destruction of real lives; that Sade's advocacy and celebration of rape and battery have been history's sustaining themes. Sade's spectacular endurance as a cultural force has been because of, not despite, the virulence of the sexual violence toward women in both his work and his life. Sade's work embodies the common values and desires of men. Described in terms of its "excesses," as it often is, the power of Sade's work in exciting the imaginations of men is lost. Nothing in Sade's work takes place outside the realm of common male belief. In story and discourse, Sade's conception of romance is this: "I've already told you: the only way to a woman's heart is along the path of torment. I know none other as sure." Sade's conception of sexuality is this:

> . . . there is no more selfish passion than lust; none that is severer in its demands; smitten stiff by desire, 'tis with yourself you must be solely concerned, and as for the object that serves you, it must always be considered as some sort of victim, destined to that passion's fury. Do not all passions require victims?

These convictions are ordinary, expressed often in less grand language, upheld in their rightness by the application of male-supremacist law especially in the areas of rape, battery, and reproduction; they are fully consonant with the practices (if not the preachments) of ordinary men with ordinary women. Had Sade's work—boring, repetitive, ugly as it is—not embodied these common values, it would long ago have been forgotten. Had Sade himself—a sexual terrorist, a sexual tyrant—not embodied in

---

Michel Foucault on Sade and Classicism:

[*Juliette*] closes the Classical age upon itself, just as *Don Quixote* had opened it. And though it is true that this is the last language still contemporaneous with Rousseau and Racine, though it is the last discourse that undertakes to 'represent', to *name,* we are well enough aware that it simultaneously reduces this ceremony to the utmost precision (it calls things by their strict name, thus eliminating the space occupied by rhetoric) and extends it to infinity (by naming everything, including the slightest of possibilities, for they are all traversed in accordance with the Universal Characteristic of Desire). Sade attains the end of Classical discourse and thought. He holds sway precisely upon their frontier. After him, violence, life and death, desire, and sexuality will extend, below the level of representation, an immense expanse of shade which we are now attempting to recover, as far as we can, in our discourse, in our freedom, in our thought. But our thought is so brief, our freedom so enslaved, our discourse so repetitive, that we must face the fact that that expanse of shade below is really a bottomless sea. The prosperities of *Juliette* are still more solitary—and endless.

Michel Foucault, in his The Order of Things: An Archaeology of the Human Sciences, *Pantheon, 1970.*

his life these same values, he would not have excited the twisted, self-righteous admiration of those who have portrayed him as revolutionary, hero, martyr (or, in the banal prose of Richard Gilman, "the first compelling enunciator in modern times of the desire to be other than what society determined, to act otherwise than existing moral structures coerced one into doing").

Sade's importance, finally, is not as dissident or deviant: it is as Everyman, a designation the power-crazed aristocrat would have found repugnant but one that women, on examination, will find true. In Sade, the authentic equation is revealed: the power of the pornographer is the power of the rapist/batterer is the power of the man.

Joan DeJean   (essay date 1984)

SOURCE: "Inside the Sadean Fortress: *Les 120 journées de Sodome,*" in *Literary Fortifications: Rousseau, Laclos, Sade,* Princeton University Press, 1984, pp. 263-326.

[*DeJean has published several books on French literature of the seventeenth and eighteenth centuries and on literature by and about women. In the following excerpt, she considers the relationship of* The 120 Days of Sodom *to the Classical literary tradition.*]

The invitation to a literary feast that Sade has his narrator extend to the reader [in the introduction to ***The 120 Days of Sodom***] is representative of just that strain in Sade's work to which recent critics have been most sensitive, Sade's rejection of convention and his invitation to literary liberation. Furthermore, the portrait of Sade as author implicit in these lines also conforms to the image that lies behind recent criticism of his works: Sade as author is the literary equivalent of Sade the liberator of the Bastille. Part of the recent fascination with Sade results from critical admiration for an author so confident of his philosophical and textual superiority that he can invite his reader— just as he invited the crowds that gathered outside the Bastille within earshot of his prison cell—to join him in tearing down the fortress, even when the fortress is his own construction rather than a prison symbolic of the system of authority that had deprived him of his freedom for so many years.

The current vision of Sade has its origin in part in the Surrealist fascination with this *auteur maudit.* One document that testifies eloquently to the power of that fascination, Man Ray's "Portrait imaginaire du marquis de Sade" (1938), also betrays the limits of the legend of Sade the liberating author. In the Man Ray portrait, the figure of Sade (shown from the shoulders up) dominates the image. The marquis is looking at a fortress in the background. The fortress is under siege; clearly the Bastille is being stormed. Yet the portrait represents far more than the triumph of a revolutionary spirit over the forces of oppression. Man Ray's most striking insight is his representation of the figure of Sade as a construction of stones, of the same stones that compose both the fortress under siege and its protective outworks: the divine marquis is himself a fortress. Man Ray's portrait illustrates above all Sade's paradoxical position, simultaneously inside and outside the fortress. Sade is made of the same material as the Ancien Régime.

The truth of Man Ray's vision is also borne out by Sade's *oeuvre.* The novels of the Ancien Régime's illustrious prisoner are too often viewed as a marginal manifestation of the archetypal Enlightenment drive. They are said to announce our modernity even as they bring down the fortress of Classical literature by throwing light on the dark areas repressed by earlier novelists. While this view is faithful to Sade's self portrait as author—witness the address of the *120* to the reader—it can account neither for Sade's views of his literary predecessors, including his (alleged) jealousy of Laclos, nor for the shape he chose for at least certain of his fictions, notably the (in)famous *120.* Sade is an essentially equivocal author: he speaks simultaneously with two voices, a voice of liberation and a voice of control. The effect of this second voice on his fiction will be my principal subject here. I will take up Man Ray's suggestion that Sade was made of the same building blocks as the Ancien Régime. From this perspective, it becomes clear that Sade intended his fiction to be viewed not as a rupture with previous literary tradition but as its culminating point. Sade, the great rebel outcast, was trying not to destroy the great tradition of the French novel, but to continue it. The marquis foresaw what has become the prevailing view of the history of the early French novel, with Lafayette's *La Princesse de Clèves* as that novel's origin, and the *Liaisons dangereuses* as its culmination. . . .

"Sade parvient au bout du discours et de la pensée classiques," in Foucault's evaluation. "Il règne exactement à leur limite" *(Les Mots et les choses).* His statement is as intriguingly ambiguous as Man Ray's "portrait imaginaire." On the one hand, it contains in germ the philosophy that motivates the dominant tradition of recent Sade criticism: Sade must be situated "au bout du discours . . . classique" because he marks a sort of voluntary return of all the truths repressed in this discourse. This would seem to be the meaning of another of Foucault's striking formulations about Sade: "Il n'y a pas d'ombre chez Sade" *(Histoire de la folie),* a formulation that could serve as an epigraph for many recent readings of the divine marquis. For example, Foucault has been echoed by Roger [in *Sade: La Philosophie dans le pressoir,* 1976] "Sade ne ménage aucun recoin obscur au récit."

But this is to comment on only one aspect of Foucault's intuition. It is not sufficient to say that Sade brought all of Classicism's skeletons out of the closet. The marquis is not only a rebel striving to outdo the Classical model by pointing out its weaknesses. He is at the same time Classicism's heir, built of the same stones as the fortress of the Ancien Régime. It is only logical that the relationship between Sade's fiction and the novelistic models of the French Classical age must be more problematic than is generally allowed. For example, the incipit of the *120* openly proclaims its author's admiration for the Golden Age of French literature—"la fin de ce règne [Louis XIV's], si sublime d'ailleurs." Sade's own works of prose fiction have often been compared to the novelistic masterpiece of the Sun King's reign. Lely suggests [in *Vie du marquis de Sade*] that *La Princesse de Clèves* may have served as a model for ***Adélaïde de Brunswick;*** Béatrice Didier contends [in *Sade: une écriture du désir,* 1976] that "on trouve de curieuses analogies entre ***La Marquise de***

Ganges et *La Princesse de Clèves.*" Such analogies are frequently encountered, and they are "curious" indeed, for the reader never knows which interpretation of Foucault's evaluation may be invoked to explain them.

The *120* provides the best illustration of what might be termed Sade's aggressive eulogy of Classical discourse. For example, its incipit follows the model established for the French novel by Lafayette's masterpiece. The opening of *La Princesse de Clèves* situates the novel in the last years of a reign. The novel's first business is to introduce the reader to the principal characters of that declining rule and to inform the reader about the structure of its waning power. The *120* repeats this pattern, but the "tone" that governs its repetition is not easily classified. Sade's choice of historical setting for the *120* and his careful mapping out of the actors and the strategies that govern the libertine court within a court cannot be viewed as a parody of the founding text of the Classical French novel. Here, as at every moment when the Sadean text aligns itself most closely with Classical discourse, the point of textual contact is signaled by a sort of narrative bravado that initially seems *almost* comic. Yet the purpose of the incipit of the *120* does not run counter to that of its predecessor. The beginning of Sade's novel is closer to a positive appraisal of Lafayette's understanding of the workings of power, but an appraisal that, nevertheless, makes clear that the insights it is prepared to offer are keener than those of its precursor.

In *Sade, Fourier, Loyola,* Barthes reminds us that the burnt-out, frozen landscape of Sade's fiction is not, for all its awesome timelessness, a-historical. Unlike the fairy tale and the science-fiction story, which also unfold in minimalist settings, the Sadean novel does not reject history. "Les aventures sadiennes ne sont pas fabuleuses: elles se passent dans un monde réel, contemporain de la jeunesse de Sade, à savoir la société de Louis XV." For the *120,* Sade shifts the setting from Louis XV's reign to the last years of Louis XIV's, only a slightly greater distancing. He revives the model for "historical" fiction established by *La Princesse de Clèves* by choosing a narrative that unfolds in the not too distant past, but in a past nevertheless just outside the collective memory of the writer's contemporaries. The exceptional precision with which the historical setting is inscribed into the incipit of the *120* is clearly intended to attract the reader's attention. . . .

In the *120,* Sade matches his historical distancing with a form of what might be termed architectural distancing. The result of this process is a fictive architecture that repeats the relationship, already noted in the novel, of dissonant alignment with regard to the structures of French Classicism. Critics have often contrasted the two types of châteaux created to shelter the Sadean passion plays. They note first the gracious and open *demeures* of eighteenth-century inspiration, such as Mme de Saint-Ange's country home in which the "instituteurs immoraux" of *La Philosophie dans le boudoir* devote themselves to the task of Eugénie's education. This is a château gracious enough to contain so feminine a space as a "boudoir délicieux," and a château so open that, as their pupil Eugénie remarks on several occasions, newcomers are able to enter that boudoir with great ease.

These elegant dwellings stand in sharp contrast to the fortresses surrounded by thick walls in concentric circles, of which Silling is perhaps the "classic" representative. Hénaff interprets this second type of château as intended to "convoquer d'un coup tous les signes de la forteresse féodale avec ses implications historiques" [in *L'Invention du corps libertin,* 1978]. He sees the Sadean *château fort* as emblematic of the feudal system, and contends that the *120* grants a privileged position to the fortress, and therefore to the feudal system it is intended to represent, because of the unlimited powers that system conferred on the nobility, powers the libertines reappropriate behind Silling's walls. Hénaff offers no justification for choosing to ignore Sade's own historical setting of his fiction, a setting that marks off far more restricted chronological limits for the *120.* Sade situates his novel just after the apex of the French monarchy in a decidedly post-feudal atmosphere in which nobles and financiers conspire to bring down the monarchy in order to create a paradise doomed to self-destruction. The period that serves as the historical setting for the *120* also provides a model for the defensive architecture of its fortress.

Silling is actually the polar opposite of the medieval defensive enterprise. Apparently challenging its enemies to renounce their offensive position at the sight of its collective

Imaginary portrait of the Marquis de Sade, by Man Ray.

might, the medieval fortress makes an open display of its protective layers. The libertine fortress is no virile projection surmounting a pinnacle: the descriptions of its systems of protection note no towers jutting up over its walls to complete its domination of the landscape. On the contrary, Silling is camouflaged in the center of a forest, sunken first in a valley and then projecting even deeper "dans le fond des entrailles de la terre." The libertines burrow so deep into the earth for Silling's protection that Didier speaks of "le symbolisme utérin du château qui se manifeste par son caractère essentiellement souterrain de creusement infini." The Sadean fortified place erected at Silling has the hidden, devious, even discreet, nature of its defenses in common with Vaubanian fortifications. The Classical French fortress sits close to the earth, has its elaborate trenchwork dug into the ground. Its defenses are therefore so obliquely deceptive that the full panoply of its protective barriers is only visible from above. . . .

But the Sadean fortified place is more than a realization of Vauban's dream. . . .

It never occurred to Vauban to include more about the day-to-day existence of those left inside the fortress than the amounts of the various commodities they might consume. Those responsible for the defense of the fortified place are no more than statistics for him. In the *120,* Sade's demonstration of the greatness of Vauban's system, the perspective on the siege traditional in military strategy is reversed. The story is told from the point of view of the defenders of the fortress, yet the reader is never asked to look out in the direction of the attacking forces. On the contrary, our vision is directed inside the fortress, and not on account of the possibility of attack from within, but because in the *120* the scope of life inside the fortress is explored as an end in itself. When Sade fills in an area left blank in Vauban's treatises, he sheds light on the paradox shaped in the "Idée sur les romans," his positioning of literary genius at the intersection of natural inspiration and revenge for humiliation.

The opening paragraph of the *120* can be read as a confirmation of Vauban's assessment of the balance of power in France at the end of Louis XIV's reign: the "fin de ce règne" was weakened by too many wars, and these wars were characterized by too blind an indulgence in offensive strategy; the Sun King should have protected his kingdom against internal ravages, from the creeping power of "leeches." Sade situates the novel he composed on the eve of the Revolution at what he views as the limit of Classical French military strategy. The operation of Vauban's theoretically flawless system of defenses is rendered impotent because a monarch has become libertinism's puppet.

Following the model established by Lafayette in *La Princesse de Clèves,* Sade realigns history in order to make a place in it for his fiction. His rewriting betrays his dream of omnipotence. As his story begins, his characters have already brought France's Golden Age to its knees; in the *120* they will profit from the lessons to be learned from Louis le Grand's weakness in order to make their defenses airtight. The creator of the quatrumvirate implies that his literary production likewise stands at the logical conclusion of Classical aesthetics. The *120* will be *the* master-

work of the aesthetics of Classicism because it is purified of the weakness inherent in the literary products of the Age of Louis XIV—their authors' refusal to come to grips with the strategy on which they are founded. Sade's novel tells the story of a libertine war: "Comme ce tableau réglait . . . toutes les opérations de la campagne, nous avons cru nécessaire d'en donner copie au lecteur." The novel that recounts that story is itself an act of warfare, the ultimate attempt to win the battle of/with Classicism, a last skirmish fought just as the Ancien Régime was breathing its last.

The *120* is the most Classical of Sade's novels. For his libertine utopia, the marquis rejects both the picaresque dispersal he adopts in *Justine* and *Juliette* and the epistolary polyphony chosen for *Aline et Valcour* in favor of an eminently contained and single-minded vision. The product of this repression of novelistic excess is Sade's blueprint for the novel. In the *120,* Sade takes his reader inside the Classical fortress and shows him the ultimate manifestation of natural proliferation controlled by systematization. Sade's tabulating strategy is both more excessive and more rigorous than that of either Rousseau or Laclos. He uses his calculating rigor to make explicit a vision that previous literary fortifiers had only demonstrated implicitly: the Classical utopia is a fortress.

The *120* may be the ultimate work of prison literature. It was composed in a cell in the Bastille shortly before the French Revolution (1785). Moreover, it is a fiction confined by the limits of the paper on which it was written, since in order to protect it from his captors Sade wrote it on strips of paper that were rolled up and hidden between the stones of his cell wall. Under the circumstances, it seems almost inconceivable that the dream created by the prisoner is in fact a mirror image of the panopticon in which he created it: the *120* is truly the literary equivalent of the stones between which it was camouflaged. Sade is the first (literary) fortifier to portray life inside the fortress. And when he reverses the perspective on siege warfare, he reveals a *mise en abyme.* The external state of siege—which remains purely mythical in the *120,* since there is never the slightest indication of any plan to attack Silling—contains an internal state of siege, which in turn unfolds around the "heart" of the libertine enterprise, a prison cell.

In *Emile* and *Julie,* the *mise en abyme* mirrors a situation among characters: an *infans in machina* reveals the true goal of (adult) strategy. In Sade's carceral master text, the reflection in the self-conscious mirror is architectural. A place of confinement and a center of offensive/defensive strategy is built around a miniature reproduction of itself. Silling's fortification within a fortification is a *cachot,* the torture chamber hidden in the bowels of the fortified place and Silling's true inner sanctum. . . .

The fortified place within the fortified place is the only true libertine "home": "Il était chez lui." And the home the libertine creates for himself is a prison, a prison designed simultaneously to keep out and to keep in. The *cachot* in the bowels of Silling lies at the heart of the Classical drive to systematize.

The narrator of the *120* informs his readers that when they have finished taking away all the pieces of his novel "tout aura trouvé sa place." He would have the reader believe that the structure of the *120* is neither permanent nor definitive and that the place of Sade's book is elsewhere. It will be "à sa place" when it has been disassembled and its constitutive elements have been reassimilated into other systems. Yet Sade's invitation to a beheading cannot be reconciled with the insistence on strategy, system, and calculation that dominates the *120.* Sade is merely echoing the rhetoric of liberation developed by previous defensive novelists as a smokescreen for their own strategic obsessions. In fact the *120* conveys its author's conception of the proper place of fiction and demonstrates that the novel itself—and everything in it—is "à sa place," in its proper place. That place is obviously at the culminating point of the tradition of the Classical French novel, for the admiration Sade voiced for Lafayette and Rousseau in the "Idée sur les romans" was sincere. . . .

In the *120,* Sade develops computation and combination as an alternative to the developmental unfolding and temporal sequence that normally serve to structure the novel. In a parallel move, Sade subverts the traditional elements that constitute a novel's setting by limiting geographical and architectural description to a form of ordered placement. Thus, he creates what might be termed a flattened or metonymic topography for this encyclopedia. In the *120,* situation in space means quite simply a particular type of framing, the placement of an activity in a certain place in a certain room—in other words, in its proper place. It is essential to note that Sade does not ask his readers to imagine the spaces of Silling, to give them a three-dimensional status in their minds. Instead, he literalizes the notion of space in the novel. The rooms in the libertine fortress are only architectural drawings, and the only space they occupy is on a page; setting means inscription of an activity in the blank areas of a two-dimensional backdrop.

In *Sade, Fourier, Loyola,* Barthes stresses the importance of theatricality in Sade's novels. The obsession with the theatrical is of course evident in the *120,* but here Sade subjects theatricality to the same code that flattens and distributes spatialization in the novel. Silling's theater is a memory theater, to borrow the term devised in the 1530s by Guilio Camillo to characterize the enterprise that Frances Yates describes so eloquently in *The Art of Memory.* As Yates reconstructs it, Camillo's Renaissance theater had nothing to do with drama or staging. The term refers to a backdrop on which, faithful to the centuries-old tradition of memory arts, Camillo proposed to inscribe written clues that would enable the viewer (the spectator of the memory theater) to reconstruct subjects for oratory. Camillo's theater can be interpreted as a visualization or a making concrete of all the arts of memory. From the outset, practitioners of the memory arts had instructed their students in the technique of spatially situating the concepts crucial to their discourse. During their orations, they were to imagine themselves in a familiar architectural space and to *place* their key rhetorical points in the interstices (between the columns, etc.) of that space.

When Camillo actually built such a space for memory, he was attempting to realize the full potential of the art of memory. He was not trying simply to teach a method that could be applied to individual situations. He intended instead to construct a fixed space that would house a system of actual written clues or stimuli so complete that it would permit any orator who had mastered it to stand in his theater and not only make any speech he wished but make it perfectly. As Yates points out, Camillo's contemporaries considered the potentialities of his theater so awesome that they made ever greater claims for it. For example, a visitor to Padua wrote Erasmus in 1532 that the spectator admitted to the theater and its secret became instantly the equal of the greatest master of oratory, Cicero, able to discourse on any subject as fluently as he.

Other arts of memory—that of Raymond Lull for example—are more scientifically abstract, more mathematical than Camillo's theatrical theory. If I choose to compare his memory art to Sade's encyclopedic monument to libertine passion, it is because of the extraordinary reputation Camillo enjoyed in his day for allegedly having brought a system to absolute perfection, for having attained status as a systematizer comparable to that enjoyed by Vauban. Indeed, the parallels between Camillo's career and Vauban's are striking. According to Yates, Camillo's contemporaries, like Vauban's, considered him "a divine man of whom divine things are expected" (p. 132). Moreover, in both cases these expectations were sustained despite the fact that few of their contemporaries were ever able to judge their work firsthand. Camillo displayed a wooden model of his theater—roughly the equivalent of the scale models of Vauban's fortifications—to a chosen few in Venice and in Paris, but he, like Vauban, was never to write any more than fragments of the great book that his supporters believed would preserve his secret for posterity. However, Camillo, also like Vauban, never intended to share his art (and therefore his "omnipotence") with the general public. He had planned to reveal his secret to only one man, also a king of France (in his case François I). Finally, Camillo, like Vauban, attained a type of mythic status, since his fame continued to grow after his death—in Yates's analysis, "in spite of, or perhaps because of, the fragmentary nature of his achievement." This, then, is the position reserved for those who can control the union of system and secret language, who are able, in Sade's terms, to uncover the natural code of spontaneous signals. And this is the type of legendary status Sade had in mind for his own memory theater, ***Les 120 Journées de Sodome.***

The points of comparison between Camillo's theater of memory and Sade's encyclopedic monument to libertine passion are numerous. Both are totalizing systems—like the reputed supreme master of the memory art, Sade sought to create a vehicle capable of "tout dire," "tout analyser." In the *120,* Sade constructed the literary equivalent of Camillo's legendary theater: in the interspaces of Silling's two-dimensional combinatory architecture, he was able to arrange *in order* the ultimate discourse on libertine life. Sadean architecture is flattened and geometrical because its sole function is to aid computation in the creation of an all-inclusive, flawless system, a system that, once perfected, will enable its practitioner to build a theater of memory in any space (even in a prison cell in the Bastille) and in that theater to re-create the perfect libertine discourse—without recourse to the treacherous *brouillons* to which Sade so frequently alludes.

One of the spaces inside Silling's concentric circles is described in a particularly detailed manner, the "champ de bataille des combats projetés," that is, "un cabinet d'assemblée, destiné aux narrations des historiennes." This attention is fully justified. In the *120* the *story* of sexual deviations comes to dominate the enactment of these "passions," so the room in which the verbal accounts take place becomes the real theater of war. The discussion of the room's topology is prolonged by a description of the participants' disposition around the half-circle in which the encyclopedia is created: the *historienne* on call "se trouvait alors placée comme est l'acteur sur un théâtre, et les auditeurs, placés dans les niches, se trouvaient l'être comme on l'est à l'amphithéâtre."

Sade uses the storytelling situation familiar from all the collections of *nouvelles nouvelles* (revived earlier in the eighteenth century by, for example, Marivaux in *La Voiture embourbée*) to give the *120* the "Classical" narrative distance and passivity Rousseau and Laclos found in the epistolary form. We do not witness most of the action directly; instead we see it thirdhand, as the libertines themselves are already listeners, voyeuristically imagining the "horrors" of the action on the basis of the storytelling by the *conteuses*. There is no action in most of the *120*, only a twice told, doubly controlled tale of an accounting for past events. Sade's (memory) theater, like Camillo's (and like French Classical theater), is a theater of words rather than events. Combatants in the novel's battle for memory are required either to tell or to listen to a story, with the members of the quatrumvirate, the novel's heroes and the masters of Silling's defenses, choosing the passive role of listeners and spectators. The four *historiennes* are substitute figures for Sade, who is telling his story, all their stories, on a rolled-up manuscript, "cette grande bande," inside a somewhat smaller and more solitary half-circle than that dominated by his female avatars in Silling—his prison cell in the Bastille. Even the time slots they reserve for storytelling almost coincide. The *conteuses* tell their tales of passion every day from six until ten o'clock in the evening; we know from Sade's annotations that he completed the *rouleau manuscrit* by writing from seven until ten o'clock each evening (on only thirty-four consecutive days).

Just as the *120* takes us back to a primitive union between storytelling and calculation, so it reveals an original and equally fundamental complicity on memory's part, a complicity that is evident in the story of the invention of memory arts, as Yates reconstructs it from various accounts. Simonides of Ceos, credited from antiquity with the invention of a system of memory aids, is said to have come upon this system in a manner relevant to Sade's tale of a four-month-long *grande bouffe* that was always already poised on the brink of disaster. The father of the Classical art of memory was a poet. At a banquet in Thessaly, Simonides recited a lyric poem that praised both his host, a nobleman named Scopas, and the twin gods, Castor and Pollux. Afterwards, his host refused to honor the contract that was

to govern the poet's performance. He paid Simonides only half the price they had agreed upon for his poem, informing him that he could turn to the twin gods to settle the rest of their account. Shortly thereafter, a messenger informed the poet that two men wished to speak to him outside. Simonides followed the messenger from the banquet hall and during his absence the roof fell in, crushing his host and all his guests to death. Their bodies were maimed beyond recognition, and it was only because Simonides remembered exactly where each had been seated at the banquet table that the relatives were able to identify the bodies. Thus, the means chosen by Castor and Pollux to pay for their share of the panegyric gave Simonides the basis for the art of memory.

The story of the bard's mastery of the mnemonic art has much in common with the tale in the *120*. In both cases, memory (defined as the ability to list in order, to recount, to account for) is born of violence. The poet's task is to reconstruct the final banquet before the holocaust. The *120* is situated at the end of Louis XIV's reign, characterized by Sade as a period of financial and physical "exhaustion," and just before what he sees as the regent's attempt to "faire rendre gorge à cette multitude de [sangsues]," from among whom he chooses the heroes of his novel. In both cases, memory is used to give account of a scene of violence, to provide a listing of bodies in pieces. In both cases, the poet adds up the maimed and those crushed beyond recognition, those who, in a sense, have no identity other than their place on the tally sheet. As one of his concluding gestures, the narrator of the *120* offers his reader a series of "recapitulative" tables that neatly provide the calculation of those "massacrés avant le premier mars dans les premières orgies," as well as the "sujets . . . immolés . . . depuis le premier mars."

Furthermore, in both these tales of conquest by memory, the poet is a survivor, not an infrequent phenomenon in "commemorative" literature—witness the examples of the bard spared from the *Odyssey's* final massacre and of "seigneur Gilles" who survives the slaughter at Roncevaux to tell Roland's tale. What is noteworthy about the survivors of the banquet of memory is that they are not innocent of responsibility for the bloody tales they live to tell. In these cases, memory is also an accounting in the sense of a settling of a score. Although those who recount Simonides' experience, from Cicero to Martianus to Yates, fail to comment on this aspect of his activity, the story of the invention of the memory art demonstrates that the violence that provides the poet's inspiration is in fact the poet's own act of revenge. When Castor and Pollux destroy both his patron and his public, they are acting as a projection of Simonides' desires.

Sade's encyclopedic novel is also an immense pedagogical treatise, his version of a "traité d'éducation naturelle." In all Sade's extended fictions, the libertines share an interest in pedagogy and the cast of characters frequently contains an "instituteur." However, in the *120* pedagogy is far more than an interest: it is the novel's central concern. The novel's didactic passion is reflected in its pedagogical subtitle, "L'Ecole du libertinage." "Il s'agit essentiellement d'une société éducative," in Barthes's formulation, "ou plus exactement d'une société-école (et même d'une société internat)." Thus all the controls the narrator and the *historiennes* exercise over their stories are justified as essential to the advancement of pedagogical concerns.

The narrator alleges that he includes so many tables of calculation just to maintain the reader's interest. For example, he explains the purpose of the "Tableau des projects du reste du voyage": "Il nous a semblé que, sachant après l'avoir lu la destination des sujets, il prendrait plus d'intérêt aux sujets dans le reste des opérations." According to his theory, the perfectly informed reader, the reader who has all the information about the characters, their environment, and their actions clearly laid out for him, the reader who therefore feels totally in control of the story he is reading, this reader is not likely to put that story down before he has learned all there is to learn from it. To make his point perfectly clear, the narrator even includes at the end of this "tableau" a résumé of its contents, a listing of the listings in the event that the length and complexity of the original entry had created any confusion in the reader's mind.

Nor is the pedagogical combination of repetition and recapitulation limited to this occurrence. The narrator includes résumés of all his most important résumés. "[C]et arrangement, qu'il est à propos de récapituler pour la facilité du lecteur," so he describes his strategy to keep his reader with him through the complexities of the libertines' marital arrangements. Perhaps the most remarkable occurrence of this technique of doubling involves the presentation of the novel's cast of characters. Initially, the characters are described at some length and in an exceptionally detailed and systematic manner. After this first overview of the actors in the *120*'s drama, the reader finds himself at least as well-equipped to identify the principal characters as he would be after reading the first sixty pages of any other novel. He cannot but be slightly puzzled to encounter at this point a repetition in shortened form of the basic information about the cast of characters labeled "Personnages du roman de l'Ecole du libertinage." "A mesure que l'on recontrera un nom qui embarrassera dans les récits, on pourra recourir à cette table et, plus haut, aux portraits étendus, si cette légère esquisse ne suffit pas à rappeler ce qui aura été dit." Ever the pedagogue, the narrator of the *120* is careful to point out that should any reader find himself in a difficult situation and unable to remember one of the characters, he has only to turn back to the handy résumés.

Never has the task of reading been made so effortless. The narrator's technique is pedagogically sound, and through the combined effects of his tables and the system of cataloguing he employs, it is seemingly impossible for his reader to miss anything or to be even momentarily lost or confused. The dominant narrative ideology of Sadean fiction thus appears to be the antithesis of the code governing any work that could be termed modernist; the narrator of the *120* desires above all to make his tale as clear and as undemanding as possible. It is inevitable that the reader should wonder why Sade created a narrator so concerned with sharing control of his narrative with his reader and why Sade and his narrator are so interested in the question of the reader's sense of security.

Only once do the narrator's comments on the repetitions he so obviously relishes hint at an explanation for his concern. He contends that his pedagogical simplifications of his text are necessary to ensure the reader's *jouissance*. Just before he launches into the proclamation of the "code de lois" that governs life at Silling, the narrator pauses for an apostrophe to "notre lecteur," "qui, d'après l'exacte description que nous lui avons faite du tout, n'aura plus maintenant qu'à suivre légèrement et voluptueusement le récit, sans que rien trouble son intelligence ou vienne embarrasser sa mémoire." The Sadean narrator's version of the *texte de jouissance* is a narrative so well controlled that its reader will never find it necessary to make the slightest effort to recollect its details or to ponder its complexities. The narrator explains his attention to order and completeness as essential for the reader's liberation, as if the slightest movement in the direction of active participation in the "making" of the text would be fatal to the proper appreciation of it.

However, an obvious result of the form of reader passivity the narrator prescribes is a reluctance on the part of the reader to give up that passive stance in order to form an interpretation of the work. The insistence in the *120* on catalogues and computations is intended to "liberate" the reader from his usual hermeneutic concerns to the extent that he will eventually relinquish an essential part of the imaginative space generally permitted him by fiction. The *120*'s author/narrator refuses to allow the reader to forget or to become confused. In the process, he also attempts to deny him any interpretive freedom, the right to step out of the line the narrator traces for his reading. Under the guise of making life easier for his reader, the *120*'s authorial dictator moves to take over the reader's space.

"Au langage de la maîtrise, lié à celui de la propriété, de l'accaparement," Roger contends, "s'oppose directement le flot continu et dépersonnalisé du texte sadien, où la multitude des locateurs interchangeables font du langage, non le bien de quelques-uns, mais la production de tous." What Roger calls "le flot continu et dépersonnalisé du texte sadien" is one of the most striking features of the *120;* it is this "neutralization" of language that explains the reader's difficulty in remembering and the narrator's compulsion to repeat. But it is impossible to accept Roger's assessment of this language as unpoliced, communally shared, and liberated from the "commander/obéir" dialectic that stymied the progress of the tutor's student in *Emile*.

Instead of exhilaration, the depersonalized flow of Sadean language only produces a numbing effect on the reader being harangued by it. The linguistic leveling process operative in the *120* takes the novel beyond pedagogy to didacticism, and the drive to impose at any cost the ideology serviced by this neutered voice destroys such potentially deviant forces as individualized psychology. The nondifferentiated Sadean language is neither liberated nor liberating: "le flot continu et dépersonnalisé" is indicative of the uncontested reign of the master teacher's language. The Sadean discourse can in no way be considered an attempt to share the speaker's traditional power with his audience, to become truly dialogic. The fact that all those in power sound alike and speak with the same language restrains the reader's urge to identification or projection. The dominant discourse in the *120* is a monolithic force that seeks to hold Sade's reader in check, to turn him into the victim of the master who has thought of everything.

Granted, readerly freedom is an elusive affair at best. No author, not even the author of the most extreme modernist texts, creates a text supple enough to allow the reader absolute interpretive freedom and accords his reader license to make of his work what he will. Yet this is just what the Sadean narrator-authorial projection claims to do—"C'est à toi à le prendre et à laisser le reste"; "choisis et laisse le reste." On the basis of these pronouncements, the *120*'s potential reader would imagine that he was about to embark on an experience with fiction in which he would be encouraged to be as active and creative a reader as possible. The image the *120* seeks to project of itself is of a type of narrative that corresponds to Benjamin's definition of storytelling [in *Illuminations*, 1968], that is, a fiction that does not attempt to lead the reader through its narration from beginning to end. "It is half the art of story-telling to keep a story free from explanation as one reproduces it," Benjamin affirms. "It is left up to [the reader] to interpret things the way he understands them, and thus the narrative achieves an amplitude that information lacks." For Benjamin, the appeal of storytelling lies in the space it leaves the reader to flesh out the narrative with his interpretive vision. He views such fiction as analogous to the city for Baudelaire's *flâneur,* as constructs open to their observer's personal contribution.

The fiction Sade shapes in the *120* is anything but a flexible construct, a set of building blocks put out for the reader to rearrange and reshape into a personal interpretation of the *120*'s story. The narrator holds out to the reader the freedom to use any of the encyclopedic building blocks he may find useful to construct his own encyclopedia. He then makes it clear that as he has arranged them, these blocks form a complete and perfectly ordered entity. Like the master's language, the *120*'s numbered passions add up to a monolithic structure, a narrative ruled by a pedagogical order so authoritarian that only a foolhardy participant at the *120*'s banquet could imagine that its narrator/author meant his invitation to deconstruct his edifice to be take literally. The *120* is powerfully and indelibly marked by its author's struggle to bring it to structural perfection: Sade provides a fitting *mise en abyme* of his authorial activity in the image of his libertines erecting barriers around themselves so flawless that "il ne devenait même plus possible de reconnaître où avaient été les portes."

In *Les Liaisons dangereuses,* Merteuil, a self-proclaimed "new Delilah," betrays the man she typecasts as a "modern-day Samson," Valmont. She cannot fail to know the end of the Biblical story she adopts as her "emblem," that is, that Samson will take revenge for his victimization by pulling the house down, crushing himself to death along with all the observers of his humiliation (the new Delilah, like her Biblical namesake, escapes, but she is obliged to

flee the world of action—and of literature). Simonides also displaces his revenge by confiding it to the pugilistic twin gods (literally his enemy twins?). He, like Merteuil and unlike Samson, is not caught when the roof caves in, for the ultimate revenge of the poet with mnemonic gifts is to live to tell the tale of his victimization and his subsequent settling of accounts. Sade's narrator is cleverer still. His victimization has already taken place when his performance begins. He is, according to the logic of the "Idée sur les romans," in the novelist's proper place, "à la juste distance où il faut qu'il soit pour étudier les hommes." From this distance, he is able to control not only the outcome of the literary banquet, but its disposition as well. He invites the guests and shows them to their places at the table in the storytelling theater. He then proceeds to regale them with a tale of mastery that, as far as narrator and author are concerned, is actually a tale that demonstrates memory's power of control—six hundred passions (or very nearly so) all tidily put in their places, rolled up tightly, and tucked away between the stones, the stones destined to come tumbling down only a few days after the new Camillo is taken away.

Sade describes the *120* to his reader as "l'histoire d'un magnifique repas où six cents plats divers s'offrent à ton appétit." The reader may see Sade's novel as an invitation to a pleasure party; he may view its violence as aesthetically pleasing; but these ways of writing violence out of the Sadean text underestimate its goal. Memory is murderous. All those who are guests at the banquet at which the poet of memory performs have a sword of Damocles suspended over their heads, for the writer with mnemonic gifts also possesses death dealing powers.

Lawrence W. Lynch   (essay date 1984)

SOURCE: "Sade and His Critics," in *The Marquis de Sade,* Twayne Publishers, 1984, pp. 122-32.

[*Lynch has published several books and articles on eighteenth-century French literature. In this excerpt, he reviews the influence of Sade's writings and his critical reception in the nineteenth and twentieth centuries.*]

Sade in the Nineteenth Century

Sade's last three contributions to literature, the trilogy of historical novels, did not attract much attention, a fact that is quite understandable when one recalls that two of them remained unpublished until 1953-54. But Sade's reputation had already been fixed at the turbulent conclusion of the eighteenth century, and we have seen ample proof of its "infamous" nature. Furthermore, when we compare the literary trends which dominated the first part of the nineteenth century to the content of Sadian fiction, we can readily understand the relative silence on him before 1860. Although the restored Bourbon regime and the July monarchy were not as overtly stifling as their counterparts in England, they were no more receptive to Sade's intensity than revolutionary Paris had been. Claude Duchet's article, "L'Image de Sade à l'époque romantique," explains Sade's anonymity for almost fifty years. Other than the 1834 study by Jules Janin on Sade, which was condemnatory and which drew enough public attention to justify a separate reprint, the Marquis de Sade was relegated to infrequent quips and references in journals and personal diaries. Such is the case with Benjamin Constant, who observed in a note in his *Journal intime* in 1804: "The novel *Justine* is not in the least an exaggeration of human corruption." Curiously, Sade himself had foreseen the unflattering treatment which his best work would receive when, together with the name of his nemesis Villeterque, he cited those of Mme. de Genlis, Chateaubriand, and La Harpe in his **Notes littéraires.** In 1840, the young Flaubert recommended to Ernest Chevalier: "Read the Marquis de Sade and read him to the last page of the last volume; that will complete your moral education." In contrast, Stendhal limited himself to several uncomplimentary associations between Sade, Eugène Sue, and François Cenci, in 1834.

A few years later, Sainte-Beuve, one of the greatest literary critics of them all, published an item entitled "Quelques vérités sur la situation en littérature" in the *Revue des deux mondes.* After citing traces of Sade's influence on several writers of the period, Sainte-Beuve set forth this observation: "I dare ascertain, without fear of being contradicted, that Byron and Sade—and I beg forgiveness for the association—are perhaps the two greatest sources of inspiration for our moderns, the first being ostensibly visible, the second clandestine, but not too clandestine." Sainte-Beuve's judgment is astute for two reasons: its date (1 July 1843) marks the beginning of an increase in visibility for Sade, and second, his presence in the latter part of the nineteenth century and the first decades of the twentieth century was felt primarily among poets. The most frequently cited instance is that of Algernon Swinburne, who came to know Sade through the intermediary of Lord Houghton, the latter having provided the poet with pornographic works of all kinds, including some by Sade. In a letter to Houghton of July 1865, Swinburne recognized his debt to the French author: "The poet, thinker and man of the world from whom the theology of my poem ["Atalanta"] is derived was greater than Byron. . . . He indeed, fatalist or not, saw to the bottom of gods and men." Swinburne also wrote a long poem in French, "Charenton en 1810" (written in 1861, published in 1951), and an "Apologie de Sade," also in French (written in 1916, printed for private circulation).

It is among the poets of the latter nineteenth century that one would expect to find the greatest recognition of Sade's importance, and such is precisely the case with Baudelaire and Verlaine. Baudelaire, the father of modern poetry who emphasized sensations and sensitivity, the diabolic and the occult in his unprecedented and unrivaled verse, did not dwell at any length on his debt to Sade. In his "Projets et Notes diverses," however, he wrote one memorable sentence: "One must always come back to Sade, by that I mean to *Natural Man,* in order to explain evil." Verlaine was more explicit, in four lines from the poem "A Gabriel Vicaire":

> I am a sensualist, you are another.
> But you, gentle, riant, a Gaulois and a half.
> While I am the shadow of the Marquis de Sade,
>   and this I am

> Among the occasional false and naive airs of a
>   good apostle.

Verlaine's personal anxieties and sexual frustrations and eccentricities cannot be totally attributed to his reading the Marquis de Sade; the same can be said of Swinburne. We prefer to think that some of the more refined literary and philosophical aspects of his volumes were involved in the process of influencing later authors, but detailed studies of this type of influence have yet to be done.

Sade in the Twentieth Century

The poets of the first part of the twentieth century continued to stress the importance of the Marquis de Sade in the formation of their literary ideas and their manner of expression. This applies to the most unique poet of the first two decades of this century, Guillaume Apollinaire, who was directly responsible for resurrecting Sade. In 1909, Apollinaire prefaced a partial edition of Sade, *L'Oeuvre du Marquis de Sade, pages choisies,* with a fifty-seven-page essay entitled "Le Divin Marquis." In it, he wrote a biographical sketch of Sade, provided synopses of his major writings, corrected the denunciations and misconceptions of Sade which had surfaced in the preceding century, and concluded with a citation from Sade: "I address myself only to people capable of understanding me, and these people will read me without danger." Apollinaire's approach to Sade inaugurated a positive trend that has continued to the present. We have already indicated the 1904 edition of **Les 120 Journées de Sodome** by Iwan Bloch, which associated Sade with Krafft-Ebing and his *Psychopathia sexualis.* The positive trend was pursued foremost by two scholars, Gilbert Lely and Maurice Heine, whose efforts resulted in several major editions of Sade's works and included a wealth of material previously unedited. Lely was so taken with the importance of Sade and so obsessed with his efforts at restoring him to dignity that he reputedly left a place setting, albeit a vacant one, for Sade at his dining table. His encyclopedic contributions to Sade studies culminate with a poem, "Sade," and which concludes thus:

> We believe in the revolt of Rimbaud, in that of
>   Lautréamont and of Sade.
> We believe in the value of Poetry, of Love and
>   of Liberty.
> We believe in the Surrealist Revolution.

Paperback editions of Sade continue to appear regularly in France, notably in the *10/18* series. The 1957 Pauvert edition of Sade's opus, and the ensuing trial which ended in the deletion of the more controversial writings, are symptomatic of the continually troubled reception of the "Divine Marquis" by the public. Regarding that trial, one should at least mention that testimony in favor of the unexpurgated publication of Sade was given by writers such as Georges Bataille, André Breton, Jean Cocteau, and Jean Paulhan. The indebtedness of Breton and other poets to Sade antedates 1957 by many years, however. Sade was indeed the "Right Person for Surrealism." Emphasizing revolt, nihilism, and a search for new orientations in art by means of outrage and shock tactics, these writers appropriately singled out Sade as one of their apostles. In the first *Manifeste du Surréalisme* (1924), Breton included

Sade in his famous enumeration of precursors: Sade was "surrealistic in Sadism," as Swift was in mischief, Chateaubriand in exoticism, and so on. In the second *Manifeste* (1930), Breton eulogized Sade again for the perfect integrity of his thought and life. He continued to praise Sade in his *Anthologie de l'humour noir,* and later made it known that the "Exposition inteRnatiOnale du Surréalisme, 1959-1960" had been organized under the aegis of the Marquis de Sade.

Other members of the surrealist group continued the homage which Breton paid to Sade. René Char published a "Homage à D. A. F. de Sade" in 1931, and identified Sade and Lautréamont as the cornerstones of his system of thought. Similarly, Paul Eluard explained Sade's insistence on virtue punished as an effort to return man to his primitive instincts, as opposed to the respect of traditional Christian values, which only perpetuated moral enslavement (*Evidence poétique,* 1939). Sade's name and his radical literature entered not only the polemical writings of dadaism and surrealism; he also penetrated the realm of painting. René Magritte executed an interpretation of *La Philosophie dans le boudoir,* and Man Ray painted a stylized portrait of Sade in which the rugged stones of the Bastille fortress are blended into the subject's face. . . .

The specific questions of direct influence by Sade on modern writers, both French and non-French, are yet to be answered. One of the more obvious areas where such influence should be found is in the theatrical writings of Antonin Artaud; according to Ronald Hayman, Artaud's idea for a Theater of Cruelty was based on Sade's principles. But before a comprehensive account can be made of the degree of Sade's penetration into the ideas and expressions of major contemporary writers, we must content ourselves with occasional manifestations of indebtedness. Such is the case with Albert Camus who, like Baudelaire, briefly but poignantly acknowledged the importance of Sade: "With him really began the history and the tragedy of our times." Aldous Huxley's evaluation of Sade is almost identical. In his note on Sade in *Ends and Means,* he wrote: "De Sade's philosophy was the philosophy of meaninglessness carried to its logical conclusion. Life was without significance. . . . His books are of permanent interest and value because they contain a kind of *reductio ad absurdum* of revolutionary theory. . . . De Sade is the only completely consistent and thorough-going revolutionary of history." When one recalls the pessimistic social and political atmosphere of 1930-40, one can appreciate why the name of Sade was quoted in this manner by Huxley and Camus.

More recently, two leaders of the *nouveau roman* phenomenon of the 1950-60 period contributed essays on Sade: Alain Robbe-Grillet and André Pieyre de Mandiargues. Sade has even been commemorated in film. Luis Buñuel's 1930 surrealist film, *L'Age d'or,* contains a scene derived from *Les 120 Journées de Sodome.* In that scene, the Duc de Blangis appears as a Christ-like figure who offers help to a young girl. For this scene and others, the film elicited such a scandal that it was withdrawn from public circulation in 1934. Similar to the 1957 trial of the Pauvert company, the surrealists circulated a questionnaire defending the Buñuel film; it was signed by Aragon, Breton, Char, Dali, Eluard, Ernst, Man Ray, Tzara, and others. In 1975, the Italian cinema director Pasolini produced a film entitled *Salo, ou les 120 Journées de Sodome.* As one can easily imagine, the life and legend of the Marquis de Sade have also fostered the production of a series of x-rated films (*Justine, De Sade*).

One of the most penetrating accounts written on Sade by modern authors is Simone de Beauvoir's *Faut-it brûler Sade?* Together with the insights mentioned previously in the course of this study, Beauvoir compares Sade's biographic and literary situation to that of Oscar Wilde, another author whose personal behavior and writings were viewed as being so outrageous that public humiliation and ruin were the results. The case of Wilde shows that even one hundred years after Sade, unconventional private behavior, when made public (what is labeled *outrage aux moeurs* in France), can entail the most dire of consequences for an author.

Since 1945, the number of books and articles written on Sade has multiplied rapidly, each year witnessing dozens of essays, commemorative issues in serials, and books. It is no mere coincidence that some of the most perceptive and most highly regarded analyses of him have been from the structuralist point of view. The cyclical nature of Sade's fiction, his verbal aggression, and the need to say all about the previously ineffable, make Sade a likely candidate for such an approach. As indicated in the discussion of Sade's philosophical treatises, the structuralist psychologist Jacques Lacan was the first to point out the kinship between Kant's *Critique of Practical Reason* and Sade's thought, and the relationship between crime and pleasure derived therefrom. Roland Barthes, in his essay "L'Arbre du crime" (in the winter 1967 edition of *Tel Quel* devoted to Sade), and in his *Sade, Fourier, Loyola,* used a topical approach to identify the significance of *things* in Sade's linguistic system: food, clothing, mirrors, among others. Pierre Klossowski has been cited twice in the course of this study. If we had to reduce his abundant criticism on Sade to several cardinal points, they would be the following: (1) the relationships between the Sadian conscience, God, and fellowman are negative, but to the extent that these negations are real, they introduce the very notions which they suppress; without the notions of God and fellowman as points of attack, there can be no Sadian conscience; (2) Sade's use of the word *vertu,* as is amply done in *Justine, La Nouvelle Justine,* and *Juliette,* does not automatically translate as its closest equivalent "virtue," but rather as a primordial virginity which is the focus of Sadian oppression; (3) the idea of *delectatio morosa,* that is, the desire for death by those who are incapable of finding it, is frequently manifested in Sadian characters, and again, a seemingly negative exponent becomes a positive, creative one.

Two other critics of structuralist affiliation have contributed significantly to our understanding of Sade today. Georges Bataille, who testified at the Pauvert trial in 1957, prefaced *La Nouvelle Justine* with an essay, "Sade et l'homme normal" (6:45-65). Like Barthes and Klossowski, Betaille concentrates on Sade's *langage;* using *La*

Philosophie dans le boudoir as his point of reference, Bataille arrives at a different conclusion. Since the language of normal men opposes the expression of violence, violence itself must be suspended when the discursive element of Sade assumes priority, and the resultant situation is, as illustrated in *La Philosophie dans le boudoir* (and in all of Sade's other extreme works), the dual structure of action (sex) interrupted by lengthy philosophical discourse. According to Bataille, Sade's language is more than that of a man revolting against confinement or against a few particulars; it is an assault against all of humanity.

The only major nineteenth-century writer not examined previously and who felt the influence of Sade is Lautréamont (Isadore Ducasse). In another monumental work of Sadian criticism, *Lautréamont et Sade* (1963), Maurice Blanchot is less preoccupied with the question of direct influence than with affinities between the two, although he does list obvious areas of influence. Like Philippe Sollers, in his 1967 *Tel Quel* article "Sade dans le texte," Blanchot concentrates on a passage of vital importance in *Juliette,* where Clairwil offers her definition of the perfect crime:

> I would like, said Clairwil, to find a crime whose everlasting effect would continue to act, even when I would no longer be acting, so that there would not be one single moment in my life, even when asleep, during which I would not be the cause of some disturbance, and this disturbance could extend to the point of causing general corruption or so formal a disruption that its effect would be prolonged beyond the limit of my life.

To this desire of the utopian, self-perpetuating crime, Juliette responds: "In order to complete this project, my angel, I responded, I see few alternatives other than what can be called moral assassination, which is realized through counsel, through writing, or through action." From this and other *élans* of verbal rebellion, we can see why Sade has had a captive audience among recent critics and why, as early as 1909, writers like Apollinaire spoke of Juliette as a new woman with "wings" who breaks loose from the rest of humanity . . . Sade's depictions of human sexuality, femininity, and masculinity are at times as credible as Lautréamont's hero Maldoror, who copulates with a female shark. We have already seen that to the extent that Sade was fascinated with feminine beauty, his numerous portraits of women pose many problems of credibility. Sade's violence is indeed that of language. If he were interpreted literally, there would be no survivors left to read him.

Sade's violence is indeed that of language. If he were interpreted literally, there would be no survivors left to read him.

—Lawrence W. Lynch

For these and other reasons, it is not surprising that the majority of studies on Sade which have appeared in the last few years have been authored primarily by women. The problem of cruelty to women in his fiction is bound to provoke reactions of one form or another. . . . [These recent studies] are not necessarily feminist criticisms; nor are they merely "corrected" views of Sade's treatment of women. Alice Laborde has traced the evolution of Sade's most famous work from the draft of *Les Infortunes de la vertu* through the definitive *Justine* and *La Nouvelle Justine,* and has also shown that to the degree that the text is amplified, its plausibility decreases. Béatrice Didier has explained the nature and function of the *château intérieur* motif in Sade's principal works. . . .

Dictionaries and biographies have a rather significant role in determining the manner in which an author becomes known to the general public. In the third chapter of this study, the hostility against Sade of Michaud's *Biographie universelle* was noted, and even against the relatively innocuous texts *Aline et Valcour* and *Isabelle de Bavière.* The publication date of Michaud's biography (1854) shows that its negativity corresponds to the generally hostile reception of Sade at that time. The *Petit Larousse* dictionary is probably the most popular of all French dictionaries. Its encyclopedic section contained no entry on Sade until 1935. That particular edition tersely introduced Sade with: "Sade (Marquis de), famous for his morbidly obscene novels, born in Paris (1740-1814)." The *Petit Larousse* entries on Sade improved commensurately with his restoration to dignity through the efforts of writers cited in the preceding paragraphs. The 1969 version of the same dictionary was remarkably more favorable to Sade; its entry, which remained virtually unchanged until 1980, read: "Sade (D. A. F., Marquis de) French writer, born in Paris (1740-1814). His novels depict characters obsessed with the demonic pleasure of making innocent victims suffer, but the importance of his works derives from his presentation therein of the revolt of free men against God and society." Even the reservations concerning demonic cruelty and the persecution of the innocent have disappeared in the revised 1981 edition of the same popular dictionary: "Sade (Marquis de). French writer born in Paris (1740-1814). His work, which is both the theory and illustration of sadism, constitutes the pathological double of naturalist and liberal philosophies of the Age of Enlightenment." This newest entry goes so far as to cite two of Sade's creations, *Justine* and *La Philosophie dans le boudoir.* The gradual evolution in the entries from a mass-distributed dictionary may seem to be a trivial detail, but it also demonstrates the general ideological progress made in Sade commentaries. . . .

Obviously, Sade's letters do not have the historical or literary significance of the correspondence of Voltaire or that of Rousseau, for example. But the almost three hundred of his letters which have survived deal with a vast range of subjects and temperaments, and include satire, parody, and scatology. They are an accurate source of reflections of the real man. His correspondence was submitted to a fate which recalls that of many of his other writings; it was published for the first time in 1929 by Paul Bourdin, who disdainfully qualified the letters with the remark: "I never succeed in taking him [Sade] seriously." Gilbert Lely eventually produced a more complete and more reliable edition of these letters. Those of the beginning of Sade's first long period of incarceration (1777-90) witness the agony of imprisonment: "Never . . . has my blood or my mind been able to bear total confinement." His protests against isolation recall the grim despair of the victims of Ste.-Marie des-bois: "I am alone here, I am at the limit of the world, removed from all eyes, without any creature ever being able to reach me." . . .

Perhaps writing was the "perfect crime" for the Marquis de Sade, as he had Juliette observe so bluntly. Since he already faced indefinite isolation for debaucheries which were left unpunished when others of his stature committed them, and since the ire and disgrace felt by his mother-in-law was continued by his own family, he could not be punished any further, and spent the two decades following 1781 writing books which provoke the most vociferous reactions today. His personal letters of the 1790-1800 period show only that he was obsessed with survival and monetary solvency—a trait which may explain the scope and intensity of *La Nouvelle Justine* and *Juliette.* In the final stage of his imprisonment (1802-14), he was still denying the authorship of *Justine,* the point of departure for the pornographic expansions mentioned and concentrated mainly on obtaining official pardon. But the image of Sade as the author of the "infamous" *Justine* was so firmly established even then that the remark which he flippantly made to his lawyer Gaufridy in 1775, that "not one cat will be beaten in the province without people saying: *it was the Marquis de Sade,"* remains fairly valid for his reception by posterity.

Robert F. O'Reilly   (essay date 1987)

SOURCE: "Language and the Transcendent Subject in Three Works of the Marquis de Sade: *Les 120 journées de Sodome, La Philosophie dans le boudoir,* and *Justine,"* in *Studies on Voltaire and the Eighteenth Century,* Vol. 249, 1987, pp. 399-406.

[*In the following excerpt, O'Reilly examines contradictions in Sade's concept of the self as reflected in his rhetorical practices.*]

In his pioneering work on Sade [*Sade, Fourier, Loyola,* 1971], Roland Barthes focused attention on Sade's use of language, a context within which such problems as the readability and paradoxes of Sade's texts were resolved into a code that Barthes offered as appropriate to a reading of Sade. However, the shift away from structuralism in recent years has entailed a move away from the study of language as a closed and self-referential system to the study of discourse or language seized as utterance involving speaking and writing subjects as well as readers and listeners [according to Terry Eagleton, *Literary Theory,* 1983]. While Barthes's discussion of Sade was revelatory at the time, the post-structural period invites new readings of Sade's works with a view to their textuality or dialogic nature. Post-structural criticism takes into account the various social, philosophical, and linguistic factors that inform discourse, and therefore offers a critical strategy that is particularly appropriate to the study of Sade as well as

other eighteenth-century French writers whose works often tended to blur the borders between literature and philosophy. While Barthes's discussion demonstrated that the Sadean discourse reveals a system of relays between the libertine's rhetoric and the erotic scene or between logos and eros, the present study will concentrate on certain rhetorical practices in Sade's books that place in question Barthes's conclusions regarding the self-referential nature of Sade's texts.

Rhetorical practices in Sade's works contain inherent contradictions that mirror the libertine's dualistic conception of the self. They address the reader and at the same time reject the effort at communication by interrupting and violating traditional modes of communication. The libertine's use of language reflects the circular and static condition of Sade's books and his thought. Since the libertine's desire for transcendence is constantly at odds with his efforts and need to communicate, each utterance exposes an unworkable and paradoxical conception of man.

The libertine's rhetorical practices define an unstable and uneasy relationship in Sade's works where the libertine's dream of transcendence struggles for a coexistence with the empirical reality of communicative practices. Just as the libertine always professes an emotional indifference with regard to his victims in order to maintain his position of dominance, so too each utterance in Sade's books attempts to preserve the libertine's freedom from the reader from within the 'always already' nature of language. Each time that the libertine speaks he is confronted by the impossible situation of being hopelessly enmeshed in deterministic philosophical and linguistic systems that his rhetoric nevertheless attempts to control. Therefore, Sade's rhetoric is always vigilant in order to resist absorption in the expected and the ordinary, and by interrogating the readers' implicit social, philosophical, and literary assumptions, Sade's rhetoric seeks a problematic accommodation between the libertine's exalted concept of the self and the human need to speak in the first place.

Sade's heroes go through the motions of mouthing many of the respected and popular concerns of the *philosophe* movement in eighteenth-century France. Yet they are always acutely aware that such notions are opposed to the very concept that they have of their freedom. The materialist ideas of Sade's characters echo the philosophical tradition of the atomists beginning with Lucretius and as developed by the materialists of the day. The libertine espouses the determinist's claim that man is a machine that nature 'meut à son gré'. Philosophically speaking, the libertine's efforts to ground a concept of 'libertinage' or freedom in a deterministic system is contradictory, since the philosophical system threatens the very notion of freedom that it claims to support. Sade's heroes recognise that they are caught up in a deterministic philosophy that threatens their dream of transcendence. They realise that their freedom always risks being absorbed by social, philosophical, and linguistic systems that are already in place. Therefore, the libertine uses certain rhetorical strategies that oppose commonplace communicative practices in order to preserve his concept of the self.

In *Les 120 journées de Sodome* Curval's expression of the

libertine's frustrated desire for the absolute from within a deterministic context points to the failure of eighteenth-century thought to resolve successfully this dualistic conception of man's nature. Curval's solution involves a crime against nature of such a magnitude that it would obliterate nature and thus free the libertine from his enslavement. . . .

Curval's desire to destroy nature and to impose a general silence restates the broader philosophical question. How can the Sadean subject reconcile his aspirations for the absolute with the reality of a natural law that limits his freedom? For Curval, as well as for Sade's other heroes, nature is a constant reminder of man's finite status. Language discloses the same weakness in the libertine's need to communicate or speak in the first place. The conflict or tension between the libertine's realisation of his finite nature and his desire to rise above that finitude is especially reproduced in his rhetorical practices which repeatedly resist being absorbed in predetermined linguistic categories. The contradictions between man's desires and the reality of the human condition articulated by Curval in this passage are constantly reflected in the libertine's language. Curval's desire to destroy nature and to free himself from her dominion is recreated throughout Sade's texts in the confrontation between Sade's heroes and the reader. The libertine employs a linguistic system that successfully communicates with the reader but that also strives to free itself from the always already nature of language by breaking down traditional communicative practices.

For example, it is not surprising when the libertine's victims use the vocative, particularly since they are often appealing to their captors for justice and mercy. However, when incorporated into the libertine's discourse, apostrophe seems at first glance to be an inappropriate transgression of the libertine's principles. After all, to apostrophise is no longer to command from a position of strength but to implore someone to yield to one's wishes. Since there is very little question in Sade's books of treating victims as anything other than as submissive and mute objects, the libertine's sincerity must always be placed in brackets especially when an emotional tone of voice is employed. The libertine's use of the vocative cannot be an indication of concern for the victim or an invitation to engage the victim in discussion, since the libertine has always done his utmost to reduce his victims to the most abject states of dependency. Victims in Sade's texts are always completely deprived of their rights to choose and often even of their rights to respond even when the libertine seems to be inviting them to do so. The libertine's repetitive pleas to his victims are also something more than just a mocking and cynical imitation of the supplicant victims' cries of distress. Instead, the libertine's use of the vocative suggests that the libertine does not have the victim in mind at all when he apostrophises but views the reader as the intended receiver of his emotional message. The use of apostrophe particularly during philosophical arguments confirms the suspicion that logical and dispassionate philosophical discussions never have a very high priority in Sade's books. As a rhetorical device apostrophe always masquerades as something which it is not. The vocative poses as a plea or a prayer aimed at capturing the reader's attention at one level of communication, but it is always a carefully calculated linguistic strategy which intends to reimpose the libertine's dominance over the reader through a subversion of the usual operations of the figure. 'O Thérèse,' expostulates Cœur-de-Fer in the midst of an attack on religion, 'de quel poids doivent être ces raisons sur un esprit examinateur et philosophe? Eh! non, Thérèse, non, toutes ces atrocités-là ne sont pas faites pour nous guider. Détestons ces horreurs, Thérèse; que les outrages les mieux constatés cimentent le mépris qui leur est si bien dû' (*Justine*, iii. 115-16). The emotional appeal to Thérèse is especially ironic coming from a man named Cœur-de-Fer whose harshness and brutality are already firmly inscribed in his name. In the mouth of Cœur-de-Fer, the vocative cannot be taken at face value as a sincere effort to establish some emotional rapport with the victim. However, if apostrophe is viewed as a cynical and calculated inversion of the roles of master and slave, of subject and object, it becomes another means of tormenting the victim, this time linguistically. While such linguistic forms of torture cohere with the libertine's aim of total domination over his victims, they also possess a surplus of meaning in a world where the libertine already commands his domains totally. Thus the libertine must also have the reader in mind as the receiver of his message, and apostrophe becomes a linguistic means of entrapping the reader in the libertine's critical gaze.

Traditionally apostrophe operates through an emotional appeal to collapse the distance separating the subject from the object, so that some rapprochement of subject and object can be effected. The libertine seems to acknowledge deliberately and consciously the presence of his reader by appealing to him as another subject or as an equal. It is precisely at those moments when the libertine appears to be voicing some dependency on the reader, by creating a bond between himself and his listener through an impassioned speech, that he is also using language in a critical mode.

When apostrophe is juxtaposed to the figure of interrogation, it becomes a duplicitous and cynical prelude to a reenactment or repetition of the libertine's exercise of power over the reader, in this instance through the use of rhetorical questions. The libertine's use of apostrophe is always ironic because it announces a false collusion and bonding between the speaking subject and the intended receiver of the message. Apostrophe remains seductive because of traditional assumptions that the reader brings to the figure. And even though the reader may never believe in or accept at face value the libertine's radical social message, the reader is compelled through the libertine's use of language to read in a particular mode and to conceive of the libertine's character and designs in a certain way.

The interrogative part of the sentence underscores the libertine's parodic and ironic use of the vocative. Interrogation in the same sentence as apostrophe abolishes any sympathetic collusion between the libertine and his reader, since it immediately reconstitutes the distance separating the libertine from his victim by insisting on the reader's status as object and the libertine's as subject. Interrogation points to the libertine's intention to reimpose himself upon his victim and reader by (dis)closing his argument in a manner that ultimately imposes a silence because it does not invite any response or discussion. Indeed, the flattery of being included among those so-called 'enquiring and philosophical minds' is mocking if addressed to Justine since she has no choice at all in the matter of her enslavement. And when that flattery is addressed to the reader, it is equally contemptuous, since it is a critical indictment of all those readers who fail to recognise that a cherished ideal of enlightenment philosophy is under attack. Any appeal to philosophical discussion or debate is rendered meaningless especially when framed in the context of such rhetorical tactics as apostrophe and interrogation. Instead of positing conventional philosophical discourse as a method of investigation and persuasion, the libertine's particularly cynical use of the notion of 'esprit examinateur et philosophe' underscores his contempt for and ridicule of traditional philosophical systems. Instead, the libertine seeks to reconcile the tension between his ideal of freedom and the use of a traditional figure by ridiculing the reader's dependency on certain conventions of language.

The use of the imperative mood in the last two sentences of the passage completes the picture of the unrelenting and calculating libertine who literally bullies his readers into submission through his language. The imperious tone is progressively developed in direct relationship to the subversiveness of the libertine's social project which is a vigorous attack on religion. In this particular rhetorical context, the libertine's social message has the effect of asserting its independence from the approval or disapproval of the reader because language has already been used to impose a silence and to transform the role of the reader into that of a mute and perhaps stunned observer.

The logic of this passage describes a linguistic strategy that is often employed in Sade's works. The passage uses a conventional rhetorical device in order to undermine and finally to displace traditional notions regarding the operation of certain linguistic practices. Thus the libertine's use of apostrophe turns against a traditional use of apostrophe by parodying its own rhetorical operations especially when it collides with the figure of interrogation. Finally the language of the passage is organised to compel the reader towards the radical social conclusion that emerges when interrogation and the imperative are used as weapons in an attack on religion. Ultimately, the libertine's rhetoric is always directed towards his project of reproducing an image of the self as a free creature who is nevertheless speaking from within the confines of a linguistic system. The success of this linguistic project depends on a parodic use of the conventions of language that allows the libertine to communicate with the reader and at the same time to criticise those very modes of communication.

The conclusion of the Duc de Blangis's harangue to the so-called 'êtres faibles et enchaînés', who have been imprisoned in the château of Silling, presents a still clearer illustration that the intended receiver of the libertine's message is the reader and not a character in a novel. . . .

After having done his best for several pages to convince

the 'êtres faibles et enchaînés' that any form of escape or freedom from the château is futile, the Duke's monologue takes an unexpected turn in tone as he suddenly concludes his diatribe with an invitation to his victims to consider freely and openly the truth of the ideas that he has just done his best to force upon them. Clearly the Duke's invitation is quite meaningless if viewed as a serious effort to open a dialogue with his victims. After all he has already spoken for several pages without inviting commentary and has made it clear that his victims have no choice at all in the matter of their imprisonment. Instead the Duke's invitation is directed at the reader. When the Sadean hero appears to be engaging in a meaningless and superfluous discussion with his victims, he is in fact engaged in a power struggle with the reader.

The Duke's suggestion to the reader to reason with him, contained in the phrase 'décidez vous-mêmes', subtly undermines a seemingly generous and open offer to reason by framing the invitation in the imperious tone of the imperative mood. A similarly ironic rhetorical pattern can be discerned operating throughout this passage in the libertine's apparent willingness to entertain a discussion of the possibility of the existence of God while at the same time excluding and subverting that possibility by means of certain linguistic practices.

A sequence of conditional clauses in the passage functions simultaneously to include and to exclude the participation of the reader in the debate over the (non)existence of God. By placing the question of God's existence in the 'si' clause of the conditional sentence, the libertine has already exposed the hypothetical nature of that existence by putting its reality in doubt. The conditional proposition proposes a hypothesis that the libertine presents as already contrary to fact. The principal clauses are phrased as questions that seem to invite a response from the reader, a participation in the philosophical debate over the (non) existence of God. However, the series of questions represents an ongoing rhetorical strategy to encourage the reader's attention in the debate even though the reality of God's existence has already been posited as imaginary by its expression in the conditional proposition. Repetition of the rhetorical question 'permettrait-il' in the principal clause of the conditional sentences already imposes the libertine's conclusion on the reader by answering its own query regarding the reality of God's existence. The sequence of rhetorical questions diminishes all the more forcefully the already hypothetical nature of that possibility. Also, instead of framing the principal clause negatively to state those activities that could not transpire in the presence of God's existence, the libertine's rhetorical questions have the effect of drawing the reader's attention to the hypothetical or unreal aspects of the conditional proposition, by answering the very question that it poses so disingenuously.

The Duke's invitation to the reader to decide for himself the question of God's existence or to participate in open debate was never intended as a serious consideration of the reader's point of view. It has become instead a carefully orchestrated linguistic assault on the readers' social, philosophical, and linguistic values. What seems to begin as a hypothetical discussion of the existence of God is transformed into a reassertion of the libertine's certainty regarding the nonexistence of God and becomes a further illustration of his skill in imposing his domination over the reader through a manipulation of language.

Ellipses of the conditional proposition throughout the remainder of the passage are an additional rhetorical manœuvre that suppresses quite literally the existence of God by an absolute exclusion of subsequent mention of the word God in the conditional proposition. Thus the libertine's extraordinary mastery of the subtleties of language has created a linguistic situation that reflects and responds to Curval's concerns regarding the libertine's finite powers when confronted by the example of nature's powers. By suppressing linguistically the existence of God in his harangue to the reader, the libertine's rhetoric has become a disguised technique for challenging the reader's moral and linguistic assumptions and at the same time of projecting an image of the libertine as an autonomous and independent creature.

In *La Philosophie dans le boudoir,* even more obviously than in the other two works we have examined, Sade's language contests Barthes's conclusions regarding the reciprocity of the libertine's rhetoric and the erotic scene. Since there is no one in need of instruction in *La Philosophie dans le boudoir* language is always directed outwardly towards the libertine's battle with the reader. *La Philosophie dans le boudoir* has only willing accomplices. Even Eugénie, whose education is at least in theory the object of Dolmancé's instructions, is quickly converted to a liking for libertinism. . . . Thus we need to look elsewhere in order to discover the intended receiver of the libertine's message. . . .

Rhetorical practices in Sade's books are informed by an underlying paradoxical conception of man. Sade's language reveals an impossible dilemma for those individuals who try to support an ideal of freedom, authority, and scientific objectivity within the context of a deterministic conception of man's place in his world. The libertine's rhetoric points to a conception of man as an enslaved sovereign whose language is a tortuous exercise in attempting to reconcile the irreconcilable. When the Sadean hero uses such powerful rhetorical devices as apostrophe, interrogation, and the imperative he does so self-consciously in order to impose a silence that coheres with his dream of the self as an autonomous creation. Repetition of similar rhetorical strategies in Sade's works is the clearest sign of the impasse or aporia that results as each utterance restates a paradoxical and unworkable conception of man. Since each new effort by the libertine to communicate confirms his finite nature, each new attempt must also strive to deny that finitude. While the libertine's rhetorical practices undertake to subvert the very operations of language that make it intelligible to the reader, they reveal simultaneously an unresolvable dualistic conception of man as a creature who aspires to absolute mastery and control of his environment but who is repeatedly threatened by absorption in the world he seeks to master.

The only imaginable language that might possibly suit Curval's desire to outrage nature and free the libertine from its dominion would be a non-communicative one that is made up of meaningless utterances. Such a language would be free from the linguistic and social traditions that inform all forms of discourse. This would, of course, be an impossible language to conceive, since it would imply the destruction of language in its refusal to communicate. Ironically, at those moments when the libertine's passion reduces his words to unintelligible mutterings, he emerges as a more individuated representation of an autonomous force within a deterministic conception of nature than he does when he employs his rhetoric to mask but never resolve the inherent duality of his situation.

Colette V. Michael   (essay date 1989)

SOURCE: "The Rhetoric of Excess and the Excesses of Sadian Rhetoric: From the Cosmic to the Comic," in *Studies on Voltaire and the Eighteenth Century,* Vol. 265, 1989, pp. 1277-82.

[*The author of numerous books on French literature, ethics, philosophy, and women's rights, Michael has published several books and articles on the Marquis de Sade. In this excerpt, she suggests that Sade uses irony and comic effects to distance the reader from his text.*]

Sade never killed anyone, nor was he ever convicted of murder, but it is said that he committed, after his death, the perfect crime, one that perpetuates itself each time one of his readers is shocked or outraged by his writings. Sade published his first book at the age of 51; it is unlikely that he would have become a writer had he not been imprisoned for some thirty years of his life. But in his own way, Sade freed himself through his writings and vicariously lived the free lives of his heroes. That type of freedom knew no boundaries and led him to say more than had ever been said before, to excess.

These excesses have meanings especially as a description of a complete structure relating to sexology. In a first-rate article published in 1977 in *Obliques,* Marcel Henaff suggested that Sade tried to say it all in the *120 Days of Sodom,* but that this simple formula is paradoxical; on the one hand, states Henaff, to say it all means to englobe the totality of the signified; and on the other, to say it all might mean not hide anything, thus go beyond any limits, therefore to excess. Marcel Henaff also contends, and quite rightly so, that telling of an occurrence of sexual perversion as a fictional event removes it from the realm of the scientific; yet adding to the recitative all possible aspects of sexual perversions turns the entire enterprise into an encyclopedia. We all know that the eighteenth century had a mania, a thirst for encyclopedias. Sade then, according to Henaff, simply added one more type: an encyclopedia of perversions. What is most interesting in that repertory of passions and perversion is that the degree of suffering created in us by reading them is inversely proportional to the number read. The greater number, the smaller the pain, if any, it creates in humans. A corollary which is less obvious is a demonstration of man's incapacity for suffering.

Again and again Sade sets his libertines, intent on sensual and sexual pleasure, in very restricted surroundings, in a utopia of unrestricted evil. Yet, out of this hidden, forsaken, foreboding place emerges an unwelcome truth. The sufferings that a person really can feel or even understand are his own. Humans can react-perhaps even suffer-upon hearing the news that the girl next door has been raped. Just as a human reacts-and suffers-when watching the dramatisation of a family's tragedy in the 'Holocaust'. To say that one million families suffered the same fate does not relatively have as strong an impact, because statistics convey essentially very little. The tragedy takes on a cosmic dimension. A scholar, Jean Hallier, suggested in an article published in *La Table ronde* in 1954 that the sadian heroes are basically impotent because they fail to be gratified by sensual pleasures but that their greatest failure is their inability to suffer. There is no other suffering in sadism than not to be able to suffer. To a great extent, this is also true of Sade's readers for whom the situation must be dramatised, must be particularised. Yet, Sade plays a subtle trick on his reader, so conditioned by pre-set values. Taking one single example from *Justine* (1791), a very brief semiotic analysis of one passage will be made to look at Sade's treatment of a particular case.

Justine or the misfortunes of virtue, is the first work published during Sade's lifetime and the second version of the work. It was well-received and during the ten years that followed, it was re-edited six times. Justine and her sister Juliette were orphaned at 12 and 15 respectively and each ventured into the world with opposite principles, Justine as a proponent of virtue while Juliette plunged heartily into vice. Everything succeeds for Juliette, while Justine is submitted to every kind of ignominy and indignity. Through it all she keeps her faith and she is rewarded for that faith, not by eternal paradise, but by being struck by lightning, as if, suggests Anne Lacombe, her virtue were an offence to nature which handed her a cosmic punishment. Now, mind you, Justine has been held prisoner, beaten, been witness and involuntary party to murder and has barely escaped being experimented upon by a surgeon; she gets lost in a threatening forest, when lo and behold, there looms in the distance a monastery, Saint-Mary-in-the-Woods. She presents herself at God's door, she reports, and with some reluctance and kind words a monk lets her into the church. When she has answered his questions, he leads her towards the depth of the church, which turns out to be a den of iniquities. She later reports what happened to a friend thus:

> 'On your knees', the monk said to me, 'I am
>   going to whip your titties.'
> 'My titties, oh! my Father!'
> 'Yes, those two lubricious masses, which never
>   excite me but I wish to use them thus', and
>   upon saying this, he squeezed them, he com-
>   pressed them violently.
> 'Oh Father! They are so delicate! You will kill
>   me!'

An entire article, it seems, could be written on just that passage. First one can see several semantic extensions. The word 'Father' is the second word of the Lord's prayer; as such it could considered an invocation, maybe even the act of conjuring evil if it were not juxtaposed to 'oh!' but to something like 'help me'. Father is also an appellation for both a man of the church and a parent. Considering the second meaning opens all kind of interpretations leading to incest, a subject which Sade wrote much about.

'On your knees': an amplification of the meaning of this expression could also suggest several denotations. First, it is the position of one who prays, and secondly, the position of one who begs: Justine is on her knees not in order to pray or to beg. But as she is in church, by order of the priest, 'on her knees' is a very satirical commentary on religious ritual. Although the usual behaviour associated with church attendance remains, the cause here is totally irrelevent and irreverent. Constructed is an absurd relationship between cause and effect. It is incongruous, black humour at its best. There is, by the way, a very short review entitled 'Le fou rire du marquis de Sade', but essays on the comic of Sade are virtually non-existent.

Now, if one looks at that dialogue from the syntactic point of view, simply with regard to the relations between the signs, and without reference to their meanings, 'Oh! my Father' or 'Oh Father' takes on several values which could even be 'Oh my love!' Does that not suggest an analysis of the unconscious as advocated by Lacan? Perhaps this would show that Sade identified himself with Justine and that he was, not a sadist, but a masochist.

Yet another way of looking at this passage is simply from the pragmatic point of view, with regard to the use of the language. This leads back to excesses. 'My Father!' is a sign of respect toward a holy man. Such a naïve acceptance of brutality, of undue torture, renders the whole episode comical. It is comical through excess of respect. We cannot sympathise. We cannot suffer for her. No in-depth study of the comical in Sade exists to date, but it is not possible to take such utterances seriously. How could a woman being raped by a priest exclaim: 'Oh my Father'? This shows how pernicious Sade can be. A reader might be so busy screaming 'pornography!' that he might not see that we are being taken in by Sade who is playing a joke on us, and a monumental irreverent one.

A sadian utopia is a realm where evil and vice have a totally free reign. The sadian libertine operates within the limits he himself sets, in this case an out-of-the-way monastery. Fulfilling a double purpose, this is both a refuge from pursuers and a prison for those inside. In a brilliant study [*Le Marquis de Sade,* 1968] Jean-Jacques Brochier has suggested that this closed space sets up a new order, that of the language. The paradox is that Sade manages to show by an investigation set within these confines that certain behavioural traits generally attributed to man in society are not only erroneous but completely arbitrary. In this I share the views of Yvon Belaval who, in an article published in *Cahiers du Sud* in 1947, stated that the works of Sade are a questioning of man's destiny: first, a demystification, a de-mythology—this was also suggested by Alice Laborde [in *L'Esprit créateur,* 1975]—then the construction of a new different view of man and his function-or place-in the universe.

In Sade's work man's inhumanity to man becomes a metaphysical question; how could such evil be possible? Incestuous orgies, meaningless torture, and wanton cruelty fill some of his books—not all of them—but with an ironic overstatement, Sade puts a distance between us and his prose so that in a way his contentions are not painful. These horrendous descriptions, quite foreign to us, are so clinically atrocious that they take on a cosmic dimension. By the same token, Sade saw the potentiality for creating suffering with a particular, specific case of a good person repeatedly in trouble. Justine is a virtuous girl whose faith never abandons her. But she talks when she should scream and is constantly at the wrong place at just the right time. Again with an ironic overstatement and an incongruous sense of humour, Sade destroys this capacity for suffering in us. The comic, from Sade's expert pen, becomes a new type of lethal weapon, as yet virtually ignored in most of his work, as pernicious as it is timeless.

David B. Morris   (essay date 1990)

SOURCE: "The Marquis de Sade and the Discourses of Pain: Literature and Medicine at the Revolution," in *The Languages of Psyche: Mind and Body in Enlightenment Thought, Clark Library Lectures 1985-1986,* edited by G. S. Rousseau, University of California Press, 1990, pp. 291-330.

[*Morris is an American literary critic who has also published studies on eighteenth-century English poetry. In the following excerpt, he explores Sade's use and transformation of contemporary ideas about pain and the social and political implications of this aspect of Sade's work.*]

My purpose in this essay is to explore Sade's literary treatment of pain, especially as his works consume and transform the conventional vocabularies in which pain was discussed. Foremost among these vocabularies—which included theology and libertinism as well as law—was medicine. Thus my specific focus will concern Sade's transvaluations of medical knowledge. Sade did not simply appropriate a scientific vocabulary borrowed from eighteenth-century medicine and (to varying degrees) evident in the work of contemporary British and Continental writers, for whom the "life" or "nature" imitated in the novel now proved inextricable from the language of Enlightenment science. Sade's transvaluations alter what they appropriate. His borrowings from scientific sources are not the most characteristic feature of his style, but they have not passed unnoticed. (In 1968 Jean Deprun published an important essay entitled "Sade et la philosophie biologique de son temps.") It nevertheless needs to be emphasized that Sadean transvaluations employ biomedical language and concepts in ways that ultimately estrange them from the scientific and humanitarian labor of eighteenth-century medicine. Medicine in Sade is so thoroughly transvalued that it comes to constitute the appropriately unstable foundation for an otherwise foundationless libertine world, where reason always leads back toward the irrational, where clear and graspable truths grow indistinct and unsteady as they encounter the dark, corrosive, liberating power of desire. Pain for Sade is far more than (as we tend to consider it) a medical subject, and after Sade pain would never be quite the same. . . .

Pain in Sade's writing is notoriously associated with its traditional opposite, pleasure. As important and far less obvious, however, is the Sadean bond that unites pain with truth. Sade is never more at home in the Enlightenment than when he joins the unmasking philosophers who sought to demystify every form of intellectual humbug, but he immediately resumes his isolated stance in equating truth (a specifically masculine version of truth) with physical pain. The libertine monk Clément argues in *Justine:* "There is no more lively sensation than that of pain; its impressions are certain and dependable, they never deceive as may those of the pleasure women perpetually feign and almost never experience." An almost identical argument, with its implicit phallocentric anxieties, appears in Sade's companion novel, *Juliette,* where the arch libertine Saint-Fond declares: "I've never cared much about seeing pleasure's lineaments writ over a woman's countenance. They're too equivocal, too unsure; I prefer the signs of pain, which are more dependable by far." These passages suggest that there is more to the libertine obsession with pain than an exotic, eccentric, sexual taste. Pain not only affirms (a clearly uncertain) male superiority and mastery. It also assumes the character of a sign-system that—in contrast with the slipperiness attributed to language and to appearances (no doubt to women as well)—establishes a direct, if limited, correspondence with truth. It communicates an authenticity that Sade's libertine heroes and heroines see everywhere eluding them in a world dominated by deceit, custom, equivocation, timidity, and ignorance. Here, pain for Sade has already absorbed a range of meaning that distinguishes it from merely random agonies or from meaningless sensation. Already we have entered the unstable realm of Sadean transvaluations, where familiar words and actions take on unfamiliar significance, even as libertine sexual pleasure adopts the unexpected vocabulary of screams and rage. It is a realm where medicine too cannot remain unchanged. . . .

Ignored as the symptom of temporary dysfunction and dismissed as the chastising pedagogue of traditional ethics, pain for Sade emerges in a new and primary role as coextensive with the truth of the body. Pain, that is, informs us truly about the state of the body. Further, this information gains immeasurable importance because the body's truth comes to define the limits of whatever Sade holds as true. It is, in effect, the sole truth in a world where every other foundation of knowledge ultimately dissolves into falsehood or uncertainty. Thus, even though Sade thoroughly alters the status of pain within medicine, medicine provides him with the knowledge indispensable for understanding the truth of the body. Sometimes this truth reflects little more than the general Enlightenment fascination with the discovery of natural facts, disentangled from theological corruptions or learned error. Medicine, for example, holds a purely positive, demystifying function in *Philosophy in the Bedroom,* where the willing ingenue Eugénie—as an introduction to her ensuing libertine education—receives a lecture in male and female anatomy, which might have come directly from a medical textbook (or indirectly from a medical textbook, through the libertine tradition in which such anatomy lectures were a recurrent narrative device). Here again Sade typically converts medicine from a healing and instructive art to an erotic practice. He seems to have understood a sense in which the penetrating gaze holds sexual as well as medical implications. As in the modern soap opera, sexuality and medicine prove inextricably entangled.

The Enlightenment emphasis upon medicine as a science—a practice grounded in experiment and in observable fact—proves fundamentally equivocal in Sade's work. Science matters to the libertine mind mainly as it permits or advances sexual practices that depend on cruelty. Thus the vivisection common to French medical experiments on animals reappears in Sade's work as a technique for generating pleasure. In *Justine* the libertine surgeon Rodin, an eminent technologist who extols "the progress of science," discovers in the probing, cutting, agonizing penetrations of (pre-anesthetic) surgery a lure that proves wholly erotic. When Rodin asserts that the science of anatomy will never reach its "ultimate state of perfection" until he has examined a child of fourteen or fifteen who has died a cruel death, experienced readers of Sade know instantly that this high-minded passion for scientific progress conceals a sexual aim and that the victim of Rodin's excited, protracted vivisection will be his own beautiful daugther. Reduced to a mechanical technology for penetrating the body, medicine serves the libertine world less for relieving pain than for inflicting it. Like the ghoulish aristocrat in *Justine* who manages to achieve orgasm only by repeatedly bleeding his young wife in a vampirish simulation of phlebotomy, Sade's libertines find their ultimate erotic stimulation in blood, which is transformed from medical fact to sexual marker. The balms that miraculously restore Justine and other long-suffering victims of libertinage belong not to Enlightenment pharmacology but to primitive traditions of magic, where drugs are among the standard accoutrement of eroticism. Their Sadean purpose is simply to prepare the victim for new episodes of sexual pain.

The same process of transvaluation in Sade's work that renders medicine erotic also helps to eroticize and to medicalize pain. The most significant result of this process is not the pornographic description that it makes possible. (Sade, of course, did not invent erotic cruelty but rather refined and elaborated it within the contours of his libertine system.) Placing pain within a medical context offers Sade the insuperable advantage of thereby silencing and effectively refuting other discourses traditionally concerned with human suffering. In Sade, as in American courtrooms and hospitals, medicine has a tendency to overrule or to dominate alternative systems of thought, so that priest and judge defer to the wisdom of medical testimony. Because medicine in Sade carries the authority of Enlightenment science, it breaks free from the literary heritage that portrays the doctor as a greedy quack. Indeed, Sade's libertine surgeon Rodin is an anti-quack: a wealthy man-of-science whose reasoning is formidable. In its relentless appeal to the facts of human anatomy and physiology, medicine as Sade employs it thoroughly displaces the more speculative discussions of pain that had been a traditional employment of philosophers and theologians. The Sadean libertine ultimately empties virtue and vice (or sin and innocence) of their familiar content in classical and Christian writing, where our attraction to pleasure and aversion from pain seem changeless, natural, God-given responses that provide a foundation for the ethical life. In

one sense, Sade exposes the unforeseen conclusions that follow from a Benthamite reliance upon pleasure and pain as a philosophical bedrock for ethics. In another sense, all traditional foundations crumble in Sade when virtue and vice are redefined as cultural artifacts characterized by their greater or lesser powers to stimulate the nervous system. Medicine, as various Enlightenment *philosophes* had predicted, now gives direction to philosophical thought.

Theology fares even worse than philosophy at the hands of Sade's libertine medicine. The voluminous Christian meditations on human suffering might be said to take their origin from the iconography of the cross and from the prophetic words of Isaiah: "With his pain we are healed" (54:4). Pain in Augustinian theology enters the world with original sin, but Christian pain is ultimately redemptive. Christ suffers so that man might find eternal life. The body suffers in order that the soul might be saved. Sade's contemptuous and relentless assault on Christianity as "incompatible with the libertarian system" includes his parodic transvaluation of Christian attitudes toward redemptive suffering. In fact, his fullest response to this pervasive Christian reading of pain is simply the plot of *Justine.* The innocent Justine's faith in God and her love of virtue are the qualities that generate each new episode of outrage and violence, as if the novel—far from reflecting picaresque randomness—were a demonstration in logic. Sade contrives Justine's imitation of Christ to establish the absence of redemptive suffering. The world that she encounters inside the church mirrors exactly the libertine cruelties that she meets everywhere else. There is no inside, no outside. Even when she escapes from the debauched monks at St. Mary-in-the-Wood, Justine simply encounters their doubles wherever she turns.

Sade's equivocal representation of Enlightenment medicine mirrors an ambivalence in his treatment of Christianity. It is possible that Sadean atheism—so vocal and jubilant as to undermine its own claims—expresses (as Pierre Klossowski has argued [in *Sade mon prochain,* 1947]) his unacknowledged need for God. It is certain that Christianity contains for Sade, as if despite itself, a hidden ground for affirmation. What Sade affirms in Christianity is not its doctrines but its historical concern with pain, from original sin, martyrdom, and self-flagellation to inquisitorial torture and the torment of the damned. The final episode of *120 Days of Sodom* thus provides a culminating image of Sade's secular transvaluation of Christianity in the horrifying erotic carnage of a pastime called "The Hell Game"—complete with impersonated demons and agonized sinners. By comparison, the parody of Christian pain in *Justine* seems oblique and almost subtle. In Sade's work, theology—like philosophy—provides only a mocking, empty, archaic language for interpreting pain, no match for the up-to-date physiology of nerve impulses and electrical fluids. As Justine suffers each new excruciating episode of sexual abuse, her suffering leads nowhere, illuminates nothing, redeems no one.

Sade's transvaluations of medical knowledge will grow clearer if we focus upon two specific passages from *Juliette* and *Justine.* The first brings us openly to a question at the heart of Sade's work. How is it, asks the libertine statesman Saint-Fond, that we arrive at pleasure through the sight of others undergoing pain and, stranger still, through suffering pain ourselves? To this central problem in Sade's fiction—which might seem so complex as to evoke cloudbanks of obscure evasions—Saint-Fond's fellow libertine Noirceuil delivers an absolutely explicit reply. Like similar demystifying exercises of Enlightenment reason, it begins by citing the error it proposes to unmask, quoted in the exact words of the Port-Royal Jansenist theologian Pierre Nicole:

> "Pain, logically defined, is nothing other than a sentiment of hostility in the soul toward the body it animates, the which it signifies through certain movements that conflict with the body's physical organization." So says Nicole, who perceived in man an ethereal substance, which he called soul, and which he differentiated from the material substance we call body. I, however, who will have none of this frivolous stuff and who consider man as something on the order of an absolutely material plant, I shall simply say that pain is the consequence of a defective relationship between objects foreign to us and the organic molecules composing us; in such wise that instead of composing harmoniously with those that make up our neural fluids, as they do in the commotion of pleasure, the atoms emanating from these foreign objects strike them aslant, crookedly, sting them, repulse them, and never fuse with them. Still, though the effects are negative, they are effects nonetheless, and whether it be pleasure or pain brewing in us, you will always have a certain impact upon the neural fluids.

Although Noirceuil and Nicole are both French, they speak in effect two different languages. Noirceuil's confident talk of atoms, organic molecules, and neural fluids—however garbled by the standards of twentieth-century science—represents an effort to silence theology by invoking as a superior or superseding discourse the empirical language of Enlightenment medicine. Behind their use of these two distinct languages or systems of discourse stand two utterly opposed visions of man. Nicole's theological paradigm of pain requires the concept of an eternal, immaterial soul at odds with a material, ephemeral body. By contrast, for Noirceuil pain becomes the occasion for asserting a materialism so comprehensive that it denies substantial differences separating bodies from minds or souls. As another libertine philosopher explains: "All we attribute to the soul is all simply the effect of matter." . . .

Pain as it concerns nerve fibers and neural fluids—not the welfare of an immaterial soul or the effects of original sin—is the explicit subject of a second passage I wish to examine, from the novel ***Justine***. Here again we can observe how medicine functions for Sade in providing a language opposed to the discourse of theology, but it is the erotic implications of his dryly technical language that deserve special attention. The passage, which appears as a note attached to a speech by Justine's libertine temptress Dubois, sounds less like novelistic talk than like textbook physiology and opens with a hyperbole typical of Sade, which perhaps only an anatomist could take seriously:

> There is no part of the human body more interesting than the nerve. . . . Life and indeed the entire harmony of the body as a machine depend on the nerves. From them come sensations and pleasures, thoughts and ideas; they constitute, briefly, the center of the whole human structure. The soul is located there, that is to say the principle of life, which dies out among animals, which grows and declines in them, and is by consequence wholly material.

> The nerves are imagined to be tubes destined to carry the animal spirits into the organs to which they are distributed and to report back to the brain the impressions of external objects on these organs.

Let me interrupt the passage to make two brief comments. First, the word translated here (and generally in Sade) as "pain" is *"la douleur."* *"Douleur"* retains its traditional contrast with *"peine"* (also translated as "pain"), which implies physical injury or indefinite harm with no accompanying mental or emotional anguish. It is precisely the mental and emotional suffering of their victims—which includes the victims' awareness of their victimization—that makes Sade's libertines vastly prefer *douleur* to *peine*. Second, in defining the soul as the "principle of life" Sade remains securely within the boundaries of libertine materialism. There is no real difference—merely a change in vocabulary—between Noirceuil's vision of man as an "absolutely material plant" and the view, expressed in Sade's note, that the body is a "machine" animated by a life force. (Again, La Mettrie could provide Sade with a source for *both* metaphors: each pointing toward the same restrictive range of meaning.) In other writers, the metaphorical shift from machine to plant might well reflect conceptual changes important to medical and scientific controversies of the time, measuring the distance separating an older, strictly mechanistic physiology from the newer, vitalist physiology centered in Montpellier; in Sade's hands, however, both metaphors—plant and machine—equally serve to exclude the possibility of an immaterial spirit that survives independent of the body.

Sade's abandonment of the Christian and Cartesian immaterial soul is unmistakable as the note continues. Whether we attribute the note to author, character, or impersonated editor, its physiological language explains that the nervous system alone provides everything necessary to account for the experience of pleasure and pain:

> An intense inflammation excites to an extraordinary degree the animal spirits that flow into the nerve tubes which, in turn, induce pleasure. If the inflammation occurs on the genitals or nearby parts, this explains the pleasures imparted by blows, stabbings, pinches or floggings. From the extreme influence of the mental on the physical comes likewise the painful or agreeable shock of the animal spirits, by reason of the mental sensation one receives. From all this it follows that with such principles and philosophy—with the total annihilation of prejudice—one can extend unbelievably (as we have said elsewhere) the sphere of one's sensations.

This passage does not contain the sort of writing that immediately springs to mind when someone mentions Sade, yet it is almost as typical of Sadean narrative as scenes of sexual cruelty. Sadean eroticism establishes its difference from unreflective violence—violence unconscious of its own nature—by insisting upon the replacement of antiquated theological doctrine with up-to-date, physiological fact.

Fact, we should recognize, plays a different role in Sadean narrative from that which it plays in scientific and medical writing. Thus the reader who seeks to extract a single, self-consistent Sadean physiology will go wrong exactly in the manner of readers seeking a unified, self-consistent Sadean philosophy. Sade's characters employ—and frequently mix—elements drawn from quite different systems of physiology. Pain may be explained with reference to stinging atoms, to excited animal spirits, to stretched nerve fibers, to irritated tissue. There is some reason for feeling that Sade has brewed up a gigantic, simmering soup of fact in which pieces borrowed from widely disparate sources—early and late—float around together in suspension. What matters to Sade is not whether his characters have access to a final truth of science (too many questions are still in doubt) but whether their facts support a demystified vision of man. The passage we have just encountered, for example, might have come nearly verbatim from the celebrated encyclopedist, philosopher, atheist, and materialist d'Holbach. The exact source of Sade's facts, however, is far less important than their implications within his vastly heterogeneous narrative texture. When we examine what "follows" from the often mixed-up facts of Sadean physiology, it will soon be clear that the now antiquated vocabulary of hollow nerve tubes and of racing animal spirits entailed serious—even deadly—consequences.

Pain belongs at the center of Sadean eroticism because, as I have suggested, it serves as a comprehensive metaphor for truth. The truth that it affirms, however, appears from the perspective of theology or of ordinary life to be simply outrage, perversion, and scandalous error. As Georges Bataille writes of Sade: "He went as far as the imagination allows: there was nothing respectable which he did not mock, nothing pure which he did not soil, nothing joyful which he did not frighten." Sade's truth is in effect the negation of beliefs so basic to normal human life that we regard them as self-evidently true. The only self-evident truth in Sade's world, however, is the truth of the body, and it is pain that serves as spokesman for the body's truth. Pain for Sade is what we cannot deny, cannot evade, cannot forswear, while pleasure inevitably deceives, rhetoric beguiles, and logic unweaves its own constructions with the cunning of a false Penelope.

The truth of the body is, of course, exactly what Enlightenment medicine undertook to disclose, finding its most potent instrument and symbol in the newly routine practice of autopsy. Yet, Sade did not stop with the eroticized versions of anatomy and surgery we have seen him employ. Biomedical learning also provided crucial support for his explorations into previously unexplored areas of human sexual behavior, where the truth of the body makes itself known as desire. Pornography, of course, is an ancient and mostly superficial art dedicated to the description of sexual acts. Before Sade, however, never in the history of the novel had a writer employed the license of pornography to create such a blinding, exhaustive vision of desire freed from its normal social constraints. The truth of desire for Sade leads both through and beyond the description of sexual acts to a comprehensive yet flexible system in which bodies, minds, and politics are complexly interlocked. If we follow the sequence leading from body to mind to politics, we will be better prepared to understand how Sade employs pain as the ultimate figure of desire.

The body constitutes for Sade not just the indispensable locus of sexual behavior but, far more important, the force that defines and determines our sexuality. Thus Sade's work posits as a central dogma that we live out a sexual destiny imposed not by God, not by gender, not by culture, but solely by the nerves and tissues of our individual bodies. He once wrote to his wife that his outrageous manner of thought "holds with my existence" (as he put it): "with the way I am made."

In Sade, physiology is destiny. What mankind calls virtue and vice (so runs the libertine argument) reflects merely the facts of biochemical fate. "Our constitution, our scheme, our organs, the flow of liquids, the animal spirits' energy," declares a typical Sadean libertine, "such are the physical causes which in the same hour make for the Tituses and the Neros." Sodomy and pyromania in effect are hardwired in the body. This conviction, which implicitly absolves Sade's libertines from the moral censure that only adds zest to their crimes, appeals for its support to the same progressive spirit of inquiry underlying Enlightenment medicine. As the dissolute monk Clément concludes, after laborious reference to the language of fluids, fibers, blood, and animal spirits: "When the study of anatomy reaches perfection they will without any trouble be able to demonstrate the relationship of the human constitution to the [sexual] tastes which it affects." Anyone foolish enough to punish a libertine will discover that it cannot be done. A taste for pain—like the monks' delight in blaspheming a God whom they believe not to exist—stands fully comprehensible for Sade as a proven truth of the libertine body, inscribed in a personal biology of nerves, tissues, and membranes.

The body in Sade's work sometimes seems entirely detached from mind, like the adjacent blocks of pornographic description and of argumentative reasoning that provide the alternating structure of his books. But the apparent separation of mind and body is always a temporary state or narrative illusion that conceals their fundamental unity. Mind . . . is not for Sade alien to the body, opposed in an irreconcilable division. In fact, we should recall Delbène's assertion to Juliette that it is the body which feels, suffers, enjoys, judges, and *thinks*. The concept of a thinking body is Sade's response to the Cartesian dualism that rigorously opposes material bodies and immaterial thoughts. Sade's libertine system, on the contrary, considers body and mind equally material, although they differ in the same degree as steam might differ from ice. Mind and body are for Sade not just equally material but also (as they were, surprisingly, for Descartes) mutually interactive. The mind relies wholly for its contents—"all sensations, knowledge and ideas" (as Sade noted in *Justine*)—upon the impulses that it receives through the nervous system. What complicates this far from original psychology—which Sade might have borrowed from various empiricist philosophers, including his near contemporary Condillac—is his insistence that the sensations communicated through our nerves and fibers may in turn be altered radically by our thoughts, as if mind triumphed over matter.

The triumph of mind over matter in Sade is figurative ("as if ")—not literal or actual—because, as we have seen, the libertine system regards mind as material: mind cannot literally triumph over itself. In this uncompromising materialism, Sade resembles such modern thinkers as John Searle, who in *Minds, Brains and Science* (1984) dismisses the traditional mind/body problem as a false dilemma or non-problem. (For Searle, thinking is caused by and realized in functions of the brain, much as digestion is caused by and realized in functions of the stomach. He compares the mind/body problem to a digestion/stomach problem, finding them both equally comical and futile enterprises for philosophy.) What sets Sade apart from many materialists and monists, both ancient and modern, is the enormous power that he grants to consciousness or thought in reshaping the ways in which we normally experience our bodies. Mind, that is, possesses for Sade sufficient force to overrule or to alter organic responses (such as the response to pain) usually considered natural. The experience of pain, despite its organic basis in the functioning of the nervous system, may be changed, radically, by the intervention of mind, thus altering the almost physical revulsion normal in contemplating such typical Sadean practices as incest, torture, and the consumption of excrement. In imparting to the libertine body a dynamic (almost unlimited) power of change, mind thoroughly complicates Sade's description of physiology as destiny. Our physiology—through its union with mind—includes the potential for remaking our destinies.

Pain, like pleasure, in effect expands or contracts according to the play of the libertine mind. This play of mind is especially remarkable in Sade for harmonizing or reconciling the two normally antithetical powers of reason and imagination. Reason makes its most notorious appearance in the endless Sadean dissertations justifying libertine erotic tastes. Reason indeed proves a formal requirement of libertine sexuality in Sade, regularly preceding and following each episode of debauchery with an erudite harangue, and for dedicated libertines such as Juliette this Sadean dissertation serves less as an excuse or rationale than as an aphrodisiac. Her sodomite activities with the pope on the high altar of St. Peter's do not inflame her more than the thought of hearing his private lecture on the propriety of murder. Sade is among the few major writers to explore an eroticism of reason. It is not simply that his libertines reason about sexual topics or acts. Reasoning itself—as a mode of personal power—holds erotic attractions. (Juliette: "I loved Noirceuil for his libertinage, for his mental qualities: I was not by any means captivated by his person.") Reason confers attractions as palpable as any of Sade's impossibly rounded buttocks or sensual perfections. In this office reason complements rather than op-

poses the work of imagination. It is important to recognize that imagination, like reason, has been assigned specific responsibilities or labor in Sade's erotic economy, which depends on mind for its more obvious fleshy exchanges. In Saint-Fond's aphorism: "The imagination's fire must set the furnace of the senses alight."

The power of the imagination to inflame the senses depends on the unity of mind and body basic to Sade's outlook, wherein sensuality is never merely an affair of the senses. This reciprocal interpenetration of mental and of physical states had preoccupied several innovative physicians among Sade's contemporaries, especially Cabanis and Alibert, who sought to understand the mind's power over specific bodily conditions. For Sade, the reciprocity linking the realms of the *"physique"* and *"moral"* (to cite the French terms commonly employed to indicate differences between bodily and mental states) extended even to the relationship between text and reader. He anticipates that the imaginative, mental stimulation of reading will excite measurable, physiological changes in the reader. (In *120 Days of Sodom* the narrator explains: "Many of the extravagances you are about to see illustrated will doubtless displease you, yes, I am well aware of it, but there are amongst them a few which will warm you to the point of costing you some fuck, and that, reader, is all we ask of you.") In addition to authorizing this pornographic variant of reader-response criticism, the regulating power of imagination makes itself felt in the aesthetic arrangements inseparable from Sadean eroticism. Rarely are passions satisfied in a chaotic haste and tangle. Sexual partners and groups observe a carefully discussed choreography. Setting—like the elaborate theatrical scene specially constructed at the chateau Silling—often requires costly and ingenious preparations. Crimes are seldom merely perpetrated but rather lovingly premeditated with an artistic attention to minor details, and libertines who survive long enough frequently develop a brilliant flair for spontaneous dramatic gestures, as when Juliette (after climbing to the summit of a volcano) decides to cast a tiresome companion into the bowels of the earth and then follows this gothic performance with impromptu copulations staged imaginatively on the very brink of the gaping crater.

It is the imagination that permits Sade to approach the perfect freedom represented by libertinage: a freedom whereby nature as well as society may be overcome. Sade once defended himself by explaining that while he had imagined every possible form of sexual crime, he had not performed everything he imagined. He was a libertine but not a criminal. Yet, he also composed the speech in which a libertine—distressed at the idea of crimes limited to a single lifetime—is urged to consider the "moral crime" of writing, whereby the imagination permits a writer to extend corrupting fantasies far into the future. For Sade, our imagination—both in its intensity and in its tastes—depends on our physiology (on "the peculiar organization a particular individual is endowed with"), but our physiology thereby contains the power to remake both ourselves and the world. As the dissolute monk Clément expresses Sade's dark version of Romantic idealism: "Objects have no value for us save that which our imagination imparts to them." Pain, when objectified in a suffering victim, proves to be a supreme example of the imagination's power to transform *anything* into pleasure.

The imagination's power to transvalue (or to drain of value) the conventional world of objects and of bodies holds implications that extend beyond individual bodies or minds to politics. Political power is implicit in the imaginative capacity to reshape the world according to our own desires, at least when Sade's libertines possess the wealth, guile, and social standing that permit them to impose their desires upon other persons. The political implications of Sadean eroticism are not farfetched or oblique, as the recent history of feminist readings of Sade makes unmistakably clear. My choice here is not to focus on what might be called—somewhat metaphorically—Sade's sexual politics. The representation of women in Sade's novels, with its sources in social and economic structures as oppressive as any libertine desire, is a subject that leads far beyond the scope of this essay and that Angela Carter has discussed brilliantly at book length. Consistent with a study centering on transvaluations of medical knowledge, my focus concerns the less apparent moments when Sade takes as his subject, directly or indirectly, politics construed in its literal sense as the art or condition of government.

Sade's sexual themes are so prominent, so overwhelming, that they tend to obscure his representations of political power. Yet, he recognized a close link between sexuality and government. For example, he insisted upon a social and political significance in fiction where critics for generations have reported finding only sensationalism and debauchery. In his **Reflections on the Novel** (1800), Sade had high praise for Matthew Lewis's gothic extravaganza *The Monk,* observing that it was "the inevitable result of the revolutionary shocks which all of Europe has suffered." **Philosophy in the Bedroom** places Sade's secluded libertines within a historical setting where incendiary pamphlets are distributed openly outside the palace of Equality. One such pamphlet Sade actually incorporates in his text—the famous libertine manifesto *Yet Another Effort, Frenchmen, If You Would Become Republicans,* with its guidelines for a utopian state in which legitimate forms of personal freedom now include prostitution, incest, rape, sodomy, and murder. From his cell in the Bastille Sade was a firsthand spectator of the gathering Revolutionary shock (the authorities removed him for inciting passers-by); during his less than four years of freedom after the fall of the Bastille, he held for a time the improbable office of assessor or judge on one of the innumerable Revolutionary committees; and upon his rearrest in 1793, the house in which he was temporarily imprisoned became the location for a guillotine, where some eighteen hundred victims of the Terror were executed. For Sade, who defined the novel as "the representation of secular customs" and who spent most of his adult life imprisoned because of his unorthodox tastes and writings, it would be hard indeed to avoid observing the link between sexual practice and political power.

Politics for Sade is closely and inseparably related to what he regards as the truth of the body. "The Body Politic," as one of his libertine heroes asserts, "should be governed by the same rules that apply to the Body Physical." More is at work here than the spell of analogy. Sadean politics is not just indirectly linked to the body through a physiology that includes the imagination. The body for Sade— through its nerves, fibers, and animal spirits—directly authorizes a larger, encompassing distribution of social power. "Stripping people of their liberty amuses me," explains one libertine, "I like holding captives." "Man likes to command," reports another, "to be obeyed, to surround himself with slaves compelled to satisfy him." Although Sade professed to distinguish between what he called "absurd political despotism" and the "delightful despotism" of the libertine, French political life under the ancien régime finds its perfect miniaturization (as Roland Barthes has observed) in the despotic power which Sade's libertines exercise over their powerless victims. Thus in a note to **Juliette** Sade writes that one of his grasping libertine statesmen resembles "those monsters that abounded under the *ancien régime* and personified it." This sexualized, social, and absolute power authorized by the body amounts to what we might call a politics of sensibility.

Sensibility, of course, is a crucial concept in late-eighteenth-century medicine and literature, where it permitted the development of a tightly woven argument about that favorite Enlightenment object of study, human nature. This argument, so pervasive that it operated usually in abbreviated versions accepted or offered as an unspoken assumption, rested on the belief shared by Sadean libertines that our sensibility or power of feeling depends ultimately upon the refinement of our individual nervous system. The stages of this argument have been reconstructed by G. S. Rousseau in the following series: "(A) the soul is limited to the brain, (B) the brain performs the entirety of its work through the nerves, (C) the more 'exquisite' and 'delicate' one's nerves are, morphologically speaking, the greater the ensuing degree of sensibility and imagination, (D) refined people and other persons of fashion are born with more 'exquisite' anatomies, the tone and texture of their nervous systems more 'delicate' than those of the lower classes." All we need in order to transform this physiological argument into a politics of sensibility is the conclusion supplied in a fascinating essay by Christopher Lawrence. Lawrence shows in a detailed study of Scottish Enlightenment thought [*Natural Order: Historical Studies of Scientific Culture,* 1979] how the argument based on physiology was employed to advance the political and social interests of an autocratic, landed minority, whose heightened capacity for exquisite feeling supposedly earned them a natural right as governors and custodians of power in a backward land.

Sade—in the transvaluations he so often performed upon Enlightenment thought—effectively converted the politics of sensibility into a sexual despotism based on pain. Understood solely as a phenomenon of nerves and tissues, pain supplies the foundation for a Sadean politics in which mastery requires that other people suffer. If the Enlightenment man of feeling—whose acute sensitivity to pain was legendary—implicitly lent support to the political suppression of persons whose sensibility was deemed less delicate, Sade's libertines argue openly that their individual powers of feeling give them an absolute right over other people. "I affirm," declares the libertine statesman Saint-Fond, "that the fundamental, profoundest, and keenest penchant in man is incontestably to enchain his fellow creatures and to tyrannize them with all his might." Pain, however, plays a curious double role in this Sadean tyranny. Sade emphasizes that a taste for cruelty depends on a particularly sensitive nervous system, so that women—according to the libertine argument—are especially cruel. ("The extreme delicacy of their fibers, the prodigious sensitivity of their organs," explains a Sadean annotation, "cause them to go a great deal farther than men in this direction.") At the same time, the disposition for inflicting pain also requires a paradoxical deadening of the emotions in order that cruelty might be enjoyed to the utmost. It is said of Madame Clairwil—"the most exceptional libertine of her century"—that for lack of sensibility she had no equal: "she indeed prided herself on never having shed a tear."

The paradox of libertine sensibility—simultaneously hypersensitive and numb—may be traced ultimately to the Sadean monism of body and mind. It is the body's "organization"—to use Sade's favorite biological term—that ensures our leaning toward what the world calls virtue or vice. Thus, in comparing women with men, Sade repeats the familiar argument that physiology is destiny. ("Their organs are more finely constructed, their sensitivity profounder, their nerves more irascible: barbarity is not a trait of the individual of inferior sensibility.") The libertine's superior sensibility, nonetheless, requires for the perfection of barbarism a complementary mental development. Sade's libertines therefore take particular care to harden their sensibilities against the normal pity or distress we are disposed to feel at the sight of human suffering. They cultivate the *apathy*—a rational indifference to feeling—which Max Horkheimer and Theodore W. Adorno identify as a basic strain of Enlightenment thought: what Kant called "a necessary presupposition of virtue."

Sadean apathy is a necessary deadening of the emotions and elevation of reason that finds its significance not as a goal or end of conduct—and certainly not as a presupposition of virtue—but as one stage in a dialectic of pain. Because Sadean libertines must deaden their feelings in order to feel more intensely, their condition bears less resemblance to a generalized, Stoic apathy (in which reason everywhere dominates passion) than to a highly selective, local anesthesia (which eliminates only a specific band or zone of feeling, while thereby heightening the sensation that remains). Specific emotions such as pity are eradicated to assure a cold detachment; reason is magnified; imagination inflames the senses. Thus Sadean libertines encourage the tendency they discover within themselves for enjoying the intensest shocks to the nervous system that accompany both their own pain and the spectacle of pain in others. A body politic governed by the same rules that apply to the libertine body will find apathy a necessary precondition of social life. Selective anesthesia is perhaps what permits every ruling elite to transform its own principles and sensibility into a license for oppression. Sade's libertine societies are unique not in their brutality but in their undeceived awareness and open enjoyment of the suffering they inflict.

The twofold libertine education of the feelings—simultaneously hardening the sensibility to pity and enlarging its relish for pain—issues finally in the murderous supremacy which Saint-Fond and his fellow libertines accept as their natural right. In the sexualized torture they inflict upon their victims, Sade's libertines reveal how pain serves so often to reify or give visible shape to the political power that, as Elaine Scarry has argued [in *The Body in Pain: The Making and Unmaking of the World,* 1985], is always implicitly or explicitly claimed by the torturer. Unquestionably, the pain that Sade's work emphasizes is closely linked to social conventions of gender, so that women (represented by the pious, submissive, piteous Justine) are its normal site. Even Sade's emancipated libertine woman—as we see in Juliette—depends, like his male libertines, on a supply of victims who are usually powerless and mostly female. In Sade's work, however, the politics of sensibility does not coincide exactly with a conventional sexual politics, in which males are invariably oppressors and women victims. Power in Sade in ultimately genderless, and gender sometimes grows as shifty as pain. The ultimate libertine erotic adventure—death—seems finally beyond gender, a mode of autoeroticism in which pleasure transcends distinctions of female and male. Like the brigand chief Roland, who trusts Justine to cut the rope, submissively, just when he hangs himself, the libertine mind makes use of gender in order to seek a state more archaic and indistinct, where social and biological differences between male and female dissolve in an erotic embrace of death. The victims of Sade's libertines—often mutilated past all recognition—divide simply into the dead and the about-to-die. In Sade's transvaluation of Enlightenment norms, the politics of sensibility leads logically to the androgynous or bisexual libertine witch Durand and to the final extension of undifferentiated, tyrannous power that she contemplates: genocide.

It was not tyranny, however, but revolution that provided for Sade the political metaphor best summarizing the meanings he discovered in pain. Sade settles for tyranny, we might say, because it represents a durable substitute for the transient purity of revolution. Revolution for Sade is the anarchic dream of absolute freedom realized in the moment when an established government falls and its successor has not yet come into being. In the temporary release from all law and all authority, it confronts us with a condition of utter ambiguity as the state dissolves into an elemental, inchoate, and primal disorder. "Lawful rule," as a Sadean libertine explains, "is inferior to anarchy: the greatest proof whereof is the government's obligation to plunge the State into anarchy whenever it wishes to frame a new constitution. To abrogate its former laws it is driven to establish a revolutionary regime in which there are no laws at all. The revolutionary regime is by definition unstable and transitional. It soon calls forth a new state with new laws and new authority, where absolute freedom is once again merely a dream. Indeed, politics as a social practice—as the day-to-day art of government—held almost no interest for Sade compared to the intoxicating and almost purely theoretical moment of revolution when all government dissolves. It is this moment of complete freedom and utter ambiguity when ordinary structures fly apart that fascinated Sade. Like the tumultuous moment of orgasm for Sadean libertines, it provides an image of the terrifying, exhilarating vertigo that ensues when human beings live fully the consequences of their own desire. Pain, I suggest, comes to signify for Sade the vast and never wholly communicable ambiguity that he understands as implicit in the truth of desire.

Desire is an overworked topic in literary criticism of the novel, but it is also the central point to which Sade's treatment of body, mind, and politics continually returns. Within the almost limitless perimeters set by desire, what concerns me here is a quite limited, concluding issue: the relation of desire to pain. Indeed, Sadean desire seems nearly unique in selecting pain as its favored object. Sade's paradoxical argument—making pain a source of pleasure—in effect profoundly revises several powerful traditions that precede, but by no means predict, his work. In Sade, the ancient erotic topos of the lover's pain—a pain the lover half-enjoys because its poignancy and its intensity seem inseparable from love—reappears completely altered: love simply vanishes (along with religion) as a source of libertine feeling. Eros for Sade has little or nothing to do with Cupid. Similarly, Sade turns on its head the Socratic theory that desire always presupposes a painful lack or absence. (For Socrates, at least in the earlier dialogues, pain activates and accompanies desire, disappearing when desire attains its object, much as the pangs of hunger disappear after one eats.) Sadean pain not only arouses and accompanies desire but also satisfies it—or, more accurately, promises to satisfy it. Pain thus achieves a special value for Sade exactly in proportion to its capacity for *resisting* disappearance. It is something to be cherished and enjoyed and protracted: an additive that both prolongs and even replaces lesser modes of pleasure. Indeed, in its quest for permanence, Sadean desire no longer flees from absence and pain but actively courts them. It recognizes in pain the promise of an ultimate and unending and undeceiving satisfaction.

The Sadean embrace of pain is not merely a search for intense sensation. Desire, in seeking pain, seeks more than the satisfaction of carnal appetite, which is why bodies alone (gluttonously consumed) are never enough for Sade's libertines: they demand reasons and meanings as well. The two main clusters of meaning enfolded within the experience of Sadean pain should be now quite familiar. First, there is pain defined (against powerful religious and ethical traditions) strictly as an event of the central nervous system, measured through the shock that it delivers to the body and described in a biomedical language of neural fluids, animal spirits, and hollow nerve tubes. The social and sexual implications of this Sadean perspective on pain are, as I have tried to indicate, far-reaching. Second, there is the libertine insistence that pain somehow unites us with truth. Pleasure deceives, pain informs. Pleasure is always doubtful, pain provides certainty. Pain, as I have argued, is regarded as expressing the truth of the body, and the truth of the body proves coextensive with the normally suppressed, repressed, and openly denied truth of desire. It is now necessary to complicate this picture, briefly but unmercifully.

Sadean desire, which we might define as a normally un-

heard and unheeded voice prior to all laws and all authority, always returns to pain—as if to its source or origin. Explanations for this recurrent pattern no doubt require an awareness that pain and desire share exactly the same structure within the libertine system. Pain, as we have seen, promises absolute certainty, a bedrock for belief that cannot be questioned because it is self-evidently true, an unfeigned and unambiguous speech uttered as if involuntarily by the body, a forced confession. At the same time, this bedrock truth proves far less firm than it appears. Within the libertine body, pain swiftly and imperceptibly passes into its opposite, pleasure, in a process that is never simply or solely a reversal, as if pleasure now meant pain, and pain pleasure. Their relation is more unstable, fluid, and shifting. For Descartes, the physiological differences between pleasure and pain involve potentially measurable changes in nerve fibers. In the sensation of pleasure, the fibers are merely stretched, while pain finds them strained and torn. (Quite different organs are also involved in exciting the joy of pleasure and despondency of pain.) For Sade, the physiological differences between pleasure and pain involve potentially measurable changes in "the neural fluid particles which circulate in the hollow of our nerves." Yet the differences that for Descartes seemed absolute and binding now for Sade appear relatively ambiguous. Inscribed on the victims of libertine cruelties, the signs of pain may still look certain. Within the libertine body, however, pleasure and pain no longer hold their normative role of opposites but commingle in uncertain and changing patterns. Like desire, pain for Sade leads away from clarities.

Pain in Sade is not just the object of desire but in some sense its double. Sadean desire is thus drawn to pain as to its own mirror image. What they share fundamentally is a negative power to block satisfaction, to prevent any firm or final accommodation with meaning. Sade's libertines obsessively follow the instructions of desire but discover (in or through satiety) a perpetual dissatisfaction, lack of fulfillment, the void from which desire springs anew. "Nothing measures up to the stature of my desires," explains a voracious female libertine, whose usual debaucheries continue for twenty-four hours and reduce her genitals to what she calls "an open wound": "a hash." Desire—in seeking satisfaction through pain—remains unappeasable. The monk Clément, after putting Justine through a terrifying sexual ordeal indistinguishable from torture, regrets that her vividly physical sufferings are inevitably "a very pale image of what one should really like to do." Behind the breathtaking atrocities Sade's libertines perform there lies an unattainable—perhaps even unknowable—level of cruelty that always defeats them. Like pain, desire reserves to itself something that finally remains always unspoken, beyond or against language. In this sense Sade's work is a sea of horrors in which pain continually seeks and perpetually fails to drain dry the unspeakable.

Anyone who wishes to explore the assumptions underlying four decades of quite extraordinary French writing on Sade should begin with the belief that Sadean horrors represent an assault on the unspeakable. Simone de Beauvoir puts it this way: "He is trying to communicate an experience whose distinguishing characteristic is, nevertheless, a tendency to be incommunicable." Maurice Blanchot writes of Sade: "Everything which is said is clear, but seems to be at the mercy of something left unsaid"; "everything *is* expressed, is revealed, but also everything is plunged back again into the obscurity of unformulated and inexpressible thoughts." Georges Bataille comments: "The evident monotony of Sade's books is due to the decision to subordinate literature to the expression of an inexpressible event." This consensus does not guarantee that its claim is correct, but it both defines a basis for the modern revaluation of Sade and helps to suggest why Sadean desire—in its endless torrent of repetitive images and words—finds in pain an appropriate vehicle for a quest characteristic of Romantic writing: the pursuit of the inexpressible. Pain in Sade draws to itself the speechless, erotic mysteries culminating and cohering in the embrace of death.

In its intrinsic contact with the inexpressible and the unspeakable, pain takes Sade far beyond the medicine of his day, when madness and unreason were still locked within the secure (if no longer absolute) classical confinement that Michel Foucault describes in *Madness and Civilization.* Foucault reads Sade as a figure of the late Enlightenment who exposes a truth that Enlightenment medicine mostly resisted. "Sadism," he writes, "is not a name finally given to a practice as old as Eros; it is a massive cultural fact which appeared precisely at the end of the eighteenth century, and which constitutes one of the greatest conversions of Western imagination: unreason transformed into delirium of the heart, madness of desire, the insane dialogue of love and death in the limitless presumption of appetite." Sade, I would guess, is among the crucial, ambiguous monuments that Foucault's unfinished history of sexuality would unavoidably reconsider. In such a reconsideration, Sade should appear not as the author of a few vast, unreadable pornographic novels but as an almost impersonal force giving voice to a newly transformed discourse on the erotic life. It is not only as a sign of mastery or as a well-recognized surrogate for death—with its speechless mysteries and sensual affiliations—that pain served Sade. Modern clinical treatment now frequently begins with the Sadean assumption that pain is always solitary and private, full of sound but essentially inarticulate, a measure of the immense distance that separates individuals. Against cultural pieties proclaiming a human community, an almost infinite space opens between the person in pain and the comforters or tormenters who stand close by. Not even the physician or research scientist who seeks to relieve pain, tracing its shared vocabulary and redefining the biochemistry of the brain, can as yet successfully collapse the distance. Words and knowledge carry poorly across this abyss. Pain, as one modern treatment center advises its staff, is "anything that the patient says it is." "Pain," wrote Emily Dickinson, "has an Element of Blank." The blankness, the anythingness of pain, especially its power to summon up experience ultimately inaccessible to language, its power to engage ambiguities too slippery for even the slickest libertine reasoners: these are among the meanings with which Sade endowed the mechanical rush of animal spirits through hollow, fibrous nerves.

Scott Carpenter   (essay date 1991)

SOURCE: "Sade and the Problem of Closure: Keeping Philosophy in the Bedroom," in *Neophilologus,* Vol. LXXV, No. 4, October, 1991, pp. 519-28.

[In this excerpt, Carpenter examines Sade's violations of the Classical principle of closure, particularly in Philosophy in the Bedroom, *as a threat to "the notion of ideology as such."]*

As Michel Foucault has demonstrated, the Classical age had mastered the art of excluding from society its undesirables, be they the criminal, the deranged, or the physically or politically abnormal. But Sade, half *grand seigneur,* half Revolutionary, straddled the boundary between the social and the antisocial. His contacts and influence made total seclusion impossible. As much as the authorities, egged on by Sade's venomous mother-in-law, tried to hermetically seal the marquis behind the walls of his cells, he always managed to make himself heard. Sometimes this was in the form of a more or less secret correspondence, by which (among other things) he arranged a series of escapes. Twice he eluded the death sentence. These escapades resulted in his internment in increasingly secure quarters, measures which smacked of surprising severity for someone of Sade's modest infractions. What becomes clear is that Sade was not merely a victim of the ancien régime's official moral code. First of all, his earliest offenses— including sodomy, blasphemy, lacing candies with Spanish fly, and adulterous relations with his sister-in-law— were generally overlooked in Sade's time when the perpetrator was a nobleman. Second, Sade was imprisoned under three separate governments of very different ideological platforms: the ancien régime, the Revolutionary Convention, and the Empire. The threat Sade posed— whatever it was—seems to transcend individual ideologies. Indeed, insofar as ideology is always an essentially closed structure, Sade's refusal to submit to physical, legal, or literary containment would seem to threaten the notion of ideology as such.

What emerges from this rapid overview is that Sade made a career out of upsetting the notions of closure and enclosure that were so essential to the Classical age, and this tendency marks his literary production as well. More than a mere reflection of this practice, his writing was constitutive of it. At times writing remained Sade's only connection with the outside world, and while awaiting the opportunity to smuggle packages out, he had saved whole manuscripts from confiscation by hiding them in cracks in the prison walls. More than a mere symbol of his irrepressibility, Sade's writings reenacted the problematization of closure that had rendered the author so undesirable, and this literary reenactment was to draw censure that would outlive its author: regularly banned throughout the 19th century, Sade's works faced their last court challenge in 1957 when the publisher J-J Pauvert produced the ***Oeuvres complètes.***

This problematization amounts at least to a challenging of the classical desire for totalization and wholeness, and of its concomitant policy of excluding those elements which frustrate this desire. Sade's relationship to the Classical age is profoundly ambiguous. Both product and victim of his era, he might be said to write with both hands, demonstrating thematically a desire for closure while simultaneously resisting it. Somewhat superficially such a conflict might be cited in the difficulties Sade experienced in simply drawing his works to a close. The plan for *Les 120 journées de Sodome* was structurally typical of the Enlightenment in that it proposed an exhaustive, encyclopedic cataloguing of 600 passions, but only a quarter of these were ever brought to completion. More dramatic was Sade's continual re-opening of the novels in the *Justine* cycle as he expanded *Les Infortunes de la vertu* into *Justine,* later enlarging it for *La Nouvelle Justine,* to which he appended the massive *Histoire de Juliette, sa soeur.*

This resistance to conclude would appear incongruous in a literary corpus that, as Barthes and others have convincingly demonstrated, thematically privileges closure. The château de Silling (in *Les Cent vingt journées*), for example, figures as the libertine sanctuary par excellence and serves as the model for the isolated chambers of the Jus-

Frontispiece from an early edition of Sade's works, showing his own castle of La Coste and three fortresses in which he was imprisoned.

tine novels. . . . Regulated by a strict code of rules, impenetrable from the outside, inescapable from within, the château de Silling seems to represent the ideal of absolute closure. However, even within this paradigmatic fortress, the forces of confinement are not inviolate. Infractions of the rigid code are regularly noted, and at one point even an escape is contemplated. Furthermore, although the return route is described as impracticable without the wooden bridge burnt upon arrival sixteen members of the troupe inexplicably make their way back to Paris. In *Justine* this "leakage" is even more flagrant, for the progression of the novel relies on Justine's repeated escapes from the supposedly secure confines of libertine society.

One witnesses, then, in Sade a conflict between a plan or theory of closure and the practical impossibility of this theory's adequate application, and this conflict appears in the various dimensions of literary history, philosophy, textual themes, and language itself. Present throughout Sade's work, it emerges most forcefully in a text that explicitly tries to join theory and practice, that works to introduce commentary into the sanctuary of libertine activity.

La Philosophie dans le boudoir, written between 1782 and 1789, is a sort of libertine complement to Rousseau's *Emile.* It presents the sensual and moral re-education of the young Eugénie de Mistival who, having recently completed her convent education, has come secretly to Mme de Saint-Ange for initiation into the ways of libertinism. During the course of the seven vaguely theatrical dialogues that take place in her boudoir, Mme de Saint-Ange enlists the aid of her brother and lover, the Chevalier de Mirvel; that of a libertine maestro, Dolmancé; and that of a few servants as the need arises. Eugénie's education will consist of a thorough indoctrination into libertine theory, punctuated by involvement in a series of increasingly scabrous acts. Inserted within the fifth dialogue is a vast political tract, or pamphlet, entitled "Français encore un effort si vous voulez être républicains," which serves to summarize the teachings of Dolmancé. The tale ends in paroxysm when Eugénie's mother arrives to rescue her daughter, only to be tortured by her and subsequently infected with a deadly pox.

Meticulously constructed, the dialogues never deviate from the lessons at hand, and at the outset they seem to conform entirely to the classical aesthetic of wholeness, even satisfying the unities of time, place, and action. Even the political pamphlet that occupies a quarter of the text corresponds precisely to Dolmancé's libertine theories. This rigorous adherence to narrative unity is the first sign of Sade's commitment to a classical mode of domination, illustrating the paradoxical nature of a libertinism that has nothing to do with freedom. In spite of accepted beliefs, it becomes clear that *libertinage* is neither reckless nor merely sensual: the crescendo of staged and timed orgiastic events is the result of precise organization.

The drive toward closure manifests itself here as a concern for self-sufficiency or independence, for the "perfection" of the libertine-in-training. Eugénie's education can only be rounded out by an understanding of the theoretical foundations of libertine practice . . .

Dolmancé and Saint-Ange insist throughout on the importance of closure and self-containment. Thus, in the tradition of the libertine sanctuary, Mme de Saint-Ange's secret boudoir is divided from the world. . . . Indeed, the overriding concept in libertinism is, not surprisingly, that of satisfaction, both in the sense of fulfilling desire and in the corresponding filling of gaps, of orifices. Just as Dolmancé fills in the lacunae in Eugénie's bourgeois education, so he orchestrates the scenes in which she learns to make use of every orifice and recess her body has to offer. . . .

Furthermore, dramatic development in **La Philosophie dans le boudoir** depends on the full sexual exploitation of a given number of participants. Once the initial triad has accomplished all possible configurations, a need is created for a new player. Happily supplementing the group is the Chevalier, Saint-Ange's brother and sometimes mate. Dolmancé indicates that he arrives just in time to respond to a new demand, that of a practical demonstration. . . .

The demonstration given, the foursome engages in some of the strenuous sexual gymnastics typical of Sade, which result in a new satisfaction, and a renewed need for expansion. For this they enlist Augustin, Mme de Saint-Ange's provincial but well-equipped gardener. As the numbers increase, so does the level of violence: the Chevalier accepts the job of brutally raping Eugénie, which precedes her sensual beating by Dolmancé and her "impaling" by the gigantic Augustin. In this context it seems natural that the philosophical discussion should turn to the heightened pleasure of victimization, and even murder. With the current configurations exhausted, and this new desire kindled, a victim is sought. The felicitous arrival of Mme de Mistival, Eugénie's mother, will provide one, and her torture satisfies this last impulse as it, too, marks the drive toward closure, bringing into action all six of the players.

Yet the increase in violence is more than just a dramatic heightening of action and obscenity, corresponding to a desire to *épater le bourgeois* (although this is undoubtedly present as well). This escalation is instead a symptom of the conflict that subtends Sade's strange utopia.

On one hand Sade imitates the gesture of exclusion effected by the dominant ideology, and he seems to strive for a closure so complete that it would lead to virtual autonomy and self—sufficiency. The closed space of Mme de Saint-Ange's boudoir serves not only to protect, but also to *conserve*. In the Sadean dream of plenitude, nothing is lost, and libertine activity—in spite of what would appear to be quite exhausting antics—is not one of unchecked *dépense*. Although the regular introduction of characters serves as a sort of dramatic refueling, the "Sade machine" strives to function like a perpetual motion machine. The very number of orgasms (and they are best counted by the score) attests to a conservation of libertine energy. Bodies are not mere vessels expelling their fluids, but insofar as they are generally joined, they become *vases communicants*: fluids pass back and forth, but are never to leave the closed system. . . .

This opposition to loss, especially when it has to do with the loss of sperm, is quite properly a resistance to *dissemi-*

nation in any form. That this resistance extends beyond the realm of bodily fluids and into the body of language is evidenced by the presence of the lengthy political tract, "Français, encore un effort si vous voulez être républicains," which is inserted in the text to serve as a consolidation of Dolmancé's intermittent teachings. . . . More important, there is a tendency in Sade to try to restrict the dissemination inherent to language itself. Barthes [in *Sade, Fourier, Loyola,* 1971] has discussed how Sade disdains the suggestive deferments of the "strip-tease" indeed, his determination is to present the body stripped of all veils, in all its immediacy. In contrast to some of his earlier writings (see the snake in **"Le Serpent"**), *La Philosophie dans le boudoir* generally disdains sexual symbolization and strives to narrow the gap between sign and referent. In short, in Sade, *il faut appeler une chatte une chatte*. Or better, one would avoid conventional language, with its ambiguities and deferred meanings, altogether. The ideal Sadean act takes place in silence.

The drive toward total closure requires such measures. Classical thought posited the sign as an absence, as a mark pointing to a meaning, or referent, that is always elsewhere (*Les Mots et les choses*). Sade desires to create an enclosed, self-contained language, one that does not point "away" or "outside" of itself, and the only way to achieve this is for him to rupture the hymen that marries the signifier to a conventional signified. Dolmancé's instruction works to methodically annihilate reference and signification, convincingly demonstrating to Eugénie that words such as God, law, right, and wrong point to nothing, and have no existence except in the materiality of the words themselves. Similarly, the normally reliable bond between sign and referent, which would assert that words such as brother and lover are not interchangeable, is violated by the fact that the Chevalier is both of these to his sister. Sade further devalues referents as he arranges carnal scenes that become nearly impossible to picture. . . .

Finally, conventional language proves inadequate for the representation of what Sade construes as meaning itself. In the midst of one of Mme de Saint-Ange's orgasms, the narrator interrupts her onomatopoeic groans to comment on the monotony of a language that fails to capture the jubilation of the moment: "*Augustin, Dolmancé et le chevalier font chorus; la crainte d'être monotone nous empêche de rendre des expressions qui, dans de tels instants, se ressemblent toutes.*" . . . Similarly, when Dolmancé leads Augustin off into the next room, the act he is to perform entirely escapes referential language—"mais, en vérité, cela ne peut pas se dire" and thus cannot be represented in the text.

As Dolmancé dismantles the notion of linguistic reference, he privileges the materiality—one might say the corporeality—of the signifier. Indeed, characters in **La Philosophie dans le boudoir** only have meaning as bodies, and then only when they have been inserted into what becomes an unusual kind of "signifying chain," whose meaning, in the form of *jouissance,* is not "elsewhere," but is immediately present in the body once the chain is complete. In this configuration, Dolmancé acts as the master syntactician of Sadean language. His philosophy does not transcend the material world, but anchors meaning in the enclosed presence of the bedroom.

The problem in Sade's libertine world, however, is that the utopian plenitude is never quite complete, is never fully realized. There remain throughout traces of a lack, of a dissatisfaction, of a gap that calls to be filled. This is not just the gap implied by Sade's own narration, which becomes unavoidably referential as it points us to a bedroom which is not present around us. It also mars the closures within and constituting the libertine sanctuary. The perpetual motion machine requires the elimination of entropy; however, no single assemblage of bodies is capable of meeting this condition. There is always a loose "end," a body that is disseminating pleasure without recuperating it. . . .

The constant gap prompts the entrance of the characters, each of whom is summoned in an attempt to close the circle. Such a circle, however, would be an ultimate, unsurpassable limit, and it is clear that Dolmancé is not drawn to such a barrier. Restrictions are valuable only to the extent that they are not absolute. . . . Resistance, as that which defines a physical (or here: sexual) object, is clearly desirable: the tightness of Eugénie's virgin orifices heightens her pleasure (and that of her partners) as she is "perforated" by the progressively larger members of Dolmancé, the Chevalier, and Augustin. However, total resistance would destroy pleasure, as "penetration" and "perforation" would no longer be possible. Total closure could only be understood as death.

This becomes apparent at the story's climax, when the libertine sanctuary suffers an intrusion, and one which attempts to reassert conventional representation. When Mme de Mistival enters the scene and orders Eugénie to obey her, she invokes her legal and moral rights as a parent. Nowhere is the emptiness of conventional language more evident, for the power implied by these rights resides, unfortunately, *elsewhere,* and once in the bedroom, Mme de Mistival exists only as a body at the mercy of a more immediate authority. Originally condemned to death by her daughter and the other libertines, Mme de Mistival would appear destined to serve as the example of Dolmancé's and Sade's ideal of total closure, occurring appropriately at the close of the novel. Yet this first sentence is not carried out. Instead, Dolmancé has his valet, Lapierre, inject Mme de Mistival with his diseased semen, and the contaminated openings are sewn shut to prevent evaporation. Furthermore, her lips are sealed in effect by the letter of authorization issued by her libertine husband.

In spite of this grotesque suturing job, the rape of Mme de Mistival constitutes another kind of "leakage." Injected with a libertine pox, she is sent back out into society, the very incarnation of the libertine contaminant that is leaking into and corrupting the social body. Paradoxically, it is a contagion that, by infecting society, purifies the libertine practice, just as Lapierre is to be cured by infusing his illness into such a healthy specimen. . . . This improbable cure could only be realized by relativizing the standards for measuring health and illness: in an infected society, Lapierre would figure as normal, and libertinism would be the law of the land.

It is precisely the fear of this kind of leakage, and of the subsequent contamination, that dictated the constant repression of Sade and his work. For Sade undermined the presuppositions and underlying categories of classical thought, and as Robert Darnton has illustrated, this challenging of the limits that constitute meaning is an exceptionally dangerous practice—especially in a society that had so successfully protected the way it organized the world by reducing its challengers to silence. Most of the undesirables of the Classical age were easily and effectively repressed because they failed to appropriate the discourse of the society that had excluded them; they led separate existences in asylums and prisons. Excluded, Sade nevertheless maintained his voice in society, attacking it from within, and perverting the morality of the society that had produced him. However, far more unsettling than the threat of a leakage of Sadean *morality* was the possibility of such a leakage into the realm of politics or ideology. In *La Philosophie dans le boudoir* this was a very real consideration, for in fact, Mme de Mistival is not the only object to escape from the confines of the boudoir. There is also the novelistic account, the book, *La Philosophie dans le boudoir,* which is itself injected with a venom, that of its political tract.

"Français, encore un effort si vous voulez être républicains" is atypical of Sade's libertine treatises in that it addresses the general public rather than the secret community of libertines. Unlike the code of rules drawn up in *Les 120 journées de Sodome,* which operated as a social pact within the libertine community, "Français, encore un effort . . ." calls for anarchy in the fullest sense of the term. Sade is writing against the grain of the original social pact, the *contrat social,* which was Rousseau's device for guaranteeing order in society. For Rousseau, each individual surrendered his own sovereignty only to the extent that he gained sovereignty over his fellow man, thus establishing a kind of balance and interdependence among men. Sade's pamphlet urges a return to a state of nature preceding any such pact, one that distributes power not according to any "divine right" (the nominal justification of the *ancien régime*) or even according to organized democracy (the theoretical goal of the Revolutionary forces); instead, Sade's utopia is governed by what he sees as the law of nature, which is to say no law at all. Might makes right. According to "Français encore un effort" such might could never be institutionalized in the form of any kind of régime: instead, power is decentralized and would change hands often, with each successful challenge mounted against it. It is the antithesis of society as both the ancien régime and the *philosophes* had conceived of it, devoid of ethical considerations. Thus the subjugation of women, which Sade describes as part of this utopia, arises less from any moral stance than from the premise of superior masculine strength. Advocating the abolition of law (after all, the author argues, murder helps to check overpopulation and theft helps to redistribute wealth) and the dissolution of social bonds (for marriage can be seen to constitute an immoral act of "possession"), the tract follows the example of Lapierre's pox, threatening to circulate within and corrupt the body politic. This is not just a threat to the ideology of the ancien régime, or to those of the Revolution or the Empire, but to the very notion of ideology in general.

Fredric Jameson, in *The Political Unconscious,* has characterized ideology as an essentially closed system. A strategy of containment, it tries to impose itself as right, moral, healthy, and authoritative, and any politics of leakage or contamination must be viewed as dangerously subversive. Sade is doubly so, for beyond denouncing a particular form of repression, he resists all attempts at containment. His strategy is very nearly counter-ideological, for the theories expounded in "Français, encore un effort . . . " undermine the current dominant culture, and they aim to undercut the very possibility of ideological hegemony. For ideology is an irreducibly social construct, and Sade's political pamphlet pushes for a dissolution of the codes and bonds that constitute the social body, leading to the return to "nature." Herein lies Sade's threat to society, more radical than anything envisioned by the *philosophes.* Clearly no régime could tolerate such an unpalatable program unless it could neutralize it by containment or exclusion, and as *La Philosophie dans le boudoir* so admirably illustrates, Sade always struggled to prevent this neutralization.

This simultaneous obsession with and subversion of closure was to mark the battles Sade waged against even those forces that supersede ideological repression and physical confinement: most notably, the absolute closure of death. Popular memory, largely inspired by Man Ray's famous portrait of the marquis, would have Sade embrace the silence of the tomb. The legend placed at the bottom of this painting, borrowed from Sade's last will and testament, reads: "afin que les traces de ma tombe disparaissent de dessus de la surface de la terre, comme je me flatte que ma mémoire s'effacera de l'esprit des hommes. . . ." But the line ends with an ellipsis; even Man Ray's quotation of this supposed embrace of closure is not closed. Predictably, Sade had appended an exclusion: no trace should subsist in the minds of men: "excepté néanmoins," he continued, "du petit nombre de ceux qui ont bien voulu m'aimer jusqu'au dernier moment et dont j'emporte un bien doux souvenir au tombeau." Of course, the trace that remains is Sade's writing, texts like *La Philosophie dans le boudoir,* which were to continue to circulate and infect. In the end, it was this intractable politics of contamination that predicated his repression by all sectors. Ironically, if only Sade's orgies, philosophy, and political epidemic had been successfully and hermetically sealed in the Bastille, in the grave, or in the bedroom, they would have remained entirely harmless.

Frances Ferguson   (essay date 1991)

SOURCE: "Sade and the Pornographic Legacy," in *Representations,* No. 36, Fall, 1991, pp. 1-21.

[*In this excerpt, Ferguson discusses* Philosophy in the Bedroom *as an "antimetaphysical" and "anticultural" political dialogue and relates elements of the text to French policy regarding the national debt.*]

In the discussion that follows, I shall be, essentially, taking up various aspects of the view that Sade attempts in *Philosophy in the Bedroom* to write a political dialogue that

would be as material—as physical and as unmetaphysical—as possible. In that sense, understanding pornography as a genre with specific claims embedded in its medium seems important. For pornography's medium—or its heuristic medium—would avoid representational metaphysics; it would write in bodies (as in the passage at the beginning of the *Philosophy* in which Madame de Saint-Ange offers herself up as an instructional aid, the living embodiment of an anatomy chart).

In addition to arguing that Sade's interest in the pornographic is generally antimetaphysical, however, I shall also be claiming that Sade's *Philosophy in the Bedroom* is specifically anticultural. Culture, coming in the *Philosophy* to represent the transmissibility of civil society from one generation to another, that is, comes to amount to a notion of intergenerational inheritance that emerges specifically in the context of the French politics of the national debt. The legacy of the French Revolution, in the terms of Sade's *Philosophy,* is at least as much a dissemination of indebtedness as of entitlement, as individuals come to secure equal rights by means of a national process of buying out individual inheritances (church lands as well as the public offices that had, by virtue of being bought and sold and by virtue of being treated as heritable, been converted into property) with public funds. The attempt to maximize intragenerational equality, that is, becomes the vehicle for promoting intergenerational inequality, for inaugurating the national debt as the emblem of the modern state as illimitable shared responsibilities.

Recently Sadean pornography has been of interest to historians of the French Revolutionary period . . . because it participates in the eighteenth century's discovery that politics could be waged by sexual means. Sexuality, in this view, is less physical than symbolic. Pornographic pamphlets and cartoons, particularly those directed against the royal family, made private sexual acts look like public crimes. If their sexuality made Louis XVI and Marie Antoinette look human rather than divine, Louis's rumored sexual impotence and Marie Antoinette's supposed incest with the Dauphin made them look less than human, as if sexual abnormality clearly vitiated any claims to legitimate inheritance of sovereign power. Pornography, on this account, collapses the king's two bodies into one, exposing the noncorporeal body as a sham and indicting the royal family of libertinage; their sexual excesses assimilated themselves to the same pattern of pretension that had enabled the king to claim two bodies instead of the one that is standard issue for the rest of mankind.

Within the context of the growing political exploitation of pornography during the last years of the *ancien régime,* that is, it makes sense for Sade to have been incarcerated for libertinage. Thus, for historians uncovering the politics of pornography, Sade's protest in his famous letter of 20 February 1781 appears more than a little disingenuous:

> Yes, I admit I am a libertine and in that area I
> have imagined everything that can be imagined.
> But I have absolutely not acted out everything
> that I imagined nor do I intend to. I am a libertine, but I am not a criminal or a murderer.

If the logic of political pornography of the period is to annihilate the royalist claim to a nonphysical body, the politics of pornography makes libertinage itself a crime. Yet the analogy between political liberty and sexual liberty does not completely explain Sade's versatility as an equal-opportunity offender and his remarkable ability to return to prison under the old regime and the new, under the monarchy, the Republic, the Consulate, and the Empire. If the crime of the pornographer against the monarchy is to decry the royal presumption to a metaphysical body, his crime against the Republic is the charge that it has consistently attacked the wrong target. Where the Republic has attacked bodies that seem associated with the illusions of religion, monarchy, and feudal property rights, Sade suggests an implicit conservatism even in this approach. The gothic illusions that had accompanied various physical entities, that is, may attach to the progressive as well as to the royalist position.

Sade's dogged materialism, his dispatching of spirit and presenting nature as merely matter in motion without recourse to any metaphysical external cause, suggests the difficulty of assimilating him to a particular progressive or regressive politics. In the twentieth century the rediscovery of Sade has involved a second position—an enthusiasm for the sexuality of his texts that examines the aesthetics of a writing that eschews what I am calling metaphysics by appeal to individual privacy. Blanchot's account [in *Lautréamont et Sade,* 1949] of the inevitable egoism of sexual experience can thus be read as an insistence upon Sade's pornography as establishing an ineradicable domain of solitude. However much the modern democratic state may nationalize and publicize, Sadean pornography announces the limits of the public arena. However much sexual pleasure in Sade relies upon the presence of others, it nonetheless remains, for Blanchot, supremely private. Sexual pleasure comes to be the epitome of the bodily sensation as absolutely ungeneralizable (nontranscendental) experience.

Indeed, as Bataille builds upon Blanchot's reading of Sade [in *Erotisue; Death and Sensuality,* 1986, and *Literature and Evil,* 1990] the notion of sexual pleasure as a version of contact without communication becomes increasingly clear. Those characters whom Bataille titles "sovereign beings" demonstrate not merely that one person's sexual pleasure does not operate to disseminate sexual pleasure to his/her partner(s); they also indicate the ways in which sexuality continually reinaugurates societal inequality. The sovereign being, that is, happily produces the pain of his/her partner for the sake of his own pleasure. As the most private of all private experience, sexual pleasure makes tyrants of us all, because it constitutes an assertion that one's pleasure does not rest on a transmission of pleasure (a solicitious regard for one's partner[s] as expressed in the question "Was it good for you?"). From an entirely non-Bataillean perspective, pornography might register a kind of equality by undressing people and making bodies rather than clothing or any external ornament the focus of attention. From a Bataillean perspective, pornography does not stress equality by dwelling on the fact that all persons, whatever else they may have, have bodies. Instead, it insists that inequality begins with the body, as the pain or discomfort of the "superior individual's" sexual partner

comes to look like an essential rather than an accidental part of that pleasure. As Bataille puts it in *Erotism:*

> The kind of sexuality he [Sade] has in mind runs counter to the desires of other people . . . ; they are to be victims, not partners. De Sade makes his heroes uniquely self-centred; the partners are denied any rights at all: this is the key to his system. . . . Communion between the participants is a limiting factor and it must be ruptured before the true violent nature of eroticism can be seen, whose translation into practice corresponds with the notion of the sovereign man. The man subject to no restraints of any kind falls on his victims with the devouring fury of a vicious hound.

As Bataille elaborates the argument, Sadean pornography not only reveals the fundamental equivalence of sexuality and violence; it also comes to represent an inequality absolutely fundamental to even the apparently egalitarian republican state. Thus, even though Bataille sees Sade as, in part, having "sided with the Revolution and criticised the monarchy," he also sees Sadean pornography as providing a consolation for the loss of that monarchy. Sadean pornography becomes the aesthetic replacement for monarchical glory. Indeed, Bataille continues this line of argument by affirming that Sade "exploited the infinite possibilities of literature and propounded to his readers the concept of a sovereign type of humanity whose privileges would not have to be agreed upon by the masses"—and which, for Bataille, is important precisely because they could not be agreed upon by even two persons, much less the masses.

The place of pornography becomes abundantly if ambivalently clear. Pornography, as the absolute opposite to even vestigial notions of contract that control many nineteenth-century accounts of aesthetic experience, registers the possibility of material affect. It alters the terms of exchange for the contract of pleasure, insisting that it was never designed to create equality or equilibrium but rather to identify inequality, violence, and sexuality. Sexuality for Sade merely is the inherent motion of matter, with that motion being so much a property or attribute as to render any external motive or spirit conspicuously redundant. And as such motion, it is as inimical to equality as it is indifferent to a divinity.

All acts of heterosexual intercourse thus look as inequitable as Catherine MacKinnon and Andrea Dworkin have claimed that they are. Bataille had made the egoism of sexuality appear an invalidation of the social contract as such—until, of course, the symbolic significance of the sovereign individual came to function as a collective social myth that did not so much challenge society as sustain it. The "infinite possibilities of literature," that is, resurrect the religious, royalist, and feudal standards that the egoistic sexual self would seem to have renounced. Pornography writes the story of sexuality as inequality, an inequality that is intrinsic to every sexual act involving more than one person. . . .

But if the means of reproduction themselves carry the taint of inequality, that end—the continued generation of persons—constitutes for Sade an even more massive inequality, one in which we recruit the unconsenting for society and continually announce the simultaneous hold of the social contract on persons who succeed one another. Writing an educational treatise that would conform to our own current accounts of sexual harassment, Sade presents *Philosophy in the Bedroom* as if the inequality of sexual acts were an inequality so mild as to constitute a veritable antidote to the inequality of human succession.

What is pornographic about Sadean pornography is not, or not merely, that it establishes the limits to communication in language or the limits to equality in sexuality. It is, rather, that pornography would, with the privacy and self-shattering self-interest of sexuality, undo a metaphysics that is always extending matter in time and space to create causes and histories as if matter could not, did not, take care of itself.

This antimetaphysical position emerges, most conspicuously, in the pamphlet, *Yet Another Effort Frenchmen, If You Would Be Republicans,* that Sade encapsulates in the *Philosophy.* In the latter half of the *Philosophy,* Dolmancé, the arch libertine, introduces the pamphlet that he has supposedly bought just that morning outside the Palace of Equality and offers it to the group. It ought, "if one can believe the title," to provide an answer to the question Eugénie, the initiate, has been invited to ask—"Whether manners are truly necessary in a governed society, whether their influence has any weight with the national genius." What is, in other words, the place of custom in civil society?

This pamphlet makes its appearance *ex machina.* As if it were an antitype to the objects in *Robinson Crusoe* that exist almost as pretexts for anticipation and regret, for budgeting and recalculation, the pamphlet appears on the scene to make the very existence of objects identical to their immediate use. If Defoe sets Crusoe to an endless process of taking inventory, the pamphlet's sudden appearance, by contrast, indicates a peculiar fact about the Sadean scene: for all that one knows it to be a world of privilege with recognizable class configurations—which make Madame de Saint-Ange and her gardener Augustin equals only for the space of the sexual contract that they continually negotiate in their contact—there is no excess. The *Philosophy,* that is, presents a remarkably uncluttered and indeed Spartan decor. While the interior spaces may emblematize as relentless an enclosure as Barthes has said they do, they involve no housekeeping. Indeed, part of the point of the enclosed spaces is to keep people from imagining the transportation of objects across the boundaries of the particular rooms they occupy. Likewise, the characters, remarkably undecorated and oblivious to fashion, do not acquire or accumulate, do not dress for success or pack for tomorrow.

To frame the matter differently, as the pamphlet suddenly materializes almost out of thin air we see yet another manifestation of Sade's commitment to tracking metaphysics to its physical bases. For a pamphlet, a whip, or a dildo to emerge as always ready to hand but never in the way, as there when you want it and never needing to be fumbled with or searched for, is for material objects to have lost that annoying character of temporal duration that continually harnesses them to the most metaphysical lines of argument.

Sadean pornography, that is, does not consist (or does not merely consist) in treating persons as thought they were things, mere objects to be subordinated by the Sadean "sovereign individuals," in Bataille's phrase. Rather, it involves treating persons as though they were things—and as though things were especially volatile entities, the materialism of a relentlessly idealist world in which things ceased to exist when people left the room. Rousseau had written in the *Emile* of the importance of objects in educating a child, because objects do not respond to the child's will, do not accommodate or yield to the child's demands. Sade depicts this situation in reverse—objects come only when they are called, like the pamphlet that appears only when a question has been asked. An object of infinite politeness, the pamphlet speaks only when spoken to.

Thus, even though the pamphlet never becomes equal to its audience in the sense of their being similar kinds of things, things that might be mistaken for one another, it epitomizes Sade's thinking about equality in two ways—as statement and as example. As statement, it rehearses the arguments of Sadean equality (one owes nothing to one's parents because they invested no labor in one's production; a woman's husband has no property right in her not because a woman has, like any other individual, inalienable property rights in herself, but because every man has a property right in her; and so on). The equalities that it states, that is, are both temporary and limited. As example, it is similarly temporary and limited. It appears, is read, is approved, and disappears. While it represents positions so compatible with Dolmancé's that it could have been written by him, it is a pamphlet of anonymous authorship. The parallels with Sade's refusal to attach his name to various works (including the *Philosophy,* which appeared in 1795 as "a posthumous work" by the also anonymous author of *Justine*) may make this look merely circumstantial, or like a clever joke on the political and judicial climate in which Sade wrote. Anonymous authorship was, after all, a gesture toward avoiding the blame for writing that kept accruing to Sade's account and kept him in one prison or another for twenty-seven years. It was, also and more importantly, a strategy for avoiding the patronymic, the passing on of the name as if identity, either for human or literary progeny, could be transmitted.

This is to say that the *Philosophy* continually elaborates the difficulties of living in the material world as a problem of inheritance. Edmund Burke had written in his *Reflections on the Revolution in France* of 1790 that we wish to derive everything as an inheritance from our ancestors, and the French Revolutionaries had conceived the state as salvageable if one could, among other things, reconfigure property relations. For Sade, heritability was a rather more basic issue, involving as it did for him a challenge to both the duty-based and the rights-based versions of the social contract. For if the Burkean account clearly converted custom into an emanation of nature on the basis of the inevitable connectedness of generations, the revolutionary account was unsatisfactory because it represented too slight an adjustment to the relation between law and custom. Eugénie's question, that is, was an infinitely more serious one than either the antirevolutionaries or the revolutionaries were prepared to admit: "Je voudrais savoir si les moeurs sont vraiment nécessaires dans un gouvernement, si leur influence est de quelque poids sur le génie d'une nation" (in the lame translation of the Grove Press edition, "I should like to know whether manners are truly necessary in a governed society . . ."). She does not ask if laws are necessary to a law-governed society.

As the *Philosophy* proceeds to address the question, it comes to appear in a still more radical form—Are customs themselves supportable in a law-governed society? Or, isn't it the whole function of law to replace custom? Sade's pamphlet's call for a "few laws" that should be "good ones" may, in its insistent vagueness, be directed against the revolutionaries' efforts to coordinate the variety of laws governing marriage, divorce, children, and inheritance into a single unified system for the nation. But instead of making the Burkean argument for custom as the expression of nature, Sade makes custom itself the antagonist of nature, on the basis of an attack on the family as itself unnatural, as the point at which nature ceases being nature and becomes instead customary.

Just as objects become metaphysical in the process of becoming property, so laws become metaphysical in the process of becoming custom. Custom, in short, is the name of an overextended law. In its Burkean form, custom treats nature as if it were civil society, as if the existence of land could come to count as an argument for the existence of persons whose merely nominal connection to landed property gave them authority less because of their being persons than because of their being emanations of the land. Custom represents the ghostly version of nature, the point at which the entire interest of nature for Sade— its physicality—gets lost.

In the wake of the Revolution, the system of feudal rights and duties had been abolished. The Revolution, on this evidence, looked like the end to feudalism that Georges Lefebvre's modernization hypothesis has maintained that it was: the Revolution was effect in part as an acknowledgment of the rising middle class in its attack on inherited claims to offices and property rights. It curtailed obligations to the feudal lord as a landed, human version of religious illusion.

Yet the aspect of the Revolution that many recent historians have explored—its attempt to formulate and promulgate a new symbolic culture—must have looked to Sade like a peculiarly self-vitiating gesture. From Sade's standpoint, the problem with feudalism was not the systematic inequity of its operation or its favoritism for the nobility. It was, in the end, that it read one physical entity, land existing in nature, as if its connection to persons could be sustained in their absence, and another physical entity, a person, as if its connection to other persons could have similar metaphysical persistence. Society remains feudal, for Sade, so long as its notions of property and the family cede duration and extension to persons.

This is as much as to say that for Sade the project of the *Philosophy* is essentially rather than accidentally pornographic.

If Andrea Dworkin emphasizes pornography as "writing on the bodies of whores," Sade's bedroom more and less explicitly repudiates nonpornographic, symbolic writing that can operate by incorporeal means. The message of antifeudalism, then, is not (or not merely) that the ancient aristocracy and the old system of land tenure was unjust. It is, on Sade's account, that any nonpornographic society is illusory and injust. A nonpornographic society, in short, continually emphasizes custom as a storage system that eviscerates the very bodies that seemed to be its basis. Even as the republican constitution extended the vote to "over half the adult male population; or to more than two-thirds of those over the required age of twenty-five, it enabled those voters to vote only for electors whose eligibility for office depended upon their being a version of self-storage. For the electors were not merely to have the means to supply their needs; they were defined as those whose property specifically constituted an accumulation of labor. In cities of more than 6,000 inhabitants, one could qualify as an elector by owning "real property assessed on the tax rolls at an annual income value equivalent to 200 days' unskilled labor," or by leasing "a dwelling worth an annual income value (or rental) of 150 days' labor." In smaller cities and towns the amount of stored labor that was required was less, but the same principle obtained. If the feudal lord was no longer able to treat a laboring peasant as his accumulated savings, the Revolution produced governmental equality by making property holding the freedom that was based directly on one's own industry. This reallocation of governmental access limited the heritability of property in office. It did so, however, by substituting a metaphysical and unavailable self for a physical self; in basing political privilege less on use than on the ability to forestall need, it also established the individual as his own potential heir. Property bespoke freedom, that is, precisely by denying the freedom to use.

Although the reform of the criminal code had taken precedence over that of the civil code, the outline of the civil code was perceptible from a very early stage of the Convention's discussion. "Three things are necessary and sufficient to man in society: to be master of his person; to have the means to satisfy his needs; to be able to dispose, in his own best interest, of his person and his goods. All civil rights resolve themselves thus to those of liberty, property, and contract." As the Assembly's legislation circumscribed paternal prerogatives and provided for the equal division of estates among heirs, it substantiated those principles in the name of equality. The fraternity of the Revolution was the equality of brothers, specifically conceived as an equality that neither paternal authority nor birth order should constrain. By the custom of united succession, equal shares in the real property of a deceased had been consolidated in one heir, the eldest son in France succeeding to the burgesses' tenements (just as the youngest son in England succeeded to tenancy). Thus, primogeniture reproduced within generations the very inequality that paternal authority had produced between them.

In the revolutionary period, and . . . even more importantly in the prerevolutionary period, the attack on property involved in part an attack on the gross imbalances in the distribution of property and prosperity. It was an imbalance most strikingly apparent when the peasantry found itself with an increased tax burden in the 1780s (as the government tried to fund its payments on the debt it had assumed to support, among other things, its participation in the American Revolution) and when that increased tax burden coincided with "poor to catastrophic" harvests "almost everywhere" in 1788. For even though the nobility had felt tax increases very keenly (as the capitation, the "head tax," fell upon everyone with a body), it had also been able to pass along even the burden of that tax by raising agricultural rents. The most basic right that the Convention registered—a citizen's right to have the means to satisfy his needs—was a strictly material right, the claim for a person as a body to maintain itself. From that physical right would seem to be derived the right to self-sovereignty, the right to be master of one's body. Had the body gained a self through use, through supplying its own needs, the physical economy would have been sustained. With the use of property to designate the self-sovereignty, however, the individual could only configure itself as anticipated need.

The reformulation of the person/property distinction in the prerevolutionary and revolutionary periods was, as has been frequently observed, a break with feudalism. And feudalism looked Gothic not merely because it represented an inheritance from the medieval period but because its systematic workings had converted property from a concrete to a conspicuously immaterial notion. In Doyle's words, "Long before the eighteenth century lordship and ownership had ceased to be synonymous." Feudalism had come to mean that a seigneur had rights that were only erratically related to his property rights. "It was rare to find a lord who did not own any of the land over which he exercised rights; but it was equally rare to find a lord who exercised rights only over his own land. Among the rights of lordship that would be challenged by the revolutionary reforms, none were more significant than the rights of access or use that enabled a lord to hunt and shoot; to establish monopolies in milling, baking, and wine pressing; and, most importantly, to levy dues (exact duties).

In its ability to call on the rights of use or access, lordship represented the social and economic form of the relationship to objects that I described earlier. For though it related to property, it had the peculiar advantage of enabling one to treat property as most perfectly one's own when one didn't own it—one didn't have to own it but could instead invoke a right to the duties of those who did. As the tax rates increased in the 1780s, they exposed the competition between rights of sovereignty and rights of ownership in a particularly graphic way. It was not merely that the nobility enjoyed exemptions from more taxes than the peasantry, or that they were taxed at a disproportionately low rate in relation to their abilities to pay. It was, more importantly, that the feudal duties made their taxes the peasant landowners' taxes. If the Lockean account of property distinguished property from nature on the basis of the investment of one's labor in it, seigneurial rights

constituted a heritable right to reward without labor. Sovereignty was, in short, the demand for the satisfaction of one's needs without any obligation to anticipate those needs. Rights of sovereignty converted other people into the functional equivalent of one's own forethought. While Crusoe must continually ration his property to himself, doling out portions that create immediate scarcity for the sake of his anticipated future needs, the feudal sovereign has a right in other people's property that is the material equivalent of anticipation. Other people and their labor become his savings account.

It is, then, as an attack on the metaphysics that underwrites both the landed and the laboring versions of inheritance that Sade stakes his argument for use. Rather than extending the rights to property and public office that had attached to the nobility, he would extend the only seigneurial right of any value—the right to access, to use. In the *Philosophy,* moreover, the right to sexual use contends directly with the family. The family and sexuality are sharply distinguished in Sade's bedroom, not merely because parental authority (and specifically paternal authority) operates as the same kind of metaphysical projection as religion and royalism. Rather, the family builds metaphysics into nature. Making generation look like a consequence—an inheritance—of sex, it makes sexuality look assimilable to heritability.

Generation, in short, continually operates less as an inconvenience or necessary risk that always attends properly pornographic sexuality than as an essential statement of injustice. This injustice does not, however, involve Sade's extreme sensitivity to what for Burke and even for Freud is a lamentable fact of human existence, that persons, being born of other persons, inevitably discern the limits of their own independence. Rather, generation, for Sade, becomes unjust at the moment at which one person's existence comes to seem the consequence of another person's intention.

As Dolmancé reads the rights of birth, they involve neither an inheritance of property nor an inheritance of property rights in children: "We owe nothing to our parents." Eugénie has suggested that the satisfaction of individual needs may yield to ties of affection . . . , and Dolmancé counters by supplanting the social contract with coition. "So long as the act of coition lasts, I may, to be sure, continue in need of that object, in order to participate in the act; but once it is over and I am satisfied, what, I wonder, will attach the results of this commerce to me?" Sexual partners "who, exclusively thoughtful of their own pleasure," begin to call themselves spouses or parents may be praised for having given one life or blamed for "having given us nothing but an unhappy and unhealthy existence." Parental authority converts mere temporal priority into a claim to property rights in an individual. Fear (in this case, fear on the part of parents) causes them to create themselves as (former) gods: "These latter relationships [of marriage and consanguinity] were the results of the terror of parents who dreaded lest they be abandoned in old age"; "The politic attentions they show us when we are in our infancy have no object but to make them deserving of the same consideration when they are become old. Parenthood, in sum, involves a contractual structure in which an accident (conception) is misrepresented as an intention, and inequality is insisted upon by the contract itself. The trade is always of one party's incapacity for the other's capacity, the weakness of the child or the aged for the strength of an able-bodied adult.

It is in the context of such a critique of implicit contract, the contract of custom, that one can understand the catalogue that Dolmancé and Madame de Saint-Ange compile of family relationships—a list of pretenders to other people's bodies. Women cannot be mothers, because "that which we women furnish has a merely elaborative function" and because "the child born of the father's blood owes filial tenderness to him alone" on account of the father's having been alone in desiring "our birth." Men, similarly, cannot be fathers, because conception operates by chance. Indeed, a man's inability to cause procreation at will becomes the basis for the impossibility of his denying his paternity to any child of a sexual partner. As Madame de Saint-Ange puts it to Eugénie, "Provided I sleep with my husband, provided his semen flows to the depths of my womb, should I see ten men at the same time I consort with him, nothing will ever be able to prove to him that the child I bear does not belong to him." If any claim to paternity is to be allowed, all possible attributions of paternity cease to be deniable. "Immediately it can be his, it is his." Although parental relationships continually invoke the language of intentional causes and obligated effects, the cause-and-effect relationship can only be achieved in the sexual exchange itself. Nature produces children by accident; sexual partners produce one another by use.

The sequence of disqualified relationships continually seems to award rights in a child more to fathers than to mothers, more to mothers than to fathers, more to children themselves—only to issue in the disqualification of all intergenerational and nonsimultaneous relationships as a basis for heritability. The family, as a unit spanning generations, ceases to exist—which means that the incest Sade proposes to counterbalance the family comes as an illusory remedy to an illusory wrong. On the one hand, biological connection looks impossible to establish, so that sexual acts that offend against biological connection look equally impossible to establish. On the other hand, Sade insists that both history and nature sanction incest. First, biblical history adduces the case of Adam as the most tightly wound case of incest imaginable, a version of partial onanism or sex with one's own body part. Second, nature not only tolerates the continued existence of an anonymous incestuous friend of Dolmancé's but enables him to produce sexual partners almost at will.

> One of my friends has the habit of living with the girl he had by his own mother; not a week ago he deflowered a thirteen-year-old boy, fruit of his commerce with this girl; in a few years' time, this same lad will wed his mother: such are my friend's wishes; he is readying for them all a destiny analogous to the projects he delights in and his intentions, I know very well, are yet to enjoy what this marriage will bring to bear.

Incest makes this genealogical tree (could one quite diagram it) not so much foreshortened as increasingly flat-

tened. The man sleeps with his mother to produce a daughter; the man sleeps with this daughter to produce a son; the man sleeps with this son—as if the point of sexuality were to erase cross-generational inequality. The man who sleeps with his son is, for the space of their intercourse, equal to his son, even though he is simultaneously father of his son and also grandfather of this same son on the maternal side. Dolmancé has rehearsed the most basic genetic argument for incest: the appeal of incest . . . lies in its approximation of equality: "If, in a word, love is born of resemblance, where may it be more perfect than between brother and sister, between father and daughter?" Resemblance as likeness approaches sameness or equivalence. Yet the movement from the *intra*generational pair—brother and sister—to the *inter*generational pair— father and daughter—progressively strains the notion of resemblance. The pleasures of "carnal connection with the family," in sum, do not so much rely upon the inherent appeal of resemblance as they create resemblance. Only, that is, in terms of the systemic equivalence of each of the individual elements in the sexual arrangements that Sade disposes does a woman resemble a man and a child resemble her parent.

Incest enables the lateralization of the vertical hierarchy produced by generation. If the Republic's abolition of the law of primogeniture made it possible for all heirs to succeed equally to an estate, incest makes it possible to end the tyranny of succession by identifying the benefactor with the beneficiary, the settler with the heir. The significance of incest in the **Philosophy,** then, is that it demonstrates exactly why the French need "yet another effort" to "become republicans." The Republic had attacked the notion of heritable office, but it had at the same time left the basic structure of heritability intact. Public office had been opened to ability rather than heritability as the republicans attempted to equalize the relationships between members of the same generation. Yet just as heritable property in office had been abolished with the one hand, heritability had been incalculably strengthened on the other. The state, in ending the venality of public offices (through which members of the bourgeoisie had entered the nobility at a profit to the royal treasury), had foreclosed a crucial source of income. The seizure of church lands and the issuing of *assignats* backed by that church land attempted to replace some of those funds. This was the financial situation that Burke was responding to when he saw the confiscation of church land and the paper money economy as creating an abstract and inflationary system that attempted an impossible break with the fact of human successive generation. For Sade the problem must have seemed both different and more severe. Even though France had supported an extremely high level of government borrowing for two decades, the venality—the vendibility—of public office had served in the first place to make public office holding the privilege of birth and to make wealth the privilege of manufacturing the privilege of birth. Public offices that were purchasable and, thus, heritable by virtue of not having been themselves inherited had, in addition to providing an (admittedly narrow) avenue for upward social mobility, tended to disguise the publicness, the omnipresence and nonexclusiveness, of the national debt. The debt, as something that the king could pay in part by minting new men in exchange for their money, looked like monarchical and ministerial debt. As the Republic abolished the sale of heritable office, however, it explicitly established the debt as national and secured the abolition of such heritable office by funding it through an announced nationalization of the debt. Heritable office was thus replaced by heritable debt, in the foundation of "a consolidated national debt, the *Grand Livre de la dette publique,*" in August of 1793.

More than one commentator has referred to national debts as inaugurating civil society generally, and many have traced to classical times the use of a national debt for funding such extraordinary expenses as wars. Yet however time-honored the basic structure of national indebtedness may be, for the France of the 1790s in which Sade wrote the **Philosophy in the Bedroom,** the explicit nationalization of the debt makes the state itself insist upon replacing heritable property with heritable debt. The national debt, that is, makes the state's power ineluctable. As intergenerational debt, it operates with a violence that is no less illimitable for being abstract. Against the Sadean account of sexual violence that enforces inequities and insists upon the right of men to compel women's submission "not exclusively . . . but temporarily," the nationalized debt becomes the sign of the inevitable inequality of the modern state, whose contract is most binding precisely on account of its applying only to those who could not, by definition, have had any part in its formulation.

In 1783 Sade had written angrily from prison objecting to the fact that his eldest son, Louis-Marie de Sade, had been named sub-lieutenant in the Rohan-Soubise Regiment. Instead of complaining that his son had not received a properly exalted position, Sade protested the appointment because his son was not a legacy. He, the marquis, had wanted Louis-Marie to serve in his old regiment and wear the same cavalry uniform he had worn. This rather extreme insistence on heritability—on intergenerational hand-me-downs—waned, however, in the 1790s. In 1792, another son, Donatien-Claude-Armand de Sade, aide-de-camp of the marquis de Toulongeon, deserted, and Sade legally disavowed his son's emigration. This gesture was, on some level, purely expedient. The Republic had decreed that parents were responsible for the actions of their children, and Sade had, as it were, to divorce himself from his son in order to escape legal liability for his son's actions. On the argument of the **Philosophy,** Sade's disavowal could not, however, have been purely expedient. For the **Philosophy** insists that intergenerational inheritance—whether forward, from fathers to sons, or backward, from sons to fathers—inaugurates political culture as the essentially metaphysical, the diametrical opposite to a pornography that knows how to keep its place.

Julie Candler Hayes   (essay date 1991)

SOURCE:"Sade," in *Identity and Ideology: Diderot, Sade, and the Serious Genre,* John Benjamins Publishing Company, 1991, pp. 105-30.

[*In the following excerpt, Hayes examines the role of con-flicting ideologies in Sade's plays and novels, concentrating in particular on his disruption of structure and meaning.*]

The plays have known a strange history, even among the many odd histories of Sade's texts. Refused by theater directors, hidden in libraries, walled up in a room of the Sade family château, censored even by the editor of Sade's complete works, the plays might be thought to contain a message as bitterly powerful as anything in the novels or in the drama they indirectly inspired, Peter Weiss's *Marat/Sade.* Great was the general disappointment when the eighteen sentimental pieces were published in 1970, and even the most positive accounts of them tended to skim over them in order to arrive at the "theatricality" of the more interesting novels.

Sade's editor, Gilbert Lely, had scant regard for the plays "écrites dans le genre larmoyant du plus mauvais Diderot. . . . " Posterity has persisted in regarding both Diderot and Sade as literary giants even as it turned away from their theater as something unsuited to the "modernity" of the other works and hence unworthy of attention. But there is nothing to be gained by such excision: to the contrary. If one cannot "recognize Sade" in his plays, then clearly there is more to be known about Sade than previously thought. Fortunately, several critics have recently taken another look at what [Chantal Thomas] has called the "excessive conformity" in Sade's plays, where the more disturbing elements of his major works appear not to be as alien as once thought.

The very conventionality of the plays is interesting. Public productions that they aspire to be, Sade's plays and related texts—prefaces, letters, commentary—represent some of his most self-conscious writing. Here he is constantly taking stock of himself as a dramatist, confronting his predecessors, comparing and defending his work against theirs. The plays are beset with an overwhelming alterity, haunted by the presence of other writers, imaginary audiences, both real and supposed critics; they bespeak a slavish devotion to theatrical conventions and norms. Tracing the references is complicated, however, because the supposedly objective prefaces and commentaries are as intricate as any product of Freudian dreamwork—the relationships Sade draws between his plays and those of his predecessors are subject to distortion, displacement, and outright denial.

It is useful to be aware of the circumstances of the plays' composition and their very real intertexts before examining the account which Sade himself gives of the process. Sade's material and imaginary literary relations help clarify his approach to the production of meaning in literature and in literary history.

Thorough examination of the plays and their prefaces firmly establishes Sade the dramatist in the company of the other sentimental playwrights as a demystifyer of the idea of individual identity. However, whereas Diderot in particular expresses the desirability of the self's integration into a harmonious system of relationships, Sade's work is wracked by a conflict between the dispersion of identity on the one hand and a tremendous will to selfhood (or originality, or Godhood) on the other. The conflict proceeds on several levels. Relationships within the dramas all bear an odd tendency toward a distortion of family relationships through incest and parricide; in the prefaces the plays themselves become elements in a similarly distorted system of relationships between Sade and the other writers whom he sees as his rivals. From one point of view, it is possible to say that, despite a superficial allegiance to certain conventions of the bourgeois theater, Sade's plays are profoundly disturbed by undercurrents which belie the surface ideology, resulting in a breakdown of the aesthetic and social structures upon which they are based. From another point of view, it might appear that Sade is simply pushing the limits of the eccentric logic that characterizes the genre in general. Similar patterns occur in Sade's critical reflections in his dramatic prefaces, in which his attempt at rewriting literary history and creating his niche in the hierarchy of the writers who have preceded him succeeds only in distorting all such relationships and repeating the disturbances present in the plays. The problem would repeat itself *ad infinitum* in the novels, where larger-than-life libertines pursue their rivalry with God through endless desire and endless frustration.

"CE SERAIT POUR MOI UN GRAND PLAISIR . . . DE VOIR JOUER MES OUVRAGES": PLAYS

Sade's dramatic activity spanned his life and cannot be discounted as an aberration of either youth or age. Some scholars have attempted to be rid of the problem posed by what they tend to see as the polarization of stances in such works as *Juliette* and *Oxtiern* by relegating the plays to the category of "merely public" productions meant to cover up the more "personal" clandestine—and hence more "authentic"—novels, stories, and dialogues. There are a number of things wrong with such a view, not the least of which is that it transposes a late twentieth-century appreciation of "public" and "personal" on works from a period which perceived those notions quite differently. It furthermore seems unwise to make claims for so rigid a binary opposition in a body of writing in which rigid values and absolute positions rarely survive.

Sade, it is true, fostered this separation to a certain extent with such letters as the one he wrote to the abbé Amblet in April 1784, touching on his dramatic ambitions:

> Ce serait pour moi un grand plaisir, sans doute, de voir jouer mes ouvrages à Paris, et si je parvenais à réussir, la réputation d'esprit que je me procurerais ferait peut-être oublier les travers de ma jeunesse et me réhabiliterait dans un sens. . . .

The problem, obviously, is that we know no more regarding which "side" was the more "authentic" one for Sade: were his "public" writings only a wash for his "*travers*" or conversely were his scandalous texts the result of a publisher's ploy? The issue of Sade's repeated denials of *Justine* is complex; violent denunciations of the novel appear even in the marquis's personal notebooks. In any case, the "public" writings (like *Aline et Valcour,* which Sade was not ashamed to send to Reinaud, or, for that matter, like the theater) also have their scandalous side, even if they lack the crudeness of expression of *Juliette.* Sade's scandalous side and Sade's bourgeois side are about as separate as *le côté de chez Swann* and *le côté de Guermantes,* and our interpretation of either "side" must change in light of this fact.

Not merely a cover for illicit literary activities, the plays betray a passion going beyond a love of respectability or admiration for Molière; the theater is an object of desire pursued as ardently by Sade as Justine is pursued by the denizens of an evil world.

Sade's plays situate themselves in a context of unfulfillment and desire for mastery. Sade would like to "find himself" as a dramatist, and to this end he trims, polishes, rewrites, and analyzes his plays over and over again. He attempts all genres and carefully notes the extent to which he has imitated others and the points at which his practice differs from dramatic norms. In the prefaces and correspondence one is reminded how important the notion of genre was to Sade, how conscious he was of other writers, rivals, and critics, and what difficulty he had in being original. "[J]e suis enfoncé dans mon cabinet au milieu de Molière, Destouches, Marivaux, Boissy, Regnard, que je regarde, considère, admire, et que je n'atteins jamais." Sade's place as a dramatist is thus already defined by others, contemporaries as well as predecessors, and he must either resign himself to imitating them or show that they were imperfect, so that he may improve on them, rid himself of them. Incest and parricide, two of the main structures for relationships in his erotic works, influence these intra-literary relationships as well.

Sade's theater is striking not only because of the energy that the would-be playwright put into it, but also from his methodical, even encyclopedic approach to genres and conventions. Sade tried his hand at everything: seven comedies, six dramas, one tragedy, one *scène lyrique,* and one vaudeville. To this one must add *La Ruse de l'amour,* which is itself an anthology of different genres: a high comedy or "pièce de caractère," a tragedy, a *drame anglais,* an *opéracomique,* a *comédie-féerie,* and a concluding *ballet-pantomime.*

As for the genre which influenced Sade the most, his approach can be seen in many respects as a subversion of bourgeois drama. It seems clear from a look at those plays which Sade himself classed as dramas that what counted in his eyes were either the trappings of the so-called *drame anglais*—murders, imprisonments, poison, and even ghosts—or the titillating family entanglements of the French *genre sérieux.* Insofar as the significance of the *drame* for such theoreticians as Diderot, Beaumarchais, and Mercier lay in its depiction of relationships and its evocation of the profoundly harmonious interaction of the social order, Sade's theater must be seen as something rather different. Just as his *comédie de caractère* reveals a vortex of irrationality as its "character," so Sade's bourgeois drama reflects anything but a harmonious social order. Relationships are confused, blurred, and distorted; family ties are threatened on the one hand with undercurrents of incest and on the other with suggestions of parricide. On the other hand, the plays' attempt to negate or subvert relationships is in a sense itself subverted by their obsessive return to relationships as the basis of the drama.

Furthermore, insofar as the genre's aesthetic is one of movement, dispersion, and the breaking of barriers, Sade can be seen as having had a profond intuition of its "equivocations."

In Sade, whether in the letters, critical prefaces, plays, dialogues, or novels, no one is free from the *système de rapports* defining every member of any group. This scheme of things, which operates so smoothly in the works of earlier writers, here undergoes a crucial modification. The Durvals and the Dorvals of La Chaussée and Diderot knew their moments of renunciation and solitude, but always came to realize the importance and intrinsic worth of an eventual integration in the social group. Sade's characters and even Sade himself, as the protagonist of the letters, prefaces, and notebooks, all find themselves in an unresolvable conflict with the system. Harmoniously related members of familial systems no longer, Sade's characters are trapped by conventions and clichés which distort the most basic relationships. Distancing and clarification of *rapports,* however needed, never occur. Instead, relationships blur and become uncomfortably close: lovers discover that they are brother and sister and then that they are not; parents forget who their children are and either fall in love with them or try to destroy them. Individual identity is sought in vain, lost in the confusion, as is that rational ideal, the family structure.

Order here is finally a matter of dramatic and generic convention and does not stem from any internal coherency. Diderot's exteriorizing social fable here operates on another level. These plays bespeak an attempt to produce autonomous works of art that results in a blind adherence to established theatrical traditions and clichés, a desire to write that is subsumed in the desire to be seen as a writer. Despite years of strenuous efforts and countless letters to theater directors, Sade never succeeded in realizing this particular fantasy. Their moralizing denouements notwithstanding, his plays were routinely rejected for lack of *bienséance.* Whether censored by public officials or repressed by a personal aesthetic, the disturbances responsible for the power of Sade's best-known writing here, too, begin to weaken the structures of thought and morality.

Sade's dramas are all to some extent family dramas, and all are to a greater or lesser extent based on delusions and distortions of the basic family relationships. These disturbances occur most notably in the *rapports* binding character to character and play to genre. Such confusion and ambiguity are already manifest in the early sketch *Le Mariage du siècle.* Showing the ruin of a family through the imprudent marriage of a daughter, the sketch is clearly in the lineage of the *drame anglais:* stabbings and murders follow constantly upon one another, the imprisoned heroine dies of poison, and the hero, fatally enamored of an unscrupulous courtesan (reminiscent of Millwood in Lillo's *The London Merchant*), eventually commits suicide in order to escape *Macbeth*-like ghosts from his past. Apart from the gothic decor, very little in the play makes sense; few motives are given for the bizarre actions of the characters, and the roles and attitudes of the minor characters are left in a haze. More important, apparently, were the requisite "English" elements, the gloom, the ghosts, the poison. Relationships are emphasized as required by the plot; but a brother can disappear altogether and a father be imprisoned and die (seemingly the consequence of his daughter's imprudence) without either creating much stir. *L'Egarement de l'infortune* similarly distorts family relationships. Derval, driven to desperation by poverty, robs an old man and is sentenced to death for his crime, only to be belatedly recognized as the son of his victim (they have been separated only two years) as he awaits execution. The same insight reveals the villain of the piece, a young libertine bent on persecuting Derval and seducing his wife, to be none other than Derval's brother.

Generally, the instability of relationships takes two forms in Sade's plays. In *Oxtiern, Jeanne Laisné, L'Egarement de l'infortune, Le Mariage du siècle,* and *Le Prévaricateur* the relationships among family members are marked by an often murderous strife. In *Le Prévaricateur* and *Franchise et trahison* even the absence of the father causes endless difficulties for the children. *Henriette et Saint-Clair* and *Le Misanthrope par amour,* on the other hand, bring sister and brother, father and daughter, dangerously close and blur family ties with the suggestion of incest. In all cases, the question of parenthood is crucial, just as the suppression of parental and filial ties is deadly.

Preoccupation with the father's role and rebellion against his authority are common enough themes in the serious genre and form part of the natural order of things in Diderot's work, particularly in *Le Père de famille.* That play and *Le Fils naturel* furnish images of disorder erupting in the absence of the father, whose eventual return coincides with the reestablishment of the social and familial order. In Sade, the fathers are disguised and their identities unknown, yet the conflict between the generations continues unabated and with unwonted violence, as in Derval's attack on Merville in *L'Egarement* and the Colonel's duel with his daughter in *Oxtiern.* (We should note that in the short story version in *Les Crimes de l'amour,* he kills her.) The Colonel's mistake echoes that of Tancred, who murders his lover, Clorinda, when Sade attempts a *scène lyrique.* The father dies as a result of his daughter's ill-advised marriage in *Le Mariage du siècle,* as we have seen. All the plays in *La Ruse de l'amour* are concerned with "les malheurs menaçant un père qui sacrifie sa fille à son ambition," and one of them, *Cléontine* (later expanded into *Fanni ou les effets du désespoir*) is a full-fledged *drame anglais,* replete with prison, madness, poison, and suicide. There, the father tries to force his daughter to marry a man who is almost a carbon copy of himself. The treacherous father of *Euphémie de Melun* takes arms against his homeland, only to find his daughter in the opposing army (the Tancred-*Oxtiern* scenario again). Euphémie, it might be noted, loves only her cousin, a childhood companion she calls her "frère d'armes." The *Suborneur* presents a father and daughter nearly brought to ruin through failure to communicate and an overwillingness to heed the lies of a false friend, a situation that recurs in *Franchise et trahison,* which recounts the perils faced by a mother and her daughter during the absence and presumed death of the father, as they attempt to unravel the web of lies spun by the father's usurper. In the historical tragedy *Jeanne Laisné,* the daughter fights to save the city that her father has betrayed. In *Le Prévaricateur,* a saintly father is refused alms by his evil, ungrateful son.

All the plays end with suitably virtuous regrets, repentances, and, whenever possible, reparations, but something still seems amiss. Ideal fatherhood, like ideal truth and justice in *Tartuffe,* has been missing from the action too long to be extremely convincing when all relationships are hastily reestablished in the denouement. One feels there to be something hollow and unfortunate in so many fortuitous triumphs of virtue and order, when all before has been unmotivated confusion. This is perhaps the reason so many theater directors found the plays wanting in *bienséance.* Unlike the Diderot's plays, in which the ideal of a social order is never really lost from view, and despite an equally great obsession with *rapports,* Sade's plays succeed through inconsistencies and trivialized morality in weakening the *rapports* rather than in upholding them. The relationships are no less important for the violence inflicted on them, as we shall see.

Their importance is particularly evident in those plays where love does as much violence to the *système de rapports* as does strife, where incest spreads the same disorder as hate. Already in *Le Fils naturel,* incest functions as the physical correlative of Dorval's antisocial tendencies, the bodily substratum of his broken promises. Much has been written on Sade's fascination with incest and its possibilities as a privileged instrument for perforating the social order. Society depends on exogamy, the possibility of relationships based on a free exchange between groups whose members, particularly women, are defined by their role in the system of exchange. By reducing the importance of the individual, exchange strengthens the importance of the hierarchical group. Incest constitutes on the one hand the ultimate refusal of the system, since when incestuous couples renounce the society of others and bask instead in the narcissistic glow of a mirror image, the social structure begins to fall apart. At the same time, insofar as incest is appreciated for its value as transgression, it presupposes and upholds the system, since the crime can have no meaning if the structure is not respected.

Le Misanthrope par amour flirts with incest and although it eventually upholds the rules of *bienséance* it ironically does so only to the detriment of the social order. The hero Desfrancs has fallen in love with his ward Sophie, whom he alone knows to be his own daughter. The guilt he suffers from this shameful sentiment has made him a recluse; throughout the play his main occupation is attempting to marry her off to his old friend Anselme. She has known Anselme all her life, but feels for him only a sort of *amour-estime*—filial feelings, of a sort. She is considerably more smitten with her guardian. She resists marriage with an "outsider" as hotly as Eugénie de Franval, the heroine of Sade's incest parable in *Les Crimes de l'amour.* . . . As for Desfrancs, his "misanthropy" ill conceals feelings of guilt and dissatisfaction. The *système* he refuses to accept and the *raison* by which he will not be duped are, of course, the structures of the incest taboo. Fortunately, the play's rapid conclusion reveals the old friend Anselme to be Sophie's father and fulfills Desfrancs's wish that the *sys-*

tème be changed. Such an alteration of the structures of kinship is surely a blow to the reign of *raison.* . . . Yet there remains something shocking in the denouement. Sophie and Desfrancs remain an isolated pair of identical souls (she considers herself his "imparfaite apparence"), and they neatly escape separation and integration into the marital system of exchange: incest, by any other name. . . .

Sade's plays are thus as concerned with *rapports* as any; as in Diderot's work, the relationships in question are mainly familial. Paternity remains a crucial, overwhelming attribute. "Je suis père," says the unknown wanderer in the fourth act of *Henriette,* before revealing anything else about himself. Fascination with this subject is scarcely limited to Sade or Diderot; in an age preoccupied with the structures of society and the individual's place in that structure, the patriarchal family functioned as a microcosm of humanity. Diderot exemplifies this approach. In Sade, something seems awry. The emphasis on *rapports* is as omnipresent as ever; the plots are for the most part based on familial relationships. Yet the *rapports* themselves become twisted and confused. Fathers, mothers, sisters, and brothers fumble blindly and mistake one another for enemies or for friends. The practice may be voluntary, as when Saint-Clair and his father address each other as *ami* (so do Eugénie de Franval and her father). The blurring of relationships leads to a blurring of meaning. The relationships between Sophie and Desfrancs, Henriette and Saint-Clair, as well as those between the parents and children of *Fanni, L'Egarement, Le Mariage du siècle,* and the others, are ambiguous, and the meaning of the plays is unclear.

At the same time, the notion of identity has become more problematic than ever. Pierre Klossowski's oft-cited description [in *Sade mon Prochain,* 1967] of Sade's characters as "somnambules en plein jour" is an apt description of the characters in the *théâtre de rêve.* After the weakening and confusion of relationships, nothing is left for the characters except incomprehension and meaninglessness—"death," decides Saint-Clair. Where can meaning be found? Meaning is a function of the social order, and the social order is founded on a coherent and repeatable structure, the key to which lies in the succession from the parents to the children. But what is a father who abandons his family, who accepts changelings for children, who pushes his daughter to suicide, or who marries her? What are children who mistake their fathers for someone else, attacking them in the street, refusing them aid? The system ceases to make sense as it once did in Diderot's plays, where the social structure might evoke a certain meaning, in the sense of a plan for action, despite "equivocations."

In Sade's plays, events are not governed by the organizational rules of society, nor even by the less defined "laws of nature," but by something more obscure—"providence impénétrable"—Sade's synonym for the absurd and unreasonable. To penetrate this providence is to see that Sade's inconsistent and absurd characters in no way bespeak a comprehensible "identity," any more than their situations augur for confidence in a functional social system. They bespeak a centuries-old theatrical tradition of pure heroines, passionate heroes, wise old men, virtue rewarded, and vice condemned. They bespeak an idea that if one wants to be a playwright, then one must write plays, and if one must write plays, then there are certain kinds of plays which one must write. The normative and dramatic structures in the plays are virtually incoherent because the plays themselves are props in a larger drama, where the playwright is just as implicated in a *système de rapports* as any of his characters. . . .

"DES ENFANTEMENTS DE CHIMERES": LETTERS AND NOVELS

The plays and the prefaces reveal a Sade to whom we are unaccustomed, who nevertheless remains oddly familiar. These works from the first half of Sade's literary career reveal the formation of a strong and disruptive literary sensibility which has not yet found its ideal form of expression. Consciously or not, in his plays Sade is taking all the commonplaces of his period and distorting them just slightly, in a language awash with virtue and sensibility. The conventions, however, no longer find themselves at home; the social harmony which the bourgeois theater attempts to mirror is cast into doubt. At the end of **Le Fils naturel,** incest is averted and the social system saved; at the end of the **Misanthrope** and **Henriette,** literal incest is averted, but only at the price of the social order. In the prefaces, Sade's relationships with other writers are equally ambiguous: he claims kinship when he has the least right to, and denies it in plain contradiction to evidence. Sade's plays and Sade's literary genealogy as presented in the prefaces are in their way studies in the dispersion of meaning, as the earlier works were studies in the disintegration of the self. They are also studies in frustration; try as he might, Sade never attained a place alongside Molière, Gresset, Destouches, and Regnard, with or without Diderot as part of the company. It was necessary to try something else.

That something else was the novel, a new form and one less encumbered by predecessors (especially if one could forget Diderot and Laclos, vilify Restif, and pretend to direct descendance from Richardson and Rousseau).

The remaining part of this essay will explore some similarities between Sade's novelistic aims and his dramatic ones. Before discussing the novels, however, I want to digress briefly in order to examine a little collection of documents which have a direct bearing on any notions one might form of meaning in Sade. These are the letters written mainly from Vincennes between 1779 and 1784, an extremely dark time in the life of the marquis. Imprisoned by his mother-in-law, the Présidente de Montreuil, on a *lettre de cachet,* Sade was totally without any means for knowing when he was to be released, or even when he would be permitted visits or walks. Most of his communication with the outside world came through letters. In the early years of his imprisonment, Sade endured what later he was to inflict on countless fictive characters. Tormented by the evil genius of the Présidente, closed off from the world, he wrote, "Il me semble que toute la nature soit morte pour moi." This was in 1777. A year later his letters began to take another turn. Going on a careless phrase in a letter from the marquise, he began to calculate what her words might mean in terms of his imprisonment, as if she

were the keeper of the secret tauntingly suggested in her letter. At first he was able to see the improbability of such hidden messages. . . . Shortly thereafter, the calculations became increasingly important in the letters, and the marquis more and more firmly convinced that his wife and other correspondents were hiding some vital truth from him through the so-called *signaux* and *chiffres.* . . . At other times, Sade was so deeply involved in his *système chiffral* that one loses all sense of his meaning. . . . Anything might furnish material for his calculations—dates, word-counts, repeated events, times of day, even puns (as when "il vint le quatre" produced 24, "vingt-quatre"; or "cesse"—and by extension "fin"—gave 16, "seize"). Sade claims that his enemies, jailers, mother-in-law, and wife are taunting him with "signals" and "ciphers"—deliriously conceived signs that he thought would reveal the date of his release from prison. The privileged audience for his ravings is his wife, whose letters become the proving ground for the exercise of a manic variety of reader-response criticism. Refusing any possibility of authorial intentions, Sade appropriates her utterances and subjects them to the painful machinery of some exotic interpretive conventions. The marquise is no longer in control of her own discourse; she pleads and protests, but her meaning is invariably distorted, translated into ciphers, turned against her. The letters are also physically overwritten. Sade fills the margins with calculations, denials, obscenities, and aggressive commentary. . . .

Epistolary power has its limits. Sade remains in prison and no message, no date of release, is uncovered. Yet his dazzling manipulations of the conventions of communication reveal something of the arbitrary and contingent nature of language and meaning better than analysis could have done. Sade appears to have discovered that unnerving power of language that Lacan described [in *Écrits I,* 1966] as "la possibilité que j'ai, justement dans la mesure où . . . cette langue existe, de m'en servir pour signifier *tour autre chose* que ce qu'elle dit. . . ." This then is Sade's revenge, the subjugation and violation of language itself.

There are clear parallels between the violence done to Mme de Sade's utterances, the breakdown of traditional structures in the plays, and the distortion of literary relationships apparent in the dramatic commentary. In every case, Sade has brought the basic conventions to light and either deliberately abused them or used them in a way which renders them incoherent, a practice consistent with the approach to writing we encounter in his better-known texts.

Controlled by invisible forces, the world utterly "dead to him," incapable of knowing anything regarding his future, Sade invented a wholly arbitrary system of *signaux* and *chiffres* which came to represent his understanding of reality. And as I have mentioned, it was during this period that Sade wrote the majority of his plays. In the plays, as in the letters of this period, the reader is confronted by a peculiar world of relationships and signs which somehow ought to yield meaning and yet which don't, quite. Banality, indiscriminate use of convention, and subversive undercurrents replace the orderly vision of the workings of society that we found earlier; here, as in Diderot's plays, disorder threatens, but in Sade's plays disorder is never totally done away with. The relationships structuring "normal" society, between parents and children, siblings, lovers, here are called into question and left in uncertainty. Ever the close reader, Sade would seem to have sensed the *drame's* possibilities and puzzles. But where Diderot dreamed the infinite regress of relationality, Sade experiments with a theater of frustrated nostalgia. One senses a strong desire for normalcy running through his moralizing plays, just as one senses a desperate wish for the reassurance of knowledge and certainty in the letters from Vincennes.

What follows are some reflections on the role of *rapports* in Sade's fiction. As has been suggested, the gap between those infamous novels and the plays "d'eau-rose"—his phrase—is less wide than generally assumed. Sade put his frustration to work in the novels. The stifling constraints of convention and *bienséance* which order the plays become in the novels an exquisite machine—quite unlike Diderot's infinite machine—and their author holds the key to the prison of words which had fettered him before.

In this closed, unnatural world, *rapports* and categorizations are all that define the various characters, particularly in the many model societies found in the novels: the monastery of Sainte-Marie-des-bois, the Château de Silling, numberless forts and châteaux. Justine and her companions in distress are not noted for their individuality. Each is "faite à peindre," and the reader is quickly lost amid the profusion of perfect young bodies and ideal innocence. As the monks at Sainte-Marie-des-bois are chiefly defined by their sexual preferences, so the prisoners too are characterized by the roles which they are forced to perform. The exercise in classification reaches its extreme in *Les Cent-Vingt Journées,* in which the victims are chosen to fulfill pre-arranged sets of Femmes, Historiennes, Duègnes, Jeunes Filles, Jeunes Garçons, Fouteurs. The distinguishing qualities of the young girls and boys are their noble births and family connections—"fille d'un gentilhomme de Berry," "page du roi," and so on. No other distinctions are possible. . . .

The individual controls neither identity nor destiny; the *rapports* which have hitherto governed existence have all been changed, rules and rituals substituted for custom and family ties. . . . Former ties were based on "nature" and on bourgeois domesticity. Now these same *liens* are corrupted and given new perverted significance. Blangis's denial notwithstanding, it is clear that these ties are, if not *sacrés,* then certainly indispensable. The value of the libertines' wives, Constance, Adelaïde, Aline, and Julie, stems largely from the fact that they are also their daughters, so that abusing them permits the confection of simultaneous crimes: adultery, sodomy, incest, and so on.

The variable nature of *rapports* is understood in *Les Infortunes de la vertu* in the passage concerning the "other tower" of Sainte-Marie-des-bois. The imprisoned women have no knowledge of any possible life beyond the regulations which govern their every moment. . . . Nothing beyond the daily routine, nothing that happens to women who leave the prison, is known. The "other tower" intensifies the experience. Has each woman her counterpart in

another, invisible, tower? Like speculation on the plurality of worlds, the possibility that Sophie and her comrades may not be alone in their distress offers no solace but instead renders their existence more problematic than ever. Do the monks have other slaves in other towers, or are Sophie and her friends utterly alone? The inability to understand the system of *rapports* contributes to the ambiguity and terror of their situation.

Many are the passages in which Justine and other victims attempt to combat their persecutors by calling on "natural law" and what they consider to be inalienable rights and unbreakable ties among family and friends. . . . [Like *La Philosophie dans le boudoir,*] Justine's tale is also a long recounting of the inevitable contradiction of her beliefs in the social order by the libertine's eloquently destructive rhetoric, which prefers theft to property rights, treachery to gratitude, and blasphemy to reverence for God.

Like Blangis, the libertines delight in the rupture of all ties and contracts, and if their victims are primarily concerned with establishing relationships based on reason and nature, they themselves are motivated by precisely the opposite drive. In his classic essay on Sade [*Lautréamont et Sade,* 1963], Maurice Blanchot viewed the refusal of all *rapports* as the chief characteristic of the libertine hero. . . . As Blanchot recognizes, the libertines encounter considerable difficulty in upholding this stance. They constantly experience the inescapability of *rapports.* The libertine's involvement with others is most evident in the numerous pacts created with other libertines; although shaky in *Juliette,* such pacts hold in *Justine* and in *Les Cent-Vingt Journées.* The rulers of Silling can scarcely be said to be "unique"—the libertine slogan—save insofar as one speaks of their entire group; otherwise they are identified, like their victims, by social roles (aristocrat, judge, bishop, financier) and by family ties (fathers, husbands, sons-in-law). No amount of concentration on the apathy of the libertine and the nothingness of the victim allows escape from the problem of *rapports.*

The libertines succeed neither in the quest for uniqueness nor in the search for mastery. Beyond their reach there is always an Other. . . . So the individual has not greatly changed in the passage from Sade's theater to his novels. Identity dissolves in a relational alterity; the relational structures are bereft of sense. Even if the author would refuse this wholesale dispersion of individuals into a larger hierarchy, all efforts to impose another *système social* or *dramatique* come to nothing. The libertine's frustration manifests itself in insatiable desire. . . .

Sade discovered that the contest with God could not be won through opposition or destruction, but that it had to be accomplished through repetition, the perversion of creation. The real revolt does not depend on the amount of damage that the libertines perpetrate on the bodies of their victims or the sensibilities of their readers, but in a deconstruction of the order of things. God's order is Nature: reason, causality, logic. The libertine denies this nature and reduces meaning and final cause to "le mouvement perpétuel de la matière" (*Juliette*) and universal indifference.

Sade's handwriting and signature, from a letter to his aunt.

The resulting system, although devoid of logic or reason, is anything but anarchic. Nothing could be more strictly regimented than the libertine utopias at Sainte-Marie-des-bois or Silling. The former develops gradually from Omphale's sketchy account in *Les Infortunes de la vertu,* in which details concerning life in the monastery are hazy . . . , to *La Nouvelle Justine,* in which the same speech takes on the form and language of a code of law. As the regulations become more complex, life correspondingly becomes less ambiguous; the "other tower" disappears from the text and the fate of the women who leave the seraglio becomes much clearer. Similar sets of rules exist in *Juliette,* but neither it nor *Justine* equals *Les Cent-Vingt Journées,* in which the arithmetical precision of the rules determines the form of the book. Far from helping us to discover rationality, as did the creation of relationships and structures in Diderot's *réseau social,* Sade's social contracts return us instead to the insane *système chiffral* of the prison letters.

God and Justine presumably want to make sense. The libertines do not believe sense to be possible, and in their despair create structures of non-sense, eschew fairness and conventional logic, and plunge the reader into a contradictory, regimented, and repetitive world where the ideal symmetry of the ritual belies the essential incoherence of the whole. The whole is incoherent because it is isolated . . . and a supposed basis for relationships, pacts which may or may not obtain. . . . Meaning gives way to a series of rules, rites, and postures that signify no more than the 16s and 4s of the letters from Vincennes. At the heart of the structure is a hollow place, for these highly organized systems of signification bear no meaning. . . .

The frequently criticized "monotony" of Sade's novels provides the substance of his literary technique and the foundation for his major works, beginning with the elaborate rituals of *Les Cent-Vingt Journées,* all performed in quadruplicate, varied only in intensity, governed by arbitrary laws. Repetition need not come to an end within the individual work; Sade repeated other writers and also himself, returning to anecdotes to create stories and pillaging stories to create other stories, novels, and plays. The most impressive instance is doubtless his tireless rewriting of the philosophical tale *Les Infortunes de la vertu* as *Justine ou les Malheurs de la vertu* and the immense *Nouvelle Justine ou les Malheurs de la vertu suivie de l'Histoire de Juliette ou les Prospérités du vice,* a work whose scope rivals the projected *Cent-Vingt Journées* as apparently did the lost *Journées de Florbelle.* Sade spent his life writing and rewriting one huge recursive work, his *œuvres complètes.*

The destructive force of all this repetition is clearly evident in the three versions of *Justine.* With precision and delicacy Sade uses the same opening passage to demonstrate two utterly opposed things: the first two versions present the story of Justine and her sister to "prove" one point and the third purports to "prove" exactly the opposite. Rather than choose one stance as being "Sade's," one should appreciate the futility of such a choice. Hence no work of Sade's is "atypical": Sade must be understood in the light of the boundless contradictions which arise when one considers all his works together.

The theater is important in this respect because it is there that something is the most obviously amiss in the slippage between the plaintive moralizing, the requisite conventions, and the subversive undercurrents of passion and destruction. What is noteworthy in terms of Sade's shortcomings as a dramatist is not only his repeating himself, showing yet again how incapable he was of fitting his expression to conventional aesthetics and morality, but also the way in which this incapacity manifests itself. Sade does not attack his enemies, meaning, and Western logic, according to the rules (the rules of Western logic), which require meeting force with equal or greater force and battling to prove where the greater strength lies. Sade begins instead from a position of weakness, even passivity, as when in the correspondence he reverses the positions of power as well as the relationship of message sent to message received. By refusing to play by the rules, he posits the rules' absurdity.

Similarly, the Sade we see in the plays and prefaces has a somewhat comic role, that of the eager incompetent "au milieu de Molière, Destouches, Marivaux, Boissy, Regnard. . . ." Nevertheless, something is amiss even in this apparently simple scheme. Sade's weakness is both feigned and serious, both sad and comic—how could the divine marquis be worried about competition from a Boissy, even a Destouches? But it is this very weakness which casts the entire program in an ironic light and which also indicates the fragility of a "normal" view of literary history. Everything is as it is perceived, and all perception is subject to misprision, even subversion. Sade performs the same operation on the positive values of literary history, its hierarchies and relationships that he imposes on morality, communication, and logic: he displaces, reverses, subverts, seduces the institutions which consider themselves the intact repositories of knowledge and power. Like the relationships in the plays (or elsewhere) the kinship structures here are non-functional, marred by passion and repression. Meaning and representation have once again eluded the reader, who is left amid a profusion of conflicting signs and references to a world of texts and conventions which they do not suffice to explain.

The blurring of relationships in the plays and prefaces leads to a blurring of meaning. The plays themselves remain opaque, unclear, annoying, and ambiguous; critics continue to disagree over the significance of the theater in Sade's life. Although more clearly in evidence than ever, systems have ceased to make sense. The distortion of relationships and subsequent disintegration of meaning, the subversive rupture between the surface ideology and the dramatic *discours,* mark these plays as indeed belonging to their author. It is damaging to the destructive force of Sade's writing to separate it into "real" or clandestine writing (the novels) and "inauthentic" or public writing (the plays). To the contrary, the conjunction of the "moral" Sade and the "immoral" Sade produces a greater disruption of sense than that of any individual work.

Barthes saw the importance of this conjunction and its effect on language in the moralizing footnotes that grace Sade's most libertine texts. . . . The discursive complexity of Sade's theater is thrown into sharpest relief when one realizes that during the years of his greatest dramatic output Sade was also living through his experience of the *système chiffral.* These were the years of Sade's formation as a writer, the period in which he learned just how arbitrary a signifying system—whether linguistic, aesthetic, or normative—could be.

Whatever else it may be, Sade's work is not polemical. It marks the end of all possible polemics, shows the absurdity of argument and reasoning. This is the realization informing both his forgotten theater and his perennially disturbing novels. If the theater failed, it was primarily because of its lack of direction. Sade cannot write plays like Molière or Gresset because he has neither their technique nor their world view. His plays remain faltering, unoriginal, ambiguous. In his novels, Sade would put his sensibilities to another use.

Commenting on Foucault's evaluation of Sade as the writer who put an end to classical notions of representation, Marcel Hénaff [in *Sade: L'Invention du corps libertin,* 1978] echoes Horkheimer and Adorno's thesis that Sade is the "scandalous prolongation" of Enlightenment and *la pensée classique.* And yet, nothing could be less totalizing than Sade's work and his staging of the death of totality. It is not the sleep of reason which produced Sade's monsters, but reason itself which became monstrous. Sade did not win any cosmological struggle through either the blasphemies or the immoral moralizing of his libertines; he degrades the struggle into an exercise in the exploitation and manipulation of structures and relationships. What kills is his deadly attachment to the normal, the banal. The theater reveals the necessary place of "bourgeois" morality in Sade's writing: the conflicting ideologies, the repetitions, the systematizing, and the suppression all point to a disintegration of language and sense. Despite many recognizable features, Sade's sentimental drama fails to convey the meaning that the genre once was thought to contain, and yet it is he nonetheless who most fully exploits the genre's capacity for equivocation. Therein perhaps lies his original attraction to it. His is the move that brings the

---

Annie Le Brun on Sade's letters:

On one particularly tender day, Sade wrote a letter to his wife, beginning with the words: "Fresh piglet of my thoughts." I hope that one day there will be a woman who can dream of receiving a love letter that begins as well, for the whole world is thereby laid at her feet, and freedom—real freedom, freedom as lived by Juliette—is rolled out before her like a carpet. I shall not discuss Sade's letters here. I recommended only that you read them when very much alone.

Annie Le Brun, in her Sade: A Sudden Abyss, *City Light Books, 1990.*

system down. One might say as much of his approach to the novel or to language itself. Through repetition, regimentation, and contradiction, he sucks all meaning from the great rational body of language and exceeds the reveries of libidinous destruction of Curval and Juliette. Here lies his revolt, a denial of principles, structures, meanings. God created by naming all things; Sade, like Proust's artist Elstir, rivaled God by taking the names away.

Thomas DiPiero   (essay date 1992)

SOURCE: "Justine and the Discourse of the (Other) Master," in *Dangerous Truths & Criminal Passions: The Evolution of the French Novel, 1569-1791.* Stanford University Press, 1992, pp. 333-74.

[*In his book* Dangerous Truths & Criminal Passions, *DiPiero argues that the novel arose as a medium of resistance to accepted literary genres and to the ideological assumptions they served to legitimize. In the following excerpt, he suggests that Sade's narrative strategies in* Justine *expose the constructed nature of discourse and ideology.*]

In the marquis de Sade's *Justine ou les malheurs de la vertu* we will see [a] protagonist employ the discursive mode she learns from others. She not only represents herself with the express intent to seduce, but she threatens the security of bourgeois patriarchy's system of values. . . .

Despite critics' claims that *Justine* is a novel "in which nothing has been spared," the narrator who opens the work before handing narrative responsibility over to Justine implicitly addresses the possibility of achieving narrative mastery, the complete discursive control over the articulation and interpretation of texts. In the first sentence of the novel, he disavows the feasibility of representing the world completely.

> The very masterpiece of philosophy would be to develop the means Providence employs to arrive at the ends she designs for man, and from this construction to deduce some rules of conduct acquainting this two-footed individual with the manner wherein he must proceed along life's thorny way, forewarned of the strange caprices of that fatality they denominate by twenty different titles, and all unavailingly, for it has not yet been scanned nor defined.

It is impossible, the narrator states, to represent everything. People might be better off if they could understand and explain nature and thus avoid the "strange caprices" that befall them; so far, however, no one has succeeded in domesticating nature, or in giving it a name whereby one could know and comprehend its system. If there were a masterpiece of philosophy—but the narrator reveals his skepticism in his use of the conditional mood—it would reveal nature as final cause, and demonstrate the system according to which it deals with people. The paradox here is that articulating that which escapes naming might make us feel more secure, but even with twenty different names the mysteries of nature still elude our understanding. Naming unveils and simultaneously dissimulates because it establishes specific discursive structures not only as adequate or realistic representations of actual social practice,

but also, as we will see, as substitutes for those practices themselves. . . .

Barthes [in *Tel Quel,* Winter, 1967] calls Justine an "ambiguous victim endowed with narrating speech." Justine is the victim of a great many violent crimes, which certainly makes her seem a victim, but because she speaks she possesses what we have determined to be a very significant libertine characteristic: the manipulation of language. In fact, Justine's use of language is remarkably similar to the libertines'. "The master is the one who speaks, who disposes of language in its entirety," Barthes wrote. For three hundred pages, almost the entire *récit* of the novel, Justine is in control—she narrates, and she controls the scene. Not only is she the novel's principal narrator, but every time she meets a libertine she narrates the story of her life thus far: "And then I told in detail all of my ills" "[the first president judge] heard with interest the tale of my misfortunes" "I relate the horrors whereof I was simultaneously an observer and object." If libertines are those who speak and those who take pleasure in all sorts of sensation, Justine is indeed an ambiguous victim; in fact, as I will show, she looks very much like a libertine. If Justine does not derive some sort of benefit from the sensations the libertines evoke in her, it is hard to imagine why, after having learned the consequences, she continues to tell her tale.

Since the libertines can only occupy the master's position by opposing the principles of virtue and defining themselves against an other, it seems logical to ask whether Justine defines herself in opposition to the libertines. As she tells her tale, Justine takes no positions and she has no philosophies of virtue; she only ever contradicts libertine sophistry. If she is virtuous, then, it is to the extent that she attempts to be the other of vice. Yet, Justine rarely, if ever, resists the libertines. She *says* that she is virtuous, but her actions belie her words. Situations frequently arise in which Justine has the power to escape her tormentors' clutches, but more often than not she passes them by. . . .

Justine knows only one way to be virtuous, and that is to tell people that she is. She rarely performs or takes responsibility for a selfless virtuous act: in most instances in which Justine helps another it is for the benefits she can reap. In fact, she remarks early in the novel that "people are not esteemed save in reason of the aid and benefits one imagines may be had of them," and Justine herself seems to subscribe to this platitude. After Rodin burns the brand of the thief on Justine's shoulder and thus prevents her from turning him in to the authorities, Justine flees, leaving poor Rosalie, Rodin's daughter, to be vivisected.

> Anyone else might have been little impressed by the menace; what would I have to fear as soon as I found the means to prove that what I had just suffered had been the work not of a tribunal but of criminals? But my weakness, my natural timidity, the frightful memory of what I had undergone at Paris and recollections of the château de Bressac—it all stunned me, terrified me; I thought only of flight, and was far more stirred by anguish at having to abandon an innocent victim to those two villains, who were without doubt ready to immolate her, than I was touched by my own ills.

Underscoring how unlike anyone else she is, Justine says that leaving Rosalie aggrieves her but she makes no move to help her; the only action she foresees is *proving*—that is, telling or explaining—her innocence.

Justine's most protracted attempt to tell of her innocence is the novel's *récit* itself. Except for fifteen paragraphs, the novel is composed of Justine's narrative to Corville and Lorsange. Justine encounters Corville and Lorsange when on her way to Paris for the confirmation of the death penalty she received in Lyon for having killed the baby in the fire. Lorsange and Corville ask her to tell them the story of her life, and since they appear rich and influential, Justine decides to oblige them. Attempting to charge her tale with all the pathos and abjection she can, Justine begins. Calling herself Thérèse in order to defend her family's honor, she prefaces her story with a disclaimer, informing her listeners that her narrative is transgressive: "To recount you the story of my life, Madame . . . is to offer you the most striking example of innocence oppressed, is to accuse the hand of Heaven, is to bear complaint against the Supreme Being's will, is, in a sense, to rebel against His sacred designs. . . . I dare not. . . .' Tears gathered in this interesting girl's eyes and, after having given vent to them for a moment, she began her recitation in these terms." From the very beginning of Justine's narrative we can see some of the tricks she picked up from libertine narration. Barthes and Sollers [in *Tel Quel*, Winter, 1967] showed that the libertine use of language went beyond simple representation, and actually became criminal itself: as Sollers showed, telling became an act, the accomplishing of a crime. In the first sentences she utters, Justine accomplishes a transgression merely by her use of language: she claims that to recount equals to accuse and to bear complaint; to tell her story, she says, is to rebel against God's will. She turns a speech situation into a speech act because narrating her story, she avers, perpetrates an offense. Pausing only a moment to let the transgressive elements of her tale register with her audience, she plunges enthusiastically into the story.

Justine pauses a half-dozen or so times during her narrative, punctuating the *récit* with reminders that telling the story is transgressive: "Oh, Madame, I shall not attempt to represent the infamies of which I was at once victim and witness." With a little encouragement, however, she narrates the libertines' attempt to inscribe their marks of violence on Thérèse, the principal character in Justine's story. Justine's hesitations accomplish more than simply signaling to her audience that the tale is violent and that the very telling is blameworthy, however. Perhaps realizing that repeated description of events can cause her listeners' attention to wander, Justine incites them, through her hesitations, to inscribe their own marks of violence on her heroine Thérèse: "You will permit me, Madame, . . . to conceal a part of the obscene details of this odious ritual; allow your imagination to figure all that debauch can dictate to villains in such instances . . . and indeed it still will not have but a faint idea of what was done in those initial orgies." Justine gives them all the material they need to complete the story, but cannily telling them that what really happened is far worse than what she narrates, she gets them to supply for themselves the erotic details

and to write their own endings to the story she begins. To keep her listeners actively involved, she frequently breaks her tale off: "But how can I abuse your patience by relating these new horrors? Have I not already more than soiled your imagination with infamous recitations? Dare I hazard additional ones? 'Yes, Thérèse,' Monsieur de Corville put in, 'yes, we insist upon these details.' " Justine's narrative strategies here resemble the libertines' to the extent that she informs her listeners that transgression is about to occur, and also to the extent that she redefines herself as victim by inciting her listeners to violate her mentally as they imagine scenes of violence she must have undergone.

Justine's use of language is equivalent to that of the libertines. The libertines, unable to achieve their goal of self-affirmation and plenitude, need language to define themselves over and against an other. The same is true of Justine. In order to assure maximum reaction from their addresses, the libertines describe the violence about to occur. The same is true of Justine, who hesitates before telling her audience the explicit aspects of her tale, and who reveals that even narrating her story is an affront to God. The libertines proceed by describing their acts of violence to Justine, and then inscribing their marks on her. The same is true of Justine, who incites her listeners to perform mental violence on her as she sets up a scene and then leaves the conclusion to them. But while the libertines use language as a means to *jouissance* and the concomitant narcissistic unity, Justine's narrative, despite making her seem the epitome of virtue and integrity, actually effects a radical split in her subjectivity. If the image of virtue she presents to her listeners seems designed to evoke their pity and provoke them to help her—which they finally do—the reality of Justine, the woman behind the image, is more complex and elusive than her representation of herself would suggest. Justine portrays herself, in the figure of Thérèse, as absolutely other to vice and libertinism, but as we will now see, Justine and Thérèse are not simply different names for the same woman: the two are radically different in their otherness and resistance to libertinism.

Klossowski argues that Justine is the paradigm of virtue and that her function in the novel is to throw the libertines into relief. Maintaining that she is no more complex than the image of virtue that the libertines and Corville and Lorsange receive from her narrative, he claims that the libertines manage to reach her in the deepest recesses of her being. He argues that Sade portrays Justine as "always equal to herself" and that Sade exploits the distress "of a consciousness reduced to its last defenses at the point at which it sees its inviolate self-possession threatened, in the representation that the self has of its own integrity, while consciousness always remains inseparable from the body lost to its eye." Yet, I would have to argue that Justine cannot be "equal to herself," because she depicts herself as a text, a collection of episodes, indeed a *récit*. Her complexity arises from the disjunction separating her life from the representation of it. Using the pseudonym Thérèse, she constructs a narrative other that necessarily differs substantially from her reality. She only describes episodes that cause her to appear virtuous because she is the other of libertinism. Her ordeals last more than thirteen years, and enough certainly happens to Justine over the course of these years to give her material for her tale. But Justine tells not "the story of [her] life," which is what she claims to be doing; she only tells the story of her troubles and of her resistance to the libertines. On at least four occasions Justine collapses periods of up to four years into one sentence ("I had remained four years in this household unrelentingly persecuted by the same sorrows,") and she never tells any episode in her thirteen-year journey unless it is hideously violent and morally degrading. She admits that some amusing anecdotes exist in her repertory, but the necessity of detailing her misfortunes takes precedence: "Were my cruel situation to permit me to amuse you for an instant, Madame, when I must think of nothing but gaining your compassion, I should dare describe some of the symptoms of avarice I witnessed while in that house." By her own admission events occurred in Justine's life that do not contribute to the image she tries to project. Her narrative self does not correspond to her reality; Justine constructs her narrated self—Thérèse—with a very particular point in mind: to move her listeners to pity (*attendrir*). Justine is not, consequently, portrayed "equal to herself," as Klossowski claims, and Thérèse becomes an alienated, textual manifestation of Justine. . . .

Justine is concerned with the perlocutionary force of her tale, and she seems never to worry that her story might appear exaggerated or untrue. Justine strives to move her audience to pity, and the strategy she has chosen for doing so involves portraying Thérèse, her narrated self, as the incarnation of virtue. Thérèse is the undauntable other of libertinism whose spirit the libertines never succeed in breaking. Her story consists of nothing but repeated episodes of violence, and her virtue appears greater with each encounter because she never ceases to offer resistance. Justine and Thérèse differ in one significant respect, however. The more violence Thérèse suffers in Justine's story, the greater her virtue and her resistance to corruption seem to be. The real woman Justine, however, the narrator who lived through these ordeals, had an entirely different kind of resistance, one essential to the pathos of the story she constructs. That resistance is a specifically physical resistance. If we look closely at Justine's encounters with the libertines, we see that she is repeatedly violated because she offers strong moral *and* physical resistance. That is, everyone who meets Justine is taken with her remarkable beauty, and one of the reasons why the libertines find her so attractive as a victim is that her body appears fresh and virginal, and hence ripe for transgression. Even after repeated scenes of violence, even after being raped, branded, beaten, and infibulated, Justine's body is none the worse for wear. All marks on Justine's body mysteriously disappear—even her hymen grows back. At the end of her ordeals Justine is still described as a woman with "the loveliest figure imaginable, the most noble, the most agreeable, the most interesting visage, in brief, there were there all the charms of a sort to please."

The significance of Justine's inability to retain a trace of the marks of violence inscribed on her is paramount if she is to appear as the quintessence of virtue. Since the strength of her virtue is in direct proportion to the amount of violence she undergoes, it figures that Justine must be violated as often as possible if she is to appear the other of libertinism. Yet, if her body showed signs of wear, the transgression involved in each violation would be less, particularly since the libertines violate whatever offers greatest resistance. The narrated, textual Thérèse thus differs from Justine in its ability to retain the marks or memory of violence. By creating the textual Thérèse, Justine constitutes a means by which the traces of violence she underwent can be recorded and inscribed in the memory of her audience. The more violence they hear she underwent, the more they construe her as the apotheosis of virtue. Justine's description of her resistance to vice in the figure of Thérèse in this way makes virtue—as we saw was the case with libertine vice—a specifically discursive phenomenon.

Consequently, Justine's story of Thérèse foregrounds a form of *vraisemblance.* Despite the fact that it is physically impossible for anyone to have lived through the ordeals Justine describes, much less to remain beautiful and innocent to boot, the tale retains an affective and ideological register clearly endorsing bourgeois patriarchy's conception of feminine sexuality and, consequently, moral rectitude. The story of Thérèse is not realistic in any traditional sense, but it is *vraisemblable,* since in the abstract and globalizing conception of virtue it highlights a determined political vision of the way things ought to be. Strikingly, then, Justine's version of virtue, which depends on the narrative construction of Thérèse as the unrealistic yet ideologically plausible apotheosis of virtue, is rhetorically equivalent to libertine vice. It is a discursive construction with no sound philosophical or moral basis, and it exists solely as the negation of its other.

Justine and her libertine tormentors are engaged in a dialectical struggle in which neither virtue nor vice has any positive characteristics. Each exists solely as the negation of its other, and each requires the support of a discursive representation in order to smooth over the gaps implicit in its logical and ideological composition. Both Justine and the libertines depend on the narrated figure Thérèse to fill in the holes in their philosophical narratives. The libertines need to inscribe their violence on Thérèse in order to annihilate her and approach the consummation of their own *jouissance,* and Justine must mark Thérèse so that her tale will attain the level of *vraisemblance* required to convey the pathos she specifies early on. Justine and the libertines are consequently engaged in a rhetorical struggle, one concerned less with the ideology of virtue and more with the narrative structure of ideology.

Justine and the libertines compete in telling different stories about Thérèse. The novel could go on forever, like *Le Roman bourgeois,* except for the *deus ex machina* that terminates Justine's life. Up until the moment of Justine's death, the novel is a battle of conflicting philosophies, with each side sharpening and refining its point of view with no possible resolution in sight. Justine's narrative winds down to the point at which she met Mme de Lorsange and M. de Corville when, as in a labyrinthine heroic novel, she discovers that Mme de Lorsange is her sister Juliette. Justine and Juliette retire to the latter's château, where Justine receives all the loving attention she ever wanted. One day a storm appears.

Lightning glitters, shakes, hail slashes down, winds blow wrathfully, heaven's fire convulses the clouds, in the most hideous manner makes them to seethe; it seems as if Nature were wearied out of patience with what she has wrought, as if she were ready to confound all the elements that she might wrench new forms from them. Terrified, Madame de Lorsange begs her sister to make all haste and close the shutters; anxious to calm her, Thérèse dashes to the windows which are already being broken; she would do battle with the wind, she gives a minute's flight, is driven back and at that instant a blazing thunderbolt reaches her where she stands in the middle of the room; at that moment a burst of lightning lays her flat in the middle of the room. . . . The unhappy Thérèse has been struck in such wise hope itself can no longer subsist for her; the lightning entered her right breast, found the heart, and after having consumed her chest and face, burst out through her belly.

Where no mortal had succeeded in reaching Justine and leaving a trace on her virginal body, in a flash nature inscribes its mark on her and annihilates her, thus putting to an end in as random a fashion possible the antagonistic relationship she entertained with the libertines.

The arbitrary conclusion to Justine's life represents more than simply Sade's only way out of the impossibly antagonistic relationship he had created, however. The final inscription of violence on the victim's body is a literal and metaphoric dis-figurement of the character Justine. The lightning permanently deforms the beautiful young woman, thus accomplishing the feat Justine's antagonists failed to perform. Correlatively and more importantly, however, the marks left on Justine's body by a non-intentional, indeliberate force obliterate her figurative incarnation in the form of the narrated Thérèse: eliminating the discrepancy between the woman and her self-representation, the force of nature that marks and kills her immediately extricates her from the dialectical and antagonistic relationship with vice.

In concert with the opening paragraph of *Justine,* then, the title character's death shows nature as final cause. Indeterminate because it lies outside of any discursive configuration capable of containing it, nature as a force of the Real lacks any ideological dimension. Yet, the conclusion of *Justine* underscores the determinate work of interpretation that ascribes to any act a meaningful and finite sense: Juliette reads the marks on her sister Justine's body, and she inserts the woman's life into the narrative and ideological paradigm that the tale's *vraisemblance* was designed to construe. "The miserable thing was hideous to look upon; Monsieur de Corville orders that she be borne away. . . . 'No,' says Madame de Lorsange, getting to her feet with the utmost calm; 'no, leave her here before my eyes, Monsieur, I have got to contemplate her in order to be confirmed in the resolves I have just taken.'" Juliette contemplates her sister's disfigured body, and reads in the hideous marks the unambiguous proof that nature demands people's adherence to the principles of virtue. Her interpretation of her sister's gruesome death is that straying from the path of virtue might provide one with a few

chimeric rewards here on earth, but the true road to felicity lies in austere virtue. Juliette goes off to become a Carmelite, and the horrible example of her sister's death leads her to become "the example of order and edification, as much by her great piety as by the wisdom of her mind and the regularity of her manners."

The conclusion of Justine's pitiful life strikes Juliette as too significant not to be meaningful. The story seems to close on a highly charged, resolute note: the miscreant Juliette sees the light and reforms her life. She thinks she recognizes the will of nature in the marks it inscribed on Justine's body, and as she contemplates the corpse, she pronounces these final words:

> The unheard-of sufferings this luckless creature has experienced although she has always respected her duties, have something about them which is too extraordinary for me not to open my eyes upon my own self; think not I am blinded by that false-gleaming felicity which, in the course of Thérèse's adventures, we have seen enjoyed by the villains who battened upon her. These caprices of Heaven's hand are enigmas it is not for us to sound, but which ought never seduce us.

Juliette abandons vice and embraces virtue, it seems, solely because of the natural phenomenon that disfigured and killed her sister. She interprets the definitive marks left on Justine by the bolt of lightning as the unequivocal proof that the moral of her sister's story unambiguously advocated virtue, and furthermore that this moral represents a divine will. In addition, Juliette continues to refer to Justine as Thérèse, even though she knows her true identity, as if to emphasize the discursively constructed nature of both her life and her virtue. Juliette observes the bizarre yet nevertheless natural phenomenon of her sister's untimely death, and forces it into one of the narrative paradigms that Justine's tale offers.

Juliette's interpretation of Justine's story matches the one prescribed by the novel's external narrator. This narrator, who opens the novel and who assumes control after Justine's death near its conclusion, apologizes for having written a didactic work whose lesson may be difficult to absorb:

> Doubtless it is cruel to have to describe, on the one hand, a host of ills overwhelming a sweet-tempered and sensitive woman who, as best she is able, respects virtue, and, on the other, the affluence of prosperity of those who crush and mortify this same woman. But were there nevertheless some good engendered of the demonstration, would one have to repent of making it? Ought one be sorry for having established a fact whence there resulted, for the wise man who reads to some purpose, so useful a lesson of submission to providential decrees and the fateful warning that it is often to recall us to our duties that Heaven strikes down beside us the person who seems to us best to have fulfilled his own?

The opening paragraphs of the work situate the novel within the didactic critical tradition that had evolved to shield fiction against charges of illegitimacy or moral indecency. In addition, the unequivocal interpretation concerning bourgeois virtue's moral and political superiority that the narrator's posturing intimates all reasonable readers will advocate situates the novel in the tradition of heroic fiction's master narratives. Juliette's interpretation of her sister's life, sanctioned by the novel's external narrator, strips Justine of her personal specificity and makes of her a purely abstract, emblematic figure of bourgeois conceptions of virtue.

The conclusion of *Justine* highlights the hermeneutic processes implicated by the story Justine tells and by the tradition of the moral exemplum to which the work belongs. Juliette insists on seeing a moral significance in her sister's natural death, and she inscribes the young woman's life in the ideology of bourgeois patriarchal virtue. *Justine* consequently resembles *La Princesse de Clèves* and *La Religieuse* to the extent that it objectifies a valorized interpretive practice and underscores the limits of its ability to negotiate contemporary political and moral reality. Where *La Princesse de Clèves* and *La Religieuse* foreground the failure of literary convention and the concomitant demystification of fiction's mechanisms, however, *Justine* undertakes a dismantling of the politics supporting a privileged model of *vraisemblance*. It uncovers the resilience of a determinate ideological system to appear natural even when the narrative episodes it contains could scarcely be more preposterous.

Unlike many of his predecessors who ceaselessly repeated that their narratives were true, Sade never claims that *Justine* is referentially accurate. He ironically maintains, rather, that the violent narrative episodes he relates are essential to impart the moral lesson that virtue is better than vice. However, Sade never depicts any actions in *Justine* that might be construed as virtuous—except, perhaps, the heroine's resistance to libertine sophistry. Since we have seen, however, that libertine vice and Justine's virtue constitute themselves exclusives through the negation of their other, it is equally possible to interpret vice as the libertine attempt to resist the oppressive ideology of bourgeois notions of virtue, a classbased political philosophy designed to keep the disenfranchised powerless. *Justine* unsettles the traditional bourgeois conception of virtue, a conception based primarily on sexual restraint and the respect of property, and it demonstrates the extent to which an individual's body and his or her access to pleasure have become a marketable commodity and, consequently, a form of property whose circulation can be rigidly controlled. Sade's libertines strive to break free from the politically determined apprehension of their own bodies and of the pleasures that traverse them; their failure to achieve unmediated access to the complete repertory of their own sensations, however, rehearses the narrator's early warning that all attempts to erect self-contained and self-present systems are doomed to failure. Sade's libertines rely on narrative constructions to transgress their victims and increase their own pleasure; their own access to the truth they propound is consequently restricted to language's capacity to represent the ideological systems they strive to breach. The idea of truth in *Justine* is not only relational and contingent upon the dialectic between vice and virtue, but it is constructed at every step of the way,

from the philosophical explanations of transgression to the physical mutilation of Justine's body, uniquely through narrative.

Sade's novel depicts individualism as it is constructed only through the transgression of existing social laws. His libertines strive to upset their victims' sense of virtue by disfiguring the stability of the philosophical language used to support it and consequently wrenching them free of the social bonds uniting them to their fellow humans. Paradoxically, delivery from social bonds constitutes both the source of *jouissance* for the libertines, who strive to become absolutely unique, and the epitome of torture for Thérèse, who requires a sense of identity with her fellow human beings in order for her conception of virtue to make sense. Libertines can only accomplish optimum transgression and retain the linguistic and physical mastery that ensues by expounding their philosophies and by narrating the scenes to transpire; in addition, their mastery relies on a disfiguring of language. Consequently, their quest for pleasure and mastery depends on a dual dialectic linking the opposition between the individual and the social to that opposing mimetic and poetic uses of language. That is, libertines first establish themselves as the masters of language by deploying standard tools of rhetoric and sophistry in order to upset their victims' stable conceptions of truth, a process that disconnects their victims from their own social realities. Demonstrating that language can shape and re-form reality as much as it can refer to it, they isolate their victims and strip them of all social identity. The ensuing physical mutilation pits consecrated individuals against one another. The victims inevitably lose the battle because they define themselves as victims: not to do so would rob them of the only sense of identity remaining to them.

Justine, however, retains her identity throughout these horrendous ordeals and it is primarily because she has appropriated libertine mastery of language. Telling her story to each of the libertines she meets, she constructs a narrated persona on whom she heaps the repeated scenes of abuse that contribute to construing her as the apotheosis of virtue. Thérèse consequently seduces the libertines because she presents an unsounded depth of material ripe for transgression. Justine as narrator enjoys a mastery of language similar to the libertines' because she remains in control of discourse's constative function by directing her audience to inscribe their own marks of violence on Thérèse. The pathetic figure that emerges is purely an effect of language. Destabilizing narrative's referential capacity, Justine avers in the very first words she speaks to Corville and Lorsange that her story is, in fact, a blasphemous speech act that questions God's sacred intentions. Thus, Justine's language reproduces the libertines' in its dual dialectical construction. Seducing her listeners into believing that her narrative contains a truth-value joining her to the social construction of virtue, she nevertheless withholds the information that reveals her individualistic and poetic use of language.

Justine's tale is a protracted seduction designed to project to her listeners an image corresponding to their desire, and she obfuscates the crucial difference on which her narrative depends between telling the truth and constructing it. That is, the story must appear referentially accurate if her virtue is to appear intact, but the tale derives its rhetorical strength by liberating itself from a purely constative register so that the play of language may construct a pathetic figure based not on truth but on listeners' desire. *Justine* consequently hypostatizes the representational indeterminacy characteristic of eighteenth-century French fiction: it sketches out the zone of conflict between ideologically incompatible positions, and situates its narrative at the precise juncture where their epistemological preconditions meet. Vice and virtue in *Justine* are discursively formulated, both depending on the logic of the narrative in which they appear. Neither enjoys an a priori preeminence, and both are shown to be truths constructed through a poetic use of language in which the constative dimension is overshadowed by language's power to construct meaning in the social world it putatively describes. The work's narrative, from which the external narrator indicates readers should draw their own conclusions about the benefits of virtue, consequently establishes a polemical tension between the competing ideologies it puts forth, as well as a continuing ambivalence concerning its own truth-value. Its title character imitates and subsequently appropriates libertine mastery of language in an attempt to direct reader response toward her own putative virtue. Justine's attempt to speak an unequivocal master discourse bereft of a figurative dimension open to interpretation is thwarted, however, at the novel's close. The bolt of lightning that disfigures her and the call for interpretation of her life that it seems to issue refigure her language, effectively summoning a reevaluation of her story and the ostensible stability of the master's language.

Justine flirts with the possibility of an unequivocal, master discourse of narrative and philosophy whose stable referentiality would reproduce in unmediated fashion the truth of the events or analytic systems to which it refers. The work's random and nonsensical conclusion, however, renders the master's position untenable, and it consequently contests the putatively natural ascendancy of any of its ideological positions. Although *Justine* claims to follow in the tradition of the didactic tale whose self-evident moral promotes reigning conceptions of virtue, it ironically undermines that claim by highlighting its immaterial basis. Projecting to different classes of readers the lesson they have been historically and culturally conditioned to recognize, the novel deftly skirts the issue of political or moral absolutism by allowing the traditional moral reading to coincide with the philosophically and politically more astute one. Those associated with this latter reading receive the author's sardonic nod of approval for recognizing that political or moral truth is a construction of received narrative traditions, and they can claim for that very reason the privileged position of interpretive superiority—at least temporarily. Sade's novel incites the critically astute to assert their own smug attitude of "political correctness" by pointing out the obfuscated operations of political hegemony on the unknowing folks who blindly respect its teachings.

This last position is a difficult one to escape, however, even if it is easy to criticize. Clearly my own account of Sade's

fiction . . . cannot escape similar charges of critical and political blindness. To bracket a specific interpretation and reveal its shortcomings is, of course, to attempt to occupy the master's position. To assert the legitimacy of one's own historical narrative—be it of a literary genre, the history of interpretation, or the sociopolitical events constituting war or revolution—is to attempt to foreclose interpretation and to privilege an expressive causality that one simply "found" in the raw data analyzed. The master's position, as must by now be all too clear, is an untenable one. As Diderot's *Religieuse* demonstrates, each tale and every history can always be re-framed and re-contextualized. The position of mastery is always a resolutely political one, since it strives to make its own accounts and claims appear natural and unconstructed. Readers of *Justine* who understand that its truth extends beyond the level of its narrative and is constituted instead on the level of its discourse—where the very notion of truth is constructed in the first place—are those who come closest to reading the work "entièrement."

FURTHER READING

Bibliography

Michael, Colette Verger. *The Marquis de Sade: The Man, His Works, and His Critics.* New York: Garland, 1986, 428 p.
    Annotated bibliography of books by and about Sade, covering works published through 1983.

Criticism

Airaksinen, Timo. *Of Glamor, Sex and De Sade.* Wakefield, N.H.: Longwood Academic, 1991, 220 p.
    A philosophical examination of issues involved in reading the works of Sade.

Fink, Beatrice C. "Ambivalence in the Gynogram: Sade's Utopian Woman." *Woman and Literature* 7, No. 1 (Winter 1979): 24-37.
    Examines contradictions in Sade's treatment of female characters, particularly in *Aline et Valcour.*

Gallop, Jane. *Intersections: A Reading of Sade with Bataille, Blanchot, and Klossowski.* Lincoln: University of Nebraska Press, 1981, 135 p.
    Intertextual reading of Sade and three of his most influential critics that identifies common philosophical and strategic ground between Sade and "antihumanist" (structuralist and poststructuralist) criticism.

Hackel, Roberta J. *De Sade's Quantitative Moral Universe: Of Irony, Rhetoric, and Boredom.* The Hague: Mouton, 1976, 101 p.
    Analyzes ways in which Sade manipulates vocabulary and style in order to invert conventional moral values.

Harari, Josué V. *Scenarios of the Imaginary: Theorizing the French Enlightenment.* Ithaca: Cornell University Press, 1987, 240 p.
    An investigation of the relationship between literary the-

ory and the imaginary, in which two chapters examine Sade's theory of writing.

Laborde, Alice M. "The Problem of Sexual Equality in Sadean Prose." In *French Women and the Age of Enlightenment.* Edited by Samia I. Spencer. Bloomington: Indiana University Press, 1984, pp. 332-44.

   A reading of *Philosophy in the Bedroom* as a plea for sexual equality between men and women.

Le Brun, Annie. *Sade — A Sudden Abyss.* Translated by Camille Naish. San Francisco: City Light Books, 1990, 220 p.

   An extended meditation on Sade's life and works, originally published as the introduction to the 1985 French edition of Sade's complete works co-edited by Le Brun and Jean-Jacques Pauvert.

Stockinger, Jacob. "Homosexuality and the French Enlightenment." In *Homosexualities and French Literature: Cultural Contexts/Critical Texts.* Edited by George Stambolian and Elaine Marks. Ithaca: Cornell University Press, 1979, 387 p.

   Section on Sade examines mutual influences between his work and an emerging tradition of homosexual literature.

Van Den Abbeele, Georges. "Sade, Foucault, and the Scene of Enlightenment Lucidity." *Stanford French Review* XI, No. 1 (Spring 1987): 7-16.

   Uses Michel Foucault's reading of Sade as the basis for a critique of Foucault's interpretative practice.

Additional coverage of Sade's life and career is contained in the following source published by Gale Research: *Nineteenth-Century Literature Criticism,* Vol. 3.

Nineteenth-Century Literature Criticism

Cumulative Indexes
Volumes 1-47

How to Use This Index

The main references

```
Calvino, Italo
    1923-1985.....CLC 5, 8, 11, 22, 33, 39,
                                73; SSC 3
```

list all author entries in the following Gale Literary Criticism series:

BLC = *Black Literature Criticism*
CLC = *Contemporary Literary Criticism*
CLR = *Children's Literature Review*
CMLC = *Classical and Medieval Literature Criticism*
DA = *DISCovering Authors*
DC = *Drama Criticism*
HLC = *Hispanic Literature Criticism*
LC = *Literature Criticism from 1400 to 1800*
NCLC = *Nineteenth-Century Literature Criticism*
PC = *Poetry Criticism*
SSC = *Short Story Criticism*
TCLC = *Twentieth-Century Literary Criticism*
WLC = *World Literature Criticism, 1500 to the Present*

The cross-references

```
See also CANR 23; CA 85-88;
    obituary CA 116
```

list all author entries in the following Gale biographical and literary sources:

AAYA = *Authors & Artists for Young Adults*
AITN = *Authors in the News*
BEST = *Bestsellers*
BW = *Black Writers*
CA = *Contemporary Authors*
CAAS = *Contemporary Authors Autobiography Series*
CABS = *Contemporary Authors Bibliographical Series*
CANR = *Contemporary Authors New Revision Series*
CAP = *Contemporary Authors Permanent Series*
CDALB = *Concise Dictionary of American Literary Biography*
CDBLB = *Concise Dictionary of British Literary Biography*
DLB = *Dictionary of Literary Biography*
DLBD = *Dictionary of Literary Biography Documentary Series*
DLBY = *Dictionary of Literary Biography Yearbook*
HW = *Hispanic Writers*
JRDA = *Junior DISCovering Authors*
MAICYA = *Major Authors and Illustrators for Children and Young Adults*
MTCW = *Major 20th-Century Writers*
NNAL = *Native North American Literature*
SAAS = *Something about the Author Autobiography Series*
SATA = *Something about the Author*
YABC = *Yesterday's Authors of Books for Children*

Literary Criticism Series
Cumulative Author Index

Aldiss, Brian W(ilson)
1925- .... **CLC 5, 14, 40**
See also CA 5-8R; CAAS 2; CANR 5, 28;
DLB 14; MTCW; SATA 34

Alegria, Claribel 1924-............ **CLC 75**
See also CA 131; CAAS 15; HW

Alegria, Fernando 1918-.......... **CLC 57**
See also CA 9-12R; CANR 5, 32; HW

Aleichem, Sholom .... **TCLC 1, 35**
See also Rabinovitch, Sholem

Aleixandre, Vicente 1898-1984 ... **CLC 9, 36**
See also CA 85-88; 114; CANR 26;
DLB 108; HW; MTCW

Alepoudelis, Odysseus
See Elytis, Odysseus

Aleshkovsky, Joseph 1929-
See Aleshkovsky, Yuz
See also CA 121; 128

Aleshkovsky, Yuz .... **CLC 44**
See also Aleshkovsky, Joseph

Alexander, Lloyd (Chudley) 1924- .. **CLC 35**
See also AAYA 1; CA 1-4R; CANR 1, 24,
38; CLR 1, 5; DLB 52; JRDA; MAICYA;
MTCW; SATA 3, 49

Alfau, Felipe 1902-............... **CLC 66**
See also CA 137

Alger, Horatio, Jr. 1832-1899..... **NCLC 8**
See also DLB 42; SATA 16

Algren, Nelson 1909-1981 .... **CLC 4, 10, 33**
See also CA 13-16R; 103; CANR 20;
CDALB 1941-1968; DLB 9; DLBY 81,
82; MTCW

Ali, Ahmed 1910-................ **CLC 69**
See also CA 25-28R; CANR 15, 34

Alighieri, Dante 1265-1321 .... **CMLC 3**

Allan, John B.
See Westlake, Donald E(dwin)

Allen, Edward 1948-.............. **CLC 59**

Allen, Paula Gunn 1939-.......... **CLC 84**
See also CA 112; 143; NNAL

Allen, Roland
See Ayckbourn, Alan

Allen, Sarah A.
See Hopkins, Pauline Elizabeth

Allen, Woody 1935- .... **CLC 16, 52**
See also AAYA 10; CA 33-36R; CANR 27,
38; DLB 44; MTCW

Allende, Isabel 1942- .... **CLC 39, 57; HLC**
See also CA 125; 130; HW; MTCW

Alleyn, Ellen
See Rossetti, Christina (Georgina)

Allingham, Margery (Louise)
1904-1966 .... **CLC 19**
See also CA 5-8R; 25-28R; CANR 4;
DLB 77; MTCW

Allingham, William 1824-1889 ... **NCLC 25**
See also DLB 35

Allison, Dorothy E. 1949- .... **CLC 78**
See also CA 140

Allston, Washington 1779-1843.... **NCLC 2**
See also DLB 1

Almedingen, E. M. .... **CLC 12**
See also Almedingen, Martha Edith von
See also SATA 3

Almedingen, Martha Edith von 1898-1971
See Almedingen, E. M.
See also CA 1-4R; CANR 1

Almqvist, Carl Jonas Love
1793-1866 .... **NCLC 42**

Alonso, Damaso 1898-1990 .... **CLC 14**
See also CA 110; 131; 130; DLB 108; HW

Alov
See Gogol, Nikolai (Vasilyevich)

Alta 1942-...................... **CLC 19**
See also CA 57-60

Alter, Robert B(ernard) 1935-...... **CLC 34**
See also CA 49-52; CANR 1

Alther, Lisa 1944-.............. **CLC 7, 41**
See also CA 65-68; CANR 12, 30; MTCW

Altman, Robert 1925-............. **CLC 16**
See also CA 73-76; CANR 43

Alvarez, A(lfred) 1929-.......... **CLC 5, 13**
See also CA 1-4R; CANR 3, 33; DLB 14,
40

Alvarez, Alejandro Rodriguez 1903-1965
See Casona, Alejandro
See also CA 131; 93-96; HW

Amado, Jorge 1912-..... **CLC 13, 40; HLC**
See also CA 77-80; CANR 35; DLB 113;
MTCW

Ambler, Eric 1909-............ **CLC 4, 6, 9**
See also CA 9-12R; CANR 7, 38; DLB 77;
MTCW

Amichai, Yehuda 1924- ...... **CLC 9, 22, 57**
See also CA 85-88; MTCW

Amiel, Henri Frederic 1821-1881 .. **NCLC 4**

Amis, Kingsley (William)
1922- .. **CLC 1, 2, 3, 5, 8, 13, 40, 44; DA**
See also AITN 2; CA 9-12R; CANR 8, 28;
CDBLB 1945-1960; DLB 15, 27, 100, 139;
MTCW

Amis, Martin (Louis)
1949- .... **CLC 4, 9, 38, 62**
See also BEST 90:3; CA 65-68; CANR 8,
27; DLB 14

Ammons, A(rchie) R(andolph)
1926- .... **CLC 2, 3, 5, 8, 9, 25, 57**
See also AITN 1; CA 9-12R; CANR 6, 36;
DLB 5; MTCW

Amo, Tauraatua i
See Adams, Henry (Brooks)

Anand, Mulk Raj 1905-........... **CLC 23**
See also CA 65-68; CANR 32; MTCW

Anatol
See Schnitzler, Arthur

Anaya, Rudolfo A(lfonso)
1937-................ **CLC 23; HLC**
See also CA 45-48; CAAS 4; CANR 1, 32;
DLB 82; HW 1; MTCW

Andersen, Hans Christian
1805-1875 .. **NCLC 7; DA; SSC 6; WLC**
See also CLR 6; MAICYA; YABC 1

Anderson, C. Farley
See Mencken, H(enry) L(ouis); Nathan,
George Jean

Anderson, Jessica (Margaret) Queale
.... **CLC 37**
See also CA 9-12R; CANR 4

Anderson, Jon (Victor) 1940- .... **CLC 9**
See also CA 25-28R; CANR 20

Anderson, Lindsay (Gordon)
1923-...................... **CLC 20**
See also CA 125; 128

Anderson, Maxwell 1888-1959 ..... **TCLC 2**
See also CA 105; DLB 7

Anderson, Poul (William) 1926- .... **CLC 15**
See also AAYA 5; CA 1-4R; CAAS 2;
CANR 2, 15, 34; DLB 8; MTCW;
SATA 39

Anderson, Robert (Woodruff)
1917-...................... **CLC 23**
See also AITN 1; CA 21-24R; CANR 32;
DLB 7

Anderson, Sherwood
1876-1941 .... **TCLC 1, 10, 24; DA;
SSC 1; WLC**
See also CA 104; 121; CDALB 1917-1929;
DLB 4, 9, 86; DLBD 1; MTCW

Andouard
See Giraudoux, (Hippolyte) Jean

Andrade, Carlos Drummond de ...... **CLC 18**
See also Drummond de Andrade, Carlos

Andrade, Mario de 1893-1945..... **TCLC 43**

Andreas-Salome, Lou 1861-1937... **TCLC 56**
See also DLB 66

Andrewes, Lancelot 1555-1626 .... **LC 5**

Andrews, Cicily Fairfield
See West, Rebecca

Andrews, Elton V.
See Pohl, Frederik

Andreyev, Leonid (Nikolaevich)
1871-1919 .... **TCLC 3**
See also CA 104

Andric, Ivo 1892-1975 .... **CLC 8**
See also CA 81-84; 57-60; CANR 43;
MTCW

Angelique, Pierre
See Bataille, Georges

Angell, Roger 1920-.............. **CLC 26**
See also CA 57-60; CANR 13, 44

Angelou, Maya
1928- .... **CLC 12, 35, 64, 77; BLC; DA**
See also AAYA 7; BW 2; CA 65-68;
CANR 19, 42; DLB 38; MTCW;
SATA 49

Annensky, Innokenty Fyodorovich
1856-1909 .... **TCLC 14**
See also CA 110

Anon, Charles Robert
See Pessoa, Fernando (Antonio Nogueira)

Anouilh, Jean (Marie Lucien Pierre)
1910-1987 ...... **CLC 1, 3, 8, 13, 40, 50**
See also CA 17-20R; 123; CANR 32;
MTCW

Anthony, Florence
See Ai

Anthony, John
See Ciardi, John (Anthony)

Anthony, Peter
See Shaffer, Anthony (Joshua); Shaffer,
Peter (Levin)

Anthony, Piers 1934-............ **CLC 35**
  See also AAYA 11; CA 21-24R; CANR 28;
  DLB 8; MTCW

Antoine, Marc
  See Proust, (Valentin-Louis-George-Eugene-)
  Marcel

Antoninus, Brother
  See Everson, William (Oliver)

Antonioni, Michelangelo 1912-..... **CLC 20**
  See also CA 73-76; CANR 45

Antschel, Paul 1920-1970
  See Celan, Paul
  See also CA 85-88; CANR 33; MTCW

Anwar, Chairil 1922-1949 .... **TCLC 22**
  See also CA 121

Apollinaire, Guillaume .. **TCLC 3, 8, 51; PC 7**
  See also Kostrowitzki, Wilhelm Apollinaris
  de

Appelfeld, Aharon 1932- .... **CLC 23, 47**
  See also CA 112; 133

Apple, Max (Isaac) 1941-........ **CLC 9, 33**
  See also CA 81-84; CANR 19; DLB 130

Appleman, Philip (Dean) 1926-..... **CLC 51**
  See also CA 13-16R; CAAS 18; CANR 6,
  29

Appleton, Lawrence
  See Lovecraft, H(oward) P(hillips)

Apteryx
  See Eliot, T(homas) S(tearns)

Apuleius, (Lucius Madaurensis)
  125(?)-175(?)............... **CMLC 1**

Aquin, Hubert 1929-1977......... **CLC 15**
  See also CA 105; DLB 53

Aragon, Louis 1897-1982....... **CLC 3, 22**
  See also CA 69-72; 108; CANR 28;
  DLB 72; MTCW

Arany, Janos 1817-1882........ **NCLC 34**

Arbuthnot, John 1667-1735.......... **LC 1**
  See also DLB 101

Archer, Herbert Winslow
  See Mencken, H(enry) L(ouis)

Archer, Jeffrey (Howard) 1940-.... **CLC 28**
  See also BEST 89:3; CA 77-80; CANR 22

Archer, Jules 1915- .... **CLC 12**
  See also CA 9-12R; CANR 6; SAAS 5;
  SATA 4

Archer, Lee
  See Ellison, Harlan

Arden, John 1930- .... **CLC 6, 13, 15**
  See also CA 13-16R; CAAS 4; CANR 31;
  DLB 13; MTCW

Arenas, Reinaldo
  1943-1990 .... **CLC 41; HLC**
  See also CA 124; 128; 133; HW

Arendt, Hannah 1906-1975 .... **CLC 66**
  See also CA 17-20R; 61-64; CANR 26;
  MTCW

Aretino, Pietro 1492-1556 .... **LC 12**

Arghezi, Tudor.................... **CLC 80**
  See also Theodorescu, Ion N.

Arguedas, Jose Maria
  1911-1969 .... **CLC 10, 18**
  See also CA 89-92; DLB 113; HW

Argueta, Manlio 1936-............ **CLC 31**
  See also CA 131; HW

Ariosto, Ludovico 1474-1533........ **LC 6**

Aristides
  See Epstein, Joseph

Aristophanes
  450B.C.-385B.C.... **CMLC 4; DA; DC 2**

Arlt, Roberto (Godofredo Christophersen)
  1900-1942 .... **TCLC 29; HLC**
  See also CA 123; 131; HW

Armah, Ayi Kwei 1939-.... **CLC 5, 33; BLC**
  See also BW 1; CA 61-64; CANR 21;
  DLB 117; MTCW

Armatrading, Joan 1950-.......... **CLC 17**
  See also CA 114

Arnette, Robert
  See Silverberg, Robert

Arnim, Achim von (Ludwig Joachim von
  Arnim) 1781-1831 .... **NCLC 5**
  See also DLB 90

Arnim, Bettina von 1785-1859.... **NCLC 38**
  See also DLB 90

Arnold, Matthew
  1822-1888 ..... **NCLC 6, 29; DA; PC 5;**
                               WLC
  See also CDBLB 1832-1890; DLB 32, 57

Arnold, Thomas 1795-1842 ...... **NCLC 18**
  See also DLB 55

Arnow, Harriette (Louisa) Simpson
  1908-1986 .... **CLC 2, 7, 18**
  See also CA 9-12R; 118; CANR 14; DLB 6;
  MTCW; SATA 42, 47

Arp, Hans
  See Arp, Jean

Arp, Jean 1887-1966.............. **CLC 5**
  See also CA 81-84; 25-28R; CANR 42

Arrabal
  See Arrabal, Fernando

Arrabal, Fernando 1932- ... **CLC 2, 9, 18, 58**
  See also CA 9-12R; CANR 15

Arrick, Fran.................... **CLC 30**

Artaud, Antonin 1896-1948 ..... **TCLC 3, 36**
  See also CA 104

Arthur, Ruth M(abel) 1905-1979.... **CLC 12**
  See also CA 9-12R; 85-88; CANR 4;
  SATA 7, 26

Artsybashev, Mikhail (Petrovich)
  1878-1927 .... **TCLC 31**

Arundel, Honor (Morfydd)
  1919-1973 .... **CLC 17**
  See also CA 21-22; 41-44R; CAP 2;
  CLR 35; SATA 4, 24

Asch, Sholem 1880-1957 .... **TCLC 3**
  See also CA 105

Ash, Shalom
  See Asch, Sholem

Ashbery, John (Lawrence)
  1927- ...... **CLC 2, 3, 4, 6, 9, 13, 15, 25,**
                           41, 77
  See also CA 5-8R; CANR 9, 37; DLB 5;
  DLBY 81; MTCW

Ashdown, Clifford
  See Freeman, R(ichard) Austin

Ashe, Gordon
  See Creasey, John

Ashton-Warner, Sylvia (Constance)
  1908-1984 .... **CLC 19**
  See also CA 69-72; 112; CANR 29; MTCW

Asimov, Isaac
  1920-1992 ...... **CLC 1, 3, 9, 19, 26, 76**
  See also BEST 90:2; CA 1-4R; 137;
  CANR 2, 19, 36; CLR 12; DLB 8;
  DLBY 92; JRDA; MAICYA; MTCW;
  SATA 1, 26, 74

Astley, Thea (Beatrice May)
  1925- .... **CLC 41**
  See also CA 65-68; CANR 11, 43

Aston, James
  See White, T(erence) H(anbury)

Asturias, Miguel Angel
  1899-1974 .... **CLC 3, 8, 13; HLC**
  See also CA 25-28; 49-52; CANR 32;
  CAP 2; DLB 113; HW; MTCW

Atares, Carlos Saura
  See Saura (Atares), Carlos

Atheling, William
  See Pound, Ezra (Weston Loomis)

Atheling, William, Jr.
  See Blish, James (Benjamin)

Atherton, Gertrude (Franklin Horn)
  1857-1948 .... **TCLC 2**
  See also CA 104; DLB 9, 78

Atherton, Lucius
  See Masters, Edgar Lee

Atkins, Jack
  See Harris, Mark

Atticus
  See Fleming, Ian (Lancaster)

Atwood, Margaret (Eleanor)
  1939- ..... **CLC 2, 3, 4, 8, 13, 15, 25, 44,**
              84; DA; PC 8; SSC 2; WLC
  See also AAYA 12; BEST 89:2; CA 49-52;
  CANR 3, 24, 33; DLB 53; MTCW;
  SATA 50

Aubigny, Pierre d'
  See Mencken, H(enry) L(ouis)

Aubin, Penelope 1685-1731(?)........ **LC 9**
  See also DLB 39

Auchincloss, Louis (Stanton)
  1917- .... **CLC 4, 6, 9, 18, 45**
  See also CA 1-4R; CANR 6, 29; DLB 2;
  DLBY 80; MTCW

Auden, W(ystan) H(ugh)
  1907-1973 ...... **CLC 1, 2, 3, 4, 6, 9, 11,**
                14, 43; DA; PC 1; WLC
  See also CA 9-12R; 45-48; CANR 5;
  CDBLB 1914-1945; DLB 10, 20; MTCW

Audiberti, Jacques 1900-1965 ...... **CLC 38**
  See also CA 25-28R

Audubon, John James
  1785-1851 .... **NCLC 47**

Auel, Jean M(arie) 1936-.......... **CLC 31**
  See also AAYA 7; BEST 90:4; CA 103;
  CANR 21

Auerbach, Erich 1892-1957 .... **TCLC 43**
  See also CA 118

Augier, Emile 1820-1889 .... **NCLC 31**

Barker, Howard 1946- .... **CLC 37**
See also CA 102; DLB 13

Barker, Pat 1943-................. **CLC 32**
See also CA 117; 122

Barlow, Joel 1754-1812 .... **NCLC 23**
See also DLB 37

Barnard, Mary (Ethel) 1909-........ **CLC 48**
See also CA 21-22; CAP 2

Barnes, Djuna
1892-1982 ... **CLC 3, 4, 8, 11, 29; SSC 3**
See also CA 9-12R; 107; CANR 16; DLB 4,
9, 45; MTCW

Barnes, Julian 1946-.............. **CLC 42**
See also CA 102; CANR 19; DLBY 93

Barnes, Peter 1931- .... **CLC 5, 56**
See also CA 65-68; CAAS 12; CANR 33,
34; DLB 13; MTCW

Baroja (y Nessi), Pio
1872-1956 .... **TCLC 8; HLC**
See also CA 104

Baron, David
See Pinter, Harold

Baron Corvo
See Rolfe, Frederick (William Serafino
Austin Lewis Mary)

Barondess, Sue K(aufman)
1926-1977 .... **CLC 8**
See also Kaufman, Sue
See also CA 1-4R; 69-72; CANR 1

Baron de Teive
See Pessoa, Fernando (Antonio Nogueira)

Barres, Maurice 1862-1923 ...... **TCLC 47**
See also DLB 123

Barreto, Afonso Henrique de Lima
See Lima Barreto, Afonso Henrique de

Barrett, (Roger) Syd 1946- .... **CLC 35**

Barrett, William (Christopher)
1913-1992 .... **CLC 27**
See also CA 13-16R; 139; CANR 11

Barrie, J(ames) M(atthew)
1860-1937 .... **TCLC 2**
See also CA 104; 136; CDBLB 1890-1914;
CLR 16; DLB 10, 141; MAICYA;
YABC 1

Barrington, Michael
See Moorcock, Michael (John)

Barrol, Grady
See Bograd, Larry

Barry, Mike
See Malzberg, Barry N(athaniel)

Barry, Philip 1896-1949.......... **TCLC 11**
See also CA 109; DLB 7

Bart, Andre Schwarz
See Schwarz-Bart, Andre

Barth, John (Simmons)
1930- ...... **CLC 1, 2, 3, 5, 7, 9, 10, 14,
27, 51; SSC 10**
See also AITN 1, 2; CA 1-4R; CABS 1;
CANR 5, 23; DLB 2; MTCW

Barthelme, Donald
1931-1989 ...... **CLC 1, 2, 3, 5, 6, 8, 13,
23, 46, 59; SSC 2**
See also CA 21-24R; 129; CANR 20;
DLB 2; DLBY 80, 89; MTCW; SATA 7,
62

Barthelme, Frederick 1943-........ **CLC 36**
See also CA 114; 122; DLBY 85

Barthes, Roland (Gerard)
1915-1980 .... **CLC 24, 83**
See also CA 130; 97-100; MTCW

Barzun, Jacques (Martin) 1907- .... **CLC 51**
See also CA 61-64; CANR 22

Bashevis, Isaac
See Singer, Isaac Bashevis

Bashkirtseff, Marie 1859-1884 ... **NCLC 27**

Basho
See Matsuo Basho

Bass, Kingsley B., Jr.
See Bullins, Ed

Bass, Rick 1958-................. **CLC 79**
See also CA 126

Bassani, Giorgio 1916-............ **CLC 9**
See also CA 65-68; CANR 33; DLB 128;
MTCW

Bastos, Augusto (Antonio) Roa
See Roa Bastos, Augusto (Antonio)

Bataille, Georges 1897-1962 ...... **CLC 29**
See also CA 101; 89-92

Bates, H(erbert) E(rnest)
1905-1974 .... **CLC 46; SSC 10**
See also CA 93-96; 45-48; CANR 34;
MTCW

Bauchart
See Camus, Albert

Baudelaire, Charles
1821-1867 ..... **NCLC 6, 29; DA; PC 1;
WLC**

Baudrillard, Jean 1929-........... **CLC 60**

Baum, L(yman) Frank 1856-1919 ... **TCLC 7**
See also CA 108; 133; CLR 15; DLB 22;
JRDA; MAICYA; MTCW; SATA 18

Baum, Louis F.
See Baum, L(yman) Frank

Baumbach, Jonathan 1933-....... **CLC 6, 23**
See also CA 13-16R; CAAS 5; CANR 12;
DLBY 80; MTCW

Bausch, Richard (Carl) 1945- ...... **CLC 51**
See also CA 101; CAAS 14; CANR 43;
DLB 130

Baxter, Charles 1947-.......... **CLC 45, 78**
See also CA 57-60; CANR 40; DLB 130

Baxter, George Owen
See Faust, Frederick (Schiller)

Baxter, James K(eir) 1926-1972 .... **CLC 14**
See also CA 77-80

Baxter, John
See Hunt, E(verette) Howard, Jr.

Bayer, Sylvia
See Glassco, John

Baynton, Barbara 1857-1929 ...... **TCLC 57**

Beagle, Peter S(oyer) 1939-......... **CLC 7**
See also CA 9-12R; CANR 4; DLBY 80;
SATA 60

Bean, Normal
See Burroughs, Edgar Rice

Beard, Charles A(ustin)
1874-1948 .... **TCLC 15**
See also CA 115; DLB 17; SATA 18

Beardsley, Aubrey 1872-1898 ..... **NCLC 6**

Beattie, Ann
1947- .... **CLC 8, 13, 18, 40, 63; SSC 11**
See also BEST 90:2; CA 81-84; DLBY 82;
MTCW

Beattie, James 1735-1803 .... **NCLC 25**
See also DLB 109

Beauchamp, Kathleen Mansfield 1888-1923
See Mansfield, Katherine
See also CA 104; 134; DA

Beaumarchais, Pierre-Augustin Caron de
1732-1799 .... **DC 4**

**Beauvoir, Simone (Lucie Ernestine Marie
Bertrand) de**
1908-1986 .... **CLC 1, 2, 4, 8, 14, 31, 44,
50, 71; DA; WLC**
See also CA 9-12R; 118; CANR 28;
DLB 72; DLBY 86; MTCW

Becker, Jurek 1937-............ **CLC 7, 19**
See also CA 85-88; DLB 75

Becker, Walter 1950-............... **CLC 26**

Beckett, Samuel (Barclay)
1906-1989 ...... **CLC 1, 2, 3, 4, 6, 9, 10,
11, 14, 18, 29, 57, 59, 83; DA; SSC 16;
WLC**
See also CA 5-8R; 130; CANR 33;
CDBLB 1945-1960; DLB 13, 15;
DLBY 90; MTCW

Beckford, William 1760-1844 .... **NCLC 16**
See also DLB 39

Beckman, Gunnel 1910-........... **CLC 26**
See also CA 33-36R; CANR 15; CLR 25;
MAICYA; SAAS 9; SATA 6

Becque, Henri 1837-1899......... **NCLC 3**

Beddoes, Thomas Lovell
1803-1849 .... **NCLC 3**
See also DLB 96

Bedford, Donald F.
See Fearing, Kenneth (Flexner)

Beecher, Catharine Esther
1800-1878 .... **NCLC 30**
See also DLB 1

Beecher, John 1904-1980.......... **CLC 6**
See also AITN 1; CA 5-8R; 105; CANR 8

Beer, Johann 1655-1700............. **LC 5**

Beer, Patricia 1924-.............. **CLC 58**
See also CA 61-64; CANR 13; DLB 40

Beerbohm, Henry Maximilian
1872-1956 .... **TCLC 1, 24**
See also CA 104; DLB 34, 100

Beerbohm, Max
See Beerbohm, Henry Maximilian

Begiebing, Robert J(ohn) 1946-..... **CLC 70**
See also CA 122; CANR 40

Behan, Brendan
1923-1964 .... **CLC 1, 8, 11, 15, 79**
See also CA 73-76; CANR 33;
CDBLB 1945-1960; DLB 13; MTCW

Behn, Aphra
1640(?)-1689 .... **LC 1; DA; DC 4; WLC**
See also DLB 39, 80, 131

Behrman, S(amuel) N(athaniel)
1893-1973 .... **CLC 40**
See also CA 13-16; 45-48; CAP 1; DLB 7,
44

Besant, Annie (Wood) 1847-1933 ... **TCLC 9**
See also CA 105

Bessie, Alvah 1904-1985. . . . . **CLC 23**
See also CA 5-8R; 116; CANR 2; DLB 26

Bethlen, T. D.
See Silverberg, Robert

Beti, Mongo. . . . . **CLC 27; BLC**
See also Biyidi, Alexandre

Betjeman, John
1906-1984 . . . . **CLC 2, 6, 10, 34, 43**
See also CA 9-12R; 112; CANR 33;
CDBLB 1945-1960; DLB 20; DLBY 84;
MTCW

Bettelheim, Bruno 1903-1990 . . . . . . **CLC 79**
See also CA 81-84; 131; CANR 23; MTCW

Betti, Ugo 1892-1953 . . . . **TCLC 5**
See also CA 104

Betts, Doris (Waugh) 1932-. . . . **CLC 3, 6, 28**
See also CA 13-16R; CANR 9; DLBY 82

Bevan, Alistair
See Roberts, Keith (John Kingston)

Bialik, Chaim Nachman
1873-1934 . . . . **TCLC 25**

Bickerstaff, Isaac
See Swift, Jonathan

Bidart, Frank 1939- . . . . **CLC 33**
See also CA 140

Bienek, Horst 1930-. . . . . **CLC 7, 11**
See also CA 73-76; DLB 75

Bierce, Ambrose (Gwinett)
1842-1914(?) . . . . **TCLC 1, 7, 44; DA;**
                                          SSC 9; WLC
See also CA 104; 139; CDALB 1865-1917;
DLB 11, 12, 23, 71, 74

Billings, Josh
See Shaw, Henry Wheeler

Billington, (Lady) Rachel (Mary)
1942- . . . . **CLC 43**
See also AITN 2; CA 33-36R; CANR 44

Binyon, T(imothy) J(ohn) 1936- . . . . **CLC 34**
See also CA 111; CANR 28

Bioy Casares, Adolfo
1914- . . . . . . **CLC 4, 8, 13; HLC; SSC 17**
See also CA 29-32R; CANR 19, 43;
DLB 113; HW; MTCW

Bird, C.
See Ellison, Harlan

Bird, Cordwainer
See Ellison, Harlan

Bird, Robert Montgomery
1806-1854 . . . . **NCLC 1**

Birney, (Alfred) Earle
1904- . . . . **CLC 1, 4, 6, 11**
See also CA 1-4R; CANR 5, 20; DLB 88;
MTCW

Bishop, Elizabeth
1911-1979 . . . . . . **CLC 1, 4, 9, 13, 15, 32;**
                                                   DA; PC 3
See also CA 5-8R; 89-92; CABS 2;
CANR 26; CDALB 1968-1988; DLB 5;
MTCW; SATA 24

Bishop, John 1935-. . . . . **CLC 10**
See also CA 105

Bissett, Bill 1939-. . . . . **CLC 18**
See also CA 69-72; CAAS 19; CANR 15;
DLB 53; MTCW

Bitov, Andrei (Georgievich) 1937-. . . **CLC 57**
See also CA 142

Biyidi, Alexandre 1932-
See Beti, Mongo
See also BW 1; CA 114; 124; MTCW

Bjarme, Brynjolf
See Ibsen, Henrik (Johan)

Bjornson, Bjornstjerne (Martinius)
1832-1910 . . . . **TCLC 7, 37**
See also CA 104

Black, Robert
See Holdstock, Robert P.

Blackburn, Paul 1926-1971 . . . . . . **CLC 9, 43**
See also CA 81-84; 33-36R; CANR 34;
DLB 16; DLBY 81

Black Elk 1863-1950 . . . . **TCLC 33**
See also CA 144

Black Hobart
See Sanders, (James) Ed(ward)

Blacklin, Malcolm
See Chambers, Aidan

Blackmore, R(ichard) D(oddridge)
1825-1900 . . . . **TCLC 27**
See also CA 120; DLB 18

Blackmur, R(ichard) P(almer)
1904-1965 . . . . **CLC 2, 24**
See also CA 11-12; 25-28R; CAP 1; DLB 63

Black Tarantula, The
See Acker, Kathy

Blackwood, Algernon (Henry)
1869-1951 . . . . **TCLC 5**
See also CA 105

Blackwood, Caroline 1931- . . . . **CLC 6, 9**
See also CA 85-88; CANR 32; DLB 14;
MTCW

Blade, Alexander
See Hamilton, Edmond; Silverberg, Robert

Blaga, Lucian 1895-1961 . . . . **CLC 75**

Blair, Eric (Arthur) 1903-1950
See Orwell, George
See also CA 104; 132; DA; MTCW;
SATA 29

Blais, Marie-Claire
1939- . . . . **CLC 2, 4, 6, 13, 22**
See also CA 21-24R; CAAS 4; CANR 38;
DLB 53; MTCW

Blaise, Clark 1940-. . . . . **CLC 29**
See also AITN 2; CA 53-56; CAAS 3;
CANR 5; DLB 53

Blake, Nicholas
See Day Lewis, C(ecil)
See also DLB 77

Blake, William
1757-1827 . . . . . **NCLC 13, 37; DA; WLC**
See also CDBLB 1789-1832; DLB 93;
MAICYA; SATA 30

Blasco Ibanez, Vicente
1867-1928 . . . . **TCLC 12**
See also CA 110; 131; HW; MTCW

Blatty, William Peter 1928-. . . . . **CLC 2**
See also CA 5-8R; CANR 9

Bleeck, Oliver
See Thomas, Ross (Elmore)

Blessing, Lee 1949-. . . . . **CLC 54**

Blish, James (Benjamin)
1921-1975 . . . . **CLC 14**
See also CA 1-4R; 57-60; CANR 3; DLB 8;
MTCW; SATA 66

Bliss, Reginald
See Wells, H(erbert) G(eorge)

Blixen, Karen (Christentze Dinesen)
1885-1962
See Dinesen, Isak
See also CA 25-28; CANR 22; CAP 2;
MTCW; SATA 44

Bloch, Robert (Albert) 1917-. . . . . . . **CLC 33**
See also CA 5-8R; CANR 5; DLB 44;
SATA 12

Blok, Alexander (Alexandrovich)
1880-1921 . . . . **TCLC 5**
See also CA 104

Blom, Jan
See Breytenbach, Breyten

Bloom, Harold 1930- . . . . **CLC 24**
See also CA 13-16R; CANR 39; DLB 67

Bloomfield, Aurelius
See Bourne, Randolph S(illiman)

Blount, Roy (Alton), Jr. 1941- . . . . . **CLC 38**
See also CA 53-56; CANR 10, 28; MTCW

Bloy, Leon 1846-1917. . . . . **TCLC 22**
See also CA 121; DLB 123

Blume, Judy (Sussman) 1938-. . . **CLC 12, 30**
See also AAYA 3; CA 29-32R; CANR 13,
37; CLR 2, 15; DLB 52; JRDA;
MAICYA; MTCW; SATA 2, 31, 79

Blunden, Edmund (Charles)
1896-1974 . . . . **CLC 2, 56**
See also CA 17-18; 45-48; CAP 2; DLB 20,
100; MTCW

Bly, Robert (Elwood)
1926- . . . . **CLC 1, 2, 5, 10, 15, 38**
See also CA 5-8R; CANR 41; DLB 5;
MTCW

Boas, Franz 1858-1942. . . . . **TCLC 56**
See also CA 115

Bobette
See Simenon, Georges (Jacques Christian)

Boccaccio, Giovanni
1313-1375 . . . . **CMLC 13; SSC 10**

Bochco, Steven 1943-. . . . . **CLC 35**
See also AAYA 11; CA 124; 138

Bodenheim, Maxwell 1892-1954 . . . **TCLC 44**
See also CA 110; DLB 9, 45

Bodker, Cecil 1927- . . . . **CLC 21**
See also CA 73-76; CANR 13, 44; CLR 23;
MAICYA; SATA 14

Boell, Heinrich (Theodor)
1917-1985 . . . . **CLC 2, 3, 6, 9, 11, 15, 27,**
                                          32, 72; DA; WLC
See also CA 21-24R; 116; CANR 24;
DLB 69; DLBY 85; MTCW

Boerne, Alfred
See Doeblin, Alfred

Bogan, Louise 1897-1970. . . . . **CLC 4, 39, 46**
See also CA 73-76; 25-28R; CANR 33;
DLB 45; MTCW

Bogarde, Dirk .... **CLC 19**
  See also Van Den Bogarde, Derek Jules
    Gaspard Ulric Niven
  See also DLB 14

Bogosian, Eric 1953- .... **CLC 45**
  See also CA 138

Bograd, Larry 1953-............... **CLC 35**
  See also CA 93-96; SATA 33

Boiardo, Matteo Maria 1441-1494 .... **LC 6**

Boileau-Despreaux, Nicolas
  1636-1711 .... **LC 3**

Boland, Eavan (Aisling) 1944-... **CLC 40, 67**
  See also CA 143; DLB 40

Bolt, Lee
  See Faust, Frederick (Schiller)

Bolt, Robert (Oxton) 1924-........ **CLC 14**
  See also CA 17-20R; CANR 35; DLB 13;
    MTCW

Bombet, Louis-Alexandre-Cesar
  See Stendhal

Bomkauf
  See Kaufman, Bob (Garnell)

Bonaventura.................... **NCLC 35**
  See also DLB 90

Bond, Edward 1934-...... **CLC 4, 6, 13, 23**
  See also CA 25-28R; CANR 38; DLB 13;
    MTCW

Bonham, Frank 1914-1989........ **CLC 12**
  See also AAYA 1; CA 9-12R; CANR 4, 36;
    JRDA; MAICYA; SAAS 3; SATA 1, 49,
    62

Bonnefoy, Yves 1923-........ **CLC 9, 15, 58**
  See also CA 85-88; CANR 33; MTCW

Bontemps, Arna(ud Wendell)
  1902-1973 .... **CLC 1, 18; BLC**
  See also BW 1; CA 1-4R; 41-44R; CANR 4,
    35; CLR 6; DLB 48, 51; JRDA;
    MAICYA; MTCW; SATA 2, 24, 44

Booth, Martin 1944-.............. **CLC 13**
  See also CA 93-96; CAAS 2

Booth, Philip 1925-............... **CLC 23**
  See also CA 5-8R; CANR 5; DLBY 82

Booth, Wayne C(layson) 1921- ..... **CLC 24**
  See also CA 1-4R; CAAS 5; CANR 3, 43;
    DLB 67

Borchert, Wolfgang 1921-1947 ..... **TCLC 5**
  See also CA 104; DLB 69, 124

Borel, Petrus 1809-1859........ **NCLC 41**

Borges, Jorge Luis
  1899-1986 ... **CLC 1, 2, 3, 4, 6, 8, 9, 10,
    13, 19, 44, 48, 83; DA; HLC; SSC 4;
                                        WLC**
  See also CA 21-24R; CANR 19, 33;
    DLB 113; DLBY 86; HW; MTCW

Borowski, Tadeusz 1922-1951 ...... **TCLC 9**
  See also CA 106

Borrow, George (Henry)
  1803-1881 .... **NCLC 9**
  See also DLB 21, 55

Bosman, Herman Charles
  1905-1951 .... **TCLC 49**

Bosschere, Jean de 1878(?)-1953... **TCLC 19**
  See also CA 115

Boswell, James
  1740-1795 .... **LC 4; DA; WLC**
  See also CDBLB 1660-1789; DLB 104, 142

Bottoms, David 1949-............. **CLC 53**
  See also CA 105; CANR 22; DLB 120;
    DLBY 83

Boucicault, Dion 1820-1890...... **NCLC 41**

Boucolon, Maryse 1937-
  See Conde, Maryse
  See also CA 110; CANR 30

Bourget, Paul (Charles Joseph)
  1852-1935 .... **TCLC 12**
  See also CA 107; DLB 123

Bourjaily, Vance (Nye) 1922- .... **CLC 8, 62**
  See also CA 1-4R; CAAS 1; CANR 2;
    DLB 2, 143

Bourne, Randolph S(illiman)
  1886-1918 .... **TCLC 16**
  See also CA 117; DLB 63

Bova, Ben(jamin William) 1932-.... **CLC 45**
  See also CA 5-8R; CAAS 18; CANR 11;
    CLR 3; DLBY 81; MAICYA; MTCW;
    SATA 6, 68

Bowen, Elizabeth (Dorothea Cole)
  1899-1973 ...... **CLC 1, 3, 6, 11, 15, 22;
                                        SSC 3**
  See also CA 17-18; 41-44R; CANR 35;
    CAP 2; CDBLB 1945-1960; DLB 15;
    MTCW

Bowering, George 1935-........ **CLC 15, 47**
  See also CA 21-24R; CAAS 16; CANR 10;
    DLB 53

Bowering, Marilyn R(uthe) 1949-... **CLC 32**
  See also CA 101

Bowers, Edgar 1924- .... **CLC 9**
  See also CA 5-8R; CANR 24; DLB 5

Bowie, David .... **CLC 17**
  See also Jones, David Robert

Bowles, Jane (Sydney)
  1917-1973 .... **CLC 3, 68**
  See also CA 19-20; 41-44R; CAP 2

Bowles, Paul (Frederick)
  1910- .... **CLC 1, 2, 19, 53; SSC 3**
  See also CA 1-4R; CAAS 1; CANR 1, 19;
    DLB 5, 6; MTCW

Box, Edgar
  See Vidal, Gore

Boyd, Nancy
  See Millay, Edna St. Vincent

Boyd, William 1952-........ **CLC 28, 53, 70**
  See also CA 114; 120

Boyle, Kay
  1902-1992 ..... **CLC 1, 5, 19, 58; SSC 5**
  See also CA 13-16R; 140; CAAS 1;
    CANR 29; DLB 4, 9, 48, 86; DLBY 93;
    MTCW

Boyle, Mark
  See Kienzle, William X(avier)

Boyle, Patrick 1905-1982......... **CLC 19**
  See also CA 127

Boyle, T. C.
  See Boyle, T(homas) Coraghessan

Boyle, T(homas) Coraghessan
  1948- .... **CLC 36, 55; SSC 16**
  See also BEST 90:4; CA 120; CANR 44;
    DLBY 86

Boz
  See Dickens, Charles (John Huffam)

Brackenridge, Hugh Henry
  1748-1816 .... **NCLC 7**
  See also DLB 11, 37

Bradbury, Edward P.
  See Moorcock, Michael (John)

Bradbury, Malcolm (Stanley)
  1932- .... **CLC 32, 61**
  See also CA 1-4R; CANR 1, 33; DLB 14;
    MTCW

Bradbury, Ray (Douglas)
  1920- ... **CLC 1, 3, 10, 15, 42; DA; WLC**
  See also AITN 1, 2; CA 1-4R; CANR 2, 30;
    CDALB 1968-1988; DLB 2, 8; MTCW;
    SATA 11, 64

Bradford, Gamaliel 1863-1932..... **TCLC 36**
  See also DLB 17

Bradley, David (Henry, Jr.)
  1950- .... **CLC 23; BLC**
  See also BW 1; CA 104; CANR 26; DLB 33

Bradley, John Ed(mund, Jr.)
  1958- .... **CLC 55**
  See also CA 139

Bradley, Marion Zimmer 1930-..... **CLC 30**
  See also AAYA 9; CA 57-60; CAAS 10;
    CANR 7, 31; DLB 8; MTCW

Bradstreet, Anne
  1612(?)-1672 .... **LC 4; DA; PC 10**
  See also CDALB 1640-1865; DLB 24

Bragg, Melvyn 1939- .... **CLC 10**
  See also BEST 89:3; CA 57-60; CANR 10;
    DLB 14

Braine, John (Gerard)
  1922-1986 .... **CLC 1, 3, 41**
  See also CA 1-4R; 120; CANR 1, 33;
    CDBLB 1945-1960; DLB 15; DLBY 86;
    MTCW

Brammer, William 1930(?)-1978 .... **CLC 31**
  See also CA 77-80

Brancati, Vitaliano 1907-1954..... **TCLC 12**
  See also CA 109

Brancato, Robin F(idler) 1936- ..... **CLC 35**
  See also AAYA 9; CA 69-72; CANR 11,
    45; CLR 32; JRDA; SAAS 9; SATA 23

Brand, Max
  See Faust, Frederick (Schiller)

Brand, Millen 1906-1980.......... **CLC 7**
  See also CA 21-24R; 97-100

Branden, Barbara .... **CLC 44**

Brandes, Georg (Morris Cohen)
  1842-1927 .... **TCLC 10**
  See also CA 105

Brandys, Kazimierz 1916- .... **CLC 62**

Branley, Franklyn M(ansfield)
  1915- .... **CLC 21**
  See also CA 33-36R; CANR 14, 39;
    CLR 13; MAICYA; SAAS 16; SATA 4,
    68

Brathwaite, Edward (Kamau)
1930- .... **CLC 11**
See also BW 2; CA 25-28R; CANR 11, 26;
DLB 125

Brautigan, Richard (Gary)
1935-1984 .... **CLC 1, 3, 5, 9, 12, 34, 42**
See also CA 53-56; 113; CANR 34; DLB 2,
5; DLBY 80, 84; MTCW; SATA 56

Braverman, Kate 1950- .... **CLC 67**
See also CA 89-92

Brecht, Bertolt
1898-1956 ...... **TCLC 1, 6, 13, 35; DA;**
DC 3; WLC
See also CA 104; 133; DLB 56, 124; MTCW

Brecht, Eugen Berthold Friedrich
See Brecht, Bertolt

Bremer, Fredrika 1801-1865 ..... **NCLC 11**

Brennan, Christopher John
1870-1932 .... **TCLC 17**
See also CA 117

Brennan, Maeve 1917- .... **CLC 5**
See also CA 81-84

Brentano, Clemens (Maria)
1778-1842 .... **NCLC 1**

Brent of Bin Bin
See Franklin, (Stella Maraia Sarah) Miles

Brenton, Howard 1942- .... **CLC 31**
See also CA 69-72; CANR 33; DLB 13;
MTCW

Breslin, James 1930-
See Breslin, Jimmy
See also CA 73-76; CANR 31; MTCW

Breslin, Jimmy .... **CLC 4, 43**
See also Breslin, James
See also AITN 1

Bresson, Robert 1907- .... **CLC 16**
See also CA 110

Breton, Andre 1896-1966... **CLC 2, 9, 15, 54**
See also CA 19-20; 25-28R; CANR 40;
CAP 2; DLB 65; MTCW

Breytenbach, Breyten 1939(?)- .. **CLC 23, 37**
See also CA 113; 129

Bridgers, Sue Ellen 1942- .... **CLC 26**
See also AAYA 8; CA 65-68; CANR 11,
36; CLR 18; DLB 52; JRDA; MAICYA;
SAAS 1; SATA 22

Bridges, Robert (Seymour)
1844-1930 .... **TCLC 1**
See also CA 104; CDBLB 1890-1914;
DLB 19, 98

Bridie, James .... **TCLC 3**
See also Mavor, Osborne Henry
See also DLB 10

Brin, David 1950- .... **CLC 34**
See also CA 102; CANR 24; SATA 65

Brink, Andre (Philippus)
1935- .... **CLC 18, 36**
See also CA 104; CANR 39; MTCW

Brinsmead, H(esba) F(ay) 1922- .... **CLC 21**
See also CA 21-24R; CANR 10; MAICYA;
SAAS 5; SATA 18, 78

Brittain, Vera (Mary)
1893(?)-1970 .... **CLC 23**
See also CA 13-16; 25-28R; CAP 1; MTCW

Broch, Hermann 1886-1951 ...... **TCLC 20**
See also CA 117; DLB 85, 124

Brock, Rose
See Hansen, Joseph

Brodkey, Harold 1930- .... **CLC 56**
See also CA 111; DLB 130

Brodsky, Iosif Alexandrovich 1940-
See Brodsky, Joseph
See also AITN 1; CA 41-44R; CANR 37;
MTCW

Brodsky, Joseph .. **CLC 4, 6, 13, 36, 50; PC 9**
See also Brodsky, Iosif Alexandrovich

Brodsky, Michael Mark 1948- ..... **CLC 19**
See also CA 102; CANR 18, 41

Bromell, Henry 1947- .... **CLC 5**
See also CA 53-56; CANR 9

Bromfield, Louis (Brucker)
1896-1956 .... **TCLC 11**
See also CA 107; DLB 4, 9, 86

Broner, E(sther) M(asserman)
1930- .... **CLC 19**
See also CA 17-20R; CANR 8, 25; DLB 28

Bronk, William 1918- .... **CLC 10**
See also CA 89-92; CANR 23

Bronstein, Lev Davidovich
See Trotsky, Leon

Bronte, Anne 1820-1849 .... **NCLC 4**
See also DLB 21

Bronte, Charlotte
1816-1855 ... **NCLC 3, 8, 33; DA; WLC**
See also CDBLB 1832-1890; DLB 21

Bronte, (Jane) Emily
1818-1848 .... **NCLC 16, 35; DA; PC 8;**
WLC
See also CDBLB 1832-1890; DLB 21, 32

Brooke, Frances 1724-1789 .... **LC 6**
See also DLB 39, 99

Brooke, Henry 1703(?)-1783 .... **LC 1**
See also DLB 39

Brooke, Rupert (Chawner)
1887-1915 .... **TCLC 2, 7; DA; WLC**
See also CA 104; 132; CDBLB 1914-1945;
DLB 19; MTCW

Brooke-Haven, P.
See Wodehouse, P(elham) G(renville)

Brooke-Rose, Christine 1926- ...... **CLC 40**
See also CA 13-16R; DLB 14

Brookner, Anita 1928- ...... **CLC 32, 34, 51**
See also CA 114; 120; CANR 37; DLBY 87;
MTCW

Brooks, Cleanth 1906-1994 .... **CLC 24**
See also CA 17-20R; 145; CANR 33, 35;
DLB 63; MTCW

Brooks, George
See Baum, L(yman) Frank

Brooks, Gwendolyn
1917- ...... **CLC 1, 2, 4, 5, 15, 49; BLC;**
DA; PC 7; WLC
See also AITN 1; BW 2; CA 1-4R;
CANR 1, 27; CDALB 1941-1968;
CLR 27; DLB 5, 76; MTCW; SATA 6

Brooks, Mel .... **CLC 12**
See also Kaminsky, Melvin
See also DLB 26

Brooks, Peter 1938- .... **CLC 34**
See also CA 45-48; CANR 1

Brooks, Van Wyck 1886-1963...... **CLC 29**
See also CA 1-4R; CANR 6; DLB 45, 63,
103

Brophy, Brigid (Antonia)
1929- .... **CLC 6, 11, 29**
See also CA 5-8R; CAAS 4; CANR 25;
DLB 14; MTCW

Brosman, Catharine Savage 1934-.... **CLC 9**
See also CA 61-64; CANR 21

Brother Antoninus
See Everson, William (Oliver)

Broughton, T(homas) Alan 1936- ... **CLC 19**
See also CA 45-48; CANR 2, 23

Broumas, Olga 1949- .... **CLC 10, 73**
See also CA 85-88; CANR 20

Brown, Charles Brockden
1771-1810 .... **NCLC 22**
See also CDALB 1640-1865; DLB 37, 59,
73

Brown, Christy 1932-1981 .... **CLC 63**
See also CA 105; 104; DLB 14

Brown, Claude 1937- .... **CLC 30; BLC**
See also AAYA 7; BW 1; CA 73-76

Brown, Dee (Alexander) 1908- .. **CLC 18, 47**
See also CA 13-16R; CAAS 6; CANR 11,
45; DLBY 80; MTCW; SATA 5

Brown, George
See Wertmueller, Lina

Brown, George Douglas
1869-1902 .... **TCLC 28**

Brown, George Mackay 1921-.... **CLC 5, 48**
See also CA 21-24R; CAAS 6; CANR 12,
37; DLB 14, 27, 139; MTCW; SATA 35

Brown, (William) Larry 1951-...... **CLC 73**
See also CA 130; 134

Brown, Moses
See Barrett, William (Christopher)

Brown, Rita Mae 1944-..... **CLC 18, 43, 79**
See also CA 45-48; CANR 2, 11, 35;
MTCW

Brown, Roderick (Langmere) Haig-
See Haig-Brown, Roderick (Langmere)

Brown, Rosellen 1939- .... **CLC 32**
See also CA 77-80; CAAS 10; CANR 14, 44

Brown, Sterling Allen
1901-1989 .... **CLC 1, 23, 59; BLC**
See also BW 1; CA 85-88; 127; CANR 26;
DLB 48, 51, 63; MTCW

Brown, Will
See Ainsworth, William Harrison

Brown, William Wells
1813-1884 .... **NCLC 2; BLC; DC 1**
See also DLB 3, 50

Browne, (Clyde) Jackson 1948(?)-... **CLC 21**
See also CA 120

Browning, Elizabeth Barrett
1806-1861 ..... **NCLC 1, 16; DA; PC 6;**
WLC
See also CDBLB 1832-1890; DLB 32

Browning, Robert
1812-1889 . . . . NCLC 19; DA; PC 2
See also CDBLB 1832-1890; DLB 32;
YABC 1

Browning, Tod 1882-1962 . . . . CLC 16
See also CA 141; 117

Bruccoli, Matthew J(oseph) 1931- . . CLC 34
See also CA 9-12R; CANR 7; DLB 103

Bruce, Lenny . . . . CLC 21
See also Schneider, Leonard Alfred

Bruin, John
See Brutus, Dennis

Brulard, Henri
See Stendhal

Brulls, Christian
See Simenon, Georges (Jacques Christian)

Brunner, John (Kilian Houston)
1934- . . . . CLC 8, 10
See also CA 1-4R; CAAS 8; CANR 2, 37;
MTCW

Bruno, Giordano 1548-1600 . . . . LC 27

Brutus, Dennis 1924- . . . . CLC 43; BLC
See also BW 2; CA 49-52; CAAS 14;
CANR 2, 27, 42; DLB 117

Bryan, C(ourtlandt) D(ixon) B(arnes)
1936- . . . . CLC 29
See also CA 73-76; CANR 13

Bryan, Michael
See Moore, Brian

Bryant, William Cullen
1794-1878 . . . . NCLC 6, 46; DA
See also CDALB 1640-1865; DLB 3, 43, 59

Bryusov, Valery Yakovlevich
1873-1924 . . . . TCLC 10
See also CA 107

Buchan, John 1875-1940 . . . . TCLC 41
See also CA 108; 145; DLB 34, 70; YABC 2

Buchanan, George 1506-1582 . . . . LC 4

Buchheim, Lothar-Guenther 1918- . . . CLC 6
See also CA 85-88

Buchner, (Karl) Georg
1813-1837 . . . . NCLC 26

Buchwald, Art(hur) 1925- . . . . CLC 33
See also AITN 1; CA 5-8R; CANR 21;
MTCW; SATA 10

Buck, Pearl S(ydenstricker)
1892-1973 . . . . CLC 7, 11, 18; DA
See also AITN 1; CA 1-4R; 41-44R;
CANR 1, 34; DLB 9, 102; MTCW;
SATA 1, 25

Buckler, Ernest 1908-1984 . . . . CLC 13
See also CA 11-12; 114; CAP 1; DLB 68;
SATA 47

Buckley, Vincent (Thomas)
1925-1988 . . . . CLC 57
See also CA 101

Buckley, William F(rank), Jr.
1925- . . . . CLC 7, 18, 37
See also AITN 1; CA 1-4R; CANR 1, 24;
DLB 137; DLBY 80; MTCW

Buechner, (Carl) Frederick
1926- . . . . CLC 2, 4, 6, 9
See also CA 13-16R; CANR 11, 39;
DLBY 80; MTCW

Buell, John (Edward) 1927- . . . . CLC 10
See also CA 1-4R; DLB 53

Buero Vallejo, Antonio 1916- . . . CLC 15, 46
See also CA 106; CANR 24; HW; MTCW

Bufalino, Gesualdo 1920(?)- . . . . CLC 74

Bugayev, Boris Nikolayevich 1880-1934
See Bely, Andrey
See also CA 104

Bukowski, Charles
1920-1994 . . . . CLC 2, 5, 9, 41, 82
See also CA 17-20R; 144; CANR 40;
DLB 5, 130; MTCW

Bulgakov, Mikhail (Afanas'evich)
1891-1940 . . . . TCLC 2, 16
See also CA 105

Bulgya, Alexander Alexandrovich
1901-1956 . . . . TCLC 53
See also Fadeyev, Alexander
See also CA 117

Bullins, Ed 1935- . . . . CLC 1, 5, 7; BLC
See also BW 2; CA 49-52; CAAS 16;
CANR 24; DLB 7, 38; MTCW

Bulwer-Lytton, Edward (George Earle Lytton)
1803-1873 . . . . NCLC 1, 45
See also DLB 21

Bunin, Ivan Alexeyevich
1870-1953 . . . . TCLC 6; SSC 5
See also CA 104

Bunting, Basil 1900-1985 . . . . CLC 10, 39, 47
See also CA 53-56; 115; CANR 7; DLB 20

Bunuel, Luis 1900-1983 . . CLC 16, 80; HLC
See also CA 101; 110; CANR 32; HW

Bunyan, John 1628-1688 . . LC 4; DA; WLC
See also CDBLB 1660-1789; DLB 39

Burford, Eleanor
See Hibbert, Eleanor Alice Burford

Burgess, Anthony
. CLC 1, 2, 4, 5, 8, 10, 13, 15, 22, 40, 62,
81
See also Wilson, John (Anthony) Burgess
See also AITN 1; CDBLB 1960 to Present;
DLB 14

Burke, Edmund
1729(?)-1797 . . . . LC 7; DA; WLC
See also DLB 104

Burke, Kenneth (Duva)
1897-1993 . . . . CLC 2, 24
See also CA 5-8R; 143; CANR 39; DLB 45,
63; MTCW

Burke, Leda
See Garnett, David

Burke, Ralph
See Silverberg, Robert

Burney, Fanny 1752-1840 . . . . NCLC 12
See also DLB 39

Burns, Robert
1759-1796 . . . . . . LC 3; DA; PC 6; WLC
See also CDBLB 1789-1832; DLB 109

Burns, Tex
See L'Amour, Louis (Dearborn)

Burnshaw, Stanley 1906- . . . . . CLC 3, 13, 44
See also CA 9-12R; DLB 48

Burr, Anne 1937- . . . . CLC 6
See also CA 25-28R

Burroughs, Edgar Rice
1875-1950 . . . . TCLC 2, 32
See also AAYA 11; CA 104; 132; DLB 8;
MTCW; SATA 41

Burroughs, William S(eward)
1914- . . . . CLC 1, 2, 5, 15, 22, 42, 75;
DA; WLC
See also AITN 2; CA 9-12R; CANR 20;
DLB 2, 8, 16; DLBY 81; MTCW

Burton, Richard F. 1821-1890 . . . . NCLC 42
See also DLB 55

Busch, Frederick 1941- . . . CLC 7, 10, 18, 47
See also CA 33-36R; CAAS 1; CANR 45;
DLB 6

Bush, Ronald 1946- . . . . CLC 34
See also CA 136

Bustos, F(rancisco)
See Borges, Jorge Luis

Bustos Domecq, H(onorio)
See Bioy Casares, Adolfo; Borges, Jorge
Luis

Butler, Octavia E(stelle) 1947- . . . . . CLC 38
See also BW 2; CA 73-76; CANR 12, 24,
38; DLB 33; MTCW

Butler, Robert Olen (Jr.) 1945- . . . . . CLC 81
See also CA 112

Butler, Samuel 1612-1680 . . . . LC 16
See also DLB 101, 126

Butler, Samuel
1835-1902 . . . . . . TCLC 1, 33; DA; WLC
See also CA 143; CDBLB 1890-1914;
DLB 18, 57

Butler, Walter C.
See Faust, Frederick (Schiller)

Butor, Michel (Marie Francois)
1926- . . . . CLC 1, 3, 8, 11, 15
See also CA 9-12R; CANR 33; DLB 83;
MTCW

Buzo, Alexander (John) 1944- . . . . . . CLC 61
See also CA 97-100; CANR 17, 39

Buzzati, Dino 1906-1972 . . . . CLC 36
See also CA 33-36R

Byars, Betsy (Cromer) 1928- . . . . CLC 35
See also CA 33-36R; CANR 18, 36; CLR 1,
16; DLB 52; JRDA; MAICYA; MTCW;
SAAS 1; SATA 4, 46

Byatt, A(ntonia) S(usan Drabble)
1936- . . . . CLC 19, 65
See also CA 13-16R; CANR 13, 33;
DLB 14; MTCW

Byrne, David 1952- . . . . CLC 26
See also CA 127

Byrne, John Keyes 1926-
See Leonard, Hugh
See also CA 102

Byron, George Gordon (Noel)
1788-1824 . . . . . . NCLC 2, 12; DA; WLC
See also CDBLB 1789-1832; DLB 96, 110

C. 3. 3.
See Wilde, Oscar (Fingal O'Flahertie Wills)

Caballero, Fernan 1796-1877 . . . . . NCLC 10

Cabell, James Branch 1879-1958 . . . TCLC 6
See also CA 105; DLB 9, 78

Cary, (Arthur) Joyce (Lunel)
1888-1957 . . . . TCLC 1, 29
See also CA 104; CDBLB 1914-1945;
DLB 15, 100

Casanova de Seingalt, Giovanni Jacopo
1725-1798 . . . . LC 13

Casares, Adolfo Bioy
See Bioy Casares, Adolfo

Casely-Hayford, J(oseph) E(phraim)
1866-1930 . . . . TCLC 24; BLC
See also BW 2; CA 123

Casey, John (Dudley) 1939- . . . . CLC 59
See also BEST 90:2; CA 69-72; CANR 23

Casey, Michael 1947- . . . . CLC 2
See also CA 65-68; DLB 5

Casey, Patrick
See Thurman, Wallace (Henry)

Casey, Warren (Peter) 1935-1988 . . . CLC 12
See also CA 101; 127

Casona, Alejandro . . . . CLC 49
See also Alvarez, Alejandro Rodriguez

Cassavetes, John 1929-1989 . . . . CLC 20
See also CA 85-88; 127

Cassill, R(onald) V(erlin) 1919- . . . CLC 4, 23
See also CA 9-12R; CAAS 1; CANR 7, 45;
DLB 6

Cassity, (Allen) Turner 1929- . . . . CLC 6, 42
See also CA 17-20R; CAAS 8; CANR 11;
DLB 105

Castaneda, Carlos 1931(?)- . . . . CLC 12
See also CA 25-28R; CANR 32; HW;
MTCW

Castedo, Elena 1937- . . . . CLC 65
See also CA 132

Castedo-Ellerman, Elena
See Castedo, Elena

Castellanos, Rosario
1925-1974 . . . . CLC 66; HLC
See also CA 131; 53-56; DLB 113; HW

Castelvetro, Lodovico 1505-1571 . . . . . LC 12

Castiglione, Baldassare 1478-1529 . . . LC 12

Castle, Robert
See Hamilton, Edmond

Castro, Guillen de 1569-1631 . . . . LC 19

Castro, Rosalia de 1837-1885 . . . . . NCLC 3

Cather, Willa
See Cather, Willa Sibert

Cather, Willa Sibert
1873-1947 . . . . TCLC 1, 11, 31; DA;
                                    SSC 2; WLC
See also CA 104; 128; CDALB 1865-1917;
DLB 9, 54, 78; DLBD 1; MTCW;
SATA 30

Catton, (Charles) Bruce
1899-1978 . . . . CLC 35
See also AITN 1; CA 5-8R; 81-84;
CANR 7; DLB 17; SATA 2, 24

Cauldwell, Frank
See King, Francis (Henry)

Caunitz, William J. 1933- . . . . CLC 34
See also BEST 89:3; CA 125; 130

Causley, Charles (Stanley) 1917- . . . . . CLC 7
See also CA 9-12R; CANR 5, 35; CLR 30;
DLB 27; MTCW; SATA 3, 66

Caute, David 1936- . . . . CLC 29
See also CA 1-4R; CAAS 4; CANR 1, 33;
DLB 14

Cavafy, C(onstantine) P(eter) . . . . . . TCLC 2, 7
See also Kavafis, Konstantinos Petrou

Cavallo, Evelyn
See Spark, Muriel (Sarah)

Cavanna, Betty . . . . CLC 12
See also Harrison, Elizabeth Cavanna
See also JRDA; MAICYA; SAAS 4;
SATA 1, 30

Caxton, William 1421(?)-1491(?) . . . . . LC 17

Cayrol, Jean 1911- . . . . CLC 11
See also CA 89-92; DLB 83

Cela, Camilo Jose
1916- . . . . CLC 4, 13, 59; HLC
See also BEST 90:2; CA 21-24R; CAAS 10;
CANR 21, 32; DLBY 89; HW; MTCW

Celan, Paul . . . . . . CLC 10, 19, 53, 82; PC 10
See also Antschel, Paul
See also DLB 69

Celine, Louis-Ferdinand
. . . . CLC 1, 3, 4, 7, 9, 15, 47
See also Destouches, Louis-Ferdinand
See also DLB 72

Cellini, Benvenuto 1500-1571 . . . . LC 7

Cendrars, Blaise
See Sauser-Hall, Frederic

Cernuda (y Bidon), Luis
1902-1963 . . . . CLC 54
See also CA 131; 89-92; DLB 134; HW

Cervantes (Saavedra), Miguel de
1547-1616 . . . . . . LC 6, 23; DA; SSC 12;
                                                  WLC

Cesaire, Aime (Fernand)
1913- . . . . CLC 19, 32; BLC
See also BW 2; CA 65-68; CANR 24, 43;
MTCW

Chabon, Michael 1965(?)- . . . . CLC 55
See also CA 139

Chabrol, Claude 1930- . . . . CLC 16
See also CA 110

Challans, Mary 1905-1983
See Renault, Mary
See also CA 81-84; 111; SATA 23, 36

Challis, George
See Faust, Frederick (Schiller)

Chambers, Aidan 1934- . . . . CLC 35
See also CA 25-28R; CANR 12, 31; JRDA;
MAICYA; SAAS 12; SATA 1, 69

Chambers, James 1948-
See Cliff, Jimmy
See also CA 124

Chambers, Jessie
See Lawrence, D(avid) H(erbert Richards)

Chambers, Robert W. 1865-1933 . . . TCLC 41

Chandler, Raymond (Thornton)
1888-1959 . . . . TCLC 1, 7
See also CA 104; 129; CDALB 1929-1941;
DLBD 6; MTCW

Chang, Jung 1952- . . . . CLC 71
See also CA 142

Channing, William Ellery
1780-1842 . . . . NCLC 17
See also DLB 1, 59

Chaplin, Charles Spencer
1889-1977 . . . . CLC 16
See also Chaplin, Charlie
See also CA 81-84; 73-76

Chaplin, Charlie
See Chaplin, Charles Spencer
See also DLB 44

Chapman, George 1559(?)-1634 . . . . . . LC 22
See also DLB 62, 121

Chapman, Graham 1941-1989 . . . . . . CLC 21
See also Monty Python
See also CA 116; 129; CANR 35

Chapman, John Jay 1862-1933 . . . . . TCLC 7
See also CA 104

Chapman, Walker
See Silverberg, Robert

Chappell, Fred (Davis) 1936- . . . . CLC 40, 78
See also CA 5-8R; CAAS 4; CANR 8, 33;
DLB 6, 105

Char, Rene(-Emile)
1907-1988 . . . . CLC 9, 11, 14, 55
See also CA 13-16R; 124; CANR 32;
MTCW

Charby, Jay
See Ellison, Harlan

Chardin, Pierre Teilhard de
See Teilhard de Chardin, (Marie Joseph)
Pierre

Charles I 1600-1649 . . . . LC 13

Charyn, Jerome 1937- . . . . CLC 5, 8, 18
See also CA 5-8R; CAAS 1; CANR 7;
DLBY 83; MTCW

Chase, Mary (Coyle) 1907-1981 . . . . . . DC 1
See also CA 77-80; 105; SATA 17, 29

Chase, Mary Ellen 1887-1973 . . . . CLC 2
See also CA 13-16; 41-44R; CAP 1;
SATA 10

Chase, Nicholas
See Hyde, Anthony

Chateaubriand, Francois Rene de
1768-1848 . . . . NCLC 3
See also DLB 119

Chatterje, Sarat Chandra 1876-1936(?)
See Chatterji, Saratchandra
See also CA 109

Chatterji, Bankim Chandra
1838-1894 . . . . NCLC 19

Chatterji, Saratchandra . . . . TCLC 13
See also Chatterje, Sarat Chandra

Chatterton, Thomas 1752-1770 . . . . LC 3
See also DLB 109

Chatwin, (Charles) Bruce
1940-1989 . . . . CLC 28, 57, 59
See also AAYA 4; BEST 90:1; CA 85-88;
127

Chaucer, Daniel
See Ford, Ford Madox

Chaucer, Geoffrey
1340(?)-1400 . . . . LC 17; DA
See also CDBLB Before 1660

Chaviaras, Strates 1935-
 See Haviaras, Stratis
 See also CA 105

Chayefsky, Paddy .... **CLC 23**
 See also Chayefsky, Sidney
 See also DLB 7, 44; DLBY 81

Chayefsky, Sidney 1923-1981
 See Chayefsky, Paddy
 See also CA 9-12R; 104; CANR 18

Chedid, Andree 1920-............. **CLC 47**
 See also CA 145

Cheever, John
 1912-1982 ...... **CLC 3, 7, 8, 11, 15, 25,
 64; DA; SSC 1; WLC**
 See also CA 5-8R; 106; CABS 1; CANR 5,
 27; CDALB 1941-1968; DLB 2, 102;
 DLBY 80, 82; MTCW

Cheever, Susan 1943-.......... **CLC 18, 48**
 See also CA 103; CANR 27; DLBY 82

Chekhonte, Antosha
 See Chekhov, Anton (Pavlovich)

Chekhov, Anton (Pavlovich)
 1860-1904 ..... **TCLC 3, 10, 31, 55; DA;
 SSC 2; WLC**
 See also CA 104; 124

Chernyshevsky, Nikolay Gavrilovich
 1828-1889 .... **NCLC 1**

Cherry, Carolyn Janice 1942-
 See Cherryh, C. J.
 See also CA 65-68; CANR 10

Cherryh, C. J. .... **CLC 35**
 See also Cherry, Carolyn Janice
 See also DLBY 80

Chesnutt, Charles W(addell)
 1858-1932 .... **TCLC 5, 39; BLC; SSC 7**
 See also BW 1; CA 106; 125; DLB 12, 50,
 78; MTCW

Chester, Alfred 1929(?)-1971....... **CLC 49**
 See also CA 33-36R; DLB 130

Chesterton, G(ilbert) K(eith)
 1874-1936 .... **TCLC 1, 6; SSC 1**
 See also CA 104; 132; CDBLB 1914-1945;
 DLB 10, 19, 34, 70, 98; MTCW;
 SATA 27

Chiang Pin-chin 1904-1986
 See Ding Ling
 See also CA 118

Ch'ien Chung-shu 1910-........... **CLC 22**
 See also CA 130; MTCW

Child, L. Maria
 See Child, Lydia Maria

Child, Lydia Maria 1802-1880 .... **NCLC 6**
 See also DLB 1, 74; SATA 67

Child, Mrs.
 See Child, Lydia Maria

Child, Philip 1898-1978 .... **CLC 19, 68**
 See also CA 13-14; CAP 1; SATA 47

Childress, Alice
 1920- .... **CLC 12, 15; BLC; DC 4**
 See also AAYA 8; BW 2; CA 45-48;
 CANR 3, 27; CLR 14; DLB 7, 38; JRDA;
 MAICYA; MTCW; SATA 7, 48

Chislett, (Margaret) Anne 1943-.... **CLC 34**

Chitty, Thomas Willes 1926-....... **CLC 11**
 See also Hinde, Thomas
 See also CA 5-8R

Chomette, Rene Lucien 1898-1981
 See Clair, Rene
 See also CA 103

Chopin, Kate .... **TCLC 5, 14; DA; SSC 8**
 See also Chopin, Katherine
 See also CDALB 1865-1917; DLB 12, 78

Chopin, Katherine 1851-1904
 See Chopin, Kate
 See also CA 104; 122

Chretien de Troyes
 c. 12th cent. - .... **CMLC 10**

Christie
 See Ichikawa, Kon

Christie, Agatha (Mary Clarissa)
 1890-1976 ...... **CLC 1, 6, 8, 12, 39, 48**
 See also AAYA 9; AITN 1, 2; CA 17-20R;
 61-64; CANR 10, 37; CDBLB 1914-1945;
 DLB 13, 77; MTCW; SATA 36

Christie, (Ann) Philippa
 See Pearce, Philippa
 See also CA 5-8R; CANR 4

Christine de Pizan 1365(?)-1431(?) .... **LC 9**

Chubb, Elmer
 See Masters, Edgar Lee

Chulkov, Mikhail Dmitrievich
 1743-1792 .... **LC 2**

Churchill, Caryl 1938-......... **CLC 31, 55**
 See also CA 102; CANR 22; DLB 13;
 MTCW

Churchill, Charles 1731-1764........ **LC 3**
 See also DLB 109

Chute, Carolyn 1947-............. **CLC 39**
 See also CA 123

Ciardi, John (Anthony)
 1916-1986 .... **CLC 10, 40, 44**
 See also CA 5-8R; 118; CAAS 2; CANR 5,
 33; CLR 19; DLB 5; DLBY 86;
 MAICYA; MTCW; SATA 1, 46, 65

Cicero, Marcus Tullius
 106B.C.-43B.C............... **CMLC 3**

Cimino, Michael 1943-............ **CLC 16**
 See also CA 105

Cioran, E(mil) M. 1911-........... **CLC 64**
 See also CA 25-28R

Cisneros, Sandra 1954-...... **CLC 69; HLC**
 See also AAYA 9; CA 131; DLB 122; HW

Clair, Rene...................... **CLC 20**
 See also Chomette, Rene Lucien

Clampitt, Amy 1920- .... **CLC 32**
 See also CA 110; CANR 29; DLB 105

Clancy, Thomas L., Jr. 1947-
 See Clancy, Tom
 See also CA 125; 131; MTCW

Clancy, Tom..................... **CLC 45**
 See also Clancy, Thomas L., Jr.
 See also AAYA 9; BEST 89:1, 90:1

Clare, John 1793-1864 .... **NCLC 9**
 See also DLB 55, 96

Clarin
 See Alas (y Urena), Leopoldo (Enrique
 Garcia)

Clark, Al C.
 See Goines, Donald

Clark, (Robert) Brian 1932-....... **CLC 29**
 See also CA 41-44R

Clark, Curt
 See Westlake, Donald E(dwin)

Clark, Eleanor 1913- .... **CLC 5, 19**
 See also CA 9-12R; CANR 41; DLB 6

Clark, J. P.
 See Clark, John Pepper
 See also DLB 117

Clark, John Pepper 1935- .... **CLC 38; BLC**
 See also Clark, J. P.
 See also BW 1; CA 65-68; CANR 16

Clark, M. R.
 See Clark, Mavis Thorpe

Clark, Mavis Thorpe 1909-........ **CLC 12**
 See also CA 57-60; CANR 8, 37; CLR 30;
 MAICYA; SAAS 5; SATA 8, 74

Clark, Walter Van Tilburg
 1909-1971 .... **CLC 28**
 See also CA 9-12R; 33-36R; DLB 9;
 SATA 8

Clarke, Arthur C(harles)
 1917- ...... **CLC 1, 4, 13, 18, 35; SSC 3**
 See also AAYA 4; CA 1-4R; CANR 2, 28;
 JRDA; MAICYA; MTCW; SATA 13, 70

Clarke, Austin 1896-1974......... **CLC 6, 9**
 See also CA 29-32; 49-52; CAP 2; DLB 10,
 20

Clarke, Austin C(hesterfield)
 1934-............. **CLC 8, 53; BLC**
 See also BW 1; CA 25-28R; CAAS 16;
 CANR 14, 32; DLB 53, 125

Clarke, Gillian 1937-............. **CLC 61**
 See also CA 106; DLB 40

Clarke, Marcus (Andrew Hislop)
 1846-1881 .... **NCLC 19**

Clarke, Shirley 1925-............. **CLC 16**

Clash, The
 See Headon, (Nicky) Topper; Jones, Mick;
 Simonon, Paul; Strummer, Joe

Claudel, Paul (Louis Charles Marie)
 1868-1955 ....TCLC 2, 10
 See also CA 104

Clavell, James (duMaresq)
 1925-..................... **CLC 6, 25**
 See also CA 25-28R; CANR 26; MTCW

Cleaver, (Leroy) Eldridge
 1935- .... **CLC 30; BLC**
 See also BW 1; CA 21-24R; CANR 16

Cleese, John (Marwood) 1939- ..... **CLC 21**
 See also Monty Python
 See also CA 112; 116; CANR 35; MTCW

Cleishbotham, Jebediah
 See Scott, Walter

Cleland, John 1710-1789 .... **LC 2**
 See also DLB 39

Clemens, Samuel Langhorne 1835-1910
 See Twain, Mark
 See also CA 104; 135; CDALB 1865-1917;
 DA; DLB 11, 12, 23, 64, 74; JRDA;
 MAICYA; YABC 2

Cleophil
 See Congreve, William

Clerihew, E.
See Bentley, E(dmund) C(lerihew)

Clerk, N. W.
See Lewis, C(live) S(taples)

Cliff, Jimmy.....................**CLC 21**
See also Chambers, James

Clifton, (Thelma) Lucille
1936-..............**CLC 19, 66; BLC**
See also BW 2; CA 49-52; CANR 2, 24, 42;
CLR 5; DLB 5, 41; MAICYA; MTCW;
SATA 20, 69

Clinton, Dirk
See Silverberg, Robert

Clough, Arthur Hugh 1819-1861.. **NCLC 27**
See also DLB 32

Clutha, Janet Paterson Frame 1924-
See Frame, Janet
See also CA 1-4R; CANR 2, 36; MTCW

Clyne, Terence
See Blatty, William Peter

Cobalt, Martin
See Mayne, William (James Carter)

Coburn, D(onald) L(ee) 1938-...... **CLC 10**
See also CA 89-92

Cocteau, Jean (Maurice Eugene Clement)
1889-1963 .... **CLC 1, 8, 15, 16, 43; DA;**
WLC
See also CA 25-28; CANR 40; CAP 2;
DLB 65; MTCW

Codrescu, Andrei 1946-........... **CLC 46**
See also CA 33-36R; CAAS 19; CANR 13,
34

Coe, Max
See Bourne, Randolph S(illiman)

Coe, Tucker
See Westlake, Donald E(dwin)

Coetzee, J(ohn) M(ichael)
1940-................. **CLC 23, 33, 66**
See also CA 77-80; CANR 41; MTCW

Coffey, Brian
See Koontz, Dean R(ay)

Cohen, Arthur A(llen)
1928-1986 .... **CLC 7, 31**
See also CA 1-4R; 120; CANR 1, 17, 42;
DLB 28

Cohen, Leonard (Norman)
1934-..................... **CLC 3, 38**
See also CA 21-24R; CANR 14; DLB 53;
MTCW

Cohen, Matt 1942-............... **CLC 19**
See also CA 61-64; CAAS 18; CANR 40;
DLB 53

Cohen-Solal, Annie 19(?)-......... **CLC 50**

Colegate, Isabel 1931-........... **CLC 36**
See also CA 17-20R; CANR 8, 22; DLB 14;
MTCW

Coleman, Emmett
See Reed, Ishmael

Coleridge, Samuel Taylor
1772-1834 .... **NCLC 9; DA; WLC**
See also CDBLB 1789-1832; DLB 93, 107

Coleridge, Sara 1802-1852....... **NCLC 31**

Coles, Don 1928- .... **CLC 46**
See also CA 115; CANR 38

Colette, (Sidonie-Gabrielle)
1873-1954 ...... **TCLC 1, 5, 16; SSC 10**
See also CA 104; 131; DLB 65; MTCW

Collett, (Jacobine) Camilla (Wergeland)
1813-1895 .... **NCLC 22**

Collier, Christopher 1930-......... **CLC 30**
See also CA 33-36R; CANR 13, 33; JRDA;
MAICYA; SATA 16, 70

Collier, James L(incoln) 1928-..... **CLC 30**
See also CA 9-12R; CANR 4, 33; CLR 3;
JRDA; MAICYA; SATA 8, 70

Collier, Jeremy 1650-1726.......... **LC 6**

Collins, Hunt
See Hunter, Evan

Collins, Linda 1931-.............. **CLC 44**
See also CA 125

Collins, (William) Wilkie
1824-1889 .... **NCLC 1, 18**
See also CDBLB 1832-1890; DLB 18, 70

Collins, William 1721-1759 .... **LC 4**
See also DLB 109

Colman, George
See Glassco, John

Colt, Winchester Remington
See Hubbard, L(afayette) Ron(ald)

Colter, Cyrus 1910-.............. **CLC 58**
See also BW 1; CA 65-68; CANR 10;
DLB 33

Colton, James
See Hansen, Joseph

Colum, Padraic 1881-1972......... **CLC 28**
See also CA 73-76; 33-36R; CANR 35;
MAICYA; MTCW; SATA 15

Colvin, James
See Moorcock, Michael (John)

Colwin, Laurie (E.)
1944-1992 .... **CLC 5, 13, 23, 84**
See also CA 89-92; 139; CANR 20;
DLBY 80; MTCW

Comfort, Alex(ander) 1920-........ **CLC 7**
See also CA 1-4R; CANR 1, 45

Comfort, Montgomery
See Campbell, (John) Ramsey

Compton-Burnett, I(vy)
1884(?)-1969 ...... **CLC 1, 3, 10, 15, 34**
See also CA 1-4R; 25-28R; CANR 4;
DLB 36; MTCW

Comstock, Anthony 1844-1915 .... **TCLC 13**
See also CA 110

Conan Doyle, Arthur
See Doyle, Arthur Conan

Conde, Maryse 1937-............. **CLC 52**
See also Boucolon, Maryse
See also BW 2

Condillac, Etienne Bonnot de
1714-1780 .... **LC 26**

Condon, Richard (Thomas)
1915- .... **CLC 4, 6, 8, 10, 45**
See also BEST 90:3; CA 1-4R; CAAS 1;
CANR 2, 23; MTCW

Congreve, William
1670-1729 ... **LC 5, 21; DA; DC 2; WLC**
See also CDBLB 1660-1789; DLB 39, 84

Connell, Evan S(helby), Jr.
1924-................. **CLC 4, 6, 45**
See also AAYA 7; CA 1-4R; CAAS 2;
CANR 2, 39; DLB 2; DLBY 81; MTCW

Connelly, Marc(us Cook)
1890-1980 .... **CLC 7**
See also CA 85-88; 102; CANR 30; DLB 7;
DLBY 80; SATA 25

Connor, Ralph .... **TCLC 31**
See also Gordon, Charles William
See also DLB 92

Conrad, Joseph
1857-1924 .... **TCLC 1, 6, 13, 25, 43, 57;**
DA; SSC 9; WLC
See also CA 104; 131; CDBLB 1890-1914;
DLB 10, 34, 98; MTCW; SATA 27

Conrad, Robert Arnold
See Hart, Moss

Conroy, Pat 1945-.............. **CLC 30, 74**
See also AAYA 8; AITN 1; CA 85-88;
CANR 24; DLB 6; MTCW

Constant (de Rebecque), (Henri) Benjamin
1767-1830 .... **NCLC 6**
See also DLB 119

Conybeare, Charles Augustus
See Eliot, T(homas) S(tearns)

Cook, Michael 1933- .... **CLC 58**
See also CA 93-96; DLB 53

Cook, Robin 1940-............... **CLC 14**
See also BEST 90:2; CA 108; 111;
CANR 41

Cook, Roy
See Silverberg, Robert

Cooke, Elizabeth 1948- .... **CLC 55**
See also CA 129

Cooke, John Esten 1830-1886..... **NCLC 5**
See also DLB 3

Cooke, John Estes
See Baum, L(yman) Frank

Cooke, M. E.
See Creasey, John

Cooke, Margaret
See Creasey, John

Cooney, Ray .... **CLC 62**

Cooper, Henry St. John
See Creasey, John

Cooper, J. California............... **CLC 56**
See also AAYA 12; BW 1; CA 125

Cooper, James Fenimore
1789-1851 .... **NCLC 1, 27**
See also CDALB 1640-1865; DLB 3;
SATA 19

Coover, Robert (Lowell)
1932- ..... **CLC 3, 7, 15, 32, 46; SSC 15**
See also CA 45-48; CANR 3, 37; DLB 2;
DLBY 81; MTCW

Copeland, Stewart (Armstrong)
1952-....................... **CLC 26**

Coppard, A(lfred) E(dgar)
1878-1957 .... **TCLC 5**
See also CA 114; YABC 1

Coppee, Francois 1842-1908 ...... **TCLC 25**

Coppola, Francis Ford 1939-....... **CLC 16**
See also CA 77-80; CANR 40; DLB 44

Corbiere, Tristan 1845-1875 . . . . . NCLC 43

Corcoran, Barbara 1911- . . . . CLC 17
    See also CA 21-24R; CAAS 2; CANR 11,
    28; DLB 52; JRDA; SATA 3, 77

Cordelier, Maurice
    See Giraudoux, (Hippolyte) Jean

Corelli, Marie 1855-1924 . . . . TCLC 51
    See also Mackay, Mary
    See also DLB 34

Corman, Cid . . . . CLC 9
    See also Corman, Sidney
    See also CAAS 2; DLB 5

Corman, Sidney 1924-
    See Corman, Cid
    See also CA 85-88; CANR 44

Cormier, Robert (Edmund)
    1925- . . . . CLC 12, 30; DA
    See also AAYA 3; CA 1-4R; CANR 5, 23;
    CDALB 1968-1988; CLR 12; DLB 52;
    JRDA; MAICYA; MTCW; SATA 10, 45

Corn, Alfred (DeWitt III) 1943- . . . . CLC 33
    See also CA 104; CANR 44; DLB 120;
    DLBY 80

Cornwell, David (John Moore)
    1931- . . . . CLC 9, 15
    See also le Carre, John
    See also CA 5-8R; CANR 13, 33; MTCW

Corso, (Nunzio) Gregory 1930- . . . CLC 1, 11
    See also CA 5-8R; CANR 41; DLB 5, 16;
    MTCW

Cortazar, Julio
    1914-1984 . . . . . . CLC 2, 3, 5, 10, 13, 15,
                          33, 34; HLC; SSC 7
    See also CA 21-24R; CANR 12, 32;
    DLB 113; HW; MTCW

Corwin, Cecil
    See Kornbluth, C(yril) M.

Cosic, Dobrica 1921- . . . . CLC 14
    See also CA 122; 138

Costain, Thomas B(ertram)
    1885-1965 . . . . CLC 30
    See also CA 5-8R; 25-28R; DLB 9

Costantini, Humberto
    1924(?)-1987 . . . . CLC 49
    See also CA 131; 122; HW

Costello, Elvis 1955- . . . . CLC 21

Cotter, Joseph Seamon Sr.
    1861-1949 . . . . TCLC 28; BLC
    See also BW 1; CA 124; DLB 50

Couch, Arthur Thomas Quiller
    See Quiller-Couch, Arthur Thomas

Coulton, James
    See Hansen, Joseph

Couperus, Louis (Marie Anne)
    1863-1923 . . . . TCLC 15
    See also CA 115

Coupland, Douglas 1961- . . . . CLC 85
    See also CA 142

Court, Wesli
    See Turco, Lewis (Putnam)

Courtenay, Bryce 1933- . . . . CLC 59
    See also CA 138

Courtney, Robert
    See Ellison, Harlan

Cousteau, Jacques-Yves 1910- . . . . . . CLC 30
    See also CA 65-68; CANR 15; MTCW;
    SATA 38

Coward, Noel (Peirce)
    1899-1973 . . . . CLC 1, 9, 29, 51
    See also AITN 1; CA 17-18; 41-44R;
    CANR 35; CAP 2; CDBLB 1914-1945;
    DLB 10; MTCW

Cowley, Malcolm 1898-1989 . . . . CLC 39
    See also CA 5-8R; 128; CANR 3; DLB 4,
    48; DLBY 81, 89; MTCW

Cowper, William 1731-1800 . . . . NCLC 8
    See also DLB 104, 109

Cox, William Trevor 1928- . . . CLC 9, 14, 71
    See also Trevor, William
    See also CA 9-12R; CANR 4, 37; DLB 14;
    MTCW

Cozzens, James Gould
    1903-1978 . . . . CLC 1, 4, 11
    See also CA 9-12R; 81-84; CANR 19;
    CDALB 1941-1968; DLB 9; DLBD 2;
    DLBY 84; MTCW

Crabbe, George 1754-1832 . . . . NCLC 26
    See also DLB 93

Craig, A. A.
    See Anderson, Poul (William)

Craik, Dinah Maria (Mulock)
    1826-1887 . . . . NCLC 38
    See also DLB 35; MAICYA; SATA 34

Cram, Ralph Adams 1863-1942 . . . . TCLC 45

Crane, (Harold) Hart
    1899-1932 . . . . TCLC 2, 5; DA; PC 3;
                                             WLC
    See also CA 104; 127; CDALB 1917-1929;
    DLB 4, 48; MTCW

Crane, R(onald) S(almon)
    1886-1967 . . . . CLC 27
    See also CA 85-88; DLB 63

Crane, Stephen (Townley)
    1871-1900 . . . . TCLC 11, 17, 32; DA;
                                   SSC 7; WLC
    See also CA 109; 140; CDALB 1865-1917;
    DLB 12, 54, 78; YABC 2

Crase, Douglas 1944- . . . . CLC 58
    See also CA 106

Crashaw, Richard 1612(?)-1649 . . . . . . LC 24
    See also DLB 126

Craven, Margaret 1901-1980 . . . . . . CLC 17
    See also CA 103

Crawford, F(rancis) Marion
    1854-1909 . . . . TCLC 10
    See also CA 107; DLB 71

Crawford, Isabella Valancy
    1850-1887 . . . . NCLC 12
    See also DLB 92

Crayon, Geoffrey
    See Irving, Washington

Creasey, John 1908-1973 . . . . CLC 11
    See also CA 5-8R; 41-44R; CANR 8;
    DLB 77; MTCW

Crebillon, Claude Prosper Jolyot de (fils)
    1707-1777 . . . . LC 1

Credo
    See Creasey, John

Creeley, Robert (White)
    1926- . . . . . CLC 1, 2, 4, 8, 11, 15, 36, 78
    See also CA 1-4R; CAAS 10; CANR 23, 43;
    DLB 5, 16; MTCW

Crews, Harry (Eugene)
    1935- . . . . CLC 6, 23, 49
    See also AITN 1; CA 25-28R; CANR 20;
    DLB 6, 143; MTCW

Crichton, (John) Michael
    1942- . . . . CLC 2, 6, 54
    See also AAYA 10; AITN 2; CA 25-28R;
    CANR 13, 40; DLBY 81; JRDA;
    MTCW; SATA 9

Crispin, Edmund . . . . CLC 22
    See also Montgomery, (Robert) Bruce
    See also DLB 87

Cristofer, Michael 1945(?)- . . . . CLC 28
    See also CA 110; DLB 7

Croce, Benedetto 1866-1952 . . . . . . TCLC 37
    See also CA 120

Crockett, David 1786-1836 . . . . NCLC 8
    See also DLB 3, 11

Crockett, Davy
    See Crockett, David

Crofts, Freeman Wills
    1879-1957 . . . . TCLC 55
    See also CA 115; DLB 77

Croker, John Wilson 1780-1857 . . NCLC 10
    See also DLB 110

Crommelynck, Fernand 1885-1970 . . CLC 75
    See also CA 89-92

Cronin, A(rchibald) J(oseph)
    1896-1981 . . . . CLC 32
    See also CA 1-4R; 102; CANR 5; SATA 25,
    47

Cross, Amanda
    See Heilbrun, Carolyn G(old)

Crothers, Rachel 1878(?)-1958 . . . . . TCLC 19
    See also CA 113; DLB 7

Croves, Hal
    See Traven, B.

Crowfield, Christopher
    See Stowe, Harriet (Elizabeth) Beecher

Crowley, Aleister . . . . TCLC 7
    See also Crowley, Edward Alexander

Crowley, Edward Alexander 1875-1947
    See Crowley, Aleister
    See also CA 104

Crowley, John 1942- . . . . CLC 57
    See also CA 61-64; CANR 43; DLBY 82;
    SATA 65

Crud
    See Crumb, R(obert)

Crumarums
    See Crumb, R(obert)

Crumb, R(obert) 1943- . . . . CLC 17
    See also CA 106

Crumbum
    See Crumb, R(obert)

Crumski
    See Crumb, R(obert)

Crum the Bum
    See Crumb, R(obert)

Crunk
See Crumb, R(obert)

Crustt
See Crumb, R(obert)

Cryer, Gretchen (Kiger) 1935-...... **CLC 21**
See also CA 114; 123

Csath, Geza 1887-1919.......... **TCLC 13**
See also CA 111

Cudlip, David 1933-.............. **CLC 34**

Cullen, Countee
1903-1946 ...... **TCLC 4, 37; BLC; DA**
See also BW 1; CA 108; 124;
CDALB 1917-1929; DLB 4, 48, 51;
MTCW; SATA 18

Cum, R.
See Crumb, R(obert)

Cummings, Bruce F(rederick) 1889-1919
See Barbellion, W. N. P.
See also CA 123

Cummings, E(dward) E(stlin)
1894-1962 ...... **CLC 1, 3, 8, 12, 15, 68;**
DA; PC 5; WLC 2
See also CA 73-76; CANR 31;
CDALB 1929-1941; DLB 4, 48; MTCW

Cunha, Euclides (Rodrigues Pimenta) da
1866-1909 .... **TCLC 24**
See also CA 123

Cunningham, E. V.
See Fast, Howard (Melvin)

Cunningham, J(ames) V(incent)
1911-1985 .... **CLC 3, 31**
See also CA 1-4R; 115; CANR 1; DLB 5

Cunningham, Julia (Woolfolk)
1916- .... **CLC 12**
See also CA 9-12R; CANR 4, 19, 36;
JRDA; MAICYA; SAAS 2; SATA 1, 26

Cunningham, Michael 1952- .... **CLC 34**
See also CA 136

Cunninghame Graham, R(obert) B(ontine)
1852-1936 .... **TCLC 19**
See also Graham, R(obert) B(ontine)
Cunninghame
See also CA 119; DLB 98

Currie, Ellen 19(?)-.............. **CLC 44**

Curtin, Philip
See Lowndes, Marie Adelaide (Belloc)

Curtis, Price
See Ellison, Harlan

Cutrate, Joe
See Spiegelman, Art

Czaczkes, Shmuel Yosef
See Agnon, S(hmuel) Y(osef Halevi)

Dabrowska, Maria (Szumska)
1889-1965 .... **CLC 15**
See also CA 106

Dabydeen, David 1955- .... **CLC 34**
See also BW 1; CA 125

Dacey, Philip 1939- .... **CLC 51**
See also CA 37-40R; CAAS 17; CANR 14,
32; DLB 105

Dagerman, Stig (Halvard)
1923-1954 .... **TCLC 17**
See also CA 117

Dahl, Roald 1916-1990..... **CLC 1, 6, 18, 79**
See also CA 1-4R; 133; CANR 6, 32, 37;
CLR 1, 7; DLB 139; JRDA; MAICYA;
MTCW; SATA 1, 26, 73; SATA-Obit 65

Dahlberg, Edward 1900-1977... **CLC 1, 7, 14**
See also CA 9-12R; 69-72; CANR 31;
DLB 48; MTCW

Dale, Colin.................... **TCLC 18**
See also Lawrence, T(homas) E(dward)

Dale, George E.
See Asimov, Isaac

Daly, Elizabeth 1878-1967........ **CLC 52**
See also CA 23-24; 25-28R; CAP 2

Daly, Maureen 1921-............. **CLC 17**
See also AAYA 5; CANR 37; JRDA;
MAICYA; SAAS 1; SATA 2

Damas, Leon-Gontran 1912-1978 ... **CLC 84**
See also BW 1; CA 125; 73-76

Daniel, Samuel 1562(?)-1619....... **LC 24**
See also DLB 62

Daniels, Brett
See Adler, Renata

Dannay, Frederic 1905-1982 .... **CLC 11**
See also Queen, Ellery
See also CA 1-4R; 107; CANR 1, 39;
DLB 137; MTCW

D'Annunzio, Gabriele
1863-1938 .... **TCLC 6, 40**
See also CA 104

d'Antibes, Germain
See Simenon, Georges (Jacques Christian)

Danvers, Dennis 1947-........... **CLC 70**

Danziger, Paula 1944- .... **CLC 21**
See also AAYA 4; CA 112; 115; CANR 37;
CLR 20; JRDA; MAICYA; SATA 30,
36, 63

Dario, Ruben 1867-1916 .... **TCLC 4; HLC**
See also CA 131; HW; MTCW

Darley, George 1795-1846........ **NCLC 2**
See also DLB 96

Daryush, Elizabeth 1887-1977.... **CLC 6, 19**
See also CA 49-52; CANR 3; DLB 20

Daudet, (Louis Marie) Alphonse
1840-1897 .... **NCLC 1**
See also DLB 123

Daumal, Rene 1908-1944........ **TCLC 14**
See also CA 114

Davenport, Guy (Mattison, Jr.)
1927- .... **CLC 6, 14, 38; SSC 16**
See also CA 33-36R; CANR 23; DLB 130

Davidson, Avram 1923-
See Queen, Ellery
See also CA 101; CANR 26; DLB 8

Davidson, Donald (Grady)
1893-1968 .... **CLC 2, 13, 19**
See also CA 5-8R; 25-28R; CANR 4;
DLB 45

Davidson, Hugh
See Hamilton, Edmond

Davidson, John 1857-1909....... **TCLC 24**
See also CA 118; DLB 19

Davidson, Sara 1943-.............. **CLC 9**
See also CA 81-84; CANR 44

Davie, Donald (Alfred)
1922-................ **CLC 5, 8, 10, 31**
See also CA 1-4R; CAAS 3; CANR 1, 44;
DLB 27; MTCW

Davies, Ray(mond Douglas) 1944- .. **CLC 21**
See also CA 116

Davies, Rhys 1903-1978.......... **CLC 23**
See also CA 9-12R; 81-84; CANR 4;
DLB 139

Davies, (William) Robertson
1913- ..... **CLC 2, 7, 13, 25, 42, 75; DA;**
WLC
See also BEST 89:2; CA 33-36R; CANR 17,
42; DLB 68; MTCW

Davies, W(illiam) H(enry)
1871-1940 .... **TCLC 5**
See also CA 104; DLB 19

Davies, Walter C.
See Kornbluth, C(yril) M.

Davis, Angela (Yvonne) 1944-...... **CLC 77**
See also BW 2; CA 57-60; CANR 10

Davis, B. Lynch
See Bioy Casares, Adolfo; Borges, Jorge
Luis

Davis, Gordon
See Hunt, E(verette) Howard, Jr.

Davis, Harold Lenoir 1896-1960.... **CLC 49**
See also CA 89-92; DLB 9

Davis, Rebecca (Blaine) Harding
1831-1910 .... **TCLC 6**
See also CA 104; DLB 74

Davis, Richard Harding
1864-1916 .... **TCLC 24**
See also CA 114; DLB 12, 23, 78, 79

Davison, Frank Dalby 1893-1970 ... **CLC 15**
See also CA 116

Davison, Lawrence H.
See Lawrence, D(avid) H(erbert Richards)

Davison, Peter (Hubert) 1928- ..... **CLC 28**
See also CA 9-12R; CAAS 4; CANR 3, 43;
DLB 5

Davys, Mary 1674-1732.............. **LC 1**
See also DLB 39

Dawson, Fielding 1930- .... **CLC 6**
See also CA 85-88; DLB 130

Dawson, Peter
See Faust, Frederick (Schiller)

Day, Clarence (Shepard, Jr.)
1874-1935 .... **TCLC 25**
See also CA 108; DLB 11

Day, Thomas 1748-1789............. **LC 1**
See also DLB 39; YABC 1

Day Lewis, C(ecil)
1904-1972 .... **CLC 1, 6, 10**
See also Blake, Nicholas
See also CA 13-16; 33-36R; CANR 34;
CAP 1; DLB 15, 20; MTCW

Dazai, Osamu .... **TCLC 11**
See also Tsushima, Shuji

de Andrade, Carlos Drummond
See Drummond de Andrade, Carlos

Deane, Norman
See Creasey, John

de Beauvoir, Simone (Lucie Ernestine Marie Bertrand)
See Beauvoir, Simone (Lucie Ernestine Marie Bertrand) de

de Brissac, Malcolm
See Dickinson, Peter (Malcolm)

de Chardin, Pierre Teilhard
See Teilhard de Chardin, (Marie Joseph) Pierre

Dee, John 1527-1608 . . . . **LC 20**

Deer, Sandra 1940- . . . . **CLC 45**

De Ferrari, Gabriella . . . . **CLC 65**

Defoe, Daniel
1660(?)-1731 . . . . **LC 1; DA; WLC**
See also CDBLB 1660-1789; DLB 39, 95, 101; JRDA; MAICYA; SATA 22

de Gourmont, Remy
See Gourmont, Remy de

de Hartog, Jan 1914- . . . . **CLC 19**
See also CA 1-4R; CANR 1

de Hostos, E. M.
See Hostos (y Bonilla), Eugenio Maria de

de Hostos, Eugenio M.
See Hostos (y Bonilla), Eugenio Maria de

Deighton, Len . . . . **CLC 4, 7, 22, 46**
See also Deighton, Leonard Cyril
See also AAYA 6; BEST 89:2; CDBLB 1960 to Present; DLB 87

Deighton, Leonard Cyril 1929-
See Deighton, Len
See also CA 9-12R; CANR 19, 33; MTCW

Dekker, Thomas 1572(?)-1632 . . . . . . **LC 22**
See also CDBLB Before 1660; DLB 62

de la Mare, Walter (John)
1873-1956 . . **TCLC 4, 53; SSC 14; WLC**
See also CDBLB 1914-1945; CLR 23; DLB 19; SATA 16

Delaney, Franey
See O'Hara, John (Henry)

Delaney, Shelagh 1939- . . . . **CLC 29**
See also CA 17-20R; CANR 30; CDBLB 1960 to Present; DLB 13; MTCW

Delany, Mary (Granville Pendarves)
1700-1788 . . . . **LC 12**

Delany, Samuel R(ay, Jr.)
1942- . . . . **CLC 8, 14, 38; BLC**
See also BW 2; CA 81-84; CANR 27, 43; DLB 8, 33; MTCW

De La Ramee, (Marie) Louise 1839-1908
See Ouida
See also SATA 20

de la Roche, Mazo 1879-1961 . . . . . . **CLC 14**
See also CA 85-88; CANR 30; DLB 68; SATA 64

Delbanco, Nicholas (Franklin)
1942- . . . . **CLC 6, 13**
See also CA 17-20R; CAAS 2; CANR 29; DLB 6

del Castillo, Michel 1933- . . . . **CLC 38**
See also CA 109

Deledda, Grazia (Cosima)
1875(?)-1936 . . . . **TCLC 23**
See also CA 123

Delibes, Miguel . . . . **CLC 8, 18**
See also Delibes Setien, Miguel

Delibes Setien, Miguel 1920-
See Delibes, Miguel
See also CA 45-48; CANR 1, 32; HW; MTCW

DeLillo, Don
1936- . . . . . **CLC 8, 10, 13, 27, 39, 54, 76**
See also BEST 89:1; CA 81-84; CANR 21; DLB 6; MTCW

de Lisser, H. G.
See De Lisser, Herbert George
See also DLB 117

De Lisser, Herbert George
1878-1944 . . . . **TCLC 12**
See also de Lisser, H. G.
See also BW 2; CA 109

Deloria, Vine (Victor), Jr. 1933- . . . . **CLC 21**
See also CA 53-56; CANR 5, 20; MTCW; SATA 21

Del Vecchio, John M(ichael)
1947- . . . . **CLC 29**
See also CA 110; DLBD 9

de Man, Paul (Adolph Michel)
1919-1983 . . . . **CLC 55**
See also CA 128; 111; DLB 67; MTCW

De Marinis, Rick 1934- . . . . **CLC 54**
See also CA 57-60; CANR 9, 25

Demby, William 1922- . . . . **CLC 53; BLC**
See also BW 1; CA 81-84; DLB 33

Demijohn, Thom
See Disch, Thomas M(ichael)

de Montherlant, Henry (Milon)
See Montherlant, Henry (Milon) de

Demosthenes 384B.C.-322B.C. . . . **CMLC 13**

de Natale, Francine
See Malzberg, Barry N(athaniel)

Denby, Edwin (Orr) 1903-1983 . . . . . **CLC 48**
See also CA 138; 110

Denis, Julio
See Cortazar, Julio

Denmark, Harrison
See Zelazny, Roger (Joseph)

Dennis, John 1658-1734 . . . . **LC 11**
See also DLB 101

Dennis, Nigel (Forbes) 1912-1989 . . . . **CLC 8**
See also CA 25-28R; 129; DLB 13, 15; MTCW

De Palma, Brian (Russell) 1940- . . . . **CLC 20**
See also CA 109

De Quincey, Thomas 1785-1859 . . . **NCLC 4**
See also CDBLB 1789-1832; DLB 110; 144

Deren, Eleanora 1908(?)-1961
See Deren, Maya
See also CA 111

Deren, Maya . . . . **CLC 16**
See also Deren, Eleanora

Derleth, August (William)
1909-1971 . . . . **CLC 31**
See also CA 1-4R; 29-32R; CANR 4; DLB 9; SATA 5

Der Nister 1884-1950 . . . . **TCLC 56**

de Routisie, Albert
See Aragon, Louis

Derrida, Jacques 1930- . . . . **CLC 24**
See also CA 124; 127

Derry Down Derry
See Lear, Edward

Dersonnes, Jacques
See Simenon, Georges (Jacques Christian)

Desai, Anita 1937- . . . . **CLC 19, 37**
See also CA 81-84; CANR 33; MTCW; SATA 63

de Saint-Luc, Jean
See Glassco, John

de Saint Roman, Arnaud
See Aragon, Louis

Descartes, Rene 1596-1650 . . . . **LC 20**

De Sica, Vittorio 1901(?)-1974 . . . . . **CLC 20**
See also CA 117

Desnos, Robert 1900-1945 . . . . **TCLC 22**
See also CA 121

Destouches, Louis-Ferdinand
1894-1961 . . . . **CLC 9, 15**
See also Celine, Louis-Ferdinand
See also CA 85-88; CANR 28; MTCW

Deutsch, Babette 1895-1982 . . . . **CLC 18**
See also CA 1-4R; 108; CANR 4; DLB 45; SATA 1, 33

Devenant, William 1606-1649 . . . . **LC 13**

Devkota, Laxmiprasad
1909-1959 . . . . **TCLC 23**
See also CA 123

De Voto, Bernard (Augustine)
1897-1955 . . . . **TCLC 29**
See also CA 113; DLB 9

De Vries, Peter
1910-1993 . . . . **CLC 1, 2, 3, 7, 10, 28, 46**
See also CA 17-20R; 142; CANR 41; DLB 6; DLBY 82; MTCW

Dexter, Martin
See Faust, Frederick (Schiller)

Dexter, Pete 1943- . . . . **CLC 34, 55**
See also BEST 89:2; CA 127; 131; MTCW

Diamano, Silmang
See Senghor, Leopold Sedar

Diamond, Neil 1941- . . . . **CLC 30**
See also CA 108

di Bassetto, Corno
See Shaw, George Bernard

Dick, Philip K(indred)
1928-1982 . . . . **CLC 10, 30, 72**
See also CA 49-52; 106; CANR 2, 16; DLB 8; MTCW

Dickens, Charles (John Huffam)
1812-1870 . . . . . **NCLC 3, 8, 18, 26; DA; SSC 17; WLC**
See also CDBLB 1832-1890; DLB 21, 55, 70; JRDA; MAICYA; SATA 15

Dickey, James (Lafayette)
1923- . . . . **CLC 1, 2, 4, 7, 10, 15, 47**
See also AITN 1, 2; CA 9-12R; CABS 2; CANR 10; CDALB 1968-1988; DLB 5; DLBD 7; DLBY 82, 93; MTCW

Dickey, William 1928-1994 . . . . . . **CLC 3, 28**
See also CA 9-12R; 145; CANR 24; DLB 5

Dickinson, Charles 1951- . . . . **CLC 49**
See also CA 128

Dickinson, Emily (Elizabeth)
1830-1886 .. NCLC 21; DA; PC 1; WLC
See also CDALB 1865-1917; DLB 1;
SATA 29

Dickinson, Peter (Malcolm)
1927- .... CLC 12, 35
See also AAYA 9; CA 41-44R; CANR 31;
CLR 29; DLB 87; JRDA; MAICYA;
SATA 5, 62

Dickson, Carr
See Carr, John Dickson

Dickson, Carter
See Carr, John Dickson

Diderot, Denis 1713-1784 .... LC 26

Didion, Joan 1934-..... CLC 1, 3, 8, 14, 32
See also AITN 1; CA 5-8R; CANR 14;
CDALB 1968-1988; DLB 2; DLBY 81,
86; MTCW

Dietrich, Robert
See Hunt, E(verette) Howard, Jr.

Dillard, Annie 1945-............ CLC 9, 60
See also AAYA 6; CA 49-52; CANR 3, 43;
DLBY 80; MTCW; SATA 10

Dillard, R(ichard) H(enry) W(ilde)
1937- .... CLC 5
See also CA 21-24R; CAAS 7; CANR 10;
DLB 5

Dillon, Eilis 1920-................ CLC 17
See also CA 9-12R; CAAS 3; CANR 4, 38;
CLR 26; MAICYA; SATA 2, 74

Dimont, Penelope
See Mortimer, Penelope (Ruth)

Dinesen, Isak.......... CLC 10, 29; SSC 7
See also Blixen, Karen (Christentze
Dinesen)

Ding Ling........................ CLC 68
See also Chiang Pin-chin

Disch, Thomas M(ichael) 1940-... CLC 7, 36
See also CA 21-24R; CAAS 4; CANR 17,
36; CLR 18; DLB 8; MAICYA; MTCW;
SAAS 15; SATA 54

Disch, Tom
See Disch, Thomas M(ichael)

d'Isly, Georges
See Simenon, Georges (Jacques Christian)

Disraeli, Benjamin 1804-1881 .. NCLC 2, 39
See also DLB 21, 55

Ditcum, Steve
See Crumb, R(obert)

Dixon, Paige
See Corcoran, Barbara

Dixon, Stephen 1936-..... CLC 52; SSC 16
See also CA 89-92; CANR 17, 40; DLB 130

Dobell, Sydney Thompson
1824-1874 .... NCLC 43
See also DLB 32

Doblin, Alfred.................. TCLC 13
See also Doeblin, Alfred

Dobrolyubov, Nikolai Alexandrovich
1836-1861 .... NCLC 5

Dobyns, Stephen 1941-............ CLC 37
See also CA 45-48; CANR 2, 18

Doctorow, E(dgar) L(aurence)
1931- ..... CLC 6, 11, 15, 18, 37, 44, 65
See also AITN 2; BEST 89:3; CA 45-48;
CANR 2, 33; CDALB 1968-1988; DLB 2,
28; DLBY 80; MTCW

Dodgson, Charles Lutwidge 1832-1898
See Carroll, Lewis
See also CLR 2; DA; MAICYA; YABC 2

Dodson, Owen (Vincent)
1914-1983 .... CLC 79; BLC
See also BW 1; CA 65-68; 110; CANR 24;
DLB 76

Doeblin, Alfred 1878-1957....... TCLC 13
See also Doblin, Alfred
See also CA 110; 141; DLB 66

Doerr, Harriet 1910- .... CLC 34
See also CA 117; 122

Domecq, H(onorio) Bustos
See Bioy Casares, Adolfo; Borges, Jorge
Luis

Domini, Rey
See Lorde, Audre (Geraldine)

Dominique
See Proust, (Valentin-Louis-George-Eugene-)
Marcel

Don, A
See Stephen, Leslie

Donaldson, Stephen R. 1947-....... CLC 46
See also CA 89-92; CANR 13

Donleavy, J(ames) P(atrick)
1926- .... CLC 1, 4, 6, 10, 45
See also AITN 2; CA 9-12R; CANR 24;
DLB 6; MTCW

Donne, John
1572-1631 .... LC 10, 24; DA; PC 1
See also CDBLB Before 1660; DLB 121

Donnell, David 1939(?)-........... CLC 34

Donoso (Yanez), Jose
1924- .... CLC 4, 8, 11, 32; HLC
See also CA 81-84; CANR 32; DLB 113;
HW; MTCW

Donovan, John 1928-1992 .... CLC 35
See also CA 97-100; 137; CLR 3;
MAICYA; SATA 29

Don Roberto
See Cunninghame Graham, R(obert)
B(ontine)

Doolittle, Hilda
1886-1961 ..... CLC 3, 8, 14, 31, 34, 73;
DA; PC 5; WLC
See also H. D.
See also CA 97-100; CANR 35; DLB 4, 45;
MTCW

Dorfman, Ariel 1942-.... CLC 48, 77; HLC
See also CA 124; 130; HW

Dorn, Edward (Merton) 1929-... CLC 10, 18
See also CA 93-96; CANR 42; DLB 5

Dorsan, Luc
See Simenon, Georges (Jacques Christian)

Dorsange, Jean
See Simenon, Georges (Jacques Christian)

Dos Passos, John (Roderigo)
1896-1970 ...... CLC 1, 4, 8, 11, 15, 25,
34, 82; DA; WLC
See also CA 1-4R; 29-32R; CANR 3;
CDALB 1929-1941; DLB 4, 9; DLBD 1;
MTCW

Dossage, Jean
See Simenon, Georges (Jacques Christian)

Dostoevsky, Fedor Mikhailovich
1821-1881 ...... NCLC 2, 7, 21, 33, 43;
DA; SSC 2; WLC

Doughty, Charles M(ontagu)
1843-1926 .... TCLC 27
See also CA 115; DLB 19, 57

Douglas, Ellen.................... CLC 73
See also Haxton, Josephine Ayres;
Williamson, Ellen Douglas

Douglas, Gavin 1475(?)-1522........ LC 20

Douglas, Keith 1920-1944 .... TCLC 40
See also DLB 27

Douglas, Leonard
See Bradbury, Ray (Douglas)

Douglas, Michael
See Crichton, (John) Michael

Douglass, Frederick
1817(?)-1895 .... NCLC 7; BLC; DA;
WLC
See also CDALB 1640-1865; DLB 1, 43, 50,
79; SATA 29

Dourado, (Waldomiro Freitas) Autran
1926- .... CLC 23, 60
See also CA 25-28R; CANR 34

Dourado, Waldomiro Autran
See Dourado, (Waldomiro Freitas) Autran

Dove, Rita (Frances)
1952- .... CLC 50, 81; PC 6
See also BW 2; CA 109; CAAS 19;
CANR 27, 42; DLB 120

Dowell, Coleman 1925-1985........ CLC 60
See also CA 25-28R; 117; CANR 10;
DLB 130

Dowson, Ernest Christopher
1867-1900 .... TCLC 4
See also CA 105; DLB 19, 135

Doyle, A. Conan
See Doyle, Arthur Conan

Doyle, Arthur Conan
1859-1930 .... TCLC 7; DA; SSC 12;
WLC
See also CA 104; 122; CDBLB 1890-1914;
DLB 18, 70; MTCW; SATA 24

Doyle, Conan
See Doyle, Arthur Conan

Doyle, John
See Graves, Robert (von Ranke)

Doyle, Roddy 1958(?)-............ CLC 81
See also CA 143

Doyle, Sir A. Conan
See Doyle, Arthur Conan

Doyle, Sir Arthur Conan
See Doyle, Arthur Conan

Dr. A
See Asimov, Isaac; Silverstein, Alvin

Drabble, Margaret
    1939- . . . . **CLC 2, 3, 5, 8, 10, 22, 53**
    See also CA 13-16R; CANR 18, 35;
      CDBLB 1960 to Present; DLB 14;
      MTCW; SATA 48

Drapier, M. B.
    See Swift, Jonathan

Drayham, James
    See Mencken, H(enry) L(ouis)

Drayton, Michael 1563-1631 . . . . **LC 8**

Dreadstone, Carl
    See Campbell, (John) Ramsey

Dreiser, Theodore (Herman Albert)
    1871-1945 . . . . . . **TCLC 10, 18, 35; DA;**
                       WLC
    See also CA 106; 132; CDALB 1865-1917;
      DLB 9, 12, 102, 137; DLBD 1; MTCW

Drexler, Rosalyn 1926- . . . . **CLC 2, 6**
    See also CA 81-84

Dreyer, Carl Theodor 1889-1968. . . . **CLC 16**
    See also CA 116

Drieu la Rochelle, Pierre(-Eugene)
    1893-1945 . . . . **TCLC 21**
    See also CA 117; DLB 72

Drinkwater, John 1882-1937 . . . . . **TCLC 57**
    See also CA 109; DLB 10, 19

Drop Shot
    See Cable, George Washington

Droste-Hulshoff, Annette Freiin von
    1797-1848 . . . . **NCLC 3**
    See also DLB 133

Drummond, Walter
    See Silverberg, Robert

Drummond, William Henry
    1854-1907 . . . . **TCLC 25**
    See also DLB 92

Drummond de Andrade, Carlos
    1902-1987 . . . . **CLC 18**
    See also Andrade, Carlos Drummond de
    See also CA 132; 123

Drury, Allen (Stuart) 1918- . . . . **CLC 37**
    See also CA 57-60; CANR 18

Dryden, John
    1631-1700 . . . **LC 3, 21; DA; DC 3; WLC**
    See also CDBLB 1660-1789; DLB 80, 101,
      131

Duberman, Martin 1930- . . . . **CLC 8**
    See also CA 1-4R; CANR 2

Dubie, Norman (Evans) 1945- . . . . . . **CLC 36**
    See also CA 69-72; CANR 12; DLB 120

Du Bois, W(illiam) E(dward) B(urghardt)
    1868-1963 . . . . . . **CLC 1, 2, 13, 64; BLC;**
                      DA; WLC
    See also BW 1; CA 85-88; CANR 34;
      CDALB 1865-1917; DLB 47, 50, 91;
      MTCW; SATA 42

Dubus, Andre 1936- . . . **CLC 13, 36; SSC 15**
    See also CA 21-24R; CANR 17; DLB 130

Duca Minimo
    See D'Annunzio, Gabriele

Ducharme, Rejean 1941- . . . . **CLC 74**
    See also DLB 60

Duclos, Charles Pinot 1704-1772 . . . . . **LC 1**

Dudek, Louis 1918- . . . . **CLC 11, 19**
    See also CA 45-48; CAAS 14; CANR 1;
      DLB 88

Duerrenmatt, Friedrich
    1921-1990 . . . . . . **CLC 1, 4, 8, 11, 15, 43**
    See also CA 17-20R; CANR 33; DLB 69,
      124; MTCW

Duffy, Bruce (?)- . . . . **CLC 50**

Duffy, Maureen 1933- . . . . **CLC 37**
    See also CA 25-28R; CANR 33; DLB 14;
      MTCW

Dugan, Alan 1923- . . . . **CLC 2, 6**
    See also CA 81-84; DLB 5

du Gard, Roger Martin
    See Martin du Gard, Roger

Duhamel, Georges 1884-1966 . . . . **CLC 8**
    See also CA 81-84; 25-28R; CANR 35;
      DLB 65; MTCW

Dujardin, Edouard (Emile Louis)
    1861-1949 . . . . **TCLC 13**
    See also CA 109; DLB 123

Dumas, Alexandre (Davy de la Pailleterie)
    1802-1870 . . . . **NCLC 11; DA; WLC**
    See also DLB 119; SATA 18

Dumas, Alexandre
    1824-1895 . . . . **NCLC 9; DC 1**

Dumas, Claudine
    See Malzberg, Barry N(athaniel)

Dumas, Henry L. 1934-1968 . . . . . **CLC 6, 62**
    See also BW 1; CA 85-88; DLB 41

du Maurier, Daphne
    1907-1989 . . . . **CLC 6, 11, 59**
    See also CA 5-8R; 128; CANR 6; MTCW;
      SATA 27, 60

Dunbar, Paul Laurence
    1872-1906 . . . . . . **TCLC 2, 12; BLC; DA;**
                  PC 5; SSC 8; WLC
    See also BW 1; CA 104; 124;
      CDALB 1865-1917; DLB 50, 54, 78;
      SATA 34

Dunbar, William 1460(?)-1530(?) . . . . **LC 20**

Duncan, Lois 1934- . . . . **CLC 26**
    See also AAYA 4; CA 1-4R; CANR 2, 23,
      36; CLR 29; JRDA; MAICYA; SAAS 2;
      SATA 1, 36, 75

Duncan, Robert (Edward)
    1919-1988 . . . . **CLC 1, 2, 4, 7, 15, 41, 55;**
                        PC 2
    See also CA 9-12R; 124; CANR 28; DLB 5,
      16; MTCW

Dunlap, William 1766-1839 . . . . **NCLC 2**
    See also DLB 30, 37, 59

Dunn, Douglas (Eaglesham)
    1942- . . . . **CLC 6, 40**
    See also CA 45-48; CANR 2, 33; DLB 40;
      MTCW

Dunn, Katherine (Karen) 1945- . . . . . **CLC 71**
    See also CA 33-36R

Dunn, Stephen 1939- . . . . **CLC 36**
    See also CA 33-36R; CANR 12; DLB 105

Dunne, Finley Peter 1867-1936. . . . **TCLC 28**
    See also CA 108; DLB 11, 23

Dunne, John Gregory 1932- . . . . **CLC 28**
    See also CA 25-28R; CANR 14; DLBY 80

Dunsany, Edward John Moreton Drax
    Plunkett 1878-1957
    See Dunsany, Lord
    See also CA 104; DLB 10

Dunsany, Lord . . . . **TCLC 2**
    See also Dunsany, Edward John Moreton
      Drax Plunkett
    See also DLB 77

du Perry, Jean
    See Simenon, Georges (Jacques Christian)

Durang, Christopher (Ferdinand)
    1949- . . . . **CLC 27, 38**
    See also CA 105

Duras, Marguerite
    1914- . . . . . . **CLC 3, 6, 11, 20, 34, 40, 68**
    See also CA 25-28R; DLB 83; MTCW

Durban, (Rosa) Pam 1947- . . . . **CLC 39**
    See also CA 123

Durcan, Paul 1944- . . . . **CLC 43, 70**
    See also CA 134

Durkheim, Emile 1858-1917 . . . . . . **TCLC 55**

Durrell, Lawrence (George)
    1912-1990 . . . . **CLC 1, 4, 6, 8, 13, 27, 41**
    See also CA 9-12R; 132; CANR 40;
      CDBLB 1945-1960; DLB 15, 27;
      DLBY 90; MTCW

Durrenmatt, Friedrich
    See Duerrenmatt, Friedrich

Dutt, Toru 1856-1877. . . . . **NCLC 29**

Dwight, Timothy 1752-1817. . . . . . **NCLC 13**
    See also DLB 37

Dworkin, Andrea 1946- . . . . **CLC 43**
    See also CA 77-80; CANR 16, 39; MTCW

Dwyer, Deanna
    See Koontz, Dean R(ay)

Dwyer, K. R.
    See Koontz, Dean R(ay)

Dylan, Bob 1941- . . . . . . **CLC 3, 4, 6, 12, 77**
    See also CA 41-44R; DLB 16

Eagleton, Terence (Francis) 1943-
    See Eagleton, Terry
    See also CA 57-60; CANR 7, 23; MTCW

Eagleton, Terry . . . . **CLC 63**
    See also Eagleton, Terence (Francis)

Early, Jack
    See Scoppettone, Sandra

East, Michael
    See West, Morris L(anglo)

Eastaway, Edward
    See Thomas, (Philip) Edward

Eastlake, William (Derry) 1917- . . . . . **CLC 8**
    See also CA 5-8R; CAAS 1; CANR 5;
      DLB 6

Eastman, Charles A(lexander)
    1858-1939 . . . . **TCLC 55**
    See also YABC 1

Eberhart, Richard (Ghormley)
    1904- . . . . **CLC 3, 11, 19, 56**
    See also CA 1-4R; CANR 2;
      CDALB 1941-1968; DLB 48; MTCW

Eberstadt, Fernanda 1960- . . . . **CLC 39**
    See also CA 136

Faust, Frederick (Schiller)
1892-1944(?) .... **TCLC 49**
See also CA 108

Faust, Irvin 1924-................ **CLC 8**
See also CA 33-36R; CANR 28; DLB 2, 28;
DLBY 80

Fawkes, Guy
See Benchley, Robert (Charles)

Fearing, Kenneth (Flexner)
1902-1961 .... **CLC 51**
See also CA 93-96; DLB 9

Fecamps, Elise
See Creasey, John

Federman, Raymond 1928- ...... **CLC 6, 47**
See also CA 17-20R; CAAS 8; CANR 10,
43; DLBY 80

Federspiel, J(uerg) F. 1931-........ **CLC 42**

Feiffer, Jules (Ralph) 1929-.... **CLC 2, 8, 64**
See also AAYA 3; CA 17-20R; CANR 30;
DLB 7, 44; MTCW; SATA 8, 61

Feige, Hermann Albert Otto Maximilian
See Traven, B.

Feinberg, David B. 1956-......... **CLC 59**
See also CA 135

Feinstein, Elaine 1930-............ **CLC 36**
See also CA 69-72; CAAS 1; CANR 31;
DLB 14, 40; MTCW

Feldman, Irving (Mordecai) 1928-.... **CLC 7**
See also CA 1-4R; CANR 1

Fellini, Federico 1920-1993 ..... **CLC 16, 85**
See also CA 65-68; 143; CANR 33

Felsen, Henry Gregor 1916- .... **CLC 17**
See also CA 1-4R; CANR 1; SAAS 2;
SATA 1

Fenton, James Martin 1949-....... **CLC 32**
See also CA 102; DLB 40

Ferber, Edna 1887-1968........... **CLC 18**
See also AITN 1; CA 5-8R; 25-28R; DLB 9,
28, 86; MTCW; SATA 7

Ferguson, Helen
See Kavan, Anna

Ferguson, Samuel 1810-1886..... **NCLC 33**
See also DLB 32

Ferling, Lawrence
See Ferlinghetti, Lawrence (Monsanto)

Ferlinghetti, Lawrence (Monsanto)
1919(?)-........ **CLC 2, 6, 10, 27; PC 1**
See also CA 5-8R; CANR 3, 41;
CDALB 1941-1968; DLB 5, 16; MTCW

Fernandez, Vicente Garcia Huidobro
See Huidobro Fernandez, Vicente Garcia

Ferrer, Gabriel (Francisco Victor) Miro
See Miro (Ferrer), Gabriel (Francisco
Victor)

Ferrier, Susan (Edmonstone)
1782-1854 .... **NCLC 8**
See also DLB 116

Ferrigno, Robert 1948(?)-.......... **CLC 65**
See also CA 140

Feuchtwanger, Lion 1884-1958 ..... **TCLC 3**
See also CA 104; DLB 66

Feuillet, Octave 1821-1890 ...... **NCLC 45**

Feydeau, Georges (Leon Jules Marie)
1862-1921 .... **TCLC 22**
See also CA 113

Ficino, Marsilio 1433-1499 .... **LC 12**

Fiedeler, Hans
See Doeblin, Alfred

Fiedler, Leslie A(aron)
1917-.................. **CLC 4, 13, 24**
See also CA 9-12R; CANR 7; DLB 28, 67;
MTCW

Field, Andrew 1938-.............. **CLC 44**
See also CA 97-100; CANR 25

Field, Eugene 1850-1895 .... **NCLC 3**
See also DLB 23, 42, 140; MAICYA;
SATA 16

Field, Gans T.
See Wellman, Manly Wade

Field, Michael .... **TCLC 43**

Field, Peter
See Hobson, Laura Z(ametkin)

Fielding, Henry
1707-1754 .... **LC 1; DA; WLC**
See also CDBLB 1660-1789; DLB 39, 84,
101

Fielding, Sarah 1710-1768........... **LC 1**
See also DLB 39

Fierstein, Harvey (Forbes) 1954- ... **CLC 33**
See also CA 123; 129

Figes, Eva 1932-................. **CLC 31**
See also CA 53-56; CANR 4, 44; DLB 14

Finch, Robert (Duer Claydon)
1900-.................... **CLC 18**
See also CA 57-60; CANR 9, 24; DLB 88

Findley, Timothy 1930-........... **CLC 27**
See also CA 25-28R; CANR 12, 42;
DLB 53

Fink, William
See Mencken, H(enry) L(ouis)

Firbank, Louis 1942-
See Reed, Lou
See also CA 117

Firbank, (Arthur Annesley) Ronald
1886-1926 .... **TCLC 1**
See also CA 104; DLB 36

Fisher, M(ary) F(rances) K(ennedy)
1908-1992 .... **CLC 76**
See also CA 77-80; 138; CANR 44

Fisher, Roy 1930-................ **CLC 25**
See also CA 81-84; CAAS 10; CANR 16;
DLB 40

Fisher, Rudolph
1897-1934 .... **TCLC 11; BLC**
See also BW 1; CA 107; 124; DLB 51, 102

Fisher, Vardis (Alvero) 1895-1968.... **CLC 7**
See also CA 5-8R; 25-28R; DLB 9

Fiske, Tarleton
See Bloch, Robert (Albert)

Fitch, Clarke
See Sinclair, Upton (Beall)

Fitch, John IV
See Cormier, Robert (Edmund)

Fitzgerald, Captain Hugh
See Baum, L(yman) Frank

FitzGerald, Edward 1809-1883 .... **NCLC 9**
See also DLB 32

Fitzgerald, F(rancis) Scott (Key)
1896-1940 ...... **TCLC 1, 6, 14, 28, 55;**
DA; SSC 6; WLC
See also AITN 1; CA 110; 123;
CDALB 1917-1929; DLB 4, 9, 86;
DLBD 1; DLBY 81; MTCW

Fitzgerald, Penelope 1916-... **CLC 19, 51, 61**
See also CA 85-88; CAAS 10; DLB 14

Fitzgerald, Robert (Stuart)
1910-1985 .... **CLC 39**
See also CA 1-4R; 114; CANR 1; DLBY 80

FitzGerald, Robert D(avid)
1902-1987 .... **CLC 19**
See also CA 17-20R

Fitzgerald, Zelda (Sayre)
1900-1948 .... **TCLC 52**
See also CA 117; 126; DLBY 84

Flanagan, Thomas (James Bonner)
1923-.................... **CLC 25, 52**
See also CA 108; DLBY 80; MTCW

Flaubert, Gustave
1821-1880 .... **NCLC 2, 10, 19; DA;**
SSC 11; WLC
See also DLB 119

Flecker, (Herman) James Elroy
1884-1915 .... **TCLC 43**
See also CA 109; DLB 10, 19

Fleming, Ian (Lancaster)
1908-1964 .... **CLC 3, 30**
See also CA 5-8R; CDBLB 1945-1960;
DLB 87; MTCW; SATA 9

Fleming, Thomas (James) 1927- .... **CLC 37**
See also CA 5-8R; CANR 10; SATA 8

Fletcher, John Gould 1886-1950... **TCLC 35**
See also CA 107; DLB 4, 45

Fleur, Paul
See Pohl, Frederik

Flooglebuckle, Al
See Spiegelman, Art

Flying Officer X
See Bates, H(erbert) E(rnest)

Fo, Dario 1926-.................. **CLC 32**
See also CA 116; 128; MTCW

Fogarty, Jonathan Titulescu Esq.
See Farrell, James T(homas)

Folke, Will
See Bloch, Robert (Albert)

Follett, Ken(neth Martin) 1949- .... **CLC 18**
See also AAYA 6; BEST 89:4; CA 81-84;
CANR 13, 33; DLB 87; DLBY 81;
MTCW

Fontane, Theodor 1819-1898 ..... **NCLC 26**
See also DLB 129

Foote, Horton 1916-.............. **CLC 51**
See also CA 73-76; CANR 34; DLB 26

Foote, Shelby 1916- .... **CLC 75**
See also CA 5-8R; CANR 3, 45; DLB 2, 17

Forbes, Esther 1891-1967......... **CLC 12**
See also CA 13-14; 25-28R; CAP 1;
CLR 27; DLB 22; JRDA; MAICYA;
SATA 2

Forche, Carolyn (Louise)
1950- . . . . **CLC 25, 83; PC 10**
See also CA 109; 117; DLB 5

Ford, Elbur
See Hibbert, Eleanor Alice Burford

Ford, Ford Madox
1873-1939 . . . . **TCLC 1, 15, 39, 57**
See also CA 104; 132; CDBLB 1914-1945;
DLB 34, 98; MTCW

Ford, John 1895-1973. . . . . **CLC 16**
See also CA 45-48

Ford, Richard 1944- . . . . **CLC 46**
See also CA 69-72; CANR 11

Ford, Webster
See Masters, Edgar Lee

Foreman, Richard 1937-. . . . . **CLC 50**
See also CA 65-68; CANR 32

Forester, C(ecil) S(cott)
1899-1966 . . . . **CLC 35**
See also CA 73-76; 25-28R; SATA 13

Forez
See Mauriac, Francois (Charles)

Forman, James Douglas 1932-. . . . . . **CLC 21**
See also CA 9-12R; CANR 4, 19, 42;
JRDA; MAICYA; SATA 8, 70

Fornes, Maria Irene 1930-. . . . . . **CLC 39, 61**
See also CA 25-28R; CANR 28; DLB 7;
HW; MTCW

Forrest, Leon 1937- . . . . **CLC 4**
See also BW 2; CA 89-92; CAAS 7;
CANR 25; DLB 33

Forster, E(dward) M(organ)
1879-1970 . . . . . **CLC 1, 2, 3, 4, 9, 10, 13,
15, 22, 45, 77; DA; WLC**
See also AAYA 2; CA 13-14; 25-28R;
CANR 45; CAP 1; CDBLB 1914-1945;
DLB 34, 98; DLBD 10; MTCW;
SATA 57

Forster, John 1812-1876 . . . . **NCLC 11**
See also DLB 144

Forsyth, Frederick 1938-. . . . . . **CLC 2, 5, 36**
See also BEST 89:4; CA 85-88; CANR 38;
DLB 87; MTCW

Forten, Charlotte L. . . . . **TCLC 16; BLC**
See also Grimke, Charlotte L(ottie) Forten
See also DLB 50

Foscolo, Ugo 1778-1827 . . . . **NCLC 8**

Fosse, Bob . . . . **CLC 20**
See also Fosse, Robert Louis

Fosse, Robert Louis 1927-1987
See Fosse, Bob
See also CA 110; 123

Foster, Stephen Collins
1826-1864 . . . . **NCLC 26**

Foucault, Michel
1926-1984 . . . . **CLC 31, 34, 69**
See also CA 105; 113; CANR 34; MTCW

Fouque, Friedrich (Heinrich Karl) de la Motte
1777-1843 . . . . **NCLC 2**
See also DLB 90

Fournier, Henri Alban 1886-1914
See Alain-Fournier
See also CA 104

Fournier, Pierre 1916- . . . . **CLC 11**
See also Gascar, Pierre
See also CA 89-92; CANR 16, 40

Fowles, John
1926- . . . . **CLC 1, 2, 3, 4, 6, 9, 10, 15, 33**
See also CA 5-8R; CANR 25; CDBLB 1960
to Present; DLB 14, 139; MTCW;
SATA 22

Fox, Paula 1923-. . . . . **CLC 2, 8**
See also AAYA 3; CA 73-76; CANR 20,
36; CLR 1; DLB 52; JRDA; MAICYA;
MTCW; SATA 17, 60

Fox, William Price (Jr.) 1926- . . . . . **CLC 22**
See also CA 17-20R; CAAS 19; CANR 11;
DLB 2; DLBY 81

Foxe, John 1516(?)-1587 . . . . **LC 14**

Frame, Janet . . . . **CLC 2, 3, 6, 22, 66**
See also Clutha, Janet Paterson Frame

France, Anatole . . . . **TCLC 9**
See also Thibault, Jacques Anatole Francois
See also DLB 123

Francis, Claude 19(?)- . . . . **CLC 50**

Francis, Dick 1920- . . . . **CLC 2, 22, 42**
See also AAYA 5; BEST 89:3; CA 5-8R;
CANR 9, 42; CDBLB 1960 to Present;
DLB 87; MTCW

Francis, Robert (Churchill)
1901-1987 . . . . **CLC 15**
See also CA 1-4R; 123; CANR 1

Frank, Anne(lies Marie)
1929-1945 . . . . **TCLC 17; DA; WLC**
See also AAYA 12; CA 113; 133; MTCW;
SATA 42

Frank, Elizabeth 1945-. . . . . **CLC 39**
See also CA 121; 126

Franklin, Benjamin
See Hasek, Jaroslav (Matej Frantisek)

Franklin, Benjamin 1706-1790. . . **LC 25; DA**
See also CDALB 1640-1865; DLB 24, 43,
73

Franklin, (Stella Maraia Sarah) Miles
1879-1954 . . . . **TCLC 7**
See also CA 104

Fraser, (Lady) Antonia (Pakenham)
1932- . . . . **CLC 32**
See also CA 85-88; CANR 44; MTCW;
SATA 32

Fraser, George MacDonald 1925-. . . . **CLC 7**
See also CA 45-48; CANR 2

Fraser, Sylvia 1935-. . . . . **CLC 64**
See also CA 45-48; CANR 1, 16

Frayn, Michael 1933-. . . . . . **CLC 3, 7, 31, 47**
See also CA 5-8R; CANR 30; DLB 13, 14;
MTCW

Fraze, Candida (Merrill) 1945-. . . . . **CLC 50**
See also CA 126

Frazer, J(ames) G(eorge)
1854-1941 . . . . **TCLC 32**
See also CA 118

Frazer, Robert Caine
See Creasey, John

Frazer, Sir James George
See Frazer, J(ames) G(eorge)

Frazier, Ian 1951-. . . . . **CLC 46**
See also CA 130

Frederic, Harold 1856-1898. . . . . . **NCLC 10**
See also DLB 12, 23

Frederick, John
See Faust, Frederick (Schiller)

Frederick the Great 1712-1786 . . . . . . **LC 14**

Fredro, Aleksander 1793-1876. . . . . **NCLC 8**

Freeling, Nicolas 1927- . . . . **CLC 38**
See also CA 49-52; CAAS 12; CANR 1, 17;
DLB 87

Freeman, Douglas Southall
1886-1953 . . . . **TCLC 11**
See also CA 109; DLB 17

Freeman, Judith 1946-. . . . . **CLC 55**

Freeman, Mary Eleanor Wilkins
1852-1930 . . . . **TCLC 9; SSC 1**
See also CA 106; DLB 12, 78

Freeman, R(ichard) Austin
1862-1943 . . . . **TCLC 21**
See also CA 113; DLB 70

French, Marilyn 1929-. . . . . . **CLC 10, 18, 60**
See also CA 69-72; CANR 3, 31; MTCW

French, Paul
See Asimov, Isaac

Freneau, Philip Morin 1752-1832. . **NCLC 1**
See also DLB 37, 43

Freud, Sigmund 1856-1939 . . . . **TCLC 52**
See also CA 115; 133; MTCW

Friedan, Betty (Naomi) 1921- . . . . . . **CLC 74**
See also CA 65-68; CANR 18, 45; MTCW

Friedman, B(ernard) H(arper)
1926- . . . . **CLC 7**
See also CA 1-4R; CANR 3

Friedman, Bruce Jay 1930-. . . . **CLC 3, 5, 56**
See also CA 9-12R; CANR 25; DLB 2, 28

Friel, Brian 1929-. . . . . **CLC 5, 42, 59**
See also CA 21-24R; CANR 33; DLB 13;
MTCW

Friis-Baastad, Babbis Ellinor
1921-1970 . . . . **CLC 12**
See also CA 17-20R; 134; SATA 7

Frisch, Max (Rudolf)
1911-1991 . . . . . **CLC 3, 9, 14, 18, 32, 44**
See also CA 85-88; 134; CANR 32;
DLB 69, 124; MTCW

Fromentin, Eugene (Samuel Auguste)
1820-1876 . . . . **NCLC 10**
See also DLB 123

Frost, Frederick
See Faust, Frederick (Schiller)

Frost, Robert (Lee)
1874-1963 . . . . **CLC 1, 3, 4, 9, 10, 13, 15,
26, 34, 44; DA; PC 1; WLC**
See also CA 89-92; CANR 33;
CDALB 1917-1929; DLB 54; DLBD 7;
MTCW; SATA 14

Froude, James Anthony
1818-1894 . . . . **NCLC 43**
See also DLB 18, 57, 144

Froy, Herald
See Waterhouse, Keith (Spencer)

Fry, Christopher 1907-. . . . . . . **CLC 2, 10, 14**
See also CA 17-20R; CANR 9, 30; DLB 13;
MTCW; SATA 66

Frye, (Herman) Northrop
1912-1991 . . . . CLC 24, 70
See also CA 5-8R; 133; CANR 8, 37;
DLB 67, 68; MTCW

Fuchs, Daniel 1909-1993 . . . . CLC 8, 22
See also CA 81-84; 142; CAAS 5;
CANR 40; DLB 9, 26, 28; DLBY 93

Fuchs, Daniel 1934- . . . . CLC 34
See also CA 37-40R; CANR 14

Fuentes, Carlos
1928- . . . . . . CLC 3, 8, 10, 13, 22, 41, 60;
DA; HLC; WLC
See also AAYA 4; AITN 2; CA 69-72;
CANR 10, 32; DLB 113; HW; MTCW

Fuentes, Gregorio Lopez y
See Lopez y Fuentes, Gregorio

Fugard, (Harold) Athol
1932- . . . . CLC 5, 9, 14, 25, 40, 80; DC 3
See also CA 85-88; CANR 32; MTCW

Fugard, Sheila 1932- . . . . CLC 48
See also CA 125

Fuller, Charles (H., Jr.)
1939- . . . . CLC 25; BLC; DC 1
See also BW 2; CA 108; 112; DLB 38;
MTCW

Fuller, John (Leopold) 1937- . . . . CLC 62
See also CA 21-24R; CANR 9, 44; DLB 40

Fuller, Margaret . . . . NCLC 5
See also Ossoli, Sarah Margaret (Fuller
marchesa d')

Fuller, Roy (Broadbent)
1912-1991 . . . . CLC 4, 28
See also CA 5-8R; 135; CAAS 10; DLB 15,
20

Fulton, Alice 1952- . . . . CLC 52
See also CA 116

Furphy, Joseph 1843-1912 . . . . TCLC 25

Fussell, Paul 1924- . . . . CLC 74
See also BEST 90:1; CA 17-20R; CANR 8,
21, 35; MTCW

Futabatei, Shimei 1864-1909 . . . . . TCLC 44

Futrelle, Jacques 1875-1912 . . . . . . TCLC 19
See also CA 113

Gaboriau, Emile 1835-1873 . . . . . . NCLC 14

Gadda, Carlo Emilio 1893-1973 . . . . CLC 11
See also CA 89-92

Gaddis, William
1922- . . . . CLC 1, 3, 6, 8, 10, 19, 43
See also CA 17-20R; CANR 21; DLB 2;
MTCW

Gaines, Ernest J(ames)
1933- . . . . CLC 3, 11, 18; BLC
See also AITN 1; BW 2; CA 9-12R;
CANR 6, 24, 42; CDALB 1968-1988;
DLB 2, 33; DLBY 80; MTCW

Gaitskill, Mary 1954- . . . . CLC 69
See also CA 128

Galdos, Benito Perez
See Perez Galdos, Benito

Gale, Zona 1874-1938 . . . . TCLC 7
See also CA 105; DLB 9, 78

Galeano, Eduardo (Hughes) 1940- . . . CLC 72
See also CA 29-32R; CANR 13, 32; HW

Galiano, Juan Valera y Alcala
See Valera y Alcala-Galiano, Juan

Gallagher, Tess 1943- . . . . CLC 18, 63; PC 9
See also CA 106; DLB 120

Gallant, Mavis
1922- . . . . CLC 7, 18, 38; SSC 5
See also CA 69-72; CANR 29; DLB 53;
MTCW

Gallant, Roy A(rthur) 1924- . . . . CLC 17
See also CA 5-8R; CANR 4, 29; CLR 30;
MAICYA; SATA 4, 68

Gallico, Paul (William) 1897-1976 . . . CLC 2
See also AITN 1; CA 5-8R; 69-72;
CANR 23; DLB 9; MAICYA; SATA 13

Gallup, Ralph
See Whitemore, Hugh (John)

Galsworthy, John
1867-1933 . . . . TCLC 1, 45; DA; WLC 2
See also CA 104; 141; CDBLB 1890-1914;
DLB 10, 34, 98

Galt, John 1779-1839 . . . . NCLC 1
See also DLB 99, 116

Galvin, James 1951- . . . . CLC 38
See also CA 108; CANR 26

Gamboa, Federico 1864-1939 . . . . . . TCLC 36

Gann, Ernest Kellogg 1910-1991 . . . . CLC 23
See also AITN 1; CA 1-4R; 136; CANR 1

Garcia, Cristina 1958- . . . . CLC 76
See also CA 141

Garcia Lorca, Federico
1898-1936 . . . . TCLC 1, 7, 49; DA;
DC 2; HLC; PC 3; WLC
See also CA 104; 131; DLB 108; HW;
MTCW

Garcia Marquez, Gabriel (Jose)
1928- . . . . CLC 2, 3, 8, 10, 15, 27, 47, 55,
68; DA; HLC; SSC 8; WLC
See also AAYA 3; BEST 89:1, 90:4;
CA 33-36R; CANR 10, 28; DLB 113;
HW; MTCW

Gard, Janice
See Latham, Jean Lee

Gard, Roger Martin du
See Martin du Gard, Roger

Gardam, Jane 1928- . . . . CLC 43
See also CA 49-52; CANR 2, 18, 33;
CLR 12; DLB 14; MAICYA; MTCW;
SAAS 9; SATA 28, 39, 76

Gardner, Herb . . . . CLC 44

Gardner, John (Champlin), Jr.
1933-1982 . . . . . CLC 2, 3, 5, 7, 8, 10, 18,
28, 34; SSC 7
See also AITN 1; CA 65-68; 107;
CANR 33; DLB 2; DLBY 82; MTCW;
SATA 31, 40

Gardner, John (Edmund) 1926- . . . . . CLC 30
See also CA 103; CANR 15; MTCW

Gardner, Noel
See Kuttner, Henry

Gardons, S. S.
See Snodgrass, W(illiam) D(e Witt)

Garfield, Leon 1921- . . . . CLC 12
See also AAYA 8; CA 17-20R; CANR 38,
41; CLR 21; JRDA; MAICYA; SATA 1,
32, 76

Garland, (Hannibal) Hamlin
1860-1940 . . . . TCLC 3
See also CA 104; DLB 12, 71, 78

Garneau, (Hector de) Saint-Denys
1912-1943 . . . . TCLC 13
See also CA 111; DLB 88

Garner, Alan 1934- . . . . CLC 17
See also CA 73-76; CANR 15; CLR 20;
MAICYA; MTCW; SATA 18, 69

Garner, Hugh 1913-1979 . . . . CLC 13
See also CA 69-72; CANR 31; DLB 68

Garnett, David 1892-1981 . . . . CLC 3
See also CA 5-8R; 103; CANR 17; DLB 34

Garos, Stephanie
See Katz, Steve

Garrett, George (Palmer)
1929- . . . . CLC 3, 11, 51
See also CA 1-4R; CAAS 5; CANR 1, 42;
DLB 2, 5, 130; DLBY 83

Garrick, David 1717-1779 . . . . LC 15
See also DLB 84

Garrigue, Jean 1914-1972 . . . . CLC 2, 8
See also CA 5-8R; 37-40R; CANR 20

Garrison, Frederick
See Sinclair, Upton (Beall)

Garth, Will
See Hamilton, Edmond; Kuttner, Henry

Garvey, Marcus (Moziah, Jr.)
1887-1940 . . . . TCLC 41; BLC
See also BW 1; CA 120; 124

Gary, Romain . . . . CLC 25
See also Kacew, Romain
See also DLB 83

Gascar, Pierre . . . . CLC 11
See also Fournier, Pierre

Gascoyne, David (Emery) 1916- . . . . CLC 45
See also CA 65-68; CANR 10, 28; DLB 20;
MTCW

Gaskell, Elizabeth Cleghorn
1810-1865 . . . . NCLC 5
See also CDBLB 1832-1890; DLB 21, 144

Gass, William H(oward)
1924- . . . CLC 1, 2, 8, 11, 15, 39; SSC 12
See also CA 17-20R; CANR 30; DLB 2;
MTCW

Gasset, Jose Ortega y
See Ortega y Gasset, Jose

Gates, Henry Louis, Jr. 1950- . . . . . . CLC 65
See also BW 2; CA 109; CANR 25; DLB 67

Gautier, Theophile 1811-1872 . . . . . NCLC 1
See also DLB 119

Gawsworth, John
See Bates, H(erbert) E(rnest)

Gaye, Marvin (Penze) 1939-1984 . . . CLC 26
See also CA 112

Gebler, Carlo (Ernest) 1954- . . . . CLC 39
See also CA 119; 133

Gee, Maggie (Mary) 1948- . . . . CLC 57
See also CA 130

Gee, Maurice (Gough) 1931- . . . . CLC 29
See also CA 97-100; SATA 46

Gelbart, Larry (Simon) 1923- . . . CLC 21, 61
See also CA 73-76; CANR 45

Goldberg, Anatol 1910-1982 .... **CLC 34**
See also CA 131; 117

Goldemberg, Isaac 1945- .... **CLC 52**
See also CA 69-72; CAAS 12; CANR 11,
32; HW

Golding, William (Gerald)
1911-1993 .... **CLC 1, 2, 3, 8, 10, 17, 27,
58, 81; DA; WLC**
See also AAYA 5; CA 5-8R; 141;
CANR 13, 33; CDBLB 1945-1960;
DLB 15, 100; MTCW

Goldman, Emma 1869-1940 ...... **TCLC 13**
See also CA 110

Goldman, Francisco 1955- .... **CLC 76**

Goldman, William (W.) 1931- .... **CLC 1, 48**
See also CA 9-12R; CANR 29; DLB 44

Goldmann, Lucien 1913-1970 ...... **CLC 24**
See also CA 25-28; CAP 2

Goldoni, Carlo 1707-1793 .... **LC 4**

Goldsberry, Steven 1949- .... **CLC 34**
See also CA 131

Goldsmith, Oliver
1728-1774 .... **LC 2; DA; WLC**
See also CDBLB 1660-1789; DLB 39, 89,
104, 109, 142; SATA 26

Goldsmith, Peter
See Priestley, J(ohn) B(oynton)

Gombrowicz, Witold
1904-1969 .... **CLC 4, 7, 11, 49**
See also CA 19-20; 25-28R; CAP 2

Gomez de la Serna, Ramon
1888-1963 .... **CLC 9**
See also CA 116; HW

Goncharov, Ivan Alexandrovich
1812-1891 .... **NCLC 1**

Goncourt, Edmond (Louis Antoine Huot) de
1822-1896 .... **NCLC 7**
See also DLB 123

Goncourt, Jules (Alfred Huot) de
1830-1870 .... **NCLC 7**
See also DLB 123

Gontier, Fernande 19(?)- .... **CLC 50**

Goodman, Paul 1911-1972 .... **CLC 1, 2, 4, 7**
See also CA 19-20; 37-40R; CANR 34;
CAP 2; DLB 130; MTCW

Gordimer, Nadine
1923- .... **CLC 3, 5, 7, 10, 18, 33, 51, 70;
DA; SSC 17**
See also CA 5-8R; CANR 3, 28; MTCW

Gordon, Adam Lindsay
1833-1870 .... **NCLC 21**

Gordon, Caroline
1895-1981 ... **CLC 6, 13, 29, 83; SSC 15**
See also CA 11-12; 103; CANR 36; CAP 1;
DLB 4, 9, 102; DLBY 81; MTCW

Gordon, Charles William 1860-1937
See Connor, Ralph
See also CA 109

Gordon, Mary (Catherine)
1949- .... **CLC 13, 22**
See also CA 102; CANR 44; DLB 6;
DLBY 81; MTCW

Gordon, Sol 1923- .... **CLC 26**
See also CA 53-56; CANR 4; SATA 11

Gordone, Charles 1925- .... **CLC 1, 4**
See also BW 1; CA 93-96; DLB 7; MTCW

Gorenko, Anna Andreevna
See Akhmatova, Anna

Gorky, Maxim .... **TCLC 8; WLC**
See also Peshkov, Alexei Maximovich

Goryan, Sirak
See Saroyan, William

Gosse, Edmund (William)
1849-1928 .... **TCLC 28**
See also CA 117; DLB 57, 144

Gotlieb, Phyllis Fay (Bloom)
1926- .... **CLC 18**
See also CA 13-16R; CANR 7; DLB 88

Gottesman, S. D.
See Kornbluth, C(yril) M.; Pohl, Frederik

Gottfried von Strassburg
fl. c. 1210- .... **CMLC 10**
See also DLB 138

Gould, Lois .... **CLC 4, 10**
See also CA 77-80; CANR 29; MTCW

Gourmont, Remy de 1858-1915 .... **TCLC 17**
See also CA 109

Govier, Katherine 1948- .... **CLC 51**
See also CA 101; CANR 18, 40

Goyen, (Charles) William
1915-1983 .... **CLC 5, 8, 14, 40**
See also AITN 2; CA 5-8R; 110; CANR 6;
DLB 2; DLBY 83

Goytisolo, Juan
1931- .... **CLC 5, 10, 23; HLC**
See also CA 85-88; CANR 32; HW; MTCW

Gozzano, Guido 1883-1916 .... **PC 10**
See also DLB 114

Gozzi, (Conte) Carlo 1720-1806 .. **NCLC 23**

Grabbe, Christian Dietrich
1801-1836 .... **NCLC 2**
See also DLB 133

Grace, Patricia 1937- .... **CLC 56**

Gracian y Morales, Baltasar
1601-1658 .... **LC 15**

Gracq, Julien .... **CLC 11, 48**
See also Poirier, Louis
See also DLB 83

Grade, Chaim 1910-1982 .... **CLC 10**
See also CA 93-96; 107

Graduate of Oxford, A
See Ruskin, John

Graham, John
See Phillips, David Graham

Graham, Jorie 1951- .... **CLC 48**
See also CA 111; DLB 120

Graham, R(obert) B(ontine) Cunninghame
See Cunninghame Graham, R(obert)
B(ontine)
See also DLB 98, 135

Graham, Robert
See Haldeman, Joe (William)

Graham, Tom
See Lewis, (Harry) Sinclair

Graham, W(illiam) S(ydney)
1918-1986 .... **CLC 29**
See also CA 73-76; 118; DLB 20

Graham, Winston (Mawdsley)
1910- .... **CLC 23**
See also CA 49-52; CANR 2, 22, 45;
DLB 77

Grant, Skeeter
See Spiegelman, Art

Granville-Barker, Harley
1877-1946 .... **TCLC 2**
See also Barker, Harley Granville
See also CA 104

Grass, Guenter (Wilhelm)
1927- ..... **CLC 1, 2, 4, 6, 11, 15, 22, 32,
49; DA; WLC**
See also CA 13-16R; CANR 20; DLB 75,
124; MTCW

Gratton, Thomas
See Hulme, T(homas) E(rnest)

Grau, Shirley Ann
1929- .... **CLC 4, 9; SSC 15**
See also CA 89-92; CANR 22; DLB 2;
MTCW

Gravel, Fern
See Hall, James Norman

Graver, Elizabeth 1964- .... **CLC 70**
See also CA 135

Graves, Richard Perceval 1945- .... **CLC 44**
See also CA 65-68; CANR 9, 26

Graves, Robert (von Ranke)
1895-1985 ...... **CLC 1, 2, 6, 11, 39, 44,
45; PC 6**
See also CA 5-8R; 117; CANR 5, 36;
CDBLB 1914-1945; DLB 20, 100;
DLBY 85; MTCW; SATA 45

Gray, Alasdair 1934- .... **CLC 41**
See also CA 126; MTCW

Gray, Amlin 1946- .... **CLC 29**
See also CA 138

Gray, Francine du Plessix 1930- .... **CLC 22**
See also BEST 90:3; CA 61-64; CAAS 2;
CANR 11, 33; MTCW

Gray, John (Henry) 1866-1934 .... **TCLC 19**
See also CA 119

Gray, Simon (James Holliday)
1936- .... **CLC 9, 14, 36**
See also AITN 1; CA 21-24R; CAAS 3;
CANR 32; DLB 13; MTCW

Gray, Spalding 1941- .... **CLC 49**
See also CA 128

Gray, Thomas
1716-1771 ...... **LC 4; DA; PC 2; WLC**
See also CDBLB 1660-1789; DLB 109

Grayson, David
See Baker, Ray Stannard

Grayson, Richard (A.) 1951- .... **CLC 38**
See also CA 85-88; CANR 14, 31

Greeley, Andrew M(oran) 1928- .... **CLC 28**
See also CA 5-8R; CAAS 7; CANR 7, 43;
MTCW

Green, Brian
See Card, Orson Scott

Green, Hannah
See Greenberg, Joanne (Goldenberg)

Green, Hannah .... **CLC 3**
See also CA 73-76

Green, Henry.................... CLC 2, 13
See also Yorke, Henry Vincent
See also DLB 15

Green, Julian (Hartridge) 1900-
See Green, Julien
See also CA 21-24R; CANR 33; DLB 4, 72;
MTCW

Green, Julien................ CLC 3, 11, 77
See also Green, Julian (Hartridge)

Green, Paul (Eliot) 1894-1981...... CLC 25
See also AITN 1; CA 5-8R; 103; CANR 3;
DLB 7, 9; DLBY 81

Greenberg, Ivan 1908-1973
See Rahv, Philip
See also CA 85-88

Greenberg, Joanne (Goldenberg)
1932-..................... CLC 7, 30
See also AAYA 12; CA 5-8R; CANR 14,
32; SATA 25

Greenberg, Richard 1959(?)-....... CLC 57
See also CA 138

Greene, Bette 1934-.............. CLC 30
See also AAYA 7; CA 53-56; CANR 4;
CLR 2; JRDA; MAICYA; SAAS 16;
SATA 8

Greene, Gael.................... CLC 8
See also CA 13-16R; CANR 10

Greene, Graham
1904-1991 .... CLC 1, 3, 6, 9, 14, 18, 27,
37, 70, 72; DA; WLC
See also AITN 2; CA 13-16R; 133;
CANR 35; CDBLB 1945-1960; DLB 13,
15, 77, 100; DLBY 91; MTCW; SATA 20

Greer, Richard
See Silverberg, Robert

Greer, Richard
See Silverberg, Robert

Gregor, Arthur 1923-.............. CLC 9
See also CA 25-28R; CAAS 10; CANR 11;
SATA 36

Gregor, Lee
See Pohl, Frederik

Gregory, Isabella Augusta (Persse)
1852-1932 .... TCLC 1
See also CA 104; DLB 10

Gregory, J. Dennis
See Williams, John A(lfred)

Grendon, Stephen
See Derleth, August (William)

Grenville, Kate 1950-............. CLC 61
See also CA 118

Grenville, Pelham
See Wodehouse, P(elham) G(renville)

Greve, Felix Paul (Berthold Friedrich)
1879-1948
See Grove, Frederick Philip
See also CA 104; 141

Grey, Zane 1872-1939 .... TCLC 6
See also CA 104; 132; DLB 9; MTCW

Grieg, (Johan) Nordahl (Brun)
1902-1943 .... TCLC 10
See also CA 107

Grieve, C(hristopher) M(urray)
1892-1978 .... CLC 11, 19
See also MacDiarmid, Hugh
See also CA 5-8R; 85-88; CANR 33;
MTCW

Griffin, Gerald 1803-1840 .... NCLC 7

Griffin, John Howard 1920-1980.... CLC 68
See also AITN 1; CA 1-4R; 101; CANR 2

Griffin, Peter 1942- .... CLC 39
See also CA 136

Griffiths, Trevor 1935-......... CLC 13, 52
See also CA 97-100; CANR 45; DLB 13

Grigson, Geoffrey (Edward Harvey)
1905-1985 .... CLC 7, 39
See also CA 25-28R; 118; CANR 20, 33;
DLB 27; MTCW

Grillparzer, Franz 1791-1872...... NCLC 1
See also DLB 133

Grimble, Reverend Charles James
See Eliot, T(homas) S(tearns)

Grimke, Charlotte L(ottie) Forten
1837(?)-1914
See Forten, Charlotte L.
See also BW 1; CA 117; 124

Grimm, Jacob Ludwig Karl
1785-1863 .... NCLC 3
See also DLB 90; MAICYA; SATA 22

Grimm, Wilhelm Karl 1786-1859 .. NCLC 3
See also DLB 90; MAICYA; SATA 22

Grimmelshausen, Johann Jakob Christoffel
von 1621-1676 .... LC 6

Grindel, Eugene 1895-1952
See Eluard, Paul
See also CA 104

Grisham, John 1955(?)- .... CLC 84
See also CA 138

Grossman, David 1954-........... CLC 67
See also CA 138

Grossman, Vasily (Semenovich)
1905-1964 .... CLC 41
See also CA 124; 130; MTCW

Grove, Frederick Philip .... TCLC 4
See also Greve, Felix Paul (Berthold
Friedrich)
See also DLB 92

Grubb
See Crumb, R(obert)

Grumbach, Doris (Isaac)
1918-................ CLC 13, 22, 64
See also CA 5-8R; CAAS 2; CANR 9, 42

Grundtvig, Nicolai Frederik Severin
1783-1872 .... NCLC 1

Grunge
See Crumb, R(obert)

Grunwald, Lisa 1959-............. CLC 44
See also CA 120

Guare, John 1938- .... CLC 8, 14, 29, 67
See also CA 73-76; CANR 21; DLB 7;
MTCW

Gudjonsson, Halldor Kiljan 1902-
See Laxness, Halldor
See also CA 103

Guenter, Erich
See Eich, Guenter

Guest, Barbara 1920-............. CLC 34
See also CA 25-28R; CANR 11, 44; DLB 5

Guest, Judith (Ann) 1936-....... CLC 8, 30
See also AAYA 7; CA 77-80; CANR 15;
MTCW

Guild, Nicholas M. 1944-.......... CLC 33
See also CA 93-96

Guillemin, Jacques
See Sartre, Jean-Paul

Guillen, Jorge 1893-1984.......... CLC 11
See also CA 89-92; 112; DLB 108; HW

Guillen (y Batista), Nicolas (Cristobal)
1902-1989 ..... CLC 48, 79; BLC; HLC
See also BW 2; CA 116; 125; 129; HW

Guillevic, (Eugene) 1907-.......... CLC 33
See also CA 93-96

Guillois
See Desnos, Robert

Guiney, Louise Imogen
1861-1920 .... TCLC 41
See also DLB 54

Guiraldes, Ricardo (Guillermo)
1886-1927 .... TCLC 39
See also CA 131; HW; MTCW

Gunn, Bill .... CLC 5
See also Gunn, William Harrison
See also DLB 38

Gunn, Thom(son William)
1929-........... CLC 3, 6, 18, 32, 81
See also CA 17-20R; CANR 9, 33;
CDBLB 1960 to Present; DLB 27;
MTCW

Gunn, William Harrison 1934(?)-1989
See Gunn, Bill
See also AITN 1; BW 1; CA 13-16R; 128;
CANR 12, 25

Gunnars, Kristjana 1948-.......... CLC 69
See also CA 113; DLB 60

Gurganus, Allan 1947-............ CLC 70
See also BEST 90:1; CA 135

Gurney, A(lbert) R(amsdell), Jr.
1930- .... CLC 32, 50, 54
See also CA 77-80; CANR 32

Gurney, Ivor (Bertie) 1890-1937... TCLC 33

Gurney, Peter
See Gurney, A(lbert) R(amsdell), Jr.

Guro, Elena 1877-1913........... TCLC 56

Gustafson, Ralph (Barker) 1909-.... CLC 36
See also CA 21-24R; CANR 8, 45; DLB 88

Gut, Gom
See Simenon, Georges (Jacques Christian)

Guthrie, A(lfred) B(ertram), Jr.
1901-1991 .... CLC 23
See also CA 57-60; 134; CANR 24; DLB 6;
SATA 62; SATA-Obit 67

Guthrie, Isobel
See Grieve, C(hristopher) M(urray)

Guthrie, Woodrow Wilson 1912-1967
See Guthrie, Woody
See also CA 113; 93-96

Guthrie, Woody................... CLC 35
See also Guthrie, Woodrow Wilson

Hemingway, Ernest (Miller)
    1899-1961 .... **CLC 1, 3, 6, 8, 10, 13, 19,**
        30, 34, 39, 41, 44, 50, 61, 80; DA; SSC 1;
                                    WLC
    See also CA 77-80; CANR 34;
        CDALB 1917-1929; DLB 4, 9, 102;
        DLBD 1; DLBY 81, 87; MTCW

Hempel, Amy 1951- .... **CLC 39**
    See also CA 118; 137

Henderson, F. C.
    See Mencken, H(enry) L(ouis)

Henderson, Sylvia
    See Ashton-Warner, Sylvia (Constance)

Henley, Beth .... **CLC 23**
    See also Henley, Elizabeth Becker
    See also CABS 3; DLBY 86

Henley, Elizabeth Becker 1952-
    See Henley, Beth
    See also CA 107; CANR 32; MTCW

Henley, William Ernest
    1849-1903 .... **TCLC 8**
    See also CA 105; DLB 19

Hennissart, Martha
    See Lathen, Emma
    See also CA 85-88

Henry, O. .... **TCLC 1, 19; SSC 5; WLC**
    See also Porter, William Sydney

Henry, Patrick 1736- .... **LC 25**
    See also CA 145

Henryson, Robert 1430(?)-1506(?).... **LC 20**

Henry VIII 1491-1547 .... **LC 10**

Henschke, Alfred
    See Klabund

Hentoff, Nat(han Irving) 1925- ..... **CLC 26**
    See also AAYA 4; CA 1-4R; CAAS 6;
        CANR 5, 25; CLR 1; JRDA; MAICYA;
        SATA 27, 42, 69

Heppenstall, (John) Rayner
    1911-1981 .... **CLC 10**
    See also CA 1-4R; 103; CANR 29

Herbert, Frank (Patrick)
    1920-1986 ...... **CLC 12, 23, 35, 44, 85**
    See also CA 53-56; 118; CANR 5, 43;
        DLB 8; MTCW; SATA 9, 37, 47

Herbert, George 1593-1633 .... **LC 24; PC 4**
    See also CDBLB Before 1660; DLB 126

Herbert, Zbigniew 1924- .... **CLC 9, 43**
    See also CA 89-92; CANR 36; MTCW

Herbst, Josephine (Frey)
    1897-1969 .... **CLC 34**
    See also CA 5-8R; 25-28R; DLB 9

Hergesheimer, Joseph
    1880-1954 .... **TCLC 11**
    See also CA 109; DLB 102, 9

Herlihy, James Leo 1927-1993 ...... **CLC 6**
    See also CA 1-4R; 143; CANR 2

Hermogenes fl. c. 175- .... **CMLC 6**

Hernandez, Jose 1834-1886 ...... **NCLC 17**

Herrick, Robert
    1591-1674 .... **LC 13; DA; PC 9**
    See also DLB 126

Herring, Guilles
    See Somerville, Edith

Herriot, James 1916- .... **CLC 12**
    See also Wight, James Alfred
    See also AAYA 1; CANR 40

Herrmann, Dorothy 1941- .... **CLC 44**
    See also CA 107

Herrmann, Taffy
    See Herrmann, Dorothy

Hersey, John (Richard)
    1914-1993 .... **CLC 1, 2, 7, 9, 40, 81**
    See also CA 17-20R; 140; CANR 33;
        DLB 6; MTCW; SATA 25;
        SATA-Obit 76

Herzen, Aleksandr Ivanovich
    1812-1870 .... **NCLC 10**

Herzl, Theodor 1860-1904 .... **TCLC 36**

Herzog, Werner 1942- .... **CLC 16**
    See also CA 89-92

Hesiod c. 8th cent. B.C.- .... **CMLC 5**

Hesse, Hermann
    1877-1962 .... **CLC 1, 2, 3, 6, 11, 17, 25,**
                        69; DA; SSC 9; WLC
    See also CA 17-18; CAP 2; DLB 66;
        MTCW; SATA 50

Hewes, Cady
    See De Voto, Bernard (Augustine)

Heyen, William 1940- .... **CLC 13, 18**
    See also CA 33-36R; CAAS 9; DLB 5

Heyerdahl, Thor 1914- .... **CLC 26**
    See also CA 5-8R; CANR 5, 22; MTCW;
        SATA 2, 52

Heym, Georg (Theodor Franz Arthur)
    1887-1912 .... **TCLC 9**
    See also CA 106

Heym, Stefan 1913- .... **CLC 41**
    See also CA 9-12R; CANR 4; DLB 69

Heyse, Paul (Johann Ludwig von)
    1830-1914 .... **TCLC 8**
    See also CA 104; DLB 129

Hibbert, Eleanor Alice Burford
    1906-1993 .... **CLC 7**
    See also BEST 90:4; CA 17-20R; 140;
        CANR 9, 28; SATA 2; SATA-Obit 74

Higgins, George V(incent)
    1939- .... **CLC 4, 7, 10, 18**
    See also CA 77-80; CAAS 5; CANR 17;
        DLB 2; DLBY 81; MTCW

Higginson, Thomas Wentworth
    1823-1911 .... **TCLC 36**
    See also DLB 1, 64

Highet, Helen
    See MacInnes, Helen (Clark)

Highsmith, (Mary) Patricia
    1921- .... **CLC 2, 4, 14, 42**
    See also CA 1-4R; CANR 1, 20; MTCW

Highwater, Jamake (Mamake)
    1942(?)- .... **CLC 12**
    See also AAYA 7; CA 65-68; CAAS 7;
        CANR 10, 34; CLR 17; DLB 52;
        DLBY 85; JRDA; MAICYA; SATA 30,
        32, 69

Hijuelos, Oscar 1951- ...... **CLC 65; HLC**
    See also BEST 90:1; CA 123; HW

Hikmet, Nazim 1902(?)-1963 .... **CLC 40**
    See also CA 141; 93-96

Hildesheimer, Wolfgang
    1916-1991 .... **CLC 49**
    See also CA 101; 135; DLB 69, 124

Hill, Geoffrey (William)
    1932- .... **CLC 5, 8, 18, 45**
    See also CA 81-84; CANR 21;
        CDBLB 1960 to Present; DLB 40;
        MTCW

Hill, George Roy 1921- .... **CLC 26**
    See also CA 110; 122

Hill, John
    See Koontz, Dean R(ay)

Hill, Susan (Elizabeth) 1942- .... **CLC 4**
    See also CA 33-36R; CANR 29; DLB 14,
        139; MTCW

Hillerman, Tony 1925- .... **CLC 62**
    See also AAYA 6; BEST 89:1; CA 29-32R;
        CANR 21, 42; SATA 6

Hillesum, Etty 1914-1943 .... **TCLC 49**
    See also CA 137

Hilliard, Noel (Harvey) 1929- ...... **CLC 15**
    See also CA 9-12R; CANR 7

Hillis, Rick 1956- .... **CLC 66**
    See also CA 134

Hilton, James 1900-1954 .... **TCLC 21**
    See also CA 108; DLB 34, 77; SATA 34

Himes, Chester (Bomar)
    1909-1984 .... **CLC 2, 4, 7, 18, 58; BLC**
    See also BW 2; CA 25-28R; 114; CANR 22;
        DLB 2, 76, 143; MTCW

Hinde, Thomas .... **CLC 6, 11**
    See also Chitty, Thomas Willes

Hindin, Nathan
    See Bloch, Robert (Albert)

Hine, (William) Daryl 1936- .... **CLC 15**
    See also CA 1-4R; CAAS 15; CANR 1, 20;
        DLB 60

Hinkson, Katharine Tynan
    See Tynan, Katharine

Hinton, S(usan) E(loise)
    1950- .... **CLC 30; DA**
    See also AAYA 2; CA 81-84; CANR 32;
        CLR 3, 23; JRDA; MAICYA; MTCW;
        SATA 19, 58

Hippius, Zinaida .... **TCLC 9**
    See also Gippius, Zinaida (Nikolayevna)

Hiraoka, Kimitake 1925-1970
    See Mishima, Yukio
    See also CA 97-100; 29-32R; MTCW

Hirsch, E(ric) D(onald), Jr. 1928-... **CLC 79**
    See also CA 25-28R; CANR 27; DLB 67;
        MTCW

Hirsch, Edward 1950- .... **CLC 31, 50**
    See also CA 104; CANR 20, 42; DLB 120

Hitchcock, Alfred (Joseph)
    1899-1980 .... **CLC 16**
    See also CA 97-100; SATA 24, 27

Hitler, Adolf 1889-1945 .... **TCLC 53**
    See also CA 117

Hoagland, Edward 1932- .... **CLC 28**
    See also CA 1-4R; CANR 2, 31; DLB 6;
        SATA 51

Hoban, Russell (Conwell) 1925-. . **CLC 7, 25**
See also CA 5-8R; CANR 23, 37; CLR 3;
DLB 52; MAICYA; MTCW; SATA 1,
40, 78

Hobbs, Perry
See Blackmur, R(ichard) P(almer)

Hobson, Laura Z(ametkin)
1900-1986 . . . . **CLC 7, 25**
See also CA 17-20R; 118; DLB 28;
SATA 52

Hochhuth, Rolf 1931-. . . . . **CLC 4, 11, 18**
See also CA 5-8R; CANR 33; DLB 124;
MTCW

Hochman, Sandra 1936-. . . . . **CLC 3, 8**
See also CA 5-8R; DLB 5

Hochwaelder, Fritz 1911-1986. . . . . . **CLC 36**
See also CA 29-32R; 120; CANR 42;
MTCW

Hochwalder, Fritz
See Hochwaelder, Fritz

Hocking, Mary (Eunice) 1921-. . . . . **CLC 13**
See also CA 101; CANR 18, 40

Hodgins, Jack 1938-. . . . . **CLC 23**
See also CA 93-96; DLB 60

Hodgson, William Hope
1877(?)-1918 . . . . **TCLC 13**
See also CA 111; DLB 70

Hoffman, Alice 1952-. . . . . **CLC 51**
See also CA 77-80; CANR 34; MTCW

Hoffman, Daniel (Gerard)
1923-. . . . . **CLC 6, 13, 23**
See also CA 1-4R; CANR 4; DLB 5

Hoffman, Stanley 1944-. . . . . **CLC 5**
See also CA 77-80

Hoffman, William M(oses) 1939-. . . **CLC 40**
See also CA 57-60; CANR 11

Hoffmann, E(rnst) T(heodor) A(madeus)
1776-1822 . . . . **NCLC 2; SSC 13**
See also DLB 90; SATA 27

Hofmann, Gert 1931-. . . . . **CLC 54**
See also CA 128

Hofmannsthal, Hugo von
1874-1929 . . . . **TCLC 11; DC 4**
See also CA 106; DLB 81, 118

Hogan, Linda 1947-. . . . . **CLC 73**
See also CA 120; CANR 45

Hogarth, Charles
See Creasey, John

Hogg, James 1770-1835. . . . . **NCLC 4**
See also DLB 93, 116

Holbach, Paul Henri Thiry Baron
1723-1789 . . . . **LC 14**

Holberg, Ludvig 1684-1754 . . . . **LC 6**

Holden, Ursula 1921-. . . . . **CLC 18**
See also CA 101; CAAS 8; CANR 22

Holderlin, (Johann Christian) Friedrich
1770-1843 . . . . **NCLC 16; PC 4**

Holdstock, Robert
See Holdstock, Robert P.

Holdstock, Robert P. 1948-. . . . . **CLC 39**
See also CA 131

Holland, Isabelle 1920-. . . . . **CLC 21**
See also AAYA 11; CA 21-24R; CANR 10,
25; JRDA; MAICYA; SATA 8, 70

Holland, Marcus
See Caldwell, (Janet Miriam) Taylor
(Holland)

Hollander, John 1929-. . . . . . **CLC 2, 5, 8, 14**
See also CA 1-4R; CANR 1; DLB 5;
SATA 13

Hollander, Paul
See Silverberg, Robert

Holleran, Andrew 1943(?)-. . . . . **CLC 38**
See also CA 144

Hollinghurst, Alan 1954-. . . . . **CLC 55**
See also CA 114

Hollis, Jim
See Summers, Hollis (Spurgeon, Jr.)

Holmes, John
See Souster, (Holmes) Raymond

Holmes, John Clellon 1926-1988. . . . **CLC 56**
See also CA 9-12R; 125; CANR 4; DLB 16

Holmes, Oliver Wendell
1809-1894 . . . . **NCLC 14**
See also CDALB 1640-1865; DLB 1;
SATA 34

Holmes, Raymond
See Souster, (Holmes) Raymond

Holt, Victoria
See Hibbert, Eleanor Alice Burford

Holub, Miroslav 1923-. . . . . **CLC 4**
See also CA 21-24R; CANR 10

Homer c. 8th cent. B.C.-. . . . . **CMLC 1; DA**

Honig, Edwin 1919-. . . . . **CLC 33**
See also CA 5-8R; CAAS 8; CANR 4, 45;
DLB 5

Hood, Hugh (John Blagdon)
1928-. **CLC 15, 28**
See also CA 49-52; CAAS 17; CANR 1, 33;
DLB 53

Hood, Thomas 1799-1845. . . . . **NCLC 16**
See also DLB 96

Hooker, (Peter) Jeremy 1941-. . . . . . **CLC 43**
See also CA 77-80; CANR 22; DLB 40

Hope, A(lec) D(erwent) 1907-. . . . **CLC 3, 51**
See also CA 21-24R; CANR 33; MTCW

Hope, Brian
See Creasey, John

Hope, Christopher (David Tully)
1944-. . . . . **CLC 52**
See also CA 106; SATA 62

Hopkins, Gerard Manley
1844-1889 . . . . **NCLC 17; DA; WLC**
See also CDBLB 1890-1914; DLB 35, 57

Hopkins, John (Richard) 1931-. . . . . . **CLC 4**
See also CA 85-88

Hopkins, Pauline Elizabeth
1859-1930 . . . . **TCLC 28; BLC**
See also BW 2; CA 141; DLB 50

Hopkinson, Francis 1737-1791 . . . . . . **LC 25**
See also DLB 31

Hopley-Woolrich, Cornell George 1903-1968
See Woolrich, Cornell
See also CA 13-14; CAP 1

Horatio
See Proust, (Valentin-Louis-George-Eugene-)
Marcel

Horgan, Paul 1903-. . . . . **CLC 9, 53**
See also CA 13-16R; CANR 9, 35;
DLB 102; DLBY 85; MTCW; SATA 13

Horn, Peter
See Kuttner, Henry

Hornem, Horace Esq.
See Byron, George Gordon (Noel)

Horovitz, Israel 1939-. . . . . **CLC 56**
See also CA 33-36R; DLB 7

Horvath, Odon von
See Horvath, Oedoen von
See also DLB 85, 124

Horvath, Oedoen von 1901-1938. . . **TCLC 45**
See also Horvath, Odon von
See also CA 118

Horwitz, Julius 1920-1986. . . . . **CLC 14**
See also CA 9-12R; 119; CANR 12

Hospital, Janette Turner 1942-. . . . . **CLC 42**
See also CA 108

Hostos, E. M. de
See Hostos (y Bonilla), Eugenio Maria de

Hostos, Eugenio M. de
See Hostos (y Bonilla), Eugenio Maria de

Hostos, Eugenio Maria
See Hostos (y Bonilla), Eugenio Maria de

Hostos (y Bonilla), Eugenio Maria de
1839-1903 . . . . **TCLC 24**
See also CA 123; 131; HW

Houdini
See Lovecraft, H(oward) P(hillips)

Hougan, Carolyn 1943-. . . . . **CLC 34**
See also CA 139

Household, Geoffrey (Edward West)
1900-1988 . . . . **CLC 11**
See also CA 77-80; 126; DLB 87; SATA 14,
59

Housman, A(lfred) E(dward)
1859-1936 . . . . . . **TCLC 1, 10; DA; PC 2**
See also CA 104; 125; DLB 19; MTCW

Housman, Laurence 1865-1959 . . . . . **TCLC 7**
See also CA 106; DLB 10; SATA 25

Howard, Elizabeth Jane 1923-. . . **CLC 7, 29**
See also CA 5-8R; CANR 8

Howard, Maureen 1930-. . . . . . **CLC 5, 14, 46**
See also CA 53-56; CANR 31; DLBY 83;
MTCW

Howard, Richard 1929-. . . . . . **CLC 7, 10, 47**
See also AITN 1; CA 85-88; CANR 25;
DLB 5

Howard, Robert Ervin 1906-1936. . . **TCLC 8**
See also CA 105

Howard, Warren F.
See Pohl, Frederik

Howe, Fanny 1940-. . . . . **CLC 47**
See also CA 117; SATA 52

Howe, Irving 1920-1993. . . . . **CLC 85**
See also CA 9-12R; 141; CANR 21;
DLB 67; MTCW

Howe, Julia Ward 1819-1910 . . . . . **TCLC 21**
See also CA 117; DLB 1

Howe, Susan 1937-. . . . . **CLC 72**
See also DLB 120

Howe, Tina 1937-. . . . . **CLC 48**
See also CA 109

Howell, James 1594(?)-1666 . . . . LC **13**

Howells, W. D.
See Howells, William Dean

Howells, William D.
See Howells, William Dean

Howells, William Dean
1837-1920 . . . . **TCLC 7, 17, 41**
See also CA 104; 134; CDALB 1865-1917;
DLB 12, 64, 74, 79

Howes, Barbara 1914- . . . . CLC **15**
See also CA 9-12R; CAAS 3; SATA 5

Hrabal, Bohumil 1914- . . . . CLC **13, 67**
See also CA 106; CAAS 12

Hsun, Lu . . . . TCLC **3**
See also Shu-Jen, Chou

Hubbard, L(afayette) Ron(ald)
1911-1986 . . . . CLC **43**
See also CA 77-80; 118; CANR 22

Huch, Ricarda (Octavia)
1864-1947 . . . . TCLC **13**
See also CA 111; DLB 66

Huddle, David 1942- . . . . CLC **49**
See also CA 57-60; DLB 130

Hudson, Jeffrey
See Crichton, (John) Michael

Hudson, W(illiam) H(enry)
1841-1922 . . . . TCLC **29**
See also CA 115; DLB 98; SATA 35

Hueffer, Ford Madox
See Ford, Ford Madox

Hughart, Barry 1934- . . . . CLC **39**
See also CA 137

Hughes, Colin
See Creasey, John

Hughes, David (John) 1930- . . . . CLC **48**
See also CA 116; 129; DLB 14

Hughes, (James) Langston
1902-1967 . . . . . CLC 1, 5, 10, 15, 35, 44;
BLC; DA; DC 3; PC 1; SSC 6; WLC
See also AAYA 12; BW 1; CA 1-4R;
25-28R; CANR 1, 34; CDALB 1929-1941;
CLR 17; DLB 4, 7, 48, 51, 86; JRDA;
MAICYA; MTCW; SATA 4, 33

Hughes, Richard (Arthur Warren)
1900-1976 . . . . CLC **1, 11**
See also CA 5-8R; 65-68; CANR 4;
DLB 15; MTCW; SATA 8, 25

Hughes, Ted
1930- . . . . CLC 2, 4, 9, 14, 37; PC 7
See also CA 1-4R; CANR 1, 33; CLR 3;
DLB 40; MAICYA; MTCW; SATA 27,
49

Hugo, Richard F(ranklin)
1923-1982 . . . . CLC **6, 18, 32**
See also CA 49-52; 108; CANR 3; DLB 5

Hugo, Victor (Marie)
1802-1885 . . NCLC **3, 10, 21; DA; WLC**
See also DLB 119; SATA 47

Huidobro, Vicente
See Huidobro Fernandez, Vicente Garcia

Huidobro Fernandez, Vicente Garcia
1893-1948 . . . . TCLC **31**
See also CA 131; HW

Hulme, Keri 1947- . . . . CLC **39**
See also CA 125

Hulme, T(homas) E(rnest)
1883-1917 . . . . TCLC **21**
See also CA 117; DLB 19

Hume, David 1711-1776 . . . . LC **7**
See also DLB 104

Humphrey, William 1924- . . . . CLC **45**
See also CA 77-80; DLB 6

Humphreys, Emyr Owen 1919- . . . . . CLC **47**
See also CA 5-8R; CANR 3, 24; DLB 15

Humphreys, Josephine 1945- . . . . CLC **34, 57**
See also CA 121; 127

Hungerford, Pixie
See Brinsmead, H(esba) F(ay)

Hunt, E(verette) Howard, Jr.
1918- . . . . CLC **3**
See also AITN 1; CA 45-48; CANR 2

Hunt, Kyle
See Creasey, John

Hunt, (James Henry) Leigh
1784-1859 . . . . NCLC **1**

Hunt, Marsha 1946- . . . . CLC **70**
See also BW 2; CA 143

Hunt, Violet 1866-1942 . . . . TCLC **53**

Hunter, E. Waldo
See Sturgeon, Theodore (Hamilton)

Hunter, Evan 1926- . . . . CLC **11, 31**
See also CA 5-8R; CANR 5, 38; DLBY 82;
MTCW; SATA 25

Hunter, Kristin (Eggleston) 1931- . . . CLC **35**
See also AITN 1; BW 1; CA 13-16R;
CANR 13; CLR 3; DLB 33; MAICYA;
SAAS 10; SATA 12

Hunter, Mollie 1922- . . . . CLC **21**
See also McIlwraith, Maureen Mollie
Hunter
See also CANR 37; CLR 25; JRDA;
MAICYA; SAAS 7; SATA 54

Hunter, Robert (?)-1734 . . . . LC **7**

Hurston, Zora Neale
1903-1960 . . . . CLC **7, 30, 61; BLC; DA;
SSC 4**
See also BW 1; CA 85-88; DLB 51, 86;
MTCW

Huston, John (Marcellus)
1906-1987 . . . . CLC **20**
See also CA 73-76; 123; CANR 34; DLB 26

Hustvedt, Siri 1955- . . . . CLC **76**
See also CA 137

Hutten, Ulrich von 1488-1523 . . . . LC **16**

Huxley, Aldous (Leonard)
1894-1963 . . . . . CLC **1, 3, 4, 5, 8, 11, 18,
35, 79; DA; WLC**
See also AAYA 11; CA 85-88; CANR 44;
CDBLB 1914-1945; DLB 36, 100;
MTCW; SATA 63

Huysmans, Charles Marie Georges
1848-1907
See Huysmans, Joris-Karl
See also CA 104

Huysmans, Joris-Karl . . . . TCLC **7**
See also Huysmans, Charles Marie Georges
See also DLB 123

Hwang, David Henry
1957- . . . . CLC **55; DC 4**
See also CA 127; 132

Hyde, Anthony 1946- . . . . CLC **42**
See also CA 136

Hyde, Margaret O(ldroyd) 1917- . . . CLC **21**
See also CA 1-4R; CANR 1, 36; CLR 23;
JRDA; MAICYA; SAAS 8; SATA 1, 42,
76

Hynes, James 1956(?)- . . . . CLC **65**

Ian, Janis 1951- . . . . CLC **21**
See also CA 105

Ibanez, Vicente Blasco
See Blasco Ibanez, Vicente

Ibarguengoitia, Jorge 1928-1983 . . . . CLC **37**
See also CA 124; 113; HW

Ibsen, Henrik (Johan)
1828-1906 . . . . TCLC **2, 8, 16, 37, 52;
DA; DC 2; WLC**
See also CA 104; 141

Ibuse Masuji 1898-1993 . . . . CLC **22**
See also CA 127; 141

Ichikawa, Kon 1915- . . . . CLC **20**
See also CA 121

Idle, Eric 1943- . . . . CLC **21**
See also Monty Python
See also CA 116; CANR 35

Ignatow, David 1914- . . . . . . CLC **4, 7, 14, 40**
See also CA 9-12R; CAAS 3; CANR 31;
DLB 5

Ihimaera, Witi 1944- . . . . CLC **46**
See also CA 77-80

Ilf, Ilya . . . . TCLC **21**
See also Fainzilberg, Ilya Arnoldovich

Immermann, Karl (Lebrecht)
1796-1840 . . . . NCLC **4**
See also DLB 133

Inclan, Ramon (Maria) del Valle
See Valle-Inclan, Ramon (Maria) del

Infante, G(uillermo) Cabrera
See Cabrera Infante, G(uillermo)

Ingalls, Rachel (Holmes) 1940- . . . . . CLC **42**
See also CA 123; 127

Ingamells, Rex 1913-1955 . . . . TCLC **35**

Inge, William Motter
1913-1973 . . . . CLC **1, 8, 19**
See also CA 9-12R; CDALB 1941-1968;
DLB 7; MTCW

Ingelow, Jean 1820-1897 . . . . NCLC **39**
See also DLB 35; SATA 33

Ingram, Willis J.
See Harris, Mark

Innaurato, Albert (F.) 1948(?)- . . CLC **21, 60**
See also CA 115; 122

Innes, Michael
See Stewart, J(ohn) I(nnes) M(ackintosh)

Ionesco, Eugene
1912-1994 . . . . CLC **1, 4, 6, 9, 11, 15, 41;
DA; WLC**
See also CA 9-12R; 144; MTCW; SATA 7;
SATA-Obit 79

Iqbal, Muhammad 1873-1938 . . . . . TCLC **28**

Ireland, Patrick
See O'Doherty, Brian

Iron, Ralph
See Schreiner, Olive (Emilie Albertina)

Irving, John (Winslow)
1942- .... **CLC 13, 23, 38**
See also AAYA 8; BEST 89:3; CA 25-28R;
CANR 28; DLB 6; DLBY 82; MTCW

Irving, Washington
1783-1859 .... **NCLC 2, 19; DA; SSC 2;
WLC**
See also CDALB 1640-1865; DLB 3, 11, 30,
59, 73, 74; YABC 2

Irwin, P. K.
See Page, P(atricia) K(athleen)

Isaacs, Susan 1943- .... **CLC 32**
See also BEST 89:1; CA 89-92; CANR 20,
41; MTCW

Isherwood, Christopher (William Bradshaw)
1904-1986 .... **CLC 1, 9, 11, 14, 44**
See also CA 13-16R; 117; CANR 35;
DLB 15; DLBY 86; MTCW

Ishiguro, Kazuo 1954- ...... **CLC 27, 56, 59**
See also BEST 90:2; CA 120; MTCW

Ishikawa Takuboku
1886(?)-1912 .... **TCLC 15; PC 10**
See also CA 113

Iskander, Fazil 1929- .... **CLC 47**
See also CA 102

Ivan IV 1530-1584 .... **LC 17**

Ivanov, Vyacheslav Ivanovich
1866-1949 .... **TCLC 33**
See also CA 122

Ivask, Ivar Vidrik 1927-1992 ...... **CLC 14**
See also CA 37-40R; 139; CANR 24

Jackson, Daniel
See Wingrove, David (John)

Jackson, Jesse 1908-1983 .... **CLC 12**
See also BW 1; CA 25-28R; 109; CANR 27;
CLR 28; MAICYA; SATA 2, 29, 48

Jackson, Laura (Riding) 1901-1991
See Riding, Laura
See also CA 65-68; 135; CANR 28; DLB 48

Jackson, Sam
See Trumbo, Dalton

Jackson, Sara
See Wingrove, David (John)

Jackson, Shirley
1919-1965 ..... **CLC 11, 60; DA; SSC 9;
WLC**
See also AAYA 9; CA 1-4R; 25-28R;
CANR 4; CDALB 1941-1968; DLB 6;
SATA 2

Jacob, (Cyprien-)Max 1876-1944 ... **TCLC 6**
See also CA 104

Jacobs, Jim 1942- .... **CLC 12**
See also CA 97-100

Jacobs, W(illiam) W(ymark)
1863-1943 .... **TCLC 22**
See also CA 121; DLB 135

Jacobsen, Jens Peter 1847-1885 .. **NCLC 34**

Jacobsen, Josephine 1908- .... **CLC 48**
See also CA 33-36R; CAAS 18; CANR 23

Jacobson, Dan 1929- .... **CLC 4, 14**
See also CA 1-4R; CANR 2, 25; DLB 14;
MTCW

Jacqueline
See Carpentier (y Valmont), Alejo

Jagger, Mick 1944- .... **CLC 17**

Jakes, John (William) 1932- .... **CLC 29**
See also BEST 89:4; CA 57-60; CANR 10,
43; DLBY 83; MTCW; SATA 62

James, Andrew
See Kirkup, James

James, C(yril) L(ionel) R(obert)
1901-1989 .... **CLC 33**
See also BW 2; CA 117; 125; 128; DLB 125;
MTCW

James, Daniel (Lewis) 1911-1988
See Santiago, Danny
See also CA 125

James, Dynely
See Mayne, William (James Carter)

James, Henry
1843-1916 ..... **TCLC 2, 11, 24, 40, 47;
DA; SSC 8; WLC**
See also CA 104; 132; CDALB 1865-1917;
DLB 12, 71, 74; MTCW

James, M. R.
See James, Montague (Rhodes)

James, Montague (Rhodes)
1862-1936 .... **TCLC 6; SSC 16**
See also CA 104

James, P. D. .... **CLC 18, 46**
See also White, Phyllis Dorothy James
See also BEST 90:2; CDBLB 1960 to
Present; DLB 87

James, Philip
See Moorcock, Michael (John)

James, William 1842-1910 ..... **TCLC 15, 32**
See also CA 109

James I 1394-1437 .... **LC 20**

Jameson, Anna 1794-1860 ...... **NCLC 43**
See also DLB 99

Jami, Nur al-Din 'Abd al-Rahman
1414-1492 .... **LC 9**

Jandl, Ernst 1925- .... **CLC 34**

Janowitz, Tama 1957- .... **CLC 43**
See also CA 106

Jarrell, Randall
1914-1965 .... **CLC 1, 2, 6, 9, 13, 49**
See also CA 5-8R; 25-28R; CABS 2;
CANR 6, 34; CDALB 1941-1968; CLR 6;
DLB 48, 52; MAICYA; MTCW; SATA 7

Jarry, Alfred 1873-1907 .... **TCLC 2, 14**
See also CA 104

Jarvis, E. K.
See Bloch, Robert (Albert); Ellison, Harlan;
Silverberg, Robert

Jeake, Samuel, Jr.
See Aiken, Conrad (Potter)

Jean Paul 1763-1825 .... **NCLC 7**

Jefferies, (John) Richard
1848-1887 .... **NCLC 47**
See also DLB 98, 141; SATA 16

Jeffers, (John) Robinson
1887-1962 .... **CLC 2, 3, 11, 15, 54; DA;
WLC**
See also CA 85-88; CANR 35;
CDALB 1917-1929; DLB 45; MTCW

Jefferson, Janet
See Mencken, H(enry) L(ouis)

Jefferson, Thomas 1743-1826 .... **NCLC 11**
See also CDALB 1640-1865; DLB 31

Jeffrey, Francis 1773-1850 .... **NCLC 33**
See also DLB 107

Jelakowitch, Ivan
See Heijermans, Herman

Jellicoe, (Patricia) Ann 1927- ...... **CLC 27**
See also CA 85-88; DLB 13

Jen, Gish .... **CLC 70**
See also Jen, Lillian

Jen, Lillian 1956(?)-
See Jen, Gish
See also CA 135

Jenkins, (John) Robin 1912- .... **CLC 52**
See also CA 1-4R; CANR 1; DLB 14

Jennings, Elizabeth (Joan)
1926- .... **CLC 5, 14**
See also CA 61-64; CAAS 5; CANR 8, 39;
DLB 27; MTCW; SATA 66

Jennings, Waylon 1937- .... **CLC 21**

Jensen, Johannes V. 1873-1950 .... **TCLC 41**

Jensen, Laura (Linnea) 1948- ...... **CLC 37**
See also CA 103

Jerome, Jerome K(lapka)
1859-1927 .... **TCLC 23**
See also CA 119; DLB 10, 34, 135

Jerrold, Douglas William
1803-1857 .... **NCLC 2**

Jewett, (Theodora) Sarah Orne
1849-1909 .... **TCLC 1, 22; SSC 6**
See also CA 108; 127; DLB 12, 74;
SATA 15

Jewsbury, Geraldine (Endsor)
1812-1880 .... **NCLC 22**
See also DLB 21

Jhabvala, Ruth Prawer
1927- .... **CLC 4, 8, 29**
See also CA 1-4R; CANR 2, 29; DLB 139;
MTCW

Jiles, Paulette 1943- .... **CLC 13, 58**
See also CA 101

Jimenez (Mantecon), Juan Ramon
1881-1958 .... **TCLC 4; HLC; PC 7**
See also CA 104; 131; DLB 134; HW;
MTCW

Jimenez, Ramon
See Jimenez (Mantecon), Juan Ramon

Jimenez Mantecon, Juan
See Jimenez (Mantecon), Juan Ramon

Joel, Billy .... **CLC 26**
See also Joel, William Martin

Joel, William Martin 1949-
See Joel, Billy
See also CA 108

John of the Cross, St. 1542-1591 .... **LC 18**

Johnson, B(ryan) S(tanley William)
1933-1973 .... **CLC 6, 9**
See also CA 9-12R; 53-56; CANR 9;
DLB 14, 40

Johnson, Benj. F. of Boo
See Riley, James Whitcomb

Johnson, Benjamin F. of Boo
See Riley, James Whitcomb

Johnson, Charles (Richard)
1948- .... CLC **7, 51, 65; BLC**
See also BW 2; CA 116; CAAS 18;
CANR 42; DLB 33

Johnson, Denis 1949-............. CLC **52**
See also CA 117; 121; DLB 120

Johnson, Diane 1934-........ CLC **5, 13, 48**
See also CA 41-44R; CANR 17, 40;
DLBY 80; MTCW

Johnson, Eyvind (Olof Verner)
1900-1976 .... CLC **14**
See also CA 73-76; 69-72; CANR 34

Johnson, J. R.
See James, C(yril) L(ionel) R(obert)

Johnson, James Weldon
1871-1938 .... TCLC **3, 19; BLC**
See also BW 1; CA 104; 125;
CDALB 1917-1929; CLR 32; DLB 51;
MTCW; SATA 31

Johnson, Joyce 1935-............. CLC **58**
See also CA 125; 129

Johnson, Lionel (Pigot)
1867-1902 .... TCLC **19**
See also CA 117; DLB 19

Johnson, Mel
See Malzberg, Barry N(athaniel)

Johnson, Pamela Hansford
1912-1981 .... CLC **1, 7, 27**
See also CA 1-4R; 104; CANR 2, 28;
DLB 15; MTCW

Johnson, Samuel
1709-1784 .... LC **15; DA; WLC**
See also CDBLB 1660-1789; DLB 39, 95,
104, 142

Johnson, Uwe
1934-1984 .... CLC **5, 10, 15, 40**
See also CA 1-4R; 112; CANR 1, 39;
DLB 75; MTCW

Johnston, George (Benson) 1913- ... CLC **51**
See also CA 1-4R; CANR 5, 20; DLB 88

Johnston, Jennifer 1930-........... CLC **7**
See also CA 85-88; DLB 14

Jolley, (Monica) Elizabeth 1923- ... CLC **46**
See also CA 127; CAAS 13

Jones, Arthur Llewellyn 1863-1947
See Machen, Arthur
See also CA 104

Jones, D(ouglas) G(ordon) 1929-.... CLC **10**
See also CA 29-32R; CANR 13; DLB 53

Jones, David (Michael)
1895-1974 .... CLC **2, 4, 7, 13, 42**
See also CA 9-12R; 53-56; CANR 28;
CDBLB 1945-1960; DLB 20, 100; MTCW

Jones, David Robert 1947-
See Bowie, David
See also CA 103

Jones, Diana Wynne 1934- .... CLC **26**
See also AAYA 12; CA 49-52; CANR 4,
26; CLR 23; JRDA; MAICYA; SAAS 7;
SATA 9, 70

Jones, Edward P. 1950-........... CLC **76**
See also BW 2; CA 142

Jones, Gayl 1949-.......... CLC **6, 9; BLC**
See also BW 2; CA 77-80; CANR 27;
DLB 33; MTCW

Jones, James 1921-1977.... CLC **1, 3, 10, 39**
See also AITN 1, 2; CA 1-4R; 69-72;
CANR 6; DLB 2, 143; MTCW

Jones, John J.
See Lovecraft, H(oward) P(hillips)

Jones, LeRoi .... CLC **1, 2, 3, 5, 10, 14**
See also Baraka, Amiri

Jones, Louis B. .... CLC **65**
See also CA 141

Jones, Madison (Percy, Jr.) 1925- ... CLC **4**
See also CA 13-16R; CAAS 11; CANR 7

Jones, Mervyn 1922- .... CLC **10, 52**
See also CA 45-48; CAAS 5; CANR 1;
MTCW

Jones, Mick 1956(?)- .... CLC **30**

Jones, Nettie (Pearl) 1941- .... CLC **34**
See also BW 2; CA 137

Jones, Preston 1936-1979 .... CLC **10**
See also CA 73-76; 89-92; DLB 7

Jones, Robert F(rancis) 1934-....... CLC **7**
See also CA 49-52; CANR 2

Jones, Rod 1953- .... CLC **50**
See also CA 128

Jones, Terence Graham Parry
1942- .... CLC **21**
See also Jones, Terry; Monty Python
See also CA 112; 116; CANR 35; SATA 51

Jones, Terry
See Jones, Terence Graham Parry
See also SATA 67

Jones, Thom 1945(?)-............. CLC **81**

Jong, Erica 1942-...... CLC **4, 6, 8, 18, 83**
See also AITN 1; BEST 90:2; CA 73-76;
CANR 26; DLB 2, 5, 28; MTCW

Jonson, Ben(jamin)
1572(?)-1637 .... LC **6; DA; DC 4; WLC**
See also CDBLB Before 1660; DLB 62, 121

Jordan, June 1936-.......... CLC **5, 11, 23**
See also AAYA 2; BW 2; CA 33-36R;
CANR 25; CLR 10; DLB 38; MAICYA;
MTCW; SATA 4

Jordan, Pat(rick M.) 1941- .... CLC **37**
See also CA 33-36R

Jorgensen, Ivar
See Ellison, Harlan

Jorgenson, Ivar
See Silverberg, Robert

Josephus, Flavius c. 37-100 ...... CMLC **13**

Josipovici, Gabriel 1940-........ CLC **6, 43**
See also CA 37-40R; CAAS 8; DLB 14

Joubert, Joseph 1754-1824 .... NCLC **9**

Jouve, Pierre Jean 1887-1976...... CLC **47**
See also CA 65-68

Joyce, James (Augustine Aloysius)
1882-1941 ...... TCLC **3, 8, 16, 35; DA;
SSC 3; WLC**
See also CA 104; 126; CDBLB 1914-1945;
DLB 10, 19, 36; MTCW

Jozsef, Attila 1905-1937.......... TCLC **22**
See also CA 116

Juana Ines de la Cruz 1651(?)-1695 ... LC **5**

Judd, Cyril
See Kornbluth, C(yril) M.; Pohl, Frederik

Julian of Norwich 1342(?)-1416(?) .... LC **6**

Just, Ward (Swift) 1935-......... CLC **4, 27**
See also CA 25-28R; CANR 32

Justice, Donald (Rodney) 1925- .. CLC **6, 19**
See also CA 5-8R; CANR 26; DLBY 83

Juvenal c. 55-c. 127 .... CMLC **8**

Juvenis
See Bourne, Randolph S(illiman)

Kacew, Romain 1914-1980
See Gary, Romain
See also CA 108; 102

Kadare, Ismail 1936- .... CLC **52**

Kadohata, Cynthia. .... CLC **59**
See also CA 140

Kafka, Franz
1883-1924 .... TCLC **2, 6, 13, 29, 47, 53;
DA; SSC 5; WLC**
See also CA 105; 126; DLB 81; MTCW

Kahanovitsch, Pinkhes
See Der Nister

Kahn, Roger 1927-............... CLC **30**
See also CA 25-28R; CANR 44; SATA 37

Kain, Saul
See Sassoon, Siegfried (Lorraine)

Kaiser, Georg 1878-1945 .... TCLC **9**
See also CA 106; DLB 124

Kaletski, Alexander 1946-......... CLC **39**
See also CA 118; 143

Kalidasa fl. c. 400- .... CMLC **9**

Kallman, Chester (Simon)
1921-1975 .... CLC **2**
See also CA 45-48; 53-56; CANR 3

Kaminsky, Melvin 1926-
See Brooks, Mel
See also CA 65-68; CANR 16

Kaminsky, Stuart M(elvin) 1934- ... CLC **59**
See also CA 73-76; CANR 29

Kane, Paul
See Simon, Paul

Kane, Wilson
See Bloch, Robert (Albert)

Kanin, Garson 1912-.............. CLC **22**
See also AITN 1; CA 5-8R; CANR 7;
DLB 7

Kaniuk, Yoram 1930-............. CLC **19**
See also CA 134

Kant, Immanuel 1724-1804 ...... NCLC **27**
See also DLB 94

Kantor, MacKinlay 1904-1977 ...... CLC **7**
See also CA 61-64; 73-76; DLB 9, 102

Kaplan, David Michael 1946- ...... CLC **50**

Kaplan, James 1951- .... CLC **59**
See also CA 135

Karageorge, Michael
See Anderson, Poul (William)

Karamzin, Nikolai Mikhailovich
1766-1826 .... NCLC **3**

Karapanou, Margarita 1946-....... CLC **13**
See also CA 101

Karinthy, Frigyes 1887-1938...... TCLC **47**

Karl, Frederick R(obert) 1927-..... CLC **34**
See also CA 5-8R; CANR 3, 44

Kastel, Warren
See Silverberg, Robert

Kataev, Evgeny Petrovich 1903-1942
See Petrov, Evgeny
See also CA 120

Kataphusin
See Ruskin, John

Katz, Steve 1935- .... **CLC 47**
See also CA 25-28R; CAAS 14; CANR 12;
DLBY 83

Kauffman, Janet 1945- .... **CLC 42**
See also CA 117; CANR 43; DLBY 86

Kaufman, Bob (Garnell)
1925-1986 .... **CLC 49**
See also BW 1; CA 41-44R; 118; CANR 22;
DLB 16, 41

Kaufman, George S. 1889-1961 ..... **CLC 38**
See also CA 108; 93-96; DLB 7

Kaufman, Sue .... **CLC 3, 8**
See also Barondess, Sue K(aufman)

Kavafis, Konstantinos Petrou 1863-1933
See Cavafy, C(onstantine) P(eter)
See also CA 104

Kavan, Anna 1901-1968 ...... **CLC 5, 13, 82**
See also CA 5-8R; CANR 6; MTCW

Kavanagh, Dan
See Barnes, Julian

Kavanagh, Patrick (Joseph)
1904-1967 .... **CLC 22**
See also CA 123; 25-28R; DLB 15, 20;
MTCW

Kawabata, Yasunari
1899-1972 ..... **CLC 2, 5, 9, 18; SSC 17**
See also CA 93-96; 33-36R

Kaye, M(ary) M(argaret) 1909- ..... **CLC 28**
See also CA 89-92; CANR 24; MTCW;
SATA 62

Kaye, Mollie
See Kaye, M(ary) M(argaret)

Kaye-Smith, Sheila 1887-1956 ..... **TCLC 20**
See also CA 118; DLB 36

Kaymor, Patrice Maguilene
See Senghor, Leopold Sedar

Kazan, Elia 1909- .... **CLC 6, 16, 63**
See also CA 21-24R; CANR 32

Kazantzakis, Nikos
1883(?)-1957 .... **TCLC 2, 5, 33**
See also CA 105; 132; MTCW

Kazin, Alfred 1915- .... **CLC 34, 38**
See also CA 1-4R; CAAS 7; CANR 1, 45;
DLB 67

Keane, Mary Nesta (Skrine) 1904-
See Keane, Molly
See also CA 108; 114

Keane, Molly .... **CLC 31**
See also Keane, Mary Nesta (Skrine)

Keates, Jonathan 19(?)- .... **CLC 34**

Keaton, Buster 1895-1966 .... **CLC 20**

Keats, John
1795-1821 ... **NCLC 8; DA; PC 1; WLC**
See also CDBLB 1789-1832; DLB 96, 110

Keene, Donald 1922- .... **CLC 34**
See also CA 1-4R; CANR 5

Keillor, Garrison .... **CLC 40**
See also Keillor, Gary (Edward)
See also AAYA 2; BEST 89:3; DLBY 87;
SATA 58

Keillor, Gary (Edward) 1942-
See Keillor, Garrison
See also CA 111; 117; CANR 36; MTCW

Keith, Michael
See Hubbard, L(afayette) Ron(ald)

Keller, Gottfried 1819-1890 ...... **NCLC 2**
See also DLB 129

Kellerman, Jonathan 1949- .... **CLC 44**
See also BEST 90:1; CA 106; CANR 29

Kelley, William Melvin 1937- ...... **CLC 22**
See also BW 1; CA 77-80; CANR 27;
DLB 33

Kellogg, Marjorie 1922- .... **CLC 2**
See also CA 81-84

Kellow, Kathleen
See Hibbert, Eleanor Alice Burford

Kelly, M(ilton) T(erry) 1947- .... **CLC 55**
See also CA 97-100; CANR 19, 43

Kelman, James 1946- .... **CLC 58**

Kemal, Yashar 1923- .... **CLC 14, 29**
See also CA 89-92; CANR 44

Kemble, Fanny 1809-1893 .... **NCLC 18**
See also DLB 32

Kemelman, Harry 1908- .... **CLC 2**
See also AITN 1; CA 9-12R; CANR 6;
DLB 28

Kempe, Margery 1373(?)-1440(?) ..... **LC 6**

Kempis, Thomas a 1380-1471 .... **LC 11**

Kendall, Henry 1839-1882 .... **NCLC 12**

Keneally, Thomas (Michael)
1935- ...... **CLC 5, 8, 10, 14, 19, 27, 43**
See also CA 85-88; CANR 10; MTCW

Kennedy, Adrienne (Lita)
1931- .... **CLC 66; BLC**
See also BW 2; CA 103; CABS 3;
CANR 26; DLB 38

Kennedy, John Pendleton
1795-1870 .... **NCLC 2**
See also DLB 3

Kennedy, Joseph Charles 1929-
See Kennedy, X. J.
See also CA 1-4R; CANR 4, 30, 40;
SATA 14

Kennedy, William 1928- ... **CLC 6, 28, 34, 53**
See also AAYA 1; CA 85-88; CANR 14,
31; DLB 143; DLBY 85; MTCW;
SATA 57

Kennedy, X. J. .... **CLC 8, 42**
See also Kennedy, Joseph Charles
See also CAAS 9; CLR 27; DLB 5

Kent, Kelvin
See Kuttner, Henry

Kenton, Maxwell
See Southern, Terry

Kenyon, Robert O.
See Kuttner, Henry

Kerouac, Jack ..... **CLC 1, 2, 3, 5, 14, 29, 61**
See also Kerouac, Jean-Louis Lebris de
See also CDALB 1941-1968; DLB 2, 16;
DLBD 3

Kerouac, Jean-Louis Lebris de 1922-1969
See Kerouac, Jack
See also AITN 1; CA 5-8R; 25-28R;
CANR 26; DA; MTCW; WLC

Kerr, Jean 1923- .... **CLC 22**
See also CA 5-8R; CANR 7

Kerr, M. E. .... **CLC 12, 35**
See also Meaker, Marijane (Agnes)
See also AAYA 2; CLR 29; SAAS 1

Kerr, Robert .... **CLC 55**

Kerrigan, (Thomas) Anthony
1918- .... **CLC 4, 6**
See also CA 49-52; CAAS 11; CANR 4

Kerry, Lois
See Duncan, Lois

Kesey, Ken (Elton)
1935- ...... **CLC 1, 3, 6, 11, 46, 64; DA;
WLC**
See also CA 1-4R; CANR 22, 38;
CDALB 1968-1988; DLB 2, 16; MTCW;
SATA 66

Kesselring, Joseph (Otto)
1902-1967 .... **CLC 45**

Kessler, Jascha (Frederick) 1929- .... **CLC 4**
See also CA 17-20R; CANR 8

Kettelkamp, Larry (Dale) 1933- .... **CLC 12**
See also CA 29-32R; CANR 16; SAAS 3;
SATA 2

Keyber, Conny
See Fielding, Henry

Keyes, Daniel 1927- .... **CLC 80; DA**
See also CA 17-20R; CANR 10, 26;
SATA 37

Khanshendel, Chiron
See Rose, Wendy

Khayyam, Omar
1048-1131 .... **CMLC 11; PC 8**

Kherdian, David 1931- .... **CLC 6, 9**
See also CA 21-24R; CAAS 2; CANR 39;
CLR 24; JRDA; MAICYA; SATA 16, 74

Khlebnikov, Velimir .... **TCLC 20**
See also Khlebnikov, Viktor Vladimirovich

Khlebnikov, Viktor Vladimirovich 1885-1922
See Khlebnikov, Velimir
See also CA 117

Khodasevich, Vladislav (Felitsianovich)
1886-1939 .... **TCLC 15**
See also CA 115

Kielland, Alexander Lange
1849-1906 .... **TCLC 5**
See also CA 104

Kiely, Benedict 1919- .... **CLC 23, 43**
See also CA 1-4R; CANR 2; DLB 15

Kienzle, William X(avier) 1928- .... **CLC 25**
See also CA 93-96; CAAS 1; CANR 9, 31;
MTCW

Kierkegaard, Soren 1813-1855.... **NCLC 34**

Killens, John Oliver 1916-1987..... **CLC 10**
See also BW 2; CA 77-80; 123; CAAS 2;
CANR 26; DLB 33

Killigrew, Anne 1660-1685.......... **LC 4**
See also DLB 131

Kim
See Simenon, Georges (Jacques Christian)

Kincaid, Jamaica 1949- ... **CLC 43, 68; BLC**
See also BW 2; CA 125

King, Francis (Henry) 1923- ..... **CLC 8, 53**
See also CA 1-4R; CANR 1, 33; DLB 15,
139; MTCW

King, Martin Luther, Jr.
1929-1968 .... **CLC 83; BLC; DA**
See also BW 2; CA 25-28; CANR 27, 44;
CAP 2; MTCW; SATA 14

King, Stephen (Edwin)
1947- ...... **CLC 12, 26, 37, 61; SSC 17**
See also AAYA 1; BEST 90:1; CA 61-64;
CANR 1, 30; DLB 143; DLBY 80;
JRDA; MTCW; SATA 9, 55

King, Steve
See King, Stephen (Edwin)

Kingman, Lee .... **CLC 17**
See also Natti, (Mary) Lee
See also SAAS 3; SATA 1, 67

Kingsley, Charles 1819-1875 ..... **NCLC 35**
See also DLB 21, 32; YABC 2

Kingsley, Sidney 1906- .... **CLC 44**
See also CA 85-88; DLB 7

Kingsolver, Barbara 1955- ...... **CLC 55, 81**
See also CA 129; 134

Kingston, Maxine (Ting Ting) Hong
1940- .... **CLC 12, 19, 58**
See also AAYA 8; CA 69-72; CANR 13,
38; DLBY 80; MTCW; SATA 53

Kinnell, Galway
1927- .... **CLC 1, 2, 3, 5, 13, 29**
See also CA 9-12R; CANR 10, 34; DLB 5;
DLBY 87; MTCW

Kinsella, Thomas 1928- .... **CLC 4, 19**
See also CA 17-20R; CANR 15; DLB 27;
MTCW

Kinsella, W(illiam) P(atrick)
1935- .... **CLC 27, 43**
See also AAYA 7; CA 97-100; CAAS 7;
CANR 21, 35; MTCW

Kipling, (Joseph) Rudyard
1865-1936 ...... **TCLC 8, 17; DA; PC 3;**
SSC 5; WLC
See also CA 105; 120; CANR 33;
CDBLB 1890-1914; DLB 19, 34, 141;
MAICYA; MTCW; YABC 2

Kirkup, James 1918- .... **CLC 1**
See also CA 1-4R; CAAS 4; CANR 2;
DLB 27; SATA 12

Kirkwood, James 1930(?)-1989 ...... **CLC 9**
See also AITN 2; CA 1-4R; 128; CANR 6,
40

Kis, Danilo 1935-1989 .... **CLC 57**
See also CA 109; 118; 129; MTCW

Kivi, Aleksis 1834-1872 .... **NCLC 30**

Kizer, Carolyn (Ashley)
1925- .... **CLC 15, 39, 80**
See also CA 65-68; CAAS 5; CANR 24;
DLB 5

Klabund 1890-1928 .... **TCLC 44**
See also DLB 66

Klappert, Peter 1942- .... **CLC 57**
See also CA 33-36R; DLB 5

Klein, A(braham) M(oses)
1909-1972 .... **CLC 19**
See also CA 101; 37-40R; DLB 68

Klein, Norma 1938-1989 .... **CLC 30**
See also AAYA 2; CA 41-44R; 128;
CANR 15, 37; CLR 2, 19; JRDA;
MAICYA; SAAS 1; SATA 7, 57

Klein, T(heodore) E(ibon) D(onald)
1947- .... **CLC 34**
See also CA 119; CANR 44

Kleist, Heinrich von
1777-1811 .... **NCLC 2, 37**
See also DLB 90

Klima, Ivan 1931- .... **CLC 56**
See also CA 25-28R; CANR 17

Klimentov, Andrei Platonovich 1899-1951
See Platonov, Andrei
See also CA 108

Klinger, Friedrich Maximilian von
1752-1831 .... **NCLC 1**
See also DLB 94

Klopstock, Friedrich Gottlieb
1724-1803 .... **NCLC 11**
See also DLB 97

Knebel, Fletcher 1911-1993 .... **CLC 14**
See also AITN 1; CA 1-4R; 140; CAAS 3;
CANR 1, 36; SATA 36; SATA-Obit 75

Knickerbocker, Diedrich
See Irving, Washington

Knight, Etheridge
1931-1991 .... **CLC 40; BLC**
See also BW 1; CA 21-24R; 133; CANR 23;
DLB 41

Knight, Sarah Kemble 1666-1727 ..... **LC 7**
See also DLB 24

Knister, Raymond 1899-1932 ...... **TCLC 56**
See also DLB 68

Knowles, John
1926- .... **CLC 1, 4, 10, 26; DA**
See also AAYA 10; CA 17-20R; CANR 40;
CDALB 1968-1988; DLB 6; MTCW;
SATA 8

Knox, Calvin M.
See Silverberg, Robert

Knye, Cassandra
See Disch, Thomas M(ichael)

Koch, C(hristopher) J(ohn) 1932- ... **CLC 42**
See also CA 127

Koch, Christopher
See Koch, C(hristopher) J(ohn)

Koch, Kenneth 1925- .... **CLC 5, 8, 44**
See also CA 1-4R; CANR 6, 36; DLB 5;
SATA 65

Kochanowski, Jan 1530-1584 .... **LC 10**

Kock, Charles Paul de
1794-1871 .... **NCLC 16**

Koda Shigeyuki 1867-1947
See Rohan, Koda
See also CA 121

Koestler, Arthur
1905-1983 .... **CLC 1, 3, 6, 8, 15, 33**
See also CA 1-4R; 109; CANR 1, 33;
CDBLB 1945-1960; DLBY 83; MTCW

Kogawa, Joy Nozomi 1935- .... **CLC 78**
See also CA 101; CANR 19

Kohout, Pavel 1928- .... **CLC 13**
See also CA 45-48; CANR 3

Koizumi, Yakumo
See Hearn, (Patricio) Lafcadio (Tessima
Carlos)

Kolmar, Gertrud 1894-1943 ...... **TCLC 40**

Konrad, George
See Konrad, Gyoergy

Konrad, Gyoergy 1933- ...... **CLC 4, 10, 73**
See also CA 85-88

Konwicki, Tadeusz 1926- ..... **CLC 8, 28, 54**
See also CA 101; CAAS 9; CANR 39;
MTCW

Koontz, Dean R(ay) 1945- .... **CLC 78**
See also AAYA 9; BEST 89:3, 90:2;
CA 108; CANR 19, 36; MTCW

Kopit, Arthur (Lee) 1937- .... **CLC 1, 18, 33**
See also AITN 1; CA 81-84; CABS 3;
DLB 7; MTCW

Kops, Bernard 1926- .... **CLC 4**
See also CA 5-8R; DLB 13

Kornbluth, C(yril) M. 1923-1958 .... **TCLC 8**
See also CA 105; DLB 8

Korolenko, V. G.
See Korolenko, Vladimir Galaktionovich

Korolenko, Vladimir
See Korolenko, Vladimir Galaktionovich

Korolenko, Vladimir G.
See Korolenko, Vladimir Galaktionovich

Korolenko, Vladimir Galaktionovich
1853-1921 .... **TCLC 22**
See also CA 121

Kosinski, Jerzy (Nikodem)
1933-1991 .... **CLC 1, 2, 3, 6, 10, 15, 53,
70**
See also CA 17-20R; 134; CANR 9; DLB 2;
DLBY 82; MTCW

Kostelanetz, Richard (Cory) 1940- .. **CLC 28**
See also CA 13-16R; CAAS 8; CANR 38

Kostrowitzki, Wilhelm Apollinaris de
1880-1918
See Apollinaire, Guillaume
See also CA 104

Kotlowitz, Robert 1924- .... **CLC 4**
See also CA 33-36R; CANR 36

Kotzebue, August (Friedrich Ferdinand) von
1761-1819 .... **NCLC 25**
See also DLB 94

Kotzwinkle, William 1938- ... **CLC 5, 14, 35**
See also CA 45-48; CANR 3, 44; CLR 6;
MAICYA; SATA 24, 70

Kozol, Jonathan 1936- .... **CLC 17**
See also CA 61-64; CANR 16, 45

Kozoll, Michael 1940(?)- .... **CLC 35**

Kramer, Kathryn 19(?)- .... **CLC 34**

Kramer, Larry 1935- .... **CLC 42**
See also CA 124; 126

Krasicki, Ignacy 1735-1801 .... **NCLC 8**

Krasinski, Zygmunt 1812-1859 .... **NCLC 4**

Kraus, Karl 1874-1936 .... **TCLC 5**
See also CA 104; DLB 118

Kreve (Mickevicius), Vincas
1882-1954 .... **TCLC 27**

Kristeva, Julia 1941- .... **CLC 77**

Kristofferson, Kris 1936- .... **CLC 26**
See also CA 104

Krizanc, John 1956- .... **CLC 57**

Krleza, Miroslav 1893-1981........ **CLC 8**
See also CA 97-100; 105

Kroetsch, Robert 1927- ...... **CLC 5, 23, 57**
See also CA 17-20R; CANR 8, 38; DLB 53;
MTCW

Kroetz, Franz
See Kroetz, Franz Xaver

Kroetz, Franz Xaver 1946- .... **CLC 41**
See also CA 130

Kroker, Arthur 1945- .... **CLC 77**

Kropotkin, Peter (Aleksieevich)
1842-1921 .... **TCLC 36**
See also CA 119

Krotkov, Yuri 1917- .... **CLC 19**
See also CA 102

Krumb
See Crumb, R(obert)

Krumgold, Joseph (Quincy)
1908-1980 .... **CLC 12**
See also CA 9-12R; 101; CANR 7;
MAICYA; SATA 1, 23, 48

Krumwitz
See Crumb, R(obert)

Krutch, Joseph Wood 1893-1970.... **CLC 24**
See also CA 1-4R; 25-28R; CANR 4;
DLB 63

Krutzch, Gus
See Eliot, T(homas) S(tearns)

Krylov, Ivan Andreevich
1768(?)-1844 .... **NCLC 1**

Kubin, Alfred 1877-1959 .... **TCLC 23**
See also CA 112; DLB 81

Kubrick, Stanley 1928-............ **CLC 16**
See also CA 81-84; CANR 33; DLB 26

Kumin, Maxine (Winokur)
1925- .... **CLC 5, 13, 28**
See also AITN 2; CA 1-4R; CAAS 8;
CANR 1, 21; DLB 5; MTCW; SATA 12

Kundera, Milan
1929- .... **CLC 4, 9, 19, 32, 68**
See also AAYA 2; CA 85-88; CANR 19;
MTCW

Kunene, Mazisi (Raymond) 1930-... **CLC 85**
See also BW 1; CA 125; DLB 117

Kunitz, Stanley (Jasspon)
1905- .... **CLC 6, 11, 14**
See also CA 41-44R; CANR 26; DLB 48;
MTCW

Kunze, Reiner 1933-............. **CLC 10**
See also CA 93-96; DLB 75

Kuprin, Aleksandr Ivanovich
1870-1938 .... **TCLC 5**
See also CA 104

Kureishi, Hanif 1954(?)-........... **CLC 64**
See also CA 139

Kurosawa, Akira 1910-........... **CLC 16**
See also AAYA 11; CA 101

Kushner, Tony 1957(?)- .... **CLC 81**
See also CA 144

Kuttner, Henry 1915-1958........ **TCLC 10**
See also CA 107; DLB 8

Kuzma, Greg 1944-................ **CLC 7**
See also CA 33-36R

Kuzmin, Mikhail 1872(?)-1936 .... **TCLC 40**

Kyd, Thomas 1558-1594....... **LC 22; DC 3**
See also DLB 62

Kyprianos, Iossif
See Samarakis, Antonis

La Bruyere, Jean de 1645-1696...... **LC 17**

Lacan, Jacques (Marie Emile)
1901-1981 .... **CLC 75**
See also CA 121; 104

Laclos, Pierre Ambroise Francois Choderlos
de 1741-1803 .... **NCLC 4**

La Colere, Francois
See Aragon, Louis

Lacolere, Francois
See Aragon, Louis

La Deshabilleuse
See Simenon, Georges (Jacques Christian)

Lady Gregory
See Gregory, Isabella Augusta (Persse)

Lady of Quality, A
See Bagnold, Enid

La Fayette, Marie (Madelaine Pioche de la
Vergne Comtes 1634-1693....... **LC 2**

Lafayette, Rene
See Hubbard, L(afayette) Ron(ald)

Laforgue, Jules 1860-1887........ **NCLC 5**

Lagerkvist, Paer (Fabian)
1891-1974 .... **CLC 7, 10, 13, 54**
See also Lagerkvist, Par
See also CA 85-88; 49-52; MTCW

Lagerkvist, Par
See Lagerkvist, Paer (Fabian)
See also SSC 12

Lagerloef, Selma (Ottiliana Lovisa)
1858-1940 .... **TCLC 4, 36**
See also Lagerlof, Selma (Ottiliana Lovisa)
See also CA 108; SATA 15

Lagerlof, Selma (Ottiliana Lovisa)
See Lagerloef, Selma (Ottiliana Lovisa)
See also CLR 7; SATA 15

La Guma, (Justin) Alex(ander)
1925-1985 .... **CLC 19**
See also BW 1; CA 49-52; 118; CANR 25;
DLB 117; MTCW

Laidlaw, A. K.
See Grieve, C(hristopher) M(urray)

Lainez, Manuel Mujica
See Mujica Lainez, Manuel
See also HW

Lamartine, Alphonse (Marie Louis Prat) de
1790-1869 .... **NCLC 11**

Lamb, Charles
1775-1834 .... **NCLC 10; DA; WLC**
See also CDBLB 1789-1832; DLB 93, 107;
SATA 17

Lamb, Lady Caroline 1785-1828.. **NCLC 38**
See also DLB 116

Lamming, George (William)
1927- .... **CLC 2, 4, 66; BLC**
See also BW 2; CA 85-88; CANR 26;
DLB 125; MTCW

L'Amour, Louis (Dearborn)
1908-1988 .... **CLC 25, 55**
See also AITN 2; BEST 89:2; CA 1-4R;
125; CANR 3, 25, 40; DLBY 80; MTCW

Lampedusa, Giuseppe (Tomasi) di ... **TCLC 13**
See also Tomasi di Lampedusa, Giuseppe

Lampman, Archibald 1861-1899 .. **NCLC 25**
See also DLB 92

Lancaster, Bruce 1896-1963........ **CLC 36**
See also CA 9-10; CAP 1; SATA 9

Landau, Mark Alexandrovich
See Aldanov, Mark (Alexandrovich)

Landau-Aldanov, Mark Alexandrovich
See Aldanov, Mark (Alexandrovich)

Landis, John 1950-............. **CLC 26**
See also CA 112; 122

Landolfi, Tommaso 1908-1979... **CLC 11, 49**
See also CA 127; 117

Landon, Letitia Elizabeth
1802-1838 .... **NCLC 15**
See also DLB 96

Landor, Walter Savage
1775-1864 .... **NCLC 14**
See also DLB 93, 107

Landwirth, Heinz 1927-
See Lind, Jakov
See also CA 9-12R; CANR 7

Lane, Patrick 1939- .... **CLC 25**
See also CA 97-100; DLB 53

Lang, Andrew 1844-1912......... **TCLC 16**
See also CA 114; 137; DLB 98, 141;
MAICYA; SATA 16

Lang, Fritz 1890-1976 .... **CLC 20**
See also CA 77-80; 69-72; CANR 30

Lange, John
See Crichton, (John) Michael

Langer, Elinor 1939- .... **CLC 34**
See also CA 121

Langland, William
1330(?)-1400(?) .... **LC 19; DA**

Langstaff, Launcelot
See Irving, Washington

Lanier, Sidney 1842-1881 .... **NCLC 6**
See also DLB 64; MAICYA; SATA 18

Lanyer, Aemilia 1569-1645 .... **LC 10**

Lao Tzu .... **CMLC 7**

Lapine, James (Elliot) 1949-....... **CLC 39**
See also CA 123; 130

Larbaud, Valery (Nicolas)
1881-1957 .... **TCLC 9**
See also CA 106

Lardner, Ring
See Lardner, Ring(gold) W(ilmer)

Lardner, Ring W., Jr.
See Lardner, Ring(gold) W(ilmer)

Lardner, Ring(gold) W(ilmer)
1885-1933 .... **TCLC 2, 14**
See also CA 104; 131; CDALB 1917-1929;
DLB 11, 25, 86; MTCW

Leiber, Fritz (Reuter, Jr.)
1910-1992 . . . . **CLC 25**
See also CA 45-48; 139; CANR 2, 40;
DLB 8; MTCW; SATA 45;
SATA-Obit 73

Leimbach, Martha 1963-
See Leimbach, Marti
See also CA 130

Leimbach, Marti . . . . **CLC 65**
See also Leimbach, Martha

Leino, Eino . . . . **TCLC 24**
See also Loennbohm, Armas Eino Leopold

Leiris, Michel (Julien) 1901-1990 . . . **CLC 61**
See also CA 119; 128; 132

Leithauser, Brad 1953-. . . . . **CLC 27**
See also CA 107; CANR 27; DLB 120

Lelchuk, Alan 1938-. . . . . **CLC 5**
See also CA 45-48; CANR 1

Lem, Stanislaw 1921-. . . . . . . **CLC 8, 15, 40**
See also CA 105; CAAS 1; CANR 32;
MTCW

Lemann, Nancy 1956-. . . . . **CLC 39**
See also CA 118; 136

Lemonnier, (Antoine Louis) Camille
1844-1913 . . . . **TCLC 22**
See also CA 121

Lenau, Nikolaus 1802-1850 . . . . . . **NCLC 16**

L'Engle, Madeleine (Camp Franklin)
1918- . . . . **CLC 12**
See also AAYA 1; AITN 2; CA 1-4R;
CANR 3, 21, 39; CLR 1, 14; DLB 52;
JRDA; MAICYA; MTCW; SAAS 15;
SATA 1, 27, 75

Lengyel, Jozsef 1896-1975. . . . . **CLC 7**
See also CA 85-88; 57-60

Lennon, John (Ono)
1940-1980 . . . . **CLC 12, 35**
See also CA 102

Lennox, Charlotte Ramsay
1729(?)-1804 . . . . **NCLC 23**
See also DLB 39

Lentricchia, Frank (Jr.) 1940-. . . . . . **CLC 34**
See also CA 25-28R; CANR 19

Lenz, Siegfried 1926-. . . . . **CLC 27**
See also CA 89-92; DLB 75

Leonard, Elmore (John, Jr.)
1925- . . . . **CLC 28, 34, 71**
See also AITN 1; BEST 89:1, 90:4;
CA 81-84; CANR 12, 28; MTCW

Leonard, Hugh. . . . . **CLC 19**
See also Byrne, John Keyes
See also DLB 13

Leopardi, (Conte) Giacomo (Talegardo
Francesco di Sales Save
1798-1837 . . . . **NCLC 22**

Le Reveler
See Artaud, Antonin

Lerman, Eleanor 1952-. . . . . **CLC 9**
See also CA 85-88

Lerman, Rhoda 1936-. . . . . **CLC 56**
See also CA 49-52

Lermontov, Mikhail Yuryevich
1814-1841 . . . . **NCLC 47**

Leroux, Gaston 1868-1927. . . . . **TCLC 25**
See also CA 108; 136; SATA 65

Lesage, Alain-Rene 1668-1747. . . . . . . **LC 2**

Leskov, Nikolai (Semyonovich)
1831-1895 . . . . **NCLC 25**

Lessing, Doris (May)
1919- . . . . . **CLC 1, 2, 3, 6, 10, 15, 22, 40;**
DA; SSC 6
See also CA 9-12R; CAAS 14; CANR 33;
CDBLB 1960 to Present; DLB 15, 139;
DLBY 85; MTCW

Lessing, Gotthold Ephraim
1729-1781 . . . . **LC 8**
See also DLB 97

Lester, Richard 1932-. . . . . **CLC 20**

Lever, Charles (James)
1806-1872 . . . . **NCLC 23**
See also DLB 21

Leverson, Ada 1865(?)-1936(?) . . . . **TCLC 18**
See also Elaine
See also CA 117

Levertov, Denise
1923- . . . . . . **CLC 1, 2, 3, 5, 8, 15, 28, 66**
See also CA 1-4R; CAAS 19; CANR 3, 29;
DLB 5; MTCW

Levi, Jonathan. . . . . **CLC 76**

Levi, Peter (Chad Tigar) 1931-. . . . . **CLC 41**
See also CA 5-8R; CANR 34; DLB 40

Levi, Primo
1919-1987 . . . . **CLC 37, 50; SSC 12**
See also CA 13-16R; 122; CANR 12, 33;
MTCW

Levin, Ira 1929-. . . . . **CLC 3, 6**
See also CA 21-24R; CANR 17, 44;
MTCW; SATA 66

Levin, Meyer 1905-1981 . . . . **CLC 7**
See also AITN 1; CA 9-12R; 104;
CANR 15; DLB 9, 28; DLBY 81,
SATA 21, 27

Levine, Norman 1924-. . . . . **CLC 54**
See also CA 73-76; CANR 14; DLB 88

Levine, Philip 1928-. . **CLC 2, 4, 5, 9, 14, 33**
See also CA 9-12R; CANR 9, 37; DLB 5

Levinson, Deirdre 1931-. . . . . **CLC 49**
See also CA 73-76

Levi-Strauss, Claude 1908- . . . . **CLC 38**
See also CA 1-4R; CANR 6, 32; MTCW

Levitin, Sonia (Wolff) 1934- . . . . **CLC 17**
See also CA 29-32R; CANR 14, 32; JRDA;
MAICYA; SAAS 2; SATA 4, 68

Levon, O. U.
See Kesey, Ken (Elton)

Lewes, George Henry
1817-1878 . . . . **NCLC 25**
See also DLB 55, 144

Lewis, Alun 1915-1944. . . . . **TCLC 3**
See also CA 104; DLB 20

Lewis, C. Day
See Day Lewis, C(ecil)

Lewis, C(live) S(taples)
1898-1963 . . . . . **CLC 1, 3, 6, 14, 27; DA;**
WLC
See also AAYA 3; CA 81-84; CANR 33;
CDBLB 1945-1960; CLR 3, 27; DLB 15,
100; JRDA; MAICYA; MTCW;
SATA 13

Lewis, Janet 1899-. . . . . **CLC 41**
See also Winters, Janet Lewis
See also CA 9-12R; CANR 29; CAP 1;
DLBY 87

Lewis, Matthew Gregory
1775-1818 . . . . **NCLC 11**
See also DLB 39

Lewis, (Harry) Sinclair
1885-1951 . . . . . **TCLC 4, 13, 23, 39; DA;**
WLC
See also CA 104; 133; CDALB 1917-1929;
DLB 9, 102; DLBD 1; MTCW

Lewis, (Percy) Wyndham
1884(?)-1957 . . . . **TCLC 2, 9**
See also CA 104; DLB 15

Lewisohn, Ludwig 1883-1955. . . . . . **TCLC 19**
See also CA 107; DLB 4, 9, 28, 102

Lezama Lima, Jose 1910-1976 . . . **CLC 4, 10**
See also CA 77-80; DLB 113; HW

L'Heureux, John (Clarke) 1934-. . . . **CLC 52**
See also CA 13-16R; CANR 23, 45

Liddell, C. H.
See Kuttner, Henry

Lie, Jonas (Lauritz Idemil)
1833-1908(?) . . . . **TCLC 5**
See also CA 115

Lieber, Joel 1937-1971. . . . . **CLC 6**
See also CA 73-76; 29-32R

Lieber, Stanley Martin
See Lee, Stan

Lieberman, Laurence (James)
1935- . . . . **CLC 4, 36**
See also CA 17-20R; CANR 8, 36

Lieksman, Anders
See Haavikko, Paavo Juhani

Li Fei-kan 1904-
See Pa Chin
See also CA 105

Lifton, Robert Jay 1926-. . . . . **CLC 67**
See also CA 17-20R; CANR 27; SATA 66

Lightfoot, Gordon 1938-. . . . . **CLC 26**
See also CA 109

Lightman, Alan P. 1948-. . . . . **CLC 81**
See also CA 141

Ligotti, Thomas 1953- . . . . **CLC 44; SSC 16**
See also CA 123

Liliencron, (Friedrich Adolf Axel) Detlev von
1844-1909 . . . . **TCLC 18**
See also CA 117

Lilly, William 1602-1681. . . . . **LC 27**

Lima, Jose Lezama
See Lezama Lima, Jose

Lima Barreto, Afonso Henrique de
1881-1922 . . . . **TCLC 23**
See also CA 117

Limonov, Eduard. . . . . **CLC 67**

Lin, Frank
See Atherton, Gertrude (Franklin Horn)

Lincoln, Abraham   1809-1865.....   **NCLC 18**

Lind, Jakov . . . .   **CLC 1, 2, 4, 27, 82**
See also Landwirth, Heinz
See also CAAS 4

Lindbergh, Anne (Spencer) Morrow
   1906- . . . .   **CLC 82**
See also CA 17-20R; CANR 16; MTCW;
   SATA 33

Lindsay, David   1878-1945 . . . .   **TCLC 15**
See also CA 113

Lindsay, (Nicholas) Vachel
   1879-1931 . . . .   **TCLC 17; DA; WLC**
See also CA 114; 135; CDALB 1865-1917;
   DLB 54; SATA 40

Linke-Poot
See Doeblin, Alfred

Linney, Romulus   1930- . . . .   **CLC 51**
See also CA 1-4R; CANR 40, 44

Linton, Eliza Lynn   1822-1898. . . .   **NCLC 41**
See also DLB 18

Li Po   701-763 . . . .   **CMLC 2**

Lipsius, Justus   1547-1606 . . . .   **LC 16**

Lipsyte, Robert (Michael)
   1938- . . . .   **CLC 21; DA**
See also AAYA 7; CA 17-20R; CANR 8;
   CLR 23; JRDA; MAICYA; SATA 5, 68

Lish, Gordon (Jay)   1934- . . . .   **CLC 45**
See also CA 113; 117; DLB 130

Lispector, Clarice   1925-1977 . . . . . .   **CLC 43**
See also CA 139; 116; DLB 113

Littell, Robert   1935(?)- . . . .   **CLC 42**
See also CA 109; 112

Little, Malcolm   1925-1965
See Malcolm X
See also BW 1; CA 125; 111; DA; MTCW

Littlewit, Humphrey Gent.
See Lovecraft, H(oward) P(hillips)

Litwos
See Sienkiewicz, Henryk (Adam Alexander
   Pius)

Liu E   1857-1909 . . . .   **TCLC 15**
See also CA 115

Lively, Penelope (Margaret)
   1933- . . . .   **CLC 32, 50**
See also CA 41-44R; CANR 29; CLR 7;
   DLB 14; JRDA; MAICYA; MTCW;
   SATA 7, 60

Livesay, Dorothy (Kathleen)
   1909- . . . .   **CLC 4, 15, 79**
See also AITN 2; CA 25-28R; CAAS 8;
   CANR 36; DLB 68; MTCW

Livy   c. 59B.C.-c. 17 . . . .   **CMLC 11**

Lizardi, Jose Joaquin Fernandez de
   1776-1827 . . . .   **NCLC 30**

Llewellyn, Richard
See Llewellyn Lloyd, Richard Dafydd
   Vivian
See also DLB 15

Llewellyn Lloyd, Richard Dafydd Vivian
   1906-1983 . . . .   **CLC 7, 80**
See also Llewellyn, Richard
See also CA 53-56; 111; CANR 7;
   SATA 11, 37

Llosa, (Jorge) Mario (Pedro) Vargas
See Vargas Llosa, (Jorge) Mario (Pedro)

Lloyd Webber, Andrew   1948-
See Webber, Andrew Lloyd
See also AAYA 1; CA 116; SATA 56

Llull, Ramon   c. 1235-c. 1316 . . . . .   **CMLC 12**

Locke, Alain (Le Roy)
   1886-1954 . . . .   **TCLC 43**
See also BW 1; CA 106; 124; DLB 51

Locke, John   1632-1704 . . . .   **LC 7**
See also DLB 101

Locke-Elliott, Sumner
See Elliott, Sumner Locke

Lockhart, John Gibson
   1794-1854 . . . .   **NCLC 6**
See also DLB 110, 116, 144

Lodge, David (John)   1935- . . . .   **CLC 36**
See also BEST 90:1; CA 17-20R; CANR 19;
   DLB 14; MTCW

Loennbohm, Armas Eino Leopold   1878-1926
See Leino, Eino
See also CA 123

Loewinsohn, Ron(ald William)
   1937- . . . .   **CLC 52**
See also CA 25-28R

Logan, Jake
See Smith, Martin Cruz

Logan, John (Burton)   1923-1987 . . . . .   **CLC 5**
See also CA 77-80; 124; CANR 45; DLB 5

Lo Kuan-chung   1330(?)-1400(?) . . . . . .   **LC 12**

Lombard, Nap
See Johnson, Pamela Hansford

London, Jack . .   **TCLC 9, 15, 39; SSC 4; WLC**
See also London, John Griffith
See also AITN 2; CDALB 1865-1917;
   DLB 8, 12, 78; SATA 18

London, John Griffith   1876-1916
See London, Jack
See also CA 110; 119; DA; JRDA;
   MAICYA; MTCW

Long, Emmett
See Leonard, Elmore (John, Jr.)

Longbaugh, Harry
See Goldman, William (W.)

Longfellow, Henry Wadsworth
   1807-1882 . . . .   **NCLC 2, 45; DA**
See also CDALB 1640-1865; DLB 1, 59;
   SATA 19

Longley, Michael   1939- . . . .   **CLC 29**
See also CA 102; DLB 40

Longus   fl. c. 2nd cent. - . . . .   **CMLC 7**

Longway, A. Hugh
See Lang, Andrew

Lopate, Phillip   1943- . . . .   **CLC 29**
See also CA 97-100; DLBY 80

Lopez Portillo (y Pacheco), Jose
   1920- . . . .   **CLC 46**
See also CA 129; HW

Lopez y Fuentes, Gregorio
   1897(?)-1966 . . . .   **CLC 32**
See also CA 131; HW

Lorca, Federico Garcia
See Garcia Lorca, Federico

Lord, Bette Bao   1938- . . . .   **CLC 23**
See also BEST 90:3; CA 107; CANR 41;
   SATA 58

Lord Auch
See Bataille, Georges

Lord Byron
See Byron, George Gordon (Noel)

Lorde, Audre (Geraldine)
   1934-1992 . . . .   **CLC 18, 71; BLC**
See also BW 1; CA 25-28R; 142; CANR 16,
   26; DLB 41; MTCW

Lord Jeffrey
See Jeffrey, Francis

Lorenzo, Heberto Padilla
See Padilla (Lorenzo), Heberto

Loris
See Hofmannsthal, Hugo von

Loti, Pierre . . . .   **TCLC 11**
See also Viaud, (Louis Marie) Julien
See also DLB 123

Louie, David Wong   1954- . . . .   **CLC 70**
See also CA 139

Louis, Father M.
See Merton, Thomas

Lovecraft, H(oward) P(hillips)
   1890-1937 . . . .   **TCLC 4, 22; SSC 3**
See also CA 104; 133; MTCW

Lovelace, Earl   1935- . . . .   **CLC 51**
See also BW 2; CA 77-80; CANR 41;
   DLB 125; MTCW

Lovelace, Richard   1618-1657 . . . .   **LC 24**
See also DLB 131

Lowell, Amy   1874-1925 . . . .   **TCLC 1, 8**
See also CA 104; DLB 54, 140

Lowell, James Russell   1819-1891 . .   **NCLC 2**
See also CDALB 1640-1865; DLB 1, 11, 64,
   79

Lowell, Robert (Traill Spence, Jr.)
   1917-1977 . . .   **CLC 1, 2, 3, 4, 5, 8, 9, 11,
                  15, 37; DA; PC 3; WLC**
See also CA 9-12R; 73-76; CABS 2;
   CANR 26; DLB 5; MTCW

Lowndes, Marie Adelaide (Belloc)
   1868-1947 . . . .   **TCLC 12**
See also CA 107; DLB 70

Lowry, (Clarence) Malcolm
   1909-1957 . . . .   **TCLC 6, 40**
See also CA 105; 131; CDBLB 1945-1960;
   DLB 15; MTCW

Lowry, Mina Gertrude   1882-1966
See Loy, Mina
See also CA 113

Loxsmith, John
See Brunner, John (Kilian Houston)

Loy, Mina . . . .   **CLC 28**
See also Lowry, Mina Gertrude
See also DLB 4, 54

Loyson-Bridet
See Schwob, (Mayer Andre) Marcel

Lucas, Craig 1951- .... **CLC 64**
See also CA 137

Lucas, George 1944- .... **CLC 16**
See also AAYA 1; CA 77-80; CANR 30;
SATA 56

Lucas, Hans
See Godard, Jean-Luc

Lucas, Victoria
See Plath, Sylvia

Ludlam, Charles 1943-1987 ..... **CLC 46, 50**
See also CA 85-88; 122

Ludlum, Robert 1927- .... **CLC 22, 43**
See also AAYA 10; BEST 89:1, 90:3;
CA 33-36R; CANR 25, 41; DLBY 82;
MTCW

Ludwig, Ken .... **CLC 60**

Ludwig, Otto 1813-1865 .... **NCLC 4**
See also DLB 129

Lugones, Leopoldo 1874-1938 ..... **TCLC 15**
See also CA 116; 131; HW

Lu Hsun 1881-1936 .... **TCLC 3**

Lukacs, George .... **CLC 24**
See also Lukacs, Gyorgy (Szegeny von)

Lukacs, Gyorgy (Szegeny von) 1885-1971
See Lukacs, George
See also CA 101; 29-32R

Luke, Peter (Ambrose Cyprian)
1919- .... **CLC 38**
See also CA 81-84; DLB 13

Lunar, Dennis
See Mungo, Raymond

Lurie, Alison 1926- .... **CLC 4, 5, 18, 39**
See also CA 1-4R; CANR 2, 17; DLB 2;
MTCW; SATA 46

Lustig, Arnost 1926- .... **CLC 56**
See also AAYA 3; CA 69-72; SATA 56

Luther, Martin 1483-1546 .... **LC 9**

Luzi, Mario 1914- .... **CLC 13**
See also CA 61-64; CANR 9; DLB 128

Lynch, B. Suarez
See Bioy Casares, Adolfo; Borges, Jorge
Luis

Lynch, David (K.) 1946- .... **CLC 66**
See also CA 124; 129

Lynch, James
See Andreyev, Leonid (Nikolaevich)

Lynch Davis, B.
See Bioy Casares, Adolfo; Borges, Jorge
Luis

Lyndsay, Sir David 1490-1555 ...... **LC 20**

Lynn, Kenneth S(chuyler) 1923- .... **CLC 50**
See also CA 1-4R; CANR 3, 27

Lynx
See West, Rebecca

Lyons, Marcus
See Blish, James (Benjamin)

Lyre, Pinchbeck
See Sassoon, Siegfried (Lorraine)

Lytle, Andrew (Nelson) 1902- ...... **CLC 22**
See also CA 9-12R; DLB 6

Lyttelton, George 1709-1773 .... **LC 10**

Maas, Peter 1929- .... **CLC 29**
See also CA 93-96

Macaulay, Rose 1881-1958 ..... **TCLC 7, 44**
See also CA 104; DLB 36

Macaulay, Thomas Babington
1800-1859 .... **NCLC 42**
See also CDBLB 1832-1890; DLB 32, 55

MacBeth, George (Mann)
1932-1992 .... **CLC 2, 5, 9**
See also CA 25-28R; 136; DLB 40; MTCW;
SATA 4; SATA-Obit 70

MacCaig, Norman (Alexander)
1910- .... **CLC 36**
See also CA 9-12R; CANR 3, 34; DLB 27

MacCarthy, (Sir Charles Otto) Desmond
1877-1952 .... **TCLC 36**

MacDiarmid, Hugh
.... **CLC 2, 4, 11, 19, 63; PC 9**
See also Grieve, C(hristopher) M(urray)
See also CDBLB 1945-1960; DLB 20

MacDonald, Anson
See Heinlein, Robert A(nson)

Macdonald, Cynthia 1928- ...... **CLC 13, 19**
See also CA 49-52; CANR 4, 44; DLB 105

MacDonald, George 1824-1905 ..... **TCLC 9**
See also CA 106; 137; DLB 18; MAICYA;
SATA 33

Macdonald, John
See Millar, Kenneth

MacDonald, John D(ann)
1916-1986 .... **CLC 3, 27, 44**
See also CA 1-4R; 121; CANR 1, 19;
DLB 8; DLBY 86; MTCW

Macdonald, John Ross
See Millar, Kenneth

Macdonald, Ross ..... **CLC 1, 2, 3, 14, 34, 41**
See also Millar, Kenneth
See also DLBD 6

MacDougal, John
See Blish, James (Benjamin)

MacEwen, Gwendolyn (Margaret)
1941-1987 .... **CLC 13, 55**
See also CA 9-12R; 124; CANR 7, 22;
DLB 53; SATA 50, 55

Macha, Karel Hynek 1810-1846 .. **NCLC 46**

Machado (y Ruiz), Antonio
1875-1939 .... **TCLC 3**
See also CA 104; DLB 108

Machado de Assis, Joaquim Maria
1839-1908 .... **TCLC 10; BLC**
See also CA 107

Machen, Arthur .... **TCLC 4**
See also Jones, Arthur Llewellyn
See also DLB 36

Machiavelli, Niccolo 1469-1527 .. **LC 8; DA**

MacInnes, Colin 1914-1976 ...... **CLC 4, 23**
See also CA 69-72; 65-68; CANR 21;
DLB 14; MTCW

MacInnes, Helen (Clark)
1907-1985 .... **CLC 27, 39**
See also CA 1-4R; 117; CANR 1, 28;
DLB 87; MTCW; SATA 22, 44

Mackay, Mary 1855-1924
See Corelli, Marie
See also CA 118

Mackenzie, Compton (Edward Montague)
1883-1972 .... **CLC 18**
See also CA 21-22; 37-40R; CAP 2;
DLB 34, 100

Mackenzie, Henry 1745-1831 .... **NCLC 41**
See also DLB 39

Mackintosh, Elizabeth 1896(?)-1952
See Tey, Josephine
See also CA 110

MacLaren, James
See Grieve, C(hristopher) M(urray)

Mac Laverty, Bernard 1942- .... **CLC 31**
See also CA 116; 118; CANR 43

MacLean, Alistair (Stuart)
1922-1987 .... **CLC 3, 13, 50, 63**
See also CA 57-60; 121; CANR 28; MTCW;
SATA 23, 50

Maclean, Norman (Fitzroy)
1902-1990 .... **CLC 78; SSC 13**
See also CA 102; 132

MacLeish, Archibald
1892-1982 .... **CLC 3, 8, 14, 68**
See also CA 9-12R; 106; CANR 33; DLB 4,
7, 45; DLBY 82; MTCW

MacLennan, (John) Hugh
1907-1990 .... **CLC 2, 14**
See also CA 5-8R; 142; CANR 33; DLB 68;
MTCW

MacLeod, Alistair 1936- .... **CLC 56**
See also CA 123; DLB 60

MacNeice, (Frederick) Louis
1907-1963 .... **CLC 1, 4, 10, 53**
See also CA 85-88; DLB 10, 20; MTCW

MacNeill, Dand
See Fraser, George MacDonald

Macpherson, (Jean) Jay 1931- ...... **CLC 14**
See also CA 5-8R; DLB 53

MacShane, Frank 1927- .... **CLC 39**
See also CA 9-12R; CANR 3, 33; DLB 111

Macumber, Mari
See Sandoz, Mari(e Susette)

Madach, Imre 1823-1864 .... **NCLC 19**

Madden, (Jerry) David 1933- .... **CLC 5, 15**
See also CA 1-4R; CAAS 3; CANR 4, 45;
DLB 6; MTCW

Maddern, Al(an)
See Ellison, Harlan

Madhubuti, Haki R.
1942- .... **CLC 6, 73; BLC; PC 5**
See also Lee, Don L.
See also BW 2; CA 73-76; CANR 24;
DLB 5, 41; DLBD 8

Maepenn, Hugh
See Kuttner, Henry

Maepenn, K. H.
See Kuttner, Henry

Maeterlinck, Maurice 1862-1949 ... **TCLC 3**
See also CA 104; 136; SATA 66

Maginn, William 1794-1842 ...... **NCLC 8**
See also DLB 110

Mahapatra, Jayanta 1928- .... **CLC 33**
See also CA 73-76; CAAS 9; CANR 15, 33

Mahfouz, Naguib (Abdel Aziz Al-Sabilgi)
    1911(?)-
    See Mahfuz, Najib
    See also BEST 89:2; CA 128; MTCW

Mahfuz, Najib . . . . CLC 52, 55
    See also Mahfouz, Naguib (Abdel Aziz
        Al-Sabilgi)
    See also DLBY 88

Mahon, Derek   1941- . . . . CLC 27
    See also CA 113; 128; DLB 40

Mailer, Norman
    1923- . . . . . . CLC 1, 2, 3, 4, 5, 8, 11, 14,
                        28, 39, 74; DA
    See also AITN 2; CA 9-12R; CABS 1;
        CANR 28; CDALB 1968-1988; DLB 2,
        16, 28; DLBD 3; DLBY 80, 83; MTCW

Maillet, Antonine   1929- . . . . CLC 54
    See also CA 115; 120; DLB 60

Mais, Roger   1905-1955 . . . . TCLC 8
    See also BW 1; CA 105; 124; DLB 125;
        MTCW

Maistre, Joseph de   1753-1821 . . . . NCLC 37

Maitland, Sara (Louise)   1950- . . . . . . CLC 49
    See also CA 69-72; CANR 13

Major, Clarence
    1936- . . . . CLC 3, 19, 48; BLC
    See also BW 2; CA 21-24R; CAAS 6;
        CANR 13, 25; DLB 33

Major, Kevin (Gerald)   1949- . . . . CLC 26
    See also CA 97-100; CANR 21, 38;
        CLR 11; DLB 60; JRDA; MAICYA;
        SATA 32

Maki, James
    See Ozu, Yasujiro

Malabaila, Damiano
    See Levi, Primo

Malamud, Bernard
    1914-1986 . . . . . . CLC 1, 2, 3, 5, 8, 9, 11,
                    18, 27, 44, 78, 85; DA; SSC 15; WLC
    See also CA 5-8R; 118; CABS 1; CANR 28;
        CDALB 1941-1968; DLB 2, 28;
        DLBY 80, 86; MTCW

Malaparte, Curzio   1898-1957 . . . . . TCLC 52

Malcolm, Dan
    See Silverberg, Robert

Malcolm X . . . . CLC 82; BLC
    See also Little, Malcolm

Malherbe, Francois de   1555-1628 . . . . . LC 5

Mallarme, Stephane
    1842-1898 . . . . NCLC 4, 41; PC 4

Mallet-Joris, Francoise   1930- . . . . . . CLC 11
    See also CA 65-68; CANR 17; DLB 83

Malley, Ern
    See McAuley, James Phillip

Mallowan, Agatha Christie
    See Christie, Agatha (Mary Clarissa)

Maloff, Saul   1922- . . . . CLC 5
    See also CA 33-36R

Malone, Louis
    See MacNeice, (Frederick) Louis

Malone, Michael (Christopher)
    1942- . . . . CLC 43
    See also CA 77-80; CANR 14, 32

Malory, (Sir) Thomas
    1410(?)-1471(?) . . . . LC 11; DA
    See also CDBLB Before 1660; SATA 33, 59

Malouf, (George Joseph) David
    1934- . . . . CLC 28
    See also CA 124

Malraux, (Georges-)Andre
    1901-1976 . . . . . . CLC 1, 4, 9, 13, 15, 57
    See also CA 21-22; 69-72; CANR 34;
        CAP 2; DLB 72; MTCW

Malzberg, Barry N(athaniel)   1939- . . . CLC 7
    See also CA 61-64; CAAS 4; CANR 16;
        DLB 8

Mamet, David (Alan)
    1947- . . . . CLC 9, 15, 34, 46; DC 4
    See also AAYA 3; CA 81-84; CABS 3;
        CANR 15, 41; DLB 7; MTCW

Mamoulian, Rouben (Zachary)
    1897-1987 . . . . CLC 16
    See also CA 25-28R; 124

Mandelstam, Osip (Emilievich)
    1891(?)-1938(?) . . . . TCLC 2, 6
    See also CA 104

Mander, (Mary) Jane   1877-1949 . . . TCLC 31

Mandiargues, Andre Pieyre de . . . . . . CLC 41
    See also Pieyre de Mandiargues, Andre
    See also DLB 83

Mandrake, Ethel Belle
    See Thurman, Wallace (Henry)

Mangan, James Clarence
    1803-1849 . . . . NCLC 27

Maniere, J.-E.
    See Giraudoux, (Hippolyte) Jean

Manley, (Mary) Delariviere
    1672(?)-1724 . . . . LC 1
    See also DLB 39, 80

Mann, Abel
    See Creasey, John

Mann, (Luiz) Heinrich   1871-1950 . . . TCLC 9
    See also CA 106; DLB 66

Mann, (Paul) Thomas
    1875-1955 . . . . TCLC 2, 8, 14, 21, 35, 44;
                        DA; SSC 5; WLC
    See also CA 104; 128; DLB 66; MTCW

Manning, David
    See Faust, Frederick (Schiller)

Manning, Frederic   1887(?)-1935 . . . TCLC 25
    See also CA 124

Manning, Olivia   1915-1980 . . . . . . CLC 5, 19
    See also CA 5-8R; 101; CANR 29; MTCW

Mano, D. Keith   1942- . . . . CLC 2, 10
    See also CA 25-28R; CAAS 6; CANR 26;
        DLB 6

Mansfield, Katherine
    . . . . TCLC 2, 8, 39; SSC 9; WLC
    See also Beauchamp, Kathleen Mansfield

Manso, Peter   1940- . . . . CLC 39
    See also CA 29-32R; CANR 44

Mantecon, Juan Jimenez
    See Jimenez (Mantecon), Juan Ramon

Manton, Peter
    See Creasey, John

Man Without a Spleen, A
    See Chekhov, Anton (Pavlovich)

Manzoni, Alessandro   1785-1873 . . NCLC 29

Mapu, Abraham (ben Jekutiel)
    1808-1867 . . . . NCLC 18

Mara, Sally
    See Queneau, Raymond

Marat, Jean Paul   1743-1793 . . . . LC 10

Marcel, Gabriel Honore
    1889-1973 . . . . CLC 15
    See also CA 102; 45-48; MTCW

Marchbanks, Samuel
    See Davies, (William) Robertson

Marchi, Giacomo
    See Bassani, Giorgio

Margulies, Donald . . . . CLC 76

Marie de France   c. 12th cent. - . . . . CMLC 8

Marie de l'Incarnation   1599-1672 . . . . LC 10

Mariner, Scott
    See Pohl, Frederik

Marinetti, Filippo Tommaso
    1876-1944 . . . . TCLC 10
    See also CA 107; DLB 114

Marivaux, Pierre Carlet de Chamblain de
    1688-1763 . . . . LC 4

Markandaya, Kamala . . . . CLC 8, 38
    See also Taylor, Kamala (Purnaiya)

Markfield, Wallace   1926- . . . . CLC 8
    See also CA 69-72; CAAS 3; DLB 2, 28

Markham, Edwin   1852-1940 . . . . . . TCLC 47
    See also DLB 54

Markham, Robert
    See Amis, Kingsley (William)

Marks, J
    See Highwater, Jamake (Mamake)

Marks-Highwater, J
    See Highwater, Jamake (Mamake)

Markson, David M(errill)   1927- . . . . CLC 67
    See also CA 49-52; CANR 1

Marley, Bob . . . . CLC 17
    See also Marley, Robert Nesta

Marley, Robert Nesta   1945-1981
    See Marley, Bob
    See also CA 107; 103

Marlowe, Christopher
    1564-1593 . . . . . LC 22; DA; DC 1; WLC
    See also CDBLB Before 1660; DLB 62

Marmontel, Jean-Francois
    1723-1799 . . . . LC 2

Marquand, John P(hillips)
    1893-1960 . . . . CLC 2, 10
    See also CA 85-88; DLB 9, 102

Marquez, Gabriel (Jose) Garcia
    See Garcia Marquez, Gabriel (Jose)

Marquis, Don(ald Robert Perry)
    1878-1937 . . . . TCLC 7
    See also CA 104; DLB 11, 25

Marric, J. J.
    See Creasey, John

Marrow, Bernard
    See Moore, Brian

Marryat, Frederick   1792-1848 . . . . NCLC 3
    See also DLB 21

Marsden, James
    See Creasey, John

Marsh, (Edith) Ngaio
    1899-1982 .... **CLC 7, 53**
    See also CA 9-12R; CANR 6; DLB 77;
    MTCW

Marshall, Garry   1934- .... **CLC 17**
    See also AAYA 3; CA 111; SATA 60

Marshall, Paule
    1929- .... **CLC 27, 72; BLC; SSC 3**
    See also BW 2; CA 77-80; CANR 25;
    DLB 33; MTCW

Marsten, Richard
    See Hunter, Evan

Martha, Henry
    See Harris, Mark

Martial   40-104 .... **PC 10**

Martin, Ken
    See Hubbard, L(afayette) Ron(ald)

Martin, Richard
    See Creasey, John

Martin, Steve   1945- .... **CLC 30**
    See also CA 97-100; CANR 30; MTCW

Martin, Violet Florence
    1862-1915 .... **TCLC 51**

Martin, Webber
    See Silverberg, Robert

Martindale, Patrick Victor
    See White, Patrick (Victor Martindale)

Martin du Gard, Roger
    1881-1958 .... **TCLC 24**
    See also CA 118; DLB 65

Martineau, Harriet   1802-1876.... **NCLC 26**
    See also DLB 21, 55; YABC 2

Martines, Julia
    See O'Faolain, Julia

Martinez, Jacinto Benavente y
    See Benavente (y Martinez), Jacinto

Martinez Ruiz, Jose   1873-1967
    See Azorin; Ruiz, Jose Martinez
    See also CA 93-96; HW

Martinez Sierra, Gregorio
    1881-1947 .... **TCLC 6**
    See also CA 115

Martinez Sierra, Maria (de la O'LeJarraga)
    1874-1974 .... **TCLC 6**
    See also CA 115

Martinsen, Martin
    See Follett, Ken(neth Martin)

Martinson, Harry (Edmund)
    1904-1978 .... **CLC 14**
    See also CA 77-80; CANR 34

Marut, Ret
    See Traven, B.

Marut, Robert
    See Traven, B.

Marvell, Andrew
    1621-1678 ..... **LC 4; DA; PC 10; WLC**
    See also CDBLB 1660-1789; DLB 131

Marx, Karl (Heinrich)
    1818-1883 .... **NCLC 17**
    See also DLB 129

Masaoka Shiki. .... **TCLC 18**
    See also Masaoka Tsunenori

Masaoka Tsunenori   1867-1902
    See Masaoka Shiki
    See also CA 117

Masefield, John (Edward)
    1878-1967 .... **CLC 11, 47**
    See also CA 19-20; 25-28R; CANR 33;
    CAP 2; CDBLB 1890-1914; DLB 10;
    MTCW; SATA 19

Maso, Carole   19(?)- .... **CLC 44**

Mason, Bobbie Ann
    1940- .... **CLC 28, 43, 82; SSC 4**
    See also AAYA 5; CA 53-56; CANR 11,
    31; DLBY 87; MTCW

Mason, Ernst
    See Pohl, Frederik

Mason, Lee W.
    See Malzberg, Barry N(athaniel)

Mason, Nick   1945- .... **CLC 35**

Mason, Tally
    See Derleth, August (William)

Mass, William
    See Gibson, William

Masters, Edgar Lee
    1868-1950 ...... **TCLC 2, 25; DA; PC 1**
    See also CA 104; 133; CDALB 1865-1917;
    DLB 54; MTCW

Masters, Hilary   1928- .... **CLC 48**
    See also CA 25-28R; CANR 13

Mastrosimone, William   19(?)- ...... **CLC 36**

Mathe, Albert
    See Camus, Albert

Matheson, Richard Burton   1926- ... **CLC 37**
    See also CA 97-100; DLB 8, 44

Mathews, Harry   1930- .... **CLC 6, 52**
    See also CA 21-24R; CAAS 6; CANR 18,
    40

Mathews, John Joseph   1894-1979... **CLC 84**
    See also CA 19-20; 142; CANR 45; CAP 2

Mathias, Roland (Glyn)   1915- ...... **CLC 45**
    See also CA 97-100; CANR 19, 41; DLB 27

Matsuo Basho   1644-1694. .... **PC 3**

Mattheson, Rodney
    See Creasey, John

Matthews, Greg   1949- .... **CLC 45**
    See also CA 135

Matthews, William   1942- .... **CLC 40**
    See also CA 29-32R; CAAS 18; CANR 12;
    DLB 5

Matthias, John (Edward)   1941- ...... **CLC 9**
    See also CA 33-36R

Matthiessen, Peter
    1927- .... **CLC 5, 7, 11, 32, 64**
    See also AAYA 6; BEST 90:4; CA 9-12R;
    CANR 21; DLB 6; MTCW; SATA 27

Maturin, Charles Robert
    1780(?)-1824 .... **NCLC 6**

Matute (Ausejo), Ana Maria
    1925- .... **CLC 11**
    See also CA 89-92; MTCW

Maugham, W. S.
    See Maugham, W(illiam) Somerset

Maugham, W(illiam) Somerset
    1874-1965 ...... **CLC 1, 11, 15, 67; DA;**
                                              SSC 8; WLC
    See also CA 5-8R; 25-28R; CANR 40;
    CDBLB 1914-1945; DLB 10, 36, 77, 100;
    MTCW; SATA 54

Maugham, William Somerset
    See Maugham, W(illiam) Somerset

Maupassant, (Henri Rene Albert) Guy de
    1850-1893 .... **NCLC 1, 42; DA; SSC 1;**
                                                          WLC
    See also DLB 123

Maurhut, Richard
    See Traven, B.

Mauriac, Claude   1914- .... **CLC 9**
    See also CA 89-92; DLB 83

Mauriac, Francois (Charles)
    1885-1970 .... **CLC 4, 9, 56**
    See also CA 25-28; CAP 2; DLB 65;
    MTCW

Mavor, Osborne Henry   1888-1951
    See Bridie, James
    See also CA 104

Maxwell, William (Keepers, Jr.)
    1908- .... **CLC 19**
    See also CA 93-96; DLBY 80

May, Elaine   1932- .... **CLC 16**
    See also CA 124; 142; DLB 44

Mayakovski, Vladimir (Vladimirovich)
    1893-1930 .... **TCLC 4, 18**
    See also CA 104

Mayhew, Henry   1812-1887 ...... **NCLC 31**
    See also DLB 18, 55

Maynard, Joyce   1953- .... **CLC 23**
    See also CA 111; 129

Mayne, William (James Carter)
    1928- .... **CLC 12**
    See also CA 9-12R; CANR 37; CLR 25;
    JRDA; MAICYA; SAAS 11; SATA 6, 68

Mayo, Jim
    See L'Amour, Louis (Dearborn)

Maysles, Albert   1926- .... **CLC 16**
    See also CA 29-32R

Maysles, David   1932- .... **CLC 16**

Mazer, Norma Fox   1931- .... **CLC 26**
    See also AAYA 5; CA 69-72; CANR 12,
    32; CLR 23; JRDA; MAICYA; SAAS 1;
    SATA 24, 67

Mazzini, Guiseppe   1805-1872 .... **NCLC 34**

McAuley, James Phillip
    1917-1976 .... **CLC 45**
    See also CA 97-100

McBain, Ed
    See Hunter, Evan

McBrien, William Augustine
    1930- .... **CLC 44**
    See also CA 107

McCaffrey, Anne (Inez)   1926- ...... **CLC 17**
    See also AAYA 6; AITN 2; BEST 89:2;
    CA 25-28R; CANR 15, 35; DLB 8;
    JRDA; MAICYA; MTCW; SAAS 11;
    SATA 8, 70

McCann, Arthur
    See Campbell, John W(ood, Jr.)

Montagu, Elizabeth 1917- .... **NCLC 7**
See also CA 9-12R

Montagu, Mary (Pierrepont) Wortley
1689-1762 .... **LC 9**
See also DLB 95, 101

Montagu, W. H.
See Coleridge, Samuel Taylor

Montague, John (Patrick)
1929- .... **CLC 13, 46**
See also CA 9-12R; CANR 9; DLB 40;
MTCW

Montaigne, Michel (Eyquem) de
1533-1592 .... **LC 8; DA; WLC**

Montale, Eugenio 1896-1981... **CLC 7, 9, 18**
See also CA 17-20R; 104; CANR 30;
DLB 114; MTCW

Montesquieu, Charles-Louis de Secondat
1689-1755 .... **LC 7**

Montgomery, (Robert) Bruce 1921-1978
See Crispin, Edmund
See also CA 104

Montgomery, L(ucy) M(aud)
1874-1942 .... **TCLC 51**
See also AAYA 12; CA 108; 137; CLR 8;
DLB 92; JRDA; MAICYA; YABC 1

Montgomery, Marion H., Jr. 1925- .. **CLC 7**
See also AITN 1; CA 1-4R; CANR 3;
DLB 6

Montgomery, Max
See Davenport, Guy (Mattison, Jr.)

Montherlant, Henry (Milon) de
1896-1972 .... **CLC 8, 19**
See also CA 85-88; 37-40R; DLB 72;
MTCW

Monty Python
See Chapman, Graham; Cleese, John
(Marwood); Gilliam, Terry (Vance); Idle,
Eric; Jones, Terence Graham Parry; Palin,
Michael (Edward)
See also AAYA 7

Moodie, Susanna (Strickland)
1803-1885 .... **NCLC 14**
See also DLB 99

Mooney, Edward 1951-
See Mooney, Ted
See also CA 130

Mooney, Ted .... **CLC 25**
See also Mooney, Edward

Moorcock, Michael (John)
1939- .... **CLC 5, 27, 58**
See also CA 45-48; CAAS 5; CANR 2, 17,
38; DLB 14; MTCW

Moore, Brian
1921- .... **CLC 1, 3, 5, 7, 8, 19, 32**
See also CA 1-4R; CANR 1, 25, 42; MTCW

Moore, Edward
See Muir, Edwin

Moore, George Augustus
1852-1933 .... **TCLC 7**
See also CA 104; DLB 10, 18, 57, 135

Moore, Lorrie .... **CLC 39, 45, 68**
See also Moore, Marie Lorena

Moore, Marianne (Craig)
1887-1972 .... **CLC 1, 2, 4, 8, 10, 13, 19,**
47; DA; PC 4
See also CA 1-4R; 33-36R; CANR 3;
CDALB 1929-1941; DLB 45; DLBD 7;
MTCW; SATA 20

Moore, Marie Lorena 1957-
See Moore, Lorrie
See also CA 116; CANR 39

Moore, Thomas 1779-1852....... **NCLC 6**
See also DLB 96, 144

Morand, Paul 1888-1976 .... **CLC 41**
See also CA 69-72; DLB 65

Morante, Elsa 1918-1985........ **CLC 8, 47**
See also CA 85-88; 117; CANR 35; MTCW

Moravia, Alberto....... **CLC 2, 7, 11, 27, 46**
See also Pincherle, Alberto

More, Hannah 1745-1833 .... **NCLC 27**
See also DLB 107, 109, 116

More, Henry 1614-1687............. **LC 9**
See also DLB 126

More, Sir Thomas 1478-1535 .... **LC 10**

Moreas, Jean.................... **TCLC 18**
See also Papadiamantopoulos, Johannes

Morgan, Berry 1919- .... **CLC 6**
See also CA 49-52; DLB 6

Morgan, Claire
See Highsmith, (Mary) Patricia

Morgan, Edwin (George) 1920-..... **CLC 31**
See also CA 5-8R; CANR 3, 43; DLB 27

Morgan, (George) Frederick
1922- .... **CLC 23**
See also CA 17-20R; CANR 21

Morgan, Harriet
See Mencken, H(enry) L(ouis)

Morgan, Jane
See Cooper, James Fenimore

Morgan, Janet 1945- .... **CLC 39**
See also CA 65-68

Morgan, Lady 1776(?)-1859...... **NCLC 29**
See also DLB 116

Morgan, Robin 1941-............... **CLC 2**
See also CA 69-72; CANR 29; MTCW

Morgan, Scott
See Kuttner, Henry

Morgan, Seth 1949(?)-1990 .... **CLC 65**
See also CA 132

Morgenstern, Christian
1871-1914 .... **TCLC 8**
See also CA 105

Morgenstern, S.
See Goldman, William (W.)

Moricz, Zsigmond 1879-1942 ..... **TCLC 33**

Morike, Eduard (Friedrich)
1804-1875 .... **NCLC 10**
See also DLB 133

Mori Ogai .... **TCLC 14**
See also Mori Rintaro

Mori Rintaro 1862-1922
See Mori Ogai
See also CA 110

Moritz, Karl Philipp 1756-1793 ...... **LC 2**
See also DLB 94

Morland, Peter Henry
See Faust, Frederick (Schiller)

Morren, Theophil
See Hofmannsthal, Hugo von

Morris, Bill 1952-............... **CLC 76**

Morris, Julian
See West, Morris L(anglo)

Morris, Steveland Judkins 1950(?)-
See Wonder, Stevie
See also CA 111

Morris, William 1834-1896....... **NCLC 4**
See also CDBLB 1832-1890; DLB 18, 35, 57

Morris, Wright 1910-... **CLC 1, 3, 7, 18, 37**
See also CA 9-12R; CANR 21; DLB 2;
DLBY 81; MTCW

Morrison, Chloe Anthony Wofford
See Morrison, Toni

Morrison, James Douglas 1943-1971
See Morrison, Jim
See also CA 73-76; CANR 40

Morrison, Jim .... **CLC 17**
See also Morrison, James Douglas

Morrison, Toni
1931-.. **CLC 4, 10, 22, 55, 81; BLC; DA**
See also AAYA 1; BW 2; CA 29-32R;
CANR 27, 42; CDALB 1968-1988;
DLB 6, 33, 143; DLBY 81; MTCW;
SATA 57

Morrison, Van 1945- .... **CLC 21**
See also CA 116

Mortimer, John (Clifford)
1923- .... **CLC 28, 43**
See also CA 13-16R; CANR 21;
CDBLB 1960 to Present; DLB 13;
MTCW

Mortimer, Penelope (Ruth) 1918-.... **CLC 5**
See also CA 57-60; CANR 45

Morton, Anthony
See Creasey, John

Mosher, Howard Frank 1943-...... **CLC 62**
See also CA 139

Mosley, Nicholas 1923-........ **CLC 43, 70**
See also CA 69-72; CANR 41; DLB 14

Moss, Howard
1922-1987 .... **CLC 7, 14, 45, 50**
See also CA 1-4R; 123; CANR 1, 44;
DLB 5

Mossgiel, Rab
See Burns, Robert

Motion, Andrew 1952-............ **CLC 47**
See also DLB 40

Motley, Willard (Francis)
1909-1965 .... **CLC 18**
See also BW 1; CA 117; 106; DLB 76, 143

Motoori, Norinaga 1730-1801 .... **NCLC 45**

Mott, Michael (Charles Alston)
1930- .... **CLC 15, 34**
See also CA 5-8R; CAAS 7; CANR 7, 29

Mowat, Farley (McGill) 1921- ..... **CLC 26**
See also AAYA 1; CA 1-4R; CANR 4, 24,
42; CLR 20; DLB 68; JRDA; MAICYA;
MTCW; SATA 3, 55

Moyers, Bill 1934-............... **CLC 74**
See also AITN 2; CA 61-64; CANR 31

Mphahlele, Es'kia
See Mphahlele, Ezekiel
See also DLB 125

Mphahlele, Ezekiel 1919- . . . . . **CLC 25; BLC**
See also Mphahlele, Es'kia
See also BW 2; CA 81-84; CANR 26

Mqhayi, S(amuel) E(dward) K(rune Loliwe)
1875-1945 . . . . **TCLC 25; BLC**

Mr. Martin
See Burroughs, William S(eward)

Mrozek, Slawomir 1930- . . . . **CLC 3, 13**
See also CA 13-16R; CAAS 10; CANR 29;
MTCW

Mrs. Belloc-Lowndes
See Lowndes, Marie Adelaide (Belloc)

Mtwa, Percy (?)- . . . . **CLC 47**

Mueller, Lisel 1924- . . . . **CLC 13, 51**
See also CA 93-96; DLB 105

Muir, Edwin 1887-1959 . . . . **TCLC 2**
See also CA 104; DLB 20, 100

Muir, John 1838-1914 . . . . **TCLC 28**

Mujica Lainez, Manuel
1910-1984 . . . . **CLC 31**
See also Lainez, Manuel Mujica
See also CA 81-84; 112; CANR 32; HW

Mukherjee, Bharati 1940- . . . . **CLC 53**
See also BEST 89:2; CA 107; CANR 45;
DLB 60; MTCW

Muldoon, Paul 1951- . . . . **CLC 32, 72**
See also CA 113; 129; DLB 40

Mulisch, Harry 1927- . . . . **CLC 42**
See also CA 9-12R; CANR 6, 26

Mull, Martin 1943- . . . . **CLC 17**
See also CA 105

Mulock, Dinah Maria
See Craik, Dinah Maria (Mulock)

Munford, Robert 1737(?)-1783 . . . . **LC 5**
See also DLB 31

Mungo, Raymond 1946- . . . . **CLC 72**
See also CA 49-52; CANR 2

Munro, Alice
1931- . . . . **CLC 6, 10, 19, 50; SSC 3**
See also AITN 2; CA 33-36R; CANR 33;
DLB 53; MTCW; SATA 29

Munro, H(ector) H(ugh) 1870-1916
See Saki
See also CA 104; 130; CDBLB 1890-1914;
DA; DLB 34; MTCW; WLC

Murasaki, Lady . . . . **CMLC 1**

Murdoch, (Jean) Iris
1919- . . . . . . **CLC 1, 2, 3, 4, 6, 8, 11, 15,
22, 31, 51**
See also CA 13-16R; CANR 8, 43;
CDBLB 1960 to Present; DLB 14;
MTCW

Murnau, Friedrich Wilhelm
See Plumpe, Friedrich Wilhelm

Murphy, Richard 1927- . . . . **CLC 41**
See also CA 29-32R; DLB 40

Murphy, Sylvia 1937- . . . . **CLC 34**
See also CA 121

Murphy, Thomas (Bernard) 1935- . . . **CLC 51**
See also CA 101

Murray, Albert L. 1916- . . . . **CLC 73**
See also BW 2; CA 49-52; CANR 26;
DLB 38

Murray, Les(lie) A(llan) 1938- . . . . . **CLC 40**
See also CA 21-24R; CANR 11, 27

Murry, J. Middleton
See Murry, John Middleton

Murry, John Middleton
1889-1957 . . . . **TCLC 16**
See also CA 118

Musgrave, Susan 1951- . . . . **CLC 13, 54**
See also CA 69-72; CANR 45

Musil, Robert (Edler von)
1880-1942 . . . . **TCLC 12**
See also CA 109; DLB 81, 124

Musset, (Louis Charles) Alfred de
1810-1857 . . . . **NCLC 7**

My Brother's Brother
See Chekhov, Anton (Pavlovich)

Myers, Walter Dean 1937- . . . **CLC 35; BLC**
See also AAYA 4; BW 2; CA 33-36R;
CANR 20, 42; CLR 4, 16, 35; DLB 33;
JRDA; MAICYA; SAAS 2; SATA 27, 41,
71

Myers, Walter M.
See Myers, Walter Dean

Myles, Symon
See Follett, Ken(neth Martin)

Nabokov, Vladimir (Vladimirovich)
1899-1977 . . . . . **CLC 1, 2, 3, 6, 8, 11, 15,
23, 44, 46, 64; DA; SSC 11; WLC**
See also CA 5-8R; 69-72; CANR 20;
CDALB 1941-1968; DLB 2; DLBD 3;
DLBY 80, 91; MTCW

Nagai Kafu . . . . **TCLC 51**
See also Nagai Sokichi

Nagai Sokichi 1879-1959
See Nagai Kafu
See also CA 117

Nagy, Laszlo 1925-1978 . . . . **CLC 7**
See also CA 129; 112

Naipaul, Shiva(dhar Srinivasa)
1945-1985 . . . . **CLC 32, 39**
See also CA 110; 112; 116; CANR 33;
DLBY 85; MTCW

Naipaul, V(idiadhar) S(urajprasad)
1932- . . . . **CLC 4, 7, 9, 13, 18, 37**
See also CA 1-4R; CANR 1, 33;
CDBLB 1960 to Present; DLB 125;
DLBY 85; MTCW

Nakos, Lilika 1899(?)- . . . . **CLC 29**

Narayan, R(asipuram) K(rishnaswami)
1906- . . . . **CLC 7, 28, 47**
See also CA 81-84; CANR 33; MTCW;
SATA 62

Nash, (Fredric) Ogden 1902-1971 . . **CLC 23**
See also CA 13-14; 29-32R; CANR 34;
CAP 1; DLB 11; MAICYA; MTCW;
SATA 2, 46

Nathan, Daniel
See Dannay, Frederic

Nathan, George Jean 1882-1958 . . . **TCLC 18**
See also Hatteras, Owen
See also CA 114; DLB 137

Natsume, Kinnosuke 1867-1916
See Natsume, Soseki
See also CA 104

Natsume, Soseki . . . . **TCLC 2, 10**
See also Natsume, Kinnosuke

Natti, (Mary) Lee 1919-
See Kingman, Lee
See also CA 5-8R; CANR 2

Naylor, Gloria
1950- . . . . **CLC 28, 52; BLC; DA**
See also AAYA 6; BW 2; CA 107;
CANR 27; MTCW

Neihardt, John Gneisenau
1881-1973 . . . . **CLC 32**
See also CA 13-14; CAP 1; DLB 9, 54

Nekrasov, Nikolai Alekseevich
1821-1878 . . . . **NCLC 11**

Nelligan, Emile 1879-1941 . . . . **TCLC 14**
See also CA 114; DLB 92

Nelson, Willie 1933- . . . . **CLC 17**
See also CA 107

Nemerov, Howard (Stanley)
1920-1991 . . . . **CLC 2, 6, 9, 36**
See also CA 1-4R; 134; CABS 2; CANR 1,
27; DLB 6; DLBY 83; MTCW

Neruda, Pablo
1904-1973 . . . . . **CLC 1, 2, 5, 7, 9, 28, 62;
DA; HLC; PC 4; WLC**
See also CA 19-20; 45-48; CAP 2; HW;
MTCW

Nerval, Gerard de 1808-1855 . . . . . . **NCLC 1**

Nervo, (Jose) Amado (Ruiz de)
1870-1919 . . . . **TCLC 11**
See also CA 109; 131; HW

Nessi, Pio Baroja y
See Baroja (y Nessi), Pio

Nestroy, Johann 1801-1862 . . . . . . **NCLC 42**
See also DLB 133

Neufeld, John (Arthur) 1938- . . . . . . **CLC 17**
See also AAYA 11; CA 25-28R; CANR 11,
37; MAICYA; SAAS 3; SATA 6

Neville, Emily Cheney 1919- . . . . **CLC 12**
See also CA 5-8R; CANR 3, 37; JRDA;
MAICYA; SAAS 2; SATA 1

Newbound, Bernard Slade 1930-
See Slade, Bernard
See also CA 81-84

Newby, P(ercy) H(oward)
1918- . . . . **CLC 2, 13**
See also CA 5-8R; CANR 32; DLB 15;
MTCW

Newlove, Donald 1928- . . . . **CLC 6**
See also CA 29-32R; CANR 25

Newlove, John (Herbert) 1938- . . . . . **CLC 14**
See also CA 21-24R; CANR 9, 25

Newman, Charles 1938- . . . . **CLC 2, 8**
See also CA 21-24R

Newman, Edwin (Harold) 1919- . . . . **CLC 14**
See also AITN 1; CA 69-72; CANR 5

Newman, John Henry
1801-1890 . . . . **NCLC 38**
See also DLB 18, 32, 55

Newton, Suzanne 1936- . . . . **CLC 35**
See also CA 41-44R; CANR 14; JRDA;
SATA 5, 77

O'Donovan, Michael John
1903-1966 .... **CLC 14**
See also O'Connor, Frank
See also CA 93-96

Oe, Kenzaburo 1935- .... **CLC 10, 36**
See also CA 97-100; CANR 36; MTCW

O'Faolain, Julia 1932- .... **CLC 6, 19, 47**
See also CA 81-84; CAAS 2; CANR 12;
DLB 14; MTCW

O'Faolain, Sean
1900-1991 .... **CLC 1, 7, 14, 32, 70;**
SSC 13
See also CA 61-64; 134; CANR 12;
DLB 15; MTCW

O'Flaherty, Liam
1896-1984 .... **CLC 5, 34; SSC 6**
See also CA 101; 113; CANR 35; DLB 36;
DLBY 84; MTCW

Ogilvy, Gavin
See Barrie, J(ames) M(atthew)

O'Grady, Standish James
1846-1928 .... **TCLC 5**
See also CA 104

O'Grady, Timothy 1951- .... **CLC 59**
See also CA 138

O'Hara, Frank
1926-1966 .... **CLC 2, 5, 13, 78**
See also CA 9-12R; 25-28R; CANR 33;
DLB 5, 16; MTCW

O'Hara, John (Henry)
1905-1970 .... **CLC 1, 2, 3, 6, 11, 42;**
SSC 15
See also CA 5-8R; 25-28R; CANR 31;
CDALB 1929-1941; DLB 9, 86; DLBD 2;
MTCW

O Hehir, Diana 1922- .... **CLC 41**
See also CA 93-96

Okigbo, Christopher (Ifenayichukwu)
1932-1967 ..... **CLC 25, 84; BLC; PC 7**
See also BW 1; CA 77-80; DLB 125;
MTCW

Olds, Sharon 1942- .... **CLC 32, 39, 85**
See also CA 101; CANR 18, 41; DLB 120

Oldstyle, Jonathan
See Irving, Washington

Olesha, Yuri (Karlovich)
1899-1960 .... **CLC 8**
See also CA 85-88

Oliphant, Laurence
1829(?)-1888 .... **NCLC 47**
See also DLB 18

Oliphant, Margaret (Oliphant Wilson)
1828-1897 .... **NCLC 11**
See also DLB 18

Oliver, Mary 1935- .... **CLC 19, 34**
See also CA 21-24R; CANR 9, 43; DLB 5

Olivier, Laurence (Kerr)
1907-1989 .... **CLC 20**
See also CA 111; 129

Olsen, Tillie
1913- .... **CLC 4, 13; DA; SSC 11**
See also CA 1-4R; CANR 1, 43; DLB 28;
DLBY 80; MTCW

Olson, Charles (John)
1910-1970 ..... **CLC 1, 2, 5, 6, 9, 11, 29**
See also CA 13-16; 25-28R; CABS 2;
CANR 35; CAP 1; DLB 5, 16; MTCW

Olson, Toby 1937- .... **CLC 28**
See also CA 65-68; CANR 9, 31

Olyesha, Yuri
See Olesha, Yuri (Karlovich)

Ondaatje, (Philip) Michael
1943- .... **CLC 14, 29, 51, 76**
See also CA 77-80; CANR 42; DLB 60

Oneal, Elizabeth 1934-
See Oneal, Zibby
See also CA 106; CANR 28; MAICYA;
SATA 30

Oneal, Zibby .... **CLC 30**
See also Oneal, Elizabeth
See also AAYA 5; CLR 13; JRDA

O'Neill, Eugene (Gladstone)
1888-1953 ...... **TCLC 1, 6, 27, 49; DA;**
WLC
See also AITN 1; CA 110; 132;
CDALB 1929-1941; DLB 7; MTCW

Onetti, Juan Carlos 1909-1994 ... **CLC 7, 10**
See also CA 85-88; 145; CANR 32;
DLB 113; HW; MTCW

O Nuallain, Brian 1911-1966
See O'Brien, Flann
See also CA 21-22; 25-28R; CAP 2

Oppen, George 1908-1984 .... **CLC 7, 13, 34**
See also CA 13-16R; 113; CANR 8; DLB 5

Oppenheim, E(dward) Phillips
1866-1946 .... **TCLC 45**
See also CA 111; DLB 70

Orlovitz, Gil 1918-1973 .... **CLC 22**
See also CA 77-80; 45-48; DLB 2, 5

Orris
See Ingelow, Jean

Ortega y Gasset, Jose
1883-1955 .... **TCLC 9; HLC**
See also CA 106; 130; HW; MTCW

Ortiz, Simon J(oseph) 1941- .... **CLC 45**
See also CA 134; DLB 120

Orton, Joe .... **CLC 4, 13, 43; DC 3**
See also Orton, John Kingsley
See also CDBLB 1960 to Present; DLB 13

Orton, John Kingsley 1933-1967
See Orton, Joe
See also CA 85-88; CANR 35; MTCW

Orwell, George
.... **TCLC 2, 6, 15, 31, 51; WLC**
See also Blair, Eric (Arthur)
See also CDBLB 1945-1960; DLB 15, 98

Osborne, David
See Silverberg, Robert

Osborne, George
See Silverberg, Robert

Osborne, John (James)
1929- .... **CLC 1, 2, 5, 11, 45; DA; WLC**
See also CA 13-16R; CANR 21;
CDBLB 1945-1960; DLB 13; MTCW

Osborne, Lawrence 1958- .... **CLC 50**

Oshima, Nagisa 1932- .... **CLC 20**
See also CA 116; 121

Oskison, John Milton
1874-1947 .... **TCLC 35**
See also CA 144

Ossoli, Sarah Margaret (Fuller marchesa d')
1810-1850
See Fuller, Margaret
See also SATA 25

Ostrovsky, Alexander
1823-1886 .... **NCLC 30**

Otero, Blas de 1916-1979......... **CLC 11**
See also CA 89-92; DLB 134

Otto, Whitney 1955-.............. **CLC 70**
See also CA 140

Ouida .... **TCLC 43**
See also De La Ramee, (Marie) Louise
See also DLB 18

Ousmane, Sembene 1923- .... **CLC 66; BLC**
See also BW 1; CA 117; 125; MTCW

Ovid 43B.C.-18(?).......... **CMLC 7; PC 2**

Owen, Hugh
See Faust, Frederick (Schiller)

Owen, Wilfred (Edward Salter)
1893-1918 ...... **TCLC 5, 27; DA; WLC**
See also CA 104; 141; CDBLB 1914-1945;
DLB 20

Owens, Rochelle 1936-............. **CLC 8**
See also CA 17-20R; CAAS 2; CANR 39

Oz, Amos 1939- ... **CLC 5, 8, 11, 27, 33, 54**
See also CA 53-56; CANR 27; MTCW

Ozick, Cynthia
1928- .... **CLC 3, 7, 28, 62; SSC 15**
See also BEST 90:1; CA 17-20R; CANR 23;
DLB 28; DLBY 82; MTCW

Ozu, Yasujiro 1903-1963 .... **CLC 16**
See also CA 112

Pacheco, C.
See Pessoa, Fernando (Antonio Nogueira)

Pa Chin .... **CLC 18**
See also Li Fei-kan

Pack, Robert 1929-............... **CLC 13**
See also CA 1-4R; CANR 3, 44; DLB 5

Padgett, Lewis
See Kuttner, Henry

Padilla (Lorenzo), Heberto 1932-... **CLC 38**
See also AITN 1; CA 123; 131; HW

Page, Jimmy 1944-............... **CLC 12**

Page, Louise 1955-.............. **CLC 40**
See also CA 140

Page, P(atricia) K(athleen)
1916- .... **CLC 7, 18**
See also CA 53-56; CANR 4, 22; DLB 68;
MTCW

Paget, Violet 1856-1935
See Lee, Vernon
See also CA 104

Paget-Lowe, Henry
See Lovecraft, H(oward) P(hillips)

Paglia, Camille (Anna) 1947-....... **CLC 68**
See also CA 140

Paige, Richard
See Koontz, Dean R(ay)

Pakenham, Antonia
See Fraser, (Lady) Antonia (Pakenham)

Palamas, Kostes 1859-1943 .... **TCLC 5**
See also CA 105

Palazzeschi, Aldo 1885-1974 ...... **CLC 11**
See also CA 89-92; 53-56; DLB 114

Paley, Grace 1922- .... **CLC 4, 6, 37; SSC 8**
See also CA 25-28R; CANR 13; DLB 28;
MTCW

Palin, Michael (Edward) 1943- ..... **CLC 21**
See also Monty Python
See also CA 107; CANR 35; SATA 67

Palliser, Charles 1947- .... **CLC 65**
See also CA 136

Palma, Ricardo 1833-1919 .... **TCLC 29**

Pancake, Breece Dexter 1952-1979
See Pancake, Breece D'J
See also CA 123; 109

Pancake, Breece D'J .... **CLC 29**
See also Pancake, Breece Dexter
See also DLB 130

Panko, Rudy
See Gogol, Nikolai (Vasilyevich)

Papadiamantis, Alexandros
1851-1911 .... **TCLC 29**

Papadiamantopoulos, Johannes 1856-1910
See Moreas, Jean
See also CA 117

Papini, Giovanni 1881-1956 ...... **TCLC 22**
See also CA 121

Paracelsus 1493-1541 .... **LC 14**

Parasol, Peter
See Stevens, Wallace

Parfenie, Maria
See Codrescu, Andrei

Parini, Jay (Lee) 1948- .... **CLC 54**
See also CA 97-100; CAAS 16; CANR 32

Park, Jordan
See Kornbluth, C(yril) M.; Pohl, Frederik

Parker, Bert
See Ellison, Harlan

Parker, Dorothy (Rothschild)
1893-1967 .... **CLC 15, 68; SSC 2**
See also CA 19-20; 25-28R; CAP 2;
DLB 11, 45, 86; MTCW

Parker, Robert B(rown) 1932- ...... **CLC 27**
See also BEST 89:4; CA 49-52; CANR 1,
26; MTCW

Parkin, Frank 1940- .... **CLC 43**

Parkman, Francis, Jr.
1823-1893 .... **NCLC 12**
See also DLB 1, 30

Parks, Gordon (Alexander Buchanan)
1912- .... **CLC 1, 16; BLC**
See also AITN 2; BW 2; CA 41-44R;
CANR 26; DLB 33; SATA 8

Parnell, Thomas 1679-1718 .... **LC 3**
See also DLB 94

Parra, Nicanor 1914- .... **CLC 2; HLC**
See also CA 85-88; CANR 32; HW; MTCW

Parrish, Mary Frances
See Fisher, M(ary) F(rances) K(ennedy)

Parson
See Coleridge, Samuel Taylor

Parson Lot
See Kingsley, Charles

Partridge, Anthony
See Oppenheim, E(dward) Phillips

Pascoli, Giovanni 1855-1912 ...... **TCLC 45**

Pasolini, Pier Paolo
1922-1975 .... **CLC 20, 37**
See also CA 93-96; 61-64; DLB 128;
MTCW

Pasquini
See Silone, Ignazio

Pastan, Linda (Olenik) 1932- ...... **CLC 27**
See also CA 61-64; CANR 18, 40; DLB 5

Pasternak, Boris (Leonidovich)
1890-1960 ...... **CLC 7, 10, 18, 63; DA;
PC 6; WLC**
See also CA 127; 116; MTCW

Patchen, Kenneth 1911-1972 ... **CLC 1, 2, 18**
See also CA 1-4R; 33-36R; CANR 3, 35;
DLB 16, 48; MTCW

Pater, Walter (Horatio)
1839-1894 .... **NCLC 7**
See also CDBLB 1832-1890; DLB 57

Paterson, A(ndrew) B(arton)
1864-1941 .... **TCLC 32**

Paterson, Katherine (Womeldorf)
1932- .... **CLC 12, 30**
See also AAYA 1; CA 21-24R; CANR 28;
CLR 7; DLB 52; JRDA; MAICYA;
MTCW; SATA 13, 53

Patmore, Coventry Kersey Dighton
1823-1896 .... **NCLC 9**
See also DLB 35, 98

Paton, Alan (Stewart)
1903-1988 ...... **CLC 4, 10, 25, 55; DA;
WLC**
See also CA 13-16; 125; CANR 22; CAP 1;
MTCW; SATA 11, 56

Paton Walsh, Gillian 1937-
See Walsh, Jill Paton
See also CANR 38; JRDA; MAICYA;
SAAS 3; SATA 4, 72

Paulding, James Kirke 1778-1860 .. **NCLC 2**
See also DLB 3, 59, 74

Paulin, Thomas Neilson 1949-
See Paulin, Tom
See also CA 123; 128

Paulin, Tom .... **CLC 37**
See also Paulin, Thomas Neilson
See also DLB 40

Paustovsky, Konstantin (Georgievich)
1892-1968 .... **CLC 40**
See also CA 93-96; 25-28R

Pavese, Cesare 1908-1950 .... **TCLC 3**
See also CA 104; DLB 128

Pavic, Milorad 1929- .... **CLC 60**
See also CA 136

Payne, Alan
See Jakes, John (William)

Paz, Gil
See Lugones, Leopoldo

Paz, Octavio
1914- ...... **CLC 3, 4, 6, 10, 19, 51, 65;
DA; HLC; PC 1; WLC**
See also CA 73-76; CANR 32; DLBY 90;
HW; MTCW

Peacock, Molly 1947- .... **CLC 60**
See also CA 103; DLB 120

Peacock, Thomas Love
1785-1866 .... **NCLC 22**
See also DLB 96, 116

Peake, Mervyn 1911-1968 .... **CLC 7, 54**
See also CA 5-8R; 25-28R; CANR 3;
DLB 15; MTCW; SATA 23

Pearce, Philippa .... **CLC 21**
See also Christie, (Ann) Philippa
See also CLR 9; MAICYA; SATA 1, 67

Pearl, Eric
See Elman, Richard

Pearson, T(homas) R(eid) 1956- .... **CLC 39**
See also CA 120; 130

Peck, Dale 1968(?)- .... **CLC 81**

Peck, John 1941- .... **CLC 3**
See also CA 49-52; CANR 3

Peck, Richard (Wayne) 1934- ...... **CLC 21**
See also AAYA 1; CA 85-88; CANR 19,
38; CLR 15; JRDA; MAICYA; SAAS 2;
SATA 18, 55

Peck, Robert Newton 1928- .... **CLC 17; DA**
See also AAYA 3; CA 81-84; CANR 31;
JRDA; MAICYA; SAAS 1; SATA 21, 62

Peckinpah, (David) Sam(uel)
1925-1984 .... **CLC 20**
See also CA 109; 114

Pedersen, Knut 1859-1952
See Hamsun, Knut
See also CA 104; 119; MTCW

Peeslake, Gaffer
See Durrell, Lawrence (George)

Peguy, Charles Pierre
1873-1914 .... **TCLC 10**
See also CA 107

Pena, Ramon del Valle y
See Valle-Inclan, Ramon (Maria) del

Pendennis, Arthur Esquir
See Thackeray, William Makepeace

Penn, William 1644-1718 .... **LC 25**
See also DLB 24

Pepys, Samuel
1633-1703 .... **LC 11; DA; WLC**
See also CDBLB 1660-1789; DLB 101

Percy, Walker
1916-1990 .... **CLC 2, 3, 6, 8, 14, 18, 47,
65**
See also CA 1-4R; 131; CANR 1, 23;
DLB 2; DLBY 80, 90; MTCW

Perec, Georges 1936-1982 .... **CLC 56**
See also CA 141; DLB 83

Pereda (y Sanchez de Porrua), Jose Maria de
1833-1906 .... **TCLC 16**
See also CA 117

Pereda y Porrua, Jose Maria de
See Pereda (y Sanchez de Porrua), Jose
Maria de

Peregoy, George Weems
See Mencken, H(enry) L(ouis)

Perelman, S(idney) J(oseph)
1904-1979 ... **CLC 3, 5, 9, 15, 23, 44, 49**
See also AITN 1, 2; CA 73-76; 89-92;
CANR 18; DLB 11, 44; MTCW

Peret, Benjamin 1899-1959 .... **TCLC 20**
See also CA 117

Peretz, Isaac Loeb 1851(?)-1915... **TCLC 16**
See also CA 109

Peretz, Yitzkhok Leibush
See Peretz, Isaac Loeb

Perez Galdos, Benito 1843-1920 ... **TCLC 27**
See also CA 125; HW

Perrault, Charles 1628-1703 .... **LC 2**
See also MAICYA; SATA 25

Perry, Brighton
See Sherwood, Robert E(mmet)

Perse, St.-John .... **CLC 4, 11, 46**
See also Leger, (Marie-Rene Auguste) Alexis
Saint-Leger

Peseenz, Tulio F.
See Lopez y Fuentes, Gregorio

Pesetsky, Bette 1932- .... **CLC 28**
See also CA 133; DLB 130

Peshkov, Alexei Maximovich 1868-1936
See Gorky, Maxim
See also CA 105; 141; DA

Pessoa, Fernando (Antonio Nogueira)
1888-1935 .... **TCLC 27; HLC**
See also CA 125

Peterkin, Julia Mood 1880-1961.... **CLC 31**
See also CA 102; DLB 9

Peters, Joan K. 1945- .... **CLC 39**

Peters, Robert L(ouis) 1924- .... **CLC 7**
See also CA 13-16R; CAAS 8; DLB 105

Petofi, Sandor 1823-1849........ **NCLC 21**

Petrakis, Harry Mark 1923- .... **CLC 3**
See also CA 9-12R; CANR 4, 30

Petrarch 1304-1374................. **PC 8**

Petrov, Evgeny .... **TCLC 21**
See also Kataev, Evgeny Petrovich

Petry, Ann (Lane) 1908- ...... **CLC 1, 7, 18**
See also BW 1; CA 5-8R; CAAS 6;
CANR 4; CLR 12; DLB 76; JRDA;
MAICYA; MTCW; SATA 5

Petursson, Halligrimur 1614-1674 .... **LC 8**

Philipson, Morris H. 1926- .... **CLC 53**
See also CA 1-4R; CANR 4

Phillips, David Graham
1867-1911 .... **TCLC 44**
See also CA 108; DLB 9, 12

Phillips, Jack
See Sandburg, Carl (August)

Phillips, Jayne Anne
1952- .... **CLC 15, 33; SSC 16**
See also CA 101; CANR 24; DLBY 80;
MTCW

Phillips, Richard
See Dick, Philip K(indred)

Phillips, Robert (Schaeffer) 1938-... **CLC 28**
See also CA 17-20R; CAAS 13; CANR 8;
DLB 105

Phillips, Ward
See Lovecraft, H(oward) P(hillips)

Piccolo, Lucio 1901-1969......... **CLC 13**
See also CA 97-100; DLB 114

Pickthall, Marjorie L(owry) C(hristie)
1883-1922 .... **TCLC 21**
See also CA 107; DLB 92

Pico della Mirandola, Giovanni
1463-1494 .... **LC 15**

Piercy, Marge
1936- .... **CLC 3, 6, 14, 18, 27, 62**
See also CA 21-24R; CAAS 1; CANR 13,
43; DLB 120; MTCW

Piers, Robert
See Anthony, Piers

Pieyre de Mandiargues, Andre 1909-1991
See Mandiargues, Andre Pieyre de
See also CA 103; 136; CANR 22

Pilnyak, Boris .... **TCLC 23**
See also Vogau, Boris Andreyevich

Pincherle, Alberto 1907-1990 ... **CLC 11, 18**
See also Moravia, Alberto
See also CA 25-28R; 132; CANR 33;
MTCW

Pinckney, Darryl 1953- .... **CLC 76**
See also BW 2; CA 143

Pindar 518B.C.-446B.C.......... **CMLC 12**

Pineda, Cecile 1942-............... **CLC 39**
See also CA 118

Pinero, Arthur Wing 1855-1934 ... **TCLC 32**
See also CA 110; DLB 10

Pinero, Miguel (Antonio Gomez)
1946-1988 .... **CLC 4, 55**
See also CA 61-64; 125; CANR 29; HW

Pinget, Robert 1919- .... **CLC 7, 13, 37**
See also CA 85-88; DLB 83

Pink Floyd
See Barrett, (Roger) Syd; Gilmour, David;
Mason, Nick; Waters, Roger; Wright,
Rick

Pinkney, Edward 1802-1828 ..... **NCLC 31**

Pinkwater, Daniel Manus 1941- .... **CLC 35**
See also Pinkwater, Manus
See also AAYA 1; CA 29-32R; CANR 12,
38; CLR 4; JRDA; MAICYA; SAAS 3;
SATA 46, 76

Pinkwater, Manus
See Pinkwater, Daniel Manus
See also SATA 8

Pinsky, Robert 1940- .... **CLC 9, 19, 38**
See also CA 29-32R; CAAS 4; DLBY 82

Pinta, Harold
See Pinter, Harold

Pinter, Harold
1930- ..... **CLC 1, 3, 6, 9, 11, 15, 27, 58,
73; DA; WLC**
See also CA 5-8R; CANR 33; CDBLB 1960
to Present; DLB 13; MTCW

Pirandello, Luigi
1867-1936 ...... **TCLC 4, 29; DA; WLC**
See also CA 104

Pirsig, Robert M(aynard)
1928- .... **CLC 4, 6, 73**
See also CA 53-56; CANR 42; MTCW;
SATA 39

Pisarev, Dmitry Ivanovich
1840-1868 .... **NCLC 25**

Pix, Mary (Griffith) 1666-1709 .... **LC 8**
See also DLB 80

Pixerecourt, Guilbert de
1773-1844 .... **NCLC 39**

Plaidy, Jean
See Hibbert, Eleanor Alice Burford

Planche, James Robinson
1796-1880 .... **NCLC 42**

Plant, Robert 1948- .... **CLC 12**

Plante, David (Robert)
1940- .... **CLC 7, 23, 38**
See also CA 37-40R; CANR 12, 36;
DLBY 83; MTCW

Plath, Sylvia
1932-1963 ..... **CLC 1, 2, 3, 5, 9, 11, 14,
17, 50, 51, 62; DA; PC 1; WLC**
See also CA 19-20; CANR 34; CAP 2;
CDALB 1941-1968; DLB 5, 6; MTCW

Plato 428(?)B.C.-348(?)B.C.... **CMLC 8; DA**

Platonov, Andrei .... **TCLC 14**
See also Klimentov, Andrei Platonovich

Platt, Kin 1911- .... **CLC 26**
See also AAYA 11; CA 17-20R; CANR 11;
JRDA; SAAS 17; SATA 21

Plick et Plock
See Simenon, Georges (Jacques Christian)

Plimpton, George (Ames) 1927-..... **CLC 36**
See also AITN 1; CA 21-24R; CANR 32;
MTCW; SATA 10

Plomer, William Charles Franklin
1903-1973 .... **CLC 4, 8**
See also CA 21-22; CANR 34; CAP 2;
DLB 20; MTCW; SATA 24

Plowman, Piers
See Kavanagh, Patrick (Joseph)

Plum, J.
See Wodehouse, P(elham) G(renville)

Plumly, Stanley (Ross) 1939- ...... **CLC 33**
See also CA 108; 110; DLB 5

Plumpe, Friedrich Wilhelm
1888-1931 .... **TCLC 53**
See also CA 112

Poe, Edgar Allan
1809-1849 ..... **NCLC 1, 16; DA; PC 1;
SSC 1; WLC**
See also CDALB 1640-1865; DLB 3, 59, 73,
74; SATA 23

Poet of Titchfield Street, The
See Pound, Ezra (Weston Loomis)

Pohl, Frederik 1919- .... **CLC 18**
See also CA 61-64; CAAS 1; CANR 11, 37;
DLB 8; MTCW; SATA 24

Poirier, Louis 1910-
See Gracq, Julien
See also CA 122; 126

Poitier, Sidney 1927-.............. **CLC 26**
See also BW 1; CA 117

Polanski, Roman 1933- .... **CLC 16**
See also CA 77-80

Poliakoff, Stephen 1952- .... **CLC 38**
See also CA 106; DLB 13

Pynchon, Thomas (Ruggles, Jr.)
1937- ..... CLC 2, 3, 6, 9, 11, 18, 33, 62, 72; DA; SSC 14; WLC
See also BEST 90:2; CA 17-20R; CANR 22; DLB 2; MTCW

Qian Zhongshu
See Ch'ien Chung-shu

Qroll
See Dagerman, Stig (Halvard)

Quarrington, Paul (Lewis) 1953-.... CLC 65
See also CA 129

Quasimodo, Salvatore 1901-1968 ... CLC 10
See also CA 13-16; 25-28R; CAP 1; DLB 114; MTCW

Queen, Ellery.................... CLC 3, 11
See also Dannay, Frederic; Davidson, Avram; Lee, Manfred B(ennington); Sturgeon, Theodore (Hamilton); Vance, John Holbrook

Queen, Ellery, Jr.
See Dannay, Frederic; Lee, Manfred B(ennington)

Queneau, Raymond
1903-1976 .... CLC 2, 5, 10, 42
See also CA 77-80; 69-72; CANR 32; DLB 72; MTCW

Quevedo, Francisco de 1580-1645.... LC 23

Quiller-Couch, Arthur Thomas
1863-1944 .... TCLC 53
See also CA 118; DLB 135

Quin, Ann (Marie) 1936-1973 .... CLC 6
See also CA 9-12R; 45-48; DLB 14

Quinn, Martin
See Smith, Martin Cruz

Quinn, Simon
See Smith, Martin Cruz

Quiroga, Horacio (Sylvestre)
1878-1937 .... TCLC 20; HLC
See also CA 117; 131; HW; MTCW

Quoirez, Francoise 1935-........ CLC 9
See also Sagan, Francoise
See also CA 49-52; CANR 6, 39; MTCW

Raabe, Wilhelm 1831-1910 .... TCLC 45
See also DLB 129

Rabe, David (William) 1940-... CLC 4, 8, 33
See also CA 85-88; CABS 3; DLB 7

Rabelais, Francois
1483-1553 .... LC 5; DA; WLC

Rabinovitch, Sholem 1859-1916
See Aleichem, Sholom
See also CA 104

Radcliffe, Ann (Ward) 1764-1823 .. NCLC 6
See also DLB 39

Radiguet, Raymond 1903-1923 .... TCLC 29
See also DLB 65

Radnoti, Miklos 1909-1944 .... TCLC 16
See also CA 118

Rado, James 1939-............... CLC 17
See also CA 105

Radvanyi, Netty 1900-1983
See Seghers, Anna
See also CA 85-88; 110

Rae, Ben
See Griffiths, Trevor

Raeburn, John (Hay) 1941-........ CLC 34
See also CA 57-60

Ragni, Gerome 1942-1991 .... CLC 17
See also CA 105; 134

Rahv, Philip 1908-1973 .... CLC 24
See also Greenberg, Ivan
See also DLB 137

Raine, Craig 1944- .... CLC 32
See also CA 108; CANR 29; DLB 40

Raine, Kathleen (Jessie) 1908- ... CLC 7, 45
See also CA 85-88; DLB 20; MTCW

Rainis, Janis 1865-1929 .... TCLC 29

Rakosi, Carl.................... CLC 47
See also Rawley, Callman
See also CAAS 5

Raleigh, Richard
See Lovecraft, H(oward) P(hillips)

Rallentando, H. P.
See Sayers, Dorothy L(eigh)

Ramal, Walter
See de la Mare, Walter (John)

Ramon, Juan
See Jimenez (Mantecon), Juan Ramon

Ramos, Graciliano 1892-1953 ..... TCLC 32

Rampersad, Arnold 1941-........ CLC 44
See also BW 2; CA 127; 133; DLB 111

Rampling, Anne
See Rice, Anne

Ramuz, Charles-Ferdinand
1878-1947 .... TCLC 33

Rand, Ayn
1905-1982 ...... CLC 3, 30, 44, 79; DA; WLC
See also AAYA 10; CA 13-16R; 105; CANR 27; MTCW

Randall, Dudley (Felker)
1914- .... CLC 1; BLC
See also BW 1; CA 25-28R; CANR 23; DLB 41

Randall, Robert
See Silverberg, Robert

Ranger, Ken
See Creasey, John

Ransom, John Crowe
1888-1974 .... CLC 2, 4, 5, 11, 24
See also CA 5-8R; 49-52; CANR 6, 34; DLB 45, 63; MTCW

Rao, Raja 1909-.............. CLC 25, 56
See also CA 73-76; MTCW

Raphael, Frederic (Michael)
1931-................... CLC 2, 14
See also CA 1-4R; CANR 1; DLB 14

Ratcliffe, James P.
See Mencken, H(enry) L(ouis)

Rathbone, Julian 1935- .... CLC 41
See also CA 101; CANR 34

Rattigan, Terence (Mervyn)
1911-1977 .... CLC 7
See also CA 85-88; 73-76; CDBLB 1945-1960; DLB 13; MTCW

Ratushinskaya, Irina 1954-........ CLC 54
See also CA 129

Raven, Simon (Arthur Noel)
1927-...................... CLC 14
See also CA 81-84

Rawley, Callman 1903-
See Rakosi, Carl
See also CA 21-24R; CANR 12, 32

Rawlings, Marjorie Kinnan
1896-1953 .... TCLC 4
See also CA 104; 137; DLB 9, 22, 102; JRDA; MAICYA; YABC 1

Ray, Satyajit 1921-1992........ CLC 16, 76
See also CA 114; 137

Read, Herbert Edward 1893-1968.... CLC 4
See also CA 85-88; 25-28R; DLB 20

Read, Piers Paul 1941- ...... CLC 4, 10, 25
See also CA 21-24R; CANR 38; DLB 14; SATA 21

Reade, Charles 1814-1884 .... NCLC 2
See also DLB 21

Reade, Hamish
See Gray, Simon (James Holliday)

Reading, Peter 1946- .... CLC 47
See also CA 103; DLB 40

Reaney, James 1926-............. CLC 13
See also CA 41-44R; CAAS 15; CANR 42; DLB 68; SATA 43

Rebreanu, Liviu 1885-1944 .... TCLC 28

Rechy, John (Francisco)
1934-.......... CLC 1, 7, 14, 18; HLC
See also CA 5-8R; CAAS 4; CANR 6, 32; DLB 122; DLBY 82; HW

Redcam, Tom 1870-1933 .... TCLC 25

Reddin, Keith.................... CLC 67

Redgrove, Peter (William)
1932-..................... CLC 6, 41
See also CA 1-4R; CANR 3, 39; DLB 40

Redmon, Anne................... CLC 22
See also Nightingale, Anne Redmon
See also DLBY 86

Reed, Eliot
See Ambler, Eric

Reed, Ishmael
1938- ... CLC 2, 3, 5, 6, 13, 32, 60; BLC
See also BW 2; CA 21-24R; CANR 25; DLB 2, 5, 33; DLBD 8; MTCW

Reed, John (Silas) 1887-1920 ...... TCLC 9
See also CA 106

Reed, Lou........................ CLC 21
See also Firbank, Louis

Reeve, Clara 1729-1807 .... NCLC 19
See also DLB 39

Reich, Wilhelm 1897-1957........ TCLC 57

Reid, Christopher (John) 1949-..... CLC 33
See also CA 140; DLB 40

Reid, Desmond
See Moorcock, Michael (John)

Reid Banks, Lynne 1929-
See Banks, Lynne Reid
See also CA 1-4R; CANR 6, 22, 38; CLR 24; JRDA; MAICYA; SATA 22, 75

Reilly, William K.
See Creasey, John

Reiner, Max
See Caldwell, (Janet Miriam) Taylor
(Holland)

Reis, Ricardo
See Pessoa, Fernando (Antonio Nogueira)

Remarque, Erich Maria
1898-1970 . . . . **CLC 21; DA**
See also CA 77-80; 29-32R; DLB 56;
MTCW

Remizov, A.
See Remizov, Aleksei (Mikhailovich)

Remizov, A. M.
See Remizov, Aleksei (Mikhailovich)

Remizov, Aleksei (Mikhailovich)
1877-1957 . . . . **TCLC 27**
See also CA 125; 133

Renan, Joseph Ernest
1823-1892 . . . . **NCLC 26**

Renard, Jules 1864-1910 . . . . **TCLC 17**
See also CA 117

Renault, Mary . . . . **CLC 3, 11, 17**
See also Challans, Mary
See also DLBY 83

Rendell, Ruth (Barbara) 1930- . . **CLC 28, 48**
See also Vine, Barbara
See also CA 109; CANR 32; DLB 87;
MTCW

Renoir, Jean 1894-1979 . . . . **CLC 20**
See also CA 129; 85-88

Resnais, Alain 1922- . . . . **CLC 16**

Reverdy, Pierre 1889-1960 . . . . **CLC 53**
See also CA 97-100; 89-92

Rexroth, Kenneth
1905-1982 . . . . . . **CLC 1, 2, 6, 11, 22, 49**
See also CA 5-8R; 107; CANR 14, 34;
CDALB 1941-1968; DLB 16, 48;
DLBY 82; MTCW

Reyes, Alfonso 1889-1959 . . . . **TCLC 33**
See also CA 131; HW

Reyes y Basoalto, Ricardo Eliecer Neftali
See Neruda, Pablo

Reymont, Wladyslaw (Stanislaw)
1868(?)-1925 . . . . **TCLC 5**
See also CA 104

Reynolds, Jonathan 1942- . . . . **CLC 6, 38**
See also CA 65-68; CANR 28

Reynolds, Joshua 1723-1792 . . . . **LC 15**
See also DLB 104

Reynolds, Michael Shane 1937- . . . . **CLC 44**
See also CA 65-68; CANR 9

Reznikoff, Charles 1894-1976 . . . . **CLC 9**
See also CA 33-36; 61-64; CAP 2; DLB 28,
45

Rezzori (d'Arezzo), Gregor von
1914- . . . . **CLC 25**
See also CA 122; 136

Rhine, Richard
See Silverstein, Alvin

Rhodes, Eugene Manlove
1869-1934 . . . . **TCLC 53**

R'hoone
See Balzac, Honore de

Rhys, Jean
1890(?)-1979 . . . . **CLC 2, 4, 6, 14, 19, 51**
See also CA 25-28R; 85-88; CANR 35;
CDBLB 1945-1960; DLB 36, 117; MTCW

Ribeiro, Darcy 1922- . . . . **CLC 34**
See also CA 33-36R

Ribeiro, Joao Ubaldo (Osorio Pimentel)
1941- . . . . **CLC 10, 67**
See also CA 81-84

Ribman, Ronald (Burt) 1932- . . . . **CLC 7**
See also CA 21-24R

Ricci, Nino 1959- . . . . **CLC 70**
See also CA 137

Rice, Anne 1941- . . . . **CLC 41**
See also AAYA 9; BEST 89:2; CA 65-68;
CANR 12, 36

Rice, Elmer (Leopold)
1892-1967 . . . . **CLC 7, 49**
See also CA 21-22; 25-28R; CAP 2; DLB 4,
7; MTCW

Rice, Tim 1944- . . . . **CLC 21**
See also CA 103

Rich, Adrienne (Cecile)
1929- . . . . **CLC 3, 6, 7, 11, 18, 36, 73, 76;
PC 5**
See also CA 9-12R; CANR 20; DLB 5, 67;
MTCW

Rich, Barbara
See Graves, Robert (von Ranke)

Rich, Robert
See Trumbo, Dalton

Richards, David Adams 1950- . . . . . . **CLC 59**
See also CA 93-96; DLB 53

Richards, I(vor) A(rmstrong)
1893-1979 . . . . **CLC 14, 24**
See also CA 41-44R; 89-92; CANR 34;
DLB 27

Richardson, Anne
See Roiphe, Anne (Richardson)

Richardson, Dorothy Miller
1873-1957 . . . . **TCLC 3**
See also CA 104; DLB 36

Richardson, Ethel Florence (Lindesay)
1870-1946
See Richardson, Henry Handel
See also CA 105

Richardson, Henry Handel . . . . **TCLC 4**
See also Richardson, Ethel Florence
(Lindesay)

Richardson, Samuel
1689-1761 . . . . **LC 1; DA; WLC**
See also CDBLB 1660-1789; DLB 39

Richler, Mordecai
1931- . . . . **CLC 3, 5, 9, 13, 18, 46, 70**
See also AITN 1; CA 65-68; CANR 31;
CLR 17; DLB 53; MAICYA; MTCW;
SATA 27, 44

Richter, Conrad (Michael)
1890-1968 . . . . **CLC 30**
See also CA 5-8R; 25-28R; CANR 23;
DLB 9; MTCW; SATA 3

Riddell, J. H. 1832-1906 . . . . **TCLC 40**

Riding, Laura . . . . **CLC 3, 7**
See also Jackson, Laura (Riding)

Riefenstahl, Berta Helene Amalia 1902-
See Riefenstahl, Leni
See also CA 108

Riefenstahl, Leni . . . . **CLC 16**
See also Riefenstahl, Berta Helene Amalia

Riffe, Ernest
See Bergman, (Ernst) Ingmar

Riggs, (Rolla) Lynn 1899-1954 . . . . **TCLC 56**
See also CA 144

Riley, James Whitcomb
1849-1916 . . . . **TCLC 51**
See also CA 118; 137; MAICYA; SATA 17

Riley, Tex
See Creasey, John

Rilke, Rainer Maria
1875-1926 . . . . **TCLC 1, 6, 19; PC 2**
See also CA 104; 132; DLB 81; MTCW

Rimbaud, (Jean Nicolas) Arthur
1854-1891 . . . . . **NCLC 4, 35; DA; PC 3;
WLC**

Rinehart, Mary Roberts
1876-1958 . . . . **TCLC 52**
See also CA 108

Ringmaster, The
See Mencken, H(enry) L(ouis)

Ringwood, Gwen(dolyn Margaret) Pharis
1910-1984 . . . . **CLC 48**
See also CA 112; DLB 88

Rio, Michel 19(?)- . . . . **CLC 43**

Ritsos, Giannes
See Ritsos, Yannis

Ritsos, Yannis 1909-1990 . . . . . **CLC 6, 13, 31**
See also CA 77-80; 133; CANR 39; MTCW

Ritter, Erika 1948(?)- . . . . **CLC 52**

Rivera, Jose Eustasio 1889-1928 . . . **TCLC 35**
See also HW

Rivers, Conrad Kent 1933-1968 . . . . . . **CLC 1**
See also BW 1; CA 85-88; DLB 41

Rivers, Elfrida
See Bradley, Marion Zimmer

Riverside, John
See Heinlein, Robert A(nson)

Rizal, Jose 1861-1896 . . . . **NCLC 27**

Roa Bastos, Augusto (Antonio)
1917- . . . . **CLC 45; HLC**
See also CA 131; DLB 113; HW

Robbe-Grillet, Alain
1922- . . . . . . **CLC 1, 2, 4, 6, 8, 10, 14, 43**
See also CA 9-12R; CANR 33; DLB 83;
MTCW

Robbins, Harold 1916- . . . . **CLC 5**
See also CA 73-76; CANR 26; MTCW

Robbins, Thomas Eugene 1936-
See Robbins, Tom
See also CA 81-84; CANR 29; MTCW

Robbins, Tom . . . . **CLC 9, 32, 64**
See also Robbins, Thomas Eugene
See also BEST 90:3; DLBY 80

Robbins, Trina 1938- . . . . **CLC 21**
See also CA 128

Roberts, Charles G(eorge) D(ouglas)
1860-1943 . . . . **TCLC 8**
See also CA 105; CLR 33; DLB 92;
SATA 29

Roberts, Kate   1891-1985 . . . . **CLC 15**
See also CA 107; 116

Roberts, Keith (John Kingston)
1935- . . . . **CLC 14**
See also CA 25-28R

Roberts, Kenneth (Lewis)
1885-1957 . . . . **TCLC 23**
See also CA 109; DLB 9

Roberts, Michele (B.)   1949- . . . . **CLC 48**
See also CA 115

Robertson, Ellis
See Ellison, Harlan; Silverberg, Robert

Robertson, Thomas William
1829-1871 . . . . **NCLC 35**

Robinson, Edwin Arlington
1869-1935 . . . . **TCLC 5; DA; PC 1**
See also CA 104; 133; CDALB 1865-1917;
DLB 54; MTCW

Robinson, Henry Crabb
1775-1867 . . . . **NCLC 15**
See also DLB 107

Robinson, Jill   1936- . . . . **CLC 10**
See also CA 102

Robinson, Kim Stanley   1952- . . . . . . **CLC 34**
See also CA 126

Robinson, Lloyd
See Silverberg, Robert

Robinson, Marilynne   1944- . . . . **CLC 25**
See also CA 116

Robinson, Smokey . . . . **CLC 21**
See also Robinson, William, Jr.

Robinson, William, Jr.   1940-
See Robinson, Smokey
See also CA 116

Robison, Mary   1949- . . . . **CLC 42**
See also CA 113; 116; DLB 130

Rod, Edouard   1857-1910 . . . . **TCLC 52**

Roddenberry, Eugene Wesley   1921-1991
See Roddenberry, Gene
See also CA 110; 135; CANR 37; SATA 45

Roddenberry, Gene . . . . **CLC 17**
See also Roddenberry, Eugene Wesley
See also AAYA 5; SATA-Obit 69

Rodgers, Mary   1931- . . . . **CLC 12**
See also CA 49-52; CANR 8; CLR 20;
JRDA; MAICYA; SATA 8

Rodgers, W(illiam) R(obert)
1909-1969 . . . . **CLC 7**
See also CA 85-88; DLB 20

Rodman, Eric
See Silverberg, Robert

Rodman, Howard   1920(?)-1985 . . . . . **CLC 65**
See also CA 118

Rodman, Maia
See Wojciechowska, Maia (Teresa)

Rodriguez, Claudio   1934- . . . . **CLC 10**
See also DLB 134

Roelvaag, O(le) E(dvart)
1876-1931 . . . . **TCLC 17**
See also CA 117; DLB 9

Roethke, Theodore (Huebner)
1908-1963 . . . . . . **CLC 1, 3, 8, 11, 19, 46**
See also CA 81-84; CABS 2;
CDALB 1941-1968; DLB 5; MTCW

Rogers, Thomas Hunton   1927- . . . . . **CLC 57**
See also CA 89-92

Rogers, Will(iam Penn Adair)
1879-1935 . . . . **TCLC 8**
See also CA 105; 144; DLB 11

Rogin, Gilbert   1929- . . . . **CLC 18**
See also CA 65-68; CANR 15

Rohan, Koda . . . . **TCLC 22**
See also Koda Shigeyuki

Rohmer, Eric . . . . **CLC 16**
See also Scherer, Jean-Marie Maurice

Rohmer, Sax . . . . **TCLC 28**
See also Ward, Arthur Henry Sarsfield
See also DLB 70

Roiphe, Anne (Richardson)
1935- . . . . **CLC 3, 9**
See also CA 89-92; CANR 45; DLBY 80

Rojas, Fernando de   1465-1541 . . . . . **LC 23**

**Rolfe, Frederick (William Serafino Austin
Lewis Mary)**   1860-1913 . . . . . **TCLC 12**
See also CA 107; DLB 34

Rolland, Romain   1866-1944 . . . . . . **TCLC 23**
See also CA 118; DLB 65

Rolvaag, O(le) E(dvart)
See Roelvaag, O(le) E(dvart)

Romain Arnaud, Saint
See Aragon, Louis

Romains, Jules   1885-1972 . . . . **CLC 7**
See also CA 85-88; CANR 34; DLB 65;
MTCW

Romero, Jose Ruben   1890-1952 . . . **TCLC 14**
See also CA 114; 131; HW

Ronsard, Pierre de   1524-1585 . . . . **LC 6**

Rooke, Leon   1934- . . . . **CLC 25, 34**
See also CA 25-28R; CANR 23

Roper, William   1498-1578 . . . . **LC 10**

Roquelaure, A. N.
See Rice, Anne

Rosa, Joao Guimaraes   1908-1967 . . . **CLC 23**
See also CA 89-92; DLB 113

Rose, Wendy   1948- . . . . **CLC 85**
See also CA 53-56; CANR 5; NNAL;
SATA 12

Rosen, Richard (Dean)   1949- . . . . **CLC 39**
See also CA 77-80

Rosenberg, Isaac   1890-1918 . . . . . . **TCLC 12**
See also CA 107; DLB 20

Rosenblatt, Joe . . . . **CLC 15**
See also Rosenblatt, Joseph

Rosenblatt, Joseph   1933-
See Rosenblatt, Joe
See also CA 89-92

Rosenfeld, Samuel   1896-1963
See Tzara, Tristan
See also CA 89-92

Rosenthal, M(acha) L(ouis)   1917- . . . **CLC 28**
See also CA 1-4R; CAAS 6; CANR 4;
DLB 5; SATA 59

Ross, Barnaby
See Dannay, Frederic

Ross, Bernard L.
See Follett, Ken(neth Martin)

Ross, J. H.
See Lawrence, T(homas) E(dward)

Ross, Martin
See Martin, Violet Florence
See also DLB 135

Ross, (James) Sinclair   1908- . . . . **CLC 13**
See also CA 73-76; DLB 88

Rossetti, Christina (Georgina)
1830-1894 . . . **NCLC 2; DA; PC 7; WLC**
See also DLB 35; MAICYA; SATA 20

Rossetti, Dante Gabriel
1828-1882 . . . . **NCLC 4; DA; WLC**
See also CDBLB 1832-1890; DLB 35

Rossner, Judith (Perelman)
1935- . . . . **CLC 6, 9, 29**
See also AITN 2; BEST 90:3; CA 17-20R;
CANR 18; DLB 6; MTCW

Rostand, Edmond (Eugene Alexis)
1868-1918 . . . . **TCLC 6, 37; DA**
See also CA 104; 126; MTCW

Roth, Henry   1906- . . . . **CLC 2, 6, 11**
See also CA 11-12; CANR 38; CAP 1;
DLB 28; MTCW

Roth, Joseph   1894-1939 . . . . **TCLC 33**
See also DLB 85

Roth, Philip (Milton)
1933- . . . . . . **CLC 1, 2, 3, 4, 6, 9, 15, 22,
31, 47, 66; DA; WLC**
See also BEST 90:3; CA 1-4R; CANR 1, 22,
36; CDALB 1968-1988; DLB 2, 28;
DLBY 82; MTCW

Rothenberg, Jerome   1931- . . . . **CLC 6, 57**
See also CA 45-48; CANR 1; DLB 5

Roumain, Jacques (Jean Baptiste)
1907-1944 . . . . **TCLC 19; BLC**
See also BW 1; CA 117; 125

Rourke, Constance (Mayfield)
1885-1941 . . . . **TCLC 12**
See also CA 107; YABC 1

Rousseau, Jean-Baptiste   1671-1741 . . . **LC 9**

Rousseau, Jean-Jacques
1712-1778 . . . . **LC 14; DA; WLC**

Roussel, Raymond   1877-1933 . . . . . **TCLC 20**
See also CA 117

Rovit, Earl (Herbert)   1927- . . . . **CLC 7**
See also CA 5-8R; CANR 12

Rowe, Nicholas   1674-1718 . . . . **LC 8**
See also DLB 84

Rowley, Ames Dorrance
See Lovecraft, H(oward) P(hillips)

Rowson, Susanna Haswell
1762(?)-1824 . . . . **NCLC 5**
See also DLB 37

Roy, Gabrielle   1909-1983 . . . . **CLC 10, 14**
See also CA 53-56; 110; CANR 5; DLB 68;
MTCW

Rozewicz, Tadeusz   1921- . . . . **CLC 9, 23**
See also CA 108; CANR 36; MTCW

Ruark, Gibbons   1941- . . . . **CLC 3**
See also CA 33-36R; CANR 14, 31;
DLB 120

Rubens, Bernice (Ruth)   1923- . . . **CLC 19, 31**
See also CA 25-28R; CANR 33; DLB 14;
MTCW

Rudkin, (James) David 1936- ...... **CLC 14**
See also CA 89-92; DLB 13

Rudnik, Raphael 1933-............. **CLC 7**
See also CA 29-32R

Ruffian, M.
See Hasek, Jaroslav (Matej Frantisek)

Ruiz, Jose Martinez............... **CLC 11**
See also Martinez Ruiz, Jose

Rukeyser, Muriel
1913-1980 .... **CLC 6, 10, 15, 27**
See also CA 5-8R; 93-96; CANR 26;
DLB 48; MTCW; SATA 22

Rule, Jane (Vance) 1931-......... **CLC 27**
See also CA 25-28R; CAAS 18; CANR 12;
DLB 60

Rulfo, Juan 1918-1986.... **CLC 8, 80; HLC**
See also CA 85-88; 118; CANR 26;
DLB 113; HW; MTCW

Runeberg, Johan 1804-1877...... **NCLC 41**

Runyon, (Alfred) Damon
1884(?)-1946 .... **TCLC 10**
See also CA 107; DLB 11, 86

Rush, Norman 1933-.............. **CLC 44**
See also CA 121; 126

Rushdie, (Ahmed) Salman
1947- .... **CLC 23, 31, 55**
See also BEST 89:3; CA 108; 111;
CANR 33; MTCW

Rushforth, Peter (Scott) 1945- ..... **CLC 19**
See also CA 101

Ruskin, John 1819-1900......... **TCLC 20**
See also CA 114; 129; CDBLB 1832-1890;
DLB 55; SATA 24

Russ, Joanna 1937-.............. **CLC 15**
See also CA 25-28R; CANR 11, 31; DLB 8;
MTCW

Russell, (Henry) Ken(neth Alfred)
1927- .... **CLC 16**
See also CA 105

Russell, Willy 1947-.............. **CLC 60**

Rutherford, Mark................ **TCLC 25**
See also White, William Hale
See also DLB 18

Ryan, Cornelius (John) 1920-1974 ... **CLC 7**
See also CA 69-72; 53-56; CANR 38

Ryan, Michael 1946- .... **CLC 65**
See also CA 49-52; DLBY 82

Rybakov, Anatoli (Naumovich)
1911- .... **CLC 23, 53**
See also CA 126; 135; SATA 79

Ryder, Jonathan
See Ludlum, Robert

Ryga, George 1932-1987 .... **CLC 14**
See also CA 101; 124; CANR 43; DLB 60

S. S.
See Sassoon, Siegfried (Lorraine)

Saba, Umberto 1883-1957 .... **TCLC 33**
See also CA 144; DLB 114

Sabatini, Rafael 1875-1950 .... **TCLC 47**

Sabato, Ernesto (R.)
1911- .... **CLC 10, 23; HLC**
See also CA 97-100; CANR 32; HW;
MTCW

Sacastru, Martin
See Bioy Casares, Adolfo

Sacher-Masoch, Leopold von
1836(?)-1895 .... **NCLC 31**

Sachs, Marilyn (Stickle) 1927- .... **CLC 35**
See also AAYA 2; CA 17-20R; CANR 13;
CLR 2; JRDA; MAICYA; SAAS 2;
SATA 3, 68

Sachs, Nelly 1891-1970 .... **CLC 14**
See also CA 17-18; 25-28R; CAP 2

Sackler, Howard (Oliver)
1929-1982 .... **CLC 14**
See also CA 61-64; 108; CANR 30; DLB 7

Sacks, Oliver (Wolf) 1933- .... **CLC 67**
See also CA 53-56; CANR 28; MTCW

Sade, Donatien Alphonse Francois Comte
1740-1814 .... **NCLC 47**

Sadoff, Ira 1945-.................. **CLC 9**
See also CA 53-56; CANR 5, 21; DLB 120

Saetone
See Camus, Albert

Safire, William 1929-............. **CLC 10**
See also CA 17-20R; CANR 31

Sagan, Carl (Edward) 1934-....... **CLC 30**
See also AAYA 2; CA 25-28R; CANR 11,
36; MTCW; SATA 58

Sagan, Francoise .... **CLC 3, 6, 9, 17, 36**
See also Quoirez, Francoise
See also DLB 83

Sahgal, Nayantara (Pandit) 1927-... **CLC 41**
See also CA 9-12R; CANR 11

Saint, H(arry) F. 1941- .... **CLC 50**
See also CA 127

St. Aubin de Teran, Lisa 1953-
See Teran, Lisa St. Aubin de
See also CA 118; 126

Sainte-Beuve, Charles Augustin
1804-1869 .... **NCLC 5**

Saint-Exupery, Antoine (Jean Baptiste Marie Roger) de
1900-1944 .... **TCLC 2, 56; WLC**
See also CA 108; 132; CLR 10; DLB 72;
MAICYA; MTCW; SATA 20

St. John, David
See Hunt, E(verette) Howard, Jr.

Saint-John Perse
See Leger, (Marie-Rene Auguste) Alexis
Saint-Leger

Saintsbury, George (Edward Bateman)
1845-1933 .... **TCLC 31**
See also DLB 57

Sait Faik .... **TCLC 23**
See also Abasiyanik, Sait Faik

Saki .... **TCLC 3; SSC 12**
See also Munro, H(ector) H(ugh)

Sala, George Augustus .... **NCLC 46**

Salama, Hannu 1936-............. **CLC 18**

Salamanca, J(ack) R(ichard)
1922- .... **CLC 4, 15**
See also CA 25-28R

Sale, J. Kirkpatrick
See Sale, Kirkpatrick

Sale, Kirkpatrick 1937- .... **CLC 68**
See also CA 13-16R; CANR 10

Salinas (y Serrano), Pedro
1891(?)-1951 .... **TCLC 17**
See also CA 117; DLB 134

Salinger, J(erome) D(avid)
1919- ...... **CLC 1, 3, 8, 12, 55, 56; DA;
SSC 2; WLC**
See also AAYA 2; CA 5-8R; CANR 39;
CDALB 1941-1968; CLR 18; DLB 2, 102;
MAICYA; MTCW; SATA 67

Salisbury, John
See Caute, David

Salter, James 1925- .... **CLC 7, 52, 59**
See also CA 73-76; DLB 130

Saltus, Edgar (Everton)
1855-1921 .... **TCLC 8**
See also CA 105

Saltykov, Mikhail Evgrafovich
1826-1889 .... **NCLC 16**

Samarakis, Antonis 1919- .... **CLC 5**
See also CA 25-28R; CAAS 16; CANR 36

Sanchez, Florencio 1875-1910..... **TCLC 37**
See also HW

Sanchez, Luis Rafael 1936-........ **CLC 23**
See also CA 128; HW

Sanchez, Sonia 1934-... **CLC 5; BLC; PC 9**
See also BW 2; CA 33-36R; CANR 24;
CLR 18; DLB 41; DLBD 8; MAICYA;
MTCW; SATA 22

Sand, George
1804-1876 ...... **NCLC 2, 42; DA; WLC**
See also DLB 119

Sandburg, Carl (August)
1878-1967 .... **CLC 1, 4, 10, 15, 35; DA;
PC 2; WLC**
See also CA 5-8R; 25-28R; CANR 35;
CDALB 1865-1917; DLB 17, 54;
MAICYA; MTCW; SATA 8

Sandburg, Charles
See Sandburg, Carl (August)

Sandburg, Charles A.
See Sandburg, Carl (August)

Sanders, (James) Ed(ward) 1939- ... **CLC 53**
See also CA 13-16R; CANR 13, 44;
DLB 16

Sanders, Lawrence 1920-.......... **CLC 41**
See also BEST 89:4; CA 81-84; CANR 33;
MTCW

Sanders, Noah
See Blount, Roy (Alton), Jr.

Sanders, Winston P.
See Anderson, Poul (William)

Sandoz, Mari(e Susette)
1896-1966 .... **CLC 28**
See also CA 1-4R; 25-28R; CANR 17;
DLB 9; MTCW; SATA 5

Saner, Reg(inald Anthony) 1931- .... **CLC 9**
See also CA 65-68

Sannazaro, Jacopo 1456(?)-1530...... **LC 8**

Sansom, William 1912-1976....... **CLC 2, 6**
See also CA 5-8R; 65-68; CANR 42;
DLB 139; MTCW

Santayana, George 1863-1952..... **TCLC 40**
See also CA 115; DLB 54, 71

Scott, Walter
1771-1832 .... **NCLC 15; DA; WLC**
See also CDBLB 1789-1832; DLB 93, 107,
116, 144; YABC 2

Scribe, (Augustin) Eugene
1791-1861 .... **NCLC 16**

Scrum, R.
See Crumb, R(obert)

Scudery, Madeleine de 1607-1701 ..... **LC 2**

Scum
See Crumb, R(obert)

Scumbag, Little Bobby
See Crumb, R(obert)

Seabrook, John
See Hubbard, L(afayette) Ron(ald)

Sealy, I. Allan 1951- .... **CLC 55**

Search, Alexander
See Pessoa, Fernando (Antonio Nogueira)

Sebastian, Lee
See Silverberg, Robert

Sebastian Owl
See Thompson, Hunter S(tockton)

Sebestyen, Ouida 1924- .... **CLC 30**
See also AAYA 8; CA 107; CANR 40;
CLR 17; JRDA; MAICYA; SAAS 10;
SATA 39

Secundus, H. Scriblerus
See Fielding, Henry

Sedges, John
See Buck, Pearl S(ydenstricker)

Sedgwick, Catharine Maria
1789-1867 .... **NCLC 19**
See also DLB 1, 74

Seelye, John 1931- .... **CLC 7**

Seferiades, Giorgos Stylianou 1900-1971
See Seferis, George
See also CA 5-8R; 33-36R; CANR 5, 36;
MTCW

Seferis, George .... **CLC 5, 11**
See also Seferiades, Giorgos Stylianou

Segal, Erich (Wolf) 1937- .... **CLC 3, 10**
See also BEST 89:1; CA 25-28R; CANR 20,
36; DLBY 86; MTCW

Seger, Bob 1945- .... **CLC 35**

Seghers, Anna .... **CLC 7**
See also Radvanyi, Netty
See also DLB 69

Seidel, Frederick (Lewis) 1936- ..... **CLC 18**
See also CA 13-16R; CANR 8; DLBY 84

Seifert, Jaroslav 1901-1986 ..... **CLC 34, 44**
See also CA 127; MTCW

Sei Shonagon c. 966-1017(?) ...... **CMLC 6**

Selby, Hubert, Jr. 1928- ..... **CLC 1, 2, 4, 8**
See also CA 13-16R; CANR 33; DLB 2

Selzer, Richard 1928- .... **CLC 74**
See also CA 65-68; CANR 14

Sembene, Ousmane
See Ousmane, Sembene

Senancour, Etienne Pivert de
1770-1846 .... **NCLC 16**
See also DLB 119

Sender, Ramon (Jose)
1902-1982 .... **CLC 8; HLC**
See also CA 5-8R; 105; CANR 8; HW;
MTCW

Seneca, Lucius Annaeus
4B.C.-65 .... **CMLC 6**

Senghor, Leopold Sedar
1906- .... **CLC 54; BLC**
See also BW 2; CA 116; 125; MTCW

Serling, (Edward) Rod(man)
1924-1975 .... **CLC 30**
See also AITN 1; CA 65-68; 57-60; DLB 26

Serna, Ramon Gomez de la
See Gomez de la Serna, Ramon

Serpieres
See Guillevic, (Eugene)

Service, Robert
See Service, Robert W(illiam)
See also DLB 92

Service, Robert W(illiam)
1874(?)-1958 ...... **TCLC 15; DA; WLC**
See also Service, Robert
See also CA 115; 140; SATA 20

Seth, Vikram 1952- .... **CLC 43**
See also CA 121; 127; DLB 120

Seton, Cynthia Propper
1926-1982 .... **CLC 27**
See also CA 5-8R; 108; CANR 7

Seton, Ernest (Evan) Thompson
1860-1946 .... **TCLC 31**
See also CA 109; DLB 92; JRDA; SATA 18

Seton-Thompson, Ernest
See Seton, Ernest (Evan) Thompson

Settle, Mary Lee 1918- .... **CLC 19, 61**
See also CA 89-92; CAAS 1; CANR 44;
DLB 6

Seuphor, Michel
See Arp, Jean

**Sevigne, Marie (de Rabutin-Chantal) Marquise
de** 1626-1696 .... **LC 11**

Sexton, Anne (Harvey)
1928-1974 .... **CLC 2, 4, 6, 8, 10, 15, 53;
DA; PC 2; WLC**
See also CA 1-4R; 53-56; CABS 2;
CANR 3, 36; CDALB 1941-1968; DLB 5;
MTCW; SATA 10

Shaara, Michael (Joseph Jr.)
1929-1988 .... **CLC 15**
See also AITN 1; CA 102; DLBY 83

Shackleton, C. C.
See Aldiss, Brian W(ilson)

Shacochis, Bob .... **CLC 39**
See also Shacochis, Robert G.

Shacochis, Robert G. 1951-
See Shacochis, Bob
See also CA 119; 124

Shaffer, Anthony (Joshua) 1926- .... **CLC 19**
See also CA 110; 116; DLB 13

Shaffer, Peter (Levin)
1926- .... **CLC 5, 14, 18, 37, 60**
See also CA 25-28R; CANR 25;
CDBLB 1960 to Present; DLB 13;
MTCW

Shakey, Bernard
See Young, Neil

Shalamov, Varlam (Tikhonovich)
1907(?)-1982 .... **CLC 18**
See also CA 129; 105

Shamlu, Ahmad 1925- .... **CLC 10**

Shammas, Anton 1951- .... **CLC 55**

Shange, Ntozake
1948- .... **CLC 8, 25, 38, 74; BLC; DC 3**
See also AAYA 9; BW 2; CA 85-88;
CABS 3; CANR 27; DLB 38; MTCW

Shanley, John Patrick 1950- .... **CLC 75**
See also CA 128; 133

Shapcott, Thomas William 1935- ... **CLC 38**
See also CA 69-72

Shapiro, Jane .... **CLC 76**

Shapiro, Karl (Jay) 1913- .. **CLC 4, 8, 15, 53**
See also CA 1-4R; CAAS 6; CANR 1, 36;
DLB 48; MTCW

Sharp, William 1855-1905 .... **TCLC 39**

Sharpe, Thomas Ridley 1928-
See Sharpe, Tom
See also CA 114; 122

Sharpe, Tom .... **CLC 36**
See also Sharpe, Thomas Ridley
See also DLB 14

Shaw, Bernard .... **TCLC 45**
See also Shaw, George Bernard
See also BW 1

Shaw, G. Bernard
See Shaw, George Bernard

Shaw, George Bernard
1856-1950 .... **TCLC 3, 9, 21; DA; WLC**
See also Shaw, Bernard
See also CA 104; 128; CDBLB 1914-1945;
DLB 10, 57; MTCW

Shaw, Henry Wheeler
1818-1885 .... **NCLC 15**
See also DLB 11

Shaw, Irwin 1913-1984 .... **CLC 7, 23, 34**
See also AITN 1; CA 13-16R; 112;
CANR 21; CDALB 1941-1968; DLB 6,
102; DLBY 84; MTCW

Shaw, Robert 1927-1978 .... **CLC 5**
See also AITN 1; CA 1-4R; 81-84;
CANR 4; DLB 13, 14

Shaw, T. E.
See Lawrence, T(homas) E(dward)

Shawn, Wallace 1943- .... **CLC 41**
See also CA 112

Sheed, Wilfrid (John Joseph)
1930- .... **CLC 2, 4, 10, 53**
See also CA 65-68; CANR 30; DLB 6;
MTCW

Sheldon, Alice Hastings Bradley
1915(?)-1987
See Tiptree, James, Jr.
See also CA 108; 122; CANR 34; MTCW

Sheldon, John
See Bloch, Robert (Albert)

Shelley, Mary Wollstonecraft (Godwin)
1797-1851 .... **NCLC 14; DA; WLC**
See also CDBLB 1789-1832; DLB 110, 116;
SATA 29

Shelley, Percy Bysshe
1792-1822 .... **NCLC 18; DA; WLC**
See also CDBLB 1789-1832; DLB 96, 110

Shepard, Jim 1956-............. **CLC 36**
See also CA 137

Shepard, Lucius 1947-........... **CLC 34**
See also CA 128; 141

Shepard, Sam
1943-........ **CLC 4, 6, 17, 34, 41, 44**
See also AAYA 1; CA 69-72; CABS 3;
CANR 22; DLB 7; MTCW

Shepherd, Michael
See Ludlum, Robert

Sherburne, Zoa (Morin) 1912-...... **CLC 30**
See also CA 1-4R; CANR 3, 37; MAICYA;
SAAS 18; SATA 3

Sheridan, Frances 1724-1766........ **LC 7**
See also DLB 39, 84

Sheridan, Richard Brinsley
1751-1816 ... **NCLC 5; DA; DC 1; WLC**
See also CDBLB 1660-1789; DLB 89

Sherman, Jonathan Marc.......... **CLC 55**

Sherman, Martin 1941(?)-......... **CLC 19**
See also CA 116; 123

Sherwin, Judith Johnson 1936-... **CLC 7, 15**
See also CA 25-28R; CANR 34

Sherwood, Frances 1940-......... **CLC 81**

Sherwood, Robert E(mmet)
1896-1955 .... **TCLC 3**
See also CA 104; DLB 7, 26

Shestov, Lev 1866-1938.......... **TCLC 56**

Shiel, M(atthew) P(hipps)
1865-1947 .... **TCLC 8**
See also CA 106

Shiga, Naoya 1883-1971.......... **CLC 33**
See also CA 101; 33-36R

Shilts, Randy 1951-1994 .... **CLC 85**
See also CA 115; 127; 144; CANR 45

Shimazaki Haruki 1872-1943
See Shimazaki Toson
See also CA 105; 134

Shimazaki Toson................. **TCLC 5**
See also Shimazaki Haruki

Sholokhov, Mikhail (Aleksandrovich)
1905-1984 .... **CLC 7, 15**
See also CA 101; 112; MTCW; SATA 36

Shone, Patric
See Hanley, James

Shreve, Susan Richards 1939-...... **CLC 23**
See also CA 49-52; CAAS 5; CANR 5, 38;
MAICYA; SATA 41, 46

Shue, Larry 1946-1985........... **CLC 52**
See also CA 145; 117

Shu-Jen, Chou 1881-1936
See Hsun, Lu
See also CA 104

Shulman, Alix Kates 1932- ...... **CLC 2, 10**
See also CA 29-32R; CANR 43; SATA 7

Shuster, Joe 1914- .... **CLC 21**

Shute, Nevil...................... **CLC 30**
See also Norway, Nevil Shute

Shuttle, Penelope (Diane) 1947- ..... **CLC 7**
See also CA 93-96; CANR 39; DLB 14, 40

Sidney, Mary 1561-1621 .... **LC 19**

Sidney, Sir Philip 1554-1586.... **LC 19; DA**
See also CDBLB Before 1660

Siegel, Jerome 1914- .... **CLC 21**
See also CA 116

Siegel, Jerry
See Siegel, Jerome

Sienkiewicz, Henryk (Adam Alexander Pius)
1846-1916 .... **TCLC 3**
See also CA 104; 134

Sierra, Gregorio Martinez
See Martinez Sierra, Gregorio

Sierra, Maria (de la O'LeJarraga) Martinez
See Martinez Sierra, Maria (de la
O'LeJarraga)

Sigal, Clancy 1926-............... **CLC 7**
See also CA 1-4R

Sigourney, Lydia Howard (Huntley)
1791-1865 .... **NCLC 21**
See also DLB 1, 42, 73

Siguenza y Gongora, Carlos de
1645-1700 .... **LC 8**

Sigurjonsson, Johann 1880-1919... **TCLC 27**

Sikelianos, Angelos 1884-1951 .... **TCLC 39**

Silkin, Jon 1930- .... **CLC 2, 6, 43**
See also CA 5-8R; CAAS 5; DLB 27

Silko, Leslie (Marmon)
1948-.................. **CLC 23, 74; DA**
See also CA 115; 122; CANR 45; DLB 143

Sillanpaa, Frans Eemil 1888-1964... **CLC 19**
See also CA 129; 93-96; MTCW

Sillitoe, Alan
1928-.......... **CLC 1, 3, 6, 10, 19, 57**
See also AITN 1; CA 9-12R; CAAS 2;
CANR 8, 26; CDBLB 1960 to Present;
DLB 14, 139; MTCW; SATA 61

Silone, Ignazio 1900-1978 .... **CLC 4**
See also CA 25-28; 81-84; CANR 34;
CAP 2; MTCW

Silver, Joan Micklin 1935- .... **CLC 20**
See also CA 114; 121

Silver, Nicholas
See Faust, Frederick (Schiller)

Silverberg, Robert 1935- .... **CLC 7**
See also CA 1-4R; CAAS 3; CANR 1, 20,
36; DLB 8; MAICYA; MTCW; SATA 13

Silverstein, Alvin 1933- .... **CLC 17**
See also CA 49-52; CANR 2; CLR 25;
JRDA; MAICYA; SATA 8, 69

Silverstein, Virginia B(arbara Opshelor)
1937- .... **CLC 17**
See also CA 49-52; CANR 2; CLR 25;
JRDA; MAICYA; SATA 8, 69

Sim, Georges
See Simenon, Georges (Jacques Christian)

Simak, Clifford D(onald)
1904-1988 .... **CLC 1, 55**
See also CA 1-4R; 125; CANR 1, 35;
DLB 8; MTCW; SATA 56

Simenon, Georges (Jacques Christian)
1903-1989 .... **CLC 1, 2, 3, 8, 18, 47**
See also CA 85-88; 129; CANR 35;
DLB 72; DLBY 89; MTCW

Simic, Charles 1938-... **CLC 6, 9, 22, 49, 68**
See also CA 29-32R; CAAS 4; CANR 12,
33; DLB 105

Simmons, Charles (Paul) 1924-..... **CLC 57**
See also CA 89-92

Simmons, Dan 1948-.............. **CLC 44**
See also CA 138

Simmons, James (Stewart Alexander)
1933-....................... **CLC 43**
See also CA 105; DLB 40

Simms, William Gilmore
1806-1870 .... **NCLC 3**
See also DLB 3, 30, 59, 73

Simon, Carly 1945-.............. **CLC 26**
See also CA 105

Simon, Claude 1913-....... **CLC 4, 9, 15, 39**
See also CA 89-92; CANR 33; DLB 83;
MTCW

Simon, (Marvin) Neil
1927-........... **CLC 6, 11, 31, 39, 70**
See also AITN 1; CA 21-24R; CANR 26;
DLB 7; MTCW

Simon, Paul 1942(?)- .... **CLC 17**
See also CA 116

Simonon, Paul 1956(?)- .... **CLC 30**

Simpson, Harriette
See Arnow, Harriette (Louisa) Simpson

Simpson, Louis (Aston Marantz)
1923-.................. **CLC 4, 7, 9, 32**
See also CA 1-4R; CAAS 4; CANR 1;
DLB 5; MTCW

Simpson, Mona (Elizabeth) 1957-... **CLC 44**
See also CA 122; 135

Simpson, N(orman) F(rederick)
1919- .... **CLC 29**
See also CA 13-16R; DLB 13

Sinclair, Andrew (Annandale)
1935-...................... **CLC 2, 14**
See also CA 9-12R; CAAS 5; CANR 14, 38;
DLB 14; MTCW

Sinclair, Emil
See Hesse, Hermann

Sinclair, Iain 1943-.............. **CLC 76**
See also CA 132

Sinclair, Iain MacGregor
See Sinclair, Iain

Sinclair, Mary Amelia St. Clair 1865(?)-1946
See Sinclair, May
See also CA 104

Sinclair, May................. **TCLC 3, 11**
See also Sinclair, Mary Amelia St. Clair
See also DLB 36, 135

Sinclair, Upton (Beall)
1878-1968 ...... **CLC 1, 11, 15, 63; DA;
WLC**
See also CA 5-8R; 25-28R; CANR 7;
CDALB 1929-1941; DLB 9; MTCW;
SATA 9

Singer, Isaac
See Singer, Isaac Bashevis

Singer, Isaac Bashevis
1904-1991 .... **CLC 1, 3, 6, 9, 11, 15, 23,
38, 69; DA; SSC 3; WLC**
See also AITN 1, 2; CA 1-4R; 134;
CANR 1, 39; CDALB 1941-1968; CLR 1;
DLB 6, 28, 52; DLBY 91; JRDA;
MAICYA; MTCW; SATA 3, 27;
SATA-Obit 68

Souster, (Holmes) Raymond
1921- .... CLC 5, 14
See also CA 13-16R; CAAS 14; CANR 13,
29; DLB 88; SATA 63

Southern, Terry 1926- .... CLC 7
See also CA 1-4R; CANR 1; DLB 2

Southey, Robert 1774-1843 .... NCLC 8
See also DLB 93, 107, 142; SATA 54

Southworth, Emma Dorothy Eliza Nevitte
1819-1899 .... NCLC 26

Souza, Ernest
See Scott, Evelyn

Soyinka, Wole
1934- ...... CLC 3, 5, 14, 36, 44; BLC;
DA; DC 2; WLC
See also BW 2; CA 13-16R; CANR 27, 39;
DLB 125; MTCW

Spackman, W(illiam) M(ode)
1905-1990 .... CLC 46
See also CA 81-84; 132

Spacks, Barry 1931- .... CLC 14
See also CA 29-32R; CANR 33; DLB 105

Spanidou, Irini 1946- .... CLC 44

Spark, Muriel (Sarah)
1918- .... CLC 2, 3, 5, 8, 13, 18, 40;
SSC 10
See also CA 5-8R; CANR 12, 36;
CDBLB 1945-1960; DLB 15, 139; MTCW

Spaulding, Douglas
See Bradbury, Ray (Douglas)

Spaulding, Leonard
See Bradbury, Ray (Douglas)

Spence, J. A. D.
See Eliot, T(homas) S(tearns)

Spencer, Elizabeth 1921- .... CLC 22
See also CA 13-16R; CANR 32; DLB 6;
MTCW; SATA 14

Spencer, Leonard G.
See Silverberg, Robert

Spencer, Scott 1945- .... CLC 30
See also CA 113; DLBY 86

Spender, Stephen (Harold)
1909- .... CLC 1, 2, 5, 10, 41
See also CA 9-12R; CANR 31;
CDBLB 1945-1960; DLB 20; MTCW

Spengler, Oswald (Arnold Gottfried)
1880-1936 .... TCLC 25
See also CA 118

Spenser, Edmund
1552(?)-1599 .... LC 5; DA; PC 8; WLC
See also CDBLB Before 1660

Spicer, Jack 1925-1965 ...... CLC 8, 18, 72
See also CA 85-88; DLB 5, 16

Spiegelman, Art 1948- .... CLC 76
See also AAYA 10; CA 125; CANR 41

Spielberg, Peter 1929- .... CLC 6
See also CA 5-8R; CANR 4; DLBY 81

Spielberg, Steven 1947- .... CLC 20
See also AAYA 8; CA 77-80; CANR 32;
SATA 32

Spillane, Frank Morrison 1918-
See Spillane, Mickey
See also CA 25-28R; CANR 28; MTCW;
SATA 66

Spillane, Mickey .... CLC 3, 13
See also Spillane, Frank Morrison

Spinoza, Benedictus de 1632-1677 .... LC 9

Spinrad, Norman (Richard) 1940-... CLC 46
See also CA 37-40R; CAAS 19; CANR 20;
DLB 8

Spitteler, Carl (Friedrich Georg)
1845-1924 .... TCLC 12
See also CA 109; DLB 129

Spivack, Kathleen (Romola Drucker)
1938- .... CLC 6
See also CA 49-52

Spoto, Donald 1941- .... CLC 39
See also CA 65-68; CANR 11

Springsteen, Bruce (F.) 1949- ...... CLC 17
See also CA 111

Spurling, Hilary 1940- .... CLC 34
See also CA 104; CANR 25

Squires, (James) Radcliffe
1917-1993 .... CLC 51
See also CA 1-4R; 140; CANR 6, 21

Srivastava, Dhanpat Rai 1880(?)-1936
See Premchand
See also CA 118

Stacy, Donald
See Pohl, Frederik

Stael, Germaine de
See Stael-Holstein, Anne Louise Germaine
Necker Baronn
See also DLB 119

Stael-Holstein, Anne Louise Germaine Necker
Baronn 1766-1817 .... NCLC 3
See also Stael, Germaine de

Stafford, Jean 1915-1979 ... CLC 4, 7, 19, 68
See also CA 1-4R; 85-88; CANR 3; DLB 2;
MTCW; SATA 22

Stafford, William (Edgar)
1914-1993 .... CLC 4, 7, 29
See also CA 5-8R; 142; CAAS 3; CANR 5,
22; DLB 5

Staines, Trevor
See Brunner, John (Kilian Houston)

Stairs, Gordon
See Austin, Mary (Hunter)

Stannard, Martin 1947- .... CLC 44
See also CA 142

Stanton, Maura 1946- .... CLC 9
See also CA 89-92; CANR 15; DLB 120

Stanton, Schuyler
See Baum, L(yman) Frank

Stapledon, (William) Olaf
1886-1950 .... TCLC 22
See also CA 111; DLB 15

Starbuck, George (Edwin) 1931-.... CLC 53
See also CA 21-24R; CANR 23

Stark, Richard
See Westlake, Donald E(dwin)

Staunton, Schuyler
See Baum, L(yman) Frank

Stead, Christina (Ellen)
1902-1983 .... CLC 2, 5, 8, 32, 80
See also CA 13-16R; 109; CANR 33, 40;
MTCW

Stead, William Thomas
1849-1912 .... TCLC 48

Steele, Richard 1672-1729 .... LC 18
See also CDBLB 1660-1789; DLB 84, 101

Steele, Timothy (Reid) 1948-....... CLC 45
See also CA 93-96; CANR 16; DLB 120

Steffens, (Joseph) Lincoln
1866-1936 .... TCLC 20
See also CA 117

Stegner, Wallace (Earle)
1909-1993 .... CLC 9, 49, 81
See also AITN 1; BEST 90:3; CA 1-4R;
141; CAAS 9; CANR 1, 21; DLB 9;
DLBY 93; MTCW

Stein, Gertrude
1874-1946 ...... TCLC 1, 6, 28, 48; DA;
WLC
See also CA 104; 132; CDALB 1917-1929;
DLB 4, 54, 86; MTCW

Steinbeck, John (Ernst)
1902-1968 ...... CLC 1, 5, 9, 13, 21, 34,
45, 75; DA; SSC 11; WLC
See also AAYA 12; CA 1-4R; 25-28R;
CANR 1, 35; CDALB 1929-1941; DLB 7,
9; DLBD 2; MTCW; SATA 9

Steinem, Gloria 1934-............. CLC 63
See also CA 53-56; CANR 28; MTCW

Steiner, George 1929-............. CLC 24
See also CA 73-76; CANR 31; DLB 67;
MTCW; SATA 62

Steiner, K. Leslie
See Delany, Samuel R(ay, Jr.)

Steiner, Rudolf 1861-1925........ TCLC 13
See also CA 107

Stendhal
1783-1842 ..... NCLC 23, 46; DA; WLC
See also DLB 119

Stephen, Leslie 1832-1904........ TCLC 23
See also CA 123; DLB 57, 144

Stephen, Sir Leslie
See Stephen, Leslie

Stephen, Virginia
See Woolf, (Adeline) Virginia

Stephens, James 1882(?)-1950...... TCLC 4
See also CA 104; DLB 19

Stephens, Reed
See Donaldson, Stephen R.

Steptoe, Lydia
See Barnes, Djuna

Sterchi, Beat 1949-............... CLC 65

Sterling, Brett
See Bradbury, Ray (Douglas); Hamilton,
Edmond

Sterling, Bruce 1954-............. CLC 72
See also CA 119; CANR 44

Sterling, George 1869-1926 .... TCLC 20
See also CA 117; DLB 54

Stern, Gerald 1925-............... CLC 40
See also CA 81-84; CANR 28; DLB 105

Stern, Richard (Gustave) 1928-... CLC 4, 39
See also CA 1-4R; CANR 1, 25; DLBY 87

Sternberg, Josef von 1894-1969..... CLC 20
See also CA 81-84

Sterne, Laurence
1713-1768 . . . . **LC 2; DA; WLC**
See also CDBLB 1660-1789; DLB 39

Sternheim, (William Adolf) Carl
1878-1942 . . . . **TCLC 8**
See also CA 105; DLB 56, 118

Stevens, Mark 1951- . . . . **CLC 34**
See also CA 122

Stevens, Wallace
1879-1955 . . . . **TCLC 3, 12, 45; DA;**
PC 6; WLC
See also CA 104; 124; CDALB 1929-1941;
DLB 54; MTCW

Stevenson, Anne (Katharine)
1933- . . . . **CLC 7, 33**
See also CA 17-20R; CAAS 9; CANR 9, 33;
DLB 40; MTCW

Stevenson, Robert Louis (Balfour)
1850-1894 . . . . **NCLC 5, 14; DA;**
SSC 11; WLC
See also CDBLB 1890-1914; CLR 10, 11;
DLB 18, 57, 141; JRDA; MAICYA;
YABC 2

Stewart, J(ohn) I(nnes) M(ackintosh)
1906- . . . . **CLC 7, 14, 32**
See also CA 85-88; CAAS 3; MTCW

Stewart, Mary (Florence Elinor)
1916- . . . . **CLC 7, 35**
See also CA 1-4R; CANR 1; SATA 12

Stewart, Mary Rainbow
See Stewart, Mary (Florence Elinor)

Stifle, June
See Campbell, Maria

Stifter, Adalbert 1805-1868 . . . . . . **NCLC 41**
See also DLB 133

Still, James 1906- . . . . **CLC 49**
See also CA 65-68; CAAS 17; CANR 10,
26; DLB 9; SATA 29

Sting
See Sumner, Gordon Matthew

Stirling, Arthur
See Sinclair, Upton (Beall)

Stitt, Milan 1941- . . . . **CLC 29**
See also CA 69-72

Stockton, Francis Richard 1834-1902
See Stockton, Frank R.
See also CA 108; 137; MAICYA; SATA 44

Stockton, Frank R. . . . . **TCLC 47**
See also Stockton, Francis Richard
See also DLB 42, 74; SATA 32

Stoddard, Charles
See Kuttner, Henry

Stoker, Abraham 1847-1912
See Stoker, Bram
See also CA 105; DA; SATA 29

Stoker, Bram . . . . **TCLC 8; WLC**
See also Stoker, Abraham
See also CDBLB 1890-1914; DLB 36, 70

Stolz, Mary (Slattery) 1920- . . . . **CLC 12**
See also AAYA 8; AITN 1; CA 5-8R;
CANR 13, 41; JRDA; MAICYA;
SAAS 3; SATA 10, 71

Stone, Irving 1903-1989 . . . . **CLC 7**
See also AITN 1; CA 1-4R; 129; CAAS 3;
CANR 1, 23; MTCW; SATA 3;
SATA-Obit 64

Stone, Oliver 1946- . . . . **CLC 73**
See also CA 110

Stone, Robert (Anthony)
1937- . . . . **CLC 5, 23, 42**
See also CA 85-88; CANR 23; MTCW

Stone, Zachary
See Follett, Ken(neth Martin)

Stoppard, Tom
1937- . . . . . . **CLC 1, 3, 4, 5, 8, 15, 29, 34,**
63; DA; WLC
See also CA 81-84; CANR 39;
CDBLB 1960 to Present; DLB 13;
DLBY 85; MTCW

Storey, David (Malcolm)
1933- . . . . **CLC 2, 4, 5, 8**
See also CA 81-84; CANR 36; DLB 13, 14;
MTCW

Storm, Hyemeyohsts 1935- . . . . **CLC 3**
See also CA 81-84; CANR 45

Storm, (Hans) Theodor (Woldsen)
1817-1888 . . . . **NCLC 1**

Storni, Alfonsina
1892-1938 . . . . **TCLC 5; HLC**
See also CA 104; 131; HW

Stout, Rex (Todhunter) 1886-1975 . . . **CLC 3**
See also AITN 2; CA 61-64

Stow, (Julian) Randolph 1935- . . **CLC 23, 48**
See also CA 13-16R; CANR 33; MTCW

Stowe, Harriet (Elizabeth) Beecher
1811-1896 . . . . **NCLC 3; DA; WLC**
See also CDALB 1865-1917; DLB 1, 12, 42,
74; JRDA; MAICYA; YABC 1

Strachey, (Giles) Lytton
1880-1932 . . . . **TCLC 12**
See also CA 110; DLBD 10

Strand, Mark 1934- . . . . . . **CLC 6, 18, 41, 71**
See also CA 21-24R; CANR 40; DLB 5;
SATA 41

Straub, Peter (Francis) 1943- . . . . . . **CLC 28**
See also BEST 89:1; CA 85-88; CANR 28;
DLBY 84; MTCW

Strauss, Botho 1944- . . . . **CLC 22**
See also DLB 124

Streatfeild, (Mary) Noel
1895(?)-1986 . . . . **CLC 21**
See also CA 81-84; 120; CANR 31;
CLR 17; MAICYA; SATA 20, 48

Stribling, T(homas) S(igismund)
1881-1965 . . . . **CLC 23**
See also CA 107; DLB 9

Strindberg, (Johan) August
1849-1912 . . . . . . **TCLC 1, 8, 21, 47; DA;**
WLC
See also CA 104; 135

Stringer, Arthur 1874-1950 . . . . **TCLC 37**
See also DLB 92

Stringer, David
See Roberts, Keith (John Kingston)

Strugatskii, Arkadii (Natanovich)
1925-1991 . . . . **CLC 27**
See also CA 106; 135

Strugatskii, Boris (Natanovich)
1933- . . . . **CLC 27**
See also CA 106

Strummer, Joe 1953(?)- . . . . **CLC 30**

Stuart, Don A.
See Campbell, John W(ood, Jr.)

Stuart, Ian
See MacLean, Alistair (Stuart)

Stuart, Jesse (Hilton)
1906-1984 . . . . **CLC 1, 8, 11, 14, 34**
See also CA 5-8R; 112; CANR 31; DLB 9,
48, 102; DLBY 84; SATA 2, 36

Sturgeon, Theodore (Hamilton)
1918-1985 . . . . **CLC 22, 39**
See also Queen, Ellery
See also CA 81-84; 116; CANR 32; DLB 8;
DLBY 85; MTCW

Sturges, Preston 1898-1959 . . . . **TCLC 48**
See also CA 114; DLB 26

Styron, William
1925- . . . . **CLC 1, 3, 5, 11, 15, 60**
See also BEST 90:4; CA 5-8R; CANR 6, 33;
CDALB 1968-1988; DLB 2, 143;
DLBY 80; MTCW

Suarez Lynch, B.
See Bioy Casares, Adolfo; Borges, Jorge
Luis

Su Chien 1884-1918
See Su Man-shu
See also CA 123

Sudermann, Hermann 1857-1928 . . **TCLC 15**
See also CA 107; DLB 118

Sue, Eugene 1804-1857 . . . . **NCLC 1**
See also DLB 119

Sueskind, Patrick 1949- . . . . **CLC 44**
See also Suskind, Patrick

Sukenick, Ronald 1932- . . . . . **CLC 3, 4, 6, 48**
See also CA 25-28R; CAAS 8; CANR 32;
DLBY 81

Suknaski, Andrew 1942- . . . . **CLC 19**
See also CA 101; DLB 53

Sullivan, Vernon
See Vian, Boris

Sully Prudhomme 1839-1907 . . . . . . **TCLC 31**

Su Man-shu . . . . **TCLC 24**
See also Su Chien

Summerforest, Ivy B.
See Kirkup, James

Summers, Andrew James 1942- . . . . . **CLC 26**

Summers, Andy
See Summers, Andrew James

Summers, Hollis (Spurgeon, Jr.)
1916- . . . . **CLC 10**
See also CA 5-8R; CANR 3; DLB 6

Summers, (Alphonsus Joseph-Mary Augustus)
Montague 1880-1948 . . . . **TCLC 16**
See also CA 118

Sumner, Gordon Matthew 1951- . . . . **CLC 26**

Surtees, Robert Smith
1803-1864 . . . . **NCLC 14**
See also DLB 21

Susann, Jacqueline 1921-1974 . . . . **CLC 3**
See also AITN 1; CA 65-68; 53-56; MTCW

Torsvan, Traven
See Traven, B.

Tournier, Michel (Edouard)
1924- .... **CLC 6, 23, 36**
See also CA 49-52; CANR 3, 36; DLB 83;
MTCW; SATA 23

Tournimparte, Alessandra
See Ginzburg, Natalia

Towers, Ivar
See Kornbluth, C(yril) M.

Townsend, Sue 1946- .... **CLC 61**
See also CA 119; 127; MTCW; SATA 48,
55

Townshend, Peter (Dennis Blandford)
1945- .... **CLC 17, 42**
See also CA 107

Tozzi, Federigo 1883-1920....... **TCLC 31**

Traill, Catharine Parr
1802-1899 .... **NCLC 31**
See also DLB 99

Trakl, Georg 1887-1914.......... **TCLC 5**
See also CA 104

Transtroemer, Tomas (Goesta)
1931- .... **CLC 52, 65**
See also CA 117; 129; CAAS 17

Transtromer, Tomas Gosta
See Transtroemer, Tomas (Goesta)

Traven, B. (?)-1969............. **CLC 8, 11**
See also CA 19-20; 25-28R; CAP 2; DLB 9,
56; MTCW

Treitel, Jonathan 1959- .... **CLC 70**

Tremain, Rose 1943-.............. **CLC 42**
See also CA 97-100; CANR 44; DLB 14

Tremblay, Michel 1942-........... **CLC 29**
See also CA 116; 128; DLB 60; MTCW

Trevanian........................ CLC 29
See also Whitaker, Rod(ney)

Trevor, Glen
See Hilton, James

Trevor, William
1928- .... **CLC 7, 9, 14, 25, 71**
See also Cox, William Trevor
See also DLB 14, 139

Trifonov, Yuri (Valentinovich)
1925-1981 .... **CLC 45**
See also CA 126; 103; MTCW

Trilling, Lionel 1905-1975 .... **CLC 9, 11, 24**
See also CA 9-12R; 61-64; CANR 10;
DLB 28, 63; MTCW

Trimball, W. H.
See Mencken, H(enry) L(ouis)

Tristan
See Gomez de la Serna, Ramon

Tristram
See Housman, A(lfred) E(dward)

Trogdon, William (Lewis) 1939-
See Heat-Moon, William Least
See also CA 115; 119

Trollope, Anthony
1815-1882 ...... **NCLC 6, 33; DA; WLC**
See also CDBLB 1832-1890; DLB 21, 57;
SATA 22

Trollope, Frances 1779-1863 ..... **NCLC 30**
See also DLB 21

Trotsky, Leon 1879-1940........ **TCLC 22**
See also CA 118

Trotter (Cockburn), Catharine
1679-1749 .... **LC 8**
See also DLB 84

Trout, Kilgore
See Farmer, Philip Jose

Trow, George W. S. 1943-........ **CLC 52**
See also CA 126

Troyat, Henri 1911-............. **CLC 23**
See also CA 45-48; CANR 2, 33; MTCW

Trudeau, G(arretson) B(eekman) 1948-
See Trudeau, Garry B.
See also CA 81-84; CANR 31; SATA 35

Trudeau, Garry B................. CLC 12
See also Trudeau, G(arretson) B(eekman)
See also AAYA 10; AITN 2

Truffaut, Francois 1932-1984...... **CLC 20**
See also CA 81-84; 113; CANR 34

Trumbo, Dalton 1905-1976 .... **CLC 19**
See also CA 21-24R; 69-72; CANR 10;
DLB 26

Trumbull, John 1750-1831....... **NCLC 30**
See also DLB 31

Trundlett, Helen B.
See Eliot, T(homas) S(tearns)

Tryon, Thomas 1926-1991 ...... **CLC 3, 11**
See also AITN 1; CA 29-32R; 135;
CANR 32; MTCW

Tryon, Tom
See Tryon, Thomas

Ts'ao Hsueh-ch'in 1715(?)-1763....... **LC 1**

Tsushima, Shuji 1909-1948
See Dazai, Osamu
See also CA 107

Tsvetaeva (Efron), Marina (Ivanovna)
1892-1941 .... **TCLC 7, 35**
See also CA 104; 128; MTCW

Tuck, Lily 1938-................ **CLC 70**
See also CA 139

Tu Fu 712-770.................... **PC 9**

Tunis, John R(oberts) 1889-1975 ... **CLC 12**
See also CA 61-64; DLB 22; JRDA;
MAICYA; SATA 30, 37

Tuohy, Frank..................... CLC 37
See also Tuohy, John Francis
See also DLB 14, 139

Tuohy, John Francis 1925-
See Tuohy, Frank
See also CA 5-8R; CANR 3

Turco, Lewis (Putnam) 1934- ... **CLC 11, 63**
See also CA 13-16R; CANR 24; DLBY 84

Turgenev, Ivan
1818-1883 ...... **NCLC 21; DA; SSC 7;
WLC**

Turgot, Anne-Robert-Jacques
1727-1781 .... **LC 26**

Turner, Frederick 1943-.......... **CLC 48**
See also CA 73-76; CAAS 10; CANR 12,
30; DLB 40

Tutu, Desmond M(pilo)
1931- .... **CLC 80; BLC**
See also BW 1; CA 125

Tutuola, Amos 1920- ... **CLC 5, 14, 29; BLC**
See also BW 2; CA 9-12R; CANR 27;
DLB 125; MTCW

Twain, Mark
... **TCLC 6, 12, 19, 36, 48; SSC 6; WLC**
See also Clemens, Samuel Langhorne
See also DLB 11, 12, 23, 64, 74

Tyler, Anne
1941- .... **CLC 7, 11, 18, 28, 44, 59**
See also BEST 89:1; CA 9-12R; CANR 11,
33; DLB 6, 143; DLBY 82; MTCW;
SATA 7

Tyler, Royall 1757-1826.......... **NCLC 3**
See also DLB 37

Tynan, Katharine 1861-1931 ...... **TCLC 3**
See also CA 104

Tyutchev, Fyodor 1803-1873 ..... **NCLC 34**

Tzara, Tristan .... CLC 47
See also Rosenfeld, Samuel

Uhry, Alfred 1936-............... **CLC 55**
See also CA 127; 133

Ulf, Haerved
See Strindberg, (Johan) August

Ulf, Harved
See Strindberg, (Johan) August

Ulibarri, Sabine R(eyes) 1919- ..... **CLC 83**
See also CA 131; DLB 82; HW

Unamuno (y Jugo), Miguel de
1864-1936 .... **TCLC 2, 9; HLC; SSC 11**
See also CA 104; 131; DLB 108; HW;
MTCW

Undercliffe, Errol
See Campbell, (John) Ramsey

Underwood, Miles
See Glassco, John

Undset, Sigrid
1882-1949 .... **TCLC 3; DA; WLC**
See also CA 104; 129; MTCW

Ungaretti, Giuseppe
1888-1970 .... **CLC 7, 11, 15**
See also CA 19-20; 25-28R; CAP 2;
DLB 114

Unger, Douglas 1952-............. **CLC 34**
See also CA 130

Unsworth, Barry (Forster) 1930-.... **CLC 76**
See also CA 25-28R; CANR 30

Updike, John (Hoyer)
1932- ...... **CLC 1, 2, 3, 5, 7, 9, 13, 15,
23, 34, 43, 70; DA; SSC 13; WLC**
See also CA 1-4R; CABS 1; CANR 4, 33;
CDALB 1968-1988; DLB 2, 5, 143;
DLBD 3; DLBY 80, 82; MTCW

Upshaw, Margaret Mitchell
See Mitchell, Margaret (Munnerlyn)

Upton, Mark
See Sanders, Lawrence

Urdang, Constance (Henriette)
1922- .... **CLC 47**
See also CA 21-24R; CANR 9, 24

Uriel, Henry
See Faust, Frederick (Schiller)

Uris, Leon (Marcus) 1924-....... **CLC 7, 32**
See also AITN 1, 2; BEST 89:2; CA 1-4R;
CANR 1, 40; MTCW; SATA 49

Urmuz
See Codrescu, Andrei

Ustinov, Peter (Alexander) 1921- .... **CLC 1**
See also AITN 1; CA 13-16R; CANR 25;
DLB 13

Vaculik, Ludvik 1926- .... **CLC 7**
See also CA 53-56

Valdez, Luis (Miguel)
1940- .... **CLC 84; HLC**
See also CA 101; CANR 32; DLB 122; HW

Valenzuela, Luisa 1938-... **CLC 31; SSC 14**
See also CA 101; CANR 32; DLB 113; HW

Valera y Alcala-Galiano, Juan
1824-1905 .... **TCLC 10**
See also CA 106

Valery, (Ambroise) Paul (Toussaint Jules)
1871-1945 .... **TCLC 4, 15; PC 9**
See also CA 104; 122; MTCW

Valle-Inclan, Ramon (Maria) del
1866-1936 .... **TCLC 5; HLC**
See also CA 106; DLB 134

Vallejo, Antonio Buero
See Buero Vallejo, Antonio

Vallejo, Cesar (Abraham)
1892-1938 .... **TCLC 3, 56; HLC**
See also CA 105; HW

Valle Y Pena, Ramon del
See Valle-Inclan, Ramon (Maria) del

Van Ash, Cay 1918- .... **CLC 34**

Vanbrugh, Sir John 1664-1726 ...... **LC 21**
See also DLB 80

Van Campen, Karl
See Campbell, John W(ood, Jr.)

Vance, Gerald
See Silverberg, Robert

Vance, Jack .... **CLC 35**
See also Vance, John Holbrook
See also DLB 8

Vance, John Holbrook 1916-
See Queen, Ellery; Vance, Jack
See also CA 29-32R; CANR 17; MTCW

Van Den Bogarde, Derek Jules Gaspard Ulric
Niven 1921-
See Bogarde, Dirk
See also CA 77-80

Vandenburgh, Jane .... **CLC 59**

Vanderhaeghe, Guy 1951- .... **CLC 41**
See also CA 113

van der Post, Laurens (Jan) 1906-... **CLC 5**
See also CA 5-8R; CANR 35

van de Wetering, Janwillem 1931-.. **CLC 47**
See also CA 49-52; CANR 4

Van Dine, S. S. .... **TCLC 23**
See also Wright, Willard Huntington

Van Doren, Carl (Clinton)
1885-1950 .... **TCLC 18**
See also CA 111

Van Doren, Mark 1894-1972..... **CLC 6, 10**
See also CA 1-4R; 37-40R; CANR 3;
DLB 45; MTCW

Van Druten, John (William)
1901-1957 .... **TCLC 2**
See also CA 104; DLB 10

Van Duyn, Mona (Jane)
1921- .... **CLC 3, 7, 63**
See also CA 9-12R; CANR 7, 38; DLB 5

Van Dyne, Edith
See Baum, L(yman) Frank

van Itallie, Jean-Claude 1936-...... **CLC 3**
See also CA 45-48; CAAS 2; CANR 1;
DLB 7

van Ostaijen, Paul 1896-1928 ..... **TCLC 33**

Van Peebles, Melvin 1932- ...... **CLC 2, 20**
See also BW 2; CA 85-88; CANR 27

Vansittart, Peter 1920-........... **CLC 42**
See also CA 1-4R; CANR 3

Van Vechten, Carl 1880-1964 ...... **CLC 33**
See also CA 89-92; DLB 4, 9, 51

Van Vogt, A(lfred) E(lton) 1912-..... **CLC 1**
See also CA 21-24R; CANR 28; DLB 8;
SATA 14

Varda, Agnes 1928- .... **CLC 16**
See also CA 116; 122

Vargas Llosa, (Jorge) Mario (Pedro)
1936- .... **CLC 3, 6, 9, 10, 15, 31, 42, 85;**
DA; HLC
See also CA 73-76; CANR 18, 32, 42; HW;
MTCW

Vasiliu, Gheorghe 1881-1957
See Bacovia, George
See also CA 123

Vassa, Gustavus
See Equiano, Olaudah

Vassilikos, Vassilis 1933-......... **CLC 4, 8**
See also CA 81-84

Vaughan, Henry 1621-1695........ **LC 27**
See also DLB 131

Vaughn, Stephanie................ **CLC 62**

Vazov, Ivan (Minchov)
1850-1921 .... **TCLC 25**
See also CA 121

Veblen, Thorstein (Bunde)
1857-1929 .... **TCLC 31**
See also CA 115

Vega, Lope de 1562-1635........... **LC 23**

Venison, Alfred
See Pound, Ezra (Weston Loomis)

Verdi, Marie de
See Mencken, H(enry) L(ouis)

Verdu, Matilde
See Cela, Camilo Jose

Verga, Giovanni (Carmelo)
1840-1922 .... **TCLC 3**
See also CA 104; 123

Vergil 70B.C.-19B.C. .... **CMLC 9; DA**

Verhaeren, Emile (Adolphe Gustave)
1855-1916 .... **TCLC 12**
See also CA 109

Verlaine, Paul (Marie)
1844-1896 .... **NCLC 2; PC 2**

Verne, Jules (Gabriel)
1828-1905 .... **TCLC 6, 52**
See also CA 110; 131; DLB 123; JRDA;
MAICYA; SATA 21

Very, Jones 1813-1880.......... **NCLC 9**
See also DLB 1

Vesaas, Tarjei 1897-1970......... **CLC 48**
See also CA 29-32R

Vialis, Gaston
See Simenon, Georges (Jacques Christian)

Vian, Boris 1920-1959 .... **TCLC 9**
See also CA 106; DLB 72

Viaud, (Louis Marie) Julien 1850-1923
See Loti, Pierre
See also CA 107

Vicar, Henry
See Felsen, Henry Gregor

Vicker, Angus
See Felsen, Henry Gregor

Vidal, Gore
1925- ..... **CLC 2, 4, 6, 8, 10, 22, 33, 72**
See also AITN 1; BEST 90:2; CA 5-8R;
CANR 13, 45; DLB 6; MTCW

Viereck, Peter (Robert Edwin)
1916-.................... **CLC 4**
See also CA 1-4R; CANR 1; DLB 5

Vigny, Alfred (Victor) de
1797-1863 .... **NCLC 7**
See also DLB 119

Vilakazi, Benedict Wallet
1906-1947 .... **TCLC 37**

Villiers de l'Isle Adam, Jean Marie Mathias
Philippe Auguste Comte
1838-1889 .... **NCLC 3; SSC 14**
See also DLB 123

Vinci, Leonardo da 1452-1519...... **LC 12**

Vine, Barbara .... **CLC 50**
See also Rendell, Ruth (Barbara)
See also BEST 90:4

Vinge, Joan D(ennison) 1948-...... **CLC 30**
See also CA 93-96; SATA 36

Violis, G.
See Simenon, Georges (Jacques Christian)

Visconti, Luchino 1906-1976....... **CLC 16**
See also CA 81-84; 65-68; CANR 39

Vittorini, Elio 1908-1966...... **CLC 6, 9, 14**
See also CA 133; 25-28R

Vizinczey, Stephen 1933-.......... **CLC 40**
See also CA 128

Vliet, R(ussell) G(ordon)
1929-1984 .... **CLC 22**
See also CA 37-40R; 112; CANR 18

Vogau, Boris Andreyevich 1894-1937(?)
See Pilnyak, Boris
See also CA 123

Vogel, Paula A(nne) 1951-......... **CLC 76**
See also CA 108

Voight, Ellen Bryant 1943-........ **CLC 54**
See also CA 69-72; CANR 11, 29; DLB 120

Voigt, Cynthia 1942- .... **CLC 30**
See also AAYA 3; CA 106; CANR 18, 37,
40; CLR 13; JRDA; MAICYA;
SATA 33, 48, 79

Voinovich, Vladimir (Nikolaevich)
1932-.................... **CLC 10, 49**
See also CA 81-84; CAAS 12; CANR 33;
MTCW

Voloshinov, V. N.
See Bakhtin, Mikhail Mikhailovich

Warwick, Jarvis
See Garner, Hugh

Washington, Alex
See Harris, Mark

Washington, Booker T(aliaferro)
1856-1915 .... **TCLC 10; BLC**
See also BW 1; CA 114; 125; SATA 28

Washington, George 1732-1799 ...... **LC 25**
See also DLB 31

Wassermann, (Karl) Jakob
1873-1934 .... **TCLC 6**
See also CA 104; DLB 66

Wasserstein, Wendy
1950- .... **CLC 32, 59; DC 4**
See also CA 121; 129; CABS 3

Waterhouse, Keith (Spencer)
1929- .... **CLC 47**
See also CA 5-8R; CANR 38; DLB 13, 15;
MTCW

Waters, Roger 1944- .... **CLC 35**

Watkins, Frances Ellen
See Harper, Frances Ellen Watkins

Watkins, Gerrold
See Malzberg, Barry N(athaniel)

Watkins, Paul 1964- .... **CLC 55**
See also CA 132

Watkins, Vernon Phillips
1906-1967 .... **CLC 43**
See also CA 9-10; 25-28R; CAP 1; DLB 20

Watson, Irving S.
See Mencken, H(enry) L(ouis)

Watson, John H.
See Farmer, Philip Jose

Watson, Richard F.
See Silverberg, Robert

Waugh, Auberon (Alexander) 1939- ... **CLC 7**
See also CA 45-48; CANR 6, 22; DLB 14

Waugh, Evelyn (Arthur St. John)
1903-1966 ...... **CLC 1, 3, 8, 13, 19, 27,
44; DA; WLC**
See also CA 85-88; 25-28R; CANR 22;
CDBLB 1914-1945; DLB 15; MTCW

Waugh, Harriet 1944- .... **CLC 6**
See also CA 85-88; CANR 22

Ways, C. R.
See Blount, Roy (Alton), Jr.

Waystaff, Simon
See Swift, Jonathan

Webb, (Martha) Beatrice (Potter)
1858-1943 .... **TCLC 22**
See also Potter, Beatrice
See also CA 117

Webb, Charles (Richard) 1939- ...... **CLC 7**
See also CA 25-28R

Webb, James H(enry), Jr. 1946- .... **CLC 22**
See also CA 81-84

Webb, Mary (Gladys Meredith)
1881-1927 .... **TCLC 24**
See also CA 123; DLB 34

Webb, Mrs. Sidney
See Webb, (Martha) Beatrice (Potter)

Webb, Phyllis 1927- .... **CLC 18**
See also CA 104; CANR 23; DLB 53

Webb, Sidney (James)
1859-1947 .... **TCLC 22**
See also CA 117

Webber, Andrew Lloyd .... **CLC 21**
See also Lloyd Webber, Andrew

Weber, Lenora Mattingly
1895-1971 .... **CLC 12**
See also CA 19-20; 29-32R; CAP 1;
SATA 2, 26

Webster, John 1579(?)-1634(?) .... **DC 2**
See also CDBLB Before 1660; DA; DLB 58;
WLC

Webster, Noah 1758-1843 .... **NCLC 30**

Wedekind, (Benjamin) Frank(lin)
1864-1918 .... **TCLC 7**
See also CA 104; DLB 118

Weidman, Jerome 1913- .... **CLC 7**
See also AITN 2; CA 1-4R; CANR 1;
DLB 28

Weil, Simone (Adolphine)
1909-1943 .... **TCLC 23**
See also CA 117

Weinstein, Nathan
See West, Nathanael

Weinstein, Nathan von Wallenstein
See West, Nathanael

Weir, Peter (Lindsay) 1944- .... **CLC 20**
See also CA 113; 123

Weiss, Peter (Ulrich)
1916-1982 .... **CLC 3, 15, 51**
See also CA 45-48; 106; CANR 3; DLB 69,
124

Weiss, Theodore (Russell)
1916- .... **CLC 3, 8, 14**
See also CA 9-12R; CAAS 2; DLB 5

Welch, (Maurice) Denton
1915-1948 .... **TCLC 22**
See also CA 121

Welch, James 1940- .... **CLC 6, 14, 52**
See also CA 85-88; CANR 42

Weldon, Fay
1933(?)- .... **CLC 6, 9, 11, 19, 36, 59**
See also CA 21-24R; CANR 16;
CDBLB 1960 to Present; DLB 14;
MTCW

Wellek, Rene 1903- .... **CLC 28**
See also CA 5-8R; CAAS 7; CANR 8;
DLB 63

Weller, Michael 1942- .... **CLC 10, 53**
See also CA 85-88

Weller, Paul 1958- .... **CLC 26**

Wellershoff, Dieter 1925- .... **CLC 46**
See also CA 89-92; CANR 16, 37

Welles, (George) Orson
1915-1985 .... **CLC 20, 80**
See also CA 93-96; 117

Wellman, Mac 1945- .... **CLC 65**

Wellman, Manly Wade 1903-1986 .. **CLC 49**
See also CA 1-4R; 118; CANR 6, 16, 44;
SATA 6, 47

Wells, Carolyn 1869(?)-1942 ...... **TCLC 35**
See also CA 113; DLB 11

Wells, H(erbert) G(eorge)
1866-1946 .... **TCLC 6, 12, 19; DA;
SSC 6; WLC**
See also CA 110; 121; CDBLB 1914-1945;
DLB 34, 70; MTCW; SATA 20

Wells, Rosemary 1943- .... **CLC 12**
See also CA 85-88; CLR 16; MAICYA;
SAAS 1; SATA 18, 69

Welty, Eudora
1909- ...... **CLC 1, 2, 5, 14, 22, 33; DA;
SSC 1; WLC**
See also CA 9-12R; CABS 1; CANR 32;
CDALB 1941-1968; DLB 2, 102, 143;
DLBY 87; MTCW

Wen I-to 1899-1946 .... **TCLC 28**

Wentworth, Robert
See Hamilton, Edmond

Werfel, Franz (V.) 1890-1945 ...... **TCLC 8**
See also CA 104; DLB 81, 124

Wergeland, Henrik Arnold
1808-1845 .... **NCLC 5**

Wersba, Barbara 1932- .... **CLC 30**
See also AAYA 2; CA 29-32R; CANR 16,
38; CLR 3; DLB 52; JRDA; MAICYA;
SAAS 2; SATA 1, 58

Wertmueller, Lina 1928- .... **CLC 16**
See also CA 97-100; CANR 39

Wescott, Glenway 1901-1987 .... **CLC 13**
See also CA 13-16R; 121; CANR 23;
DLB 4, 9, 102

Wesker, Arnold 1932- .... **CLC 3, 5, 42**
See also CA 1-4R; CAAS 7; CANR 1, 33;
CDBLB 1960 to Present; DLB 13;
MTCW

Wesley, Richard (Errol) 1945- .... **CLC 7**
See also BW 1; CA 57-60; CANR 27;
DLB 38

Wessel, Johan Herman 1742-1785 .... **LC 7**

West, Anthony (Panther)
1914-1987 .... **CLC 50**
See also CA 45-48; 124; CANR 3, 19;
DLB 15

West, C. P.
See Wodehouse, P(elham) G(renville)

West, (Mary) Jessamyn
1902-1984 .... **CLC 7, 17**
See also CA 9-12R; 112; CANR 27; DLB 6;
DLBY 84; MTCW; SATA 37

West, Morris L(anglo) 1916- ..... **CLC 6, 33**
See also CA 5-8R; CANR 24; MTCW

West, Nathanael
1903-1940 ..... **TCLC 1, 14, 44; SSC 16**
See also CA 104; 125; CDALB 1929-1941;
DLB 4, 9, 28; MTCW

West, Owen
See Koontz, Dean R(ay)

West, Paul 1930- .... **CLC 7, 14**
See also CA 13-16R; CAAS 7; CANR 22;
DLB 14

West, Rebecca 1892-1983 .. **CLC 7, 9, 31, 50**
See also CA 5-8R; 109; CANR 19; DLB 36;
DLBY 83; MTCW

Westall, Robert (Atkinson)
1929-1993 . . . . CLC 17
See also AAYA 12; CA 69-72; 141;
CANR 18; CLR 13; JRDA; MAICYA;
SAAS 2; SATA 23, 69; SATA-Obit 75

Westlake, Donald E(dwin)
1933- . . . . CLC 7, 33
See also CA 17-20R; CAAS 13; CANR 16,
44

Westmacott, Mary
See Christie, Agatha (Mary Clarissa)

Weston, Allen
See Norton, Andre

Wetcheek, J. L.
See Feuchtwanger, Lion

Wetering, Janwillem van de
See van de Wetering, Janwillem

Wetherell, Elizabeth
See Warner, Susan (Bogert)

Whalen, Philip   1923- . . . . CLC 6, 29
See also CA 9-12R; CANR 5, 39; DLB 16

Wharton, Edith (Newbold Jones)
1862-1937 . . . . . . TCLC 3, 9, 27, 53; DA;
SSC 6; WLC
See also CA 104; 132; CDALB 1865-1917;
DLB 4, 9, 12, 78; MTCW

Wharton, James
See Mencken, H(enry) L(ouis)

Wharton, William (a pseudonym)
. . . . CLC 18, 37
See also CA 93-96; DLBY 80

Wheatley (Peters), Phillis
1754(?)-1784 . . . . LC 3; BLC; DA; PC 3;
WLC
See also CDALB 1640-1865; DLB 31, 50

Wheelock, John Hall   1886-1978 . . . . CLC 14
See also CA 13-16R; 77-80; CANR 14;
DLB 45

White, E(lwyn) B(rooks)
1899-1985 . . . . CLC 10, 34, 39
See also AITN 2; CA 13-16R; 116;
CANR 16, 37; CLR 1, 21; DLB 11, 22;
MAICYA; MTCW; SATA 2, 29, 44

White, Edmund (Valentine III)
1940- . . . . CLC 27
See also AAYA 7; CA 45-48; CANR 3, 19,
36; MTCW

White, Patrick (Victor Martindale)
1912-1990 . . CLC 3, 4, 5, 7, 9, 18, 65, 69
See also CA 81-84; 132; CANR 43; MTCW

White, Phyllis Dorothy James   1920-
See James, P. D.
See also CA 21-24R; CANR 17, 43; MTCW

White, T(erence) H(anbury)
1906-1964 . . . . CLC 30
See also CA 73-76; CANR 37; JRDA;
MAICYA; SATA 12

White, Terence de Vere
1912-1994 . . . . CLC 49
See also CA 49-52; 145; CANR 3

White, Walter F(rancis)
1893-1955 . . . . TCLC 15
See also White, Walter
See also BW 1; CA 115; 124; DLB 51

White, William Hale   1831-1913
See Rutherford, Mark
See also CA 121

Whitehead, E(dward) A(nthony)
1933- . . . . CLC 5
See also CA 65-68

Whitemore, Hugh (John)   1936- . . . . . CLC 37
See also CA 132

Whitman, Sarah Helen (Power)
1803-1878 . . . . NCLC 19
See also DLB 1

Whitman, Walt(er)
1819-1892 . . . . . NCLC 4, 31; DA; PC 3;
WLC
See also CDALB 1640-1865; DLB 3, 64;
SATA 20

Whitney, Phyllis A(yame)   1903- . . . . CLC 42
See also AITN 2; BEST 90:3; CA 1-4R;
CANR 3, 25, 38; JRDA; MAICYA;
SATA 1, 30

Whittemore, (Edward) Reed (Jr.)
1919- . . . . CLC 4
See also CA 9-12R; CAAS 8; CANR 4;
DLB 5

Whittier, John Greenleaf
1807-1892 . . . . NCLC 8
See also CDALB 1640-1865; DLB 1

Whittlebot, Hernia
See Coward, Noel (Peirce)

Wicker, Thomas Grey   1926-
See Wicker, Tom
See also CA 65-68; CANR 21

Wicker, Tom . . . . CLC 7
See also Wicker, Thomas Grey

Wideman, John Edgar
1941- . . . . CLC 5, 34, 36, 67; BLC
See also BW 2; CA 85-88; CANR 14, 42;
DLB 33, 143

Wiebe, Rudy (Henry)   1934- . . . CLC 6, 11, 14
See also CA 37-40R; CANR 42; DLB 60

Wieland, Christoph Martin
1733-1813 . . . . NCLC 17
See also DLB 97

Wiene, Robert   1881-1938 . . . . TCLC 56

Wieners, John   1934- . . . . CLC 7
See also CA 13-16R; DLB 16

Wiesel, Elie(zer)
1928- . . . . CLC 3, 5, 11, 37; DA
See also AAYA 7; AITN 1; CA 5-8R;
CAAS 4; CANR 8, 40; DLB 83;
DLBY 87; MTCW; SATA 56

Wiggins, Marianne   1947- . . . . CLC 57
See also BEST 89:3; CA 130

Wight, James Alfred   1916-
See Herriot, James
See also CA 77-80; SATA 44, 55

Wilbur, Richard (Purdy)
1921- . . . . CLC 3, 6, 9, 14, 53; DA
See also CA 1-4R; CABS 2; CANR 2, 29;
DLB 5; MTCW; SATA 9

Wild, Peter   1940- . . . . CLC 14
See also CA 37-40R; DLB 5

Wilde, Oscar (Fingal O'Flahertie Wills)
1854(?)-1900 . . . . TCLC 1, 8, 23, 41; DA;
SSC 11; WLC
See also CA 104; 119; CDBLB 1890-1914;
DLB 10, 19, 34, 57, 141; SATA 24

Wilder, Billy . . . . CLC 20
See also Wilder, Samuel
See also DLB 26

Wilder, Samuel   1906-
See Wilder, Billy
See also CA 89-92

Wilder, Thornton (Niven)
1897-1975 . . . . . . CLC 1, 5, 6, 10, 15, 35,
82; DA; DC 1; WLC
See also AITN 2; CA 13-16R; 61-64;
CANR 40; DLB 4, 7, 9; MTCW

Wilding, Michael   1942- . . . . CLC 73
See also CA 104; CANR 24

Wiley, Richard   1944- . . . . CLC 44
See also CA 121; 129

Wilhelm, Kate . . . . CLC 7
See also Wilhelm, Katie Gertrude
See also CAAS 5; DLB 8

Wilhelm, Katie Gertrude   1928-
See Wilhelm, Kate
See also CA 37-40R; CANR 17, 36; MTCW

Wilkins, Mary
See Freeman, Mary Eleanor Wilkins

Willard, Nancy   1936- . . . . CLC 7, 37
See also CA 89-92; CANR 10, 39; CLR 5;
DLB 5, 52; MAICYA; MTCW;
SATA 30, 37, 71

Williams, C(harles) K(enneth)
1936- . . . . CLC 33, 56
See also CA 37-40R; DLB 5

Williams, Charles
See Collier, James L(incoln)

Williams, Charles (Walter Stansby)
1886-1945 . . . . TCLC 1, 11
See also CA 104; DLB 100

Williams, (George) Emlyn
1905-1987 . . . . CLC 15
See also CA 104; 123; CANR 36; DLB 10,
77; MTCW

Williams, Hugo   1942- . . . . CLC 42
See also CA 17-20R; CANR 45; DLB 40

Williams, J. Walker
See Wodehouse, P(elham) G(renville)

Williams, John A(lfred)
1925- . . . . CLC 5, 13; BLC
See also BW 2; CA 53-56; CAAS 3;
CANR 6, 26; DLB 2, 33

Williams, Jonathan (Chamberlain)
1929- . . . . CLC 13
See also CA 9-12R; CAAS 12; CANR 8;
DLB 5

Williams, Joy   1944- . . . . CLC 31
See also CA 41-44R; CANR 22

Williams, Norman   1952- . . . . CLC 39
See also CA 118

Williams, Tennessee
1911-1983 . . . . . CLC 1, 2, 5, 7, 8, 11, 15,
19, 30, 39, 45, 71; DA; DC 4; WLC
See also AITN 1, 2; CA 5-8R; 108;
CABS 3; CANR 31; CDALB 1941-1968;
DLB 7; DLBD 4; DLBY 83; MTCW

Wright, Judith (Arandell)
1915- . . . . CLC 11, 53
See also CA 13-16R; CANR 31; MTCW;
SATA 14

Wright, L(aurali) R. 1939- . . . . CLC 44
See also CA 138

Wright, Richard (Nathaniel)
1908-1960 . . . . CLC 1, 3, 4, 9, 14, 21, 48,
74; BLC; DA; SSC 2; WLC
See also AAYA 5; BW 1; CA 108;
CDALB 1929-1941; DLB 76, 102;
DLBD 2; MTCW

Wright, Richard B(ruce) 1937- . . . . . . CLC 6
See also CA 85-88; DLB 53

Wright, Rick 1945- . . . . CLC 35

Wright, Rowland
See Wells, Carolyn

Wright, Stephen Caldwell 1946- . . . . CLC 33
See also BW 2

Wright, Willard Huntington 1888-1939
See Van Dine, S. S.
See also CA 115

Wright, William 1930- . . . . CLC 44
See also CA 53-56; CANR 7, 23

Wu Ch'eng-en 1500(?)-1582(?) . . . . LC 7

Wu Ching-tzu 1701-1754 . . . . LC 2

Wurlitzer, Rudolph 1938(?)- . . . CLC 2, 4, 15
See also CA 85-88

Wycherley, William 1641-1715 . . . . LC 8, 21
See also CDBLB 1660-1789; DLB 80

Wylie, Elinor (Morton Hoyt)
1885-1928 . . . . TCLC 8
See also CA 105; DLB 9, 45

Wylie, Philip (Gordon) 1902-1971 . . . CLC 43
See also CA 21-22; 33-36R; CAP 2; DLB 9

Wyndham, John . . . . CLC 19
See also Harris, John (Wyndham Parkes
Lucas) Beynon

Wyss, Johann David Von
1743-1818 . . . . NCLC 10
See also JRDA; MAICYA; SATA 27, 29

Yakumo Koizumi
See Hearn, (Patricio) Lafcadio (Tessima
Carlos)

Yanez, Jose Donoso
See Donoso (Yanez), Jose

Yanovsky, Basile S.
See Yanovsky, V(assily) S(emenovich)

Yanovsky, V(assily) S(emenovich)
1906-1989 . . . . CLC 2, 18
See also CA 97-100; 129

Yates, Richard 1926-1992 . . . . . CLC 7, 8, 23
See also CA 5-8R; 139; CANR 10, 43;
DLB 2; DLBY 81, 92

Yeats, W. B.
See Yeats, William Butler

Yeats, William Butler
1865-1939 . . . . . TCLC 1, 11, 18, 31; DA;
WLC
See also CA 104; 127; CANR 45;
CDBLB 1890-1914; DLB 10, 19, 98;
MTCW

Yehoshua, A(braham) B.
1936- . . . . CLC 13, 31
See also CA 33-36R; CANR 43

Yep, Laurence Michael 1948- . . . . . . CLC 35
See also AAYA 5; CA 49-52; CANR 1;
CLR 3, 17; DLB 52; JRDA; MAICYA;
SATA 7, 69

Yerby, Frank G(arvin)
1916-1991 . . . . CLC 1, 7, 22; BLC
See also BW 1; CA 9-12R; 136; CANR 16;
DLB 76; MTCW

Yesenin, Sergei Alexandrovich
See Esenin, Sergei (Alexandrovich)

Yevtushenko, Yevgeny (Alexandrovich)
1933- . . . . CLC 1, 3, 13, 26, 51
See also CA 81-84; CANR 33; MTCW

Yezierska, Anzia 1885(?)-1970 . . . . . CLC 46
See also CA 126; 89-92; DLB 28; MTCW

Yglesias, Helen 1915- . . . . CLC 7, 22
See also CA 37-40R; CANR 15; MTCW

Yokomitsu Riichi 1898-1947 . . . . . . TCLC 47

Yonge, Charlotte (Mary)
1823-1901 . . . . TCLC 48
See also CA 109; DLB 18; SATA 17

York, Jeremy
See Creasey, John

York, Simon
See Heinlein, Robert A(nson)

Yorke, Henry Vincent 1905-1974 . . . CLC 13
See also Green, Henry
See also CA 85-88; 49-52

Yoshimoto, Banana . . . . CLC 84
See also Yoshimoto, Mahoko

Yoshimoto, Mahoko 1964-
See Yoshimoto, Banana
See also CA 144

Young, Al(bert James)
1939- . . . . CLC 19; BLC
See also BW 2; CA 29-32R; CANR 26;
DLB 33

Young, Andrew (John) 1885-1971 . . . . CLC 5
See also CA 5-8R; CANR 7, 29

Young, Collier
See Bloch, Robert (Albert)

Young, Edward 1683-1765 . . . . LC 3
See also DLB 95

Young, Marguerite 1909- . . . . CLC 82
See also CA 13-16; CAP 1

Young, Neil 1945- . . . . CLC 17
See also CA 110

Yourcenar, Marguerite
1903-1987 . . . . CLC 19, 38, 50
See also CA 69-72; CANR 23; DLB 72;
DLBY 88; MTCW

Yurick, Sol 1925- . . . . CLC 6
See also CA 13-16R; CANR 25

Zabolotskii, Nikolai Alekseevich
1903-1958 . . . . TCLC 52
See also CA 116

Zamiatin, Yevgenii
See Zamyatin, Evgeny Ivanovich

Zamyatin, Evgeny Ivanovich
1884-1937 . . . . TCLC 8, 37
See also CA 105

Zangwill, Israel 1864-1926 . . . . TCLC 16
See also CA 109; DLB 10, 135

Zappa, Francis Vincent, Jr. 1940-1993
See Zappa, Frank
See also CA 108; 143

Zappa, Frank . . . . CLC 17
See also Zappa, Francis Vincent, Jr.

Zaturenska, Marya 1902-1982 . . . . CLC 6, 11
See also CA 13-16R; 105; CANR 22

Zelazny, Roger (Joseph) 1937- . . . . . CLC 21
See also AAYA 7; CA 21-24R; CANR 26;
DLB 8; MTCW; SATA 39, 57

Zhdanov, Andrei A(lexandrovich)
1896-1948 . . . . TCLC 18
See also CA 117

Zhukovsky, Vasily 1783-1852 . . . . NCLC 35

Ziegenhagen, Eric . . . . CLC 55

Zimmer, Jill Schary
See Robinson, Jill

Zimmerman, Robert
See Dylan, Bob

Zindel, Paul 1936- . . . . CLC 6, 26; DA
See also AAYA 2; CA 73-76; CANR 31;
CLR 3; DLB 7, 52; JRDA; MAICYA;
MTCW; SATA 16, 58

Zinov'Ev, A. A.
See Zinoviev, Alexander (Aleksandrovich)

Zinoviev, Alexander (Aleksandrovich)
1922- . . . . CLC 19
See also CA 116; 133; CAAS 10

Zoilus
See Lovecraft, H(oward) P(hillips)

Zola, Emile (Edouard Charles Antoine)
1840-1902 . . . . . . TCLC 1, 6, 21, 41; DA;
WLC
See also CA 104; 138; DLB 123

Zoline, Pamela 1941- . . . . CLC 62

Zorrilla y Moral, Jose 1817-1893 . . NCLC 6

Zoshchenko, Mikhail (Mikhailovich)
1895-1958 . . . . TCLC 15; SSC 15
See also CA 115

Zuckmayer, Carl 1896-1977 . . . . CLC 18
See also CA 69-72; DLB 56, 124

Zuk, Georges
See Skelton, Robin

Zukofsky, Louis
1904-1978 . . . . CLC 1, 2, 4, 7, 11, 18
See also CA 9-12R; 77-80; CANR 39;
DLB 5; MTCW

Zweig, Paul 1935-1984 . . . . CLC 34, 42
See also CA 85-88; 113

Zweig, Stefan 1881-1942 . . . . TCLC 17
See also CA 112; DLB 81, 118

Literary Criticism Series
Cumulative Topic Index

This index lists all topic entries in the Gale Literary Criticism Series *Classical and Medieval Literature Criticism, Contemporary Literary Criticism, Literature Criticism from 1400 to 1800, Nineteenth-Century Literature Criticism,* and *Twentieth-Century Literary Criticism.*

Topic Index

NCLC Cumulative Nationality Index

Ghalib **39**

IRISH
Allingham, William **25**
Banim, John **13**
Banim, Michael **13**
Boucicault, Dion **41**
Carleton, William **3**
Croker, John Wilson **10**
Darley, George **2**
Edgeworth, Maria **1**
Ferguson, Samuel **33**
Griffin, Gerald **7**
Jameson, Anna **43**
Le Fanu, Joseph Sheridan **9**
Lever, Charles (James) **23**
Maginn, William **8**
Mangan, James Clarence **27**
Maturin, Charles Robert **6**
Moore, Thomas **6**
Morgan, Lady **29**
O'Brien, Fitz-James **21**

ITALIAN
Foscolo, Ugo **8**
Gozzi, (Conte) Carlo **23**
Leopardi, (Conte) Giacomo **22**
Manzoni, Alessandro **29**
Mazzini, Guiseppe **34**
Nievo, Ippolito **22**

JAPANESE
Motoori, Norinaga **45**

LITHUANIAN
Mapu, Abraham (ben Jekutiel) **18**

MEXICAN
Lizardi, Jose Joaquin Fernandez de **30**

NORWEGIAN
Collett, (Jacobine) Camilla (Wergeland) **22**
Wergeland, Henrik Arnold **5**

POLISH
Fredro, Aleksander **8**
Krasicki, Ignacy **8**
Krasinski, Zygmunt **4**
Mickiewicz, Adam **3**
Norwid, Cyprian Kamil **17**
Slowacki, Juliusz **15**

ROMANIAN
Eminescu, Mihail **33**

RUSSIAN
Aksakov, Sergei Timofeyvich **2**
Bakunin, Mikhail (Alexandrovich) **25**
Bashkirtseff, Marie **27**
Belinski, Vissarion Grigoryevich **5**
Chernyshevsky, Nikolay Gavrilovich **1**
Dobrolyubov, Nikolai Alexandrovich **5**
Dostoevsky, Fedor Mikhailovich **2, 7, 21, 33, 43**
Gogol, Nikolai (Vasilyevich) **5, 15, 31**
Goncharov, Ivan Alexandrovich **1**
Herzen, Aleksandr Ivanovich **10**
Karamzin, Nikolai Mikhailovich **3**
Krylov, Ivan Andreevich **1**
Lermontov, Mikhail Yuryevich **5**
Leskov, Nikolai (Semyonovich) **25**
Nekrasov, Nikolai Alekseevich **11**

Ostrovsky, Alexander **30**
Pisarev, Dmitry Ivanovich **25**
Pushkin, Alexander (Sergeyevich) **3, 27**
Saltykov, Mikhail Evgrafovich **16**
Smolenskin, Peretz **30**
Turgenev, Ivan **21**
Tyutchev, Fyodor **34**
Zhukovsky, Vasily **35**

SCOTTISH
Baillie, Joanna **2**
Beattie, James **25**
Campbell, Thomas **19**
Ferrier, Susan (Edmonstone) **8**
Galt, John **1**
Hogg, James **4**
Jeffrey, Francis **33**
Lockhart, John Gibson **6**
Mackenzie, Henry **41**
Oliphant, Margaret (Oliphant Wilson) **11**
Scott, Walter **15**
Stevenson, Robert Louis (Balfour) **5, 14**
Thomson, James **18**
Wilson, John **5**

SPANISH
Alarcon, Pedro Antonio de **1**
Caballero, Fernan **10**
Castro, Rosalia de **3**
Espronceda, Jose de **39**
Larra (y Sanchez de Castro), Mariano Jose de **17**
Tamayo y Baus, Manuel **1**
Zorrilla y Moral, Jose **6**

SWEDISH
Almqvist, Carl Jonas Love **42**
Bremer, Fredrika **11**
Tegner, Esaias **2**

SWISS
Amiel, Henri Frederic **4**
Keller, Gottfried **2**
Wyss, Johann David Von **10**

Nationality Index

Title Index